Bisel's

Pennsylvania Municipal Lawsource®

AF870280

Twenty-second Edition

The Collected Municipal Statutes, Regulations, Rules, First Class Township, Second Class Township, Third Class City and Borough Codes

By

DARRELL M. ZASLOW

and

LEVI S. ZASLOW

GEORGE T. BISEL COMPANY, INC.

710 S. WASHINGTON SQUARE

PHILADELPHIA GTB **PENNSYLVANIA**

www.bisel.com

Printed in United States of America

Library of Congress Catalog Card Number: 97-078244

ISBN: 1-887024-27-1
ISSN: 2160-3227

HOW TO USE

First refer to main text herein, then check any current supplement, using same reference numbers. New material subsequent to publication of original text is contained in later supplements and text revisions. SINCE LAWS AND CODE REFERENCES CHANGE QUITE FREQUENTLY, ALWAYS CHECK THE TIMELINESS AND APPLICABILITY OF THE STATUTES AND CODE CONTAINED HEREIN.

FOR QUESTIONS ABOUT THIS PUBLICATION,
CALL TOLL FREE 1-800-247-3526

Contact the Bisel Editorial Department directly with your questions and suggestions by e-mail at tonyd@bisel.com

PRACTICE TITLES AVAILABLE FROM BISEL

BASIC REFERENCE SETS/FORMS

Dunlap-Hanna PA Forms (Litigation and Transactional), 14 Vols with CD-ROM

Dunlap-Hanna PA Forms, CD-ROM (1 Year Service)

Sell and Stefanoni PA Keystone, Lawyer's Desk Library of Practice, 8 Vols or CD-ROM

ESTATE ADMINISTRATION/PLANNING

Weinberg, PA Estate Planning & Drafting, 3 Vols or CD-ROM

Grossman & Smith, PA Inheritance & Estate Tax or CD-ROM

Smith, Grossman & Hollinger, PA Fiduciary Guide

Aker, PA Probate, Estates & Fiduciaries Code or CD-ROM

Aker, Law of Wills in PA or CD-ROM

Bregy, PA Intestate, Wills & Estates Provisions of the PEF Code

Grossman, PA Orphans' Court Lawsource

Hunter, Orphans' Court Commonplace Set, 8 Vols

Remick's PA Orphans' Court Practice, 7 Vols

Steinbacher & Stahl, PA Trust Guide

Steinbacher & Stahl, PA Special Needs Planning Guide

REAL ESTATE PRACTICE

Friedman, Ladner PA Real Estate Law, 2 Vols

Glazer, PA Community Association Law & Practice

Friedman, PA Landlord-Tenant Law

Zaslow, Wilson & Zaslow, PA Real Estate Tax Sales & Municipal Claims

Ryan, PA Zoning Law & Practice, 2 Vols or CD-ROM

Snitzer, PA Eminent Domain

Emmons, PA Real Estate Brokerage Law & Practice, 2 Vols

Zaslow, PA Real Estate Lawsource

FAMILY LAW PRACTICE

PA Family Law Update Newsletter (Monthly)

Zulick & Zanan, PA Support Practice

Zulick & Zanan, PA Divorce Code Annotated

Bertin, PA Child Custody

Zanan, PA Domestic Relations Lawsource

PA Family Law E-Reporter

WORKERS' COMPENSATION/EMPLOYMENT

Barbieri, Poorman, Seelig, & Pond PA Workers' Compensation, 3 Vols

Zanan, PA Workers' Compensation Lawsource

PA Workers' Compensation Update Newsletter (Monthly)

PA Labor and Employment Lawsource

PA Unemployment Compensation Lawsource

CONSTITUTIONAL LAW

Gormley, The Pennsylvania Constitution

ADR

Creo, Alternative Dispute Resolution

CRIMINAL LAW/MOTOR VEHICLES

Evangelista, PA Criminal Trial Guide, 2 Vols

Sherman & Vogrin, PA Driving Under the Influence Law and Practice, 2 Vols

Laub & Evangelista's PA Manual of Civil and Criminal Penalties and Sentences

MacIntyre & Evangelista, PA Crimes Code & Criminal Law

PA Criminal Law Update Newsletter (Monthly)

Zanan, PA Motor Vehicle Insurance Lawsource

Zanan, Motor Vehicle Operation Lawsource

Meyer, PA Vehicle Code Annotated

Zanan & Kempner, PA Vehicle Negligence

Di Pietro, PA Juvenile Delinquency Law

Ricca & Zanan, PA ARD/Expungement Handbook

PA Vehicle Law E-Reporter

CIVIL PRACTICE/TRIAL

Feldman, Kempner PA Trial Guide (Civil), 7 Vols

- PA Trial Guide—Evidence or CD-ROM
- PA Trial Guide—Procedure
- PA Trial Guide—Damages, Death Actions & Consortium
- PA Trial Guide—Professional Malpractice
- PA Trial Guide—Product Liability

Stefanoni, PA Civil Practice Handbook

Rothman, McCarter & English, NJ Civil Practice Handbook

Rich, Zanan, & Ruff, PA Damages—Personal Injury Verdicts & Settlements

Dempsey, PA Negligence

Kempner & Zanan, Discovery Lawsource

Wettick, PA Forms for Rules of Civil Procedure

Guben & Zanan, PA Animal Law

MUNICIPAL PRACTICE

Zaslow, PA Municipal Lawsource

BUSINESS LAW PRACTICE

Sell & Clark, PA Business Corporations

Clark & Sell, PA Business Associations Lawsource

Clark & Sell, PA Nonprofit Corporations and Charities Lawsource

Carter, PA Consumer Law

Kempner, PA Consumer Lawsource

Best, PA Insurance Law

Kogan, Bisel's BUSINESSMAKER™ PA Business Entity Creation Software

Carobus, PA Debt Collection

Zanan, PA Bankruptcy Lawsource

ELDER LAW PRACTICE

Gerhard, PA Medicaid—Long-Term Care

Gerhard, PA Medicaid—Long-Term Care Lawsource

Pearson & Cowart, The Law of Financial Abuse and Exploitation

Preface to the Twenty-second Edition

January, 2025

The various prefaces to this Municipal Lawsource repeatedly exhort local, national, and international governments to dedicate and rededicate to the difficult and worthy task of self-governance. Self-governance for the benefit of all. We must never accept such a critical task with cynicism or defeat. To the contrary, no matter how deep the divisions may seem, seeking broad coalitions of understanding and friendship is always possible. This holds true from the most local of politics to international divides. There are limitless examples in the recent and distant past. Indeed, in the most trying of times, President Abraham Lincoln reminded us in his first inaugural address: "I am loath to close. We are not enemies, but friends. We must not be enemies. Though passion may have strained it must not break our bonds of affection. The mystic chords of memory, stretching from every battlefield and patriot grave to every living heart and hearthstone all over this broad land, will yet swell the chorus of the Union, when again touched, as surely they will be, by the better angels of our nature." And so may it be today that each of us, and those with whom government is trusted, must recall—or discover in the first instance—the affection for our fellows and be guided by good sense, good judgment, and our good nature.

Numerous statutory revisions throughout the 2024 legislative season are included in this volume. It is this author's hope that, starting with our local governments, we can set a positive model for local, national, and international governments on the critical functions of government for the benefit of all.

As always, we thank the reader and welcome any suggestions for inclusion or other improvements to this Municipal Lawsource.

Preface to the Twenty-first Edition

January, 2024

In words that could have been written today, in 2007 the Preface to the Sixth Edition of this Municipal Lawsource lamented that the state of the "world is in turmoil. Lawlessness is absurdly rampant across much of the globe. We see issues arising, profound issues of war and destruction, which are global in scope. Yet it is at the municipal level that destruction unfolds, and it is there that law must start. It is in the towns and cities of the world that human beings are made to suffer, and societies collapse." For this reason, and many others, the Preface observed that it "is now more critical than ever that we dedicate and rededicate ourselves to the difficult and worthy task of self-governance."

The 2023 political season was defined by partisan gridlock in Harrisburg. The essentially evenly divided General Assembly halted to a standstill for much of the year. As a result, the House remained out of session for part of the year, it took many months to agree to a budget, and months after that to sign it into law. In fact, the budget was not signed into law until December 14, 2023, which is more than five months after the deadline. Along with the budget came dozens of bills in a marathon session. With shared goals, the spirit of compromise, and an eye towards improving the lives of the people whose lives government affects, great things are possible in Pennsylvania and beyond. Good and wise governance and decision-making at the local, state, national, and international level is critical. It is our hope that we dedicate and rededicate ourselves to the difficult and worthy task of self-governance.

As always, we thank the reader and welcome any suggestions for inclusion or other improvements to this Municipal Lawsource.

Levi S. Zaslow, Esq.

Preface to the Twentieth Edition

December, 2022

This edition of the Pennsylvania Municipal Lawsource presents a major milestone. Originally published in 1998, this is the twentieth edition of this publication, which now spans the course of 25 years. In the midst of global, national, statewide, and local issues—both large and small—the law governing Pennsylvania municipalities is constantly in motion. The General Assembly enacts, revises, and repeals statutes on a constant, seemingly endless basis and regulations are frequently revised. Through it all, this publication has become an indispensable guide for those whose practice touches Pennsylvania municipalities.

This most recent edition contains revisions to the Local Tax Enabling Act, Local Tax Collection Law, Uniform Construction Code Regulations, land banks, and numerous other statutory and regulatory provisions throughout. Gratitude is expressed to the readers of this publication and those who have provided feedback on this and prior editions. Suggestions for inclusion or other improvements to this Municipal Lawsource are always welcome and encouraged.

Levi S. Zaslow, Esq.

Preface to the Nineteenth Edition

December, 2021

If 2020 was a year like no other in recent memory, 2021 followed fast on its heels. January 6 is now a day that will be etched in history. The violence and breach of the United States Capitol that day disrupted a joint session of the U.S. Congress that was in the process of ascertaining and counting the electoral votes related to the 2020 presidential election. According to the United States Attorney's Office, "since January 6, more than 700 individuals have been arrested in nearly all 50 states for crimes related to the breach of the U.S. Capitol, including over 220 individuals charged with assaulting or impeding law enforcement. The investigation remains ongoing." The country is still grappling with the effects and consequences from that day.

Meanwhile, COVID-19 still dominates the headlines and our daily lives. As of the date of this publication there have been an estimated 815,423 deaths in the United States and 5,386,666 worldwide attributed to the virus. An estimated 8,861,449,091 total vaccine doses have been administered, which represents over 48% of the world population. COVID-19 "variants," "surges," and "waves" are now common references. The world hopes for a full return to health, safety, and normalcy soon.

However, the basic work and functions of government continue. Once again, the General Assembly has continued to enact and amend Pennsylvania's statutes. Thus, in preparing for the next generation of wireless networks, Pennsylvania has enacted the Small Wireless Facilities Deployment Act, which is designed to stimulate wireless and 5G deployment. It has a direct effect on Pennsylvania municipalities. The Sunshine Act, Municipality Authorities Act, and other statutory provisions were also amended and are presented in this edition. Suggestions for inclusion or other improvements to this Municipal Lawsource are always welcome and encouraged.

Levi S. Zaslow, Esq.

Preface to the Eighteenth Edition

December, 2020

2020 was a year like no other in recent memory. The COVID-19 pandemic raged across the globe and the world unmistakably changed. As of the date of this publication there have been an estimated 317,656 deaths in the United States and 1,692,210 deaths worldwide attributed to the virus. In addition to the direct effects of the virus, states and municipalities have ordered lockdowns, shutdowns, social distancing, and limitations on the size of gatherings. It has touched virtually everything, including schools, houses of worship, worksites, sports venues, and courthouses.

The court system and litigation were certainly not spared. Courthouses nationwide were temporarily physically closed or have been operating in a limited capacity. Some litigants, particularly civil litigants, may have their cases delayed for years. But our system of justice does not stop. The courts, judges, attorneys, and litigants have adapted. Remote depositions by electronic means have become commonplace and remote trials and court proceedings are frequent.

But there is hope on the horizon. The FDA has recently issued two Emergency Use Authorizations for COVID-19 vaccines. Under Operation Warp Speed, the vaccine is currently being shipped around the country and is just starting to be administered. Nationally, Joseph R. Biden is President-elect and inherits the task of battling the virus. The battle for the U.S. Senate is at its apex, with the Georgia runoff election right around the corner.

Through it all, the General Assembly has continued its work of enacting and amending Pennsylvania's statutes. Perhaps most significantly, the General Assembly passed significant legislation intended to modernize and recodify the First Class Township Code, which had not been done in 70 years. The Local Government Commission's Executive Summary describes this as a years-long endeavor to remove obsolete provisions, incorporate language to reflect case law and current practices, standards and requirements, update archaic language or language in conflict with other statutes, consolidate common subjects, and add some language, as relevant, that had been part of previous significant recodifications (the Borough Code, Third Class City Code, and Second Class Township Code).

The newly-amended, recodified, and modernized First Class Township Code is presented in this edition. This edition also includes the new Municipality Condemnation Order Act and numerous revisions to the statutes throughout. Suggestions for inclusion or other improvements to this Municipal Lawsource are always welcome and encouraged.

Levi S. Zaslow, Esq.

Preface to the Seventeenth Edition

January, 2020

The country remains divided on significant issues of national politics and foreign relations. The United States House of Representatives has voted to impeach the President of the United States. As this Seventeenth Edition goes to press, the Articles of Impeachment have yet to be turned over to the United States Senate for trial. The partisan divide is easily seen in Pennsylvania, with each of its eighteen House representatives voting on party lines: an even 9-9. A member of the earliest sessions of the House of Representatives once wrote concerning an address by President George Washington and the reply by the House that "[b]oth contain some divine molasses." President Washington, on January 14, 1790, expressed his hope and confidence that Congress be "directed by an enlightened and virtuous zeal for the happiness of our country." Good government, relations amongst the various branches of government, and the relationship between the government and the people are matters of longstanding debate and of critical importance.

The Preface to the Ninth Edition of this book expresses that, "[a]s ever, the legislative quest for good government, though sometimes quixotic, proceeds." Thus, while critical matters of national and international importance continue to be debated, the General Assembly continues to enact, revise, and amend Pennsylvania's statutes and rules, all of which have a direct impact on municipalities and the day-to-day lives of its residents. These numerous revisions are reflected in this volume. In addition to the many statutory revisions, this volume also includes new chapters for relevant statutes useful to practitioners and government officials, including the Abandoned and Blighted Property Conservatorship Act, a new definition for "blight," and the statutory provisions for Intergovernmental Cooperation. Suggestions for inclusion or other improvements to this Municipal Lawsource are always welcome.

Levi S. Zaslow, Esq.

Preface to the Sixteenth Edition

December, 2018

In national politics, the political parties continue to play their great game of thrones – or at least maneuver for seats in Congress and on the Supreme Court. Debates have swirled around the country on national and international matters, including foreign policy, border security, immigration, health care, Supreme Court nominations, and a host of other important issues. Yet, from the earliest days of the Roman *municipia* to the current day municipalities, local governments have had a direct impact on the lives of the citizenry, from local politics, taxes, revenue from public lands, and numerous other issues. Thus, while the major national debates go on and on, politics at the local level continue to be of critical importance in our day-to-day lives. Revisions to the Local Tax Enabling Act, rules of procedure, land banks, and municipal codes, among other statutory revisions, are all reflected in the current volume. As always, suggestions for inclusion or other improvements to this Municipal Lawsource are always welcome.

Levi S. Zaslow, Esq.

Preface to the Fifteenth Edition

December, 2017

The publication of the Fifteenth Edition of Bisel's Pennsylvania Municipal Lawsource is bittersweet. Shortly after the publication of the last edition, the author and compiler of the fourteen prior editions of this book, Darrell M. Zaslow, Esq., tragically passed away. We mourn that loss every day. Beloved by so many, the loss is shared by family, friends, colleagues, and countless others who were fortunate enough to know him or benefit from his works.

Among his many talents, he was a tremendous scholar, advocate, and author. He wrote or compiled at least five books, including this Municipal Lawsource. The collected statutes, rules, and regulations governing municipalities collected in this work have benefited countless attorneys, government officials, private citizens, and other professionals in accessing and understanding the laws governing Pennsylvania municipalities. Both the practice of law and local governance have improved as a direct result of this book. Without the work and diligence of Darrell M. Zaslow, this book would simply not exist in its current form.

I was fortunate to collaborate closely on the fifth and sixth editions of this book and returning to author this edition was like reuniting with an old, close, and not-forgotten friend. Indeed, the General Assembly continues its noble work and new statutes are enacted, old statutes are updated, and rules and regulations continue to be promulgated. Thus, the continuous need to update and recompile this book. We always welcome ideas or suggestions for inclusions or other improvements.

While it would be impossible to thank each person who made this book and my practice of law possible, I would like to express gratitude to: my incredible, caring, and understanding wife Shoshana; my wonderful children Zechariah, Tehilla, and Akiva; my parents Darrell and Sherri Zaslow; my parents-in-law Abbe and Adena Mendlowitz; my grandparents and grandparents-in-law; the Honorable Althea M. Handy, Associate Judge of the Circuit Court for Baltimore City; my law partners at Joseph, Greenwald & Laake, P.A.; and Tony DiGioia, Esq., Editor-in-Chief of the George T. Bisel Company, Inc. Each of them has provided guidance and support in their own way and gratitude is expressed to each of them.

Levi S. Zaslow, Esq.

Preface to the Fourteenth Edition

December, 2016

This season of the Municipal Law produced a political shocker. Actually it was a shocker for all those in the political world except for one person: that is the Commander-in-Chief, the Hon. Donald J. Trump. He obviously knew what was happening and had his hand on the pulse of the nation. It is a seismic change in the world of local and national politics, with a ripple effect down to every level. Whether a person supported Mr. Trump or supported another candidate, very few people even of the most savvy nature can lay claim that they saw it coming. Who knows if there will be other seismic shifts yet to come, but for the time being it is clear that Donald J. Trump is the President of the United States of America, and he is of course wished well in his ability to provide for this great nation. All persons of good feeling will wish the best to the new administration and hope the United States of America will prosper for the benefit of all Americans and the world.

Notwithstanding enormous political upheaval, the basic level politics of the United States proceeds as it always has and will. The Commonwealth of Pennsylvania, providing the best kind of government for the people at the most basic level, will continue to implement numerous new laws and modifications as are always occurring with municipal law. The laws of Pennsylvania are implemented with a new series of laws on a number of levels, each one making subtle changes in the way the Commonwealth of Pennsylvania governs us at the local level. The state legislature continues to change the laws which govern at our local level, each intended for improvements in the many changes which have occurred. May our efforts at the local level be mirrored at all levels of government.

Darrell M. Zaslow, Esq.

Preface to the Thirteenth Edition

December, 2015

It is ironic as this book goes to press, incorporating inter alia new enactments relative to tax collection, that the Commonwealth of Pennsylvania is severely overdue in enacting a budget delineating how the taxes so collected are to be spent. Collections and spending, however, proceed apace. The effort to consolidate the state's statutes again results in certain critical Codes being rewritten and renumbered. The process of land development procedures as always receives attention by the Legislature, in efforts to improve the process for both municipalities and developers. Pennsylvania's Uniform Construction Code continues to increase its impact and applicability, with new enactments declaring the primacy of that Code as to the construction, alteration, repair, and occupancy of all buildings and structures. On the national scene a new presidential election cycle is heating up, with issues of international and domestic terrorism filling the airwaves; meanwhile local government struggles to pay its bills, police its streets, and provide for the general welfare. In accordance with the conventional wisdom that all politics is local, the action of a local Board or Council can have an impact far surpassing the most tumultuous events which bombard the average person through their phone, tablet, or TV. As always it is Municipal Law which intimately impacts the daily lives of citizens where they live.

Darrell M. Zaslow, Esq.

Preface to the Twelfth Edition

December, 2014

Reenactment and recodification of several of the Codes, with numerous changes and additions interspersed, will require some adjustment by practitioners used to the prior long-standing citations. Both substantive and stylistic changes have been incorporated by new legislation, as well as total relocation of key provisions. Regulations governing land development, municipal authorities, and taxation have likewise been modified. Wholesale changes in government occurred in 2014, including legislative leadership and the directive of the voters retiring the sitting Governor. The impact of these significant political changes on legislation has yet to be felt. Whether the result will be gridlock or a platform of major change will be apparent as the new Governor and legislative leaders commence their terms.

Darrell M. Zaslow, Esq.

Preface to the Eleventh Edition

December, 2013

Enactments relative to the new reality of electronic communication are finding the way into law, resulting in new statutes applying to e-notice permissions and requirements. While newspapers remain a mainstay of notices, at expense to municipal government, the world of the web at last begins to exert influence in the codes. In an apparent recognition of market realities, and in an attempt to assist development, the issuance of certain governmental permits have received statutory extension. Whether the general stimulation needed for economic growth will return the Commonwealth to full prosperity remains to be seen. Newly effective enactments in the township codes have changed longstanding nomenclature regarding tax collectors. In general, the governance of local municipalities continues as a focus of legislative intent in order to maintain each of the codes and statutes in this volume in up to date fashion, functioning smoothly for government, citizens, and developers.

Darrell M. Zaslow, Esq.

Preface to the Tenth Edition

November, 2012

The state of the nation and the world continues in profound economic malaise and increasing polarization between nations. Violent civil wars have flared, and only somewhat less violent civil wars, termed as national "springtimes", have occurred since the last edition of this Lawsource was published. Within our own country, polarization increased as well, and while Democrats and Republicans are thankfully not in actual combat, the 2012 election season was a close resemblance. All eyes of the country are upon the newly re-elected President, in the hopes that we can somehow spearhead a rejuvenation of national strength.

In the meantime, in the world of Municipal law, local governments are faced with increasing service demands and decreasing revenues. The legislative machinery churns ever forward, with significant changes enacted in many of the important Codes contained in this book, including most notably the Borough Code. Other important modifications also occurred, including sections of the First and Second Township Codes, the Authorities Act, and the Municipalities Planning Code. The continuing efforts to improve Pennsylvania's increasingly decrepit housing stock resulted in the enacted of a Land Bank law, which seeks to empower local government with the ability to acquire and oversee rejuvenation of vacant, abandoned, and tax-delinquent property.

The discovery in Pennsylvania of new sources of oil and gas, coupled with new methods of extraction of those precious resources from the ground deed below, have resulted in a new industry returning to the State, on a scale perhaps not seen since the first discovery of oil in northwestern Pennsylvania and the booming oil rush of the 1860's. The contentious Pennsylvania statute regulating the "fracking" industry, governing the interplay between state and local governments, appears in this Lawsource for the first time. It remains to be seen how the tension will play out between state revenues, private industry, and what had previously thought to be the nearly inviolate zoning power of local government.

Darrell M. Zaslow, Esq.

Preface to the Ninth Edition

December, 2011

The economic status of the state, the nation, and indeed the world being mediocre at best, the legislative machinery continues its efforts to somehow enact improvement. Over the last legislative sessions the hiring and firing of police and fire apparatus operators has been modified, having impact in many municipalities. The ongoing wars in which the country expends valuable resources have precipitated modifications to municipal hiring practices of Veterans. The value of the dollar being diminished, and the cost of government increasing, the legislature has seen fit to nearly double municipal expenditures permissible without bids.

The growing concern over the deteriorated nature of property and neighborhoods prompted the legislative concept that punishment of the owners of distressed property will somehow correct the problem. It likely will not, as the problem is much more severe, and the solutions need to be much better conceptualized. Significant money is being thrown away by government on ineffective solutions. A bigger picture needs to emerge. In any case the legislature enacted a law granting power to punish property owners whose properties do not meet standards. Municipalities may take advantage and correct some blight here and there, yet without really assisting the economic and financial inability of many to keep their homes up to snuff. Abandonment and deterioration will continue to be rampant.

The ever-expanding horizons of electronic life has resulted in other enactments to streamline municipal functioning, including new permission to conduct public auctions of personal property owned by a municipality by means of an online auction. And so E-Bay style activities come to local government. Continuing efforts to save townships considerable money by allowing on-line publication of Public Notices has not yet occurred as of publication of this Ninth Edition of the *Municipal Lawsource*. It appears that private advertisers have largely abandoned newspapers as a profitable source of advertising; the taxpayers, by virtue of Public Notices mandated by law, are at present funding what remains of paper news. This is likely to change in the near future, as websites inexorably supplant newsprint.

Concern over the misbehavior of elected officials has prompted the legislature to increase the penalties for violation of the Sunshine Act. The undersigned compiler of this book recently had the privilege of arguing, and succeeding, in the case of *Alexseev and HAPCO v. City of Philadelphia*, 8 A.3d 311, wherein the City Council claimed immunity from the public comment law which governs every other municipality in the Commonwealth. After losing at the Common Pleas level, and again at the Commonwealth Court, it was gratifying for the Supreme Court to permit the appeal and overturn the lower courts. As a result Philadelphia must now hear public comment from its residents. In any case, the penalties for purposeful Sunshine Act violations have been fortified.

Numerous other changes are incorporated throughout the statutory materials in this volume. As ever, the legislative quest for good government, though sometimes quixotic, proceeds.

Darrell M. Zaslow, Esq.

Preface to the Eighth Edition

December, 2009

With this eighth edition of Municipal Lawsource we welcome Pennsylvania's 53 Third Class Cities. From the colonial days of Chester, Lancaster, Easton and

York to the present, 3rd Class Cities have served as home and government for many of Pennsylvania's citizens. Altoona and Reading grew with the railroad, while Johnstown, Bethlehem, Clairton and Coatesville were strengthened with steel. Allentown, Erie, Wilkes-Barre, and our capital city of Harrisburg, each has its own unique history and special flavor of government. We trust this volume will assist in fine governance for their residents.

This eighth edition of Municipal Lawsource is also the first in what may be viewed in later times as a new era. The election of a new president coincided with the most unfortunate downturn in the economics of the nation since the Great Depression. While many families face foreclosure and uncertain employment circumstances, the impact on government has become equally severe. Funds are short, and the need to raise taxes and cut services threatens to interfere with the quality of life. The federal government continues to exercise its prerogative to spend the money of several generations yet unborn. At the local level, the dangerous luxury of deficit spending is not an option. Municipal officials agonize over spending and taxing, yet the best buy for the money is at the municipal level.

The Uniform Construction Code continues to have significant impact. With this eighth edition of Municipal Lawsource we see the establishment of a "Uniform Construction Code Review & Advisory Council". Taxation being an ever-present issue, the Local Tax Enabling Act is the subject of constant tinkering, which together with other changes affecting municipal law generally are all reflected in the volume.

Darrell M. Zaslow, Esq.

Preface to the Seventh Edition

October, 2008

It is a goal of good government to operate in full public view. While not every governmental action can safely be made in the rays of glorious sunshine, most activity of elected officials is enhanced if the public is privy to the decision-making. Citizen access to the documents and records of government makes democracy a successful community affair. This is especially true at the local government level.

In recognition of the dynamic of government–citizen relations, the Pennsylvania legislature, among many other municipal law amendments, has enacted a new Right-to-Know law. The new legislation is intended to enhance citizen access to the books and records of their community. The law, approved on February 14, 2008, will be fully effective on January 1, 2009. Certain of the new law's provisions are effective immediately. Practitioners in the area of local government are likely to be confronted with innumerable questions regarding the impact and interpretation of the law.

It is certain that questions will arise not only in the halls of local government, but that ultimately many of those questions will spill over into the Courts. The battle over the bill was hard fought, and fraught with significant practical problems. Real issues of concern were raised by all of the parties interested in the legislation. Activists sought the maximum release of information; advocates for local government sought restraint on release of documents where security of the public, or sensitivity to private issues, could arise. Local governments were, and are, concerned about the requirements of the new open-records law and the impact on already overworked staff.

The prior open-records law, first enacted in 1957, generated many court cases. It is likely that the new law will likewise engender decades worth of disputes.

With the good will of citizens and elected officials alike, however, the continued success of our unique American self-government is assured.

The Law, living up to her name as a jealous mistress, saw enactment of critical changes to the Local Tax Enabling Act just as final proofs were being prepared for this seventh edition. The new law substantially changes the way Pennsylvania's local income taxes are collected. After years of study, and negotiations between the government and the business community, the new law consolidates collection of earned income taxes at the county level. Significant administrative reforms are to be implemented. The new enactment establishes a tax collection committee in each county district. Each political subdivision imposing an earned income tax will appoint one voting delegate, with the intended result being the streamlining of tax collection, and a cost savings to all. Solicitors, private lawyers, and laypeople alike will of course be called upon to iron out many disputes and discrepancies as they arise.

As a final blow to publishing timelines, the Legislature, as this book went to press enacted yet another attempt to deal with the issue of challenges to procedurally invalid ordinances under the Municipalities Planning Code. Having spent, and still spending, an enormous amount of time in Court on an issue revolving around procedural invalidity of an important ordinance, the enormity of the problem is obvious. The presses were proverbially stopped, and the Legislature's recent attempt to deal with the issue is incorporated in this volume. It is unclear whether the latest legislative attempt to purportedly protect political subdivisions from their own procedural errors will succeed. The last two attempts were declared unconstitutional by the Supreme Court.

Darrell M. Zaslow, Esq.

Preface to the Sixth Edition

April, 2007

It is now more critical than ever that we dedicate and rededicate ourselves to the difficult and worthy task of self-governance. The world is in turmoil. Lawlessness is absurdly rampant across much of the globe. We see issues arising, profound issues of war and destruction, which are global in scope. Yet it is at the municipal level that destruction unfolds, and it is there that law must start. It is in the towns and cities of the world that human beings are made to suffer, and societies collapse. We see it is no longer the day of the great battlefield, of two opposing armies, fought in a far-off field. Today's wars are fought at the municipal level, where the people live. Bombs in the streets and marketplace, they think violence to be virtue, as if mayhem would ever improve their lot.

Here in the townships and cities of Pennsylvania, and throughout the other States, we have good and fortune. We continue to cherish the values that have ennobled us, and prospered us, since the first days of our nation and state. The Common Law traditions of our society are as dynamic as ever, and we continue to protect, and be protected by, our Constitutions. May this mode of American self-government ever sustain us, with liberty, with justice, and with peace.

This sixth edition of the Municipal Law Source has been fully redesigned to aid the user, and several important new sections have been added. The statutes necessary to the practitioner of Municipal Law have been grouped into five broad subject-areas. The side margins will assist in locating a particular statute. The right hand margin of each page highlights the main subject area; flipping through the left hand margin within each main subject area should facilitate speedy arrival at the statute.

An editor is in many ways like the hand of Heaven-finding the errors, and correcting them. In that regard, the editorial devotion of Tony DiGioia, Editor-in-chief of the publisher, is unsurpassed in professionalism and personal warmth. Aided by Frank Coyne in painstaking perusal of every section and word, their efforts are vital to final publication in finished form. Our thanks also to Stephen P. Imms, Jr., Esq., practicing up in Harleysville, for his kind words regarding the usefulness of this book, and suggestion for inclusion of material. Ideas for improvement are always appreciated.

This book again takes advantage of the excellent assistance in research and preparation offered by Mr. Levi Zaslow, a student at the University of Baltimore School of Law, Managing Editor of the University of Baltimore Law Forum, and National Trial Competition Trial Team Member. Levi Zaslow's joint participation in the legal details and creativity of this publication has enhanced the work, and is very much appreciated. From the barristers of Old England to the bar associations of the 21st century, lawyers have been the leaven of the law. It is the attorney-at-law who kneads esoteric legal concepts into the living of life. We *Juris Doctors,* who know the law and are agile practitioners of it, make the law work. We look forward to Levi Zaslow joining us at the Bar, and sharing in that glorious task.

Darrell M. Zaslow, Esq.

Preface to the Fifth Edition

October, 2005

Once again the greatness of America, and the Commonwealth of Pennsylvania, is evident in the ongoing legislative effort to improve society at our most basic level of government. While much of the world is engaged in war and the battle against terrorist violence, here at home solid Municipal Law continues to improve our communities. If only the evil ones in this world would concentrate on the nuts and bolts of good local government, instead of seeking to do harm to others! Perhaps they would find that building first-rate government, while hard work fraught with difficulties and disagreements, is the solution to the well being of all of our citizens and families.

The preface to the 4th edition of this Lawsource lamented the need to include a new chapter, *Counterterrorism Planning,* as a result of the infamous attacks of September 11th. As this preface to this 5th edition of the Municipal Lawsource goes to print, the country is reeling from the effects of Hurricane Katrina, which utterly destroyed New Orleans and many municipalities in other states, and Hurricanes Rita and Wilma struck with similar fury. The fury of many in the country over the alleged unpreparedness of government to deal with these natural disasters prompted inclusion herein of the Pennsylvania law governing *Local Emergency Management Services.* We pray that such emergencies, natural or otherwise, will never affect us, but preparedness is second only to prayer in averting catastrophe.

It is a particular honor to acknowledge the significant contribution of Mr. Levi Zaslow to this 5th edition of Bisel's Municipal Lawsource. It was Levi Zaslow, presently a student at the University of Baltimore School of Law, who expended the extensive and intensive effort required to examine and meticulously update the thousands of statutory sections appearing in this volume. Levi's precise and excellent workmanship, and his many suggestions for implementing improvements to the book's format, will be appreciated by the many lawyers and other professionals who have come to rely upon this Lawsource in their daily practice of municipal law. As always, we welcome and request any corrections, and suggestions for inclusion of additional materials.

Preface to the Fourth Edition

October, 2004

The span of two years since publication of the last edition of this municipal Lawsource has witnessed extraordinary change in the world. On the home front, the Legislature continues to tinker with our Statutes, ever seeking the proper balance between individual and municipal rights and responsibilities. New regulations governing housing construction, published statewide for the first time in Pennsylvania's history, are intended to provide safety and uniformity in the construction burgeoning around our region. In the area of land use, skyrocketing land and home values have placed new pressures on the planning and growth of communities. It is part of the strength of our Commonwealth and our Nation that we seek to comtemplate and enact good laws, and search for the best methods of government.

Concern for the religious belief of all residents of the Commonwealth prompted enactment of the *Religious Freedom Protection Act*. The Act seeks to insure that state and local governments will not substantially burden the free exercise of religion without compelling justification. The legislature announced that all of its laws, heretofore or hereafter enacted, and all laws enacted by all municipalities, other than the Construction Code, shall be construed so as to avoid the imposition of substantial burdens on religious practices.

While the legislature was devoting its talents to enactment of laws to protect freedom, others in the world were dedicating themselves to evil lawlessness. The new world and its post September 11th, 2001 war and violence has had an impact upon municipalities in our State, prompting passage of the *Counterterrorism Planning, Preparedness, and Response Act*. The Act incorporates our Pennsylvania municipalities into the search for security. While the legislature was devoting its talents to enactment of laws to protect freedom, it became sadly necessarily to also protect against the purveyors of terror. The mundane aspects of Municipal law pale in comparison to the disdain for life and law now raging over the global community. May our legislatures and boards and councils have the luxury of tinkering with the niceties of our municipal law, in a world of peace through justice and law.

Preface to the Third Edition

August, 2002

The legislature continues to refine the laws governing local municipalities in the Commonwealth of Pennsylvania. Certain changes in the law will have a significant effect upon the everyday lives of the residents of our townships and boroughs, such as new provisions of the Municipalities Planning Code mandating zoning permission for home-based business activities. The Open Records Law, an important gatekeeper between citizens and their local government, was completely revamped just as this third edition goes to press. Significant litigation is likely to result, as local governments balance what is all too frequently a penchant for secrecy in some municipalities, against what are all too often unnecessarily incessant demands for information by local gadflies. The public has a right to know, but government has the burden of functioning both forthrightly and efficiently. It is a tough balance on the scales of justice.

Other changes will affect the practitioner of municipal law. These changes include, at long last, an attempt to renumber the Municipalities Authorities Act, which up until now boasted perhaps the longest and most incomprehensible sequence of sections and subsections of any law on the books. It is hoped that the new codification will allow practicing attorneys to find the law without using an abacus. Citations in the prior law, such as 306(B)(t)(1)(iii)(A)(III) should be illegal. The new codification is somewhat better, although it has already been amended in several sections to correct problems discovered in the initial enactment. More such discrepancies are likely to surface, and practitioners are urged to contact their state representatives to suggest improvements.

New enactments relative to Code Enforcement and Neighborhood Improvement Districts reflect legislative attempts at problem solving, using appropriate carrots and sticks. All of the enactments are intended to improve the quality of life for the residents of Pennsylvania. It is a hope shared by all that the Law will contribute to that end.

Preface to the Second Edition

September, 2000

This second edition of ***The Pennsylvania Municipal Lawsource*** incorporates changes recently enacted in the various codes and statutes governing the day-to-day life of local municipalities, including a new Law which may significantly affect many Townships and Boroughs. The Construction Code Act, for the first time in Pennsylvania history, now requires certain minimum building standards and contains procedures for townships wishing to grandfather prior codes, or enact codes at variance with the 1999 BOCA code. Developers and their attorneys may wish to examine provisions of the Act which provide for a limited right of appeal of overly stringent building codes within the first 30 days of ordinance enactment.

Also newly included in the ***Lawsource*** is the Pennsylvania Municipal Authorities Act, which was requested by several esteemed members of the Bar after review of the book's first edition, including Gilbert High, Esq., of Norristown, and Edward Rudolph, Esq., of Bensalem. Out in Emporium, Pa., Paul Malizia, Esq., who requested inclusion of the Public Contracts-Bidding Law, avoided service as a municipal solicitor for 15 years before succumbing to the lure and lunacy of becoming The Township Solicitor. Their input for enhancing the value of this publication is appreciated, as are any and all suggestions for revisions or inclusion of other materials.

Significant amendments to The Municipalities Planning Code, effective August 22, 2000, empower multi-municipal planning and comprehensive plans. The impact of these amendments, touted as the most comprehensive in 30 years, remains to be seen.

Original Preface

February, 1998

The great freedoms of our democracy initially sprout where the grass roots grow. Local government is responsible for the streets where we live, the centers where we shop, the businesses where we work, and the places where we play and pray. Pennsylvania municipalities have a long and proud history of implementing the American way, and a primary source of this success is Pennsylvania Municipal Law.

The need for a consolidated compilation of the relevant laws governing Pennsylvania Municipalities became apparent during service as Solicitor for Bensalem, Bucks County, the largest Second Class Township in Pennsylvania. Proper preparedness for meetings of the township Council often required attendance with a brief case full of books.

This book is intended for the four groups participating in local government. *Lawyers,* whether representing the government, business interests, or citizens, need to appear in public with the law at their fingertips. The second group, *elected officials,* place an over-reliance on the lawyers. Good government is more likely when elected and appointed officials also know the laws by which they govern the rest of us. The third group, the many *citizens* who actively participate in and monitor their local government, should likewise be well armed with accurate statutes. The law should never be the property of just the lawyers and officials. The fourth group, *the local press,* might augment their attempts at accurate reporting with the law in hand.

Local Government is significantly enhanced when all four groups—the lawyers, the officials, the citizens, and the press have ready access to the laws by which we govern ourselves at the local level. Bisel's Municipal Lawsource attempts to answer that need.

The author expresses gratitude to the Township of Bensalem, where good Government is a shared value and a frequently achieved goal. Gratitutde is likewise expressed to those without whom this book, the practice of law, and life in general would be impossible: especially Lewis A. Walder, Esq., mentor, partner, and friend; my ever pleasant and diligent secretary, Stacie A. Roberts; Tony DiGioia, Esq., Editor in Chief of the Bisel Co.; my honored parents; my wife, Sherri for her willing acceptance of that jealous mistress, the law; our four wonderful children, Dorie, Janna, Levi & Joshua; and lastly, inadequate gratitude is expressed to the Source of All Law, for the blessing of opportunity to prepare this manuscript.

Darrell M. Zaslow
Attorney-at-Law

TABLE OF CONTENTS
(Condensed)

TABLE OF CONTENTS
(Detailed)

PART I
ETHICS, RECORDS, AND OPEN MEETINGS

CHAPTER 1
SUNSHINE ACT
OPEN MEETINGS LAW
65 Pa.C.S. §§ 701–716

CHAPTER 2
RIGHT-TO-KNOW LAW; INSPECTION, COPYING, AND DISPOSITION OF RECORDS

CHAPTER 2.1
RIGHT-TO-KNOW LAW
65 P.S. §§ 67.101–67.3104

TABLE OF CONTENTS—ETHICS, RECORDS, OPEN MEETINGS

CHAPTER 2.2

DISPOSITION OF RECORDS

53 P.S. §§ 1381–1389

CHAPTER 2.3

MUNICIPAL DEED REGISTRATION ACT

21 P.S. § 338.3

CHAPTER 3

PUBLIC OFFICIAL AND EMPLOYEE ETHICS ACT CONFLICTS OF INTEREST; OATH OF OFFICE

65 Pa.C.S. §§ 1101–1113

65 P.S. § 410

53 Pa.C.S. § 1141

PART II
TAXATION

CHAPTER 4

LOCAL TAX ENABLING ACT

53 P.S. §§ 6924.101–6924.901

CHAPTER 1

PRELIMINARY PROVISIONS

CHAPTER 2

[Reserved]

CHAPTER 3

LOCAL TAXES

CHAPTER 4

OPTIONAL OCCUPATION TAX ELIMINATION

CHAPTER 5

CONSOLIDATED COLLECTION OF LOCAL INCOME TAXES

CHAPTER 6

[Reserved]

CHAPTER 7

COLLECTION OF DELINQUENT TAXES

CHAPTER 8

[Reserved]

Table of Contents
Part I Ch. 1–3 Ethics, Records, Open Meetings
Part II Ch. 4–10 Taxation
Part III Ch. 11–18 Torts, Contracts & Civil Rules
Part IV Ch. 19–24 Zoning & Planning
Part V Ch. 25–30 Construction and Emergency Codes
Part VI Ch. 31–39 Municipal Codes
Index

CHAPTER 9
MISCELLANEOUS PROVISIONS

CHAPTER 5

LOCAL TAX COLLECTION LAW
72 P.S. §§ 5511.1–5511.42

CHAPTER 6

LOCAL GOVERNMENT UNIT DEBT ACT

53 Pa. C.S. §§ 8001 et seq.

Sec.

CHAPTER 7

OPTIONAL OCCUPATION TAX ELIMINATION ACT

53 P.S. §§ 6927.1–6927.9

[REPEALED]

Table of Contents
Part I Ch. 1–3 Ethics, Records, Open Meetings
Part II Ch. 4–10 Taxation
Part III Ch. 11–18 Torts, Contracts & Civil Rules
Part IV Ch. 19–24 Zoning & Planning
Part V Ch. 25–30 Construction and Emergency Codes
Part VI Ch. 31–39 Municipal Codes
Index

CHAPTER 8

LOCAL TAXPAYERS BILL OF RIGHTS

58 Pa.C.S. §§ 8421-8438

CHAPTER 9

NEIGHBORHOOD IMPROVEMENT DISTRICT ACT

73 P.S. §§ 831–840

CHAPTER 10

RESIDENTIAL VISITABILITY DESIGN TAX CREDIT ACT

72 P.S. § 4751-101 to § 4751-106

PART III
TORTS, CONTRACTS, AND CIVIL RULES

CHAPTER 11

TORT CLAIMS ACT

42 Pa.C.S. §§ 8501–8564

CHAPTER 12

CONTRACTS FOR PUBLIC WORKS

62 Pa.C.S. §§ 3902–3942

Sec.

NONRECEIPT OF BIDS

73 P.S. §§ 1641–1644

CHAPTER 13

ELECTRONIC BIDDING BY LOCAL GOVERNMENT UNITS

62 Pa.C.S. §§ 4601–4604

Sec.

CHAPTER 14

PUBLIC WORKS CONTRACTORS' BONDS

8 P.S. §§ 191 et seq.

CHAPTER 15

PREVAILING WAGE ACT

43 P.S. §§ 165-1 et seq.

CHAPTER 16

LIMITATION OF ACTIONS AND APPEALS GENERALLY

42 Pa.C.S. §§ 5522, 5524, 5571, & 5572

Table of Contents
Part I Ch. 1–3 Ethics, Records, Open Meetings
Part II Ch. 4–10 Taxation
Part III Ch. 11–18 Torts, Contracts & Civil Rules
Part IV Ch. 19–24 Zoning & Planning
Part V Ch. 25–30 Construction and Emergency Codes
Part VI Ch. 31–39 Municipal Codes
Index

CHAPTER 17

PENNSYLVANIA RULES OF CIVIL PROCEDURE
ACTION IN MANDAMUS

CHAPTER 18

PENNSYLVANIA RULES OF CIVIL PROCEDURE
THE COMMONWEALTH AND POLITICAL SUBDIVISIONS AS PARTIES

PART IV
ZONING AND PLANNING

CHAPTER 19

PENNSYLVANIA MUNICIPALITIES PLANNING CODE
53 P.S. §§ 10101–11202

ARTICLE I. GENERAL PROVISIONS

TABLE OF CONTENTS—PART IV

ARTICLE II. PLANNING AGENCIES

ARTICLE III. COMPREHENSIVE PLAN

ARTICLE IV. OFFICIAL MAP

ARTICLE V. SUBDIVISION AND LAND DEVELOPMENT

ARTICLE VII-A. TRADITIONAL NEIGHBORHOOD DEVELOPMENT

ARTICLE VIII. ZONING CHALLENGES; GENERAL PROVISIONS [REPEALED]

ARTICLE VIII-A. JOINT MUNICIPAL ZONING

ARTICLE IX. ZONING HEARING BOARD AND OTHER ADMINISTRATIVE PROCEEDINGS

ARTICLE X. APPEALS [REPEALED]

ARTICLE X-A. APPEALS TO COURT

ARTICLE XI. INTERGOVERNMENTAL COOPERATIVE PLANNING AND IMPLEMENTATION AGREEMENTS

ARTICLE XI-A. WASTEWATER PROCESSING COOPERATIVE PLANNING

ARTICLE XII. REPEALS

CHAPTER 19.1

WIRELESS BROADBAND COLLOCATION ACT

53 P.S. §§ 11702.1–11702.6

Sec.

CHAPTER 21-A
GAS AND OIL

LOCAL ORDINANCES RELATING TO OIL AND GAS OPERATION

58 Pa.C.S. §§ 3301–3309

Sec.

CHAPTER 21-B
REGULATION OF LOCAL AGRICULTURE

3 Pa.C.S. §§ 311–522

CHAPTER 3

LOCAL REGULATION

Subchapter

Subchapter A
Preliminary Provisions

Sec.

Subchapter B
Normal Agricultural Operations

Sec.

CHAPTER 5

NUTRIENT MANAGEMENT AND ODOR MANAGEMENT

CHAPTER 22

OPEN SPACE LANDS ACQUISITION AND PRESERVATION

32 P.S. §§ 5001–5013

CHAPTER 22.1

LAND BANKS

68 Pa.C.S. §§ 2101–2120

CHAPTER 23

CONSERVATION AND PRESERVATION EASEMENTS ACT

32 P.S. §§ 5051–5059

CHAPTER 24

RELIGIOUS ISSUES

CHAPTER 24.1

RELIGIOUS LAND USE AND INSTITUTIONALIZED PERSONS ACT OF 2000

42 U.S.C. §§ 2000cc et seq. (Federal Law)

CHAPTER 24.2

PENNSYLVANIA RELIGIOUS FREEDOM PROTECTION ACT

ACT NO. 2002–214

71 P.S. §§ 2401–2408

PART V
CONSTRUCTION AND EMERGENCY CODES

CHAPTER 25

CONSTRUCTION CODE ACT

35 P.S. §§ 7210.101–7210.1103

Chapter 1. Preliminary Provisions

Chapter 3. Uniform Construction Code

Chapter 5. Adoption and Enforcement by Municipalities

Table of Contents
Part I Ch. 1–3 Ethics, Records, Open Meetings
Part II Ch. 4–10 Taxation
Part III Ch. 11–18 Torts, Contracts & Civil Rules
Part IV Ch. 19–24 Zoning & Planning
Part V Ch. 25–30 Construction and Emergency Codes
Part VI Ch. 31–39 Municipal Codes
Index

CHAPTER 26

UNIFORM CONSTRUCTION CODE REGULATIONS

Title 34: The Pennsylvania Code

Chapter 401. TRAINING AND CERTIFICATION OF CODE ADMINISTRATORS

Chapter 403. ADMINISTRATION

GENERALLY

STANDARDS

PERMIT AND INSPECTION PROCESS FOR COMMERCIAL CONSTRUCTION

PERMIT AND INSPECTION PROCESS FOR RESIDENTIAL BUILDINGS

DEPARTMENT, MUNICIPAL AND THIRD-PARTY ENFORCEMENT FOR NONCOMPLIANCE

MUNICIPAL ELECTION

BOARD OF APPEALS

DEPARTMENT ENFORCEMENT

Chapter 405. ELEVATORS AND OTHER LIFTING DEVICES

STAGE, ORCHESTRA AND ORGAN CONSOLE ELEVATORS

CHAPTER 27.1

MUNICIPAL CODE AND ORDINANCE COMPLIANCE ACT AND BLIGHT

68 P.S. §§ 1081–1083

CHAPTER 27.2

MUNICIPALITY CONDEMNATION ORDER ACT

53 P.S. §§ 4271–4277

CHAPTER 27.3

FAILURE TO COMPLY WITH A CODE REQUIREMENT

53 Pa.C.S. § 6115

CHAPTER 27.4

NEIGHBORHOOD BLIGHT RECLAMATION AND REVITALIZATION ACT

53 Pa.C.S. § 6101-6145

Chapter 61. Neighborhood Blight Reclamation and Revitalization

CHAPTER 27.5

ABANDONED AND BLIGHTED PROPERTY CONSERVATORSHIP ACT

68 P.S. §§ 1101–1111

CHAPTER 27.6

BLIGHTED PROPERTY—DEFINITION

CHAPTER 28

SOCIAL SECURITY NUMBER PRIVACY ACT

71 P.S. §§ 2601–2608

CHAPTER 29

COUNTERTERRORISM PLANNING, PREPAREDNESS AND RESPONSE ACT

35 P.S. §§ 2140.101–303

Chapter 1. General Provisions

Chapter 2. Counterterrorism Planning, Preparedness and Response

Chapter 3. Public Health Emergency Measures

CHAPTER 30

EMERGENCY MANAGEMENT SERVICES CODE

35 Pa. C.S. §§ 7101–7111

35 Pa. C.S. §§ 7501–7515

PART VI

MUNICIPAL CODES

CHAPTER 31

MUNICIPALITY AUTHORITIES ACT

53 Pa.C.S. §§ 5601–5623

CHAPTER 32

WATER SERVICES ACT

53 P.S. §§ 3102.101 et seq.

Chapter 1. Preliminary Provisions

Chapter 3. Municipal Authority Approval of Actions

Chapter 5. Water Utilities

Chapter 40. Miscellaneous Provisions

CHAPTER 33

HOME RULE AND OPTIONAL PLANS GOVERNMENT

53 Pa.C.S. §§ 2901–3171

Chapter 29. General Provisions

Subchapter A. Preliminary Provisions

Subchapter B. Procedure for Adoption of Home Rule Charter or Optional Plan of Government

Subchapter B. Treasurer

Subchapter C. Appointment Power and Personnel

Subchapter D. Filling Vacancies in Elected Office

Subchapter E. Legislation by Council.

Subchapter F. Audit and Control

Subchapter G. Transition to Optional Plan Government.

Subchapter H. Repeal of Optional Plan

CHAPTER 34

FIRST CLASS TOWNSHIP CODE

53 P.S. §§ 55101 to 58502

Sec.

ARTICLE I. PRELIMINARY PROVISIONS

TABLE OF CONTENTS—FIRST CLASS TOWNSHIP CODE

ARTICLE II. CLASSIFICATION, CREATION, REESTABLISHMENT AND CHANGE OF NAME OF TOWNSHIPS

ARTICLE II.I. CHANGE OF NAME OF TOWNSHIP OF FIRST CLASS

ARTICLE III. TOWNSHIP LINES AND BOUNDARIES [REPEALED]

ARTICLE IV. WARDS

ARTICLE V. ELECTION OF OFFICERS; VACANCIES IN OFFICE

ARTICLE VI. GENERAL PROVISIONS RELATING TO TOWNSHIP OFFICERS

ARTICLE VII. TOWNSHIP COMMISSIONERS

ARTICLE VIII. TOWNSHIP TREASURER

ARTICLE VIII REPEALED effective January 6, 2014

ARTICLE VIII-A. APPOINTED TOWNSHIP TREASURER

ARTICLE VIII-B. TAX COLLECTOR

ARTICLE IX. TOWNSHIP SECRETARY

ARTICLE X. AUDITORS

ARTICLE XI. CONTROLLER

ARTICLE XII. TOWNSHIP SOLICITOR

ARTICLE XIII. TOWNSHIP ENGINEER

ARTICLE XIII-A. TOWNSHIP MANAGER

ARTICLE XIII-B. VETERANS' AFFAIRS

ARTICLE XIV. POLICE

ARTICLE XV. CORPORATE POWERS

ARTICLE XV-A. REAL ESTATE REGISTRY

ARTICLE XVI. PUBLIC HEALTH

ARTICLE XVII. FINANCE AND TAXATION

ARTICLE XVIII. CONTRACTS

ARTICLE XIX. EMINENT DOMAIN; ASSESSMENT OF DAMAGES AND BENEFITS

ARTICLE XX. STREETS AND HIGHWAYS

ARTICLE XXI. BOUNDARY ROADS AND STREETS

ARTICLE XXII. BRIDGES

ARTICLE XXIII. SIDEWALKS

ARTICLE XXIV. SANITARY SEWERS AND DRAINS

ARTICLE XXV. COLLECTION BY INSTALMENT OF THE COST OF STREET, CURB, SIDEWALK AND SEWER IMPROVEMENTS

ARTICLE XXV-A. ASSESSMENTS FOR PUBLIC IMPROVEMENTS

ARTICLE XXVI. REVOLVING FUND FOR STREET AND SEWER IMPROVEMENTS

ARTICLE XXVII. WATER SUPPLY

ARTICLE XXX-A. LAND SUBDIVISION

ARTICLE XXXI. ZONING

ARTICLE XXXI-A. UNIFORM CONSTRUCTION CODE, PROPERTY MAINTENANCE CODE AND RESERVED POWERS

ARTICLE XXXII. TOWNSHIP PLANNING COMMISSION

ARTICLE XXXIII. ENFORCEMENT OF ORDINANCES

CHAPTER 35

SECOND CLASS TOWNSHIP CODE

53 P.S. §§ 65101–68701

Sec.

ARTICLE XI. TOWNSHIP SOLICITOR

ARTICLE XII. TOWNSHIP ENGINEER

ARTICLE XIII. TOWNSHIP MANAGER

ARTICLE XIV. COUNTY AND STATE ASSOCIATIONS OF TOWNSHIPS

ARTICLE XV. CORPORATE POWERS

ARTICLE XXII. PARKS, RECREATION CENTERS AND FORESTS

ARTICLE XXIII. ROADS, STREETS, BRIDGES AND HIGHWAYS

ARTICLE XXIV. SIDEWALKS, FOOTPATHS AND CURBS

ARTICLE XXV. SANITARY SEWERS

ARTICLE XXVI. WATER SUPPLY

ARTICLE XXVII. STORM WATER MANAGEMENT PLANS AND FACILITIES

ARTICLE XXVIII. MANUFACTURE AND SALE OF ELECTRICITY

ARTICLE XXIX. SHADE TREE COMMISSION

ARTICLE XXX. BOARD OF HEALTH

ARTICLE XXXI. CONTRACTS

ARTICLE XXXII. TAXATION AND FINANCE

ARTICLE XXXIII. COLLECTION OF ASSESSMENTS

ARTICLE XXXIV. EMINENT DOMAIN; ASSESSMENT OF DAMAGES AND BENEFITS

ARTICLE XXXV. VIOLATION OF ACT GENERALLY

ARTICLE XXXVI. ACTIONS BY TOWNSHIPS

ARTICLE XXXVII. REPEALS

CHAPTER 36

THE BOROUGH CODE

8 Pa.C.S.A. §§ 101–3501

Chapter 1. Preliminary Provisions

Chapter 7. Associations and Organizations

Chapter 8. Elections of Officers

Subchapter A. General Provisions

Subchapter B. Members of Council

Subchapter C. Mayor (Reserved)

Subchapter D. Auditors (Reserved)

Subchapter E. Controller (Reserved)

Subchapter F. Assessors (Reserved)

Subchapter G. Tax Collector (Reserved)

Chapter 9. Vacancies in Office

Chapter 10. Powers and Duties of Elected Officials

Subchapter A. Council

Chapter 11. Powers, Duties and Rights of Appointed Officers and Employees

Subchapter A. General Provisions

Subchapter B. Treasurer

Subchapter C. Secretary

Subchapter D. Solicitor

Subchapter E. Police

Subchapter F. Police Pension Fund in Boroughs Having Police Force of Less Than Three Members

Subchapter G. Manager

Subchapter H. Planning Commission (Reserved)

Subchapter I. Mine and Quarry Inspection and Surface Support (Reserved)

Subchapter J. Civil Service for Police and Fire Apparatus Operators

Chapter 15. Eminent Domain, Assessment of Damages and Damages for Injury to Property

Subchapter A. General Provisions Relating to Eminent Domain

Subchapter B. Procedure for Assessment of Benefits by Viewers (Reserved)

Subchapter C. Damages for Injury to Property

Chapter 16. Land Subdivision (Reserved)

Chapter 17. Streets

Subchapter A. General Provisions

Subchapter B. Plan of Streets

Subchapter C. Laying Out Streets

Subchapter D. Opening, Acceptance and Vacation of Streets

Subchapter E. Vacating Streets (Reserved)

Subchapter F. Straightening and Relocating Streets

Subchapter G. Improvement of Borough Streets

Chapter 26. Wharves and Docks

Chapter 27. Recreation Places, Shade Trees and Forests

Subchapter A. Parks and Playgrounds

Subchapter B. Shade Trees

Subchapter C. Forests

Chapter 28. Cemeteries

Chapter 29. Licenses and License Fees

Chapter 29A. Veterans' Affairs

Subchapter A. Pennsylvania National Guard

Subchapter B. Support of Veterans' Organizations

Chapter 30. Real Estate Registry (Reserved)

Chapter 31. Health and Sanitation

Chapter 32. Zoning (Reserved)

Chapter 32A. Uniform Construction Code, Property Maintenance Code and Reserved Powers

Chapter 33. Ordinances

Subchapter A. General Provisions

Subchapter B. Enforcement

Chapter 34. Actions by and Against Boroughs (Reserved)

Chapter 35. Acts of Assembly Repealed and Saving Clause

CHAPTER 37-A

THIRD CLASS CITY CODE

11 Pa.C.S. §§ 101–14702

Chapter 101. Preliminary Provisions

Chapter 102. Procedures for Incorporation

Chapter 103. Change of Corporate Title

Chapter 112A. City Administrator

Chapter 114. City Treasurer

Chapter 115. City Engineer

Chapter 116. City Solicitor

Chapter 117. City Controller and Independent Auditor

Subchapter A. City Controller

Subchapter B. Independent Auditor

Chapter 118. Accounts and Finances

Chapter 119. Contracts

Chapter 120. Police Force

Chapter 121. Fire Bureau

Chapter 122. Surveys and Surface Support in Coal Mining Areas

Chapter 123. Public Health

Subchapter A. Board of Health

Subchapter B. Public Nuisances Detrimental to Public Health

Subchapter C. Corporations Acting as Boards of Health

Subchapter D. Penalty

Chapter 124. Corporate Powers

Chapter 132. Sanitary Sewers

Chapter 134. Watercourses, Flood Protection Projects and Storm Water Systems

Chapter 135. Utility Service

Chapter 136. Public Buildings and Works

Chapter 137. Parks, Playgrounds and Recreation Centers

Chapter 141A. Uniform Construction Code, Property Maintenance Code and Reserved Powers

Chapter 142. Aeronautics

Chapter 143. Pensions

Subchapter A. Police

Subchapter B. Firefighters

Subchapter C. Pension For Employees Other Than Police Officers and City-Paid Firefighters

CHAPTER 37-B

OPTIONAL THIRD CLASS CITY CHARTER LAW

53 P.S. § 41101–41625

ARTICLE V. COUNCIL-MANAGER PLAN

ARTICLE VI. GENERAL PROVISIONS COMMON TO OPTIONAL PLANS

CHAPTER 38

INTERGOVERNMENTAL COOPERATION

53 Pa.C.S. §§ 2301-2317

Title 53

Chapter 23. General Provisions

Subchapter A. Intergovernmental Cooperation

Sec.

CHAPTER 39

RESIDENCY DURING MILITARY SERVICE

53 Pa.C.S. § 1142

Sec.

PART I

ETHICS, RECORDS, AND OPEN MEETINGS

Chapter 1. Sunshine Act: Open Meetings Law
Chapter 2. Right-To-Know Law: Inspection and Copying of Records
Chapter 3. Public Official and Employee Ethics Act; Oath of Office

CHAPTER 1

SUNSHINE ACT: OPEN MEETINGS LAW[1]

65 Pa. C.S. §§ 701–716

Requiring public agencies to hold certain meetings and hearings open to the public; and providing penalties.

TABLE OF CONTENTS

§ 701. Short title.

This act shall be known and may be cited as the Sunshine Act.

§ 702. Legislative findings and declaration.

(a) Findings.—The General Assembly finds that the right of the public to be present at all meetings of agencies and to witness the deliberation, policy formulation and decisionmaking of agencies is vital to the enhancement and

1. 1998, Oct. 15, P.L. 729, No. 93 § 1.

proper functioning of the democratic process and that secrecy in public affairs undermines the faith of the public in government and the public's effectiveness in fulfilling its role in a democratic society.

(b) Declarations.—The General Assembly hereby declares it to be the public policy of this Commonwealth to insure the right of its citizens to have notice of and the right to attend all meetings of agencies at which any agency business is discussed or acted upon as provided in this act.

§ 703. Definitions.

The following words and phrases when used in this act shall have the meanings given to them in this section unless the context clearly indicates otherwise:

"Administrative action." The execution of policies relating to persons or things as previously authorized or required by official action of the agency adopted at an open meeting of the agency. The term does not, however, include the deliberation of agency business.

"Agency." The body, and all committees thereof authorized by the body to take official action or render advice on matters of agency business, of all the following: the General Assembly, the executive branch of the government of this Commonwealth, including the Governor's Cabinet when meeting on official policymaking business, any board, council, authority or commission of the Commonwealth or of any political subdivision of the Commonwealth or any State, municipal, township or school authority, school board, school governing body, commission, the boards of trustees of all State-aided colleges and universities, the councils of trustees of all State-owned colleges and universities, the boards of trustees of all State-related universities and all community colleges or similar organizations created by or pursuant to a statute which declares in substance that the organization performs, or has for its purpose the performance of, an essential governmental function and through the joint action of its members exercises governmental authority and takes official action. The term shall include the governing board of any nonprofit corporation which by a mutually binding legal written agreement with a community college or State-aided, State-owned or State-related institution of higher education is granted legally enforceable supervisory and advisory powers regarding the degree programs of the institution of higher education. The term does not include a caucus nor a meeting of an ethics committee created under rules of the Senate or House of Representatives. (amended 2004, July 15, P.L. 743, No. 88 §1)

"Agency business." The framing, preparation, making or enactment of laws, policy or regulations, the creation of liability by contract or otherwise or the adjudication of rights, duties and responsibilities, but not including administrative action.

"Caucus." A gathering of members of a political party or coalition which is held for purposes of planning political strategy and holding discussions designed to prepare the members for taking official action in the General Assembly.

"Conference." Any training program or seminar, or any session arranged by State or Federal agencies for local agencies, organized and conducted for the sole purpose of providing information to agency members on matters directly related to their official responsibilities.

"Deliberation." The discussion of agency business held for the purpose of making a decision.

"Emergency meeting." A meeting called for the purpose of dealing with a real or potential emergency involving a clear and present danger to life or property.

"Executive session." A meeting from which the public is excluded, although the agency may admit those persons necessary to carry out the purpose of the meeting.

"Litigation." Any pending, proposed or current action or matter subject to appeal before a court of law or administrative adjudicative body, the decision of which may be appealed to a court of law.

"Meeting." Any prearranged gathering of an agency which is attended or participated in by a quorum of the members of an agency held for the purpose of deliberating agency business or taking official action.

"Official action."

(1) Recommendations made by an agency pursuant to statute, ordinance or executive order.

(2) The establishment of policy by an agency.

(3) The decisions on agency business made by an agency.

(4) The vote taken by an agency on any motion, proposal, resolution, rule, regulation, ordinance, report or order.

"Political subdivision." Any county, city, borough, incorporated town, township, school district, intermediate unit, vocational school district or county institution district.

"Public notice."

(1) For a meeting:

(i) Publication of notice of the place, date and time of a meeting in a newspaper of general circulation, as defined by 45 Pa.C.S. § 101 (relating to definitions), which is published and circulated in the political subdivision where the meeting will be held, or in a newspaper of general circulation which has a bona fide paid circulation in the political subdivision equal to or greater than any newspaper published in the political subdivision.

(ii) Posting a notice of the place, date and time of a meeting prominently at the principal office of the agency holding the meeting or at the public building in which the meeting is to be held.

(iii) Giving notice to parties under section 709(c) (relating to public notice).

(2) For a recessed or reconvened meeting:

(i) Posting a notice of the place, date and time of the meeting prominently at the principal office of the agency holding the meeting or at the public building in which the meeting is to be held.

(ii) Giving notice to parties under section 709(c).

"Special meeting." A meeting scheduled by an agency after the agency's regular schedule of meetings has been established.

§ 704. Open meetings.

Official action and deliberations by a quorum of the members of an agency shall take place at a meeting open to the public unless closed under section 707 (relating to exceptions to open meetings), 708 (relating to executive sessions) or 712 (relating to General Assembly meetings covered).

§ 705. Recording of votes.

In all meetings of agencies, the vote of each member who actually votes on any resolution, rule, order, regulation, ordinance or the setting of official policy must be publicly cast and, in the case of roll call votes, recorded.

§ 706. Minutes of meetings, public records and recording of meetings.

Written minutes shall be kept of all open meetings of agencies. The minutes shall include:

(1) The date, time and place of the meeting.

Table of Contents
Part I Ch. 1–3 Ethics, Records, Open Meetings
Part II Ch. 4–10 Taxation
Part III Ch. 11–18 Torts, Contracts & Civil Rules
Part IV Ch. 19–24 Zoning & Planning
Part V Ch. 25–30 Construction and Emergency Codes
Part VI Ch. 31–39 Municipal Codes
Index

(2) The names of members present.

(3) The substance of all official actions and a record by individual member of the roll call votes taken.

(4) The names of all citizens who appeared officially and the subject of their testimony.

§ 707. Exceptions to open meetings.

(a) Executive session.—An agency may hold an executive session under section 708 (relating to executive sessions).

(b) Conference.—An agency is authorized to participate in a conference which need not be open to the public. Deliberation of agency business may not occur at a conference.

(c) Certain working sessions.—Boards of auditors may conduct working sessions not open to the public for the purpose of examining, analyzing, discussing and deliberating the various accounts and records with respect to which such boards are responsible, so long as official action of a board with respect to such records and accounts is taken at a meeting open to the public and subject to the provisions of this chapter.

§ 708. Executive sessions.

(a) Purpose.—An agency may hold an executive session for one or more of the following reasons:

(1) To discuss any matter involving the employment, appointment, termination of employment, terms and conditions of employment, evaluation of performance, promotion or disciplining of any specific prospective public officer or employee or current public officer or employee employed or appointed by the agency, or former public officer or employee, provided, however, that the individual employees or appointees whose rights could be adversely affected may request, in writing, that the matter or matters be discussed at an open meeting. The agency's decision to discuss such matters in executive session shall not serve to adversely affect the due process rights granted by law, including those granted by Title 2 of the Pennsylvania Consolidated Statutes (relating to administrative law and procedure). The provisions of this paragraph shall not apply to any meeting involving the appointment or selection of any person to fill a vacancy in any elected office.

(2) To hold information, strategy and negotiation sessions related to the negotiation or arbitration of a collective bargaining agreement or, in the absence of a collective bargaining unit, related to labor relations and arbitration.

(3) To consider the purchase or lease of real property up to the time an option to purchase or lease the real property is obtained or up to the time an agreement to purchase or lease such property is obtained if the agreement is obtained directly without an option.

(4) To consult with its attorney or other professional advisor regarding information or strategy in connection with litigation or with issues on which identifiable complaints are expected to be filed.

(5) To review and discuss agency business which, if conducted in public, would violate a lawful privilege or lead to the disclosure of information or confidentiality protected by law, including matters related to the initiation and conduct of investigations of possible or certain violations of the law and quasi-judicial deliberations.

(6) For duly constituted committees of a board or council of trustees of a State-owned, State-aided or State-related college or university or community college or of the Board of Governors of the State System of Higher Education to discuss matters of academic admission or standings.

(7) To discuss, plan or review matters and records that are deemed necessary for emergency preparedness, protection of public safety and security of all property in a manner that if disclosed would be reasonably likely to jeopardize or threaten public safety or preparedness or public protection.

(b) Procedure.—The executive session may be held during an open meeting, at the conclusion of an open meeting, or may be announced for a future time. The reason for holding the executive session must be announced at the open meeting occurring immediately prior or subsequent to the executive session. If the executive session is not announced for a future specific time, members of the agency shall be notified 24 hours in advance of the time of the convening of the meeting specifying the date, time, location and purpose of the executive session.

(c) Limitation.—Official action on discussions held pursuant to subsection (a) shall be taken at an open meeting. Nothing in this section or section 707 (relating to exceptions to open meetings) shall be construed to require that any meeting be closed to the public, nor shall any executive session be used as a subterfuge to defeat the purposes of section 704 (relating to open meetings).

§ 709. Public notice.

(a) Meetings.—An agency shall give public notice of its first regular meeting of each calendar or fiscal year not less than three days in advance of the meeting and shall give public notice of the schedule of its remaining regular meetings. An agency shall give public notice of each special meeting or each rescheduled regular or special meeting at least 24 hours in advance of the time of the convening of the meeting specified in the notice. Public notice is not required in the case of an emergency meeting or a conference. Professionl licensing boards within the Bureau of Professional and Occupational Affairs of the Department of State of the Commonwealth shall include in the public notice each matter involving a proposal to revoke, suspend or restrict a license.

(b) Notice.—With respect to any provision of this act that requires public notice to be given by a certain date, the agency, to satisfy its legal obligation, must give the notice in time to allow it to be published or circulated within the political subdivision where the principal office of the agency is located or the meeting will occur before the date of the specified meeting.

(c) Copies.—In addition to the public notice required by this section, the agency holding a meeting shall supply, upon request, copies of the public notice thereof to any newspaper of general circulation in the political subdivision in which the meeting will be held, to any radio or television station which regularly broadcasts into the political subdivision and to any interested parties if the newspaper, station or party provides the agency with a stamped, self-addressed envelope prior to the meeting.

(c.1) Notification of agency business to be considered.—

(1) In addition to any public notice required under this section, an agency shall provide the following notification of agency business to be considered at a meeting as follows:

(i) If the agency has a publicly accessible Internet website, the agency shall post the agenda, which includes a listing of each matter of agency business that will be or may be the subject of deliberation or official action at the meeting, on the website no later than 24 hours in advance of the time of the convening of the meeting.

(ii) The agency shall post the agenda, which includes a listing of each matter of agency business that will be or may be the subject of deliberation or official action at the meeting, at the location of the meeting and at the principal office of the agency.

(iii) The agency shall make available to individuals in attendance at the meeting copies of the agenda, which include a listing of each matter of agency

Table of Contents
Part I Ch. 1–3 Ethics, Records, Open Meetings
Part II Ch. 4–10 Taxation
Part III Ch. 11–18 Torts, Contracts & Civil Rules
Part IV Ch. 19–24 Zoning & Planning
Part V Ch. 25–30 Construction and Emergency Codes
Part VI Ch. 31–39 Municipal Codes
Index

business that will be or may be the subject of deliberation or official action at the meeting.

(2) This subsection shall not apply to a conference or a working session under section 707 (relating to exceptions to open meetings) or an executive session under section 708 (relating to executive sessions).

(d) Meetings of General Assembly in Capitol Complex.—Notwithstanding any provision of this section to the contrary, in case of sessions of the General Assembly, all meetings of legislative committees held within the Capitol Complex where bills are considered, including conference committees, all legislative hearings held within the Capitol Complex where testimony is taken and all meetings of legislative commissions held within the Capitol Complex, the requirement for public notice thereof shall be complied with if, not later than the preceding day:

(1) The supervisor of the newsroom of the State Capitol Building in Harrisburg is supplied for distribution to the members of the Pennsylvania Legislative Correspondents Association with a minimum of 30 copies of the notice of the date, time and place of each session, meeting or hearing or the notice is provided via electronic means to an email address designated by the Pennsylvania Legislative Correspondents Association.

(2) There is a posting of the copy of the notice at public places within the Main Capitol Building designated by the Secretary of the Senate and the Chief Clerk of the House of Representatives or the notice is posted on the publicly accessible Internet website of the General Assembly.

(e) Announcement.—Notwithstanding any provision of this act to the contrary, committees may be called into session in accordance with the provisions of the Rules of the Senate or the House of Representatives and an announcement by the presiding officer of the Senate or the House of Representatives. The announcement shall be made in open session of the Senate or the House of Representatives.

§ 710. Rules and regulations for conduct of meetings.

Nothing in this act shall prohibit the agency from adopting, by official action, the rules and regulations necessary for the conduct of its meetings and the maintenance of order. The rules and regulations shall not be made to violate the intent of this act.

§ 710.1. Public participation.

(a) General rule.—Except as provided in subsection (d), the board or council of a political subdivision or of an authority created by a political subdivision shall provide a reasonable opportunity at each advertised regular meeting and advertised special meeting for residents of the political subdivision or of the authority created by a political subdivision or for taxpayers of the political subdivision or of the authority created by a political subdivision or for both to comment on matters of concern, official action or deliberation which are or may be before the board or council prior to taking official action. The board or council has the option to accept all public comment at the beginning of the meeting. If the board or council determines that there is not sufficient time at a meeting for residents of the political subdivision or of the authority created by a political subdivision or for taxpayers of the political subdivision or of the authority created by a political subdivision or for both to comment, the board or council may defer the comment period to the next regular meeting or to a special meeting occurring in advance of the next regular meeting.[2]

---

2. Final (fourth) sentence of subsection in enrolled bill dropped, which read: "The board or counsel has the option to accept all public comment at the beginning of the meeting." (The second sentence of subsection in enrolled bill states: "The board or council has the option to accept all public comment at the beginning of the meeting.")

(b) Limitation on judicial relief.—If a board or council of a political subdivision or an authority created by a political subdivision has complied with the provisions of subsection (a), the judicial relief under section 713 (relating to business transacted at unauthorized meeting void) shall not be available on a specific action solely on the basis of lack of comment on that action.

(c) Objection.—Any person has the right to raise an objection at any time to a perceived violation of this chapter at any meeting of a board or council of a political subdivision or an authority created by a political subdivision.

(d) Exception.—The board or council of a political subdivision or of an authority created by a political subdivision which had, before January 1, 1993, established a practice or policy of holding special meetings solely for the purpose of public comment in advance of advertised regular meetings shall be exempt from the provisions of subsection (a).

(10.1 added June 15, 1993, P.L. 95, No. 20)

§ 711. Use of equipment during meetings.

(a) Recording devices.—Except as provided in subsection (b), a person attending a meeting of an agency shall have the right to use recording devices to record all the proceedings. Nothing in this section shall prohibit the agency from adopting and enforcing reasonable rules for their use under section 710 (relating to rules and regulations for conduct of meetings).

(b) Rules of the Senate and House of Representatives.—The Senate and House of Representatives may adopt rules governing the recording or broadcast of their sessions and meetings and hearings of committees.

§ 712. General Assembly meetings covered.

Notwithstanding any other provision, for the purpose of this act, meetings of the General Assembly which are covered are as follows: All meetings of committees where bills are considered, all hearings where testimony is taken and all sessions of the Senate and the House of Representatives. Not included in the intent of this act are caucuses or meetings of any ethics committee created pursuant to the Rules of the Senate or the House of Representatives.

§ 712.1. Notification of agency business required and exceptions.

(a) Official action.—Except as provided in subsection (b), (c), (d) or (e), an agency may not take official action on a matter of agency business at a meeting if the matter was not included in the notification required under section 709(c.1) (relating to public notice).

(b) Emergency business.—An agency may take official action at a regularly scheduled meeting or an emergency meeting on a matter of agency business relating to a real or potential emergency involving a clear and present danger to life or property regardless of whether public notice was given for the meeting.

(c) Business arising within 24 hours before meeting.—An agency may take official action on a matter of agency business that is not listed on a meeting agenda if:

(1) the matter arises or is brought to the attention of the agency within the 24-hour period prior to the meeting; and

(2) the matter is de minimis in nature and does not involve the expenditure of funds or entering into a contract or agreement by the agency.

(d) Business arising during meeting.—If, during the conduct of a meeting, a resident or taxpayer brings a matter of agency business that is not listed on the meeting agenda to the attention of the agency, the agency may take official action to refer the matter to staff, if applicable, for the purpose of researching the matter for inclusion on the agenda of a future meeting, or, if the matter is de minimis in nature and does not involve the expenditure of funds or entering into a contract or agreement, the agency may take official action on the matter.

(e) Changes to agenda.—

(1) Upon majority vote of the individuals present and voting during the conduct of a meeting, an agency may add a matter of agency business to the agenda. The reasons for the changes to the agenda shall be announced at the meeting before any vote is conducted to make the changes to the agenda. The agency may subsequently take official action on the matter added to the agenda. The agency shall post the amended agenda on the agency's publicly accessible Internet website, if available, and at the agency's principal office location no later than the first business day following the meeting at which the agenda was changed.

(2) This subsection shall not apply to a conference or a working session under section 707 (relating to exceptions to open meetings) or an executive session under section 708 (relating to executive sessions).

(f) Minutes.—If action is taken upon a matter of agency business added to the agenda under this section, the minutes of the meeting shall reflect the substance of the matter added, the vote on the addition and the announced reasons for the addition.

§ 713. Business transacted at unauthorized meeting void.

A legal challenge under this act shall be filed within 30 days from the date of a meeting which is open, or within 30 days from the discovery of any action that occurred at a meeting which was not open at which this[3] chapter was violated, provided that, in the case of a meeting which was not open, no legal challenge may be commenced more than one year from the date of said meeting. The court may enjoin any challenged action until a judicial determination of the legality of the meeting at which the action was adopted is reached. Should the court determine that the meeting did not meet the requirements of this chapter, it may in its discretion find that any or all official action taken at the meeting shall be invalid. Should the court determine that the meeting met the requirements of this chapter, all official action taken at the meeting shall be fully effective.

§ 714. Penalty.

(a) Fines and costs.—Any member of any agency who participates in a meeting with the intent and purpose by that member of violating this chapter commits a summary offense and shall, upon conviction, be sentenced to pay:

(1) For a first offense, the costs of prosecution plus a fine of at least $100 and, in the discretion of the sentencing authority, of not more than $1,000.

(2) For a second or subsequent offense, the costs of prosecution plus a fine of at least $500 and, in the discretion of the sentencing authority, of not more than $2,000.

(b) Payment.—An agency shall not make a payment on behalf of or reimburse a member of an agency for a fine or cost resulting from the member's violation of this section.

§ 714.1 Attorney fees.

If the court determines that an agency willfully or with wanton disregard violated a provision of this chapter, in whole or in part, the court shall award the prevailing party reasonable attorney fees and costs of litigation or an appropriate portion of the fees and costs. If the court finds that the legal challenge was

3. "the" in enrolled bill.

of a frivolous nature or was brought with no substantial justification, the court shall award the prevailing party reasonable attorney fees and costs of litigation or an appropriate portion of the fees and costs.

§ 715. Jurisdiction and venue of judicial proceedings.

The Commonwealth Court shall have original jurisdiction of actions involving State agencies and the courts of common pleas shall have original jurisdiction of actions involving other agencies to render declaratory judgments or to enforce this act, by injunction or other remedy deemed appropriate by the court. The action may be brought by any person where the agency whose act is complained of is located or where the act complained of occurred.

§ 716. Confidentiality.

All acts and parts of acts are repealed insofar as they are inconsistent herewith, excepting those statutes which specifically provide for the confidentiality of information. Those deliberations or official actions which, if conducted in public, would violate a lawful privilege or lead to the disclosure of information or confidentiality protected by law, including matter related to the investigation of possible or certain violations of the law and quasi-judicial deliberations, shall not fall within the scope of this chapter.

Table of Contents
Part I Ch. 1–3 Ethics, Records, Open Meetings
Part II Ch. 4–10 Taxation
Part III Ch. 11–18 Torts, Contracts & Civil Rules
Part IV Ch. 19–24 Zoning & Planning
Part V Ch. 25–30 Construction and Emergency Codes
Part VI Ch. 31–39 Municipal Codes
Index

CHAPTER 2

RIGHT-TO-KNOW LAW; INSPECTION, COPYING, AND DISPOSITION OF RECORDS

Chapter 2.1

RIGHT-TO-KNOW LAW

65 P.S. §§ 67.101–67.3104

TABLE OF CONTENTS

Table of Contents
Part I Ch. 1–3 Ethics, Records, Open Meetings
Part II Ch. 4–10 Taxation
Part III Ch. 11–18 Torts, Contracts & Civil Rules
Part IV Ch. 19–24 Zoning & Planning
Part V Ch. 25–30 Construction and Emergency Codes
Part VI Ch. 31–39 Municipal Codes
Index

The General Assembly of the Commonwealth of Pennsylvania hereby enacts as follows:

CHAPTER 1
PRELIMINARY PROVISIONS

§ 101. Short title.

This act shall be known and may be cited as the Right-to-Know Law.

§ 102. Definitions.

The following words and phrases when used in this act shall have the meanings given to them in this section unless the context clearly indicates otherwise:

"Administrative proceeding." A proceeding by an agency the outcome of which is required to be based on a record or documentation prescribed by law or in which a statute or regulation is particularized in application to individuals. The term includes an appeal.

"Agency." A Commonwealth agency, a local agency, a judicial agency or a legislative agency.

"Aggregated data." A tabulation of data which relate to broad classes, groups or categories so that it is not possible to distinguish the properties of individuals within those classes, groups or categories.

"Appeals officer." As follows:

(1) For a Commonwealth agency or a local agency, the appeals officer designated under section 503(a).

(2) For a judicial agency, the individual designated under section 503(b).

(3) For a legislative agency, the individual designated under section 503(c).

(4) For the Attorney General, State Treasurer, Auditor General and local agencies in possession of criminal investigative records, the individual designated under section 503(d).

"Commonwealth agency." Any of the following:

(1) Any office, department, authority, board, multistate agency or commission of the executive branch; an independent agency; and a State-affiliated entity. The term includes:

(i) The Governor's Office.

(ii) The Office of Attorney General, the Department of the Auditor General and the Treasury Department.

(iii) An organization established by the Constitution of Pennsylvania, a statute or an executive order which performs or is intended to perform an essential governmental function.

(2) The term does not include a judicial or legislative agency.

"Confidential proprietary information." Commercial or financial information received by an agency:

(1) which is privileged or confidential; and

(2) the disclosure of which would cause substantial harm to the competitive position of the person that submitted the information.

"Financial record." any of the following:

(1) Any account, voucher or contract dealing with:

(i) the receipt or disbursement of funds by an agency; or

(ii) an agency's acquisition, use or disposal of services, supplies, materials, equipment or property.

(2) The salary or other payments or expenses paid to an officer or employee of an agency, including the name and title of the officer or employee.

(3) A financial audit report. the term does not include work papers underlying an audit.

"Homeland security." Governmental actions designed to prevent, detect, respond to and recover from acts of terrorism, major disasters and other emergencies, whether natural or manmade. The term includes activities relating to the following:

(1) emergency preparedness and response, including preparedness and response activities by volunteer medical, police, emergency management, hazardous materials and fire personnel;

(2) intelligence activities;

(3) critical infrastructure protection;

(4) border security;

(5) ground, aviation and maritime transportation security;

(6) biodefense;

(7) detection of nuclear and radiological materials; and

(8) research on next-generation securities technologies.

"Independent agency." Any board, commission or other agency or officer of the Commonwealth, that is not subject to the policy supervision and control of the Governor. The term does not include a legislative or judicial agency.

"Judicial agency." A court of the Commonwealth or any other entity or office of the unified judicial system.

"Legislative agency." Any of the following:

(1) The Senate.

(2) The House of Representatives.

(3) The Capitol Preservation Committee.

(4) The Center for Rural Pennsylvania.

(5) The Joint Legislative Air and Water Pollution Control and Conservation Committee.

(6) The Joint State Government Commission.

(7) The Legislative Budget and Finance Committee.

(8) The Legislative Data Processing Committee.

(9) The Independent Regulatory Review Commission.

(10) The Legislative Reference Bureau.

(11) The Local Government Commission.

(12) The Pennsylvania Commission on Sentencing.

(13) The Legislative Reapportionment Commission.

(14) The Legislative Office of Research Liaison.

(15) The legislative audit advisory commission.

"Legislative record." Any of the following relating to a legislative agency or a standing committee, subcommittee or conference committee of a legislative agency:

(1) A financial record.

(2) A bill or resolution that has been introduced and amendments offered thereto in committee or in legislative session, including resolutions to adopt or amend the rules of a chamber.

(3) Fiscal notes.

(4) A cosponsorship memorandum.

(5) The journal of a chamber.

(6) The minutes of, record of attendance of members at a public hearing or a public committee meeting and all recorded votes taken in a public committee meeting.

(7) The transcript of a public hearing when available.

(8) Executive nomination calendars.

(9) The rules of a chamber.

(10) A record of all recorded votes taken in a legislative session.

(11) Any administrative staff manuals or written policies.

(12) An audit report prepared pursuant to the act of June 30, 1970 (P.L.442, No.151) entitled, "An act implementing the provisions of Article VIII, section 10 of the Constitution of Pennsylvania, by designating the Commonwealth officers who shall be charged with the function of auditing the financial transactions after the occurrence thereof of the Legislative and Judicial branches of the government of the Commonwealth, establishing a Legislative Audit Advisory Commission, and imposing certain powers and duties on such commission."

(13) Final or annual reports required by law to be submitted to the General Assembly.

(14) Legislative Budget and Finance Committee reports.

(15) Daily Legislative Session Calendars and marked calendars.

(16) A record communicating to an agency the official appointment of a legislative appointee.

(17) A record communicating to the appointing authority the resignation of a legislative appointee.

(18) Proposed regulations, final-form regulations and final-omitted regulations submitted to a legislative agency.

(19) The results of public opinion surveys, polls, focus groups, marketing research or similar efforts designed to measure public opinion funded by a legislative agency.

"Local agency." Any of the following:

(1) Any political subdivision, intermediate unit, charter school, cyber charter school or public trade or vocational school.

(2) Any local, intergovernmental, regional or municipal agency, authority, council, board, commission or similar governmental entity.

"Office of Open Records." The Office of Open Records established in section 1310.

"Personal financial information." An individual's personal credit, charge or debit card information; bank account information; bank, credit or financial statements; account or PIN numbers and other information relating to an individual's personal finances.

"Privilege." The attorney-work product doctrine, the attorney-client privilege, the doctor-patient privilege, the speech and debate privilege or other privilege recognized by a court interpreting the laws of this Commonwealth.

"Public record." A record, including a financial record, of a Commonwealth or local agency that:

(1) is not exempt under section 708;

(2) is not exempt from being disclosed under any other Federal or State law or regulation or judicial order or decree; or

(3) is not protected by a privilege.

"Record." Information, regardless of physical form or characteristics, that documents a transaction or activity of an agency and that is created, received or retained pursuant to law or in connection with a transaction, business or activity of the agency. The term includes a document, paper, letter, map, book, tape, photograph, film or sound recording, information stored or maintained electronically and a data-processed or image- processed document.

"Requester." A person that is a legal resident of the United States and requests a record pursuant to this act. The term includes an agency.

"Response." Access to a record or an agency's written notice to a requester granting, denying or partially granting and partially denying access to a record.

"Social services." Cash assistance and other welfare benefits, medical, mental and other health care services, drug and alcohol treatment, adoption services, vocational services and training, occupational training, education services, counseling services, workers' compensation services and unemployment compensation services, foster care services, services for the elderly, services for individuals with disabilities and services for victims of crimes and domestic violence.

"State-affiliated entity." A Commonwealth authority or Commonwealth entity. The term includes the Pennsylvania Higher Education Assistance Agency and any entity established thereby, the Pennsylvania Gaming Control Board, the Pennsylvania Game Commission, the Pennsylvania Fish and Boat Commission, the Pennsylvania Housing Finance Agency, the Pennsylvania Municipal Retirement Board, the State System of Higher Education, a community college, the Pennsylvania Turnpike Commission, the Pennsylvania Public Utility Commission, the Pennsylvania Infrastructure Investment Authority, the State Public School Building Authority, the Pennsylvania Interscholastic Athletic Association and the Pennsylvania Educational Facilities Authority. The term does not include a State-related institution.

"State-related institution." Includes:

(1) Temple University.

(2) The University of Pittsburgh.

(3) The Pennsylvania State University.

(4) Lincoln University.

"Terrorist act." A violent or life-threatening act that violates the criminal laws of the United States or any state and appears to be intended to:

(1) intimidate or coerce a civilian population;

(2) influence the policy of a government; or

(3) affect the conduct of a government by mass destruction, assassination or kidnapping.

"Trade secret." Information, including a formula, drawing, pattern, compilation, including a customer list, program, device, method, technique or process that:

(1) derives independent economic value, actual or potential, from not being generally known to and not being readily ascertainable by proper means by other persons who can obtain economic value from its disclosure or use; and

(2) is the subject of efforts that are reasonable under the circumstances to maintain its secrecy.

The term includes data processing software obtained by an agency under a licensing agreement prohibiting disclosure.

CHAPTER 3

REQUIREMENTS AND PROHIBITIONS

§ 301. Commonwealth agencies.

(a) Requirement.—A Commonwealth agency shall provide public records in accordance with this act.

(b) Prohibition.—A Commonwealth agency may not deny a requester access to a public record due to the intended use of the public record by the requester unless otherwise provided by law.

§ 302. Local agencies.

(a) Requirement.—A local agency shall provide public records in accordance with this act.

(b) Prohibition.—A local agency may not deny a requester access to a public record due to the intended use of the public record by the requester unless otherwise provided by law.

§ 303. Legislative agencies.

(a) Requirement.—A legislative agency shall provide legislative records in accordance with this act.

(b) Prohibition.—A legislative agency may not deny a requester access to a legislative record due to the intended use of the legislative record by the requester.

§ 304. Judicial agencies.

(a) Requirement.—A judicial agency shall provide financial records in accordance with this act or any rule or order of court providing equal or greater access to the records.

(b) Prohibition.—A judicial agency may not deny a requester access to a financial record due to the intended use of the financial record by the requester.

§ 305. Presumption.

(a) General rule.—A record in the possession of a Commonwealth agency or local agency shall be presumed to be a public record. The presumption shall not apply if:

Chapter 3 Public Official and Employee Ethics Law Conflicts of Interests
Chapter 2.3 Municipal Deed Registration
Chapter 2.2 Disposition of Records
Chapter 2.1 Right-to-Know Law
Chapter 1 Sunshine Act: Open Meetings Law

(1) the record is exempt under section 708;

(2) the record is protected by a privilege; or

(3) the record is exempt from disclosure under any other Federal or State law or regulation or judicial order or decree.

(b) Legislative records and financial records.—A legislative record in the possession of a legislative agency and a financial record in the possession of a judicial agency shall be presumed to be available in accordance with this act. The presumption shall not apply if:

(1) the record is exempt under section 708;

(2) the record is protected by a privilege; or

(3) the record is exempt from disclosure under any other Federal or State law, regulation or judicial order or decree.

§ 306. Nature of document.

Nothing in this act shall supersede or modify the public or nonpublic nature of a record or document established in Federal or State law, regulation or judicial order or decree.

CHAPTER 5
ACCESS

§ 501. Scope of chapter.

This chapter applies to all agencies.

§ 502. Open-records officer.

(a) Establishment.—

(1) An agency shall designate an official or employee to act as the open-records officer.

(2) For a legislative agency other than the Senate or the House of Representatives, the open-records officer designated by the Legislative Reference Bureau shall serve as the open-records officer. Notwithstanding paragraph (1), a political party caucus of a legislative agency may appoint an open-records officer under this section.

(b) Functions.—

(1) The open-records officer shall receive requests submitted to the agency under this act, direct requests to other appropriate persons within the agency or to appropriate persons in another agency, track the agency's progress in responding to requests and issue interim and final responses under this act.

(2) Upon receiving a request for a public record, legislative record or financial record, the open-records officer shall do all of the following:

(i) Note the date of receipt on the written request.

(ii) Compute the day on which the five-day period under section 901 will expire and make a notation of that date on the written request.

(iii) Maintain an electronic or paper copy of a written request, including all documents submitted with the request until the request has been fulfilled. If the request is denied, the written request shall be maintained for 30 days or, if an appeal is filed, until a final determination is issued under section 1101(b) or the appeal is deemed denied.

(iv) Create a file for the retention of the original request, a copy of the response, a record of written communications with the requester and a copy of other communications. This subparagraph shall only apply to Commonwealth agencies.

§ 503. Appeals officer.

(a) Commonwealth agencies and local agencies.—Except as provided in subsection (d), the Office of Open Records established under section 1310 shall designate an appeals officer under section 1101(a)(2) for all:

(1) Commonwealth agencies; and

(2) local agencies.

(b) Judicial agencies.—A judicial agency shall designate an appeals officer to hear appeals under Chapter 11.

(c) Legislative agencies.—

(1) Except as set forth in paragraph (2), the Legislative Reference Bureau shall designate an appeals officer to hear appeals under Chapter 11 for all legislative agencies.

(2) Each of the following shall designate an appeals officer to hear appeals under Chapter 11:

(i) The Senate.

(ii) The House of Representatives.

(d) Law enforcement records and Statewide officials.—

(1) The Attorney General, State Treasurer and Auditor General shall each designate an appeals officer to hear appeals under Chapter 11.

(2) The district attorney of a county shall designate one or more appeals officers to hear appeals under Chapter 11 relating to access to criminal investigative records in possession of a local agency of that county. The appeals officer designated by the district attorney shall determine if the record requested is a criminal investigative record.

§ 504. Regulations and policies.

(a) Authority.—An agency may promulgate regulations and policies necessary for the agency to implement this act. The Office of Open Records may promulgate regulations relating to appeals involving a Commonwealth agency or local agency.

(b) Posting.—The following information shall be posted at each agency and, if the agency maintains an Internet website, on the agency's Internet website:

(1) Contact information for the open-records officer.

(2) Contact information for the Office of Open Records or other applicable appeals officer.

(3) A form which may be used to file a request.

(4) Regulations, policies and procedures of the agency relating to this act.

§ 505. Uniform form.

(a) Commonwealth and local agencies.—The Office of Open Records shall develop a uniform form which shall be accepted by all Commonwealth and local agencies in addition to any form used by the agency to file a request under this act. The uniform form shall be published in the Pennsylvania Bulletin and on the Office of Open Record's Internet website.

(b) Judicial agencies.—A judicial agency or the Administrative Office of Pennsylvania Courts may develop a form to request financial records or may accept a form developed by the Office of Open Records.

(c) Legislative agencies.—A legislative agency may develop a form to request legislative records or may accept the form developed by the Office of Open Records.

§ 506. Requests.

(a) Disruptive requests.—

(1) An agency may deny a requester access to a record if the requester has made repeated requests for that same record and the repeated requests have placed an unreasonable burden on the agency.

(2) A denial under this subsection shall not restrict the ability to request a different record.

(b) Disaster or potential damage.—

(1) An agency may deny a requester access:

(i) when timely access is not possible due to fire, flood or other disaster; or

(ii) to historical, ancient or rare documents, records, archives and manuscripts when access may, in the professional judgment of the curator or custodian of records, cause physical damage or irreparable harm to the record.

(2) To the extent possible, the contents of a record under this subsection shall be made accessible to a requester even when the record is physically unavailable.

(c) Agency discretion.—An agency may exercise its discretion to make any otherwise exempt record accessible for inspection and copying under this chapter, if all of the following apply:

(1) Disclosure of the record is not prohibited under any of the following:

(i) Federal or State law or regulation.

(ii) Judicial order or decree.

(2) The record is not protected by a privilege.

(3) The agency head determines that the public interest favoring access outweighs any individual, agency or public interest that may favor restriction of access.

(d) Agency possession.—

(1) A public record that is not in the possession of an agency but is in the possession of a party with whom the agency has contracted to perform a governmental function on behalf of the agency, and which directly relates to the governmental function and is not exempt under this act, shall be considered a public record of the agency for purposes of this act.

(2) Nothing in this act shall be construed to require access to any other record of the party in possession of the public record.

(3) A request for a public record in possession of a party other than the agency shall be submitted to the open records officer of the agency. Upon a determination that the record is subject to access under this act, the open records officer shall assess the duplication fee established under section 1307(b) and upon collection shall remit the fee to the party in possession of the record if the party duplicated the record.

§ 507. Retention of records.

Nothing in this act shall be construed to modify, rescind or supersede any record retention policy or disposition schedule of an agency established pursuant to law, regulation, policy or other directive.

CHAPTER 7
PROCEDURE

§ 701. Access.

(a) General rule.—Unless otherwise provided by law, a public record, legislative record or financial record shall be accessible for inspection and duplication in accordance with this act. A record being provided to a requester shall be provided in the medium requested if it exists in that medium; otherwise, it shall be provided in the medium in which it exists. Public records, legislative records or financial records shall be available for access during the regular business hours of an agency.

(b) Construction.—Nothing in this act shall be construed to require access to any computer either of an agency or individual employee of an agency.

§ 702. Requests.

Agencies may fulfill verbal, written or anonymous verbal or written requests for access to records under this act. If the requester wishes to pursue the relief and remedies provided for in this act, the request for access to records must be a written request.

§ 703. Written requests.

A written request for access to records may be submitted in person, by mail, by e-mail, by facsimile or, to the extent provided by agency rules, any other electronic means. A written request must be addressed to the open-records officer designated pursuant to section 502. Employees of an agency shall be directed to forward requests for records to the open-records officer. A written request should identify or describe the records sought with sufficient specificity to enable the agency to ascertain which records are being requested and shall include the name and address to which the agency should address its response. A written request need not include any explanation of the requester's reason for requesting or intended use of the records unless otherwise required by law.

§ 704. Electronic access.

(a) General rule.—In addition to the requirements of section 701, an agency may make its records available through any publicly accessible electronic means.

(b) Response.—

(1) In addition to the requirements of section 701, an agency may respond to a request by notifying the requester that the record is available through publicly accessible electronic means or that the agency will provide access to inspect the record electronically.

(2) If the requester is unwilling or unable to access the record electronically, the requester may, within 30 days following receipt of the agency notification, submit a written request to the agency to have the record converted to paper. The agency shall provide access to the record in printed form within five days of the receipt of the written request for conversion to paper.

§ 705. Creation of record.

When responding to a request for access, an agency shall not be required to create a record which does not currently exist or to compile, maintain, format or organize a record in a manner in which the agency does not currently compile, maintain, format or organize the record.

§ 706. Redaction.

If an agency determines that a public record, legislative record or financial record contains information which is subject to access as well as information which is not subject to access, the agency's response shall grant access to the information which is subject to access and deny access to the information which is not subject to access. If the information which is not subject to access is an integral part of the public record, legislative record or financial record and cannot be separated, the agency shall redact from the record the information which is not subject to access, and the response shall grant access to the information which is subject to access. The agency may not deny access to the record if the information which is not subject to access is able to be redacted. Information which an agency redacts in accordance with this subsection shall be deemed a denial under Chapter 9.

§ 707. Production of certain records.

(a) General rule.—If, in response to a request, an agency produces a record that is not a public record, legislative record or financial record, the agency shall notify any third party that provided the record to the agency, the person that is the subject of the record and the requester.

(b) Requests for trade secrets.—An agency shall notify a third party of a request for a record if the third party provided the record and included a written statement signed by a representative of the third party that the record contains a trade secret or confidential proprietary information. Notification shall be provided within five business days of receipt of the request for the record. The third party shall have five business days from receipt of notification from the agency to provide input on the release of the record. The agency shall deny the request for the record or release the record within ten business days of the provision of notice to the third party and shall notify the third party of the decision.

(c) Transcripts.—

(1) Prior to an adjudication becoming final, binding and nonappealable, a transcript of an administrative proceeding shall be provided to a requester by the agency stenographer or a court reporter, in accordance with agency procedure or an applicable contract.

(2) Following an adjudication becoming final, binding and nonappealable, a transcript of an administrative proceeding shall be provided to a requester in accordance with the duplication rates established in section 1307(b).

§ 708. Exceptions for public records.

(a) Burden of proof.—

(1) The burden of proving that a record of a Commonwealth agency or local agency is exempt from public access shall be on the Commonwealth agency or local agency receiving a request by a preponderance of the evidence.

(2) The burden of proving that a legislative record is exempt from public access shall be on the legislative agency receiving a request by a preponderance of the evidence.

(3) The burden of proving that a financial record of a judicial agency is exempt from public access shall be on the judicial agency receiving a request by a preponderance of the evidence.

(b) Exceptions.—Except as provided in subsections (c) and (d), the following are exempt from access by a requester under this act:

(1) A record the disclosure of which:

(i) would result in the loss of Federal or State funds by an agency or the Commonwealth; or

(ii) would be reasonably likely to result in a substantial and demonstrable risk of physical harm to or the personal security of an individual.

(2) A record maintained by an agency in connection with the military, homeland security, national defense, law enforcement or other public safety activity that if disclosed would be reasonably likely to jeopardize or threaten public safety or preparedness or public protection activity or a record that is designated classified by an appropriate Federal or State military authority.

(3) A record, the disclosure of which creates a reasonable likelihood of endangering the safety or the physical security of a building, public utility, resource, infrastructure, facility or information storage system, which may include:

(i) documents or data relating to computer hardware, source files, software and system networks that could jeopardize computer security by exposing a vulnerability in preventing, protecting against, mitigating or responding to a terrorist act;

(ii) lists of infrastructure, resources and significant special events, including those defined by the Federal Government in the National Infrastructure Protections, which are deemed critical due to their nature and which result from risk analysis; threat assessments; consequences assessments; antiterrorism protective measures and plans; counterterrorism measures and plans; and security and response needs assessments; and

(iii) building plans or infrastructure records that expose or create vulnerability through disclosure of the location, configuration or security of critical systems, including public utility systems, structural elements, technology, communication, electrical, fire suppression, ventilation, water, wastewater, sewage and gas systems.

(4) A record regarding computer hardware, software and networks, including administrative or technical records, which, if disclosed, would be reasonably likely to jeopardize computer security.

(5) A record of an individual's medical, psychiatric or psychological history or disability status, including an evaluation, consultation, prescription, diagnosis or treatment; results of tests, including drug tests; enrollment in a health care program or program designed for participation by persons with disabilities, including vocation rehabilitation, workers' compensation and unemployment compensation; or related information that would disclose individually identifiable health information.

(6) (i) The following personal identification information:

(A) A record containing all or part of a person's Social Security number; driver's license number; personal financial information; home, cellular or personal telephone numbers; personal e- mail addresses; employee number or other confidential personal identification number.

(B) A spouse's name; marital status, beneficiary or dependent information.

(C) The home address of a law enforcement officer or judge.

(ii) Nothing in this paragraph shall preclude the release of the name, position, salary, actual compensation or other payments or expenses, employment contract, employment-related contract or agreement and length of service of a public official or an agency employee.

(iii) An agency may redact the name or other identifying information relating to an individual performing an undercover or covert law enforcement activity from a record.

(7) The following records relating to an agency employee:

(i) A letter of reference or recommendation pertaining to the character or qualifications of an identifiable individual, unless it was prepared in relation to the appointment of an individual to fill a vacancy in an elected office or an appointed office requiring Senate confirmation.

(ii) A performance rating or review.

(iii) The result of a civil service or similar test administered by a Commonwealth agency, legislative agency or judicial agency. The result of a civil service or similar test administered by a local agency shall not be disclosed if restricted by a collective bargaining agreement. Only test scores of individuals who obtained a passing score on a test administered by a local agency may be disclosed.

(iv) The employment application of an individual who is not hired by the agency.

(v) Workplace support services program information.

(vi) Written criticisms of an employee.

(vii) Grievance material, including documents related to discrimination or sexual harassment.

(viii) Information regarding discipline, demotion or discharge contained in a personnel file. This subparagraph shall not apply to the final action of an agency that results in demotion or discharge.

(ix) An academic transcript.

(8) (i) A record pertaining to strategy or negotiations relating to labor relations or collective bargaining and related arbitration proceedings. This subparagraph shall not apply to a final or executed contract or agreement between the parties in a collective bargaining procedure.

(ii) In the case of the arbitration of a dispute or grievance under a collective bargaining agreement, an exhibit entered into evidence at an arbitration proceeding, a transcript of the arbitration or the opinion. This subparagraph shall not apply to the final award or order of the arbitrator in a dispute or grievance procedure.

(9) The draft of a bill, resolution, regulation, statement of policy, management directive, ordinance or amendment thereto prepared by or for an agency.

(10) (i) A record that reflects:

(A) The internal, predecisional deliberations of an agency, its members, employees or officials or predecisional deliberations between agency members, employees or officials and members, employees or officials of another agency, including predecisional deliberations relating to a budget recommendation, legislative proposal, legislative amendment, contemplated or proposed policy or course of action or any research, memos or other documents used in the predecisional deliberations.

(B) The strategy to be used to develop or achieve the successful adoption of a budget, legislative proposal or regulation.

(ii) Subparagraph (i)(A) shall apply to agencies subject to 65 Pa.C.S. Ch. 7 (relating to open meetings) in a manner consistent with 65 Pa.C.S. Ch. 7. A record which is not otherwise exempt from access under this act and which is presented to a quorum for deliberation in accordance with 65 Pa.C.S. Ch. 7 shall be a public record.

(iii) This paragraph shall not apply to a written or Internet application or other document that has been submitted to request Commonwealth funds.

(iv) This paragraph shall not apply to the results of public opinion surveys, polls, focus groups, marketing research or similar effort designed to measure public opinion.

(11) A record that constitutes or reveals a trade secret or confidential proprietary information.

(12) Notes and working papers prepared by or for a public official or agency employee used solely for that official's or employee's own personal use, including telephone message slips, routing slips and other materials that do not have an official purpose.

(13) Records that would disclose the identity of an individual who lawfully makes a donation to an agency unless the donation is intended for or restricted to providing remuneration or personal tangible benefit to a named public of-

ficial or employee of the agency, including lists of potential donors compiled by an agency to pursue donations, donor profile information or personal identifying information relating to a donor.

(14) Unpublished lecture notes, unpublished manuscripts, unpublished articles, creative works in progress, research- related material and scholarly correspondence of a community college or an institution of the State System of Higher Education or a faculty member, staff employee, guest speaker or student thereof.

(15) (I) Academic transcripts.

(II) Examinations, examination questions, scoring keys or answers to examinations. this subparagraph shall include licensing and other examinations relating to the qualifications of an individual and to examinations given in primary and secondary schools and institutions of higher education.

(16) A record of an agency relating to or resulting in a criminal investigation, including:

(i) Complaints of potential criminal conduct other than a private criminal complaint.

(ii) Investigative materials, notes, correspondence, videos and reports.

(iii) A record that includes the identity of a confidential source or the identity of a suspect who has not been charged with an offense to whom confidentiality has been promised.

(iv) A record that includes information made confidential by law or court order.

(v) Victim information, including any information that would jeopardize the safety of the victim.

(vi) A record that, if disclosed, would do any of the following:

(A) Reveal the institution, progress or result of a criminal investigation, except the filing of criminal charges.

(B) Deprive a person of the right to a fair trial or an impartial adjudication.

(C) Impair the ability to locate a defendant or codefendant.

(D) Hinder an agency's ability to secure an arrest, prosecution or conviction.

(E) Endanger the life or physical safety of an individual.

This paragraph shall not apply to information contained in a police blotter as defined in 18 Pa.C.S. § 9102 (relating to definitions) and utilized or maintained by the Pennsylvania State Police, local, campus, transit or port authority police department or other law enforcement agency or in a traffic report except as provided under 75 Pa.C.S. § 3754(b) (relating to accident prevention investigations).

(17) A record of an agency relating to a noncriminal investigation, including:

(i) Complaints submitted to an agency.

(ii) Investigative materials, notes, correspondence and reports.

(iii) A record that includes the identity of a confidential source, including individuals subject to the act of December 12, 1986 (P.L.1559, No.169), known as the Whistleblower Law.

(iv) A record that includes information made confidential by law.

(v) Work papers underlying an audit.

(vi) A record that, if disclosed, would do any of the following:

(A) Reveal the institution, progress or result of an agency investigation, except the imposition of a fine or civil penalty, the suspension, modification or revocation of a license, permit, registration, certification or similar authorization issued by an agency or an executed settlement agreement unless the agreement is determined to be confidential by a court.

(B) Deprive a person of the right to an impartial adjudication.

(C) Constitute an unwarranted invasion of privacy.

(D) Hinder an agency's ability to secure an administrative or civil sanction.

(E) Endanger the life or physical safety of an individual.

(18) (i) Records or parts of records, except time response logs, pertaining to audio recordings, telephone or radio transmissions received by emergency dispatch personnel, including 911 recordings.

(ii) This paragraph shall not apply to a 911 recording, or a transcript of a 911 recording, if the agency or a court determines that the public interest in disclosure outweighs the interest in nondisclosure.

(19) DNA and RNA records.

(20) An autopsy record of a coroner or medical examiner and any audiotape of a postmortem examination or autopsy, or a copy, reproduction or facsimile of an autopsy report, a photograph, negative or print, including a photograph or videotape of the body or any portion of the body of a deceased person at the scene of death or in the course of a postmortem examination or autopsy taken or made by or caused to be taken or made by the coroner or medical examiner. This exception shall not limit the reporting of the name of the deceased individual and the cause and manner of death.

(21) (i) Draft minutes of any meeting of an agency until the next regularly scheduled meeting of the agency.

(ii) Minutes of an executive session and any record of discussions held in executive session.

(22) (i) The contents of real estate appraisals, engineering or feasibility estimates, environmental reviews, audits or evaluations made for or by an agency relative to the following:

(A) The leasing, acquiring or disposing of real property or an interest in real property.

(B) The purchase of public supplies or equipment included in the real estate transaction.

(C) Construction projects.

(ii) This paragraph shall not apply once the decision is made to proceed with the lease, acquisition or disposal of real property or an interest in real property or the purchase of public supply or construction project.

(23) Library and archive circulation and order records of an identifiable individual or groups of individuals.

(24) Library archived and museum materials, or valuable or rare book collections or documents contributed by gift, grant, bequest or devise, to the extent of any limitations imposed by the donor as a condition of the contribution.

(25) A record identifying the location of an archeological site or an endangered or threatened plant or animal species if not already known to the general public.

(26) A proposal pertaining to agency procurement or disposal of supplies, services or construction prior to the award of the contract or prior to the opening and rejection of all bids; financial information of a bidder or offeror requested in an invitation for bid or request for proposals to demonstrate the

bidder's or offeror's economic capability; or the identity of members, notes and other records of agency proposal evaluation committees established under 62 Pa.C.S. § 513 (relating to competitive sealed proposals).

(27) A record or information relating to a communication between an agency and its insurance carrier, administrative service organization or risk management office. This paragraph shall not apply to a contract with an insurance carrier, administrative service organization or risk management office or to financial records relating to the provision of insurance.

(28) A record or information:

(i) identifying an individual who applies for or receives social services; or

(ii) relating to the following:

(A) the type of social services received by an individual;

(B) an individual's application to receive social services, including a record or information related to an agency decision to grant, deny, reduce or restrict benefits, including a quasi-judicial decision of the agency and the identity of a caregiver or others who provide services to the individual; or

(C) eligibility to receive social services, including the individual's income, assets, physical or mental health, age, disability, family circumstances or record of abuse.

(29) Correspondence between a person and a member of the General Assembly and records accompanying the correspondence which would identify a person that requests assistance or constituent services. This paragraph shall not apply to correspondence between a member of the General Assembly and a principal or lobbyist under 65 Pa.C.S. Ch. 13A (relating to lobbyist disclosure).

(30) A record identifying the name, home address or date of birth of a child 17 years of age or younger.

(c) Financial records.—The exceptions set forth in subsection (b) shall not apply to financial records, except that an agency may redact that portion of a financial record protected under subsection (b)(1), (2), (3), (4), (5), (6), (16) or (17). an agency shall not disclose the identity of an individual performing an undercover or covert law enforcement activity.

(d) Aggregated data.—The exceptions set forth in subsection (b) shall not apply to aggregated data maintained or received by an agency, except for data protected under subsection (b)(1), (2), (3), (4) or (5).

(e) Construction—In determining whether a record is exempt from access under this section, an agency shall consider and apply each exemption separately.

CHAPTER 9
AGENCY RESPONSE

§ 901. General rule.

Upon receipt of a written request for access to a record, an agency shall make a good faith effort to determine if the record requested is a public record, legislative record or financial record and whether the agency has possession, custody or control of the identified record, and to respond as promptly as possible under the circumstances existing at the time of the request. All applicable fees shall be paid in order to receive access to the record requested. The time for response shall not exceed five business days from the date the written request is received by the open-records officer for an agency. If the agency fails to send the response within five business days of receipt of the written request for access, the written request for access shall be deemed denied.

§ 902. Extension of time.

(a) Determination.—Upon receipt of a written request for access, the open-records officer for an agency shall determine if one of the following applies:

(1) the request for access requires redaction of a record in accordance with section 706;

(2) the request for access requires the retrieval of a record stored in a remote location;

(3) a timely response to the request for access cannot be accomplished due to bona fide and specified staffing limitations;

(4) a legal review is necessary to determine whether the record is a record subject to access under this act;

(5) the requester has not complied with the agency's policies regarding access to records;

(6) the requester refuses to pay applicable fees authorized by this act; or

(7) the extent or nature of the request precludes a response within the required time period.

(b) Notice.—

(1) Upon a determination that one of the factors listed in subsection (a) applies, the open-records officer shall send written notice to the requester within five business days of receipt of the request for access under subsection (a).

(2) The notice shall include a statement notifying the requester that the request for access is being reviewed, the reason for the review, a reasonable date that a response is expected to be provided and an estimate of applicable fees owed when the record becomes available. If the date that a response is expected to be provided is in excess of 30 days, following the five business days allowed for in section 901, the request for access shall be deemed denied unless the requester has agreed in writing to an extension to the date specified in the notice.

(3) If the requester agrees to the extension, the request shall be deemed denied on the day following the date specified in the notice if the agency has not provided a response by that date.

§ 903. Denial.

If an agency's response is a denial of a written request for access, whether in whole or in part, the denial shall be issued in writing and shall include:

(1) A description of the record requested.

(2) The specific reasons for the denial, including a citation of supporting legal authority.

(3) The typed or printed name, title, business address, business telephone number and signature of the open-records officer on whose authority the denial is issued.

(4) Date of the response.

(5) The procedure to appeal the denial of access under this act.

§ 904. Certified copies.

If an agency's response grants a request for access, the agency shall, upon request, provide the requester with a certified copy of the record if the requester pays the applicable fees under section 1307.

§ 905. Record discard.

If an agency response to a requester states that copies of the requested records are available for delivery at the office of an agency and the requester fails to retrieve the records within 60 days of the agency's response, the agency may dispose of any copies which have not been retrieved and retain any fees paid to date.

CHAPTER 11
APPEAL OF AGENCY DETERMINATION

§ 1101. Filing of appeal.

(a) Authorization.—

(1) If a written request for access to a record is denied or deemed denied, the requester may file an appeal with the Office of Open Records or judicial, legislative or other appeals officer designated under section 503(d) within 15 business days of the mailing date of the agency's response or within 15 business days of a deemed denial. The appeal shall state the grounds upon which the requester asserts that the record is a public record, legislative record or financial record and shall address any grounds stated by the agency for delaying or denying the request.

(2) Except as provided in section 503(d), in the case of an appeal of a decision by a Commonwealth agency or local agency, the Office of Open Records shall assign an appeals officer to review the denial.

(b) Determination.—

(1) Unless the requester agrees otherwise, the appeals officer shall make a final determination which shall be mailed to the requester and the agency within 30 days of receipt of the appeal filed under subsection (a).

(2) If the appeals officer fails to issue a final determination within 30 days, the appeal is deemed denied.

(3) Prior to issuing a final determination, a hearing may be conducted. The determination by the appeals officer shall be a final order. The appeals officer shall provide a written explanation of the reason for the decision to the requester and the agency.

(c) Direct interest.—

(1) A person other than the agency or requester with a direct interest in the record subject to an appeal under this section may, within 15 days following receipt of actual knowledge of the appeal but no later than the date the appeals officer issues an order, file a written request to provide information or to appear before the appeals officer or to file information in support of the requester's or agency's position.

(2) The appeals officer may grant a request under paragraph (1) if:

(i) no hearing has been held;

(ii) the appeals officer has not yet issued its order; and

(iii) the appeals officer believes the information will be probative.

(3) Copies of the written request shall be sent to the agency and the requester.

§ 1102. Appeals officers.

(a) Duties.—An appeals officer designated under section 503 shall do all of the following:

(1) Set a schedule for the requester and the open- records officer to submit documents in support of their positions.

(2) Review all information filed relating to the request. The appeals officer may hold a hearing. A decision to hold or not to hold a hearing is not appealable. The appeals officer may admit into evidence testimony, evidence and documents that the appeals officer believes to be reasonably probative and relevant to an issue in dispute. The appeals officer may limit the nature and extent of evidence found to be cumulative.

(3) Consult with agency counsel as appropriate.

(4) Issue a final determination on behalf of the Office of Open Records or other agency.

(b) Procedures.—The Office of Open Records, a judicial agency, a legislative agency, the Attorney General, Auditor General, State Treasurer or district attorney may adopt procedures relating to appeals under this chapter.

(1) If an appeal is resolved without a hearing, 1 Pa. Code Pt. II (relating to general rules of administrative practice and procedure) does not apply except to the extent that the agency has adopted these chapters in its regulations or rules under this subsection.

(2) If a hearing is held, 1 Pa. Code Pt. II shall apply unless the agency has adopted regulations, policies or procedures to the contrary under this subsection.

(3) In the absence of a regulation, policy or procedure governing appeals under this chapter, the appeals officer shall rule on procedural matters on the basis of justice, fairness and the expeditious resolution of the dispute.

CHAPTER 13
JUDICIAL REVIEW

§ 1301. Commonwealth agencies, legislative agencies and judicial agencies.

(a) General rule.—Within 30 days of the mailing date of the final determination of the appeals officer relating to a decision of a Commonwealth agency, a legislative agency or a judicial agency issued under section 1101(b) or the date a request for access is deemed denied, a requester or the agency may file a petition for review or other document as might be required by rule of court with the Commonwealth Court. The decision of the court shall contain findings of fact and conclusions of law based upon the evidence as a whole. The decision shall clearly and concisely explain the rationale for the decision.

(b) Stay.—A petition for review under this section shall stay the release of documents until a decision under subsection (a) is issued.

§ 1302. Local agencies.

(a) General rule.—Within 30 days of the mailing date of the final determination of the appeals officer relating to a decision of a local agency issued under section 1101(b) or of the date a request for access is deemed denied, a requester or local agency may file a petition for review or other document as required by rule of court with the court of common pleas for the county where the local agency is located. The decision of the court shall contain findings of fact and conclusions of law based upon the evidence as a whole. The decision shall clearly and concisely explain the rationale for the decision.

(b) Stay.—A petition for review under this section shall stay the release of documents until a decision under subsection (a) is issued.

§ 1303. Notice and records.

(a) Notice.—An agency, the requester and the Office of Open Records or designated appeals officer shall be served notice of actions commenced in accordance

Chapter 3
Public Official and Employee Ethics Law
Conflicts of Interests
Chapter 2.3
Municipal Deed
Registration
Chapter 2.2
Disposition of
Records
Chapter 2.1
Right-to-Know Law
Chapter 1
Sunshine Act: Open Meetings Law

with section 1301 or 1302 and shall have an opportunity to respond in accordance with applicable court rules.

(b) Record on appeal.—The record before a court shall consist of the request, the agency's response, the appeal filed under section 1101, the hearing transcript, if any, and the final written determination of the appeals officer.

§ 1304. Court costs and attorney fees.

(a) Reversal of agency determination.—If a court reverses the final determination of the appeals officer or grants access to a record after a request for access was deemed denied, the court may award reasonable attorney fees and costs of litigation or an appropriate portion thereof to a requester if the court finds either of the following:

(1) the agency receiving the original request willfully or with wanton disregard deprived the requester of access to a public record subject to access or otherwise acted in bad faith under the provisions of this act; or

(2) the exemptions, exclusions or defenses asserted by the agency in its final determination were not based on a reasonable interpretation of law.

(b) Sanctions for frivolous requests or appeals.—The court may award reasonable attorney fees and costs of litigation or an appropriate portion thereof to an agency or the requester if the court finds that the legal challenge under this chapter was frivolous.

(c) Other sanctions.—Nothing in this act shall prohibit a court from imposing penalties and costs in accordance with applicable rules of court.

§ 1305. Civil penalty.

(a) Denial of access.—A court may impose a civil penalty of not more than $1,500 if an agency denied access to a public record in bad faith.

(b) Failure to comply with court order.—An agency or public official who does not promptly comply with a court order under this act is subject to a civil penalty of not more than $500 per day until the public records are provided.

§ 1306. Immunity.

(a) General rule.—Except as provided in sections 1304 and 1305 and other statutes governing the release of records, no agency, public official or public employee shall be liable for civil penalties resulting from compliance or failure to comply with this act.

(b) Schedules.—No agency, public official or public employee shall be liable for civil or criminal damages or penalties under this act for complying with any written public record retention and disposition schedule.

§ 1307. Fee limitations.

(a) Postage.—Fees for postage may not exceed the actual cost of mailing.

(b) Duplication.—

(1) Fees for duplication by photocopying, printing from electronic media or microfilm, copying onto electronic media, transmission by facsimile or other electronic means and other means of duplication shall be established:

(i) by the Office of Open Records, for Commonwealth agencies and local agencies;

(ii) by each judicial agency; and

(iii) by each legislative agency.

(2) The fees must be reasonable and based on prevailing fees for comparable duplication services provided by local business entities.

(3) Fees for local agencies may reflect regional price differences.

(4) The following apply to complex and extensive data sets, including geographic information systems or integrated property assessment lists.

(i) Fees for copying may be based on the reasonable market value of the same or closely related data sets.

(ii) Subparagraph (i) shall not apply to:

(A) a request by an individual employed by or connected with a newspaper or magazine of general circulation, weekly publication, press association or radio or television station, for the purpose of obtaining information for publication or broadcast; or

(B) a request by a nonprofit organization for the conduct of educational research.

(iii) Information obtained under subparagraph (ii) shall be subject to paragraphs (1), (2) and (3).

(c) Certification.—An agency may impose reasonable fees for official certification of copies if the certification is at the behest of the requester and for the purpose of legally verifying the public record.

(d) Conversion to paper.—If a record is only maintained electronically or in other nonpaper media, duplication fees shall be limited to the lesser of the fee for duplication on paper or the fee for duplication in the original media as provided by subsection (b) unless the requester specifically requests for the record to be duplicated in the more expensive medium.

(e) Enhanced electronic access.—If an agency offers enhanced electronic access to records in addition to making the records accessible for inspection and duplication by a requester as required by this act, the agency may establish user fees specifically for the provision of the enhanced electronic access, but only to the extent that the enhanced electronic access is in addition to making the records accessible for inspection and duplication by a requester as required by this act. The user fees for enhanced electronic access may be a flat rate, a subscription fee for a period of time, a per-transaction fee, a fee based on the cumulative time of system access or any other reasonable method and any combination thereof. The user fees for enhanced electronic access must be reasonable, must be approved by the Office of Open Records and may not be established with the intent or effect of excluding persons from access to records or duplicates thereof or of creating profit for the agency.

(f) Waiver of fees.—An agency may waive the fees for duplication of a record, including, but not limited to, when:

(1) the requester duplicates the record; or

(2) the agency deems it is in the public interest to do so.

(g) Limitations.—Except as otherwise provided by statute, no other fees may be imposed unless the agency necessarily incurs costs for complying with the request, and such fees must be reasonable. No fee may be imposed for an agency's review of a record to determine whether the record is a public record, legislative record or financial record subject to access in accordance with this act.

(h) Prepayment.—Prior to granting a request for access in accordance with this act, an agency may require a requester to prepay an estimate of the fees authorized under this section if the fees required to fulfill the request are expected to exceed $100.

§ 1308. Prohibition.

A policy or regulation adopted under this act may not include any of the following:

(1) A limitation on the number of records which may be requested or made available for inspection or duplication.

Table of Contents | Part I Ch. 1–3 Ethics, Records, Open Meetings | Part II Ch. 4–10 Taxation | Part III Ch. 11–18 Torts, Contracts & Civil Rules | Part IV Ch. 19–24 Zoning & Planning | Part V Ch. 25–30 Construction and Emergency Codes | Part VI Ch. 31–39 Municipal Codes | Index

(2) A requirement to disclose the purpose or motive in requesting access to records.

§ 1309. Practice and procedure.

The provisions of 2 Pa.C.S. (relating to administrative law and procedure) shall not apply to this act unless specifically adopted by regulation or policy.

§ 1310. Office of Open Records.

(a) Establishment.—There is established in the Department of Community and Economic Development an Office of Open Records. The office shall do all of the following:

(1) Provide information relating to the implementation and enforcement of this act.

(2) Issue advisory opinions to agencies and requesters.

(3) Provide annual training courses to agencies, public officials and public employees on this act and 65 Pa.C.S. Ch. 7 (relating to open meetings).

(4) Provide annual, regional training courses to local agencies, public officials and public employees.

(5) Assign appeals officers to review appeals of decisions by Commonwealth agencies or local agencies, except as provided in section 503(d), filed under section 1101 and issue orders and opinions. The office shall employ or contract with attorneys to serve as appeals officers to review appeals and, if necessary, to hold hearings on a regional basis under this act. Each appeals officer must comply with all of the following:

(i) Complete a training course provided by the Office of Open Records prior to acting as an appeals officer.

(ii) If a hearing is necessary, hold hearings regionally as necessary to ensure access to the remedies provided by this act.

(iii) Comply with the procedures under section 1102(b).

(6) Establish an informal mediation program to resolve disputes under this act.

(7) Establish an Internet website with information relating to this act, including information on fees, advisory opinions and decisions and the name and address of all open records officers in this Commonwealth.

(8) Conduct a biannual review of fees charged under this act.

(9) Annually report on its activities and findings to the Governor and the General Assembly. The report shall be posted and maintained on the Internet website established under paragraph (7).

(b) Executive director.—Within 90 days of the effective date of this section, the Governor shall appoint an executive director of the office who shall serve for a term of six years. Compensation shall be set by the Executive Board established under section 204 of the act of April 9, 1929 (P.L.177, No.175), known as The Administrative Code of 1929. The executive director may serve no more than two terms.

(c) Limitation.—The executive director shall not seek election nor accept appointment to any political office during his tenure as executive director and for one year thereafter.

(d) Staffing.—The executive director shall appoint attorneys to act as appeals officers and additional clerical, technical and professional staff as may be appropriate and may contract for additional services as necessary for the performance of the executive director's duties. The compensation of attorneys and other staff shall be set by the Executive Board. The appointment of attorneys shall not be subject to the act of October 15, 1980 (P.L.950, No.164), known as the Commonwealth Attorneys Act.

(e) Duties.—The executive director shall ensure that the duties of the Office of Open Records are carried out and shall monitor cases appealed to the Office of Open Records.

(f) Appropriation.—The appropriation for the office shall be in a separate line item and shall be under the jurisdiction of the executive director.

CHAPTER 15
STATE-RELATED INSTITUTIONS

§ 1501. Definition.

As used in this chapter, "State-related institution" means any of the following:

(1) Temple University.

(2) The University of Pittsburgh.

(3) The Pennsylvania State University.

(4) Lincoln University.

§ 1502. Filing.

No later than May 30 of each year, unless otherwise provided under this chapter, a State-related institution shall file the information set forth in section 1503 as required under section 1504.

§ 1503. Contents of filing.

(a) Information included.—The filing required under section 1502 shall include the following:

(1) Except as provided in paragraph (4), all information required by Form 990 or an equivalent form of the United States Department of the Treasury, Internal Revenue Service, entitled the Return of Organization Exempt From Income Tax, regardless of whether the State-related institution is required to file the form by the Federal Government.

(2) The salaries of all officers and directors of the State-related institution.

(3) The highest 25 salaries paid to employees of the institution that are not included under paragraph (2)and, for a State-related institution with 2,500 employees or more, the next highest 175 salaries paid to employees of the institution that are not included under paragraph (2). Faculty members' salaries shall be presented in salary ranges.

(4) The filing shall not include information relating to individual donors.

(5) Revenue and expenditure budgets of the State-related institution's academic and administrative support units for the current fiscal year.

(6) The actual revenue and expenditures for the prior year.

(7) For any defined project or program which is the subject of a specific line item appropriation from the General Fund, the State-related institution shall disclose the following:

(i) Revenue and expenditure budgets of the defined program or project for the current fiscal year.

(ii) The actual revenue and expenditures of the defined program or project for the prior year.

(8) The revenue and expenditures of any auxiliary enterprise which is directly funded in whole or in part by tuition or a State appropriation for the current fiscal year.

(9) The most recent audited financial statement for the State-related institution.

Table of Contents
Part I Ch. 1–3 Ethics, Records, Open Meetings
Part II Ch. 4–10 Taxation
Part III Ch. 11–18 Torts, Contracts & Civil Rules
Part IV Ch. 19–24 Zoning & Planning
Part V Ch. 25–30 Construction and Emergency Codes
Part VI Ch. 31–39 Municipal Codes
Index

(10) The following information for the prior fiscal year for each academic or administrative support unit, for each defined project or program and for an auxiliary enterprise:

(i) The number of employees by academic rank.

(ii) The number of administrators, staff, clerical and technical service employees, by classification.

(iii) Median and mean salary by academic rank.

(iv) Median and mean salaries of administrators, staff, clerical and technical service employees, by classification.

(v) Nonsalary compensation as a percentage of salary. Nonsalary compensation shall include:

(A) Medical benefits.

(B) Life insurance benefits.

(C) Pension benefits.

(D) Leave benefits.

(E) Employer Social Security payments.

(F) Workers' compensation benefits.

(vi) A statement of the State-related institution's retirement policies.

(vii) A policy statement relating to a reduction of tuition for employees' family members.

(viii) A list by academic or administrative support unit in the aggregate of the expenses of travel, subsistence and lodging, whether provided or reimbursed.

(b) Providing information.—Each State-related institution shall provide full, complete and accurate information as may be required by the Department of Education or the chairperson or minority chairperson of the Appropriations Committee of the Senate or the chairperson or minority chairperson of the Appropriations Committee of the House of Representatives.

(c) Financial statements.—Each State-related institution shall present and report its financial statements required under the provisions of this act in accordance with:

(1) The generally accepted accounting principles as prescribed by the National Association of College and University Business Officers, the American Institute of Certified Public Accountants or by another recognized authoritative body.

(2) The Commonwealth of Pennsylvania Budget Instructions for the State System of Higher Education, State-Related Universities and Non-State-Related Colleges and Universities.

(3) The financial reporting policies and standards promulgated by the Commonwealth of Pennsylvania and by the Federal Government that apply to the State-related institutions.

(d) Appropriations.—

(1) In a year a State-related institution receives an appropriation, a report shall be submitted prior to September 1 and shall cover the 12-month period beginning with the summer term of the preceding year. The report shall include:

(i) The following counts and distributions for each term during the period:

(A) The definition and number of:

(I) Faculty members employed full time.

(II) Faculty members employed part time.

(III) Full-time students enrolled in a graduate course.

(IV) Full-time students enrolled in an undergraduate course.

(V) Part-time students enrolled in a graduate course.

(VI) Part-time students enrolled in an undergraduate course.

(B) The total number of:

(I) Undergraduate student credit hours, divided into lower division and upper division course levels.

(II) Graduate student credit hours, divided into three course levels: master's, first professional and doctoral.

(C) The number of different courses scheduled by level of instruction and the number of sections of individual instruction scheduled by level of instruction, each further subdivided by two-digit Classification of Instructional Program (CIP) categories of instructional programs of higher education as defined by the National Center for Education Statistics, United States Department of Education.

(D) The number of terms scheduled and the dates of the terms.

(ii) For the summer term and the following academic year in total and for each two-digit CIP program category:

(A) A classification of faculty members or other professional employees by title, including:

(I) Professor.

(II) Associate professor.

(III) Assistant professor.

(IV) Instructor.

(V) Lecturer.

(VI) Research associate.

(VII) Librarian and academic administrator.

(B) Faculty members or other professional employees under each title to be subdivided into teaching and nonteaching.

(C) Each set of faculty members or other professional employees to be further subdivided by full-time or part-time employment.

(D) The following aggregates for each subdivided classification:

(I) The number of faculty and other professional employees and the full-time equivalence in instructional and noninstructional functions.

(II) The sum of credits assigned to undergraduate classroom courses and the sum of credits assigned to graduate classroom courses taught divided into lower division, upper division, master's, first professional and doctoral course levels.

(III) The sum of credits assigned to undergraduate individual instruction courses and the sum of credits assigned to graduate individual instruction courses taught divided into lower division, upper division, master's, first professional and doctoral course levels.

(IV) The sum of undergraduate classroom student credit hours and the sum of graduate classroom student credit hours generated, divided into lower division, upper division, master's, first professional and doctoral course levels.

(V) The sum of undergraduate individual instruction student credit hours and the sum of graduate individual instruction student credit hours generated, divided into lower division, upper division, master's, first professional and doctoral course levels.

(VI) The total salary paid for instructional functions and for non-instructional functions and the amount of salary paid for each of these functions from State-related institution funds, Federal funds and other funds.

(iii) For each term of the period covered for each faculty member employed full-time identified by two-digit CIP program category and title, the report shall contain an analysis of the average hours per week spent:

(A) In State-related-institution-related activities, stating specifically hours spent in undergraduate classroom contact and graduate classroom contact hours spent in preparation.

(B) In research.

(C) In public service.

(2) The report covering the 12-month period shall include for each program of the State-related institution:

(i) Minimum number of credits required for a baccalaureate and a master's degree.

(ii) Number of bachelor's, master's, first professional and doctoral degrees awarded for the previous five years and those estimates for that year.

(e) Minutes.—Each State-related institution shall make a copy of the minutes of each public meeting of the institution's board of trustees available for public inspection in the institution's library in print format and online on the institution's publicly accessible Internet website. The minutes shall be maintained in print and online for no fewer than 20 years.

(f) Data systems report.—Each State-related institution shall make a copy of the institution's integrated postsecondary education data systems report available for public inspection in the institution's library in print format and online on the institution's publicly accessible Internet website.

§ 1504. Requirements for information in filings.

A State-related institution shall make the information required under section 1502 accessible to the public in accordance with the following:

(1) The information shall be posted online on the institution's publicly accessible Internet website in a searchable, sortable and downloadable database format that is freely accessible by the public. To the extent possible, a State-related institution shall post the information online in a similar manner in order to facilitate easy public review. The information of prior years shall be maintained for no fewer than 10 years.

(2) The information shall be maintained in print format in the institution's library for no fewer than 10 years.

(3) The information shall be provided in electronic format to the Department of Education and the Joint State Government Commission.

(4) The information shall be provided in print format to the General Assembly and to each of the State regional library resource centers.

§ 1505. Contracts.

(a) Scope.—By May 30 of each year, a State-related institution shall file with the Governor's Office, the Secretary of the Senate, the Chief Clerk of the House of Representatives and the State Library an annual list of contracts in excess of $5,000 for the purchase of all goods and third-party services.

(b) Contents.—The list shall include all of the following:

(1) Date of execution.

(2) Amount of the contract.

(3) Beginning date of the contract.

(4) End date of the contract, if applicable.

(5) The name and address of the vendor.

(6) Subject matter of the contract.

(c) Privilege.—This section shall not apply to a contract for services protected by a privilege.

(d) Evidence.—This section:

(1) Shall apply to a purchase order evidencing new obligations.

(2) Shall not apply to a purchase order evidencing fulfillment of an existing contract.

(e) Posting.—Information under this section shall be posted and maintained on the institution's publicly accessible Internet website.

CHAPTER 17
STATE CONTRACT INFORMATION

§ 1701. Submission and retention of contracts.

(a) General rule.—Whenever any Commonwealth agency, legislative agency or judicial agency shall enter into any contract involving any property, real, personal or mixed of any kind or description or any contract for personal services where the consideration involved in the contract is $5,000 or more, a copy of the contract shall be filed with the Treasury Department within ten days after the contract is fully executed on behalf of the Commonwealth agency, legislative agency or judicial agency or otherwise becomes an obligation of the Commonwealth agency, legislative agency or judicial agency. The provisions of this chapter shall not apply to contracts for services protected by a privilege. The provisions of this chapter shall not apply to a purchase order evidencing fulfillment of an existing contract but shall apply to a purchase order evidencing new obligations. The following shall apply:

(1) Each Commonwealth agency, legislative agency and judicial agency shall submit contracts in a form and structure mutually agreed upon by the Commonwealth agency, legislative agency or judicial agency and the State Treasurer.

(2) The Treasury Department may require each Commonwealth agency, legislative agency or judicial agency to provide a summary with each contract, which shall include the following:

(i) Date of execution.

(ii) Amount of the contract.

(iii) Beginning date of the contract.

(iv) End date of the contract, if applicable.

(v) Name of the agency entering into the contract.

(vi) The name of all parties executing the contract.

(vii) Subject matter of the contract.

Each agency shall create and maintain the data under this paragraph in an ASCII-delimited text file, spreadsheet file or other file provided by Treasury Department regulation.

(b) Retention.—Every contract filed pursuant to subsection

(a) shall remain on file with the Treasury Department for a period of not less than four years after the end date of the contract.

(c) Accuracy.—Each Commonwealth agency, legislative agency and judicial agency is responsible for verifying the accuracy and completeness of the information that it submits to the State Treasurer. The contract provided to the Treasury Department pursuant to this chapter shall be redacted in accordance with applicable provisions of this act by the agency filing the contract to the Treasury Department.

(d) Applicability.—The provisions of this act shall not apply to copies of contracts submitted to the Treasury Department, the Office of Auditor General or other agency for purposes of audits and warrants for disbursements under section 307, 401, 402 or 403 of the act of April 9, 1929 (P.L.343, No.176), known as The Fiscal Code.

§ 1702. Public availability of contracts.

(a) General rule.—The Treasury Department shall make each contract filed pursuant to section 1701 available for public inspection either by posting a copy of the contract on the Treasury Department's publicly accessible Internet website or by posting a contract summary on the department's publicly accessible Internet website.

(b) Posting.—The Treasury Department shall post the information received pursuant to this chapter in a manner that allows the public to search contracts or contract summaries by the categories enumerated in section 1701(a)(2).

(c) Request to review or receive copy of contract.—The Treasury Department shall maintain a page on its publicly accessible Internet website that includes instructions on how to review a contract on the Internet website.

(d) Paper copy.—A paper copy of a contract may be requested from the agency that executed the contract in accordance with this act.

CHAPTER 31
MISCELLANEOUS PROVISIONS

§ 3101. Applicability.

This act shall apply to requests for information made after december 31, 2008.

§ 3101.1. RELATION TO OTHER LAWS.

If the provisions of this act regarding access to records conflict with any other federal or state law, the provisions of this act shall not apply.

§ 3101.2. Severability.

All provisions of this act are severable.

§ 3102. Repeals.

Repeals are as follows:

(1) The General Assembly declares as follows:

(i) The repeal under paragraph (2)(i) is necessary to effectuate Chapter 17.

(ii) The repeals under paragraph (2)(ii) and (iii) are necessary to effectuate this act.

(2) The following acts and parts of acts are repealed:

(i) Section 1104 of the act of April 9, 1929 (P.L.177, No.175), known as The Administrative Code of 1929.

(ii) The act of June 21, 1957 (P.L.390, No.212), referred to as the Right-to-Know Law.

(iii) 62 Pa.C.S. § 106.

§ 3103. References.

Notwithstanding 1 Pa.C.S. § 1937(b), a reference in a statute or regulation to the act of June 21, 1957 (P.L.390, No.212), referred to as the Right-to-Know Law, shall be deemed a reference to this act.

§ 3104. Effective date.

This act shall take effect as follows:

(1) The following provisions shall take effect immediately:

(i) Sections 101, 102 and 1310.

(ii) This section.

(2) Chapters 15 and 17 and sections 3102(1)(i) and 3102(2)(i) shall take effect july 1, 2008.

(3) The remainder of this act shall take effect january 1, 2009.

Chapter 2.2
DISPOSITION OF RECORDS
53 P.S. §§ 1381–1389

TABLE OF CONTENTS

Sec.

§ 1381. Short title and scope of subchapter.

(a) Short title of subchapter.—This subchapter shall be known and may be cited as the Municipal Records Act.

(b) Scope of subchapter.—This subchapter applies to the following entities:

(1) A city of the third class, borough, incorporated town, township of the first class or township of the second class, including any municipal corporation as described in this paragraph which has adopted a home rule charter.

(2) Municipal authorities created by any municipal corporation which is subject to this subchapter.

This subchapter does not apply to cities of the first class, second class or second class A.

§ 1382. Definitions.

The following words and phrases when used in this subchapter shall have the meanings given to them in this section unless the context clearly indicates otherwise:

"Commission." The Pennsylvania Historical and Museum Commission.

"Committee." The Local Government Records Committee.

"Public records." Any papers, books, maps, photographs or other documentary materials, regardless of physical form or characteristics, made or received by an entity under law or in connection with the exercise of its powers and the discharge of its duties.

§ 1383. Disposition of public records.

Public records may be disposed of if the disposition is in conformity with schedules and regulations which are promulgated by the committee as established by section 1385 (relating to Local Government Records Committee).

§ 1384. Proposed retention and disposal schedules.

The commission, in cooperation with the several associations of municipal officials and related Commonwealth agencies, shall make a study of public records and shall prepare proposed retention and disposition schedules for submission to the committee for its approval and advise each of them of all applicable operative schedules and prepare updates of these schedules as needed. No such schedule shall be operative unless approved by the committee.

§ 1385. Local Government Records Committee.

(a) Establishment.—There shall be established under the commission the Local Government Records Committee which shall consist of the Auditor General, the State Treasurer, the General Counsel, the Executive Director of the Pennsylvania Historical and Museum Commission, the Secretary of Community and Economic Development and five other members to be appointed by the Governor to represent each of the following municipal associations: the League of Cities, the State Association of Boroughs, the State Association of Township Commissioners, the State Association of Township Supervisors and the Municipal Authorities' Association. Each ex officio member of the committee may designate in writing a representative to act in place of the member. The Secretary of Community and Economic Development shall serve as chairman, and the executive director of the commission shall serve as secretary. Meetings of the committee shall be at the call of the chairman.

(b) Powers and duties.—The committee shall have the powers and duties vested in and imposed upon it by this subchapter and shall promulgate regulations not inconsistent with law necessary to adequately effectuate its powers and duties.

§ 1386. Effect of approval of schedule.

(a) Disposition generally.—Whenever a schedule is approved by the committee, a copy shall be filed with the commission which shall, through appropriate means, notify the entities that the schedule has been approved. Upon such notification, the schedule becomes effective and may be acted upon by them until superseded by a subsequent duly approved schedule. Each entity shall declare its intent to follow the schedule by ordinance or resolution. Each individual act of disposition shall be approved by resolution of the governing body.

(b) Disposition of permanent retention records.—Original records scheduled for permanent retention may be disposed of if, in addition to the procedures listed in this section, the entity generates and maintains a copy of the original in conformance with section 1388 (relating to recording and copying records) and receives written permission from the commission to dispose of the records. Written permission from the commission is required only for disposition actions involving records scheduled for permanent retention, records not listed on the schedules and records selected for transfer to the State Archives.

§ 1387. Nonliability of official.

An official shall not be held liable on his official bond for damages for loss or in any other manner, civil or criminal, because of the disposition of public records pursuant to the provisions of this subchapter.

§ 1388. Recording and copying records.

(a) Authorized methods.—Records may be recorded or copied in conformance with section 1 of the act of May 9, 1949 (P.L. 908, No. 250),[1] entitled "An act relating to public records of political subdivisions other than cities and counties of the first class; authorizing the recording and copying of documents, plats, papers and instruments of writing by photostatic, photographic, microfilm or other mechanical process, and the admissibility thereof and enlargements thereof in evidence; providing for the storage of duplicates and sale of microfilm copies of official records and for the destruction of other records deemed valueless; and providing for the services of the Department of Property and Supplies to political subdivisions," and applicable policies, standards and procedures adopted by the committee.

(b) Evidence of records.—Upon disposition of any public records under this subchapter, the copy shall be receivable in evidence in any court or proceeding and shall have the same force and effect as though the original public record had been produced and proved.

§ 1389. Applicability of other statutes.

This subchapter is intended as a supplement to existing statutes. The existing statutes which provide for destruction may be utilized by officials in lieu of compliance with this subchapter. Nothing in this subchapter shall prevent officials from retaining records longer than the periods which may be provided in schedules approved by the committee.

Chapter 2.3

MUNICIPAL DEED REGISTRATION ACT

21 P.S. § 338.3

§ 338.3 Registration of deeds generally

(a) General rule.—Notwithstanding any other provision of law or ordinance or resolution to the contrary, after the effective date of this act, any requirement that a deed or conveyance be registered with a municipality shall be satisfied by either of the following:

(1) Registration by the owner or agent in accordance with section 4.[2]

(2) The obtaining of information necessary for registration of the deed or conveyance by the municipality, in lieu of registration under paragraph (1), in accordance with section 5.[3]

(b) Prohibition.—A municipality shall not require that registration of a deed be made prior to the recordation of the original deed with the recorder of deeds.

---

1. 65 P.S. § 63.1.
2. 21 P.S. § 338.4.
3. 21 P.S. § 338.5.

CHAPTER 3

PUBLIC OFFICIAL AND EMPLOYEE ETHICS ACT[1]; OATH OF OFFICE

65 Pa.C.S. § 1101–1113
65 P.S. § 410
53 Pa.C.S. § 1141

TABLE OF CONTENTS

---

§ 1101. Short title of chapter.

This chapter shall be known and may be cited as the Public Official and Employee Ethics Act.

§ 1101.1. Purpose.

(a) Declarations.—The Legislature hereby declares that public office is a public trust and that any effort to realize personal financial gain through public office other than compensation provided by law is a violation of that trust. In order to strengthen the faith and confidence of the people of this Commonwealth in their government, the Legislature further declares that the people have a right to be assured that the financial interests of holders of or nominees or candidates for public office do not conflict with the public trust. Because public confidence in government can best be sustained by assuring the people of the impartiality and honesty of public officials, this chapter shall be liberally construed to promote complete financial disclosure as specified in this chapter. Furthermore, it is recognized that clear guidelines are needed in order to guide public officials and employees in their actions. Thus, the General Assembly by this chapter intends to define as clearly as possible those areas which represent conflict with the public trust.

(b) Recognition.—It is recognized that many public officials, including most local officials and members of the General Assembly, are citizen-officials who bring to their public office the knowledge and concerns of ordinary citizens and

---

1. Act of 1998, P.L. 729, No. 93.

Table of Contents
Part I Ch. 1–3 Ethics, Records, Open Meetings
Part II Ch. 4–10 Taxation
Part III Ch. 11–18 Torts, Contracts & Civil Rules
Part IV Ch. 19–24 Zoning & Planning
Part V Ch. 25–30 Construction and Emergency Codes
Part VI Ch. 31–39 Municipal Codes
Index

taxpayers. They should not be discouraged from maintaining their contacts with their community through their occupations and professions. Thus, in order to foster maximum compliance with its terms, this chapter shall be administered in a manner that emphasizes guidance to public officials and public employees regarding the ethical standards established by this chapter.

(c) Legislative intent.—It is the intent of the General Assembly that this chapter be administered by an independent commission composed of members who are cognizant of the responsibilities and burdens of public officials and employees and who have demonstrated an interest in promoting public confidence in government.

§ 1102. Definitions.

The following words and phrases when used in this chapter shall have, unless the context clearly indicates otherwise, the meanings given to them in this section:

"Advice." Any directive of the chief counsel of the State Ethics Commission issued under section 1107(11) (relating to powers and duties of commission) and based exclusively on prior commission opinions, this chapter, regulations promulgated pursuant to this chapter and court opinions which interpret this chapter.

"Aggregate." The total of all gifts received from a single source as provided in section 1105(b)(6) (relating to statement of financial interests).

"Authority of office or employment." The actual power provided by law, the exercise of which is necessary to the performance of duties and responsibilities unique to a particular public office or position of public employment.

"Business." Any corporation, partnership, sole proprietorship, firm, enterprise, franchise, association, organization, self-employed individual, holding company, joint stock company, receivership, trust or any legal entity organized for profit.

"Business with which he is associated." Any business in which the person or a member of the person's immediate family is a director, officer, owner, employee or has a financial interest.

"Candidate." Any individual who seeks nomination or election to public office by vote of the electorate, other than a judge of elections, inspector of elections or official of a political party, whether or not such individual is nominated or elected. An individual shall be deemed to be seeking nomination or election to such office if he has:

(1) received a contribution or made an expenditure or given his consent for any other person or committee to receive a contribution or make an expenditure for the purpose of influencing his nomination or election to such office, whether or not the individual has announced the specific office for which he will seek nomination or election at the time the contribution is received or the expenditure is made; or

(2) taken the action necessary under the laws of this Commonwealth to qualify himself for nomination or election to such office.

The term shall include individuals nominated or elected as write-in candidates unless they resign such nomination or elected office within 30 days of having been nominated or elected.

"Commission." The State Ethics Commission.

"Confidential information." Information not obtainable from reviewing a public document or from making inquiry to a publicly available source of information.

"Conflict" or "conflict of interest." Use by a public official or public employee of the authority of his office or employment or any confidential information received through his holding public office or employment for the private pecuniary benefit of himself, a member of his immediate family or a business with which he or a member of his immediate family is associated. The term does not include an action having a de minimis economic impact or which affects to the same degree a class consisting of the general public or a subclass consisting of an industry, occupation or other group which includes the public official or public employee, a member of his immediate family or a business with which he or a member of his immediate family is associated.

"Contract." An agreement or arrangement for the acquisition, use or disposal by the Commonwealth or a political subdivision of consulting or other services or of supplies, materials, equipment, land or other personal or real property. The term shall not mean an agreement or arrangement between the State or political subdivision as one party and a public official or public employee as the other party, concerning his expense, reimbursement, salary, wage, retirement or other benefit, tenure or other matters in consideration of his current public employment with the Commonwealth or a political subdivision.

"De minimis economic impact." An economic consequence which has an insignificant effect.

"Executive-level State employee." The Governor, Lieutenant Governor, cabinet members, deputy secretaries, the Governor's office staff, any State employee with discretionary powers which may affect the outcome of a State agency's decision in relation to a private corporation or business or any employee who by virtue of his job function could influence the outcome of such a decision.

"Financial interest." Any financial interest in a legal entity engaged in business for profit which comprises more than 5% of the equity of the business or more than 5% of the assets of the economic interest in indebtedness.

"Findings report." An initial report containing findings of fact as determined by the State Ethics Commission's investigation but not containing any conclusions of law or any determination of whether there has been a violation of law.

"Frivolous complaint." A complaint filed in a grossly negligent manner without basis in law or fact.

"Gift." Anything which is received without consideration of equal or greater value. The term shall not include a political contribution otherwise reported as required by law or a commercially reasonable loan made in the ordinary course of business.

"Governmental body." Any department, authority, commission, committee, council, board, bureau, division, service, office, officer, administration, legislative body or other establishment in the executive, legislative or judicial branch of a state, a nation or a political subdivision thereof or any agency performing a governmental function.

"Governmental body with which a public official or public employee is or has been associated." The governmental body within State government or a political subdivision by which the public official or employee is or has been employed or to which the public official or employee is or has been appointed or elected and subdivisions and offices within that governmental body.

"Honorarium." Payment made in recognition of published works, appearances, speeches and presentations and which is not intended as consideration for the value of such services which are nonpublic occupational or professional in nature. The term does not include tokens presented or provided which are of de minimis economic impact.

"Immediate family." A parent, spouse, child, brother or sister.

"Income." Any money or thing of value received or to be received as a claim on future services or in recognition of services rendered in the past, whether in the form of a payment, fee, salary, expense, allowance, forbearance, forgiveness, interest, dividend, royalty, rent, capital gain, reward, severance payment, proceeds from the sale of a financial interest in a corporation, professional corporation, partnership or other entity resulting from termination or withdrawal

Table of Contents
Part I Ch. 1–3 Ethics, Records, Open Meetings
Part II Ch. 4–10 Taxation
Part III Ch. 11–18 Torts, Contracts & Civil Rules
Part IV Ch. 19–24 Zoning & Planning
Part V Ch. 25–30 Construction and Emergency Codes
Part VI Ch. 31–39 Municipal Codes
Index

therefrom upon assumption of public office or employment or any other form of recompense or any combination thereof. The term refers to gross income and includes prize winnings and tax-exempt income. The term does not include gifts, governmentally mandated payments or benefits, retirement, pension or annuity payments funded totally by contributions of the public official or employee, or miscellaneous, incidental income of minor dependent children.

"Indirect interest in real estate." Any business entity the assets of which are 80% or more in real property.

"Ministerial action." An action that a person performs in a prescribed manner in obedience to the mandate of legal authority, without regard to or the exercise of the person's own judgment as to the desirability of the action being taken.

"Nominee." Any person whose name has been submitted to a public official or governmental body vested with the power to finally confirm or reject proposed appointments to public office or employment.

"Nonministerial actions." An action in which the person exercises his own judgment as to the desirability of the action taken.

"Opinion." A directive of the State Ethics Commission issued pursuant to section 1107(10) (relating to powers and duties of commission) setting forth a public official's or public employee's duties under this chapter.

"Order." A directive of the State Ethics Commission issued pursuant to section 1107(13) (relating to powers and duties of commission) at the conclusion of an investigation which contains findings of fact, conclusions of law and penalties.

"Person." A business, governmental body, individual, corporation, union, association, firm, partnership, committee, club or other organization or group of persons.

"Political contribution." Any advance, conveyance, deposit, distribution, transfer of funds, loan, payment, pledge, purchase of a ticket to a testimonial or similar fund-raising affair, or subscription of money or anything of value, except volunteer services, in connection with a political campaign, and any contract, agreement, promise or other obligations, whether or not legally enforceable, to make a political contribution.

"Political subdivision." Any county, city, borough, incorporated town, township, school district, vocational school, county institution district, and any authority, entity or body organized by the aforementioned.

"Public employee." Any individual employed by the Commonwealth or a political subdivision who is responsible for taking or recommending official action of a nonministerial nature with regard to:

(1) contracting or procurement;

(2) administering or monitoring grants or subsidies;

(3) planning or zoning;

(4) inspecting, licensing, regulating or auditing any person; or

(5) any other activity where the official action has an economic impact of greater than a de minimis nature on the interests of any person.

The term shall not include individuals who are employed by this Commonwealth or any political subdivision thereof in teaching as distinguished from administrative duties.

"Public official." Any person elected by the public or elected or appointed by a governmental body or an appointed official in the executive, legislative or judicial branch of this Commonwealth or any political subdivision thereof, provided that it shall not include members of advisory boards that have no authority to expend public funds other than reimbursement for personal expense or to otherwise exercise the power of the State or any political subdivision thereof.

"Represent." To act on behalf of any other person in any activity which includes, but is not limited to, the following: personal appearances, negotiations, lobbying and submitting bid or contract proposals which are signed by or contain the name of a former public official or public employee.

"Solicitor." A person elected or appointed to the office of solicitor for the political subdivision.

"Source." Any person who is a provider of an item reportable under section 1105 (relating to statement of financial interests).

"State consultant." A person who, as an independent contractor, performs professional, scientific, technical or advisory service for an agency of this Commonwealth, and who receives a fee, honorarium or similar compensation for such services. A State consultant is not an executive-level employee.

§ 1103. Restricted activities.

(a) Conflict of interest.—No public official or public employee shall engage in conduct that constitutes a conflict of interest.

(b) Seeking improper influence.—No person shall offer or give to a public official, public employee or nominee or candidate for public office or a member of his immediate family or a business with which he is associated, anything of monetary value, including a gift, loan, political contribution, reward or promise of future employment based on the offeror's or donor's understanding that the vote, official action or judgment of the public official or public employee or nominee or candidate for public office would be influenced thereby.

(c) Accepting improper influence.—No public official, public employee or nominee or candidate for public office shall solicit or accept anything of monetary value, including a gift, loan, political contribution, reward or promise of future employment, based on any understanding of that public official, public employee or nominee that the vote, official action or judgment of the public official or public employee or nominee or candidate for public office would be influenced thereby.

(d) Honorarium.—No public official or public employee shall accept an honorarium.

(e) Contingent and severance payments.—

(1) No person shall solicit or accept a severance payment or anything of monetary value contingent upon the assumption or acceptance of public office or employment.

(2) This subsection shall not prohibit:

(i) Payments received pursuant to an employment agreement in existence prior to the time a person becomes a candidate or is notified by a member of a transition team, a search committee or a person with appointive power that he is under consideration for public office or makes application for public employment.

(ii) Receipt of a salary, fees, severance payment or proceeds resulting from the sale of a person's interest in a corporation, professional corporation, partnership or other entity resulting from termination or withdrawal therefrom upon the assumption or acceptance of public office or employment.

(3) Payments made or received pursuant to paragraph (2)(i) and (ii) shall not be based on the agreement, written or otherwise, that the vote or official action of the prospective public official or employee would be influenced thereby.

(f) Contract.—No public official or public employee or his spouse or child or any business in which the person or his spouse or child is associated shall enter into any contract valued at $500 or more with the governmental body with which the public official or public employee is associated or any subcontract valued at $500 or more with any person who has been awarded a contract with the governmental body with which the public official or public employee is associated, unless the contract has been awarded through an open and public process, including prior public notice and subsequent public disclosure of all proposals considered and contracts awarded. In such a case, the public official or public employee shall not have any supervisory or overall responsibility for the implementation or administration of the contract. Any contract or subcontract made in violation of this subsection shall be voidable by a court of competent jurisdiction if the suit is commenced within 90 days of the making of the contract or subcontract.

(g) Former official or employee.—No former public official or public employee shall represent a person, with promised or actual compensation, on any matter before the governmental body with which he has been associated for one year after he leaves that body. **AUTHOR'S NOTE:** In the case of ***Shaulis v. Penn. St. Ethics Com'n*** **833 A.2d 123, (Pa 2003)** the Pennsylvania Supreme Court held §1103(g) unconstitutional as applied to former government employees who are attorneys.

(h) Misuse of statement of financial interest.—No person shall use for any commercial purpose information copied from statements of financial interests required by this chapter or from lists compiled from such statements.

(i) Former executive-level employee.—No former executive-level State employee may for a period of two years from the time that he terminates employment with this Commonwealth be employed by, receive compensation from, assist or act in a representative capacity for a business or corporation that he actively participates in recruiting to this Commonwealth or that he actively participated[2] in inducing to open a new plant, facility or branch in this Commonwealth or that he actively participated in inducing to expand an existent plant or facility within this Commonwealth, provided that the above prohibition shall be invoked only when the recruitment or inducement is accomplished by a grant or loan of money or a promise of a grant or loan of money from the Commonwealth to the business or corporation recruited or induced to expand.

(j) Voting conflict.—Where voting conflicts are not otherwise addressed by the Constitution of Pennsylvania or by any law, rule, regulation, order or ordinance, the following procedure shall be employed. Any public official or public employee who in the discharge of his official duties would be required to vote on a matter that would result in a conflict of interest shall abstain from voting and, prior to the vote being taken, publicly announce and disclose the nature of his interest as a public record in a written memorandum filed with the person responsible for recording the minutes of the meeting at which the vote is taken, provided that whenever a governing body would be unable to take any action on a matter before it because the number of members of the body required to abstain from voting under the provisions of this section makes the majority or other legally required vote of approval unattainable, then such members shall be permitted to vote if disclosures are made as otherwise provided herein. In the case of a three-member governing body of a political subdivision, where one member has abstained from voting as a result of a conflict of interest and the remaining two members of the governing body have cast opposing votes, the member who has abstained shall be permitted to vote to break the tie vote if disclosure is made as otherwise provided herein.

§ 1104. Statement of financial interests required to be filed.

(a) Public official or public employee.—Each public official of the Commonwealth shall file a statement of financial interests for the preceding calendar year with the commission no later than May 1 of each year that he holds such a

2. "participates" in enrolled bill.

position and of the year after he leaves such a position. Each public employee and public official of the Commonwealth shall file a statement of financial interests for the preceding calendar year with the department, agency, body or bureau in which he is employed or to which he is appointed or elected no later than May 1 of each year that he holds such a position and of the year after he leaves such a position. Any other public employee or public official shall file a statement of financial interests with the governing authority of the political subdivision by which he is employed or within which he is appointed or elected no later than May 1 of each year that he holds such a position and of the year after he leaves such a position. Persons who are full-time or part-time solicitors for political sudivisions are required to file under this section.

(b) Candidate.—

(1) Any candidate for a State-level public office shall file a statement of financial interests for the preceding calendar year with the commission on or before the last day for filing a petition to appear on the ballot for election. A copy of the statement of financial interests shall also be appended to such petition.

(2) Any candidate for county-level or local office shall file a statement of financial interests for the preceding calendar year with the governing authority of the political subdivision in which he is a candidate on or before the last day for filing a petition to appear on the ballot for election. A copy of the statement of financial interests shall also be appended to such petition.

(3) No petition to appear on the ballot for election shall be accepted by the respective State or local election officials unless the petition has appended thereto a statement of financial interests as set forth in paragraphs (1) and (2). Failure to file the statement in accordance with the provisions of this chapter shall, in addition to any other penalties provided, be a fatal defect to a petition to appear on the ballot.

(c) Nominee.—Each State-level nominee for public office shall file a statement of financial interests for the preceding calendar year with the commission and with the official or body that is vested with the power of confirmation at least ten days before the official or body shall approve or reject the nomination. Each nominee for a county-level or local office shall file a statement of financial interests for the preceding calendar year with the governing authority of the political subdivision in which he or she is a nominee and, if different, with the official or body that is vested with the power of confirmation at least ten days before the official or body shall approve or reject the nomination.

(d) Failure to file required statement.—No public official shall be allowed to take the oath of office or enter or continue upon his duties, nor shall he receive compensation from public funds, unless he has filed a statement of financial interests as required by this chapter.

(e) Public inspection and copying.—All statements of financial interests filed pursuant to the provisions of this chapter shall be made available for public inspection and copying during regular office hours, and copying facilities shall be made available at a charge not to exceed actual cost.

§ 1105. Statement of financial interests.

(a) Form.—The statement of financial interests filed pursuant to this chapter shall be on a form prescribed by the commission. All information requested on the statement shall be provided to the best of the knowledge, information and belief of the person required to file and shall be signed under oath or equivalent affirmation.

(b) Required information.—The statement shall include the following information for the prior calendar year with regard to the person required to file the statement:

(1) Name, address and public position.

(2) Occupation or profession.

(3) Any direct or indirect interest in any real estate which was sold or leased to the Commonwealth, any of its agencies or political subdivisions, or purchased[3] or leased from the Commonwealth, any of its agencies or political subdivisions, or which was the subject of any condemnation proceedings by the Commonwealth, any of its agencies or political subdivisions.

(4) The name and address of each creditor to whom is owed in excess of $6,500 and the interest rate thereon. However, loans or credit extended between members of the immediate family and mortgages securing real property which is the principal or secondary residence of the person filing shall not be included.

(5) The name and address of any direct or indirect source of income totalling in the aggregate $1,300 or more. However, this provision shall not be construed to require the divulgence of confidential information protected by statute or existing professional codes of ethics or common law privileges.

(6) The name and address of the source and the amount of any gift or gifts valued in the aggregate at $250 or more and the circumstances of each gift. This paragraph shall not apply to a gift or gifts received from a spouse, parent, parent by marriage, sibling, child, grandchild, other family member or friend when the circumstances make it clear that the motivation for the action was a personal or family relationship. However, for the purposes of this paragraph, the term "friend" shall not include a registered lobbyist or an employee of a registered lobbyist.

(7) The name and address of the source and the amount of any payment for or reimbursement of actual expenses for transportation and lodging or hospitality received in connection with public office or employment where such actual expenses for transportation and lodging or hospitality exceed $650 in the course of a single occurrence. This paragraph shall not apply to expenses reimbursed by a governmental body or to expenses reimbursed by an organization or association of public officials or employees of political subdivisions which the public official or employee serves in an official capacity.

(8) Any office, directorship or employment of any nature whatsoever in any business entity.

(9) Any financial interest in any legal entity engaged in business for profit.

(10) The identity of any financial interest in a business with which the reporting person is or has been associated in the preceding calendar year which has been transferred to a member of the reporting person's immediate family.

(c) Reporting amounts.—Except where an amount is required to be reported pursuant to subsection (b)(6) and (7), the statement of financial interests need not include specific amounts for the items required to be listed.

(d) Cost-of-living adjustments.—On a biennial basis the commission shall review the dollar amounts set forth in this section and may increase these amounts to such rates as are deemed reasonable for assuring appropriate disclosure. The commission shall publish any such adjusted threshold amounts in the Pennsylvania Bulletin.

§ 1106. State Ethics Commission.

(a) Continuation of commission.—The State Ethics Commission established under the act of October 4, 1978 (P.L. 883, No. 170),[4] referred to as the Public Official and Employee Ethics Law, is continued and shall be composed of seven members. The President pro tempore of the Senate, the Minority Leader of the

3. "subdivisions; purchased" in enrolled bill.

4. 65 P.S. § 401 et seq.

Senate, the Speaker of the House and the Minority Leader of the House shall each appoint one member. Three members shall be appointed by the Governor without confirmation. No more than two of the members appointed by the Governor shall be of the same political party. No appointee shall have served as an officer in a political party for one year prior to his appointment.

(b) Term of service.—Members of the commission shall serve for terms of three years, except that members shall continue to serve until their successors are appointed and qualified.

(c) Maximum number of terms.—No member shall be appointed to more than two full three-year terms on the commission.

(d) Prohibited activities.—No individual while a member or employee of the commission shall:

(1) hold or campaign for any other public office;

(2) hold office in any political party or political committee;

(3) actively participate in or contribute to any political campaign;

(4) directly or indirectly attempt to influence any decision by a governmental body, other than a court of law or as a representative of the commission on a matter within the jurisdiction of the commission; or

(5) be employed by the Commonwealth or a political subdivision in any other capacity, whether or not for compensation.

(e) Vacancy.—A majority of the commission by resolution shall declare vacant the position on the commission of any member who takes part in activities prohibited by subsection (d). An individual appointed to fill a vacancy occurring other than by the expiration of a term of office shall be appointed for the unexpired term of the member he succeeds and is eligible for appointment to two full three-year terms thereafter. Any vacancy occurring on the commission shall be filled within 30 days in the manner in which that position was originally filled.

(f) Election of chairman and vice chairman.—The commission shall elect a chairman and a vice chairman. The vice chairman shall act as chairman in the absence of the chairman or in the event of a vacancy in that position.

(g) Quorum.—Four members of the commission shall constitute a quorum and except as provided in section 1108(g) (relating to investigations by commission), the votes of a majority of the members present are[5] required for any action or recommendation of the commission. The chairman or any four members of the commission may call a meeting provided that advance written notice is mailed to each member and to any person who requests notice of such meetings.

(h) Compensation.—Members of the commission shall be compensated at a rate of $250 per day and shall receive reimbursement for their actual and necessary expenses while performing the business of the commission.

(i) Staff.—The commission shall employ an executive director, a chief counsel and such other staff as are necessary to carry out its duties pursuant to this chapter. The executive director shall be responsible for the administrative operations of the commission and shall perform such other duties as may be delegated or assigned to him by the commission, except that the commission shall not delegate the making of regulations to the executive director. The chief counsel shall be the chief legal officer of the commission. The commission may obtain the services of experts and consultants as necessary to carry out its duties pursuant to this chapter. The State Treasurer and the Attorney General shall make available to the commission such personnel, facilities and other assistance as the commission may request.

5. "is" in enrolled bill.

(j) **Regulations.**—The commission shall develop regulations that provide for a code of conduct to govern the activities and ethical standards of its members, which code shall subject the members of the commission to no less than is required for public officials or public employees under this chapter.

§ 1107. Powers and duties of commission

In addition to other powers and duties prescribed by law, the commission shall:

(1) Prescribe and publish rules and regulations to carry out the provisions of this chapter.

(2) Prescribe forms for statements and reports required to be filed by this chapter and furnish such forms to persons required to file such statements and reports.

(3) Prepare and publish guidelines setting forth recommended uniform methods of accounting and reporting for use by persons required to file statements and reports by this chapter.

(4) Accept and file any information voluntarily supplied that exceeds the requirements of this chapter.

(5) Inspect statements of financial interests which have been filed in order to ascertain whether any reporting person has failed to file such a statement or has filed a deficient statement. If, upon inspection, it is determined that a reporting person has failed to file a statement of financial interests or that any statement which has been filed fails to conform with the requirements of section 1105 (relating to statement of financial interests), then the commission shall in writing notify the person. Such notice shall state in detail the deficiency and the penalties for failure to file or for filing a deficient statement of financial interests.

(6) Provide that statements and reports filed with the commission be made available for public inspection and copying during regular office hours and provide that copying facilities be made available at a charge not to exceed actual cost and advise other State and local agencies of the provisions of this paragraph.

(7) Compile and maintain an index of all reports and statements filed with the commission to facilitate public access to such reports and statements and instruct other State and local agencies which receive and file financial interest statements in the maintenance of systems which facilitate public access to such statements.

(8) Prepare and publish annual summaries of statements and reports filed with the commission.

(9) Preserve statements and reports filed with the commission for a period of five years from date of receipt and advise other State and local agencies which receive and store financial interest statements to preserve such statements for a period of five years from date of receipt.

(10) Issue to any person upon such person's request or to the appointing authority or employer of that person upon the request of such appointing authority or employer an opinion with respect to such person's duties under this chapter. The commission shall, within 14 days, either issue the opinion or advise the person who made the request whether an opinion will be issued. No person who acts in good faith on an opinion issued to him by the commission shall be subject to criminal or civil penalties for so acting, provided that the material facts are as stated in the opinion request. The commission's opinion shall be public records and may from time to time be published. The person requesting the opinion may, however, require that the opinion shall contain such deletions and changes as shall be necessary to protect the identity of the persons involved.

(11) Provide written advice to any person or the appointing authority or employer of such person, upon their request with respect to such person's duties under this chapter. Such advice shall be provided within 21 working days of the request, provided that the time may be extended for good cause. It shall be a complete defense in any enforcement proceeding initiated by the commission, and evidence of good faith conduct in any other civil or criminal proceeding, if the requester, at least 21 working days prior to the alleged violation, requested written advice from the commission in good faith, disclosed truthfully all the material facts and committed the acts complained of either in reliance on the advice or because of the failure of the commission to provide advice within 21 days of the request or such later extended time. The person requesting the advice may, however, require that the advice shall contain such deletions and changes as shall be necessary to protect the identity of the persons involved.

(12) Initiate an inquiry, pursuant to section 1108(a) (relating to investigations by commission), where a complaint has not been filed but where there is a reasonable belief that a conflict may exist.

(13) Issue findings, reports and orders relating to investigations initiated pursuant to section 1108, which set forth the alleged violation, findings of fact and conclusions of law. An order may include recommendations to law enforcement officials. Any order resulting from a finding that a public official or public employee has obtained a financial gain in violation of this chapter may require the restitution plus interest of that gain to the appropriate governmental body. The commission or the Office of Attorney General shall have standing to apply to the Commonwealth Court to seek enforcement of an order requiring such restitution. This restitution requirement shall be in addition to any other penalties provided for in this chapter.

(14) Hold hearings, take testimony, issue subpoenas and compel the attendance of witnesses.

(15) Make recommendations to law enforcement officials either for criminal prosecution or dismissal of charges arising out of violations of this chapter.

(16) Prepare and publish special reports, educational materials, and technical studies to further the purposes of this chapter.

(17) Prepare and publish, prior to June 1 of each year, an annual report summarizing the activities of the commission.

(18) Transmit, free of charge, copies of each order, advice and opinion which has become a matter of public record quarterly to the law library of each county, one public library in each county, the State Library, the State Senate Library, each authority appointing commission members under this chapter, the Pennsylvania Association of County Commissioners, the Pennsylvania Association of Boroughs, the Pennsylvania State Association of Township Supervisors, the Pennsylvania State Association of Township Commissioners, the Pennsylvania School Boards Association and the Pennsylvania League of Cities.

(19) Hold at least two public hearings each year, of which at least one shall be held in Harrisburg and at least one shall be held in a location other than Harrisburg, to seek input from persons and organizations who represent any individual subject to the provisions of this chapter and from other interested parties.

§ 1108. Investigations by commission.

(a) **Preliminary inquiry.**—Upon a complaint signed under penalty of perjury by any person or upon its own motion, the commission, through its executive director, shall conduct a preliminary inquiry into any alleged violation of this

Table of Contents
Part I Ch. 1–3 Ethics, Records, Open Meetings
Part II Ch. 4–10 Taxation
Part III Ch. 11–18 Torts, Contracts & Civil Rules
Part IV Ch. 19–24 Zoning & Planning
Part V Ch. 25–30 Construction and Emergency Codes
Part VI Ch. 31–39 Municipal Codes
Index

chapter. The commission shall keep information, records and proceedings relating to a preliminary inquiry confidential. The commission shall, however, have the authority to refer the case to law enforcement officials during a preliminary inquiry or anytime thereafter without providing notice to the subject of the inquiry. The commission shall complete its preliminary inquiry within 60 days of its initiation.

(b) Termination of preliminary inquiry.—If a preliminary inquiry fails to establish reason to believe that this chapter has been violated, the commission shall terminate the inquiry and so notify the complainant and the person who had been the subject of the inquiry. If the commission determines that a complaint is frivolous, it shall so state.

(c) Initiation of investigation.—If a preliminary inquiry establishes reason to believe that this chapter has been violated, the commission may, through its executive director, initiate an investigation to determine if there has been a violation. The commission shall keep information, records and proceedings relating to an investigation confidential until a final determination is made, except as otherwise provided in subsection (g). No investigation may be commenced until the person who is the subject of the investigation has been notified and provided a general statement of the alleged violation or violations of the chapter and other applicable statutes with respect to such investigation. Service of notice is complete upon mailing which shall be by certified or registered mail. The commission shall notify the complainant within 72 hours of the commencement of an investigation, and, thereafter, the commission shall advise the complainant and the person who is the subject of the investigation of the status of the investigation at least every 90 days until the investigation is terminated. The commission shall, within 180 days of the initiation of an investigation, either terminate the investigation pursuant to subsection (d) or issue a findings report pursuant to subsection (e). Upon a showing by the executive director of the need for extension of this period, the commission may extend an investigation for up to two 90-day periods, provided that each 90-day extension shall be approved by a majority vote of members present. In no event shall a findings report be issued later than 360 days after initiation of an investigation.

(d) Termination of investigation.—If an investigation conducted under this chapter indicates that no violation has been committed, the commission shall immediately terminate the investigation and send written notice of such determination to the complainant and the person who was the subject of the investigation.

(e) Findings report.—The commission, upon the completion of an investigation, shall issue a findings report to the subject of the investigation setting forth the pertinent findings of fact. The subject shall have the right to respond to said findings and to request an evidentiary hearing on said matter. The commission shall grant any request for a hearing. Said hearing shall be held in Harrisburg or, at the request of the subject, in either Philadelphia or Pittsburgh. Any response to the findings report must either admit or deny by corresponding number and letter the pertinent facts set forth. The subject of the investigation shall have access to any evidence intended to be used by the commission at the hearing and any exculpatory evidence developed by the commission in the course of its investigation. Matters not specifically denied in the response shall be deemed admitted. The response must be filed within 30 days of the issuance of the findings report unless the time period is extended by the commission for good cause shown. Hearings conducted upon request shall be instituted within 45 days after the filing of the response.

(f) Final order.—Within 30 days of the receipt by the commission of the hearing record or, if no hearing is to be held, within 30 days of the receipt by the commission of the response to the findings report, the commission shall issue an order which shall be final. Upon receipt of a final order, the subject shall have the right to file a petition for reconsideration in accordance with the regulations of the commission.

(g) Procedure for hearing.—Hearings conducted pursuant to this section shall be closed to the public unless the subject requests an open hearing. Any person who appears before the commission shall have all of the due process rights, privileges and responsibilities of a party or witness appearing before an administrative agency of this Commonwealth. All witnesses summoned for such hearings shall receive reimbursement for reasonable expenses in accordance with 42 Pa.C.S. § 5903 (relating to compensation and expenses of witnesses). At the conclusion of a hearing concerning an alleged violation and in a timely manner, the commission shall deliberate on the evidence and determine whether there has been a violation of this chapter. At least four members of the commission present at a meeting must find a violation by clear and convincing proof. The names of the members finding a violation and the names of those dissenting and abstaining shall be listed in the order. The determination of the commission, in the form of a final order and findings of fact, shall be a matter of public record.

(h) Availability of final orders, files and records.—Orders which become final in accordance with the provisions of this section shall be available as public documents, but the files and records of the commission relating to the case shall remain confidential.

(i) Appeal.—Any person aggrieved by an opinion or order which becomes final in accordance with the provisions of this chapter who has direct interest in such opinion or order shall have the right to appeal therefrom in accordance with law and general rules.

(j) Retaliation prohibited.—No public official or public employee shall discharge any official or employee or change his official rank, grade or compensation or deny him a promotion or threaten to do so for filing a complaint with or providing information to the commission or testifying in any commission proceeding. No member of the commission and no employee of the commission shall discharge any employee of the commission or change his official rank, grade or compensation or threaten to do so for providing any information about the internal operations of the commission, not required by law to be kept secret, to any legislator or legislative staff member or testifying in any legislative proceeding.

(k) Confidentiality.—As a general rule, no person shall disclose or acknowledge to any other person any information relating to a complaint, preliminary inquiry, investigation, hearing or petition for reconsideration which is before the commission. However, a person may disclose or acknowledge to another person matters held confidential in accordance with this subsection when the matters pertain to any of the following:

(1) final orders of the commission as provided in subsection (h);

(2) hearings conducted in public pursuant to subsection (g);

(3) for the purpose of seeking advice of legal counsel;

(4) filing an appeal from a commission order;

(5) communicating with the commission or its staff, in the course of a preliminary inquiry, investigation, hearing or petition for reconsideration by the commission;

(6) consulting with a law enforcement official or agency for the purpose of initiating, participating in or responding to an investigation or prosecution by the law enforcement official or agency;

(7) testifying under oath before a governmental body or a similar body of the United States of America;

(8) any information, records or proceedings relating to a complaint, preliminary inquiry, investigation, hearing or petition for reconsideration which the person is the subject of; or

(9) such other exceptions as the commission by regulation may direct.

(l) Frivolous complaints and wrongful disclosure.—If a public official or public employee has reason to believe the complaint is frivolous as defined by this chapter, or without probable cause and made primarily for a purpose other than that of reporting a violation of this chapter, or a person publicly disclosed or caused to be disclosed that a complaint against the public official or public employee has been filed with the commission, the public official or public employee shall notify the commission and the commission, through its executive director, shall conduct an investigation.

(m) Limitation of time.—The commission may conduct an investigation within five years after the alleged occurrence of any violation of this chapter.

§ 1109. Penalties.

(a) Restricted activities violation.—Any person who violates the provisions of section 1103(a), (b) and (c) (relating to restricted activities) commits a felony and shall, upon conviction, be sentenced to pay a fine of not more than $10,000 or to imprisonment for not more than five years, or both.

(b) Financial interests statement violation.—Any person who violates the provisions of section 1103(d) through (j), 1104 (relating to statement of financial interests required to be filed) or 1105(a) (relating to statement of financial interests) commits a misdemeanor and shall, upon conviction, be sentenced to pay a fine of not more than $1,000 or to imprisonment for not more than one year, or both.

(c) Treble damages.—Any person who obtains financial gain from violating any provision of this chapter, in addition to any other penalty provided by law, shall pay a sum of money equal to three times the amount of the financial gain resulting from such violation into the State Treasury or the treasury of the political subdivision. Treble damages shall not be assessed against a person who acted in good faith reliance on the advice of legal counsel.

(d) Impeachment and disciplinary action.—The penalties prescribed in this chapter do not limit the power of either House of the Legislature to discipline its own members or impeach a public official and do not limit the power of agencies or commissions to discipline officials or employees.

(e) Other violations of chapter.—Any person who violates the confidentiality of a commission proceeding pursuant to section 1108 (relating to investigations by commission) commits a misdemeanor and shall, upon conviction, be sentenced to pay a fine of not more than $1,000 or to imprisonment for not more than one year, or both. Any person who engages in retaliatory activity proscribed by section 1108(j) commits a misdemeanor and, in addition to any other penalty provided by law, shall, upon conviction, be sentenced to pay a fine of not more than $1,000 or to imprisonment for not more than one year, or both. Any person who willfully affirms or swears falsely in regard to any material matter before a commission proceeding pursuant to section 1108 commits a felony and shall, upon conviction, be sentenced to pay a fine of not more than $5,000 or to imprisonment for not more than five years, or both.

(f) Civil penalty.—In addition to any other civil remedy or criminal penalty provided for in this chapter, the commission may, after notice has been served in accordance with section 1107(5) (relating to powers and duties of commission) and upon a majority vote of its members, levy a civil penalty upon any person subject to this chapter who fails to file a statement of financial interests in a timely manner or who files a deficient statement of financial interests, at a rate of not more than $25 for each day such statement remains delinquent or deficient. The maximum penalty payable under this paragraph is $250.

(g) Reliance on solicitor's opinion.—A public official of a political subdivision who acts in good faith reliance on a written, nonconfidential opinion of the solicitor of the political subdivision or upon an opinion of the solicitor of the political subdivision, publicly stated at an open meeting of the political subdivision and recorded in the official minutes of the meeting, shall not be subject to the penalties provided for in subsections (a) and (b) nor for the treble damages provided for in subsection (c). However, this subsection shall not apply in situations where the solicitor's opinion has been rendered under duress or where the parties seeking and rendering the solicitor's opinion have colluded to purposefully commit a violation of this chapter.

§ 1110. Wrongful use of chapter.

(a) Liability.—A person who signs a complaint alleging a violation of this chapter against another is subject to liability for wrongful use of this chapter if:

(1) the complaint was frivolous, as defined by this chapter, or without probable cause and made primarily for a purpose other than that of reporting a violation of this chapter; or

(2) he publicly disclosed or caused to be disclosed that a complaint against a person had been filed with the commission.

(b) Probable cause.—A person who signs a complaint alleging a violation of this chapter has probable cause for doing so if he reasonably believes in the existence of the facts upon which the claim is based and either:

(1) reasonably believes that under those facts the complaint may be valid under this chapter; or

(2) believes to this effect in reliance upon the advice of counsel, sought in good faith and given after full disclosure of all relevant facts within his knowledge and information.

(c) Commission procedures.—When the commission determines that a complainant has violated the provisions set forth in subsection (a), the commission, upon receiving a written request from the subject of the complaint, shall provide the name and address of the complainant to said subject. If the commission determines that a complainant has not violated the provisions of subsection (a), the commission shall notify the subject accordingly. The subject shall have the right to appeal the commission's determination, and the commission shall schedule an appeal hearing. The subject shall show cause why the complainant violated the provisions of this section. If the commission grants the appeal, the commission shall immediately release the complainant's name and address to the subject. If the commission denies the appeal, it shall present evidence why the complainant's name and address shall not be released.

(d) Damages.—When the essential elements of an action brought pursuant to this section have been established, the plaintiff is entitled to recover for the following:

(1) The harm to his reputation by a defamatory matter alleged as the basis of the proceeding.

(2) The expenses, including any reasonable attorney fees, that he has reasonably incurred in proceedings before the commission.

(3) Any specific pecuniary loss that has resulted from the proceedings.

(4) Any emotional distress that has been caused by the proceedings.

(5) Any punitive damages according to law in appropriate cases.

§ 1111. Supplemental provisions.

Any governmental body may adopt requirements to supplement this chapter, provided that no such requirements shall in any way be less restrictive than the chapter.

§ 1112. Conflict of law.

Except as otherwise provided in Chapter 13 (relating to lobby regulation and disclosure), if the provisions of this chapter conflict with any other statute, ordinance, regulation or rule, the provisions of this chapter shall control.

§ 1113. Severability.

If any provision of this chapter, or the application thereof to any person or circumstance is held invalid, the validity of the remainder of this chapter and the application of such provisions to other persons and circumstances shall not be affected thereby.

Note: Act 93 of 1998 repealed sections 401–409 and 410.1–413 of the Ethics Act. Section 410, CONSTABLES, was not repealed, and remains effective. See 65 P.S. 410

§ 410. Constables.

Nothing in this act, or in any other law or court rule shall be construed to prohibit any constable from also being an officer of a political body or political party as such terms are defined in the act of June 3, 1937 (P.L. 1333, No. 320),[6] known as the "Pennsylvania Election Code," and the same may hold the office of a county, State or national committee of any political party, and may run for and hold any elective office, and may participate in any election day activities.

53 Pa.C.S. § 1141. Form of oaths of office.

Whenever an elected or appointed official of a municipality is required to take, subscribe or file an oath or affirmation of office, the oath or affirmation shall be in the form prescribed in this section, as follows:

I do solemnly swear (or affirm) that I will support, obey and defend the Constitution of the United States and the Constitution of this Commonwealth and that I will discharge the duties of my office with fidelity.

6. 25 P.S. § 2600 et seq.

PART II
TAXATION

CHAPTER 4
LOCAL TAX ENABLING ACT[1]
53 P.S. §§ 6924.101–6924.901

Act Repealed in Part

Section 23 of Act 1986, July 2, P.L. 318, No. 77, repealed parts of this Act insofar as it is inconsistent with said act.

Section 4(a) of Act 1996, July 11, P.L. 602, No. 102 (amending 53 P.S. § 25942 and adding 53 P.S. § 25059), repealed parts of this Act insofar as it is inconsistent with that act.

Amendments to sections 2, 2.2, 2.3, 5.1, 8, 10, 22.4, & 22.5, enacted pursuant to Act 2004, Dec. 1, P.L. 1729, No. 222, apply to taxes levied for tax years commencing on or after January 1, 2005.

Amendments to sections 10, 13V(h), 21, 22.1, 22.2, & 22.3, enacted pursuant to 2004, Nov. 30, P.L. 1520, No. 192, are effective January 30, 2005.

Section 6 of the act of December 1, 2004 (P.L.1729, No.222), entitled "An act amending the act of December 31, 1965 (P.L.1257, No.511)" is repealed effective June 21, 2007.

Prior Section 53 P.S. § 6909 was repealed insofar as inconsistent with 53 P.S. § 6926.351, pursuant to 2006, June 27, P.L. 1873, No. 1 (Spec. Sess. No. 1), § 5005(2), imd. effective.

TABLE OF CONTENTS

CHAPTER 1
PRELIMINARY PROVISIONS

CHAPTER 2
[Reserved]

1. Act of 1965, P.L. 1257, No. 511.

LOCAL TAX ENABLING ACT

CHAPTER 3
LOCAL TAXES

Sec.

CHAPTER 4
OPTIONAL OCCUPATION TAX ELIMINATION

Sec.

CHAPTER 5
CONSOLIDATED COLLECTION OF LOCAL INCOME TAXES

Sec.

CHAPTER 6

[Reserved]

CHAPTER 7

COLLECTION OF DELINQUENT TAXES

CHAPTER 8

[Reserved]

CHAPTER 9

MISCELLANEOUS PROVISIONS

CHAPTER 1

PRELIMINARY PROVISIONS

§ 6924.101. Short title.

This act shall be known and may be cited as "The Local Tax Enabling Act."

CHAPTER 2

[RESERVED]

CHAPTER 3

LOCAL TAXES

6924.305. Vacation of tax ordinances and resolutions by state tax measures.
6924.306. Advertisement of intention to adopt tax ordinance or resolution.
6924.307. Rate, amount, court approval; revision of budget.
6924.308. Second class city parking tax rates.
6924.309. Appeals by taxpayers.
6924.310. Filing of certified copies of ordinances and resolutions.
6924.311. Limitations on rates of specific taxes.
6924.312. Register for and withholding of local services taxes.
6924.312.1. (Reserved).
6924.313. Collection of taxes.
6924.314. (Reserved).
6924.315. Audits of taxes other than earned income taxes.
6924.316. (Reserved).
6924.317. Payment of tax to other political subdivisions or states as credit or deduction; withholding tax.
6924.318. Personal property.
6924.319. Limitation on assessment.
6924.320. Tax limitations.
6924.6924.321.–328. (Reserved).
6924.329. Legal representation.
6924.330. Restricted use.

§ 6924.301. Definitions.—

(a) The following words and phrases when used in this chapter shall have the meanings given to them in this section unless the context clearly indicates otherwise:

"Contingent fee audit" means an audit of a taxpayer's books and records for which the collection fee is based on a percentage of tax assessed or collected, or both.

"Family farm corporation" means a Pennsylvania corporation at least seventy-five percent of the assets of which are devoted to the business of agriculture, which business, for the purposes of this definition, shall not be deemed to include:

(i) recreational activities, such as, but not limited to, hunting, fishing, camping, skiing, show competition or racing;

(ii) the raising, breeding or training of game animals or game birds, fish, cats, dogs or pets or animals intended for use in sporting or recreational activities;

(iii) fur farming;

(iv) stockyard and slaughterhouse operations; or

(v) manufacturing or processing operations of any kind: Provided, however, That at least seventy-five percent of all of the stock of the corporation must be owned by members of the same family.

"Members of the same family" means an individual, such individual's brothers and sisters, the brothers and sisters of such individual's parents and grandparents, the ancestors and lineal descendents of any of the foregoing and a spouse of any of the foregoing. Individuals related by the half blood or by legal adoption shall be treated as if they were related by the whole blood.

"Private collection agency" means a business entity or person appointed to audit taxpayers and collect delinquent taxes.

(b) As used in this chapter, the terms "business entity," "earned income," "employer," "net profits," "private agency" "agency", public agency", and "tax bureau" shall have the same meanings as those terms are given in section 501.

§ 6924.301.1. Delegation of taxing powers and restrictions thereon.

(a) The duly constituted authorities of the following political subdivisions, cities of the second class, cities of the second class A, cities of the third class, boroughs, towns, townships of the first class, townships of the second class, school districts of the second class, school districts of the third class, and school districts of the fourth class, in all cases including independent school districts may, in their discretion, by ordinance or resolution, for general revenue purposes, levy, assess and collect or provide for the levying, assessment and collection of such taxes as they shall determine on persons, transactions, occupations, privileges, subjects and personal property within the limits of such political subdivisions, and upon the transfer of real property, or of any interest in real property, situate within the political subdivision levying and assessing the tax, regardless of where the instruments making the transfers are made, executed or delivered or where the actual settlements on such transfer take place. The taxing authority may provide that the transferee shall remain liable for any unpaid realty transfer taxes imposed by virtue of this chapter.

(a.1)(1) A local taxing authority may levy a tax on the privilege of doing business in the jurisdiction of the local taxing authority if:

(i) the privilege is exercised by conducting transactions in the jurisdiction of the levying local taxing authority for all or part of fifteen or more calendar days within the calendar year; or

(ii) the privilege is exercised through a base of operations in the jurisdiction of the levying local taxing authority. The gross receipts subject to this tax shall not include any receipts subject to a tax measured by such gross receipts which is imposed under subparagraph (i).

(2) As used in this subsection, the term "base of operations" shall mean an actual, physical and permanent place of business from which a taxpayer manages, directs and controls its business activities at that location.

(b) Each local taxing authority may, by ordinance or resolution, exempt any person whose total income from all sources is less than twelve thousand dollars ($12,000) per annum from the per capita or similar head tax, occupation tax or earned income tax, or any portion thereof, and may adopt regulations for the processing of claims for exemptions.

(c) (1) Each political subdivision levying the local services tax shall exempt the following persons from the local services tax:

(i) Any person who has served in any war or armed conflict in which the United States was engaged and is honorably discharged or released under honorable circumstances from active service if, as a result of military service, the person is blind, paraplegic or a double or quadruple amputee or has a service-connected disability declared by the United States Veterans' Administration or its successor to be a total one hundred percent permanent disability.

(ii) Any person who serves as a member of a reserve component of the armed forces and is called to active duty at any time during the taxable year.

(2) For purposes of this subsection, "reserve component of the armed forces" shall mean the United States Army Reserve, United States Navy Reserve, United States Marine Corps Reserve, United States Coast Guard Reserve, United States Air Force Reserve, the Pennsylvania Army National Guard or the Pennsylvania Air National Guard.

(d) Each political subdivision levying the local services tax at a rate exceeding ten dollars ($10) shall, and each political subdivision levying the local services tax at a rate of ten dollars ($10) or less may, by ordinance or resolution, exempt any person from the local services tax whose total earned income and net profits from all sources within the political subdivision is less than twelve thousand dollars ($12,000) for the calendar year in which the local services tax is levied.

(e) (1) A person seeking to claim an exemption from the local services tax may annually file an exemption certificate with the political subdivision levying the tax and with the person's employer affirming that the person reasonably expects to receive earned income and net profits from all sources within the political subdivision of less than twelve thousand dollars ($12,000) in the calendar year for which the exemption certificate is filed. In the event the political subdivision utilizes a tax collection officer pursuant to section 10[1] of this act, the political subdivision shall provide a copy of the exemption certificate to that officer. The exemption certificate shall have attached to it a copy of all the employe's last pay stubs or W-2 forms from employment within the political subdivision for the year prior to the fiscal year for which the employe is requesting to be exempted from the local services tax. Upon receipt of the exemption certificate and until otherwise instructed by the political subdivision levying the tax or except as required by clause (2), the employer shall not withhold the tax from the person during the calendar year or the remainder of the calendar year for which the exemption certificate applies. Employers shall ensure that the exemption certificate forms are readily available to employes at all times and shall furnish each new employe with a form at the time of hiring. The Department of Community and Economic Development shall develop and make available to political subdivisions and employers uniform exemption certificates required by this clause.

(2) With respect to a person who claimed an exemption for a given calendar year from the local services tax, upon notification to an employer by the person or by the political subdivision that the person has received earned income and net profits from all sources within that political subdivision equal to or in excess of twelve thousand dollars ($12,000) in that calendar year or that the person is otherwise ineligible for the tax exemption for that calendar year, or upon an employer's payment to the person of earned income within that political subdivision in an amount equal to or in excess of twelve thousand dollars ($12,000) in that calendar year, an employer shall withhold the local services tax from the person under clause (3).

(3) If a person who claimed an exemption for a given calendar year from the local services tax becomes subject to the tax for the calendar year under clause (2), the employer shall withhold the tax for the remainder of that calendar year. The employer shall withhold from the person, for the first payroll period after receipt of the notification under clause (2), a lump sum equal to the amount of tax that was not withheld from the person due to the exemption claimed by the person under this subsection, plus the per payroll amount due for that first payroll period. The amount of tax withheld per payroll period for the remaining payroll periods in that calendar year shall be the same amount withheld for other employes. In the event the employment of a person subject to withholding of the tax under this clause is subsequently severed in that calendar year, the person shall be liable for any outstanding balance of tax due, and the political subdivision levying the tax may pursue collection under this act.

(4) Except as provided in clause (2), it is the intent of this subsection that employers shall not be responsible for investigating exemption certificates, monitoring tax exemption eligibility or exempting any employe from a local services tax.

(f) Such local authorities shall not have authority by virtue of this act:

(1) To levy, assess and collect or provide for the levying, assessment and collection of any tax on the transfer of real property when the transfer is by will or mortgage or the intestate laws of this Commonwealth or on a transfer by the owner of previously occupied residential premises to a builder of new residential premises when such previously occupied residential premises is taken in trade by such builder as part of the consideration from the purchaser of a new previously unoccupied single family residential premises or on a transfer between corporations operating housing projects pursuant to the housing and redevelopment assistance law and the shareholders thereof, or on a transfer between nonprofit industrial development agencies and industrial corporations purchasing from them, or on transfer to or from nonprofit industrial development agencies, or on a transfer between husband and wife, or on a transfer between persons who were previously husband and wife but who have since been divorced; provided such transfer is made

1. Editor's Note: should probably be "section 313" not "section 10." Error in enrolled bill.

within three months of the date of the granting of the final decree in divorce, or the decree of equitable distribution of marital property, whichever is later, and the property or interest therein, subject to such transfer, was acquired by the husband and wife, or husband or wife, prior to the granting of the final decree in divorce, or on a transfer between parent and child or the spouse of such a child, or between parent and trustee for the benefit of a child or the spouse of such child, or on a transfer between a grandparent and grandchild or the spouse of such grandchild, or on a transfer between brother and sister or brother and brother or sister and sister or the spouse of such brother or sister, or on a transfer to a conservancy which possesses a tax-exempt status pursuant to section 501(c)(3) of the Internal Revenue Code[2], and which has as its primary purpose the preservation of land for historic, recreational, scenic, agricultural or open space opportunities, by and between a principal and straw party for the purpose of placing a mortgage or ground rent upon the premises, or on a correctional deed without consideration, or on a transfer to the United States, the Commonwealth of Pennsylvania, or to any of their instrumentalities, agencies or political subdivisions, by gift, dedication or deed in lieu of condemnation, or deed of confirmation in connection with condemnation proceedings, or reconveyance by the condemning body of the property condemned to the owner of record at the time of condemnation which reconveyance may include property line adjustments provided said reconveyance is made within one year from the date of condemnation; or leases or lease transactions;[3] or on a conveyance to a trustee under a recorded trust agreement for the express purpose of holding title in trust as security for a debt contracted at the time of the conveyance under which the trustee is not the lender and requiring the trustee to make reconveyance to the grantor-borrower upon the repayment of the debt, or a transfer within a family from a sole proprietor family member to a family farm corporation, or in any sheriff sale instituted by a mortgagee in which the purchaser of said sheriff sale is the mortgagee who instituted said sale, or on a privilege, transaction, subject, occupation or personal property which is now or does hereafter become subject to a State tax or license fee;

(2) To levy, assess or collect a tax on the gross receipts from utility service of any person or company whose rates and services are fixed and regulated by the Pennsylvania Public Utility Commission or on any public utility services rendered by any such person or company or on any privilege or transaction involving the rendering of any such public utility service;

(3) Except on sales of admission to places of amusement, other than on sales of admission to professional baseball events in a city of the third class with a population of not less than one hundred six thousand and not more than one hundred seven thousand based on the 2000 Federal decennial census, or on sales or other transfers of title or possession of property, to levy, assess or collect a tax on the privilege of employing such tangible property as is now or does hereafter become subject to a State tax; and for the purposes of this clause, real property rented for camping purposes shall not be considered a place of amusement.

(4) To levy, assess and collect a tax on goods and articles manufactured in such political subdivision or on the by-products of manufacture, or on minerals, timber, natural resources and farm products produced in such political subdivision or on the preparation or processing thereof for use or market, or on any privilege, act or transaction related to the business of manufacturing, the production, preparation or processing of minerals, timber and natural resources, or farm products, by manufacturers, by producers and by farmers with respect to the goods, articles and products of their own manufacture, production or growth, or on any privilege, act or transaction relating to the

2. 26 U.S.C. § 501(c)(3).

3. the restriction of authority to levy a tax on lease transaction does not apply to municipalities imposing a tax on leases or lease transactions prior to July 1, 2008.

business of processing by-products of manufacture, or on the transportation, loading, unloading or dumping or storage of such goods, articles, products or by-products; except that local authorities may levy, assess and collect a local services tax and taxes on the occupation, per capita and earned income or net profits of natural persons engaged in the above activities whether doing business as individual proprietorship or as members of partnerships or other associations;

(5) To levy, assess or collect a tax on salaries, wages, commissions, compensation and earned income of nonresidents of the political subdivisions: Provided, That this limitation (5) shall apply only to school districts of the second, third and fourth classes;

(6) To levy, assess or collect a tax on personal property subject to taxation by counties or on personal property owned by persons, associations and corporations specifically exempted by law from taxation under the county personal property tax law: Provided, That this limitation (6) shall not apply to cities of the second class;

(7) To levy, assess or collect a tax on membership in or membership dues, fees or assessment of charitable, religious, beneficial or nonprofit organizations including but not limited to sportsmens, recreational, golf and tennis clubs, girl and boy scout troops and councils;

(8) To levy, assess or collect any tax on a mobilehome or house trailer subject to a real property tax unless the same tax is levied, assessed and collected on other real property in the political subdivision.

(9) To levy, assess or collect any tax on individuals for the privilege of engaging in an occupation except that such a tax, to be known as the local services tax, may be levied, assessed and collected only by the political subdivision of the taxpayer's place of employment. The following apply:

(i) If a local services tax is levied at a combined rate exceeding ten dollars ($10) in a calendar year, a person subject to the local services tax shall be assessed a pro rata share of the tax for each payroll period in which the person is engaging in an occupation. The pro rata share of the tax assessed on the person for a payroll period shall be determined by dividing the combined rate of the local services tax levied for the calendar year by the number of payroll periods established by the employer for the calendar year. For purposes of determining the pro rata share, an employer shall round down the amount of the tax collected each payroll period to the nearest one-hundredth of a dollar. Collection of the local services tax levied under this subclause shall be made on a payroll period basis for each payroll period in which the person is engaging in an occupation, except as provided in subclause (v).

(ii) If a school district levied an emergency and municipal services tax on the effective date of this subclause, the school district may continue to levy the local services tax in the same amount the school district collected on the effective date of this subclause. However, if a municipality located in whole or in part within the school district subsequently levies the local services tax, the school district may only collect five dollars ($5) on persons employed within the municipality each calendar year. A school district that did not levy an emergency and municipal services tax on the effective date of this subclause shall be prohibited from levying the local services tax. If a school district and a municipality located in whole or in part within the school district both levy a local services tax at a combined rate exceeding ten dollars ($10), the school district's pro rata share of the aggregate local services taxes levied on persons employed within the municipality shall be collected by the municipality or its tax officer based on payroll periods as provided under subclause (i) and shall be paid to the school district on a quarterly basis within sixty days of receipt by the municipality or its tax officer.

(iii) Except as provided in subclause (ii), no person shall be subject to the payment of the local services tax by more than one political subdivision during each payroll period as established by subclause (iv).

(iv) With respect to a person subject to the local services tax at a combined rate exceeding ten dollars ($10), the situs of the tax shall be the place of employment on the first day the person becomes subject to the tax during each payroll period. With respect to a person subject to the local services tax at a combined rate of not more than ten dollars ($10), the situs of the tax shall be the place of employment determined as of the day the person first becomes subject to the tax during the calendar year. In the event a person is engaged in more than one occupation, that is, concurrent employment, or an occupation which requires the person working in more than one political subdivision during a payroll period, the priority of claim to collect the local services tax shall be in the following order: first, the political subdivision in which a person maintains the person's principal office or is principally employed; second, the political subdivision in which the person resides and works, if the tax is levied by that political subdivision; and third, the political subdivision in which a person is employed and which imposes the tax nearest in miles to the person's home.

(v) In the case of concurrent employment, an employer shall refrain from withholding the local services tax if the employe provides a recent pay statement from a principal employer that includes the name of the employer, the length of the payroll period and the amount of the local services tax withheld and a statement from the employe that the pay statement is from the employe's principal employer and the employe will notify other employers of a change in principal place of employment within two weeks of its occurrence. The Department of Community and Economic Development shall develop a uniform employe statement form.

(vi) The local services tax shall be no more than fifty-two dollars ($52) on each person for each calendar year, irrespective of the number of political subdivisions within which a person may be employed. A political subdivision shall provide a taxpayer a receipt of payment upon request by the taxpayer.

(vii) Political subdivisions shall adopt regulations for the processing of refund claims for overpaid local services taxes for any calendar year. The regulations shall be consistent with 53 Pa.C.S. § 8425 (relating to refunds of overpayments) and 8426 (relating to interest on overpayment). Refunds made within seventy-five days of a refund request or seventy-five days after the last day the employer is required to remit the local services tax for the last quarter of the calendar year under section 9[4] of this act, whichever is later, shall not be subject to interest imposed under 53 Pa.C.S. § 8426. Political subdivisions shall only provide refunds for amounts overpaid in a calendar year that exceed one dollar ($1).

(viii) The Department of Community and Economic Development shall provide suggested forms and technical assistance to facilitate the administration of the local services tax for political subdivisions and reduce the burden of implementation, accounting and compliance for employers and taxpayers.

(ix) For purposes of this clause, "combined rate" shall mean the aggregate annual rate of the local services tax levied by a school district and a municipality located in whole or in part within the school district.

(10) To levy, assess or collect a tax on admissions to motion picture theatres: Provided, That this limitation (10) shall not apply to cities of the second class.

(11) To levy, assess or collect a tax on the construction of or improvement to residential dwellings or upon the application for or issuance of permits for the construction of or improvements to residential dwellings.

4. Editor's Note: should probably be "section 312" not "section 9." Error in enrolled bill.

(12) To levy, assess and collect a mercantile or business privilege tax on gross receipts or part thereof which are: (i) discounts allowed to purchasers as cash discounts for prompt payment of their bills; (ii) charges advanced by a seller for freight, delivery or other transportation for the purchaser in accordance with the terms of a contract of sale; (iii) received upon the sale of an article of personal property which was acquired by the seller as a trade-in to the extent that the gross receipts in the sale of the article taken in trade does not exceed the amount of trade-in allowance made in acquiring such article; (iv) refunds, credits or allowances given to a purchaser on account of defects in goods sold or merchandise returned; (v) Pennsylvania sales tax; (vi) based on the value of exchanges or transfers between one seller and another seller who transfers property with the understanding that property of an identical description will be returned at a subsequent date; however, when sellers engaged in similar lines of business exchange property and one of them makes payment to the other in addition to the property exchanged, the additional payment received may be included in the gross receipts of the seller receiving such additional cash payments; (vii) of sellers from sales to other sellers in the same line where the seller transfers the title or possession at the same price for which the seller acquired the merchandise; or (viii) transfers between one department, branch or division of a corporation or other business entity of goods, wares and merchandise to another department, branch or division of the same corporation or business entity and which are recorded on the books to reflect such interdepartmental transactions.

(13) To levy, assess or collect an amusement or admissions tax on membership, membership dues, fees or assessments, donations, contributions or monetary charges of any character whatsoever paid by the general public, or a limited or selected number thereof, for such persons to enter into any place, indoors or outdoors, to engage in any activities, the predominant purpose or nature of which is exercise, fitness, health maintenance, improvement or rehabilitation, health or nutrition education, or weight control.

(14) Except by cities of the second class, to levy, assess or collect a tax on payroll amounts generated as a result of business activity.

(15) Except by cities of the second class in which a sports stadium or arena that has received public funds in connection with its construction or maintenance is located, to levy, assess and collect a publicly funded facility usage fee upon those nonresident individuals who use such facility to engage in an athletic event or otherwise render a performance for which they receive remuneration.

(16) To levy, assess or collect an amusement or admissions tax on the charge imposed upon a patron for the sale of admission to or for the privilege of admission to a bowling alley or bowling lane to engage in one or more games of bowling.

(17) To levy, assess or collect an amusement or admission tax based on a charge imposed for the movement of passengers by a for-profit railroad that operates as a common carrier of freight subject to the jurisdiction of the United States Surface Transportation Board if the freight constitutes a majority of the movements handled by the railroad measured by both income and volume and the for-profit railroad transports more than 20,000 revenue carloads annually while offering tourist or passenger service.

§ 6924.302. Recapture of tax.

(a) Notwithstanding the provisions of section 301.1(f)(1), if any stock of a family farm corporation is transferred to a person who is not a family member within ten years from the date of the conveyance from a sole proprietor family member to a family farm corporation, the tax imposed by this article shall become immediately due and payable.

§ 6924.303. Payroll tax.

A city of the second class may levy, assess or collect a tax that does not exceed fifty-five hundredths percent on payroll amounts generated as a result of an employer conducting business activity within a city of the second class. For purposes of a payroll tax levied, assessed or collected by a city of the second class, the business activity shall be directly attributable to activity within a city of the second class. For purposes of computation of the payroll tax imposed pursuant to this section, the payroll amount attributable to the city shall be determined by applying an apportionment factor to total payroll expense based on that portion of payroll expense which the total number of days an employe, partner, member, shareholder or other individual works within the city bears to the total number of days such employe or person works within and outside of the city.

(a.1) A charitable organization that qualifies for tax exemption pursuant to the act of November 26, 1997 (P.L. 508, No. 55), 10 P.S. § 371] known as the "Institutions of Purely Public Charity Act," shall calculate the tax that would otherwise be attributable to the city, but shall only pay the tax on that portion of its payroll expense attributable to business activity for which a tax may be imposed pursuant to section 511 of the Internal Revenue Code of 1986 (Public Law 99-514, 26 U.S.C. § 1 et seq.). If the charity has purchased or is operating branches, affiliates, subsidiaries or other business entities that do not independently meet the standards of the "Institutions of Purely Public Charity Act," the tax shall be paid on the payroll attributable to such for-profit branches, affiliates or subsidiaries, whether or not the employes are leased or placed under the auspices of the charity's umbrella or parent organization. Nothing in this subsection shall restrict the ability of a charitable organization to contract with the city to provide services to the city in lieu of some or all taxes due under this section.

(b) For purposes of the payroll tax assessed pursuant to this section, an employer is conducting business within a city of the second class if the employer engages, hires, employs or contracts with one or more individuals as employes and, in addition, the employer does at least one of the following:

(1) maintains a fixed place of business within the city;

(2) owns or leases real property within the city for purposes of such business;

(3) maintains a stock of tangible personal property in the city for sale in the ordinary course of such business;

(4) conducts continuous solicitation within the city related to such business; or

(5) utilizes the streets of the city in connection with the operation of such business other than transportation through the city

(c) All employers in a city of the second class shall file quarterly returns and make quarterly payments as provided for by ordinance enacted by a city of the second class. Every employer making a return shall certify the correctness thereof. A city of the second class may audit, examine or inspect the books, records or accounts of all employers subject to the tax imposed pursuant to this section.

(d) A city of the second class may enact ordinances and regulations necessary to implement this section. The ordinance levying the tax authorized by this section shall permanently replace the city's existing mercantile tax and shall reduce the business privilege tax rate as follows:

(1) In tax years 2005 and 2006, the business privilege tax shall be two mills.

(2) In tax years 2007, 2008 and 2009, the business privilege tax shall be one mill unless the revenues collected from the payroll expense tax exceed fifty million five hundred thousand dollars ($50,500,000) in any fiscal year, at which time the business privilege tax shall be replaced for the subsequent fiscal year. After the phaseout of the business privilege tax, all amounts of moneys in excess of fifty million five hundred thousand dollars ($50,500,000) shall be used by the city of the second class to further accelerate the reduction of the tax imposed by the city of the second class on parking as provided in section 308.

(3) In tax year 2010 and thereafter, the business privilege tax may not be imposed.

(e) All taxes, additions and penalties collected pursuant to this section shall be used by a city of the second class exclusively for the general revenue purposes of the city.

(f) An employer shall not offset the amount of tax paid pursuant to this section by reducing compensation or benefits paid to employes.

(g) A city of the second class may bring suit for the recovery of taxes due and unpaid under this section. Any suit brought to recover the tax imposed by this section shall be commenced within three years after such tax is due or within three years after the declaration or return has been filed, whichever is later: Provided, however, That this limitation shall not prevent the institution of a suit for the collection of any tax due or determined to be due in the following cases:

(1) Where no declaration or return was filed by any person although a declaration or return was required to be filed by him under provisions of this section, there shall be no limitation.

(2) Where an examination of the declaration or return filed by any person or of other evidence relating to such declaration or return in the possession of the city of the second class reveals a fraudulent evasion of taxes, there shall be no limitation.

(3) In the case of substantial understatement of tax liability of twenty-five percent or more and no fraud, suit shall be begun within six years.

(4) This section shall not be construed to limit the governing body from recovering delinquent taxes by any other means provided by law, with the exception of contingent fee audits by a private collection agency, which shall be prohibited.

(h) If for any reason the payroll tax is not paid when due, interest at the rate of six percent per annum on the amount of said tax and an additional penalty of one percent of the amount of the unpaid tax for each month or fraction thereof during which the tax remains unpaid shall be added and collected. Where suit is brought for the recovery of any such tax, the employer shall, in addition, be liable for the costs of collection and the interest and penalties herein imposed. A city of the second class may, by ordinance or resolution, establish a one-time period during which interest or interest and penalties that would otherwise be imposed for the nonreporting or underreporting of payroll tax liabilities or for the nonpayment of payroll taxes previously imposed and due shall be waived in total or in part if the taxpayer voluntarily files delinquent returns and pays the taxes in full during the period so established.

(i) In addition to any other additions, penalties or enforcement proceedings provided for by ordinance of a city of the second class or a law of this Commonwealth for the collection and enforcement of taxes or the submission of information to a government entity:

(1) Any employer who wilfully makes any false or untrue statement on the employer's return commits a misdemeanor of the second degree and shall, upon conviction, be sentenced to pay a fine of not more than two thousand dollars ($2,000) or to imprisonment for not more than two years, or both.

(2) Any employer who wilfully fails or refuses to file a return required by this section commits a misdemeanor of the third degree and shall, upon conviction, be sentenced to pay a fine of not more than one thousand dollars ($1,000) or to imprisonment for not more than one year, or both.

(3) Any person who wilfully fails or refuses to appear before the collector in person with the employer's books, records or accounts for examination when required under the provisions of this section or of an ordinance to do so, or who wilfully refuses to permit inspection of the books, records or accounts of any employer in the person's custody or control when the right to make such inspection by the collector is requested, commits a misdemeanor and shall, upon conviction, be sentenced to pay a fine of not more than five hundred dollars ($500) or to imprisonment for not more than six months, or both.

(j) As used in this section:

"Employer" means all persons conducting business activity within a city of the second class except for a governmental entity.

"Payroll amounts" means all amounts paid by an employer as salaries, wages, commissions, bonuses, net earnings and incentive payments, whether based on profits or otherwise, fees and similar remuneration for services rendered, whether directly or through an agent and whether in cash, in property or the right to receive property.

§ 6924.304. Nonresident sports facility usage fee.

A city of the second class in which is located a sports stadium or arena that has received public funds in connection with its construction or maintenance may enact a publicly funded facility usage fee upon those nonresident individuals who use such facility to engage in an athletic event or otherwise render a performance for which they receive remuneration. The fee may be a flat dollar amount or a percentage of the individual's income attributable to such individual's usage of the facility. If the fee is a percentage, it may not exceed three percent of the earned income of the individual attributable to the usage of the facility. If any fee is imposed, those individuals liable for the fee shall be exempt from any earned income tax imposed by the city of the second class pursuant to this chapter and any such tax imposed under section 652.1 of the act of March 10, 1949 (P.L. 30, No. 14), [24 P.S. § 6-652.1] known as the "Public School Code of 1949." Should a court of competent jurisdiction determine this provision to be invalid for any reason, persons subject to the publicly funded facility usage fee shall not be exempt from any previously applicable earned income tax.

§ 6924.305. Vacation of tax ordinances and resolutions by state tax measures.

If, subsequent to the passage of any ordinance or resolution under the authority of this chapter, the General Assembly shall impose a tax or license fee on any privilege, transactions, subject or occupation, or on personal property or on sales of admission to places of amusement or on sales or other transfer of title or possession of property taxed by any such political subdivision hereunder, the act of Assembly imposing the State tax or license fee thereon shall automatically vacate the ordinance or resolution passed under the authority of this chapter as to all taxes accruing subsequent to the end of the current fiscal year of such political subdivision. It is the intention of this section to confer upon such political subdivision the power to levy, assess and collect taxes upon any and all subjects of taxation, except as above restricted and limited, which the Commonwealth has power to tax but which it does not tax or license, subject only to the foregoing provision that any tax or license shall automatically terminate at the end of the current fiscal year of the political subdivision.

§ 6924.306. Advertisement of intention to adopt tax ordinance or resolution.

Prior to the passage of any ordinance or the adoption of any resolution imposing a tax or license fee under the authority hereunder granted, such political subdivision shall give notice of the intention to pass such ordinance or adopt such resolution. Such notice shall be given in addition to all other notices required by law to be given and shall set forth the substantial nature of the tax or license fee to be imposed by the proposed ordinance or resolution, the reason which, in the judgment of the officials of the subdivision, necessitates the imposition of the tax, and the amount of revenue estimated to be derived from the tax. Publication of such notice shall be made by advertisement once a week for three weeks in a newspaper of general circulation within such political subdivision if there is such newspaper and, if there is not, then such publication shall be made in a newspaper of general circulation within the county in which the advertising political subdivision is located.

Every such tax shall continue in force on a calendar or fiscal year basis, as the case may be, without annual reenactment unless the rate of the tax is subsequently changed.

§ 6924.307. Rate, amount, court approval; revision of budget.

Any tax imposed under this chapter shall not be subject to any limitations under existing laws as to rate or amount or as to the necessity of securing court approval or as to budgetary requirements. Any city, borough or township imposing a tax under this chapter may revise its budget during any fiscal year by increasing or making additional appropriations from funds to be provided from such tax.

The ordinance or resolution may be passed or adopted prior to the beginning of the fiscal year and prior to the preparation of the budget when desirable.

Every ordinance or resolution which imposed a tax under the authority of this chapter shall be passed or adopted, if for a school district, during the period other school taxes are required by law to be levied and assessed by such district. Each ordinance and resolution shall state that it is enacted under the authority of this chapter, known as "The Local Tax Enabling Act."

§ 6924.308. Second class city parking tax rates.

The rate of the tax imposed on parking transactions shall not differ from the rate contained in City of Pittsburgh Ordinance Number 43-2003 as of January 1, 2004, except as follows:

(1) In tax year 2007, the rate of tax shall not exceed 45%.

(2) In tax year 2008, the rate of tax shall not exceed 40%.

(3) In tax year 2009, the rate of tax shall not exceed 37.5%.

(4) In tax year 2010, the rate of tax shall not exceed 35% as existed prior to the adoption of the ordinance.

§ 6924.309. Appeals by taxpayers.

No tax levied for the first time by any political subdivision to which this chapter applies shall go into effect until thirty days from the time of the adoption of the ordinance or resolution levying the tax. Within said thirty days, taxpayers representing twenty-five percent or more of the total valuation of real estate in the political subdivision as assessed for taxation purposes, or taxpayers of the political subdivision not less than twenty-five in number aggrieved by the ordinance or resolution shall have the right to appeal therefrom to the court of quarter sessions of the county upon giving bond with sufficient security in the amount of five hundred dollars ($500), approved by the court, to prosecute the appeal with effect and for the payment of costs. The petition shall set forth the objections to the tax and the facts in support of such objections, and shall be accompanied by the affidavit of at least five of the petitioners that the averments of the petition are true and the petition is not filed for the purpose of delay.

No such appeal shall act as a supersedeas unless specifically allowed by the court to which the appeal is taken or a judge thereof.

Immediately upon the filing of any such petition, the petitioners shall serve a copy of the petition and any rule granted by the court upon the president, chairman, secretary or clerk of the legislative body levying the tax.

The court shall fix a day for a hearing not less than fifteen days nor more than thirty days after the filing of the petition. Notice of the time of such hearing shall be given to all interested parties as the court shall direct. The court shall promptly hear and dispose of the appeal.

It shall be the duty of the court to declare the ordinance and the tax imposed thereby to be valid unless it concludes that the ordinance is unlawful or finds that the tax imposed is excessive or unreasonable; but the court shall not interfere with the reasonable discretion of the legislative body in selecting the subjects or fixing the rates of the tax. The court may declare invalid all or any portion of the ordinance or of the tax imposed or may reduce the rates of tax.

§ 6924.310. Filing of certified copies of ordinances and resolutions.

When an ordinance or a resolution is first passed or adopted by a political subdivision imposing a tax or license fee under the authority of this chapter, an exact printed or typewritten copy thereof, certified to by the secretary of the taxing body, shall be filed with the Department of Community and Economic Development within fifteen days after the same becomes effective.

Any secretary or person acting as the clerk or secretary of the taxing body of any political subdivision during the meeting at which an ordinance or resolution imposing a tax or license fee is passed or adopted as herein provided who shall fail to file the certified copy or statement relative thereto with the Department of Community and Economic Development as herein required, shall, upon summary conviction thereof in the county in which the political subdivision is located, be sentenced to pay a fine of not less than five dollars ($5) nor more than twenty-five dollars ($25), and the costs of prosecution.

§ 6924.311. Limitations on rates of specific taxes.

No taxes levied under the provisions of this chapter shall be levied by any political subdivision on the following subjects exceeding the rates specified in this section:

(1) Per capita, poll or other similar head taxes, ten dollars ($10).

(2) On each dollar of the whole volume of business transacted by wholesale dealers in goods, wares and merchandise, one mill, by retail dealers in goods, wares and merchandise and by proprietors of restaurants or other places where food, drink and refreshments are served, one and one-half mills; except in cities of the second class, where rates shall not exceed one mill on wholesale dealers and two mills on retail dealers and proprietors. No such tax shall be levied on the dollar volume of business transacted by wholesale and retail dealers derived from the resale of goods, wares and merchandise, taken by any dealer as a trade-in or as part payment for other goods, wares and merchandise, except to the extent that the resale price exceeds the trade-in allowance. When a political subdivision which currently levies, assesses or collects a mercantile or business privilege tax on gross receipts under section 533 of the act of December 13, 1988 (P.L. 1121, No. 145),[5] known as the "Local Tax Reform Act," merges with one or more political subdivisions to form a new political subdivision on or after August 1, 2008, the new political subdivision may levy that mercantile or business privilege tax in the first year following the merger at a rate necessary to generate the same revenues generated in the last fiscal year that the merging political subdivision generated before the merger. Such rate shall remain in effect for the new political subdivision in subsequent years, but the revenue-neutral limitation shall only apply to the first year following the merger. If the merging political subdivision had previously shared the rate of taxation with another political subdivision, the nonmerging political subdivision which had shared the rate is capped at the rate it was previously levying.[6]

(3) On wages, salaries, commissions and other earned income of individuals, one percent.

(4) On retail sales involving the transfer of title or possession of tangible personal property, two percent.

(5) On the transfer of real property, one percent

(6) On admissions to places of amusement, athletic events and the like, and on motion picture theatres in cities of the second class, ten percent.

(7) Flat rate occupation taxes not using a millage or percentage as a basis, ten dollars ($10).

---

5. 72 P.S. § 4750.533.

6. Note that by Act 39 of 2013 Section 311(2) as to mercantile or business privilege tax due amended retroactively to July 1, 2012

Chapter 10 Residential Design Tax Credit
Chapter 9 Neighborhood Improvement
Chapter 8 Local Taxpayers Bill of Rights
Chapter 7 Occupation Tax Elimination Act
Chapter 6 Local Government Unit Debt Act
Chapter 5 Local Tax Collection Law
Chapter 4 Local Tax Enabling Act

(8) Local services taxes, fifty-two dollars ($52).

(9) On admissions to ski facilities, ten percent. The tax base upon which the tax shall be levied shall not exceed forty percent of the cost of the lift ticket. The lift ticket shall include all costs of admissions to the ski facility.

(10) On admissions to golf courses, ten percent. The tax base upon which the tax shall be levied shall not exceed forty percent of the greens fee. The greens fee shall include all costs of admissions to the golf course.

(11) Deleted by 2004, Dec. 1, P.L. 1729, No. 222, § 3, imd. effective.

(12) On payrolls, fifty-five hundredths percent.

Except as otherwise provided in this chapter, at any time two political subdivisions shall impose any one of the above taxes on the same person, subject, business, transaction or privilege, located within both such political subdivisions, during the same year or part of the same year, under the authority of this act then the tax levied by a political subdivision under the authority of this chapter shall, during the time such duplication of the tax exists, except as hereinafter otherwise provided, be one-half of the rate, as above limited, and such one-half rate shall become effective by virtue of the requirements of this chapter from the day such duplication becomes effective without any action on the part of the political subdivision imposing the tax under the authority of this chapter. When any one of the above taxes has been levied under the provisions of this chapter by one political subdivision and a subsequent levy is made either for the first time or is revived after a lapse of time by another political subdivision on the same person, subject, business, transaction or privilege at a rate that would make the combined levies exceed the limit allowed by this subdivision, the tax of the second political subdivision shall not become effective until the end of the fiscal year for which the prior tax was levied, unless:

(1) Notice indicating its intention to make such levy is given to the first taxing body by the second taxing body as follows: (i) when the notice is given to a school district it shall be given at least forty-five days prior to the last day fixed by law for the levy of its school taxes; (ii) when given to any other political subdivision it shall be prior to the first day of January immediately preceding, or if a last day for the adoption of the budget is fixed by law, at least forty-five days prior to such last day; or

(2) Unless the first taxing body shall indicate by appropriate resolution its desire to waive notice requirements in which case the levy of the second taxing body shall become effective on such date as may be agreed upon by the two taxing bodies.

It is the intent and purpose of this provision to limit rates of taxes referred to in this section so that the entire burden of one tax on a person, subject, business, transaction or privilege shall not exceed the limitations prescribed in this section: Provided, however, That any two political subdivisions which impose any one of the above taxes, on the same person, subject, business, transaction or privilege during the same year or part of the same year may agree among themselves that, instead of limiting their respective rates to one-half of the maximum rate herein provided, they will impose respectively different rates, the total of which shall not exceed the maximum rate as above permitted.

Notwithstanding the provisions of this section, any city of the second class A may enact a tax upon wages, salaries, commissions and other earned income of individuals resident therein, not exceeding one percent, even though a school district levies a similar tax on the same person provided that the aggregate of both taxes does not exceed two percent.

§ 6924.312. Register for and withholding of local services taxes.

It shall be the duty of the Department of Community and Economic Development to have available an official continuing register supplemented annually of all earned income and local services taxes levied under authority of this chapter. The register and its supplements, hereinafter referred to as the register, shall list such jurisdictions levying earned income and local services taxes, the rate of the tax as stated in the tax levying ordinance or resolution, and the effective rate on resident and nonresident taxpayers, if different from the stated rate because of a coterminous levy, the name and address of the officer responsible for administering the collection of the tax and from whom information, forms for reporting and copies of rules and regulations are available. With each jurisdiction listed, all jurisdictions making coterminous levies shall also be noted and their tax rates shown.

Information for the register shall be furnished by the secretary of each taxing body to the Department of Community and Economic Development in such manner and on such forms as the Department of Community and Economic Development may prescribe. The information must be received by the Department of Community and Economic Development by certified mail not later than May 31 of each year to show new tax enactments, repeals and changes. Failure to comply with this date for filing may result in the omission of the levy from the register for that year. Failure of the Department of Community and Economic Development to receive information of taxes continued without change may be construed by the department to mean that the information contained in the previous register remains in force.

The Department of Community and Economic Development shall have the register with such annual supplements as may be required by new tax enactments, repeals or changes available upon request not later than July 1 of each year. The effective period for each register shall be from July 1 of the year in which it is issued to June 30 of the following year.

Employers shall not be required by any local ordinance to withhold from the wages, salaries, commissions or other compensation of their employes any tax imposed under the provisions of this act, which is not listed in the register, or make reports of wages, salaries, commissions or other compensation in connection with taxes not so listed: Provided, That if the register is not available by July 1, the register of the previous year shall continue temporarily in effect for an additional period not to exceed one year. The provisions of this section shall not affect the liability of any taxpayer for taxes lawfully imposed under this act.

Ordinances or resolutions imposing local services taxes under authority of this chapter may contain provisions requiring employers doing business within the jurisdiction of the political subdivision imposing the tax to withhold the tax from the compensation of those of their employes who are subject to the tax: Provided, That no employer shall be held liable for failure to withhold earned income taxes or for the payment of such withheld tax money to a political subdivision other than the political subdivision entitled to receive such money if such failure to withhold or such incorrect transmittal of withheld taxes arises from incorrect information as to the employe's place of residence submitted by the employe: And provided further, That no employer shall be held liable for failure to withhold the local services tax or for the payment of the withheld tax money to a political subdivision if the failure to withhold taxes arises from incorrect information submitted by the employe as to the employe's place or places of employment, the employe's principal office or where the employe is principally employed: And provided further, That an employer shall not be liable for payment of the local services tax in an amount exceeding the amount withheld by the employer if the employer complies with the provisions of section 301.1(e) and (f)(9) and remits the amount so withheld in accordance with this section: And provided further, That the local services tax shall be applicable to employment in the period beginning January 1, of the current year and ending December 31 of the current year, except that taxes imposed for the first time shall become effective from January 1 of the year specified in the ordinance or resolution, and the tax shall continue in force on a calendar year basis: And provided further, That employers shall be required to remit the local services taxes thirty days after the end of each quarter of a calendar year.

Chapter 10 Residential Design Tax Credit
Chapter 9 Neighborhood Improvement
Chapter 8 Local Taxpayers Bill of Rights
Chapter 7 Occupation Tax Elimination Act
Chapter 6 Local Government Unit Debt Act
Chapter 5 Local Tax Collection Law
Chapter 4 Local Tax Enabling Act

§ 6924.312.1. [Reserved].

§ 6924.313. Collection of taxes.

(a) Administrative Personnel; Joint Agreements.—

(1) Except as provided in section 506, any political subdivision is hereby authorized to provide by ordinance or resolution for the creation or designation of tax bureaus or the appointment and compensation of a political subdivision, public employe, tax bureau or public or private agency for the assessment and collection of taxes imposed under authority of this chapter. Each ordinance or resolution under this section authorizing a political subdivision, public employe, tax bureau or public or private agency to act in the capacity and with the authority of a tax collector shall continue in force without annual reauthorization unless otherwise repealed or revoked by the political subdivision or unless otherwise provided by this act.

(2) Except as provided in section 506, political subdivisions imposing taxes under authority of this chapter are authorized to make joint agreements for the collection of such taxes or any of them. The same political subdivision, tax bureau or public or private agency may be employed by two or more political subdivisions to collect any taxes imposed by them under authority of this chapter.

(b) Single Collector for Earned Income Taxes When Certain School Districts Impose Such Taxes.—Except as provided in subsection (c), whenever a school district of the second, third or fourth class shall be established pursuant to section 296, act of March 10, 1949 (P.L. 30), [24 P.S. § 2-296] known as the "Public School Code of 1949," added August 8, 1963 (P.L. 564), and such school district shall levy, assess and collect or provide for the levying, assessment and collection of a tax upon earned income, such school district and all cities, boroughs, towns and townships within its geographical limits which levy, assess and collect or provide for the levying, assessment and collection of a tax upon earned income, may on January 1, 1967, or as soon thereafter as the school district shall provide for the levying, assessment and collection of taxes upon earned income, select one person or agency to collect the taxes upon earned income imposed by all such political subdivisions. In selecting such person or agency, each political subdivision shall share in the selection upon a basis agreed upon by each political subdivision, or in the absence of any agreement on the basis of voting according to the proportion that the population of each bears to the entire population of the combined collection district, according to the latest official Federal census, and the majority of such votes cast shall determine the person or agency selected to collect the taxes. The provisions of this paragraph shall not prohibit school districts and other political subdivisions which levy, assess and collect or provide for the levying, assessment and collection of taxes upon earned income, under authority of this act, from selecting the same person or agency to collect such tax upon earned income in an area larger than the geographical limits of a school district established pursuant to section 296 of the "Public School Code of 1949."

(c) Single Tax Collector in Certain Home Rule Municipality.—In a municipality having a population under the 2000 Federal decennial census of at least forty thousand and less than ninety thousand located in a second class county and which municipality has adopted a home rule charter under 53 Pa.C.S. Pt. III Subpt. E [53 Pa.C.S.A. § 2901 et seq.] (relating to home rule and optional plan government) , the person or persons appointed by the board of school directors for the school district in which the municipality is located as collector or collectors of taxes levied by the school district under this act shall also serve as the collector or collectors of taxes levied by the municipality under this act.

§ 6924.314. [Reserved].

§ 6924.315. Audits of taxes other than earned income taxes.

The books, accounts and records of tax collectors pursuant to this chapter, other than taxes levied, assessed and collected upon earned income, shall be audited, adjusted and settled in the manner prescribed by law for the auditing, adjusting and settling of accounts of persons receiving or expending funds of the political subdivision which has levied, assessed and collected the taxes pursuant to this chapter, other than taxes levied, assessed and collected upon earned income.

§ 6924.316. [Reserved].

§ 6924.317. Payment of tax to other political subdivisions or states as credit or deduction; withholding tax.

(a) Payment of any tax to any political subdivision pursuant to an ordinance or resolution passed or adopted prior to the effective date of this act shall be credited to and allowed as a deduction from the liability of taxpayers for any like tax respectively on salaries, wages, commissions, other compensation or on net profits of businesses, professions or other activities and for any income tax imposed by any other political subdivision of this Commonwealth under the authority of this act.

(b) Payment of any tax on salaries, wages, commissions, other compensation or on net profits of business, professions or other activities to a political subdivision by residents thereof pursuant to an ordinance or resolution passed or adopted under the authority of this act shall be credited to and allowed as a deduction from the liability of such persons for any other like tax respectively on salaries, wages, commissions, other compensation or on net profits of businesses, professions or other activities imposed by any other political subdivision of this Commonwealth under the authority of this act.

(c) Payment of any tax on income to any political subdivision by residents thereof pursuant to an ordinance or resolution passed or adopted under the authority of this act shall, to the extent that such income includes salaries, wages, commissions, other compensation or net profits of businesses, professions or other activities, but in such proportion as hereinafter set forth, be credited to and allowed as a deduction from the liability of such persons for any other tax on salaries, wages, commissions, other compensation or on net profits of businesses, professions, or other activities imposed by any other political subdivision of this Commonwealth under the authority of this chapter.

(d) Payment of any tax on income to any state or to any political subdivision thereof by residents thereof, pursuant to any State or local law, shall, to the extent that such income includes salaries, wages, commissions, or other compensation or net profits of businesses, professions or other activities but in such proportions as hereinafter set forth, be credited to and allowed as a deduction from the liability of such person for any other tax on salaries, wages, commissions, other compensation or net profits of businesses, professions or other activities imposed by any political subdivision of this Commonwealth under the authority of this act if residents of the political subdivision in Pennsylvania receive credits and deductions of a similar kind to a like degree from the tax on income imposed by the other state or political subdivision thereof.

(e) Payment of any tax on income to any State other than Pennsylvania or to any political subdivision located outside the boundaries of this Commonwealth, by residents of a political subdivision located in Pennsylvania shall, to the extent that such income includes salaries, wages, commissions, or other compensation or net profits of businesses, professions or other activities but in such proportions as hereinafter set forth, be credited to and allowed as a deduction from the liability of such person for any other tax on salaries, wages, commissions, other compensation or net profits of businesses, professions or other activities imposed by any political subdivision of this Commonwealth under the authority of this act.

(f) Where a credit or a deduction is allowable in any of the several cases hereinabove provided, it shall be allowed in proportion to the concurrent periods for which taxes are imposed by the other state or respective political subdivisions, but not in excess of the amount previously paid for a concurrent period.

(g) No credit or deduction shall be allowed against any tax on earned income imposed under authority of this act to the extent of the amount of credit or deduction taken for the same period by the taxpayer against any income tax imposed by the Commonwealth of Pennsylvania under section 314 of the act of March 4,

1971 (P.L.6, No.2) known as the "Tax Reform Code of 1971," on account of taxes imposed on income by other states or by their political subdivisions.

§ 6924.318. Personal property.

Any assessment of a tax on personal property of a decedent shall include all property owned, held or possessed by a decedent, which should have been returned by him for taxation for any former year or years not exceeding five years prior to the year in which the decedent died. Wherever any personal property taxable under the provisions of this act, was owned by a decedent at the time of this death and is held by his executor or administrator, return of such personal property shall be made and the tax paid, if such decedent was domiciled at the time of his death in the political subdivision imposing the tax, notwithstanding the residence or location of such executor or administrator or of any beneficiary, or the place which such securities are kept.

§ 6924.319. Limitation on assessment.

No assessment may be made of any earned income tax imposed under this act more than five years after the date on which such tax should have been filed, including extended due dates, except where a fraudulent return has been filed.

§ 6924.320. Tax limitations.

(a) Over-all Limit of Tax Revenues.—The aggregate amount of all taxes imposed by any political subdivision under this section and in effect during any fiscal year shall not exceed an amount equal to the product obtained by multiplying the latest total market valuation of real estate in such political subdivision, as determined by the board for the assessment and revision of taxes or any similar board established by the assessment laws which determines market values of real estate within the political subdivision, by twelve mills. In school districts of the second class, third class and fourth class and in any political subdivision within a county where no market values of real estate have been determined by the board for the assessment and revision of taxes, or any similar board, the aggregate amount of all taxes imposed under this section and in effect during any fiscal year shall not exceed an amount equal to the product obtained by multiplying the latest total market valuation of real estate in such school district, or other political subdivision, as certified by the State Tax Equalization Board, by twelve mills. In school districts of the third and fourth class, taxes imposed on sales involving the transfer of real property shall not be included in computing the aggregate amount of taxes for any fiscal year in which one hundred or more new homes or other major improvements on real estate were constructed in the school district.

The aggregate amount of all taxes imposed by any independent school district under this section during any fiscal year shall not exceed an amount equal to the product obtained by multiplying the latest total valuation of real estate in such district by fifteen mills.

(b) Reduction of Rates Where Taxes Exceed Limitations; Use of Excess Moneys.—If, during any fiscal year, it shall appear that the aggregate revenues from taxes levied and collected under the authority of this chapter will materially exceed the limitations imposed by this chapter, the political subdivision shall forthwith reduce the rate or rates of such tax or taxes to stay within such limitations as nearly as may be. Any one or more persons liable for the payment of taxes levied and collected under the authority of this chapter shall have the right to complain to the court of common pleas of the county in an action of mandamus to compel compliance with the preceding provision of this subsection. Tax moneys levied and collected in any fiscal year in excess of the limitations imposed by this chapter shall not be expended during such year, but shall be deposited in a separate account in the treasury of the political subdivision for expenditure in the following fiscal year. The rates of taxes imposed under this chapter for the following fiscal year shall be so fixed that the revenues thereby produced, together with the excess tax moneys on deposit as aforesaid, shall not exceed the limitations imposed by this chapter.

(c) Domicile.—An individual who does not meet the domicile requirements for the purpose of determining and paying the tax provided under Article III of the act of March 4, 1971 (P.L.6, No.2), known as the "Tax Reform Code of 1971," shall be deemed to not meet the domicile requirements for local tax purposes.

(d) Local Tax Limitations.—The calculation of the aggregate amount of all taxes imposed under this section shall not include the following:

(1) Any revenues derived from a tax rate in excess of the tax rates authorized under this chapter which is levied under the act of July 10, 1987 (P.L.246, No.47), known as the "Municipalities Financial Recovery Act," or the act of December 18, 1984 (P.L.1005, No.205), known as the "Municipal Pension Plan Funding Standard and Recovery Act."

(2) Any revenues derived from the levy of a tax by a home rule municipality in compliance with 53 Pa.C.S. § 2962(b) (relating to limitation on municipal powers).

§ 6924.321–328. [Reserved].

§ 6924.329. Legal Representation.

When bringing a suit under any provision of this chapter, the taxing district or the person, public employe or private agency designated by the taxing district shall be represented by an attorney.

§ 6924.330. Restricted Use.

(a) Any municipality deriving funds from the local services tax may only use the funds for:

(1) Emergency services, which shall include emergency medical services, police services and/or fire services.

(2) Road construction and/or maintenance.

(3) Reduction of property taxes.

(4) Property tax relief through implementation of a homestead and farmstead exclusion in accordance with 53 Pa.C.S. Ch. 85 Subch. F (relating to homestead property exclusion).

(a.1) A municipality shall use no less than twenty-five percent of the funds derived from the local services tax for emergency services.

(b) In the event that a municipality decides to implement a homestead and farmstead exclusion for purposes of providing property tax relief in accordance with subsection (a)(4), the following shall apply:

(1) The decision to provide a homestead and farmstead exclusion shall be made, by ordinance, prior to December 1, with the homestead and farmstead exclusion to take effect for the fiscal year beginning the first day of January following adoption of the ordinance. Upon adopting an ordinance in accordance with this paragraph, a municipality shall, by first class mail, notify the assessor, as defined in 53 Pa.C.S. § 8582 (relating to definitions), of its decision to provide a homestead and farmstead exclusion.

(2) The assessor shall provide a municipality that will be imposing a homestead and farmstead exclusion in accordance with subsection (a)(4) with a certified report, as provided in 53 Pa.C.S. § 8584(i) (relating to administration and procedure), listing information regarding homestead and farmstead properties in the municipality as determined pursuant to applications filed with the assessor in connection with this or any other law under which a homestead or farmstead exclusion has been adopted. In the year in which an ordinance is adopted in accordance with paragraph (1), the assessor shall provide the certified report after being notified by the municipality of its decision to provide a homestead and farmstead exclusion. In each succeeding year, the assessor shall provide the certified report by December 1 or at the same time the tax duplicate is certified to the municipality, whichever occurs first. Any duty placed on an assessor in accordance with this paragraph shall be in addition to

those established in 53 Pa.C.S. Ch. 85 Subch. F and the act of June 27, 2006 (1st Sp.Sess. P.L.1873, No.1), known as the "Taxpayer Relief Act."

(3) Only homestead or farmstead properties identified in the certified report of the assessor obtained in any year shall be eligible to receive the exclusion for the next fiscal year.

(4) In the year in which a municipality adopts the ordinance evidencing its decision to implement a homestead and farmstead exclusion, the municipality shall notify by first class mail the owner of each parcel of residential property within the municipality which is not approved as a homestead or farmstead property or for which the approval is due to expire of the following:

(i) That the homestead and farmstead exclusion program is to be implemented to provide property tax relief as authorized by subsection (a)(4), beginning in the next fiscal year.

(ii) That only properties currently identified in the certified report of the assessor as having been approved in whole or in part as homestead or farmstead properties shall be entitled to an exclusion in the next fiscal year.

(iii) That owners of properties that have not been approved by the assessor as homestead or farmstead properties may file an application in accordance with 53 Pa.C.S. § 8584(a) by the annual application deadline of March 1 in order to qualify for the program in the year following the next fiscal year.

(5) The one-time notice required by paragraph (4) may be combined and made together with the annual notice required by paragraph (7) or with an annual notice by a coterminous political subdivision that has implemented a homestead and farmstead exclusion.

(6) In the year in which the initial decision to provide a homestead and farmstead exclusion is made and in each succeeding year, a municipality shall, by resolution, fix the dollar amount that is to be excluded from the assessed value of each homestead and farmstead property for the next fiscal year, consistent with 53 Pa.C.S. §§ 8583 (relating to exclusion for homestead property) and 8586 (relating to limitations). This determination of the amount of the homestead and farmstead exclusion shall be made, after receipt of the tax duplicate and the certified report from the assessor, at the time the governing body of a municipality determines the municipal budget and estimates revenues to be derived from the local services tax for the next fiscal year.

(7) Each year after the year in which the municipality implements a homestead and farmstead exclusion and no later than one hundred twenty days prior to the application deadline, the municipality shall give notice of the existence of the municipality's homestead and farmstead exclusion program; the need to file an application in accordance with 53 Pa.C.S. § 8584(a) in order to qualify for the program; and the application deadline, which, notwithstanding 53 Pa.C.S. § 8584(b), shall be December 15. This annual notice, which shall be given by first class mail, need only be sent to the owner of each parcel of residential property in the municipality which is not approved as homestead or farmstead property or for which the approval is due to expire.

(c) For purposes of this section, the term "municipality" does not include a school district.

CHAPTER 4
OPTIONAL OCCUPATION TAX ELIMINATION

Sec.

6924.401. Scope of chapter
6924.402. Definitions
6924.403. Occupation tax replacement generally
6924.404. Income tax rate limits
6924.405. Occupation tax prohibited

§ 6924.401. Scope of chapter

This chapter relates to optional occupation tax elimination.

§ 6924.402. Definitions

The following words and phrases when used in this chapter shall have the meanings given to them in this section unless the context clearly indicates otherwise:

"Earned income tax." A tax on earned income and net profits levied under this act or a tax on earned income and net profits levied under the act of June 27, 2006 (1st Sp.Sess., P.L. 1873, No. 1),[1] known as the Taxpayer Relief Act.

"Election officials." The county board of elections of a county.

"Governing body." A city council, borough council, incorporated town council, board of township commissioners, board of township supervisors, a governing council of a home rule municipality or optional plan municipality, a governing council of any similar general purpose unit of government which may hereafter be created by statute or a board of school directors of a school district.

"Income tax." An earned income tax or a personal income tax imposed under this chapter.

"Occupation tax." A tax based upon an assessed valuation of a particular trade, occupation or profession. The term includes a tax imposed on a flat rate on all trades, occupations or professions. The term does not include a tax upon persons employed in a taxing district, commonly known as an occupational privilege tax.

"Personal income tax." A tax on income enumerated under section 303 of the act of March 4, 1971 (P.L. 6, No. 2),[2] known as the Tax Reform Code of 1971, as determined by the Department of Revenue, subject to any correction or fraud, evasion or error as finally determined by the Commonwealth and levied pursuant to the act of June 27, 2006 (1st Sp.Sess., P.L. 1873, No. 1), known as the Taxpayer Relief Act.

"Political subdivision." Any city, borough, incorporated town, township or school district.

"Taxpayer Relief Act." The act of June 27, 2006 (1st Sp.Sess., P.L. 1873, No. 1), known as the Taxpayer Relief Act.

§ 6924.403. Occupation tax replacement generally

A political subdivision that levies an occupation tax may replace the revenues provided by the occupation tax by increasing the rate of the income tax as provided in this chapter.

§ 6924.404. Income tax rate limits

(a) Income tax rate limits.—For the first fiscal year beginning after approval of the referendum under section 407,[3] and each fiscal year thereafter, the governing body of a political subdivision using the procedures authorized by this chapter shall be authorized to impose an income tax at a rate not exceeding the maximum income tax rate as calculated under subsection (b) or (b.1).

(b) Calculation of maximum earned income tax rate.—The maximum earned income tax rate shall be determined by taking the sum of the rates calculated under paragraphs (1) and (2) and limited by paragraph (3):

---

1. 53 P.S. § 6926.101 et seq.
2. 72 P.S. § 7303.
3. 53 P.S. § 6924.407.

Table of Contents | Part I Ch. 1–3 Ethics, Records, Open Meetings | Part II Ch. 4–10 Taxation | Part III Ch. 11–18 Torts, Contracts & Civil Rules | Part IV Ch. 19–24 Zoning & Planning | Part V Ch. 25–30 Construction and Emergency Codes | Part VI Ch. 31–39 Municipal Codes | Index

(1) The rate of the earned income tax that would have resulted in the collection by the political subdivision of an amount equal to the amount collected from the occupation tax. The calculation by a school district under this paragraph shall be made using actual revenue collections for the fiscal year ending in 2002. The calculation by a municipality under this paragraph shall be made using actual revenue collections for the calendar year ending December 31, 2001.

(2) The rate at which the earned income tax was collected by a school district for the fiscal year ending in 2002 or the rate at which the earned income tax was collected by a municipality for the calendar year ending December 31, 2001.

(3) The tax rate determined under paragraphs (1) and (2) shall be rounded off to the nearest increment of ten hundredths of one percent.

The maximum rate of the earned income tax calculated under this subsection shall not be subject to the limits on the earned income tax specified under section 311(3).[4]

(b.1) Calculation of maximum income tax rate.—The maximum income tax rate for a school district that levied an occupation tax for the fiscal year ending in 2009, or a municipality that levied an occupation tax for the calendar year ending December 31, 2008, shall be determined by taking the sum of the rates calculated under paragraphs (1) and (2) and limited by paragraph (3):

(1) The rate of the income tax that would have resulted in the collection by the political subdivision of an amount equal to the amount collected from the occupation tax. The calculation by a school district under this paragraph shall be made using actual revenue collections for the fiscal year ending in 2009. The calculation by a municipality under this paragraph shall be made using actual revenue collections for the calendar year ending December 31, 2008.

(2) The rate at which the income tax was collected by a school district for the fiscal year ending in 2009 or the rate at which an earned income tax was collected by a municipality for the calendar year ending December 31, 2008.

(3) The tax rate determined under paragraphs (1) and (2) shall be rounded off to the nearest increment of ten hundredths of one percent.

The maximum rate of the income tax calculated under this subsection shall not be subject to the limits on the earned income tax specified under section 311(3).

(c) Other rates of taxation.—If a municipality or school district, both of which impose an earned income tax on the same individual under this act or the Taxpayer Relief Act and both of which are limited to or have agreed upon a division of the tax rate in accordance with section 311 or 304[5] of the Taxpayer Relief Act, and the municipality or school district receives voter approval under section 407 and opts to increase the rate of income tax in excess of that limit or agreement, then the municipality or school district which does not receive voter approval shall remain subject to that limit or agreement.

§ 6924.405. Occupation tax prohibited

(a) General rule.—For the first fiscal year beginning after approval of the referendum required under section 407[6] and each fiscal year thereafter, a political subdivision is prohibited from levying, assessing or collecting an occupation tax.

---

4. 53 P.S. § 6924.311.

5. 53 P.S. §§ 6924.311, 6924.304.

6. 53 P.S. § 6924.407.

(b) Occupation assessment tax roll.—In a county where no political subdivision levies the tax, the county shall not be required under the provisions of this or another statute to maintain the occupation assessment tax roll.

(c) Applicability.—This section shall not apply to the collection of delinquent occupation taxes.

§ 6924.406. Resolution required

The governing body may seek authority to increase the maximum limits of the income tax by adopting a resolution to place a referendum on the ballot pursuant to section 407.[7] The governing body shall transmit a copy of the resolution to the appropriate election officials. Prior to approving the resolution, the governing body shall:

(1) Give public notice of its intent to adopt the resolution in the manner provided under section 306.[8]

(2) Conduct at least one public hearing regarding eliminating the occupation tax and increasing the maximum rate of the income tax.

§ 6924.407. Binding referendum

(a) Referendum to be held.—A political subdivision may increase the maximum rate of the income tax only by obtaining the approval of the electorate of the affected political subdivision in a public referendum at the general or municipal election preceding the fiscal year when the maximum rate of the income tax will be increased. The election officials shall cause a question to be placed on the ballot at the first general or municipal election occurring at least 90 days after their receipt of the resolution required under section 406.[9]

(b) Contents of question.—The referendum question must state the maximum rate of the income tax calculated under section 404[10] and that the additional revenue generated by an increase in the income tax will be used to eliminate the occupation tax. The question shall be in clear language that is readily understandable by a layperson. For the purpose of illustration, a referendum question may be framed as follows:

Do you favor increasing the rate of the (earned or personal) income tax to a maximum of X%, with the requirement that the increase be used to eliminate the occupation tax?

(c) Vote.—If a majority of the electors voting on the question vote "yes," then the governing body shall be authorized to implement an increase in the income tax pursuant to section 404 and shall be required to eliminate the occupation tax as required under section 405.[11] If a majority of the electors voting on the question vote "no," the governing body shall have no authority to increase the rate of the income tax above the maximum rate otherwise provided by law.

(d) Voting proceedings.—Proceedings under this section shall be in accordance with the provisions of the act of June 3, 1937 (P.L. 1333, No. 320),[12] known as the Pennsylvania Election Code.

§ 6924.408. Applicability

This chapter shall apply to political subdivisions which levy an occupation tax on the date of enactment of this section.

7. 53 P.S. § 6924.407.
8. 53 P.S. § 6924.306.
9. 53 P.S. § 6924.406.
10. 53 P.S. § 6924.404.
11. 53 P.S. § 6924.405.
12. 25 P.S. § 2601 et seq.

§ 6924.409. Applicability of personal income tax

Nothing in this chapter shall be construed to authorize a municipality to levy, assess or collect a personal income tax. The authority to levy, assess or collect a personal income tax shall only apply to a school district in which a board of school directors sought to impose a personal income tax under section 321(c) of the Taxpayer Relief Act[13] and the referendum under section 331.2 or 332[14] of the Taxpayer Relief Act is approved by the electorate under the Taxpayer Relief Act.

CHAPTER 5

CONSOLIDATED COLLECTION OF LOCAL INCOME TAXES

Sec.

§ 6924.501. Definitions.

The following words and phrases when used in this chapter shall have the meanings given to them in this section unless the context clearly indicates otherwise:

"Article XIII tax officer." The tax officer authorized by a political subdivision to collect income taxes levied prior to January 1, 2012.

"Business." An enterprise, activity, profession or any other undertaking of an unincorporated nature conducted for profit or ordinarily conducted for profit whether by a person, partnership, association or any other entity.

"Business entity." A sole proprietorship, corporation, joint-stock association or company, partnership, limited partnership, limited liability company, association, business trust, syndicate or other commercial or professional activity organized under the laws of this Commonwealth or any other jurisdiction.

"Certified public accountant" or "public accountant." certified public accountant, public accountant or firm, as provided for in the act of May 26, 1947 (P.L.318, No.140), known as the CPA Law.

"Claim." A written demand for payment made by a tax officer or tax collection district for income taxes collected by another tax officer or tax collection district.

"Corporation." A corporation or joint stock association organized under the laws of the United States, the Commonwealth of Pennsylvania or any other state,

---

13. 53 P.S. § 6926.321.

14. 53 P.S. §§ 6926.331.2, 6926.332

territory, foreign country or dependency. The term shall include an entity which is classified as a corporation for Federal income tax purposes.

"Current year." The calendar year for which the tax is levied.

"Department." The Department of Community and Economic Development of the Commonwealth.

"Domicile." The place where a person lives and has a permanent home and to which the person has the intention of returning whenever absent. Actual residence is not necessarily domicile, for domicile is the fixed place of abode which, in the intention of the taxpayer, is permanent rather than transitory. Domicile is the voluntarily fixed place of habitation of a person, not for a mere special or limited purpose, but with the present intention of making a permanent home, until some event occurs to induce the person to adopt some other permanent home. In the case of a business, domicile is that place considered as the center of business affairs and the place where its functions are discharged.

"Earned income." The compensation as required to be reported to or as determined by the Department of Revenue under section 303 of the act of March 4, 1971 (P.L.6, No.2), known as the Tax Reform Code of 1971, and rules and regulations promulgated under that section subject to the following:

(1) Employee business expenses as reported to or determined by the Department of Revenue under Article III of the Tax Reform Code of 1971 shall constitute allowable deductions in determining earned income.

(2) The term does not include:

(i) Wages or compensation paid to individuals on active military service, regardless of whether it is earned for active military service inside or outside this Commonwealth.

(ii) Offsets for business losses.

(iii) The amount of any housing allowance provided to a member of the clergy.

(3) For purposes of collection of earned income and net profits taxes under this chapter and for crediting purposes under section 317, the term shall include all taxes on earned income or net profits whether authorized by this act or any other law of this Commonwealth unless the law expressly provides otherwise.

"Earned income and net profits tax." The tax levied by apolitical subdivision on earned income and net profits.

"Effective local services tax rate." The actual local services tax rate levied by a political subdivision on taxpayers based on the total of all local services taxes imposed under this act and all other acts, adjusted under section 311.

"Effective income tax rate." The actual tax rate levied by apolitical subdivision on a taxpayer based on the total of all income taxes imposed under this act and all other acts, adjusted under section 311.

"Employer." A person, business entity or other entity, employing one or more persons for a salary, wage, commission or other compensation. The term includes the Commonwealth, a political subdivision and an instrumentality or public authority of either. For purposes of penalties under this chapter, the term includes a corporate officer.

"Farming." Includes all activities that are farming for purposes of section 325 of the act of March 4, 1971 (P.L.6, No.2), known as the Tax Reform Code of 1971.

"Income tax." Except as set forth in section 511(b), an earned income and net profits tax, personal income tax or other tax that is assessed on the income of a taxpayer levied by a political subdivision under the authority of this act or any other act.

"Joint tax collection committee." An entity formed by two or more tax collection committees for the purpose of income tax collection in more than one tax collection district.

"Local services tax." A tax on individuals for the privilege of engaging in an occupation that is levied, assessed and collected only by the political subdivision of the taxpayer's place of employment under the authority of this act or any other act.

"Municipality." A city of the second class, city of the second class A, city of the third class, borough, town, township of the first class or township of the second class.

"Net profits." The net income from the operation of a business, other than a corporation, as required to be reported to or as determined by the Department of Revenue under section 303 of the act of March 4, 1971 (P.L.6, No.2), known as the Tax Reform Code of 1971, and rules and regulations promulgated under that section. The term does not under any of the following paragraphs:

(1) income which:

(i) is not paid for services provided; and

(ii) is in the nature of earnings from an investment.

(2) income which represents:

(i) any gain on the sale of farm machinery;

(ii) any gain on the sale of livestock held 12 Months or more for draft, breeding or dairy purposes; or

(iii) any gain on the sale of other capital assets of a farm.

"Nonresident." A person or business domiciled outside the political subdivision levying the tax and performing services within the political subdivision levying the tax for at least 90 or more consecutive days.

"Nonresident tax." An income tax levied by a municipality on a nonresident who has performed services within the political subdivision levying the tax for at least 90 or more consecutive days.

"Official register." The part of the tax register that includes withholding tax rates as provided in section 511(a)(3).

"Person." A natural person.

"Political subdivision." A city of the second class, city of the second class A, city of the third class, borough, town, township of the first class, township of the second class, school district of the first class A, school district of the second class, school district of the third class, school district of the fourth class or municipal authority.

"Preceding year." The calendar year before the current year.

"Private agency." A business entity or person appointed as a tax officer by a tax collection committee.

"Public agency." Any and all public bodies, authorities, agencies, instrumentalities, political subdivisions, intermediate units, councils, boards, commissions or similar governmental entities.

"Resident." A person or business domiciled in the political subdivision levying the tax.

"Resident tax." An income tax levied by:

(1) a municipality on a resident of that municipality; or

(2) a school district on a resident of that school district.

"Resident tax officer." The tax officer administering and collecting income taxes for the tax collection district in which a taxpayer is domiciled.

"Succeeding year." The calendar year following the current year.

"Tax bureau." A public nonprofit entity established for the administration and collection of taxes.

"Tax collection committee." The committee established to govern each tax collection district for the purpose of income tax collection. The term shall include a joint tax collection committee.

"Tax collection district." A tax collection district established under section 504.

"Tax officer." A political subdivision, public employee, tax bureau, county, except a county of the first class, or private agency which administers and collects income taxes for one or more tax collection districts. Unless otherwise specifically provided, for purposes of the obligations of an employer, the term shall mean the tax officer for the tax collection district within which the employer is located, or, if an employer maintains workplaces in more than one district, the tax officer for each such district with respect to employees principally employed therein.

"Tax records." Tax returns, supporting schedules, correspondence with auditors or taxpayers, account books and other documents, including electronic records, obtained or created by the tax officer to administer or collect a tax under this act. The term includes documents required by section 509(e). The term "electronic records" includes data and information inscribed on a tangible medium or stored in an electronic or other medium and which is retrievable in perceivable form.

"Tax register." A database of all county, municipal and school tax rates available on the Internet as provided in section 511(a)(1).

"Taxable income." Includes:

(1) In the case of an earned income and net profits tax, earned income and net profits.

(2) In the case of a personal income tax, income enumerated in section 303 of the act of March 4, 1971 (P.L.6,No.2), known as the Tax Reform Code of 1971, as reported to and determined by the Department of Revenue, subject to correction for fraud, evasion or error, as finally determined by the Commonwealth.

"Taxpayer." A person or business required under this act to file a return of an income tax or to pay an income tax. The term includes a person or business that filed a return of taxable income during the prior year but that had no taxable income during the current year and was required by the tax collector to file a final return indicating why the person or business no longer has taxable income. The term does not include a person or business with no taxable income, which person or business shall not be required to file a return of income or to pay an income tax under this act.

"Withholding tax." An income tax or a local services tax levied by a political subdivision under the authority of this act or any other act, or any other tax levied by a municipality or school district for which employer withholding may be required under this act or any other act.

§ 6924.502. Declaration and payment of income taxes.

(a) Application.—

(1) Income taxes shall be applicable to taxable income earned or received based on the method of accounting used by the taxpayer in the period beginning January 1 of the current year and ending December 31 of the current year; except that taxes imposed for the first time and changes to existing tax rates shall become effective on January 1 or July 1, as specified in the ordinance or resolution, and the tax shall continue in force on a calendar year or taxpayer fiscal year basis, without annual reenactment, unless the rate of the tax is subsequently changed.

(2) For a taxpayer whose fiscal year is not a calendar year, the tax officer shall establish deadlines for filing, reporting and payment of taxes which provide time periods equivalent to those provided for a calendar year taxpayer.

(b) Partial domicile.—The taxable income subject to tax of a taxpayer who is domiciled in a political subdivision for only a portion of the tax year shall be an amount equal to the taxpayer's taxable income multiplied by a fraction, the numerator of which is the number of calendar months during the tax year that the individual is domiciled in the political subdivision, and the denominator of which is 12. A taxpayer shall include in the numerator any calendar month during which

Chapter 10 Residential Design Tax Credit
Chapter 9 Neighborhood Improvement
Chapter 8 Local Taxpayers Bill of Rights
Chapter 7 Occupation Tax Elimination Act
Chapter 6 Local Government Unit Debt Act
Chapter 5 Local Tax Collection Law
Chapter 4 Local Tax Enabling Act

the taxpayer is domiciled for more than half the calendar month. A day that a taxpayer's domicile changes shall be included as a day the individual is in the new domicile and not the old domicile. If the number of days in the calendar month in which the individual lived in the old and new domiciles are equal, the calendar month shall be included in calculating the number of months in the new domicile.

(c) **Declaration and payment.**—Except as provided in subsections (a)(2) and (d), taxpayers shall declare and pay income taxes as follows:

(1) Every taxpayer shall make and file with the resident tax officer, a final return showing the amount of taxable income received during the period beginning January 1 of the current year and ending December 31 of the current year, the total amount of tax due on the taxable income, the amount of tax paid, the amount of tax that has been withheld under section 512 and the balance of tax due. All amounts reported shall be rounded to the nearest whole dollar. At the time of filing the final return, the taxpayer shall pay the resident tax officer the balance of the tax due or shall make demand for refund or credit in the case of overpayment. Taxpayers may use the Annual Local Earned Income Tax Return form available from the department's publicly accessible Internet website to file the final return.

(2) (i) Every taxpayer making net profits shall, by April 15 of the current year, make and file with the resident tax officer a declaration of the taxpayer's estimated net profits during the period beginning January 1 and ending December 31 of the current year, and shall pay to the resident tax officer in four equal quarterly installments the tax due on the estimated net profits. The first installment shall be paid at the time of filing the declaration, and the other installments shall be paid on or before July 15 of the current year, October 15 of the current year and January 15 of the succeeding year, respectively.

(ii) Any taxpayer who first anticipates any net profit after April 15 of the current year shall make and file the declaration required on or before July 15 of the current year, October 15 of the current year or January 15 of the succeeding year, whichever date next follows the date on which the taxpayer first anticipates such net profit, and shall pay to the resident tax officer in equal installments the tax due on or before the quarterly payment dates that remain after the filing of the declaration.

(iii) Every taxpayer shall make and file with the resident tax officer a final return showing the amount of net profits earned or received based on the method of accounting used by the taxpayer during the period beginning January 1 of the current year, and ending December 31 of the current year, the total amount of tax due on the net profits and the total amount of tax paid. At the time of filing the final return, the taxpayer shall pay to the resident tax officer the balance of tax due or shall make demand for refund or credit in the case of overpayment. Any taxpayer may, in lieu of paying the fourth quarterly installment of the estimated tax, elect to make and file with the resident tax officer on or before January 31 of the succeeding year, the final return.

(iv) The department, in consultation with the Department of Revenue, shall provide by regulation for the filing of adjusted declarations of estimated net profits and for the payments of the estimated tax in cases where a taxpayer who has filed the declaration required under this subsection anticipates additional net profits not previously declared or has overestimated anticipated net profits.

(v) Every taxpayer who discontinues business prior to December 31 of the current year, shall, within 30 days after the discontinuance of business, file a final return as required under this paragraph and pay the tax due.

(3) Every taxpayer who receives any other taxable income not subject to withholding under section 512(3) shall make and file with the resident tax officer a quarterly return on or before April 15 of the current year, July 15 of the current year, October 15 of the current year, and January 15 of the

succeeding year, setting forth the aggregate amount of taxable income not subject to withholding by the taxpayer during the three-month periods ending March 31 of the current year, June 30 of the current year, September 30 of the current year, and December 31 of the current year, respectively, and subject to income tax, together with such other information as the department may require. Every taxpayer filing a return shall, at the time of filing the return, pay to the resident tax officer the amount of income tax due. The department shall establish criteria under which the tax officer may waive the quarterly return and payment of the income tax and permit a taxpayer to file the receipt of taxable income on the taxpayer's annual return and pay the income tax due on or before April 15 of the succeeding year.

(4) The filing deadline of a final return under paragraphs (1) and (2)(iii) shall coincide with the filing deadline for a tax return under section 330(a) of the act of March 4, 1971 (P.L. 6, No. 2), known as the Tax Reform Code of 1971. If any date prescribed in this section for filing or payment of tax should fall on a Saturday, Sunday or legal holiday, the taxpayer may file or make payment on the next business day.

(5) Every taxpayer subject to the declaration and payment provisions under this section shall be deemed to have met the requirements and therefore not be subject to a penalty so long as one of the following safe harbor exceptions is met:

(i) Make four equal, timely estimated payments equal to 100% of the prior year's tax less any earned income tax withheld for the current year.

(ii) Make four equal, timely estimated payments equal to 90% of the current year's tax less any earned income tax withheld for the current year.

(d) Filing of estimated tax by taxpayers whose major source of gross income is from farming.—Notwithstanding any other provision of this section, a declaration of estimated tax of an individual having an estimated gross income from farming for the taxable year which is at least two-thirds of his total estimated gross income for the taxable year may be filed at any time on or before January 15 of the succeeding year, but if the farmer files a final return and pays the entire tax by March 1, the return may be considered as his declaration due on or before January 15.

(e) Restrictions.—In administering the provisions of this section, no political subdivision, tax collection committee or tax officer may:

(1) Prohibit a taxpayer from filing any return or declaration required under this section in person or by first class mail.

(2) Prohibit a taxpayer from filing any local income tax return form, estimated tax return form or other form related to any filing required under this section that has been posted by the department on its publicly accessible Internet website.

(3) Impose a penalty for failing to timely file a quarterly estimated tax return for which no payment of estimated tax was due, as shown in the taxpayer's annual income tax return.

(4) Impose a penalty on a taxpayer unless it has issued a letter that notifies the taxpayer that the taxpayer is required to take corrective action within 30 days and failure to take corrective action will result in a penalty being imposed on the taxpayer.

§ 6924.503. (Reserved).

§ 6924.504. Tax collection districts.

(a) General rule.—A tax collection district is established in each county, except a county of the second class, for purposes of collecting income taxes. The geographic boundaries of a tax collection district shall be coterminous with the county in which it is created, except as provided in this section. A school district located in more than one county shall be included in the tax collection district with the greatest share of the school district's population based on the 2000 Federal Decennial Census. A municipality shall be included in the tax collection district in which its school district is located. If a municipality is located in more than one school district, each of which is in a different tax collection district, the portion of the municipality in each school district shall be included in the tax collection district for that school district. The department shall establish a list of all tax collection districts and the political subdivisions in each tax collection district. By January 16, 2009, the list shall be transmitted to the Legislative Reference Bureau for publication in the Pennsylvania Bulletin; and by January 28, 2009, the list shall be made available on the department's Internet website.

(b) Counties of the second class.—Each county of the second class with a population of over 1,000,000 persons, and which also contains a city of the second class, shall be divided into four tax collection districts, each to be as consistent as practicable with the general rules pertaining to municipalities and school districts contained in subsection (a), and to be further established as follows:

(1) One district shall be comprised of a city of the second class and any municipality and school district geographically located within the boundaries of such city.

(2) The remainder of the county shall be divided into three tax collection districts of relatively equal population which contain coterminous municipalities and school districts that are bordered by the county boundaries and by commercially navigable rivers which are at least 100 miles in length.

(3) The department shall develop a map and a list of all tax collection districts in each county of the second class and the political subdivisions in each tax collection district. By January 16, 2009, the list shall be transmitted to the Legislative Reference Bureau for publication in the Pennsylvania Bulletin and by January 28, 2009, the list shall be made available on the department's Internet website.

(c) Existing consolidated collection arrangements: notwithstanding the provisions of subsection (a), in any county in which, on the effective date of this section, all political subdivisions levying an income tax, including a county school district located partially outside of but contiguous to the county, are served by one existing tax bureau, the county tax collection district shall also include such a school district and all of its component municipalities in the event a tax collection committee is established for that county pursuant to section 505(m).

§ 6924.505. Tax collection committees.

(a) General rule.— Subject to the provisions of subsection (m), each tax collection district shall be governed by a tax collection committee constituted and operated as set forth in this section. Meetings of the tax collection committee shall be conducted under 65 Pa.C.S. Ch. 7 (relating to open meetings) and the act of June 21, 1957 (P.L.390, No.212), referred to as the Right-to-Know Law.

(a.1) Duties.—A tax collection committee has the following duties:

(1) To keep records of all votes and other actions taken by the tax collection committee.

(2) To appoint and oversee a tax officer for the tax collection district as provided in section 507(a).

(3) To set the compensation of the tax officer under section 507(c).

(4) To require, hold, set and review the tax officer's bond required by section 509(d).

(5) To establish the manner and extent of financing of the tax collection committee.

(6) To adopt, amend and repeal bylaws for the management of its affairs consistent with subsection (f) and regulations under section 508.

(7) To adopt, amend and repeal policies and procedures consistent with the regulations under section 508 for the administration of income taxes within the tax collection district. The procedures shall supersede any contrary resolutions or ordinances adopted by a political subdivision and no additional forms, policies or procedures may be adopted other than those promulgated by the department unless permitted by the department under subsection (a.3). This authority shall not be construed to permit a tax collection committee to change the rate or subject of any tax.

(a.2) Powers.—A tax collection committee has the following powers:

(1) To adopt, amend and repeal resolutions to carry out its powers and duties under this section.

(2) To create a tax bureau and to provide for its operation and administration. The department shall, upon request of a tax collection committee, provide technical assistance to the tax collection committee in the creation of a tax bureau.

(3) To enter into contracts as necessary.

(4) To appoint a director for the tax collection committee and other employees as necessary and to fix their compensation.

(5) To retain counsel, auditors and other consultants or advisors to render professional services as necessary.

(6) To acquire, lease, rent or dispose of real or personal property.

(7) To enter into agreements with one or more other tax collection committees to form a joint tax collection committee. Such agreements may assign to a joint tax collection committee some or all of the powers and duties enumerated in subsection (a.1) and this subsection with respect to all tax collection districts from which the joint tax collection committee is formed.

(8) To sue and be sued, and complain and defend in all courts.

(9) To borrow money, accept grants, incur indebtedness and issue notes, debentures and other obligations to evidence borrowing for the purposes for which it is organized in an amount not to exceed 50% of the total revenues anticipated in the following fiscal year.

(a.3) Form.—Beginning January 1, 2020, in administering this act, no political subdivision, tax collection committee or tax officer may use any form other than that which is promulgated by the department unless, for religious reasons, the department expressly grants an exception to this requirement.

(b) Delegates.—

(1) The governing body of each political subdivision within a tax collection district that imposed an income tax prior to July 1, 2009, shall appoint one voting delegate and one or more alternates to represent the political subdivision on the tax collection committee by September 15, 2009. The governing body of each political subdivision that after June 30, 2009, imposes an income tax for the first time shall appoint one voting delegate and one or more alternates to represent the political subdivision on the tax collection committee. A voting delegate or alternate shall serve at the pleasure of the governing body of the political subdivision.

(2) The governing body of each political subdivision within a tax collection district that prior to July 1, 2009, does not impose an income tax may appoint one nonvoting delegate and one or more alternates to represent the political subdivision on the tax collection committee. If, after June 30, 2009, the political subdivision imposes an income tax, the nonvoting delegate shall become a voting delegate to represent the political subdivision on the tax collection committee.

Chapter 10 Residential Design Tax Credit
Chapter 9 Neighborhood Improvement
Chapter 8 Local Taxpayers Bill of Rights
Chapter 7 Occupation Tax Elimination Act
Chapter 6 Local Government Unit Debt Act
Chapter 5 Local Tax Collection Law
Chapter 4 Local Tax Enabling Act

(b.1) Quorum.—Unless otherwise provided for in the bylaws of a tax collection committee, a majority of the delegates of a tax collection committee appointed under subsection (b)(1) constitutes a quorum. A quorum must be present in order to take official action.

(b.2) Lack of quorum at first meeting. If a quorum is not present at the first meeting, the chair of the governing body of the county in which the tax collection district is located or the chair's designee shall reschedule the meeting within three weeks. The chair or the chair's designee shall provide, by first class mail, notice of the rescheduled meeting to the department and to the governing bodies of all political subdivisions in the tax collection district on a form prescribed by the department. The form shall include the date, time and location of there scheduled meeting and a notice that the delegates present at the rescheduled meeting shall constitute a quorum. There scheduled meeting shall be deemed to be the first meeting for purposes of this chapter.

(c) Voting rights.—

(1) Only a delegate appointed by the governing body of apolitical subdivision may represent a political subdivision at a tax collection committee meeting. If a delegate cannot be present for a tax collection committee meeting, the alternate appointed under this section may represent the political subdivision. Each delegate or alternate shall be entitled to vote upon any action authorized or required of the tax collection committee under this chapter.

(2) For the first meeting of the tax collection committee, actions of the tax collection committee shall be determined by a majority vote of those delegates present. Votes shall be weighted among the governing bodies of the member political subdivisions according to the following formula: 50% shall be allocated according to the proportional population of each political subdivision in proportion to the population of each tax collection district as determined by the most recent Federal decennial census data and 50% shall be weighted in direct proportion to income tax revenues collected in each political subdivision, based on each political subdivision's most recent annual financial report submitted to the department or the Department of Education. For subsequent meetings, votes shall be taken in accordance with this paragraph unless the bylaws provide otherwise.

(3) No later than September 1, 2009, the department shall calculate the weighted vote for each political subdivision within each tax collection district based on the formula specified in paragraph (2). By July 1 of the year following the first meeting, and of each year thereafter, each tax collection committee shall recalculate the weighted vote unless the bylaws provide for a more frequent recalculation.

(4) If a political subdivision within the tax collection district imposes an income tax for the first time, the tax collection committee shall recalculate the weighted vote or other method of voting under the bylaws.(d) First meeting schedule.—The first meeting of the tax collection committee in each tax collection district shall be on or before November 15, 2009. The chair of the county commissioners or the chief executive of the county in which the tax collection district is primarily located or the chair's designee shall schedule the first meeting of the tax collection committee and shall provide, at least 21 days before the meeting, public notice, as required by 65 Pa.C.S. § 703(relating to definitions), and notice by first class mail by September 15, 2009, to the department and to the governing body of each political subdivision located in the tax collection district.

(e) First meeting agenda.—The chair of the county commissioners or the chair's designee or the chief executive of the county or his designee shall convene the first meeting of the tax collection committee, conduct the meeting and record all votes until a chairperson, vice chairperson and secretary are elected by the tax collection committee. The voting delegates of the tax collection committee shall elect a chairperson and a vice chairperson, each of whom must be duly appointed voting delegates, and a secretary who need not be a duly appointed voting delegate. The chairperson shall schedule meetings, set the agenda, conduct meetings, record votes and perform other duties as determined by the tax collection committee. The secretary shall maintain the minutes and records of the tax collection committee and provide public notices and all notices to each delegate and alternate appointed to the tax collection committee.

(f) Bylaws.—No later than April 15, 2010, the delegates of each tax collection committee shall adopt bylaws to govern the tax collection committee and notify the department within 30 days of adoption. The department shall provide sample bylaws to the tax collection committee. Written notice shall be provided to each delegate and alternate delegate that the adoption or amendment of bylaws will be considered at a meeting. Notice shall include copies of the proposed bylaws or amendments. The bylaws for each tax collection committee shall provide for the following:

(1) Rules of procedure, quorum requirements, voting rights and provisions for managing the affairs of the tax collection committee.

(2) A list of officers, their terms and powers and a process for their election.

(3) Meetings, including special meetings.

(4) The process for adopting and amending bylaws.

(5) The procedure for the addition of new political subdivisions to the tax collection committee.

(g) Officers.—Upon the election of any new officers, the tax collection committee shall notify the department within 30 days and shall provide the department with the name and address of each officer.

(h) Audits of taxes received and disbursed.—

(1) By the end of each calendar year, the tax collection committee shall provide for at least one examination for each calendar year of the books, accounts, financial statements, compliance reports and records of the tax officer by a certified public accountant or public accountant approved by the tax collection committee. The examination shall be conducted on a calendar-year basis. An examination conducted on any other basis shall not be accepted by the department, and failure to comply with this requirement shall be considered noncompliance with this act resulting in the imposition of penalties under section 510. The examination shall include an audit of all records relating to the cash basis receipt and disbursement of all public money by the tax officer, a reconciliation of the monthly reports required by section 509(b), an analysis of the bond amount under section 509(d) and an analysis of the collection fees charged to the tax collection committee. In the case of a private agency, the examination shall not include payroll and other proprietary information. The examination shall be conducted according to generally accepted governmental auditing standards.

(2) The certified public accountant or public accountant shall issue a report, on a calendar-year basis and in a format prescribed by the department, to the tax collection committee, which shall include an auditor's opinion letter, a financial statement for the year ending December 31, a reconciliation of the monthly reports required by section 509(b) with the receipts and disbursements on a calendar-year basis, a summary of collection fees charged to the tax collection committee on a calendar-year basis, a report on the tax officer's compliance with this act, a list of any findings of noncompliance with this act and a copy of a management letter if one is issued by the auditor. If there are findings of noncompliance, a copy of the report shall be filed with the Department of the Auditor General and the department. A copy of the report shall be filed with all political subdivisions within the tax collection district and the department on or before September 1 of the succeeding year. The department may make available on its Internet website summary data from the reports

filed under this subsection. The department may reject any report which is not in the proper format and does not meet the requirements of this paragraph. Failure to correct the submission within 30 days of the rejection shall constitute noncompliance with this act and result in the imposition of penalties under section 510.

(i) **Applicability of statutes.—**Each tax collection committee shall be subject to the provisions of the following:

(1) The Right-to-Know Law.

(2) The act of July 19, 1957 (P.L.1017, No.451), known as the State Adverse Interest Act.

(3) 65 Pa.C.S. Ch. 7 (relating to open meetings).

(4) 65 Pa.C.S. Ch. 11 (relating to ethics standards and financial disclosure).

(j) **Appeals board.—**

(1) By June 1, 2010, each tax collection committee shall establish an appeals board comprised of a minimum of three delegates or, in the case of a tax collection committee established pursuant to subsection (m), a minimum of three residents of the county.

(2) A determination of the tax officer relating to the assessment, collection, refund, withholding, remittance or distribution of income taxes may be appealed to the appeals board by a taxpayer, employer, political subdivision or another tax collection district.

(3) All appeals, other than those brought under subsection (k), shall be conducted in a manner consistent with 53 Pa.C.S. §§ 8431 (relating to petitions), 8432(relating to practice and procedure), 8433 (relating to decisions), 8434 (relating to appeals) and 8435 (relating to equitable and legal principles to apply).

(4) A tax collection committee may enter into agreement with another tax collection committee to establish a joint appeals board.

(5) No member of an appeals board or joint appeals board may be a tax officer or an employee, agent or attorney for a tax officer.

(6) An appeals board appointed pursuant to this section shall constitute a joint local tax appeals board as provided for in 53 Pa.C.S. § 8430 (relating to administrative appeals) for purposes of taxes collected under the supervision of the appointing tax collection committee.

(k) **Mediation and appeals of tax collector actions.—**

(1) Any dispute among the affected parties involving a10% or greater deviation from taxes received in the previous tax year shall be subject to mandatory mediation under this section, in accordance with regulations and guidelines to be adopted by the department. A dispute involving less than the 10% threshold may be the subject of voluntary mediation in accordance with regulations and guidelines to be adopted by the department.

(2) One or more affected political subdivisions shall give written notice to the tax collection committee and the department of its desire to submit the disputed matter to mediation by the department. Thereafter, the affected political subdivisions, tax collection committee and tax officer shall submit to mediation to which the following provisions shall apply:

(i) Within 20 days of submission of the written notice, the affected political subdivisions, tax collection committee and tax officer shall each submit to the mediator and each other party to the mediation a statement of no more than five pages, stating the position of such party as to the disputed and undisputed facts and issues in the case and whether prior settlement negotiations have occurred.

(ii) Within 30 days of submission of the written notice, the department shall determine whether the dispute meets the threshold conditions for mandatory mediation under paragraph (1), which decision shall be final and not appealable. Notice of such determination shall be given in writing to all affected parties.

(iii) If the mediator determines that the dispute meets the threshold conditions of paragraph (1), a mediation shall be commenced in accordance with procedures established under guidelines adopted by the department. The mediation efforts shall be completed no later than 30 days following the notice that the dispute has met the threshold requirement of paragraph (1), unless the time period is extended by mutual agreement of the parties to the mediation. The parties shall have any official authorized to settle the matter on their behalf available at the mediation. At the discretion of the mediator, the mediation may be held via telephonic communication or in person.

(iv) The mediation sessions shall be closed to the public and shall not be subject to the requirements of 65Pa.C.S. Ch. 7 (relating to open meetings).

(v) No offers or statements made in a mediation session, excluding the final written settlement agreement, if any, shall be admissible as evidence in any subsequent judicial or administrative proceedings in accordance with the provisions of 42 Pa.C.S. § 5949(relating to confidential mediation communications and documents).

(vi) If a settlement is reached during the mediation, the department shall prepare a written settlement agreement and obtain all necessary signatures of the parties within 30 days of the agreement of the parties to settle the issue. The settlement agreement shall be binding upon the parties to the agreement. Such settlement agreement shall be subject to the provisions of the Right-to-Know Law. Such agreements shall be admissible as evidence in any subsequent judicial or administrative proceedings in accordance with the provisions of the Pennsylvania Rules of Court, the Pennsylvania Rules of Evidence and 42 Pa.C.S. § 5949.

(vii) If the mediation has not resulted in a written agreement signed by the parties as provided in subparagraph (vi), the mediation shall be deemed to have been unsuccessful unless all parties and the department agree in writing to extend the mediation. The mediator shall have the right to determine that the mediation has been unsuccessful and to terminate the mediation if the parties have not executed a settlement agreement by the ending date of the extension, or any further extension agreeable to the affected parties and the mediator.

(viii) Costs incurred by the department for amendatory mediation under this section shall be equitably assessed by the department against the parties to the mediation. The assessment of costs shall be final and not appealable.

(3) The department shall adopt guidelines to further provide for the mandatory and voluntary mediation processes in this subsection.

(l) Annual budget required.—

(1) Each tax collection committee shall adopt an annual budget providing for compensation of the tax officer and other expenses of operating the tax collection district.

(2) The expenses of operating the tax collection district shall be shared among and paid by all political subdivisions within the tax collection district that are represented by voting delegates on the tax collection committee and shall be weighted in direct proportion to income tax revenues collected in each participating political subdivision based on the political subdivision's most recent annual audit report required under this section.

Table of Contents
Part I Ch. 1–3 Ethics, Records, Open Meetings
Part II Ch. 4–10 Taxation
Part III Ch. 11–18 Torts, Contracts & Civil Rules
Part IV Ch. 19–24 Zoning & Planning
Part V Ch. 25–30 Construction and Emergency Codes
Part VI Ch. 31–39 Municipal Codes
Index

Chapter 10 Residential Design Tax Credit
Chapter 9 Neighborhood Improvement
Chapter 8 Local Taxpayers Bill of Rights
Chapter 7 Occupation Tax Elimination Act
Chapter 6 Local Government Unit Debt Act
Chapter 5 Local Tax Collection Law
Chapter 4 Local Tax Enabling Act

(m) Committee establishment in counties with existing consolidated collection arrangements.—in any county in which, on the effective date of this section, all political subdivisions levying an income tax, including a county school district located partially outside of but contiguous to the county, are served by one existing tax bureau and that tax bureau is governed by a single governing entity created solely by the action of the school districts located wholly within and one or more partially outside of but contiguous to that county, such existing governing entity shall constitute the tax collection committee for that county and school district provided a majority of the governing bodies of the political subdivisions served by such tax bureau and within the tax collection district as defined in section 504(c) adopt uniform resolutions on or before July 1, 2009, designating said governing entity as the county tax collection committee for purposes of this act. In the event such a majority is not achieved, the establishment of a tax collection committee for that county and such school district shall proceed as otherwise provided for in this section. The following apply:

(1) A tax collection committee established pursuant to this subsection shall not be subject to any of the following:

(i) subsection (b).

(ii) subsection (b.1).

(iii) subsection (b.2).

(iv) subsection (c).

(v) subsection (d).

(vi) subsection (e).

(vii) subsection (f), except that the substance of bylaws utilized by such a tax collection committee shall address the subjects enumerated therein.

(viii) subsection (l)(2).

(2) all of the following requirements shall be deemed to have been met without the necessity of further action by a tax collection committee established pursuant to this subsection:

(i) the initial adoption of bylaws otherwise required of a tax collection committee under subsection (a.1)(6).

(ii) the initial adoption of policies and procedures

Otherwise required of a tax collection committee under Subsection (a.1)(7).

(3) in addition to the withdrawal options for political subdivisions under section 510(h), each political subdivision governed by a tax collection committee established pursuant to this subsection may, within the 90-day period ending November 15, 2013, and November 15 every fourth year thereafter, adopt and file with the department and the tax collection committee a resolution evidencing its desire to withdraw from governance by such tax collection committee as of January 1 of the second succeeding calendar year. The following apply:

(i) if a majority of the governing bodies of such political subdivisions adopt resolutions evidencing a desire to withdraw, a new tax collection committee shall be established in accordance with subparagraph (iii).

(ii) if a majority of the governing bodies of such political subdivisions fail to adopt resolutions evidencing a desire to withdraw from governance by the tax collection committee established pursuant to this subsection, such governance shall continue as before for all political subdivisions.

(iii) the department shall promulgate appropriate regulations governing the establishment of a new county tax collection committee necessitated by the action of political subdivisions under this paragraph in withdrawing from a tax collection committee established pursuant to this subsection.

Among other things, such regulations shall provide for voting rights, quorum requirements, meeting requirements, meeting agendas, bylaw requirements and other items as provided for in this section and other parts of this act dealing with the initial establishment of tax collection committees, to the extent warranted, and shall establish the time frame and schedule within which any and all actions necessary to establish such a new tax collection committee are to be effectuated to ensure a timely and efficient transfer of tax collection and governance responsibilities.

§ 6924.506. Tax officer.

(a) Collection and administration.—Notwithstanding any other provision of law to the contrary, income taxes shall be collected and administered by one tax officer in each tax collection district appointed under section 507(a). Two or more tax collection districts may appoint the same tax officer. If two or more tax collection districts form a joint tax collection committee, the joint tax collection committee shall appoint a single tax officer.

(b) Standards.—A tax collection committee may not appoint a tax officer that:

(1) has been convicted of a felony involving fraud, extortion or dishonesty in any jurisdiction;

(2) has engaged in conduct which significantly adversely reflects on the applicant's credibility, honesty or integrity;

(3) is unable to obtain the bond required by section 509(d);

(4) has not satisfied the mandatory education requirements under section 508(e); or

(5) does not meet the qualifications and requirements established by the department under section 508(f).

§ 6924.507. Appointment of tax officer.

(a) Appointment.—By September 15, 2010, each tax collection committee shall appoint a tax officer by resolution and shall notify the department of the appointment, including the tax officer's name, address and telephone number and any other information required by the department within ten days of the appointment. The name, telephone number and address of the tax officer appointed shall be added to the official register and shall be effective for the assessment, collection and administration of income taxes levied, imposed and collected in fiscal years beginning on and after January 1, 2012. If the position of tax officer becomes vacant, the tax collection committee shall appoint a new tax officer by resolution.

(b) Court selection.—

(1) If a tax collection committee has not appointed a tax officer under subsection (a) or if a tax officer ceases to hold office and a successor has not been appointed within 30 days of the vacancy, the tax collection committee shall immediately notify the department and shall submit the names of at least two nominees for the position of tax officer to the court of common pleas in the county in which the tax collection district is located. The court shall select a tax officer from among the nominees submitted by the tax collection committee.

(2) If the tax collection committee fails to submit nominees in accordance with this subsection, any political subdivision within the tax collection district may, after notifying the department, petition the court to select a tax officer. The court may provide for other persons to submit nominations for the position of tax officer. The court may select a tax officer from among the nominees.

(3) In the event that a tax officer is to be selected by the court under this subsection, the department shall inform the court of the time frame by which an appointment of a tax officer is needed and of upcoming deadlines which the tax officer must meet in order to timely fulfill the duties of appointment.

(4) Upon the selection of a tax officer by the court, the tax collection committee shall appoint the person selected.

(c) Compensation.—The tax officer shall receive reasonable compensation for services and expenses as determined by the tax collection committee. At the discretion of the tax collection committee, the tax officer may be permitted to withhold the amount of the tax officer's compensation from income taxes collected, if the monthly reports required by section 509(b)submitted by the tax officer include an accounting for all compensation withheld.

(d) Written agreement.—Except when a tax collection committee establishes a tax bureau under section 505(a.2)(2), all appointments of a tax officer shall be made pursuant to a written agreement between the tax officer and the tax collection committee. The agreement shall be approved by the committee by resolution.

(e) Eligibility of existing tax collection entities.—Notwithstanding any provision of law to the contrary, it shall not be regarded as a conflict of interest for a delegate or alternate to participate in discussions and voting of the tax collection committee relating to the appointment of a tax officer, solely on the basis that the delegate or alternate also is an employee or member of the governing body of an existing tax bureau or other public tax collection entity which is under consideration for appointment as the tax officer or which has submitted a proposal for appointment as tax officer, or is an employee or member of the governing body of a political subdivision participating in such an existing tax bureau or other public tax collection entity.

§ 6924.508. Powers and duties of the department.

(a) Additional powers.—In addition to the powers and duties provided for in this act, the department, in consultation with the Department of Revenue, shall prescribe standardized forms, reports, notices, returns and schedules and shall promulgate regulations as necessary to carry out the provisions of this act.

(b) Temporary regulations.—The department may promulgate temporary regulations, for a period of two years, as necessary, which shall be published in the Pennsylvania Bulletin. The temporary regulations promulgated by the department shall expire no later than three years following the effective date of this part or upon promulgation of regulations as generally provided by law. The temporary regulations shall not be subject to any of the following;

(1) Sections 201, 202, 203 and 204 of the act of July 31, 1968 (P.L.769, No.240), referred to as the CommonwealthDocuments Law.

(2) The act of June 25, 1982 (P.L.633, No.181), known as the Regulatory Review Act.

(c) Interim regulations.—Until promulgation of the temporary or permanent regulations under this section, rules and regulations in use by tax officers under the former Division V(c) of section 13 shall remain valid.

(d) Departmental study.—

(1) Immediately upon the earliest effective date of this section, the department shall commence a study of existing local earned income tax collection methods and practices within this Commonwealth, with particular attention to the practices and methods of previously existing cooperative collection bureaus established by one or more political subdivisions, for the purpose of identifying, collecting and comparing those practices, methods, structures, procedures, regulations, software, information systems, governance alternatives, risk management strategies and other characteristics that appear to promote the greatest likelihood of effectiveness, cost efficiency, loss prevention and willing intergovernmental cooperation.

(2) No later than December 31, 2009, the department shall furnish each tax collection committee a report of the findings and recommendations result-

ing from the study, including sample bylaws, procedures, regulations, forms, agreements, requests for proposals for the selection of tax officers, requests for proposals for the procurement of software systems and other critical systems and other appropriate samples.

(3) As a part of the study, the department shall also investigate and report upon the feasibility of contracting on a Statewide basis for the development and/or procurement of appropriate software systems that may be adopted and purchased by county tax collection districts or their appointed tax officers through the Commonwealth's cooperative purchasing programs.

(4) Nothing in this subsection shall be construed to authorize the department to compel the disclosure of information that is confidential, proprietary or a trade secret.

(e) Mandatory education for tax officers.—Persons and entities seeking or maintaining appointment as tax officers shall complete mandatory education as a prerequisite for their appointment and, for continuing appointment, not less than annually. The department shall provide the mandatory education and shall adopt regulations, guidelines and procedures for the mandatory education sufficient to meet the requirements of this act.

(f) Establishment of qualifications and requirements.—

(1) The department shall, by regulation, establish the qualifications and requirements a tax officer must meet prior to being appointed and must meet for continuing appointment.

(2) A tax collection committee may establish additional qualifications and requirements a tax officer must meet prior to being appointed and must meet for continuing appointment.

(g) Oversight.—The department shall oversee all tax collection committees, tax collectors and tax collection offices. In exercising this duty, the department shall:

(1) Provide the public with a method to report tax collection issues.

(2) Ensure that all ordinances, rules, regulations and forms adopted in the collection of the earned income and net profits taxes are those promulgated by the department.

§ 6924.509. Powers and duties of tax officer.

(a) Tax collection.—In addition to any other power and duty conferred upon a tax officer in this act, it shall be the duty of the tax officer:

(1) To collect, reconcile, administer and enforce income taxes imposed on residents and nonresidents of each political subdivision included in the tax collection district.

(2) To receive and distribute income taxes and to enforce withholding by employers located in the tax collection district.

(3) To receive income taxes distributed by tax officers for other tax collection districts.

(4) To distribute income taxes to political subdivisions as required by section 513.

(5) To comply with all regulations adopted by the department under this act and all resolutions, policies and procedures adopted by the tax collection committee.

(6) To invest all income taxes in the custody of the tax officer in authorized investments, subject to the approval of the tax collection committee. The tax officer shall observe the standard of care that would be observed by a prudent person dealing with property of another. For the purposes of this paragraph, the term "authorized investment" shall include all of the following:

(i) Short-term obligations of the United States Government or its agencies or instrumentalities which are backed by the full faith and credit of the United States or are rated in the highest category by a nationally recognized statistical rating organization.

(ii) Deposits in savings accounts, time deposits, share accounts or certificates of deposit of institutions, insured by the Federal Deposit Insurance Corporation or the National Credit Union Share Insurance Fund, or their successor agencies, to the extent that the accounts are insured and, for the amount above the insured maximum, that collateral, free from other liens, for the amount is pledged by the depository institution.

(iii) Deposits in investment pools established by the State Treasurer or established by local governments pursuant to 53 Pa.C.S. Ch. 23 Subch. A (relating to intergovernmental cooperation) and related statutes, provided that the investment pools are rated in the highest category by a nationally recognized statistical rating organization.

(iv) Repurchase agreements which are fully collateralized by obligations of the United States Government or its agencies or instrumentalities, which are free from other liens and backed by the full faith and credit of the United States or are rated in the highest category by a nationally recognized statistical rating organization.

(7) To distribute income generated from investments authorized under paragraph (6) as determined by the tax collection committee.

(b) Monthly reports.—

(1) The tax officer shall, within 20 days after the end of each month, provide a written report, on forms prescribed by the department, to the secretary of the tax collection committee and to the secretary of each political subdivision in the tax collection district for which taxes were collected during the previous month.

(2) The report shall include a breakdown of all income taxes, income generated from investments under subsection (a)(6), penalties, costs and other money received, collected, expended and distributed for each political subdivision served by the tax officer and of all money distributed to tax officers for other tax collection districts.

(3) The report shall also include a calendar year-to-date total column of all the items enumerated in paragraph (2).

(4) In addition to the duty imposed under paragraph (1), a copy of the December monthly report shall be filed with the department.

(c) Overpayments.—A tax officer shall refund, under 53Pa.C.S. §§ 8425 (relating to refunds of overpayments) and 8426(relating to interest on overpayment), on petition of and proof by the taxpayer, income taxes paid in excess of income taxes rightfully due.

(d) Bonds.—Prior to initiating any official duties, each tax officer shall give and acknowledge a bond to the appointing tax collection committee as follows:

(1) The tax collection committee shall fix the amount of the bond in an amount equal to the maximum amount of taxes that may be in the possession of the tax officer at any given time or an amount sufficient, in combination with fiscal controls, insurance and other risk management and loss prevention measures used by the tax collection district, to secure the financial responsibility of the tax officer in accordance with guidelines adopted by the department. The amount of the bond shall be revised annually by the tax collection committee based upon the annual examination required under section 505(h).

(2) Each bond shall be joint and several, with one or more corporate sureties, which shall be surety companies authorized to do business in this Commonwealth and licensed by the Insurance Department.

(3) Each bond shall be conditioned upon the completion of all of the following by the tax officer's employees and appointees:

(i) The faithful execution of all duties required of the tax officer.

(ii) The just and faithful accounting or payment over of all moneys and balances paid to, received or held by the tax officer by virtue of the office in accordance with law.

(iii) The delivery of all tax records or other official items held in right as the tax officer to the tax officer's successor in office.

(4) Each bond shall be taken in the name of the tax collection district and shall be for the use of the tax collection district appointing the tax officer, and for the use of any other political subdivision or tax collection district for which income taxes shall be collected or distributed in case of a breach of any conditions of the bond by the acts or neglect of the principal on the bond.

(5) A tax collection committee or any political subdivision may sue upon the bond for the payment or distribution of income taxes.

(6) Each bond shall contain the name of the surety company bound on the bond.

(7) The tax collection committee may, upon cause shown and due notice to the tax officer and the tax officer's sureties, require or allow the substitution or the addition of a surety company acceptable to the tax collection committee for the purpose of making the bond sufficient in amount, without releasing the sureties first approved from any accrued liability or previous action on the bond.

(8) The tax collection committee shall designate the custodian of the bond.

(9) The tax officer shall file copies of all bonds in effect with each political subdivision in the tax collection district.

(10) A copy of all bonds in effect shall be made available upon request and at no cost to the department or to a tax collection district or political subdivision seeking payment or distribution of income taxes authorized by this act.

(e) **Records.**—It shall be the duty of the tax officer to keep a record showing the amount of income taxes received from each taxpayer or other tax officer, the date of receipt, the amount and date of all other moneys received or distributed and any other information required by the department. All tax records shall be the property of the political subdivision and the tax collection district in which the taxes were collected. The tax collection district and tax officer shall retain all tax records as directed by the tax collection committee and, when applicable, in accordance with retention and disposition schedules established by the Local Government Records Committee of the Pennsylvania Historical and Museum Commission under 53 Pa.C.S. Ch. 13 Subch. F (relating to records). Tax records under this subsection may be retained electronically as permitted bylaw.

(f) **Employer and taxpayer audits.**—

(1) In order to verify the accuracy of any income tax declaration or return or, if no declaration or return was filed, to ascertain the income tax due, the tax officer and the tax officer's designated employees may examine or audit the records pertaining to income taxes due of any of the following:

(i) An employer.

(ii) A taxpayer.

(iii) A person whom the tax officer reasonably believes to be an employer or taxpayer.

(2) The examination or audit conducted by the tax officer and the tax officer's designated employees shall conform to the requirements set forth in 53 Pa.C.S. Ch. 84,Subch. C (relating to local taxpayers bill of rights).

(3) Every employer and taxpayer or other person whom the tax officer reasonably believes to be an employer or taxpayer shall provide to the tax officer and the tax officer's designated employees the means, facilities and opportunity for the examination and investigation authorized under paragraph (1).

(4) For purposes of this subsection, the term "records" shall include any books, papers, and relevant Federal or State tax returns and accompanying schedules, or supporting documentation for any income taxable under this act.

(g) Exchange of information.—

(1) The tax officer of each tax collection district shall ensure that the tax collection district enters into an agreement with the Department of Revenue for the exchange of information as necessary for the collection of income taxes.

(2) The Department of Revenue may enter into agreements with each tax collection district and shall establish procedures under which tax collection, filing and other taxpayer and locality information in its custody will be made available to tax officers for purposes of collection, reconciliation and enforcement no later than one year after the deadline for filing returns for the tax year in question.

(h) Actions for collection of income taxes.—The tax officer may file an action in the name of a political subdivision within the tax collection district for the recovery of income taxes due to the political subdivision and unpaid. Nothing in this subsection shall affect the authority of a political subdivision to file an action in its own name for collection of income taxes under this chapter. This subsection shall not be construed to limit a tax officer, a tax collection district or political subdivision from recovering delinquent income taxes by any other means provided by this act. Actions for collection of income taxes shall be subject to the following:

(1) Except as set forth in paragraph (2) or (4), an action brought to recover income taxes must be commenced within three years of the later of the date:

(i) the income taxes are due;

(ii) the declaration or return has been filed; or

(iii) of a redetermination of compensation or net profits by the Department of Revenue.

(2) If there is substantial understatement of income tax liability of 25% or more and there is no fraud, an action must be commenced within six years.

(3) Except as set forth in paragraph (4)(ii), (iii) or (iv), an action by a tax officer for recovery of an erroneous refund must be commenced as follows:

(i) Except as set forth in subparagraph (ii), within two years after making the refund.

(ii) If it appears that any part of the refund was induced by fraud or misrepresentation of material fact, within five years after making the refund.

(4) There is no limitation of action if any of the following apply:

(i) A taxpayer fails to file a declaration or return required under this act.

(ii) An examination of a declaration or return or of other evidence in the possession of the tax officer relating to the declaration or return reveals a fraudulent evasion of income taxes.

(iii) An employer has deducted income taxes under section 512 and has failed to pay the amount deducted to the tax officer.

(iv) An employer has intentionally failed to make deductions required by this act.

(i) Interest and penalties.—

(1) Except as provided in paragraph (2), if the income tax is not paid when due, interest at the rate the taxpayer is required to pay to the Commonwealth under section 806 of the act of April 9, 1929 (P.L.343, No.176), known as The

Fiscal Code, on the amount of the income tax, and an additional penalty of 1% of the amount of the unpaid income tax for each month or fraction of a month during which the income tax remains unpaid shall be added and collected but the amount shall not exceed 15% in the aggregate. Where an action is brought for the recovery of the income tax, the taxpayer liable for the income tax shall, in addition, be liable for the costs of collection, interest and penalties.

(2) The department may establish conditions under which a tax officer, with the concurrence of the tax collection committee, may abate interest or penalties that would otherwise be imposed for the nonreporting or underreporting of income tax liabilities or for the nonpayment of income taxes previously imposed and due if the taxpayer voluntarily files delinquent returns and pays the income taxes in full.

(3) The provisions of paragraph (2) shall not affect or terminate any petitions, investigations, prosecutions or other proceedings pending under of this chapter, or prevent the commencement or further prosecution of any proceedings by the proper authorities for violations of this act. No proceedings shall, however, be commenced on the basis of delinquent returns filed pursuant to subsection (h) if the returns are determined to be substantially true and correct and the income taxes are paid in full within the prescribed time.

(j) Fines and penalties for violations.—

(1) Any taxpayer who fails, neglects or refuses to make any declaration or return required by this chapter, any employer who fails, neglects or refuses to register, keep or supply records or returns required by section 512 or to pay the income tax deducted from employees, or fails, neglects or refuses to deduct or withhold the income tax from employees, any taxpayer or employer who refuses to permit the tax officer appointed by a tax collection committee or an employee or agent of the tax officer to examine books, records and papers, and any taxpayer or employer who knowingly makes any incomplete, false or fraudulent return, or attempts to do anything whatsoever to avoid the full disclosure of the amount of income in order to avoid the payment of income taxes shall, upon conviction thereof, be sentenced to pay a fine of not more than $2,500 for each offense and reasonable costs, and in default of payment of said fine and costs, to imprisonment for not more than six months.

(2) Any employer required under this chapter to collect, account for and distribute income taxes who willfully fails to collect or truthfully account for and distribute income taxes, commits a misdemeanor and shall, upon conviction, be sentenced to pay a fine not exceeding $25,000 or to imprisonment not exceeding two years, or both.

(3) The penalties imposed under this subsection shall be in addition to any other costs and penalties imposed by this act.

(4) The failure of any person to obtain forms required for making the declaration or returns required by this act shall not excuse the person from making the declaration or return.

(k) Collection.—In addition to the powers and duties enumerated in this section, when designated by the tax collection committee a tax officer may collect other taxes levied pursuant to this act, the act of June 27, 2006 (1st Sp.Sess., P.L.1873, No.1), known as the Taxpayer Relief Act, or other statutory law.

§ 6924.510. Fines and penalties against tax officers.

(a) Distribution of nonresident taxes.—A tax collection district or a political subdivision that brings an action under subsection (e) with respect to distribution of income taxes under section 513 may seek equitable relief from a tax officer, including an accounting of all undistributed income taxes and monetary damages, in the form of recovery of the income taxes not previously distributed plus interest calculated from the date that the income taxes should have been distributed. In addition, the court may impose a civil penalty not to exceed $2,500 for each quarter for which income taxes were not distributed in accordance with section 513, plus reasonable costs and attorney fees. If a tax officer fails to distribute income taxes to the appropriate political subdivision as required under section 513 for four consecutive tax quarters, the court may impose a civil penalty not to exceed $5,000. In addition, the court may impose a fine not to exceed $100 per day for every day past the deadline that a tax officer does not respond to a claim under section 513(b).

(b) Monthly reports and audits of income taxes.—If a tax officer fails to submit the report required under section 509(b), a tax collection district or a political subdivision entitled to receive the report may bring an action in the court of common pleas of the county in which the tax collection district is primarily located. The court may impose a civil penalty of $20 a day for each day that the report is overdue, not to exceed $500. If an examination submitted under section 505(h) includes any findings of noncompliance, the court may impose an additional civil penalty of not less than $500 but not more than $2,500.

(c) Failure of duty.—An action may be brought against the tax officer to compel the performance of duties required by this chapter or imposed by regulations adopted pursuant to this chapter, including the duty to deliver all tax records and other official items held in right as tax officer to the tax officer's successor. Upon a finding of failure to perform a duty, the court may impose a penalty not to exceed $5,000; and the tax officer may be held liable for the cost of reproducing tax records if they are lost or cannot be delivered.

(d) Other violations.—A tax officer who violates any other provision of this act shall be subject to a civil penalty of up to $2,500 for each violation.

(e) Actions against a tax officer.—An action against a tax officer for a violation of this chapter may be brought by a tax collection district or a political subdivision for which the tax officer collects income taxes, a political subdivision or tax collection committee owed income taxes by the tax officer or by a surety.

(f) Rescinded appointment.—

(1) A tax collection committee shall temporarily remove a tax officer if a criminal action is commenced against the tax officer for an offense which would constitute a violation of the standards of office under section 506(b). If the tax officer is convicted or pleads guilty or nolo contendere in the action, the tax collection committee shall rescind the appointment and remove the tax officer permanently.

(2) A tax collection committee may remove or rescind the appointment of a tax officer where the tax officer or an employee or agent of the tax officer violates the provisions under section 514(b).

(3) A tax collection committee may remove or rescind the appointment of a tax officer for cause.

(4) A tax collection committee may not retain a tax officer who has been penalized under subsection (a), (b), (c)or (d) more than three times or who fails to satisfy the requirements under section 506.

(g) Interpretation.—A tax officer shall not be considered a debt collector for purposes of the act of March 28, 2000(P.L.23, No.7), known as the Fair Credit Extension Uniformity Act. Except as otherwise authorized in this act, a tax officer shall be subject to the restrictions and prohibitions imposed on creditors. Notwithstanding the provisions of the Fair Credit Extension Uniformity Act, this act shall supersede any restrictions and prohibitions on creditors otherwise applicable under the Fair Credit Extension Uniformity Act.

(h) Withdrawal from tax collection district.—

(1) In an action brought by a political subdivision under this section after January 1, 2014, the court may, in addition to other available remedies, grant

a request by the political subdivision to withdraw from the tax collection district for good cause, provided the court determines, after hearing, that all of the following conditions exist:

(i) The political subdivision has suffered loss in income tax revenues that is directly and primarily attributable to the willful and continued failure of the tax officer or tax collection committee to comply with the provisions of this act.

(ii) The tax collection committee has failed to take reasonable measures to correct the deficiencies in the performance of the tax officer and otherwise assure compliance with the requirements of this act.

(iii) The political subdivision and the tax collection committee have engaged in good faith mediation before a special master appointed by the court, but nonetheless have failed to reach agreement about alternative corrective measures in lieu of withdrawal of the political subdivision from the tax collection district.

(iv) Other relief available that could be ordered by the court would not be adequate to provide a reasonable prospect of compliance by the tax officer and tax collection committee with the requirements of this act and that withdrawal of the political subdivision from the tax collection district is otherwise in the best interests of the political subdivision, taxpayers and employers.

(2) (i) In the event the court grants a request by apolitical subdivision under this section to withdraw from the tax collection district in which it is located, the governing body of the political subdivision may withdraw by adopting a resolution to that effect and appointing a tax officer to collect the income tax levied by that political subdivision, effective for the next calendar year beginning at least six months after the adoption of such resolution.

(ii) With respect to the income tax levied by that political subdivision, a tax officer appointed pursuant to this paragraph shall have the same powers and duties as a tax officer appointed by a tax collection district and all other requirements of this act pertaining to the functions and qualifications of tax collection districts and tax officers, and the related obligations of employers and taxpayers shall apply equally to the political subdivision, its governing body and a tax officer appointed by that political subdivision.

§ 6924.511. Tax registers.

(a) Requirement.—The department shall maintain a tax register and an official register. All of the following shall apply:

(1) The department shall maintain a tax register on the department's Internet website. Information for the tax register shall be furnished by each county and each political subdivision to the department as prescribed by the department. The department shall continuously update the tax register.

(2) As part of the tax register under paragraph (1), the department shall maintain an official register. The requirement to maintain an official register in accordance with this section shall supersede the requirements for an official register in any act.

(3) The official register shall be organized by municipality and shall list:

(i) Each municipality and coterminous school district.

(ii) The effective income tax rate on taxpayers who reside in the municipality.

(iii) The effective income tax rate on taxpayers who reside in the school district.

(iv) The combined municipal and school district income tax rate on taxpayers residing in each municipality.

Table of Contents | Part I Ch. 1–3 Ethics, Records, Open Meetings | Part II Ch. 4–10 Taxation | Part III Ch. 11–18 Torts, Contracts & Civil Rules | Part IV Ch. 19–24 Zoning & Planning | Part V Ch. 25–30 Construction and Emergency Codes | Part VI Ch. 31–39 Municipal Codes | Index

(v) The income tax rate on taxpayers working within the municipality.

(vi) Whether an income tax is a personal income tax levied under the act of June 27, 2006 (1st Sp.Sess., P.L.1873, No.1), known as the Taxpayer Relief Act, or any other act.

(vii) The effective emergency and municipal services tax rate on taxpayers working within the municipality.

(viii) The effective emergency and municipal services tax rate on taxpayers working within the school district.

(ix) The combined municipal and school district emergency and municipal services tax rate.

(x) The amount of any other withholding tax.

(xi) The name, telephone number, address, e-mail and Internet address, where available, of the tax officer responsible for administering the collection of the tax.

(xii) Any other information deemed necessary by the department.

(4) Each year the department shall update and officially release withholding tax rates on the official register on June 15 and December 15. Tax rates released on June 15 shall become effective July 1. Tax rates released on December 15 shall become effective January 1 of the following year. The department may revise the notification, official release and effective dates of the register for good cause. Six months prior to the revision, the department shall notify each affected political subdivision of the revision and shall publish notice of the revision in the Pennsylvania Bulletin.

(5) Information for the official register shall be furnished by each political subdivision to the department as prescribed by the department and shall include a copy of the ordinance or resolution enacting, repealing or changing the tax. The department shall be notified of changes to the official register as follows:

(i) New withholding tax enactments, repeals and changes shall be received by the department no later than June 1 to require withholding of a new tax, withholding at a new rate or to suspend withholding of such tax effective July 1 of that year. All new withholding tax enactments, repeals and changes received by the department by June 1 shall be officially released by the department June 15 and become effective July 1. Failure of the department to receive information by June 1 from political subdivisions regarding current withholding tax rates, new withholding tax enactments, repeals and changes shall be construed by the department to mean that the information contained in the previous December 15 release of the official register is still in force. Information received by the department after June 1 but before December 1 shall be officially released on December 15.

(ii) New withholding tax enactments, repeals and changes shall be received by the department no later than December 1 to require withholding of a new tax, withholding at a new rate or to suspend withholding of such tax effective January 1 of the following year. All new withholding tax enactments, repeals and changes-received by the department by December 1 shall be officially released by the department on December 15 and become effective January 1 of the following year. Failure of the department to receive information by December 1 from political subdivisions regarding current withholding tax rates, new withholding tax enactments, repeals and changes shall be construed by the department to mean that the information contained in the previous June 15 release of the official register is still in force. Information received by the department after December 1 but before June 1 shall be officially released on June 15.

(6) (i) Employers shall not be required to deduct from compensation of their employees or make reports of compensation in connection with any withholding tax that is not released on the official register as of June 15 and December 15 of each year as provided in paragraphs (4) and (5), unless the political subdivision imposing the tax has provided written notice to the employer of the tax or tax rate and the withholding requirement.

(ii) Notwithstanding any law to the contrary, no political subdivision or tax officer may require any employer to deduct a withholding tax at a rate or amount that is not released on the official register, unless the political subdivision imposing the tax has provided written notice to the employer of the tax or tax rate and the withholding requirement.

(iii) The provisions of this paragraph shall not affect the liability of any taxpayer for withholding taxes lawfully imposed under this act.

(7) An employer may withhold at the most recently available rate on the tax register even if such rate is different than the tax rate released on the official register as provided in paragraphs (4) and (5), provided that an employer shall not be required to withhold at a tax rate that is not released on the official register, unless the political subdivision imposing the tax has provided written notice to the employer of the current tax rate.

(8) No employer shall be held liable for failure to withhold an income tax from an employee if the failure to withhold the income tax arises from incorrect information submitted by the employee as to the employee's place of residence.

(9) No employer shall be held liable for failure to withhold the emergency and municipal services tax or for the payment of tax money withheld to a tax officer if the failure to withhold the taxes arises from incorrect information submitted by the employee as to the employee's place of employment, the employee's principal office or where the employee is principally employed.

(b) Definition.—As used in this section, notwithstanding section 501, the terms "income tax" and "withholding tax" include a tax assessed on the income of a taxpayer and levied by a municipality under the act of August 5, 1932 (Sp. Sess., P.L.45, No.45), referred to as the Sterling Act.

§ 6924.512. Withholding and remittance.

(a) General rule.—For taxable years commencing on and after January 1, 2012, or earlier taxable years if specified by a tax collection district, income taxes shall be withheld, remitted and reported as follows:

(1) Every employer having an office, factory, workshop, branch, warehouse or other place of business within a tax collection district who employs one or more persons, other than domestic servants, for a salary, wage, commission or other compensation, who has not previously registered, shall, within 15 days after becoming an employer, register with the tax officer the name and address of the employer and such other information as the department may require.

(2) An employer shall require each new employee to complete a certificate of residency form, which shall be an addendum to the Federal Employee's Withholding Allowance Certificate (Form W-4). An employer shall also require any employee who changes their address or domicile to complete a certificate of residency form. Upon request, certificate of residency forms shall be provided by the department. The certificate of residency form shall provide information to help identify the political subdivisions where an employee lives and works.

(3) Every employer having an office, factory, workshop, branch, warehouse or other place of business within a tax collection district that employs one or more persons, other than domestic servants, for a salary, wage, commission or

Table of Contents
Part I Ch. 1–3 Ethics, Records, Open Meetings
Part II Ch. 4–10 Taxation
Part III Ch. 11–18 Torts, Contracts & Civil Rules
Part IV Ch. 19–24 Zoning & Planning
Part V Ch. 25–30 Construction and Emergency Codes
Part VI Ch. 31–39 Municipal Codes
Index

Chapter 10 Residential Design Tax Credit
Chapter 9 Neighborhood Improvement
Chapter 8 Local Taxpayers Bill of Rights
Chapter 7 Occupation Tax Elimination Act
Chapter 6 Local Government Unit Debt Act
Chapter 5 Local Tax Collection Law
Chapter 4 Local Tax Enabling Act

other compensation, shall, at the time of payment, deduct from the compensation due each employee employed at such place of business the greater of the employee's resident tax or the employee's nonresident tax as released in the official register under section 511. In the case of employees with temporary job assignments, the employer shall withhold and remit the following taxes:

(i) Employees working for less than 90 consecutive days at a job location, the greater of the employee's resident tax or the employee's nonresident tax based on the location of the permanent home office of the employer.

(ii) Employees working for 90 or more consecutive days at a job location, the greater of the employee's resident tax or the employee's nonresident tax based on the job location.

(iii) Employees working in the City of Philadelphia shall be exempt from the provisions of this section to the extent they are subject to the act of August 5, 1932 (Sp.Sess., P.L.45, No.45), referred to as the Sterling Act.

(4) Except as set forth in paragraph (5), by the last day of the month following the end of each calendar quarter, every employer shall file a quarterly return and pay the amount of income taxes deducted during the preceding calendar quarter to the tax officer for the place of employment of each employee. The form shall show the name, address and Social Security number of each employee, the compensation of the employee during the preceding three-month period, the income tax deducted from the employee, the political subdivisions imposing the income tax upon the employee, the total compensation of all employees during the preceding calendar quarter, the total income tax deducted from the employees and paid with the return and any other information prescribed by the department.

(5) Notwithstanding paragraph (4), the provisions of this paragraph shall apply if an employer has more than one place of employment in more than one tax collection district. On or before the last day of the month succeeding the month for which the return required by paragraph (4) is due, the employer may file the return and pay the total amount of income taxes deducted from employees in all work locations during the preceding month to the tax officer for either the tax collection district in which the employer's payroll operations are located or as determined by the department. The return and income taxes deducted shall be filed and paid electronically. The employer must file a notice of intention to file combined returns and make combined payments with the tax officer for each place of employment at least one month before filing its first combined return or making its first combined payment. This paragraph shall not be construed to change the location of an employee's place of employment for purposes of nonresident tax liability.

(6) Any employer who for two of the preceding four quarterly periods has failed to deduct the proper income tax, or any part of the income tax, or has failed to pay over the proper amount of income tax as required by paragraph (3) to the tax collection district, may be required by the tax officer to file returns and pay the income tax monthly. In such cases, payments of income tax shall be made to the tax officer on or before the last day of the month succeeding the month for which the income tax was withheld.

(7) On or before February 28 of the succeeding year, every employer shall file with the tax officer where income taxes have been deducted and remitted pursuant to paragraph (3):

(i) An annual return showing, for the period beginning January 1 of the current year and ending December 31 of the current year, the total amount of compensation paid, the total amount of income tax deducted, the total amount of income tax paid to the tax officer and any other information prescribed by the department.

(ii) An individual withholding statement, which may be integrated with the Federal Wage and Tax Statement (Form W-2), for each employee employed during all or any part of the period beginning January 1 of the current year and ending December 31 of the current year, setting forth the address and Social Security number, the amount of compensation paid to the employee during the period, the amount of income tax deducted, the numerical code prescribed by the department representing the political subdivision of the employee's work location and, in the case where an employer has made an election under paragraph (5) to file with a single tax officer, the two-digit code representing the tax collection district to whose tax officer the withheld taxes were remitted in the format of xxxxxx-xx and any other information required by the department. Every employer shall furnish one copy of the individual withholding statement to the employee for whom it is filed.

(8) Any employer who discontinues business prior to December 31 of the current year shall, within 30 days after the discontinuance of business, file returns and withholding statements required under this section and pay the income tax due.

(9) Except as otherwise provided in section 511, an employer who willfully or negligently fails or omits to make the deductions required by this subsection shall be liable for payment of income taxes which the employer was required to withhold to the extent that the income taxes have not been recovered from the employee. The failure or omission of any employer to make the deductions required by this section shall not relieve any employee from the payment of the income tax or from complying with the requirements for filing of declarations and returns.

(b) Date of filing.—If any date prescribed in this section for filing or payment of tax should fall on a Saturday, Sunday or legal holiday, the filing or payment may be performed on the next business day.

§ 6924.513. Distribution of income taxes.

(a) General rule.—Subject to subsection (b), all of the following apply:

(1) Unless otherwise agreed to or required by the tax collection committee, distribution of income taxes from a tax officer to political subdivisions within the tax collection district or to other tax collection districts shall be as follows:

(i) Income taxes received from employers prior to April 1, 2013, under section 512(4) shall be distributed within 60 days of the later of:

(A) receipt; or

(B) the deadline for payment under section 512(4).

(ii) Income taxes received from employers on or after April 1, 2013, under section 512(4) shall be distributed within 30 days of the later of:

(A) receipt; or

(B) the deadline for payment under section 512(4).

(iii) Income taxes received from employers under section 512(5) shall be distributed within 30 days of the last day of the month following receipt.

(iv) Income taxes received from taxpayers and other tax collection districts prior to April 1, 2013, shall be distributed within 60 days of receipt.

(v) Income taxes received from taxpayers and other tax collection districts on or after April 1, 2013, shall be distributed within 30 days of receipt.

(2) Income taxes received from employers, taxpayers or other tax collection districts shall be distributed based on the information submitted by the employers, taxpayers or tax collection districts. It shall not be permissible to base the distribution of income taxes on any method not expressly authorized by act of the General Assembly.

(3) A tax officer shall maintain a record of all income taxes distributed under this section, which shall include all of the information required in the reports under section 512(4) and (5), the date of distribution, the political subdivision or tax officer to which the income taxes are distributed and any other information required by the department. The record shall be provided to another tax collection district at the time of distribution.

(4) A tax officer who, within two years after receiving an income tax payment after reasonable efforts meeting conditions established by the tax collection committee, cannot identify the political subdivision entitled to the income tax payment shall make payment to the municipality in which the income tax was collected.

(b) Other tax collection districts.—In addition to subsection (a), for distribution of income taxes to other tax collection districts, the following shall apply:

(1) If nonresident taxes are not distributed to the appropriate tax officer as required under subsection (a)(1),a tax officer may make a claim for income taxes attributable to residents of the tax collection district served by that tax officer. The tax officer for the tax collection district against which a claim is made shall, within 30 days:

(i) pay the claim if it is undisputed; or

(ii) respond in writing stating the reasons why the claim cannot be paid.

(2) If the tax officer for the tax collection district against which the claim is made does not act under paragraph (1)(i) or (ii), the tax officer making the claim may bring an action in the court of common pleas in the county in which the tax collection district with the claim is primarily located for both the amount of the claim and interest at the rate provided for in 53 Pa.C.S. § 8426 (relating to interest on overpayment) from the date which the income taxes were received from the taxpayer, employer or other tax officer. Notwithstanding any other law to the contrary, an action under this paragraph must be brought within seven years after the claim is made.

(c) Codes.—Employers and tax officers shall use political subdivision and tax collection district codes prescribed by the department.

(d) Fee prohibition.—No tax officer, political subdivision or tax collection district shall be required to pay a fee or commission to another tax collection district on account of income taxes distributed under this section.

§ 6924.514. Confidentiality.

(a) General rule.—Any information gained by a tax officer or any employee or agent of a tax officer or of the tax collection committee as a result of any declarations, returns, investigations, hearings or verifications shall be confidential tax information.

(b) Prohibited conduct.—It shall be unlawful, except for official purposes or as provided by law, for the Commonwealth, any political subdivision, tax collection committee member, tax officer, or employee or agent of a tax officer or tax collection committee to do any of the following:

(1) Divulge or make known confidential tax information.

(2) Permit confidential tax information or a book containing an abstract or particulars of the abstract to be seen or examined by any person.

(3) Print, publish or otherwise make known any confidential tax information.

(c) Penalties.—A person that violates subsection (b) commits a misdemeanor of the third degree and shall, upon conviction, be sentenced to pay a fine of not more than $2,500 or to imprisonment for not more than one year, or both. If the offender is a member of the tax collection committee, the member shall be removed from the tax collection committee. If the offender is an employee of a tax collection committee or apolitical subdivision, the employee shall be discharged from employment. The offender shall pay the costs of prosecution.

§ 6924.515. Transition.

(a) Fines and penalties against tax officers.—

(1) A political subdivision which brings an action under former Division V(h) of section 13 may seek equitable relief from a tax officer, including an accounting of all undistributed income taxes and monetary damages, in the form of recovery of the income taxes not previously distributed. In addition, the court may impose a civil penalty not to exceed $2,500 for each quarter for which income taxes were not distributed in accordance with former Division V(h) of section 13, plus reasonable costs and attorney fees.

(2) If a tax officer fails to distribute income taxes to the appropriate political subdivision as required under former Division V(h) of section 13 for four consecutive quarters, the court may impose a civil penalty not to exceed $5,000.

(3) An action may be brought against the tax officer to compel the performance of duties required by Chapter 3 or former section 13 or imposed by regulations adopted pursuant to Chapter 5, including the duty to deliver all tax records and other official items held in right as tax officer to the tax officer's successor. Upon a finding of failure to perform a duty, the court may impose a penalty not to exceed $5,000; and the tax officer may be held liable for the cost or reproducing tax records if they are lost or cannot be delivered.

(4) An Article XIII tax officer who violates any other provision of this section or former section 13 shall be subject to a civil penalty of up to $2,500 for each violation.

(5) An action against an Article XIII tax officer for a violation of this act may be brought by a political subdivision for which the Article XIII tax officer collects income taxes, a political subdivision owed income taxes by the Article XIII tax officer or by a surety that is liable because of the violation.

(6) A political subdivision shall remove or rescind the appointment of an Article XIII tax officer who has been penalized more than three times under paragraph (1), (2), (3)or (4).

(b) Transition.—

(1) (i) The governing body of each political subdivision which imposed an income tax prior to January 1, 2011, shall do all of the following:

(A) Determine by November 1, 2010, whether the Article XIII tax officer or the newly appointed tax officer shall collect 2011 income taxes.

(B) Notify the department by December 1, 2010, of the determination under clause (A) in accordance with section 511(a)(5).

(ii) Every employer shall remit 2011 income taxes and file the quarterly and annual reports required by former Division IV(b) and (c) of section 13 to either the Article XIII tax officer or the newly appointed tax officer, as determined by the appropriate political subdivision and released on the official register in accordance with section 511.

(2) By July 1, 2011, each tax collection committee shall develop a plan to transition from the provisions of former section 13 to the provisions of sections 512 and 513, and from the Article XIII tax officer to the newly appointed tax officer for 2012 income taxes.

(3) The Article XIII tax officer shall deliver all tax records to the political subdivision and the newly appointed tax officer by June 30, 2012, unless otherwise agreed to by the political subdivision and the newly appointed tax officer.

(4) Any delinquent income taxes or reports from 2011, or previous years which have not been remitted or provided to the Article XIII tax officer by June 30, 2012, shall become the responsibility of the newly appointed tax officer. Apolitical subdivision which has made other provisions for the collection of delinquent income taxes or reports for 2011 or previous years shall notify the newly appointed tax officer.

(5) Beginning with the first quarter of 2012, employers shall remit income taxes withheld and make reports as required by section 512 to the newly appointed tax officer.

(c) Definitions.—The following words and phrases when used in this section shall have the meanings given to them in this subsection unless the context clearly indicates otherwise:

"Newly appointed tax officer." A tax officer appointed under section 507(a) responsible for the collection of 2012 income taxes.

§ 6924.516. Regulatory conflict.

In the event of a conflict between a regulation under this chapter and a regulation under the act of June 27, 2006 (1st Sp.Sess., P.L.1873, No.1), known as the Taxpayer Relief Act, in the area of tax collection, the regulation under this chapter shall prevail.

§ 6924.517. Audit and evaluation.

(a) General rule.—Before 2017, the Legislative Budget and Finance Committee shall conduct an audit and evaluation of the impact of this chapter and consolidated collection of local income taxes. The committee shall consult with the Auditor General in the course of its audit and evaluation. The audit and evaluation shall:

(1) Determine the extent to which income tax revenue losses have been minimized or eliminated by the implementation of uniform collection standards and a countywide income tax collection system.

(2) Determine whether consolidated collection and standardized withholding and remittance of local income taxes as required in section 512 has simplified the system, reduced fragmentation and reduced the burden of withholding, remitting and distributing the local income tax for employers.

(3) Determine if tax compliance is simpler, easier, fairer and less time-consuming for taxpayers.

(4) Determine whether the tax collection system under this chapter is more efficient than the prior system.

(5) Determine if tax collection committees are exercising their powers and duties under section 505

effectively.

(6) Determine the extent to which cooperation and coordination exists among tax officers and tax collection districts.

(7) Determine whether authorized investments under 509(a)(6) and the bonding requirements under section 509(d) provide sufficient protection to income tax collections.

(8) Determine whether nonresident and resident taxes are being properly distributed among tax collection districts within this Commonwealth and to political subdivisions within each tax collection district.

(9) Determine whether the reporting, audit, accountability, transparency and oversight requirements for taxes collected, distributed and administered in this chapter are adequate and being met within and among tax collection districts.

(10) Determine if the appeals boards created under section 505(j) are impartial, fair and effective.

(11) Determine whether the penalties against tax officers under section 510 are effective and the extent to which tax officers are in compliance with the rules and regulations required by this chapter, and identify any tax officers that are in substantial noncompliance with these rules and regulations.

(12) Determine whether the agreements under section 509(g) have been approved by the Department of Revenue and each tax collection district, and that the exchange of information is reciprocal, timely and useful.

(13) Determine whether the interest, penalties and fines under section 509(i) and (j) are appropriate and adequate.

(14) Recommend needed improvements to the system.

(b) Filing requirement.—Copies of the audit findings of the Legislative Budget and Finance Committee under subsection (a) shall be filed with the chair of the Finance Committee of the Senate, the chair of the Finance Committee of the House of Representatives, the department, the Auditor General and with each tax collection committee.

CHAPTER 6
[RESERVED]

CHAPTER 7
COLLECTION OF DELINQUENT TAXES

§ 6924.701. Definitions.—As used in this chapter:

"Business entity" means a sole proprietorship, corporation, joint-stock association or company, partnership, limited partnership, limited liability company, association, business trust, syndicate or other commercial or professional activity organized under the laws of this Commonwealth or any other jurisdiction.

"Employer" means a person, business entity or other entity, including the Commonwealth, its political subdivisions and instrumentalities and public authorities, employing one or more persons for a salary, wage, commission or other compensation.

"Private agency" means a business entity or person appointed as a tax collector by a political subdivision.

§ 6924.701.1. Distress and sale of goods and chattels of taxpayer.

Every tax collector under Chapter 3 and tax officer under Chapter 5 shall have power, in case of the neglect or refusal of any person, or business entity to make payment of the amount of any tax due from the person or business entity, after two months from the date of the tax notice, to levy the amount of such tax, any penalty due thereon and costs, not exceeding costs and charges allowed constables for similar services by distress and sale of the goods and chattels of such delinquent, wherever situate or found, upon giving at least ten days' public notice of such sale, by posting ten written or printed notices, and by one advertisement in a newspaper of general circulation published in the county.

No failure to demand or collect any taxes by distress and sale of goods and chattels shall invalidate any return made, or lien filed for nonpayment of taxes, or any tax sale for the collection of taxes.

§ 702. Collection of delinquent per capita, occupation, occupational privilege, emergency and municipal services, local services and income taxes from employers, etc.

The tax collector under Chapter 3 and the tax officer under Chapter 5 shall demand, receive and collect from all employers, other than the Commonwealth, employing persons owing delinquent per capita, occupation, or occupational privilege taxes under Chapter 3 or emergency and municipal services, local services and income taxes under Chapter 5, or whose spouse owes delinquent per capita, occupation or occupational privilege taxes under Chapter 3 or emergency and municipal services, local services and income taxes under Chapter 5, or having in possession unpaid commissions or earnings belonging to any person or persons owing delinquent per capita, occupation or occupational privilege taxes under Chapter 3 or emergency and municipal services, local services and income taxes under Chapter 5, or whose spouse owes delinquent per capita, occupation or occupational privilege taxes under Chapter 3 or emergency and municipal services, local services and income taxes under Chapter 5, upon the presentation of a written notice and demand certifying that the information contained therein is true and correct and containing the name of the taxable or the spouse thereof and the amount of tax due. Upon the presentation of such written notice and demand, it shall be the duty of any employer to deduct from the wages, commissions or earnings of such individual employes, then owing or that shall within sixty days thereafter become due, or from any unpaid commissions or earnings of any such taxable in the employer's possession, or that shall within sixty days thereafter come into the employer's possession, a sum sufficient to pay the respective amount of the delinquent taxes and costs, shown upon the written notice or demand, and to pay the same to the tax collector of the taxing district or to the tax officer for the tax collection district in which such delinquent tax was levied within sixty days after such notice shall have been given. No more than ten percent of the wages, commissions or earnings of the delinquent taxpayer or spouse thereof may be deducted at any one time for delinquent taxes and costs. The employer shall be entitled to deduct from the moneys collected from each employe the costs incurred from the extra bookkeeping necessary to record such transactions, not exceeding two percent of the amount of money so collected and paid over to the tax collector or tax officer. Upon the failure of any employer to deduct the amount of such taxes or to pay the same over to the tax collector or tax officer, less the cost of bookkeeping involved in such transaction, as herein provided, within the time hereby required, the employer shall forfeit and pay the amount of such tax for each such taxable whose taxes are not withheld and paid over, or that are withheld and not paid over together with a penalty of ten percent added thereto, to be recovered by an action of assumpsit in a suit to be instituted by the tax collector or tax officer, or by the proper authorities of the taxing district or tax collection district, as debts of like amount are now by law recoverable, except that such person shall not have the benefit of any stay of execution or exemption law. The tax collector or tax officer shall not proceed against a spouse or the spouse's employer until the tax collector or tax officer has pursued collection remedies against the delinquent taxpayer and his employer under this section.

§ 6924.703. Collection of delinquent per capita, occupation, occupational privilege, emergency and municipal services, local services and income taxes from the Commonwealth.

Upon presentation of a written notice and demand under oath or affirmation, to the State Treasurer or any other fiscal officer of the State, or its boards, authorities, agencies or commissions, it shall be the duty of the treasurer or officer to deduct from the wages then owing, or that shall within sixty days thereafter become due to any employe, a sum sufficient to pay the respective amount of the delinquent per capita, occupation or occupational privilege, emergency and municipal services, local services under Chapter 3 and income taxes under Chapter 5 and costs shown on the written notice. The same shall be paid to the tax collector or the tax officer of the tax collection district of the taxing district in which said delinquent tax was levied within sixty days after such notice shall have been given.

§ 6924.704. Notice.

The tax collector or tax officer shall, at least fifteen days prior to the presentation of a written notice and demand to the State Treasurer or other fiscal officer of the State, or to any employer, notify the taxpayer owing the delinquent tax by registered or certified mail that a written notice and demand shall be presented to the taxpayer's employer unless such tax is paid. The return receipt card for certified or registered mail shall be marked delivered to addressee only, and the cost of notification by certified or registered mail shall be added to the costs for collecting taxes.

§ 6924.705. Collection of taxes by suit.

(a) Each taxing district or person, public employe or private agency designated by the taxing district under Chapter 3 and each tax officer under Chapter 5 shall have power to collect unpaid taxes from the persons owing such taxes by suit in assumpsit or other appropriate remedy. Upon each such judgment, execution may be issued without any stay or benefit of any exemption law. The right to collect unpaid taxes under the provisions of this section shall not be affected by the fact that such taxes have been entered as liens in the office of the prothonotary, or the fact that the property against which they were levied has been returned to the county commissioners for taxes for prior years.

(b) (1) All taxes deducted and withheld from employes pursuant to this chapter or under cover of this chapter, plus any penalties and interest with respect thereto, shall constitute a trust fund for the political subdivision and shall be enforceable against such employer, his representative or any other person receiving any such fund.

(2) When suit is brought for the recovery of any such tax, the person liable therefore shall, in addition, be liable for the costs of collection and the interest and penalties herein imposed.

§ 6924.706. Penalties.

(a) Except as otherwise provided in the case of any tax levied and assessed upon income, any such political subdivision shall have power to prescribe and enforce reasonable penalties for the nonpayment, within the time fixed for their payment, of taxes imposed under authority of this act.

(b) If for any reason any tax levied and assessed upon income by any such political subdivision is not paid when due, interest and penalties as provided in section 509(i) shall be added and collected. When suit is brought for the recovery of any such tax, the person liable therefor shall, in addition, be liable for the costs of collection and the interest and penalties herein imposed.

(c) In addition to any other power provided by this act, a tax collector or officer may abate any penalty imposed under any provision of this act.

§ 6924.707. Costs of collection of delinquent per capita, occupation, occupational privilege and earned income taxes.

(a) A bureau, political subdivision or private agency designated by a governing body of a political subdivision or a tax collection district to collect and administer per capita, occupation or occupational privilege, emergency and municipal services, local services taxes under Chapter 3 or income taxes under Chapter 5 may impose and collect the reasonable costs incurred to provide notices of delinquency or to implement similar procedures utilized to collect delinquent taxes from a taxpayer as approved by the governing body of the political subdivision or the tax collection committee. Reasonable costs collected may be retained by the tax collector under Chapter 3 or the tax officer under Chapter 5. An itemized accounting of all costs collected shall be remitted to the political subdivision or the tax collection committee on an annual basis.

(b) Costs related to the collection of unpaid per capita, occupation, occupational privilege, emergency and municipal services or local services taxes may only be assessed, levied and collected for five years from the last day of the calendar year in which the tax was due.

(c) A delinquent taxpayer may not bring an action for reimbursement, refund or elimination of reasonable costs of collection assessed or imposed prior to the effective date of this section. Additional costs may not be assessed on delinquent taxes collected prior to the effective date of this section.

(d) A contingent fee audit may not be conducted in the collection of delinquent taxes.

§ 6924.708. Clarification of existing law.

The addition of section 707 of this act is intended as a clarification of existing law and is not intended to:

(1) establish new rights or enlarge existing rights of political subdivisions or employes or agents of political subdivisions; or

(2) establish new obligations or enlarge existing obligations of taxpayers.

Municipal Lawsource Note to Act no. 2007-7, Senate Bill 218, PN 1056, titled "An Act amending the act of December 31, 1965 (P.L.1257, No.511), known as The Local Tax Enabling Act, providing for local services taxes; repealing provisions relating to emergency and municipal services taxes and to continuation of occupational privilege taxes; and making editorial changes" included the following sections 10, 11, 12, and 13, impacting upon the Local Tax Enabling Act as follows:

Section 10. Any ordinance or resolution providing for the levying, assessment or collection of a tax on individuals for the privilege of engaging in an occupation which has been enacted by a political subdivision prior to December 1, 2004, shall continue in full force and effect, without reenactment, as if such tax had been levied, assessed or collected as a local services tax under section 2(9) 2(F)(9) of the act. All references in any ordinance or resolution to a tax on the privilege of engaging in an occupation shall be deemed to be a reference to a local services tax for the purposes of the act. Section 11. All emergency and municipal services taxes levied for the calendar year beginning on January 1, 2007, shall remain in effect for the calendar year beginning on January 1, 2007, and ending December 31, 2007, and are not otherwise altered.

Section 12. The following shall apply:

(1) Except as provided in paragraph (2), the amendment or addition of the following provisions shall apply to taxes levied for calendar year 2008 and each year thereafter:

(i) The amendment of section 2 of the act.

(ii) The amendment of section 8 of the act.

(iii) The amendment of section 9 of the act, except for any editorial amendment changing the reference from the Department of Community Affairs to the Department of Community and Economic Development.

(iv) The amendment of section 19 of the act.

(v) The amendment of section 20 of the act.

(vi) The amendment of section 22.1 of the act.

(vii) The amendment of section 22.4 of the act.

(viii) The amendment of section 22.5 of the act.

(ix) The addition of section 22.6 of the act.

(2) The amendment of the introductory paragraph of section 2 of the act shall not apply, until January 1, 2009, (2) AS MUCH OF THE REDESIGNATION AS SUBSECTION (D) OF THE INTRODUCTORY PARAGRAPH OF SECTION 2 OF THE ACT, INCLUDING THE AMENDMENT OF THAT PROVISION, SHALL NOT APPLY UNTIL JANUARY 1, 2009, to a municipality which reduced its real estate property tax by at least 25% upon adoption of an ordinance pursuant to the act of December 1, 2004 (P.L.1729, No.222), entitled "An act amending the act of December 31, 1965 (P.L.1257, No.511), entitled 'An act empowering cities of the second class, cities of the second class A, cities of the third class, boroughs, towns, townships of the first class, townships of the second class, school districts of the second class, school districts of the third class and school districts of the fourth class including independent school districts, to levy, assess, collect or to provide for the levying, assessment and collection of certain taxes subject to maximum limitations for general revenue purposes; authorizing the establishment of bureaus and the appointment and compensation of officers, agencies and employes to assess and collect such taxes; providing for joint collection of certain taxes, prescribing certain definitions and other provisions for taxes levied and assessed upon earned income, providing for annual audits and for collection of delinquent taxes, and permitting and requiring penalties to be imposed and enforced, including penalties for disclosure of confidential information, providing an appeal from the ordinance or resolution levying such taxes to the court of quarter sessions and to the Supreme Court and Superior Court,' further providing for delegation of taxing powers and restrictions thereon; providing for nonresident sports facility usage fee, for parking tax rates and for payroll taxes; further providing for limitations on rates of specific taxes and for the appointment of a single collector of taxes; further providing for the applicability of petitions under the act of July 10, 1987 (P.L.246, No.47), known as the Municipalities Financial Recovery Act; and making a repeal."

Section 13. Repeals are as follows:

(1) The General Assembly declares that the repeal under paragraph (2) is necessary to effectuate the amendment of section 2(9) of the act.

(2) Section 6 of the act of December 1, 2004 (P.L.1729, No.222), entitled "An act amending the act of December 31, 1965 (P.L.1257, No.511), entitled 'An act empowering cities of the second class, cities of the second class A, cities of the third class, boroughs, towns, townships of the first class, townships

of the second class, school districts of the second class, school districts of the third class and school districts of the fourth class including independent school districts, to levy, assess, collect or to provide for the levying, assessment and collection of certain taxes subject to maximum limitations for general revenue purposes; authorizing the establishment of bureaus and the appointment and compensation of officers, agencies and employes to assess and collect such taxes; providing for joint collection of certain taxes, prescribing certain definitions and other provisions for taxes levied and assessed upon earned income, providing for annual audits and for collection of delinquent taxes, and permitting and requiring penalties to be imposed and enforced, including penalties for disclosure of confidential information, providing an appeal from the ordinance or resolution levying such taxes to the court of quarter sessions and to the Supreme Court and Superior Court,' further providing for delegation of taxing powers and restrictions thereon; providing for nonresident sports facility usage fee, for parking tax rates and for payroll taxes; further providing for limitations on rates of specific taxes and for the appointment of a single collector of taxes; further providing for the applicability of petitions under the act of July 10, 1987 (P.L.246, No.47), known as the Municipalities Financial Recovery Act; and making a repeal," is repealed.

CHAPTER 8
[RESERVED]

CHAPTER 9
MISCELLANEOUS PROVISIONS

§ 6924.901. Repeals.

(a)(1) The act of June 25, 1947 (P.L. 1145), [53 P.S. §§ 6851 to 6857] entitled, as amended, "An act empowering cities of the second class, cities of the second class A, cities of the third class, boroughs, towns, townships of the first class, townships of the second class, school districts of the second class, school districts of the third class and school districts of the fourth class to levy, assess, and collect or to provide for the levying, assessment and collection of certain additional taxes subject to maximum limitations for general revenue purposes; authorizing the establishment of bureaus and the appointment and compensation of officers and employes to assess and collect such taxes; and permitting penalties to be imposed and enforced; providing an appeal from the ordinance or resolution levying such taxes to the court of quarter sessions and to the Supreme Court and Superior Court," is repealed.

(2) All other acts and parts of acts are repealed in so far as they are inconsistent herewith.

(b) The following acts and parts of acts are repealed to the extent specified:

(1) Section 224 of the act of April 9, 1929 (P.L.177, No.175), known as The Administrative Code of 1929, insofar as it is inconsistent with this act.

(2) The act of August 24, 1961 (P.L.1135, No.508), referred to as the First Class A School District Earned Income Tax Act, insofar as it is inconsistent with this act.

(3) Sections 322, 326, 351 and 5004.1 of the act of June 27, 2006 (1st Sp.Sess., P.L.1873, No.1), known as the Taxpayer Relief Act, insofar as it is inconsistent with this act.

Misc. Occupation Taxes assessed prior to December 1, 2004 [Act 32 2008 section 37]

Any ordinance or resolution providing for the levying, assessment or collection of a tax on individuals for the privilege of engaging in an occupation which has been enacted by a political subdivision prior to December 1, 2004, shall continue in full force and effect, without reenactment, as if such tax had been levied, assessed or collected as a local services tax under section 301.1(f)(9) of the act. All references in any ordinance or resolution to a tax on the privilege of engaging in an occupation shall be deemed to be a reference to a local services tax for the purposes of the act.

Misc. Emergency and municipal services taxes levied beginning January 1, 2007 [Act 32 2008 section 38]

All emergency and municipal services taxes levied for the calendar year beginning on January 1, 2007, shall remain in effect for the calendar year beginning on January 1, 2007, and ending December 31, 2007, and are not otherwise altered.

Misc. Application of Act [Act 32 2008 section 39]

This act shall apply as follows:

(1) The following provisions shall not apply to an Article XIII tax officer with respect to income taxes levied before January 1, 2012:

(i) The amendment of section 10 of the act.

(ii) The repeal of section 11 of the act.

(2) The repeal of divisions (II), (III), (IV), (V), (VI), (VII), (VIII) and (IX) of section 13 of the act[1] shall not apply to income taxes levied and collected prior to January 1, 2012.

(3) Except as set forth in paragraph (4) and sections 508 and 515 of the act, the addition of Chapter 5 of the act shall apply to income taxes levied and collected after December 31, 2011.

(4) The addition of section 511 of the act shall apply to the official register released June 15, 2008, and each year thereafter.

Misc. Effective date. [Act 32 2008 section 40]

This act shall take effect as follows:

(1) The following provisions shall take effect January 1, 2012:

(i) The amendment of section 10 of the act.[2]

(ii) The repeal of section 11 of the act.[3]

(2) The amendment of section 13 of the act[4] shall take effect June 30, 2012.

(3) The remainder of this act shall take effect immediately.

1. [former section titled Earned Income Tax]
2. [Collection of Taxes]
3. [Audits of Earned Income Taxes]
4. [Collection of Taxes]

CHAPTER 5

LOCAL TAX COLLECTION LAW

72 P.S. §§ 5511.1–5511.42

TABLE OF CONTENTS

§ 1. Short title.

This act shall be known and may be cited as the "Local Tax Collection Law."

§ 2. Definitions.

The words—

"Duplicate" shall mean a listing of the valuations of persons and property within a taxing district taxable for the applicable year and may include a computerized billing register of annual taxes. It shall be prepared or derived from the county assessment roll and, after being certified as accurate by the taxing district, shall be used by the tax collector to notify the persons whose names appear thereon of the valuations and identification of the properties or persons taxed, the rates of taxes and the amount of tax due. A duplicate can be in a written, typographical, photostatic, photographic, microphotographic, microfilm, microcard, miniature photographic, optical electronic or other form which comprises a durable medium and from which an accurate reproduction can be made.

"Tax Collector" or **"Elected Tax Collector"** shall include every person duly elected or appointed to collect all taxes, levied by any political subdivision included in the provisions of this act, including the treasurers of cities of the third class, elected collectors of taxes in townships of the first class and county collectors of taxes in counties of the third, fourth, fifth, sixth, seventh and eighth class who have been designated to collect county and institution district taxes in cities of the third class and county treasurers in counties of the fourth, fifth, sixth, seventh and eighth class who have been designated to collect county taxes in municipalities existing or organized under 53 Pa.C.S. Pt. III Subpt. E (relating to home rule and optional plan government[1]) that have eliminated the elective office of tax collector and county treasurers in counties of the third, fourth, fifth, sixth, seventh and eighth class who have been designated to collect taxes under section 4.4 of this act. The term includes a person authorized to collect taxes under section 4.2 of this act.

"Taxing District" shall include counties (except counties of the first or second class), county institution districts (except in counties of the second class), cities of the third class, boroughs, towns, townships and school districts of the second, third and fourth classes, and vocational school districts. The term "Taxing District" shall also include a city of the second class A for the purposes of sections 10 and 11 of this act.

"Taxes" shall include all taxes levied and assessed by taxing districts except those levied and assessed under authority of the act of June 25, 1947 (P.L. 1145), as amended,[2] and shall also include the penalties and interest imposed thereon.

§ 3. Application of act.

(a) All of the provisions of this act relating to county taxes shall also, without specific reference thereto, relate and apply to county institution district taxes, except in counties of the second class.

(b) All of the provisions of this act shall apply to all taxes covered by the provisions of this act heretofore levied and remaining uncollected, as well as to all such taxes hereafter levied.

(c)(1) Except as provided in clauses (2) and (3), none of the provisions of this act shall apply to any county of the first or second class, city of the first or second class or second class A, or to any school district of the first class, or school district in a city of the second class A.

(2) The provisions of sections 10 and 11 of this act shall apply to cities of the second class A.

(3) The provisions of section 10(f) shall apply to school districts of the first class, school districts in cities of the second class A and all other school districts.

1. 53 Pa.C.S. § 2901 et seq.
2. 53 P.S. § 6851 et seq.

(d) The provisions of this act shall not repeal or supply any local or special act.

(e) This act does not include, and shall not be construed to repeal, any provisions of any law providing for the return of uncollected taxes to the county commissioners and the sale of real property bound thereby by the county treasurer or by a city treasurer nor to the entry and enforcement of liens for unpaid taxes.

§ 4. Bonds of tax collectors.

(a) In cities of the third class the treasurer, as tax collector for the various taxing districts, shall give bond secured and conditioned as provided by the laws relating to such cities. Cities of the third class may join in joint bidding with other municipalities for bonds of tax collectors. The joint bidding of the bonds shall be subject to all provisions of this act not inconsistent with the requirement of joint bidding.

(b) In boroughs, towns and townships of the first or second class, the elected tax collector shall be the collector of borough, town or township taxes, as the case may be, and of county, county institution district, school district and vocational school district taxes. He shall, before he enters upon the duties of his office, take and subscribe an oath of office and file the same in the office of the clerk of the court of common pleas of the county. He shall enter into one surety bond to the Commonwealth for all taxes to be collected by him, in an amount to be fixed by the court of common pleas of the county, which amount shall never exceed the estimated amount of taxes charged in the duplicates to be delivered to him in one year. Such bond may, at the option of the tax collector, be an annual bond or may cover the full term of office for which the tax collector shall have been elected. Such bond shall have thereon at least one bonding company, and the sufficiency of the sureties on the bond shall be approved by the court of common pleas at any time prior to the delivery of a tax duplicate to the tax collector. The bond shall be filed in the office of the clerk of the court of common pleas on or before the fifteenth day of March of the year in which the tax collector qualifies for office and annually thereafter, except where the first bond given by the tax collector covers the full term of office for which he was elected. Should any of the taxing districts be of the opinion, at any time, that the bond given by the tax collector is not sufficient in amount, or as to the surety thereon, the said taxing district may apply to the court by petition to have the tax collector furnish additional bond in the manner provided by this section. Thereupon the tax collector shall furnish such additional bond, if any, as the court of common pleas may prescribe, but not exceeding the limitation as to the amount hereinbefore prescribed: Provided, That where taxes for borough purposes are collected by an appointee of council the bond shall be as may be prescribed by council. The board of commissioners of any county by resolution adopted no later than November 1 of the prior year may authorize and require for the following year the joint bidding by the board of commissioners of bonds for all tax collectors for the county and for boroughs, incorporated towns and townships of the first or second class, and school districts and vocational school districts within the county. The joint bidding of the bonds shall be subject to all provisions of this act not inconsistent with the requirement of joint bidding.

(b.1) In boroughs, towns and townships of the second class, and after the thirty-first day of December, one thousand nine hundred fifty-three, in townships of the first class, the premium on the bond shall be paid by the respective taxing districts. Each taxing district shall be liable to pay that percentage of the bond premium as the total taxes charged in the duplicate of the taxing district bears to the total taxes charged in the duplicate of all of the taxing districts. In any case where a tax collector is required to furnish additional bond the premium on such additional bond shall be paid by the taxing district which petitioned the court for the additional bond. Prior to the first day of January, one thousand nine hundred fifty-four, where the surety on a tax collector's bond in a township of the first class is a bonding company, any taxing district may pay its percentage of the bond premium as above provided.

(c) In boroughs, towns and townships of the first or second class, the condition of the bond shall be that the collector as tax collector for the borough, town or township, as the case may be, and for the county, the county institution district, school district and vocational school district shall account for and pay over all taxes, penalties and interest received and collected by him to the taxing districts entitled thereto.

(d) The tax collector of boroughs, towns and townships of the first or second class and his sureties shall be discharged from further liability on his bond for the taxes charged in a duplicate delivered to him as soon as all tax items contained in the said duplicate are either—(1) collected and paid over to the proper taxing district; or (2) certified to the taxing authority for entry as liens in the office of the prothonotary; or (3) returned to the county commissioners for sale of the real estate by the county treasurer; or (4) in the case of occupation, poll and per capita and personal property taxes accounted for by the payment over, or by exoneration, which shall be granted by the taxing district upon oath or affirmation by the tax collector that he has complied with section twenty of this act: Provided, however, That the tax collector and his sureties shall not be discharged of their liability under the provisions of this subsection if the tax collector has in fact collected such taxes but has failed to pay the same over to the proper taxing district.

(e) The bond given by a borough, town or first or second class township tax collector shall be for the use of the borough, town or first or second class township, as the case may be, and for the county, the county institution district, school district and vocational school district.

(f) In case where a tax collector shall be appointed in a borough, town or township of the first or second class to fill a vacancy in said office, or where the elected tax collector shall have failed to qualify, or to furnish bond, or where a tax collector shall have failed to settle a duplicate, as provided in section thirty-one of this act, the person appointed in accordance with existing laws, including an individual, corporation or the county treasurer to collect such taxes, shall give bond secured and conditioned as above provided; where a township of the first or second class or a school district shall in such cases exercise its power to appoint a separate tax collector to collect its taxes, such appointee shall give bond secured and conditioned as above provided.

(g) The bond of any county treasurer in counties of the third, fourth, fifth, sixth, seventh and eighth class shall be fixed by the county commissioners. The premium on any such bond shall be paid by the county. The condition of the bond shall be that the county treasurer, as collector of taxes for the county and county institution district as provided for in section 2, shall account for and pay over all taxes, penalties and interest received and collected by him to the county and county institution district. The county treasurer in third, fourth, fifth, sixth, seventh and eighth class counties and his sureties shall be discharged from further liability on his bond for the taxes charged in a duplicate delivered to him as soon as all tax items contained in the said duplicate are either (1) collected and paid over to the county, or (2) certified to the county commissioners for entry as liens in the office of the prothonotary or as claims in the tax claim bureau as the case may be, or (3) returned to the county commissioners for sale of the real estate by the county treasurer, or (4) in the case of occupation, poll and per capita and personal property taxes accounted for by the payment over or by exoneration which shall be granted by the county commissioners, upon oath or affirmation by the county treasurer that he has complied with section twenty of this act: Provided, That the county treasurer in third, fourth, fifth, sixth, seventh and eighth class counties and his sureties shall not be discharged of their liability under the provisions of this subsection if the county treasurer has in fact collected such taxes but has failed to pay the same over to the county. The bond given by a county treasurer in third, fourth, fifth, sixth, seventh and eighth class counties shall be for the use of the county and county institution district.

(h) Notwithstanding any other act to the contrary, joint bidding of bonds of tax collectors shall be subject to the requirements of counties for advertising of bids for contracts or purchases, except that the provisions relating to minimum amount of expenditure shall not apply.

(i) The approval of a deputy tax collector by a tax collector's surety required under section 22(b) shall be provided to each taxing district served by the tax collector and shall not be required to be filed in the office of the clerk of the court of common pleas.

§ 4a. Interim basic and continuing education programs for tax collectors

(a) The department, in consultation with the Pennsylvania State Tax Collectors' Association, shall adopt and implement programs of basic training, examination and qualification of tax collectors and of continuing education to be met by persons qualified as tax collectors as condition for renewal. The department may contract with a third party to provide the basic training, examination, qualification and continuing education.

(a.1)(1) The basic training program shall include, but not be limited to, the following courses:

(i) Procedures for collecting taxes.

(ii) This act and other statutes related to the imposition and collection of taxes.

(iii) Auditing.

(iv) Accounting.

(v) Ethics.

(vi) Computerization.

(vii) Recent court decisions affecting the imposition and collection of taxes.

(2) As a prerequisite to taking a qualification examination, the individual shall complete the basic training program authorized by the department.

(3)(i) An individual shall have the option to sit for any qualification examination relating to the basic education program.

(ii) No individual shall obtain qualification unless that individual has passed a basic qualification examination.

(iii) An individual who passes the basic qualification examination shall be known as a qualified tax collector.

(a.2) The department shall:

(1) Make certain a qualified tax collector certificate is issued to an individual who passes the basic qualification examination. The certificate shall expire one year from the date of issuance but may be renewed for subsequent consecutive years upon the completion of mandatory continuing education in accordance with subsection (b).

(2) Maintain a register that lists all qualified tax collectors. The register shall be open to public inspection and copying upon payment of a nominal fee.

(3) Provide once each year a list of all qualified tax collectors on the department's publicly accessible Internet website.

(4) Determine and approve reasonable fees for the training program and for testing and qualification. The individual shall bear the cost of the program, testing and qualification unless the political subdivision agrees to pay for the cost in whole or in part.

(a.3) It shall be unlawful on or after the effective date of this subsection for any individual to hold himself out as being qualified in training under this section unless the individual holds a current, valid certificate.

(a.4) Deleted by 2014, Oct. 22, P.L. 2604, No. 164, § 1, effective in one year [Oct. 22, 2015].

(a.5) to (a.7) Deleted by 2015, Oct. 22, P.L. ___, No. 48, § 2, effective Oct. 22, 2015.

(a.8) Nothing in this section shall prevent any individual from participating in the department's basic training program and obtaining qualification.

(b) Each qualified tax collector shall be required to obtain six hours of mandatory continuing education during each year of his term of office.

(c) The topics for continuing education shall include, but not be limited to, the following:

(1) Accounting.

(2) Auditing.

(3) Computerization.

(4) Ethics.

(5) Procedures for collecting taxes.

(6) Recent court decisions affecting the imposition and collection of taxes.

(7) The local tax collection laws and other statutes related to the imposition and collection of taxes.

(d) The department shall inform qualified tax collectors of the continuing education requirement upon issuance of certificates.

(e) Renewal of qualification shall be on an annual basis upon completion of continuing education requirements as set forth in this section. The collectors shall bear the cost of the program and qualification unless the political subdivision agrees to pay for the cost in whole or in part.

(f) A record of all qualified tax collectors shall be kept by the department and shall be open to public inspection and copying upon payment of a nominal fee.

(g) Deleted by 2014, Oct. 22, P.L. 2604, No. 164, § 1, effective in one year [Oct. 22, 2015].

(g.1) Deleted by 2015, Oct. 22, P.L. ___, No. 48, § 2, effective Oct. 22, 2015.

(g.2) This section shall not apply to a person who has served eight or more terms as a tax collector.

(g.3) This section shall expire December 31, 2016.

(h) The following words and phrases when used in this section shall have the meanings given to them in this subsection unless the context clearly indicates otherwise:

"Department" shall mean the Department of Community and Economic Development of the Commonwealth.

"Qualified tax collector" shall mean a person who holds a current valid certificate of qualification issued by the Department of Community and Economic Development.

"Tax collector" shall mean a person duly elected or appointed to collect real property taxes levied by a political subdivision, other than a county, including the following:

(1) A tax collector in a borough, incorporated town or township of the first or second class.

(2) A treasurer of a city of the third class in that person's capacity as tax collector.

(3) An employe or official who has been designated to collect real property taxes in a municipality, other than a county, existing or organized under 53 Pa.C.S. Pt. III Subpt. E (relating to home rule and optional plan government) which municipality has eliminated the elective office of tax collector.

§ 4b. Joint tax collection district.

(a) Notwithstanding any other law to the contrary, where a vacancy exists in the office of tax collector in a taxing district, the governing body of the taxing district may, by ordinance or resolution, enter into an agreement with the governing body of an adjoining or conveniently located taxing district for the joint collection of taxes under this act. Two or more taxing districts may enter into an agreement under this section.

(b) The tax collector in the adjoining or conveniently located taxing district must agree to serve as the tax collector for the joint tax collection district for the remainder of the person's term before an agreement under subsection (a) is implemented. If the tax collector agrees to collect taxes in the joint tax collection district, notice of the agreement and a copy of the ordinance or resolution adopted under this section shall be provided to the county board of elections. Following the expiration of the term of office of a person agreeing to collect taxes under this subsection, a person shall be elected as tax collector by the electors of the joint tax collection district.

(c) A taxing district that is a party to an agreement under this section may withdraw from the joint tax collection district by providing notice of its intention to withdraw to the other parties to the agreement and to the county board of elections. To be effective, notice must be received before the end of the calendar year preceding the next election for tax collector in the joint tax collection district.

(d) An ordinance or resolution adopted by the governing body of a taxing district under this section shall specify:

(1) The conditions of agreement.

(2) The duration of the term of the agreement.

(3) The purpose and objectives of the agreement, including the powers and scope of authority delegated under the agreement.

(e) Court approval shall not be required for taxing districts to enter into an agreement under this section.

§ 4c. Tax collection records.

(a) A tax collector during the time that he or she holds the office of tax collector shall maintain and have legal custody of tax collection records that are not in the custody of a taxing district.

(b) Nothing in this section shall prevent a person who formerly held the office of tax collector from maintaining copies of tax collection records that may be necessary for purposes of any subsequent audit, tax certification or other required service or for defending against claims for liability that may be made against the former tax collector. Unless a court, upon a rule to show cause, shall extend the time, copies of tax collection records shall not be retained by a person who formerly held the office of tax collector or his representative for more than five years from the completion of the final audit for the last year in which the person who formerly held the office of tax collector was responsible for the collection of taxes. All copies of tax collection records held by the former tax collector or his representative shall be returned to the taxing district within the time period provided in this subsection.

(c) This section shall not be construed to do any of the following:

(1) Make a tax collector an "agency" or authorize requests of the tax collector for records pursuant to the act of June 21, 1957 (P.L. 390, No. 212),[3] referred to as the Right-to-Know Law.

(2) Alter or amend any law concerning the confidentiality of tax collection records.

3. 65 P.S. § 66.1 et seq.

(d) No person who formerly held the office of tax collector shall intentionally and unlawfully deny legal custody or otherwise impair the availability of tax collection records by refusing to transfer possession of the records to a taxing district or its tax collector.

(e) As used in this section, the term "tax collection records" shall mean records to which access is required by a tax collector in order to carry out the duties under this act and which are among the categories of tax collection records that are to be maintained in conformity with disposition and retention schedules and regulations that are promulgated by the Local Government Records Committee in accordance with 53 Pa.C.S. Ch. 13 Subch. F (relating to records).

§ 4d. Collection of Municipal Taxes by County Treasurer.

(a) Notwithstanding any law, if, as a result of a vacancy in the office of elected tax collector in a municipality within a county of the third, fourth, fifth, sixth, seventh or eighth class, the county treasurer has been appointed or directed by the county commissioners to bill and collect all county and county institution district taxes within the municipality under section 1701.1(b.2) of the act of August 9, 1955 (P.L.323, No. 130), [16 P.S. § 1701.1] known as "The County Code," the governing body of the municipality and the county commissioners may by agreement provide that the county treasurer shall have the duties and responsibilities of billing and collecting all taxes levied by the municipality.

(b) An agreement under subsection (a) shall be effective only through the end of the calendar year in which a successor tax collector is elected in accordance with law and shall provide that the compensation that otherwise would be attributable to the billing and collection of municipal taxes within the municipality be paid to the county treasurer's office. Court approval shall not be required for the execution of an agreement.

(c) Prior to executing an agreement under subsection (a), the governing body of the municipality and the county commissioners shall each adopt a resolution specifying:

(1) The conditions of agreement.

(2) That the duration of the term of the agreement is as specified under subsection (b).

(3) The purpose and objectives of the agreement, including the powers and scope of authority delegated under the agreement.

(d) As used in this section, the term "municipality" shall mean a borough, town or township.

§ 4e. Criminal history record information.

(a) An individual filing a nomination petition or papers for the office of tax

(a) An individual filing a nomination petition or papers for the office of tax collector to the county board of elections under the act of June 3, 1937 (P.L. 1333, No. 320), known as the "Pennsylvania Election Code," shall include the following information obtained within one year prior to filing the petition or papers:

(1) In accordance with 18 Pa.C.S. Ch. 91 (relating to criminal history record information), a report of criminal history record information from the Pennsylvania State Police. The dissemination of criminal history record information to an individual filing a nomination petition or papers for the office of tax collector shall be governed by 18 Pa.C.S. § 9121(b)(2) (relating to general regulations).

(2) If an individual filing a nomination petition or papers who for the two years immediately preceding the filing of the petition or papers has not been a resident of this Commonwealth, the individual shall submit a report of Federal criminal history record information obtained pursuant to 28 CFR Pt. 16, Subpt. C (relating to production of FBI identification records in response to written requests by subjects thereof).

(3) An individual who is elected to the office of tax collector for the term of office beginning January 1, 2016, shall submit the information required under paragraph (1) or (2) to the municipality for which the tax collector was elected before the individual is scheduled to take the oath of office as prescribed by law. If the tax collector does not submit the required information before the date the individual is scheduled to take the oath, the office of tax collector shall be deemed vacant.

(a.1) An individual whose name did not appear on the ballot but has received sufficient votes under section 1405 of the "Pennsylvania Election Code" to be issued a certificate of election by the county board of elections as the successful candidate for the office of tax collector shall, within thirty days of the certification, provide to the county board of elections the following information obtained within one year prior to certification by the county board of elections:

(1) In accordance with 18 Pa.C.S. Ch. 91, a report of criminal history record information from the Pennsylvania State Police. The dissemination of criminal history record information to an individual certified by the county board of elections for the office of tax collector shall be governed by 18 Pa.C.S. § 9121(b)(2).

(2) If an individual who for the two years immediately preceding certification by the county board of elections for the office of tax collector has not been a resident of this Commonwealth, the individual shall submit a report of Federal criminal history record information obtained pursuant to 28 CFR Pt. 16, Subpt. C.

(a.2) An individual who is appointed to fill a vacancy in the office of tax collector shall provide to each taxing district served by that tax collector the following information obtained within thirty days of appointment:

(1) In accordance with 18 Pa.C.S. Ch. 91, a report of criminal history record information from the Pennsylvania State Police. The dissemination of criminal history record information to an individual appointed to the office of tax collector shall be governed by 18 Pa.C.S. § 9121(b)(2).

(2) If an individual is appointed to the office of tax collector who for the two years immediately preceding the appointment has not been a resident of this Commonwealth, the individual shall submit a report of Federal criminal history record information obtained pursuant to 28 CFR Pt. 16, Subpt. C.

(a.3) An individual appointed to collect taxes under an agreement provided by sections 4.2 and 4.4 shall not be subject to the criminal history requirements of this section.

(b)(1) The criminal history record information received by the county board of elections under (a) or (a.1) shall be considered a part of the nomination petition or papers in accordance with section 308 of the "Pennsylvania Election Code." A Social Security number or other personal identification information under section 708(b)(6)(i) of the act of February 14, 2008 (P.L. 6, No. 3), known as the "Right-to-Know Law," shall be redacted from the criminal history record information prior to being released pursuant to a request under the "Right-to-Know Law."

(2) The criminal history record information received by a taxing district under subsection (a.2) shall be subject to the "Right-to-Know Law." A Social Security number or other personal identification information under section 708(b)(6)(i) of the "Right-to-Know Law" shall be redacted from the criminal history record information prior to being released pursuant to a request under the "Right-to-Know Law."

(c) [Deleted by Act 48 of 2015].

(d) An individual who fails to meet the applicable requirements under subsection (a) or (a.1) shall not be qualified to hold the office of tax collector.

(e) In no case shall an individual submit a nomination petition or papers for the office of tax collector if the individual's criminal history record information indicates the individual has been convicted of any of the following:

(1) An offense under any of the following:

(i) 18 Pa.C.S. Ch. 35 (relating to burglary and other criminal intrusion).

(ii) 18 Pa.C.S. Ch. 37 (relating to robbery).

(iii) 18 Pa.C.S. Ch. 39 (relating to theft and related offenses).

(iv) 18 Pa.C.S. Ch. 41 (relating to forgery and fraudulent practices).

(v) 18 Pa.C.S. Pt. II Art. E (relating to offenses against public administration).

(vi) 18 Pa.C.S. Ch. 76 Subch. B (relating to hacking and similar offenses).

(2) A Federal or out-of-State offense similar in nature to the offenses listed in clause (1).

(f) An objection to the nomination petition based on the conditions outlined in subsection (e) may be filed in accordance with section 977 of the "Pennsylvania Election Code."

(g) No member of a county board of elections shall be held civilly liable for any action directly related to good faith compliance with this section.

(g.1) This section shall not apply to an individual filing a nomination petition or papers for a second or subsequent term in the office of tax collector.

(h) As used in this section, the term "tax collector" shall have the same meaning as in section 4.6.

§ 4f. Permanent basic and continuing education programs for tax collectors.

(a) The department, in consultation with the Pennsylvania State Tax Collectors' Association and four tax collectors selected by the department who are not members of a Statewide association and are selected from different regions of this Commonwealth, shall adopt and implement programs of basic training, examination and qualification of tax collectors and of continuing education to be met by persons qualified as tax collectors as condition for renewal. The department may contract with a third party to provide the basic training, examination qualification and continuing education.

(b)(1) The basic training program shall include, but not be limited to, the following courses:

(i) Procedures for collecting taxes.

(ii) This act, the act of July 7, 1947 (P.L.1368, No.542), known as the Real Estate Tax Sale Law, the act of December 31, 1965 (P.L.1257, No.511), known as The Local Tax Enabling Act, and other statutes related to the imposition and collection of taxes.

(iii) Auditing.

(iv) Accounting.

(v) Ethics.

(vi) Computerization.

(vii) Recent court decisions affecting the imposition and collection of taxes.

(viii) Assessments.

(2) As a prerequisite to taking a qualification examination, the individual shall complete the basic training program authorized by the department.

(3)(i) After successfully completing the basic training program, an individual shall sit for the qualification examination relating to the basic training program.

(ii) No individual shall obtain qualification unless that individual has passed a basic qualification examination.

(iii) An individual who passes the basic qualification examination shall be known as a qualified tax collector and may not be required to retake the basic qualification examination.

(iv) An individual who, on the effective date of this section, is holding the office of tax collector shall be known as a qualified tax collector.

(c) The department shall:

(1) Make certain a qualified tax collector certificate is issued to an individual who passes the basic qualification examination or is an individual described in subsection (b)(3)(iv) and shall provide notification of the certification, electronically or by mail, to the municipal secretary or clerk of the political subdivision for which the individual was elected.

(2) Maintain a register that lists all qualified tax collectors. The register shall be open to public inspection and copying upon payment of a nominal fee.

(3) Provide once each year a list of all qualified TAX collectors on the department's publicly accessible Internet website.

(4) Determine and approve reasonable fees for the training program and for testing and qualification. The fees may not in the aggregate exceed $250. The individual shall bear the cost of the program, testing and qualification unless the political subdivision agrees to pay for the cost in whole or in part.

(5) Develop, implement and maintain an online training and testing program as an alternative option for individuals in lieu of in-classroom instruction and testing. The department may provide the training via compact disc. The testing shall be conducted in an online or a classroom setting. Nothing in this clause shall preclude the department from contracting with a third party to develop, implement or maintain the online training or testing program or to develop, produce or distribute the training compact disc.

(d) It shall be unlawful on or after the effective date of this subsection for any individual to hold himself out as being qualified in training under this section unless the individual holds a valid certificate.

(e)(1) Except as provided in clause (2), before taking the oath of office, an individual elected to the office of tax collector shall complete the basic training program provided by the department and pass the basic qualification examination in accordance with this section.

(2) If an individual is not a qualified tax collector on the date he is scheduled to take the oath, the office of tax collector shall be deemed vacant.

(3)(i) If an individual is appointed to fill a vacancy in the office of tax collector, the individual shall have sixty days to become a qualified tax collector. If the appointee fails to become a qualified tax collector within the time required, the office shall be deemed vacant.

(ii) Notwithstanding subclause (i), and if there is less than one year remaining in the term of the office of tax collector when a vacancy occurs in the office, the individual appointed as tax collector is not required to become a qualified tax collector.

(4) A tax collector subject to clause (2) that seeks reelection to the office of tax collector for a subsequent term must become a qualified TAX collector.

(5) Nothing in this section shall preclude an individual from retaking the qualification examination prior to taking the oath of office for the office of tax collector if the individual failed the qualification examination on a prior attempt.

(f) This section shall not preclude filling a vacancy in the office of tax collector by:

(1) A municipality entering into an agreement with the county commissioners under section 4.4 for the county treasurer to collect the taxes levied by the municipality.

(2) A taxing district forming a joint tax collection district in accordance with section 4.2.

(3) Any other method of filling a vacancy in the office of tax collector provided by law.

(g) For the purposes of this section, a county treasurer who collects taxes for a municipality in accordance with an agreement under section 4.4 shall not be considered a tax collector under this section.

(h) A tax collector in office on the effective date of this subsection shall be considered a qualified tax collector under this section and issued a qualified tax collector certificate by the department and added to the list of qualified tax collectors.

(i) Each qualified tax collector shall be required to obtain two hours of mandatory continuing education during his four-year term of office.

(j) The topics for continuing education may include any of the topics of the courses listed under subsection (b)(1).

(k) The department shall inform qualified tax collectors of the continuing education requirement upon issuance of certificates.

(k.1) The Pennsylvania State Tax Collectors' Association and any other organization or individual may offer continuing education courses. Each course offered shall be reviewed and approved by the department to ensure the course complies with the criteria in subsection (j). Attendance at an annual meeting of the Pennsylvania State Tax Collectors' Association or a similar organization that includes an educational component shall qualify as one hour of continuing education.

(l)(1) Renewal of qualification shall be completed prior to the tax collector's final year in office, upon completion of continuing education requirements as set forth in this section. The tax collector shall bear the cost of the program and qualification unless the municipality agrees to pay for the cost in whole or in part.

(2) The department shall issue a renewed qualified tax collector certificate to each tax collector upon the tax collector's successful completion of the continuing education requirements.

(m) Within thirty days of the department issuing a renewed qualified tax collector certificate to a tax collector, the department shall, electronically or by mail, provide a copy of the renewed qualified tax collector certificate to the municipal secretary or clerk of the municipality for which the tax collector was elected.

(n) If the tax collector fails to successfully complete the continuing education requirements, the tax collector shall be deemed ineligible to be placed on the ballot for the office of tax collector at the end of the tax collector's current term of office.

(o) The department shall bear the costs of subsection (c)(5). The Governor shall annually recommend an appropriation to the General Assembly from the General Fund in an amount sufficient to cover the costs incurred by the department in carrying out the certification and training program.

(p) The following words and phrases when used in this section shall have the meanings given to them in this subsection unless the context clearly indicates otherwise:

"Department" shall mean the Department of Community and Economic Development of the Commonwealth.

"Qualified tax collector" shall mean a person who holds a current valid certificate of qualification issued by the Department of Community and Economic Development.

"Tax collector" shall mean a person duly elected or appointed to collect real property taxes levied by a political subdivision, other than a county, including the following:

(1) A tax collector in a borough, incorporated town or township of the first or second class.

(2) A treasurer of a city of the third class in that person's capacity as tax collector.

(3) An employe or official who has been designated to collect real property taxes in a municipality, other than a county, existing or organized under 53 Pa.C.S. Pt. III Subpt. E (relating to home rule and optional plan government), which municipality has eliminated the elective office of tax collector.

§ 5. Tax collector's warrant.

A duplicate when issued to a tax collector shall constitute his warrant for the collection of the taxes levied and assessed therein, and such warrant shall remain in force until the complete settlement of all taxes in such duplicate as provided in this act. This section shall be construed to apply to duplicates heretofore issued.

§ 5a. Interim assessment; duplicate; warrant.

(a) When a duplicate is issued after an interim assessment, it shall constitute the elected tax collector's warrant for the collection of the taxes levied and assessed therein.

(b) Notwithstanding the complete and final settlement to be completed in accordance with section 26, the following shall apply to taxes due upon a duplicate issued after an interim assessment:

(1) If the whole amount is paid within two months after the date of the tax notice, a discount of at least two per centum from the amount of such tax shall apply.

(2) If paid within four months after the date of the tax notice, no penalty may be imposed and said taxes shall not be considered delinquent even if the payment occurs after December 31.

(3) If, as of December 31, taxes remain unpaid and less than four months have elapsed since the date of the tax notice, the taxing district shall reissue the duplicate to the elected tax collector in order to permit the taxpayer four months from the date of the tax notice to pay said taxes before either a penalty is imposed or a delinquency is declared.

§ 6. Notices of taxes.

When any duplicate of taxes assessed is issued and delivered by any taxing district to the tax collector, he shall within thirty days after receiving the tax duplicate, unless such time shall be extended by the taxing district, notify every taxable whose name appears on such duplicate: Provided, however, That a tax notice shall be sent to every taxable whose name appears on the duplicate not later than the first day of July following receipt of the tax duplicate, or not later than fifteen days after the duplicate of taxes assessed is issued and delivered by the taxing district to the tax collector if such delivery is after the sixteenth day of June: And provided further, That municipalities that have adopted a home rule charter under the act of April 13, 1972 (P.L.184, No.62), known as the "Home Rule Charter and Optional Plans Law," may establish a different date for the sending of tax notices to taxables. Such notice shall contain—(1) the date of the tax notice; (2) the rate or rates of taxation; (3) the valuation and identification of the real property of such taxpayer; (4) the occupation valuation of such taxpayer, if any; (5) the several amounts of real and personal property and personal taxes for which said taxpayer is liable for the current year; (6) the total amount of said taxes; (7) a statement that such taxes are due and payable; (8) a request for payment thereof. A separate notice shall be issued for each parcel of real property of a taxable. Personal property and personal taxes may be included on any one of such tax notices. Such notice shall further designate a place and time where the taxes shall be paid and state the time during which an abatement of tax will be allowed, when full amount of tax will be collected, and when an additional percentage will be added as a penalty. Such notice shall be mailed or delivered to the last known post office address of each of said taxables. Any such notice may include information as to taxes levied by two or more taxing districts.

The Department of Community and Economic Development shall prepare a uniform form of tax notice and supply specimen copies thereof to the county commissioners of the several counties for distribution to tax collectors.

[Compiler's note: this section effective October 22, 2015]

§ 7. Effect of Failure to Receive Tax Notice.

(a) Failure to receive notice shall not relieve any taxpayer from the payment of any taxes imposed by any taxing district, and such taxpayer shall be charged with his taxes as though he had received notice.

(b) (1) Notwithstanding any other provision of law, a taxing district shall, within ninety days of the effective date of this subsection,[4] by ordinance or resolution, require a tax collector to waive additional charges for real estate taxes beginning in the first tax year after the effective date of this subsection, if the taxpayer does all of the following:

(i) provides a waiver request of additional charges to the tax collector in possession of the claim within twelve months of a qualifying event;

(ii) attests that a notice was not received;

(iii) provides the tax collector in possession of the claim with one of the following:

(A) a copy of the deed showing the date of real property transfer; or

(B) a copy of the title following the acquisition of a mobile or manufactured home subject to taxation as real estate showing the date of issuance or a copy of an executed lease agreement between the owner of a mobile or manufactured home and the owner of a parcel of land on which the mobile or manufactured home will be situated showing the date the lease commences; and

(iv) pays the face value amount of the tax notice for the real estate tax with the waiver request.

(2) The Department of Community and Economic Development shall develop and make available to each taxing district a form by which a taxpayer may request a waiver of additional charges under this section, which shall include a space for attestation by the taxpayer.

(3) A taxpayer granted a waiver and paying real estate tax as provided in this subsection shall not be subject to an action at law or in equity for an additional charge, and any claim existing or lien filed for an additional charge shall be deemed satisfied.

(4) A tax collector that accepts a waiver and payment in good faith in accordance with this subsection shall not be personally liable for any amount due or arising from the real estate tax that is the subject in the waiver.

(5) As used in this section, the following words and phrases shall have the meanings given to them in this subsection unless the context clearly indicates otherwise:

The term "additional charge" shall mean any interest, fee, penalty or charge accruing to and in excess of the face amount of the real estate tax as provided in the real estate tax notice.

The term "qualifying event" shall mean:

(i) For purposes of real property, the date of transfer of ownership.

(ii) For purposes of manufactured or mobile homes, the date of transfer of ownership or the date a lease agreement commences for the original loca-

4. Subsec. (b) added by 2022, July 11, P.L. 701, No. 57, § 1, effective in 90 days [Oct. 11, 2022].

tion or relocation of a mobile or manufactured home on a parcel of land not owned by the owner of the mobile or manufactured home. The term does not include the renewal of a lease for the same location.

The term "tax collector" shall mean a tax collector as defined in section 2,[5] a delinquent tax collector as provided in section 26.1,[6] the tax claim bureau or an alternative collector of taxes as provided in the act of July 7, 1947 (P.L.1368, No.542),[7] known as the "Real Estate Tax Sale Law," an employee, agent or assignee authorized to collect the tax, a purchaser of claim for the tax or any other person authorized by law or contract to secure collection of, or take any action at law or in equity against, the person or property of the taxpayer for the real estate tax or amounts, liens or claims derived from the real estate tax.

§ 8. Affidavit as to notice.

Before any allowance is made by any taxing district, or by the auditing authority thereof, for commissions due the tax collector, he shall make an affidavit setting forth that he has complied with the provisions of this act in respect to notice to taxpayers.

§ 9. Expenses paid by taxing districts.

The expenses of postage and printing of any notice required by this act shall be paid by the taxing districts.

§ 10. Discounts; penalties; notice.

(a) The rates of discounts and penalties on taxes shall be established by the taxing district. All taxpayers subject to the payment of taxes, assessed by any taxing district, shall be entitled to a discount of at least two per centum from the amount of such tax upon making payment of the whole amount thereof within two months after the date of the tax notice. All taxpayers, who shall fail to make payment of any such taxes charged against them for four months after the date of the tax notice, shall be charged a penalty of up to ten per centum which penalty shall be added to the taxes by the tax collector and be collected by him. The provisions of this section shall apply to cities of the second class A.

(b) If a taxpayer has not paid taxes on real estate within four months after the date of the tax notice, the tax collector shall send by first class mail the following notice in bold print capital letters to the taxpayer:

YOUR REAL ESTATE TAXES HAVE NOT BEEN PAID ON TIME, AND A PENALTY HAS BEEN ADDED TO THE AMOUNT YOU OWE. IF NOT PAID BY DECEMBER 31, YOUR REAL ESTATE TAXES WILL BE DELINQUENT. IF YOU HAVE ANY QUESTIONS, PLEASE CONTACT (NAME OF TAX COLLECTOR) BY MAIL AT (ADDRESS) OR BY TELEPHONE AT (TELEPHONE NUMBER). IF YOUR REAL ESTATE TAXES ARE TO BE PAID FROM AN ESCROW ACCOUNT ESTABLISHED IN CONNECTION WITH YOUR MORTGAGE, YOU SHOULD CONTACT THE COMPANY MANAGING YOUR ESCROW ACCOUNT.

(c) Failure to receive notice as required by subsection (b) shall not relieve any taxpayer from the payment of any taxes imposed by any taxing district.

(d) For purposes of determining if payment is timely made in order either to qualify for a discount or to avoid a penalty, the following shall apply:

(1) Whenever the last day of a period during which payment may be made at a discount or without penalty shall fall on Saturday or Sunday or on any day made a legal holiday by the laws of this Commonwealth or of the United States, payment shall be considered timely if it is tendered or postmarked by the United States Postal Service on the succeeding secular or business day.

5. 72 P.S. § 5511.2.
6. 72 P.S. § 5511.26a.
7. 72 P.S. § 5860.101 et seq.

(2) A tax collector shall not refuse to accept payment tendered or postmarked by the United States Postal Service in a timely manner pursuant to this subsection.

(e) A tax collector shall not refuse to accept payment tendered or postmarked by the United States Postal Service by December 31, but nothing in this section shall be construed as limiting the authority of a tax collector to set a date, not earlier than December 15, after which personal checks will no longer be accepted for payment of taxes and penalty.

(f) Notwithstanding the provisions of this section, for the school year that begins July 1, 2020, the board of directors of a school district may by majority vote, by resolution, extend the time period that qualifies taxpayers for a discount or waive a penalty for failure to make timely payment of any such taxes on real estate charged against them, or both. If a board of school directors of a school district adopts such resolution, the school board shall immediately deliver the resolution to the tax collector via mail or electronic mail and the tax collector shall, in consultation with the board of school directors, modify the contents of the notice required under subsection (b) accordingly and may send an additional notice explaining the provisions of such resolution.

§ 11. Installment payment of taxes.

(a) Any taxing district shall have power to provide by ordinance or resolution for the collection and payment of its taxes in not more than four installments. Where payment of taxes is made on the installment basis, no abatement or discount shall be allowed on said taxes.

(b)(1) Any such ordinance or resolution shall set forth the number of installments in which taxes shall be paid and the dates when the respective installments become due and delinquent. Notwithstanding the complete and final settlement made in accordance with section 26, a taxing district may set installment payment dates subsequent to December 31. The unpaid installments shall not be considered delinquent if paid on or before the respective installment dates established by ordinance or resolution of the taxing district. To each installment on the date when it becomes delinquent, a penalty of up to ten per centum shall be added, which shall be collected by the tax collector. No further penalties, except as hereinafter provided, shall be added to any installment of taxes, unless one or more installments remain unpaid, and the lands upon which such installments are due are returned under existing laws to the county commissioners for nonpayment of taxes, or in case a lien for such unpaid installment or installments is filed under existing laws in the office of the prothonotary, in which case, the additional penalty or interest provided for by such existing return and lien laws shall apply.

(2) If a taxing district has set installment payment dates subsequent to December 31, the following shall apply:

(i) Installment payments subsequent to December 31 of the year in which the taxes are levied shall be collected by the elected tax collector.

(ii) The elected tax collector shall, upon the certification over to him of installments remaining unpaid, proceed to collect the same from the persons respectively charged therewith, for which purpose he shall have all the authority and power now vested by law in any tax collector for the collection of such taxes. The taxing district issuing the original warrants shall issue an additional warrant to the collector of installment payments.

(iii) Installments to be made on or before December 31 of the year in which taxes are levied shall be collected by the elected tax collector. The elected tax collector shall be allowed a credit for the total amount of all uncollected, nonlienable installments not required to be paid by December 31 and this amount shall be identified and carried forward on the reporting form prepared by the Department of Community and Economic Development in accordance with this act as nonlienable installments to be collected by the installment collector.

(iv) The elected tax collector shall be paid such commissions or compensation at the same rate on installment payments as is paid for the collection of taxes generally. Such commissions or compensation shall be paid by proper orders drawn on the taxing district. Every elected tax collector shall be responsible and accountable to the taxing district for all such taxes collected by the tax collector, and the final accounts and records, returns and payments, and duplicates shall be audited annually in the year in which the installments are collected in like manner and in accordance with the laws pertaining to tax collections.

(c)(1) The payment of the first installment by a taxpayer before the same becomes delinquent shall conclusively evidence an intention to pay his taxes on the installment plan, as provided by said ordinance or resolution.

(2) If installment payments are permitted subsequent to December 31 of the year in which taxes are levied, a taxpayer shall evidence his intention to make installment payments of taxes after December 31 either by the timely payment to the tax collector of a first installment before December 31 or, if the first payment is not due before December 31, by notifying the elected tax collector in writing of his intention to make installment payments.

(d) Where a taxpayer shall fail to evidence an intention to pay on the installment plan, as hereinbefore provided, his taxes shall become due and payable and be collected as elsewhere provided in this act, subject to the discounts and penalties provided thereby.

(e) The provisions of this section shall apply to cities of the second class A.

§ 12. Payment of taxes by joint-tenants, etc.

Any joint tenant, tenant in common, or coparcener of real property shall have the right to pay his proportionate part of the amount of taxes due thereon. It shall be the duty of the tax collector to receive and receipt for the same. The interest of any such joint tenant, tenant in common, or coparcener, shall not be affected by any proceeding or sale to enforce payment of taxes on the other interests in said land.

§ 13. Collectors required to be in attendance.

The tax collector shall in person, or by some person duly authorized, be in attendance for the purpose of receiving and receipting for taxes on at least three days of each week during the last two weeks of the period or periods during which discounts are allowed, at his residence or some other appropriate place, to be designated by him in the tax notice.

§ 14. Tax receipts.

The tax collectors shall furnish each person on the payment of taxes from a book containing a stub, or from a bill containing a stub, or carbon copy to be furnished at the expense of the taxing district or districts, a numbered receipt setting out the date of payment, name of taxpayer, the district in which the taxpayer is assessed, the amount of real and personal property and personal taxes paid, stated separately, and in the case of taxes on real property, identifying the property. A separate receipt shall be issued for each parcel of real property. On the stub or bill a memorandum shall be made, in ink, of the number of the receipt and giving the same information as was given in the receipt.

Where payment of taxes is made by mail, a receipt shall be required to be furnished only if the taxpayer shall enclose with the payment a self-addressed and stamped envelope for the return of the receipt.

The Department of Community Affairs shall prepare a uniform form of tax receipt and supply specimen copies thereof to the county commissioners of the several counties for distribution to tax collectors.

§ 15. Receiving county taxes not assessed and adding names to duplicates prohibited.

It shall not be lawful for any county treasurer, county commissioner or any tax collector, nor for any other person, on his or their behalf, to receive payment or give any receipt for the payment of any taxes that have not been duly assessed and returns of said assessment made according to law, nor shall any such treasurer, commissioner or tax collector, or other person on his or their behalf, receive payment or give any receipt for the payment of any taxes, from the collection of which the tax collector has been exonerated according to law. But where the tax collector has been so exonerated, such taxes shall remain payable to the taxing district. Except as hereinafter otherwise provided, it shall not be lawful for any county commissioner, or for any other person on his behalf, to add any name to the duplicate return or list of taxables made or furnished by the assessor or assistant assessors of any township, ward or district.

§ 16. Adding names to duplicates.

In case the tax collector or a deputy tax collector shall at any time find, within the taxing district, any resident or inhabitant above the age of eighteen years whose name does not appear upon the duplicate of such taxing district, he shall report the name of such person forthwith to the assessor who made the assessment used by the taxing district.

The assessor shall thereupon promptly certify the said name to the taxing district which made the assessment, which shall then promptly certify such name to the tax collector reporting such name. If the taxing authorities of any taxing district shall at any time find, within the district, any resident or inhabitant above the age of eighteen years whose name does not appear upon the duplicate of the taxing district, it may, by resolution, determine that the name of such person belongs on the tax assessment list and on the tax duplicate and certify the same to the tax collector with direction to collect the proper taxes from such person for the current year and for the preceding year or the two preceding years, if he was liable for such taxes under existing law. The taxing authorities shall at the same time certify such name to the county board for the assessment and revision of taxes or other authority charged with the duty of making the assessment used by the taxing district.

Upon receiving any name as aforesaid, the tax collector shall add the name and assessment of such person to the duplicate of the proper taxing district and proceed to collect the tax or taxes assessed against such person as herein provided.

§ 17. Distress and sale of goods and chattels of taxpayer.

Every tax collector shall have power, in case of the neglect or refusal of any person, copartnership, association, or corporation, to make payment of the amount of any tax due by him, after two months from the date of the tax notice, to levy the amount of such tax, any penalty due thereon, and costs, not exceeding costs and charges allowed constables for similar services, by distress and sale of the goods and chattels of such delinquent, wherever situate or found, provided the distraint levy includes written notice thereon that, within ten days after the date of the levy, the alleged delinquent may appear at the office of the district magistrate in the district in which the goods and chattels are located and demand a hearing on the merits of the claim and also upon giving public notice of such sale, at least twenty days after the date of the levy or at least ten days after any hearing on the merits in which the alleged delinquent is adjudged delinquent, by posting ten written or printed notices, and by one advertisement in a newspaper of general circulation published in the county.

No failure to demand or collect any taxes by distress and sale of goods and chattels shall invalidate any return made, or lien filed for nonpayment of taxes, or any tax sale for the collection of taxes.

§ 18. Collection of taxes from occupants of real estate by distress.

Any person occupying real property shall be liable to pay all the taxes levied, becoming due and payable thereon, and the goods and chattels belonging to such person, or belonging to any other and found on the premises, shall be liable to distress and sale for the nonpayment of any taxes assessed upon such real property, during his possession and occupancy, and remaining unpaid, in like manner, as if they were the goods and chattels of the owner of such real property, and having so paid such taxes or any part thereof, the occupant of such real property may by action of debt, or otherwise, recover said taxes from his landlord, or person liable therefor, or at his election, may defalcate the amount thereof in the payment of the rent due his landlord.

§ 19. Collection of tax on real property out of rent payable by tenant.

In case any person who is the owner of real estate neglects or refuses to pay any tax levied against such real property, the tax collector of such taxes may any time thereafter notify in writing the tenant in possession of any such real property, that the owner thereof has failed to pay such tax, and request the payment of such tax together with any penalties and interest due thereon by such tenant out of any rent money then due and owing, or thereafter to become due and owing to such delinquent taxpayer. Upon receipt of such notice from the tax collector, the tenant in possession of any such real property shall deduct from any rent that is then, or may thereafter become due and owing to such delinquent owner, the amount of such delinquent tax and the penalties and interest due thereon, and pay the same over to the collector of such taxes. The proper receipt for such taxes and penalties and interest, if any, paid to the tax collector by any tenant shall be a good and sufficient voucher to offset any claim that such delinquent taxpayer may have against such tenant for any rent to the amount thereof.

§ 20. Collection of per capita, poll and occupation taxes from employers, etc.

The tax collector shall demand, receive and collect from all corporations, political subdivisions, associations, companies, firms or individuals, employing persons owing per capita, poll or occupation taxes, or having in possession unpaid commissions or earnings belonging to any person or persons owing per capita, poll or occupation taxes, upon the presentation of a written notice and demand containing the name of the taxable and the amount of tax due. Upon the presentation of such written notice and demand, it shall be the duty of any such corporation, political subdivision, association, company, firm or individual to deduct from the wages, commissions or earnings of such individual employes, then owing or that shall within sixty days thereafter become due, or from any unpaid commissions or earnings of any such taxable in its or his possession, or that shall within sixty days thereafter come into its or his possession, a sum sufficient to pay the respective amount of the per capita, poll or occupation taxes, and costs, shown upon the written notice or demand, and to pay the same to the tax collector of the taxing district in which such delinquent tax was levied within sixty days after such notice shall have been given; such corporation, political subdivision, association, firm or individual shall be entitled to deduct from the moneys collected from each employe the costs incurred from the extra bookkeeping necessary to record such transactions, not exceeding two per centum of the amount of money so collected and paid over to the tax collector. Upon the failure of any such corporation, political subdivision, association, company, firm or individual to deduct the amount of such taxes or to pay the same over to the tax collector, less the cost of bookkeeping involved in such transaction, as herein provided, within the time hereby required, such corporation, political subdivision, association, company, firm or individual shall forfeit and pay the amount of such tax for each such taxable whose taxes are not withheld and paid over, or that are withheld and not paid over together with a penalty of ten per centum added thereto, to be recovered by an action of assumpsit in a suit to be instituted by the tax collector, or by the proper authorities of the taxing district, as debts of like amount are now by law recoverable, except that such persons shall not have the benefit of any stay of execution or exemption law. The tax collector shall not proceed against a spouse or his employer until he has pursued collection remedies against the delinquent taxpayer and his employer under this section.

§ 20a. Collection of per capita and occupation taxes from the Commonwealth.

Upon presentation of a written notice and demand to the State Treasurer or any other fiscal officer of the State, or its boards, authorities, agencies or commissions, it shall be the duty of the Treasurer or officer to deduct from the wages then owing, or that shall within sixty days thereafter become due to any employe, a sum sufficient to pay the respective amount of the per capita or occupation taxes and costs shown on the written notice. The same shall be paid to the tax collector of the taxing district in which said delinquent tax was levied within sixty days after such notice shall have been given.

§ 21. Collection of taxes by suit.

(a) A tax collector may institute a suit in assumpsit against a delinquent taxable for the collection of any real property taxes due and unpaid after the fifteenth day of May of the year following the year for which the taxes were levied and assessed if—(1) the property against which such taxes were levied has not been returned to the county commissioners; and (2) such taxes have not been certified for entry of liens; and (3) such taxes are not held in the custody of a court as herein provided. Execution may be had upon any such judgment recovered without any stay or benefit of any exemption law.

(b) In addition to all other remedies provided by this act, each taxing district shall have power to collect unpaid taxes from the persons owing such taxes by suit in assumpsit or other appropriate remedy. To each judgment obtained for such taxes there shall be added a penalty of ten per centum together with costs of suit. Upon each such judgment, execution may be issued without any stay or benefit of any exemption law. The right of each such taxing district to collect unpaid taxes under the provisions of this subsection shall not be affected by the fact that such taxes have been entered as liens in the office of the prothonotary, or the fact that the property against which they were levied has been returned to the county commissioners for taxes for prior years.

(c) In addition to the fine or imprisonment provided by subsection (b) of section 7.1, act of June 26, 1931 (P.L. 1379), any person violating subsection (a) of section 7.1 of said act shall be liable in a civil action or actions to any tax collector or taxing district in an amount equal to the taxes that said district would have imposed upon such property during the time it was erroneously listed as exempt, together with interest at the rate of six per centum per annum. In case of a dispute as to the assessment that would have applied from time to time, the same shall be determined by the court without proceedings by the board.

§ 22. Deputy tax collectors.

(a)(1) A tax collector may, with the approval of a taxing district and his surety, deputize in writing one or more deputy tax collectors, who, when so deputized, shall be authorized to receive and collect any or all of the taxes in like manner and with like authority as the tax collector appointing them. Any tax collector, appointing any deputy collector, shall be responsible for and account to the taxing district for all taxes received or collected by his deputy.

(2) The surety bond entered into by the tax collector pursuant to section 4 shall also be deemed to cover all taxes collected by a deputy tax collector appointed under this section. Any claims made on the bond arising from the actions of a deputy tax collector shall become the responsibility of the tax collector.

(b) Notwithstanding subsection (a), at a minimum at the beginning of the tax collector's term, a tax collector shall, with the approval of a municipality for which the tax collector was elected and the tax collector's surety, appoint an individual as a deputy tax collector who shall collect and settle taxes during any incapacitation of the tax collector. The deputy tax collector shall collect and settle taxes for the duration of the tax collector's incapacitation, unless the taxing district determines action under section 4.2 or 4.4 is necessary. As used in this subsection, the term "incapacitation" shall mean temporarily or permanently impaired by reason of physical illness, physical disability, mental illness, mental deficiency or other cause to the extent that the person lacks sufficient understanding or capacity to make or communicate responsible decisions concerning the collection and settlement of taxes.

(c) Nothing in this subsection shall be construed to preclude a quo warranto action regarding the incapacitated tax collector's right to hold office.

(d) A tax collector shall provide a copy of the appointment of the deputy appointed pursuant to subsection (b) to each taxing district served by the tax collector.

(e) Any vacancy in the office of tax collector shall be filled as otherwise provided in law.

§ 23. Collection of unseated land tax in certain counties.

All taxes on unseated lands, except in counties of the seventh and eighth classes, shall be collected in the same manner and at the same time, as provided by this act, for the collection of taxes on seated lands.

§ 24. Collection of unseated land taxes in seventh and eighth class counties.

(a) In counties of the seventh and eighth classes, taxes charged upon unseated lands shall be certified and returned by the several taxing districts levying the same to the county commissioners on or before April first of each year.

The county commissioners shall certify such returns to the county treasurer, whose duty it shall be to receive the taxes contained in such returns.

(b) All taxes levied upon unseated lands shall be paid to the county treasurer by the owner or owners of such unseated lands within the year for which the same are levied. In case of the refusal or failure of any owner or owners of such unseated lands to pay the taxes so levied within the year for which the same are levied and collectible, then interest at the rate of six per centum per annum shall be charged upon the amount of said taxes, or any part thereof, remaining due and unpaid from and after the first day of the year following that for which said taxes were levied, until the same has been paid in full, or the land sold as provided by law for the sale of unseated lands.

(c) When taxes upon unseated lands are paid to a county treasurer by the owners or claimants of said lands, it shall be the duty of the county treasurer to enter such payments upon the proper book kept by him for the purpose, and, if requested by the person paying such taxes, give a certified copy under the official seal of said county treasurer of the entries in such book, specifying the name of the person or persons as whose property such lands are taxed, the location of such lands, the number of the warrant, and the number of acres or other description thereof, the kind and amount of taxes assessed thereon and so paid, the date of payment of the same, and the name of the person or persons paying the said taxes and for whose use the same are paid. The county treasurer shall be entitled to receive therefor from the person demanding the receipt or certified copy the sum of twenty-five cents.

(d) It shall be the duty of the county treasurer on receiving the said taxes, or any part thereof, and not before, to pay over the amount thereof to the taxing districts, who shall respectively be entitled to the same.

§ 25. Collection and payment over of taxes.

The tax collector shall keep a correct account of all moneys collected by him as taxes under the authority of any duplicate or duplicates in his possession. He shall mark "paid" on each duplicate, at the name of each taxable, the amount of taxes paid and the date on which payment was made.

The tax collector shall on or before the tenth day of each month, or more frequently if required by ordinance or resolution of the taxing district, provide a true, verified statement, in writing on a form approved by the Department of Community and Economic Development, to the secretary or clerk of the taxing district or, in the case of cities of the third class, to the director of accounts and finance for all taxes collected for such taxing district during the previous month or period, giving the names of taxables, the amount collected from each, along with discounts granted or penalties applied, if any, and the total amount of taxes received, discounts granted and penalties applied. The tax collector shall include with each statement made under this section a reconciled monthly tax collector's report for each type of tax collected for each taxing district. The report shall be reconciled from the tax duplicates to the amount of taxes remaining to be collected. A taxing district may require the elected tax collector to provide it with additional information supplementing that set forth on the form approved by the Department of Community and Economic Development.

If a tax collector does not provide the statement, including the reconciled reports, within the prescribed period, the taxing district may impose a late filing fee in accordance with this section. Such fee shall not exceed twenty dollars for each day or part of a day, excluding Saturdays, Sundays and holidays, for the first six days that a statement with reconciled reports is overdue, and such fee shall not exceed ten dollars for each day or part of a day, excluding Saturdays, Sundays and holidays, for each day after such sixth day that a statement with reconciled reports is overdue. The maximum fee payable with respect to a single statement with reconciled reports shall not exceed two hundred fifty dollars. If a taxing district determines that there is a reasonable cause for failure to timely file the statement with reconciled reports under this section, the taxing district may waive the late filing fees. A taxing district shall receive an overdue statement with reconciled reports even if any late filing fee due has not been paid, but the statement with reconciled reports shall not be considered filed until all fees have been paid. No further late filing fees shall be incurred, notwithstanding the fact that the statement with reconciled reports is not considered filed.

The collector shall pay over on or before the tenth day of each month, or more often if required by ordinance or resolution of the taxing district, to the treasurer of the taxing district all moneys collected as taxes during the previous month or period and take his receipt for the same.

The tax collector shall, at any time on demand of any taxing district, exhibit any duplicate in his possession showing the uncollected taxes as of any date.

§ 26. Settlement of duplicates; audit.

(a) By January fifteenth, the tax collector shall make a final and complete settlement of all taxes for the prior calendar year with the proper authority of the taxing district. In the settlement of such taxes, the tax collector shall be allowed a credit for the following:

(1) for all taxes collected and paid over;

(2) for all uncollected, nonlienable installments carried forward and certified for collection by the elected tax collector in accordance with section 11;

(3) for all unpaid taxes certified by the tax collector to the taxing district for collection as delinquent taxes as authorized by law;

(4) for unpaid taxes resulting from an interim assessment where, as of December 31, taxes remain unpaid and less than four months have elapsed since the date of the tax notice;

(5) for all unpaid taxes upon real property, which real property shall have been returned to the county commissioners as provided by law, or shall have

been certified to the taxing district, or its solicitor, for the entry of liens in the office of the prothonotary; and

(6) in the case of occupation, poll and per capita taxes, for taxes accounted for by exonerations, which shall be granted by the taxing district upon oath or affirmation that he has complied with section twenty of this act.

In all taxing districts which have authorized installment payments to be made after December 31 of the year in which taxes are levied, all unpaid installments of taxes upon real property shall be certified by the elected tax collector to the taxing district, together with a proper description of the property upon which the same is levied, at the time of complete and final settlement. All unpaid installments so certified to the taxing district shall be collected by the elected tax collector in accordance with section 11.

Upon final and complete settlement of a tax duplicate, a tax collector shall take an oath or affirmation in writing and subscribed by the tax collector, that he has made a true and just return of all taxes collected by him. Such oath or affirmation shall be administered by the officer of the taxing district empowered to make settlement, who shall have power to administer the same, and shall be filed with such officer.

(b)(1) The final accounts and monthly or other periodic returns and payments of a tax collector for county taxes collected for a county of the third, fourth, fifth, sixth, seventh or eighth class in counties with an elected controller may be audited by the controller. If the controller does not conduct this audit, clause (2) shall apply.

(2) The provisions of this clause shall apply to all taxing districts except counties in which an audit is conducted by a county controller in accordance with clause (1). (i) The tax collector's final accounts and records, monthly or other periodic returns and payments and duplicates shall be audited annually by the controller or auditors of the taxing district or, at the request of the taxing district, by an independent certified public accountant or public accountant. (ii) If the audit is conducted by the controller or auditors of the taxing district, the audit shall be conducted in accordance with the laws of the Commonwealth applicable to the taxing district. (iii) If the audit is conducted by a certified public accountant or public accountant, the audit shall be conducted in accordance with generally accepted auditing standards.

(3) Nothing in this act or any other law shall prohibit local taxing districts from cooperating in conducting a simultaneous audit of any tax collector serving the taxing districts. Taxing districts may enter into agreements whereby the elected auditor or controller of one taxing district or a designated certified public accountant or public accountant may conduct a simultaneous audit on behalf of each taxing district.

§ 26a. Delinquent tax collector.

(a) Subject to the conditions in subsection (b), in a county, city of the third class, borough, town or township governed by this act, the elected tax collector shall serve as a delinquent tax collector for the collection of delinquent taxes in accordance with and provided with the same powers, rights, privileges, duties and obligations as are set forth in section 686 of the act of March 10, 1949 (P.L. 30, No. 14),[4] known as the "Public School Code of 1949."

(b)(1) In a taxing district governed by this section that is also subject to the act of July 7, 1947 (P.L. 1368, No. 542),[5] known as the "Real Estate Tax Sale

8. 24 P.S. § 6-686.

9. 72 P.S. §§ 5860.101 et seq.

Table of Contents
Part I Ch. 1–3 Ethics, Records, Open Meetings
Part II Ch. 4–10 Taxation
Part III Ch. 11–18 Torts, Contracts & Civil Rules
Part IV Ch. 19–24 Zoning & Planning
Part V Ch. 25–30 Construction and Emergency Codes
Part VI Ch. 31–39 Municipal Codes
Index

Law," the tax collector shall serve as a delinquent tax collector in accordance with subsection (a) only until the date established in accordance with section 306 of the "Real Estate Tax Sale Law"[6] for the return to the county tax claim bureau.

(2) In a taxing district governed by this section that is not subject to the "Real Estate Tax Sale Law," the tax collector shall serve as delinquent tax collector in accordance with subsection (a) only until the date established by the governing body of the taxing district.

§ 27. Recovery of taxes paid over by tax collector.

In case a tax collector pays the taxes levied against any real property or personal taxes without having collected the same, he shall be entitled to collect the same from the person who is liable therefor so long as his warrant remains in force, or in the case of real property have the taxes filed as a lien to his use in the office of the prothonotary, if the period for the filing of such lien has not expired.

§ 28. Expiration of term of third class city treasurer and county treasurer.

Upon the expiration of the term of office of the city treasurer of any city of the third class or a county treasurer, in case any of the taxes he was commanded to collect remain unpaid, he shall turn over the unpaid or delinquent taxes to his successor in office, who shall have power to collect the same in the same manner as in the case of the treasurer to whom warrants were first issued. Before such duplicates are surrendered to a successor, the tax accounts of the outgoing treasurer shall be adjusted and balanced to the satisfaction of the incoming treasurer and the respective taxing authorities, before any release of the bond of the outgoing treasurer shall be given.

§ 29. Collection of taxes after expiration of office.

Any tax collector and his sureties, except a treasurer of a city of the third class, upon the expiration of his term of office shall be responsible for the collection and payment over of the unpaid taxes charged in duplicates in his possession and for the final and complete settlement of such duplicates in the manner provided by this act.

§ 30. Collection of taxes by legal representatives of deceased collector.

The executors or administrators of any deceased tax collector, except a treasurer of a city of the third class and except a county treasurer of any county of the third, fourth, fifth, sixth, seventh or eighth class designated to collect county and institution district taxes in cities of the third class, and except a county treasurer of any county of the fourth, fifth, sixth, seventh and eighth class designated to collect county taxes in municipalities existing or organized under the act of April 13, 1972 (P.L. 184, No. 62), known as the "Home Rule Charter and Optional Plans Law,"[7] that have eliminated the elective office of tax collector, shall have the same powers to enforce collection of unpaid taxes as the collector would have if living, and for that purpose, may employ a suitable person to act for them in the execution of the warrants with all the powers possessed by the deceased collector.

§ 31. Failure to settle duplicates.

Unless settlement of a duplicate is made by a tax collector of a borough, town or township of the second class, or by any tax collector of school taxes in the manner provided by this act, he shall not be entitled to the duplicate or duplicates of any taxing district with which settlement has not been so made for any succeeding year during his term, and a tax collector shall be appointed in his stead in the manner provided by law.

---

10. 72 P.S. § 5860.306.
11. 53 P.S. § 1-101 et seq.

§ 32. Compensation to be made by warrant.

All payments made by any taxing district to any such tax collector for compensation or expenses incident to his serving as tax collector, shall be made by proper warrants or orders drawn upon the treasurer. It shall be unlawful for any such tax collector to deduct funds for his compensation or expenses as tax collector or treasurer from any taxing district funds in his possession.

§ 33. Compensation and expenses of tax collector in cities of the third class shared.

For the collection of city, county institution district and school taxes in a city of the third class, the city treasurer, as tax collector, shall be paid an annual salary, which salary shall be fixed before the election of the city treasurer jointly by taxing authorities, other than the institution district whose taxes are collected under the provisions of this act. In the case of newly created cities, the said salary shall be fixed by said taxing authorities before any tax duplicates are delivered to the city treasurer. In fixing the salary of the tax collector the taxing authorities fixing the same shall each be assigned one vote, which one vote shall be divided into fractions, assigning an equal fraction of one vote to each member of the same taxing authority, and a majority of all the fractional votes cast shall govern.

The tax collector of each city of the third class shall appoint all necessary deputies, clerks and assistants whose number and salaries shall be fixed jointly by the taxing districts in the same manner as hereinbefore provided for the fixing of the salary of the tax collector. Said deputies, clerks and assistants shall give fidelity bond payable to the Commonwealth for the use of the city, county institution district and school district, conditioned on the faithful accounting and payment over of all tax moneys received by them.

Each city of the third class shall provide and furnish for the tax collector at his office, as city treasurer, suitable office space, light, heat, furniture and janitor service.

The salaries of the tax collector and his deputies, clerks and assistants shall be paid monthly or semi-monthly in equal proportions by the city, the county and the school district in the same manner as other officers of said city, county and school district under such arrangement as to payment as may be agreed upon between said taxing districts.

The salaries of the city treasurer as tax collector, his deputies, clerks and assistants, as fixed under the provisions of this section, shall in each case be considered as salary or compensation for purposes of any pension or retirement act in effect in such city and the taxing authorities, other than the institution district, shall contribute, pay or guarantee to the pension or retirement fund the amount which, according to law, the city is required to contribute, pay or guarantee to such fund by reason of the fact that the salaries herein provided for are considered as salaries or compensation of such employes for the calculation of pension or retirement rights and liabilities. Each taxing district may annually set aside, apportion and appropriate out of all taxes and income a sum sufficient for such payments or guarantees.

The salaries of the deputies, clerk and assistants of the city treasurer, as tax collector, as fixed under the provisions of this section, shall in each case be considered as salary or compensation paid by the city for the purposes of any pension or retirement act in effect in such city, and the taxing authorities, other than such city, or an institution district, shall pay to the said city their respective pro rata share of the amount paid by the city to said fund.

The taxing authorities, other than the institution district, shall be required to pay in the proportions hereinafter prescribed the premium on the bonds, required to be given by law, by the tax collector and his deputies, clerks and assistants to the Commonwealth.

The taxing authorities, other than the institution district, shall, in equal proportions, pay the cost of stationery, supplies, printing, notices, postage, telephone service, office equipment and incidental expenses necessarily incurred in the conduct of the tax collector's office; these expenses to be determined by a board consisting of one representative from each such taxing authority to be appointed by such taxing authority.

In sharing the cost of premium on bonds the city, county and school district shall each pay such portion thereof as the amount of taxes on its duplicate delivered to the city treasurer for collection bears to the total amount of the taxes on the duplicates of all said taxing districts delivered to the treasurer for collection. The proportionate shares of the above costs to be paid by the said taxing districts under the provisions of this amendment shall commence on the date when this act becomes effective, shall be calculated on the tax duplicates delivered to the city treasurer in the year one thousand nine hundred forty-nine, and shall be paid according to such initial calculation for a period of twelve months. At the end of such twelve month period and at the end of each twelve month period thereafter, new pro rata shares shall be calculated on the tax duplicates delivered to the city treasurer during the calendar year in which such period ended and shall be paid for the twelve months following.

Provisions of this section shall not apply with respect to county and county institution district taxes in counties of the third, fourth, fifth, sixth, seventh or eighth class having appointed a county treasurer to assume responsibility for the billing and collection of county and county institution district taxes in cities of the third class nor to county taxes in counties of the fourth, fifth, sixth, seventh and eighth class having appointed a county treasurer to assume responsibility for the billing and collection of county taxes in municipalities existing or organized under the act of April 13, 1972 (P.L. 184, No. 62), known as the "Home Rule Charter and Optional Plans Law,"[8] that have eliminated the elective office of tax collector.

§ 34. Compensation of tax collector in first class townships.

(a) The township tax collector shall receive for his duties as tax collector for the township, a sum equal to five per centum of all township taxes received or collected from the township unless a different rate or annual compensation shall be fixed by ordinance of the township commissioners: Provided, That in no case shall the total compensation from the township exceed the sum of ten thousand dollars. The township tax collector shall be allowed such actual printing and postage expenses as shall be incurred in performing the duties prescribed in this act.

(b) The following shall apply:

(1) For the collection of county and institution district taxes, compensation shall be fixed by the county commissioners, and shall not exceed five per centum of the amount collected.

(2) For the collection of school district taxes, compensation shall be fixed by the board of school directors, and shall not exceed five per centum of the amount collected. The total cost of such collection shall be reported annually to the Superintendent of Public Instruction and shall be published in his report.

(3) For the collection of county, institution district and school taxes, the tax collector shall be allowed by the respective taxing authorities actual and needful expenditures for printing, postage, books, blanks and forms.

§ 35. Compensation of tax collector in boroughs and townships of the second class.

(a) The tax collector in boroughs and townships of the second class shall receive compensation as provided for herein.

12. 53 P.S. § 1-101 et seq.

(1) For the collection of county, institution district, borough taxes and township taxes in townships of the second class with three thousand or more residents, salary, wages or a commission on all such taxes are to be fixed by the respective taxing authorities levying such taxes, not exceeding five per centum of the amount collected.

(2) For the collection of township taxes in townships of the second class with less than three thousand residents, salary, wages or a commission on all such taxes are to be fixed by the board of supervisors, not exceeding ten per centum of the amount collected.

(3) In the case of school district taxes, the commission or compensation of the tax collector shall be determined by the board of school directors, and the total cost of such collection shall be reported annually to the Secretary of Education and shall be published in his report.

(b) Notwithstanding the provisions of section 36.1 or subsection (a)(2), if a millage reduction adopted by the board of supervisors in townships of the second class with less than three thousand residents will decrease the amount of compensation received by a tax collector who is compensated on a commission basis, the board of supervisors may by ordinance at any time increase the commission to the level required to compensate the tax collector in an amount equal to the compensation that would have been received under the former commission prior to the millage decrease.

(c) For the collection of county, institution district, school district, borough and township taxes, the tax collector shall be allowed by the respective taxing authorities, actual and needful expenditures for printing, postage, books, blanks and forms.

§ 36. Compensation for collection of vocational school district taxes.

The compensation of the collectors of vocational school district taxes shall be fixed by the board of directors of vocational schools.

§ 36a. Increase or reduction of compensation.

When any taxing district or taxing authorities propose to either raise or reduce the compensation or salary for the office of an elected tax collector, such action shall be by ordinance or resolution, finally passed or adopted prior to the fifteenth day of February of the year of the municipal election.

Section 6 of 2012, Oct. 24, P.L. 1318, No. 166, provides that "[t]he provisions of section 36.1 of the act [72 P.S. § 5511.36a] shall not apply to the initial term of office of a tax collector elected to replace a township treasurer in a first class township but shall apply to all other terms of office and all township tax collectors elected thereafter in that township."

§ 36b. Compensation for interim tax bills.

(a) In fixing tax collector compensation in accordance with this act, a taxing district shall provide a method whereby a tax collector will receive additional remuneration for work related to collection efforts with regard to taxes levied and assessed upon a duplicate issued after an interim assessment.

(b) The additional compensation required in subsection (a) may be based on the issuance of an interim bill or calculated in any other manner permitted by this act.

§ 37. Exonerations.

Taxing districts shall at all times make exonerations for uncollectible occupation, poll and per capita taxes, mistakes, indigent persons, unseated lands, deaths, removals, et cetera, as to them shall appear just and reasonable. The chief clerk or secretary, as the case may be, of each taxing district shall enter in a book or books, to be kept for that purpose, the names of all persons exonerated, together with the reason why, the amount of the tax, and date when made, and give to the tax collector a certificate directed to the proper treasurer, stating the nature of the tax and the amount exonerated in order to make settlement accordingly. The list of exonerations shall remain in force until the taxing district

Table of Contents
Part I Ch. 1–3 Ethics, Records, Open Meetings
Part II Ch. 4–10 Taxation
Part III Ch. 11–18 Torts, Contracts & Civil Rules
Part IV Ch. 19–24 Zoning & Planning
Part V Ch. 25–30 Construction and Emergency Codes
Part VI Ch. 31–39 Municipal Codes
Index

upon information received from the tax collector or for other valid reasons, shall rescind or change the list. When a tax collector has been exonerated from the collection of any tax, such action shall not in any way have the effect of discharging or limiting the liability of the taxable, but all methods of enforcing collection of taxes shall continue as though no exoneration had been made.

§ 38. Advertising names of persons exonerated.

Taxing districts may, at the expense of the district, advertise once a week for not longer than three weeks in a newspaper of general circulation in the district, the names of all persons who have been exonerated from the payment of their taxes.

§ 39. Defaulting tax collectors; embezzlement; penalty.

If any person charged with the collection, safekeeping or transfer of any taxes under this act, shall convert or appropriate the moneys so collected, or any part thereof, to his own use, in any way whatever, or shall use by the way of investment, in any kind of property or merchandise, any portion of the money so collected by him, and shall prove a defaulter or fail to pay over the same, or any part thereof, at the time and place required by this act to the person legally authorized to demand and receive the same, shall be guilty of embezzlement, and every such tax collector and every other person aiding or abetting or being in any way accessory to such act, and being thereof convicted, shall be sentenced to undergo imprisonment, not exceeding five years, or to pay a fine, not exceeding five thousand dollars, or both, at the discretion of the court.

§ 40. Collection of taxes by sureties of defaulting or deceased collectors.

(a) When any tax collector shall default in the payment of the taxes charged on the duplicates, either by embezzlement, negligence or failure to collect such taxes within the time prescribed by this act, it shall be lawful for the surety or sureties on his bond to demand from the tax collector the tax duplicates in which said sureties are interested, and the tax collector shall turn over to his said sureties such duplicates of the various taxing districts for which he is collector.

(b) If the tax collector shall fail, neglect or refuse to turn over such duplicates, upon demand made by his surety or sureties, it shall be lawful for the surety or sureties to present a petition to the court of common pleas of the county in which such tax collector resides, setting forth the fact that such collector has defaulted in making collections. The court being satisfied that such default has been made shall make an order to compel the tax collector to turn over to his sureties, the tax duplicates upon which the sureties are liable.

(b-1) When any tax collector shall have died and no executor or administrator, within fifteen (15) days thereafter, has been appointed to administer his estate, the surety or sureties on his bond shall have the right and power, after petitioning the court of common pleas of the county in which such deceased tax collector resided, and after the said court has entered an order granting the prayer of the said petition, to take over the tax duplicates in which said sureties are interested, and to proceed to collect the taxes remaining unpaid upon such duplicates in accordance with the provisions of this section until such time as an executor or administrator of the estate of the deceased tax collector shall be appointed, at which time the said surety or sureties shall file an accounting of such collections in the court where the said order was entered and shall pay such undistributed funds to said executor or administrator.

(c) The holders of such duplicates shall have the right to appoint a collector for such period of time as herein provided to collect the taxes remaining unpaid upon such duplicates. Any collector so appointed shall have all the authority and power under the warrant issued to the original collector vested by this act. The authorities, issuing said warrants, may issue an additional warrant to the collector of such delinquent taxes upon request of such sureties.

(d) The provisions of any law extending the time, or any warrant for the collection of taxes on duplicates, shall likewise extend to the collection of taxes on such delinquent tax duplicates.

(e) Whenever the surety or sureties on the bond of any defaulting or deceased tax collector shall, under the provisions of this section, undertake to collect delinquent taxes, charged in any duplicate delivered to such defaulting or deceased tax collector, by distress and sale of the goods and chattels of the delinquent, or shall distrain on the goods and chattels of any person who shall allege that the taxes with which he stands charged have actually been paid, or that such person whose goods and chattels have been distrained upon shall deny liability for such taxes, then in either event, the taxpayer may petition the court of quarter sessions of the county for a stay of any such sale of goods and chattels distrained upon setting forth the reasons therefor.

The court shall have power to stay such sale pending a hearing of the matter. The court shall have power to fix a day for hearing of which due notice shall be given the surety or sureties of such defaulting or deceased tax collector, as the court may prescribe.

(f) If the court, after hearing, shall be of the opinion that a taxpayer has actually paid such taxes, or is not liable for the taxes with which he stands charged on the duplicate, it shall direct satisfaction to be entered on such duplicate by the surety or sureties.

(g) The surety or sureties on the bond of any such defaulting or deceased tax collector or any taxpayer shall have the right, upon demand made, to have a jury pass upon the question whether or not a taxpayer has paid taxes with which he stands charged, and if the jury shall find such taxes have been so paid, the court shall direct the surety or sureties to enter satisfaction on the duplicate.

§ 41. Judgment on liability of collector of taxes; appeals; execution.

(a) In all cases where, in any settlement of the accounts of any tax collector, the taxing district or the auditing authority thereof, shall subject a tax collector to any liability, a certificate under the hands and seals of the corporate authorities, shall be filed in the office of the prothonotary of the court of common pleas of the county, stating the amount due and unpaid by such tax collector. Notice thereof shall be given by the taxing district, by registered mail, to such tax collector and his sureties.

(b) It shall be the duty of the prothonotary to enter such certificate on his docket. Such certificate shall from such entry have the same force and effect as a judgment of the court of common pleas, and execution may be issued thereon as on judgments for the amount remaining unpaid at any time after the entry aforesaid.

(c) Within thirty days of the date of such notice, any tax collector or his sureties, may appeal to the court of common pleas of the proper county from such judgment. No such appeal shall be allowed by the court, unless the appellant shall enter into good and sufficient bond with two sureties or a surety company in such amount as the court shall fix, conditioned to prosecute such appeal, and to pay such sum of money as shall appear to be due on the final determination of the proceedings on said appeal. The court shall thereupon issue a rule on the taxing district to show cause why such judgment should not be opened or stricken from the record for reasons set forth in the petition. An answer to any such petition and rule shall be filed by the taxing district within thirty days from the date of the service of the rule. Service of the rule shall be made in such manner as the court may direct. The issues joined on the petition, and answer thereto, shall be tried by the court and jury, unless a jury trial shall be waived by both parties.

(d) In case the appellant does not recover final judgment in court more favorable to him than the amount of the judgment, he shall pay all costs that may accrue on his appeal, but if he should recover in court a final judgment more

Chapter 10 Residential Design Tax Credit
Chapter 9 Neighborhood Improvement
Chapter 8 Local Taxpayers Bill of Rights
Chapter 7 Occupation Tax Elimination Act
Chapter 6 Local Government Unit Debt Act
Chapter 5 Local Tax Collection Law
Chapter 4 Local Tax Enabling Act

favorable than the original judgment, then the taxing district shall pay the costs that may accrue on such appeal.

(e) If no appeal is entered, or if an appeal is entered and no security given, as herein required, or if upon such appeal, judgment is given against the tax collector in any amount, execution may issue in like manner as on judgments for the amount due, and recourse may be had against the sureties of such tax collector.

§ 42. Penalty.

(a) Any tax collector failing to comply with the provisions of section thirteen of this act, and any tax collector, treasurer or commissioner who violates any of the provisions of section fourteen of this act, shall be sentenced to pay a fine of not more than five hundred dollars, or be sentenced to imprisonment for not more than six months, or both, at the discretion of the court.

(b) A person who formerly held the office of tax collector who unlawfully and intentionally impairs the availability of tax collection records in violation of section 4.3(d)[9] commits a misdemeanor of the second degree.

13. 72 P.S. § 5511.4c.

CHAPTER 6
LOCAL GOVERNMENT UNIT DEBT ACT

53 Pa. C.S. §§ 8001 et seq.

TABLE OF CONTENTS

Sec.

---

§ 8001. Short title, scope and applicability of subpart.

(a) Short title of subpart.—This subpart shall be known and may be cited as the Local Government Unit Debt Act.

(b) Scope of subpart.—This subpart shall apply to all local government units.

(c) Exemption of bonds and notes from taxation in this Commonwealth.—This section is the Commonwealth's pledge to and agreement with a person, firm, corporation or Federal agency subscribing to or acquiring any bonds or notes, including tax anticipation notes issued by any local government unit under this subpart, the act of June 25, 1941 (P.L. 159, No. 87),[1] known as the Municipal Borrowing Law, or the act of July 12, 1972 (P.L. 781, No. 185),[2]

1. 53 P.S. § 6101 et seq. (repealed).

known as the Local Government Unit Debt Act, that the bonds or notes, their transfer and the income therefrom, including any profits made on their sale, shall be free from taxation for State and local purposes within this Commonwealth. This exemption does not apply to gift, inheritance, succession or estate taxes or any other taxes not levied directly on the bonds or notes, their transfer, the income therefrom or the realization of profits on their sale. The exemption under this subsection of profits made on the sale of bonds or notes does not apply to bonds or notes issued on or after February 1, 1994 (the effective date of section 2901 of the act of March 4, 1971 (P.L. 6, No. 2),[3] known as the Tax Reform Code of 1971.)

(d) Exclusive procedure.—A local government unit may borrow money on bonds or notes, including tax anticipation notes, only as provided in this subpart. This subpart provides an exclusive and uniform system on the subjects covered by this subpart.

§ 8002. Definitions.

(a) Classification of debt.—With respect to classifications of debt and subject to additional definitions contained in subsequent provisions of this subpart which are applicable to specific provisions of this subpart, the following words and phrases when used in this subpart shall have the meanings given to them in this section unless the context clearly indicates otherwise:

"Debt." The amount of all obligations for the payment of money incurred by the local government unit, whether due and payable in all events, or only upon the performances of work, possession of property as lessee, rendering of services by others or other contingency, except the following:

(1) Current obligations for the full payment of which current revenues have been appropriated, including tax anticipation notes, and current payments for the funding of pension plans.

(2) Obligations under contracts for supplies, services and pensions allocable to current operating expenses of future years in which the supplies are to be expended or furnished, the services rendered or the pensions paid.

(3) Rentals or payments payable in future years under leases, guaranties, subsidy contracts or other forms of agreement not evidencing the acquisition of capital assets. This exception shall not apply to rentals or payments under any instruments which would constitute lease rental debt but for the fact that the lessor or obligee is not an entity described in section 8004(a)(1) (relating to when lease or other agreement evidences acquisition of capital asset).

(4) Interest or assumed taxes payable on bonds or notes which interest or taxes are not yet overdue.

(5) Obligations incurred and payments, including periodic scheduled payments and termination payments, payable pursuant to a qualified interest rate management agreement.

"Electoral debt." All net debt incurred with the assent of the electors, given as provided in this subpart whether issued by a local government unit or through an authority.

"Lease rental debt." The principal amount of authority bonds or notes or bonds or notes of another local government unit to be repaid from payments of the local government unit made pursuant to leases, guaranties, subsidy contracts or other forms of agreement where those payments are or may be made out of the tax and other general revenues of a local government unit under

2. 53 P.S. § 6780-1 et seq.

3. 72 P.S. § 9101 et seq.

leases, guaranties, subsidy contracts or other forms of agreement which evidence the acquisition of capital assets, excluding any amount which has been approved by the electors.

"Net lease rental debt." A portion of lease rental debt as determined under Subchapter B (relating to limitations on debt of local government units).

"Net nonelectoral debt." A portion of nonelectoral debt as determined in accordance with Subchapter B (relating to limitations on debt of local government units).

"Nonelectoral debt." All debt determined as provided in this subpart, incurred or authorized to be incurred, except electoral debt and lease rental debt, in each case whether authorized before or after July 12, 1972, and whether before or after the debt is incurred.

(b) Exclusions from debt.—With respect to exclusions from any particular category of debt and subject to additional definitions contained in subsequent provisions of this subpart which are applicable to specific provisions of this subpart, the following words and phrases when used in this subpart shall have the meanings given to them in this section unless the context clearly indicates otherwise:

"Self-liquidating debt." Debt payable solely from rents, rates or other charges to the ultimate users of the project, to be financed in whole or in part by that debt, or payable solely from special levies or assessments of benefits lawfully earmarked exclusively for that purpose. The term also includes debt or any portion thereof at the time qualified as self-liquidating pursuant to this subpart, whether or not solely payable from those sources. The term **"ultimate users"** includes the local government unit itself only where its use of the project is incidental to the use of the project by other users.

"Subsidized debt." The amount of debt which is self-liquidating to the local government unit because the annual debt service on the amount for the fiscal year next following the time of determination will be covered by one of the following:

(1) Payments of subsidies on account of the cost of the project or on account of operations, but measured by the cost of the project, or which will be covered by capital account reimbursements, which subsidies or reimbursements will be paid by either the Commonwealth or the Federal Government, or both, where such payments under the legislation in force at the time of determination are stated to be of a recurring nature, if the Commonwealth or the Federal Government shall have preliminarily or finally qualified the project for the subsidy or reimbursement, all as determined under section 8024 (relating to exclusion of subsidized debt from net nonelectoral debt or net lease rental debt).

(2) Payments under a subsidy contract with another local government unit or under a subsidy contract with an authority and the amount is lawful lease rental debt as to the other local government unit as determined under section 8024.

(c) Other definitions.—Subject to additional definitions contained in subsequent provisions of this subpart which are applicable to specific provisions of this subpart, the following words and phrases when used in this subpart shall have the meanings given to them in this section unless the context clearly indicates otherwise:

"Accountant." A certified public accountant or public accountant or a firm of either of them.

"Authority." An authority or nonprofit corporation organized under any statute by or on behalf of the Commonwealth or any local government unit or jointly by any one or more of them.

Table of Contents | Part I Ch. 1–3 Ethics, Records, Open Meetings | Part II Ch. 4–10 Taxation | Part III Ch. 11–18 Torts, Contracts & Civil Rules | Part IV Ch. 19–24 Zoning & Planning | Part V Ch. 25–30 Construction and Emergency Codes | Part VI Ch. 31–39 Municipal Codes | Index

"Bond or note." Any instrument issued by a local government unit imposing an obligation for the repayment of money borrowed, but not including a guaranty endorsed on an instrument issued by an authority. Unless otherwise indicated, the term does not include tax anticipation notes. A bond or a note which is a security as defined in 13 Pa.C.S. Div. 8 (relating to investment securities) shall be governed by 13 Pa.C.S. Div. 8, and every other bond or note shall be governed by 13 Pa.C.S. Div. 3 (relating to negotiable instruments), except in each case as otherwise provided in this subchapter.

"Borrowing base." The annual arithmetic average of the total revenues for the three full fiscal years ended next preceding the date of the incurring of nonelectoral debt or lease rental debt as set forth in a certificate stating the total revenues in each of these years and stating the average, executed by the authorized officials of the local government unit or by an independent accountant. If, within that three-year period, there has been an expansion or contraction of the territorial or functional jurisdiction of a local government unit through transfer, merger, annexation or assumption, in whole or in part, in relation to another local government unit or an authority, the borrowing base shall be calculated as if the expansion or contraction had occurred within or prior to the commencement of the three-year period in the manner as the statutes, charter provisions or court decree provide or direct or, in the absence of those provisions, as the department approves.

"Department." The Department of Community and Economic Development of the Commonwealth.

"General obligation." In the title of a bond or note, means a bond or note for the payment of which the full faith, credit and taxing power of the local government unit is pledged, for the payment of which the local government unit has entered into the required covenant under section 8104 (relating to covenant to pay bonds or notes or a guaranty), and for the payment of which no specific revenues are pledged.

"Governing body." The authorities in each local government unit authorized by law to levy taxes or fix the tax rate of the local government unit. The term also includes the school board of a school district and the board or officers authorized to make binding commitments for joint local government units, even though that body has no power to levy taxes.

"Guaranteed revenue." In the title of a bond or note, means a bond or note of a local government unit payable in whole or in part from pledged revenues, but which becomes wholly or partly a general obligation of the local government unit, as guarantor in the event of deficiency in the pledged revenues.

"Guaranty." A guaranty, whether conditional or unconditional and whether full or partial, to or for the benefit of holders of bonds or notes of the local government unit or holders of bonds or notes or other obligations of an authority or another local government unit, of the payment of the principal of and interest on the bonds or notes, the premium, if any, and assumed taxes, if any, on those obligations.

"Incur" or "incurred." When used with respect to debt, means the point in time when, in the case of debt assented to by the electors, the assent has been given, and, in the case of nonelectoral or other debt the first ordinance or in the case of small borrowings under section 8109 (relating to small borrowing for capital purposes), the resolution authorizing the debt has been finally enacted or adopted, unless the authority for the debt has been canceled or terminated as provided in this subpart. Final enactment or adoption means the final act necessary to make an ordinance or resolution, as the case may be, effective pursuant to all requirements of law, including any necessary approval by a mayor or other executive officer or failure of action by the mayor or officer within a specified statutory time limit, or passage over the veto of a mayor or of the officer, but does not include any required advertising subsequent to the date of adoption by the governing body of the local governing unit.

"Independent financial advisor." A person or entity experienced in the financial aspects and risks of interest rate management agreements who is retained by a local government unit to advise the local government unit with respect to a qualified interest rate management agreement. The independent financial advisor may not be the other party or an affiliate or agent of the other party on a qualified interest rate management agreement with respect to which the independent financial advisor is advising a local government unit. For purposes of sections 8281(b)(2) and (e)(5) (relating to qualified interest rate management agreements), the independent financial advisor may be retained by a public authority.

"Interest rate management plan." A written plan prepared or reviewed by an independent financial advisor with respect to a qualified interest rate management agreement, which includes:

(1) A schedule listing the amount of debt outstanding for each outstanding debt issue of the local government unit and the expected annual debt service on that debt. In the case of variable rate debt, the schedule shall set forth the estimated annual debt service thereon and annual debt service on the debt calculated at the maximum rate specified for the variable rate debt.

(2) A schedule listing the notional amounts outstanding of each previously executed qualified interest rate management agreement which is then in effect.

(3) A schedule listing all consulting, advisory, brokerage or similar fees, paid or payable by the local government unit in connection with the qualified interest rate management agreement, and a schedule of any finder's fees, consulting fees or brokerage fees, paid or payable by the other party in connection with the qualified interest rate management agreement.

(4) A schedule listing the estimated and maximum periodic scheduled payments to be paid by the local government unit and to be received by the local government unit from the other party in each year during the term of the qualified interest rate management agreement.

(5) An analysis of the interest rate risk, basis risk, termination risk, credit risk, market-access risk and other risks of entering into the qualified interest rate management agreement. This paragraph includes schedules of the estimated and maximum scheduled periodic payments which would be due under the qualified interest rate management agreement.

(6) An analysis of the interest rate risk, basis risk, termination risk, credit risk, market-access risk and other risks to the local government unit of the net payments due for all debt outstanding and all qualified interest rate management agreements of the local government unit. This paragraph includes schedules of the estimated and maximum net payments of total debt service and scheduled, periodic, net payments, which would be due under all of the qualified interest rate management agreements.

(7) The local government unit's plan to monitor interest rate risk, basis risk, termination risk, credit risk, market-access risk and other risks. This paragraph includes the valuation of the market or termination value of all outstanding qualified interest rate management agreements.

"Issue." All bonds authorized to be sold in respect of a particular project, whether authorized to be sold at one time or from time to time in one or more series.

"Local government unit." A county, county institution district, city, borough, incorporated town, township, school district or any similar, general or limited purpose unit of local government or any unit created by joint action of two or more local government units which is authorized to be created by law. The term does not include a city or county of the first class, an authority as defined in this section or any unit created by joint action of two or more local government units which have not been granted by statute the power to issue bonds. The term includes school districts of the first class presently operating under a home rule charter or home rule charter supplement and the provisions of this subpart shall govern over inconsistent charter provisions.

"Ordinance." The formal action of a local government unit, whether, under the law applicable to the local government unit, the action is taken by ordinance or by resolution, to which the requirements of section 8003 (relating to advertisement and effectiveness of ordinances) applies.

"Project." Includes any of the following:

(1) Items of construction, acquisition, extraordinary maintenance or repair which have been undertaken by a local government unit.

(2) Preliminary studies, surveying, planning, testing or design work for any undertaking described in paragraph (1).

(3) Lands or rights in land to be acquired.

(4) Furnishings, machinery, apparatus or equipment normally classified as capital items, but these items must have a useful life of five years or more if financed separately and not as a part of a construction or acquisition project.

(5) The local government unit's share of the cost of a project undertaken jointly with one or more other local government units or the Commonwealth or one of its agencies.

(6) County-wide revision of assessment of real property.

(7) Funding of all or any portion of a reserve, or a contribution toward a combined reserve, pool or other arrangement, relating to self-insurance, which has been established by one or more local government units, pursuant to 42 Pa.C.S. § 8564 (relating to liability insurance and self-insurance), up to, but not exceeding, the amount provided in section 8007 (relating to cost of project).

(8) Funding of an unfunded actuarial accrued liability or a portion of an unfunded actuarial accrued liability.

(9) Funding or refunding of debt incurred for any or all of the foregoing purposes.

(10) Any combination of any or all of the foregoing as any or all of the above may be designated as a project by the governing body for the financing of which it desires to incur debt.

(11) Any deficit to be funded by bonds or notes as provided in this subpart or the creation of a revolving fund for specific improvements.

(12) Where a local government unit has adopted a capital budget, any unfunded portion of the capital budget selected by ordinance for current funding.

"Qualified interest rate management agreement." An agreement, including a confirmation evidencing a transaction effected under a master agreement, entered into by a local government unit in accordance with and fulfilling the requirements of section 8281 (relating to qualified interest rate management agreements), which agreement in the judgment of the local government unit is designed to manage interest rate risk or interest cost of the local government unit on any debt a local government unit is authorized to incur under this subpart, including, but not limited to, swaps, interest rate caps, collars, corridors, ceiling and floor agreements, forward agreements, float agreements and other similar arrangements which in the judgment of the local government unit will assist the local government unit in managing the interest rate risk or interest cost of the local government unit.

"Resolution." A formal action of a governmental unit other than an ordinance, whether, under the law applicable to the local government unit, the action is taken by ordinance or by resolution, to which section 8003 (relating to advertisement and effectiveness of ordinances) does not apply.

"Revenue." In the title of a bond or note not preceded by the word guaranteed, means a bond or note payable solely from user charges, rates, revenues, rentals, fees, special assessments and receipts pledged for the purpose.

"Series." All the bonds or notes to be sold and delivered at one time in respect of one project or of any two or more projects which have been combined for purposes of financing or where the bonds or notes have been combined for sale as provided in this subpart.

"Sinking fund." The special fund created pursuant to section 8221 (relating to creation of sinking funds and deposits, reserves and surplus funds) for the payment of the principal of and interest on bonds or notes, premium, if any, and assumed taxes, if any, or for the payment of a guaranty.

"Tax anticipation notes." Notes issued in anticipation of taxes, in anticipation of revenues or in anticipation of both as designated in the notes.

"Total revenues." All moneys received by the local government unit in a fiscal year from whatever source derived, except the following:

(1) Subsidies or reimbursements from the Federal Government or from the Commonwealth measured by the cost of, or given or paid on account of, a particular project financed by debt.

(2) Project revenues, rates, receipts, user charges, special assessments and special levies which are or will be pledged or budgeted for specific self-liquidating debt, or for payments under leases, guaranties, subsidy contracts or other forms of agreement which could constitute lease rental debt except that the payments are payable solely from these sources, but that portion thereof that has been returned to or retained by the local government unit shall not be excluded.

(3) Interest on moneys in sinking funds, reserves and other funds, which interest is pledged or budgeted for the payment or security of outstanding debt, and interest on bond or note proceeds, if similarly pledged.

(4) Grants and gifts in aid of or measured by the construction or acquisition of specified projects.

(5) Proceeds from the disposition of capital assets, and other nonrecurring items including bond or note proceeds not considered income under generally accepted municipal accounting principles.

"Unfunded actuarial accrued liability." With respect to a local government unit retirement system, pension plan or pension trust fund, the excess of the actuarial accrued liability over the actuarial value of assets of the retirement system, pension plan or pension trust fund, computed as follows:

(1) In the case of a local government unit that is subject to the act of December 18, 1984 (P.L. 1005, No. 205),[4] known as the Municipal Pension Plan Funding Standard and Recovery Act, in accordance with the requirements of that act.

(2) In the case of a local government unit that is not subject to the Municipal Pension Plan Funding Standard and Recovery Act, in accordance with the applicable laws for that local government unit regarding minimum funding requirements for the unit's retirement system, pension plan or pension trust fund or, if there are no such laws, in accordance with the ordinance, resolution

4. 53 P.S. § 895.101 et seq.

or contract under which the local government unit participates in the retirement system, pension plan or pension trust fund.

In the case of a local government unit that participates in a retirement system, pension plan or pension trust fund for employees of more than one local government unit, including an association of local government units cooperating under Subchapter A of Chapter 23 (relating to intergovernmental cooperation), the term includes the local government unit's pro rata share of the total unfunded actuarial accrued liability of the retirement system, pension plan or pension trust fund, as the pro rata share may be determined under the applicable laws or, if there are no applicable laws, under the ordinance, resolution or contract under which the local government unit participates in the retirement system, pension plan or pension trust fund.

§ 8003. Advertisement and effectiveness of ordinances.

(a) Advertisement of ordinances.—Notwithstanding any other statute to the contrary, an ordinance required to be adopted by this subpart shall be advertised not less than three nor more than 30 days prior to its enactment. The advertisement shall appear once in a newspaper of general circulation in the area of the local government unit, shall set forth a summary of the contents of the ordinance and shall state that a copy of the full proposed text thereof may be examined by any citizen in the office of the secretary of the local government unit at the address and during the reasonable hours stated in the advertisement.

(b) Notice of enactment.—Not later than 15 days after the final enactment of the ordinance, a notice of the enactment shall be advertised once in a newspaper of general circulation in the local government unit. This notice shall state:

(1) Briefly, the substance of any amendments made during final passage, and, where applicable:

(i) in respect of lease rental debt the range of lease rental payments; and

(ii) in other cases, the price bid for bonds or notes and the range of interest rates named in the successful bid.

(2) That the final text of the ordinance as enacted may be examined by any citizen in the office of the secretary of the local government unit at the address and during the reasonable hours stated in the notice.

(c) Effectiveness of ordinance.—The ordinance shall be valid and effective for all purposes on the fifth day after the second advertisement. The second advertisement shall be conclusive, so far as concerns the effectiveness of the ordinance or the validity of any debt incurred, as to the existence of all matters recited or referred to therein unless an action questioning the validity or effectiveness has been filed in timely manner as provided in this subpart, but the conclusiveness shall not affect the liability of any person for failure to permit inspection. No other or different publication shall be required notwithstanding the provisions of any other statute.

§ 8004. When lease or other agreement evidences acquisition of capital asset.

(a) General rule.—A lease, guaranty, subsidy contract or other agreement entered into by a local government unit shall evidence the acquisition of a capital asset if:

(1) the lessee or obligor is a local government unit and the lessor or obligee is an authority organized under any law of this Commonwealth, another local government unit, a nonprofit corporation, the State Public School Building Authority or other agency or authority of the Commonwealth;

(2) the payments, or any portion thereof, which are payable in a subsequent fiscal year or subsequent fiscal years and which are applicable to debt service requirements or capital costs are payable, whether in all events or only upon

the happening of certain events, under the terms of the instrument from the tax or general revenues of the local government unit; and

(3) upon termination of the lease guaranty, subsidy contract or other agreement or upon dissolution of the lessor or obligee, whether before or after the termination of the lease, title to the subject project or premises or a given part thereof or undivided interest therein, shall or, at the option of the local government unit, may vest by agreement or operation of law in the local government unit or in the Commonwealth.

(b) Agreement exceeding useful life of asset.—A lease, guaranty, subsidy contract or other form of agreement entered into by a local government unit shall also evidence the acquisition of a capital asset if the payments to be made in a subsequent fiscal year or subsequent fiscal years applicable to debt service requirements or capital costs are payable, whether in all events or only upon the happening of certain events, under the provisions of the instrument from the tax or general revenues of the local government unit and the term of the instrument is equal to or exceeds the useful life of the asset, regardless of the nature of the lessor or obligee.

§ 8005. Classification and authority to issue bonds and notes.

(a) Classification.—Bonds or notes prior to the authorization thereof shall be classified by the issuing local government unit as one of the following three types of obligation:

(1) General obligation bonds or notes.

(2) Guaranteed revenue bonds or notes.

(3) Revenue bonds or notes.

(b) Guaranteed revenue bonds or notes.—Guaranteed revenue bonds or notes may have either a general or a limited guaranty as the governing body of the local government unit may determine, but if the guaranty is less than a full unconditional guaranty, the title of the bond or note shall contain the word "limited" before the word "guaranteed." The guaranty of the local government may be of its own revenue bonds or notes or of the revenue bonds or notes of an authority or another local government unit subject, however, to the provisions of subsection (c).

(c) Authority to issue bonds and notes.—Notwithstanding any other law to the contrary, every local government unit shall have full power and authority to issue bonds or notes, and make guaranties, leases, subsidy contracts or other agreements evidencing the acquisition of capital assets payable out of taxes and other general revenues, to provide funds for and towards the cost of or the cost of completing any project or combination of projects which the local government unit is authorized to own, acquire, subsidize, operate or lease, or to participate in owning, acquiring, subsidizing, operating or leasing with others, to issue tax anticipation notes and funding bonds or notes as provided in this subpart, and to contract for insurance covering the risks of nonpayment of principal, interest and premium of bonds, notes, tax anticipation notes and guaranties.

(d) Nature of guaranty.—For the purpose of this subpart, unless debt evidenced by a guaranty has been approved as electoral debt in accordance with Subchapter C (relating to procedure for securing approval of electors), the guaranty shall be deemed to be nonelectoral debt if the local government unit guaranties its own bonds or notes and shall be deemed to be lease rental debt if it guaranties the bonds or notes of an authority or another local government unit. For the purpose of all other statutes, the guaranty shall be deemed to create debt or indebtedness of the local government unit making the guaranty.

§ 8006. Preliminary cost estimates.

Prior to the initial authorization of bonds or notes or the issuance of any guaranty to finance any project involving construction or acquisition, the governing body shall obtain realistic cost estimates through actual bids, option agreements or professional estimates from registered architects, professional engineers or other persons qualified by experience. Any local government unit may retain the services of a financial advisor. Costs of preliminary estimates and the fees of financial advisors may, if initially paid by the local government unit, be reimbursed out of the net proceeds of the issue of bonds or notes as a cost of the project.

§ 8007. Cost of project.

The cost of a project includes the amount of all payments to contractors or for the acquisition of a project or for lands, easements, rights and other appurtenances deemed necessary for the project, fees of architects, engineers, appraisers, consultants, financial advisors and attorneys incurred in connection with the project financing costs, costs of necessary printing and advertising, costs of preliminary feasibility studies and tests, cost estimates and interest on money borrowed to finance the project, if capitalized, to the date of completion of construction and, if deemed necessary, for one year thereafter, amounts to be placed in reserve funds, if any, a reasonable initial working capital for operating the project and a proper allowance for contingencies and any amount which constitutes, under generally accepted accounting principles, a cost of, and which has been determined by an independent actuary or other expert to be required for the purposes of, a reserve or a contribution toward a combined reserve, pool or other arrangement, for losses or liabilities covered by a self-insurance arrangement established by one or more local government units.

§ 8008. Home rule.

Every local government unit obtaining a home rule charter after July 12, 1972, shall be subject to the substantive provisions of this subpart applicable to it as if it were a local government unit and may adopt the procedural provisions of this subpart, by incorporation thereof by reference, in its home rule charter.

§ 8009. Guaranty funds and compulsory associations.

a) Self-insurance.—No self-insurance program funded pursuant to this subpart shall be required or permitted to join or contribute financially to any insurance insolvency guaranty fund, or similar mechanism, in this Commonwealth, nor shall any such self-insurance program funded pursuant to this subpart, or its insureds or claimants against its insureds, receive any benefit from any such fund for claims arising under the coverage provided by such self-insurance program.

(b) Exception.—When a local government unit or group of local government units obtains insurance from a self-insurance program funded pursuant to this subpart, such risks, wherever resident or located, shall not be covered by any insurance guaranty fund or similar mechanism in this Commonwealth.

Subchapter B. Limitations on Debt of Local Government Units

§ 8021. No limitation on debt approved by electors.

All debt of any classification, whenever incurred, which is approved, either before or after the debt is incurred, by majority of the votes cast upon the question of incurring the debt at a general or special election held as provided by applicable law is excluded from the nonelectoral debt or the lease rental debt, as the case may be, of a local government unit, and the limitations imposed by this subpart upon the debt of the classification shall not apply to such debt.

§ 8022. Limitations on incurring of other debt.

(a) Nonelectoral debt.—Except as provided in subsections (c), (d) and (e) and as otherwise specifically provided in this subpart, a local government unit shall not incur any new nonelectoral debt if the aggregate net principal amount of the new nonelectoral debt, together with all other net nonelectoral debt outstanding, would cause the total net nonelectoral debt of the local government unit to exceed any of the following:

(1) One hundred percent of its borrowing base in the case of a school district of the first class.

(2) Three hundred percent of its borrowing base in the case of a county.

(3) Two hundred fifty percent of its borrowing base in the case of any other local government unit.

(b) Nonelectoral debt plus lease rental debt.—Except as provided in subsections (c), (d) and (e) or as otherwise specifically provided in this subpart, in the exercise of legislative control over the budgets and expenditures of local government units and of the purposes for which tax moneys and general revenues of local government units may be expended, a local government unit shall not incur any new lease rental debt or nonelectoral debt if the aggregate net principal amount of the new debt, together with any other net nonelectoral debt and net lease rental debt then outstanding, would cause the outstanding total of net nonelectoral debt plus net lease rental debt of the local government unit to exceed any of the following:

(1) Two hundred percent of the borrowing base in the case of a school district of the first class.

(2) Four hundred percent of its borrowing base in the case of a county.

(3) Three hundred fifty percent of its borrowing base in the case of all other local government units.

(c) Self-liquidating or subsidized debt.—The limitations and prohibitions of subsections (a) and (b), referred to as the "regular debt limits," shall not apply to electoral debt; to debt excluded in computing net amounts of nonelectoral debt or of lease rental debt, as self-liquidating or because subsidized, when the exclusion is made pursuant to sections 8024 (relating to exclusion of subsidized debt from net nonelectoral debt or net lease rental debt), 8025 (relating to exclusion of self-liquidating debt evidenced by revenue bonds or notes to determine net nonelectoral debt) and 8026 (relating to exclusion of other self-liquidating debt to determine net nonelectoral debt or net lease rental debt); nor to debt incurred to fund an unfunded actuarial accrued liability except to the extent that bonds or notes issued to fund an unfunded actuarial accrued liability shall be limited to the principal amount necessary, after deduction of costs of issuance, underwriter's discount and original issue discount, to fund the unfunded actuarial accrued liability.

(d) Additional nonelectoral or lease rental debt.—Additional nonelectoral or additional lease rental debt or both in the aggregate amount of 100% of the borrowing base may be incurred by a county which has assumed countywide responsibility or, where the county has not assumed countywide responsibility, by a local government unit which has assumed responsibility for its and its adjacent areas for hospitals and other public health services, air and water pollution control, flood control, environmental protection, water distribution and supply systems, sewage and refuse collection and disposal systems, education at any level, highways, public transportation or port operations. The additional debt limit may be so utilized only to provide funds for and towards the cost of capital facilities for any or any combination of the foregoing purposes. Debt, other than electoral debt, at any time incurred for such purposes or any of them may be assigned by ordinance to this additional debt limit if the remaining borrowing capacity within the regular limits is insufficient to finance other projects deemed necessary by the governing body of the local government unit.

(e) Emergency debt.—If replacement of assets is required as a result of fire, flood, storm, war, riot, civil commotion or other catastrophe, or the replacement or any improvements are required for the prevention of dangers to health or safety, or if funds are required for the payment of tort liability not covered by insurance, or if funds are required to be used for and towards the costs of mandated installations of health, safety, antipollution, environmental protection and control facilities or of complying with other mandated Federal or State programs, a local government unit lacking sufficient remaining borrowing capacity as nonelectoral or lease rental debt or being otherwise prohibited by section 8045 (relating to effect of defeat of question) from incurring debt for the purpose, upon petition to the court of common pleas alleging the catastrophe, or the danger to health and safety, or the mandated nature of the program and the estimated costs of the proposed facilities, and upon proof thereof to the satisfaction of the court, shall be authorized, notwithstanding section 8045 or the insufficiency of nonelectoral or lease rental borrowing capacity, to incur debt, as either lease rental or nonelectoral debt, up to an additional 50% of its borrowing base, if the increase is found by the court to have been made necessary under this subsection by reason of the causes set forth in the petition. The increase, together with all outstanding other additional emergency debt which may have been previously authorized under this subsection excluding any allocated to the additional debt limit under subsection (d), shall not exceed 50% of the borrowing base. Public notice of the intention to file such a petition and of the purpose for which the additional emergency debt is to be incurred shall be given by advertisement in at least one and not more than two newspapers of general circulation and in the legal journal not less than five nor more than 20 days before the filing thereof. The additional emergency debt may be incurred only for the purposes and upon the terms approved by the court. The amount of the debt initially in excess of the regular debt limits shall not thereafter be included in computing net amounts of nonelectoral or lease rental debt.

(f) Limitations on incurring of debt by school districts.—Except for purposes of refinancing existing debt under this subpart and notwithstanding the other provisions of this section, no school district of the first class A through fourth classes shall incur any new nonelectoral debt or lease rental debt if the aggregate net principal amount of such new debt together with any other net nonelectoral debt and lease rental debt then outstanding would cause the outstanding total of net nonelectoral debt plus net lease rental debt of the school district to exceed 225% of the school district's borrowing base as defined in section 8002 (relating to definitions). This section shall apply regardless of whether there is an election by the school district under section 8703 (relating to adoption of referendum).

§ 8023. Transfer to electoral debt of debt incurred without approval of electors.

The governing body of any local government unit may, by resolution, signify a desire to have any debt theretofore incurred without the approval of the electors transferred to the electoral debt. The resolution shall direct the holding of an election for the purpose of obtaining the approval of the electors to the debt in the manner provided for securing the approval of electoral debt. The question shall be whether the remaining unpaid debt incurred without the approval of the electors for the project named in the question shall be removed from the category of nonelectoral or lease rental debt. If a majority of the votes cast upon the question at the election favor transfer to electoral debt, a certified copy of the resolution, proof of due advertisement of the election and a certified return of the election shall be filed with the department. If the department finds the proceedings to have been taken in conformity with the law, it shall endorse its approval on a duplicate original and return it to the local government unit. The debt shall thereupon be no longer classified as nonelectoral or lease rental debt.

§ 8024. Exclusion of subsidized debt from net nonelectoral debt or net lease rental debt.

(a) Filings with department.—Subsidized debt shall not be excluded from nonelectoral debt or lease rental debt, as the case may be, for the purposes of establishing net outstanding debt of either category until the following have been filed with and approved by the department:

(1) A copy, certified by the secretary of the board of the local government unit or of the authority, of the permanent or preliminary approval from the Commonwealth or from the Federal Government of the project of the related bonds or notes, or of the interest thereon, for subsidization or for reimbursement of all or part of debt service or on account of operations, but measured by the cost of the project or a certified copy of the subsidy contract with another local government unit or an authority.

(2) Evidence satisfactory to the department from the subsidizing agency as to the indicated annual amount of the subsidy.

(3) Appropriate reference to the legislation authorizing the reimbursement or subsidy indicating the legislated recurring nature of the subsidy or, in the case of a subsidy contract with another local government unit, evidence satisfactory to the department that the amount to be excluded is within the debt limitations of the other local government unit or has been approved as electoral debt.

(4) A computation, in reasonable detail, certified by the proper officers of the local government unit or of the authority, or by the financial advisor if one be retained, showing the principal amount of the bonds to be serviced by the reimbursement or subsidy, determined in the proportion that the total indicated subsidy or reimbursement to be received over the remaining life of the issue bears to the total debt service to be paid over the remaining life of the issue, computed to stated maturity or earlier mandatory call dates.

The principal amount of the bonds or notes of the local government unit of the authority which will constitute subsidized debt shall, in those instances where the subsidy is related to a percentage of lease rentals or to a percentage of sinking fund payments, in either case applicable solely to debt service, be that stated percentage of the bonds or notes. That proportion of the bonds or of lease rental debt shall be excluded as subsidized debt. The filing may be made simultaneously with the filing for the approval of the balance of the bonds then being issued or may be made or corrected at a later date.

(b) Incurring new debt.—Each time any new debt is to be incurred, if subsidized debt is to be excluded, a new certification shall be made to the department, stating one of the following:

(1) That there has been no decrease in the subsidy.

(2) That there has been a decrease, in which case the certification shall include a recomputation of the principal amount to be excluded.

(3) That there has been an increase and the local government unit desires an increased exclusion certifying all matters so changed and recomputing the principal amount to be excluded.

(c) Approval by department.—If the department approves the exclusion of the principal amount of bonds or notes or lease rental debt as being subsidized debt in accordance with this subpart, originally or upon any recertification it shall return a duplicate original of the filing to the local government unit with its approval endorsed thereon. Upon receipt of the approval by the local government unit, the principal amount of bonds shall be excluded from nonelectoral debt or lease rental debt for the purpose of determining net debt in each category.

§ 8025. Exclusion of self-liquidating debt evidenced by revenue bonds or notes to determine net nonelectoral debt.

Self-liquidating debt evidenced by revenue bonds or notes shall not be excluded from nonelectoral debt for the purpose of establishing net nonelectoral debt until the following have been filed with the department:

Table of Contents | Part I Ch. 1–3 Ethics, Records, Open Meetings | Part II Ch. 4–10 Taxation | Part III Ch. 11–18 Torts, Contracts & Civil Rules | Part IV Ch. 19–24 Zoning & Planning | Part V Ch. 25–30 Construction and Emergency Codes | Part VI Ch. 31–39 Municipal Codes | Index

(1) A statement by the proper officials of the local government unit certifying the amount of the debt, the project for which it was incurred and the nature of the revenues from which the debt is to be repaid.

(2) A certificate from a qualified professional engineer or architect, or other person qualified by experience appropriate to the project, estimating the revenues and operating expenses of the project and showing that the net revenues so estimated will be sufficient to pay the annual debt service as it falls due.

(3) An opinion of the bond counsel approving the issue to the effect that the holders of the bonds or notes have no claim upon the taxing power or tax revenues of the local government unit issuing the bonds or notes, but only claims upon the specific revenues pledged and rights to the enforcement of any covenants as to the levying or collection of rates and charges for the use of the project being financed or any covenants as to the assessment of benefits upon properties serviceable by the project as provided in the covenants with the holders of the revenue bonds.

§ 8026. Exclusion of other self-liquidating debt to determine net nonelectoral debt or net lease rental debt.

(a) Filings with department.—Self-liquidating debt shall not be excluded in determining net nonelectoral debt or net lease rental debt for the purpose of establishing net debt of either category where the debt is evidenced by general obligation bonds or notes, by bonds, notes or other obligations of an authority or of another local government unit or by a guaranty until there has been filed with and approved by the department a report to the local government unit from qualified registered engineers or architects or other persons qualified by experience appropriate to the project, setting forth:

(1) The estimated or, if available, the actual cost of construction, acquisition or improvement of the project financed or to be financed.

(2) The principal amount of the general obligation bonds or notes, the bonds, notes or obligations guaranteed or the bonds or notes of an authority or another local government unit secured by an instrument evidencing lease rental debt which are to be issued, the dates, interest rate and amounts of each stated maturity thereof and, set forth separately, the same information with respect to the outstanding bonds, notes or obligations.

(3) The amount or the estimated amount of the annual debt service for each year during the life of all the bonds, notes or obligations or the bonds or notes of an authority or another local government unit secured by an instrument evidencing lease rental debt issued and intended to be issued to finance the project.

(4) The date or estimated date of the completion of the project.

(5) The estimated net revenues of the project for each year of the remaining life of the bonds, notes or obligations with a computation showing, in reasonable detail, that the net revenues, together with other available funds to be received in respect of the project, will be sufficient in each year to pay the annual debt service, other than capitalized debt service, on the bonds, notes or obligations or a specified aggregate principal amount thereof.

(6) The qualified person's certificate that the estimates of net revenues have been computed from the person's best estimate of the gross revenues to be obtained from the rentals, rates, tolls and charges, interest to be received on reserve accounts, established or to be established by ordinance or from payments under bulk service or other contracts with other local government units or authorities for the use of the project, or the gross revenues to be received from special assessments levied to finance the project, by deducting from the gross revenues, in each year, the total estimated costs of operation and maintenance of the project chargeable against the revenues or assessments and any

State taxes assumed on such bonds or notes all based on assumptions deemed reasonable for the purpose by that person.

(7) The qualified person's further certificate that he is qualified to act with regard to the type of project being financed, stating his experience.

(b) Approval by department.—If the department approves the exclusion of the principal amount of bonds, notes or obligations or bonds or notes of an authority of another local government unit secured by an instrument evidencing lease rental debt stated in the report as being self-liquidating debt as being in accordance with law, it shall endorse its approval upon a duplicate original of the proceedings and return it to the local government unit. Upon receipt of the approval by the local government unit, the principal amount of bonds, notes or obligations shall be excluded from nonelectoral debt or net lease rental debt, as the case may be, during the period of construction and thereafter until new electoral, nonelectoral or lease rental debt is to be incurred. At that time, if the principal is to be excluded, a certification of no decrease, other than decreases resulting from the payment of bonds or notes, in the amount to be excluded shall be included in the debt statement to be filed pursuant to section 8110 (relating to debt statement). If there is a decrease, or if more of the debt is desired to be excluded as self-liquidating, a new certification shall be filed.

§ 8027. Effect of debt limitations on outstanding debt.

Notwithstanding anything in other law or in this subpart, this subpart shall not be construed to invalidate any debt which was lawful when incurred or which could have been lawfully incurred if this subpart had been in effect, whether incurred before or after the passage of this subpart, and the percentage limitations set forth in section 8022 (relating to limitations on incurring of other debt) shall be deemed increased to the extent necessary to cover such incurred debt. This subpart shall not be construed to subject any debt incurred and voted upon prior to July 12, 1972, as electoral debt to any of the limitations herein imposed by this subpart on nonelectoral debt.

§ 8028. Determination of existing net nonelectoral debt and net nonelectoral plus net lease rental debt.

(a) Gross nonelectoral and lease rental debt.—From the gross principal amount of all incurred debt shall be subtracted gross incurred electoral debt. The amount remaining shall then be separated into gross incurred nonelectoral debt and gross incurred lease rental debt.

(b) Net nonelectoral and lease rental debt.—Net nonelectoral and net lease rental debt shall then be determined by subtracting separately from gross nonelectoral debt and gross lease rental debt respectively, as may be applicable, and as the local government unit may desire to claim the following:

(1) All funds in the applicable sinking funds, whether controlled by the local government unit or by the authority which incurred the debt, reserve funds or accounts, except maintenance and replacement reserve funds or accounts, and net bond proceeds, held for the payment of the cost of a project financed by the debt, including, in each case, interest accrued thereon, but only to the extent that those funds are available for payment of the principal amount of the debt.

(2) The current appropriation for the payment of the principal of and overdue interest on the nonelectoral debt or for the payment of the net lease rental in the case of lease rental debt, except to the extent that the same has already been deposited in sinking funds.

(3) The uncollected amount of the benefits or costs or the estimates thereof which have been or are authorized to be assessed against owners of property and for which liens may be legally filed, to the extent that the assessments are available for the payment of the principal amount of the debt.

(4) The amount of delinquent taxes from prior years and other undisputed municipal liens actually filed against property less the sum of:

(i) A reserve, reasonable in amount, for so much thereof as may not be collected.

(ii) The amount thereof appropriated for current expenses in the current year's budget.

(5) The amount of self-liquidating debt, subsidized debt and debt issued to fund an unfunded actuarial accrued liability, properly excluded and concurrently excludable from each respective category being computed.

(6) The amount of surplus cash not specifically appropriated to any purpose and available for the payment of the principal amount of debt, but if this deduction is claimed, the amount so claimed may not thereafter be appropriated to any purpose except the payment of debt.

(7) All other solvent debts due the local government unit directly, the payment of which can be enforced as one of the unit's quick assets, and which have not been committed to any other purpose.

(8) The amount of any insurance coverage indemnifying the local government unit against any outstanding liability to the extent the liability is debt.

(c) **Priority of applying exclusions.**—In determining net nonelectoral debt, the amounts claimed under subsection (b)(8) shall be exclusively applicable to nonelectoral debt, and subsection (b)(4), (6) and (7) shall be first applied against nonelectoral debt, with any excess being applicable against lease rental debt.

(d) **Valuation of legal investments.**—In computing the value of any funds, all legal investments therein shall be computed at current market values.

(e) **Use of debt determinations.**—The net nonelectoral debt so determined shall be used in determining compliance with the limit imposed by section 8022(a) (relating to limitations on incurring of other debt). The sum of the net nonelectoral debt and the net lease rental debt so determined shall be used in determining compliance with the limit imposed by section 8022(b).

§ 8029. Determination of debt limits.

Whenever it is necessary to determine the limitations on the amount of nonelectoral debt, or nonelectoral debt plus lease rental debt that may be incurred by any local government unit, the appropriate percentage limitations of section 8022 (relating to limitations on incurring of other debt) shall be applied to the borrowing base of the local government unit. The certificate as to the borrowing base shall be made a part of all proceedings for the sale of bonds or notes, for the guaranty of authority obligations or for the incurring of lease rental debt and a copy shall be filed with the department as a part of all proceedings required to be filed for its approval. The borrowing base set forth in the certificate and a similar certificate as to net nonelectoral debt or net lease rental debt outstanding shall be conclusive as to the respective figures for the purposes of this subpart, upon the approval of the proceedings by the department, unless contested within the specified time limits as provided in this subpart.

Subchapter C. Procedure for Securing Approval of Electors

§ 8041. Desire resolution and expense of certain elections.

(a) **Resolution.**—Whenever the governing body of any local government unit shall determine that it is advisable to make an increase in the debt of the local government unit with the assent of the electors, or to obtain the assent of the electors to transfer any debt previously incurred without the approval of the electors to electoral debt, it shall adopt a resolution signifying that determination, calling an election for the purpose of obtaining the assent and approving the content and substantial form of notice of election.

(b) Date of election.—The date fixed shall be that of a municipal, general, primary or special election for other purposes, but if the date of the nearest of the elections is more than 90 or less than 30 days from the effective date of the desire resolution, the governing body may fix a date for a special election.

(c) Payment of expense of special election.—In the case of a special election to increase debt not held concurrently with an election for other purposes, the expense of holding the election shall be paid by the local government unit for whose benefit it is held.

§ 8042. Advertisement of election.

(a) General rule.—Notice of the election shall be given in one but not more than two newspapers of general circulation in the local government unit and in the legal journal, if any, designated by the rules of court of the county in which the local government unit is located for the publication of legal notices and advertisements. If only newspaper publication is done, the notice shall be published three times at intervals of not less than three days, but if published in a weekly newspaper and in the legal journal, it shall be published only twice, once a week for two successive weeks. The first publication in at least one newspaper shall be not less than 14 nor more than 21 days before the election, but all publications shall be after the effective date of the resolution and need not be upon the same dates in different newspapers.

(b) Content of election notice.—The election notice shall contain and state:

(1) The date upon which the election is to be held.

(2) The estimated amount of the debt to be incurred or to be approved by the electors if already incurred.

(3) The project for which the debt will be or was incurred.

(4) The estimated cost of the project.

(5) The question to be submitted to the electors at the election, which shall be substantially in the following appropriate form:

Shall debt in the sum of (insert amount) dollars for the purpose of financing (insert brief description of project) be (authorized to be incurred as) (transferred from nonelectoral debt to) debt approved by the electors?

§ 8043. Conduct of election.

(a) Certification of resolution and question.—The governing body, at least 45 days before any election called pursuant to section 8041 (relating to desire resolution and expense of certain elections) shall cause to be certified to the county board of elections of each county in which the election is to be held a copy of the desire resolution and the form of the question to be submitted to the electors.

(b) Regulation of election.—An election called pursuant to section 8041 shall be held at the place, during the hours and under the same regulations as provided by law for the holding of municipal elections. In receiving, counting and making returns of the votes cast, the inspectors, judges and clerks of the election shall be governed by the act of June 3, 1937 (P.L. 1333, No. 320),[5] known as the Pennsylvania Election Code.

(c) Qualification of electors.—At the elections, only qualified electors of the local government unit, the debt of which is to be increased or approved by the electors may vote.

5. 25 P.S. §§ 2600 et seq.

(d) Election returns.—The election officers and clerks shall make return on forms provided by the county board of elections of the votes cast on the question to the county board of elections. The county board of elections shall compute the vote and transmit a certified return thereof to the governing body of the local government unit, which shall enter the same on its minutes. If the certified return shows that a majority of those voting on the question have voted in favor thereof, irrespective of any other statute requiring a greater percentage, the local government unit shall file with the department a certified copy of the desire resolution, the certified return and proofs of publication of the notice of election, whereupon the amount of the debt so approved shall constitute electoral debt from the date of the election, subject to the provisions of section 8044 (relating to finality of result of election).

§ 8044. Finality of result of election.

Any interested party or any taxpayer may contest the validity of any election proceedings under this subchapter by filing with the court a complaint in equity, specifically alleging any errors complained of in the proceedings, and the petitioner shall have the burden of proof. If no complaint has been filed or if a complaint has been filed and has been finally dismissed, the election shall be conclusively deemed to be valid. If, prior to the timely filing of a complaint, further proceedings in connection with the incurring of the debt have been filed with the department, then any contest shall proceed by way of an appeal from the action of the department upon the proceedings. The petition or appeal provided by this section shall be the party's or the taxpayer's sole and exclusive remedies.

§ 8045. Effect of defeat of question.

If at the election the question is defeated, another election for the same purpose may not be held until 155 days have elapsed since the prior election. During the interim no bonds or notes may be issued and no lease rental debt may be incurred for such purpose, except that nonelectoral or lease rental debt may be incurred if required to complete projects already under construction, to finance a different portion or portions of a capital budget or to evidence debt incurred for purposes and pursuant to a court approval obtained in accordance with section 8022(e) (relating to limitations on incurring of other debt).

§ 8046. Issuance of bonds, notes or other instruments to evidence electoral debt.

If, at the election, the question is approved, the governing body shall issue bonds or notes as electoral debt as obligations of the local government unit or shall authorize execution and delivery of an instrument which, but for the electoral approval, would evidence lease rental debt at the times and evidencing the amounts of obligations not exceeding in the aggregate the estimated amount approved by the electors, subject to the provisions of Subchapter C of Chapter 81 (relating to provisions of bonds and notes). The bonds, notes or obligations shall continue for such term as may have been stated in the notice of election or, if none was stated, for the term the governing body determines. The initial series may be of bond anticipation notes or of notes to be refunded by a bond issue. If the governing body determines it advisable, the initial series of bonds or notes constituting a part of the issue may be for a shorter term of years, with the maturity of subsequent series stated to mature later than the last stated maturity of the preceding series for the same project. This subchapter shall not preclude the issue of additional nonelectoral debt or lease rental debt to complete the project or the issue of additional electoral debt for that purpose if authorized by a subsequent election.

§ 8047. Cancellation or termination of approval of electors.

(a) Lapse of time.—On the tenth anniversary of the date on which an assent of the electors obtained under this subpart became final, the authority to issue any or any further bonds or notes, other than as nonelectoral debt or lease rental debt subject to the limitations imposed by this subpart, shall terminate.

(b) Resolution of governing body.—The governing body of any local government unit may by resolution, without the assent of the electors, rescind or cancel, in whole or in part, the authorization to incur electoral debt for any reason stated in the resolution, and thereupon the assent of the electors shall be of no further effect. A certified copy of the resolution with proof of the due publication thereof shall be filed with the department.

§ 8048. Limitation on use of proceeds of electoral debt.

Where bonds or notes have been issued pursuant to an assent of the electors given under this subpart, the proceeds thereof shall be kept in a separate account and shall be invested and used only for the cost, including the retirement of notes previously issued for the same project with the proceeds of bonds, of the project for which the assent was obtained unless such purpose is changed as provided in this subpart. Otherwise, the proceeds shall be kept invested and used for the retirement at maturity, or earlier call date, of the fifth or any subsequent stated maturity of the relevant series of bonds or notes, unless the proceeds were previously used to purchase the bonds or notes in the open market or upon tenders at prices not exceeding the principal amount thereof plus accrued and unpaid interest to the date of purchase.

§ 8049. Manner of changing purpose of electoral debt.

If the governing body determines it to be advisable either before or after the issue of bonds or notes to use the proceeds, or any part thereof, of bonds or notes evidencing electoral debt for any purpose other than the project approved by the electors or the payment or prior redemption or purchase of bonds or notes evidencing debt incurred for the project, the governing body shall by resolution express its desire to do so, specifying the project for which the funds are proposed to be used, and shall provide for an election to be held in like manner, time and place as provided in this subchapter for elections to secure the assent of the electors to the increase of debt, except that the notice of the election shall state:

(1) The date on which such election is to be held.

(2) The date and amount of money theretofore borrowed and the project for which borrowed.

(3) The amount of money remaining unused.

(4) The new purpose for which the local government unit desires to make use of the money.

(5) The reason why the money is not being used for the purpose for which it was borrowed.

(6) The question to be submitted to the electors, which shall be substantially in the following form:

Shall the sum of (insert amount) dollars heretofore borrowed or authorized to be borrowed by this local government unit for the purpose of (state purpose) be used for the purpose of (state purpose)?

The election shall be conducted, return made thereon, notices of election published and certificates filed and recorded as provided in section 8043 (relating to conduct of election). If it appears that a majority of those voting on the question have voted in favor of using the funds for the changed purpose, irrespective of any other statute requiring a greater percentage, the funds specified may be used for the changed purpose.

CHAPTER 7

OPTIONAL OCCUPATION TAX ELIMINATION ACT

53 P.S. §§ 6927.1–6927.9

The Optional Occupation Tax Elimination Act is REPEALED. For the text of statutory material dealing with the subject matter see Chapter 4 of the LOCAL TAX ENABLING ACT 53 P.S. §§6901 et. seq., appearing in this Municipal Lawsource as Part II, Chapter 4, §§ 401–409.

CHAPTER 8

LOCAL TAXPAYERS BILL OF RIGHTS

58 Pa.C.S. §§ 8421-8438

TABLE OF CONTENTS

---

§ 8421. Short title of subchapter.

This subchapter shall be known and may be cited as the Local Taxpayers Bill of Rights Act.

§ 8422. Definitions.

The following words and phrases when used in this subchapter shall have the meanings given to them in this section unless the context clearly indicates otherwise:

"Assessment." The determination by a local taxing authority of the amount of underpayment by a taxpayer.

"Board." A board of local tax appeals established under section 8430 (relating to administrative appeals).

"Eligible tax." Any of the following, including interest and penalty provided by law, when levied by a political subdivision:

(1) Any tax authorized or permitted under the act of December 31, 1965 (P.L. 1257, No. 511), [53 P.S. § 6901 et seq] known as The Local Tax Enabling Act.

(2) Any per capita tax levied under any act.

(3) Any occupation, occupation assessment or occupation privilege tax levied under any act.

(4) Any tax on income levied under any act.

(5) Any tax measured by gross receipts levied under any act.

(6) Any tax on a privilege levied under any act.

Table of Contents
Part I Ch. 1–3 Ethics, Records, Open Meetings
Part II Ch. 4–10 Taxation
Part III Ch. 11–18 Torts, Contracts & Civil Rules
Part IV Ch. 19–24 Zoning & Planning
Part V Ch. 25–30 Construction and Emergency Codes
Part VI Ch. 31–39 Municipal Codes
Index

Chapter 10 Residential Design Tax Credit
Chapter 9 Neighborhood Improvement
Chapter 8 Local Taxpayers Bill of Rights
Chapter 7 Occupation Tax Elimination Act
Chapter 6 Local Government Unit Debt Act
Chapter 5 Local Tax Collection Law
Chapter 4 Local Tax Enabling Act

(7) Any tax on amusements or admissions levied under any act.

(8) Any tax on earned income and net profits.

"Governing body." A city council, borough council, incorporated town council, board of township commissioners, board of township supervisors, a governing council of a home rule municipality or optional plan municipality, a governing council of any similar general purpose unit of government which may hereafter be created by statute or a board of school directors of a school district.

"Local taxing authority." A political subdivision levying an eligible tax. The term shall include any officer, agent, agency, clerk, income tax officer, collector, employee or other person to whom the governing body has assigned responsibility for the audit, assessment, determination or administration of an eligible tax. The term shall not include a tax collector or collection agency who has no authority to audit a taxpayer or determine the amount of an eligible tax or whose only responsibility is to collect an eligible tax on behalf of the governing body.

"Overpayment." Any payment of tax which is determined in the manner provided by law not to be legally due.

"Taxpayer." An individual, partnership, association, corporation, limited liability company, estate, trust, trustee, fiduciary or any other entity subject to or claiming exemption from any eligible tax or under a duty to perform an act for itself or for another under or pursuant to the authority of an act providing for an eligible tax.

"Underpayment." The amount or portion of any tax determined to be legally due in the manner provided by law for which payment or remittance has not been made.

"Voluntary payment." A payment of an eligible tax made pursuant to the free will of the taxpayer. The term does not include a payment made as a result of distraint or levy or pursuant to a legal proceeding in which the local taxing authority is seeking to collect its delinquent taxes or file a claim therefor.

§ 8423. Disclosure statement.

(a) Contents.—The local taxing authority shall prepare a statement which sets forth the following in simple and nontechnical terms:

(1) The rights of a taxpayer and the obligation of the local taxing authority during an audit or an administrative review of the taxpayer's books or records.

(2) The administrative and judicial procedures by which a taxpayer may appeal or seek review of any adverse decision of the local taxing authority.

(3) The procedure for filing and processing refund claims and taxpayer complaints.

(4) The enforcement procedures.

(b) Distribution.—The local taxing authority shall notify any taxpayer contacted regarding the assessment, audit, determination, review or collection of an eligible tax of the availability of the statement under subsection (a). The local taxing authority shall make copies of the statement available to taxpayers upon request at no charge to the taxpayer, including mailing costs. The notification shall be stated as follows:

You are entitled to receive a written explanation of your rights with regard to the audit, appeal, enforcement, refund and collection of local taxes by calling (name of local taxing authority) at (telephone number) during the hours of (hours of operation).

§ 8424. Requirements for requests.

(a) Minimum time periods for taxpayer response.—

(1) The taxpayer shall have at least 30 calendar days from the mailing date to respond to requests for information by a local taxing authority. The local

taxing authority shall grant additional reasonable extensions upon application for good cause.

(2) The local taxing authority shall notify the taxpayer of the procedures to obtain an extension in its initial request.

(3) A local taxing authority shall take no lawful action against a taxpayer for the tax year in question until the expiration of the applicable response period, including extensions.

(b) Requests for prior year returns.—

(1) Except as provided in paragraph (2), an initial inquiry by a local taxing authority regarding a taxpayer's compliance with any eligible tax may include taxes required to be paid or tax returns required to be filed no more than three years prior to the mailing date of the notice.

(2) A local taxing authority may make a subsequent request for a tax return or supporting information if, after the initial request, the local taxing authority determines that the taxpayer failed to file a tax return, underreported income or failed to pay a tax for one or more of the tax periods covered by the initial request.

This subsection shall not apply if the local taxing authority has sufficient information to indicate that the taxpayer failed to file a required return or pay an eligible tax which was due more than three years prior to the date of the notice.

(c) Use of Federal tax information.—A local taxing authority may require a taxpayer to provide copies of the taxpayer's Federal individual income tax return if the local taxing authority can demonstrate that the Federal tax information is reasonably necessary for the enforcement or collection of an eligible tax and the information is not available from other available sources or the Department of Revenue.

§ 8425. Refunds of overpayments.

(a) General rule.—A taxpayer who has paid an eligible tax to a local taxing authority may file a written request with the local taxing authority for refund or credit of the eligible tax. A request for refund shall be made within three years of the due date for filing the report as extended or one year after actual payment of the eligible tax, whichever is later. If no report is required, the request shall be made within three years after the due date for payment of the eligible tax or within one year after actual payment of the eligible tax, whichever is later.

(1) For purposes of this section, a tax return filed by the taxpayer with the local taxing authority showing an overpayment of tax shall be deemed to be a written request for a cash refund unless otherwise indicated on the tax return.

(2) A request for refund under this section shall not be considered a petition under section 8430 (relating to administrative appeals) and shall not preclude a taxpayer from submitting a petition under section 8431 (relating to petitions).

(b) Notice of underpayment.—For amounts paid as a result of a notice asserting or informing a taxpayer of an underpayment, a written request for refund shall be filed with the local taxing authority within one year of the date of the payment.

§ 8426. Interest on overpayment.

(a) General rule.—All overpayments of tax due a local taxing authority, including taxes on real property, shall bear simple interest from the date of overpayment until the date of resolution.

(b) Interest rate.—Interest on overpayments shall be allowed and paid at the same rate as the Commonwealth is required to pay pursuant to section 806.1 of the act of April 9, 1929 (P.L. 343, No. 176), [72 P.S. § 806.1] known as The Fiscal Code.

(c) Exceptions.—

(1) No interest shall be allowed if an overpayment is refunded or applied against any other tax, interest or penalty due the local taxing authority within 75 days after the last date prescribed for filing the report of the tax liability or within 75 days after the date the return or report of the liability due is filed, whichever is later.

(2) Overpayments of interest or penalty shall not bear any interest.

(d) Acceptance of refund check.—The taxpayer's acceptance of the local taxing authority's check shall not prejudice any right of the taxpayer to claim any additional overpayment and interest thereon. Tender of a refund check by the local taxing authority shall be deemed to be acceptance of the check by the taxpayer for purposes of this section.

(e) Definitions.—As used in this section, the following words and phrases shall have the meanings given to them in this subsection:

"Date of overpayment." The later of the date paid or the date tax is deemed to have been overpaid as follows:

(1) Any tax actually deducted and withheld at the source shall be deemed to have been overpaid on the last day for filing the report for the tax period, determined without regard to any extension of time for filing.

(2) Any amount overpaid as estimated tax for the tax period shall be deemed to have been overpaid on the last day for filing the final report for the tax period, determined without regard to any extension of time for filing.

(3) An overpayment made before the last day prescribed for payment shall be deemed to have been paid on the last day.

(4) Any amount claimed to be overpaid with respect to which a lawful administrative review or appellate procedure is initiated shall be deemed to have been overpaid 60 days following the date of initiation of the review or procedure.

(5) Any amount shown not to be due on an amended income or earned income and net profits tax return shall be deemed to have been overpaid 60 days following the date of filing of the amended income tax return.

"Date of resolution." The date the overpayment is refunded or credited as follows:

(1) For a cash refund, a date preceding the date of the local taxing authority's refund check by not more than 30 days.

(2) For a credit for an overpayment:

(i) the date of the local taxing authority's notice to the taxpayer of the determination of the credit; or

(ii) the due date for payment of the tax against which the credit is applied, whichever first occurs. For a cash refund of a previously determined credit, interest shall be paid on the amount of the credit from a date 90 days after the filing of a request to convert the credit to a cash refund to a date preceding the date of the refund check by not more than 30 days whether or not the refund check is accepted by the taxpayer after tender.

§ 8427. Notice of basis of underpayment.

A local taxing authority shall notify the taxpayer in writing of the basis for any underpayment that the local taxing authority has determined to exist. The notification shall include:

(1) The tax period or periods for which the underpayment is asserted.

(2) The amount of the underpayment detailed by tax period.

(3) The legal basis upon which the local taxing authority has relied to determine that an underpayment exists.

(4) An itemization of the revisions made by the local taxing authority to a return or report filed by the taxpayer that results in the determination that an underpayment exists.

§ 8428. Abatement of certain interest and penalty.

(a) Errors and delays.—In the case of any underpayment, the local taxing authority may abate all or any part of interest for any period for the following:

(1) Any underpayment or tax finally determined to be due attributable in whole or in part to any error or delay by the local taxing authority in the performance of a ministerial act. For purposes of this paragraph, an error or delay shall be taken into account only if no significant aspect of the error or delay can be attributed to the taxpayer and after the local taxing authority has contacted the taxpayer in writing with respect to the underpayment of tax finally determined to be due or payable.

(2) Any payment of a tax to the extent that any error or delay in the payment is attributable to an officer, employee or agent of the local taxing authority being erroneous or dilatory in performance of a ministerial act. The local taxing authority shall determine what constitutes timely performance of ministerial acts performed under this subchapter.

(b) Abatement due to erroneous written advice by local taxing authority.—

(1) The local taxing authority shall abate any portion of any penalty or excess interest attributable to erroneous advice furnished to the taxpayer in writing by an officer, employee or agent of the local taxing authority acting in the officer's, employee's or agent's official capacity if:

(i) the written advice was reasonably relied upon by the taxpayer and was in response to specific written request of the taxpayer; and

(ii) the portion of the penalty or addition to tax or excess interest did not result from a failure by the taxpayer to provide adequate or accurate information.

(2) This subsection shall not be construed to require the local taxing authority to provide written advice to taxpayers.

§ 8429. Application of payments.

Unless otherwise specified by the taxpayer, all voluntary payments of an eligible tax shall be prioritized by the local taxing authority as follows:

(1) Tax.

(2) Interest.

(3) Penalty.

(4) Any other fees or charges.

§ 8430. Administrative appeals.

A political subdivision levying an eligible tax shall establish an administrative process to receive and make determinations on petitions from taxpayers relating to the assessment, determination or refund of an eligible tax. The administrative process shall consist of any one of the following:

(1) Review and decision or hearing and decision by a local tax appeals board appointed by the governing body. The board shall consist of at least three but not more than seven members. Qualifications for service on the board and compensation, if any, of the members shall be determined by the governing body. The governing body may enter into agreements with other political subdivisions to establish a joint local tax appeals board.

(2) Review and decision by the governing body in executive session.

Chapter 10 Residential Design Tax Credit
Chapter 9 Neighborhood Improvement
Chapter 8 Local Taxpayers Bill of Rights
Chapter 7 Occupation Tax Elimination Act
Chapter 6 Local Government Unit Debt Act
Chapter 5 Local Tax Collection Law
Chapter 4 Local Tax Enabling Act

(3) A hearing and decision by a hearing officer appointed by the governing body. The governing body shall determine the qualifications and compensation, if any, of the hearing officer.

(4) An administrative review or appeal process existing on the effective date of this chapter that is substantially similar to the procedures in paragraph (1), (2) or (3).

§ 8431. Petitions.

(a) Filing.—A petition is timely filed if the letter transmitting the petition is postmarked by the United States Postal Service on or before the final day on which the petition is required to be filed. Deadlines for filing petitions are as follows:

(1) Refund petitions shall be filed within three years after the due date for filing the report as extended or one year after actual payment of an eligible tax, whichever is later. If no report is required, the petition shall be filed within three years after the due date for payment of an eligible tax or within one year after actual payment, whichever is later.

(2) Petitions for reassessment of an eligible tax shall be filed within 90 days of the date of the assessment notice.

(b) Contents.—The governing body shall adopt regulations specifying the form and content of petitions, including the process and deadlines.

§ 8432. Practice and procedure.

Practice and procedure under this subchapter shall not be governed by 2 Pa.C.S. Chs. 5 Subch. B (relating to practice and procedure of local agencies) and 7 Subch. B (relating to judicial review of local agency action). The governing body shall adopt regulations governing practice and procedure under this subchapter.

§ 8433. Decisions.

Decisions on petitions submitted under this subchapter shall be issued within 60 days of the date a complete and accurate petition is received. Failure to act within 60 days shall result in the petition being deemed approved.

§ 8434. Appeals.

Any person aggrieved by a decision under this chapter who has a direct interest in the decision shall have the right to appeal to the court vested with the jurisdiction of local tax appeals by or pursuant to 42 Pa.C.S. (relating to judiciary and judicial procedure).

§ 8435. Equitable and legal principles to apply.

Decisions under this chapter may be made according to principles of law and equity.

§ 8436. Installment agreements.

(a) Authorization.—A local taxing authority may enter into written agreements with any taxpayer under which the taxpayer is allowed to satisfy liability for any eligible tax in installment payments if the local taxing authority determines that the agreement will facilitate collection.

(b) Extent to which agreements remain in effect.—

(1) Except as otherwise provided in this subsection, any agreement entered into by the local taxing authority under subsection (a) shall remain in effect for the term of the agreement.

(2) The local taxing authority may terminate any prior agreement entered into under subsection (a) if:

(i) information which the taxpayer provided to the local taxing authority prior to the date of the agreement was inaccurate or incomplete; or

(ii) the local taxing authority believes that collection of any eligible tax under the agreement is in jeopardy.

(3) If the local taxing authority finds that the financial condition of the taxpayer has significantly changed, the local taxing authority may alter, modify or terminate the agreement, but only if:

(i) notice of the local taxing authority's finding is provided to the taxpayer no later than 30 days prior to the date of such action; and

(ii) the notice contains the reasons why the local taxing authority believes a significant change has occurred.

(4) The local taxing authority may alter, modify or terminate an agreement entered into by the local taxing authority under subsection (a) if the taxpayer fails to do any of the following:

(i) Pay any installment at the time the installment is due under such agreement.

(ii) Pay any other tax liability at the time the liability is due.

(iii) Provide a financial condition update as requested by the local taxing authority.

(c) Prepayment permitted.—Nothing in this section shall prevent a taxpayer from prepaying in whole or in part any eligible tax under any agreement with the local taxing authority.

§ 8437. Confidentiality of tax information.

Any information gained by a local taxing authority as a result of any audit, return, report, investigation, hearing or verification shall be confidential tax information. It shall be unlawful, except for official purposes or as provided by law, for any local taxing authority to:

(1) Divulge or make known in any manner any confidential information gained in any return, investigation, hearing or verification to any person.

(2) Permit confidential tax information or any book containing any abstract or particulars thereof to be seen or examined by any person.

(3) Print, publish or make known in any manner any confidential tax information.

An offense under this section is a misdemeanor of the third degree, and, upon conviction thereof, a fine of not more than $2,500 and costs, or a term of imprisonment for not more than one year, or both, may be imposed. If the offender is an officer or employee of the local taxing authority, the officer or employee shall be dismissed from office or discharged from employment.

§ 8438. Taxes on real property.

Except as provided in section 8426 (relating to interest on overpayment), this subchapter shall not apply to any tax on real property.

CHAPTER 9

NEIGHBORHOOD IMPROVEMENT DISTRICT ACT

73 P.S. §§ 831–840

TABLE OF CONTENTS

---

§ 1. Short title.

This act shall be known and may be cited as the Neighborhood Improvement District Act.

§ 2. Legislative findings.

The General Assembly finds that:

(1) Existing tax rates in many municipalities are at or near their statutory cap.

(2) The General Fund revenue derived from these taxes many times is not sufficient to provide adequate municipal services or additional services needed in specific geographic areas within the municipality, including, but not limited to, downtown commercial districts.

(3) As a result, municipalities should be encouraged to create, where feasible and desired, assessment-based neighborhood improvement districts which would include, but not be limited to, downtown commercial districts. Designated district management associations would initiate and administer programs to promote and enhance more attractive and safer commercial, industrial, residential and mixed-use neighborhoods; economic growth; increased employment opportunities; and improved commercial, industrial, business districts and business climates.

(4) Municipalities should be given the broadest possible discretion in establishing by local ordinance the type of assessment-based programs most consistent with neighborhood needs, goals and objectives as determined and expressed by property owners in the designated district.

§ 3. Definitions.

The following words and phrases when used in this act shall have the meanings given to them in this section unless the context clearly indicates otherwise:

"Authority." A body politic and corporate, created pursuant to the act of May 2, 1945 (P.L.382, No.164), known as the Municipality Authorities Act of 1945.

"Benefited property." Those properties located within a neighborhood improvement district which profit from district improvements based on a ra-

Table of Contents
Part I Ch. 1–3 Ethics, Records, Open Meetings
Part II Ch. 4–10 Taxation
Part III Ch. 11–18 Torts, Contracts & Civil Rules
Part IV Ch. 19–24 Zoning & Planning
Part V Ch. 25–30 Construction and Emergency Codes
Part VI Ch. 31–39 Municipal Codes
Index

tional nexus test. Properties need not profit equally to be considered to have benefited.

"Bonds." The term shall include the notes, bonds and other evidence of indebtedness or obligations which each municipal corporation is authorized to issue under section 4(7).[1]

"Business improvement." In the case of neighborhood improvement district management associations created for the purpose of making improvements or providing administrative services within a neighborhood improvement district, the term shall mean those improvements needed in specific areas or to individual properties, including, but not limited to, sidewalks, retaining walls, street paving, parks, recreational equipment and facilities, open space, street lighting, parking lots, parking garages, trees and shrubbery, pedestrian walks, sewers, water lines, rest areas and the acquisition and rehabilitation or demolition of blighted buildings or structures.

"Business improvement district." A business improvement district (BID) created prior to the effective date of this act, governed by the act of May 2, 1945 (P.L. 382, No. 164), known as the Municipality Authorities Act of 1945, insofar as it relates to business improvement districts or 53 Pa.C.S. Ch. 54 (relating to business improvement districts). On or after the effective date of this act, the term shall mean a limited geographical area comprised of real property which is used for any for-profit activity involving trade and traffic, or commerce in general.

"Commercial." Relating to or associated with any for-profit activity involving trade and traffic or commerce in general.

"Construction expenditures." Property and right-of-way acquisition costs where applicable.

"Costs of improvements." The term includes architectural fees, engineering fees, attorney fees, consulting fees, professional fees, preliminary planning expenditures, feasibility study expenditures, financing costs and any other expenditures necessary and incidental to the development, construction or completion of the improvement.

"District advisory council." A committee comprised of property owners from a neighborhood improvement district established under section 7(a), for the purpose of providing guidance and direction to the neighborhood improvement district management association concerning association activities within the district.

"Industrial district." A limited, geographical area comprised of real property which is used predominantly for manufacturing, commercial or any other activity related to the distribution of goods and services and intermediate and final products, including, but not limited to, warehousing, shipping, transportation, remanufacturing, stockpiling of raw materials, repair and maintenance of machinery and equipment, storage, administration or business activities, and research and development.

"Institution." The term includes, but is not limited to, colleges, universities, schools, hospitals, museums, theaters, churches, synagogues, art centers or similar facilities.

"Institutional district." A limited, geographical area comprised predominantly of real property on which educational, health-related or cultural activities occur within buildings and structures, including, but not limited to, colleges, universities, schools, hospitals, museums, theaters, churches, synagogues and art centers.

1. "4(5)." in enrolled bill.

"Mixed-use district." A limited, geographical area comprised of real property used for any or all purposes contained within a business, residential, industrial or institutional district.

"Municipal corporation." The body or board authorized by law to enact ordinances or adopt resolutions for the particular municipality.

"Municipality." With the exception of cities of the first class, any city, borough, incorporated town, township, home rule, optional plan or optional charter municipality, located within this Commonwealth.

"Neighborhood." A limited geographic area within a municipality establishing a neighborhood improvement district, the limits of which form the neighborhood improvement district boundary.

"Neighborhood improvement." Improvements needed in specific geographic areas or to individual properties within those areas, including, but not limited to, sidewalks, retaining walls, street paving, parks, recreational equipment and facilities, open space, street lighting, parking lots, trees and shrubbery, sewers, water lines, rest areas and the acquisition and rehabilitation or demolition of deteriorated buildings or structures.

"Neighborhood improvement district." A limited geographic area within a municipality, in which a special assessment is levied on all designated property, other than tax-exempt property, for the purpose of promoting the economic and general welfare of the district and the municipality, hereinafter referred to as NID. Such districts shall be referred to generally as neighborhood improvement district (NID) and specifically as business improvement district (BID), residential improvement district (RID), industrial improvement district (IID), institutional improvement district (INID) or mixed-use improvement district (MID), depending on the type district established. A designated property may not be included in more than one neighborhood improvement district.

"Neighborhood improvement district management association." The governing body which oversees the management of neighborhood improvement districts in a municipality as established under section 5 which hereinafter shall be referred to as the NIDMA. Such body shall be incorporated as a nonprofit corporation in this Commonwealth or an authority as established pursuant to the act of May 2, 1945 (P.L. 382, No. 164), known as the Municipality Authorities Act of 1945.

"Neighborhood improvement district plan." The strategic plan for neighborhood improvements required by section 5, hereinafter referred to as NIDP, and all projects, programs and supplemental services to be provided within the district to implement the plan by the neighborhood improvement district management association.

"Neighborhood improvement district services." In the case of neighborhood improvement district management associations created for the purpose of making improvements or providing expanded services within any neighborhood business improvement districts established, the term shall include, but not be limited to, those services which improve the ability of the commercial establishments within the district to serve the consumer, such as free or reduced-fee parking for customers, transportation-related expenses, public relations programs, group advertising and district maintenance and security services. For services provided within any residential, industrial, institutional or mixed-use neighborhood improvement district, the term shall include, but not be limited to, those services which improve the ability of property owners to enjoy a safer and more attractive neighborhood through the provision of increased or expanded services, including street lighting, street cleaning, street maintenance, parks, recreational equipment and facilities, open space and/or security services.

"Nonprofit corporation." A legal entity that is incorporated within this Commonwealth and specifies in its charter or bylaws that no part of the net earnings may benefit any private shareholder or individual holding interest in such entity.

"Private security officer." Any person or firm employed by the neighborhood improvement district management association for the purpose of providing increased security or protective patrol services within the neighborhood improvement district. The term may include off-duty police officers provided that the use of such officers for this purpose is approved by the governing body of the municipality in which the neighborhood improvement district is located or the municipality where the officer is employed if different.

"Project." The acquisition, development, construction, improvement, rehabilitation, operation and/or maintenance of any building, facility, equipment or structure, by purchase, lease or contract, by a neighborhood improvement district management association to facilitate neighborhood and business improvements as authorized by this act.

"Rational nexus." The legal principle which requires that there is a rational, definable benefit which accrues to any property owner assessed a fee for said benefit in a neighborhood improvement district created under this act. All property owners within a designated neighborhood improvement district paying a special assessment fee must benefit directly or indirectly from facilities or services provided by a neighborhood improvement district management association within the neighborhood improvement district, provided, however, that property owners need not benefit equally.

"Residential district." A limited, geographical area comprised of real property consisting predominantly of buildings and structures for housing individuals and families, including, but not limited to, single family detached homes, single-family semidetached homes, townhouses, condominiums, apartments, manufactured homes, modular homes or any combination of same.

"Service area." The area within the boundaries of the neighborhood improvement district established by a municipality under this act in which the neighborhood improvement district management association provides programs, services and improvements. The term may also include an area outside of the neighborhood improvement district where services are being provided by the neighborhood improvement district management association under contract.

"Special assessment fee." The fee assessed on property owners within a neighborhood improvement district levied by the municipality establishing a neighborhood improvement district under section 4(10)[2] for the purposes of providing programs, improvements and services under section 7.

"Sunset provision." The term means a provision in the neighborhood improvement district plan, under section 5(c), establishing a neighborhood improvement district, which provides for the automatic termination of the neighborhood improvement district on a date specified in the neighborhood improvement district plan and in the municipal ordinance establishing the neighborhood improvement district. The neighborhood improvement district may be continued beyond that date, provided the municipal enabling ordinance creating the original neighborhood improvement district is reenacted, following a review of the neighborhood improvement district and the neighborhood improvement district management association programs and services provided within the neighborhood improvement district, by the municipality.

2. "4(8)." in enrolled bill.

§ 4. Powers of municipal corporation.

Every municipal corporation shall have the power:

(1) To establish within the municipality an area or areas designated as an NID.

(2) To establish an authority to administer the NID or to designate an existing community development corporation or other existing nonprofit corporation to administer same or to create a community development corporation or other nonprofit corporation to administer same under sections 6 and 7.

(3) To appropriate and expend, in accordance with the specific provisions of the municipal enabling ordinance, municipal funds as may be required to:

(i) Acquire by purchase or lease real or personal property deemed necessary to effectuate the purposes of the NID.

(ii) Prepare or have prepared preliminary planning or feasibility studies to determine needed improvements in an NID, including, but not limited to, capital improvements, traditional streetscape and building renovations, retaining walls, street paving, street lighting, parking lots, parking garages, trees and shrubbery, pedestrian walks, sewers, water lines, rest areas, acquisition, rehabilitation or demolition of blighted buildings and structures, graffiti removal, security, marketing, promotions, advertising, business retention and recruitment activities, master leasing and property management, joint advertising, research and planning as well as the provision of additional services to supplement, not replace, existing municipal services provided within the NID.

(4) To advance funds to a NIDMA as may be required to carry out the purposes of this act.

(5) To collect special property assessments on behalf of the NIDMA levied on designated property owners within the NID and to employ any legal methods to insure collection of the assessments.

(6) To acquire by gift, purchase or eminent domain, land, real property or rights-of way which may be needed for the purposes of making physical improvements within the NID.

(7) To issue bonds, notes or guarantees, in accordance with the provisions of general laws in the amounts and for the periods necessary, to finance needed improvements within any NID.

(8) To review all proposed expenditures of funds within NIDs by NIDMAs and suggest changes to same where a nonprofit corporation is the NIDMA.

(9) To include a sunset provision of no less than five years in the municipal enabling ordinance creating the NID and in the contract with the NIDMA.

(10) To levy an assessment fee on property owners located within an NID needed to finance additional supplemental programs, services and improvements to be provided or made by the NIDMA.

§ 5. Creation of neighborhood improvement district.

(a) Establishment.—

(1) The governing body of the municipality or any municipal businesses or residents or combination thereof may initiate action to establish an NID or NIDs within the municipality under this act.

(2) In the case of businesses, or residents, or both desiring to establish an NID, where the municipality has not taken action to do so, the governing body of the municipality may be petitioned to establish an NID, under the procedures provided for by this act.

Table of Contents
Part I Ch. 1–3 Ethics, Records, Open Meetings
Part II Ch. 4–10 Taxation
Part III Ch. 11–18 Torts, Contracts & Civil Rules
Part IV Ch. 19–24 Zoning & Planning
Part V Ch. 25–30 Construction and Emergency Codes
Part VI Ch. 31–39 Municipal Codes
Index

(3) In no case where the governing body of a municipality is petitioned to establish an NID under paragraph (2), shall the municipality be required to establish an NID.

(b) Specific procedures.—

(1) A copy of everything required under this section, as well as the date, location and time of any public hearing required by this act, shall be provided by the municipal corporation to all property owners and lessees of property owners located in the proposed NID at least 30 days prior to the first public hearing required by this section.

(2) At least one public hearing, no earlier than 15 days apart, for the purpose of receiving public comment from affected property owners within the proposed NID, on the proposed NIDP, shall be held by the municipality before the establishment of an NID. Notice of the hearing shall be advertised at least ten days prior thereto in a newspaper of general circulation in the municipality.

(3) Any objections by property owners within the proposed NID must be made in writing by persons representing the ownership of 40%, in numbers, of the benefited properties within the NID. Objections must be signed by the property owner and filed in the office of the clerk for the governing body of the municipality in which the NID is proposed.

(c) Contents of preliminary plan.—The plan shall include the following:

(1) A map indicating the boundaries, by street, of the proposed NID; however, a designated property may not be included in more than one NID.

(2) A written report from the municipality containing:

(i) The name of the proposed district.

(ii) A detailed description of the service areas of the proposed district.

(iii) A list of all properties to be assessed.

(iv) A list of proposed improvements within the NID, and their estimated cost.

(v) A proposed budget for the first fiscal year, including, but not limited to, the following: personnel and administration, programs and services, maintenance and operation, and capital expenditures.

(vi) The proposed revenue sources for financing all proposed improvements, programs and services.

(vii) The estimated time for implementation and completion of all proposed improvements, programs and services.

(viii) A statement identifying the administrative body which will govern and administer the NID.

(ix) Any other information, including the statutory authority, or, in the case of a nonprofit corporation, the bylaws, which describe the powers and duties of and the method for making decisions by the NIDMA.

(x) The method of determining the amount of the assessment fee to be levied on property owners within the NID under section 7.

(3) In addition, the plan shall also:

(i) Identify in detail the specific duties and responsibilities of both the NIDMA and the municipal corporation with respect to the NID.

(ii) Require that a written agreement be signed by the municipal corporation and the NIDMA describing in detail their respective duties and responsibilities.

(iii) Allow for and encourage tax-exempt property owners located within the NID to provide in-kind services or a financial contribution to the NIDMA, if not assessed, in lieu of a property assessment fee.

(iv) Require in the agreement between the municipal corporation and the NIDMA that the municipality must maintain the same level of municipal programs and services provided within the NID before NID designation as after NID designation.

(v) Allow the municipal corporation the right to include in the agreement with the NIDMA and in the enabling ordinance establishing the NID a sunset provision of no less than five years for renewal of the agreement.

(vi) Require in the agreement with the NIDMA that the municipality establishing an NID shall be responsible for the collection of all property assessment fees levied within the NID if so desired by the NIDMA.

(vii) Provide that a negative vote of at least 40% of the property owners within the NID proposed NID by filing objections with the clerk for the governing body of the municipality within 45 days of presentation of the final plan where the governing body of municipality is inclined to establish the NID.

(d) Final plan.—Prior to the establishment of an NID, the municipality shall submit a revised final plan to property owners located within the proposed NID which incorporates changes made to the plan based on comments from affected property owners within the NID provided at the public hearings or at some other time. Changes to the final plan which differ from the preliminary plan shall also be so indicated in an easily discernible method for the reader, including, but not limited to, changes being in boldfaced or italicized type.

(e) Public hearing.—At least one public hearing for the purpose of receiving public comment on any revisions to the preliminary plan made following suggestions by affected property owners within the proposed NID and reflected in the final NIDP shall be held by the municipal corporation before enacting an ordinance establishing an NID. Notice of the hearing shall be advertised at least ten days prior thereto in a newspaper of general circulation in the municipality.

(f) Veto of final plan for NID.—

(1) Following the last public hearing required under subsection (e) or under subsection (g) if an amendment to the final plan, affected property owners located within a proposed NID shall have 45 days from the date of the hearing to object to and disapprove the final plan or any amendment to the final plan under the requirements of subsection (b)(3).

(2) If 40% or more of the affected property owners within the proposed NID fail to register their disapproval of the final plan or amendment to the final plan in writing with the clerk of the governing body of the municipality in which the NID is proposed, the governing body of the municipality may, following the 45-day period, enact a municipal ordinance establishing an NID under this act or, in the case of an amendment to the final plan, adopt any amendments to the ordinance.

(g) Amendments to final plan.—

(1) The final plan may be amended by the NIDMA any time after the establishment of an NID, pursuant to the provisions of this act, upon the recommendation of the NIDMA board, provided there is concurrence with 60% of the property owners within the NID.

(2) Amendments to the final plan which also require the approval of the governing body of the municipality establishing the NID include:

(i) Substantially changed or added programs, improvements and/or services to be provided in the NID.

(ii) Increased expenditures affecting more than 25% of the total NIDMA budget for the fiscal year.

(iii) Incurring increased indebtedness.

(iv) Changing the assessment fee structure levied on property owners in the NID.

(v) Changing the legal entity (NIDMA) which provides programs, improvements and services within the NID.

(vi) Changing the NID service area boundary.

Prior to the governing body of the municipality approving any of the changes in this paragraph, the governing body shall hold at least one public hearing to determine that such changes are in the public interest as it relates to affected property owners within the NID.

(3) The municipality shall provide public notice of the hearing for any amendments, by publication of a notice in at least one newspaper having a general circulation in the NID specifying the time and the place of such hearing and the amendments to be considered. This notice shall be published once at least 10 days prior to the date of the hearing.

(4) The governing body of the municipality may within 30 days following the public hearing and at its sole discretion approve or disapprove of any amendments to the plan. If approved, such amendments shall be effective upon the date of such approval.

(5) Prior to the adoption of any amendment to the NID boundary which increases the size of the NID, any owner of property to be added to the NID shall be notified of the date, time and location of the public hearing on the proposed amendment to the final plan and provided all information required by subsection (c).

§ 6. Creation of neighborhood improvement district management association.

(a) Association designated.—When a municipality establishes an NID under this act, a neighborhood improvement district management association shall be designated by the governing body of the municipality in which the NID is to be located to administer programs, improvements and services within the NID.

(b) Administration.—

(1) NIDs created pursuant to this act shall be administered by an NIDMA which shall be an authority created pursuant to the act of May 2, 1945 (P.L. 382, No. 164), known as the Municipality Authorities Act of 1945, an existing nonprofit development corporation, an existing nonprofit corporation or a nonprofit development corporation or nonprofit corporation established by the governing body or authorized to be established by the governing body of the municipality in which the NID is to be located, to administer the NIDP.

(2) If an active nonprofit development corporation already exists within the geographic boundaries of the NID and formally indicates its interest to the governing body of the municipality to become the designated NIDMA, the governing body of the municipality shall grant that request unless 40% or

more of the affected property owners within the proposed NID register their disapproval of this designation in writing with the clerk of the governing body within a 45-day period following the formal written request for designation by the nonprofit development corporation to become the NIDMA.

(c) Powers.—An NIDMA created under this act shall assume all powers provided for in section 7 immediately upon the effective date of the municipal ordinance enacted under section 4 creating an NID.

(d) Board.—Every NIDMA shall have an administrative board.

(1) Where an authority created pursuant to the Municipality Authorities Act of 1945 serves as the NIDMA, the board shall be appointed pursuant to the Municipality Authorities Act of 1945.

(2) Where an existing nonprofit development corporation or other nonprofit corporation is to serve as the NIDMA, the board shall be appointed according to the bylaws of the NIDMA filed with the Department of State.

(3) Where a nonprofit development corporation or other nonprofit corporation is established to serve as the NIDMA for an NID, the board shall be comprised of an odd number of members, between five and nine, with at least one member representing the municipal corporation in which the NID is located.

(4) In all cases, NIDMA boards shall include a representative of property owners located in the NID, business owners located in the NID and any institutions located in the NID. Institutional members may appoint a designee to represent them. All board members need not be residents of the NID.

§ 7. Powers of neighborhood improvement district management association.

(a) General powers.—An NIDMA shall have, in addition to any other powers provided pursuant to the act of May 2, 1945 (P.L. 382, No. 164), known as the Municipality Authorities Act of 1945, where the NIDMA is an authority, or in addition to any other powers provided pursuant to the charter establishing a nonprofit development corporation or other nonprofit corporation, where the NIDMA is a nonprofit development corporation or other nonprofit corporation, the power to:

(1) Sue or be sued, implead or be impleaded, complain and defend in all courts.

(2) Employ an executive director or administrator and any necessary supporting staff or contract for the provision of same.

(3) Prepare planning or feasibility studies or contract for the preparation of same to determine needed capital improvements or administrative programs and services within the NID.

(4) Make capital improvements or provide administrative programs and services within an NID.

(5) Purchase, own, construct, renovate, develop, operate, rehabilitate, manage, sell and/or dispose of real property.

(6) Contract with existing businesses within the NID.

(7) Contract for the provision of products or services by the NIDMA to clients located inside and outside of the NID, including billing and collection of assessment fees by another NIDMA.

(8) Appropriate and expend NID funds which would include any Federal, State or municipal funds received by the NIDMA. The funds shall be expended in accordance with any specific provisions contained in the municipal enabling ordinance establishing the NID and may be used:

(i) To acquire by purchase or lease real or personal property to effectuate the purposes of this act, including making common improvements within the

NID, including, but not limited to, sidewalks, retaining walls, street paving, parks, recreational equipment and facilities, open space, street lighting, parking lots, parking garages, trees and shrubbery, pedestrian walks, sewers, water lines, rest areas and the acquisition, rehabilitation or demolition of blighted buildings or comparable structures.

(ii) To provide free or reduced-fee parking for customers of businesses within the NID, transportation-related expenditures, public relations programs, group advertising and NID maintenance and security services.

(iii) To impose special assessment fees.

(9) Solicit in-kind services or financial contributions from tax-exempt property owners within the NID in lieu of property assessment fees. This may include entering into voluntary multiyear agreements (VMAs) between the NIDMA and tax-exempt property owners located within an NID for the provision of same.

(10) Impose liens on property for the nonpayment of property assessments. NIDs administered by nonprofit corporations would have any such liens filed by the municipal corporation.

(11) Hire additional off-duty police officers or private security officers whose patrol area responsibilities would be limited to the geographical area incorporated within the designated NID service area and whose responsibility would be to support existing municipal and volunteer efforts aimed at reducing crime and improving security in the NID.

(12) Designate a district advisory committee, referred to as the DAC, for each NID established within the municipality. Each DAC shall consist of an odd number of members, between five and nine, who shall be representative of the neighborhood's character, including, but not limited to, age, sex and cultural diversity.

(b) Assessments.—

(1) The NIDMA shall, upon approval by the governing body of the municipality, have the power to assess property owners within the NID a special property assessment fee. Revenues from the fee shall be accounted for and used by the NIDMA to make improvements and provide programs and services within the NID as authorized by this act. Where the district established is a BID, the NIDMA shall have the authority to exempt residential property owners from any special assessment fees levied.

(2) All assessments authorized under this section shall be calculated using January 1 as the first day of the fiscal year.

(3) All special property assessment fees shall be based upon the estimated cost of the programs, improvements or services to be provided in such NID as stated in the final plan under section 5(d). In no case shall the aggregate amount of all fees levied by the NIDMA during the year exceed the estimated cost of proposed programs, improvements and services for the year.

(4) In the case of an NID which contains a combination of business, residential, industrial and/or institutional areas and uses, a weighted assessment may be instituted. In such case, the fee levied on property owners generally may be weighted higher for business, industrial or institutional properties than that levied on residential property owners, provided the basis for the calculation of the fee meets the rational nexus test.

(5) The total costs of improvements, programs and administrative services provided by the NIDMA shall be assessed to all designated properties within the NID by one of the following methods:

(i) An assessment determined by multiplying the total service and improvement costs by the ratio of the assessed value of the benefited property to the total assessed valuation of all designated benefited properties in the NID.

(ii) An assessment upon the several properties in the NID in proportion to benefits as ascertained by viewers appointed in accordance with law.

(iii) Any method that equitably apportions costs among benefiting properties.

(iv) In the case of improvements benefiting properties abutting the NID by the front-foot method, with equitable adjustments for corner properties and other cases provided for in the municipal ordinance. Any property which cannot be equitably assessed by the front-foot method may be assessed by any of the above methods.

(c) **Payment.**—The governing body may by ordinance authorize the payment of the assessment in equal annual or more frequent installments over such time and bearing interest at the rate specified in the municipal ordinance. If bonds have been issued and sold or notes or guarantees have been given or issued to provide for the cost of the services and improvements, the assessment in equal installments shall not be payable beyond the term for which the bonds, notes or guarantees are payable.

(d) **Liens.**—

(1) Notwithstanding the filing of the claims, all assessments which are made payable in installments shall constitute liens and encumbrances upon the respective benefited properties at the beginning of each calendar year, except as provided in subsection (c), and only in an amount equal to the sum of:

(i) the annual or other installments becoming payable in such year, with interest and penalties, if any, thereon; and

(ii) the total of all installments, with interest and penalties thereon, which became due during prior years and which remain due and unpaid at the beginning of the current year.

(2) In the case of default in the payment of any installment and interest for a period of 90 days after the payment becomes due, the assessment ordinance may provide either for the entire assessment, with accrued interest and penalties, to become due and become a lien from the due date of the installment or may provide solely for the enforcement of the claim as to the overdue installment, with interest and penalties, in which case the ordinance shall further provide that, if any installment or portion thereof remains due and unpaid for one year after it has become due and payable, then the entire assessment with accrued interest and penalties shall become due and become a lien from the due date of the installment.

(3) No action taken to enforce a claim for any installment or installments shall affect the status of any subsequent installment of the same assessment, each of which shall continue to become a lien upon the property annually pursuant to paragraph (1).

(4) The ordinance may contain any other provision relating to installment assessments which is not inconsistent with applicable law.

(5) Any owner of property against whom an assessment has been made may pay the assessment in full at any time, with accrued interest and costs thereon, and such a payment shall discharge the lien of the assessment, or installments then constituting a lien, and shall also release the claim to any later installments.

(6) Claims to secure the assessments shall be entered in the prothonotary's office of the county at the same time and in the same form and collected in the same manner as municipal tax claims are filed and collected, notwithstanding the provisions of this section as to installment payments.

Chapter 10 Residential Design Tax Credit | Chapter 9 Neighborhood Improvement | Chapter 8 Local Taxpayers Bill of Rights | Chapter 7 Occupation Tax Elimination Act | Chapter 6 Local Government Unit Debt Act | Chapter 5 Local Tax Collection Law | Chapter 4 Local Tax Enabling Act

§ 8. Dissolution of neighborhood improvement district management association and neighborhood improvement district.

(a) Conveying projects.—When any NIDMA shall have finally paid and discharged all bonds which together with the interest due thereon shall have been secured by a pledge of any of the revenues or receipts of a project, it may, subject to any agreements concerning the operation or disposition of such proj-ect and the NIDMA bylaws, convey such project or projects to the municipal corporation which established or had established the NIDMA.

(b) Request for termination.—Any request for the termination of the NID and NIDMA approved by 40% of the assessed property owners, in numbers, located in the NID shall be submitted to the governing body of the municipality in writing. The governing body shall hold a hearing on the merits of same, pursuant to section 5(b)(2) as it relates to the required procedure of holding a hearing. Such written request shall be considered by the governing body of the municipality. If the request is approved by the governing body of the municipality, then a resolution to that effect shall be filed with the Secretary of the Commonwealth, and the secretary shall note the termination of the existence on the record of incorporation and return the resolution with his or her approval shown on the resolution to the municipal corporation. Then, the property of the NIDMA shall pass to the municipal corporation, as the case may be, and the NIDMA and NID shall cease to exist. Any request for the termination of the NID and NIDMA by the governing body of the municipality in which the NID is located shall result in a hearing on the merits of same, pursuant to section 5(b)(2) as it relates to the required procedure for holding a hearing. Before the decision to terminate an NID and NIDMA is made, such termination must be approved by 40% of the assessed property owners, in numbers, located in the NID, and shall be submitted to the governing body of the municipality in writing. Such written request shall be considered by the governing body of the municipality. If the request is approved by the governing body of the municipality, then a resolution to that effect shall be filed with the Secretary of the Commonwealth, and the secretary shall note the termination of the existence on the record of incorporation and return the resolution with his or her approval shown to the municipal corporation. The property of the NIDMA shall pass to the municipal corporation, as the case may be, and the NIDMA and NID shall cease to exist.

§ 9. Annual audit; report.

The NIDMA shall annually:

(1) submit an audit of all income and expenditures to the Department of Community and Economic Development and the governing body of the municipality in which the NID is located within 120 days after the end of each fiscal year; and

(2) submit a report, including financial and programmatic information, including a summary of audit findings, to the governing body of the municipality in which the NID is located and to all assessed property owners located in the NID.

§ 10. Applicability.

(a) Existing districts.—Except as provided for in subsection (d), any existing business improvement district or downtown improvement district established prior to the effective date of this act shall remain in existence and shall be governed by the act of May 2, 1945 (P.L. 382, No. 164), known as the Municipality Authorities Act of 1945, insofar as it relates to business improvement districts or 53 Pa.C.S. Ch. 54 (relating to business improvement districts).

(b) Districts created subsequently.—Any NID established subsequent to the effective date of this act shall be governed by the provisions of this act.

(c) Previously terminated districts.—Any business improvement district or downtown improvement district in existence prior to the effective date of this act which is terminated shall, upon its reestablishment, be governed by the provisions of this act. This shall include any termination resulting from a sunset provision in any municipal agreement or ordinance.

(d) Additional requirements.—Any business improvement district or downtown improvement district in existence on the effective date of this act shall:

(1) be required to carry out any duty or responsibility imposed on NIDs under this act; and

(2) possess any additional power given to NIDs under this act without having to restructure or reorganize under this act.

Table of Contents
Part I Ch. 1–3 Ethics, Records, Open Meetings
Part II Ch. 4–10 Taxation
Part III Ch. 11–18 Torts, Contracts & Civil Rules
Part IV Ch. 19–24 Zoning & Planning
Part V Ch. 25–30 Construction and Emergency Codes
Part VI Ch. 31–39 Municipal Codes
Index

CHAPTER 10
RESIDENTIAL VISITABILITY DESIGN TAX CREDIT ACT

72 P.S. § 4751-101 to § 4751-106

TABLE OF CONTENTS

Sec.

---

§ 1. Short title.

This act shall be known and may be cited as the Residential Visitability Design Tax Credit Act.

§ 2. Construction.

This act shall be construed to further authorize local taxing authorities to provide special tax provisions for the benefit of persons who have disabilities or other infirmities and to establish minimum uniform design standards as authorized under section 2(b)(ii) of Article VIII of the Constitution of Pennsylvania.

§ 3. Definitions.

The following words and phrases when used in this act shall have the meanings given to them in this section unless the context clearly indicates otherwise:

"Acceptable slope." A variable grade measured by rise over distance.

"Circulation path." An exterior or interior way of passage from one place to another for pedestrians.

"Dwelling." A structure used as a place of habitation by a natural person. The term shall include new residential construction, existing residential construction or any commercial or industrial building that is converted for residential use.

"Eligible property owner." A person responsible for the payment of taxes on a dwelling.

"Local taxing authority." A county, city, borough, incorporated town, township, school district or home rule municipality having authority to levy real property taxes.

"No-step entry." An entry to a housing unit that has no steps or other barrier to people who have significant mobility impairment.

"Pedestrian site arrival point." A place where pedestrians may enter a dwelling site from a public right-of-way. The term typically includes sidewalks, driveways, streets, alleys and paths.

"Powder room." A toileting room having, at a minimum, a water closet and a lavatory.

"Significant mobility impairment." The disability of a person who needs assistive mobility technology in the form of a wheelchair, walker, crutches or a similar device in order to move along a circulation path.

"Visitability design." The presence of architectural design features which enhance access and usability for visitors and residents who have significant mobility impairment and which minimize the cost of full accessibility modifications, if necessary, at a later time.

§ 4. Tax credit authorized.

(a) Authorization.—The governing body of a local taxing authority which levies a tax on residential property is authorized to and may, by ordinance or resolution, provide a residential visitability design tax credit against a real property tax levied on such property. The credit may be offered to residential owners at the sole discretion of the local taxing authority, so long as the uniform design standards contained in this act are provided within the eligible residential units.

(b) Applicability.—The tax credit authorized under subsection (a) shall be limited to any new or renovated dwelling that contains visitability design features which will enhance the usability of the dwelling for persons with significant mobility impairment and which minimize the cost of full accessibility modifications, if necessary, at a later time.

(c) Amount.—The amount of the tax credit shall be determined by the governing body and shall not exceed $2,500 or the total amount of the increased amount of property taxes owed during the first five years from the time the tax credit is approved, whichever is less.

(d) Administration.—The governing body shall determine the form and manner in which any eligible property owner shall apply for the credit and may adopt rules and regulations for the approval and disapproval of applications.

§ 5. Design standards.

(a) General standards.—The architectural design of a visitable home shall comply with all of the following requirements:

(1) The path from either a vehicle parking area or a pedestrian entrance to the lot to the no-step entrance shall be firm, stable and slip resistant.

(i) The grade of the path shall not exceed the following acceptable slopes: 1:8 for slope length of five feet or less with a maximum rise of 7.5 inches; 1:10 for slope length of 12 feet or less with a maximum rise of 14.4 inches; and 1:12 for slope length of more than 12 feet.

(ii) Notwithstanding subparagraph (i), if the average slope of the property line along and contiguous to the public right-of-way exceeds a slope of 1:12, the slope of the exterior circulation path may be greater, if necessary, to provide access to the no-step entry, but it may not exceed the average slope of the property line.

(2) The residence shall provide at least one no-step entrance approachable by a firm, stable and slip-resistant path with an acceptable slope. The no-step entrance shall have a threshold of no greater than three-fourths of an inch. The no-step entrance to the residence may be located on any exterior side of the house or an entrance through the integral garage to the visitable level of the residence.

(3) All no-step entry doors must have a minimum clear open width of at least 32 inches and be equipped with lever handle hardware.

(4) Interior circulation paths on the visitable level of the dwelling must be at least 36 inches in width.

(5) All interior doorways on the visitable level of the dwelling, excluding closets and doorways to floors below the visitable level, shall have a minimum clear open width of 32 inches.

(6) Each visitable dwelling shall have a minimum of one powder room or bathroom on the visitable-level floor. The powder room shall have a 30-inch

by 48-inch minimum clear floor space contiguous to the water closet and the lavatory. The clear space under the lavatory may be included in these measurements, and clear spaces contiguous to the water closet and lavatory may overlap. Plumbing fixtures and entry room doors accessing the visitable powder room must be equipped with lever-style hardware.

(7)(i) All bathrooms and powder rooms throughout the residential unit shall have reinforcement of at least two inches by eight inches of blocking between the studs placed inside the walls for easy installation of grab bars if needed. Reinforcement shall be capable of supporting grab bars that resist shear and bending forces of 250 pounds or greater. Blocking should be centered at 34 inches from and parallel to the finished floor.

(ii) Notwithstanding subparagraph (i), in renovated homes only the walls in powder rooms or bathrooms on the visitable floor and those on floors that have the stud walls exposed as part of the renovation process need to comply with this paragraph.

(8)(i) Light switches may not be higher than 48 inches above the finished floor of the residential unit. If there are two controls for the same light, only one need be in compliance with these standards.

(ii) Notwithstanding subparagraph (i), in renovated homes only the switches on the visitable floor need to comply with this paragraph unless the electrical renovations extend beyond the visitable floor.

(b) **Modifications.**—The design standards contained in this section may not be modified or made mandatory, except as provided by the act of November 10, 1999 (P.L. 491, No. 45), 35 P.S. § 7210.101 et seq known as the Pennsylvania Construction Code Act.

§ 6. Effective date.

This act shall take effect immediately.

Approved October 28, 2006.

PART III
TORTS, CONTRACTS, AND CIVIL RULES

CHAPTER 11
THE TORT CLAIMS ACT
42 Pa.C.S. §§ 8501–8564

MATTERS AFFECTING GOVERNMENT UNITS

Subchapter

SUBCHAPTER A
GENERAL PROVISIONS
42 Pa.C.S. § 8501–8502

Sec.

---

§ 8501. Definitions.

The following words and phrases when used in this chapter shall have, unless the context clearly indicates otherwise, the meanings given to them in this section:

"Act." Includes a failure to act.

"Commonwealth party." A Commonwealth agency and any employee thereof, but only with respect to an act within the scope of his office or employment.

"Employee." Any person who is acting or who has acted on behalf of a government unit whether on a permanent or temporary basis, whether compensated or not and whether within or without the territorial boundaries of the government unit, including any volunteer fireman and any elected or appointed officer, member of a governing body or other person designated to act for the government unit. Independent contractors under contract to the government unit and their employees and agents and persons performing tasks over which the government unit has no legal right of control are not employees of the government unit.

"Injury." Includes death.

"Judicial determination." Any determination by a court of competent jurisdiction including any settlement approved by such court.

"Local agency." A government unit other than the Commonwealth government. The term includes an intermediate unit.

§ 8502. Enforcement proceedings.

(a) Venue.—Except as otherwise prescribed by general rules the venue of any action or proceeding by a Commonwealth agency to enforce any statute or regulation or order of a government unit may be laid in any court having jurisdiction of the subject matter.

(b) Bond.—Neither a Commonwealth agency nor a district attorney shall be required to give bond in connection with any application for equitable relief incident to the enforcement of any statute or regulation or order of a government unit.

SUBCHAPTER B
ACTIONS AGAINST COMMONWEALTH PARTIES

42 Pa.C.S. §§ 8521–8528

Sec.

SOVEREIGN IMMUNITY

LIMITATIONS ON DAMAGES

SOVEREIGN IMMUNITY

§ 8521. Sovereign immunity generally.

(a) General rule.—Except as otherwise provided in this subchapter, no provision of this title shall constitute a waiver of sovereign immunity for the purpose of 1 Pa.C.S. § 2310 (relating to sovereign immunity reaffirmed; specific waiver) or otherwise.

(b) Federal courts.—Nothing contained in this subchapter shall be construed to waive the immunity of the Commonwealth from suit in Federal courts guaranteed by the Eleventh Amendment to the Constitution of the United States.

§ 8522. Exceptions to sovereign immunity.

(a) Liability imposed.—The General Assembly, pursuant to section 11 of Article I of the Constitution of Pennsylvania, does hereby waive, in the instances set forth in subsection (b) only and only to the extent set forth in this subchapter and within the limits set forth in section 8528 (relating to limitations on damages), sovereign immunity as a bar to an action against Commonwealth parties, for damages arising out of a negligent act where the damages would be recoverable under the common law or a statute creating a cause of action if the injury were caused by a person not having available the defense of sovereign immunity.

(b) Acts which may impose liability.—The following acts by a Commonwealth party may result in the imposition of liability on the Commonwealth and the defense of sovereign immunity shall not be raised to claims for damages caused by:

(1) Vehicle liability.—The operation of any motor vehicle in the possession or control of a Commonwealth party. As used in this paragraph, "motor vehicle" means any vehicle which is self-propelled and any attachment thereto, including vehicles operated by rail, through water or in the air.

(2) Medical-professional liability.—Acts of health care employees of Commonwealth agency medical facilities or institutions or by a Commonwealth party who is a doctor, dentist, nurse or related health care personnel.

(3) Care, custody or control of personal property.—The care, custody or control of personal property in the possession or control of Commonwealth parties, including Commonwealth-owned personal property and property of persons held by a Commonwealth agency, except that the sovereign immunity of the Commonwealth is retained as a bar to actions on claims arising out of Commonwealth agency activities involving the use of nuclear and other radioactive equipment, devices and materials.

(4) Commonwealth real estate, highways and sidewalks.—A dangerous condition of Commonwealth agency real estate and sidewalks, including Commonwealth-owned real property, leaseholds in the possession of a Commonwealth agency and Commonwealth-owned real property leased by a Commonwealth agency to private persons, and highways under the jurisdiction of a Commonwealth agency, except conditions described in paragraph (5).

(5) Potholes and other dangerous conditions.—A dangerous condition of highways under the jurisdiction of a Commonwealth agency created by potholes or sinkholes or other similar conditions created by natural elements, except that the claimant to recover must establish that the dangerous condition created a reasonably foreseeable risk of the kind of injury which was incurred and that the Commonwealth agency had actual written notice of the dangerous condition of the highway a sufficient time prior to the event to have taken measures to protect against the dangerous condition. Property damages shall not be recoverable under this paragraph.

(6) Care, custody or control of animals.—The care, custody or control of animals in the possession or control of a Commonwealth party, including but not limited to police dogs and horses and animals incarcerated in Commonwealth agency laboratories. Damages shall not be recoverable under this paragraph on account of any injury caused by wild animals, including but not limited to bears and deer, except as otherwise provided by statute.

(7) Liquor store sales.—The sale of liquor at Pennsylvania liquor stores by employees of the Pennsylvania Liquor Control Board created by and operating under the act of April 12, 1951 (P.L.90, No.21), known as the "Liquor Code," if such sale is made to any minor, or to any person visibly intoxicated, or to any insane person, or to any person known as an habitual drunkard, or of known intemperate habit.

(8) National Guard activities.—Acts of a member of the Pennsylvania military forces.

(9) Toxoids and vaccines.—The administration, manufacture and use of a toxoid or vaccine not manufactured in this Commonwealth under the following conditions:

(i) The toxoid or vaccine is manufactured in, and available only from, an agency of another state.

(ii) The agency of the other state will not make the toxoid or vaccine available to private persons or corporations, but will only permit its sale to another state or state agency.

(iii) The agency of the other state will make the toxoid or vaccine available to the Commonwealth only if the Commonwealth agrees to indemnify, defend and save harmless that agency from any and all claims and losses which may arise against it from the administration, manufacture or use of the toxoid or vaccine.

(iv) A determination has been made by the appropriate Commonwealth agency, approved by the Governor and published in the Pennsylvania Bulletin, that the toxoid or vaccine is necessary to safeguard and protect the health of the citizens or animals of this Commonwealth.

(v) The toxoid or vaccine is distributed by a Commonwealth agency to qualified persons for ultimate use.

The Commonwealth shall make the toxoid or vaccine available to a qualified person only if the person agrees to indemnify, defend and save harmless the Commonwealth from any and all claims and losses which may arise against the Commonwealth from the manufacture, distribution, administration or use of the toxoid or vaccine.

(10) Sexual abuse.—Conduct which constitutes an offense enumerated under section 5551(7) (relating to no limitation applicable) if the injuries to the plaintiff were caused by actions or omissions of the Commonwealth party which constitute negligence.

§ 8523. Venue and process.

(a) Venue.—Actions for claims against a Commonwealth party may be brought in and only in a county in which the principal or local office of the Commonwealth party is located or in which the cause of action arose or where a transaction or occurrence took place out of which the cause of action arose. If venue is obtained in the Twelfth Judicial District (Dauphin County) solely because the principal office of the Commonwealth party is located within it, any judge of the Court of Common Pleas of Dauphin County shall have the power to transfer the action to any appropriate county where venue would otherwise lie.

(b) Process.—Service of process in the case of an action against the Commonwealth shall be made at the prinicpal or local office of the Commonwealth agency that is being sued and at the office of the Attorney General.

§ 8524. Defenses.

The following common law defenses are available:

(1) An official of a Commonwealth agency, or a member of the General Assembly or the judiciary may assert on his own behalf, or the Commonwealth may assert on his behalf, defenses which have heretofore been available to such officials.

(2) An employee of a Commonwealth agency, or a member of the General Assembly or of the judiciary may assert on his own behalf, or the Commonwealth may assert on his behalf, the defense that the employee was acting pursuant to a duty required by a statute or statutorily authorized regulation.

(3) An employee of a Commonwealth agency, or a member of the General Assembly or of the judiciary may assert on his own behalf, or the Commonwealth may assert on his behalf, the defense that the act was within the discretion granted to the employee by statute or statutorily authorized regulation.

§ 8525. Legal assistance.

When an action is brought under this subchapter against an employee of the Commonwealth government, and it is alleged that the act of the employee which gave rise to the claim was within the scope of the office or duties of the employee, the Commonwealth through the Attorney General shall defend the action, unless the Attorney General determines that the act did not occur within the scope of the office or duties of the employee. In the latter case, if it is subsequently determined that the act occurred within the scope of the office or duties of the employee, the Commonwealth shall reimburse the employee for the expense of his legal defense in such amounts as shall be determined to be reasonable by the court. If an action is brought against a Commonwealth government employee for damages on account of injury to a person or property and it is not alleged that the act of the employee which gave rise to the claim was within the scope of his office or duties, and he successfully defends the action on the basis that the act was within the scope of his office or duties, and he has given prior notice to the Attorney General and the Attorney General has refused to defend the action, he shall likewise be entitled to the reasonable expenses of the defense.

§ 8526. Counterclaim by the Commonwealth.

In any action initiated under this subchapter, the Commonwealth may set forth any cause of action or set-off which it has against the plaintiff. A counterclaim need not diminish or defeat the relief demanded by the plaintiff. It may demand relief exceeding in amount or different in kind from that demanded by the plaintiff.

§ 8527. Indemnity relating to inmate health care

The Commonwealth shall indemnify against liability a municipal corporation for a claim against the municipal corporation arising from an act or omission of the municipal corporation, its officials, its employees or agents when participating in a program for the provision of medical treatment in a health care facility to inmates from a Commonwealth correctional facility pursuant to a program authorized by the Department of Corrections. This indemnification shall not extend to claims of medical malpractice against any person nor to claims against the health care facility, its employees or agents nor to claims against the municipal corporation that are the result of gross negligence, wanton and reckless acts or intentional misconduct by the municipal corporation, its officials, employees or agents.

LIMITATIONS ON DAMAGES

§ 8528. Limitations on damages.

(a) General rule.—Actions for which damages are limited by reference to this subchapter shall be limited as set forth in this section.

(b) Amount recoverable.—Damages arising from the same cause of action or transaction or occurrence or series of causes of action or transactions or occurrences shall not exceed $250,000 in favor of any plaintiff or $1,000,000 in the aggregate.

(c) Types of damages recoverable.—Damages shall be recoverable only for:

(1) Past and future loss of earnings and earning capacity.

(2) Pain and suffering.

(3) Medical and dental expenses including the reasonable value of reasonable and necessary medical and dental services, prosthetic devices and necessary ambulance, hospital, professional nursing, and physical therapy expenses accrued and anticipated in the diagnosis, care and recovery of the claimant.

(4) Loss of consortium.

(5) Property losses, except that property losses shall not be recoverable in claims brought pursuant to section 8522(b)(5) (relating to exceptions to sovereign immunity).

(d) Exclusions.—This section shall not apply to damages awarded under section 8522(b)(10).

SUBCHAPTER C
ACTIONS AGAINST LOCAL PARTIES

42 Pa.C.S. §§ 8541–8564

Sec.

GOVERNMENTAL IMMUNITY

§ 8541. Governmental immunity generally.

Except as otherwise provided in this subchapter, no local agency shall be liable for any damages on account of any injury to a person or property caused by any act of the local agency or an employee thereof or any other person.

§ 8542. Exceptions to governmental immunity.

(a) Liability imposed.—A local agency shall be liable for damages on account of an injury to a person or property within the limits set forth in this subchapter if both of the following conditions are satisfied and the injury occurs as a result of one of the acts set forth in subsection (b):

(1) The damages would be recoverable under common law or a statute creating a cause of action if the injury were caused by a person not having available a defense under section 8541 (relating to governmental immunity generally) or section 8546 (relating to defense of official immunity); and

(2) The injury was caused by the negligent acts of the local agency or an employee thereof acting within the scope of his office or duties with respect to one of the categories listed in subsection (b). As used in this paragraph, "negligent acts" shall not include acts or conduct which constitutes a crime, actual fraud, actual malice or willful misconduct.

(b) Acts which may impose liability.—The following acts by a local agency or any of its employees may result in the imposition of liability on a local agency:

(1) Vehicle liability.—The operation of any motor vehicle in the possession or control of the local agency, provided that the local agency shall not be liable to any plaintiff that claims liability under this subsection if the plaintiff was; during the course of the alleged negligence, in flight or fleeing apprehension or resisting arrest by a police officer or knowingly aided a group, one or more of whose members were in flight or fleeing apprehension or resisting arrest by a police officer. As used in this paragraph, "motor vehicle" means any vehicle which is self-propelled and any attachment thereto, including vehicles operated by rail, through water or in the air.

(2) Care, custody or control of personal property.—The care, custody or control of personal property of others in the possession or control of the local agency. The only losses for which damages shall be recoverable under this paragraph are those property losses suffered with respect to the personal property in the possession or control of the local agency.

(3) Real property.—The care, custody or control of real property in the possession of the local agency, except that the local agency shall not be liable for damages on account of any injury sustained by a person intentionally trespassing on real property in the possession of the local agency. As used in this paragraph, "real property" shall not include:

(i) trees, traffic signs, lights and other traffic controls, street lights and street lighting systems;

(ii) facilities of steam, sewer, water, gas and electric systems owned by the local agency and located within rights-of-way;

(iii) streets; or

(iv) sidewalks.

(4) Trees, traffic controls and street lighting.—A dangerous condition of trees, traffic signs, lights or other traffic controls, street lights or street lighting systems under the care, custody or control of the local agency, except that the claimant to recover must establish that the dangerous condition created a reasonably foreseeable risk of the kind of injury which was incurred and that the local agency had actual notice or could reasonably be charged with notice under the circumstances of the dangerous condition at a sufficient time prior to the event to have taken measures to protect against the dangerous condition.

(5) Utility service facilities.—A dangerous condition of the facilities of steam, sewer, water, gas or electric systems owned by the local agency and located within rights-of-way, except that the claimant to recover must establish that the dangerous condition created a reasonably foreseeable risk of the kind of injury which was incurred and that the local agency had actual notice or could reasonably be charged with notice under the circumstances of the dangerous condition at a sufficient time prior to the event to have taken measures to protect against the dangerous condition.

(6) Streets.—

(i) A dangerous condition of streets owned by the local agency, except that the claimant to recover must establish that the dangerous condition created a reasonably foreseeable risk of the kind of injury which was incurred and that the local agency had actual notice or could reasonably be charged with notice under the circumstances of the dangerous condition at a sufficient time prior to the event to have taken measures to protect against the dangerous condition.

(ii) A dangerous condition of streets owned or under the jurisdiction of Commonwealth agencies, if all of the following conditions are met:

(A) The local agency has entered into a written contract with a Commonwealth agency for the maintenance and repair by the local agency of such streets and the contract either:

(i) has not expired or been otherwise terminated prior to the occurrence of the injury; or

(ii) if expired, contained a provision that expressly established local agency responsibility beyond the term of the contract for injuries arising out of the local agency's work.

(B) The injury and dangerous condition were directly caused by the negligent performance of its duties under such contract.

(C) The claimant must establish that the dangerous condition created a reasonably foreseeable risk of the kind of injury which was incurred and that the local agency had actual notice or could reasonably be charged with notice under the circumstances of the dangerous condition at a sufficient time prior to the event to have taken measures to protect against the dangerous condition.

(7) Sidewalks.—A dangerous condition of sidewalks within the rights-of-way of streets owned by the local agency, except that the claimant to recover must establish that the dangerous condition created a reasonably foreseeable risk of the kind of injury which was incurred and that the local agency had actual notice or could reasonably be charged with notice under the circumstances of the dangerous condition at a sufficient time prior to the event to have taken measures to protect against the dangerous condition. When a local agency is liable for damages under this paragraph by reason of its power and authority to require installation and repair of sidewalks under the care, custody and control of other persons, the local agency shall be secondarily liable only and such other persons shall be primarily liable.

(8) Care, custody or contol of animals.—The care, custody or control of animals in the possession or control of a local agency, including but not limited to police dogs and horses. Damages shall not be recoverable under this paragraph on account of any injury caused by wild animals, including but not limited to bears and deer, except as otherwise provided by statute.

(9) Sexual abuse.—Conduct which constitutes an offense enumerated under section 5551(7) (relating to no limitation applicable) if the injuries to the plaintiff were caused by actions or omissions of the local agency which constitute negligence.

(c) Limited definition.—As used in this section the amount of time reasonably required to take protective measures, including inspections required by law, shall be determined with reference to the actual equipment, personnel and facilities available to the local agency and the competing demands therefor.

(d) Evidence.—Whenever any plaintiff claims liability under subsection (b)(1), evidence is admissible to demonstrate that the plaintiff, at any time during the course of the alleged negligence, was engaged or participating in willful misconduct, including, but not limited to, the illegal possession of controlled substances, firearms or ammunition.

OFFICIAL IMMUNITY

§ 8545. Official liability generally.

An employee of a local agency is liable for civil damages on account of any injury to a person or property caused by acts of the employee which are within the scope of his office or duties only to the same extent as his employing local agency and subject to the limitations imposed by this subchapter.

§ 8546. Defense of official immunity.

In any action brought against an employee of a local agency for damages on account of an injury to a person or property based upon claims arising from, or reasonably related to, the office or the performance of the duties of the employee, the employee may assert on his own behalf, or the local agency may assert on his behalf:

(1) Defenses which are available at common law to the employee.

(2) The defense that the conduct of the employee which gave rise to the claim was authorized or required by law, or that he in good faith reasonably believed the conduct was authorized or required by law.

(3) The defense that the act of the employee which gave rise to the claim was within the policymaking discretion granted to the employee by law. For purposes of this subsection, all acts of members of the governing body of a local agency or of the chief executive officer thereof are deemed to be within the policymaking discretion granted to such person by law.

§ 8547. Legal assistance.

(a) **Mandatory provision of legal assistance generally.**—When an action is brought against an employee of a local agency for damages on account of an injury to a person or property, and it is alleged that the act of the employee which gave rise to the claim was within the scope of the office or duties of the employee, the local agency shall, upon the written request of the employee, defend the action, unless or until there is a judicial determination that such act was not within the scope of the office or duties of the employee.

(b) **Optional provision of legal assistance generally.**—When an action is brought against an employee of a local agency for damages on account of an injury to a person or property, and it is not alleged that the act of the employee which gave rise to the claim was within the scope of his office or duties, the local agency may, upon the written request of the employee, defend the action, and such undertaking to defend thereafter may be withdrawn only with the approval of the court. If the local agency has refused a written request to defend the action, and it is judicially determined that the act was, or that the employee in good faith reasonably believed that such act was, within the scope of the office or duties of the employee and did not constitute a crime, actual fraud, actual malice or willful misconduct, the local agency shall reimburse the employee for the expenses of his legal defense in such amounts as shall be determined to be reasonable by the court.

(c) **Control of litigation.**—When, pursuant to subsection (a) or subsection (b), the local agency defends an action against an employee thereof at the request of the employee, it may assume exclusive control of the defense of the employee, keeping him advised with respect thereto, and the employee shall cooperate fully with the defense, except that in situations where the legal counsel provided by the local agency determines that the interests of the employee and the local agency conflict, the local agency shall obtain the express written consent of the employee for such interested representation or shall supply independent representation.

§ 8548. Indemnity.

(a) **Indemnity by local agency generally.**—When an action is brought against an employee of a local agency for damages on account of an injury to a person or property, and he has given timely prior written notice to the local agency, and it is judicially determined that an act of the employee caused the injury and such act was, or that the employee in good faith reasonably believed that such act was, within the scope of his office or duties, the local agency shall indemnify the employee for the payment of any judgment on the suit.

(b) **Indemnity by employee generally.**—No employee of a local agency shall be liable to the local agency for any surcharge, contribution, indemnity or reimbursement for any liability incurred by the local agency for damages on account of an injury to a person or property caused by an act of the employee which was within the scope of his office or duties or which he in good faith reasonably believed to be within the scope of his office or duties. No employee of a local agency shall be liable to the local agency for any sucharge, contribution, indemnity or reimbursement for any expenses or legal fees incurred by the local agency while defending the employee against a claim for damages on account of an injury to a person or property caused by an act of the employee.

(c) Cooperation.—In any action against a local agency or an employee thereof for damages on account of an injury caused by the act of the employee in which action the employee has not fully cooperated with the local agency in the defense of the action, the provisions of subsection (b) shall not apply.

§ 8549. Limitations on damages.

In any action brought against an employee of a local agency for damages on account of an injury to a person or property in which it is judicially determined that the act of the employee caused the injury and that such act was, or that the employee in good faith reasonably believed that such act was, within the scope of his office or duties, damages shall be recoverable only within the limits set forth in this subchapter.

§ 8550. Willful misconduct.

In any action against a local agency or employee thereof for damages on account of an injury caused by the act of the employee in which it is judicially determined that the act of the employee caused the injury and that such act constituted a crime, actual fraud, actual malice or willful misconduct, the provisions of sections 8545 (relating to official liability generally), 8546 (relating to defense of official immunity), 8548 (relating to indemnity) and 8549 (relating to limitation on damages) shall not apply.

LIMITATIONS ON DAMAGES

§ 8553. Limitations on damages.

(a) General rule.—Actions for which damages are limited by reference to this subchapter shall be limited as set forth in this section.

(b) Amounts recoverable.—Damages arising from the same cause of action or transaction or occurrence or series of causes of action or transactions or occurrences shall not exceed $500,000 in the aggregate.

(c) Types of losses recognized.—Damages shall be recoverable only for:

(1) Past and future loss of earnings and earning capacity.

(2) Pain and suffering in the following instances:

(i) death; or

(ii) only in cases of permanent loss of a bodily function, permanent disfigurement or permanent dismemberment where the medical and dental expenses referred to in paragraph (3) are in excess of $1,500.

(3) Medical and dental expenses including the reasonable value of reasonable and necessary medical and dental services, prosthetic devices and necessary ambulance, hospital, professional nursing, and physical therapy expenses accrued and anticipated in the diagnosis, care and recovery of the claimant.

(4) Loss of consortium.

(5) Loss of support.

(6) Property losses.

(d) Insurance benefits.—If a claimant receives or is entitled to receive benefits under a policy of insurance other than a life insurance policy as a result of losses for which damages are recoverable under subsection (c), the amount of such benefits shall be deducted from the amount of damages which would otherwise be recoverable by such claimant.

(e) Exclusions.—This section shall not apply to damages awarded under section 8542(b)(9) (relating to exceptions to governmental immunity).

JUDGMENTS

§ 8557. Judgment as a bar.

The judgment in an action cognizable under section 8545 (relating to official liability generally) shall constitute a complete bar to any action by the claimant, by reason of the same subject matter, against the local agency of which the defendant in such action is an employee. The judgment in an action under section 8542 (relating to exceptions to governmental immunity) shall constitute a complete bar to any action by the claimant, by reason of the same subject matter, against the employee whose act gave rise to the claim.

§ 8558. Judgments against insured local agency.

If the judgment is obtained against a local agency that has procured a contract or policy of public liability insurance protection, the holder of the judgment may use the methods of collecting the judgment as are provided by the pollicy or contract and the laws of the Commonwealth to the extent of the limits of coverage provided.

§ 8559. Judgments against self-insured local agency and those not fully insured.

For the payment of any judgment obtained under the provisions of this subchapter against a local agency that is a self-insurer or not fully covered by liability insurance, the manner of paying a money judgment shall be based upon a proof of indebtedness or evidence of any estimated tax levy necessary for payment of the judgment and any other evidence or statements which the court of original jurisdiction may require. As an alternative to paying the money judgment in this manner, the court may provide for the judgment to be paid over a period of not less than one nor more than ten years. The interest rate on any judgment where payment is extended more than three years shall be at the rate prescribed by law for the first three years and at the rate of 6% for each remaining year.

POWERS OF LOCAL AGENCIES

§ 8563. General powers of local agencies.

(a) Rules and regulations.—A local agency may promulgate rules and regulations not inconsistent with this subchapter in order to implement the intent of this subchapter.

(b) Delegation of duties.—Any duties placed upon a local agency under the provisions of this subchapter may be delegated to an independent contractor by a written agreement.

§ 8564. Liability insurance and self-insurance.

(a) Purchase of liability insurance.—A local agency may purchase insurance on itself or its employees for any liability arising from the performance of their duties within the scope of their employment.

(b) Employment of risk manager.—A local agency may employ a professional risk manager whose responsibility it shall be to administer a public liability insurance program for the local agency and initiate any risk management program for the local agency and its employees.

(c) Joint action by local agency.—Any two or more local agencies may join together, enter into any agreements or jointly contract for the development of a group risk management program either through the provisions of the act of July 12, 1972 (P.L. 762, No. 180), referred to as the Intergovernmental Cooperation Law, or any other applicable statute. Any two or more local agencies may join together, enter into any agreements or jointly contract for the purchasing of public liability insurance. Any two or more local agencies may pool their public liability insurance risks through the provisions of the act of July 12, 1972 (P.L. 762, No. 180) or any other applicable statute.

(d) Insurance pooling and coinsurance.—The pooling of insurance risks, reserves, claims or losses shall not be construed to be transacting insurance nor otherwise subject local agencies to the provisions of statutes regulating insurance or insurance companies. Local agencies may be construed under a master policy and the total premium may be prorated among the local agencies. Any county may undertake a group risk management program or public liability insurance program on behalf of itself and any other local agencies covered by this subchapter within the county that wish to voluntarily participate in the programs.

(e) Self-insurance.—Any local agency may self-insure which must be funded on an annual basis by appropriations to establish a reserve for self-insurance purposes.

CHAPTER 12

CONTRACTS FOR PUBLIC WORKS

62 Pa.C.S. §§ 3902–3942

TABLE OF CONTENTS

NONRECEIPT OF BIDS

73 P.S. §§ 1641–1644

---

§ 3901. Application and purpose of chapter

(a) Application.—Except as otherwise specifically provided in this chapter, this chapter applies to contracts entered into by a government agency through competitive sealed bidding or competitive sealed proposals.

(b) Purpose of chapter.—The purpose of this chapter is to establish a uniform and mandatory system governing public contracts to the extent of the requirements set forth in this chapter and shall be construed to effectuate such purpose. The provisions of this chapter shall in no way affect the provisions of the act of August 15, 1961 (P.L. 987, No. 442), [43 P.S. § 165-1] known as the Pennsylvania Prevailing Wage Act, nor the regulations promulgated under that act, nor shall any requirements of this chapter affect any provisions of a contract to be awarded pursuant to any Federal law or regulations containing specific provisions which are different from the public contract requirements of this chapter.

§ 3902. Definitions.

The following words and phrases when used in this chapter shall have the meanings given to them in this section unless the context clearly indicates otherwise:

"Contract." A contract exceeding $50,000 for construction as defined in section 103 (relating to definitions), including heating or plumbing contracts but excluding Department of Transportation contracts under section 301(c)(1) (relating to procurement responsibility).

"Contractor." A person who enters into a contract with a government agency.

"Deficiency item." Work performed but which the design professional, the contractor or the inspector will not certify as being completed according to the contract.

"Design professional." Persons performing professional services as defined in section 901 (relating to definitions).

"Government agency." Includes any State-aided institutions.

"Inspector." The person authorized or engaged by the government agency to inspect the work performed and materials furnished pursuant to a contract to determine whether the work completed is in compliance with the contract.

"Local government unit." Any county, city, borough, incorporated town, township, school district, vocational school district, county institution, local authority or any joint or cooperative body of local government units or any instrumentality, authority or corporation thereof which has authority to enter into a contract.

"State-aided institution." Any institution which receives State funds directly or indirectly for construction as defined in section 103 (relating to definitions).

"Subcontractor." A person who has contracted to furnish labor or materials to or has performed labor for a contractor or another subcontractor in connection with a contract.

"Substantial completion." Construction that is sufficiently completed in accordance with the contract and certified by the architect or engineer of the government agency, as modified by change orders agreed to by the parties, so that the project can be used, occupied or operated for its intended use. In no event shall a project be certified as substantially complete until at least 90% of the work on the project is completed.

§ 3911. Time for awarding contract.

(a) General rule.—In the case of a contract to be entered into by a government agency through competitive sealed bidding, the contract shall be awarded to the lowest responsible and responsive bidder within 60 days of the bid opening, or all bids shall be rejected except as otherwise provided in this section.

(b) Delay.—If the award is delayed by the required approval of another government agency, the sale of bonds or the award of a grant, the contract shall be awarded to the lowest responsible and responsive bidder within 120 days of the bid opening, or all bids shall be rejected.

(c) Extensions.—Extensions of the date for the award may be made by the mutual written consent of the government agency and the lowest responsible and responsive bidder.

(d) List of bidders.—All government agencies shall be required to provide a list of the bidders and their bid amount on each contract within ten working days of the bid opening to interested parties for a fee to be determined by the government agency to cover the cost of developing such list. This requirement shall not apply to the contracting bodies of any political subdivision or local authority which has the authority to enter into a contract.

(e) Contract negotiation.—When the amount of the bid submitted by the lowest responsive and responsible bidder for a Department of General Services construction contract exceeds the verifiable contract allocation established by the Department of General Services for the contract, the department may, prior to awarding the contract, negotiate the price, work items and time requirements for the contract with the lowest responsive and responsible bidder to bring the bid within the established contract allocation.

§ 3912. Time for executing contract.

In the case of a contract entered into by a government agency through competitive sealed bidding, the contract shall be executed by the government agency within 60 days of the date that the contract is awarded.

§ 3913. Release of successful bidder.

Failure of the government agency to comply with the requirements of sections 3911 (relating to time for awarding contract) and 3912 (relating to time for executing contract) shall, unless the successful bidder waives the noncompliance by written notice to the government agency, release the successful bidder from any liability in respect to its bid or contract and entitle all bidders to the immediate return of any bonds or security deposits posted in connection with the bid or contract.

§ 3921. Retainage.

(a) Contract provision.—A contract may include a provision for the retainage of a portion of the amount due the contractor to insure the proper performance of the contract except that the sum withheld by the government agency from the contractor shall not exceed 10% of the amount due the contractor until 50% of the contract is completed. When the contract is 50% completed, one-half of the amount retained by the government agency shall be returned to the contractor. However, the architect or engineer must approve the application for payment. The contractor must be making satisfactory progress, and there must be no specific cause for greater withholding. The sum withheld by the government agency from the contractor after the contract is 50% completed shall not exceed 5% of the value of completed work based on monthly progress payment requests. In the event a dispute arises between the government agency and any prime contractor, which dispute is based upon increased costs claimed by one prime contractor occasioned by delays or other actions of another prime contractor, additional retainage in the sum of one and one-half times the amount of any possible liability may be withheld until such time as a final resolution is agreed to by all parties directly or indirectly involved unless the contractor causing the additional claim furnishes a bond satisfactory to the government agency to indemnify the agency against the claim. All money retained by the government agency may be withheld from the contractor until substantial completion of the contract.

(b) Department of General Services.—Notwithstanding subsection (a), when the Department of General Services is the government agency, the contract may include a provision for the retainage of a portion of the amount due the contractor to insure the proper performance of the contract except that the sum withheld by the department for the contractor shall not exceed 6% of the then total estimates until 50% of the contract is satisfactorily completed. The sum withheld by the department from the contractor after the contract is 50% satisfactorily completed shall not exceed 3% of the original contract amount.

§ 3922. Payment of retainage to subcontractors.

In the absence of sufficient reason, within 20 days of the receipt of payment by the contractor, the contractor shall pay all subcontractors with which it has contracted their earned share of the payment the contractor received.

Table of Contents
Part I Ch. 1–3 Ethics, Records, Open Meetings
Part II Ch. 4–10 Taxation
Part III Ch. 11–18 Torts, Contracts & Civil Rules
Part IV Ch. 19–24 Zoning & Planning
Part V Ch. 25–30 Construction and Emergency Codes
Part VI Ch. 31–39 Municipal Codes
Index

§ 3931. Performance by contractor or subcontractor.

(a) Entitlement of contractor to payment.—Performance by a contractor in accordance with the provisions of a contract shall entitle the contractor to payment by the government agency.

(b) Entitlement of subcontractor to payment.—Performance by a subcontractor in accordance with the provisions of a contract shall entitle the subcontractor to payment from the contractor with whom the subcontractor has contracted.

§ 3932. Government agency's progress payment obligations.

(a) Payments in accordance with contract.—The government agency shall pay the contractor or design professional strictly in accordance with the contract.

(b) Application for progress payments.—If the contract does not contain a term governing the time for payment, the contractor or design professional shall be entitled to make application for payment from the government agency for progress payments, and the government agency shall make payment less the applicable retainage amount as authorized in section 3921 (relating to retainage) to the contractor or design professional within 45 calendar days of the date the application for payment is received.

(c) Interest on progress payments not timely made.—Except as otherwise agreed by the parties, if any progress payment less the applicable retainage amount as authorized in section 3921 is not made to a contractor or design professional by the due date established in the contract or in subsection (b), the government agency shall pay to the contractor or design professional, in addition to the amount due, interest on the amount due, and the interest shall be computed at the rate determined by the Secretary of Revenue for interest payments on overdue taxes or the refund of taxes as provided in sections 806 and 806.1 of the act of April 9, 1929 (P.L. 343, No. 176), [72 P.S. §§ 806 and 806.1] known as The Fiscal Code.

(d) When interest payment not required.—In the event that the contract does not contain a grace period and if a contractor or design professional is not paid by the payment date required by subsection (b), no interest penalty payment required under this section shall be paid if payment is made on or before the 15th calendar day after the payment date required under this subchapter.

§ 3933. Contractors' and subcontractors' payment obligations.

(a) Performance by subcontractor entitles subcontractor to payment.—Performance by a subcontractor in accordance with the provisions of the contract shall entitle the subcontractor to payment from the party with whom the subcontractor has contracted. For purposes of this section, the contract between the contractor and subcontractor is presumed to incorporate the terms of the contract between the contractor and the government agency.

(b) Disclosure of progress payment due dates.—A contractor or subcontractor shall disclose to a subcontractor, before a subcontract is executed, the due date for receipt of progress payments from the government agency. Notwithstanding any other provisions of this subchapter, if a contractor or a subcontractor fails to accurately disclose the due date to a subcontractor, the contractor or subcontractor shall be obligated to pay the subcontractor as though the due dates established in subsection (c) were met by the government agency. This subsection shall not apply to a change in due dates because of conditions outside of the contractor's control, including, but not limited to, design changes, change orders or delays in construction due to weather conditions.

(c) Payment.—When a subcontractor has performed in accordance with the provisions of the contract, a contractor shall pay to the subcontractor, and each subcontractor shall in turn pay to its subcontractors, the full or proportional amount received for each such subcontractor's work and material, based on work completed or services provided under the subcontract, 14 days after receipt of a progress payment. Payment shall be made under this section unless it is being withheld under section 3934 (relating to withholding of payment for good faith claims).

(d) Interest due when progress payment not timely.—If any progress payment is not made to a subcontractor by the due date established in the contract or in subsection (c), the contractor shall pay to the subcontractor, in addition to the amount due, interest as computed in section 3932(c) (relating to government agency's progress payment obligations).

(e) When interest payment not required.—In the event that the contract does not contain a grace period and if a subcontractor is not paid by the payment date required by subsection (c), no interest penalty payment required under this section shall be paid if payment is made on or before the 15th calendar day after the payment date required under this subchapter.

§ 3934. Withholding of payment for good faith claims.

(a) When government agency may withhold payment.—The government agency may withhold payment for deficiency items according to terms of the contract. The government agency shall pay the contractor according to the provisions of this subchapter for all other items which appear on the application for payment and have been satisfactorily completed. The contractor may withhold payment from any subcontractor responsible for a deficiency item. The contractor shall pay any subcontractor according to the provisions of this subchapter for any item which appears on the application for payment and has been satisfactorily completed.

(b) Notification when payment withheld for deficiency item.—If a government agency withholds payment from a contractor for a deficiency item, it shall notify the contractor of the deficiency item within the time period specified in the contract or 15 calendar days of the date that the application for payment is received. If a contractor withholds payment from a subcontractor for a deficiency item, it must notify the subcontractor or supplier and the government agency of the reason within 15 calendar days of the date after receipt of the notice of the deficiency item from the government agency.

§ 3935. Penalty and attorney fees.

(a) Penalty.—If arbitration or a claim with the Board of Claims or a court of competent jurisdiction is commenced to recover payment due under this subchapter and it is determined that the government agency, contractor or subcontractor has failed to comply with the payment terms of this subchapter, the arbitrator, the Board of Claims or the court may award, in addition to all other damages due, a penalty equal to 1% per month of the amount that was withheld in bad faith. An amount shall be deemed to have been withheld in bad faith to the extent that the withholding was arbitrary or vexatious. An amount shall not be deemed to have been withheld in bad faith to the extent it was withheld pursuant to section 3934 (relating to withholding of payment for good faith claims).

(b) Attorney fees.—Notwithstanding any agreement to the contrary, the prevailing party in any proceeding to recover any payment under this subchapter may be awarded a reasonable attorney fee in an amount to be determined by the Board of Claims, court or arbitrator, together with expenses, if it is determined that the government agency, contractor or subcontractor acted in bad faith. An amount shall be deemed to have been withheld in bad faith to the extent that the withholding was arbitrary or vexatious.

§ 3936. Contracts involving Federal aid.

If any provision of this chapter conflicts with a Federal statute or regulation or with conditions attached to the receipt of Federal aid, this chapter shall not operate to prevent receipt of the Federal aid in accordance with any Federal statute or regulation.

§ 3937. Certain provisions unenforceable.

A provision in the contract making it subject to the laws of another state or requiring that any litigation, arbitration or other dispute resolution process on the contract occurs in another state shall be unenforceable.

§ 3938. Applicability.

(a) **Not applicable in certain situations.**—This subchapter shall not apply in the following situations:

(1) Section 3932 (relating to government agency's progress payment obligations) shall not apply when the Commonwealth agency's nonpayment on a particular project is caused by the failure of the General Assembly to enact a budget for the fiscal year of payment.

(2) Section 3932 shall not apply when a local government unit's nonpayment on a particular project is caused by failure of the Federal or State Government to pay funds due and payable to the local government unit.

(3) Section 3932 shall not apply when a government agency's nonpayment on a particular project is caused by the failure of the General Assembly to enact an operating budget for the fiscal year of payment or a capital budget for the capital project or by failure of the Federal, State or local government to pay funds designated or to be designated for the specific project.

(4) Nothing in this subchapter shall be construed to require payment of interest penalties by the Federal or State Government if the local government unit is liable for the interest.

(b) **Not applicable to following entities.**—This chapter shall not apply to any of the following:

(1) A municipality determined to be distressed under the act of July 10, 1987 (P.L. 246, No. 47), [53 P.S. § 11701.101] known as the Municipalities Financial Recovery Act.

(2) A school district which has been determined to be a distressed school district under section 691 of the act of March 10, 1949 (P.L. 30, No. 14), [24 P.S. § 6-691] known as the Public School Code of 1949.

(3) Repealed by 2022, July 7, P.L. 440, No. 36, § 6(2)(ii), effective in 60 days [Sept. 6, 2022].

(4) A corporate entity or school district as defined in the Pennsylvania Intergovernmental Cooperation Authority Act for Cities of the First Class.

(5) A transportation authority organized or operating under 74 Pa.C.S. Ch. 17 (relating to metropolitan transportation authorities).

§ 3939. Claims by innocent parties.

(a) **No obligation to third parties.**—The government agency shall have no obligation to any third parties for any claim.

(b) **Barred claims.**—Once a contractor has made payment to the subcontractor according to the provisions of this subchapter, future claims for payment against the contractor or the contractor's surety by parties owed payment from the subcontractor which has been paid shall be barred.

§ 3941. Substantial/final payment under contract.

(a) Contract containing provision for retainage.—A contract containing a provision for retainage as provided in section 3921 (relating to retainage) shall contain a provision requiring the architect or engineer to make final inspection within 30 days of receipt of the request of the contractor for final inspection and application for final payment. If the work is substantially completed, the architect or engineer shall issue a certificate of completion and a final certificate for payment, and the government agency shall make payment in full within 45 days except as provided in section 3921, less only one and one-half times the amount required to complete any then-remaining uncompleted minor items, which amount shall be certified by the architect or engineer and, upon receipt by the government agency of any guarantee bonds which may be required, in accordance with the contract, to insure proper workmanship for a designated period of time. The certificate given by the architect or engineer shall list in detail each uncompleted item and a reasonable cost of completion. Final payment of any amount withheld for the completion of the minor items shall be paid upon completion of the items in the certificate of the engineer or architect.

(b) Interest.—The final payment due the contractor from the government agency after substantial completion of the contract shall bear interest at a rate of 6% per annum for all contracts without provisions for retainage and at a rate of 10% per annum for all contracts with provisions for retainage, the interest to begin after the date that such payment becomes due and payable to the contractor. However, where the government agency has issued bonds to finance the project, interest shall be payable to the contractor at the rate of interest of the bond issue or at the rate of 10% per annum, whichever is less, but in no event shall the interest payable to the contractor be at a rate of interest less than the legal rate of interest.

§ 3942. Arbitration.

If a dispute should arise between the contractor and the government agency over the payment of retainages and final payment, then the dispute shall be arbitrated under the applicable terms of the contract. If the contract contains no provision for arbitration, then both parties may mutually agree to arbitrate the dispute under the rules of the American Arbitration Association or in accordance with 42 Pa.C.S. Ch. 73 (relating to arbitration). In any event, either party shall have the right of appeal from any decision and award as provided by law.

NONRECEIPT OF BIDS
73 P.S. §§ 1641–1644

§ 1641. Short title.

This act shall be known and may be cited as the Public Contract Bid Nonreceipt Act.

§ 1641.1. Nonreceipt of bids.

(a) Purchase of goods.—When a political subdivision, municipality authority or transportation authority advertises for bids on an item and no bids are received, the political subdivision, municipality authority or transportation authority shall rebid the item. If again such bids are not received, the political subdivision, municipality authority or transportation authority may purchase or enter into contracts for the purchase of any item where no bids are received from suppliers for the item within 45 days of the date of second advertisement therefor.

(b) Sale of property.—When a political subdivision, municipality authority or transportation authority is required to advertise for bids in order to sell real or personal property and no bids are received, the political subdivision, municipality authority or transportation authority may proceed as follows:

(1) The political subdivision, municipality authority or transportation authority may advertise for bids a second time.

(2) If no bids are received within 15 days of the second advertisement, the political subdivision, municipality authority or transportation authority may initiate negotiations for a private sale of the property, taking into consideration its fair market value.

(3) The political subdivision, municipality authority or transportation authority must publicly announce the identity of the parties, the sale price and a summary of the other terms and conditions relating to any proposed private sale at a regular or special meeting of its governing body.

(4) After the public announcement of the sale is made in accordance with paragraph (3), at least 30 days must elapse before a political subdivision, municipality authority or transportation authority may authorize the private sale in accordance with this subsection.

(c) Contracts for services.—When a political subdivision, municipality authority or transportation authority is required to advertise for bids in order to enter into a contract for services and no bids are received, the political subdivision, municipality authority or transportation authority may proceed as follows:

(1) The political subdivision, municipality authority or transportation authority may advertise for bids a second time.

(2) If no bids are received within 15 days of the second advertisement, the political subdivision, municipality authority or transportation authority may initiate negotiations for a contract to obtain the services previously advertised, with any provider not otherwise disqualified by law or an enactment or policy of the governing body.

(3) Prior to executing the contract, the political subdivision, municipality authority or transportation authority, at a regular or special meeting of its governing body, must publicly announce the identity of the parties, the proposed contract price and a summary of the other terms and conditions relating to any proposed contract in order to demonstrate that the services to be procured are consistent with those previously advertised.

(d) Evasion.—The penalties, civil or criminal, surcharges and other liability set forth in law, regulation or ordinance for evading an advertising requirement for bids shall apply to a member of the governing body of a political subdivision, municipality authority or transportation authority who votes for a transaction under this section with the intent to evade the advertising requirement of the applicable law, regulation or ordinance.

(e) Definition.—As used in this section, the term "services" means the furnishing of labor, time or effort by a contractor not involving the delivery of a specific end product other than drawings, specifications or reports which are merely incidental to the required performance. The term includes the routine operation or maintenance of existing structures, buildings or real property, the repair or rehabilitation of existing infrastructure and utility services or those services formerly provided by public utilities, such as electrical, telephone, water and sewage service. The term does not include employment agreements or collective bargaining agreements.

§ 1642. Applicability of act.

The provisions of this act shall apply only when such political subdivision, municipality authority or transportation authority has complied with the provisions of law as to advertising for bids and no bids were submitted.

§ 1643. Repeals.

All acts and parts of acts are repealed insofar as they are inconsistent with this act.

§ 1644. Effective date.

This act shall take effect immediately.

CHAPTER 13

ELECTRONIC BIDDING BY LOCAL GOVERNMENT UNITS

62 Pa.C.S. §§ 4601–4604

TABLE OF CONTENTS

---

§ 4601. Short title of chapter.

This chapter shall be known and may be cited as the Local Government Unit Electronic Bidding Act.

§ 4602. Definitions.

The following words and phrases when used in this chapter shall have the meanings given to them in this section unless the context clearly indicates otherwise:

"Local government unit." A county, city, borough, incorporated town, township, school district, vocational school district, county institution district, home rule municipality, local authority or any joint or cooperative body of local government units or any instrumentality, authority or corporation thereof which has authority to enter into a contract.

§ 4603. Electronic bidding.

Notwithstanding any other provision of law concerning the requirements for competitive bidding for purchases and contracts by a local government unit, a local government unit may permit the electronic submission of bids and may receive bids electronically if the local government unit has the electronic capability to maintain the confidentiality of the bid until the bid opening time.

§ 4604. Competitive electronic auction bidding.

(a) Conditions for use.—Notwithstanding any other provision of law concerning the requirements for competitive bidding for purchases and contracts, if a local government unit determines by resolution that use of competitive electronic auction bidding is in the best interests of the local government unit, a contract for supplies or services, but not for construction or design professional services, may be entered into by competitive electronic auction bidding.

(b) Invitation for bids.—An invitation for bids shall be issued and shall include a procurement description and all contractual terms, whenever practical, and conditions applicable to the procurement, including a notice that bids will be received in an electronic auction manner.

(c) Public notice.—Public notice and advertisement of the invitation for bids shall be given in the same manner as provided in the law otherwise applicable to the local government unit.

(d) Auctions.—Bids shall be accepted electronically at the time and in the manner designated in the invitation for bids. During the auction, each bidder shall have the capability to view their bid rank or the low bid price. Bidders may reduce their bid prices during the auction. At the conclusion of the auction, the record of the bid prices received and the name of each bidder shall be open to public inspection.

(e) Withdrawal of bids.—After the auction period has terminated, withdrawal of bids shall be permitted by the written determination of the local government unit when the bidder requests relief and presents credible evidence that the reason for the lower bid price was a clerical mistake, as opposed to a judgment mistake, and was actually due to an unintentional arithmetical error or an unintentional omission of a substantial quantity of work, labor, material or services made directly in the compilation of the bid. The request for relief and the supporting evidence must be received by the local government unit within a reasonable time period after the bid opening. The time period shall be specified by the local government unit.

(f) Award.—The contract shall be awarded within 60 days of the auction by written notice to the lowest responsible bidder, or all bids shall be rejected, except as otherwise provided in this section. Extensions of the date for the award may be made by mutual written consent of the local government unit and the lowest responsible bidder.

CHAPTER 14
PUBLIC WORKS CONTRACTORS' BONDS

8 P.S. § 191 et seq.

TABLE OF CONTENTS

Sec.

Section 6(b) of Act 1998-57 repealed this section insofar as it relates to Commonwealth agencies as defined in 62 Pa.C.S. § 103. 8 P.S. § 191 is repealed insofar as inconsistent with 2004, Jan. 12, P.L. 1, No. 1, imd. effective, pursuant to § 3 of that act. See 35 P.S. § 1711.

§ 1. Short title.

This act shall be known and may be cited as the "Public Works Contractors' Bond Law of 1967."

§ 2. Definitions.

As used in this act—(1) "Claimant" includes any individual, firm, partnership, association or corporation.

(2) "Contracting body" means any officer, employe, authority, board, bureau, commission, department, agency or institution of the Commonwealth of Pennsylvania or any State-aided institution, or any county, city, district, municipal corporation, municipality, municipal authority, political subdivision, school district, educational institution, borough, incorporated town, township, poor district, county institution district, other incorporated district or other public instrumentality, which has authority to contract for the construction, reconstruction, alteration or repair of any public building or other public work or public improvement, including highway work.

(3) "State-aided institution" shall mean aid include any institution which receives State funds directly or indirectly for the construction, reconstruction, alteration or repair of its buildings, works or improvements, including highway work.

§ 3. Bonds required; types; sureties; filing.

(a) Before any contract exceeding five thousand dollars ($5,000) for the construction, reconstruction, alteration or repair of any public building or other public work or public improvement, including highway work, of any contracting body is awarded to any prime contractor, such contractor shall furnish to the contracting body the following bonds, which shall become binding upon the awarding of said contract to such contractor:

(1) A performance bond at one hundred percent of the contract amount, conditioned upon the faithful performance of the contract in accordance with the plans, specifications and conditions of the contract. Such bond shall be solely for the protection of the contracting body which awarded the contract.

(2) A payment bond at one hundred percent of the contract amount. Such bond shall be solely for the protection of claimants supplying labor or materials to the prime contractor to whom the contract was awarded, or to any of his subcontractors, in the prosecution of the work provided for in such contract, and shall be conditioned for the prompt payment of all such material furnished or labor supplied or performed in the prosecution of the work. "Labor or materials" shall include public utility services and reasonable rentals of equipment, but only for periods when the equipment rented is actually used at the site.

(b) Each of such bonds shall be executed by one or more surety companies legally authorized to do business in the Commonwealth of Pennsylvania. If the contracting body is the Commonwealth of Pennsylvania or any officer, employe, board, bureau, commission, department, agency or institution thereof, such bond shall be payable to the Commonwealth of Pennsylvania. If the contracting body is other than one of those enumerated in this subsection, such bond shall be payable to such other contracting body.

(c) Each of such bonds shall be filed in the office of the contracting body which awarded the contract for which such bonds were given.

§ 3.1. Financial security required; sureties; filing.

(a) Before any contract exceeding ten thousand dollars ($10,000) for the construction, reconstruction, alteration or repair of any public building or other public work or public improvement, including highway work, of any contracting body is awarded to any prime contractor, such contractor shall furnish to the contracting body the following financial security, which shall become binding upon the awarding of said contract to such contractor:

(1) A performance bond, Federal or Commonwealth chartered lending institution irrevocable letter of credit or restrictive or escrow account in such lending institution, equal to one hundred percent of the contract amount, conditioned upon the faithful performance of the contract in accordance with the plans, specifications and conditions of the contract. Such financial security shall be solely for the protection of the contracting body which awarded the contract.

(2) A payment bond, Federal or Commonwealth chartered lending institution irrevocable letter of credit or restrictive or escrow account in such lending institution, equal to one hundred percent of the contract amount. Such financial security shall be solely for the protection of claimants supplying labor or materials to the prime contractor to whom the contract was awarded, or to any of his subcontractors, in the prosecution of the work provided for in such contract, and shall be conditioned for the prompt payment of all such material furnished or labor supplied or performed in the prosecution of the work. "Labor or materials" shall include public utility services and reasonable rentals of equipment, but only for periods when the equipment rented is actually used at the site.

(b) Any bond or other financial security under the provisions of this act shall be executed by one or more surety companies or Federal or Commonwealth chartered lending institutions, chosen by the party posting the financial security and acceptable to the contracting body, legally authorized to do business in the Commonwealth of Pennsylvania.

(c) A duplicate copy of each financial security, including bonds, shall be filed in the office of the contracting body which awarded the contract for which such bonds or financial security were given.

(d) For purposes of this section, the phrase "contracting body" shall mean any county, school district, intermediate unit, area vocational-technical school, city, borough, incorporated town, township, home-rule municipality and any authority formed under the act of May 2, 1945 (P.L. 382, No. 164), known as the "Municipality Authorities Act of 1945."[1]

(e) For the contracting body as defined in subsection (d), the provisions of this section supersede the provisions of section 3 of this act.

(f) In the case of contracts of ten thousand dollars ($10,000) or less, nothing in this section shall be construed as preventing a contracting body, prior to awarding a contract for the construction, reconstruction, alteration or repair of any public building or other public work or public improvement, including highway work, from requiring a prime contractor to furnish financial security in accordance with subsection (a).

§ 4. Actions on payment bonds; service of notice.

(a) Subject to the provisions of subsection (b) hereof, any claimant who has performed labor or furnished material in the prosecution of the work provided for in any contract for which a payment bond has been given pursuant to the provisions of subsection (a) of section 3 of this act, or for which other financial security has been given pursuant to subsection (a) of section 3.1 of this act, and who has not been paid in full therefor before the expiration of ninety days after the day on which such claimant performed the last of such labor or furnished the last of such materials for which he claims payments, may bring an action on such payment bond or other financial security in his own name, in assumpsit, to recover any amount due him for such labor or material, and may prosecute such action to final judgment and have execution on the judgment.

(b) Any claimant who has a direct contractual relationship with any subcontractor of the prime contractor who gave such payment bond or other financial security but has no contractual relationship, express or implied, with such prime contractor may bring an action on the payment bond or other financial security only if he has given written notice to such contractor within ninety days from the date on which the claimant performed the last of the labor or furnished the last of the materials for which he claims payment, stating with substantial accuracy the amount claimed and the name of the person for whom the work was performed or to whom the material was furnished.

Notice shall be served by registered or certified mail, postage prepaid, in an envelope addressed to such contractor at any place where his office is regularly maintained for the transaction of business or served in any manner in which legal process may be served in the manner now or hereafter provided by law for the service of a summons, except that such service need not be made by a public officer.

§ 5. Applicability of act.

This act shall apply whether or not the material furnished or labor performed enters into and becomes a component part of the public building or other public work or public improvement, including highway work.

§ 6. Payment bonds; certified copies furnished; requests; fee for costs; evidence.

(a) The contracting body shall furnish a certified copy of any payment bond or other financial security and the contract for which such bond or security was given to any person who makes an application for such copy and who submits an affidavit stating that:

---

1. 53 P.S. §§ 301 et seq.

(1) He has furnished material or performed labor, for the completion of the work provided for in the contract, and that he has not been fully paid for such labor or material; or

(2) He is a defendant in an action brought on a payment bond or other financial security; or

(3) He is the surety in a payment bond on which an action has been brought or is the representative of a lending institution that has issued or is maintaining financial security on which an action has been brought.

(b) Every such applicant shall pay for each certified copy a fee fixed by the contracting body to cover the actual cost of the preparation of such copy.

(c) A certified copy of any payment bond or other financial security and of the contract for which such bond or security was given shall constitute prima facie evidence of the contents, execution and delivery of the original of such bond and contract.

§ 7. Repealed. 1978, April 28, P.L. 202, No. 53, § 2(a)[1413], effective June 27, 1978.

§ 8. Specifying surety or agent; penalty.

(a) It is unlawful for any representative of a contracting body, in issuing an invitation for bids, to require that any bond specified in section 3 of this act or authorized under section 3.1 of this act be furnished by a particular surety company or through a particular agent or broker.

(b) Any person who violates the provisions of this section is guilty of a misdemeanor and upon conviction thereof shall be sentenced to pay a fine not exceeding five thousand dollars ($5,000), or undergo imprisonment for a term not exceeding five years, or both.

§ 9. Prior contract rights not affected.

All rights, duties, and obligations arising under any contract awarded pursuant to an invitation for bids issued prior to the effective date of this act, or any bond given in connection with such a contract, shall continue to be governed by the provisions of the law in effect at the time of the execution of such contract by all of the parties thereto.

§ 10. Specific repeals.

The following acts and parts of acts are repealed in so far as they are inconsistent herewith:

(1) Sections 2408 and 2409, act of April 9, 1929 (P.L. 177),[2] known as they are inconsistent herewith:

(2) The act of June 22, 1931 (P.L. 880).[3]

(3) The act of June 22, 1931 (P.L. 881).[4]

(4) Section 1905, renumbered section 1907, act of June 23, 1931 (P.L. 932), known as "The Third Class City Code,"[5] reenacted and amended June 28, 1951 (P.L. 662).

(5) The act of June 23, 1931 (P.L. 1181).[6]

(6) Section 1804, act of June 24, 1931 (P.L. 1206), known as "The First Class Township Code," reenacted and amended May 27, 1949 (P.L. 1955).

2. 71 P.S. §§ 638, 639.

3. 53 P.S. §§ 1291, 1292.

4. 53 P.S. §§ 1293-1297.

5. 53 P.S. § 36907; 53 P.S. §§ 67604, 67605.

6. 53 P.S. § 56804.

(7) Section 803, act of May 1, 1933 (P.L. 103), known as "The Second Class Township Code,"[7] reenacted and amended July 10, 1947 (P.L. 1481).

(8) Section 10, act of May 2, 1945 (P.L. 382), known as the "Municipality Authorities Act of 1945."[8]

(9) Section 404, act of June 1, 1945 (P.L. 1242), known as the "State Highway Law."[9]

(10) Sections 756 and 757, act of March 10, 1949 (P.L. 30), known as the "Public School Code of 1949."[10]

(11) Section 11, act of March 31, 1949 (P.L. 372), known as "The General State Authority Act of One Thousand Nine Hundred Forty-Nine."[11]

(12) Section 13, act of April 18, 1949 (P.L. 604), known as the "State Highway and Bridge Authority Act."[12]

(13) Section 6, act of May 27, 1953 (P.L. 244).[13]

(14) Section 2518, act of July 28, 1953 (P.L. 723), known as the "Second Class County Code."[14]

(15) Section 2318, act of August 9, 1955 (P.L. 323), known as "The County Code."[15]

(16) Section 1406, act of February 1, 1966 (P.L. 1656), known as "The Borough Code."[16]

7. 53 P.S. § 65803.
8. 53 P.S. § 312.
9. 36 P.S. § 670-404.
10. 24 P.S. §§ 7-756, 7-757.
11. 71 P.S. § 1707.11.
12. 36 P.S. § 3613.
13. 53 P.S. § 53206.
14. 16 P.S. § 5518.
15. 16 P.S. § 2318.
16. 53 P.S. § 46406.

CHAPTER 15

PREVAILING WAGE ACT

43 P.S. §§ 165-1 et seq.

TABLE OF CONTENTS

---

§ 1. Short title.

This act shall be known and may be cited as the "Pennsylvania Prevailing Wage Act".

§ 2. Definitions.

As used in this act—

(1) **"Department"** means Department of Labor and Industry of the Commonwealth of Pennsylvania.

(2) **"Locality"** means any political subdivision, or combination of the same, within the county in which the public work is to be performed. When no workmen for which a prevailing minimum wage is to be determined hereunder are employed in the locality, the locality may be extended to include adjoining political subdivisions where such workmen are employed in those crafts or trades for which there are no workmen employed in the locality as otherwise herein defined.

(3) **"Maintenance work"** means the repair of existing facilities when the size, type or extent of such facilities is not thereby changed or increased.

(4) **"Public body"** means the Commonwealth of Pennsylvania, any of its political subdivisions, any authority created by the General Assembly of the Commonwealth of Pennsylvania and any instrumentality or agency of the Commonwealth of Pennsylvania.

(5) **"Public work"** means construction, reconstruction, demolition, alteration and/or repair work other than maintenance work, done under contract and paid for in whole or in part out of the funds of a public body where the estimated cost of the total project is in excess of twenty-five thousand dol-

Table of Contents
Part I Ch. 1–3 Ethics, Records, Open Meetings
Part II Ch. 4–10 Taxation
Part III Ch. 11–18 Torts, Contracts & Civil Rules
Part IV Ch. 19–24 Zoning & Planning
Part V Ch. 25–30 Construction and Emergency Codes
Part VI Ch. 31–39 Municipal Codes
Index

lars ($25,000), but shall not include work performed under a rehabilitation or manpower training program.

(6) **"Secretary"** means the Secretary of Labor and Industry or his duly authorized deputy or representative.

(7) **"Workman"** includes laborer, mechanic, skilled and semi-skilled laborer and apprentices employed by any contractor or subcontractor and engaged in the performance of services directly upon the public work project, regardless of whether their work becomes a component part thereof, but does not include material suppliers or their employes who do not perform services at the job site.

(8) **"Work performed under a rehabilitation program"**, means work arranged by and at a State institution primarily for teaching and upgrading the skills and employment opportunities of the inmates of such institutions.

(9) **"Advisory Board"** means the board created by section 2.1 of this act.

(10) **"Appeals Board"** means the board created by section 2.2 of this act.

§ 2.1. Advisory Board, powers and duties.

(a) There is hereby created in the Department of Labor and Industry an Advisory Board consisting of seven members for the purpose of assisting the secretary in carrying out his duties under the act to which this is an amendment.

(b) Except for the member employed by the secretary, each member of the Advisory Board shall be appointed by the Governor and shall receive a compensation of thirty dollars ($30) per day for each day actually spent in the performance of his duties plus necessary expenses.

(c) Of the seven members, one shall be a representative of an association of general contractors engaged full-time in the building construction industry, one shall be a representative of an association of heavy and highway contractors engaged full time in the heavy and highway construction industry, one shall be a member of an historically established union representing labor in the building construction industry, one shall be a member of an historically established union representing labor in the heavy and highway construction industry, one shall be a member of an association representing a political subdivision, one shall be learned in the law and employed by the secretary, and one shall not be engaged in or employed by the building industry or by a public body but shall represent the general public.

(d) At least two weeks' public notice shall be given in the manner prescribed by regulation of the board prior to any meeting of the board. Four members of the board shall constitute a quorum.

(e) The Advisory Board shall have the power and duty to—

(1) Consult with the secretary at his request concerning any matter arising under the administration of this act.

(2) Advise and assist the secretary in carrying out the duties provided for him by section 7 of this act.

(3) Promulgate rules and regulations necessary to carry out the duties placed upon the board by this act.

§ 2.2. Appeals Board, powers and duties.

(a) There is hereby created in the Department of Labor and Industry an Appeals Board consisting of seven members for the purpose of hearing and determining grievances arising out of the administration of the act to which this is an amendment.

(b) Except for the member employed by the secretary, each member of the Appeals Board shall be appointed by the Governor and shall receive a compensation of thirty dollars ($30) per day for each day actually spent in the performance of his duties plus necessary expenses.

(c) Of the seven members, one shall be a representative of an association of general contractors engaged full-time in the building construction industry, one shall be a representative of an association of heavy and highway contractors engaged full time in the heavy and highway construction industry, one shall be a member of an historically established union representing labor in the building construction industry, one shall be a member of an historically established union representing labor in the heavy and highway construction industry, one shall be a member of an association representing a political subdivision, one shall be learned in the law and employed by the secretary, and one shall not be engaged in or employed by the building industry or by a public body but shall represent the general public. No member of the Advisory Board created by this amendatory act shall be appointed to the Appeals Board.

(d) Four members of the board shall constitute a quorum and the board shall neither sit for purposes of hearing any grievance nor make any determination unless a quorum is present.

(e) The Appeals Board shall have the power and duty to—

(1) Hear and determine any grievance or appeal arising out of the administration of this act.

(2) Promulgate rules and regulations necessary to carry out the duties placed upon the board by this act: Provided, however, That any such rules and regulations shall provide for notice of filing of grievances and appeals, public hearings, right of representation and all other procedures required by due process of law.

§ 3. Specifications.

The specifications for every contract for any public work to which any public body is a party, shall contain a provision stating the minimum wage rate that must be paid to the workmen employed in the performance of the contract.

§ 4. Duty of public body.

It shall be the duty of every public body which proposes the making of a contract for any project of public work to determine from the secretary the prevailing minimum wage rates which shall be paid by the contractor to the workmen upon such project. Reference to such prevailing minimum rates shall be published in the notice issued for the purpose of securing bids for such project of public work. Whenever any contract for a project of public work is entered into, the prevailing minimum wages as determined by the secretary shall be incorporated into and made a part of such contract and shall not be altered during the period such contract is in force.

§ 5. Prevailing wage.

Not less than the prevailing minimum wages as determined hereunder shall be paid to all workmen employed on public work.

§ 6. Duty of contractor.

Every contractor and subcontractor shall keep an accurate record showing the name, craft and the actual hourly rate of wage paid to each workman employed by him in connection with public work, and such record shall be preserved for two years from date of payment. The record shall be open at all reasonable hours to the inspection of the public body awarding the contract and to the secretary.

§ 7. Duty of secretary.

The secretary shall, after consultation with the advisory board, determine the general prevailing minimum wage rate in the locality in which the public work is to be performed for each craft or classification of all workmen needed to perform public work contracts during the anticipated term thereof: Provided, however, That employer and employe contributions for employe benefits pursuant to a bona fide collective bargaining agreement shall be considered an integral part of the wage rate for the purpose of determining the minimum wage rate under this act. Nothing in this act, however, shall prohibit the payment of more than the general prevailing minimum wage rate to any workman employed on public work. The secretary shall forthwith give notice by mail of all determinations of general prevailing minimum wage rates made pursuant to this section to any representative of any craft, any employer or any representative of any group of employers, who shall in writing request the secretary so to do.

§ 8. Review of rates, petition and hearing.

Any prospective bidder or his representative, any representative of any group of employers engaged in the particular type of construction, reconstruction, alteration and demolition or repair work involved, any representative of any craft or classification of workmen or the public body may, within ten days after the publication and issue of the specifications covering the particular contract for public work involved, file with the secretary a verified petition to review the determination of any such rate or rates. Within two days thereafter a copy of such petition shall be filed with the public body authorizing the public work. The petition shall set forth the facts upon which it is based. The secretary shall, upon notice to the petitioner, the public body authorizing the public work and the recognized collective bargaining representatives for the particular crafts and classifications involved, and also to all persons entitled to receive notice pursuant to subsection (a) of section 7 hereof, institute an investigation and hold a public hearing within twenty days after the filing of such petition. Within ten days thereafter, the secretary shall make a determination and transmit it, in writing, to the public body and to the interested parties. Such determination shall be final unless within ten days an appeal is filed with the Appeals Board.

Upon receipt by the public body of the notice of the filing of such petition, the public body awarding the contract or authorizing the public work shall extend the closing date for the submission of bids until five days after the final determination of the general prevailing minimum wage rates pursuant to this section and the publication of such findings.

Upon the filing of any such petition, notice thereof and of the extension of the closing date for submission of bids, shall be given forthwith by the awarding public body in a special bulletin to all interested parties as defined herein, notice shall also be given to the bidders by the awarding body of the final determination of the secretary or Appeals Board which shall also be included in the contract. The determination of the secretary or Appeals Board shall be included in the contract.

§ 9. Posting of rates.

Contractors and subcontractors performing public work for a public body subject to the provisions of this act shall post the general prevailing minimum wage rates for each craft and classification involved, as determined by the secretary, including the effective date of any changes thereof, in prominent and easily accessible places at the site of the work, or at such place or places as are used by them to pay workmen their wages.

§ 10. Duty of public body.

(a) Before final payment is made by, or on behalf of any public body of any sum or sums due on public work, it shall be the duty of the treasurer of the public body or other officer or person charged with the custody and disbursement of the funds of the public body to require the contractor and subcontractor to file statements, in writing, in form satisfactory to the secretary, certifying to the amounts then due and owing from such contractor and subcontractor, filing such statement to any and all workmen for wages due on account of public work, setting forth therein the names of the persons whose wages are unpaid and the amount due to each respectively, which statement so to be filed shall be verified by the oath of the contractor and subcontractor, as the case may be, that he has read such statement subscribed by him, knows the contents thereof and that the same is true of his own knowledge: Provided, nevertheless, That nothing herein shall impair the right of a contractor to receive final payment because of the failure of any subcontractor to comply with provisions of this act.

(b) In case any workman shall have filed a protest, in writing, within three months from the date of the occurrence of the incident complained of, with the secretary, objecting to the payment to any contractor to the extent of the amount or amounts due or to become due to the said workman for wages for labors performed on public works, thereupon, the secretary shall direct the fiscal or financial officer of the public body, or other person charged with the custody and disbursements of the funds of the public body, to deduct from the whole amount of any payment on account thereof the sum or sums admitted by any contractor in such statement or statements so filed, to be due and owing by him on account of wages earned on such public work before making payment of the amount certified for payment and may withhold the amount so deducted for the benefit of the workmen whose wages are unpaid, as shown by the verified statement filed by any contractor, and may pay directly to any workmen the amount shown to be due to him for such wages by the statements filed as hereinbefore required, thereby discharging the obligation of the contractor to the person receiving such payment to the extent of the amount thereof.

(c) Any contractor or subcontractor who shall, under oath, verify the statement required to be filed under this section, which is known to him to be false, shall be guilty of a misdemeanor, and shall, upon conviction, be sentenced to pay a fine of not exceeding two thousand five hundred dollars ($2,500) or to undergo imprisonment not exceeding five years, or both.

§ 11. Remedies and penalties.

(a) The fiscal or financial officer, or any public body having public work performed under which any workman shall have been paid less than the prevailing wage, shall forthwith notify the secretary, in writing, of the name of the person or firm failing to pay the prevailing wages.

(b) Any workman may, within three months from the date of the occurrence of the incident complained of, file a protest, in writing, with the secretary objecting to the amount of wages paid for services performed by him on public work as being less than the prevailing wages for such services.

(c) Whenever a fiscal or financial officer of any public body shall notify the secretary that any person or firm required to pay its workmen the prevailing wage under this act has failed so to do, or whenever any workman employed upon public work shall have filed a timely protest objecting that he has been paid less than prevailing wages as required by this act, it shall be the duty of and the secretary shall forthwith investigate the matter and determine whether or not there has been a failure to pay the prevailing wages and whether such failure was intentional or otherwise. In any such investigation, the secretary shall provide for an appropriate hearing upon due notice to interested parties including the workmen, the employer and their respective representative, if any.

(d) In the event that the secretary shall determine, after notice and hearing as required by this section, that any person or firm has failed to pay the prevailing wages and that such failure was not intentional, he shall afford such person or firm a reasonable opportunity to adjust the matter by making payment or providing adequate security for the payment of the amounts required to be paid under this act as prevailing wages to the workmen affected on such terms and conditions as shall be approved by the secretary.

(e) In the event that the secretary shall determine, after notice and hearing as required by this section, that any person or firm has failed to pay the prevailing wages and that such failure was intentional, he shall thereupon notify all public bodies of the name or names of such persons or firms and no contract shall be

awarded to such persons or firms or to any firm, corporation or partnership in which such persons or firms have an interest until three years have elapsed from the date of the notice to the public bodies aforesaid. The secretary may in addition thereto request the Attorney General to proceed to recover the penalties for the Commonwealth of Pennsylvania which are payable under subsection (f) of this section.

(f) Whenever it shall be determined by the secretary, after notice and hearing as required by this section, that any person or firm has failed to pay the prevailing wages and that such failure was intentional, such persons or firm shall be liable to the Commonwealth of Pennsylvania for liquidated damages, in addition to damages for any other breach of the contract in the amount of the underpayment of wages due any workman engaged in the performance of such contract.

(g) It shall not constitute a failure to pay the prevailing wage rates for the work of a particular craft or classification where the prevailing wage rates determined for a specific craft or classification has been paid, and it is asserted that one or more bona fide craft unions contend that the work should have been assigned to their members instead of the members of the specific craft to whom it was assigned or by whom it was performed.

(h) The following shall constitute substantial evidence of intentional failure to pay prevailing wage rates:

(1) Any acts of omission or commission done wilfully or with a knowing disregard of the rights of workmen resulting in the payment of less than prevailing wage rates.

(2) After there has been a finding by the secretary in the manner required by this section that any person or firm has failed to pay the prevailing wages prescribed by this act and thereafter there shall be a failure by such person or firm to pay the prevailing wages prescribed by this act, or there shall be a subsequent failure of such person or firm to comply with any opportunity to adjust any differences which shall be afforded him by the secretary.

§ 12. Failure to comply, termination.

In any case where the secretary shall have determined that any person or firm has failed to pay the prevailing wages under subsections (e) and (f) of section 11 hereof, he may direct the public body to terminate, and the public body may terminate, any such contractor's right to proceed with the public work.

§ 13. Workmen's rights.

Any workmen paid less than the rates specified in the contract shall have a right of action for the difference between the wage so paid and the wages stipulated in the contract, which right of action shall be instituted within six months from the occurrence of the event creating such right.

§ 14. Rules and regulations.

The secretary is hereby authorized and empowered to prescribe, adopt, promulgate, rescind and enforce rules and regulations pertaining to the administration and enforcement of the provisions of this act.

§ 15. Application of Act.

This act shall have no application to any public works subject to the Walsh-Healey Act the act of June 30, 1936, chapter 881, 49 Stat. 2036, 41 USCA sections 35-45, or the Davis Bacon Act, the act of March 3, 1931, 40 U.S.Code 276(a).

§ 16. Repealer.

All acts and parts of acts are repealed in so far as they are inconsistent herewith.

CHAPTER 16

LIMITATION OF ACTIONS & APPEALS GENERALLY

42 Pa.C.S. §§ 5522, 5524, 5571 & 5572

TABLE OF CONTENTS

---

§ 5522. Six months limitation.

(a) Notice prerequisite to action against government unit.

(1) Within six months from the date that any injury was sustained or any cause of action accrued, any person who is about to commence any civil action or proceeding within this Commonwealth or elsewhere against a government unit for damages on account of any injury to his person or property under Chapter 85 (relating to matters affecting government units) or otherwise shall file in the office of the government unit, and if the action is against a Commonwealth agency for damages, then also file in the office of the Attorney General, a statement in writing, signed by or in his behalf, setting forth:

(i) The name and residence address of the person to whom the cause of action has accrued.

(ii) The name and residence address of the person injured.

(iii) The date and hour of the accident.

(iv) The approximate location where the accident occurred.

(v) The name and residence or office address of any attending physician.

(2) If the statement provided for by this subsection is not filed, any civil action or proceeding commenced against the government unit more than six months after the date of injury shall be dismissed and the person to whom any such cause of action accrued for any personal injury shall be forever barred from proceeding further thereon within this Commonwealth or elsewhere. The court shall excuse noncompliance with this requirement upon a showing of reasonable excuse for failure to file such statement.

(3) In the case of a civil action or proceeding against a government unit other than the Commonwealth government:

(i) The time for giving such written notice does not include the time during which an individual injured is unable, due to incapacitation or disability from the injury, to give notice, not exceeding 90 days of incapacity.

(ii) If the injuries to an individual result in death, the time for giving notice shall commence with such death.

(iii) Failure to comply with this subsection shall not be a bar if the government unit had actual or constructive notice of the incident or condition giving rise to the claim of a person.

(b) Commencement of action required.—The following actions and proceedings must be commenced within six months:

(1) An action against any officer of any government unit for anything done in the execution of his office, except an action subject to another limitation specified in this subchapter.

(2) A petition for the establishment of a deficiency judgment following execution and delivery of the sheriff's deed for the property sold in connection with the execution proceedings referenced in the provisions of section 8103(a) (relating to deficiency judgments).

(3) Repealed. 1992, July 9, P.L. 507, No. 97, § 31, effective in one year.

(4) An action under section 4563(c) (relating to civil remedy available).

(5) An action or proceeding to set aside a judicial sale of property.

(6) A petition for redetermination of fair market value pursuant to section 8103(f.1)(4) following execution and delivery of the sheriff's deed for the property sold in connection with the execution proceedings referenced under section 8103.

(c) **Exception.**—This section shall not apply to any civil action or proceeding brought under section 8522(b)(10) (relating to exceptions to sovereign immunity) or 8542(b)(9) (relating to exceptions to governmental immunity).

§ 5524. Two year limitation.

The following actions and proceedings must be commenced within two years:

(1) An action for assault, battery, false imprisonment, false arrest, malicious prosecution or malicious abuse of process.

(2) An action to recover damages for injuries to the person or for the death of an individual caused by the wrongful act or neglect or unlawful violence or negligence of another.

(3) An action for taking, detaining or injuring personal property, including actions for specific recovery thereof.

(4) An action for waste or trespass of real property.

(5) An action upon a statute for a civil penalty or forfeiture.

(6) An action against any officer of any government unit for the nonpayment of money or the nondelivery of property collected upon on execution or otherwise in his possession.

(7) Any other action or proceeding to recover damages for injury to person or property which is founded on negligent, intentional, or otherwise tortious conduct or any other action or proceeding sounding in trespass, including deceit or fraud, except an action or proceeding subject to another limitation specified in this subchapter.

§ 5571. Appeals generally.

(a) **General rule.**—The time for filing an appeal, a petition for allowance of appeal, a petition for permission to appeal or a petition for review of a quasi-judicial order, in the Supreme Court, the Superior Court or the Commonwealth Court shall be governed by general rules. No other provision of this subchapter shall be applicable to matters subject to this subsection.

(b) **Other courts.**—Except as otherwise provided in subsections (a) and (c) and in section 5571.1 (relating to appeals from ordinances, resolutions, maps, etc.), an appeal from a tribunal or other government unit to a court or from a court to an appellate court must be commenced within 30 days after the entry of the order from which the appeal is taken, in the case of an interlocutory or final order.

(c) **Exceptions.**

(1) Election cases.—The time for appeal from an order in any matter arising under the act of June 3, 1937 (P.L. 1333, No. 320), known as the "Pennsylvania Election Code,"[1] or any other statute relating to registration or elections

1. 25 P.S. § 2601 et seq.

shall, if such statutes provide for a lesser time for appeal, be governed by the appropriate provision of such statutes.

(2) Financing cases.—The time for appeal from an order in any matter arising under the act of July 12, 1972 (P.L. 781, No. 185), known as the "Local Government Unit Debt Act,"[2] or any other statute relating to the incurring of debt by a government unit, shall if such statutes provide for a lesser time for appeal, be governed by the appropriate provision of such statutes.

(3) Probate matters.—The time for appeal from an order of a register of wills under Title 20 (relating to decedents, estates and fiduciaries) shall, if such statute provides a greater time for appeal, be governed by the appropriate provision of such statute.

(4) Execution matters.—The time for appeal from an order of any system or related personnel entered in connection with enforcement of attachments, judgments or similar process or orders shall be governed by general rule.

(d) Interlocutory appeals.—A petition for permission to appeal from an interlocutory order must be filed within 30 days after its entry.

(e) Action following grant of permission to appeal.—The period limited by this section is tolled by the filing of a petition for permission to appeal. If the petition is granted further proceedings in the matter, including any time limitations, shall be governed by general rules or rules of court, and not by the provisions of subsections (b) through (d).

(f) Cross appeals.—An appellee may be permitted by general rules or rules of court to take an appeal within the time limited by rule from an order from which another party has taken a timely appeal, notwithstanding the fact that the time otherwise limited by this section has expired.

1976, July 9, P.L. 586, No. 142, § 2, effective June 27, 1978. As amended 1978, April 28, P.L. 202, No. 53, § 10(67), effective June 27, 1978; 1980, Oct. 5, P.L. 693, No. 142, § 501(a), effective in 60 days; 2002, Dec. 9, P.L. 1705, No. 215, § 3, imd. effective.

§ 5571.1. Appeals from ordinances, resolutions, maps, etc.

(a) Applicability; court of common pleas.—

(1) This section shall apply to any appeal raising questions relating to an alleged defect in the process of, or procedure for, enactment or adoption of any ordinance, resolution, map or similar action of a political subdivision.

(2) An appeal pursuant to this section shall be to the court of common pleas.

(b) Appeals of defects in statutory procedure.—

(1) Any appeal raising questions relating to an alleged defect in statutory procedure shall be brought within 30 days of the intended effective date of the ordinance.

(2) Except as provided in subsection (c), it is the express intent of the General Assembly that this 30-day limitation shall apply regardless of the ultimate validity of the challenged ordinance.

(c) Exemption from limitation.—An appeal shall be exempt from the time limitation in subsection (b) if the party bringing the appeal establishes that, because of the particular nature of the alleged defect in statutory procedure, the application of the time limitation under subsection (b) would result in an impermissible deprivation of constitutional rights.

(d) Presumptions.—Notwithstanding any other provision of law, appeals pursuant to this section shall be subject to, and in accordance with, the following:

(1) An ordinance shall be presumed to be valid and to have been enacted or adopted in strict compliance with statutory procedure.

2. 53 Pa.C.S. § 8001 et seq.

(2) In all cases in which an appeal filed in court more than two years after the intended effective date of the ordinance is allowed to proceed in accordance with subsection (c), the political subdivision involved and residents and landowners within the political subdivision shall be presumed to have substantially relied upon the validity and effectiveness of the ordinance.

(3) An ordinance shall not be found void from inception unless the party alleging the defect in statutory procedure meets the burden of proving the elements set forth in subsection (e).

(e) Burden of proof.—Notwithstanding any other provision of law, an ordinance shall not be found void from inception except as follows:

(1) In the case of an appeal brought within the 30-day time limitation of subsection (b), the party alleging the defect must meet the burden of proving that there was a failure to strictly comply with statutory procedure.

(2) In the case of an appeal which is exempt from the 30-day time limitation in accordance with subsection (c), the party alleging the defect must meet the burden of proving each of the following:

(i) That there was a failure to strictly comply with statutory procedure.

(ii) That there was a failure to substantially comply with statutory procedure which resulted in insufficient notification to the public of impending changes in, or the existence of, the ordinance, so that the public would be prevented from commenting on those changes and intervening, if necessary, or from having knowledge of the existence of the ordinance.

(iii) That there exist facts sufficient to rebut any presumption that may exist pursuant to subsection (d)(2) that would, unless rebutted, result in a determination that the ordinance is not void from inception.

(f) Void ordinances.—A determination that an ordinance is void from inception shall not affect any previously acquired rights of property owners who have exercised good faith reliance on the validity of the ordinance prior to the determination.

(g) Definitions.—As used in this section, the following words and phrases shall have the meanings given to them in this subsection:

"Intended effective date." Notwithstanding the validity of the challenged ordinance, the effective date specified in the challenged ordinance or, if no effective date is specified, the date 60 days after the date the ordinance would have been finally adopted but for the alleged defect in the process of enactment or adoption.

"Ordinance." An ordinance, resolution, map or similar action of a political subdivision.

"Statutory procedure." The pre-enactment and post-enactment procedures prescribed by statute or ordinance in adopting an ordinance.

§ 5572. Time of entry of order

The date of service of an order of a government unit, which shall be the date of mailing if service is by mail, shall be deemed to be the date of entry of the order for the purposes of this subchapter. The date of entry of an order of a court or magisterial district judge may be specified by general rules.

Rules of Civil Procedure for District Justices

Pa.R.C.P.D.J. No. 1082(4) provides that subsections (b), (c)(4) and (f) of this section shall not be deemed suspended or affected by the Rules.

CHAPTER 17

PA. RULES OF CIVIL PROCEDURE

42 Pa.C.S. Rules 1091–1100

ACTION IN MANDAMUS

RULE 1091. CONFORMITY TO CIVIL ACTION

Except as otherwise provided in this chapter, the procedure in the action of mandamus shall be in accordance with the rules relating to a civil action.

Adopted June 25, 1946, effective Jan. 1, 1947. Amended Dec. 16, 1983, effective July 1, 1984.

RULE 1092. VENUE

(a) An action brought in a court of common pleas by the Commonwealth on the relation of the Attorney General may be brought only in

(1) the county where a political subdivision is located when the action is against the political subdivision or an officer thereof, or

(2) the county where the registered office or principal place of business of a corporation or similar entity is located when the action is against the corporation or similar entity or an officer thereof.

(b) An action brought in a court of common pleas in the name of the Commonwealth on the relation of the District Attorney may be brought against a political subdivision or an officer thereof only in the county where the political subdivision is located.

(c) An action brought in a court of common pleas in the name of a party to enforce a right or to compel performance of a public act or duty in which the party has a beneficiary interest distinct from that of the general public may be brought only in

(1) the county in which the cause of action arose when the action is against an officer, department, board, commission or instrumentality of the Commonwealth, or

(2) the county where a political subdivision is located when the action is against the political subdivision or an officer thereof, or

(3) the county where a corporation or similar entity has its registered office or principal place of business when the action is against the corporation or similar entity or an officer thereof.

Adopted June 25, 1946, effective Jan. 1, 1947. Amended Nov. 5, 1975, effective July 1, 1976; June 23, 1976, effective July 1, 1976; amended effective June 24, 1976.

Explanatory Comment—1976

The amendments to these rules governing venue are designed to conform these rules to the changes resulting from the creation of the Commonwealth Court.

The adoption of the new judicial article of the Constitution of 1968 resulted in the creation of a new court of state-wide jurisdiction, the Commonwealth Court. The jurisdiction of that Court was defined by the Appellate Court Jurisdiction Act, 17 P.S. § 211.401 [repealed; see, now, 42 Pa.C.S.A. § 761], and included exclusive jurisdiction over certain matters involving the Commonwealth, its officers and agencies and concurrent jurisdiction in other matters also involving the Commonwealth.

Rules 1092, 1112, 1503 and 2103, as originally drawn, referred to the Court of Common Pleas of Dauphin County as the venue for all such matters. With the creation of the Commonwealth Court and the change in the jurisdiction of the Court of Common Pleas of Dauphin County in these cases, amendment was required.

The amendments recognize that there are certain Commonwealth cases that must be brought only in the Commonwealth Court, other cases where the Commonwealth Court and the Courts of Common Pleas have concurrent jurisdiction and cases where only the Courts of Common Pleas have jurisdiction.

The amendments deal only with those cases where the Commonwealth Court does not have exclusive jurisdiction and an action may properly be brought in a Court of Common Pleas either because the Commonwealth Court and the Court of Common Pleas have concurrent jurisdiction or because only the Court of Common Pleas has jurisdiction. They regulate the venue in such an action in the Court of Common Pleas.

The principal effect of the amendments is the elimination of the Dauphin County court as a proper venue in all cases. The amendments of Rules 1092(c), 1112(c) and 1503(c) expressly recognize venue in the county in which the cause of action arose. In actions in equity, the Commonwealth will have the benefit of the broad venue provisions of Rule 1503(a).

RULE 1093. COMMENCEMENT OF ACTION

An action may be commenced by filing a complaint with the prothonotary.

Adopted June 25, 1946, effective January 1, 1947; amended June 27, 2017, effective October 1, 2017.

RULE 1094. PARTIES DEFENDANT

(a) When an action is commenced to compel performance of a public act or duty by a political subdivision of the Commonwealth, it shall be sufficient to name as defendants such officers in their official capacities as are concerned in the act or duty.

(b) When an action is commenced against a corporation or similar entity, it shall be joined as a defendant with the particular person or body of persons concerned in the performance of the act or duty.

(c) When a public act or duty is required to be performed by an executive or administrative department, by a departmental administrative board or commission or by an independent administrative board or commission of the Commonwealth or by a board or body of a political subdivision, it shall be sufficient to name the department, board, commission or body as the defendant without joining as a defendant the head of the department or the members of the board, commission or body.

Adopted June 25, 1946, effective Jan. 1, 1947.

RULE 1095. THE COMPLAINT

The plaintiff shall set forth in the complaint:

(1) the name and description of the plaintiff and defendant;

(2) the facts upon which plaintiff relies for the relief sought;

(3) the act or duty the defendant is required to perform and the refusal to perform it;

(4) the interest of the plaintiff in the result;

(5) the damages, if any;

(6) the want of any other adequate remedy at law;

(7) a prayer for the entry of a judgment against the defendant commanding that the defendant perform the act or duty required to be performed and for damages, if any, and costs.

Adopted June 25, 1946, effective January 1, 1947; amended April 12, 1999, effective July 1, 1999.

RULE 1096. COUNTERCLAIM

No counterclaim may be asserted.

Adopted June 25, 1946, effective Jan. 1, 1947.

RULE 1097. [RESCINDED]

Note

For service upon the Commonwealth or a political subdivision, see Rule 422.

Rescinded June 20, 1985, effective Jan. 1, 1986.

RULE 1098. PEREMPTORY JUDGMENT

At any time after the filing of the complaint, the court may enter judgment if the right of the plaintiff thereto is clear. Judgment shall not be entered without prior notice to all parties unless the exigency of the case is such as to require action before notice, in which event notice shall be given as soon as possible.

Adopted June 25, 1946, effective Jan. 1, 1947. Amended effective Nov. 19, 1974; amended March 11, 1991, effective July 1, 1991; July 28, 1995, effective Jan. 1, 1996.

Explanatory Comment—1974

Mandamus Rule 1098 was adopted in 1946 at a time when there was no general summary judgment procedure in Pennsylvania. It was appropriately titled "Summary judgment". However, in 1966, twenty years later, Rule 1035 was promulgated which introduced the general summary judgment procedure into our practice.

Several reported mandamus cases since 1966 have used the term "summary judgment" without indicating whether the plaintiff has proceeded under Rule 1098 or under Rule 1035, a distinction which might have some importance in a particular situation. Both procedures are, of course, available to a plaintiff in mandamus.

It was a simple matter to remedy the duplication of titles, and to avoid any confusion as to which procedure a particular plaintiff invoked. The Mandamus Rule was retitled to read "Peremptory Judgment". This title is accurately descriptive and is particularly appropriate because of the historic use of one ancient term "peremptory writ" in the common-law mandamus procedure, and in the old Mandamus Act.

Henceforth a plaintiff in mandamus who seeks the special remedy of Rule 1098 will move for "peremptory judgment", but if he seeks a Rule 1035 remedy, he will move for "summary judgment."

[See Explanatory Comment—1991 following Rule 235]

[See Explanatory Comment—1995 following Rule 227.1]

RULE 1099. TRIAL WITHOUT JURY

The trial of actions in mandamus by a judge sitting without a jury shall be in accordance with Rule 1038.

Adopted June 27, 1969, effective Sept. 1, 1969. Amended Dec. 16, 1983, effective July 1, 1984.

RULE 1100. SUSPENSION OF ACTS OF ASSEMBLY

Section 1 of the Act approved May 9, 1889, P.L. 154, No. 171, 52 P.S. § 1, insofar as it relates to actions of mandamus to recover bodies of entombed coal miners, is suspended in accordance with the provisions of the Constitution of 1968, Article V, Section 10(c).

Adopted March 11, 1991, effective July 1, 1991.

CHAPTER 18

PENNSYLVANIA RULES OF CIVIL PROCEDURE

42 Pa.C.S., Rules 76; 422; 2101–2125

THE COMMONWEALTH AND POLITICAL SUBDIVISIONS AS PARTIES

RULE 76. DEFINITION OF "POLITICAL SUBDIVISION"

The following words and phrases when used in the Rules of Civil Procedure shall have the following meanings, respectively, unless the context clearly indicates otherwise or the particular word or phrase is expressly defined in the chapter in which the particular rule is included:

* * *

Political subdivision–any county, city, borough, incorporated town, township, school district, vocational school district, county institution district or municipal or other local authority;

Official Note: The definition of the term "political subdivision" in this rule has no bearing upon whether a particular entity is or is not a political subdivision for substantive matters.

Author's Note: The Explanatory Comment of the year 2000 provides as follows:

The Supreme Court of Pennsylvania has amended the following rules of civil procedure: Rule 76 which contains a definition of the term "political subdivision," Rules 2126, 2151 and 2176 which provide definitions governing associations as parties and Rule 2179(a)(2) which governs venue when a corporation or similar entity is a party to an action.

Political Subdivision

The rules of civil procedure have heretofore made no provision for a municipal authority as a party. The definition of the term "political subdivision" as set forth in Definition Rule 76 has now been amended to include the phrase "municipal or other local authority." The phrase "municipal or other local authority" is derived from Section 102 of the Judicial Code and Section 101 of Title 2 of the Consolidated Statutes relating to Administrative Law and Procedure.

The primary effect of the amendment is to bring a municipal or other local authority within the chapter of rules governing the Commonwealth and Political Subdivisions as Parties and subject an authority to three rules. Under Rule 2102(b) governing the style of action, an action will be brought by or against an authority "in its name." Rule 2103(b) will limit venue to the county in which the political subdivision is located unless the Commonwealth is the plaintiff or an Act of Assembly provides otherwise. Service upon an authority will be made pursuant to subdivision (b) of Rule 422 governing service upon a political subdivision.

It is recognized that a municipal or other local authority may perform a "sovereign or governmental" function, a "business or proprietary" function or a combination of both. It is useful, however, to have a unified practice which applies to all such entities. It is therefore appropriate that municipal or other local authorities be made subject to the rules governing political subdivisions in view of their performance of sovereign or governmental functions.

The characterization of a municipal or other local authority as a political subdivision is a procedural device only. As the note to the definition states, "[t]he definition of the term 'political subdivision' in this rule has no bearing upon whether a particular entity is or is not a political subdivision for substantive matters."

RULE 422. SERVICE UPON THE COMMONWEALTH AND POLITICAL SUBDIVISIONS

(a) Service of original process upon the Commonwealth or an officer of the Commonwealth, or a department, board, commission or instrumentality of the Commonwealth, or a member thereof, shall be made at the office of the defendant and the office of the attorney general by handing a copy to the person in charge thereof.

(b) Service of original process upon a political subdivision shall be made by handing a copy to

(1) an agent duly authorized by the political subdivision to receive service of process, or

(2) the person in charge at the office of the defendant, or

(3) the mayor, or the president, chairman, secretary or clerk of the tax levying body thereof, and in counties where there is no tax levying body, the chairman or clerk of the board of county commissioners.

(c) This rule shall not apply to an appeal from an administrative determination, order or decree of such officer, department, board, commission or instrumentality.

Adopted June 20, 1985, effective Jan. 1, 1986.

RULE 2101. DEFINITION OF "ACTION"

As used in this chapter,

"action" means any civil action or proceeding brought in or appealed to any court which is subject to these rules.

Adopted June 25, 1946, effective Jan. 1, 1947; amended Dec. 16, 2003, effective July 1, 2004.

RULE 2102. STYLE OF ACTION

(a)(1) An action by the Commonwealth shall be brought in the name of the Commonwealth of Pennsylvania.

(2) An action against a Commonwealth agency or party shall be styled in the following manner: Plaintiff v. "(Name of Agency or Party) of the Commonwealth of Pennsylvania".

(b) An action shall be brought by or against a political subdivision in its name.

Adopted June 25, 1946, effective June 1, 1947. Amended effective April 18, 1975; amended July 18, 1991, effective Jan. 1, 1992.

Explanatory Comment—1991

III. Commonwealth and Political Subdivisions as Parties. Rule 2102(a) governing the style of action in suits involving the Commonwealth was promulgated in 1946, more than thirty years prior to the enactment of legislation waiving sovereign immunity as to Commonwealth parties. The original rule was drafted to refer only to actions brought by the Commonwealth but not those in which a Commonwealth party was a defendant.

Since the General Assembly waived immunity in 1978, however, there have been instances in which the plaintiff sued the Commonwealth without naming the particular Commonwealth party involved. The courts have noted a distinction between the Commonwealth and a Commonwealth party and held that it was improper to sue the Commonwealth alone as the Judicial Code, 42 Pa.C.S. § 8522(a), waived sovereign immunity as a bar to an action against "Commonwealth parties" only.

Therefore, Rule 2102 has been amended to alert and guide the bench and bar in these cases by adding new subdivision (a)(2) governing the designation of a Commonwealth party as defendant. The amendment provides that the action be captioned: Plaintiff v. "__________ (Name of Agency or Party) of the Commonwealth of Pennsylvania".

The limited scope of new Rule 2102(a)(2) reflects the limited jurisdiction of the courts of common pleas in actions against the Commonwealth or a Commonwealth party. For example, it is the Board of Claims which has the duty "to arbitrate claims against the Commonwealth arising from contracts entered into by the Commonwealth. . . . " Also, section 761 of the Judicial Code vests the Commonwealth Court with exclusive jurisdiction of actions against the "Commonwealth government" except with respect to five enumerated classes of actions including actions where sovereign immunity has been waived under Chapter 85 of that Code.

The Act of Assembly creating the Board of Claims, section 1 of the Act of May 20, 1937, P.L. 728, No. 193, as amended, 72 P.S. § 4651–1, speaks of claims against the "Commonwealth". Section 761 of the Judicial Code refers to actions or proceedings against the "Commonwealth government". Neither of these provisions use the term found in Chapter 85 of the Judicial Code, i.e., "Commonwealth party".

It is not anticipated that the new rule, in view of its limited scope, will affect actions not within the jurisdiction of the courts of common pleas or actions pursuant to statutes which do not refer to Commonwealth parties.

RULE 2103. VENUE

(a) An action brought in a court of common pleas by the Commonwealth may be brought in any county permitted by a rule of the Supreme Court.

(b) Except when the Commonwealth is the plaintiff or when otherwise provided by an Act of Assembly, an action against a political subdivision may be brought only in the county in which the political subdivision is located.

Note

For the venue of actions in mandamus and quo warranto, see Rules 1092 and 1112.

Adopted June 25, 1946, effective Jan. 1, 1947. Amended effective June 24, 1976.

RULE 2104. [RESCINDED]

Note

For service upon the Commonwealth and political subdivisions, see Rule 422.

Rescinded June 20, 1985, effective Jan. 1, 1986.

RULE 2123. ACTS OF ASSEMBLY NOT SUSPENDED

The rules governing the Commonwealth and political subdivisions as parties shall not be deemed to suspend or affect any Act of Assembly regulating the venue of actions brought by the head of an executive or administrative department or by a departmental administrative board or commission or by an independent administrative board or commission of the Commonwealth.

Former Rule 2123 rescinded and new Rule 2123 adopted June 3, 1994, effective July 1, 1994.

RULE 2124. EFFECTIVE DATE. PENDING ACTIONS

These rules shall become effective on the 1st day of January 1947, but shall not apply to actions pending at that time.

Adopted June 25, 1946, effective Jan. 1, 1947.

RULE 2125. SUSPENSION OF ACTS OF ASSEMBLY

Section 213 of the Act approved March 10, 1949, P.L. 30, Art. II, 24 P.S. § 2–213, is suspended in accordance with the provisions of the Constitution of 1968, Article V, Section 10(c).

Note

This section relates to actions by and against school districts and service upon school districts.

Former Rule 2125 rescinded and new Rule 2125 adopted June 3, 1994, effective July 1, 1994.

PART IV
ZONING AND PLANNING

CHAPTER 19
"PENNSYLVANIA MUNICIPALITIES PLANNING CODE"[1]
53 P.S. §§ 10101–11202

To empower cities of the second class A, and third class, boroughs, incorporated towns, townships of the first and second classes including those within a county of the second class and counties of the second through eighth classes, individually or jointly, to plan their development and to govern the same by zoning, subdivision and land development ordinances, planned residential development and other ordinances, by official maps, by the reservation of certain land for future public purpose and by the acquisition of such land; to promote the conservation of energy through the use of planning practices and to promote the effective utilization of renewable energy sources; providing for the establishment of planning commissions, planning departments, planning committees and zoning hearing boards, authorizing them to charge fees, make inspections and hold public hearings; providing for mediation; providing for transferable development rights; providing for appropriations, appeals to courts and penalties for violations; and repealing acts and parts of acts. (Title amended Dec. 14, 1992, P.L. 815, No. 131)

CONDENSED TABLE OF CONTENTS

For full Table of Contents, see pp. xxiv–xxviii

1. Act of 1968, P.L. 805, No. 247.

Table of Contents | Part I Ch. 1–3 Ethics, Records, Open Meetings | Part II Ch. 4–10 Taxation | Part III Ch. 11–18 Torts, Contracts & Civil Rules | Part IV Ch. 19–24 Zoning & Planning | Part V Ch. 25–30 Construction and Emergency Codes | Part VI Ch. 31–39 Municipal Codes | Index

ARTICLE I
General Provisions

53 P.S. § 10101–10110

§ 101. Short Title.—This act shall be known and may be cited as the "Pennsylvania Municipalities Planning Code."

§ 102. Effective Date.—This act shall take effect January 1, 1969.

§ 103. Construction of Act.—The provisions of this act shall not affect any act done, contract executed or liability incurred prior to its effective date, or affect any suit or prosecution pending or to be instituted, to enforce any right, rule, regulation, or ordinance or to punish any offense against any such repealed laws or against any ordinance enacted under them. All ordinances, resolutions, regulations and rules made pursuant to any act of Assembly repealed by this act shall continue in effect as if such act had not been repealed, except as the provisions are inconsistent herewith. The provisions of other acts relating to municipalities other than cities of the first and second class and counties of the second class are made a part of this act and this code shall be construed to give effect to all provisions of other acts not specifically repealed.

§ 104. Constitutional Construction.—The provisions of this act shall be severable, and if any of its provisions shall be held to be unconstitutional, the validity of any of the remaining provisions of this act shall not be affected. It is hereby declared as the legislative intention that this act would have been adopted had such unconstitutional provision not been included therein.

§ 105. Purpose of Act.—It is the intent, purpose and scope of this act to protect and promote safety, health and morals; to accomplish coordinated development; to provide for the general welfare by guiding and protecting amenity, convenience, future governmental, economic, practical, and social and cultural facilities, development and growth, as well as the improvement of governmental processes and functions; to guide uses of land and structures, type and location of streets, public grounds and other facilities; to promote the conservation of energy through the use of planning practices and to promote the effective utilization of renewable energy sources; to promote the preservation of this commonwealth's natural and historic resources and prime agricultural land; to encourage municipalities to adopt municipal or joint municipal comprehensive plans generally consistent with the county comprehensive plan; to promote small business development and foster a business-friendly environment in this Commonwealth; to ensure that municipalities adopt zoning ordinances which are generally consistent with the municipality's comprehensive plan; to encourage the preservation of prime agricultural land and natural and historic resources through easements, transfer of development rights and rezoning; to ensure that municipalities enact zoning ordinances that facilitate the present and future economic viability of existing agricultural operations in this commonwealth and do not prevent or impede the owner or operator's need to change or expand their operations in the future in order to remain viable; to encourage the revitalization of established urban centers; and to permit municipalities to minimize such problems as may presently exist or which may be foreseen and wherever the provisions of this act promote, encourage, require or authorize governing bodies to protect, preserve or conserve open land, consisting of natural resources, forests and woodlands, any actions taken to protect, preserve or conserve such land shall not be for the purposes of precluding access for forestry.

§ 106. Appropriations, Grants and Gifts.—The governing body of every municipality is hereby authorized and empowered to make such appropriations as it may see fit, to accept gifts, grants or bequests from public and private sources for the purpose of carrying out the powers and duties conferred by this act, and to enter into agreements regarding the acceptance or utilization of such grants, gifts or bequests.

§ 107. Definitions.—(a) The following words and phrases when used in this act shall have the meanings given to them in this subsection unless the context clearly indicates otherwise:

"Agricultural operation," an enterprise that is actively engaged in the commercial production and preparation for market of crops, livestock and livestock products and in the production, harvesting and preparation for market or use of agricultural, agronomic, horticultural, silvicultural and aquacultural crops and commodities. The term includes an enterprise that implements changes in production practices and procedures or types of crops, livestock, livestock products or commodities produced consistent with practices and procedures that are normally engaged by farmers or are consistent with technological development within the agricultural industry.

"Applicant," a landowner or developer, as hereinafter defined, who has filed an application for development including his heirs, successors and assigns.

"Application for development," every application, whether preliminary, tentative or final, required to be filed and approved prior to start of construction or development including but not limited to an application for a building permit, for the approval of a subdivision plat or plan or for the approval of a development plan.

"Appointing authority," the mayor in cities; the board of commissioners in counties; the council in incorporated towns and boroughs; the board of commissioners in townships of the first class; and the board of supervisors in townships of the second class; or as may be designated in the law providing for the form of government.

"Authority," a body politic and corporate created pursuant to the act of May 2, 1945 (P.L. 382, No. 164), known as the "Municipality Authorities Act of 1945."

"Center for local government services." The governor's center for local government services located within the department of community and economic development.

"City" or "cities," cities of the second class A and third class.

"Consistency," an agreement or correspondence between matters being compared which denotes a reasonable, rational, similar, connection or relationship.

"Common open space," a parcel or parcels of land or an area of water, or a combination of land and water within a development site and designed and intended for the use or enjoyment of residents of a development, not including streets, off-street parking areas, and areas set aside for public facilities.

"Conditional use," a use permitted in a particular zoning district pursuant to the provisions in Article VI.

"County," any county of the second class through eighth class. (Def. amended Dec. 14, 1992, P.L. 815, No. 131)

"County comprehensive plan," a land use and growth management plan prepared by the county planning commission and adopted by the county commissioners which establishes broad goals and criteria for municipalities to use in preparation of their comprehensive plans and land use regulation.

"Designated growth area," a region within a county or counties described in a municipal or multimunicipal plan that preferably includes and surrounds a city, borough or village, and within which residential and mixed use development is permitted or planned for at densities of one unit to the acre or more, commercial, industrial and institutional uses are permitted or planned for and public infrastructure services are provided or planned.

"Developer," any landowner, agent of such landowner, or tenant with the permission of such landowner, who makes or causes to be made a subdivision of land or a land development.

"Development of regional significance and impact," any land development that, because of its character, magnitude, or location will have substantial effect upon the health, safety, or welfare of citizens in more than one municipality.

"Development plan," the provisions for development, including a planned residential development, a plat of subdivision, all covenants relating to use, location and bulk of buildings and other structures, intensity of use or density of development, streets, ways and parking facilities, common open space and public facilities. The phrase "provisions of the development plan" when used in this act shall mean the written and graphic materials referred to in this definition.

"Electronic notice," notice given by a municipality through the Internet of the time and place of a public hearing and the particular nature of the matter to be considered at the hearing.

"Forestry," the management of forests and timberlands when practiced in accordance with accepted silvicultural principles, through developing, cultivating, harvesting, transporting and selling trees for commercial purposes, which does not involve any land development. (Def. added May 27, 1994, P.L. 251, No. 38)

"Future growth area," an area of a municipal or multimunicipal plan outside of and adjacent to a designated growth area where residential, commercial, industrial and institutional uses and development are permitted or planned at varying densities and public infrastructure services may or may not be provided, but future development at greater densities is planned to accompany the orderly extension and provision of public infrastructure services.

"General consistency, generally consistent," that which exhibits consistency.

"Governing body," the council in cities, boroughs and incorporated towns; the board of commissioners in townships of the first class; the board of supervisors in townships of the second class; the board of commissioners in counties of the second class through eighth class or as may be designated in the law providing for the form of government. (Def. amended Dec. 14, 1992, P.L. 815, No. 131)

"Land development," any of the following activities:

(1) The improvement of one lot or two or more contiguous lots, tracts or parcels of land for any purpose involving:

(i) a group of two or more residential or nonresidential buildings, whether proposed initially or cumulatively, or a single nonresidential building on a lot or lots regardless of the number of occupants or tenure; or

(ii) the division or allocation of land or space, whether initially or cumulatively, between or among two or more existing or prospective occupants by means of, or for the purpose of streets, common areas, leaseholds, condominiums, building groups or other features.

(2) A subdivision of land.

(3) Development in accordance with section 503(1.1).

"Landowner," the legal or beneficial owner or owners of land including the holder of an option or contract to purchase (whether or not such option or contract is subject to any condition), a lessee if he is authorized under the lease to exercise the rights of the landowner, or other person having a proprietary interest in land.

"Lot," a designated parcel, tract or area of land established by a plat or otherwise as permitted by law and to be used, developed or built upon as a unit.

"Mailed notice," notice given by a municipality by first class mail of the time and place of a public hearing and the particular nature of the matter to be considered at the hearing.

"Mediation," a voluntary negotiating process in which parties in a dispute mutually select a neutral mediator to assist them in jointly exploring and settling their differences, culminating in a written agreement which the parties themselves create and consider acceptable.

"Minerals," any aggregate or mass of mineral matter, whether or not coherent. The term includes, but is not limited to, limestone and dolomite, sand and gravel, rock and stone, earth, fill, slag, iron ore, zinc ore, vermiculite and clay, anthracite and bituminous coal, coal refuse, peat and crude oil and natural gas.

"Mobilehome," a transportable, single family dwelling intended for permanent occupancy, contained in one unit, or in two or more units designed to be joined into one integral unit capable of again being separated for repeated towing, which arrives at a site complete and ready for occupancy except for minor and incidental unpacking and assembly operations, and constructed so that it may be used without a permanent foundation.

"Mobilehome lot," a parcel of land in a mobilehome park, improved with the necessary utility connections and other appurtenances necessary for the erections thereon of a single mobilehome.

"Mobilehome park," a parcel or contiguous parcels of land which has been so designated and improved that it contains two or more mobilehome lots for the placement thereon of mobilehomes.

"Multimunicipal plan," a plan developed and adopted by any number of contiguous municipalities, including a joint municipal plan as authorized by this act, except that all of the municipalities participating in the plan need not be contiguous if all of them are within the same school district. . . .

"Multimunicipal planning agency," a planning agency comprised of representatives of more than one municipality and constituted as a joint municipal planning commission in accordance with Article XI, or otherwise by resolution of the participating municipalities, to address, on behalf of the participating municipalities, multimunicipal issues, including, but not limited to, agricultural and open space preservation, natural and historic resources, transportation, housing and economic development.

"Municipal authority," a body politic and corporate created pursuant to the act of May 2, 1945 (P.L. 382, No. 164), known as the "Municipality Authorities Act of 1945."

"Municipal engineer," a professional engineer licensed as such in the Commonwealth of Pennsylvania, duly appointed as the engineer for a municipality, planning agency or joint planning commission.

"Municipality," any city of the second class A or third class, borough, incorporated town, township of the first or second class, county of the second class through eighth class, home rule municipality, or any similar general purpose unit of government which shall hereafter be created by the General Assembly. (Def. amended Dec. 14, 1992, P.L. 815, No. 131)

"No-impact home-based business," a business or commercial activity administered or conducted as an accessory use which is clearly secondary to the use as a residential dwelling and which involves no customer, client or patient traffic, whether vehicular or pedestrian, pickup, delivery or removal functions to or from the premises, in excess of those normally associated with residential use. The business or commercial activity must satisfy the following requirements:

(1) The business activity shall be compatible with the residential use of the property and surrounding residential uses.

(2) The business shall employ no employees other than family members residing in the dwelling.

(3) There shall be no display or sale of retail goods and no stockpiling or inventory of a substantial nature.

Table of Contents | Part I Ch. 1–3 Ethics, Records, Open Meetings | Part II Ch. 4–10 Taxation | Part III Ch. 11–18 Torts, Contracts & Civil Rules | Part IV Ch. 19–24 Zoning & Planning | Part V Ch. 25–30 Construction and Emergency Codes | Part VI Ch. 31–39 Municipal Codes | Index

(4) There shall be no outside appearance of a business use, including, but not limited to, parking, signs or lights.

(5) The business activity may not use any equipment or process which creates noise, vibration, glare, fumes, odors or electrical or electronic interference, including interference with radio or television reception, which is detectable in the neighborhood.

(6) The business activity may not generate any solid waste or sewage discharge, in volume or type, which is not normally associated with residential use in the neighborhood.

(7) The business activity shall be conducted only within the dwelling and may not occupy more than 25% of the habitable floor area.

(8) The business may not involve any illegal activity.

"Nonconforming lot," a lot the area or dimension of which was lawful prior to the adoption or amendment of a zoning ordinance, but which fails to conform to the requirements of the zoning district in which it is located by reasons of such adoption or amendment.

"Nonconforming structure," a structure or part of a structure manifestly not designed to comply with the applicable use or extent of use provisions in a zoning ordinance or amendment heretofore or hereafter enacted, where such structure lawfully existed prior to the enactment of such ordinance or amendment or prior to the application of such ordinance or amendment to its location by reason of annexation. Such nonconforming structures include, but are not limited to, nonconforming signs.

"Nonconforming use," a use, whether of land or of structure, which does not comply with the applicable use provisions in a zoning ordinance or amendment heretofore or hereafter enacted, where such use was lawfully in existence prior to the enactment of such ordinance or amendment, or prior to the application of such ordinance or amendment to its location by reason of annexation.

"Official map," a map adopted by ordinance pursuant to Article IV.

"Planned residential development," an area of land, controlled by a landowner, to be developed as a single entity for a number of dwelling units, or combination of residential and nonresidential uses, the development plan for which does not correspond in lot size, bulk, type of dwelling, or use, density, or intensity, lot coverage and required open space to the regulations established in any one district created, from time to time, under the provisions of a municipal zoning ordinance.

"Planning agency," a planning commission, planning department, or a planning committee of the governing body.

"Plat," the map or plan of a subdivision or land development, whether preliminary or final.

"Preservation or protection," when used in connection with natural and historic resources, shall include means to conserve and safeguard these resources from wasteful or destructive use, but shall not be interpreted to authorize the unreasonable restriction of forestry, mining or other lawful uses of natural resources.

"Prime agricultural land," land used for agricultural purposes that contains soils of the first, second or third class as defined by the United States Department of Agriculture Natural Resource and Conservation Services County Soil Survey.

"Professional consultants," persons who provide expert or professional advice, including, but not limited to, architects, attorneys, certified public accountants, engineers, geologists, land surveyors, landscape architects or planners.

"Public grounds," includes:

(1) parks, playgrounds, trails, paths and other recreational areas and other public areas;

(2) sites for schools, sewage treatment, refuse disposal and other publicly owned or operated facilities; and

(3) publicly owned or operated scenic and historic sites.

"Public hearing," a formal meeting held pursuant to public notice by the governing body or planning agency, intended to inform and obtain public comment, prior to taking action in accordance with this act.

"Public infrastructure area," a designated growth area and all or any portion of a future growth area described in a county or multimunicipal comprehensive plan where public infrastructure services will be provided and outside of which such public infrastructure services will not be required to be publicly financed.

"Public infrastructure services," services that are provided to areas with densities of one or more units to the acre, which may include sanitary sewers and facilities for the collection and treatment of sewage, water lines and facilities for the pumping and treating of water, parks and open space, streets and sidewalks, public transportation and other services that may be appropriate within a growth area, but shall exclude fire protection and emergency medical services and any other service required to protect the health and safety of residents.

"Public meeting," a forum held pursuant to notice under 65 PA.C.S. Ch. 7 (relating to open meetings).

"Public notice," notice published once each week for two successive weeks in a newspaper of general circulation in the municipality. Such notice shall state the time and place of the hearing and the particular nature of the matter to be considered at the hearing. The first publication shall not be more than 30 days and the second publication shall not be less than seven days from the date of the hearing.

"Regional planning agency," a planning agency that is comprised of representatives of more than one county. Regional planning responsibilities shall include providing technical assistance to counties and municipalities, mediating conflicts across county lines and reviewing county comprehensive plans for consistency with one another.

"Renewable energy source," any method, process or substance whose supply is rejuvenated through natural processes and, subject to those natural processes, remains relatively constant, including, but not limited to, biomass conversion, geothermal energy, solar and wind energy and hydroelectric energy and excluding those sources of energy used in the fission and fusion processes.

"Rural resource area," an area described in a municipal or multimunicipal plan within which rural resource uses including, but not limited to, agriculture, timbering, mining, quarrying and other extractive industries, forest and game lands and recreation and tourism are encouraged and enhanced, development that is compatible with or supportive of such uses is permitted, and public infrastructure services are not provided except in villages.

"Special exception," a use permitted in a particular zoning district pursuant to the provisions of Articles VI and IX.

"Specific plan," a detailed plan for nonresidential development of an area covered by a municipal or multimunicipal comprehensive plan, which when approved and adopted by the participating municipalities through ordinances and agreements, supersedes all other applicable ordinances.

"State land use and growth management report," a comprehensive land use and growth management report to be prepared by the center for local government services and which shall contain information, data and conclusions regarding growth and development patterns in this commonwealth and which will offer recommendations to commonwealth agencies for coordination of executive action, regulation and programs.

"Street," includes street, avenue, boulevard, road, highway, freeway, parkway, lane, alley, viaduct and any other ways used or intended to be used by vehicular traffic or pedestrians whether public or private.

"Structure," any man-made object having an ascertainable stationary location on or in land or water, whether or not affixed to the land.

"Subdivision," the division or redivision of a lot, tract or parcel of land by any means into two or more lots, tracts, parcels or other divisions of land including changes in existing lot lines for the purpose, whether immediate or future, of lease, partition by the court for distribution to heirs or devisees, transfer of ownership or building or lot development: Provided, however, That the subdivision by lease of land for agricultural purposes into parcels of more than ten acres, not involving any new street or easement of access or any residential dwelling, shall be exempted.

"Substantially completed," where, in the judgment of the municipal engineer, at least 90% (based on the cost of the required improvements for which financial security was posted pursuant to section 509) of those improvements required as a condition for final approval have been completed in accordance with the approved plan, so that the project (sic).

"Traditional neighborhood development," an area of land typically developed for a compatible mixture of residential units for various income levels and nonresidential commercial and workplace uses, including some structures that provide for a mix of uses within the same building. Residences, shops, offices, workplaces, public buildings and parks are interwoven within the neighborhood so that all are within relatively close proximity to each other. Traditional neighborhood development is relatively compact and oriented toward pedestrian activity. It has an identifiable center and a discernible edge. The center of the neighborhood is in the form of a public park, commons, plaza, square or prominent intersection of two or more major streets. Generally, there is a hierarchy of streets laid out with an interconnected network of streets and blocks that provides multiple routes from origins to destinations and are appropriately designed to serve the needs of pedestrians and vehicles equally.

"Transferable development rights," the attaching of development rights to specified lands which are desired by a municipality to be kept undeveloped, but permitting those rights to be transferred from those lands so that the development potential which they represent may occur on other lands where more intensive development is deemed to be appropriate. (Def. amended Dec. 14, 1992, P.L. 815, No. 131)

"Variance," relief granted pursuant to the provisions of Articles VI and IX.

"Village," an unincorporated settlement that is part of a township where residential and mixed use densities of one unit to the acre or more exist or are permitted and commercial, industrial or institutional uses exist or are permitted.

"Water survey," an inventory of the source, quantity, yield and use of groundwater and surface-water resources within a municipality.

(b) The following words and phrases when used in Articles IX and X-A shall have the meanings given to them in this subsection unless the context clearly indicates otherwise:

"Board," any body granted jurisdiction under a land use ordinance or under this act to render final adjudications.

"Decision," final adjudication of any board or other body granted jurisdiction under any land use ordinance or this act to do so, either by reason of the grant of exclusive jurisdiction or by reason of appeals from determinations. All decisions shall be appealable to the court of common pleas of the county and judicial district wherein the municipality lies.

"Determination," final action by an officer, body or agency charged with the administration of any land use ordinance or applications thereunder, except the following:

(1) the governing body;

(2) the zoning hearing board; or

(3) the planning agency, only if and to the extent the planning agency is charged with final decision on preliminary or final plans under the subdivision and land development ordinance or planned residential development provisions.

Determinations shall be appealable only to the boards designated as having jurisdiction for such appeal.

"Hearing," an administrative proceeding conducted by a board pursuant to section 909.1.

"Land use ordinance," any ordinance or map adopted pursuant to the authority granted in Articles IV, V, VI and VII.

"Report," any letter, review, memorandum, compilation or similar writing made by any body, board, officer or consultant other than a solicitor to any other body, board, officer or consultant for the purpose of assisting the recipient of such report in the rendering of any decision or determination. All reports shall be deemed recommendatory and advisory only and shall not be binding upon the recipient, board, officer, body or agency, nor shall any appeal lie therefrom. Any report used, received or considered by the body, board, officer or agency rendering a determination or decision shall be made available for inspection to the applicant and all other parties to any proceeding upon request, and copies thereof shall be provided at cost of reproduction.

§ 108. Optional notice of ordinance or decision; procedural validity challenges.—

(a) it is the intent of this section to allow optional public notice of municipal action in order to provide an opportunity to challenge, in accordance with section 1002-A(b) or section 1002.1-A, the validity of an ordinance or decision on the basis that a defect in procedure resulted in a deprivation of constitutional rights, and to establish a period of limitations for raising such challenges.

(b) notice that municipal action has been taken to adopt an ordinance or enter a decision, regardless of whether the municipal action was taken before or after the effective date of this section, may be provided through publication, at any time, once each week for two successive weeks in a newspaper of general circulation in the municipality by the following:

(1) the governing body of the municipality.

(2) in the case of an ordinance, any resident or landowner in the municipality.

(3) in the case of a decision, the applicant requesting the decision or the landowner or successor in interest of the property subject to or affected by the decision.

(c) each notice shall contain the following:

(1) if the notice relates to an ordinance:

(i) the municipality's ordinance number.

(ii) a brief statement of the general content of the ordinance.

(iii) the address of the municipal building where the full text of the ordinance may be reviewed by members of the public.

(2) if the notice relates to a decision:

(i) the name of the applicant or owner of the subject property.

(ii) the street address or location of the subject property.

(iii) the file number or docket number of the decision.

(iv) a brief description of the nature of the decision.

(v) the date upon which the decision was issued.

(vi) the address of the municipal building where the full text of the decision may be reviewed by members of the public.

(3) in addition to the requirements of paragraphs (1) and (2), the publication of each notice authorized by the section shall contain a statement that the publication is intended to provide notification of an ordinance or decision and that any person claiming a right to challenge the validity of the ordinance or decision must bring a legal action within 30 days of the publication of the second notice.

(4) the person providing notice as authorized by this section shall provide proof of publication to the municipality adopting the ordinance or decision for retention with municipal records. Failure to comply with this paragraph shall not invalidate any notice provided in accordance with this section or the applicability of the period of limitation in subsection (d).

(d) notwithstanding this or any other act, in order to provide certainty of the validity of an ordinance or decision, any appeal or action contesting the validity of an ordinance based on a procedural defect in the process of enactment or the validity of a decision based on a procedural or substantive defect shall be dismissed, with prejudice, as untimely if not filed within the 30th day following the second publication of the notice authorized in this section.

(e) any appeal or action filed within the 30-day period referred to in subsection (d) shall be taken to the court of common pleas and shall be conducted in accordance with and subject to the procedures set forth in 42 PA.C.S. § 5571.1 (relating to appeals from ordinances, resolutions, maps, etc.) In the case of challenges to ordinances or section 1002.1-a in the case of challenges to decisions.

(f) where no appeal or action contesting the procedural validity of an ordinance or the procedural or substantive validity of a decision is filed within the period set forth in subsection (d), the ordinance or decision shall be deemed to be reaffirmed and reissued on the date of the second publication of the optional notice permitted under this section.

(g) an appeal shall be exempt from the time limitation in subsection (d) only if the party bringing the appeal establishes that the application of the time limitation in subsection (d) would result in an unconstitutional deprivation of due process.

(h) nothing in this section shall be construed to abrogate, repeal, extend or otherwise modify the time for appeal as set forth in section 1002-a where the appellant was a party to proceedings prior to the entry of a decision or otherwise had an adequate opportunity to bring a timely action in accordance with section 1002-a to contest the procedural validity of an ordinance or the procedural or substantive validity of a decision.

§ 109. Notice.

In any case in which mailed notice or electronic notice is required by this act, the following shall apply:

(1) An owner of a tract or parcel of land located within a municipality or an owner of the mineral rights in a tract or parcel of land within a municipality may request that the municipality provide written or electronic notice of a public hearing which may affect such tract or parcel of land.

(2) Mailed notice shall be required only if an owner of a tract or parcel of land located within a municipality or an owner of the mineral rights in a tract or parcel of land within the municipality has made a written request that the notice be mailed and has supplied the municipality with a stamped, self-addressed envelope prior to a public hearing.

(3) Electronic notice shall be required only if an owner of a tract or parcel of land located within a municipality or an owner of the mineral rights in a tract or parcel of land within the municipality has made a written request that notice be sent electronically and has supplied the municipality with an electronic address prior to a public hearing and only if that municipality maintains the capability of generating an electronic notice. An owner of a tract or parcel of land located within a municipality or an owner of the mineral rights in a tract or parcel of land within the municipality making the request and supplying an electronic address may at any time notify the municipality that the owner of the tract or parcel of land located within the municipality or the owner of the mineral rights in the tract or parcel of land within the municipality no longer will accept electronic notice, and, in that event, the municipality may no longer provide electronic notice.

(4) An owner of a tract or parcel of land located within a municipality or an owner of the mineral rights in a tract or parcel of land within the municipality who has requested a mailed notice shall be solely responsible for the number, accuracy and sufficiency of the envelopes supplied. The municipality shall not be responsible or liable if the owner of a tract or parcel of land located within a municipality or an owner of the mineral rights in a tract or parcel of land within the municipality does not provide to the municipality notice of any changes in the owner's mailing address.

(5) An owner of a tract or parcel of land located within a municipality or an owner of the mineral rights in a tract or parcel of land within the municipality who has requested electronic notice shall be solely responsible for the accuracy and functioning of the electronic address provided to the municipality. The municipality shall not be responsible or liable if the owner of a tract or parcel of land located within a municipality or an owner of the mineral rights in a tract or parcel of land within the municipality does not provide to the municipality notice of any changes to the owner's electronic address.

(6) A municipality shall deposit a mailed notice in the United States mail or provide electronic notice not more than 30 and not less than seven days prior to the scheduled date of the hearing as shown on the notice.

(7) For each public hearing, the municipal secretary or zoning officer shall prepare, sign and maintain a list of all mailed notices, mailing dates, electronic notices and electronic notice dates. The signed list shall constitute a presumption that the notice was given.

(8) The mailed notice shall be deemed received by an owner of a tract or parcel of land located within a municipality or an owner of the mineral rights in a tract or parcel of land within the municipality on the date deposited in the United States mail.

(9) The electronic notice shall be deemed received by an owner of a tract or parcel of land located within a municipality or an owner of the mineral rights in a tract or parcel of land within the municipality on the date the municipality electronically notifies the owner.

(10) Failure of an owner of a tract or parcel of land located within a municipality or an owner of the mineral rights in a tract or parcel of land within the municipality to receive a requested mailed notice or electronic notice shall not be deemed to invalidate any action or proceedings under this act.

§ 110. Certain Transmittals and Submissions to Governmental Bodies.—If this act requires a municipality, including a county, to forward, send or submit a proposed comprehensive plan or amendment or a proposed land use ordinance or amendment for review, comments or recommendations, or an adopted comprehensive plan, land use ordinance or amendment, the proposed or adopted plan, ordinance or amendment may be transmitted electronically. The transmittal may include an electronic document or a link to a publicly accessible document online, provided the electronic document is in PDF format or similar standard which accurately reproduces the original. In the event a document is required by this act to be certified, the certification shall also be transmitted electronically. The following shall apply:

(1) The municipality shall transmit documents to those electronic contacts available and reasonably appropriate for receipt of the documents. Failure of a governmental body or an officer or agent of a governmental body to receive a good faith transmittal provided in accordance with this paragraph may not be grounds to challenge the effectiveness of a plan, ordinance or amendment under this act.

(2) The municipality shall retain a written or electronic record of every transmittal and all comments and recommendations under paragraph (3).

(3) If an authorized transmittal is for comments or recommendations under this act, the comments and recommendations may be transmitted to the municipality electronically.

ARTICLE II
Planning Agencies

53 P.S. § 10201–10212

§ 201. Creation of Planning Agencies.—The governing body of any municipality shall have the power to create or abolish, by ordinance, a planning commission or planning department, or both. An ordinance which creates both a planning commission and a planning department shall specify which of the powers and duties conferred on planning agencies by this act; each shall exercise and may confer upon each additional powers, duties and advisory functions not inconsistent with this act. In lieu of a planning commission or planning department, the governing body may elect to assign the powers and duties conferred by this act upon a planning committee comprised of members appointed from the governing body. The engineer for the municipality, or an engineer appointed by the governing body, shall serve the planning agency as engineering advisor. The solicitor for the municipality, or an attorney appointed by the governing body, shall serve the planning agency as legal advisor.

§ 202. Planning Commission.—If the governing body of any municipality shall elect to create a planning commission, such commission shall have not less than three nor more than nine members. Except for elected or appointed officers or employees of the municipality, members of the commission may receive compensation in an amount fixed by the governing body. Compensation shall not exceed the rate of compensation authorized to be paid to members of the governing body. Without exception, members of the planning commission may be reimbursed for necessary and reasonable expenses. However, elected or appointed officers or employees of the municipality shall not, by reason of membership thereon, forfeit the right to exercise the powers, perform the duties or receive the compensations of the municipal offices held by them during such membership.

§ 203. Appointment, Term and Vacancy.—(a) All members of the commission shall be appointed by the appointing authority of the municipality. All such appointments shall be approved by the governing body, except where the governing body is the appointing authority.

(b) The term of each of the members of the commission shall be for four years, or until his successor is appointed and qualified, except that the terms of the members first appointed pursuant to this act shall be so fixed that on commissions of eight members or less no more than two shall be reappointed or replaced during any future calendar year, and on commissions of nine members no more than three shall be so reappointed or replaced.

(c) The chairman of the planning commission shall promptly notify the appointing authority of the municipality concerning vacancies in the commission, and such vacancy shall be filled for the unexpired term. If a vacancy shall occur otherwise than by expiration of term, it shall be filled by appointment for the unexpired term according to the terms of this article.

(d) Should the governing body of any municipality determine to increase the number of members of an already existing planning commission, the additional members shall be appointed as provided in this article. If the governing body of any municipality shall determine to reduce the number of members on any existing planning commission, such reduction shall be effectuated by allowing the terms to expire and by making no new appointments to fill the vacancy. Any reduction or increase shall be by ordinance.

(e) The governing body may appoint by resolution at least one but no more than three residents of the municipality to serve as alternate members of the planning commission. The term of office of an alternate member shall be four years. When seated pursuant to the provisions of section 207, an alternate shall be entitled to participate in all proceedings and discussions of the commission to the same and full extent as provided by law for commission members, including specifically the right to cast a vote as a voting member during the proceedings, and shall have all the powers and duties set forth in this act and as otherwise provided by law. Alternates shall not serve as a member of the zoning hearing board or as a zoning officer. Any alternate may participate in any proceeding or discussion of the commission but shall not be entitled to vote as a member of the commission nor be reimbursed pursuant to section 202 unless designated as a voting alternate member pursuant to section 207.

§ 204. Members of Existing Commissions.—(204 repealed Dec. 21, 1988, P.L. 1329, No. 170)

§ 205. Membership.—All of the members of the planning commission shall be residents of the municipality. On all planning commissions appointed pursuant to this act, a certain number of the members, designated as citizen members shall not be officers or employees of the municipality. On a commission of three members at least two shall be citizen members. On a commission of four or five members at least three shall be citizen members. On a commission of either six or seven members at least five shall be citizen members, and on commissions of either eight or nine members at least six shall be citizen members.

§ 206. Removal.—Any member of a planning commission once qualified and appointed may be removed from office for malfeasance, misfeasance or nonfeasance in office or for other just cause by a majority vote of the governing body taken after the member has received 15 days' advance notice of the intent to take such a vote. A hearing shall be held in connection with the vote if the member shall request it in writing. Any appointment to fill a vacancy created by removal shall be only for the unexpired term.

§ 207. Conduct of Business.—(a) The commission shall elect its own chairman and vice-chairman and create and fill such other offices as it may determine. Officers shall serve annual terms and may succeed themselves. The commission may make and alter by laws and rules and regulations to govern its procedures consistent with the ordinances of the municipality and the laws of the Commonwealth. The commission shall keep a full record of its business and shall annually make a written report by March 1 of each year of its activities to the governing body. Interim reports may be made as often as may be necessary, or as requested by the governing body.

(b) The chairman of the planning commission may designate alternate members of the commission to substitute for any absent member or member who has recused himself or has been disqualified by the governing body, and if, by reason of absence, recusal or disqualification of a member, a quorum is not reached, the chairman of the commission shall designate as many alternate members of the commission to sit on the commission as may be needed to reach a quorum. Any alternate member of the commission shall continue to serve on the commission in all proceedings involving the matter or case for which the alternate was initially appointed until the commission has made a final decision on the matter or case. Designation of an alternate pursuant to this section shall be made on a case-by-case basis in rotation according to declining seniority among all alternates.

§ 208. Planning Department Director.—For the administration of each planning department, the appointing authority may appoint a director of planning who shall be, in the opinion of the appointing authority, qualified for the duties of his position. Each such appointment shall be with the approval of the governing body, except where the governing body is the appointing authority. The director of planning shall be in charge of the administration of the department, and shall exercise the powers and be subject to the duties that are granted or imposed on a planning agency by this act, except that where a municipality creates both a planning commission and a planning department, the director of planning shall exercise only those powers and be subject to only those duties which are specifically conferred upon him by ordinance enacted pursuant to this article.

§ 209.1. Powers and Duties of Planning Agency.—(a) The planning agency shall at the request of the governing body have the power and shall be required to:

(1) Prepare the comprehensive plan for the development of the municipality as set forth in this act, and present it for the consideration of the governing body.

(2) Maintain and keep on file records of its action. All records and files of the planning agency shall be in the possession of the governing body.

(b) The planning agency at the request of the governing body may:

(1) Make recommendations to the governing body concerning the adoption or amendment of an official map.

(2) Prepare and present to the governing body of the municipality a zoning ordinance, and make recommendations to the governing body on proposed amendments to it as set forth in this act.

(3) Prepare, recommend and administer subdivision and land development and planned residential development regulations, as set forth in this act.

(4) Prepare and present to the governing body of the municipality a building code and a housing code and make recommendations concerning proposed amendments thereto.

(5) Do such other acts or make such studies as may be necessary to fulfill the duties and obligations imposed by this act.

(6) Prepare and present to the governing body of the municipality an environmental study.

(7) Submit to the governing body of a municipality a recommended capital improvements program.

(7.1) Prepare and present to the governing body of the municipality a water survey, which shall be consistent with the State Water Plan and any applicable water resources plan adopted by a river basin commission. The water survey shall be conducted in consultation with any public water supplier in the area to be surveyed.

(8) Promote public interest in, and understanding of, the comprehensive plan and planning.

(9) Make recommendations to governmental, civic and private agencies and individuals as to the effectiveness of the proposals of such agencies and individuals.

(10) Hold public hearings and meetings.

(10.1) Present testimony before any board.

(11) Require from other departments and agencies of the municipality such available information as relates to the work of the planning agency.

(12) In the performance of its functions, enter upon any land to make examinations and surveys with the consent of the owner.

(13) Prepare and present to the governing body of the municipality a study regarding the feasibility and practicability of using renewable energy sources in specific areas within the municipality.

(14) Review the zoning ordinance, subdivision and land development ordinance, official map, provisions for planned residential development, and such other ordinances and regulations governing the development of land no less frequently than it reviews the comprehensive plan.

§ 210. Administrative and Technical Assistance.—The appointing authority may employ administrative and technical services to aid in carrying out the provisions of this act either as consultants on particular matters or as regular employees of the municipality. A county planning agency, with the consent of its governing body may perform planning services for any municipality whose governing body requests such assistance and may enter into agreements or contracts for such work.

§ 211. Assistance.—The planning agency may, with the consent of the governing body, accept and utilize any funds, personnel or other assistance made available by the county, the Commonwealth or the Federal government or any of their agencies, or from private sources. The governing body may enter into agreements or contracts regarding the acceptance or utilization of the funds or assistance in accordance with the governmental procedures of the municipality.

§ 212. Intergovernmental Cooperation.—For the purposes of this act, the governing body may utilize the authority granted under 53 Pa.C.S. §§ 2303(a) (relating to intergovernmental cooperation authorized) and 2315 (relating to effect of joint cooperation agreements).

ARTICLE III

Comprehensive Plan

53 P.S. § 10301–10307

§ 301. Preparation of Comprehensive Plan.—(a) The municipal, multimunicipal or county comprehensive plan, consisting of maps, charts and textual matter, shall include, but need not be limited to, the following related basic elements:

(1) A statement of objectives of the municipality concerning its future development, including, but not limited to, the location, character and timing of future development, that may also serve as a statement of community development objectives as provided in section 606.

(2) A plan for land use, which may include provisions for the amount, intensity, character and timing of land use proposed for residence, industry, business, agriculture, major traffic and transit facilities, utilities, community facilities, public grounds, parks and recreation, preservation of prime agricultural lands, flood plains and other areas of special hazards and other similar uses.

(2.1) A plan to meet the housing needs of present residents and of those individuals and families anticipated to reside in the municipality, which may include conservation of presently sound housing, rehabilitation of housing in declining neighborhoods and the accommodation of expected new housing in different dwelling types and at appropriate densities for households of all income levels.

(3) A plan for movement of people and goods, which may include expressways, highways, local street systems, parking facilities, pedestrian and bikeway systems, public transit routes, terminals, airfields, port facilities, railroad facilities and other similar facilities or uses.

(4) A plan for community facilities and utilities, which may include public and private education, recreation, municipal buildings, fire and police stations,

Table of Contents | Part I Ch. 1–3 Ethics, Records, Open Meetings | Part II Ch. 4–10 Taxation | Part III Ch. 11–18 Torts, Contracts & Civil Rules | Part IV Ch. 19–24 Zoning & Planning | Part V Ch. 25–30 Construction and Emergency Codes | Part VI Ch. 31–39 Municipal Codes | Index

libraries, hospitals, water supply and distribution, sewerage and waste treatment, solid waste management, storm drainage, and flood plain management, utility corridors and associated facilities, and other similar facilities or uses.

(4.1) A statement of the interrelationships among the various plan components, which may include an estimate of the environmental, energy conservation, fiscal, economic development and social consequences on the municipality.

(4.2) A discussion of short- and long-range plan implementation strategies, which may include implications for capital improvements programming, new or updated development regulations, and identification of public funds potentially available.

(5) A statement indicating that the existing and proposed development of the municipality is compatible with the existing and proposed development and plans in contiguous portions of neighboring municipalities, or a statement indicating measures which have been taken to provide buffers or other transitional devices between disparate uses, and a statement indicating that the existing and proposed development of the municipality is generally consistent with the objectives and plans of the county comprehensive plan.

(6) A plan for the protection of natural and historic resources to the extent not preempted by federal or state law. This clause includes, but is not limited to, wetlands and aquifer recharge zones, woodland, steep slopes, prime agricultural land, flood plains, unique natural areas and historic sites. The plan shall be consistent with and may not exceed those requirements imposed under the following:

(i) Act of June 22, 1937 (P.L. 1987, No. 394), known as "The Clean Streams Law";

(ii) Act of May 31, 1945 (P.L. 1198, No. 418), known as the "Surface Mining Conservation and Reclamation Act";

(iii) Act of April 27, 1966 (1st Sp. SESS, P.L. 31, No. 1), known as "The Bituminous Mine Subsidence and Land Conservation Act";

(iv) Act of September 24, 1968 (P.L. 1040, No. 318), known as the "Coal Refuse Disposal Control Act";

(v) Act of December 19, 1984 (P.L. 1140, No. 223), known as the "Oil and Gas Act";

(vi) Act of December 19, 1984 (P.L. 1093, No. 219), known as the "Noncoal Surface Mining Conservation Act";

(vii) Act of June 30, 1981 (P.L. 128, No. 43), known as the "Agricultural Area Security Law";

(viii) Act of June 10, 1982 (P.L. 454, No. 133), Entitled "An Act Protecting Agricultural Operations from Nuisance Suits and Ordinances Under Certain Circumstances"; and

(ix) Act of May 20, 1993 (P.L. 12, No. 6), known as the "Nutrient Management Act," regardless of whether any agricultural operation within the area to be affected by the plan is a concentrated animal operation as defined under the act.

(7) In addition to any other requirement of this act, a county comprehensive plan shall:

(i) Identify land uses as they relate to important natural resources and appropriate utilization of existing minerals.

(ii) Identify current and proposed land uses which have a regional impact and significance, such as large shopping centers, major industrial parks, mines and related activities, office parks, storage facilities, large residential developments, regional entertainment and recreational complexes, hospitals, airports and port facilities.

(iii) Identify a plan for the preservation and enhancement of prime agricultural land and encourage the compatibility of land use regulation with existing agricultural operations.

(iv) Identify a plan for historic preservation.

(b) The comprehensive plan shall include a plan for the reliable supply of water, considering current and future water resources availability, uses and limitations, including provisions adequate to protect water supply sources. Any such plan shall be generally consistent with the State Water Plan and any applicable water resources plan adopted by a river basin commission. It shall also contain a statement recognizing that:

(1) Lawful activities such as extraction of minerals may impact water supply sources and such activities are governed by statutes regulating mineral extraction that specify replacement and restoration of water supplies affected by such activities.

(2) Commercial agriculture production may impact water supply sources.

(c) The municipal or multimunicipal comprehensive plan shall be reviewed at least every ten years. The municipal or multimunicipal comprehensive plan shall be sent to the governing bodies of contiguous municipalities for review and comment and shall also be sent to the center for local government services for informational purposes. The municipal or multimunicipal comprehensive plan shall also be sent to the county planning commissions or, upon request of a county planning commission, a regional planning commission when the comprehensive plan is updated or at ten-year intervals, whichever comes first, for review and comment on whether the municipal or multimunicipal comprehensive plan remains generally consistent with the county comprehensive plan and to indicate where the local plan may deviate from the county comprehensive plan.

(d) The municipal, multimunicipal or county comprehensive plan may identify those areas where growth and development will occur so that a full range of public infrastructure services, including sewer, water, highways, police and fire protection, public schools, parks, open space and other services can be adequately planned and provided as needed to accommodate growth.

§ 301.1. Energy Conservation Plan Element.—To promote energy conservation and the effective utilization of renewable energy sources, the comprehensive plan may include an energy conservation plan element which systematically analyzes the impact of each other component and element of the comprehensive plan on the present and future use of energy in the municipality, details specific measures contained in the other plan elements designed to reduce energy consumption and proposes other measures that the municipality may take to reduce energy consumption and to promote the effective utilization of renewable energy sources.

§ 301.2. Surveys by Planning Agency.—In preparing the comprehensive plan, the planning agency shall make careful surveys, studies and analyses of housing, demographic, and economic characteristics and trends; amount, type and general location and interrelationships of different categories of land use; general location and extent of transportation and community facilities; natural features affecting development; natural, historic and cultural resources; and the prospects for future growth in the municipality.

§ 301.3. Submission of Plan to County Planning Agency.—If a county planning agency has been created for the county in which the municipality is located, then at least 45 days prior to the public hearing required in section 302 on the comprehensive plan or amendment thereof, the municipality shall forward a copy of that plan or amendment to the county planning agency for its comments. At the same time, the municipality shall also forward copies of the proposed plan or amendment to all contiguous municipalities and to the local school district for their review and comments.

§ 301.4. Compliance by Counties.—(a) If a county does not have a comprehensive plan, then that county shall, within three years of the effective date of this act, and with the opportunity for the review, comment and participation of the municipalities and school districts within the respective county and contiguous counties, school districts and municipalities, prepare and adopt a comprehensive plan in accordance with the requirements of Section 301. Municipal comprehensive plans which are adopted shall be generally consistent with the adopted county comprehensive plan.

(b) County planning commissions shall publish advisory guidelines to promote general consistency with the adopted county comprehensive plan. These guidelines shall promote uniformity with respect to local planning and zoning terminology and common types of municipal land use regulations.

§ 301.5. Funding of Municipal Planning.—Priority for state grants to develop or revise comprehensive plans shall be given to those municipalities which agree to adopt comprehensive plans generally consistent with the county comprehensive plan and which agree to enact a new zoning ordinance or amendment which would fully implement the municipal comprehensive plan. No more than 25% of the total funds available for these grants shall be disbursed under priority status pursuant to this provision. Municipalities and counties shall comply with these agreements within three years. Failure to comply with the agreements shall be taken into consideration for future state funding.

§ 302. Adoption of Municipal, Multimunicipal and County Comprehensive Plans and Plan Amendments.—(a) The governing body may adopt and amend the comprehensive plan as a whole or in part. Before adopting or amending a comprehensive plan, or any part thereof, the planning agency shall hold at least one public meeting before forwarding the proposed comprehensive plan or amendment thereof to the governing body. In reviewing the proposed comprehensive plan, the governing body shall consider the comments of the county, contiguous municipalities and the school district, as well as the public meeting comments and the recommendations of the municipal planning agency. The comments of the county, contiguous municipalities and the local school district shall be made to the governing body within 45 days of receipt, by the governing body, and the proposed plan or amendment thereto shall not be acted upon until such comment is received. If, however, the contiguous municipalities and the local school district fail to respond within 45 days, the governing body may proceed without their comments.

(a.1) The governing body of the county may adopt and amend the county comprehensive plan in whole or in part. Before adopting or amending a comprehensive plan, or any part thereof, the county planning agency shall hold at least one public meeting before forwarding the proposed comprehensive plan or amendment thereof to the governing body. In reviewing the proposed comprehensive plan, the governing body shall consider the comments of municipalities and school districts within the county and contiguous school districts, municipalities and counties, as well as the public meeting comments and the recommendations of the county planning agency. The comments of the counties, municipalities and school districts shall be made to the governing body within 45 days of receipt by the governing body, and the proposed comprehensive plan or amendment thereto shall not be acted upon until such comment is received. If, however, the counties, municipalities and school districts fail to respond within 45 days, the governing body may proceed without their comments.

(b) The governing body shall hold at least one public hearing pursuant to public notice. If, after the public hearing held upon the proposed plan or amendment to the plan, the proposed plan or proposed amendment thereto is substantially revised, the governing body shall hold another public hearing, pursuant to public notice, before proceeding to vote on the plan or amendment thereto.

(c) The adoption of the comprehensive plan, or any part thereof, or any amendment thereto, shall be by resolution carried by the affirmative votes of not less than a majority of all the members of the governing body. The resolution shall refer expressly to the maps, charts, textual matter, and other matters intended to form the whole or part of the plan, and the action shall be recorded on the adopted plan or part.

(d) Counties shall in accordance with subsection (a.1) consider amendments to their comprehensive plan proposed by municipalities which are considering adoption or revision of their municipal comprehensive plans so as to achieve general consistency between the respective plans. County comprehensive plans shall be updated at least every ten years. Where two or more contiguous municipalities request amendments to a county comprehensive plan for the purpose of achieving general consistency between the municipal plans or multimunicipal plan and the county comprehensive plan, the county must accept the amendment unless good cause for their refusal is established.

§ 303. Legal Status of Comprehensive Plan Within the Jurisdiction that Adopted the Plan.—(a) Whenever the governing body, pursuant to the procedures provided in section 302, has adopted a comprehensive plan or any part thereof, any subsequent proposed action of the governing body, its departments, agencies and appointed authorities shall be submitted to the planning agency for its recommendations when the proposed action relates to:

(1) the location, opening, vacation, extension, widening, narrowing or enlargement of any street, public ground, pierhead or watercourse;

(2) the location, erection, demolition, removal or sale of any public structure located within the municipality;

(3) the adoption, amendment or repeal of an official map, subdivision and land development ordinance, zoning ordinance or provisions for planned residential development, or capital improvements program; or

(4) the construction, extension or abandonment of any water line, sewer line or sewage treatment facility.

(b) The recommendations of the planning agency including a specific statement as to whether or not the proposed action is in accordance with the objectives of the formally adopted comprehensive plan shall be made in writing to the governing body within 45 days.

(c) Notwithstanding any other provision of this act, no action by the governing body of a municipality shall be invalid nor shall the same be subject to challenge or appeal on the basis that such action is inconsistent with, or fails to comply with, the provision of a comprehensive plan.

(d) Municipal zoning, subdivision and land development regulations and capital improvement programs shall generally implement the municipal and multimunicipal comprehensive plan or, where none exists, the municipal statement of community development objectives.

§ 304. Legal Status of County Comprehensive Plans Within Municipalities.—(a) Following the adoption of a comprehensive plan or any part thereof by a county, pursuant to the procedures in section 302, any proposed action of the governing body of a municipality, its departments, agencies and appointed authorities within the county shall be submitted to the county planning agency for its recommendations if the proposed action relates to:

(1) the location, opening, vacation, extension, widening, narrowing or enlargement of any street, public ground, pierhead or watercourse;

(2) the location, erection, demolition, removal or sale of any public structures located within the municipality;

(3) the adoption, amendment or repeal of any comprehensive plan, official map, subdivision or land ordinance, zoning ordinance or provisions for planned residential development; or

(4) the construction, extension or abandonment of any water line, sewer line or sewage treatment facility.

(b) The recommendation of the planning agency shall be made to the governing body of the municipality within 45 days and the proposed action shall not be taken until such recommendation is made. If, however, the planning agency fails to act within 45 days, the governing body shall proceed without its recommendation.

§ 305. The Legal Status of Comprehensive Plans Within School Districts.—Following the adoption of a comprehensive plan or any part thereof by any municipality or county governing body, pursuant to the procedures in section 302, any proposed action of the governing body of any public school district located within the municipality or county relating to the location, demolition, removal, sale or lease of any school district structure or land shall be submitted to the municipal and county planning agencies for their recommendations at least 45 days prior to the execution of such proposed action by the governing body of the school district.

§ 306. Municipal and County Comprehensive Plans.—(a) When a municipality having a comprehensive plan is located in a county which has adopted a comprehensive plan, both the county and the municipality shall each give the plan of the other consideration in order that the objectives of each plan can be protected to the greatest extent possible.

(b) Within 30 days after adoption, the governing body of a municipality, other than a county, shall forward a certified copy of the comprehensive plan, or part thereof or amendment thereto, to the county planning agency or, in counties where no planning agency exists, to the governing body of the county in which the municipality is located.

(c) Counties shall consult with municipalities and solicit comment from school districts, municipal authorities, the center for local government services, for informational purposes, and public utilities during the process of preparing or updating a county comprehensive plan in order to determine future growth needs.

§ 307. State Land Use and Growth Management Report.—The center for local government services shall issue a land use and growth management report by the year 2005 and shall review and update the report at five-year intervals.

ARTICLE IV
Official Map

53 P.S. § 10401–10408

§ 401. Grant of Power.—(a) The governing body of each municipality shall have the power to make or cause to be made an official map of all or a portion of the municipality which may show appropriate elements or portions of elements of the comprehensive plan adopted pursuant to section 302 with regard to public lands and facilities, and which may include, but need not be limited to:

(1) Existing and proposed public streets, watercourses and public grounds, including widenings, narrowings, extensions, diminutions, openings or closing of same.

(2) Existing and proposed public parks, playgrounds and open space reservations.

(3) Pedestrian ways and easements.

(4) Railroad and transit rights-of-way and easements.

(5) Flood control basins, floodways and flood plains, storm water management areas and drainage easements.

(6) Support facilities, easements and other properties held by public bodies undertaking the elements described in section 301.

(b) For the purposes of taking action under this section, the governing body or its authorized designee may make or cause to be made surveys and maps to identify, for the regulatory purposes of this article, the location of property, trafficway alignment or utility easement by use of property records, aerial photography, photogrammetric mapping or other method sufficient for identification, description and publication of the map components. For acquisition of lands and easements, boundary descriptions by metes and bounds shall be made and sealed by a licensed surveyor.

§ 402. Adoption of the Official Map and Amendments Thereto.—(a) Prior to the adoption of the official map or part thereof, or any amendments to the official map, the governing body shall refer the proposed official map, or part thereof or amendment thereto, with an accompanying ordinance describing the proposed map, to the planning agency for review. The planning agency shall report its recommendations on said proposed official map and accompanying ordinance, part thereof, or amendment thereto within 45 days unless an extension of time shall be agreed to by the governing body. If, however, the planning agency fails to act within 45 days, the governing body may proceed without its recommendations.

(b) The county and adjacent municipalities may offer comments and recommendations during said 45-day review period in accordance with section 408. Local authorities, park boards, environmental boards and similar public bodies may also offer comments and recommendations to the governing body or planning agency if requested by same during said 45-day review period. Before voting on the enactment of the proposed ordinance and official map, or part thereof or amendment thereto, the governing body shall hold a public hearing pursuant to public notice.

(c) Following adoption of the ordinance and official map, or part thereof or amendment thereto, a copy of same, verified by the governing body, shall be submitted to the recorder of deeds of the county in which the municipality is located and shall be recorded within 60 days of the effective date. The fee for recording and indexing ordinances and amendments shall be paid by the municipality enacting the ordinance or amendment and shall be in the amount prescribed by law for the recording of ordinances by the recorder of deeds.

§ 403. Effect of Approved Plats on Official Map.—After adoption of the official map, or part thereof, all streets, watercourses and public grounds and the elements listed in section 401 on final, recorded plats which have been approved as provided by this act shall be deemed amendments to the official map. Notwithstanding any of the other terms of this article, no public hearing need be held or notice given if the amendment of the official map is the result of the addition of a plat which has been approved as provided by this act.

§ 404. Effect of Official Map on Mapped Streets, Watercourses and Public Grounds.—The adoption of any street, street lines or other public lands pursuant to this article as part of the official map shall not, in and of itself, constitute or be deemed to constitute the opening or establishment of any street nor the taking or acceptance of any land, nor shall it obligate the municipality to improve or maintain any such street or land. The adoption of proposed watercourses or public grounds as part of the official map shall not, in and of itself, constitute or be deemed to constitute a taking or acceptance of any land by the municipality.

§ 405. Buildings in Mapped Streets, Watercourses or Other Public Grounds.—For the purpose of preserving the integrity of the official map of the municipality, no permit shall be issued for any building within the lines of any street, watercourse or public ground shown or laid out on the official map. No person shall recover any damages for the taking for public use of any building or improvements constructed within the lines of any street, watercourse or public ground after the same shall have been included in the official map, and any such building or improvement shall be removed at the expense of the owner. However, when the property of which the reserved location forms a part, cannot yield a reasonable return to the owner unless a permit shall be granted, the owner may apply to the governing body for the grant of a special encroachment permit to build. Before granting any special encroachment permit authorized in this section, the governing body may submit the application for a special encroachment permit to the local planning agency and allow the planning agency 30 days for review and comment and shall give public notice and hold a public hearing at which all parties in interest shall have an opportunity to be heard. A refusal by the governing body to grant the special encroachment permit applied for may be appealed by the applicant to the zoning hearing board in the same manner, and within the same time limitation, as is provided in Article IX.

§ 406. Time Limitations on Reservations for Future Taking.—The governing body may fix the time for which streets, watercourses and public grounds on the official map shall be deemed reserved for future taking or acquisition for public use. However, the reservation for public grounds shall lapse and become void one year after an owner of such property has submitted a written notice to the governing body announcing his intentions to build, subdivide or otherwise develop the land covered by the reservation, or has made formal application for an official permit to build a structure for private use, unless the governing body shall have acquired the property or begun condemnation proceedings to acquire such property before the end of the year.

§ 407. Release of Damage Claims or Compensation.—The governing body may designate any of its agencies to negotiate with the owner of land under the following circumstances:

(1) whereon reservations are made;

(2) whereon releases of claims for damages or compensation for such reservations are required; or

(3) whereon agreements indemnifying the governing body from claims by others may be required.

Any releases or agreements, when properly executed by the governing body and the owner and recorded, shall be binding upon any successor in title.

§ 408. Notice to Other Municipalities.—(a) When any county has adopted an official map in accordance with the terms of this article, a certified copy of the map and the ordinances adopting it shall be sent to every municipality within said county. All amendments shall be sent to the aforementioned municipalities. The powers of the governing bodies of counties to adopt, amend and repeal official maps shall be limited to land and watercourses in those municipalities wholly or partly within the county which have no official map in effect at the time an official map is introduced before the governing body of the county, and until the municipal official map is in effect. The adoption of an official map by any municipality, other than a county, whose land or watercourses are subject to county official mapping, shall act as a repeal protanto of the county official map within the municipality adopting such ordinance. Notwithstanding any of the other terms or conditions of this section the county official map shall govern as to county streets and public grounds, facilities and improvements, even though such streets or public grounds, facilities and improvements are located in a municipality which has adopted an official map.

(b) When a municipality proposes to adopt an official map, or any amendment thereto, a copy of the map and the proposed ordinance adopting it, or any amendment thereto, shall be forwarded for review to the county planning agency, or if no such agency exists to the governing body of the county at the same time it is submitted for review to the municipal planning agency. The comments of the county planning agency shall be made to the governing body of the municipality within 45 days, and the proposed action shall not be taken until such comments are received. If, however, the planning agency fails to act within 45 days, the governing body may proceed without its comments.

(c) Additionally, if any municipality proposes to adopt an official map, or amendment thereto, that shows any street or public lands intended to lead into any adjacent municipality a copy of said official map or amendment shall be forwarded to such adjacent municipality for review and comment by the governing body and planning agency of the adjacent municipality. The comments of the adjacent municipality shall be made to the governing body of the municipality proposing the adoption within 45 days, and the proposed action shall not be taken until such comments are received. If, however, the adjacent municipality fails to act within 45 days, the governing body of the proposing municipality may proceed without its comments. When a municipality adopts an official map, a certified copy of the map, the ordinance adopting it and any later amendments shall be forwarded, within 30 days after adoption, to the county planning agency or, in counties where no planning agency exists, to the governing body of the county in which the municipality is located. Additionally, if any municipality adopts an official map, or amendment thereto, that shows any street or public lands intended to lead into any adjacent municipality, a certified copy of said official map or amendment shall be forwarded to such adjacent municipality.

ARTICLE V
Subdivision and Land Development
53 P.S. § 10501–10515.3

§ 501. Grant of Power.—The governing body of each municipality may regulate subdivisions and land development within the municipality by enacting a subdivision and land development ordinance. The ordinance shall require that all subdivision and land development plats of land situated within the municipality shall be submitted for approval to the governing body or, in lieu thereof, to a planning agency designated in the ordinance for this purpose, in which case any planning agency action shall be considered as action of the governing body. All powers granted herein to the governing body or the planning agency shall be exercised in accordance with the provisions of the subdivision and land development ordinance. In the case of any development governed by planned residential development provisions adopted pursuant to Article VII, however, the applicable provisions of the subdivision and land development ordinance shall be as modified by such provisions and the procedures which shall be followed in the approval of any plat, and the rights and duties of the parties thereto shall be governed by Article VII and the provisions adopted thereunder. Provisions regulating mobilehome parks shall be set forth in separate and distinct articles of any subdivision and land development ordinance adopted pursuant to Article V, or any planned residential development provisions adopted pursuant to Article VII.

§ 502. Jurisdiction of County Planning Agencies; Adoption by Reference of County Subdivision and Land Development Ordinances.—(a) When any county has adopted a subdivision and land development ordinance in accordance with the terms of this article, a certified copy of the ordinance shall be sent to every municipality within the county. All amendments shall also be sent to the aforementioned municipalities. The powers of governing bodies of counties to enact, amend and repeal subdivision and land development ordinances shall be limited to land in those municipalities wholly or partly within the county which have no subdivision and land development ordinance in effect at the time a subdivision and land development ordinance is introduced before the governing body of the county, and until the municipal subdivision and land development ordinance is in effect and a certified copy of such ordinance is filed with the county planning agency, if one exists.

(b) The enactment of a subdivision and land development ordinance by any municipality, other than a county, whose land is subject to a county subdivision and land development ordinance shall act as a repeal protanto of the county subdivision and land development ordinance within the municipality adopting such ordinance. However, applications for subdivision and land development located within a municipality having adopted a subdivision and land development ordinance as set forth in this article shall be forwarded upon receipt by the municipality to the county planning agency for review and report together with a fee sufficient to cover the costs of the review and report which fee shall be paid by the applicant: Provided, That such municipalities shall not approve such applications until the county report is received or until the expiration of 30 days from the date the application was forwarded to the county.

(c) Further, any municipality other than a county may adopt by reference the subdivision and land development ordinance of the county, and may by separate ordinance designate the county planning agency, with the county planning agency's concurrence, as its official administrative agency for review and approval of plats.

§ 502.1. Contiguous Municipalities.—(a) The county planning commission shall offer a mediation option to any municipality which believes that its citizens will experience harm as the result of an applicant's proposed subdivision or development of land in a contiguous municipality, if the municipalities agree. In exercising such an option, the municipalities shall comply with the procedures set forth in Article IX. The cost of the mediation shall be shared equally by the municipalities unless otherwise agreed. The applicant shall have the right to participate in the mediation.

(b) The governing body of the municipality may appear and comment before the governing body of a contiguous municipality and the various boards and commissions of the contiguous municipality considering a proposed subdivision, change of land use or land development.

§ 503. Contents of Subdivision and Land Development Ordinance.—The subdivision and land development ordinance may include, but need not be limited to:

(1) Provisions for the submittal and processing of plats, including the charging of review fees, and specifications for such plats, including certification as to the accuracy of plats and provisions for preliminary and final approval and for processing of final approval by stages or sections of development. Such plats and surveys shall be prepared in accordance with the act of May 23, 1945 (P.L. 913, No. 367) [63 P.S. § 148] et seq. known as the "Engineer, Land Surveyor and Geologist Registration Law," except that this requirement shall not preclude the preparation of a plat in accordance with the act of January 24, 1966 (1965 P.L. 1527, No. 535), [63 P.S. § 901] et seq. known as the "Landscape Architects' Registration Law," when it is appropriate to prepare the plat using professional services as set forth in the definition of the "practice of landscape architecture" under section 2 of that act. [63 P.S. § 902] Review fees may include reasonable and necessary charges by the municipality's professional consultants for review and report thereon to the municipality. Such review fees shall be based upon a schedule established by ordinance or resolution. Such review fees shall be reasonable and in accordance with the ordinary and customary charges for similar service in the community, but in no event shall the fees exceed the rate or cost charged by the professional consultant for comparable services to the municipality for services which are not reimbursed or otherwise imposed on applicants. Fees charged to the municipality relating to any appeal of a decision on an application shall not be considered review fees and may not be charged to an applicant.

(i) The governing body shall submit to the applicant an itemized bill showing work performed, identifying the person performing the services and the time and date spent for each task. Nothing in this subparagraph shall prohibit interim itemized billing or municipal escrow or other security requirements. In the event the applicant disputes the amount of any such review fees, the applicant shall, no later than 100 days after the date of transmittal of the bill to the applicant, notify the municipality and the municipality's professional consultant that such fees are disputed and shall explain the basis of their objections to the fees charged, in which case the municipality shall not delay or disapprove a subdivision or land development application due to the applicant's dispute over fees. Failure of the applicant to dispute a bill within 100 days shall be a waiver of the applicant's right to arbitration of that bill under section 510(g). [53 P.S. § 10510].

(ii) In the event that the municipality's professional consultant and the applicant cannot agree on the amount of review fees which are reasonable and necessary, then the applicant and the municipality shall follow the procedure for dispute resolution set forth in section 510(g), provided that the arbitrator resolving such dispute shall be of the same profession or discipline as the professional consultant whose fees are being disputed.

(iii) Subsequent to a decision on an application, the governing body shall submit to the applicant an itemized bill for review fees, specifically designated as a final bill. The final bill shall include all review fees incurred at least through the date of the decision on the application. If for any reason additional review is required subsequent to the decision, including inspections and other work to satisfy the conditions of the approval, the review fees shall be charged to the applicant as a supplement to the final bill.

(1.1) Provisions for the exclusion of certain land development from the definition of land development contained in section 107 only when such land development involves:

(i) the conversion of an existing single-family detached dwelling or single family semi-detached dwelling into not more than three residential units, unless such units are intended to be a condominium;

(ii) the addition of an accessory building, including farm buildings, on a lot or lots subordinate to an existing principal building; or

(iii) the addition or conversion of buildings or rides within the confines of an enterprise which would be considered an amusement park. For the purposes of this subclause, an amusement park is defined as a tract or area used principally as a location for permanent amusement structures or rides. This exclusion shall not apply to newly acquired acreage by an amusement park until initial plans for the expanded area have been approved by proper authorities.

(2) Provisions for insuring that:

(i) the layout or arrangement of the subdivision or land development shall conform to the comprehensive plan and to any regulations or maps adopted in furtherance thereof;

(ii) streets in and bordering a subdivision or land development shall be coordinated, and be of such widths and grades and in such locations as deemed necessary to accommodate prospective traffic, and facilitate fire protection;

(iii) adequate easements or rights-of-way shall be provided for drainage and utilities;

(iv) reservations if any by the developer of any area designed for use as public grounds shall be suitable size and location for their designated uses; and

(v) land which is subject to flooding, subsidence or underground fires either shall be made safe for the purpose for which such land is proposed to be used, or that such land shall be set aside for uses which shall not endanger life or property or further aggravate or increase the existing menace.

(3) Provisions governing the standards by which streets shall be designed, graded and improved, and walkways, curbs, gutters, street lights, fire hydrants, water and sewage facilities and other improvements shall be installed as a condition precedent to final approval of plats in accordance with the requirements of section 509. The standards shall insure that the streets be improved to such a condition that the streets are passable for vehicles which are intended to use that street: Provided, however, That no municipality shall be required to accept such streets for public dedication until the streets meet such additional standards and specifications as the municipality may require for public dedication.

(4) Provisions which take into account phased land development not intended for the immediate erection of buildings where streets, curbs, gutters, street lights, fire hydrants, water and sewage facilities and other improvements may not be possible to install as a condition precedent to final approval of plats, but will be a condition precedent to the erection of buildings on lands included in the approved plat.

(4.1) Provisions which apply uniformly throughout the municipality regulating minimum setback lines and minimum lot sizes which are based upon the availability of water and sewage, in the event the municipality has not enacted a zoning ordinance.

(5) Provisions for encouraging and promoting flexibility, economy and ingenuity in the layout and design of subdivisions and land developments, including provisions authorizing alterations in site requirements and for encouraging other practices which are in accordance with modern and evolving principles of site planning and development.

(6) Provisions for encouraging the use of renewable energy systems and energy-conserving building design.

(7) Provisions for soliciting reviews and reports from adjacent municipalities and other governmental agencies affected by the plans.

(8) Provisions for administering waivers or modifications to the minimum standards of the ordinance in accordance with section 512.1, when the literal compliance with mandatory provisions is shown to the satisfaction of the governing body or planning agency, where applicable, to be unreasonable, to cause undue hardship, or when an alternative standard can be demonstrated to provide equal or better results.

(9) Provisions for the approval of a plat, whether preliminary or final, subject to conditions acceptable to the applicant and a procedure for the applicant's acceptance or rejection of any conditions which may be imposed, including a provision that approval of a plat shall be rescinded automatically upon the applicant's failure to accept or reject such conditions within such time limit as may be established by the governing ordinance.

(10) Provisions and standards for insuring that new developments incorporate adequate provisions for a reliable, safe and adequate water supply to support intended uses within the capacity of available resources.

(11) Provisions requiring the public dedication of land suitable for the use intended; and, upon agreement with the applicant or developer, the construction of recreational facilities, the payment of fees in lieu thereof, the private reservation of the land, or a combination, for park or recreation purposes as a condition precedent to final plan approval, provided that:

(i) The provisions of this paragraph shall not apply to any plan application, whether preliminary or final, pending at the time of enactment of such provisions.

(ii) The ordinance includes definite standards for determining the proportion of a development to be dedicated and the amount of any fee to be paid in lieu thereof.

(iii) The land or fees, or combination thereof, are to be used only for the purpose of providing, acquiring, operating or maintaining park or recreational facilities reasonably accessible to the development.

(iv) The governing body has a formally adopted recreation plan, and the park and recreational facilities are in accordance with definite principles and standards contained in the subdivision and land development ordinance.

(v) The amount and location of land to be dedicated or the fees to be paid shall bear a reasonable relationship to the use of the park and recreational facilities by future inhabitants of the development or subdivision.

(vi) A fee authorized under this subsection shall, upon its receipt by a municipality, be deposited in an interest-bearing account, clearly identified as reserved for providing, acquiring, operating or maintaining park or recreational facilities. Interest earned on such accounts shall become funds of that account.

(vii) Upon request of any person who paid any fee under this subsection, the municipality shall refund such fee, plus interest accumulated thereon from the date of payment, if the municipality had used the fee paid, for a purpose other than the purposes set forth in this section.

(viii) No municipality shall have the power to require the construction of recreational facilities or the dedication of land, or fees in lieu thereof, or private reservation except as may be provided by statute.

§ 503.1 Water Supply.—Every ordinance adopted pursuant to this article shall include a provision that, if water is to be provided by means other than by private wells owned and maintained by the individual owners of lots within the subdivision or development, applicants shall present evidence to the governing body or planning agency, as the case may be, that the subdivision or development is to be supplied by a certificated public utility, a bona fide cooperative association of lot owners, or by a municipal corporation, authority or utility. A copy of a Certificate of Public Convenience from the Pennsylvania Public Utility Commission or an application for such certificate, a cooperative agreement or a commitment or agreement to serve the area in question, whichever is appropriate, shall be acceptable evidence.

§ 504. Enactment of Subdivision and Land Development Ordinance.—(a) Before voting on the enactment of a proposed subdivision and land development ordinance, the governing body shall hold a public hearing thereon pursuant to public notice. A brief summary setting forth the principal provisions of the proposed ordinance and a reference to the place within the municipality where copies of the proposed ordinance may be secured or examined shall be incorporated in the public notice. Unless the proposed subdivision and land development ordinance shall have been prepared by the planning agency, the governing body shall submit the ordinance to the planning agency at least 45 days prior to the hearing on such ordinance to provide the planning agency an opportunity to submit recommendations. If a county planning agency shall have been created for the county in which the municipality adopting the ordinance is located, then, at least 45 days prior to the public hearing on the ordinance, the municipality shall submit the proposed ordinance to said county planning agency for recommendations.

(b) Within 30 days after adoption, the governing body of a municipality, other than a county, shall forward a certified copy of the subdivision and land development ordinance to the county planning agency or, in counties where no planning agency exists, to the governing body of the county in which the municipality is located.

§ 505. Enactment of Subdivision and Land Development Ordinance Amendment.—(a) Amendments to the subdivision and land development ordinance

Table of Contents | Part I Ch. 1–3 Ethics, Records, Open Meetings | Part II Ch. 4–10 Taxation | Part III Ch. 11–18 Torts, Contracts & Civil Rules | Part IV Ch. 19–24 Zoning & Planning | Part V Ch. 25–30 Construction and Emergency Codes | Part VI Ch. 31–39 Municipal Codes | Index

shall become effective only after a public hearing held pursuant to public notice in the manner prescribed for enactment of a proposed ordinance by this article. In addition, in case of an amendment other than that prepared by the planning agency, the governing body shall submit each such amendment to the planning agency for recommendations at least 30 days prior to the date fixed for the public hearing on such proposed amendment. If a county planning agency shall have been created for the county in which the municipality proposing the amendment is located, then, at least 30 days prior to the hearing on the amendment, the municipality shall submit the proposed amendment to said county planning agency for recommendations.

(b) Within 30 days after adoption, the governing body of a municipality, other than a county, shall forward a certified copy of any amendment to the subdivision and land development ordinance to the county planning agency or, in counties where no planning agency exists, to the governing body of the county in which the municipality is located.

§ 506. Publication, Advertisement and Availability of Ordinance.—(a) Proposed subdivision and land development ordinances and amendments shall not be enacted unless notice of proposed enactment is given in the manner set forth in this section, and shall include the time and place of the meeting at which passage will be considered, a reference to a place within the municipality where copies of the proposed ordinance or amendment may be examined without charge or obtained for a charge not greater than the cost thereof. The governing body shall publish the proposed ordinance or amendment once in one newspaper of general circulation in the municipality not more than 60 days nor less than seven days prior to passage. Publication of the proposed ordinance or amendment shall include either the full text thereof or the title and a brief summary, prepared by the municipal solicitor and setting forth all the provisions in reasonable detail. If the full text is not included:

(1) A copy thereof shall be supplied to a newspaper of general circulation in the municipality at the time the public notice is published.

(2) An attested copy of the proposed ordinance shall be filed in the county law library or other county office designated by the county commissioners, who may impose a fee no greater than that necessary to cover the actual costs of storing said ordinances.

(b) In the event substantial amendments are made in the proposed ordinance or amendment, before voting upon enactment, the governing body shall, at least ten days prior to enactment, readvertise, in one newspaper of general circulation in the municipality, a brief summary setting forth all the provisions in reasonable detail together with a summary of the amendments.

(c) Subdivision and land development ordinances and amendments may be incorporated into official ordinance books by reference with the same force and effect as if duly recorded therein.

§ 507. Effect of Subdivision and Land Development Ordinance.—Where a subdivision and land development ordinance has been enacted by a municipality under the authority of this article no subdivision or land development of any lot, tract or parcel of land shall be made, no street, sanitary sewer, storm sewer, water main or other improvements in connection therewith shall be laid out, constructed, opened or dedicated for public use or travel, or for the common use of occupants of buildings abutting thereon, except in accordance with the provisions of such ordinance.

§ 508. Approval of Plats.—All applications for approval of a plat (other than those governed by Article VII), whether preliminary or final, shall be acted upon by the governing body or the planning agency within such time limits as may be fixed in the subdivision and land development ordinance but the governing body or the planning agency shall render its decision and communicate it to the applicant not later than 90 days following the date of the regular meeting of the governing body or the planning agency (whichever first reviews the application) next following the date the application is filed or after a final order of court remanding an application, provided that should the said next regular meeting occur more than 30 days following the filing of the application, or the final order of the court, the said 90-day period shall be measured from the 30th day following the day the application has been filed.

(1) The decision of the governing body or the planning agency shall be in writing and shall be communicated to the applicant personally or mailed to him at his last known address not later than 15 days following the decision.

(2) When the application is not approved in terms as filed the decision shall specify the defects found in the application and describe the requirements which have not been met and shall, in each case, cite to the provisions of the statute or ordinance relied upon.

(3) Failure of the governing body or agency to render a decision and communicate it to the applicant within the time and in the manner required herein shall be deemed an approval of the application in terms as presented unless the applicant has agreed in writing to an extension of time or change in the prescribed manner of presentation of communication of the decision, in which case, failure to meet the extended time or change in manner of presentation of communication shall have like effect.

(4) Changes in the ordinance shall affect plats as follows:

(i) From the time an application for approval of a plat, whether preliminary or final, is duly filed as provided in the subdivision and land development ordinance, and while such application is pending approval or disapproval, no change or amendment of the zoning, subdivision or other governing ordinance or plan shall affect the decision on such application adversely to the applicant and the applicant shall be entitled to a decision in accordance with the provisions of the governing ordinances or plans as they stood at the time the application was duly filed. In addition, when a preliminary application has been duly approved, the applicant shall be entitled to final approval in accordance with the terms of the approved preliminary application as hereinafter provided. However, if an application is properly and finally denied, any subsequent application shall be subject to the intervening change in governing regulations.

(ii) When an application for approval of a plat, whether preliminary or final, has been approved without conditions or approved by the applicant's acceptance of conditions, no subsequent change or amendment in the zoning, subdivision or other governing ordinance or plan shall be applied to affect adversely the right of the applicant to commence and to complete any aspect of the approved development in accordance with the terms of such approval within five years from such approval. The five-year period shall be extended for the duration of any litigation, including appeals, which prevent the commencement or completion of the development, and for the duration of any sewer or utility moratorium or prohibition which was imposed subsequent to the filing of an application for preliminary approval of a plat. In the event of an appeal filed by any party from the approval or disapproval of a plat, the five-year period shall be extended by the total time from the date the appeal was filed until a final order in such matter has been entered and all appeals have been concluded and any period for filing appeals or requests for reconsideration have expired. Provided, however, no extension shall be based upon any water or sewer moratorium which was in effect as of the date of the filing of a preliminary application.

(iii) Where final approval is preceded by preliminary approval, the aforesaid five-year period shall be counted from the date of the preliminary ap-

Table of Contents
Part I Ch. 1–3 Ethics, Records, Open Meetings
Part II Ch. 4–10 Taxation
Part III Ch. 11–18 Torts, Contracts & Civil Rules
Part IV Ch. 19–24 Zoning & Planning
Part V Ch. 25–30 Construction and Emergency Codes
Part VI Ch. 31–39 Municipal Codes
Index

proval. In the case of any doubt as to the terms of a preliminary approval, the terms shall be construed in the light of the provisions of the governing ordinances or plans as they stood at the time when the application for such approval was duly filed.

(iv) Where the landowner has substantially completed the required improvements as depicted upon the final plat within the aforesaid five-year limit, or any extension thereof as may be granted by the governing body, no change of municipal ordinance or plan enacted subsequent to the date of filing of the preliminary plat shall modify or revoke any aspect of the approved final plat pertaining to zoning classification or density, lot, building, street or utility location.

(v) In the case of a preliminary plat calling for the installation of improvements beyond the five-year period, a schedule shall be filed by the landowner with the preliminary plat delineating all proposed sections as well as deadlines within which applications for final plat approval of each section are intended to be filed. Such schedule shall be updated annually by the applicant on or before the anniversary of the preliminary plat approval, until final plat approval of the final section has been granted and any modification in the aforesaid schedule shall be subject to approval of the governing body in its discretion.

(vi) Each section in any residential subdivision or land development, except for the last section, shall contain a minimum of 25% of the total number of dwelling units as depicted on the preliminary plan, unless a lesser percentage is approved by the governing body in its discretion. Provided the landowner has not defaulted with regard to or violated any of the conditions of the preliminary plat approval, including compliance with landowner's aforesaid schedule of submission of final plats for the various sections, then the aforesaid protections afforded by substantially completing the improvements depicted upon the final plat within five years shall apply and for any section or sections, beyond the initial section, in which the required improvements have not been substantially completed within said five-year period the aforesaid protections shall apply for an additional term or terms of three years from the date of final plat approval for each section.

(vii) Failure of landowner to adhere to the aforesaid schedule of submission of final plats for the various sections shall subject any such section to any and all changes in zoning, subdivision and other governing ordinance enacted by the municipality subsequent to the date of the initial preliminary plan submission.

(5) Before acting on any subdivision plat, the governing body or the planning agency, as the case may be, may hold a public hearing thereon after public notice.

(6) No plat which will require access to a highway under the jurisdiction of the Department of Transportation shall be finally approved unless the plat contains a notice that a highway occupancy permit is required pursuant to section 420 of the act of June 1, 1945 (P.L. 1242, No. 428), known as the "State Highway Law," before driveway access to a State highway is permitted. The department shall, within sixty days of the date of receipt of an application for a highway occupancy permit, (i) approve the permit, which shall be valid thereafter unless, prior to commencement of construction thereunder, the geographic, physical or other conditions under which the permit is approved change, requiring modification or denial of the permit, in which event the department shall give notice thereof in accordance with regulations, (ii) deny the permit, (iii) return the application for additional information or correction to conform with department regulations or (iv) determine that no permit is required in which case the department shall notify the municipality and the applicant in writing. If the department shall fail to take any action within the

60-day period, the permit will be deemed to be issued. The plat shall be marked to indicate that access to the State highway shall be marked to indicate that access to the State highway shall be only as authorized by a highway occupancy permit. Neither the department nor any municipality to which permit-issuing authority has been delegated under section 420 of the "State Highway Law" shall be liable in damages for any injury to persons or property arising out of the issuance or denial of a driveway permit, or for failure to regulate any driveway. Furthermore, the municipality from which the building permit approval has been requested shall not be held liable for damages to persons or property arising out of the issuance or denial of a driveway permit by the department.

(7) The municipality may offer a mediation option as an aid in completing proceedings authorized by this section. In exercising such an option, the municipality and mediating parties shall meet the stipulations and follow the procedures set forth in Article IX.

§ 508.1. Notice to School District.—Each month a municipality shall notify in writing the superintendent of a school district in which a plan for a residential development was finally approved by the municipality during the preceding month. The notice shall include, but not be limited to, the location of the development, the number and types of units to be included in the development and the expected construction schedule of the development.

§ 509. Completion of Improvements or Guarantee Thereof Prerequisite to Final Plat Approval.—(a) No plat shall be finally approved unless the streets shown on such plat have been improved to a mud-free or otherwise permanently passable condition, or improved as may be required by the subdivision and land development ordinance and any walkways, curbs, gutters, street lights, fire hydrants, shade trees, water mains, sanitary sewers, storm sewers and other improvements as may be required by the subdivision and land development ordinance have been installed in accordance with such ordinance. In lieu of the completion of any improvements required as a condition for the final approval of a plat, including improvements or fees required pursuant to section 509(i), the subdivision and land development ordinance shall provide for the deposit with the municipality of financial security in an amount sufficient to cover the costs of such improvements or common amenities including, but not limited to, roads, storm water detention and/or retention basins and other related drainage facilities, recreational facilities, open space improvements, or buffer or screen plantings which may be required. The applicant shall not be required to provide financial security for the costs of any improvements for which financial security is required by and provided to the department of transportation in connection with the issuance of a highway occupancy permit pursuant to section 420 of the act of June 1, 1945, (P.L. 1242, No. 428), known as the "State Highway Law."

(b) When requested by the developer, in order to facilitate financing, the governing body or the planning agency, if designated, shall furnish the developer with a signed copy of a resolution indicating approval of the final plat contingent upon the developer obtaining a satisfactory financial security. The final plat or record plan shall not be signed nor recorded until the financial improvements agreement is executed. The resolution or letter of contingent approval shall expire and be deemed to be revoked if the financial security agreement is not executed within 90 days unless a written extension is granted by the governing body; such extension shall not be unreasonably withheld and shall be placed in writing at the request of the developer.

(c) Without limitation as to other types of financial security which the municipality may approve, which approval shall not be unreasonably withheld, Federal or Commonwealth chartered lending institution irrevocable letters of credit and restrictive or escrow accounts in such lending institutions shall be deemed acceptable financial security for the purposes of this section.

Table of Contents
Part I Ch. 1–3 Ethics, Records, Open Meetings
Part II Ch. 4–10 Taxation
Part III Ch. 11–18 Torts, Contracts & Civil Rules
Part IV Ch. 19–24 Zoning & Planning
Part V Ch. 25–30 Construction and Emergency Codes
Part VI Ch. 31–39 Municipal Codes
Index

(d) Such financial security shall be posted with a bonding company or Federal or Commonwealth chartered lending institution chosen by the party posting the financial security, provided said bonding company or lending institution is authorized to conduct such business within the Commonwealth.

(e) Such bond, or other security shall provide for, and secure to the public, the completion of any improvements which may be required on or before the date fixed in the formal action of approval or accompanying agreement for completion of the improvements.

(f) The amount of financial security to be posted for the completion of the required improvements shall be equal to 110% of the cost of completion estimated as of 90 days following the date scheduled for completion by the developer. Annually, the municipality may adjust the amount of the financial security by comparing the actual cost of the improvements which have been completed and the estimated cost for the completion of the remaining improvements as of the expiration of the 90th day after either the original date scheduled for completion or a rescheduled date of completion. Subsequent to said adjustment, the municipality may require the developer to post additional security in order to assure that the financial security equals but does not exceed said 110%. Any additional security shall be posted by the developer in accordance with this subsection.

(g) The amount of financial security required shall be based upon an estimate of the cost of completion of the required improvements, submitted by an applicant or developer and prepared by a professional engineer licensed as such in this Commonwealth and certified by such engineer to be a fair and reasonable estimate of such cost. The municipality, upon the recommendation of the municipal engineer, may refuse to accept such estimate for good cause shown. If the applicant or developer and the municipality are unable to agree upon an estimate, then the estimate shall be recalculated and recertified by another professional engineer licensed as such in this Commonwealth and chosen mutually by the municipality and the applicant or developer. The estimate certified by the third engineer shall be presumed fair and reasonable and shall be the final estimate. In the event that a third engineer is so chosen, fees for the services of said engineer shall be paid equally by the municipality and the applicant or developer.

(h) If the party posting the financial security requires more than one year from the date of posting of the financial security to complete the required improvements, the amount of financial security may be increased by an additional 10% for each one-year period beyond the first anniversary date from posting of financial security to an amount not exceeding 110% of the cost of completing the required improvements as reestablished on or about the expiration of the preceding one-year period by using the above bidding procedure.

(i) In the case where development is projected over a period of years, the governing body or the planning agency may authorize submission of final plats by section or stages of development subject to such requirements or guarantees as to improvements in future sections or stages of development as it finds essential for the protection of any finally approved section of the development.

(j) As the work of installing the required improvements proceeds, the party posting the financial security may request the governing body to release or authorize the release, from time to time, such portions of the financial security necessary for payment to the contractor or contractors performing the work. Any such requests shall be in writing addressed to the governing body, and the governing body shall have 45 days from receipt of such request within which to allow the municipal engineer to certify, in writing, to the governing body that such portion of the work upon the improvements has been completed in accordance with the approved plat. Upon such certification the governing body shall authorize release by the bonding company or lending institution of an amount as estimated by the municipal engineer fairly representing the value of the improvements completed or, if the governing body fails to act within said 45-day period, the governing body shall be deemed to have approved the release of funds as requested. The governing body may, prior to release at the time of completion and certification by its engineer, retain 10% of the estimated cost of the remaining improvements.

(k) Where the governing body accepts dedication of all or some of the required improvements following completion, the governing body may require the posting of financial security to secure structural integrity of said dedicated improvements as well as the functioning of said dedicated improvements in accordance with the design and specifications as depicted on the final plat for a term not to exceed 18 months from the date of acceptance of dedication. Said financial security shall be of the same type as otherwise required in this section with regard to installation of such improvements, and the amount of the financial security shall not exceed 15% of the actual cost of installation of said dedicated improvements.

(l) If water mains or sanitary sewer lines, or both, along with apparatus or facilities related thereto, are to be installed under the jurisdiction and pursuant to the rules and regulations of a public utility or municipal authority separate and distinct from the municipality, financial security to assure proper completion and maintenance thereof shall be posted in accordance with the regulations of the controlling public utility or municipal authority and shall not be included within the financial security as otherwise required by this section.

(m) If financial security has been provided in lieu of the completion of improvements required as a condition for the final approval of a plat as set forth in this section, the municipality shall not condition the issuance of building, grading or other permits relating to the erection or placement of improvements, including buildings, upon the lots or land as depicted upon the final plat upon actual completion of the improvements depicted upon the approved final plat. Moreover, if said financial security has been provided, occupancy permits for any building or buildings to be erected shall not be withheld following: the improvement of the streets providing access to and from existing public roads to such building or buildings to a mud-free or otherwise permanently passable condition, as well as the completion of all other improvements as depicted upon the approved plat, either upon the lot or lots or beyond the lot or lots in question if such improvements are necessary for the reasonable use of or occupancy of the building or buildings. Any ordinance or statute inconsistent herewith is hereby expressly repealed.

§ 510. Release from Improvement Bond.—(a) When the developer has completed all of the necessary and appropriate improvements, the developer shall notify the municipal governing body, in writing, by certified or registered mail, of the completion of the aforesaid improvements and shall send a copy thereof to the municipal engineer. The municipal governing body shall, within ten days after receipt of such notice, direct and authorize the municipal engineer to inspect all of the aforesaid improvements. The municipal engineer shall, there-upon, file a report, in writing with the municipal governing body, and shall promptly mail a copy of the same to the developer by certified or registered mail. The report shall be made and mailed within 30 days after receipt by the municipal engineer of the aforesaid authorization from the governing body; said report shall be detailed and shall indicate approval or rejection of said improvements, either in whole or in part, and if said improvements, or any portion thereof, shall not be approved or shall be rejected by the municipal engineer, said report shall contain a statement of reasons for such nonapproval or rejection.

(b) The municipal governing body shall notify the developer, within 15 days of receipt of the engineer's report, in writing by certified or registered mail of the action of said municipal governing body with relation thereto.

(c) If the municipal governing body or the municipal engineer fails to comply with the time limitation provisions contained herein, all improvements will be deemed to have been approved and the developer shall be released from all liability, pursuant to its performance guaranty bond or other security agreement.

(d) If any portion of the said improvements shall not be approved or shall be rejected by the municipal governing body, the developer shall proceed to complete the same and, upon completion, the same procedure of notification, as outlined herein, shall be followed.

(e) Nothing herein, however, shall be construed in limitation of the developer's right to contest or question by legal proceedings or otherwise, any determination of the municipal governing body or the municipal engineer.

(f) Where herein reference is made to the municipal engineer, he shall be a duly registered professional engineer employed by the municipality or engaged as a consultant thereto.

(g) The municipality may prescribe that the applicant shall reimburse the municipality for the reasonable and necessary expense incurred in connection with the inspection of improvements. The applicant shall not be required to reimburse the governing body for any inspection which is duplicative of inspections conducted by other governmental agencies or public utilities. The burden of proving that any inspection is duplicative shall be upon the objecting applicant. Such reimbursement shall be based upon a schedule established by ordinance or resolution. Such expense shall be reasonable and in accordance with the ordinary and customary fees charged by the municipality's professional consultant for work performed for similar services in the community, but in no event shall the fees exceed the rate or cost charged by the professional consultant to the municipality for comparable services when fees are not reimbursed or otherwise imposed on applicants.

(1) The governing body shall submit to the applicant an itemized bill showing the work performed in connection with the inspection of improvements performed, identifying the person performing the services and the time and date spent for each task. In the event the applicant disputes the amount of any such expense in connection with the inspection of improvements, the applicant shall, no later than 100 days after the date of transmittal of a bill for inspection services, notify the municipality and the municipality's professional consultant that such inspection expenses are disputed as unreasonable or unnecessary and shall explain the basis of their objections to the fees charged, in which case the municipality shall not delay or disapprove a request for release of financial security, a subdivision or land development application or any approval or permit related to development due to the applicant's dispute of inspection expenses. Failure of the applicant to dispute a bill within 100 days shall be a waiver of the applicant's right to arbitration of that bill under this section.

(1.1) Subsequent to the final release of financial security for completion of improvements for a subdivision or land development, or any phase thereof, the professional consultant shall submit to the governing body a bill for inspection services, specifically designated as a final bill which the governing body shall submit to the applicant. The final bill shall include inspection fees incurred through the release of financial security.

(2) If the professional consultant and the applicant cannot agree on the amount of expenses which are reasonable and necessary, then the applicant shall have the right, within 100 days of the transmittal of the final bill or supplement to the final bill to the applicant, to request the appointment of another professional consultant to serve as an arbitrator. The applicant and professional consultant whose fees are being challenged shall, by mutual agreement, appoint another professional consultant to review any bills the applicant has disputed and which remain unresolved and make a determination as to the amount thereof which is reasonable and necessary. The arbitrator shall be of the same profession as the professional consultant whose fees are being challenged.

(3) The arbitrator so appointed shall hear such evidence and review such documentation as the arbitrator in his or her sole opinion deems necessary and shall render a decision no later than 50 days after the date of appointment. Based on the decision of the arbitrator, the applicant or the professional consultant whose fees were challenged shall be required to pay any amounts necessary to implement the decision within 60 days. In the event the municipality has paid the professional consultant an amount in excess of the amount determined to be reasonable and necessary, the professional consultant shall within 60 days reimburse the excess payment.

(4) In the event that the municipality's professional consultant and applicant cannot agree upon the arbitrator to be appointed within 20 days of the request for appointment of an arbitrator, then, upon application of either party, the President Judge of the Court of Common Pleas of the judicial district in which the municipality is located (or if at the time there be no President Judge, then the senior active judge then sitting) shall appoint such arbitrator, who, in that case, shall be neither the municipality's professional consultant nor any professional consultant who has been retained by, or performed services for, the municipality or the applicant within the preceding five years.

(5) The fee of the arbitrator shall be paid by the applicant if the disputed fee is upheld by the arbitrator. The fee of the arbitrator shall be paid by the charging party if the disputed fee is $2,500 or greater than the payment decided by the arbitrator. The fee of the arbitrator shall be paid in an equal amount by the applicant and the charging party if the disputed fee is less than $2,500 of the payment decided by the arbitrator.

(6) In the event that the disputed fees have been paid and the arbitrator finds that the disputed fees are unreasonable or excessive by more than $10,000, the arbitrator shall:

(i) award the amount of the fees found to be unreasonable or excessive to the party that paid the disputed fee; and

(ii) impose a surcharge of 4% of the amount found as unreasonable or excessive to be paid to the party that paid the disputed fee.

(7) A municipality or an applicant shall have 100 days after paying a fee to dispute any fee charged as being unreasonable or excessive.

§ 511. Remedies to Effect Completion of Improvements.—In the event that any improvements which may be required have not been installed as provided in the subdivision and land development ordinance or in accord with the approved final plat the governing body of the municipality is hereby granted the power to enforce any corporate bond, or other security by appropriate legal and equitable remedies. If proceeds of such bond, or other security are insufficient to pay the cost of installing or making repairs or corrections to all the improvements covered by said security, the governing body of the municipality may, at its option, install part of such improvements in all or part of the subdivision or land development and may institute appropriate legal or equitable action to recover the moneys necessary to complete the remainder of the improvements. All of the proceeds, whether resulting from the security or from any legal or equitable action brought against the developer, or both, shall be used solely for the installation of the improvements covered by such security, and not for any other municipal purpose.

§ 512.1. Modifications.—(a) The governing body or the planning agency, if authorized to approve applications within the subdivision and land development ordinance, may grant a modification of the requirements of one or more provisions if the literal enforcement will exact undue hardship because of peculiar conditions pertaining to the land in question, provided that such modification will not be contrary to the public interest and that the purpose and intent of the ordinance is observed.

(b) All requests for a modification shall be in writing and shall accompany and be a part of the application for development. The request shall state in full the grounds and facts of unreasonableness or hardship on which the request is based, the provision or provisions of the ordinance involved and the minimum modification necessary.

(c) If approval power is reserved by the governing body, the request for modification may be referred to the planning agency for advisory comments.

(d) The governing body or the planning agency, as the case may be, shall keep a written record of all action on all requests for modifications.

§ 513. Recording Plats and Deeds.—(a) Upon the approval of a final plat, the developer shall within 90 days of such final approval or 90 days after the date of delivery of an approved plat signed by the governing body following completion of conditions imposed for such approval, whichever is later, record such plat in the office of the recorder of deeds of the county in which the municipality is located. Whenever such plat approval is required by a municipality, the recorder of deeds of the county shall not accept any plat for recording, unless such plat officially notes the approval of the governing body and review by the county planning agency, if one exists.

(b) The recording of the plat shall not constitute grounds for assessment increases until such time as lots are sold or improvements are installed on the land included within the subject plat.

§ 514. Effect of Plat Approval on Official Map.—After a plat has been approved and recorded as provided in this article, all streets and public grounds on such plat shall be, and became a part of the official map of the municipality without public hearing.

§ 515. Penalties.—(515 repealed Dec. 21, 1988, P.L. 1329, No. 170)

§ 515.1. Preventive Remedies.—(a) In addition to other remedies, the municipality may institute and maintain appropriate actions by law or in equity to restrain, correct or abate violations, to prevent unlawful construction, to recover damages and to prevent illegal occupancy of a building, structure or premises. The description by metes and bounds in the instrument of transfer or other documents used in the process of selling or transferring shall not exempt the seller or transferor from such penalties or from the remedies herein provided.

(b) A municipality may refuse to issue any permit or grant any approval necessary to further improve or develop any real property which has been developed or which has resulted from a subdivision of real property in violation of any ordinance adopted pursuant to this article. This authority to deny such a permit or approval shall apply to any of the following applicants:

(1) The owner of record at the time of such violation.

(2) The vendee or lessee of the owner of record at the time of such violation without regard as to whether such vendee or lessee had actual or constructive knowledge of the violation.

(3) The current owner of record who acquired the property subsequent to the time of violation without regard as to whether such current owner had actual or constructive knowledge of the violation.

(4) The vendee or lessee of the current owner of record who acquired the property subsequent to the time of violation without regard as to whether such vendee or lessee had actual or constructive knowledge of the violation.

As an additional condition for issuance of a permit or the granting of an approval to any such owner, current owner, vendee or lessee for the development of any such real property, the municipality may require compliance with the conditions that would have been applicable to the property at the time the applicant acquired an interest in such real property.

§ 515.2. Jurisdiction.—District justices shall have initial jurisdiction in proceedings brought under section 515.3.

§ 515.3. Enforcement Remedies.—(a) Any person, partnership or corporation who or which has violated the provisions of any subdivision or land development ordinance enacted under this act or prior enabling laws shall, upon being found liable therefor in a civil enforcement proceeding commenced by a municipality, pay a judgment of not more than $500 plus all court costs, including reasonable attorney fees incurred by the municipality as a result thereof. No judgment shall commence or be imposed, levied or payable until the date of the determination of a violation by the district justice. If the defendant neither pays nor timely appeals the judgment, the municipality may enforce the judgment pursuant to the applicable rules of civil procedure. Each day that a violation continues shall constitute a separate violation, unless the district justice determining that there has been a violation further determines that there was a good faith basis for the person, partnership or corporation violating the ordinance to have believed that there was no such violation, in which event there shall be deemed to have been only one such violation until the fifth day following the date of the determination of a violation by the district justice and thereafter each day that a violation continues shall constitute a separate violation.

(b) The court of common pleas, upon petition, may grant an order of stay, upon cause shown, tolling the per diem judgment pending a final adjudication of the violation and judgment.

(c) Nothing contained in this section shall be construed or interpreted to grant to any person or entity other than the municipality the right to commence any action for enforcement pursuant to this section.

ARTICLE V-A
Municipal Capital Improvement
53 P.S. §§ 10501-A–10508-A

(Art. added Dec. 19, 1990, P.L. 1343, No. 209)

§ 501-A. Purposes.—To further the purposes of this act in an era of increasing development and of a corresponding demand for municipal capital improvements, to insure that the cost of needed capital improvements be applied to new developments in a manner that will allocate equitably the cost of those improvements among property owners and to respond to the increasing difficulty which municipalities are experiencing in developing revenue sources to fund new capital infrastructure from the public sector, the following powers are granted to all municipalities, other than counties, which municipalities have adopted either a municipal or county comprehensive plan, subdivision and land development ordinance and zoning ordinance.

(501-A added Dec. 19, 1990, P.L. 1343, No. 209)

§ 502-A. Definitions.—The following words and phrases when used in this article shall have the meanings given to them in this section unless the context clearly indicates otherwise:

"Adjusted for family size," adjusted in a manner which results in an income eligibility level which is lower for households with fewer than four people, or higher for households with more than four people, than the base income eligibility level determined as provided in the definition of low- to moderate-income persons based upon a formula as established by the rule of the agency.

"Adjusted gross income," all wages, assets, regular cash or noncash contributions or gifts from persons outside the household, and such other resources and benefits as may be determined to be income by rule of the department, adjusted for family size, less deductions under section 62 of the Internal Revenue Code of 1986 (Public Law 99-514, 26 U.S.C. § 62 et seq.).

"Affordable," with respect to the housing unit to be occupied by low- to moderate-income persons, monthly rents or monthly mortgage payments, including property taxes and insurance, that do not exceed 30% of that amount which represents 100% of the adjusted gross annual income for households within the metropolitan statistical area (MSA) or, if not within the MSA, within the county in which the housing unit is located, divided by 12.

"Agency," the Pennsylvania Housing Finance Agency as created pursuant to the act of December 3, 1959 (P.L. 1688, No. 621), known as the "Housing Finance Agency Law."

"Department," the Department of Community Affairs of the Commonwealth.

"Existing deficiencies," existing highways, roads or streets operating at a level of service below the preferred level of service designated by the municipality, as adopted in the transportation capital improvement plan.

"Highways, roads or streets," any highways, roads or streets identified on the legally adopted municipal street or highway plan or the official map which carry vehicular traffic, together with all necessary appurtenances, including bridges, rights-of-way and traffic control improvements. The term shall not include the interstate highway system.

"Impact fee," a charge or fee imposed by a municipality against new development in order to generate revenue for funding the costs of transportation capital improvements necessitated by and attributable to new development.

"Low- to moderate-income persons," one or more natural persons or a family, the total annual adjusted gross household income of which is less than 100% of the median annual adjusted gross income for households in this Commonwealth or is less than 100% of the median annual adjusted gross income for households within the metropolitan statistical area (MSA) or, if not within the MSA, within the county in which the household is located, whichever is greater.

"New development," any commercial, industrial or residential or other project which involves new construction, enlargement, reconstruction, redevelopment, relocation or structural alteration and which is expected to generate additional vehicular traffic within the transportation service area of the municipality.

"Offsite improvements," those public capital improvements which are not onsite improvements and that serve the needs of more than one development.

"Onsite improvements," all improvements constructed on the applicant's property, or the improvements constructed on the property abutting the applicant's property necessary for the ingress or egress to the applicant's property, and required to be constructed by the applicant pursuant to any municipal ordinance, including, but not limited to, the municipal building code, subdivision and land development ordinance, PRD regulations and zoning ordinance.

"Pass-through trip," a trip which has both an origin and a destination outside the service area.

"Road improvement," the construction, enlargement, expansion or improvement of public highways, roads or streets. It shall not include bicycle lanes, bus lanes, busways, pedestrian ways, rail lines or tollways.

"Traffic or transportation engineer or planner," any person who is a registered professional engineer in this Commonwealth or is otherwise qualified by education and experience to perform traffic or transportation planning analyses of the type required in this act and who deals with the planning, geometric design and traffic operations of highways, roads and streets, their networks, terminals and abutting lands and relationships with other modes of transportation for the achievement of convenient, efficient and safe movement of goods and persons.

"Transportation capital improvements," those offsite road improvements that have a life expectancy of three or more years, not including costs for maintenance, operation or repair.

"Transportation service area," a geographically defined portion of the municipality not to exceed seven square miles of area which, pursuant to the comprehensive plan and applicable district zoning regulations, has an aggregation of sites with development potential creating the need for transportation improvements within such area to be funded by impact fees. No area may be included in more than one transportation service area.

(502-A added Dec. 19, 1990, P.L. 1343, No. 209)

§ 503-A. Grant of Power.—(a) The governing body of each municipality other than a county, in accordance with the conditions and procedures set forth in this act, may enact, amend and repeal impact fee ordinances and, thereafter, may establish, at the time of municipal approval of any new development or subdivision, the amount of an impact fee for any of the offsite public transportation capital improvements authorized by this act as a condition precedent to final plat approval under the municipality's subdivision and land development ordinance. Every ordinance adopted pursuant to this act shall include, but not be limited to, provisions for the following:

(1) The conditions and standards for the determination and imposition of impact fees consistent with the provisions of this act.

(2) The agency, body or office within the municipality which shall administer the collection, disbursement and accounting of impact fees.

(3) The time, method and procedure for the payment of impact fees.

(4) The procedure for issuance of any credit against or reimbursement of impact fees which an applicant may be entitled to receive consistent with the provisions of this act.

(5) Exemptions or credits which the municipality may choose to adopt. In this regard the municipality shall have the power to:

(i) Provide a credit of up to 100% of the applicable impact fees for all new development and growth which constitutes affordable housing to low- and moderate-income persons.

(ii) Provide a credit of up to 100% of the applicable impact fees for growth which are determined by the municipality to serve an overriding public interest.

(iii) Exempt de minimus applications from impact fee requirements. If such a policy is adopted, the definition of de minimus shall be contained in the ordinance.

(b) No municipality shall have the power to require as a condition for approval of a land development or subdivision application the construction, dedication or payment of any offsite improvements or capital expenditures of any nature whatsoever or impose any contribution in lieu thereof, exaction fee, or any connection, tapping or similar fee except as may be specifically authorized under this act.

(c) No municipality may levy an impact fee prior to the enactment of a municipal impact fee ordinance adopted in accordance with the procedures set forth in this act, except as may be specifically authorized by the provisions of this act. A transportation impact fee shall be imposed by a municipality within a service area or areas only where such fees have been determined and imposed pursuant to the standards, provisions and procedures set forth herein.

(d) Impact fees may be used for those costs incurred for improvements designated in the transportation capital improvement program which are attributable to new development, including the acquisition of land and rights-of-way; engineering, legal and planning costs; and all other costs which are directly related to road improvements within the service area or areas, including debt service. Impact fees shall not be imposed or used for costs associated with any of the following:

(1) Construction, acquisition or expansion of municipal facilities other than capital improvements identified in the transportation capital improvements plan required by this act.

(2) Repair, operation or maintenance of existing or new capital improvements.

(3) Upgrading, updating, expanding or replacing existing capital improvements to serve existing developments in order to meet stricter safety, efficiency, environmental or regulatory standards not attributable to new development.

(4) Upgrading, updating, expanding or replacing existing capital improvements to remedy deficiencies in service to existing development or fund deficiencies in existing municipal capital improvements resulting from a lack of adequate municipal funding over the years for maintenance or capital construction costs.

(5) Preparing and developing the land use assumptions, roadway sufficiency analysis and transportation capital improvement plan, except that impact fees may be used for no more than a proportionate amount of the cost of professional consultants incurred in preparing a roadway sufficiency analysis of infrastructure within a specified transportation service area, such allowable proportion to be calculated by dividing the total costs of all road improvements in the adopted transportation capital improvement program within the transportation service area attributable to projected future development within the service area, as defined in section 504-A(e)(1)(iii), by the total costs of all road improvements in the adopted transportation capital improvement program within the specific transportation service area, as defined in section 504-A.

(e) Nothing in this act shall be deemed to alter or affect a municipality's existing power to require an applicant for municipal approval of any new development or subdivision from paying for the installation of onsite improvements as provided for in a municipality's subdivision and land development ordinance as authorized by this act.

(f) No municipality may delay or deny any application for building permit, certificate-of-occupancy, development or any other approval or permit required for construction, land development, subdivision or occupancy for the reason that any project of an approved capital improvement program has not been completed.

(g) A municipality which has enacted an impact fee ordinance on or before June 1, 1990, may for a period not to exceed one year from the effective date of this article, adopt an impact fee ordinance to conform with the standards and procedures set forth in this article. Where a fee previously imposed pursuant to an ordinance in effect on June 1, 1990, for transportation improvements authorized by this article is greater than the recalculated fee due under the newly adopted ordinance, the individual who paid the fee is entitled to a refund of the difference. If the recalculated fee is greater than the previously paid fee, there shall be no additional charge.

(h) The powers provided by this section may be exercised by two or more municipalities, other than counties, which have adopted a joint municipal comprehensive plan pursuant to Article XI through a joint municipal authority, subject to the conditions and procedures set forth in this article.

§ 504-A. Transportation Capital Improvements Plan.—(a) A transporta-tion capital improvements plan shall be prepared and adopted by the governing body of the municipality prior to the enactment of any impact fee ordinance. The municipality shall provide qualified professionals to assist the transportation impact fee advisory committee or the planning commission in the preparation of the transportation capital improvements plan and calculation of the impact fees to be imposed to implement the plan in accordance with the procedures, provisions and standards set forth in this act.

(b) (1) An impact fee advisory committee shall be created by resolution of a municipality intending to adopt a transportation impact fee ordinance. The resolution shall describe the geographical area or areas of the municipality for which the advisory committee shall develop the land use assumptions and conduct the roadway sufficiency analysis studies.

(2) The advisory committee shall consist of no fewer than 7 nor more than 15 members, all of whom shall serve without compensation. The governing body of the municipality shall appoint as members of the advisory committee persons who are either residents of the municipality or conduct business within the municipality and are not employees or officials of the municipality. Not less than 40% of the members of the advisory committee shall be representatives of the real estate, commercial and residential development, and building industries. The municipality may also appoint traffic or transportation engineers or planners to serve on the advisory committee provided the appointment is made after consultation with the advisory committee members. The traffic or transportation engineers or planners appointed to the advisory committee may not be employed by the municipality for the development of or consultation on the roadway sufficiency analysis which may lead to the adoption of the transportation capital improvements plan.

(3) The governing body of the municipality may elect to designate the municipal planning commission appointed pursuant to Article II as the impact fee advisory committee. If the existing planning commission does not include members representative of the real estate, commercial and residential development and building industries at no less than 40% of the membership, the governing body of the municipality shall appoint the sufficient number of representatives of the aforementioned industries who reside in the municipality or conduct business within the municipality to serve as ad hoc voting members of the planning commission whenever such commission functions as the impact fee advisory committee.

(4) No impact fee ordinance may be invalidated as a result of any legal action challenging the composition of the advisory committee which is not brought within 90 days following the first public meeting of said advisory committee.

(5) The advisory committee shall serve in an advisory capacity and shall have the following duties:

(i) To make recommendations with respect to land use assumptions, the development of comprehensive road improvements and impact fees.

(ii) To make recommendations to approve, disapprove or modify a capital improvement program by preparing a written report containing these recommendations to the municipality.

(iii) To monitor and evaluate the implementation of a capital improvement program and the assessment of impact fees, and report annually to the municipality with respect to the same.

(iv) To advise the municipality of the need to revise or update the land use assemptions, capital improvement program or impact fees.

(c) (1) As a prerequisite to the development of the transportation capital improvements plan, the advisory committee shall develop land use assumptions for the determination of future growth and development within the designated area or areas as described by the municipal resolution and recommend its findings to the governing body. Prior to the issuance and presentation of a written report to the municipality on the recommendations for proposed land use assumptions upon which to base the development of the transportation capital improvements plan, the advisory committee shall conduct a public hearing, following the providing of proper notice in accordance with section 107, for consideration of the land use assumption proposals. Following receipt of the advisory committee report, which shall include the findings of the public hearing, the governing body of the municipality shall by resolution approve, disapprove or modify the land use assumptions recommended by the advisory committee.

(2) The land use assumptions report shall:

(i) Describe the existing land uses within the designated area or areas and the highways, roads or streets incorporated therein.

(ii) To the extent possible, reflect projected changes in land uses, densities of residential development, intensities of nonresidential development and population growth rates which may affect the level of traffic within the designated area or areas over a period of at least the next five years. These projections shall be based on an analysis of population growth rates during the prior five-year period, current zoning regulations, approved subdivision and land developments, and the future land use plan contained in the adopted municipal comprehensive plan. It may also refer to all professionally produced studies and reports pertaining to the municipality regarding such items as demographics, parks and recreation, economic development and any other study deemed appropriate by the municipality.

(3) If the municipality is located in a county which has created a county planning agency, the advisory committee shall forward a copy of their proposed land use assumptions to the county planning agency for its comments at least 30 days prior to the public hearing. At the same time, the advisory committee shall also forward copies of the proposed assumptions to all contiguous municipalities and to the local school district for their review and comments.

(d) (1) Upon adoption of the land use assumptions by the municipality, the advisory committee shall prepare, or cause to be prepared, a roadway sufficiency analysis which shall establish the existing level of infrastructure sufficiency and preferred levels of service within any designated area or areas of the municipality as described by the resolution adopted pursuant to the creation of the advisory committee. The roadway sufficiency analysis shall be prepared for any highway, road or street within the designated area or areas on which the need for road improvements attributable to projected future new development is anticipated. The municipality shall commission a traffic or transportation engineer or planner to assist the advisory committee in the preparation of the roadway sufficiency analysis. Municipalities may jointly commission such engineer or planner to assist in the preparation of multiple municipality roadway sufficiency analyses. In preparing the roadway sufficiency analysis report, the engineer may consider and refer to previously produced professional studies and reports relevant to the production of the roadway sufficiency analysis as required by this section. It shall be deemed that the roads, streets and highways not on the roadway sufficiency analysis report are not impacted by future development. The roadway sufficiency analysis shall include the following components:

(i) The establishment of existing volumes of traffic and existing levels of service.

(ii) The identification of a preferred level of service established pursuant to the following:

(A) The level of service shall be one of the categories of road service as defined by the Transportation Research Board of the National Academy of Sciences or the Institute of Transportation Engineers. The municipality may choose to select a level of service on a transportation service area basis as the preferred level of service. The preferred levels of service shall be designated by the governing body of the municipality following determination of the existing level of service as established by the roadway sufficiency analysis. If the preferred level of service is designated as greater than the existing level of service, the municipality shall be required to identify road improvements needed to correct the existing deficiencies.

(B) Following adoption of the preferred level of service, such level of service may be waived for a particular road segment or intersection if the municipality finds that one or more of the following effectively precludes provision of road improvements necessary to meet the level of service: geometric design limitations, topographic limitations or the unavailability of necessary right-of-way.

(iii) The identification of existing deficiencies which need to be remedied to accommodate existing traffic at the preferred level of service.

(iv) The specification of the required road improvements needed to bring the existing level of service to the preferred level of service.

(v) A projection of anticipated traffic volumes, with a separate determination of pass-through trips, for a period of not less than five years from the date of the preparation of the roadway sufficiency analysis based upon the land use assumptions adopted under this section.

(vi) The identification of forecasted deficiencies which will be created by "pass-through" trips.

(2) The advisory committee shall provide the governing body with the findings of the roadway sufficiency analysis. Following receipt of the advisory committee report, the governing body shall by resolution approve, disapprove or modify the roadway sufficiency analysis recommended by the advisory committee.

(e) (1) Utilizing the information provided by the land use assumption and the roadway sufficiency analysis as the basis for determination of the need for road improvements to remedy existing deficiencies and accommodate future projected traffic volumes, the advisory committee shall identify those capital projects which the municipality should consider for adoption in its transportation capital improvements plan and shall recommend the delineation of the transportation service area or areas. The capital improvement plan shall be developed in accordance with generally accepted engineering and planning practices. The capital improvement program shall include projections of all designated road improvements in the capital improvement program. The total cost of the road improvements shall be based upon estimated costs, using standard traffic engineering standards, with a 10% maximum contingency which may be added to said estimate. These costs shall include improvements to correct existing deficiencies with identified anticipated sources of funding and timetables for implementation. The transportation capital improvements plan shall include the following components:

(i) A description of the existing highways, roads and streets within the transportation service area and the road improvements required to update, improve, expand or replace such highways, roads and streets in order to meet the preferred level of service and usage and stricter safety, efficiency, environmental or regulatory standards not attributable to new development.

(ii) A plan specifying the road improvements within the transportation service area attributable to forecasted pass-through traffic so as to maintain the preferred level of service after existing deficiencies identified by the roadway sufficiency analysis have been remedied.

(iii) A plan specifying the road improvements or portions thereof within the transportation service area attributable to the projected future development, consistent with the adopted land use assumptions, in order to maintain the preferred level of service after accommodation for pass-through traffic and after existing deficiencies identified in the roadway sufficiency analysis have been remedied.

(iv) The projected costs of the road improvements to be included in the transportation capital improvements plan, calculating separately for each project by the following categories:

(A) The costs or portion thereof associated with correcting existing deficiencies as specified in subparagraph (i).

(B) The costs or portions thereof attributable to providing road improvements to accommodate forecasted pass-through trips as specified in subparagraph (ii).

(C) The costs of providing necessary road improvements or portions thereof attributable to projected future development as specified in subparagraph (iii); Provided that no more than 50% of the cost of the improvements to any highway, road or street which qualifies as a state highway or portion of the rural state highway system as provided in section 102 of the act of June 1, 1945 (P.L. 1242, No. 428), known as the "State Highway Law," may be included.

(v) A projected timetable and proposed budget for constructing each road improvement contained in the plan.

(vi) The proposed source of funding for each capital improvement included in the road plan. This shall include anticipated revenue from the Federal Government, State government, municipality, impact fees and any other source. The estimated revenue for each capital improvement in the plan which is to be provided by impact fees shall be identified separately for each project.

(2) The source of funding required for projects to remedy existing deficiencies as set forth in paragraph (1)(i) and the road improvements attributable to forecasted pass-through traffic as set forth in paragraph (1)(ii) shall be exclusive of funds generated from the assessment of impact fees.

(3) Upon the completion of the transportation capital improvements plan and prior to its adoption by the governing body of the municipality and the enactment of a municipal impact fee ordinance, the advisory committee shall hold at least one public hearing for consideration of the plan. Notification of the public hearing shall comply with the requirement of section 107. The plan shall be available for public inspection at least ten working days prior to the date of the public hearing. After presentation of the recommendation by the advisory committee or its representatives at a public meeting of the governing body, the governing body may make such changes to the plan prior to its adoption as the governing body deems appropriate following review of the public comments made at the public hearing.

(4) The governing body may periodically, but no more frequently than annually, request the impact fee advisory committee to review the capital improvements plan and impact fee charges and make recommendations for revisions for subsequent consideration and adoption by the governing body based only on the following:

(i) New subsequent development which has occurred in the municipality.

(ii) Capital improvements contained in the capital improvements plan, the construction of which has been completed.

(iii) Unavoidable delays beyond the responsibility or control of the municipality in the construction of capital improvements contained in the plan.

(iv) Significant changes in the land use assumptions.

(v) Changes in the estimated costs of the proposed transportation capital improvements, which may be recalculated by applying the construction cost index as published in the American City/County Magazine or the Engineering News Record.

(vi) Significant changes in the projected revenue from all sources listed needed for the construction of the transportation capital improvements.

(f) Any improvements to Federal-aid or State highways to be funded in part by impact fees shall require the approval of the Department of Transportation and, if necessary, the United States Department of Transportation. Nothing in this act shall be deemed to alter or diminish the powers, duties or jurisdiction of the Department of Transportation with respect to State highways or the rural State highway system.

(g) Two or more municipalities may, upon agreement, appoint a joint impact fee advisory committee which may develop roadway sufficiency analyses and transportation capital improvements plans for the participating municipalities. The members of the advisory committee must be either residents of or conduct business within one of the participating municipalities.

(504-A added Dec. 19, 1990, P.L. 1343, No. 209)

§ 505-A. Establishment and Administration of Impact Fees.—(a) (1) The impact fee for transportation capital improvements shall be based upon the total costs of the road improvements included in the adopted capital improvement plan within a given transportation service area attributable to and necessitated by new development within the service area as calculated pursuant to section 504-A(e)(1)(iv)(C), divided by the number of anticipated peak hour trips generated by all new development consistent with the adopted land use assumptions and calculated in accordance with the Trip Generation Manual published by the Institute of Transportation Engineers, fourth or subsequent edition as adopted by the municipality by ordinance or resolution to equal a per trip cost for transportation improvements within the service area.

(2) The specific impact fee for a specific new development or subdivision within the service area for road improvements shall be determined as of the date of preliminary land development or subdivision approval by multiplying the per trip cost established for the service area as determined in section 503-A(a) by the estimated number of peak-hour trips to be generated by the new development or subdivision using generally accepted traffic engineering standards.

(3) A municipality may authorize or require the preparation of a special transportation study in order to determine traffic generation or circulation for a new nonresidential development to assist in the determination of the amount of the transportation fee for such development or subdivision. The municipality shall set forth by ordinance the circumstances in which such a study should be authorized or required, provided however, that no special transportation study shall be required when there is no deviation from the land use assumptions resulting in increased density, intensity or trip generation by a particular development. A developer or municipality may, however, at any time, voluntarily prepare and submit a traffic study for a proposed development or may have such a study prepared at its expense after the development is completed to include actual trips generated by the development for use in any appeal as provided for under this act. The special transportation study shall be prepared by a qualified traffic or transportation engineer using procedures and methods established by the municipality based on generally accepted transportation planning and engineering standards. The study, where required by the municipality, shall be submitted prior to the imposition of an impact fee and shall be taken into consideration by the municipality in increasing or reducing the amount of the impact fee for the new development for the amount shown on the impact fee schedule adopted by the municipality.

(b) The governing body shall enact an impact ordinance setting forth a description of the boundaries and a fee schedule for each transportation service area. At least ten working days prior to the adoption of the ordinance at a public meeting, the ordinance shall be available for public inspection. The impact fee ordinance shall include, but not be limited to, those provisions set forth in section 503-A(a) and conform with the standards, provisions and procedures set forth in this act.

(c) (1) A municipality may give notice of its intention to adopt an impact fee ordinance by publishing a statement of such intention twice in one newspaper of general circulation in the municipality. The first publication shall not occur before the adoption of the resolution by which the municipality establishes its impact fee advisory committee. The second publication shall occur not less than one nor more than three weeks thereafter.

(2) A municipal impact fee ordinance adopted under and pursuant to this act may provide that the provisions of the ordinance may have retroactive application, for a period not to exceed 18 months after the adoption of the resolution creating an impact fee advisory committee pursuant to section 504-A(b)(1), to preliminary or tentative applications for land development, subdivision or PRD with the municipality on or after the first publication of the municipality's intention to adopt an impact fee ordinance; provided, however, that the impact fee imposed on building permits for construction of new development approved pursuant to such applications filed during the period of pendancy shall not exceed $1,000 per anticipated peak hour trip as calculated in accordance with the generally accepted traffic engineering standards as set forth under the provisions of subsection (a)(1) or the subsequently adopted fee established by the ordinance, whichever is less.

(3) No action upon an application for land development, subdivision or PRD shall be postponed, delayed or extended by the municipality because adoption of a municipal impact fee ordinance is being considered. Furthermore, the adoption of an impact fee ordinance more than 18 months after adoption of a resolution creating the impact fee advisory committee shall not be retroactive or applicable to plats submitted for preliminary or tentative approval prior to the legal publication of the proposed impact fee ordinance and any fees collected pursuant to this subsection shall be refunded to the payor of such fees; provided the adoption of the impact fee ordinance was not delayed due to the initiation of any litigation challenging the adoption of such ordinance.

(d) Any impact fees collected by a municipality pursuant to a municipal ordinance shall be deposited by the municipality into an interest-bearing fund account designated solely for impact fees, clearly identifying the transportation service area from which the fee was received. Funds collected in one transportation service area must be accounted for and expended within that transportation service area, and such funds shall only be expended for that portion of the transportation capital improvements identified as being funded by impact fees under the transportation capital improvements plan. Notwithstanding any other provisions of this act, municipalities may expend impact fees paid by an applicant on projects not contained in the adopted transportation capital improvement plan, or may provide credit against impact fees for the value of any construction projects not contained in the transportation capital improvement plan which are performed at the applicant's expense, if all of the following criteria are met:

(1) The applicant has provided written consent to use of its collected impact fees, or the provision of such credit against the applicant's impact fees, for specific transportation projects which are not included in the transportation capital improvement plan.

(2) The alternative transportation projects, whether highway or multimodal, have as their purpose the reduction of traffic congestion or the removal of vehicle trips from the roadway network.

(3) The municipality amends its transportation capital improvement plan components required by section 504-a(e)(1)(vi) to provide replacement of the collected impact fees transferred to transportation projects outside the approved transportation capital improvement plan from sources other than impact fees or developer contributions within three years of completion of the alternative projects to which the transferred fees where applied or for which credit was provided. All interest earned on such funds shall become funds of that account. The municipality shall provide that an accounting be made annually for any fund account containing impact fee proceeds and earned interest. Such accounting shall include, but not be limited to, the total funds collected, the source of the funds collected, the total amount of interest accruing on such funds and the amount of funds expended on specific transportation improvements. Notice of the availability of the results of the accounting shall be included and published as part of the annual audit required of municipalities. A copy of the report shall also be provided to the advisory committee.

(e) All transportation impact fees imposed under the terms of this act shall be payable at the time of the issuance of building permits for the applicable new development or subdivision. The municipality may not require the applicant to provide a guarantee of financial security for the payment of any transportation impact fees, except the municipality may provide for the deposit with the municipality of financial security in an amount sufficient to cover the cost of the construction of any road improvement contained in the transportation capital improvement plan which is performed by the applicant.

(f) An applicant shall be entitled to a credit against the impact fee in the amount of the fair market value of any land dedicated by the applicant to the municipality for future right-of-way, realignment or widening of any existing roadways or for the value of any construction of road improvements contained in the transportation capital improvement program which is performed at the applicant's expense. The amount of such credit for any capital improvement constructed shall be the amount allocated in the capital improvement program, including contingency factors, for such work. The fair market value of any land dedicated by the applicant shall be determined as of the date of the submission of the land development or subdivision application to the municipality.

(g) Impact fees previously collected by a municipality shall be refunded, together with earned accrued interest thereon, to the payor of such fees from the date of payment under any of the following circumstances:

(1) In the event that a municipality terminates or completes an adopted capital improvements plan for a transportation service area and there remains at the time of termination or completion undispersed funds in the accounts established for that purpose, the municipality shall provide written notice by certified mail to those persons who previously paid the fees which remain undispersed of the availability of said funds for refund of the person's proportionate share of the fund balance. The allocation of the refund shall be determined by generally accepted accounting practices. In the event that any of the funds remain unclaimed following one year after the notice, which notice shall be provided to the last known address provided by the payor of the fees to the municipality, the municipality shall be authorized to transfer any funds so remaining to any other fund in the municipality without any further obligation to refund said funds.

(2) If the municipality fails to commence construction of any transportation service area road improvements within three years of the scheduled construction date set forth in the transportation capital improvements plan, any person who paid any impact fees pursuant to that transportation capital improvements plan shall, upon written request to the municipality, receive a refund of that portion of the fee attributable to the contribution for the uncommenced road improvement, plus the interest accumulated thereon from the date of payment.

(3) If, upon completion of any road improvements project, the actual expenditures of the capital project are less than 95% of the costs properly allocable to the fee paid within the transportation service area in which the completed road improvement was adopted, the municipality shall refund the pro rata difference between the budgeted costs and the actual expenditures, including interest accumulated thereon from the date of payment, to the person or persons who paid the impact fees for such improvements.

(4) If the new development for which transportation impact fees were paid is not commenced prior to the expiration of building permits issued for the new development within the time limits established by applicable building codes within the municipality or if the building permit as issued for the new development is altered and the alteration results in a decrease in the amount of the impact fee due in accordance with the calculations set forth in subsection (a)(1). (505-A added Dec. 19, 1990, P.L. 1343, No. 209)

(h) Where an impact fee ordinance has been adopted pursuant to the other provisions of this act, the ordinance may impose an additional impact fee upon new developments which generate 1,000 or more new peak-hour trips, net of pass-by trips as defined by the current edition of the institute of transportation engineers trip generation manual, during the peak-hour period designated in the ordinance. In such case, the impact fee ordinance adopted under this act may require the applicant for such a development to perform a traffic analysis of development traffic impact on highways, roads or streets outside the transportation service area in which the development site is located but within the boundaries of the municipality or municipalities adopting a joint municipal impact fee ordinance or municipalities which are participating in a joint municipal authority authorized to impose impact fees by this article. Any such highways, roads or streets or parts thereof outside the transportation service area which will accommodate 10% or more of development traffic and 100 or more new peak-hour trips may be required to be studied, and the ordinance may require the applicant to mitigate the traffic impacts of the development on such highways, roads and streets to maintain the predevelopment conditions after completion of the development.

§ 506-A. Appeals.—(a) Any person required to pay an impact fee shall have the right to contest the land use assumptions, the development and implementation of the transportation capital improvement program, the imposition of impact fees, the periodic updating of the transportation capital improvement program, the refund of impact fees and all other matters relating to impact fees, including the constitutionality or validity of the impact fee ordinance by filing an appeal with the court of common pleas.

(b) A master may be appointed by the court to hear testimony on the issues and return the record and a transcript of the testimony, together with a report and recommendations, or the court may appoint a master to hold a nonrecord hearing and to make recommendations and return the same to the court, in which case either party may demand a hearing de novo before the court.

(c) Any cost incurred by parties in such an appeal shall be the separate responsibility of the parties.

(506-A added Dec. 19, 1990, P.L. 1343, No. 209)

§ 507-A. Prerequisites for Assessing Sewer and Water Tap-in Fees.—(a) No municipality may charge any tap-in connection or other similar fee as a condition of connection to a municipally owned sewer or water system unless such fee is calculated as provided in the applicable provisions of the act of May 2, 1945, (P.L. 382, No. 164), known as the "Municipality Authorities Act of 1945."

(b) Where a municipally owned water or sewer system is to be extended at the expense of the owner or owners of properties or where the municipality otherwise would construct the connection end or customer facilities services (other than water meter installation), the property owner or owners shall have the right to construct such extension or make such connection and install such customer facilities himself or themselves or through a subcontractor in accordance with the "Municipality Authorities Act of 1945."

(c) Where a property owner or owners construct or cause to be constructed any addition, expansion or extension to or of a sewer or water system of a municipality whereby such addition, expansion or extension provides future excess capacity to accommodate future development upon the lands of others, the municipality shall provide for the reimbursement to the property owner or owners in accordance with the provisions of the "Municipality Authorities Act of 1945."

(507-A added Dec. 19, 1990, P.L. 1343, No. 209)

§ 508-A. Joint Municipal Impact Fee Ordinance.—(a) For the purpose of permitting municipalities which cooperatively plan for their future to also provide for transportation capital improvements in a cooperative manner, the governing bodies of each municipality which has adopted a joint municipal comprehensive plan pursuant to Article XI, in accordance with the conditions and procedures set forth in this article, may cooperate with one or more municipalities to enact, amend and repeal joint transportation impact fee ordinances to accomplish the purposes of this act in accordance with this article.

(b) The procedures set forth in this article shall be applicable to the enactment of a joint municipal impact fee ordinance.

(c) Each municipality party to a joint municipal impact fee ordinance shall approve the advisory committee and shall adopt the land use assumptions, roadway sufficiency analysis, capital improvement plan, and ordinances and amendments thereto in accordance with the procedures in this article, and no such ordinance shall become effective until it has been properly adopted by all the participating municipalities.

ARTICLE VI
Zoning
53 P.S. §§ 10601–10621

§ 601. General Powers.—The governing body of each municipality, in accordance with the conditions and procedures set forth in this act, may enact, amend and repeal zoning ordinances to implement comprehensive plans and to accomplish any of the purposes of this act.

§ 602. County Powers.—The powers of the governing bodies of counties to enact, amend and repeal zoning ordinances shall be limited to land in those municipalities, wholly or partly within the county, which have no zoning ordinance in effect at the time a zoning ordinance is introduced before the governing body of the county and until the municipality's zoning ordinance is in effect. The enactment of a zoning ordinance by any municipality, other than the county, whose land is subject to county zoning shall act as a repeal protanto of the county zoning ordinance within the municipality adopting such ordinance.

§ 602.1. County Review; Dispute Resolution.—The county planning commission shall offer a mediation option to any municipality which believes that its citizens will experience harm as the result of the adoption of a zoning ordinance or an amendment to an existing zoning ordinance in a contiguous municipality, if the contiguous municipalities agree. In exercising such an option, the municipalities shall comply with the procedures set forth in Article IX. The cost of the mediation shall be shared equally by the parties, unless otherwise agreed.

§ 603. Ordinance Provisions.—(a) Zoning ordinances should reflect the policy goals of the statement of community development objectives required in section 606, and give consideration to the character of the municipality, the needs of the citizens and the suitabilities and special nature of particular parts of the municipality.

(b) Zoning ordinances, except to the extent that those regulations of mineral extraction by local ordinances and enactments have heretofore been superseded and preempted by the act of May 31, 1945 (P.L. 1198, No. 418), known as the "Surface Mining Conservation and Reclamation Act," the act of December 19, 1984 (P.L. 1093, No. 219), known as the "Noncoal Surface Mining Conservation and Reclamation Act," and the act of December 19, 1984 (P.L. 1140, No. 223), known as the "Oil and Gas Act," and to the extent that the subsidence impacts of coal extraction are regulated by the act of April 27, 1966 (1st Sp.SESS., P.L. 31, No. 1), known as "The Bituminous Mine Subsidence and Land Conservation Act," and that regulation of activities related to commercial agricultural production would exceed the requirements imposed under the act of May 20, 1993 (P.L. 12, No. 6), known as the "Nutrient Management Act," regardless of whether any agricultural operation within the area to be affected by the ordinance would be a concentrated animal operation as defined by the "Nutrient Management Act," the act of June 30, 1981 (P.L. 128, No. 43), known as the "Agricultural Area Security Law," or the act of June 10, 1982 (P.L. 454, No. 133), entitled "An Act Protecting Agricultural Operations from Nuisance Suits and Ordinances Under Certain Circumstances," or that regulation of other activities are preempted by other federal or state laws may permit, prohibit, regulate, restrict and determine:

(1) Uses of land, watercourses and other bodies of water.

(2) Size, height, bulk, location, erection, construction, repair, maintenance, alteration, razing, removal and use of structures.

(3) Areas and dimensions of land and bodies of water to be occupied by uses and structures, as well as areas, courts, yards, and other open spaces and distances to be left unoccupied by uses and structures.

(4) Density of population and intensity of use.

(5) Protection and preservation of natural and historic resources and prime agricultural land and activities.

(c) Zoning ordinances may contain:

(1) provisions for special exceptions and variances administered by the zoning hearing board, which provisions shall be in accordance with this act;

(2) provisions for conditional uses to be allowed or denied by the governing body after recommendations by the planning agency and hearing, pursuant to express standards and criteria set forth in the zoning ordinance. Notice of hearings on conditional uses shall be provided in accordance with section 908(1), and notice of the decision shall be provided in accordance with section 908(10). In allowing a conditional use, the governing body may attach such reasonable conditions and safeguards, other than those related to off-site transportation or road improvements, in addition to those expressed in the ordinance, as it may deem necessary to implement the purposes of this act and the zoning ordinance;

(2.1) Repealed.

(2.2) provisions for regulating transferable development rights, on a voluntary basis, including provisions for the protection of persons acquiring the same, in accordance with express standards and criteria set forth in the ordinance and section 619.1;

(3) provisions for the administration and enforcement of such ordinances;

(4) such other provisions as may be necessary to implement the purposes of this act;

(5) provisions to encourage innovation and to promote flexibility, economy and ingenuity in development, including subdivisions and land developments as defined in this act;

(6) provisions authorizing increases in the permissible density of population or intensity of a particular use based upon expressed standards and criteria set forth in the zoning ordinance; and

(7) provisions to promote and preserve prime agricultural land, environmentally sensitive areas and areas of historic significance.

(d) Zoning ordinances may include provisions regulating the siting, density and design of residential, commercial, industrial and other developments in order to assure the availability of reliable, safe and adequate water supplies to support the intended land uses within the capacity of available water resources.

(e) Zoning ordinances may not unduly restrict the display of religious symbols on property being used for religious purposes.

(f) Zoning ordinances may not unreasonably restrict forestry activities. To encourage maintenance and management of forested or wooded open space and promote the conduct of forestry as a sound and economically viable use of forested land throughout this commonwealth, forestry activities, including, but not limited to, timber harvesting, shall be a permitted use by right in all zoning districts in every municipality. ((f) added Dec. 14, 1992, P.L. 815, No. 131)

(g) (1) Zoning ordinances shall protect prime agricultural land and may promote the establishment of agricultural security areas.

(2) Zoning ordinances shall provide for protection of natural and historic features and resources.

(h) Zoning ordinances shall encourage the continuity, development and viability of agricultural operations. Zoning ordinances may not restrict agricultural operations or changes to or expansion of agricultural operations in geographic areas where agriculture has traditionally been present, unless the agricultural operation will have a direct adverse effect on the public health and safety. Nothing in this subsection shall require a municipality to adopt a zoning ordinance that violates or exceeds the provisions of the act of May 20, 1993 (P.L. 12, No. 6), known as the "Nutrient Management Act," the act of June 30, 1981 (P.L. 128, No. 43), known as the "Agricultural Area Security Law, " or the act of June 10, 1982 (P.L. 454, No. 133), entitled "An Act Protecting Agricultural Operations from Nuisance Suits and Ordinances Under Certain Circumstances."

(i) Zoning ordinances shall provide for the reasonable development of minerals in each municipality.

(j) Zoning ordinances adopted by municipalities shall be generally consistent with the municipal or multimunicipal comprehensive plan or, where none exists, with the municipal statement of community development objectives and the county comprehensive plan. If a municipality amends its zoning ordinance in a manner not generally consistent with its comprehensive plan, it shall concurrently amend its comprehensive plan in accordance with Article III.

(k) A municipality may amend its comprehensive plan at any time, provided that the comprehensive plan remains generally consistent with the county comprehensive plan and compatible with the comprehensive plan of abutting municipalities.

(l) Zoning ordinances shall permit no-impact home-based businesses in all residential zones of the municipality as a use permitted by right, except that such permission shall not supersede any deed restriction, covenant or agreement restricting the use of land, nor any master deed, bylaw or other document applicable to a common interest ownership community.

§ 603.1. Interpretation of Ordinance Provisions.—In interpreting the language of zoning ordinances to determine the extent of the restriction upon the use of the property, the language shall be interpreted, where doubt exists as to the intended meaning of the language written and enacted by the governing body, in favor of the property owner and against any implied extension of the restriction.

§ 604. Zoning Purposes.—The provisions of zoning ordinances shall be designed:

(1) To promote, protect and facilitate any or all of the following: the public health, safety, morals, and the general welfare; coordinated and practical community development and proper density of population; emergency management preparedness and operations, airports, and national defense facilities, the provisions of adequate light and air, access to incident solar energy, police protection, vehicle parking and loading space, transportation, water, sewerage, schools, recreational facilities, public grounds, the provision of a safe, reliable and adequate water supply for domestic, commercial, agricultural or industrial use, and other public requirements; as well as preservation of the natural, scenic and historic values in the environment and preservation of forests, wetlands, aquifers and floodplains.

(2) To prevent one or more of the following: overcrowding of land, blight, danger and congestion in travel and transportation, loss of health, life or property from fire, flood, panic or other dangers.

(3) To preserve prime agriculture and farmland considering topography, soil type and classification, and present use.

(4) To provide for the use of land within the municipality for residential housing of various dwelling types encompassing all basic forms of housing, including single-family and two-family dwellings, and a reasonable range of multifamily dwellings in various arrangements, mobile homes and mobile home parks, provided, however, that no zoning ordinance shall be deemed invalid for the failure to provide for any other specific dwelling type.

(5) To accommodate reasonable overall community growth, including population and employment growth, and opportunities for development of a variety of residential dwelling types and nonresidential uses.

§ 605. Classifications.—In any municipality, other than a county, which enacts a zoning ordinance, no part of such municipality shall be left unzoned. The provisions of all zoning ordinances may be classified so that different provisions may be applied to different classes of situations, uses and structures and to such various districts of the municipality as shall be described by a map made part of the zoning ordinance. Where zoning districts are created, all provisions shall be uniform for each class of uses or structures, within each district, except that additional classifications may be made within any district:

(1) For the purpose of making transitional provisions at and near the boundaries of districts.

(1.1) For the purpose of regulating nonconforming uses and structures.

(2) For the regulation, restriction or prohibition of uses and structures at, along or near:

(i) major thoroughfares, their intersections and interchanges, transportation arteries and rail or transit terminals;

(ii) natural or artificial bodies of water, boat docks and related facilities;

(iii) places of relatively steep slope or grade, or other areas of hazardous geological or topographic features;

(iv) public buildings and public grounds;

(v) aircraft, helicopter, rocket, and spacecraft facilities;

(vi) places having unique historical, architectural or patriotic interest or value; or

(vii) flood plain areas, agricultural areas, sanitary landfills, and other places having a special character or use affecting and affected by their surroundings.

As among several classes of zoning districts, the provisions for permitted uses may be mutually exclusive, in whole or in part.

(3) For the purpose of encouraging innovation and the promotion of flexibility, economy and ingenuity in development, including subdivisions and land developments as defined in this act, and for the purpose of authorizing increases in the permissible density of population or intensity of a particular use based upon expressed standards and criteria set forth in the zoning ordinance.

(4) For the purpose of regulating transferable development rights on a voluntary basis.

§ 606. Statement of Community Development Objectives.—Zoning ordinances enacted after the effective date of this act should reflect the policy goals of the municipality as listed in a statement of community development objectives, recognizing that circumstances can necessitate the adoption and timely pursuit of new goals and the enactment of new zoning ordinances which may neither require nor allow for the completion of a new comprehensive plan and approval of new community development objectives. This statement may be supplied by reference to the community comprehensive plan or such portions of the community comprehensive plans as may exist and be applicable or may be the statement of community development objectives provided in a statement of legislative findings of the governing body of the municipality with respect to land use; density of population; the need for housing, commerce and industry; the location and function of streets and other community facilities and utilities; the need for preserving agricultural land and protecting natural resources; and any other factors that the municipality believes relevant in describing the purposes and intent of the zoning ordinance.

§ 607. Preparation of Proposed Zoning Ordinance.—(a) The text and map of the proposed zoning ordinance, as well as all necessary studies and surveys preliminary thereto, shall be prepared by the planning agency of each municipality upon request by the governing body.

(b) In preparing a proposed zoning ordinance, the planning agency shall hold at least one public meeting pursuant to public notice and may hold additional public meetings upon such notice as it shall determine to be advisable.

(c) Upon the completion of its work, the planning agency shall present to the governing body the proposed zoning ordinance, together with recommendations and explanatory materials.

(d) The procedure set forth in this section shall be a condition precedent to the validity of a zoning ordinance adopted pursuant to this act.

(e) If a county planning agency shall have been created for the county in which the municipality adopting the ordinance is located, then at least 45 days prior to the public hearing by the local governing body as provided in section 608, the municipality shall submit the proposed ordinance to said county planning agency for recommendations.

§ 608. Enactment of Zoning Ordinance.—Before voting on the enactment of a zoning ordinance, the governing body shall hold a public hearing thereon, pursuant to public notice, and pursuant to mailed notice and electronic notice to any owner of a tract or parcel of land located within a municipality or an owner of the mineral rights in a tract or parcel of land within the municipality who has made a timely request in accordance with section 109. The vote on the enactment by the governing body shall be within 90 days after the last public hearing. Within 30 days after enactment, a copy of the zoning ordinance shall be forwarded to the county planning agency or, in counties where no planning agency exists, to the governing body of the county in which the municipality is located.

§ 608.1. Municipal Authorities and Water Companies.—(a) A municipal authority, water company or any other municipality that plans to expand water, sanitary sewer or storm sewer service via a new main extension to a proposed development that has not received any municipal approvals within the municipality shall notify the municipality by certified mail, return receipt requested, of its intention and shall provide the municipality an opportunity to provide written comment on whether the proposed expansion of service within the municipality is generally consistent with the zoning ordinance.

(b) The purpose of the requirement of this section is to provide the municipal authority, water company or any other municipality with information regarding how its decision to expand service may potentially enhance and support or conflict with or negatively impact on the land use planning of municipalities.

(c) Nothing in this section shall be construed as limiting the right of a municipal authority, water company or any other municipality to expand service as otherwise permitted by law.

(d) Except as provided in section 619.2, nothing in this act shall be construed as limiting the authority of the Pennsylvania Public Utility Commission over the implementation, location, construction and maintenance of public utility facilities. The requirement of this section shall not apply to an expansion of service by a municipal authority, water company or other municipality which is ordered by a court or a federal or state agency.

(e) As used in this section:

(1) A "decision to expand service within the municipality" shall mean a decision to expand the number of its individual service connections for distribution or collection within a municipality as a result of a main extension; but, if the number of individual service connections are not being increased, locating or acquiring transmission lines or interceptors, or wells, reservoirs, aquifers, pump stations, water storage tanks or other facilities by a municipal authority or water company in a new area of a municipality shall not be deemed an expansion of service.

(2) A "water company" shall include any person or corporation, including a municipal corporation operating beyond its corporate limits, which furnishes water to or for the public for compensation.

(f) Nothing in this section shall be construed to authorize a municipality to regulate the allocation or withdrawal of water resources by any person, municipal authority or water company that is otherwise regulated by the Pennsylvania Public Utility Commission or other federal or state agencies or statutes.

§ 609. Enactment of Zoning Ordinance Amendments.—(a) For the preparation of amendments to zoning ordinances, the procedure set forth in section 607 for the preparation of a proposed zoning ordinance shall be optional.

(b)(1) Before voting on the enactment of an amendment, the governing body shall hold a public hearing thereon, pursuant to public notice, and pursuant to mailed notice and electronic notice to an owner of a tract or parcel of land located within a municipality or an owner of the mineral rights in a tract or parcel of land within the municipality who has made a timely request in accordance with section 109. In addition, if the proposed amendment involves a zoning map change, notice of said public hearing shall be conspicuously posted by the municipality at points deemed sufficient by the municipality along the tract to notify potentially interested citizens. The affected tract or area shall be posted at least one week prior to the date of the hearing.

(2)(i) In addition to the requirement that notice be posted under clause (1), where the proposed amendment involves a zoning map change, notice of the public hearing shall be mailed by the municipality at least 30 days prior to the date of the hearing by first class mail to the addressees to which real estate tax bills are sent for all real property located within the area being rezoned, as evidenced by tax records within the possession of the municipality. The notice shall include the location, date and time of the public hearing. A good faith effort and substantial compliance shall satisfy the requirements of this subsection.

(ii) This clause shall not apply when the rezoning constitutes a comprehensive rezoning.

(c) In the case of an amendment other than that prepared by the planning agency, the governing body shall submit each such amendment to the planning agency at least 30 days prior to the hearing on such proposed amendment to provide the planning agency an opportunity to submit recommendations.

(d) If, after any public hearing held upon an amendment, the proposed amendment is changed substantially, or is revised, to include land previously not affected by it, the governing body shall hold another public hearing, pursuant to public notice, mailed notice and electronic notice, before proceeding to vote on the amendment.

(e) If a county planning agency shall have been created for the county in which the municipality proposing the amendment is located, then at least 30 days prior to the public hearing on the amendment by the local governing body, the municipality shall submit the proposed amendment to the county planning agency for recommendations.

(f) The municipality may offer a mediation option as an aid in completing proceedings authorized by this section. In exercising such an option, the municipality and mediating parties shall meet the stipulations and follow the procedures set forth in Article IX.

(g) Within 30 days after enactment, a copy of the amendment to the zoning ordinance shall be forwarded to the county planning agency or, in counties where no planning agency exists, to the governing body of the county in which the municipality is located.

§ 609.1. Procedure for Landowner Curative Amendments.—(a) A landowner who desires to challenge on substantive grounds the validity of a zoning ordinance or map or any provision thereof, which prohibits or restricts the use or development of land in which he has an interest may submit a curative amendment to the governing body with a written request that his challenge and proposed amendment be heard and decided as provided in section 916.1. The governing body shall commence a hearing thereon within 60 days of the request as provided in section 916.1. The curative amendment and challenge shall be referred to the planning agency or agencies as provided in section 609 and notice of the hearing thereon shall be given as provided in section 610 and in section 916.1.

(b) The hearing shall be conducted in accordance with section 908 and all references therein to the zoning hearing board shall, for purposes of this section be references to the governing body: provided, however, That the provisions of section 908(1.2) and (9) shall not apply and the provisions of section 916.1 shall control. If a municipality does not accept a landowner's curative amendment brought in accordance with this subsection and a court subsequently rules that the challenge has merit, the court's decision shall not result in a declaration of invalidity for the entire zoning ordinance and map, but only for those provisions which specifically relate to the landowner's curative amendment and challenge.

(c) The governing body of a municipality which has determined that a validity challenge has merit may accept a landowner's curative amendment, with or

Table of Contents
Part I Ch. 1–3 Ethics, Records, Open Meetings
Part II Ch. 4–10 Taxation
Part III Ch. 11–18 Torts, Contracts & Civil Rules
Part IV Ch. 19–24 Zoning & Planning
Part V Ch. 25–30 Construction and Emergency Codes
Part VI Ch. 31–39 Municipal Codes
Index

without revision, or may adopt an alternative amendment which will cure the challenged defects. The governing body shall consider the curative amendments, plans and explanatory material submitted by the landowner and shall also consider:

(1) the impact of the proposal upon roads, sewer facilities, water supplies, schools and other public service facilities;

(2) if the proposal is for a residential use, the impact of the proposal upon regional housing needs and the effectiveness of the proposal in providing housing units of a type actually available to and affordable by classes of persons otherwise unlawfully excluded by the challenged provisions of the ordinance or map;

(3) the suitability of the site for the intensity of use proposed by the site's soils, slopes, woodlands, wetlands, flood plains, aquifers, natural resources and other natural features;

(4) the impact of the proposed use on the site's soils, slopes, woodlands, wetlands, flood plains, natural resources and natural features, the degree to which these are protected or destroyed, the tolerance of the resources to development and any adverse environmental impacts; and

(5) the impact of the proposal on the preservation of agriculture and other land uses which are essential to public health and welfare.

§ 609.2. Procedure for Municipal Curative Amendments.—If a municipality determines that its zoning ordinance or any portion thereof is substantially invalid, it shall take the following actions:

(1) A municipality shall declare by formal action, its zoning ordinance or portions thereof substantively invalid and propose to prepare a curative amendment to overcome such invalidity. Within 30 days following such declaration and proposal the governing body of the municipality shall:

(i) By resolution make specific findings setting forth the declared invalidity of the zoning ordinance which may include:

(A) references to specific uses which are either not permitted or not permitted in sufficient quantity;

(B) reference to a class of use or uses which require revision; or

(C) reference to the entire ordinance which requires revisions.

(ii) Begin to prepare and consider a curative amendment to the zoning ordinance to correct the declared invalidity.

(2) Within 180 days from the date of the declaration and proposal, the municipality shall enact a curative amendment to validate, or reaffirm the validity of, its zoning ordinance pursuant to the provisions required by section 609 in order to cure the declared invalidity of the zoning ordinance.

(3) Upon the initiation of the procedures, as set forth in clause (1), the governing body shall not be required to entertain or consider any landowner's curative amendment filed under section 609.1 nor shall the zoning hearing board be required to give a report requested under section 909.1 or 916.1 subsequent to the declaration and proposal based upon the grounds identical to or substantially similar to those specified in the resolution required by clause (1) (a). Upon completion of the procedures as set forth in clauses (1) and (2), no rights to a cure pursuant to the provisions of sections 609.1 and 916.1 shall, from the date of the declaration and proposal, accrue to any landowner on the basis of the substantive invalidity of the unamended zoning ordinance for which there has been a curative amendment pursuant to this section.

(4) A municipality having utilized the procedures as set forth in clause (1) and (2) may not again utilize said procedure for a 36-month period following the date of the enactment of a curative amendment, or reaffirmation of the

validity of its zoning ordinance, pursuant to clause (2); provided, however, if after the date of declaration and proposal there is a substantially new duty or obligation imposed upon the municipality by virtue of a change in statute or by virtue of a Pennsylvania Appellate Court decision, the municipality may utilize the provisions of this section to prepare a curative amendment to its ordinance to fulfill said duty or obligation.

§ 610. Publication, Advertisement and Availability of Ordinances.—(a) Proposed zoning ordinances and amendments shall not be enacted unless notice of proposed enactment is given in the manner set forth in this section, and shall include the time and place of the meeting at which passage will be considered, a reference to a place within the municipality where copies of the proposed ordinance or amendment may be examined without charge or obtained for a charge not greater than the cost thereof. The governing body shall publish the proposed ordinance or amendment once in one newspaper of general circulation in the municipality not more than 60 days nor less than 7 days prior to passage. Publication of the proposed ordinance or amendment shall include either the full text thereof or the title and a brief summary, prepared by the municipal solicitor and setting forth all the provisions in reasonable detail. If the full text is not included:

(1) A copy thereof shall be supplied to a newspaper of general circulation in the municipality at the time the public notice is published.

(2) An attested copy of the proposed ordinance shall be filed in the county law library or other county office designated by the county commissioners, who may impose a fee no greater than that necessary to cover the actual costs of storing said ordinances.

(b) In the event substantial amendments are made in the proposed ordinance or amendment, before voting upon enactment, the governing body shall, at least ten days prior to enactment, readvertise, in one newspaper of general circulation in the municipality, a brief summary setting forth all the provisions in reasonable detail together with a summary of the amendments.

(c) Zoning ordinances and amendments may be incorporated into official ordinance books by reference with the same force and effect as if duly recorded therein.

§ 611. Publication After Enactment.—(611 repealed Dec. 21, 1988, P.L. 1329, No. 170)

§ 612. (none)

§ 613. Registration of Nonconforming Uses, Structures and Lots.—Zoning ordinances may contain provisions requiring the zoning officer to identify and register nonconforming uses, structures and lots, together with the reasons why the zoning officer identified them as nonconformities.

§ 614. Appointment and Powers of Zoning Officer.—For the administration of a zoning ordinance, a zoning officer, who shall not hold any elective office in the municipality, shall be appointed. The zoning officer shall meet qualifications established by the municipality and shall be able to demonstrate to the satisfaction of the municipality a working knowledge of municipal zoning. The zoning officer shall administer the zoning ordinance in accordance with its literal terms, and shall not have the power to permit any construction or any use or change of use which does not conform to the zoning ordinance. Zoning officers may be authorized to institute civil enforcement proceedings as a means of enforcement when acting within the scope of their employment.

§ 615. Zoning Appeals.—All appeals from decisions of the zoning officer shall be taken in the manner set forth in this act.

§ 616. Enforcement Penalties.—(616 repealed Dec. 21, 1988, P.L. 1329, No. 170)

§ 616.1. Enforcement Notice.—(a) If it appears to the municipality that a violation of any zoning ordinance enacted under this act or prior enabling laws has occurred, the municipality shall initiate enforcement proceedings by sending an enforcement notice as provided in this section.

(b) The enforcement notice shall be sent to the owner of record of the parcel on which the violation has occurred, to any person who has filed a written request to receive enforcement notices regarding that parcel, and to any other person requested in writing by the owner of record.

(c) An enforcement notice shall state at least the following:

(1) The name of the owner of record and any other person against whom the municipality intends to take action.

(2) The location of the property in violation.

(3) The specific violation with a description of the requirements which have not been met, citing in each instance the applicable provisions of the ordinance.

(4) The date before which the steps for compliance must be commenced and the date before which the steps must be completed.

(5) That the recipient of the notice has the right to appeal to the zoning hearing board within a prescribed period of time in accordance with procedures set forth in the ordinance.

(6) That failure to comply with the notice within the time specified, unless extended by appeal to the zoning hearing board, constitutes a violation, with possible sanctions clearly described.

(d) In any appeal of an enforcement notice to the zoning hearing board the municipality shall have the responsibility of presenting its evidence first.

(e) Any filing fee paid by a party to appeal an enforcement notice to the zoning hearing board shall be returned to the appealing party by the municipality if the zoning hearing board, or any court in a subsequent appeal, rules in the appealing party's favor.

§ 617. Causes of Action.—In case any building, structure, landscaping or land is, or is proposed to be, erected, constructed, reconstructed, altered, converted, maintained or used in violation of any ordinance enacted under this act or prior enabling laws, the governing body or, with the approval of the governing body, an officer of the municipality, or any aggrieved owner or tenant of real property who shows that his property or person will be substantially affected by the alleged violation, in addition to other remedies, may institute any appropriate action or proceeding to prevent, restrain, correct or abate such building, structure, landscaping or land, or to prevent, in or about such premises, any act, conduct, business or use constituting a violation. When any such action is instituted by a landowner or tenant, notice of that action shall be served upon the municipality at least 30 days prior to the time the action is begun by serving a copy of the complaint on the governing body of the municipality. No such action may be maintained until such notice has been given.

§ 617.1. Jurisdiction.—District justices shall have initial jurisdiction over proceedings brought under section 617.2.

§ 617.2. Enforcement Remedies.—(a) Any person, partnership or corporation who or which has violated or permitted the violation of the provisions of any zoning ordinance enacted under this act or prior enabling laws shall, upon be-ing found liable therefor in a civil enforcement proceeding commenced by a municipality, pay a judgment of not more than $500 plus all court costs, including reasonable attorney fees incurred by a municipality as a result thereof. No judgment shall commence or be imposed, levied or payable until the date of the determination of a violation by the district justice. If the defendant neither pays nor timely appeals the judgment, the municipality may enforce the judgment pursuant to the applicable rules of civil procedure. Each day that a violation continues shall constitute a separate violation, unless the district justice determining that there has been a violation further determines that there was a good faith basis for the person, partnership or corporation violating the ordinance to have believed that there was no such violation, in which event there shall be deemed to have been only one such violation until the fifth day following the date of the determination of a violation by the district justice and thereafter each day that a violation continues shall constitute a separate violation. All judgments, costs and reasonable attorney fees collected for the violation of zoning ordinances shall be paid over to the municipality whose ordinance has been violated.

(b) The court of common pleas, upon petition, may grant an order of stay, upon cause shown, tolling the per diem fine pending a final adjudication of the violation and judgment.

(c) Nothing contained in this section shall be construed or interpreted to grant to any person or entity other than the municipality the right to commence any action for enforcement pursuant to this section.

§ 617.3. Finances and Expenditures.—(a) The governing body may appropriate funds to finance the preparation of zoning ordinances and shall appropriate funds for administration, for enforcement and for actions to support or oppose, upon appeal to the courts, decisions of the zoning hearing board.

(b) The governing body shall make provision in its budget and appropriate funds for the operation of the zoning hearing board.

(c) The zoning hearing board may employ or contract for and fix the compensation of legal counsel, as the need arises. The legal counsel shall be an attorney other than the municipal solicitor. The board may also employ or contract for and fix the compensation of experts and other staff and may contract for services as it shall deem necessary. The compensation of legal counsel, experts and staff and the sums expended for services shall not exceed the amount appropriated by the governing body for this use.

(d) For the same purposes, the governing body may accept gifts and grants of money and services from private sources and from the county, State and Federal Governments.

(e) The governing body may prescribe reasonable fees with respect to the administration of a zoning ordinance and with respect to hearings before the zoning hearing board. Fees for these hearings may include compensation for the secretary and members of the zoning hearing board, notice and advertising costs and necessary administrative overhead connected with the hearing. The costs, however, shall not include legal expenses of the zoning hearing board, expenses for engineering, architectural or other technical consultants or expert witness costs.

§ 618. Finances.—(618 repealed Dec. 21, 1988, P.L. 1329, No. 170)

§ 619. Exemptions.—This article shall not apply to any existing or proposed building, or extension thereof, used or to be used by a public utility corporation, if, upon petition of the corporation, the Pennsylvania Public Utility Commission shall, after a public hearing, decide that the present or proposed situation of the building in question is reasonably necessary for the convenience or welfare of the public. It shall be the responsibility of the Pennsylvania Public Utility Commission to ensure that both the corporation and the municipality in which the building or proposed building is located have notice of the hearing and are granted an opportunity to appear, present witnesses, cross-examine witnesses presented by other parties and otherwise exercise the rights of a party to the proceedings.

§ 619.1. Transferable Development Rights.—(a) To and only to the extent a local ordinance enacted in accordance with this article and Article VII so provides, there is hereby created, as a separate estate in land, the development rights therein, and the same are declared to be severable and separately conveyable from the estate in fee simple to which they are applicable.

(b) The development rights shall be conveyed by a deed duly recorded in the office of the recorder of deeds in and for the county in which the municipality whose ordinance authorizes such conveyance is located.

(c) The recorder of deeds shall not accept for recording any such instrument of conveyance unless there is endorsed thereon the approval of the municipal governing body having zoning or planned residential development jurisdiction over the land within which the development rights are to be conveyed, dated not more than 60 days prior to the recording.

(d) No development rights shall be transferable beyond the boundaries of the municipality wherein the lands from which the development rights arise are situated, except that, in the case of a joint municipal zoning ordinance or a written agreement among two or more municipalities, development rights shall be transferable within the boundaries of the municipalities comprising the joint municipal zoning ordinance. ((d) amended Dec. 14, 1992, P.L. 815, No. 131)

§ 619.2. Effect of Comprehensive Plans and Zoning Ordinances.—(a) When a county adopts a comprehensive plan in accordance with Sections 301 and 302 and any municipalities therein have adopted comprehensive plans and zoning ordinances in accordance with Sections 301, 303(d) and 603(i), commonwealth agencies shall consider and may rely upon comprehensive plans and zoning ordinances when reviewing applications for the funding or permitting of infrastructure or facilities.

(b) The center for local government services shall work with municipalities to coordinate commonwealth agency program resources with municipal planning and zoning activities. Upon request, the center for local government services shall assist municipalities in identifying and assessing the impact of commonwealth agency decisions and their effect on municipal and multimunicipal planning and zoning. Upon the authorization of the governor, the center for local government services shall have access to information, services, functions and other resources in the possession of executive agencies under the governor's jurisdiction to fulfill its obligations under this section.

(c) When municipalities adopt a joint municipal zoning ordinance:

(1) Commonwealth agencies shall consider and may rely upon the joint municipal zoning ordinance for the funding or permitting of infrastructure or facilities.

(2) The municipalities may, by agreement, share tax revenues and fees remitted to municipalities located within the joint municipal zone.

§ 620. (repealed).

§ 621. Prohibiting the Location of Methadone Treatment Facilities in Certain Locations.[1]—(a) (1) Notwithstanding any other provision of law to the contrary and except as provided in subsection (b), a methadone treatment facility shall not be established or operated within 500 feet of an existing school, public playground, public park, residential housing area, child-care facility, church, meetinghouse or other actual place of regularly stated religious worship established prior to the proposed methadone treatment facility.

(2) The provisions of this subsection shall apply whether or not an occupancy permit or certificate of use has been issued to the owner or operator of a methadone treatment facility for a location that is within 500 feet of an exist-

1. 53 P.S. § 10621.

ing school, public playground, public park, residential housing area, child-care facility, church, meetinghouse or other actual place of regularly stated religious worship established prior to the proposed methadone treatment facility.

(b) Notwithstanding subsection (a), a methadone treatment facility may be established and operated closer than 500 feet to an existing school, public playground, public park, residential housing area, child-care facility, church, meetinghouse or other actual place of regularly stated religious worship established prior to the proposed methadone treatment facility if, by majority vote, the governing body for the municipality in which the proposed methadone treatment facility is to be located votes in favor of the issuance of an occupancy permit or certificate of use for said facility at such a location. At least 14 days prior to the governing body of a municipality voting on whether to approve the issuance of an occupancy permit or certificate of use for a methadone treatment facility at a location that is closer than 500 feet to a school, public playground, public park, residential housing area, child-care facility, church, meetinghouse or other ac-tual place of regularly stated religious worship established prior to the proposed methadone treatment facility, one or more public hearings regarding the pro-posed methadone treatment facility, one or more public hearings regarding the proposed methadone treatment facility location shall be held within the municipality following public notice. All owners of real property located within 500 feet of the proposed location shall be provided written notice of said public hearings at least 30 days prior to said public hearings occurring.

(c) This section shall not apply to a methadone treatment facility that is licensed by the Department of Health prior to May 15, 1999.

(d) As used in this section, the term "methadone treatment facility" shall mean a facility licensed by the Department of Health to use the drug methadone in the treatment, maintenance or detoxification of persons.

ARTICLE VII
Planned Residential Development
53 P.S. § 10701–10713

§ 701. **Purposes.**—In order that the purposes of this act be furthered in an era of increasing urbanization and of growing demand for housing of all types and design; to insure that the provisions of Article VI which are concerned in part with the uniform treatment of dwelling type, bulk, density, intensity and open space within each zoning district, shall not be applied to the improvement of land by other than lot by lot development in a manner that would distort the objectives of that Article VI; to encourage innovations in residential and nonresidential development and renewal so that the growing demand for housing and other development may be met by greater variety in type, design and layout of dwellings and other buildings and structures and by the conservation and more efficient use of open space ancillary to said dwelllings and uses; so that greater opportunities for better housing and recreation may extend to all citizens and residents of this Commonwealth; and in order to encourage a more efficient use of land and of public services and to reflect changes in the technology of land development so that economies secured may enure to the benefit of those who need homes and for other uses; and, in aid of these purposes, to provide a procedure which can relate the type, design and layout of residential and nonresidential development to the particular site and the particular demand for housing existing at the time of development in a manner consistent with the preservation of the property values within existing residential and nonresidential areas, and to insure that the increased flexibility of regulations over land

Chapter 24 Religious Land Use
Chapter 23 Conservation Easements
Chapter 22.1 Land Banks
Chapter 22 Open Space Lands
Chapter 21-B Regulation of Local Agriculture
Chapter 21-A Gas and Oil
Chapter 20 Bluff Recession and Setback Act
Chapter 19.2 Development Permit Extension Act
Chapter 19.1 Wireless Broadband Collocation Act
Chapter 19 Municipalities Planning Code

development authorized herein is carried out under such administrative standards and procedures as shall encourage the disposition of proposals for land development without undue delay, the following powers are granted to all municipalities.

§ 702. Grant of Power.—The governing body of each municipality may enact, amend and repeal provisions within a zoning ordinance fixing standards and conditions for planned residential development. The enactment of such provisions shall be in accordance with the procedures required for the enactment of an amendment of a zoning ordinance as provided in Article VI of this act. Pursuant to such provisions the governing body may approve, modify or disapprove any development plan within the municipality adopting such provisions or designate the planning agency as its official agency for such purposes. Such provisions shall:

(1) Specify whether the governing body, or the planning agency shall administer planned residential development provisions pursuant to the provisions of this article;

(2) Set forth the standards, conditions and regulations for a planned residential development consistent with the provisions of this article; and

(3) Set forth the procedures pertaining to the application for, hearing on and tentative and final approval of a planned residential development, which shall be consistent with the provisions of this article for such applications and hearings.

§ 702.1. Transferable Development Rights.—Municipalities electing to enact planned residential development provisions may also incorporate therein provisions for transferable development rights, on a voluntary basis, in accordance with express standards and criteria set forth in the ordinance and with the requirements of Article VI.

§ 703. Applicability of Comprehensive Plan and Statement of Community Development Objectives.—All provisions and all amendments thereto adopted pursuant to this article shall be based on and interpreted in relation to the statement of community development objectives of the zoning ordinance and may be related to either the comprehensive plan for the development of the municipality prepared under the provisions of this act or a statement of legislative findings in accordance with section 606. Every application for approval of a planned residential development either shall be based on and interpreted in relation to the statement of community development objectives, and may be related to the comprehensive plan, or shall be based on and interpreted in relation to the statement of legislative findings.

§ 704. Jurisdiction of County Planning Agencies.—(a) When any county has adopted planned residential development provisions in accordance with the terms of this article, a certified copy of such provisions shall be sent to every municipality with the county. All amendments shall also be sent to the aforementioned municipalities.

(b) The powers of governing bodies of counties to enact, amend and repeal planned residential development provisions shall not supersede any local planned residential development, zoning or subdivision and land development ordinance which is already in effect or subsequently becomes effective in any municipality within such county, provided that a certified copy of such provision is filed with the county planning agency, if one exists. However, all applications for tentative approval of planned residential development of land located within a municipality having adopted planned residential development provisions as set forth in this article shall nevertheless be referred to the county planning agency, if one exists, for study and recommendation and such county planning agency shall be required to report to such municipality within 30 days or forfeit the right to review.

§ 705. Standards and Conditions for Planned Residential Development.— (a) All provisions adopted pursuant to this article shall set forth all the standards, conditions and regulations by which a proposed planned residential development shall be evaluated, and said standards, conditions and regulations shall be consistent with the following subsections.

(b) The provisions adopted pursuant to this article shall set forth the uses permitted in a planned residential development, which uses may include but shall not be limited to:

(1) Dwelling units of any dwelling type or configuration, or any combination thereof.

(2) Those nonresidential uses deemed to be appropriate for incorporation in the design of the planned residential development.

(c) The provisions may establish regulations setting forth the timing of development among the various types of dwellings and may specify whether some or all nonresidential uses are to be built before, after or at the same time as the residential uses.

(d) The provisions adopted pursuant to this article shall establish standards governing the density, or intensity of land use, in a planned residential development. The standards may vary the density or intensity of land use, otherwise applicable to the land under the provisions of a zoning ordinance of the municipality within the planned residential development in consideration of all of the following:

(1) The amount, location and proposed use of common open space.

(2) The location and physical characteristics of the site of the proposed planned residential development.

(3) The location, design, type and use of structures proposed.

(e) In the case of a planned residential development proposed to be developed over a period of years, standards established in provisions adopted pursuant to this article may, to encourage the flexibility of housing density, design and type intended by this article:

(1) Permit a variation in each section to be developed from the density, or intensity of use, established for the entire planned residential development.

(2) Allow for a greater concentration of density or intensity of land use, within some section or sections of development, whether it be earlier or later in the development that upon others.

(3) Require that the approval of such greater concentration of density or intensity of land use for any section to be developed be offset by a smaller concentration in any completed prior stage or by an appropriate reservation of common open space on the remaining land by a grant of easement or by covenant in favor of the municipality, provided that such reservation shall, as far as practicable, defer the precise location of such common open space until an application for final approval is filed, so that flexibility of development which is a prime objective of this article, can be maintained.

(f) The standards for a planned residential development established by provisions adopted pursuant to this article may require that the common open space resulting from the application of standards for density, or intensity of land use, shall be set aside for the use and benefit of the residents in such development and may include provisions which shall determine the amount and location of said common open space and secure its improvement and maintenance for common open space use, subject, however, to the following:

(1) The municipality may, at any time and from time to time, accept the dedication of land or any interest therein for public use and maintenance, but the municipality need not require, as a condition of the approval of a planned

residential development, that land proposed to be set aside for common open space be dedicated or made available to public use. The provisions may require that the landowner provide for and establish an organization for the ownership and maintenance of the common open space, and that such organization shall not be dissolved nor shall it dispose of the common open space, by sale or otherwise (except to an organization conceived and established to own and maintain the common open space), without first offering to dedicate the same to the public.

(2) In the event that the organization established to own and maintain common open space, or any successor organization, shall at any time after establishment of the planned residential development fail to maintain the common open space in reasonable order and condition in accordance with the development plan, the municipality may serve written notice upon such organization or upon the residents of the planned residential development setting forth the manner in which the organization has failed to maintain the common open space in reasonable condition, and said notice shall include a demand that such deficiencies of maintenance be corrected within 30 days thereof, and shall state the date and place of a hearing thereon which shall be held within 14 days of the notice. At such hearing the municipality may modify the terms of the original notice as to the deficiencies and may give an extension of time within which they shall be corrected.

(3) If the deficiencies set forth in the original notice or in the modifications thereof shall not be corrected within said 30 days or any extension thereof, the municipality, in order to preserve the taxable values of the properties within the planned residential development and to prevent the common open space from becoming a public nuisance, may enter upon said common open space and maintain the same for a period of one year. Said maintenance by the municipality shall not constitute a taking of said common open space, nor vest in the public any rights to use the same.

(4) Before the expiration of said year, the municipality shall, upon its initiative or upon the request of the organization theretofore responsible for the maintenance of the common open space, call a public hearing upon notice to such organization, or to the residents of the planned residential development, to be held by the governing body or its designated agency, at which hearing such organization or the residents of the planned residential development shall show cause why such maintenance by the municipality shall not, at the option of the municipality, continue for a succeeding year. If the governing body, or its designated agency, shall determine that such organization is ready and able to maintain said common open space in reasonable condition, the municipality shall cease to maintain said common open space at the end of said year. If the governing body or its designated agency shall determine that such organization is not ready and able to maintain said common open space in a reasonable condition, the municipality may, in its discretion, continue to maintain said common open space during the next succeeding year and, subject to a similar hearing and determination, in each year thereafter.

(5) The decision of the governing body or its designated agency shall be subject to appeal to court in the same manner, and within the same time limitation, as is provided for zoning appeals by this act.

(6) The cost of such maintenance by the municipality shall be assessed ratably against the properties within the planned residential development that have a right of enjoyment of the common open space, and shall become a lien on said properties. The municipality at the time of entering upon said common open space for the purpose of maintenance shall file a notice of lien in the office of the prothonotary of the county, upon the properties affected by the lien within the planned residential development.

(g) Provisions adopted pursuant to this article may require that a planned residential development contain a minimum number of dwelling units.

(h) The authority granted a municipality by Article V to establish standards for the location, width, course and surfacing of streets, walkways, curbs, gutters, street lights, shade trees, water, sewage and drainage facilities, easements or rights-of-way for drainage and utilities, reservations of public grounds, other improvements, regulations for the height and setback as they relate to renewable energy systems and energy-conserving building design, regulations for the height and location of vegetation with respect to boundary lines, as they relate to renewable energy systems and energy-conserving building design, regulations for the type and location of renewable energy systems or their components and regulations for the design and construction of structures to encourage the use of renewable energy systems, shall be vested in the governing body or the planning agency for the purposes of this article. The standards applicable to a particular planned residential development may be different than or modifications of, the standards and requirements otherwise required of subdivisions authorized under an ordinance adopted pursuant to Article V, provided, however, that provisions adopted pursuant to this article shall set forth the limits and extent of any modifications or changes in such standards and requirements in order that a landowner shall know the limits and extent of permissible modifications from the standards otherwise applicable to subdivisions.

(i) The provisions adopted pursuant to this article shall set forth the standards and criteria by which the design, bulk and location of buildings shall be evaluated, and all such standards and criteria for any feature of a planned residential development shall be set forth in such provisions with sufficient certainty to provide reasonable criteria by which specific proposals for a planned residential development can be evaluated. All standards in such provisions shall not unreasonably restrict the ability of the landowner to relate his development plan to the particular site and to the particular demand for housing existing at the time of development.

(j) Provisions adopted pursuant to this article shall include a requirement that, if water is to be provided by means other than by private wells owned and maintained by the individual owners of lots within the planned residential development, applicants shall present evidence to the governing body or planning agency, as the case may be, that the planned residential development is to be supplied by a certificated public utility, a bona fide cooperative association of lot owners, or by a municipal corporation, authority or utility. A copy of a Certificate of Public Convenience from the Pennsylvania Public Utility Commission or an application for such certificate, a cooperative agreement, or a commitment or agreement to serve the area in question, whichever is appropriate, shall be acceptable evidence.

§ 706. Enforcement and Modification of Provisions of the Plan.—To further the mutual interest of the residents of the planned residential development and of the public in the preservation of the integrity of the development plan, as finally approved, and to insure that modifications, if any, in the development plan shall not impair the reasonable reliance of the said residents upon the provisions of the development plan, nor result in changes that would adversely affect the public interest, the enforcement and modification of the provisions of the development plan as finally approved, whether those are recorded by plat, covenant, easement or otherwise shall be subject to the following provisions:

(1) The provisions of the development plan relating to:

(i) the use, bulk and location of buildings and structures;

(ii) the quantity and location of common open space, except as otherwise provided in this article; and

(iii) the intensity of use or the density of residential units;

shall run in favor of the municipality and shall be enforceable in law or in equity by the municipality, without limitation on any powers of regulation otherwise granted the municipality by law.

(2) All provisions of the development plan shall run in favor of the residents of the planned residential development but only to the extent expressly provided in the development plan and in accordance with the terms of the development plan, and to that extent said provisions, whether recorded by plat, covenant, easement or otherwise, may be enforced at law or equity by said residents acting individually, jointly, or through an organization designated in the development plan to act on their behalf; provided, however, that no provisions of the development plan shall be implied to exist in favor of residents of the planned residential development except as to those portions of the development plan which have been finally approved and have been recorded.

(3) All those provisions of the development plan authorized to be enforced by the municipality under this section may be modified, removed, or released by the municipality, except grants or easements relating to the service or equipment of a public utility, subject to the following conditions:

(i) No such modification, removal or release of the provisions of the development plan by the municipality shall affect the rights of the residents of the planned residential development to maintain and enforce those provisions, at law or equity, as provided in this section.

(ii) No modification, removal or release of the provisions of the development plan by the municipality shall be permitted except upon a finding by the governing body or the planning agency, following a public hearing thereon pursuant to public notice called and held in accordance with the provisions of this article, that the same is consistent with the efficient development and preservation of the entire planned residential development, does not adversely affect either the enjoyment of land abutting upon or across the street from the planned residential development or the public interest, and is not granted solely to confer a special benefit upon any person.

(4) Residents of the planned residential development may, to the extent and in the manner expressly authorized by the provisions of the development plan, modify, remove or release their rights to enforce the provisions of the development plan but no such action shall affect the right of the municipality to enforce the provisions of the development plan in accordance with the provisions of this section.

§ 707. Application for Tentative Approval of Planned Residential Development.—In order to provide an expeditious method for processing a development plan for a planned residential development under the provisions adopted pursuant to the powers granted herein, and to avoid the delay and uncertainty which would arise if it were necessary to secure approval, by a multiplicity of local procedures, of a plat of subdivision as well as approval of a change in the zoning regulations otherwise applicable to the property, it is hereby declared to be in the public interest that all procedures with respect to the approval or disapproval of a development plan for a planned residential development and the continuing administration thereof shall be consistent with the following provisions:

(1) An application for tentative approval of the development plan for a planned residential development shall be filed by or on behalf of the landowner.

(2) The application for tentative approval shall be filed by the landowner in such form, upon the payment of such a reasonable fee and with such officials of the municipality as shall be designated in the provisions adopted pursuant to this article.

(3) All planning, zoning and subdivision matters relating to the platting, use and development of the planned residential development and subsequent modifications of the regulations relating thereto, to the extent such modification is vested in the municipality, shall be determined and established by the governing body or the planning agency.

(4) The provisions shall require only such information in the application as is reasonably necessary to disclose to the governing body or the planning agency:

(i) the location, size and topography of the site and the nature of the landowner's interest in the land proposed to be developed;

(ii) the density of land use to be allocated to parts of the site to be developed;

(iii) the location and size of the common open space and the form of organization proposed to own and maintain the common open space;

(iv) the use and the approximate height, bulk and location of buildings and other structures;

(v) the feasibility of proposals for water supply and the disposition of sanitary waste and storm water;

(vi) the substance of covenants, grants of easements or other restrictions proposed to be imposed upon the use of the land, buildings and structures including proposed easements or grants for public utilities;

(vii) the provisions for parking of vehicles and the location and width of proposed streets and public ways;

(viii) the required modifications in the municipal land use regulations otherwise applicable to the subject property;

(viii.1) the feasibility of proposals for energy conservation and the effective utilization of renewable energy sources; and

(ix) in the case of development plans which call for development over a period of years, a schedule showing the proposed times within which applications for final approval of all sections of the planned residential development are intended to be filed and this schedule must be updated annually, on the anniversary of its approval, until the development is completed and accepted.

(5) The application for tentative approval of a planned residential development shall include a written statement by the landowner setting forth the reasons why, in his opinion, a planned residential development would be in the public interest and would be consistent with the comprehensive plan for the development of the municipality.

(6) The application for and tentative and final approval of a development plan for a planned residential development prescribed in this article shall be in lieu of all other procedures or approvals, otherwise required pursuant to Articles V and VI of this act.

§ 708. Public Hearing.—(a) Within 60 days after the filing of an application for tentative approval of a planned residential development pursuant to this article, a public hearing pursuant to public notice on said application shall be held by the governing body or the planning agency, if designated, in the manner prescribed in Article IX.

(b) The governing body or the planning agency may continue the hearing from time to time, and where applicable, may refer the matter back to the planning agency for a report, provided, however, that in any event, the public hearing or hearings shall be concluded within 60 days after the date of the first public hearing.

(c) The municipality may offer a mediation option as an aid in completing proceedings authorized by this section and by subsequent sections in this article prior to final approval by the governing body. In exercising such an option, the municipality and mediating parties shall meet the stipulations and follow the procedures set forth in Article IX.

§ 709. The Findings.—(a) The governing body, or the planning agency, within 60 days following the conclusion of the public hearing provided for in this article or within 180 days after the date of filing of the application, whichever occurs first, shall, by official written communication, to the landowner, either:

(1) grant tentative approval of the development plan as submitted;

(2) grant tentative approval subject to specified conditions not included in the development plan as submitted; or

(3) deny tentative approval to the development plan.

Failure to so act within said period shall be deemed to be a grant of tentative approval of the development plan as submitted. In the event, however, that tentative approval is granted subject to conditions, the landowner may, within 30 days after receiving a copy of the official written communication of the governing body notify such governing body of his refusal to accept all said conditions, in which case, the governing body shall be deemed to have denied tentative approval of the development plan. In the event the landowner does not, within said period, notify the governing body of his refusal to accept all said conditions, tentative approval of the development plan, with all said conditions, shall stand as granted.

(b) The grant or denial of tentative approval by official written communication shall include not only conclusions but also findings of fact related to the specific proposal and shall set forth the reasons for the grant, with or without conditions, or for the denial, and said communication shall set forth with particularity in what respects the development plan would or would not be in the public interest, including, but not limited to, findings of fact and conclusions on the following:

(1) in those respects in which the development plan is or is not consistent with the comprehensive plan for the development of the municipality;

(2) the extent to which the development plan departs from zoning and subdivision regulations otherwise applicable to the subject property, including but not limited to density, bulk and use, and the reasons why such departures are or are not deemed to be in the public interest;

(3) the purpose, location and amount of the common open space in the planned residential development, the reliability of the proposals for maintenance and conservation of the common open space, and the adequacy or inadequacy of the amount and purpose of the common open space as related to the proposed density and type of residential development;

(4) the physical design of the development plan and the manner in which said design does or does not make adequate provision for public services, provide adequate control over vehicular traffic, and further the amenities of light and air, recreation and visual enjoyment;

(5) the relationship, beneficial or adverse, of the proposed planned residential development to the neighborhood in which it is proposed to be established; and

(6) in the case of a development plan which proposes development over a period of years, the sufficiency of the terms and conditions intended to protect the interests of the public and of the residents of the planned residential development in the integrity of the development plan.

(c) In the event a development plan is granted tentative approval, with or without conditions, the governing body may set forth in the official written communication the time within which an application for final approval of the development plan shall be filed or, in the case of a development plan which provides for development over a period of years, the periods of time within which applications for final approval of each part thereof shall be filed. Except upon the consent of the landowner, the time so established between grant of tentative approval and an application for final approval shall not be less than three months and, in the case of development over a period of years, the time between applications for final approval of each part of a plan shall not be less than 12 months.

§ 710. Status of Plan After Tentative Approval.—(a) The official written communication provided for in this article shall be certified by the municipal secretary or clerk of the governing body and shall be filed in his office, and a certified copy shall be mailed to the landowner. Where tentative approval has been granted, it shall be deemed an amendment to the zoning map, effective upon final approval, and shall be noted on the zoning map.

(b) Tentative approval of a development plan shall not qualify a plat of the planned residential development for recording nor authorize development or the issuance of any building permits. A development plan which has been given tentative approval as submitted, or which has been given tentative approval with conditions which have been accepted by the landowner (and provided that the landowner has not defaulted nor violated any of the conditions of the tentative approval), shall not be modified or revoked nor otherwise impaired by action of the municipality pending an application or applications for final approval, without the consent of the landowner, provided an application or applications for final approval is filed or, in the case of development over a period of years, provided applications are filed, within the periods of time specified in the official written communication granting tentative approval.

(c) In the event that a development plan is given tentative approval and thereafter, but prior to final approval, the landowner shall elect to abandon said development plan and shall so notify the governing body in writing, or in the event the landowner shall fail to file application or applications for final approval within the required period of time or times, as the case may be, the tentative approval shall be deemed to be revoked and all that portion of the area included in the development plan for which final approval has not been given shall be subject to those local ordinances otherwise applicable thereto as they may be amended from time to time, and the same shall be noted on the zoning map and in the records of the municipal secretary or clerk of the municipality.

§ 711. Application for Final Approval.—(a) An application for final approval may be for all the land included in a development plan or, to the extent set forth in the tentative approval, for a section thereof. Said application shall be made to the official of the municipality designated by the ordinance and within the time or times specified by the official written communication granting tentative approval. The application shall include any drawings, specifications, covenants, easements, performance bond and such other requirements as may be specified by ordinance, as well as any conditions set forth in the official written communication at the time of tentative approval. A public hearing on an application for final approval of the development plan, or part thereof, shall not be required provided the development plan, or the part thereof, submitted for final approval, is in compliance with the development plan theretofore given tentative approval and with any specified conditions attached thereto.

(b) In the event the application for final approval has been filed, together with all drawings, specifications and other documents in support thereof, and as required by the ordinance and the official written communication of tentative approval, the municipality shall, within 45 days from the date of the regular meeting of the governing body or the planning agency whichever first reviews the application, next following the date the application is filed, grant such development plan final approval. Provided, however, that should the next regular meeting occur more than 30 days following the filing of the application, the 45-day period shall be measured from the 30th day following the day the application has been filed.

(c) In the event the development plan as submitted contains variations from the development plan given tentative approval, the approving body may refuse to grant final approval and shall, within 45 days from the date of the regular meeting of the governing body or the planning agency, whichever first reviews the application, next following the date the application is filed, so advise the landowner in writing of said refusal, setting forth in said notice the reasons why one or more of said variations are not in the public interest. Provided, however, that should the next regular meeting occur more than 30 days following the filing of the application, the 45-day period shall be measured from the 30th day following the day the application has been filed. In the event of such refusal, the landowner may either:

(1) refile his application for final approval without the variations objected; or

(2) file a written request with the approving body that it hold a public hearing on his application for final approval.

If the landowner wishes to take either such alternate action he may do so at any time within which he shall be entitled to apply for final approval, or within 30 additional days if the time for applying for final approval shall have already passed at the time when the landowner was advised that the development plan was not in substantial compliance. In the event the landowner shall fail to take either of these alternate actions within said time, he shall be deemed to have abandoned the development plan. Any such public hearing shall be held pursuant to public notice within 30 days after request for the hearing is made by the landowner, and the hearing shall be conducted in the manner prescribed in this article for public hearings on applications for tentative approval. Within 30 days after the conclusion of the hearing, the approving body shall by official written communication either grant final approval to the development plan or deny final approval. The grant or denial of final approval of the development plan shall, in cases arising under this section, be in the form and contain the findings required for an application for tentative approval set forth in this article. Failure of the governing body or agency to render a decision on an application for final approval and communicate it to the applicant within the time and in the manner required by this section shall be deemed an approval of the application for final approval, as presented, unless the applicant has agreed in writing to an extension of time or change in the prescribed manner of presentation of communication of the decision, in which case, failure to meet the extended time or change in manner of presentation of communication shall have like effect.

(d) A development plan, or any part thereof, which has been given final approval shall be so certified without delay by the approving body and shall be filed of record forthwith in the office of the recorder of deeds before any development shall take place in accordance therewith. Upon the filing of record of the development plan the zoning and subdivision regulations otherwise applicable to the land included in such plan shall cease to apply thereto. Pending completion, in accordance with the time provisions stated in section 508, of said planned residential development or of that part thereof, as the case may be, that has been finally approved, no modification of the provisions of said development plan, or part thereof, as finally approved, shall be made except with the consent of the landowner. Upon approval of a final plat, the developer shall record the plat in accordance with the provisions of section 513(a) and post financial security in accordance with section 509.

(e) In the event that a development plan, or a section thereof, is given final approval and thereafter the landowner shall abandon such plan or the section thereof that has been finally approved, and shall so notify the approving body in writing; or, in the event the landowner shall fail to commence and carry out the planned residential development in accordance with the time provisions stated in section 508 after final approval has been granted, no development or further development shall take place on the property included in the development plan until after the said property is reclassified by enactment of an amendment to the municipal zoning ordinance in the manner prescribed for such amendments in Article VI.

(f) Each month a municipality shall notify in writing the superintendent of a school district in which development plans for a planned residential development were finally approved by the municipality during the preceding month. The notice shall include, but not be limited to, the location of the development, the number and types of units to be included in the development and the expected construction schedule of the development.

§ 712.1. Jurisdiction.—District justices shall have initial jurisdiction over proceedings brought under section 712.2.

§ 712.2. Enforcement Remedies.—(a) Any person, partnership or corporation, who or which has violated the planned residential development provisions of any ordinance enacted under this act or prior enabling law shall, upon being found liable therefor in a civil enforcement proceeding commenced by a municipality, pay a judgment of not more than $500 plus all court costs, including reasonable attorney fees incurred by a municipality as a result thereof. No judgment shall commence or be imposed, levied or payable until the date of the determination of a violation by the district justice. If the defendant neither pays nor timely appeals the judgment, the municipality may enforce the judgment pursuant to the appropriate rules of civil procedure. Each day that a violation continues shall constitute a separate violation, unless the district justice determining that there has been a violation further determines that there was a good faith basis for the person, partnership or corporation violating the ordinance to have believed that there was no such violation, in which event there shall be deemed to have been only one such violation until the fifth day following the date of the determination of a violation by the district justice, and thereafter each day that a violation continues shall constitute a separate violation. All judgments, costs and reasonable attorney fees collected for the violation of planned residential development provisions shall be paid over to the municipality whose ordinance has been violated.

(b) The court of common pleas, upon petition, may grant an order of stay, upon cause shown, tolling the per diem judgment pending a final adjudication of the violation and judgment.

(c) Nothing contained in this section shall be construed or interpreted to grant to any person or entity other than the municipality the right to commence any action for enforcement pursuant to this section.

§ 713. Compliance by Municipalities.—Municipalities with planned residential development ordinances shall have five years from the effective date of this amendatory act to comply with the provisions of this article.

ARTICLE VII-A
Traditional Neighborhood Development

53 P.S. §§ 10701-A–10709-M

§ 701-A. Powers and Objectives.—(a) This article grants powers to municipalities for the following purposes:

(1) To insure that the provisions of Article VI which are concerned in part with the uniform treatment of dwelling type, bulk, density, intensity and open space within each zoning district, shall not be applied to the improvement of land by other than lot by lot development in a manner that would distort the objectives of Article VI;

(2) To encourage innovations in residential and nonresidential development and renewal which makes use of a mixed use form of development so that the growing demand for housing and other development may be met by greater variety in type, design and layout of dwellings and other buildings and structures and by the conservation and more efficient use of open space ancillary to said dwellings and uses;

(3) To extend greater opportunities for better housing, recreation and access to goods, services and employment opportunities to all citizens and residents of this commonwealth;

(4) To encourage a more efficient use of land and of public services to reflect changes in the technology of land development so that economies secured may benefit those who need homes and for other uses;

(5) To allow for the development of fully integrated, mixed-use pedestrian oriented neighborhoods;

(6) To minimize traffic congestion, infrastructure costs and environmental degradation;

(7) To promote the implementation of the objectives of the municipal or multimunicipal comprehensive plan for guiding the location for growth;

(8) To provide a procedure, in aid of these purposes, which can relate the type, design and layout of residential and nonresidential development to the particular site and the particular demand for housing existing at the time of development in a manner consistent with the preservation of the property values within existing residential and nonresidential areas; and

(9) To insure that the increased flexibility of regulations over land development authorized herein is carried out under such administrative standards and procedure as shall encourage the disposition of proposals for land development without undue delay.

(b) The objectives of a traditional neighborhood development are:

(1) To establish a community which is pedestrian-oriented with a number of parks, a centrally located public commons, square, plaza, park or prominent intersection of two or more major streets, commercial enterprises and civic and other public buildings and facilities for social activity, recreation and community functions;

(2) To minimize traffic congestion and reduce the need for extensive road construction by reducing the number and length of automobile trips required to access everyday needs;

(3) To make public transit a viable alternative to the automobile by organizing appropriate building densities;

(4) To provide the elderly and the young with independence of movement by locating most daily activities within walking distance;

(5) To foster the ability of citizens to come to know each other and to watch over their mutual security by providing public spaces such as streets, parks and squares and mixed use which maximizes the proximity to neighbors at almost all times of the day;

(6) To foster a sense of place and community by providing a setting that encourages the natural intermingling of everyday uses and activities within a recognizable neighborhood;

(7) To integrate age and income groups and foster the bonds of an authentic community by providing a range of housing types, shops and workplaces; and

(8) To encourage community oriented initiatives and to support the balanced development of society by providing suitable civic and public buildings and facilities.

§ 702-A. Grant of Power.—The governing body of each municipality may enact, amend and repeal provisions of a zoning ordinance in order to fix standards and conditions for traditional neighborhood development. The provisions for standards and conditions for traditional neighborhood development shall be, except as otherwise provided in this article, consistent with Article VI and shall be included within the zoning ordinance, and the enactment of the traditional neighborhood development provisions shall be in accordance with the procedures required for the enactment of an amendment of a zoning ordinance as provided in Article VI. The provisions shall:

(1) Set forth the standards, conditions and regulations for a traditional neighborhood development consistent with this article. A zoning ordinance or amendment may authorize and provide standards, conditions and regulations for traditional neighborhood development that:

(i) designate a part or parts of the municipality as a district or districts which are reserved exclusively for traditional neighborhood development; or

(ii) permit the creation of a traditional neighborhood development in any part of the municipality or in one or more specified zoning districts.

(2) Set forth the procedures pertaining to the application for, hearing on and preliminary and final approval of a traditional neighborhood development which shall be consistent with this article for those applications and hearings.

§ 703-A. Transferable Development Rights.—Municipalities electing to enact traditional neighborhood development provisions may also incorporate provisions for transferable development rights, on a voluntary basis, in accordance with express standards and criteria set forth in the ordinance and with the requirements of Article VI.

§ 704-A. Applicability of Comprehensive Plan and Statement of Community Development Objectives.—All provisions and all amendments to the provisions adopted pursuant to this article shall be based on and interpreted in relation to the statement of community development objectives of the zoning ordinance and shall be consistent with either the comprehensive plan of the municipality or the statement of community development objectives in accordance with Section 606. Every application for the approval of a traditional neighborhood development shall be based on and interpreted in relation to the statement of community development objectives, and shall be consistent with the comprehensive plan.

§ 705-A. Forms of Traditional Neighborhood Development.—A traditional neighborhood development may be developed and applied in any of the following forms.

(1) As a new development.

(2) As an outgrowth or extension of existing development.

(3) As a form of urban infill where existing uses and structure may be incorporated into the development.

(4) In any combination or variation of the above.

§ 706-A. Standards and Conditions for Traditional Neighborhood Development.—(a) All provisions adopted pursuant to this article shall set forth all the standards, conditions and regulations by which a proposed traditional neighborhood development shall be evaluated, and those standards, conditions and regulations shall be consistent with the following subsections.

(b) The provisions adopted pursuant to this article shall set forth the uses permitted in traditional neighborhood development, which uses may include, but shall not be limited to:

Table of Contents
Part I Ch. 1–3 Ethics, Records, Open Meetings
Part II Ch. 4–10 Taxation
Part III Ch. 11–18 Torts, Contracts & Civil Rules
Part IV Ch. 19–24 Zoning & Planning
Part V Ch. 25–30 Construction and Emergency Codes
Part VI Ch. 31–39 Municipal Codes
Index

(1) Dwelling units of any dwelling type or configuration, or any combination thereof.

(2) Those nonresidential uses deemed to be appropriate for incorporation in the design of the traditional neighborhood development.

(c) The provisions may establish regulations setting forth the timing of development among the various types of dwellings and may specify whether some or all nonresidential uses are to be built before, after or at the same time as the residential uses.

(d) The provisions adopted pursuant to this article shall establish standards governing the density, or intensity of land use, in a traditional neighborhood development. The standards may vary the density or intensity of land use, otherwise applicable to the land under the provisions of a zoning ordinance of the municipality within the traditional neighborhood development. It is recommended that the provisions adopted by the municipality pursuant to this article include, but not be limited to, all of the following:

(1) The amount, location and proposed use of common open space, providing for parks to be distributed throughout the neighborhood as well as the establishment of a centrally located public commons, square, park, plaza or prominent intersection of two or more major streets.

(2) The location and physical characteristics of the site of the proposed traditional neighborhood development, providing for the retaining and enhancing, where practicable, of natural features such as wetlands, ponds, lakes, waterways, trees of high quality, significant tree stands and other significant natural features. These significant natural features should be at least partially fronted by public tracts whenever possible.

(3) The location and physical characteristics of the site of the proposed traditional neighborhood development so that it will develop out of the location of squares, parks and other neighborhood centers and subcenters. Zoning changes in building type should generally occur at mid-block rather than mid-street and buildings should tend to be zoned by compatibility of building type rather than building use. The proposed traditional neighborhood development should be designed to work with the topography of the site to minimize the amount of grading necessary to achieve a street network, and some significant high points of the site should be set aside for public tracts for the location of public buildings or other public facilities.

(4) The location, design, type and use of structures proposed, with most structures being placed close to the street at generally the equivalent of one-quarter the width of the lot or less. The distance between the sidewalk and residential dwellings should, as a general rule, be occupied by a semi-public attachment, such as a porch or, at a minimum, a covered entryway.

(5) The location, design, type and use of streets, alleys, sidewalks and other public rights-of-way with a hierarchy of streets laid out with an interconnected network of streets and blocks that provide multiple routes from origins to destinations and are appropriately designed to serve the needs of pedestrians and vehicles equally. As such, most streets, except alleys, should have sidewalks.

(6) The location for vehicular parking with the street plan providing for on street parking for most streets, with the exception of alleys. All parking lots, except where there is a compelling reason to the contrary, should be located either behind or to the side of buildings and, in most cases, should be located toward the center of blocks such that only their access is visible from adjacent streets. In most cases, structures located on lots smaller than 50 feet in width should be served by a rear alley with all garages fronting on alleys. Garages not served by an alley should be set back from the front of the house or rotated so that the garage doors do not face any adjacent streets.

(7) The minimum and maximum areas and dimensions of the properties and common open space within the proposed traditional neighborhood development and the approximate distance from the center to the edge of the traditional neighborhood development. It is recommended that the distance from the center to the edge of the traditional neighborhood development be approximately one-quarter mile or less and not more than one-half mile. Traditional neighborhood developments in excess of one-half mile distance from center to edge should be divided into two or more developments.

(8) The site plan to provide for either a natural or manmade corridor to serve as the edge of the neighborhood. When standing alone, the traditional neighborhood development should front on open space to serve as its edge. Such open space may include, but is not limited to, parks, a golf course, cemetery, farmland or natural settings such as woodlands or waterways. When adjacent to existing development the traditional neighborhood development should either front on open space, a street or roadway, or any combination hereof.

(9) The greatest density of housing and the preponderance of office and commercial uses should be located to anchor the traditional neighborhood development. If the neighborhood is adjacent to existing development or a major roadway then office, commercial and denser residential uses may be located at either the edge or the center, or both. Commercial uses located at the edge of the traditional neighborhood development may be located adjacent to similar commercial uses in order to form a greater commercial corridor.

(e) In the case of a traditional neighborhood development proposed to be developed over a period of years, standards established in provisions adopted pursuant to this article may, to encourage the flexibility of housing density, design and type intended by this article:

(1) Permit a variation in each section to be developed from the density, or intensity of use, established for the entire traditional neighborhood development.

(2) Allow for a greater concentration of density or intensity of land use, within some section or sections of development, whether it be earlier or later in the development than upon others.

(3) Require that the approval of such greater concentration of density or intensity of land use for any section to be developed be offset by a smaller concentration in any completed prior stage or by an appropriate reservation of common open space on the remaining land by a grant of easement or by covenant in favor of the municipality, provided that the reservation shall, as far as practicable, defer the precise location of such common open space until an application for final approval is filed so that flexibility of development which is a prime objective of this article can be maintained.

(f) Provisions adopted pursuant to this article may require that a traditional neighborhood development contain a minimum number of dwelling units and a minimum number of nonresidential units.

(g) (1) The authority granted a municipality by Article V to establish standards for the location, width, course and surfacing of streets, walkways, curbs, gutters, street lights, shade trees, water, sewage and drainage facilities, easements or rights-of-way for drainage and utilities, reservations of public grounds, other improvements, regulations for the height and setback as they relate to renewable energy systems and energy-conserving building design, regulations for the height and location of vegetation with respect to boundary lines, as they relate to renewable energy systems and energy-conserving building design, regulations for the type and location of renewable energy systems or their components and regulations for the design and construction of structures to encourage the use of renewable energy systems, shall be vested in the governing body or the planning agency for the purposes of this article.

(2) The standards applicable to a particular traditional neighborhood development may be different than or modifications of the standards and requirements otherwise required of subdivisions or land development authorized under an ordinance adopted pursuant to Article V, provided, however, that provisions adopted pursuant to this article shall set forth the limits and extent of any modifications or changes in such standards and requirements in order that a landowner shall know the limits and extent of permissible modifications from the standards otherwise applicable to subdivisions or land development.

§ 707-A. Sketch Plan Presentation.—The municipality may informally meet with a landowner to informally discuss the conceptual aspects of the landowner's development plan prior to the filing of the application for preliminary approval for the development plan. The landowner may present a sketch plan to the municipality for discussion purposes only, and during the discussion the municipality may make suggestions and recommendations on the design of the developmental plan which shall not be binding on the municipality.

§ 708-A. Manual of Written and Graphic Design Guidelines.—Where it has adopted provisions for traditional neighborhood development, the governing body of a municipality may provide, upon review and recommendation of the planning commission where one exists, a manual of written and graphic design guidelines. The manual may be included in or amended into the subdivision and land development ordinance, the zoning ordinance or both.

§ 708.1-A. Subdivision and Land Development Ordinance Provisions Applicable to Traditional Neighborhood Development.—The municipality may enact subdivision and land development ordinance provisions applicable to a traditional neighborhood development to address the design standards that are appropriate to a traditional neighborhood development, including, but not limited to, compactness, pedestrian orientation, street geometry or other related design features. The provisions may be included as part of any ordinance pertaining to traditional neighborhood development and may be subject to modification similar to section 512.1.

§ 709-A. Applicability of Article to Agriculture.—Zoning ordinances shall encourage the continuity, development and viability of agricultural operations. Zoning ordinances may not restrict agricultural operations or changes to or expansions of agricultural operations in geographic areas where agriculture has traditionally been present, unless the agricultural operation will have a direct adverse effect on the public health and safety. Nothing in this section shall require a municipality to adopt a zoning ordinance that violates or exceeds the provisions of the act of June 30, 1981 (P.L. 128, No. 43), known as the "Agricultural Area Security Law," the act of June 10, 1982 (P.L. 454, No. 133), entitled "An Act Protecting Agricultural Operations from Nuisance Suits and Ordinances Under Certain Circumstances," and the act of May 20, 1993 (P.L. 12, No. 6), known as the "Nutrient Management Act."

ARTICLE VIII-A
Joint Municipal Zoning

53 P.S. § 10801-A–10821-A

§ 801-A. General Powers.—(a) For the purpose of permitting municipalities which cooperatively plan for their future to also regulate future growth and change in a cooperative manner, the governing body of each municipality, in accordance with the conditions and procedures set forth in this act, may cooperate with one or more municipalities to enact, amend and repeal joint municipal zoning ordinances in order to implement joint municipal comprehensive plans and to accomplish any of the purposes of this act.

(b) A joint municipal zoning ordinance shall be based upon an adopted joint municipal comprehensive plan and shall be prepared by a joint municipal planning commission established under the provisions of this act.

§ 802-A. Relation to County and Municipal Zoning.—The enactment by any municipality of a joint municipal zoning ordinance whose land is subject to county or municipal zoning shall constitute an immediate repeal of the county or municipal zoning ordinance within the municipality adopting such ordinance as of the effective date of the joint municipal zoning ordinance.

§ 803-A. Ordinance Provisions.—Joint municipal zoning ordinances may permit, prohibit, regulate, restrict and determine and may contain the same elements as authorized for municipal zoning ordinances by section 603.

§ 804-A. Zoning Purposes.—The provisions of joint municipal zoning ordinances shall be designed to serve the same purposes for the area of its jurisdiction as is required by section 604 for municipal zoning ordinances.

§ 805-A. Classifications.—The authorizations and requirements of section 605 shall be applicable to joint municipal zoning ordinances. No area of a municipality party to a joint municipal zoning ordinance shall be left unzoned.

§ 806-A. Statement of Community Development Objectives.—(a) Every joint municipal zoning ordinance shall contain a statement of community development objectives as defined by section 606.

(b) The statement of community development objectives shall be based upon the joint municipal comprehensive plan and may be supplemented by a statement of legislative findings of the governing bodies party to the joint municipal zoning ordinance as defined by section 606.

(c) The community development objectives for a joint municipal zoning ordinance shall relate to the area within the jurisdiction of the ordinance, shall identify the community development objectives of each municipality party to the joint municipal zoning ordinance and the relationship of these objectives to those of the area and shall, in addition, include the basis for the geographic delineation of the area which the ordinance regulates.

§ 807-A. Preparation of Proposed Zoning Ordinance.—The requirements of section 607 as applicable to municipal zoning ordinances shall equally apply to the preparation of a joint municipal zoning ordinance except that:

(1) The joint municipal planning commission shall assume the preparation responsibilities of the planning agency and shall be directed by the governing bodies of the participating municipalities.

(2) At least one public meeting shall be held by the joint municipal planning commission within the area of jurisdiction of the proposed joint municipal zoning ordinance.

§ 808-A. Enactment of Zoning Ordinance.—(a) The procedural requirements of section 608 shall be applicable to the enactment of a joint municipal zoning ordinance.

(b) Each municipality party to a joint municipal zoning ordinance shall enact the ordinance and it shall not become effective until it has been properly enacted by all the participating municipalities.

(c) No municipality may withdraw from or repeal a joint municipal zoning ordinance during the first three years following the date of its enactment. If, at any time after the end of the second year following the enactment of a joint municipal zoning ordinance, a municipality wishes to repeal and withdraw from a joint municipal zoning ordinance, it shall enact an ordinance, which shall be effective no sooner than one year after its enactment, repealing the joint municipal zoning ordinance and shall provide immediately and concurrently one year's advanced written notice of its repeal and withdrawal to the governing bodies of all municipalities party to the joint municipal zoning ordinance. The repeal and withdrawal may become effective within less than one year with the unanimous approval, by ordinance, of the governing bodies of all municipalities party to the joint municipal zoning ordinance.

§ 809-A. Enactment of Zoning Ordinance Amendments.—(a) The procedural requirements for amendments to a joint municipal zoning ordinance shall be as required by section 609, except that all proposed amendments shall also be submitted to the joint municipal planning commission for review at least 30 days prior to the hearing on such proposed amendments.

(b) The governing bodies of the other participating municipalities shall submit their comments, including a specific recommendation to adopt or not to adopt the proposed amendment, to the governing body of the municipality within which the amendment is proposed no later than the date of the public hearing. Failure to provide comments shall be construed as a recommendation to adopt the proposed amendments.

(c) No amendments to the joint municipal zoning ordinance shall be effective unless all of the participating municipalities approve the amendment.

§ 810-A. Procedure for Curative Amendments.—Curative amendments shall be filed in accordance with the requirements of section 609.1 with the municipality within which the landowner's property is located: Provided, however, That the governing body before which the curative amendment is brought shall not have the power to adopt any amendment to the joint municipal zoning ordinance without the approval of the other municipalities participating in the joint municipal zoning ordinance. The challenge shall be directed to the validity of the joint municipal zoning ordinances as it applies to the entire area of its jurisdiction.

§ 811-A. Area of Jurisdiction for Challenges.—In any challenge to the validity of the joint municipal zoning ordinance, the court shall consider the validity of the ordinance as it applies to the entire area of its jurisdiction as enacted and shall not limit consideration to any single constituent municipality.

§ 812-A. Procedure for Joint Municipal Curative Amendments.—(a) The governing bodies of all the participating municipalities may declare the joint municipal zoning ordinance or portions thereof substantially invalid and prepare a municipal curative amendment pursuant to section 609.2.

(b) The provisions of section 609.2(4) shall apply to all municipalities participating in the joint municipal zoning ordinance.

(c) (1) In the case of a joint municipal curative amendment involving two or three municipalities, the municipalities shall have nine months from the date of declaration of partial or total invalidity to enact a curative amendment.

(2) Subject to the limitation contained in clause (3), where there are more than three municipality parties, the nine-month period shall be extended one additional month for each municipality in excess of three that is a party to the joint municipal zoning ordinance.

(3) Notwithstanding the additional periods provided for in clause (2), a curative amendment shall be enacted by the parties to a joint municipal zoning ordinance not later than one year from the date of declaration of partial or total invalidity.

§ 813-A. Publication, Advertisement and Availability of Ordinances.—The content of public notices and the procedures for the advertisement and enactment of joint municipal zoning ordinances and amendments shall be regulated by section 610.

§ 814-A. Registration of Nonconforming Uses.—The registration of nonconforming uses shall be as specified by section 613.

§ 815-A. Administration.—(a) The governing bodies of the municipalities adopting the joint municipal zoning ordinance may establish a joint zoning hearing board pursuant to the authority of section 904, except that:

(1) The joint municipal zoning ordinance shall either create a joint zoning hearing board to administer the entire joint municipal zoning ordinance or provide for the retention or creation of individual zoning hearing boards in each of the individual participating municipalities to administer the new joint municipal zoning ordinance as to properties located within each of the individual participating municipalities.

(2) These same procedures shall be followed by a joint zoning hearing board as set forth in Article IX for individual municipal zoning hearing boards.

(b) The joint municipal zoning ordinance shall specify the number of zoning officers to be appointed to administer the ordinance pursuant to section 614. One zoning officer may be appointed by each municipality to administer the ordinance within the municipal boundaries or a single zoning officer may be appointed to administer the ordinance throughout the jurisdiction of the ordinance.

§ 816-A. Zoning Appeals.—All rights and procedures provided in Articles IX and X-A shall pertain to joint municipal zoning.

§ 817-A. Enforcement Penalties.—Penalties for violation of a joint municipal zoning ordinance shall be as specified in section 617.1.

§ 818-A. Enforcement Remedies.—(a) Enforcement remedies shall be as specified in section 617.

(b) In addition, the provisions of a joint municipal zoning ordinance shall be binding upon the municipalities and may be enforced by appropriate remedy by any one or more of the municipalities against any other municipality party thereto.

§ 819-A. Finances.—(a) The governing body of a municipality may appropriate and receive funds for a joint municipal zoning ordinance in the same manner as authorized for a municipal zoning ordinance by section 617.2.

(b) A joint municipal zoning ordinance shall specify the manner and extent of financing the costs for administration and enforcement, including the financial responsibilities for defending legal challenges to the ordinance.

§ 820-A. Exemptions.—The exemptions for a joint municipal zoning ordinance shall be those identified by section 619.

§ 821-A. Existing Bodies.—Municipalities which, on or before the effective date of this amendatory act, established joint bodies under former Article IX-A of this act, shall have five years from the effective date of this amendatory act to comply with the provisions of this article.

ARTICLE IX

Zoning Hearing Board and Other Administrative Proceedings

53 P.S. § 10901–10917

§ 901. General Provisions.—Every municipality which has enacted or enacts a zoning ordinance pursuant to this act or prior enabling laws, shall create a zoning hearing board. As used in this article, unless the context clearly indicates otherwise, the term "board" shall refer to such zoning hearing board.

§ 902. Existing Boards of Adjustment.—(902 repealed Dec. 21, 1988, P.L. 1329, No. 170)

§ 903. Membership of Board.—(a) The membership of the board shall, upon the determination of the governing body, consist of either three or five residents of the municipality appointed by resolution by the governing body. The terms of office of a three member board shall be three years and shall be so fixed that the term of office of one member shall expire each year. The terms of office of a five member board shall be five years and shall be so fixed that the term of office of one member of a five member board shall expire each year. If a three member board is changed to a five member board, the members of the existing three member board shall continue in office until their term of office would expire under prior law.The governing body shall appoint two additional members to the board with terms scheduled to expire in accordance with the provisions of this section. The board shall promptly notify the governing body of any vacancies which occur. Appointments to fill vacancies shall be only for the unexpired portion of the term. Members of the board shall hold no other elected or appointed office in the municipality, nor shall any member be an employee of the municipality.

(b) The governing body may appoint by resolution at least one but no more than three residents of the municipality to serve as alternate members of the board. The term of office of an alternate member shall be three years. When seated pursuant to the provisions of section 906, [53 P.S. § 10906] an alternate shall be entitled to participate in all proceedings and discussions of the board to the same and full extent as provided by law for board members, including specifically the right to cast a vote as a voting member during the proceedings, and shall have all the powers and duties set forth in this act and as otherwise provided by law. Alternates shall hold no other elected or appointed office in the municipality, including service as a member of the planning commission or as a zoning officer, nor shall any alternate be an employee of the municipality. Any alternate may participate in any proceeding or discussion of the board but shall not be entitled to vote as a member of the board nor be compensated pursuant to section 907 [53 P.S. § 10907] unless designated as a voting alternate member pursuant to section 906.

§ 904. Joint Zoning Hearing Boards.—(a) Two or more municipalities may, by ordinances enacted in each, create a joint zoning hearing board in lieu of a separate board for each municipality. A joint board shall consist of two members appointed from among the residents of each municipality by its governing body.

(b) The term of office of members of joint boards shall be five years, except that of the two members first appointed from each municipality, the term of office of one member shall be three years. When any vacancies occur, the joint board shall promptly notify the governing body which appointed the member whose office has become vacant, and such governing body shall appoint a member for the unexpired portion of the term. Members of the joint board shall hold no other office in the participating municipality.

(c) Where legal counsel is desired, an attorney, other than the solicitors of the participating municipalities, may be appointed to serve as counsel to the joint zoning hearing board.

(d) In all other respects, including the appointment and seating of alternate members, joint zoning hearing boards shall be governed by provisions of this act not inconsistent with the provisions of this section.

§ 905. Removal of Members.—Any board member may be removed for malfeasance, misfeasance or nonfeasance in office or for other just cause by a majority vote of the governing body which appointed the member, taken after the member has received 15 days' advance notice of the intent to take such a vote. A hearing shall be held in connection with the vote if the member shall request it in writing.

§ 906. Organization of Board.—(a) The board shall elect from its own membership its officers, who shall serve annual terms as such and may succeed themselves. For the conduct of any hearing and the taking of any action, a quorum shall be not less than a majority of all the members of the board, but the board may appoint a hearing officer from its own membership to conduct any hearing on its behalf and the parties may waive further action by the board as provided in section 908.

(b) The chairman of the board may designate alternate members of the board to replace any absent or disqualified member, and if, by reason of absence or disqualification of a member, a quorum is not reached, the chairman of the board shall designate as many alternate members of the board to sit on the board as may be needed to reach a quorum. Any alternate member of the board shall continue to serve on the board in all proceedings involving the matter or case for which the alternate was initially appointed until the board has made a final decision on the matter or case. Designation of an alternate pursuant to this section shall be made on a case-by-case basis in rotation according to declining seniority among all alternates.

(c) The board may make, alter and rescind rules and forms for its procedure, consistent with ordinances of the municipality and laws of the Commonwealth. The board shall keep full public records of its business, which records shall be the property of the municipality, and shall submit a report of its activities to the governing body as requested by the governing body.

§ 907. Expenditures for Services.—Within the limits of funds appropriated by the governing body, the board may employ or contract for secretaries, clerks, legal counsel, consultants and other technical and clerical services. Members of the board may receive compensation for the performance of their duties, as may be fixed by the governing body, but in no case shall it exceed the rate of compensation authorized to be paid to the members of the governing body. Alternate members of the board may receive compensation, as may be fixed by the governing body, for the performance of their duties when designated as alternate members pursuant to section 906, but in no case shall such compensation exceed the rate of compensation authorized to be paid to the members of the governing body.

§ 908. Hearings.—The board shall conduct hearings and make decisions in accordance with the following requirements:

(1) Public notice shall be given and written notice shall be given to the applicant, the zoning officer, such other persons as the governing body shall designate by ordinance and to any person who has made timely request for the same. Written notices shall be given at such time and in such manner as shall be prescribed by ordinance or, in the absence of ordinance provision, by rules of the board. In addition to the written notice provided herein, written notice of said hearing shall be conspicuously posted on the affected tract of land at least one week prior to the hearing.

(1.1) The governing body may prescribe reasonable fees with respect to hearings before the zoning hearing board. Fees for said hearings may include compensation for the secretary and members of the zoning hearing board, notice and advertising costs and necessary administrative overhead connected with the hearing. The costs, however, shall not include legal expenses of the zoning hearing board, expenses for engineering, architectural or other technical consultants or expert witness costs.

(1.2) The first hearing before the board or hearing officer shall be commenced within 60 days from the date of receipt of the applicant's application, unless the applicant has agreed in writing to an extension of time. Each subsequent hearing before the board or hearing officer shall be held within 45 days of the prior hearing, unless otherwise agreed to by the applicant in writing or on the record. An applicant shall complete the presentation of his case-in-chief within 100 days of the first hearing. Upon the request of the applicant, the board or hearing officer shall assure that the applicant receives at least seven hours of hearings within the 100 days, including the first hearing. Persons opposed to the application shall complete the presentation of their opposition to the application within 100 days of the first hearing held after the completion of the applicant's case-in-chief. An applicant may, upon request, be granted additional hearings to complete his case-in-chief provided the persons opposed to the application are granted an equal number of additional hearings. Persons opposed to the application may, upon the written consent or consent on the record by the applicant and municipality, be granted additional hearings to complete their opposition to the application provided the applicant is granted an equal number of additional hearings for rebuttal.

(2) The hearings shall be conducted by the board or the board may appoint any member or an independent attorney as a hearing officer. The decision, or, where no decision is called for, the findings shall be made by the board; however, the appellant or the applicant, as the case may be, in addition to the municipality, may, prior to the decision of the hearing, waive decision or findings by the board and accept the decision or findings of the hearing officer as final.

(3) The parties to the hearing shall be the municipality, any person affected by the application who has made timely appearance of record before the board, and any other person including civic or community organizations permitted to appear by the board. The board shall have power to require that all persons who wish to be considered parties enter appearances in writing on forms provided by the board for that purpose.

(4) The chairman or acting chairman of the board or the hearing officer presiding shall have power to administer oaths and issue subpoenas to compel the attendance of witnesses and the production of relevant documents and papers, including witnesses and documents requested by the parties.

(5) The parties shall have the right to be represented by counsel and shall be afforded the opportunity to respond and present evidence and argument and cross-examine adverse witnesses on all relevant issues.

(6) Formal rules of evidence shall not apply, but irrelevant, immaterial, or unduly repetitious evidence may be excluded.

(7) The board or the hearing officer, as the case may be, shall keep a stenographic record of the proceedings. The appearance fee for a stenographer shall be shared equally by the applicant and the board. The cost of the original transcript shall be paid by the board if the transcript is ordered by the board or hearing officer or shall be paid by the person appealing from the decision of the board if such appeal is made, and in either event the cost of additional copies shall be paid by the person requesting such copy or copies. In other cases the party requesting the original transcript shall bear the cost thereof.

(8) The board or the hearing officer shall not communicate, directly or indirectly, with any party or his representatives in connection with any issue involved except upon notice and opportunity for all parties to participate, shall not take notice of any communication, reports, staff memoranda, or other materials, except advice from their solicitor, unless the parties are afforded an opportunity to contest the material so noticed and shall not inspect the site or its surroundings after the commencement of hearings with any party or his representative unless all parties are given an opportunity to be present.

(9) The board or the hearing officer, as the case may be, shall render a written decision or, when no decision is called for, make written findings on the application within 45 days after the last hearing before the board or hearing officer. Where the application is contested or denied, each decision shall be accompanied by findings of fact and conclusions based thereon together with the reasons therefor. Conclusions based on any provisions of this act or of any ordinance, rule or regulation shall contain a reference to the provision relied on and the reasons why the conclusion is deemed appropriate in the light of the facts found. If the hearing is conducted by a hearing officer, and there has been no stipulation that his decision or findings are final, the board shall make his report and recommendations available to the parties within 45 days and the parties shall be entitled to make written representations thereon to the board prior to final decision or entry of findings, and the board's decision shall be entered no later than 30 days after the report of the hearing officer. Except for challenges filed under section 916.1 where the board fails to render the decision within the period required by this subsection or fails to commence, conduct or complete the required hearing as provided in subsection (1.2), the decision shall be deemed to have been rendered in favor of the applicant unless the applicant has agreed in writing or on the record to an extension

of time. When a decision has been rendered in favor of the applicant because of the failure of the board to meet or render a decision as hereinabove provided, the board shall give public notice of said decision within ten days from the last day it could have met to render a decision in the same manner as provided in subsection (1) of this section. If the board shall fail to provide such notice, the applicant may do so. Nothing in this subsection shall prejudice the right of any party opposing the application to appeal the decision to a court of competent jurisdiction.

(10) A copy of the final decision or, where no decision is called for, of the findings shall be delivered to the applicant personally or mailed to him not later than the day following its date. To all other persons who have filed their name and address with the board not later than the last day of the hearing, the board shall provide by mail or otherwise, brief notice of the decision or findings and a statement of the place at which the full decision or findings may be examined.

§ 908.1. Mediation Option.—(a) Parties to proceedings authorized in this article and Article X-A may utilize mediation as an aid in completing such proceedings. In proceedings before the zoning hearing board, in no case shall the zoning hearing board initiate mediation or participate as a mediating party. Mediation shall supplement, not replace, those procedures in this article and Article X-A once they have been formally initiated. Nothing in this section shall be interpreted as expanding or limiting municipal police powers or as modifying any principles of substantive law.

(b) Participation in mediation shall be wholly voluntary. The appropriateness of mediation shall be determined by the particulars of each case and the willingness of the parties to negotiate. Any municipality offering the mediation option shall assure that, in each case, the mediating parties, assisted by the mediator as appropriate, develop terms and conditions for:

(1) Funding mediation.

(2) Selecting a mediator who, at a minimum, shall have a working knowledge of municipal zoning and subdivision procedures and demonstrated skills in mediation.

(3) Completing mediation, including time limits for such completion.

(4) Suspending time limits otherwise authorized in this act, provided there is written consent by the mediating parties, and by an applicant or municipal decision making body if either is not a party to the mediation.

(5) Identifying all parties and affording them the opportunity to participate.

(6) Subject to legal restraints, determining whether some or all of the mediation sessions shall be open or closed to the public.

(7) Assuring that mediated solutions are in writing and signed by the parties, and become subject to review and approval by the appropriate decision making body pursuant to the authorized procedures set forth in the other sections of this act.

(c) No offers or statements made in the mediation sessions, excluding the final written mediated agreement, shall be admissible as evidence in any subsequent judicial or administrative proceedings.

§ 909. Board's Functions: Appeal from the Zoning Officer.—(909 repealed Dec. 21, 1988, P.L. 1329, No. 170)

§ 909.1. Jurisdiction.—(a) The zoning hearing board shall have exclusive jurisdiction to hear and render final adjudications in the following matters:

(1) Substantive challenges to the validity of any land use ordinance, except those brought before the governing body pursuant to sections 609.1 and 916.1(a)(2).

(2) [Deleted 2008 Act 39]

(3) Appeals from the determination of the zoning officer, including, but not limited to, the granting or denial of any permit, or failure to act on the application therefor, the issuance of any cease and desist order or the registration or refusal to register any nonconforming use, structure or lot.

(4) Appeals from a determination by a municipal engineer or the zoning officer with reference to the administration of any flood plain or flood hazard ordinance or such provisions within a land use ordinance.

(5) Applications for variances from the terms of the zoning ordinance and flood hazard ordinance or such provisions within a land use ordinance, pursuant to section 910.2.

(6) Applications for special exceptions under the zoning ordinance or flood plain or flood hazard ordinance or such provisions within a land use ordinance, pursuant to section 912.1.

(7) Appeals from the determination of any officer or agency charged with the administration of any transfers of development rights or performance density provisions of the zoning ordinance.

(8) Appeals from the zoning officer's determination under section 916.2.

(9) Appeals from the determination of the zoning officer or municipal engineer in the administration of any land use ordinance or provision thereof with reference to sedimentation and erosion control and storm water management insofar as the same relate to development not involving Article V or VII applications.

(b) The governing body or, except as to clauses (3), (4) and (5), the planning agency, if designated, shall have exclusive jurisdiction to hear and render final adjudications in the following matters:

(1) All applications for approvals of planned residential developments under Article VII pursuant to the provisions of section 702.

(2) All applications pursuant to section 508 for approval of subdivisions or land developments under Article V. Any provision in a subdivision and land development ordinance requiring that final action concerning subdivision and land development applications be taken by a planning agency rather than the governing body shall vest exclusive jurisdiction in the planning agency in lieu of the governing body for purposes of the provisions of this paragraph.

(3) Applications for conditional use under the express provisions of the zoning ordinance pursuant to section 603(c)(2).

(4) Applications for curative amendment to a zoning ordinance pursuant to sections 609.1 and 916.1(a)(2).

(5) All petitions for amendments to land use ordinances, pursuant to the procedures set forth in section 609. Any action on such petitions shall be deemed legislative acts, provided that nothing contained in this clause shall be deemed to enlarge or diminish existing law with reference to appeals to court.

(6) Appeals from the determination of the zoning officer or the municipal engineer in the administration of any land use ordinance or provisions thereof with reference to sedimentation and erosion control and storm water management insofar as the same relate to application for land development under Article V and VII. Where such determination relates only to development not involving an Article V or VII application, the appeal from such determination of the zoning officer or the municipal engineer shall be to the zoning hearing board pursuant to subsection (a)(9). Where the applicable land use ordinance vests jurisdiction for final administration of subdivision and land development applications in the planning agency, all appeals from determinations under this paragraph shall be to the planning agency and all appeals from the decision of the planning agency shall be to court.

(7) Applications for a special encroachment permit pursuant to section 405 and applications for a permit pursuant to section 406.

§ 910. Board Functions: Challenge to the Validity of any Ordinance or Map.—(910 repealed Dec. 21, 1988, P.L. 1329, No. 170)

§ 910.1. Applicability of Judicial Remedies.—Nothing contained in this article shall be construed to deny the appellant the right to proceed directly to court where appropriate, pursuant to the Pennsylvania Rules of Civil Procedure No. 1091 (relating to action in mandamus).

§ 910.2. Zoning Hearing Board's Functions; Variances.—(a) The board shall hear requests for variances where it is alleged that the provisions of the zoning ordinance inflict unnecessary hardship upon the applicant. The board may by rule prescribe the form of application and may require preliminary application to the zoning officer. The board may grant a variance, provided that all of the following findings are made where relevant in a given case:

(1) That there are unique physical circumstances or conditions, including irregularity, narrowness, or shallowness of lot size or shape, or exceptional topographical or other physical conditions peculiar to the particular property and that the unnecessary hardship is due to such conditions and not the circumstances or conditions generally created by the provisions of the zoning ordinance in the neighborhood or district in which the property is located.

(2) That because of such physical circumstances or conditions, there is no possibility that the property can be developed in strict conformity with the provisions of the zoning ordinance and that the authorization of a variance is therefore necessary to enable the reasonable use of the property.

(3) That such unnecessary hardship has not been created by the appellant.

(4) That the variance, if authorized, will not alter the essential character of the neighborhood or district in which the property is located, nor substantially or permanently impair the appropriate use or development of adjacent property, nor be detrimental to the public welfare.

(5) That the variance, if authorized, will represent the minimum variance that will afford relief and will represent the least modification possible of the regulation in issue.

(b) In granting any variance, the board may attach such reasonable conditions and safeguards as it may deem necessary to implement the purposes of this act and the zoning ordinance.

§ 912. Board's Functions: Variances.—(912 repealed Dec. 21, 1988, P.L. 1329, No. 170)

§ 912.1. Zoning Hearing Board's Functions; Special Exception.—Where the governing body, in the zoning ordinance, has stated special exceptions to be granted or denied by the board pursuant to express standards and criteria, the board shall hear and decide requests for such special exceptions in accordance with such standards and criteria. In granting a special exception, the board may attach such reasonable conditions and safeguards, in addition to those expressed in the ordinance, as it may deem necessary to implement the purposes of this act and the zoning ordinance.

§ 913. Board's Functions: Special Exceptions.—(913 repealed Dec. 21, 1988, P.L. 1329, No. 170)

§ 913.1. Unified Appeals.—(913.1 repealed Dec. 21, 1988, P.L. 1329, No. 170)

§ 913.2. Governing Body's Functions; Conditional Uses.—(a) Where the governing body, in the zoning ordinances, has stated conditional uses to be granted or denied by the governing body pursuant to express standards and criteria, the governing body shall hold hearings on and decide requests for such conditional uses in accordance with such standards and criteria. The hearing shall be conducted by the board or the board may appoint any member or an independent

Table of Contents
Part I Ch. 1–3 Ethics, Records, Open Meetings
Part II Ch. 4–10 Taxation
Part III Ch. 11–18 Torts, Contracts & Civil Rules
Part IV Ch. 19–24 Zoning & Planning
Part V Ch. 25–30 Construction and Emergency Codes
Part VI Ch. 31–39 Municipal Codes
Index

attorney as a hearing officer. The decision or, where no decision is called for, the findings shall be made by the board. However, the appellant or the applicant, as the case may be, in addition to the municipality may, prior to the decision of the hearing, waive decision or findings by the board and accept the decision or findings of the hearing officer as final. In granting a conditional use, the governing body may attach such reasonable conditions and safeguards, in addition to those expressed in the ordinance, as it may deem necessary to implement the purposes of this act in the zoning ordinance.

(b) (1) The governing body shall render a written decision or, when no decision is called for, make written findings on the conditional use application within 45 days after the last hearing before the governing body. Where the application is contested or denied, each decision shall be accompanied by findings of fact or conclusions based thereon, together with any reasons therefor. Conclusions based on any provisions of this act or of any ordinance, rule or regulation shall contain a reference to the provision relied on and the reasons why the conclusion is deemed appropriate in the light of the facts found.

(2) Where the governing body fails to render the decision within the period required by this subsection or fails to commence, conduct or complete the required hearing as provided in section 908(1.2), the decision shall be deemed to have been rendered in favor of the applicant unless the applicant has agreed in writing or on the record to an extension of time. When a decision has been rendered in favor of the applicant because of the failure of the governing body to meet or render a decision as hereinabove provided, the governing body shall give public notice of the decision within ten days from the last day it could have met to render a decision in the same manner as required by the public notice requirements of this act. If the governing body shall fail to provide such notice, the applicant may do so.

(3) Nothing in this subsection shall prejudice the right of any party opposing the application to appeal the decision to a court of competent jurisdiction. A copy of the final decision or, where no decision is called for, of the findings shall be delivered to the applicant personally or mailed to him no later than the day following its date.

§ 913.3. Parties Appellant Before the Board.—Appeals under section 909.1(a) (1), (2), (3), (4), (7), (8) and (9) may be filed with the board in writing by the landowner affected, any officer or agency of the municipality, or any person aggrieved. Requests for a variance under section 910.2 and for special exception under section 912.1 may be filed with the board by any landowner or any tenant with the permission of such landowner.

§ 914. Parties Appellant Before Board.—(914 repealed Dec. 21, 1988, P.L. 1329, No. 170)

§ 914.1. Time Limitations.—(a) No person shall be allowed to file any proceeding with the board later than 30 days after an application for development, preliminary or final, has been approved by an appropriate municipal officer, agency or body if such proceeding is designed to secure reversal or to limit the approval in any manner unless such person alleges and proves that he had no notice, knowledge, or reason to believe that such approval had been given. If such person has succeeded to his interest after such approval, he shall be bound by the knowledge of his predecessor in interest. The failure of anyone other than the landowner to appeal from an adverse decision on a tentative plan pursuant to section 709 or from an adverse decision by a zoning officer on a challenge to the validity of an ordinance or map pursuant to section 916.2 shall preclude an appeal from a final approval except in the case where the final submission substantially deviates from the approved tentative approval.

(b) All appeals from determinations adverse to the landowners shall be filed by the landowner within 30 days after notice of the determination is issued.

§ 915. Time Limitations; Persons Aggrieved.—(915 repealed Dec. 21, 1988, P.L. 1329, No. 170)

§ 915.1. Stay of Proceedings.—(a) Upon filing of any proceeding referred to in section 913.3 and during its pendency before the board, all land development pursuant to any challenged ordinance, order or approval of the zoning officer or of any agency or body, and all official action thereunder, shall be stayed unless the zoning officer or any other appropriate agency or body certifies to the board facts indicating that such stay would cause imminent peril to life or property, in which case the development or official action shall not be stayed otherwise than by a restraining order, which may be granted by the board or by the court having jurisdiction of zoning appeals, on petition, after notice to the zoning officer or other appropriate agency or body. When an application for development, preliminary or final, has been duly approved and proceedings designed to reverse or limit the approval are filed with the board by persons other than the applicant, the applicant may petition the court having jurisdiction of zoning appeals to order such persons to post bond as a condition to continuing the proceedings before the board.

(b) After the petition is presented, the court shall hold a hearing to determine if the filing of the appeal is frivolous. At the hearing, evidence may be presented on the merits of the case. It shall be the burden of the applicant for a bond to prove the appeal is frivolous. After consideration of all evidence presented, if the court determines that the appeal is frivolous, it shall grant the petition for a bond. The right to petition the court to order the appellants to post bond may be waived by the appellee, but such waiver may be revoked by him if an appeal is taken from a final decision of the court.

(c) The question whether or not such petition should be granted and the amount of the bond shall be within the sound discretion of the court. An order denying a petition for bond shall be interlocutory. An order directing the responding party to post a bond shall be interlocutory.

(d) If an appeal is taken by a respondent to the petition for a bond from an order of the court dismissing a zoning appeal for refusal to post a bond and the appellate court sustains the order of the court below to post a bond, the respondent to the petition for a bond, upon motion of the petitioner and after hearing in the court having jurisdiction of zoning appeals, shall be liable for all reasonable costs, expenses and attorney fees incurred by the petitioner.

§ 916. Stay of Proceedings.—(916 repealed Dec. 21, 1988, P.L. 1329, No. 170)

§ 916.1. Validity of Ordinance; Substantive Questions.—(a) A landowner who, on substantive grounds, desires to challenge the validity of an ordinance or map or any provision thereof which prohibits or restricts the use or development of land in which he has an interest shall submit the challenge either:

(1) to the zoning hearing board under section 909.1(a); or

(2) to the governing body under section 909.1(b)(4), together with a request for a curative amendment under section 609.1.

(b) Persons aggrieved by a use or development permitted on the land of another by an ordinance or map, or any provision thereof, who desires to challenge its validity on substantive grounds shall first submit their challenge to the zoning hearing board for a decision thereon under section 909.1(a)(1).

(c) The submissions referred to in subsections (a) and (b) shall be governed by the following:

(1) In challenges before the zoning hearing board, the challenging party shall make a written request to the board that it hold a hearing on its challenge. The request shall contain the reasons for the challenge. Where the landowner desires to challenge the validity of such ordinance and elects to proceed by curative amendment under section 609.1, his application to the governing body

shall contain, in addition to the requirements of the written request hereof, the plans and explanatory materials describing the use or development proposed by the landowner in lieu of the use or development permitted by the challenged ordinance or map. Such plans or other materials shall not be required to meet the standards prescribed for preliminary, tentative or final approval or for the issuance of a permit, so long as they provide reasonable notice of the proposed use or development and a sufficient basis for evaluating the challenged ordinance or map in light thereof. Nothing herein contained shall preclude the landowner from first seeking a final approval before submitting his challenge.

(2) If the submission is made by the landowner to the governing body under subsection (a)(2), the request also shall be accompanied by an amendment or amendments to the ordinance proposed by the landowner to cure the alleged defects therein.

(3) If the submission is made to the governing body, the municipal solicitor shall represent and advise it at the hearing or hearings referred to in section 909.1(b)(4).

(4) The governing body may retain an independent attorney to present the defense of the challenged ordinance or map on its behalf and to present their witnesses on its behalf.

(5) Based upon the testimony presented at the hearing or hearings, the governing body or the zoning board, as the case may be, shall determine whether the challenged ordinance or map is defective, as alleged by the landowner. If a challenge heard by a governing body is found to have merit, the governing body shall proceed as provided in section 609.1. If a challenge heard by a zoning hearing board is found to have merit, the decision of the zoning hearing board shall include recommended amendments to the challenged ordinance which will cure the defects found. In reaching its decision, the zoning hearing board shall consider the amendments, plans and explanatory material submitted by the landowner and shall also consider:

(i) the impact of the proposal upon roads, sewer facilities, water supplies, schools and other public service facilities;

(ii) if the proposal is for a residential use, the impact of the proposal upon regional housing needs and the effectiveness of the proposal in providing housing units of a type actually available to and affordable by classes of persons otherwise unlawfully excluded by the challenged provisions of the ordinance or map;

(iii) the suitability of the site for the intensity of use proposed by the site's soils, slopes, woodlands, wetlands, flood plains, aquifers, natural resources and other natural features;

(iv) the impact of the proposed use on the site's soils, slopes, woodlands, wetlands, flood plains, natural resources and natural features, the degree to which these are protected or destroyed, the tolerance of the resources to development and any adverse environmental impacts; and

(v) the impact of the proposal on the preservation of agriculture and other land uses which are essential to public health and welfare.

(6) The governing body or the zoning hearing board, as the case may be, shall render its decision within 45 days after the conclusion of the last hearing.

(7) If the governing body or the zoning board, as the case may be, fails to act on the landowner's request within the time limits referred to in paragraph (6), a denial of the request is deemed to have occurred on the 46th day after the close of the last hearing.

(d) The zoning hearing board or governing body, as the case may be, shall commence its hearings within 60 days after the request is filed unless the landowner requests or consents to an extension of time.

(e) Public notice of the hearing shall include notice that the validity of the ordinance or map is in question and shall give the place where and the times when a copy of the request, including any plans, explanatory material or proposed amendments may be examined by the public.

(f) The challenge shall be deemed denied when:

(1) the zoning hearing board or governing body, as the case may be, fails to commence the hearing within the time limits set forth in subsection (d);

(2) the governing body notifies the landowner that it will not adopt the curative amendment;

(3) the governing body adopts another curative amendment which is unacceptable to the landowner; or

(4) the zoning hearing board or governing body, as the case may be, fails to act on the request 45 days after the close of the last hearing on the request, unless the time is extended by mutual consent by the landowner and municipality.

(g) Where, after the effective date of this act, a curative amendment proposal is approved by the grant of a curative amendment application by the governing body pursuant to section 909.1(b)(4) or a validity challenge is sustained by the zoning hearing board pursuant to section 909.1(a)(1) or the court acts finally on appeal from denial of a curative amendment proposal or a validity challenge, and the proposal or challenge so approved requires a further application for subdivision or land development, the developer shall have two years from the date of such approval to file an application for preliminary or tentative approval pursuant to Article V or VII. Within the two-year period, no subsequent change or amendment in the zoning, subdivision or other governing ordinance or plan shall be applied in any manner which adversely affects the rights of the applicant as granted in the curative amendment or the sustained validity challenge. Upon the filing of the preliminary or tentative plan, the provisions of section 508(4) shall apply. Where the proposal appended to the curative amendment application or the validity challenge is approved but does not require further application under any subdivision or land development ordinance, the developer shall have one year within which to file for a building permit. Within the one-year period, no subsequent change or amendment in the zoning, subdivision or other governing ordinance or plan shall be applied in any manner which adversely affects the rights of the applicant as granted in the curative amendment or the sustained validity challenge. During these protected periods, the court shall retain or assume jurisdiction for the purpose of awarding such supplemental relief as may be necessary.

(h) Where municipalities have adopted a multimunicipal comprehensive plan pursuant to Article XI but have not adopted a joint municipal ordinance pursuant to Article VIII-A and all municipalities participating in the multimunicipal comprehensive plan have adopted and are administering zoning ordinances generally consistent with the provisions of the multimunicipal comprehensive plan, and a challenge is brought to the validity of a zoning ordinance of a participating municipality involving a proposed use, then the zoning hearing board or governing body, as the case may be, shall consider the availability of uses under zoning ordinances within the municipalities participating in the multimunicipal comprehensive plan within a reasonable geographic area and shall not limit its consideration to the application of the zoning ordinance on the municipality whose zoning ordinance is being challenged.

(i) A landowner who has challenged on substantive grounds the validity of a zoning ordinance or map either by submission of a curative amendment to the governing body under subsection (a)(2) of to the zoning hearing board under section 909.1(a)(1) shall not submit any additional substantive challenges involving the same parcel, group of parcels or part thereof until such time as the status of the landowner's original challenge has been finally determined or withdrawn:

Provided, however, That if after the date of the landowner's original challenge the municipality adopts a substantially new or different zoning ordinance or zoning map, the landowner may file a second substantive challenge to the new or different zoning ordinance or zoning map under subsection (a).

§ 916.2. Procedure to Obtain Preliminary Opinion.—In order not to unreasonably delay the time when a landowner may secure assurance that the ordinance or map under which he proposed to build is free from challenge, and recognizing that the procedure for preliminary approval of his development may be too cumbersome or may be unavailable, the landowner may advance the date from which time for any challenge to the ordinance or map will run under section 914.1 by the following procedure:

(1) The landowner may submit plans and other materials describing his proposed use or development to the zoning officer for a preliminary opinion as to their compliance with the applicable ordinances and maps. Such plans and other materials shall not be required to meet the standards prescribed for preliminary, tentative or final approval or for the issuance of a building permit so long as they provide reasonable notice of the proposed use or development and a sufficient basis for a preliminary opinion as to its compliance.

(2) If the zoning officer's preliminary opinion is that the use or development complies with the ordinance or map, notice thereof shall be published once each week for two successive weeks in a newspaper of general circulation in the municipality. Such notice shall include a general description of the proposed use or development and its location, by some readily identifiable directive, and the place and times where the plans and other materials may be examined by the public. The favorable preliminary approval under section 914.1 and the time therein specified for commencing a proceeding with the board shall run from the time when the second notice thereof has been published.

§ 917. Applicability of Ordinance Amendments.—When an application for either a special exception or a conditional use has been filed with either the zoning hearing board or governing body, as relevant, and the subject matter of such application would ultimately constitute either a land development as defined in section 107 or a subdivision as defined in section 107, no change or amendment of the zoning, subdivision or other governing ordinance or plans shall affect the decision on such application adversely to the applicant, and the applicant shall be entitled to a decision in accordance with the provisions of the governing ordinances or plans as they stood at the time the application was duly filed. Provided, further, should such an application be approved by either the zoning hearing board or governing body, as relevant, applicant shall be entitled to proceed with the submission of either land development or subdivision plans within a period of six months or longer as may be approved by either the zoning hearing board or the governing body following the date of such approval in accordance with the provisions of the governing ordinances or plans as they stood at the time the application was duly filed before either the zoning hearing board or governing body, as relevant. If either a land development or subdivision plan is so filed within said period, such plan shall be subject to the provisions of section 508(1) through (4) and specifically to the time limitations of section 508(4) which shall commence as of the date of filing such land development or subdivision plan.

§ 918. Special Applicability Provisions.—A municipal zoning ordinance enacted on or before August 21, 2000, shall not be invalidated, superseded or affected by any amendatory provision of the act of June 22, 2000 (P.L. 483, No. 67), entitled "An act amending the act of July 31, 1968 (P.L. 805, No. 247), entitled, as amended, 'An act to empower cities of the second class A, and third class, boroughs, incorporated towns, townships of the first and second classes including those within a county of the second class and counties of the second through eighth classes, individually or jointly, to plan their development and to govern the same by zoning, subdivision and land development ordinances, planned residential development and other ordinances, by official maps, by the reservation of certain land for future public purpose and by the acquisition of such land; to promote the conservation of energy through the use of planning practices and to promote the effective utilization of renewable energy sources; providing for the establishment of planning commissions, planning departments, planning committees and zoning hearing boards, authorizing them to charge fees, make inspections and hold public hearings; providing for mediation; providing for transferable development rights; providing for appropriations, appeals to courts and penalties for violations; and repealing acts and parts of acts,' adding definitions; providing for intergovernmental cooperative planning and implementation agreements; further providing for repeals; and making an editorial change," or the act of June 22, 2000 (P.L. 495, No. 68), entitled "An act amending the act of July 31, 1968 (P.L. 805, No. 247), entitled, as amended, 'An act to empower cities of the second class A, and third class, boroughs, incorporated towns, townships of the first and second classes including those within a county of the second class and counties of the second through eighth classes, individually or jointly, to plan their development and to govern the same by zoning, subdivision and land development ordinances, planned residential development and other ordinances, by official maps, by the reservation of certain land for future public purpose and by the acquisition of such land; to promote the conservation of energy through the use of planning practices and to promote the effective utilization of renewable energy sources; providing for the establishment of planning commissions, planning departments, planning committees and zoning hearing boards, authorizing them to charge fees, make inspections and hold public hearings; providing for mediation; providing for transferable development rights; providing for appropriations, appeals to courts and penalties for violations; and repealing acts and parts of acts,' further providing for the purpose of the act; adding certain definitions; further providing for various matters relating to the comprehensive plan and for compliance by counties; providing for funding for municipal planning and for neighboring municipalities; further providing for certain ordinances; adding provisions relating to projects of regional impact; providing for traditional neighborhood development; further providing for grant of power, for contents of subdivision and land development ordinance, for approval of plats and for recording of plats and deeds; and providing for municipal authorities and water companies and for transferable development rights," and such ordinance provisions shall continue in full force and effect until February 21, 2001; or, provided, however, any such ordinance shall be subject to such amendatory provisions on and after February 22, 2001.

ARTICLE X
Appeals

53 P.S. § 11001–11011

(Art. repealed Dec. 21, 1988, P.L. 1329, No. 170)

§ 1001. Zoning Appeals.—(1001 repealed Dec. 21, 1988, P.L. 1329, No. 170)

§ 1002. Venue.—(1002 repealed Dec. 21, 1988, P.L. 1329, No. 170)

§ 1003. Validity of Ordinance; Procedural Questions.—(1003 repealed Dec. 21, 1988, P.L. 1329, No. 170)

§ 1004. Validity of Ordinance; Substantive Questions; Landowner Appeals.—(1004 repealed Dec. 21, 1988, P.L. 1329, No. 170)

§ 1005. Validity of Ordinance; Substantive Questions; Appeals by Persons Aggrieved.—(1005 repealed Dec. 21, 1988, P.L. 1329, No. 170)

§ 1006. Applications, Decisions and Orders Not Involving the Validity of an Ordinance; Landowner Appeals.—(1006 repealed Dec. 21, 1988, P.L. 1329, No. 170)

§ 1007. Decisions and Orders Not Involving the Validity of an Ordinance; Appeals by Persons Aggrieved.—(1007 repealed Dec. 21, 1988, P.L. 1329, No. 170)

§ 1008. Appeals to Court; Commencement; Stay of Proceedings.—(1008 repealed Dec. 21, 1988, P.L. 1329, No. 170)

§ 1009. Intervention.—(1009 repealed Dec. 21, 1988, P.L. 1329, No. 170)

§ 1010. Hearing and Argument of Zoning Appeal.—(1010 repealed Dec. 21, 1988, P.L. 1329, No. 170)

§ 1011. Judicial Relief.—(1011 repealed Dec. 21, 1988, P.L. 1329, No. 170)

ARTICLE X-A
Appeals to Court

53 P.S. § 11001-A–11006-A

§ 1001-A. Land Use Appeals.—The procedures set forth in this article shall constitute the exclusive mode for securing review of any decision rendered pursuant to Article IX or deemed to have been made under this act.

§ 1002-A. Jurisdiction and Venue on Appeal; Time for Appeal.—(a) All appeals from all land use decisions rendered pursuant to Article IX shall be taken to the court of common pleas of the judicial district wherein the land is located and shall be filed within 30 days after entry of the decision as provided in 42 Pa.C.S. § 5572 (relating to time of entry of order) or, in the case of a deemed decision, within 30 days after the date upon which notice of said deemed decision is given as set forth in section 908(9) of this act. It is the express intent of the general assembly that, except in cases in which an unconstitutional deprivation of due process would result from its application, the 30-day limitation in this section should be applied in all appeals from decisions.

(b) Challenges to the validity of a land use ordinance raising procedural questions or alleged defects in the process of enactment or adoption shall be raised by appeal taken directly to the court of common pleas of the judicial district in which the municipality adopting the ordinance is located in accordance with 42 Pa.C.S. § 5571.1 (relating to appeals from ordinances, resolutions, maps, etc.).

§ 1002.1-A. Time for appeal; procedural defects of decisions.—(a) This section shall apply to all appeals challenging the validity of a land use decision on the basis of a defect in procedures prescribed by statute or ordinance.

(b) Except as otherwise provided in section 108, all appeals challenging the validity of a decision solely on the basis of a defect in procedure shall be filed within the time period provided in section 1002-A(a) unless a party establishes each of the following:

(1) that the person filing the appeal had insufficient actual or constructive notice of the decision to permit filing an appeal within the time period provided in section 1002-A(a). Notice of a hearing prior to the entry of a decision in accordance with section 908(1), notice of a decision in accordance with section 908(10) or notice of a deemed decision provided in accordance with this act shall establish constructive notice as a matter of law in any appeal under this section.

(2) that because of the insufficient actual or constructive notice of the decision, the application of the time limitation in section 1002-A(a) would result in an impermissible deprivation of constitutional rights.

(c) appeals under this section shall only be permitted by an aggrieved person who can establish that reliance on the validity of the challenged decision resulted or could result in a use of property that directly affects such person's substantive property rights.

(d) no decision challenged in an appeal pursuant to this section shall be deemed void from inception except as follows:

(1) in the case of an appeal brought within the time period provided in section 1002-a(a), the party alleging the defect must meet the burden of proving that there was a failure to strictly comply with procedure.

(2) in the case of an appeal exempt from the time period provided in section 1002-A(a) or brought pursuant to section 108, the party alleging the defect must meet the burden of proving that because of the alleged defect in procedure alone:

(i) the public was denied notice sufficient to permit participation in the proceedings prior to the entry of the decision to the extent such participation was authorized by statute or ordinance; or

(ii) those whose substantive property rights were or could be directly affected by the entry of the decision were denied an opportunity to participate in proceedings prior to the entry of the decision.

(e) substantial compliance with notice of a hearing required prior to the entry of a decision in accordance with section 908(1) shall establish notice adequate to permit public participation as a matter of law in any appeal under this section.

(f) an adjudication that a decision is void from inception shall not affect any previously acquired rights of property owners who have exercised good faith reliance on the validity of the decision prior to the determination.

§ 1003-A. Appeals to Court; Commencement; Stay of Proceedings.—(a) Land use appeals shall be entered as of course by the prothonotary or clerk upon the filing of a land use appeal notice which concisely sets forth the grounds on which the appellant relies. The appeal notice need not be verified. The land use appeal notice shall be accompanied by a true copy thereof.

(b) Upon filing of a land use appeal, the prothonotary or clerk shall forthwith, as of course, send to the governing body, board or agency whose decision or action has been appealed, by registered or certified mail, the copy of the land use appeal notice, together with a writ of certiorari commanding said governing body, board or agency, within 20 days after receipt thereof, to certify to the court its entire record in the matter in which the land use appeal has been taken, or a true and complete copy thereof, including any transcript of testimony in existence and available to the governing body, board or agency at the time it received the writ of certiorari.

(c) If the appellant is a person other than the landowner of the land directly involved in the decision or action appealed from, the appellant, within seven days after the land use appeal is filed, shall serve a true copy of the land use appeal notice by mailing said notice to the landowner or his attorney at his last known address. For identification of such landowner, the appellant may rely upon the record of the municipality and, in the event of good faith mistakes as to such identity, may make such service nunc pro tunc by leave of court.

(d) The filing of an appeal in court under this section shall not stay the action appealed from, but the appellants may petition the court having jurisdiction of land use appeals for a stay. If the appellants are persons who are seeking to prevent a use or development of the land of another, whether or not a stay

Table of Contents | Part I Ch. 1–3 Ethics, Records, Open Meetings | Part II Ch. 4–10 Taxation | Part III Ch. 11–18 Torts, Contracts & Civil Rules | Part IV Ch. 19–24 Zoning & Planning | Part V Ch. 25–30 Construction and Emergency Codes | Part VI Ch. 31–39 Municipal Codes | Index

is sought by them, the landowner whose use or development is in question may petition the court to order the appellants to post bond as a condition to proceeding with the appeal. After the petition for posting a bond is presented, the court shall hold a hearing to determine if the filing of the appeal is frivolous. At the hearing, evidence may be presented on the merits of the case. It shall be the burden of the landowners to prove the appeal is frivolous. After consideration of all evidence presented, if the court determines that the appeal is frivolous, it shall grant the petition for posting a bond. The right to petition the court to order the appellants to post bond may be waived by the appellee, but such waiver may be revoked by him if an appeal is taken from a final decision of the court. The question of the amount of the bond shall be within the sound discretion of the court. An order denying a petition for bond shall be interlocutory. An order directing the respondent to the petition for posting a bond to post a bond shall be interlocutory. If an appeal is taken by a respondent to the petition for posting a bond from an order of the court dismissing a land use appeal for refusal to post a bond, such responding party, upon motion of petitioner and, after hearing in the court having jurisdiction of land use appeals, shall be liable for all reasonable costs, expenses and attorney fees incurred by petitioner.

§ 1004-A. Intervention.—Within the 30 days first following the filing of a land use appeal, if the appeal is from a board or agency of a municipality, the municipality and any owner or tenant of property directly involved in the action appealed from may intervene as of course by filing a notice of intervention, accompanied by proof of service of the same, upon each appellant or each appelant's counsel of record. All other intervention shall be governed by the Pennsylvania Rules of Civil Procedure.

§ 1005-A. Hearing and Argument of Land Use Appeal.—If, upon motion, it is shown that proper consideration of the land use appeal requires the presentation of additional evidence, a judge of the court may hold a hearing to receive additional evidence, may remand the case to the body, agency or officer whose decision or order has been brought up for review, or may refer the case to a referee to receive additional evidence, provided that appeals brought before the court pursuant to section 916.1 shall not be remanded for further hearings before any body, agency or officer of the municipality. If the record below includes findings of fact made by the governing body, board or agency whose decision or action is brought up for review and the court does not take additional evidence or appoint a referee to take additional evidence, the findings of the governing body, board or agency shall not be disturbed by the court if supported by substantial evidence. If the record does not include findings of fact or if additional evidence is taken by the court or by a referee, the court shall make its own findings of fact based on the record below as supplemented by the additional evidence, if any.

§ 1006-A. Judicial Relief.—(a) In a land use appeal, the court shall have power to declare any ordinance or map invalid and set aside or modify any action, decision or order of the governing body, agency or officer of the municipality brought up on appeal.

(b) Where municipalities have adopted a joint municipal comprehensive plan and enacted a zoning ordinance or ordinances consistent with the joint municipal comprehensive plan within a region pursuant to Articles VIII-A and XI, the court, when determining the validity of a challenge to such a municipality's zoning ordinance, shall consider the zoning ordinance or ordinances as they apply to the entire region and shall not limit its consideration to the application of the zoning ordinance within the boundaries of the respective municipalities.

(b)(1) Notwithstanding any provision of this section to the contrary, each municipality shall provide for reasonable coal mining activities in its zoning ordinance. [Ed. note: Acts 67 & 68 of 2000 both added (b)(1). The section above appears misplaced.]

(b)(1) Where municipalities have adopted a multimunicipal comprehensive plan pursuant to Article XI but have not adopted a joint municipal ordinance pursuant to Article VIII-A and all municipalities participating in the multimunicipal comprehensive plan have adopted and are administering zoning ordinances generally consistent with the provisions of the multimunicipal comprehensive plan, and a challenge is brought to the validity of a zoning ordinance of a participating municipality involving a proposed use, then the court shall consider the availability of uses under zoning ordinances within the municipalities participating in the multimunicipal comprehensive plan within a reasonable geographic area and shall not limit its consideration to the application of the zoning ordinance on the municipality whose zoning ordinance is being challenged.

(c) If the court finds that an ordinance or map, or a decision or order thereunder, which has been brought up for review unlawfully prevents or restricts a development or use which has been described by the landowner through plans and other materials submitted to the governing body, agency or officer of the municipality whose action or failure to act is in question on the appeal, it may order the described development or use approved as to all elements or it may order it approved as to some elements and refer other elements to the governing body, agency or officer having jurisdiction thereof for further proceedings, including the adoption of alternative restrictions, in accordance with the court's opinion and order.

(d) Upon motion by any of the parties or upon motion by the court, the judge of the court may hold a hearing or hearings to receive additional evidence or employ experts to aid the court to frame an appropriate order. If the court employs an expert, the report or evidence of such expert shall be available to any party and he shall be subject to examination or cross-examination by any party. He shall be paid reasonable compensation for his services which may be assessed against any or all of the parties as determined by the court. The court shall retain jurisdiction of the appeal during the pendency of any such further proceedings and may, upon motion of the landowner, issue such supplementary orders as it deems necessary to protect the rights of the landowner as declared in its opinion and order.

(e) The fact that the plans and other materials are not in a form or are not accompanied by other submissions which are required for final approval of the development or use in question or for the issuance of permits shall not prevent the court from granting the definitive relief authorized. The court may act upon preliminary or sketch plans by framing its decree to take into account the need for further submissions before final approval is granted.

ARTICLE XI

Intergovernmental Cooperative Planning and Implementation Agreements

53 P.S. §§ 11101–11107

§ 1101. Purposes.—It is the purpose of this article:

(1) To provide for development that is compatible with surrounding land uses and that will complement existing land development with a balance of commercial, industrial and residential uses.

(2) To protect and maintain the separate identity of Pennsylvania's communities and to prevent the unnecessary conversion of valuable and limited agricultural land.

(3) To encourage cooperation and coordinated planning among adjoining municipalities so that each municipality accommodates its share of the mul-

Table of Contents
Part I Ch. 1–3 Ethics, Records, Open Meetings
Part II Ch. 4–10 Taxation
Part III Ch. 11–18 Torts, Contracts & Civil Rules
Part IV Ch. 19–24 Zoning & Planning
Part V Ch. 25–30 Construction and Emergency Codes
Part VI Ch. 31–39 Municipal Codes
Index

timunicipal growth burden and does not induce unnecessary or premature development of rural lands.

(4) To minimize disruption of the economy and environment of existing communities.

(5) To complement the economic and transportation needs of the region and this Commonwealth.

(6) To provide for the continuation of historic community patterns.

(7) To provide for coordinated highways, public services and development.

(8) To ensure that new public water and wastewater treatment systems are constructed in areas that will result in the efficient utilization of existing systems, prior to the development and construction of new systems.

(9) To ensure that new or major extension of existing public water and wastewater treatment systems are constructed only in those areas within which anticipated growth and development can adequately be sustained within the financial and evnironmental resources of the area.

(10) To identify those areas where growth and development will occur so that a full range of public infrastructure services including sewer, water, highways, police and fire protection, public schools, parks, open space and other services can be adequately planned and provided as needed to accommodate the growth that occurs.

(11) To encourage innovations in residential, commercial and industrial development to meet growing population demands by an increased variety in type, design and layout of structures and by the conservation and more efficient use of open space ancillary to such structures.

(12) To facilitate the development of affordable and other types of housing in numbers consistent with the need for such housing as shown by existing and projected population and employment data for the region.

§ 1102. Intergovernmental Cooperative Planning and Implementation Agreements.—For the purpose of developing, adopting and implementing a comprehensive plan for the entire county or for any area within the county, the governing bodies of municipalities located within the county or counties may enter into intergovernmental cooperative agreements, as provided by 53 Pa.C.S. Ch. 23 Such. A (relating to intergovernmental cooperation), except for any provisions permitting initiative and referendum. Such agreements may also be entered into between and among counties and municipalities for areas that include municipalities in more than one county, and between and among counties, municipalities, authorities and special districts providing water and sewer facilities, transportation planning or other services within the area of a plan and with the opportunity for the active participation of State agencies and school districts. Implementation of the comprehensive plan and subdivision and zoning ordinances shall be accomplished in accordance with articles of this act.

§ 1103. County or Multimunicipal Comprehensive Plans.—(a) The comprehensive plan that is the subject of an agreement may be developed by the municipalities or at the request of the municipalities, by the county planning agency, or agencies in the case of a plan covering municipalities in more than one county, in cooperation with municipalities within the area and shall include all the elements required or authorized in section 301 for the region of the plan, including a plan to meet the housing needs of present residents and those individuals and families anticipated to reside in the area of the plan, which may include conservation of presently sound housing, rehabilitation of housing in declining neighborhoods and the accommodations of expected new housing in different dwelling types and of appropriate densities for households of all income levels. The plan may:

(1) Designate growth areas where:

(i) Orderly and efficient development to accommodate the projected growth of the area within the next 20 years is planned for residential and mixed use densities of one unit or more per acre.

(ii) Commercial, industrial and institutional uses to provide for the economic and employment needs of the area and to insure that the area has an adequate tax base are planned for.

(iii) Services to serve such development are provided or planned for.

(2) Designate potential future growth areas where future development is planned for densities to accompany the orderly extension and provision of services.

(3) Designate rural resource areas, if applicable, where:

(i) Rural resource uses are planned for.

(ii) Development at densities that are compatible with rural resource uses are or may be permitted.

(iii) Infrastructure extensions or improvements are not intended to be publicly financed by municipalities except in villages, unless the participating or affected municipalities agree that such service should be provided to an area for health or safety reasons or to accomplish one or more of the purposes set forth in section 1101.

(4) Plan for the accommodation of all categories of uses within the area of the plan, provided, however, that all uses need not be provided in every municipality, but shall be planned and provided for within a reasonable geographic area of the plan.

(5) Plan for developments of area wide significance and impact, particularly those identified in section 301(3) and (4).

(6) Plan for the conservation and enhancement of the natural, scenic, historic and aesthetic resources within the area of the plan.

(b) The county may facilitate a multimunicipal process and may enter into cooperative planning agreements with participating municipalities governing particular planning subjects and responsibilities. The planning process shall include a public participation process to assure that all governing bodies, municipal authorities, school districts and agencies, whether public or private, having jurisdiction or operating within the area of the plan and landowners and citizens affected by the plan have an opportunity to be heard prior to the public hearings required for the adoption of the plan under section 302(a).

(c) Adoption of the plan and plan amendments shall conform to the requirements of section 302, and may be reflected on the official map of each participating municipality pursuant to section 401. Where a county and municipality have developed and adopted a comprehensive county or multimunicipal plan that conforms to the requirements of this article within five years prior to the date of adoption of this article, the plan may be implemented by agreements as provided for in this article.

§ 1104. Implementation Agreements.—(a) In order to implement multimunicipal comprehensive plans, under section 1103 counties and municipalities shall have authority to enter in intergovernmental cooperative agreements.

(b) Cooperative implementation agreements shall:

(1) Establish the process that the participating municipalities will use to achieve general consistency between the county or multimunicipal comprehensive plan and zoning ordinances, subdivision and land development and capital improvement plans within participating municipalities, including adoption of conforming ordinances by participating municipalities within two years and a mechanism for resolving disputes over the interpretation of

the multimunicipal comprehensive plan and the consistency of implementing plans and ordinances.

(2) Establish a process for review and approval of developments of regional significance and impact that are proposed within any participating municipality. Subdivision and land development approval powers under this act shall only be exercised by the municipality in which the property where the approval is sought. Under no circumstances shall a subdivision or land development applicant be required to undergo more than one approval process.

(3) Establish the role and responsibilities of participating municipalities with respect to implementation of the plan, including the provision of public infrastructure services within participating municipalities as described in subsection (d), the provision of affordable housing, and purchase of real property, including rights-of-way and easements.

(4) Require a yearly report by participating municipalities to the county planning agency and by the county planning agency to the participating municipalities concerning activities carried out pursuant to the agreement during the previous year. Such reports shall include summaries of public infrastructure needs in growth areas and progress toward meeting those needs through capital improvement plans and implementing actions, and reports on development applications and dispositions for residential, commercial, and industrial development in each participating municipality for the purpose of evaluating the extent of provision for all categories of use and housing for all income levels within the region of the plan.

(5) Describe any other duties and responsibilities as may be agreed upon by the parties.

(c) Cooperative implementation agreements may designate growth areas, future growth areas and rural resource areas within the plan. The agreement shall also provide a process for amending the multimunicipal comprehensive plan and redefining the designated growth area, future growth area and rural resource area within the plan.

(d) The county may facilitate convening representatives of municipalities, municipal authorities, special districts, public utilities, whether public or private, or other agencies that provide or declare an interest in providing a public infrastructure service in a public infrastructure service area or a portion of a public infrastructure service area within a growth area, as established in a county or multimunicipal comprehensive plan, for the purpose of negotiating agreements for the provision of such services. The county may provide or contract with others to provide technical assistance, mediation or dispute resolution services in order to assist the parties in negotiating such agreements.

§ 1105. Legal Effect.—(a) Where municipalities have adopted a county plan or a multimunicipal plan is adopted under this article and the participating municipalities have conformed their local plan and ordinances to the county or multimunicipal plan by implementing cooperative agreements and adopting appropriate resolutions and ordinances, the following shall apply:

(1) Sections 916.1 and 1006-A.

(2) State agencies shall consider and may rely upon comprehensive plans and zoning ordinances when reviewing applications for the funding or permitting of infrastructure or facilities.

(3) State agencies shall consider and may give priority consideration to applications for financial or technical assistance for projects consistent with the county or multimunicipal plan.

(b) Participating municipalities that have entered into implementation agreements to carry out a county or multimunicipal plan as described in this article shall have the following additional powers:

(1) To provide by cooperative agreement for the sharing of tax revenues and fees by municipalities within the region of the plan.

(2) To adopt a transfer of development rights program by adoption of an ordinance applicable to the region of the plan so as to enable development rights to be transferred from rural resource areas in any municipality within the plan to designate growth areas in any municipality within the plan.

(c) Nothing in this article shall be construed to authorize a municipality to regulate the allocation or withdrawal of water resources by a municipal authority or water company that is otherwise regulated by the Pennsylvania Public Utility Commission or other Federal or State agencies or statutes.

(d) Except as provided in section 619.2, nothing in this article shall be construed as limiting the authority of the Pennsylvania Public Utility Commission over the implementation, location, construction and maintenance of public utility facilities and the rendering of public utility services to the public.

§ 1106. Specific Plans.—(a) Participating municipalities shall have authority to adopt a specific plan for the systematic implementation of a county or multimunicipal comprehensive plan for any nonresidential part of the area covered by the plan. Such specific plan shall include a text and a diagram or diagrams and implementing ordinances which specify all of the following in detail:

(1) The distribution, location, extent of area and standards for land uses and facilities, including design of sewage, water, drainage and other essential facilities needed to support the land uses.

(2) The location, classification and design of all transportation facilities, including, but not limited to, street and roads needed to serve the land uses described in the specific plan.

(3) Standards for population density, land coverage, building intensity and supporting services, including utilities.

(4) Standards for the preservation, conservation, development and use of natural resources, including the protection of significant open spaces, resource lands and agricultural lands within or adjacent to the area covered by the specific plan.

(5) A program of implementation including regulations, financing of the capital improvements and provisions for repealing or amending the specific plan. Regulations may include zoning, storm water, subdivision and land development, highway access and any other provisions for which municipalities are authorized by law to enact. The regulations may be amended into the county or municipal ordinances or adopted as separate ordinances. If enacted as separate ordinances for the area covered by the specific plan, the ordinances shall repeal and replace any county or municipal ordinances in effect within the area covered by the specific plan and ordinances shall conform to the provisions of the specific plan.

(b) (1) No specific plan may be adopted or amended unless the proposed plan or amendment is consistent with an adopted county or multi-municipal comprehensive plan.

(2) No capital project by any municipal authority or municipality shall be approved or undertaken, and no final plan, development plan or plat for any subdivision or development of land shall be approved unless such projects, plans or plats are consistent with the adopted specific plan.

(c) In adopting or amending a specific plan, a county and participating municipalities shall use the same procedures as provided in this article for adopting comprehensive plans and ordinances.

(d) Whenever a specific plan has been adopted, applicants for subdivision or land development approval shall be required to submit only a final plan as provided in Article V, provided that such final plan is consistent with and implements the adopted specific plan.

(e) A county or counties and participating municipalities are prohibited from assessing subdivision and land development applicants for the cost of the specific plan.

§ 1107. Saving Clause.

(a) The passage of this act and the repeal by it of any prior enabling laws relating to regional planning shall not invalidate any regional planning commission created under such other laws. This act, in such respect, shall be deemed a continuation and codification of such prior enabling laws.

(b) The amendment of this article shall not invalidate any joint municipal planning commission established under the former provisions of this article. A joint municipal planning commission shall continue to function under the amended provisions of this article.

ARTICLE XI-A

Wastewater processing cooperative planning

(Second Class-A Counties)

53 PS §§ 1101-A to 1104-A

§ 1101-A. Definitions.

The following words and phrases when used in this article shall have the meanings given to them in this section unless the context clearly indicates otherwise:

"Department." The Department of Environmental Protection of the Commonwealth.

"Wastewater system official." Either:

(1) the manager of a wastewater system; or

(2) if a manager is not employed to oversee a wastewater system, the system municipal officials of the municipality in which the wastewater system exists.

§ 1102-A. Notification requirement.

(a) Notice to wastewater systems official.—

(1) Except as provided in paragraph (2), notwithstanding any other provision of law, this section applies to a person who files an application for:

(i) development, plat approval, planned residential development or waiver of land development under this act; or

(ii) a construction permit under section 502 of the act of November 10, 1999 (P.L.491, No.45), known as the Pennsylvania Construction Code Act.

(2) This article does not apply to:

(i) an application that involves new construction or alteration or renovation of a one-family or two-family dwelling;

(ii) an application that has an approved sewer module; or

(iii) an application for which the department has issued a determination that sewage planning is not required or has granted an exemption from sewage planning.

(3) A person subject to this subsection shall provide written notification of filing the application to the wastewater system official serving the property identified in the application. A copy of the written notification shall be provided by the person to the municipality.

(b) Failure to notify.—No application subject to subsection (a) may be deemed by the municipality to be administratively complete until the municipality receives a copy of the written notification required by subsection (a).

§ 1103-A. Review by wastewater system officials.

(a) Wastewater systems review.—

(1) Upon receipt of the notification required under section 1102-A(a), the wastewater system official shall review the notification to determine the impact of the application on the wastewater system. The wastewater system official may request additional information, including a copy of the application, from the applicant.

(2) (i) Except as provided under subparagraph (ii), review by the wastewater system official shall be completed within 30 days of receipt of the notification required under section 1102-A. For good cause shown, the wastewater system official may request and the municipality shall grant an extension of up to 15 days for completion of the review.

(ii) If another statute establishes an application review period of 30 days or less, the review period and extension provided under subparagraph (i) shall not apply and the wastewater system official shall complete the review within the review period provided by that statute.

(3) If a municipality does not receive any notice from the wastewater system official within the time period provided under paragraph (2), the municipality shall proceed with the application as if the application is in compliance with the requirements of the wastewater system.

(b) Notification of results of review.—

(1) Upon completion of the review required under subsection (a), the wastewater system official shall notify the applicant and the municipality in writing of its findings, which shall include a statement regarding the expected impact of the application on the current wastewater system.

(2) If the application will cause the wastewater system to exceed its permitted capacity or will result in necessary upgrades to the wastewater system's infrastructure, the written notice of the wastewater system official shall include the specific reasons that are causing the wastewater system to exceed its permitted capacity or the necessity for upgrades to the wastewater system's infrastructure.

(c) Approval of applications.—Except for applications which are exempt from the provisions of this article as provided under section 1102-A(a)(2), a municipality may not:

(1) grant final approval of an application for development, plat approval or planned residential development under this act unless final approval is conditioned upon receipt of a waiver of or an approved exemption from sewage planning or written approval of the application is received from the wastewater system official; or

(2) approve an application for a construction permit under section 502 of the act of November 10, 1999 (P.L.491, No.45), known as the Pennsylvania Construction Code Act, unless the application has been reviewed under this section.

(d) Right of appeal.—Any person aggrieved by a decision of a wastewater system official shall be entitled to seek the remedies provided under the act of January 24, 1966 (1965 P.L.1535, No.537), known as the Pennsylvania Sewage Facilities Act.

§ 1104-A. Applicability.

This article shall apply as follows:

(1) This article shall apply to applications for development, plat approval, planned residential development, waiver of land development or construction permits if the development or construction utilizes wastewater treatment service provided by a county wastewater treatment authority incorporated in a county of the second class A.

(2) This article shall apply to all municipalities served by the authority under paragraph (1).

Table of Contents | Part I Ch. 1–3 Ethics, Records, Open Meetings | Part II Ch. 4–10 Taxation | Part III Ch. 11–18 Torts, Contracts & Civil Rules | Part IV Ch. 19–24 Zoning & Planning | Part V Ch. 25–30 Construction and Emergency Codes | Part VI Ch. 31–39 Municipal Codes | Index

ARTICLE XII

Repeals

53 P.S. § 11201–11202

§ 1201. Specific Repeals.—The following acts and parts of acts and amendments thereof are repealed to the extent hereinafter specified:

(1) Section 12, act of May 16, 1891 (P.L. 75, No. 59), entitled "An act in relation to the laying out, opening, widening, straightening, extending or vacating streets and alleys, and the construction of bridges in the several municipalities of this Commonwealth, the grading, paving, macadamizing or otherwise improving streets and alleys, providing for ascertaining the damages to private property resulting therefrom, the assessment of the damages, costs and expenses thereof upon the property benefited, and the construction of sewers and payment of the damages, costs and expenses thereof, including damages to private property resulting therefrom," as to cities of the second class A, incorporated towns and townships of the first and second class.

(2) Sections 1151, 1152, 1153, 1154, 1155, 1156, 1601, 1602, 1603, 1604, 1605, 1606, 1607, 1608, 1609, 1711, 1721, 1722, 2706, 2707, 3201, 3202, 3203, 3204, 3205, 3206, 3207, 3208, 3209 and 3210, act of February 1, 1966 (P.L. 1656, No. 581), known as "The Borough Code," absolutely.

(3) Sections 2001, 3015, 3016, 3061, 3062, 3063, 3064, 3065, 3066, 3067, 3068, 3101, 3102, 3103, 3104, 3105, 3106, 3107, 3107.1, 3107.2, 3108, 3109, 3110, 3111, 3201, 3202 and 3203, act of June 24, 1931 (P.L. 1206, No. 331), known as "The First Class Township Code," reenacted and amended May 27, 1949 (P.L. 1955, No. 569), absolutely.

(4) Sections 2901, 2902, 2903, 2904, 2905, 2906, 3701, 3702, 4001, 4002, 4003, 4004, 4005, 4006, 4101, 4102, 4103, 4104, 4105, 4106, 4107, 4110, 4111, 4112, 4113, 4114, 4120, 4121, 4122, 4123, 4124, 4125, 4126, 4127, 4128 and 4129, act of June 23, 1931 (P.L. 932, No. 317), known as "The Third Class City Code," reenacted and amended June 28, 1951 (P.L. 662, No. 164), absolutely.

(5) Sections 1201-A, 1202-A, 1203-A, 1204-A, 1205-A, 1206-A, 1207-A, 1208-A, 1907.1, 1907.2, 2001, 2002, 2003, 2004, 2005, 2006, 2007, 2008, 2009, 2010, 2051, 2052, 2053, 2054, 2055, 2056 and 2057, act of May 1, 1993 (P.L. 103, No. 69), known as "The Second Class Township Code," reenacted and amended July 10, 1947 (P.L. 1481, No. 567), absolutely.

(6) The act of April 18, 1945 (P.L. 258, No. 117), entitled "An act requiring cities, boroughs, towns and townships to notify adjacent political subdivisions of proposed streets, roads and highways leading into them," as to cities of the second A and third class, boroughs, incorporated towns and townships of the first and second class.

(7) Sections 2001, 2002, 2003, 2004, 2005, 2006, 2007, 2008, 2009, 2010, 2011, 2020, 2021, 2022, 2023, 2024, 2025, 2026, 2027, 2028, 2029, 2030, 2031, 2032, 2033, 2034, 2035, 2036, 2037, 2038 and 2039, act of August 9, 1955 (P.L. 323, No. 130), known as "The County Code," absolutely.

(8) Sections 2201 through 2211 and 2220 through 2239, act of July 28, 1953 (P.L. 723, No. 230), known as the "Second Class County Code," in so far as they relate to counties of the second class A.

§ 1202. General Repeal.—All other acts and parts of acts are repealed in so far as they are inconsistent herewith, but this act shall not repeal or modify any of the provisions of 66 Pa.C.S. Pt. I (relating to Public Utility Code), 68 Pa.C.S. Pt. II Subpt. B (relating to condominiums) or any laws administered by the Department of Transportation of the Commonwealth of Pennsylvania.

CHAPTER 19.1

WIRELESS BROADBAND COLLOCATION ACT

53 P.S. §§ 11702.1–11702.6

TABLE OF CONTENTS

---

§ 1. Short title.

This act shall be known and may be cited as the Wireless Broadband Collocation Act.

§ 2. Definitions.

The following words and phrases when used in this act shall have the meanings given to them in this section unless the context clearly indicates otherwise:

"Accessory equipment." Any equipment serving or being used in conjunction with a wireless telecommunications facility or wireless support structure. The term includes utility or transmission equipment, power supplies, generators, batteries, cables, equipment buildings, cabinets and storage sheds, shelters or similar structures.

"Antenna." Telecommunications equipment that transmits and receives electromagnetic radio signals used in the provision of all types of wireless telecommunications services.

"Application." A formal request submitted to the municipality to modify a wireless support structure, equipment compound or a wireless telecommunications facility.

"Base Station." A station at a specified site authorized to communicate with mobile stations, generally consisting of radio transceivers, antennas, coaxial cables, power supplies and other associated electronics.

"Collocation." The placement or installation of new wireless telecommunications facilities on previously approved and constructed wireless support structures, including self-supporting or guyed monopoles and towers, electrical transmission towers, water towers or any other structure not classified as a wireless support structure that can support the placement or installation of wireless telecommunications facilities if approved by the municipality. The term includes the placement, replacement or modification of accessory equipment within a previously approved equipment compound.

"Electrical transmission tower." An electrical transmission structure used to support overhead power lines consisting of 69 kilovolt or greater conducting lines, generally of steel construction and having a height of at least 75 feet. The term shall not include any utility pole having a height of less than 75 feet.

"Equipment compound." An area surrounding or adjacent to a wireless support structure within which base stations, power supplies or accessory equipment are located.

"Judiciary Act Repealer Act." The act of April 28, 1978 (P.L.202, No.53), known as the Judiciary Act Repealer Act.

"Modification" or "modify." The improvement, upgrade or expansion of existing wireless telecommunications facilities or base stations on an existing wireless support structure or the improvement, upgrade or expansion of the wireless telecommunications facilities located within an existing equipment compound, if the improvement, upgrade, expansion or replacement does not substantially change the physical dimensions of the wireless support structure.

"Municipality." Any city of the first, second, second class A or third class, borough, incorporated town, township of the first or second class, county of the second class through eighth class, home rule municipality or any similar general purpose unit of government which shall hereafter be created by the General Assembly that has adopted land use or zoning regulations.

"Pennsylvania Municipalities Planning Code." The act of July 31, 1968 (P.L.805, No.247), known as the Pennsylvania Municipalities Planning Code.

"Replacement." The replacement of existing wireless telecommunications facilities on an existing wireless support structure or within an existing equipment compound due to maintenance, repair or technological advancement with equipment composed of the same wind loading and structural loading that is substantially similar in size, weight and height as the wireless telecommunications facilities initially installed and that does not substantially change the physical dimensions of the existing wireless support structure.

"Substantial change" or "substantially change."

(1) Any increase in the height of the wireless support structure by more than 10%, or by the height of one additional antenna array with separation from the nearest existing antenna not to exceed 20 feet, whichever is greater, except that the mounting of the proposed wireless telecommunications facility may exceed the size limits set forth in this paragraph if necessary to avoid interference with existing antennas.

(2) Any further increase in the height of a wireless support structure which has already been extended by more than 10% of its originally approved height or by the height of one additional antenna array in accordance with the provisions of this act shall not occur without municipal approval.

"Water tower." A standpipe or an elevated tank situated on a support structure, both of which shall be constructed of steel, have a height of at least 75 feet and be used as a reservoir or facility to deliver water.

"Wireless support structure." A freestanding structure, such as a guyed or self-supporting monopole or tower, electrical transmission tower, water tower or other structure not classified as a wireless support structure, that could support the placement or installation of wireless telecommunications facilities if approved by the municipality.

"Wireless telecommunications facility." The set of equipment and network components, including antennas, transmitters, receivers, base stations, cabling and accessory equipment, used to provide wireless data and telecommunications services. The term shall not include the wireless support structure.

§ 3. Regulation of wireless support structures

(a) Limitations.—Municipalities that have adopted zoning ordinances and land use regulations for the placement of wireless support structures may not require any additional requirements on the applicant for the collocation on a wireless support structure or the modification of a wireless telecommunications facility that has the force or effect of:

(1) Regulating the collocation, replacement or modification of antennas, accessory equipment or wireless telecommunications facilities upon an existing wireless support structure or within an existing equipment compound.

(2) Imposing additional costs, except the appropriate and reasonable permit fees, or operating restrictions on an applicant for the replacement, collocation or modification of wireless telecommunications facilities upon existing wireless support structures or within existing equipment compounds.

(3) Requiring payment of a zoning permit fee to accompany any application, the amount of which fee is in excess of the municipality's actual, reasonable costs to review and process the application or $1,000, whichever is less.

(4) Requiring an applicant to provide justification for radio frequency need.

(5) Acting to prohibit or have the effect of prohibiting the provision of mobile service as provided in 47 U.S.C. §332 (c)(7)(B)(i) (relating to regulatory treatment of mobile services).

(6) Requiring an applicant to justify the need for or the technical, business or service characteristics of the proposed wireless telecommunications facilities.

(b) (Reserved).

§ 4. Processing of applications.

(a) General rule.—Notwithstanding the Pennsylvania Municipalities Planning Code or other land use or zoning ordinances or regulations, an application for replacement, collocation or modification of a wireless telecommunications facility or wireless support structure entitled to processing under this section shall be reviewed for conformance with the municipality's applicable building permit requirements, including requirements applicable to the added structural loading of the proposed antennas and accessory equipment, but shall not be subject to the issuance of new zoning or land use approvals or review beyond the initial zoning or land use approvals issued for the previously approved wireless support structure or wireless telecommunications facility. Replacement of wireless telecommunications facilities on existing wireless support structures or within existing equipment compounds may be performed by the applicant without obtaining building or zoning permits from the municipality.

(b) Applications.—An application shall be deemed complete when all documents, information and fees specifically enumerated in the municipality's regulations, ordinances and forms pertaining to the location, modification or operation of wireless telecommunications facilities are submitted by the applicant to the municipality. The following shall apply:

(1) Within 30 calendar days of the date an application for modification or collocation is filed with the municipality, the municipality shall notify the applicant in writing of any information required to complete the application. If additional information is required to complete the application, the time required by the applicant to provide the information shall not be counted toward the 90 calendar day review period under paragraph (2).

(2) Within 90 calendar days of the date an application for modification or collocation of a wireless telecommunications facility is filed with the municipality, unless another date is specified in a written agreement between the municipality and the applicant, the municipality shall do all of the following:

(i) Make its final decision to approve the application.

(ii) Advise the applicant in writing of its final decision.

(3) If the municipality fails to act upon an application for the modification or collocation of wireless telecommunications facilities within 90 calendar days as provided under paragraph (2), the application shall be deemed approved. If

a municipality has advised the applicant in writing that additional information is required to complete the application pursuant to paragraph (1), the time required by the applicant to provide the information shall not be counted toward the 90-day period within which the municipality's failure to act shall result in a deemed approval.

(c) Requirements.—The process under this section shall apply to all applications for modification, replacement and collocation that meet all of the following requirements:

(1) The proposed collocation, modification or replacement may not substantially change the physical dimensions of the wireless support structure to which the wireless telecommunications facilities are to be attached.

(2) The proposed collocation, modification or replacement may not further increase the height of a wireless support structure which had already been extended by more than 10% of its originally approved height or by the height of one additional antenna array; provided, however, that nothing herein shall preclude an applicant from further increasing the height of a wireless support structure which had already been extended by more than 10% of its originally approved height or by the height of one additional antenna array if permitted and approved by the municipality.

(3) The proposed collocation, modification or replacement may not increase the dimensions of the equipment compound approved by the municipality.

(4) The proposed collocation, modification or replacement complies with applicable conditions of approval applied to the initial wireless telecommunications facilities, equipment compound and wireless support structure.

(5) The proposed collocation, modification or replacement may not exceed the applicable wind loading and structural loading requirements for the wireless support structure.

§ 5. Enforcement.

(a) Appeal.—Any person adversely affected by any final action or failure to act by a municipality that is inconsistent with the provisions of this act may, within 30 days after the action or failure to act, commence an action or an appeal in the court of common pleas of the county where the wireless support structure and wireless telecommunications facility is located.

(b) Hearing.—The court shall hear and decide the action on an expedited basis and in accordance with the procedures established by the Municipalities Planning Code, 2 Pa.C.S. Chs. 5 Subch. A (relating to practice and procedure of Commonwealth agencies) and 7 Subch. A (relating to judicial review of Commonwealth agency action) or the Judiciary Act Repealer Act, as the case may be, for the disposition of land use appeals.

§ 6. Preservation of local governing authority.

Notwithstanding any other law, nothing in this act shall be construed to:

(1) Limit or preempt the scope of a municipality's review of zoning, land use or permit applications for the siting of wireless support structures.

(2) Prevent a municipality from exercising its zoning power, as provided for under the Pennsylvania Municipalities Planning Code, municipal charter, municipal enabling act or other zoning or land use ordinance or regulation.

(3) Prevent a municipality from regulating any modification or collocation that substantially changes an existing wireless support structure that is inconsistent with this act.

§ 7. Effective date.

This act shall take effect in 60 days.

Chapter 24 Religious Land Use
Chapter 23 Conservation Easements
Chapter 22.1 Land Banks
Chapter 22 Open Space Lands
Chapter 21-B Regulation of Local Agriculture
Chapter 21-A Gas and Oil
Chapter 20 Bluff Recession and Setback Act
Chapter 19.2 Development Permit Extension Act
Chapter 19.1 Wireless Broadband Collocation Act
Chapter 19 Municipalities Planning Code

CHAPTER 19.2

DEVELOPMENT PERMIT EXTENSION ACT

53 P.S. § 11703.1–11703.8

TABLE OF CONTENTS

Sec.

---

§ 11703.1. Short title.

This act shall be known and may be cited as the Development Permit Extension Act.

§ 11703.2. Definitions.

The following words and phrases when used in this act shall have the meanings given to them in this section unless the context clearly indicates otherwise:

"Approval." Any of the following:

(1) except as provided in paragraphs (2) and (3), any government agency approval, agreement, permit, including a building permit or construction permit, or other authorization or decision:

(i) allowing a development or construction project to proceed; or

(ii) relating to or affecting development, granted pursuant to a statute, regulation or ordinance adopted by a municipality, including the following:

(A) 37 Pa.C.S. (relating to historical and museums).

(B) 53 Pa.C.S. (relating to municipalities generally).

(C) 68 Pa.C.S. Pt. II Subpt. B (relating to condominiums).[1]

(D) 68 Pa.C.S. Pt. II Subpt. C (relating to cooperatives).[2]

(E) 68 Pa.C.S. Pt. II Subpt. D (relating to planned communities).[3]

(F) The act of March 7, 1901 (P.L. 20, No. 14), referred to as the Second Class City Law, as it relates to development and construction.[4]

(G) The act of May 16, 1923 (P.L. 207, No. 153), referred to as the Municipal Claim and Tax Lien Law.[5]

(H) The act of April 9, 1929 (P.L. 177, No. 175), known as The Administrative Code of 1929.[6]

---

1. 68 Pa.C.S. § 3101 et seq.
2. 68 Pa.C.S. § 4101 et seq.
3. 68 Pa.C.S. § 5101 et seq.
4. 53 P.S. § 22181 et seq.
5. 53 P.S. § 7101 et seq.
6. 71 P.S. § 51 et seq.

(I) The act of June 23, 1931 (P.L. 932, No. 317), known as The Third Class City Code, as it relates to development and construction.[7]

(J) The act of June 24, 1931 (P.L. 1206, No. 331), known as The First Class Township Code, as it relates to development and construction.[8]

(K) The act of May 1, 1933 (P.L. 103, No. 69), known as The Second Class Township Code, as it relates to development and construction.[9]

(L) The act of June 22, 1937 (P.L. 1987, No. 394), known as The Clean Streams Law.[10]

(M) The act of June 1, 1945 (P.L. 1242, No. 428), known as the State Highway Law,[11] as it relates to the issuance of highway occupancy permits which are regulated under 67 Pa. Code Ch. 441 (relating to access to and occupancy of highways by driveways and local roads) or which are affected by other laws or regulations.

(N) The act of April 21, 1949 (P.L. 665, No. 155), known as the First Class City Home Rule Act, as it relates to development and construction.[12]

(O) The act of July 28, 1953 (P.L. 723, No. 230),[13] known as the Second Class County Code.

(P) The act of August 9, 1955 (P.L. 323, No. 130), known as The County Code.[14]

(Q) The act of July 15, 1957 (P.L. 901, No. 399), known as the Optional Third Class City Charter Law, as it relates to development and construction.[15]

(R) The act of January 24, 1966 (1965 P.L. 1535, No. 537), known as the Pennsylvania Sewage Facilities Act.[16]

(S) The act of February 1, 1966 (1965 P.L. 1656, No. 581), known as The Borough Code, as it relates to development and construction.[17]

(T) The act of July 31, 1968 (P.L. 805, No. 247), known as the Pennsylvania Municipalities Planning Code.[18]

(U) The act of July 9, 1971 (P.L. 206, No. 34), known as the Improvement of Deteriorating Real Property or Areas Tax Exemption Act.[19]

(V) The act of October 4, 1978 (P.L. 851, No. 166), known as the Flood Plain Management Act.[20]

(W) The act of October 4, 1978 (P.L. 864, No. 167), known as the Storm Water Management Act.[21]

---

7. 53 P.S. § 35101 et seq.
8. 53 P.S. § 55101 et seq.
9. 53 P.S. § 65101 et seq.
10. 35 P.S. § 691.1 et seq.
11. 36 P.S. § 670-101 et seq.
12. 53 P.S. § 13101 et seq.
13. 16 P.S. § 3101 et seq.
14. 16 P.S. § 101 et seq.
15. 53 P.S. § 41101 et seq.
16. 35 P.S. § 750.1 et seq.
17. 53 P.S. § 45101 et seq.
18. 53 P.S. § 10101 et seq.
19. 72 P.S. § 4711-101 et seq.
20. 32 P.S. § 679.101 et seq.
21. 32 P.S. § 680.1 et seq.

(X) The act of November 26, 1978 (P.L. 1375, No. 325), known as the Dam Safety and Encroachments Act.[22]

(Y) The act of November 10, 1999 (P.L. 491, No. 45), known as the Pennsylvania Construction Code Act.[23]

(Z) The act of December 20, 2000 (P.L. 724, No. 99), known as the Municipal Code and Ordinance Compliance Act.[24]

(Z.1) The act of June 22, 2001 (P.L. 390, No. 29), known as the Conservation and Preservation Easements Act.[25]

(Z.2) The former act of May 16, 2002 (P.L. 315, No. 46), known as the Community Services Block Grant Act.[26]

(Z.3) The act of February 22, 2008 (P.L. 36, No. 4), entitled "An act authorizing the Department of General Services, with the concurrence of the Department of Environmental Protection, to lease to VTE Philadelphia, LP, or its nominee, land within the bed of the Delaware River in the City of Philadelphia; and affirming the authority of the General Assembly to enact certain conveyances."

(Z.4) The act of February 22, 2008 (P.L. 41, No. 5), entitled "An act authorizing the Department of General Services, with the concurrence of the Department of Environmental Protection, to lease to NCCB Associates, LP, or its nominee, land within the bed of the Delaware River in the City of Philadelphia; and affirming the authority of the General Assembly to enact certain conveyances."

(Z.5) Soil erosion and sediment control plans approved by a local soil conservation district under 25 Pa. Code Ch. 102 (relating to erosion and sediment control).

(Z.6) The National Historic Preservation Act (Public Law 89-665, 80 Stat. 915),[27] to the extent the Commonwealth has been empowered to administer, approve or otherwise authorize activities under that act.

(Z.7) The Federal Water Pollution Control Act (62 Stat. 1155, 33 U.S.C. § 1251 et seq.), to the extent the Commonwealth has been empowered to administer, approve or otherwise authorize activities under that act;

(2) in cities of the first class and agencies established by such cities, the term shall include only the issuance of a building permit, a zoning use and registration permit and any administrative approval, including an approval by a board or commission, that is a condition precedent to issuance of a building permit or zoning use and registration permit to an owner of property; or

(3) any authorization to create additional units and common elements out of convertible real estate in a condominium or planned community or otherwise relating to the right to convert convertible real estate or withdraw withdrawable real estate pursuant to 68 Pa.C.S. Pt. II Subpt. B or D.[28]

"Development." Any of the following:

---

22. 32 P.S. § 693.1 et seq.

23. 35 P.S. § 7210.101 et seq.

24. 68 P.S. § 1081 et seq.

25. 32 P.S. § 5051 et seq.

26. 62 P.S. § 2992.1 et seq.

27. 16 U.S.C. § 470 et seq.

28. 68 Pa.C.S. §§ 3101 et seq., 5101 et seq.

(1) The division of a parcel of land into two or more parcels, including a subdivision as defined in section 107 of the act of July 31, 1968 (P.L. 805, No. 247),[29] known as the Pennsylvania Municipalities Planning Code.

(2) The construction, reconstruction, conversion, structural alteration, relocation or enlargement of a building or other structure.

(3) Site preparation, including grading, earth moving activities, clearance, soil removal or movement, timber harvesting relocation, excavation, landfill and moving, depositing or storing soil, rock or earth materials.

(4) A use or change in the use of a building or other structure or change in land use.

(5) Land development, as defined in section 107 of the Pennsylvania Municipalities Planning Code, or land use.

(6) Demolition, moving or removing a building or other structure.

(7) The right to convert convertible real estate or withdraw withdrawable real estate pursuant to 68 Pa.C.S. Pt. II Subpt. B (relating to condominiums) or D (relating to planned communities).

"Extension period." The period beginning after December 31, 2008, and ending before July 2, 2016.

"Government agency." The Commonwealth, a political subdivision or an agency, department, authority, commission or board of the Commonwealth or a political subdivision. The term includes regional commissions, boards or instrumentalities with the authority to issue approvals.

§ 11703.3. Existing approval.

(a) Automatic suspension.—For an approval that is granted for or in effect between the beginning of the extension period and July 2, 2013, whether obtained before or after the beginning of the extension period, the running of the period of the approval shall be automatically suspended until July 2, 2016.

(a.1) Cities of the first class.—In cities of the first class and agencies established by such cities, the suspension provided for in subsection (a) shall be valid, for any covered approval, 20 days after the notice from the approval holder to the agency that issued the approval of the approval holder's intent to exercise his or her rights under the suspension and payment of a fee equal to 50% of the original application fee, but not to exceed $5,000. The agency that issued the approval may prescribe a form of notice.

(a.2) Limitation.—Any government approval granted after July 2, 2013, shall not be extended beyond the normal approval periods of the government agency without the permission or approval of the government agency.

(b) Duration.—The extension period established under this act shall be the maximum approval period authorized under this act and shall supersede the normal time period for approvals relating to development. Nothing in this section shall prohibit the government agency from granting additional extensions as provided by law.

(c) Riparian leases.—

(1) The time period relating to obtaining a building permit under section 1(i) of the act of February 22, 2008 (P.L. 36, No. 4), entitled "An act authorizing the Department of General Services, with the concurrence of the Department of Environmental Protection, to lease to VTE Philadelphia, LP, or its nominee, land within the bed of the Delaware River in the City of Philadelphia;

---

29. 53 P.S. § 10107.

and affirming the authority of the General Assembly to enact certain conveyances," shall be extended until January 1, 2013.

(2) The time period relating to obtaining a building permit under section 1(i) of the act of February 22, 2008 (P.L. 41, No. 5), entitled "An act authorizing the Department of General Services, with the concurrence of the Department of Environmental Protection, to lease to NCCB Associates, LP, or its nominee, land within the bed of the Delaware River in the City of Philadelphia; and affirming the authority of the General Assembly to enact certain conveyances," shall be extended until January 1, 2013.

§ 11703.4. Subsequent changes.

(a) Change in law.—A law, regulation or policy enacted, adopted or modified by a government agency during the extension period shall not have the effect of prohibiting or limiting an existing approval during the extension period.

(b) Planning code approval.—When an approval has been granted under the act of July 31, 1968 (P.L. 805, No. 247),[30] known as the Pennsylvania Municipalities Planning Code, a subsequent change in a zoning, subdivision or other governing ordinance or plan shall not apply to or affect the right of the applicant to commence or complete the activities authorized by the approval for the duration of the extension period. For purposes of this subsection, the extension period shall be extended for the duration of any litigation, including appeals, relating to an approval which prevents the completion of all or part of the activity authorized by the approval.

(c) Nonexpiration.—An action by a government agency or law to lease, license, grant or otherwise convey rights in the beds of navigable waters of the Commonwealth shall not expire for the duration of the extension period, including time limits relating to the initiation, prosecution or completion of construction. A conveyance of rights under this subsection shall not terminate during the extension period for failure to initiate, prosecute or complete construction.

§ 11703.5. Agency verification.

(a) Request for verification.—

(1) The holder or recipient of an approval may seek written verification from the issuing government agency for any of the following:

(i) The existence of a valid approval.

(ii) The expiration date of the approval under this act.

(2) The request shall set forth the approval in question and the anticipated expiration date under this act.

(b) Agency action.—Upon receipt of a request under subsection (a), the government agency shall respond in writing affirming or denying the existence of the approval, its expiration date and any issues associated with its validity within 30 days. Except in cities of the first class and agencies established by such cities, failure to respond within 30 days shall result in a deemed affirmation of the existence of the approval and expiration date set forth in the request submitted under subsection (a). The agency may charge a fee of not more than $100 for verification of a residential approval and $500 for verification of a commercial approval under this subsection.

(c) Failure to seek affirmation.—The failure of the holder of an approval to seek verification from a government agency shall not be grounds for termination, revocation or other invalidation of an approval.

30. 53 P.S. § 10101 et seq.

(d) Appeals of verification.—A dispute arising under this section shall be appealable in accordance with one of the following applicable laws:

(1) 2 Pa.C.S. § 105 (relating to local agency law).

(2) The act of July 31, 1968 (P.L. 805, No. 247),[31] known as the Pennsylvania Municipalities Planning Code.

§ 11703.6. Applicability.

(a) Exceptions.—This act shall not apply to any of the following:

(1) An approval issued to comply with Federal law, the duration or terms of expiration of which is specified or determined by Federal law.

(2) An administrative consent order or other enforcement action relating to an approval that is subject to the extension period.

(3) An approval, designation or benefit under the act of October 6, 1998 (P.L. 705, No. 92),[32] known as the Keystone Opportunity Zone, Keystone Opportunity Expansion Zone and Keystone Opportunity Improvement Zone Act.

(4) A "One-Call" determination, response or other requirement under the act of December 10, 1974 (P.L. 852, No. 287),[33] referred to as the Underground Utility Line Protection Law.

(5) The revocation or modification of an approval or extension of an approval, when the approval authorizes the modification or revocation for cause.

(6) An approval issued by the Department of Transportation, except that approvals in accordance with 67 Pa. Code Ch. 441 (relating to access to and occupancy of highways by driveways and local roads) shall be extended by the department upon the submission of a complete and accurate application throughout the extension period for one-year intervals, subject to the requirements of 67 Pa. Code Ch. 441, including modifications based on changed circumstances.

(7) An approval issued by the Department of Environmental Protection implementing 25 Pa. Code § 93.4a (relating to antidegradation) in connection with surface waters, as defined in 25 Pa. Code § 93.1 (relating to definitions), or wetlands, as defined in 25 Pa. Code § 93.1, which surface waters or wetlands, after the issuance of the approval, and during the extension period, became classified as:

(i) High Quality Waters, pursuant to 25 Pa. Code §§ 93.1 and 93.4b(a) (relating to qualifying as high quality or exceptional value waters); or

(ii) Exceptional Value Waters, pursuant to 25 Pa. Code § 93.4b(b)(1).

(8) An approval issued by the Department of Environmental Protection implementing 25 Pa. Code § 93.4a in connection with surface waters, as defined in 25 Pa. Code § 93.1, or wetlands, as defined in 25 Pa. Code § 93.1, which surface waters or wetlands are classified as Exceptional Value Waters pursuant to 25 Pa. Code § 93.4b(b)(1).

(b) Sewer and water systems.—If an approval is based upon the connection to a sanitary sewer system or water distribution system, the application of the extension period as it relates to capacity shall be contingent upon the availability of sufficient capacity of the system to accommodate the development that is the subject of the extended approval. If sufficient capacity is unavailable at the time it is required to proceed with development under the approval, priority with regard to further distribution or allocation of capacity shall be established by

31. 53 P.S. § 10101 et seq.

32. 73 P.S. § 820.101 et seq.

33. 73 P.S. § 176 et seq.

the date on which the approval was obtained. Priority relating to distribution of additional capacity shall be allocated in order of the granting of the original approval for the connection.

(c) Fee.—A government agency which issued an approval may charge a fee to extend the approval that may be no more than 25% of the original application fee. In no event may the fee be more than $5,000.

§ 11703.7. Notice.

By August 5, 2010, each affected government agency shall publish notice of applicability of the extension period to approvals granted by the government agency under this act in the Pennsylvania Bulletin.

§ 11703.8. Miscellaneous.

(a) Construction.—Nothing in this act shall be construed to modify any requirement of law that is necessary to retain Federal delegation to, or assumption by, the Commonwealth of the authority to implement a Federal law or program.

(b) Authority.—During the extension period, a government agency shall retain the authority to do all of the following:

(1) Suspend or revoke an approval for noncompliance with a written condition of the approval.

(2) Enforce conditions of approvals granted under law prior to the extension period.

(3) Enforce only those conditions in an approval issued under the act of July 31, 1968 (P.L. 805, No. 247),[34] known as the Pennsylvania Municipalities Planning Code, that are required to be performed prior to final plan approval.

34. 53 P.S. § 10101 et seq.

CHAPTER 19.3

SMALL WIRELESS FACILITIES DEPLOYMENT ACT

53 P.S. §§ 11704.1–11704.11

TABLE OF CONTENTS

---

§ 1. Short title.

This act shall be known and may be cited as the Small Wireless Facilities Deployment Act.

§ 2. Definitions.

The following words and phrases when used in this act shall have the meanings given to them in this section unless the context clearly indicates otherwise:

"Antenna." Telecommunications equipment that transmits and receives electromagnetic radio signals used in the provision of all types of wireless telecommunications services.

"Applicable codes." Any of the following:

(1) Uniform building, fire, electrical, plumbing or mechanical codes adopted by a recognized national code organization or local amendments to those codes enacted solely to address imminent threats of destruction of property or injury to persons.

(2) Local zoning, land use, streets and sidewalks, rights-of-way and permitting ordinances that comply with this act.

"Applicant." A communications service provider that submits an application.

"Application." A request submitted by an applicant to a municipality:

(1) for a permit to collocate small wireless facilities; or

(2) to approve the installation, modification or replacement of a utility pole with small wireless facilities attached.

"Cable facility." Buildings, other structures and equipment used by the owner or operator of a cable television system to provide service. As used in this definition, the term "cable system" shall have the meaning given to it in section 602(6) of the Cable Communications Policy Act of 1984 (Public Law 98-549, 47 U.S.C. § 522(7)).

"Collocation" or "collocate." To install, mount, maintain, modify or replace small wireless facilities on an existing utility pole or other wireless support structure.

"Communications facility." A set of equipment and network components, including wires and cables and associated facilities, used by a communications service provider to provide a communications service.

"Communications service provider." Any of the following:

(1) A cable operator as defined in section 602(4) of the Cable Communications Policy Act of 1984 (Public Law 98-549, 47 U.S.C. § 522(5)).

(2) A provider of information service as defined in section 3(20) of the Communications Act of 1934 (48 Stat. 1064, 47 U.S.C. § 153(24)).

(3) A telecommunications carrier as defined in section 3(44) of the Communications Act of 1934 (48 Stat. 1064, 47 U.S.C. § 153(51)).

(4) A wireless provider.

"Decorative pole." A municipal pole that is specially designed and placed for aesthetic purposes.

"FCC." The Federal Communications Commission.

"Historic district or building." A building that is or a group of buildings, properties or sites that are:

(1) Listed in the National Register of Historic Places or formally determined eligible for listing by the Keeper of the National Register.

(2) Determined to be eligible for listing by the Keeper of the National Register of Historic Places who has been delegated the authority by a Federal agency to list properties and determine their eligibility for the National Register of Historic Places in accordance with section VI.D.1.a.i-v of the Nationwide Programmatic Agreement for Review Regarding the Section 106 National Historic Preservation Act Review Process as specified under 47 CFR Pt. 1, App. C (relating to Nationwide Programmatic Agreement Regarding the Section 106 National Historic Preservation Act Review Process).

(3) Marked as a historical site by the Pennsylvania Historical and Museum Commission pursuant to 37 Pa.C.S. (relating to historical and museums).

(4) Within a historic district created pursuant to the act of June 13, 1961 (P.L.282, No.167), entitled "An act authorizing counties, cities, boroughs, incorporated towns and townships to create historic districts within their geographic boundaries; providing for the appointment of Boards of Historical Architectural Review; empowering governing bodies of political subdivisions to protect the distinctive historical character of these districts and to regulate the erection, reconstruction, alteration, restoration, demolition or razing of buildings within the historic districts."

"Micro wireless facility." A small wireless facility that:

(1) does not exceed two cubic feet in volume; and

(2) has an exterior antenna no longer than 11 inches.

"Modification" or "modify." The improvement, upgrade or replacement of a small wireless facility or an existing utility pole that does not substantially change, as defined in 47 CFR 1.6100(b)(7) (relating to wireless facility modifications), the physical dimension of the small wireless facility or utility pole.

"Municipality." Any of the following:

(1) A city of the first, second, second class A or third class.

(2) A borough.

(3) An incorporated town.

(4) A township of the first or second class.

(5) A county.

(6) A home rule municipality.

(7) A similar general purpose unit of government established by the General Assembly.

"Municipal pole." A utility pole owned, managed or operated by or on behalf of a municipality.

"Right-of-way." The area on, below or above a public roadway, highway, street, sidewalk, alley, utility easement or similar property. The term does not include a Federal interstate highway.

"Small wireless facility." The equipment and network components, including antennas, transmitters and receivers, used by a wireless provider that meet the following qualifications:

(1) Each antenna associated with the deployment is no more than three cubic feet in volume.

(2) The volume of all other equipment associated with the wireless facility, whether ground-mounted or pole-mounted, is cumulatively no more than 28 cubic feet. Any equipment used solely for the concealment of the small wireless facility shall not be included in the calculation of equipment volume under this paragraph.

"Technically feasible." By virtue of engineering or spectrum usage, the proposed placement for a small wireless facility or its design or site location can be implemented without a material reduction in the functionality of the small wireless facility.

"Utility facility." Buildings, other structures and equipment owned or operated by a public utility, as defined in 66 Pa.C.S. § 102 (relating to definitions), to provide service.

"Utility pole." A pole or similar structure that is or may be used, in whole or in part, by or for telecommunications, electric distribution, lighting, traffic control, signage or a similar function or for collocation. The term includes the vertical support structure for traffic lights but does not include wireless support structures or horizontal structures to which signal lights or other traffic control devices are attached.

"Wireless facility." As follows:

(1) Equipment at a fixed location that enables wireless service between user equipment and a communications network, including any of the following:

(i) Equipment associated with wireless services.

(ii) Radio transceivers, antennas, coaxial or fiber optic cables, regular and backup power supplies or comparable equipment, regardless of technological configuration.

(2) The term includes a small wireless facility.

(3) The term does not include any of the following:

(i) The structure or improvements on, under or within which the equipment is collocated.

(ii) The coaxial or fiber optic cables that are not immediately adjacent to or directly associated with a particular antenna.

"Wireless infrastructure provider." A person authorized by the Pennsylvania Public Utility Commission to provide telecommunications service in this Commonwealth that builds or installs wireless communication transmission equipment, wireless facilities or wireless support structures but is not a wireless services provider.

Table of Contents | Part I Ch. 1–3 Ethics, Records, Open Meetings | Part II Ch. 4–10 Taxation | Part III Ch. 11–18 Torts, Contracts & Civil Rules | Part IV Ch. 19–24 Zoning & Planning | Part V Ch. 25–30 Construction and Emergency Codes | Part VI Ch. 31–39 Municipal Codes | Index

"Wireless provider." A wireless infrastructure provider or a wireless services provider.

"Wireless services." Services, whether at a fixed location or mobile, using a licensed or unlicensed spectrum, provided to the public using wireless facilities.

"Wireless services provider." A person who provides wireless services.

"Wireless support structure." The term shall have the same meaning given to it in the act of October 24, 2012 (P.L.1501, No.191), known as the Wireless Broadband Collocation Act.

§ 3. Use of right-of-way for small wireless facilities and utility poles with small wireless facilities attached.

(a) Applicability.—The provisions of this section shall only apply to activities of a wireless provider within the right-of-way to deploy small wireless facilities and associated new utility poles with small wireless facilities attached.

(b) Exclusive use prohibited.—A municipality shall not enter into an exclusive arrangement with any person for use of the right-of-way for:

(1) collocation; or

(2) the installation, operation, modification or replacement of utility poles with small wireless facilities attached.

(c) Right-of-way rates and fees.—Subject to the fee adjustment requirements under section 7(c), a municipality shall have the right to charge an annual fee for the use of the right-of-way. An annual right-of-way fee shall not exceed $270 per small wireless facility or $270 per new utility pole with a small wireless facility unless a municipality demonstrates all of the following:

(1) The annual right-of-way fee is a reasonable approximation of the municipality's costs to manage the right-of-way.

(2) The municipality's costs under paragraph (1) are reasonable.

(3) The annual right-of-way fee is nondiscriminatory.

(d) Right of access.—

(1) Under the provisions of this act, in accordance with applicable codes, and with the permission of the owner of the structure, a wireless provider shall have the right to perform the following within the right-of-way:

(i) Collocate.

(ii) Replace an existing utility pole or install a new utility pole with attached small wireless facilities.

(2) All structures and facilities shall be installed and maintained so as not to obstruct nor hinder travel or public safety within the right-of-way or obstruct the legal use of the right-of-way by the municipality and utilities.

(e) Size limits.—

(1) Each new or modified small wireless facility installed in the right-of-way shall be installed on an existing utility pole or a new utility pole subject to the following:

(i) The installation of a small wireless facility on an existing utility pole shall not extend more than five feet above the existing utility pole.

(ii) If collocation on an existing utility pole cannot be achieved under section 4(i), a small wireless facility may be installed on a new or replacement utility pole. The maximum permitted height of the facility, which shall include the utility pole and small wireless facility, shall not be taller than 50 feet above ground level.

(2) Subject to the provisions of this act, a wireless provider may collocate or install a new utility pole with small wireless facilities attached that exceeds

these height limits by including a height limit waiver request or variances in the application. Height limit waivers or variances shall be processed subject to applicable codes.

(f) Underground district.—A wireless provider shall comply with reasonable and nondiscriminatory requirements that prohibit communications service providers from placing or installing structures in the right-of-way in an area designated solely for underground or buried cable facilities and utility facilities if the municipality:

(1) Requires all cable facilities and utility facilities, other than municipal poles and attachments, to be placed underground by a date certain that is three months prior to the submission of the application.

(2) Does not prohibit the replacement of municipal poles in the designated area.

(3) Permits wireless providers to seek a waiver of the underground requirements for the installation of a new utility pole to support small wireless facilities. Upon the submission of a request for a waiver by a wireless provider, the municipality may require a public hearing and, with the approval of the property owner, permit a waiver request. Waivers shall be addressed in a nondiscriminatory manner and in accordance with applicable codes.

(g) Historic district or building.—Except for facilities excluded from evaluation for effects on historic properties under 47 CFR 1.1307(a)(4) (relating to actions that may have a significant environmental effect, for which Environmental Assessments (EAs) must be prepared), a municipality may require reasonable, technically feasible, nondiscriminatory and technologically neutral design or concealment measures in a historic district or on historic buildings. Any design or concealment measures may not have the effect of prohibiting any provider's technology or be considered a part of the small wireless facility for purposes of the size restrictions of small wireless facilities.

(h) Design guidelines.—A municipality may develop objective design guidelines for a small wireless facility regarding the minimization of aesthetic impact in accordance with the following:

(1) The design guidelines shall be technically feasible.

(2) The design guidelines may not have the effect of prohibiting the wireless provider's technology.

(3) The design guidelines may not unreasonably discriminate among wireless providers of functionally equivalent services.

(i) Damage and repair.—A wireless provider shall repair all damage to the right-of-way or any other land so disturbed, directly caused by the activities of the wireless provider or the wireless provider's contractors and return the right-of-way in as good of condition as it existed prior to any work being done in the right-of-way by the wireless provider. If the wireless provider fails to make the repairs required by the municipality within 30 days after written notice, the municipality may perform those repairs and charge the wireless provider the reasonable, documented cost of the repairs plus a penalty not to exceed $500. The municipality may suspend the ability of an applicant to receive a new permit from the municipality until the applicant has paid the amount assessed for the repair costs and the assessed penalty. The municipality may not suspend the ability of an applicant to receive a new permit that has deposited the amount assessed for the repair costs and the assessed penalty in escrow pending an adjudication of the merits of the dispute by a court of competent jurisdiction.

(j) Communications services.—The approval of the installation, placement, maintenance or operation of a small wireless facility under this section shall not authorize the provision of any communications services without compliance with all applicable laws or the installation, placement, maintenance or operation of any communications facilities other than wireless facilities and associated utility poles in the right-of-way.

§ 4. Permitting process for small wireless facilities and utility poles within right-of-way.

(a) Applicability.—The provisions of this section shall apply to a municipality's permitting of small wireless facilities by a wireless provider or the installation, modification and replacement of utility poles with small wireless facilities attached by a wireless provider within the right-of-way.

(b) Review.—An application under this section shall be treated as a permitted use in all areas of a municipality, except underground districts in accordance with section 3(f), and reviewed by municipal staff for conformance with applicable codes. Such applications shall not be subject to discretionary zoning review, including conditional use or special exception requirements.

(c) Permits.—

(1) A municipality may require an applicant to obtain one or more permits of general applicability to perform the following within the right-of-way:

(i) Collocate, maintain and modify small wireless facilities.

(ii) Replace existing utility poles for collocation.

(iii) Install new utility poles with attached small wireless facilities.

(2) Permits of general applicability shall not apply exclusively to small wireless facilities. A municipality shall receive applications for collocation or for installation, modification or replacement of utility poles with small wireless facilities attached and process and issue permits, subject to the requirements of applicable codes. The following apply:

(i) A municipality may not directly or indirectly require an applicant to perform services or provide goods unrelated to the permit, such as in-kind contributions to the municipality, including reserving fiber, conduit or pole space for the municipality.

(ii) An applicant shall not be required to provide justification for capacity or radio frequency. An applicant may be required to:

(A) Include documentation with an application that includes construction and engineering drawings, demonstrates compliance with the criteria specified under subsection (f) and includes all necessary approvals from the pole owner.

(B) Self-certify that the filing and approval of the application is required by the wireless provider to provide additional capacity or coverage for wireless services. Nothing in this subsection shall be construed to permit a municipality to require an applicant to submit information about an applicant's business decisions with respect to its service, customer demand for service or quality of service.

(C) Include documentation showing compliance with design guidelines consistent with section 3(h).

(d) Completed application.—Within 10 business days of receiving an application, a municipality must determine and notify the applicant in writing whether the application is incomplete. If an application is incomplete, the notice must specifically identify the missing information. The processing deadline shall restart at zero on the date the applicant provides the missing information. The processing deadline may be tolled by agreement of the applicant and the municipality.

(e) **Deadlines.**—An application shall be processed on a nondiscriminatory basis and deemed approved if the municipality fails to approve or deny the application within 60 days of receipt of a complete application to collocate and within 90 days of receipt of a complete application to replace an existing utility pole or install a new utility pole with small wireless facilities attached. A permit associated with an application deemed approved under this subsection shall be deemed approved if the municipality fails to approve or deny the permit within seven business days after the date of filing the permit application with the municipality unless there is a public safety reason for the delay.

(f) **Denial.**—

(1) A municipality may deny an application under this section only if any of the following apply:

(i) The small wireless facility materially interferes with the safe operation of traffic control equipment, sight lines or clear zones for transportation or pedestrians or compliance with the Americans with Disabilities Act of 1990 (Public Law 101-336, 104 Stat. 327) or similar Federal or State standards regarding pedestrian access or movement.

(ii) The small wireless facility fails to comply with applicable codes.

(iii) The small wireless facility fails to comply with the requirements specified under this act.

(iv) The applicant fails to submit a report by a qualified engineering expert which shows that the small wireless facility will comply with applicable FCC regulations.

(2) Within the time frame established under subsection (e), the municipality shall document the basis for a denial, including the specific provisions of applicable codes on which the denial was based, and send the documentation to the applicant within five business days of the denial.

(3) The applicant may cure the deficiencies identified by the municipality and resubmit the application within 30 days of receiving the written basis for the denial without being required to pay an additional application fee. The municipality shall approve or deny the revised application within 30 days of the application being resubmitted for review or the resubmitted application shall be deemed approved 30 days after resubmission. Any subsequent review shall be limited to the deficiencies cited in the denial. If the resubmitted application addresses or changes other sections of the application that were not previously denied, the municipality shall be given an additional 15 days to review the resubmitted application and may charge an additional fee for the review.

(g) **Consolidated application.**—An applicant seeking to collocate within the jurisdiction of a single municipality shall be allowed at the applicant's discretion to file a consolidated application for collocation of multiple small wireless facilities as follows:

(1) The consolidated application does not exceed 20 small wireless facilities.

(2) The denial of one or more small wireless facilities in a consolidated application shall not delay processing of any other small wireless facilities in the same consolidated application.

(3) A single applicant may not submit more than one consolidated or 20 single applications in a 30-day period in a municipality with a population of less than 50,000. If a municipality with a population of less than 50,000 receives more than one consolidated application or 20 single applications within a 45-day period, the processing deadline shall be extended 15 days in addition to the processing deadline specified under subsection (d) to allow the municipality to complete its initial review under subsection (d).

(4) The following apply:

(i) For the purpose of counting the number of small wireless facilities each applicant has before a single municipality at a given time, small wireless facilities and poles that a wireless provider applicant has requested a third party to deploy and that are included in a pending application by the third party shall be counted as pending requests by the wireless provider applicant.

(ii) An application tolled under paragraph (3) shall count towards the total number of applications included in a consolidated application unless the application is withdrawn by the applicant. As the processing of applications is completed, the municipality shall begin processing previously tolled applications in the order in which the tolled applications were submitted, unless the applicant specifies a different order.

(h) Time limit for work.—The proposed collocation, the modification or replacement of a utility pole or the installation of a new utility pole with small wireless facilities attached for which a permit is granted under this section shall be completed within one year of the permit issuance date unless the municipality and the applicant agree in writing to extend the period.

(i) Utility poles.—When applying to install a new utility pole under this act, the municipality may require the wireless provider to demonstrate that it cannot meet the service reliability and functional objectives of the application by collocating on an existing utility pole or municipal pole instead of installing a new utility pole. The municipality may require the wireless provider to self-certify that the wireless provider has made this determination in good faith and to provide a documented summary of the basis for the determination. The wireless provider's determination shall be based on whether the wireless provider can meet the service objectives of the application by collocating on an existing utility pole or municipal pole on which:

(1) The wireless provider has the right to collocation.

(2) The collocation is technically feasible and would not impose substantial additional cost.

(3) The collocation would not obstruct or hinder travel or have a negative impact on public safety.

(j) Approval.—Approval of an application authorizes the applicant to:

(1) Collocate on an existing utility pole, modify or replace a utility pole or install a new utility pole with small wireless facilities attached as identified in the initial application.

(2) Subject to the permit requirements and the applicant's right to terminate at any time, operate and maintain small wireless facilities and any associated equipment on a utility pole covered by the permit for a period of not less than five years, which shall be renewed for two additional five-year periods if the applicant is in compliance with the criteria set forth in this act or applicable codes consistent with this act and the applicant has obtained all necessary consent from the utility pole owner.

(k) Removal of equipment.—

(1) Within 60 days of suspension or revocation of a permit due to noncompliance with this act or applicable codes consistent with this act, the applicant shall remove the small wireless facility and any associated equipment, including the utility pole and any support structures if the applicant's wireless facilities and associated equipment are the only facilities on the utility pole, after receiving adequate notice and an opportunity to cure any noncompliance.

(2) Within 90 days of the end of a permit term or an extension of the permit term, the applicant shall remove the small wireless facility and any associated equipment, including the utility pole and any support structures if the

applicant's wireless facilities and associated equipment are the only facilities on the utility pole.

(l) Moratorium prohibited.—A municipality may not institute, either expressly or de facto, a moratorium on:

(1) filing, receiving or processing applications; or

(2) issuing permits for:

(i) collocation;

(ii) modification or replacement of utility poles to support small wireless facilities; or

(iii) installation of new utility poles to support small wireless facilities.

(m) When applications not required.—

(1) A municipality shall not require an application for:

(i) Routine maintenance or repair work.

(ii) The replacement of small wireless facilities with small wireless facilities that are substantially similar or the same size or smaller and still qualify as a small wireless facility.

(iii) The installation, placement, maintenance, operation or replacement of micro wireless facilities that are strung on cables between existing utility poles by or for a communications service provider authorized to occupy the right-of-way, in compliance with the National Electrical Safety Code.

(2) A municipality may require a permit to perform work within the right-of-way for the activities under paragraph (1) or subsection (c), if applicable for work that involves excavation, closure of a sidewalk or closure of a vehicular lane. Permits shall be subject to the requirements provided in this act or applicable codes consistent with this act.

(n) Application fees.—Subject to the fee adjustment requirements under section 7(c), a municipality shall have the right to charge an application fee for the review of a permit application and plans submitted for the work to be done within the right-of-way. A municipality may charge a one-time application fee of up to the following:

(1) Five hundred dollars for an application seeking approval for no more than five collocated small wireless facilities and up to $100 for each collocated small wireless facility beyond five.

(2) One thousand dollars for an application seeking approval of a small wireless facility that requires the installation of a new or replacement utility pole.

§ 5. Access to municipal poles within right-of-way.

(a) Applicability.—The provisions of this section shall apply to activities of the wireless provider within a right-of-way.

(b) Exclusive use prohibited.—A municipality may not enter into an exclusive arrangement with any person for the right to collocate on municipal poles.

(c) Collocation.—A municipality shall allow collocation on municipal poles using the process required under this act and applicable codes unless the small wireless facility would cause structural or safety deficiencies to the municipal pole, in which case the municipality and applicant shall work together for any make-ready work or modifications or replacements that are needed to accommodate the small wireless facility. All structures and facilities shall be installed and maintained so as not to obstruct nor hinder travel or public safety within the right-of-way.

(d) Rates.—Subject to the fee adjustment requirements under section 7(c), a municipality shall not charge a wireless provider a fee to collocate on municipal poles.

(e) Implementation and make-ready work.—

(1) The rates, fees and terms and conditions for the make-ready work to collocate on a municipal pole must be nondiscriminatory, competitively neutral and commercially reasonable and must comply with this act.

(2) The municipality shall provide a good faith estimate for any make-ready work necessary to enable the municipal pole to support the requested collocation by a wireless provider, including pole replacement if necessary, within 60 days after receipt of a complete application. Make-ready work, including pole replacement, shall be completed within 60 days of written acceptance of the good faith estimate by the applicant. A municipality may require replacement of the municipal pole only if the municipality demonstrates that the collocation would make the municipal pole structurally unsound.

(3) The municipality shall not require more make-ready work than required to meet applicable codes or industry standards. Fees for make-ready work on a nonreplacement municipal pole shall not include costs related to preexisting or prior damage or noncompliance. Fees for make-ready work, including replacement, shall not exceed actual costs or the amount charged to other similarly situated communications service providers for similar work and shall not include any consultant fees or expenses that are charged on a contingency basis.

(f) Future use.—A municipality may reserve space on an existing municipal pole for future public safety or transportation uses in a documented and approved plan as adopted at the time an application is filed. A reservation of space shall not preclude collocation, the replacement of an existing utility pole or the installation of a new utility pole. If the replacement of a municipal pole is necessary to accommodate collocation and the reserved future use, the wireless provider shall pay for the replacement municipal pole and the municipal pole shall accommodate the future use.

§ 6. Local authority.

Subject to the provisions of this act and applicable Federal and State laws and regulations, nothing in this act shall be construed to:

(1) Limit or preempt the scope of a municipality's zoning, land use, planning, streets and sidewalks, rights-of-way and permitting authority as it relates to small wireless facilities.

(2) Grant the authority to a municipality to exercise zoning jurisdiction over the design, engineering, construction, installation or operation of a small wireless facility located in an interior structure or on the site of a campus, stadium or athletic facility not owned or controlled by the municipality. Nothing in this act authorizes the Commonwealth or any municipality to require small wireless facility deployment or to regulate wireless services.

§ 7. Implementation.

(a) Ordinances.—A municipality may adopt ordinances that comply with this act and shall amend existing ordinances as necessary to comply with this act. If a municipality does not adopt an ordinance that complies with this act within 60 days of the effective date of this section, applications seeking permits to collocate, modify or replace existing utility poles or install new utility poles shall be processed in compliance with this act. A municipality shall not require a wireless provider to enter into an agreement to implement this act. Nothing in this subsection shall be construed to prohibit an agreement between a municipality and a wireless provider to implement this act if nondiscriminatory and entered into voluntarily.

(b) Agreements.—All agreements between municipalities and wireless service providers that are in effect on the effective date of this act shall remain in effect, subject to any termination provisions in the agreements. When an application is submitted after the effective date of this act, a wireless provider may elect to have the rates, fees, terms and conditions established under this act apply to the small wireless facility or utility pole installed after the effective date of this act.

(c) Rate or fee adjustments.—

(1) If the FCC adjusts its levels for fees for small wireless facilities, a municipality may adjust any impacted rate or fee under sections 3(c), 4(n) or 5(d), on a pro rata basis, and consistent with the FCC's adjustment.

(2) If, in a final adjudication not subject to further appeal or to review by the United States Supreme Court, a Federal court reviewing Accelerating Wireless Broadband Deployment by Removing Barriers to Infrastructure Investment, et al., Declaratory Ruling and Third Report and Order, WT Docket No. 17-79 and WC Docket No. 17-84, FCC 18-133 (released September 27, 2018), reverses or repeals the rates outlined in that FCC order, then the monetary caps under sections (3)(c), (4)(n) and (5)(d) may increase 3% annually beginning January 1, 2021, at the discretion of a municipality.

§ 8. Indemnification.

Except for a wireless provider with an existing agreement to occupy and operate in a right-of-way, a wireless provider shall fully indemnify and hold the municipality and its officers, employees and agents harmless against any claims, lawsuits, judgments, costs, liens, expenses or fees or any other damages caused by the act, error or omission of the wireless provider or its officers, agents, employees, directors, contractors or subcontractors while installing, repairing or maintaining small wireless facilities or utility poles within the right-of-way. A wireless provider shall not be required to indemnify for an act of negligence or willful misconduct by the municipality, its elected and appointed officials, employees and agents.

§ 9. General requirements for uses of rights-of-way.

The following apply:

(1) Structures and facilities deployed by a wireless provider under this act shall be constructed, maintained and located in a manner as to not obstruct, endanger or hinder the usual travel or public safety on a right-of-way, damage or interfere with other utility facilities located within a right-of-way or interfere with the other utility's use of the utility's facilities located or to be located within the right-of-way.

(2) The construction and maintenance of structures and facilities by the wireless provider shall comply with the 2017 National Electrical Safety Code and all applicable laws, ordinances and regulations for the protection of underground and overhead utility facilities.

(3) An applicant or the applicant's affiliate shall ensure that a contractor or subcontractor performing construction, reconstruction, demolition, repair or maintenance work on a small wireless facility deployed under this act meets and attests to all of the following requirements:

(i) Maintain all valid licenses, registrations or certificates required by the Federal Government, the Commonwealth or a local government entity that is necessary to do business or perform applicable work.

(ii) Maintain compliance with the act of June 2, 1915 (P.L.736, No.338), known as the Workers' Compensation Act, the act of December 5, 1936 (2nd Sp.Sess., 1937 P.L.2897, No.1), known as the Unemployment Compensation Law, and bonding and liability insurance requirements as specified in the contract for the project.

(iii) Has not defaulted on a project, declared bankruptcy, been debarred or suspended on a project by the Federal Government, the Commonwealth or a local government entity within the previous three years.

(iv) Has not been convicted of a misdemeanor or felony relating to the performance or operation of the business of the contractor or subcontractor within the previous 10 years.

(v) Has completed a minimum of the United States Occupational Safety and Health Administration's 10-hour safety training course or similar training sufficient to prepare workers for any hazards that may be encountered during their work on the small wireless facility.

§ 10. Construction.

(a) Obligations.—Nothing in this act shall be construed to impact, modify or supersede any construction standard, engineering practice, tariff provision, collective bargaining agreement, contractual obligation or right, Federal or State law or regulation relating to facilities or equipment owned or controlled by an electric distribution company or its affiliate, a telecommunications carrier, an electric cooperative or an independent transmission company that is not a wireless provider.

(b) Definitions.—As used in this section, the following words and phrases shall have the meanings given to them in this subsection unless the context clearly indicates otherwise:

"Electric distribution company." As defined in 66 Pa.C.S. § 2803 (relating to definitions).

"Facilities." As defined in 66 Pa.C.S. § 102 (relating to definitions).

"Telecommunications carrier." As defined in 66 Pa.C.S. § 3012 (related to definitions).

§ 11. Effective date.

This act shall take effect in 60 days.

CHAPTER 20

BLUFF RECESSION AND SETBACK ACT

32 P.S. §§ 5201–5215

TABLE OF CONTENTS

---

§ 1. Short title.

This act shall be known and may be cited as the "Bluff Recession and Setback Act."

§ 2. Purpose and policy.

The policy and purpose of this act is to:

(1) Encourage planning and development in bluff areas which is consistent with sound land use practices.

(2) Protect people and property in bluff areas from the dangers and damage associated with the inevitable recession of bluffs.

(3) Prevent and eliminate urban and rural blight which results from the damages of bluff erosion and recession.

(4) Minimize the expenditure of public and private funds for shoreline protection and bluff stabilization structures and activities.

(5) Authorize a comprehensive and coordinated program to regulate development activities through the use of setback ordinances in bluff recession hazard areas, designed to preserve and restore the natural ecological systems, and to prevent continuing destruction of private property and structures.

(6) Encourage local administration and management of bluffs consistent with the Commonwealth's duty as trustee of natural resources, and the people's constitutional right to the preservation of the natural, scenic, aesthetic and historic values of the environment.

§ 3. Definitions.

The following words and phrases when used in this act shall have, unless the context clearly indicates otherwise, the meanings given to them in this section:

"Bluff." Any high bank or bold headland with a broad, precipitous cliff face, overlooking a lake.

"Bluff line." The edge or crest of the bluff.

"Bluff recession." The loss of material along the bluff face caused by the direct or indirect action by one or a combination of groundwater seepage, water currents, wind generated water waves or high water levels.

"Bluff recession hazard area." An area or zone where the rate of progressive bluff recession creates a substantial threat to the safety or stability of nearby or future structures or utility facilities.

"Bluff setback ordinance and regulations." Building codes, zoning ordinances, subdivision regulations, health regulations, special purpose ordinances, and other applications of the police power, which provide standards for the location of structures and facilities in bluff recession hazard areas.

"Department." The Department of Environmental Resources of the Commonwealth of Pennsylvania.

"Development":

(1) The improvement of one lot or two or more contiguous lots, tracts or parcels of land for any purpose involving:

(i) a group of two or more buildings; or

(ii) the division or allocation of land or space between or among two or more existing or prospective occupants by means of, or for the purpose of streets, common areas, leaseholds, condominiums, building groups or other features.

(2) A subdivision of land.

"Lake." A body of fresh water covering at least 9,000 square miles.

"Municipality." A city, borough, town or township, or any county or other governmental unit when acting as an agent thereof, or any combination thereof acting jointly.

"Person." An individual, partnership, public or private association or corporation, firm, trust estate, municipality, governmental unit, public utility or any other legal entity whatsoever which is recognized by law as the subject of rights and duties. Whenever used in any section prescribing or imposing a penalty, the term "person" shall include the members of a partnership, the officers, members, servants and agents of an association, officers, agents and servants of a corporation, but shall exclude any department, board, bureau or agency of the Commonwealth.

"Structure." Any man-made object having an ascertainable stationary location on or in land or water, whether or not affixed to the land.

"Structure life span." The useful life of the structure considering both economic and physical factors.

"Substantial improvement." Any repair, reconstruction or improvement of a structure, the cost of which equals or exceeds 50% of the market value of the structure either:

(1) before the improvement or repair is started; or

(2) if the structure has been damaged, and is being restored, before the damage occurred or any repairs, reconstructions or improvements of a structure occurring over a five-year period, the aggregate cost of which equals or exceeds 50% of the market value of the structure either:

(i) before the first improvement or repair is started; or

(ii) if the structure has been damaged, and is being restored, before the damage occurred.

For the purposes of this definition "substantial improvement" is considered to occur when the first alteration of any wall, ceiling, floor or other structure part of the building commences, whether or not that alteration affects the external dimensions of the structure. The term does not, however, include any project for improvement of a structure to comply with existing State or local health, sanitary or safety specifications which are solely necessary to assure safe living conditions; or any alterations of a structure listed on the National Register of Historic Places or a State inventory of historic places.

§ 4. Designation of areas with bluff recession hazards.

(a) The department shall conduct studies necessary to identify areas in the Commonwealth subject to bluff recession hazards.

(b) The department shall notify the chief executive officer of each municipality which is tentatively identified as containing one or more areas subject to bluff recession hazards. Each such municipality shall be invited to submit within 60 days of notification by the department any technical data or comments on the proposed identification of a bluff recession hazard. The department shall submit its report, together with the comments of the affected municipality, to the Environmental Quality Board.

(c) Following receipt of the department's report, and after public notice and public hearings, the Environmental Quality Board shall by regulation identify and designate those areas and municipalities subject to bluff recession hazards.

§ 5. Bluff setback requirements.

(a) In any area designated as having a bluff recession hazard, no person shall construct, install, or engage in substantial improvement to any structure, or any utility facility such as but not limited to water, sewage, electric, gas, oil or telephone facilities, in violation of the bluff setback requirements established pursuant to this section.

(b) The Environmental Quality Board shall, by regulation, establish minimum bluff setback requirements for bluff recession hazard areas. In setting such standards, the board shall consider the applicable bluff recession rates, the appropriate life span of various classes of structures, and other relevant factors affecting the public safety and bluff stability.

(c) The Environmental Quality Board shall adopt regulations providing standards and procedures for variances to the bluff setback requirements. Such regulations shall require at a minimum that the applicant demonstrate and the administering agency determine that:

(1) A parcel established prior to a bluff recession hazard area designation does not have adequate depth considering the minimum bluff setback requirements to provide for any reasonable use of the land; or the proposed structure or utility facilities require access to the body of water and there is no feasible alternative for obtaining such access.

(2) Sound land use practices will be applied to the design, placement, construction and use of the structure or utility facilities to control runoff, erosion and acceleration of bluff recession.

(3) The structure or utility facilities will, to the maximum extent feasible, comply with the bluff setback requirements and will otherwise be designed and constructed in a manner which adequately protects against potential dangers from bluff recession, and will incorporate all feasible measures to minimize risks to life and property.

(d) The department may grant variances to the bluff setback requirements in the period prior to formal approval of a municipal bluff setback ordinance and regulations. Following approval by the department of a municipality's bluff setback ordinance and regulations, variances shall be granted by the designated municipality.

§ 6. Municipal bluff setback regulations.

(a) Within six months following designation by the Environmental Quality Board of an area and municipality subject to bluff recession hazards, each designated municipality shall adopt or amend, and shall implement such ordinances and regulations as are necessary to regulate construction and development activities in areas subject to bluff recession hazards in a manner consistent with the minimum bluff setback requirements established pursuant to section 5. Such ordinances and regulations shall require permits for all proposed construction, installation or substantial improvement of structures, or water, sewage, electric or gas utility services located in designated bluff recession hazard areas.

(b) The adoption and administration by municipalities of bluff setback ordinances and regulations which are necessary to comply with this act shall be governed by the provisions of the act of July 31, 1968 (P.L. 805, No. 247),[1] known as the "Pennsylvania Municipalities Planning Code," or other applicable enabling legislation; provided that a municipality may adopt bluff setback ordinances and regulations for a bluff recession hazard area without adopting ordinances and regulations governing any other area of the municipality, notwithstanding any provision of the "Pennsylvania Municipalities Planning Code" or other applicable enabling legislation.

(c) No provision of this act shall be construed as in any way limiting the power of any municipality to adopt more restrictive ordinances, codes or regulations governing construction and development in bluff recession hazard areas than the minimum bluff setback requirements established pursuant to section 5.

§ 7. Department oversight of municipal compliance.

(a) The department shall review and approve all municipal bluff setback ordinances and regulations, and amendments thereto. The department shall approve the ordinances and regulations if it determines that they comply with the minimum requirements of this act. If the department disapproves an ordinance or regulation, it shall notify the affected municipality in writing, stating the reasons for disapproval.

(b) If the department fails to either approve or disapprove an ordinance or regulation, or amendment thereto, within 90 days following submission by the municipality to the department, the ordinance or regulation shall be deemed to be approved.

(c) The department shall periodically review the implementation and administration by municipalities of bluff setback ordinances and regulations in order to assure coordinated and consistent enforcement of the setback requirements established pursuant to this act.

(d) Following public notice and public hearing, the Environmental Quality Board shall adopt, and periodically review and amend, regulations establishing:

(1) Criteria and standards for the coordinated and consistent enforcement of bluff setback requirements by municipalities.

(2) Requirements and procedures for the submission, review and approval of municipal bluff setback ordinances and regulations.

(3) Requirements and procedures for maintenance of records concerning municipal implementation and administration of bluff setback ordinances and regulations, and for periodic submission of such records or reports to the department for review.

(e) Where conditions affecting a bluff recession hazard area are changed, including changes created by artificial erosion and recession control projects, the

1. 53 P.S. §§ 10101 et seq.

Environmental Quality Board shall review and as appropriate amend regulations under this section.

§ 8. Failure to adopt or implement bluff setback ordinances.

(a) The department may institute an action in mandamus in the Commonwealth Court to compel a municipality to adopt and submit bluff setback ordinances and regulations which comply with the requirements of this act.

(b) If the department finds that a municipality has failed to implement and enforce, in a consistent and effective manner, the bluff setback ordinances and regulations required by this act, the department shall provide written notice of violation to the municipality.

(c) Within 60 days of the receipt of a notice of violation, the municipality shall report to the department regarding the action which it is taking to correct the violation and to comply with the requirements of this act.

(d) If within 90 days of the receipt of a notice of violation, the department determines that the municipality has failed to comply with the requirements of this act, the department shall issue an administrative order to the municipality and its officers specifying the actions necessary to correct the violation and to achieve full compliance with the requirements of this act. Any order issued under this section shall take effect upon receipt of notice unless the other specifies otherwise.

(e) Any municipality or municipal officer who violates or fails to comply with an order of the department issued pursuant to subsection (d), from which no appeal has been taken, or which has been sustained on appeal, or which has been appealed but where no supersedeas has been granted, shall be deemed to be in contempt of such order. Upon petition and certification of such order by the department, the Commonwealth Court or the court of common pleas of the county where the municipality is located, shall, if it finds that the respondent municipality or officer is not in compliance with the order, adjudge the respondent in contempt of the order and shall assess civil penalties of an amount not less than $100 nor greater than $1,000 per violation plus $200 for each continuing day of violation. Where the respondent has not as of the date of hearing before the court complied with the order of the department or board, the court shall specifically order the respondent to immediately and fully comply with such order, and may issue any further order as may be appropriate.

§ 9. Coordination with environmental protection programs.

The department and municipalities shall coordinate the implementation of this act with the administration of the environmental protection programs for erosion and sedimentation control, stormwater management and water obstructions.

§ 10. Inspections.

(a) An agent or employee of the Department of Environmental Resources or of a municipality administering bluff setback ordinances and regulations shall have the power to, upon presentation of proper credentials:

(1) Enter any land for the purpose of surveying bluff recession hazard areas.

(2) Enter any land in a bluff recession hazard area for the purpose of ascertaining the location of structure or structures.

(3) Enter land or any structure located in a bluff recession hazard area for the purpose of ascertaining the compliance or noncompliance with the bluff setback ordinance and regulations adopted pursuant to this act.

(b) Whenever an agent or employee of the Department of Environmental Resources or a municipality charged with the enforcement of the provisions of this act has been refused access to property for the purposes of conducting a survey

Table of Contents
Part I Ch. 1–3 Ethics, Records, Open Meetings
Part II Ch. 4–10 Taxation
Part III Ch. 11–18 Torts, Contracts & Civil Rules
Part IV Ch. 19–24 Zoning & Planning
Part V Ch. 25–30 Construction and Emergency Codes
Part VI Ch. 31–39 Municipal Codes
Index

or inspection as authorized by this section or reasonably requires access to such property without prior notice to the owner, such agent or employee may apply for an inspection warrant to any Commonwealth official authorized by law to issue a search or inspection warrant to enable him or her to have access and inspect such property. It shall be sufficient probable cause to issue an inspection warrant that the inspection is necessary to properly enforce the provisions of this act.

§ 11. Grants and reimbursements to municipalities.

(a) The department is authorized to administer grants to municipalities to assist or reimburse them for costs in preparing or amending bluff setback ordinances and actual administrative enforcement and implementation costs as required by this act. Grants and reimbursements shall be made from and to the extent of Federal funding augmentation under the Federal Coastal Zone Management Act[2] as appropriated by the General Assembly for such purposes and shall be made in accordance to rules and regulations adopted by the department in accordance with the following:

The grant shall be limited to:

(i) Seventy-five per cent of the allowable costs for preparation of a bluff setback ordinance, and administrative, enforcement, and implementation costs required by this act; and revisions of a bluff setback ordinance incurred by any municipality, which prior to the effective date of this act, adopted a bluff setback ordinance.

(ii) Fifty per cent of the allowable costs for administration of an ordinance incurred by any municipality. Allowable costs for administration of bluff setback ordinance shall not include those costs which are offset by reasonable permit fees imposed by the municipality.

(b) Nothing in this section shall be construed to impair or limit application of this act to any municipality or person, or to relieve any municipality or person of duties imposed under this act.

§ 12. Criminal penalties.

(a) Any person other than the officers of a municipality, county or governmental unit who violates the requirements of section 5 or any bluff setback ordinance or regulation, is guilty of a summary offense and, upon conviction, shall be sentenced to pay a fine of not less than $100 nor more than $1,000 for each separate offense, and, in default of the payment of such fine, to imprisonment for a period of not more than 60 days. All summary proceedings under this act may be brought before any district magistrate of the county where the violation occurred, and jurisdiction is hereby conferred upon said district magistrates subject to appeal by either party in the manner provided by law. In the case of any appeal from any such conviction in the manner provided by law for appeals from summary conviction, it shall be the duty of the district attorney of the county to represent the interests of the Commonwealth.

(b) Any person who, within two years after a conviction in a summary proceeding as provided in subsection (a), violates the requirements of section 5 or any bluff setback ordinances or regulations, is guilty of a misdemeanor of the third degree and, upon conviction, shall be sentenced to pay a fine of not less than $500 nor more than $5,000 for each separate offense or to imprisonment for a period of not more than one year, or both.

(c) Each day of continued violation of any provision of this act or any bluff setback ordinances or regulation shall constitute a separate offense under subsections (a) and (b).

2. 16 U.S.C. §§ 1451 et seq.

Chapter 24 Religious Land Use
Chapter 23 Conservation Easements
Chapter 22.1 Land Banks
Chapter 22 Open Space Lands
Chapter 21-B Regulation of Local Agriculture
Chapter 21-A Gas and Oil
Chapter 20 Bluff Recession and Setback Act
Chapter 19.2 Development Permit Extension Act
Chapter 19.1 Wireless Broadband Collocation Act
Chapter 19 Municipalities Planning Code

§ 13. Civil remedies.

(a) Any activity conducted in violation of section 5,[3] or of any bluff setback ordinances or regulations adopted hereunder, is declared to be a public nuisance.

(b) Suits to restrain, prevent or abate violations of this act or any bluff setback ordinances or regulations adopted hereunder, may be instituted in equity or at law by the department, any affected county or municipality, or any aggrieved person. Except in cases of emergency where, in the opinion of the court, the circumstances of the case require immediate abatement of the unlawful conduct, the court may, in its decree, fix a reasonable time during which the person responsible for the unlawful conduct shall correct or abate the same. The expense of such proceedings shall be recoverable from the violator in such manner as may now or hereafter be provided by law.

§ 14. Appeals.

(a) Any person or municipality aggrieved by an action of the department shall have the right within 30 days of the receipt of notice of such action to appeal such action to the Environmental Hearing Board, pursuant to section 1921-A of the act of April 9, 1929 (P.L. 177, No. 175),[4] known as "The Administrative Code of 1929," and the Administrative Agency Law.

(b) An appeal of any action under this act shall not act as a supersedeas. A supersedeas may be granted by the Environmental Hearing Board upon a showing by the petitioner:

(1) that irreparable harm to the petitioner or other interested parties will result if supersedeas is denied;

(2) that there is a likelihood of the petitioner's success on the merits; and

(3) that the grant of a supersedeas will not result in irreparable harm to the Commonwealth.

The hearing board may grant such a supersedeas subject to such security as it may deem proper.

§ 15. Repealer and savings clause.

(a) All acts or parts of acts inconsistent herewith are hereby repealed to the extent of such inconsistency.

(c) The provisions of this act shall not affect any suit or prosecution pending or to be instituted to enforce any right or penalty or punish any offense under the authority of any act of Assembly or part thereof repealed by this act.

3. 32 P.S. § 5205.

4. 71 P.S. § 510-21 (repealed); see, now, 35 P.S. § 7511 et seq.

Table of Contents
Part I Ch. 1–3 Ethics, Records, Open Meetings
Part II Ch. 4–10 Taxation
Part III Ch. 11–18 Torts, Contracts & Civil Rules
Part IV Ch. 19–24 Zoning & Planning
Part V Ch. 25–30 Construction and Emergency Codes
Part VI Ch. 31–39 Municipal Codes
Index

CHAPTER 21-A

GAS AND OIL

TABLE OF CONTENTS

LOCAL ORDINANCES RELATING TO OIL AND GAS OPERATION

58 Pa.C.S. §3301–3309

LOCAL ORDINANCES RELATING TO OIL AND GAS OPERATION

58 Pa.C.S. §3301-3309

§ 3301. Definitions

The following words and phrases when used in this chapter shall have the meanings given to them in this section unless the context clearly indicates otherwise:

"Building." An occupied structure with walls and a roof within which individuals live or customarily work.

"Commission." The Pennsylvania Public Utility Commission.

"Environmental acts." All statutes enacted by the Commonwealth relating to the protection of the environment or the protection of public health, safety and welfare, that are administered and enforced by the department or by another Commonwealth agency, including an independent agency, and all Federal statutes relating to the protection of the environment, to the extent those statutes regulate oil and gas operations.

"Local government." A county, city, borough, incorporated town or township of this Commonwealth.

"Local ordinance." An ordinance or other enactment, including a provision of a home rule charter, adopted by a local government that regulates oil and gas operations.

"MPC." The act of July 31, 1968 (P.L. 805, No. 247),[1] known as the Pennsylvania Municipalities Planning Code.

"Oil and gas operations." The term includes the following:

1. 53 P.S. § 10101 et seq.

(1) well location assessment, including seismic operations, well site preparation, construction, drilling, hydraulic fracturing and site restoration associated with an oil or gas well of any depth;

(2) water and other fluid storage or impoundment areas used exclusively for oil and gas operations;

(3) construction, installation, use, maintenance and repair of:

(i) oil and gas pipelines;

(ii) natural gas compressor stations; and

(iii) natural gas processing plants or facilities performing equivalent functions; and

(4) construction, installation, use, maintenance and repair of all equipment directly associated with activities specified in paragraphs (1), (2) and (3), to the extent that:

(i) the equipment is necessarily located at or immediately adjacent to a well site, impoundment area, oil and gas pipeline, natural gas compressor station or natural gas processing plant; and

(ii) the activities are authorized and permitted under the authority of a Federal or Commonwealth agency.

"Permitted use." A use which, upon submission of written notice to and receipt of a permit issued by a zoning officer or equivalent official, is authorized to be conducted without restrictions other than those set forth in section 3304 (relating to uniformity of local ordinances).

§ 3302. Oil and gas operations regulated pursuant to Chapter 32

Except with respect to local ordinances adopted pursuant to the MPC and the act of October 4, 1978 (P.L. 851, No. 166),[2] known as the Flood Plain Management Act, all local ordinances purporting to regulate oil and gas operations regulated by Chapter 32 (relating to development) are hereby superseded. No local ordinance adopted pursuant to the MPC or the Flood Plain Management Act shall contain provisions which impose conditions, requirements or limitations on the same features of oil and gas operations regulated by Chapter 32 or that accomplish the same purposes as set forth in Chapter 32. The Commonwealth, by this section, preempts and supersedes the regulation of oil and gas operations as provided in this chapter.

§ 3303. Oil and gas operations regulated by environmental acts

Notwithstanding any other law to the contrary, environmental acts are of Statewide concern and, to the extent that they regulate oil and gas operations, occupy the entire field of regulation, to the exclusion of all local ordinances. The Commonwealth by this section, preempts and supersedes the local regulation of oil and gas operations regulated by the environmental acts, as provided in this chapter.

§ 3304. Uniformity of local ordinances

(a) General rule.—In addition to the restrictions contained in sections 3302 (relating to oil and gas operations regulated pursuant to Chapter 32) and 3303 (relating to oil and gas operations regulated by environmental acts), all local ordinances regulating oil and gas operations shall allow for the reasonable development of oil and gas resources.

(b) Reasonable development of oil and gas resources.—In order to allow the for the reasonable development of oil and gas resources, a local ordinance:

(1) Shall allow well and pipeline location assessment operations, including seismic operations and related activities conducted in accordance with all ap-

2. 32 P.S. § 679.101 et seq.

Chapter 24 Religious Land Use | Chapter 23 Conservation Easements | Chapter 22.1 Land Banks | Chapter 22 Open Space Lands | Chapter 21-B Regulation of Local Agriculture | Chapter 21-A Gas and Oil | Chapter 20 Bluff Recession and Setback Act | Chapter 19.2 Development Permit Extension Act | Chapter 19.1 Wireless Broadband Collocation Act | Chapter 19 Municipalities Planning Code plicable Federal and State laws and regulations relating to the storage and use of explosives throughout every local government.

(2) May not impose conditions, requirements or limitations on the construction of oil and gas operations that are more stringent than conditions, requirements or limitations imposed on construction activities for other industrial uses within the geographic boundaries of the local government.

(3) May not impose conditions, requirements or limitations on the heights of structures, screening and fencing, lighting or noise relating to permanent oil and gas operations that are more stringent than the conditions, requirements or limitations imposed on other industrial uses or other land development within the particular zoning district where the oil and gas operations are situated within the local government.

(4) Shall have a review period for permitted uses that does not exceed 30 days for complete submissions or that does not exceed 120 days for conditional uses.

(5) Shall authorize oil and gas operations, other than activities at impoundment areas, compressor stations and processing plants, as a permitted use in all zoning districts.

(5.1) Notwithstanding section 3215 (relating to well location restrictions), may prohibit, or permit only as a conditional use, wells or well sites otherwise permitted under paragraph (5) within a residential district if the well site cannot be placed so that the wellhead is at least 500 feet from any existing building. In a residential district, all of the following apply:

(i) A well site may not be located so that the outer edge of the well pad is closer than 300 feet from an existing building.

(ii) Except as set forth in paragraph (5) and this paragraph, oil and gas operations, other than the placement, use and repair of oil and gas pipelines, water pipelines, access roads or security facilities, may not take place within 300 feet of an existing building.

(6) Shall authorize impoundment areas used for oil and gas operations as a permitted use in all zoning districts, provided that the edge of any impoundment area shall not be located closer than 300 feet from an existing building.

(7) Shall authorize natural gas compressor stations as a permitted use in agricultural and industrial zoning districts and as a conditional use in all other zoning districts, if the natural gas compressor building meets the following standards:

(i) is located 750 feet or more from the nearest existing building or 200 feet from the nearest lot line, whichever is greater, unless waived by the owner of the building or adjoining lot; and

(ii) the noise level does not exceed a noise standard of 60dbA at the nearest property line or the applicable standard imposed by Federal law, whichever is less.

(8) Shall authorize a natural gas processing plant as a permitted use in an industrial zoning district and as conditional uses in agricultural zoning districts if all of the following apply:

(i) The natural gas processing plant building is located at the greater of at least 750 feet from the nearest existing building or at least 200 feet from the nearest lot line unless waived by the owner of the building or adjoining lot.

(ii) The noise level of the natural gas processing plant building does not exceed a noise standard of 60dbA at the nearest property line or the applicable standard imposed by Federal law, whichever is less.

(9) Shall impose restrictions on vehicular access routes for overweight vehicles only as authorized under 75 Pa.C.S. (relating to vehicles) or the MPC.

(10) May not impose limits or conditions on subterranean operations or hours of operation of compressor stations and processing plants or hours of operation for the drilling of oil and gas wells or the assembly and disassembly of drilling rigs.

(11) May not increase setback distances set forth in Chapter 32 (relating to development) or this chapter. A local ordinance may impose setback distances that are not regulated by or set forth in Chapter 32 or this chapter if the setbacks are no more stringent than those for other industrial uses within the geographic boundaries of the local government.

§ 3305. Commission

(a) Advisory opinions to municipalities.—

(1) A municipality may, prior to the enactment of a local ordinance, in writing, request the commission to review a proposed local ordinance to issue an opinion on whether it violates the MPC, this chapter or Chapter 32 (relating to development).

(2) Within 120 days of receiving a request under paragraph (1), the commission shall, in writing, advise the municipality whether or not the local ordinance violates the MPC, this chapter or Chapter 32.

(3) An opinion under this subsection shall be advisory in nature and not subject to appeal.

(b) Orders.—

(1) An owner or operator of an oil or gas operation, or a person residing within the geographic boundaries of a local government, who is aggrieved by the enactment or enforcement of a local ordinance may request the commission to review the local ordinance of that local government to determine whether it violates the MPC, this chapter or Chapter 32.

(2) Participation in the review by the commission shall be limited to parties specified in paragraph (1) and the municipality which enacted the local ordinance.

(3) Within 120 days of receiving a request under this subsection, the commission shall issue an order to determine whether the local ordinance violates the MPC, this chapter or Chapter 32.

(4) An order under this subsection shall be subject to de novo review by Commonwealth Court. A petition for review must be filed within 30 days of the date of service of the commission's order. The order of the commission shall be made part of the record before the court.

(c) Exemptions.—An opinion under subsection (a) and an order under subsection (b) shall not be subject to:

(1) 2 Pa.C.S. Ch. 5 Subch. A (relating to practice and procedure of Commonwealth agencies);

(2) 65 Pa.C.S. Ch. 7 (relating to open meetings); or

(3) 66 Pa.C.S. Ch. 3 Subch. B[3] (relating to investigations and hearings).

(d) Authority.—The commission has the following powers to carry out this chapter:

(1) Employ individuals.

(2) Issue orders.

3. 66 Pa.C.S. § 331 et seq.

(3) Promulgate regulations.

(4) Until January 1, 2013, promulgate temporary regulations. Regulations under this paragraph:

(i) shall expire no later than two years following the effective date of this section; and

(ii) are exempt from:

(A) sections 201, 202 and 203 of the act of July 31, 1968 (P.L. 769, No. 240),[4] referred to as the Commonwealth Documents Law; and

(B) the act of June 25, 1982 (P.L. 633, No. 181),[5] known as the Regulatory Review Act.

§ 3306. Civil actions

The following shall apply:

(1) Notwithstanding any provision of 42 Pa.C.S. Ch. 85 Subch. C (relating to actions against local parties),[6] any person who is aggrieved by the enactment or enforcement of a local ordinance that violates the MPC, this chapter or Chapter 32 (relating to development) may bring an action in Commonwealth Court to invalidate the ordinance or enjoin its enforcement.

(2) An aggrieved person may proceed under this section without first obtaining review of the ordinance by the commission.

(3) In an action relating to the enactment or enforcement of a local ordinance, a determination of the commission made under section 3305(b) (relating to commission) shall become part of the record before the court.

§ 3307. Attorney fees and costs

In an action brought under section 3306 (relating to civil actions), the court may do any of the following:

(1) If the court determines that the local government enacted or enforced a local ordinance with willful or reckless disregard of the MPC, this chapter or Chapter 32 (relating to development), it may order the local government to pay the plaintiff reasonable attorney fees and other reasonable costs incurred by the plaintiff in connection with the action.

(2) If the court determines that the action brought by the plaintiff was frivolous or was brought without substantial justification in claiming that the local ordinance in question was contrary to the MPC, this chapter or Chapter 32, it may order the plaintiff to pay the local government reasonable attorney fees and other reasonable costs incurred by the local government in defending the action.

§ 3308. Ineligibility

If the commission, Commonwealth Court or the Supreme Court issues an order that a local ordinance violates the MPC, this chapter or Chapter 32 (relating to development), the municipality enacting or enforcing the local ordinance shall be immediately ineligible to receive any funds collected under Chapter 23 (relating to unconventional gas well fee). The local government shall remain ineligible to receive funds under Chapter 23 until the local government amends or repeals its ordinance in accordance with this chapter or the order or determination that the local ordinance is unlawful is reversed on appeal.

4. 45 P.S. §§ 1201 to 1203.

5. 71 P.S. § 745.1 et seq.

6. 42 Pa.C.S. § 8541 et seq.

§ 3309. Applicability

(a) Ordinances.—This chapter shall apply to the enforcement of local ordinances existing on the effective date of this chapter and to the enactment or enforcement of a local ordinance enacted on or after the effective date of this chapter.

(b) Local governments.—A local government that has enacted a local ordinance relating to oil and gas operations prior to the effective date of this chapter shall have 120 days from the effective date of this chapter to review and amend an ordinance in order to comply with this chapter.

CHAPTER 21-B
REGULATION OF LOCAL AGRICULTURE
3 Pa.C.S. §§ 311–522

TABLE OF CONTENTS

CHAPTER 3
LOCAL REGULATION

SUBCHAPTER A
PRELIMINARY PROVISIONS

§ 311. Scope.

This chapter deals with local regulation of normal agricultural operations.

§ 312. Definitions.

The following words and phrases when used in this chapter shall have the meanings given to them in this section unless the context clearly indicates otherwise:

"Local government unit." A political subdivision of the Commonwealth.

"Normal agricultural operation." As defined under section 2 of the act of June 10, 1982 (P.L. 454, No. 133),[1] entitled "An act protecting agricultural operations from nuisance suits and ordinances under certain circumstances."

"Unauthorized local ordinance." An ordinance enacted or enforced by a local government unit which does any of the following:

(1) Prohibits or limits a normal agricultural operation unless the local government unit:

(i) has expressed or implied authority under State law to adopt the ordinance; and

(ii) is not prohibited or preempted under State law from adopting the ordinance.

(2) Restricts or limits the ownership structure of a normal agricultural operation.

1. 3 P.S. § 952.

Chapter 24 Religious Land Use
Chapter 23 Conservation Easements
Chapter 22.1 Land Banks
Chapter 22 Open Space Lands
Chapter 21-B Regulation of Local Agriculture
Chapter 21-A Gas and Oil
Chapter 20 Bluff Recession and Setback Act
Chapter 19.2 Development Permit Extension Act
Chapter 19.1 Wireless Broadband Collocation Act
Chapter 19 Municipalities Planning Code

SUBCHAPTER B
NORMAL AGRICULTURAL OPERATIONS

Sec.

§ 313. Certain local government unit actions prohibited.

(a) Adoption and enforcement of unauthorized local ordinances.—A local government unit shall not adopt nor enforce an unauthorized local ordinance.

(b) Existing local ordinances.—This chapter shall apply to the enforcement of local ordinances existing on the effective date of this section and to the enactment or enforcement of local ordinances enacted on or after the effective date of this section.

(c) Construction.—Notwithstanding the provisions of this section, nothing in this chapter shall be construed to diminish, expand or otherwise affect the legislative or regulatory authority of local government units under State law, including the following:

(1) Chapter 5 (relating to nutrient management and odor management).

(2) The regulation, control or permitting procedures for the land application of class A or B biosolids.

§ 314. Duties of Attorney General.

(a) Request for review.—An owner or operator of a normal agricultural operation may request the Attorney General to review a local ordinance believed to be an unauthorized local ordinance and to consider whether to bring legal action under section 315(a) (relating to right of action).

(b) Discretion.—The Attorney General has the discretion whether to bring an action under section 315(a).

(c) Response.—Within 120 days after receiving a request under subsection (a), the Attorney General shall advise the person that made the request whether or not the Attorney General will bring legal action under section 315(a). If the request under subsection (a) is in writing, the response shall be in writing.

(d) Consultation.—The secretary and the dean of the College of Agricultural Sciences at The Pennsylvania State University shall, upon request of the Attorney General, provide expert consultation regarding the nature of normal agricultural operations in this Commonwealth.

§ 315. Right of action.

(a) Attorney General action.—The Attorney General may bring an action against the local government unit in Commonwealth Court to invalidate the unauthorized local ordinance or enjoin the enforcement of the unauthorized local ordinance.

(b) Other party action.—Notwithstanding any provision of 42 Pa.C.S. Ch. 85 Subch. C (relating to actions against local parties), any person who is aggrieved by the enactment or enforcement of an unauthorized local ordinance may bring an action against the local government unit in Commonwealth Court to invalidate the unauthorized local ordinance or enjoin the enforcement of the unauthorized local ordinance.

§ 316. Commonwealth Court masters.

(a) General rule.—The Commonwealth Court may promulgate rules for the selection and appointment of masters on a full-time or part-time basis for actions brought under section 315 (relating to right of action). A master shall be a member of the bar of this Commonwealth. The number and compensation of masters shall be fixed by the Commonwealth Court and their compensation shall be paid by the Commonwealth.

(b) Hearings before masters.—The Commonwealth Court may direct that hearings in actions brought under section 315 be conducted in the first instance by the master in the manner provided for in this subchapter.

(c) Recommendations of masters.—Upon the conclusion of a hearing before a master, the master shall transmit written findings and a recommendation for disposition to the president judge. Prompt written notice and copies of the findings and recommendations shall be given to the parties to the proceeding.

(d) Rehearing before president judge.—The findings and recommendations of the master shall become the findings and order of the Commonwealth Court upon written confirmation by the president judge. A rehearing may be ordered by the president judge at any time upon cause shown.

§ 317. Attorney fees and costs.

In an action brought under section 315(b) (relating to right of action), the court may do any of the following:

(1) If the court determines that the local government unit enacted or enforced an unauthorized local ordinance with negligent disregard of the limitation of authority established under State law, it may order the local government unit to pay the plaintiff reasonable attorney fees and other litigation costs incurred by the plaintiff in connection with the action.

(2) If the court determines that the action brought by the plaintiff was frivolous or was brought without substantial justification in claiming that the local ordinance in question was unauthorized, it may order the plaintiff to pay the local government unit reasonable attorney fees and other litigation costs incurred by the local government unit in defending the action.

§ 318. Reports to General Assembly.

The Attorney General shall provide to the chairman and the minority chairman of the Senate Committee on Agricultural and Rural Affairs and the chairman and minority chairman of the Agricultural and Rural Affairs Committee of the House of Representatives an annual report to include the following:

(1) Information on how many reviews were requested, the nature of the complaints and the location of the ordinances cited.

(2) Information on how many reviews were conducted.

(3) Information on how many legal actions were brought by the Attorney General.

(4) Information on the outcome of legal actions brought by the Attorney General.

CHAPTER 5

NUTRIENT MANAGEMENT AND ODOR MANAGEMENT

---

§ 501. Scope.

This chapter relates to nutrient management and odor management.

§ 502. Declaration of legislative purpose.

The purposes of this chapter are as follows:

(1) To establish criteria, nutrient management planning requirements and an implementation schedule for the application of nutrient management measures on certain agricultural operations which generate or utilize animal manure.

(2) To provide for the development of an educational program by the State Conservation Commission in conjunction with the Cooperative Extension Service of The Pennsylvania State University, the department and conservation districts to provide outreach to the agricultural community on the proper utilization and management of nutrients on farms to prevent the pollution of surface water and groundwater.

(3) To require the State Conservation Commission, in conjunction with the Cooperative Extension Service of The Pennsylvania State University, the Department of Environmental Protection, the department and the Nutrient Management Advisory Board to develop and provide technical and financial assistance for nutrient management and alternative uses of animal manure, including a manure marketing and distribution program.

(4) To require the Department of Environmental Protection to assess the extent of nonpoint source pollution from other nutrient sources, determine the adequacy of existing authority and programs to manage those sources and make recommendations to provide for the abatement of that pollution.

(5) To require the State Conservation Commission, in conjunction with the Nutrient Management Advisory Board, to develop and administer a regulatory program requiring odor management plans addressing new and expanded animal housing facilities and manure management facilities at concentrated animal operations and concentrated animal feeding operations after July 19, 1993, and to encourage the voluntary implementation of odor management plans for other agricultural operations.

§ 503. Definitions.

The following words and phrases when used in this chapter shall have the meanings given to them in this section unless the context clearly indicates otherwise:

"AEU." Animal equivalent unit.

"AEU per acre." An animal equivalent unit per acre of cropland or acre of land suitable for application of animal manure.

"Agricultural operations." The management and use of farming resources for the production of crops, livestock or poultry.

"Animal equivalent unit." One thousand pounds live weight of livestock or poultry animals, regardless of the actual number of individual animals comprising the unit.

"Animal housing facility." A roofed structure or facility, or any portion thereof, used for occupation by livestock or poultry.

"Best management practice" or "BMP." A practice or combination of practices determined by the commission to be effective and practicable (given technological, economic and institutional considerations) to manage nutrients to protect surface and ground water, taking into account applicable nutrient requirements for crop utilization. The term includes, but is not limited to:

(1) Conservation tillage.

(2) Crop rotation.

(3) Soil testing.

(4) Manure testing.

(5) Diversions.

(6) Manure storage facilities.

(7) Storm water management practices.

(8) Nutrient application.

"Board." The Nutrient Management Advisory Board created by section 510 (relating to Nutrient Management Advisory Board).

"Commission." The State Conservation Commission established by the act of May 15, 1945 (P.L. 547, No. 217),[2] known as the Conservation District Law.

"Concentrated animal feeding operation." An agricultural operation that meets the criteria established by the Department of Environmental Protection under authority of the act of June 22, 1937 (P.L. 1987, No. 394),[3] known as The Clean Streams Law.

"Concentrated animal operation." Agricultural operations meeting the criteria established under this chapter.

"Conservation district." Any county conservation district established under the act of May 15, 1945 (P.L. 547, No. 217), known as the Conservation District Law.

"Cooperative extension." The Cooperative Extension Service of The Pennsylvania State University.

"Department." The Department of Agriculture of the Commonwealth.

"Fund." The Nutrient Management Fund.

"Manure management facility." A manure storage facility, including a permanent structure or facility, or a portion of a structure or facility, utilized for the primary purpose of containing manure. The term includes liquid manure

2. 3 P.S. §§ 849 et seq.

3. 35 P.S. §§ 691.1 et seq.

structures, manure storage ponds, component reception pits and transfer pipes, containment structures built under a confinement building, permanent stacking and composting facilities and manure treatment facilities. The term does not include the animal confinement areas of poultry houses, horse stalls, free stall barns or bedded pack animal housing systems.

"Nutrient." A substance or recognized plant nutrient, element or compound which is used or sold for its plant nutritive content or its claimed nutritive value. The term includes, but is not limited to, livestock and poultry manures, compost as fertilizer, commercially manufactured chemical fertilizers, sewage sludge or combinations thereof.

"Nutrient management plan." A written site-specific plan which incorporates best management practices to manage the use of plant nutrients for crop production and water quality protection consistent with the criteria established in sections 504 (relating to powers and duties of commission) and 506 (relating to nutrient management plans).

"Nutrient management specialist." A person satisfying the certification requirements of section 508 (relating to nutrient management certification program and odor management certification program).

"Odor management plan." A written site-specific plan identifying the practices, technologies, standards and strategies to be implemented to manage the impact of odors generated from animal housing or manure management facilities located or to be located on the site.

§ 504. Powers and duties of commission.

The commission shall have the following powers and duties:

(1) Before July 19, 1995, and periodically thereafter, to promulgate regulations, in consultation with the department, the Department of Environmental Protection and the board, establishing minimum criteria for nutrient management plans developed in accordance with section 506 (relating to nutrient management plans) and other regulatory requirements to implement this chapter. In establishing such criteria, the commission shall consult the Manure Management for Environmental Protection Manual of the Department of Environmental Protection, the Pennsylvania Agronomy Guide published by The Pennsylvania State University and the Pennsylvania Technical Guide for Soil and Water Conservation published by the United States Department of Agriculture's Soil Conservation Service. The criteria to be established pursuant to this section shall include the following:

(i) An identification of nutrients as defined by this chapter. Unless otherwise appropriate pursuant to specific criteria which shall be established by the commission, there shall be a presumption that nitrogen is the nutrient of primary concern.

(ii) The establishment of procedures to determine proper application rates of nutrients to be applied to land based on conditions of soil and levels of existing nutrients in the soil and the type of agricultural, horticultural or floricultural production to be conducted on the land.

(iii) An identification of best management practices to be utilized for proper nutrient management.

(iv) The establishment of recordkeeping requirements related to land application and distribution of nutrients.

(v) The establishment of minimum standards of construction, location, storage capacity and operation of facilities intended to be used for storage of animal manure.

(vi) The establishment of conditions under which amendments to nutrient management plans are required to be made after initial development or filing.

(vii) The establishment of special criteria which may be utilized for manure handling in emergency situations where there is an outbreak of a contagious disease.

(viii) The establishment of conditions under which changes due to unforeseen circumstances render the plan amendment process set forth in section 506(e) impracticable. Where such conditions exist, the owner or operator of an agricultural operation shall follow the procedures set forth in section 506(f).

(1.1) Within two years following the effective date of this section and periodically thereafter, to promulgate regulations, in consultation with the department, the Department of Environmental Protection and the board, establishing practices, technologies, standards, strategies and other requirements for odor management plans developed in accordance with section 509 (relating to odor management plans). The commission shall consider the following in promulgating the regulations under this paragraph:

(i) Site-specific factors such as proximity to adjoining landowners, land use of the surrounding area, type of structures proposed, species of animals, local topography and direction of the prevailing winds.

(ii) Reasonably available technology, practices, standards and strategies to manage odor impacts, considering both the practical and economic feasibility of installation and operation and the potential impacts from the facilities. Only those technologies, practices, standards and strategies that are necessary to address the offsite impacts of odors associated with these new facilities will be required to be included in the odor management plans.

(2) Prior to the adoption of regulations under paragraph (1.1), to establish interim guidelines for the operations identified in section 509.

(3) To continually evaluate emerging practices, methods and technology for utilization as best management practices and to so identify the practices, where appropriate, pursuant to paragraph (1)(iii).

(4) Beginning October 1, 2002, to evaluate the criteria for concentrated animal operations in this Commonwealth and to make appropriate changes in those criteria by regulation. Any such regulatory change related to concentrated animal operations shall require a two-thirds majority vote of the commission.

(5) Prior to the adoption of regulations under paragraph (1), to recommend, in consultation with the Department of Environmental Protection, the department and the board, interim criteria for the sole purpose of facilitating the initial development of the nutrient management certification program established by this chapter.

(6) Before July 19, 1995, to develop and implement, in cooperation with the department, the board, the Cooperative Extension Service and conservation districts, a program to provide education and technical assistance to the agricultural community and, to the extent funds are available, to provide financial assistance to existing agricultural operations for implementation of proper methods, practices, facilities and techniques for the utilization and management of nutrients on the farm to prevent the pollution of groundwater and surface water.

(7) To consult with the board as provided in section 510 (relating to Nutrient Management Advisory Board).

(8) To issue orders and take actions as are necessary to administer and enforce this chapter.

(9) To delegate administration or enforcement authority, or both, under this chapter to county conservation districts that have an adequate program and sufficient resources to accept and implement this delegation.

§ 505. Powers and duties of Department of Environmental Protection.

The Department of Environmental Protection shall have the following powers and duties:

(1) Before July 19, 1994, to make an assessment of and report to the Environmental Quality Board and the General Assembly on the extent to which malfunctioning on-lot sewage systems contribute to the pollution of waters of this Commonwealth and to identify what regulatory or legislative initiatives, if any, the Department of Environmental Protection deems necessary to abate that pollution.

(2) Before July 19, 1994, to make an assessment of and report to the Environmental Quality Board and the General Assembly on the extent to which improper water well construction contributes to groundwater pollution due to the intrusion of nutrients from the surface and to identify what regulatory or legislative initiatives, if any, the Department of Environmental Protection deems necessary to abate that pollution.

(3) Before July 19, 1995, to make an assessment of and report to the Environmental Quality Board and the General Assembly on the extent to which the application of chemical fertilizers and other plant nutrients for nonagricultural purposes contributes to the pollution of the waters of this Commonwealth and to identify what regulatory or legislative initiatives, if any, the Department of Environmental Protection deems necessary to abate that pollution.

(4) Before July 19, 1995, to make an assessment of and report to the Environmental Quality Board and the General Assembly on the extent to which nutrients from storm water runoff contribute to the pollution of waters of this Commonwealth and to identify what regulatory or legislative initiatives, if any, the Department of Environmental Protection deems necessary to abate that pollution.

(5) Before July 19, 1995, to make an assessment of and report to the Environmental Quality Board and the General Assembly on the extent to which atmospheric deposition of nutrients contribute to the pollution of the waters of this Commonwealth and to identify what regulatory or legislative initiatives, if any, the Department of Environmental Protection deems necessary to abate that pollution.

(6) To include, in the assessments in paragraphs (1) through (5), recommendations to the General Assembly for budgetary and legislative initiatives where program resources or statutory authority is not adequate to address pollution sources identified in those assessments.

(7) To provide technical and administrative assistance to the commission in carrying out its responsibilities under this chapter.

§ 506. Nutrient management plans.

(a) Concentrated animal operations.—Concentrated animal operations are those agricultural operations where the animal density exceeds two AEUs per acre on an annualized basis. Beginning October 1, 2002, the commission, in consultation with the department, the board, the Department of Environmental Protection and the Cooperative Extension Service, shall review the criteria used to identify concentrated animal operations and make appropriate changes to the definition of concentrated animal operations by regulation.

(b) Development of nutrient management plans.—The operator of any concentrated animal operation shall develop and implement a nutrient management plan consistent with the requirements of this section.

(c) Certification of plans.—All plans and plan amendments shall be developed by nutrient management specialists who shall certify that the plans are in accordance with the requirements of this chapter and the regulations promulgated under this chapter.

(d) Review procedure.—Nutrient management plans required by this section shall be submitted for review in accordance with the following schedule:

(1) For a concentrated animal operation in existence on October 1, 1997, by October 1, 1998.

(2) For a concentrated animal operation which comes into existence after October 1, 1997, by the later of:

(i) January 1, 1998; or

(ii) commencement of operations.

(3) For an agricultural operation which, because of expansion, meets the criteria for a concentrated animal operation, within three months after the date of expansion.

(e) Plan review and approval.—Plans or plan amendments required under this chapter shall be submitted to local conservation districts for review and approval or alternatively to the commission for agricultural operations located in counties not delegated administrative authority under section 504 (relating to powers and duties of commission). Any person performing the plan review must be certified in accordance with section 508 (relating to nutrient management certification program and odor management certification program). Within 90 days of receipt of a nutrient management plan or plan amendment, the reviewing agency shall either approve, modify or disapprove the plan or plan amendment. Approvals shall only be granted for those plans or plan amendments which satisfy the requirements of this chapter and the regulations promulgated under this chapter. Notice of determination to approve, modify or disapprove a plan or plan amendment shall be provided in writing to the person submitting same. Notice of a determination to modify or disapprove shall include an explanation specifically stating the reasons for modification or disapproval. If a plan or plan amendment is disapproved, the person submitting a plan or plan amendment for the first time shall have 90 days after receipt of notice of disapproval to resubmit a revised plan or plan amendment. An agricultural operation that submits a complete plan or plan amendment is authorized to implement the same if the reviewing agency fails to act within 90 days of submittal. Where the reviewing agency fails to so act and the plan or plan amendment is resubmitted and the reviewing agency again fails to act within 90 days of resubmittal, it shall be deemed approved.

(f) Amendments due to unforeseen circumstances.—Amendments to plans or to implementation of plans made after initial development or filing which satisfy the criteria established under section 504(1)(vii) shall be certified by a nutrient management specialist prior to implementation and submitted to the district within 30 days of implementation.

(g) Implementation.—A person required to develop a nutrient management plan pursuant to subsection (b) shall fully implement such plan within three years of the date such plan is approved or is deemed approved or for which implementation is otherwise authorized pursuant to subsection (e), unless extended for cause shown or by a plan amendment. The three-year implementation schedule shall be extended an additional two years for individual substantial capital improvements required under an approved plan for an operation required to submit a plan under subsection (d)(1) if:

Table of Contents
Part I Ch. 1–3 Ethics, Records, Open Meetings
Part II Ch. 4–10 Taxation
Part III Ch. 11–18 Torts, Contracts & Civil Rules
Part IV Ch. 19–24 Zoning & Planning
Part V Ch. 25–30 Construction and Emergency Codes
Part VI Ch. 31–39 Municipal Codes
Index

(1) the owner or operator demonstrates that the cost of all or part of the individual improvements for which the extension is applicable cannot be financed through available funding mechanisms; and

(2) a sum of $2,000,000 or more has not been appropriated for grants and loans to the Nutrient Management Fund created under section 512 (relating to Nutrient Management Fund), above and beyond any Chesapeake Bay nonpoint source pollution abatement moneys that may be appropriated to the fund, before October 1, 1998.

(h) Voluntary plans.—Any agricultural operation which is not a concentrated animal operation may voluntarily develop a nutrient management plan and have it reviewed pursuant to this section. To the extent possible, the commission, the Cooperative Extension Service, the department, the Department of Environmental Protection and conservation districts shall assist and promote the development of voluntary plans.

(i) Financial assistance.—Any agricultural operation receiving financial assistance under the Chesapeake Bay Nonpoint Source Pollution Abatement Program or otherwise receiving financial assistance under this chapter for the development of a nutrient management plan shall agree to develop and implement a nutrient management plan as a condition for receiving this financial assistance.

(j) Compliance plans.—Any agricultural operation found to be in violation of the act of June 22, 1937 (P.L. 1987, No. 394), known as The Clean Streams Law, may be required to submit a nutrient management plan within three months of notification thereof and implement the plan in order to prevent or abate such pollution.

(k) Transferability of plans.—A plan approved under this section shall be transferable to a subsequent owner of an agricultural operation upon notification thereof to the district unless the transfer results in operational changes requiring plan modification pursuant to the criteria established under section 504(1)(vi).

(l) Construction of section.—The density criteria for concentrated animal operations as identified in subsection (a) or as it may be subsequently modified by the commission shall only be utilized to identify those agricultural operations for which the planning requirements of this section shall apply and shall not be construed to prohibit the development or expansion of agricultural operations meeting or exceeding such criteria.

§ 507. Manure application setbacks and buffers.

(a) General rule.—Unless the commission establishes a stricter requirement by regulation, no concentrated animal operation or other agricultural operation receiving manure from a concentrated animal operation directly or indirectly through a broker or other person may mechanically land apply manure within 100 feet of surface water unless a vegetated buffer no less than 35 feet in width and meeting standards established by the Natural Resources Conservation Service is used to prevent manure runoff into the surface water.

(b) Definition.—As used in this section, the term "surface water" means a perennial or intermittent stream with a defined bed and bank, a lake or a pond.

§ 508. Nutrient management certification program and odor management certification program.

(a) Requirement.—The department shall establish, in consultation with the commission, a nutrient management certification program for the purpose of certifying individuals who have demonstrated the competency necessary to develop nutrient management plans and an odor management certification program for the purpose of certifying individuals who have demonstrated the competency necessary to develop odor management plans. The department or its designee shall develop such written testing procedures, educational requirements and examinations as it deems appropriate to carry out its responsibilities under this section. The department shall by regulation establish such fees and terms and conditions of certification as it deems appropriate. The department shall establish individual, commercial and public certification categories, including a certification category for farmers to develop and certify nutrient management plans and odor management plans for their own agricultural operations.

(b) Interim nutrient management certification program.—Until the department develops and implements a nutrient management certification program, persons having the following qualifications shall, upon request, receive interim certification from the department.

(1) the person has at least two years' experience in the development of nutrient management plans;

(2) the person is approved to develop nutrient management plans approved under the Chesapeake Bay Nonpoint Source Pollution Abatement Program, the United States Department of Agriculture's Water Quality Improvement Projects Program or other programs requiring submission and approval of a nutrient management plan, including sludge disposal under the act of July 7, 1980 (P.L. 380, No. 97),[4] known as the Solid Waste Management Act; or

(3) the person is a farmer who has been provided training and assistance in developing and implementing nutrient management plans.

(c) Nutrient management specialist.—A person shall not certify a nutrient management plan or plan amendment unless that person has first satisfied the requirements of this section.

(d) Odor management specialist.—A person shall not certify an odor management plan or plan amendment unless that person has first satisfied the applicable requirements of this section.

§ 509. Odor management plans.

(a) Requirement.—

(1) The following operations shall develop and implement an odor management plan as described in this chapter:

(i) Existing concentrated animal operations and existing concentrated animal feeding operations, when doing any of the following:

(A) Erecting or constructing a new animal housing facility or a new manure management facility. The odor management plan required by this paragraph shall be developed and implemented only with respect to the new facility.

(B) Erecting or constructing an expansion of an animal housing facility or a manure management facility. The odor management plan required by this paragraph shall be developed and implemented only with respect to the newly erected or newly constructed portion of the facility.

(ii) Existing agricultural operations which, because of an increase, resulting from expansion or construction, in the number of animals maintained at the operation, will become regulated as either a concentrated animal operation or a concentrated animal feeding operation. The odor management plan required by this paragraph shall be developed and implemented only with respect to the newly expanded or newly constructed portion of the operation.

(iii) New agricultural operations which will be regulated as either a concentrated animal operation or a concentrated animal feeding operation.

4. 35 P.S. §§ 6018.101 et seq.

Table of Contents
Part I Ch. 1–3 Ethics, Records, Open Meetings
Part II Ch. 4–10 Taxation
Part III Ch. 11–18 Torts, Contracts & Civil Rules
Part IV Ch. 19–24 Zoning & Planning
Part V Ch. 25–30 Construction and Emergency Codes
Part VI Ch. 31–39 Municipal Codes
Index

(2) The operations described in paragraph (1)(i) and (ii) shall obtain approval of their odor management plan prior to the earlier of erection or construction of new or expanded animal housing facilities or the construction of new or expanded manure management facilities.

(b) Certification of plans.—All odor management plans and plan amendments shall be developed by odor management specialists who shall certify that the plans are in accordance with the requirements of the odor management regulations promulgated under this chapter.

(c) Reviewing entities.—Odor management plans or plan amendments required by this section shall be submitted to the commission for review and approval or, at the commission's discretion, to the appropriate local conservation district for review and approval.

(d) Plan review and approval.—Any person performing the plan review must be certified in accordance with section 508 (relating to nutrient management certification program and odor management certification program). Within 90 days of receipt of an odor management plan or plan amendment, the reviewing agency shall approve or disapprove the plan or plan amendment. Approvals shall only be granted for those plans or plan amendments which satisfy the requirements of the regulations promulgated under this chapter. Notice of determination to approve or disapprove a plan or plan amendment shall be provided in writing to the person submitting same. Notice of a determination to disapprove shall include an explanation specifically stating the reasons for disapproval. If a plan or plan amendment is disapproved, the person submitting a plan or plan amendment for the first time shall have 90 days after receipt of notice of disapproval to resubmit a revised plan or plan amendment. An existing or proposed concentrated animal operation or concentrated animal feeding operation that submits a complete plan or plan amendment is authorized to implement the same if the reviewing agency fails to act within 90 days of submittal.

(e) Implementation.—A person required to have an odor management plan under this section shall fully implement the plan prior to commencing use of the new animal housing facility or animal manure facility.

(f) Voluntary plans.—Any agricultural operation which is not required to comply with subsection (a) may voluntarily develop an odor management plan and have it reviewed pursuant to this section. To the extent possible, the commission, the Cooperative Extension Service, the department, the Department of Environmental Protection and conservation districts shall assist and promote the development of voluntary plans.

(g) Transferability of plans.—A plan approved under this section shall be transferable to a subsequent owner of an agricultural operation upon notification thereof to the district unless the transfer results in operational changes requiring plan modification pursuant to the criteria established in this section.

(h) Effectiveness of the section.—The requirements of this section shall become mandatory 90 days following the effective date of the regulations promulgated under section 504(1.1) (relating to powers and duties of commission).

§ 510. Nutrient Management Advisory Board.

(a) Creation.—There is created the Nutrient Management Advisory Board. The board shall consist of 16 members appointed by the chairman of the commission and approved by a two-thirds vote of the commission. The members so appointed shall consist of six active commercial farm owners or operators representing the livestock, swine, meat poultry, egg poultry and dairy industry nominated by Statewide general farm organizations, one veterinary nutrition specialist, one representative from the feed industry, one representative from the fertilizer industry, one representative of local government, one representative of academia who shall be an agronomist or plant scientist faculty member of the school of agriculture of a Pennsylvania college or university, one representative of academia who shall be an animal science faculty member with an expertise in odor management from the school of agriculture of a college or university within this Commonwealth, one hydrologist, two citizen representatives who are not farmers and one environmental representative, all of whom shall have sufficient knowledge, experience or familiarity with agronomic practices, nutrient management practices or odor management practices and all of whom shall be residents of this Commonwealth. The six active commercial farm owners or operators shall be nominated in a manner that provides representation of the northwest, north central, northeast, southwest, south central and southeast regions of this Commonwealth, corresponding to the regions served by the Department of Environmental Protection regional offices. Two of the six active commercial farm owners or operators shall hold an active concentrated animal feeding operation permit as required by the act of June 22, 1937 (P.L.1987, No.394), known as The Clean Streams Law.

(b) Compensation.—Board members shall not receive a salary but shall be reimbursed for all reasonable and necessary expenses incurred in the performance of their duties.

(c) Meetings.—A majority of the board shall constitute a quorum. All actions of the board shall be by a majority vote. The board shall meet upon the call of the commission, but not less than semiannually, to carry out its duties under this chapter. The board shall annually select a chairman and such other officers as it deems appropriate.

(d) Duties.—The board shall review and comment on all commission proposed regulations developed to implement the provisions of this chapter. The commission shall have no power to promulgate regulations under this chapter until receipt of written comments on the proposed regulations from the board or until 90 days have expired from the date when the regulations were submitted by the commission to the board for its comments. Existing regulations shall continue until modified, superseded or repealed by the commission.

(e) Term.—The term of office for each board member shall be three years except that the commission shall stagger the initial terms of the charter members such that five shall serve for one year, five shall serve for two years and six shall serve for three years. Board members may be appointed to successive terms at the discretion of the commission, provided that no member may serve more than two three-year terms.

§ 511. Financial assistance.

(a) Loans, grants, etc.—The commission shall, to the extent funds are available, provide financial assistance in the form of loans, loan guarantees and grants for the implementation of nutrient management plans and of odor management plans for existing agricultural operations.

(b) Criteria for eligibility.—In reviewing applications for financial assistance, the commission shall consider the following:

(1) Whether the project will improve the health, safety or environment of the people of this Commonwealth and otherwise satisfy the purposes of this chapter.

(2) The cost-effectiveness of the proposed practices in comparison with other alternatives.

(3) The applicant's ability to operate or maintain the practices in a proper manner.

(c) Issuance and terms.—Subject to this section, the commission shall issue loans and set terms applicable thereto in any manner it deems appropriate. The commission may consider such factors as it deems relevant, including current market interest rates, the financial ability of the applicant to repay and the necessity to maintain the funds created hereunder in a financially sound manner. Loans may be based on the ability to repay from future revenue to be derived from

Table of Contents
Part I Ch. 1–3 Ethics, Records, Open Meetings
Part II Ch. 4–10 Taxation
Part III Ch. 11–18 Torts, Contracts & Civil Rules
Part IV Ch. 19–24 Zoning & Planning
Part V Ch. 25–30 Construction and Emergency Codes
Part VI Ch. 31–39 Municipal Codes
Index

Chapter 24 Religious Land Use
Chapter 23 Conservation Easements
Chapter 22.1 Land Banks
Chapter 22 Open Space Lands
Chapter 21-B Regulation of Local Agriculture
Chapter 21-A Gas and Oil
Chapter 20 Bluff Recession and Setback Act
Chapter 19.2 Development Permit Extension Act
Chapter 19.1 Wireless Broadband Collocation Act
Chapter 19 Municipalities Planning Code

the applicant's agricultural operation, by a mortgage or other security interest or by any other fiscal manner which the commission deems appropriate. The board shall have the power to defer principal on loans for up to 12 months. The minimum rate of interest to be paid on any loan made pursuant to this section shall be 1%.

(d) Grants.—Grants shall be made available as follows:

(1) Where funds have been made available to the commission, subject to any conditions that may have accompanied the receipt of such funds.

(2) Where the commission, in its sole discretion, determines that the financial condition of the recipient is such that repayment of a loan is unlikely and that the recipient will be financially distressed by the implementation of practices without a grant.

(e) Grants and loans.—The commission shall, where it deems appropriate and to the extent financial circumstances permit, mix grant funds with loan funds.

§ 512. Nutrient Management Fund.

(a) Establishment of fund.—There is established a special nonlapsing fund in the State Treasury to be known as the Nutrient Management Fund. All fees, fines, judgments and interest collected by the commission under this chapter shall be paid into the fund. All money placed in the fund and the interest it accrues are hereby appropriated to the commission on a continuing basis for any activities necessary to meet the requirements of this chapter.

(b) Supplements to fund.—The Nutrient Management Fund may be supplemented by moneys received from the following sources:

(1) State funds appropriated to the commission.

(2) Federal funds appropriated to the commission.

(3) Proceeds from the sale of any bonds made available to the commission.

(4) Repayment of loan principal.

(5) Payment on interest loans made by the commission.

(6) Gifts and other contributions from public and private sources.

(c) Fund administration.—The commission shall have authority to adopt procedures for the use of moneys in the fund, including the creation of accounts within the fund for the purposes of administering the loan and grant programs authorized by this chapter.

(d) Status of fund.—The Nutrient Management Fund shall not be subject to 42 Pa.C.S. Ch. 37 Subch. C (relating to judicial computer system).

(e) Deposit and use of funds.—No administrative action shall prevent the deposit of moneys into the fund in the fiscal year in which they are received. The funds shall only be used for the purposes authorized by this chapter and shall not be transferred or diverted to any other purpose by administrative action.

§ 513. Unlawful conduct.

It shall be unlawful to fail to comply with or to cause or assist in the violation of any order or any of the provisions of this chapter or the rules and regulations adopted under this chapter or to fail to comply with a nutrient management plan or an odor management plan.

§ 514. Civil penalties and remedies.

(a) Civil penalty.—In addition to proceeding under any other remedy available at law or in equity for a violation of a provision of this chapter or a rule or regulation adopted, order issued or odor management plan or nutrient management plan approved under this chapter, the commission may assess a civil penalty of not more than $500 for the first day of each offense and $100 for each additional day of continuing violation. The factors for consideration in determining the amount of the penalty are:

(1) The gravity of the violation.

(2) The potential harm to the public.

(3) The potential effect on the environment.

(4) The willfulness of the violation.

(5) Previous violations.

(6) The economic benefit to the violator for failing to comply with this chapter.

Whenever the commission finds that a violation did not cause harm to human health or an adverse effect on the environment, the commission may issue a warning in lieu of assessing a penalty where the owner or operator, upon notice, takes immediate action to resolve the violation and come into compliance. If the commission finds the nutrient pollution or the danger of nutrient pollution or the negative impacts from odor associated with new or expanded facilities results from conditions, activities or practices which are being or have been implemented in accordance with a nutrient management plan or odor management plan developed and approved pursuant to and consistent with this chapter and the regulations developed under this chapter and which is being or has been fully implemented and maintained, the owner or operator of the agricultural operation shall be exempt from the imposition of penalties under this chapter.

(b) Collection.—In cases of inability to collect the civil penalty or failure of any person to pay all or a portion of the penalty, the commission may refer the matter to the Office of General Counsel or the Office of Attorney General which shall institute an action in the appropriate court to recover the penalty. Any penalty assessed shall act as a lien on the property of the person against whom the penalty has been assessed.

(c) Civil remedies.—In addition to any other remedies provided for in this chapter, any violation of this chapter, the rules and regulations promulgated under this chapter or any order or nutrient management plan or odor management plan approved under this chapter shall be abatable in the manner provided by law or equity for the abatement of public nuisances. In addition, in order to restrain or prevent any violation of this chapter or the rules and regulations promulgated under this chapter or any order or nutrient management plan or odor management plan approved under this chapter, suits may be instituted in equity or at law in the name of the Commonwealth upon relation of the Attorney General, the General Counsel, the district attorney of any county, the solicitor of any municipality affected or the solicitor of any conservation district, provided that the General Counsel, district attorney or solicitor shall first serve notice upon the Attorney General of the intention to so proceed. These proceedings may be prosecuted in the Commonwealth Court or in the court of common pleas of the county where the activity has taken place, the condition exists or the public is affected, and, to that end, jurisdiction is hereby conferred in law and equity upon these courts. Except in cases of emergency where, in the opinion of the court, the exigencies of the case require immediate abatement of the nuisance, the court may in its decree fix a reasonable time during which the person responsible for the nuisance may make provision for the abatement of same.

(d) Equitable relief.—In cases where the circumstances require it or the public health is endangered, a mandatory preliminary injunction, special injunction or temporary restraining order may be issued upon the terms prescribed by the court, provided that notice of the application has been given to the defendant in accordance with the rules of equity practice. In any such proceeding the Attorney General, the General Counsel, the district attorney or the solicitor of any municipality or conservation district shall not be required to give bond. In any such proceeding, the court shall issue a prohibitory or mandatory preliminary injunction if it finds that the defendant is engaging in unlawful conduct as defined by this chapter or is engaged in conduct which is causing immediate and irreparable harm to the public. In addition to an injunction, the court in such equity proceeding may assess civil penalties in accordance with this section.

§ 515. Limitation of liability.

If a person is fully and properly implementing a nutrient management plan or an odor management plan approved by the local conservation district or the commission and maintained under this chapter for an agricultural operation, the implementation shall be given appropriate consideration as a mitigating factor in any civil action for penalties or damages alleged to have been caused by the management or utilization of nutrients or the abatement of odor impacts pursuant to the implementation.

§ 516. Enforcement authority; enforcement orders.

(a) Right of access.—A duly authorized agent of the commission or a conservation district shall have authority to enter any agricultural operation at reasonable times to conduct such investigations and to take such actions as are necessary to enforce the provisions of this chapter or any order, rule or regulation issued hereunder.

(b) Duty to grant access.—Any person owning or operating an agricultural operation shall grant access to any duly authorized agent of the commission or a conservation district pursuant to subsection (a) and shall not hinder, obstruct, prevent or interfere with such agents in the performance of their duties, provided, however, that agents shall perform such reasonable measures and actions as directed by the owner or operator of an agricultural operation as will reasonably and substantially prevent the spread or outbreak of contagious diseases.

(c) Orders.—The commission or any conservation district delegated enforcement authority may issue such orders as are necessary to aid in the enforcement of the provisions of this chapter. Any order issued under this section shall take effect upon notice unless the order specifies otherwise. An appeal of the order to the Environmental Hearing Board shall not act as a supersedeas, provided that, upon application for and cause shown, the hearing board may issue such a supersedeas under the rules established by the hearing board.

§ 517. Appealable actions.

Any person aggrieved by an order or other administrative action of the commission issued pursuant to this chapter shall have the right, within 30 days from actual or constructive notice of the action, to appeal the action to the Environmental Hearing Board.

§ 518. Powers reserved under existing laws.

Nothing in this chapter shall limit in any way whatever the powers conferred upon the commission, the department, the Department of Environmental Protection or a conservation district under laws other than this chapter, including, but not limited to, the act of June 22, 1937 (P.L. 1987, No. 394), known as The Clean Streams Law, and the act of July 7, 1980 (P.L. 380, No. 97), known as the Solid Waste Management Act, and common law. All such powers are preserved and may be freely exercised. A court exercising general equitable jurisdiction shall not be deprived of such jurisdiction even though a nuisance or condition detrimental to health is subject to regulation or other action by the board under this chapter.

§ 519. Preemption of local ordinances.

(a) General.—This chapter and its provisions are of Statewide concern and occupy the whole field of regulation regarding nutrient management and odor management, to the exclusion of all local regulations.

(b) Nutrient management.—No ordinance or regulation of any political subdivision or home rule municipality may prohibit or in any way regulate practices related to the storage, handling or land application of animal manure or nutrients or to the construction, location or operation of facilities used for storage of animal manure or nutrients or practices otherwise regulated by this chapter if the municipal ordinance or regulation is in conflict with this chapter and the regulations or guidelines promulgated under it.

(c) Odor management.—No ordinance or regulation of a political subdivision or home rule municipality may regulate the management of odors generated from animal housing or manure management facilities regulated by this chapter if the municipal ordinance or regulation is in conflict with this chapter and the regulations or guidelines promulgated under it.

(d) Stricter requirements.—Nothing in this chapter shall prevent a political subdivision or home rule municipality from adopting and enforcing ordinances or regulations which are consistent with and no more stringent than the requirements of this chapter and the regulations or guidelines promulgated under this chapter. No penalty shall be assessed under any such local ordinance or regulation under this subsection for any violation for which a penalty has been assessed under this chapter.

§ 520. Repeals.

All acts and parts of acts are repealed insofar as they are inconsistent with this chapter.

§ 521. Other statutes not affected.

This chapter shall not be construed as modifying, rescinding or superseding any other statute or as regulating biosolids and shall be read in pari materia with other statutes. Nothing in this chapter shall limit in any way whatever the powers conferred upon the department, the Department of Environmental Protection and the State Conservation Commission under statutes other than this chapter. All such powers are preserved and may be freely exercised.

§ 522. Regulations.

The Department of Environmental Protection is authorized to adopt such regulations as it deems necessary to its administration and enforcement of this chapter. This includes the authority to establish, by regulation, such fees as are reasonably necessary to fund the implementation and enforcement of this chapter.

Additional Provisions Upon Enactment:

Severability (a) Except as set forth in subsection (b), the provisions of this act are severable. If any provision of this act or its application to any person or circumstance is held invalid, the invalidity shall not affect other provisions or applications of this act which can be given effect without the invalid provision or application.

(b) If any provision of the addition of 3 Pa.C.S. Ch. 3 or the application of such a provision to any person or circumstance is held invalid, the following provisions are void:

(1) The addition of 3 Pa.C.S. Ch. 5.

(2) Section 3 of this act.

Repeals

(1) The General Assembly declares that the repeal under paragraph (2) is necessary to effectuate the nutrient management provisions being consolidated under this act. Repealed: PA ST 3 P.S. § 1701, 3 P.S. § 1702, 3 P.S. § 1703, 3 P.S. § 1704, 3 P.S. § 1705, 3 P.S. § 1706, 3 P.S. § 1707, 3 P.S. § 1708, 3 P.S.

Table of Contents
Part I Ch. 1–3 Ethics, Records, Open Meetings
Part II Ch. 4–10 Taxation
Part III Ch. 11–18 Torts, Contracts & Civil Rules
Part IV Ch. 19–24 Zoning & Planning
Part V Ch. 25–30 Construction and Emergency Codes
Part VI Ch. 31–39 Municipal Codes
Index

§ 1709, 3 P.S. § 1710, 3 P.S. § 1711, 3 P.S. § 1712, 3 P.S. § 1713, 3 P.S. § 1714, 3 P.S. § 1715, 3 P.S. § 1716, 3 P.S. § 1717, 3 P.S. § 1718

(2) The act of May 20, 1993 (P.L. 12, No. 6),[5] known as the Nutrient Management Act, is repealed.

Continuations

The addition of 3 Pa.C.S. Ch. 5 is a continuation of the act of May 20, 1993 (P.L. 12, No. 6), known as the Nutrient Management Act. The following apply:

(1) Except as otherwise provided in 3 Pa.C.S. Ch. 5, all activities initiated under the Nutrient Management Act shall continue and remain in full force and effect and may be completed under 3 Pa.C.S. Ch. 5. Orders, regulations, rules and decisions which were made under the Nutrient Management Act and which are in effect on the effective date of section 3 of this act shall remain in full force and effect until revoked, vacated or modified under 3 Pa.C.S. Ch. 5. Contracts and obligations entered into under the Nutrient Management Act are not affected nor impaired by the repeal of the Nutrient Management Act.

(2) Except as set forth in paragraph (3), any difference in language between 3 Pa.C.S. Ch. 5 and the Nutrient Management Act is intended only to conform to the style of the Pennsylvania Consolidated Statutes and is not intended to change or affect the legislative intent, judicial construction or administration and implementation of the Nutrient Management Act.

(3) Paragraph (2) does not apply to the addition of any of the following provisions of 3 Pa.C.S.:

(i) Section 501.

(ii) Section 502(5).

(iii) The definitions of "animal housing facility," "concentrated animal feeding operation," "manure management facility" and "odor management plan" in section 503.

(iv) Section 504(1.1) and (2).

(v) Section 506.

(vi) Section 507.

(vii) Section 508.

(viii) Section 509.

(ix) Section 510(a), (d) and (e).

(x) Section 511(a).

(xi) Section 513.

(xii) Section 514(a), (c) and (d).

(xiii) Section 515.

(xiv) Section 519.

(xv) Section 521.

(xvi) Section 522.

(4) The addition of 3 Pa.C.S. Ch. 5 does not affect the terms of office of the members of the Nutrient Management Advisory Board in office on the effective date of this paragraph.

Effective Dates

(1) The addition of 3 Pa.C.S. § 507 shall take effect in 180 days.

(2) The addition of 3 Pa.C.S. § 519(c) shall take effect on the earlier of:

5. 3 P.S. §§ 1701 et seq.

(i) the effective date of regulations promulgated under 3 Pa.C.S. § 504(1.1); or

(ii) the publication in the Pennsylvania Bulletin of interim guidelines under 3 Pa.C.S. § 504(2).

(3) The remainder of this act shall take effect immediately. Approved July 6, 2005.

Table of Contents
Part I Ch. 1–3 Ethics, Records, Open Meetings
Part II Ch. 4–10 Taxation
Part III Ch. 11–18 Torts, Contracts & Civil Rules
Part IV Ch. 19–24 Zoning & Planning
Part V Ch. 25–30 Construction and Emergency Codes
Part VI Ch. 31–39 Municipal Codes
Index

CHAPTER 22

OPEN SPACE LANDS ACQUISITION AND PRESERVATION

32 P.S. §§ 5001–5013

TABLE OF CONTENTS

Sec.

§ 5001. Statement of legislative intent.

It is the purpose of this act to clarify and broaden the existing methods by which the Commonwealth and its local government units may preserve land in or acquire land for open space uses. The Legislature finds that it is important to preserve open space and to meet needs for recreation, amenity, and conservation of natural resources, including farm land, forests, and a pure and adequate water supply. The acquisition and resale of property interests authorized by this act are hereby declared to be for the public benefit, for the advancement of the public health, safety, morals and general welfare of the citizens of the Commonwealth, and for the promotion of sound land development by preserving suitable open space and concentrating more dense development in nearby areas.

§ 5002. Definitions.

For the purpose of this act the following definitions shall apply:

(1) Open space benefits. The benefits to the citizens of the Commonwealth and its local government units which result from the preservation or restriction of the use of selected predominantly undeveloped open spaces or areas, including but not limited to: (i) the protection and conservation of water resources and watersheds, by appropriate means, including but not limited to preserving the natural cover, preventing floods and soil erosion, protecting water quality and replenishing surface and ground water supplies; (ii) the protection and conservation of forests and land being used to produce timber crops; (iii) the protection and conservation of farmland; (iv) the protection of existing or planned park, recreation or conservation sites; (v) the

protection and conservation of natural or scenic resources, including but not limited to soils, beaches, streams, flood plains, steep slopes or marshes; (vi) the protection of scenic areas for public visual enjoyment from public rights of way; (vii) the preservation of sites of historic, geologic or botanic interest; (viii) the promotion of sound, cohesive, and efficient land development by preserving open spaces between communities.

(2) Interest in real property. Any right in real property, improvements thereto or water, whatsoever, including but not limited to a fee simple, easement, remainder, future interest, transferable development right (TDR), lease, license, restriction or covenant of any sort, option or contractual interest or right concerning the use of or power to transfer property.

(3) Open space property interests. Any interest in real property acquired hereunder for the purpose of achieving open space benefits.

(4) Open space uses. Land uses which are not inconsistent with the achievement of open space benefits.

(5) Local government unit.

(i) A county;

(ii) a county authority having among the purposes for which it was created the achievement of one or more of the open space benefits set forth in this section;

(iii) a municipal corporation or any similar general purpose unit of local government; or

(iv) any unit created by joint action of two or more local government units which is now or shall hereafter be authorized to be created by the General Assembly, including cooperation by two or more local government units in accordance with the former act of July 12, 1972 (P.L. 762, No. 180), referred to as the Intergovernmental Cooperation Law, or 53 Pa.C.S. Ch. 23 Subch. A (relating to intergovernmental cooperation).

(5.1) Municipal corporation. A city, borough, incorporated town or township.

(6) Planning commission. A local board, commission or agency which has been designated by the governing body of a local government unit to establish and foster a comprehensive plan for land management and development with the local government unit.

(7) Transferable development right or TDR. The attaching of development rights to specified lands which are desired by a local government unit to be kept undeveloped, but permitting those rights to be transferred from those lands so that the development potential which they represent may occur on other lands where more intensive development is deemed to be appropriate.

§ 5003. Planning requirements.

The Department of Conservation and Natural Resources and the Department of Agriculture shall not acquire any interest in real property under the provisions of this act, unless said real property has been designated for open space uses in a resource, recreation, or land use plan submitted to and approved by the State Planning Board. A local government unit shall not acquire any interest in real property under the provisions of this act unless said real property has been designated for open space uses in a resource, recreation or land use plan recommended by the planning commission of the municipality in which the real property is located and adopted by the governing body of that municipality. Where the municipality in which the real property to be acquired is located has no planning commission, a local government unit shall not acquire any interest in real property under the provisions of this act unless said real property has been designated for open space uses in a resource, recreation or land use plan approved by the planning commission of the county in which the real property is located and adopted by the governing body of the municipality wherein the real property is located.

§ 5004. Applicability.

The Commonwealth of Pennsylvania, through the Department of Conservation and Natural Resources or the Department of Agriculture, may exercise the powers granted by this act only with the consent of the county commissioners of the county in which the real property is situated. All local government units may exercise the powers granted by this act.

§ 5005. Acquisition of interest in real property.

(a) The Commonwealth of Pennsylvania, through the Department of Conservation and Natural Resources, may acquire any interest in real property by purchase, contract, condemnation, gift, devise or otherwise, for any of the following purposes:

(1) To protect and conserve water resources and watersheds;

(2) To protect and conserve forests and land being used to produce timber crops;

(3) To protect an existing or planned park, forest, wildlife preserve, nature reserve or other recreation or conservation site by controlling the use of contiguous or nearby lands in order to protect the scenic, aesthetic or watershed values of the site;

(4) To protect and conserve natural or scenic resources, including but not limited to soils, beaches, streams, flood plains or marshes;

(5) To protect scenic areas for public visual enjoyment from public rights of way;

(6) To preserve sites of historic, geologic or botanic interest;

(7) To promote sound, cohesive, and efficient land development by preserving open spaces between communities;

(8) To limit the use of the real property so as to achieve open space benefits by reselling real property acquired in fee simple, subject to restrictive covenants or easements limiting the use thereof for the purposes specified in clauses (1) through (7) hereof.

(b) The Commonwealth of Pennsylvania, through the Department of Agriculture, may acquire any interest in real property by purchase, contract, gift, or devise for any of the following purposes:

(1) To protect and conserve farmland;

(2) To protect and conserve water resources and watersheds;

(3) To limit the use of real property so as to achieve open space benefits by reselling real property acquired in fee simple, subject to restrictive covenants or easements limiting the use thereof for the purposes specified in clauses (1) and (2) hereof.

(c)(1) A local government unit may acquire any interest in real property situate within its boundaries by purchase, contract, condemnation, gift, devise or otherwise, for any of the purposes set forth in clauses (1) through (8) of subsection (a) of this section, and may acquire any interest in real property situate within its boundaries by purchase, contract, gift or devise, for any of the purposes set forth in clause (1) of subsection (b) of this section, including limiting the use of real property to achieve open space benefits by reselling real property acquired in fee simple, subject to restrictive covenants or easements limiting the use thereof for the purposes set forth in clauses (1) through (7) of subsection (a) and clause (1) of subsection (b) of this section.

(2) During the time that real property or any interest in real property acquired by a local government unit for open space purposes in accordance with this act is held by the local government unit, the real property shall be ineligible for the purchase of agricultural conservation easements authorized in the act of June 30, 1981 (P.L. 128, No. 43),[1] known as the "Agricultural Area Security Law."

§ 5006. Public Hearing.

Interests in real property to be acquired pursuant to the provisions of this act shall be designated by the Department of Conservation and Natural Resources, the Department of Agriculture or a local government unit, whichever is acquiring them. After such designation, the said interests shall not be acquired until a public hearing is held and after notice to all owners of said interests in real property and to any local government unit in which land is situate, at which hearing the department or local government unit concerned shall set forth the interests to be taken and their proposed open space benefits. At the public hearing persons and municipalities affected by the proposed acquisition of interests in real property shall have an opportunity to present relevant evidence.

§ 5007. Property acquired in fee simple.

If the owner of the interests in real property to be acquired pursuant to the provisions of this act prefers to have the Commonwealth or the local government unit acquire the property in fee simple, the Commonwealth or the local government unit shall be required to acquire the property in fee simple. All real property acquired in fee simple by the Commonwealth, through either the Department of Conservation and Natural Resources or the Department of Agriculture under the provisions of this act, shall be offered for resale publicly in the manner provided by law within two years of the date of acquisition, subject to restrictive covenants or easements limiting the land to such open space uses as may be specified by the designating department or agency in accordance with section 6 hereof, and consistent with the resource, recreation, or land use plan established in accordance with section 4 hereof. In the case of the Commonwealth, such resales may be made without specific authority of the General Assembly and shall be through the Department of General Services at public sale in the manner provided by law.

§ 5007.1. Local taxing options.

(a) A local government unit, excluding counties and county authorities, may by ordinance impose, in addition to the statutory rate limits on real estate taxes set forth in the municipal code of that local government unit, an open space tax on real property not exceeding the millage authorized by referendum under subsection (a.3). In the alternative, a local government unit, excluding counties and county authorities, may by ordinance impose, in addition to the earned income tax rate limit set forth in the act of December 31, 1965 (P.L. 1257, No. 511),[2] known as "The Local Tax Enabling Act," an open space tax on the earned income of the residents of that local government unit not exceeding the rate authorized by referendum under subsection (a.3). Revenue from the levy may only be used for the following:

(1) to retire the indebtedness incurred in purchasing interests in real property or in making additional acquisitions of real property for the purpose of securing an open space benefit or benefits under the provisions of this act or the act of June 30, 1981 (P.L. 128, No. 43),[3] known as the "Agricultural Area Security Law";

1. 3 P.S. §§ 901 et seq.
2. 53 P.S. § 6901 et seq.
3. 3 P.S. § 901 et seq.

(2) for transactional fees that are incidental to acquisitions made in accordance with this act, including, but not limited to, costs of appraisals, legal services, title searches, document preparation, title insurance, closing fees and survey costs;

(3) for expenses necessary to prepare the resource, recreation or land use plan required under section 3;[4] or

(4)(i) annually, up to 25% of any accumulated balance of the fund from the levy authorized by referendum, to develop, improve, design, engineer and maintain property acquired for an open space benefit or benefits; or

(ii) alternatively, for purposes of allocation, the local government unit may create a maintenance fund into which the local government unit may deposit in an amount up to 25% of the annual revenue from the levy authorized by referendum, to develop, improve, design, engineer and maintain property acquired for an open space benefit or benefits.

(a.1) In no event, however, shall any revenue in a particular year be used to develop, improve, design, engineer and maintain the property acquired unless the annual debt service under subsection (a)(1) or acquisition fees under subsection (a)(2) will be satisfied. The acquisition fees shall be paid in their entirety at the time of acquisition.

(a.2) Nothing in subsection (a)(4) shall prevent a local government unit from using funds set aside for development, improvement, design, engineering and maintenance of real property for acquisition of real property to secure an open space benefit or benefits pursuant to subsection (a)(1).

(a.3) The local taxing option for an open space tax authorized by subsection (a) shall not be exercised unless the governing body of the local government unit shall by ordinance first provide for a referendum on the question of the imposition at a specific rate of the additional tax to be imposed and a majority of those voting on the referendum question vote in favor of the imposition of the tax. The additional tax shall not be repealed any sooner than five years after the imposition of the tax or when any indebtedness incurred for payment of the property or properties acquired has been repaid, whichever is later. The ordinance of the governing board of the local government unit providing for a referendum on the question shall be filed with the county board of elections. The referendum shall be governed by the provisions of the act of June 3, 1937 (P.L. 1333, No. 320),[5] known as the "Pennsylvania Election Code." The election official shall cause the question to be submitted to the electors of the local government unit at the next primary, general or municipal election occurring not less than the thirteenth Tuesday following the filing of the ordinance with the county board of elections. At such election, the question shall be submitted to the voters in the same manner as other questions are submitted under the provisions of the "Pennsylvania Election Code." The question to be placed upon the ballot shall be framed in the following form:

Do you favor the imposition of a (describe tax in millage or earned income tax rate) by (local government unit) to be used to (purpose)?

(a.4) In local government units whose electors voted in a referendum pursuant to subsection (a.3) to impose the open space tax, whether before or after the effective date of this subsection, the method of repeal of the open space tax shall be by referendum, and the procedures for the filing of the ordinance and the conduct of the referendum shall be as set forth in subsection (a.3), except the question to be placed upon the ballot shall be framed in the following form:

---

4. 32 P.S. § 5003.

5. 25 P.S. § 2600 et seq.

Chapter 24 Religious Land Use
Chapter 23 Conservation Easements
Chapter 22.1 Land Banks
Chapter 22 Open Space Lands
Chapter 21-B Regulation of Local Agriculture
Chapter 21-A Gas and Oil
Chapter 20 Bluff Recession and Setback Act
Chapter 19.2 Development Permit Extension Act
Chapter 19.1 Wireless Broadband Collocation Act
Chapter 19 Municipalities Planning Code

Do you favor the continued imposition of the (describe tax in millage or earned income tax rate) by (local government unit) to be used to (purpose)?

If the referendum question passes, the open space tax shall continue to be imposed at the rate described in the question. If the referendum question fails, the increase in the rate limit of the real estate or the earned income tax provided for by subsection (a.3) shall be repealed effective in the fiscal year following the referendum. Regardless of whether the referendum question passes or fails, a referendum on either the reimposition of the open space tax pursuant to subsection (a.3) or the continued imposition of the open space tax pursuant to this subsection shall not be held any sooner than five years after the approval or disapproval of the referendum question.

(b)(1) Any of the following categories of real property may be exempted from further millage increases:

(i) Real property in which the open space property interests have been acquired by a local government unit in accordance with this act.

(ii) Real property that is subject to an easement acquired in accordance with the "Agricultural Area Security Law."

(iii) Real property from which TDRs have been transferred and retired by a local government unit without their development potential having occurred on other lands.

(2) The exemption from further millage increases authorized by clause (1) shall become effective only if the governing body of each taxing district that imposes a tax on the real property approves the exemption either by ordinance in the case of a county or municipal corporation or by resolution in the case of a school district.

(3) The exemption from further millage increases for real property as provided for in this subsection shall be authorized only for real property qualifying for such exemption under the provisions of section 2(b)(1) of Article VIII of the Constitution of Pennsylvania.

(4) If the governing body of each taxing district so resolves, the millage freeze authorized herein shall apply to all eligible real property, whether the real property met the criteria of this subsection prior to or subsequent to the date of the ordinances and resolution imposing the millage freeze. For prior acquisitions, the date on which the millage rate shall be frozen is the date that the last of the required ordinances or resolution becomes effective. For subsequent acquisitions, the date on which the millage rate shall be frozen is the date the local government unit completes the acquisition. The governing body of each taxing district shall give prompt notice to the appropriate tax collection agent of the exact amount of the millage, the date it was frozen and each parcel to which the freeze applies.

(5) The exemptions granted under this act shall not be considered by the State Tax Equalization Board in deriving the market value of school district real property so as to reduce the subsidy to that school district or to increase the subsidy to any other school district.

§ 5007.2. Procedures to be followed in connection with acquisition of real property or open space property interests.

(a) A local government unit shall not acquire interests in real property pursuant to this act unless that local government unit has by ordinance or resolution established procedures for reviewing open space property interests considered for acquisition by the local government unit, for rating the relative desirability of interests in particular parcels of real estate and for establishing the price the local government unit will pay.

(b) When a local government unit acquires an interest in real property as authorized under the provisions of this act, it shall establish and maintain a repository of records of the interests in real property which have been or are acquired by the local government. The local government unit shall also record each interest in real property acquired by the local government unit in the office of the recorder of deeds for the county in which the real property is located.

(c) A local government unit acquiring interests in real property shall submit to the school district within which the real property is located a copy of the deed reflecting the open space property interest acquisition certified by the county recorder of deeds.

§ 5007.3. Acquisition of open space property interests on an installment basis.

A local government unit may authorize the establishment of a program to purchase open space property interests on an installment or other deferred basis. The obligation of the local government unit to make payments on an installment or other deferred basis shall not be subject to the requirements of section 602(b) or (c) of the act of July 12, 1972 (P.L. 781, No. 185),[6] known as the "Local Government Unit Debt Act." A landowner who enters into an installment agreement with a local government unit shall receive, in addition to the selling price, interest in an amount or at a rate set forth in the purchase agreement.

§ 5008. Exercise of eminent domain.

(a) Use of the power of eminent domain to acquire interests in real property for the purposes of this act shall be exercised in accordance with the provisions of the Eminent Domain Code of the Commonwealth.

(b) Notwithstanding the provisions of subsection (a) or section 5(c) local government units other than counties or county authorities may not exercise the power of eminent domain in carrying out the provisions of this act.

§ 5009. Assessment.

Any open space property interest acquired by the Commonwealth or a local government unit under this act is held for public purposes, and shall be exempt from taxation. The assessment of private interests in land subject to open space property interests under this act shall reflect any change in market value of the property which may result from the acquisition of open space property interests by the Commonwealth or a local government unit.

§ 5010. Termination or disposition of open space property interests.

(a) If the Commonwealth, through either the Department of Conservation and Natural Resources or the Department of Agriculture with the approval of the State Planning Board, or a county or county authority with the approval of its County Planning Commission, determines that it is essential for the orderly development of an area to terminate or sell open space property interests acquired under this act other than property held in fee simple, the Commonwealth or the county or county authority shall offer to transfer to the original property owner from whom said property interests other than fee simple were acquired, or his estate if the original property owner, or his estate, is the current property owner, said property interests at a price which shall be equal to the price paid by the Commonwealth or the county or county authority to the original property owner for said interests; and, if said offer is not accepted within ninety days, the Commonwealth or the county or county authority shall then sell the open space property interests at public sale in the manner provided by law. In the case of the Commonwealth, such transfer or sale may be made without specific authority of

6. 53 P.S. § 6780-252(b).

the General Assembly, and shall be through the Department of General Services at public sale in the manner provided by law.

(b) If the local government unit, excluding counties and county authorities, with the approval of the planning commission serving the municipality in which the real property is located, determines that it is essential for the orderly development of an area to terminate or sell open space property interests acquired under this act other than property held in fee simple, the local government unit shall offer to transfer to the original property owner from whom said open space property interests other than fee simple were acquired, or his estate if the original property owner or his estate is the current property owner, said property interests at a price which shall be equal to the price paid by the local government unit to the original property owner for said interests. If the local government unit's offer is not accepted within ninety days, the local government unit shall then sell the open space property interests at public sale in the manner provided by law. Before any open space property interests are disposed of by a local government unit, the officials of the local government unit must first put the question to its electorate at the time and place of any general, municipal or primary election to determine if a majority of the voters participating in said election assent to the proposed disposition of the specific open space property interests.

§ 5010.1. Transfer of development rights.

If a TDR is acquired under this act by a local government unit, it may be disposed of in any manner recommended by the planning commission and adopted by the governing body of that local government unit.

§ 5011. Utility rights of way; underground gas storage.

(a) The ownership by the Commonwealth or a local government unit of an open space property interest shall not preclude the acquisition, by lease, purchase, or eminent domain, and use of rights of way or underground gas storage rights in such property by a public utility or other body entitled to exercise the power of eminent domain. In the case of an acquisition from the Commonwealth by a body other than a public utility, such acquisition shall occur only if the State Planning Board, after public hearing with notice to the Department of Conservation and Natural Resources or the Department of Agriculture, as the case may be, shall approve such acquisition. In the case of an acquisition from a local government unit by a body other than a public utility, such acquisition shall occur only if the governing body, after public hearing with notice to the public, shall approve such acquisition. In the case of an acquisition from the Commonwealth or a local government unit by a public utility, such acquisition shall occur only if the Pennsylvania Public Utility Commission, after public hearing with notice to the Department of Conservation and Natural Resources, the Department of Agriculture or the local government unit, as the case may be, shall find that such acquisition and use are necessary or proper for the service, accommodation, convenience or safety of the public.

(b)(1) Notice of public hearing given in accordance with subsection (a) shall include a statement of the purpose of the public hearing and the date, time and place of the public hearing.

(2) In the case of notice to the appropriate department or local government unit as specified in subsection (a), the notice shall be sent by United States First Class Mail at least twenty days prior to the hearing.

(3) In all cases where a public hearing is to be held in accordance with subsection (a), notice to the public shall be given by publication one time at least twenty days prior to the hearing, in a newspaper of general circulation in the area where the open space land is located and written notice shall be conspicuously posted at points deemed sufficient by the body conducting the public

hearing to notify potentially interested citizens. The affected open space tract shall be posted at least ten days prior to the hearing.

§ 5012. Severability; inconsistent laws.

If any section, provision, or clause of this act shall be declared invalid or inapplicable to any persons or circumstances such action shall not be construed to affect the rest of the act or circumstances not so affected. All laws or portions of laws inconsistent with the policy and provisions of this act are hereby repealed to that extent.

§ 5013. Effective date.

This act shall take effect immediately.

CHAPTER 22.1
LAND BANKS

68 Pa.C.S. §§ 2101–2120

TABLE OF CONTENTS

---

§ 2101. Scope of chapter.

This chapter relates to land banks.

§ 2102. Legislative findings and purpose.

The General Assembly finds and declares that:

(1) Strong communities are important to the social and economic vitality of this Commonwealth. Whether urban, suburban or rural, many communities are struggling to cope with vacant, abandoned and tax-delinquent properties.

(2) Citizens of this Commonwealth are affected adversely by vacant, abandoned and tax-delinquent properties, including properties which have been vacated or abandoned due to mortgage foreclosure.

(3) Vacant, abandoned and tax-delinquent properties impose significant costs on neighborhoods, communities and municipalities by lowering property values, increasing fire and police protection costs, decreasing tax revenues and undermining community cohesion.

(4) There is an overriding public need to confront the problems caused by vacant, abandoned and tax-delinquent properties through the creation of new tools to enable municipalities to turn vacant, abandoned and tax-delinquent spaces into vibrant places.

(5) Land banks are one of the tools that municipalities may use to facilitate the return of vacant, abandoned and tax-delinquent properties to productive use.

(6) Land banks, if used effectively, can be a powerful tool in the fight against homelessness. Using land banks to transform vacant, abandoned or tax-delinquent properties into housing facilities for homeless individuals pro-

vides tangible benefits to municipalities, including the restoration of blighted property and the ability to provide necessary resources to one of this Commonwealth's most vulnerable populations.

§ 2103. Definitions.

The following words and phrases when used in this chapter shall have the meanings given to them in this section unless the context clearly indicates otherwise:

"Board." The board of directors of a land bank.

"Department." The Department of Community and Economic Development of the Commonwealth.

"Financial institution." A bank, savings association, operating subsidiary of a bank or savings association, credit union, association licensed to originate mortgage loans or an assignee of a mortgage or note originated by such an institution.

"Land bank." A public body and a body corporate and politic established under this chapter.

"Land bank jurisdiction."

(1) a county, a city, a borough, a township and an incorporated town with a population of more than 10,000; or

(2) two or more municipalities with populations less than 10,000 that enter into an intergovernmental cooperation agreement to establish and maintain a land bank.

"Low income." A household with total income at or below 80% of the area median income, adjusted for household size, as defined annually by the United States Department of Housing and Urban Development.

"Municipality." A county, city, borough, incorporated town, township or home rule municipality.

"Owner-occupant." A natural person with a legal or equitable ownership interest in property which was the primary residence of the person for at least three consecutive months at any point in the year preceding the date of initial delinquency.

"Real property." Land and all structures and fixtures thereon and all estates and interests in land, including easements, covenants and leaseholders.

"School district." Any of the classifications of school districts specified in section 202 of the act of March 10, 1949 (P.L.30, No.14), known as the Public School Code of 1949. The term includes, as to any real property acquired, owned or conveyed by a land bank, the school district within whose geographical jurisdiction the real property is located.

§ 2104. Creation and existence.

(a) Authority.—Subject, in a city of the first class, to the home rule charter, a land bank jurisdiction may elect to create a land bank by the adoption of an ordinance to create a binding legal obligation. The ordinance must specify the following:

(1) The name of the land bank.

(2) The number of members of the board.

(3) The names of individuals to serve as initial members of the board and the length of terms which they will serve.

(4) The qualifications, manner of selection or appointment and terms of office of members of the board.

(5) The manner by which residents will be provided an opportunity to have input into the land bank decision-making process.

(6) Policies regarding former owner-occupants who are occupying homes acquired by the land bank. These policies shall show a preference for keeping the former owner-occupants in their homes, whenever feasible.

(7) Additional terms and conditions the land bank jurisdiction deems reasonable and necessary for operation of the land bank.

(b) Filing.—The governing body of the land bank jurisdiction which creates a land bank shall file a copy of the ordinance with the department and with the Department of State. After receipt of the ordinance, the Secretary of the Commonwealth shall issue a certificate of incorporation.

(c) Combinations.—

(1) The authority under subsection (a) may be exercised in combination pursuant to an intergovernmental cooperation agreement by:

(i) more than one land bank jurisdiction; or

(ii) a land bank jurisdiction and one or more municipalities.

(2) If a land bank is established under paragraph (1), the intergovernmental cooperation agreement must specify matters identified in subsection (a).

(d) Limitation.—Except as set forth in subsection (c), if a county establishes a land bank, the land bank shall have the power to acquire real property only in those portions of the county located outside of the geographical boundaries of any other land bank established by another land bank jurisdiction located partially or entirely within the county.

(e) Participation by school district.—A school district may participate in a land bank pursuant to an intergovernmental cooperation agreement. The agreement must specify the membership, if any, of the school district on the board of the land bank and the actions of the land bank which are subject to approval by the school district.

(f) Legal status of land bank.—A land bank shall:

(1) be a public body corporate and politic; and

(2) have duration until terminated and dissolved under section 2114 (relating to dissolution of land bank).

(g) Collaboration.—A land bank, a political subdivision and another municipal entity may enter into an intergovernmental cooperation agreement relative to the operations of a land bank.

(h) Redevelopment authority.—

(1) A land bank jurisdiction located in a county of the second A, third, fourth, fifth, sixth, seventh or eighth class may, by ordinance, designate a redevelopment authority created for the jurisdiction and operating under the act of May 24, 1945 (P.L.991, No.385), known as the Urban Redevelopment Law, as land bank for the jurisdiction. The ordinance shall designate the authority as the land bank and contain the specifications of subsection (a)(5), (6) and (7). The ordinance may contain voting or approval requirements as authorized by section 2110(g) (relating to disposition of property). The ordinance shall be filed with the Department of State, which shall note it on the record of incorporation for the authority. The department shall create a model ordinance for the designation.

(2) A redevelopment authority designated under this subsection shall exercise the powers of a land bank under this chapter subject to the following:

(i) The designation shall not affect the organization, membership, eligibility, tenure and compensation of the authority board, except that voting requirements specified in sections 2105(h) (relating to board) and 2115 (relating to conflicts of interest) shall apply to proceedings under this chapter. Upon a vacancy or expiration of the term of a board member occurring after the designation, the land bank jurisdiction shall appoint a replacement to ensure compliance with the requirements of section 2105(b)(3).

(ii) Subject to subparagraph (i), the authority shall establish rules, policies and procedures consistent with this chapter for land bank activities.

(iii) The authority as land bank shall only acquire, hold and dispose of property in accordance with this chapter. Finances of the authority as land bank shall be retained and accounted for separately from finances held for other authority purposes and shall be subject to section 2119 (relating to annual audit and report).

(3) The designation of the authority as land bank may be revoked in the same manner as the dissolution of a land bank under section 2114 (relating to dissolution of land bank).

§ 2105. Board.

(a) **Membership.**—A board shall consist of an odd number of members and be not less than 5 members nor more than 11 members. Unless restricted by the actions or agreements specified in section 2104 (relating to creation and existence) and subject to the limits stated in this section, the size of the board may be adjusted in accordance with bylaws of the land bank.

(b) **Eligibility to serve on board.**—

(1) Notwithstanding any law to the contrary, a public officer shall be eligible to serve as a board member, and the acceptance of the appointment shall neither terminate nor impair that public office.

(2) A municipal employee shall be eligible to serve as a board member.

(3) An established land bank board shall include at least one voting member who:

(i) is a resident of the land bank jurisdiction;

(ii) is not a public official or municipal employee; and

(iii) maintains membership with a recognized civic organization within the land bank jurisdiction.

(4) A member removed under subsection (d)(3) shall be ineligible for reappointment to the board unless the reappointment is confirmed unanimously by the board.

(5) As used in this subsection, the term "public officer" means an individual who is elected to a municipal office.

(c) **Officers.**—The members of the board shall select annually from among their members a chair, vice chair, secretary, treasurer and other officers as the board determines.

(d) **Rules.**—The board shall establish rules on all of the following:

(1) Duties of officers under subsection (c).

(2) Attendance and participation of members in its regular and special meetings.

(3) A procedure to remove a member by a majority vote of the other members for failure to comply with a rule.

(4) Other matters necessary to govern the conduct of a land bank.

(e) **Vacancies.**—A vacancy on the board shall be filled in the same manner as the original appointment. Upon removal under subsection (d)(3), the position shall become vacant.

(f) **Compensation.**—Board members shall serve without compensation. The board may reimburse a member for expenses actually incurred in the performance of duties on behalf of the land bank.

(g) **Meetings.**—

(1) The board shall meet as follows:

(i) In regular session according to a schedule adopted by the board.

(ii) In special session:

(A) as convened by the chair; or

(B) upon written notice signed by a majority of the members.

(2) A majority of the board, excluding vacancies, constitutes a quorum. When a meeting is conducted through an Internet platform, a quorum may be established with a virtual presence of members or a combination of physical presence and virtual presence of members.

(h) Voting.—

(1) Except as set forth in paragraph (2) or (3), action of the board must be approved by the affirmative vote of a majority of the board present and voting.

(2) Action of the board on the following matters must be approved by a majority of the entire board membership:

(i) Adoption of bylaws.

(ii) Adoption of rules under subsection (d).

(iii) Hiring or firing of an employee or contractor of the land bank. This function may, by majority vote of the entire board membership, be delegated by the board to a specified officer or committee of the land bank.

(iv) Incurring of debt.

(v) Adoption or amendment of the annual budget.

(vi) Sale, lease, encumbrance or alienation of real property or personal property with a value of more than $50,000.

(3) A resolution under section 2114 (relating to dissolution of a land bank) must be approved by two-thirds of the entire board membership.

(4) A member of the board may not vote by proxy.

(5) A member may request a recorded vote on any resolution or action of the land bank.

(i) Immunity.—A land bank jurisdiction which establishes a land bank and a municipality and a school district which are parties to an intergovernmental cooperation agreement establishing a land bank shall not be liable personally on the bonds or other obligations of the land bank. Rights of creditors of a land bank shall be solely against the land bank.

§ 2106. Staff.

(a) Employees.—A land bank may employ or enter into a contract for an executive director, counsel and legal staff, technical experts and other individuals and may determine the qualifications and fix the compensation and benefits of those employees.

(b) Contracts.—A land bank may enter into a contract with a municipality for:

(1) the municipality to provide staffing services to the land bank; or

(2) the land bank to provide staffing services to the municipality.

§ 2107. Powers.—

A land bank constitutes a public body, corporate and politic, exercising public powers of the Commonwealth necessary or appropriate to carry out this chapter, including the following powers:

(1) To adopt, amend and repeal bylaws for the regulation of its affairs and the conduct of its business.

(2) To sue and be sued in its own name and be a party in a civil action. This paragraph includes an action to clear title to property of the land bank.

(3) To adopt a seal and to alter the same at pleasure.

Table of Contents | Part I Ch. 1–3 Ethics, Records, Open Meetings | Part II Ch. 4–10 Taxation | Part III Ch. 11–18 Torts, Contracts & Civil Rules | Part IV Ch. 19–24 Zoning & Planning | Part V Ch. 25–30 Construction and Emergency Codes | Part VI Ch. 31–39 Municipal Codes | Index

(4) To borrow from Federal Government funds, from the Commonwealth, from private lenders or from municipalities, as necessary, for the operation and work of the land bank.

(5) To issue negotiable revenue bonds and notes according to the provisions of this chapter.

(6) To procure insurance or guarantees from the Federal Government or the Commonwealth of the payment of debt incurred by the land bank, and to pay premiums in connection with the insurance or guarantee.

(7) To enter into contracts and other instruments necessary, incidental or convenient to the performance of its duties and the exercise of its powers. This paragraph includes intergovernmental cooperation agreements under 53 Pa.C.S. Ch. 23 Subch. A (relating to intergovernmental cooperation) for the joint exercise of powers under this chapter.

(8) To enter into contracts and intergovernmental cooperation agreements with municipalities for the performance of functions by municipalities on behalf of the land bank or by the land bank on behalf of municipalities.

(9) To make and execute contracts and other instruments necessary or convenient to the exercise of the powers of the land bank. Any contract or instrument signed shall be executed by and for the land bank if the contract or instrument is signed, including an authorized facsimile signature, by:

(i) the chair or vice chair of the land bank; and

(ii) either:

(A) the secretary or assistant secretary of the land bank; or

(B) the treasurer or assistant treasurer of the land bank.

(10) To procure insurance against losses in connection with the real property, assets or activities of the land bank.

(11) To invest money of the land bank at the discretion of the board in instruments, obligations, securities or property determined proper by the board and to name and use depositories for its money.

(12) To enter into contracts for the management of, the collection of rent from or the sale of real property of the land bank.

(13) To design, develop, construct, demolish, reconstruct, rehabilitate, renovate, relocate and otherwise improve real property or rights or interests in real property.

(14) To fix, charge and collect rents, fees and charges for the use of real property of the land bank and for services provided by the land bank.

(15) To grant or acquire licenses, easements, leases or options with respect to real property of the land bank.

(16) To enter into partnerships, joint ventures and other collaborative relationships with municipalities and other public and private entities for the ownership, management, development and disposition of real property.

(16.1) To enter into partnerships, joint ventures and other collaborative relationships with other entities, including private developers, for the conversion of vacant, abandoned, tax-delinquent or otherwise blighted property into housing facilities for homeless individuals.

(17) To organize and reorganize the executive, administrative, clerical and other departments of the land bank and to fix the duties, powers and compensation of employees, agents and consultants of the land bank.

(18) To do all other things necessary or convenient to achieve the objectives and purposes of the land bank or other law related to the purposes and responsibility of the land bank.

§ 2108. Eminent domain.—

A land bank does not possess the power of eminent domain.

§ 2109. Acquisition of property.

(a) Title to be held in its name.—A land bank shall hold in its own name all real property it acquires.

(b) Tax exemption.—

(1) Except as set forth in paragraph (2), the real property of a land bank and its income and operations are exempt from State and local tax.

(2) Paragraph (1) does not apply to real property of a land bank after the fifth consecutive year in which the real property is continuously leased to a private third party. However, real property shall continue to be exempt from State and local taxes if it is leased to a nonprofit or governmental agency at substantially less than fair market value.

(c) Methods of acquisition.—A land bank may acquire real property or interests in real property by any means on terms and conditions and in a manner the land bank considers proper.

(d) Acquisitions from municipalities.—

(1) A land bank may acquire real property by purchase contracts, lease purchase agreements, installment sales contracts and land contracts and may accept transfers from municipalities upon terms and conditions as agreed to by the land bank and the municipality.

(2) A municipality may transfer to a land bank real property and interests in real property of the municipality on terms and conditions and according to procedures determined by the municipality as long as the real property is located within the jurisdiction of the land bank.

(3) A redevelopment authority located within a land bank jurisdiction established under this chapter may, with the consent of the local governing body and without a redevelopment contract, convey property which it acquired before the effective date of this paragraph to the land bank. A conveyance under this paragraph shall be with fee simple title, free of all liens and encumbrances.

(e) Maintenance.—A land bank shall maintain all of its real property in accordance with the statutes and ordinances of the jurisdiction in which the real property is located.

(f) Prohibition.—

(1) Subject to the provisions of paragraph (2), a land bank may not own or hold real property located outside the jurisdictional boundaries of the entities which created the land bank under section 2104(c) (relating to creation and existence).

(2) A land bank may be granted authority pursuant to an intergovernmental cooperation agreement with a municipality to manage and maintain real property located within the jurisdiction of the municipality.

(g) Tax claim bureaus.—A tax claim bureau may transfer to a land bank real property of the county held by the tax claim bureau, as trustee for the county, in a repository for unsold property under section 626 of the act of July 7, 1947 (P.L.1368, No.542), known as the Real Estate Tax Sale Law.

(h) Acquisition of tax delinquent properties.—If authorized by the land bank jurisdiction which created a land bank or otherwise by intergovernmental cooperation agreement, a land bank may accept donations of real property and extinguish delinquent claims for taxes as to the property under section 5.1 of the act of May 16, 1923 (P.L.207, No.153), referred to as the Municipal Claim and Tax Lien Law, or section 303 of the Real Estate Tax Sale Law. For the purposes of this subsection, the land bank shall have all rights and obligations of the municipality provided for in section 5.1 of the Municipal Claim and Tax Lien Law and of a local taxing authority provided for in section 303 of the Real Estate Tax Sale Law.

§ 2110. Disposition of property.—

(a) Public access to inventory.—A land bank shall maintain and make available for public review and inspection an inventory of real property held by the land bank.

(b) Power.—A land bank may convey, exchange, sell, transfer, lease, grant or mortgage interests in real property of the land bank in the form and by the method determined to be in the best interests of the land bank.

(c) Consideration.—

(1) A land bank shall determine the amount and form of consideration necessary to convey, exchange, sell, transfer, lease as lessor, grant or mortgage interests in real property.

(2) Consideration may take the form of monetary payments and secured financial obligations, covenants and conditions related to the present and future use of the property, contractual commitments of the transferee and other forms of consideration as determined by the board to be in the best interest of the land bank.

(d) Policies and procedures.—

(1) A board shall determine and state in the land bank policies and procedures the general terms and conditions for consideration to be received by the land bank for the transfer of real property and interests in real property.

(2) Requirements which may be applicable to the disposition of real property and interests in real property by municipalities shall not be applicable to the disposition of real property and interests in real property by a land bank.

(e) Ranking of priorities.—

(1) A land bank jurisdiction may establish a hierarchical ranking of priorities for the use of real property conveyed by a land bank, including use for:

(i) Purely public spaces and places.

(i.1) Housing for homeless individuals.

(ii) Affordable housing.

(iii) Retail, commercial and industrial activities.

(iv) Conservation areas.

(2) The priorities established may be for the entire land bank jurisdiction or may be set according to the needs of different neighborhoods, municipalities or other locations within the land bank jurisdiction, or according to the nature of the real property.

(f) Land use plans.—A land bank shall consider all duly adopted land use plans and make reasonable efforts to coordinate the disposition of land bank real property with such land use plans.

(g) Specific voting and approval requirements.—

(1) A land bank jurisdiction may, in its ordinance creating a land bank or, in the case of multiple land bank jurisdictions and municipalities creating a single land bank in the applicable intergovernmental cooperation agreement, require that a particular form of disposition of real property or a disposition of real property located within specified jurisdictions be subject to specified voting and approval requirements of the board.

(2) Except as restricted or constrained under paragraph (1), the board may delegate to officers and employees the authority to enter into and execute agreements, instruments of conveyance and other related documents pertaining to the conveyance of real property by the land bank.

§ 2111. Financing of land bank operations.

(a) General rule.—A land bank may receive funding through grants and loans from:

(1) the Federal Government;

(2) the Commonwealth;

(3) a municipality;

(4) the land bank jurisdiction which created the land bank; and

(5) private sources.

(b) Funding.—A land bank may receive and retain payments for services rendered, for rents and leasehold payments received, for consideration for disposition of real and personal property, for proceeds of insurance coverage for losses incurred, for income from investments and for an asset and activity lawfully permitted to a land bank under this chapter.

(c) Allocated real property taxes.—

(1) A taxing jurisdiction may authorize the remittance or dedication of a portion of real property taxes collected pursuant to the laws of this Commonwealth to a land bank on real property conveyed by a land bank.

(2) Allocation of property tax revenues in accordance with this subsection, if authorized by the taxing jurisdiction, shall commence with the first taxable year following the date of conveyance and continue for a period of up to five years and may not exceed a maximum of 50% of the aggregate property tax revenues generated by the property.

(3) Remittance or dedication of real property taxes shall include the real property taxes of a school district only if the school district enters into an agreement with the land bank for the remittance or dedication.

§ 2112. Borrowing and issuance of bonds.

(a) Authority.—

(1) A land bank may issue a bond for any of its corporate purposes.

(2) The principal and interest of a bond shall be payable from the land bank's general revenue.

(3) The bond may be secured by any of the following:

(i) A pledge of revenue. This subparagraph includes a grant or contribution from:

(A) The Federal Government or a Federal agency or instrumentality.

(B) The Commonwealth, a Commonwealth agency or an instrumentality of the Commonwealth.

(ii) A mortgage of property of the land bank.

(b) Nature.—The bond must meet the requirements of 13 Pa.C.S. § 3104 (relating to negotiable instrument).

(c) Tax exempt.—A bond and the income from the bond is exempt from taxation by:

(1) the Commonwealth; or

(2) a political subdivision.

(d) Procedure.—

(1) A bond must be authorized by resolution of the board and shall be a limited obligation of the land bank.

(2) The principal and interest, costs of issuance and other costs incidental to the bond shall be payable solely from the income and revenue derived from the sale, lease or other disposition of the assets of the land bank. The land bank may secure the bond by a mortgage or other security device covering all or part of the project from which the pledged revenues may be derived.

(3) A refunding bond issued under this section:

(i) shall be payable from:

(A) a source described in this chapter; or

(B) the investment of the proceeds of the refunding bonds; and

(ii) shall not constitute an indebtedness or pledge of the general credit of a political subdivision within the meaning of a constitutional or statutory limitation of indebtedness and shall contain a recital to that effect.

(4) A bond must comply with the authorizing resolution as to:

(i) form;

(ii) denomination;

(iii) interest rate;

(iv) maturity; and

(v) execution.

(5) A bond may be subject to redemption at the option of and in the manner determined by the board in the authorizing resolution.

(e) Powers of municipalities.—A municipality may elect to guarantee, insure or otherwise become primarily or secondarily obligated on the indebtedness of a land bank subject, however, to all other provisions of law of this Commonwealth applicable to municipal indebtedness.

(f) Sale.—

(1) A bond shall be issued, sold and delivered in accordance with the terms and provisions of the authorizing resolution. The board, to effectuate its best interest, may determine the manner of sale, public or private, and the price of the bond.

(2) The resolution issuing a bond must be published in a newspaper of general circulation within the jurisdiction in which the land bank is located.

(g) Liability.—

(1) Neither the members of a land bank nor a person executing the bond shall be liable personally on the bonds by reason of the issuance of the bond.

(2) The bond or other obligation of a land bank related to a bond shall not be a debt of a municipality or of the Commonwealth. A statement to this effect shall appear on the face of the bond or obligation.

(3) On the bond or other obligation of a land bank related to a bond, all of the following apply:

(i) The Commonwealth has no liability. This subparagraph applies to the revenue and property of the Commonwealth.

(ii) A municipality has no liability. This subparagraph applies to the revenue and property of a municipality.

§ 2113. Public records and public access.

(a) Public records.—A board shall keep minutes and a record of its proceedings.

(b) Public access.—A land bank is subject to:

(1) 65 Pa.C.S. Ch. 7 (relating to open meetings); and

(2) the act of February 14, 2008 (P.L.6, No.3), known as the Right-to-Know Law.

§ 2114. Dissolution of land bank.

(a) General rule.—A land bank may be dissolved as a public body corporate and politic upon compliance with all of the following:

(1) Sixty calendar days' advance written notice of consideration of a resolution to request dissolution must:

(i) be given to the land bank jurisdiction which created the land bank;

(ii) be published in a local newspaper of general circulation; and

(iii) be sent by certified mail to the trustees of outstanding bonds of the land bank.

(2) A resolution requesting dissolution must be approved under section 2105(h)(3) (relating to board).

(b) Authority.—Upon receipt of a proper resolution described in subsection (a)(1), the land bank jurisdiction which created the land bank may dissolve the land bank by adoption of an ordinance subject to the approval of the mayor in a city or the county executive in a home rule county. If approved, the governing body of the land bank jurisdiction which created the land bank shall file a certified copy of the ordinance with the Department of State, and the Secretary of the Commonwealth shall cause the termination of the existence of the land bank to be noted on the record of incorporation. Upon such filing, the land bank shall cease to function. The Secretary of the Commonwealth shall also notify the department of the dissolution of the land bank.

(c) Transfer of assets.—Upon dissolution of the land bank, real property, personal property and other assets of the land bank shall become the assets of the municipality in which the property is located. The following shall apply:

(1) Personal property, including financial assets, of the land bank shall be divided among participating land bank jurisdictions in proportion to the population of each jurisdiction.

(2) The municipality in which real property is located shall approve the transfer of title to the municipality.

(d) Multiple jurisdictions.—If multiple land bank jurisdictions create a land bank under section 2104(c) (relating to creation and existence), the withdrawal of one or more land bank jurisdictions shall not require dissolution of the land bank unless:

(1) the intergovernmental cooperation agreement provides for dissolution in this event; and

(2) there is no land bank jurisdiction which desires to continue the existence of the land bank.

§ 2115. Conflicts of interest.

(a) State Adverse Interest Act.—The acts and decisions of members of a board and of employees of a land bank shall be subject to the act of July 19, 1957 (P.L.1017, No.451), known as the State Adverse Interest Act.

(b) Ethical standards.—Board members and land bank employees are subject to 65 Pa.C.S. Ch. 11 (relating to ethics standards and financial disclosure).

(c) Supplemental rules and guidelines.—The board may adopt:

(1) supplemental rules addressing potential conflicts of interest; and

(2) ethical guidelines for members of the board and land bank employees.

§ 2116. Construction, intent and scope.

This chapter shall be construed liberally to effectuate the legislative intent and the purposes as complete and independent authorization for the implementation of this chapter, and all powers granted shall be broadly interpreted to effectuate the intent and purposes and not as a limitation of powers.

§ 2117. Delinquent property tax enforcement.

(a) Power to discharge liens and claims.—

(1) Except as set forth in paragraph (2), a land bank may, by resolution of the board, discharge a lien or claim to its real property for tax owed to the members of the land bank.

Table of Contents
Part I Ch. 1–3 Ethics, Records, Open Meetings
Part II Ch. 4–10 Taxation
Part III Ch. 11–18 Torts, Contracts & Civil Rules
Part IV Ch. 19–24 Zoning & Planning
Part V Ch. 25–30 Construction and Emergency Codes
Part VI Ch. 31–39 Municipal Codes
Index

(2) For a land bank to discharge a lien or claim to its real property under paragraph (1) for tax owed to a school district, the governing body of the school district must approve the discharge.

(3) The land bank must file evidence of the extinguishment and dissolution of liens or claims with the county tax claim bureau, including copies of the resolution by the board, the intergovernmental agreement, receipt of payment and other necessary and appropriate documentation. This requirement must be satisfied no later than the earlier of:

(i) ten days prior to the conveyance of the property; or

(ii) within 30 days after the discharge.

(b) Remittance of payments.—To the extent that a land bank receives payments attributable to a lien or claim for real property taxes owed to a municipality or school district on property acquired by the land bank, the land bank shall remit the full amount of the payments to the municipality or school district.

(c) Procedure relating to Real Estate Tax Sale Law.—For a land bank located in a municipality which follows the act of July 7, 1947 (P.L.1368, No.542), known as the Real Estate Tax Sale Law, all of the following apply:

(1) Depending upon the time of filing, the following apply:

(i) For a tax claim filed under the Real Estate Tax Sale Law, the municipality:

(A) may direct the county tax claim bureau to assign the claim or lien to the land bank under terms mutually acceptable to the municipality and land bank; and

(B) shall otherwise confer upon the land bank the rights, privileges and remedies of an assignee under section 316 of the Real Estate Tax Sale Law.

(ii) For a tax claim to be filed under the Real Estate Tax Sale Law, a municipality which has complied with section 26 of the act of May 25, 1945 (P.L.1050, No.394), known as the Local Tax Collection Law, and section 306 of the Real Estate Tax Sale Law:

(A) may assign and transfer the claim to the land bank upon terms and conditions mutually acceptable to the municipality and the land bank; and

(B) shall otherwise confer upon the land bank the rights, privileges and remedies of an assignee under section 316 of the Real Estate Tax Sale Law.

(iii) For tax liens assigned to the land bank under subparagraph (i) or (ii), the land bank shall adopt policies providing for plans and agreements by which low-income, owner-occupant households may pay their delinquent taxes. Such plans and agreements shall take into account the household's ability to pay and shall be designed to promote the continued occupancy by that household whenever feasible.

(2) All of the following apply to upset sales:

(i) The land bank and the plaintiff in the claim may enter into an agreement for the land bank to purchase the property at the minimum amount described in section 605 of the Real Estate Tax Sale Law in the event there is no bid tendered for a higher amount than the minimum amount.

(ii) If there is an agreement under subparagraph (i) and no one bids a higher price than the minimum amount described in section 605 of the Real Estate Tax Sale Law, the property shall be sold to the land bank upon payment by the land bank for the upset sale costs and all liens, claims and subordinate encumbrances shall be discharged by the sale.

(3) All of the following apply to judicial sales:

(i) Notwithstanding section 612 of the Real Estate Tax Sale Law, the form, substance and timing of the land bank's payment of the sales price may be according to the agreement as is mutually acceptable to the plaintiff and the land bank if all of the following apply:

(A) A judicial sale is ordered pursuant to a judgment on a tax claim.

(B) The purchaser of the property is the land bank.

(C) The sales price is an amount agreed to by the land bank and the plaintiff in the claim.

(ii) The obligation of the land bank to perform in accordance with the agreement under subparagraph (i) shall be deemed to be in full satisfaction of the tax claim which was the basis for the judgment.

(iii) The land bank, as purchaser at the sale, shall have an absolute title to the property sold, free and discharged of tax and municipal claims, liens, mortgages, ground rents, charges and estates.

(4) The notice and return under sections 602 and 607(a) of the Real Estate Tax Sale Law must contain reference to a potential bid by the land bank.

(5) The deed to the land bank under sections 608 and 615 of the Real Estate Tax Sale Law shall be delivered and acknowledged and recorded within 30 days of the date of confirmation.

(6) All of the following apply to judicial sales for multiple tracts:

(i) In a petition for a judicial sale, the municipality or the land bank, if it is the holder of municipal tax liens, may combine in a single petition multiple tracts of real property if the petition and accompanying affidavits provide all of the following:

(A) Identification of each tract of real property.

(B) The identities of each party having an interest in a tract of real property.

(C) The amount of the tax liens then due and owing, together with associated interest, costs and fees.

(D) The nature of the notice of the proposed sale provided to the interested parties.

(ii) The court may authorize in a single final judgment that all or part of the real properties identified in the petition be sold free and clear of tax and municipal claims, mortgages, liens, charges and estates and ground rents.

(d) **Procedure relating to Municipal Claim and Tax Lien Law.**—For a land bank located in a municipality which follows the act of May 16, 1923 (P.L.207, No.153), referred to as the Municipal Claim and Tax Lien Law, all of the following apply:

(1) Regardless of the time of filing, the municipality:

(i) may assign and transfer a tax or municipal claim to the land bank upon terms and conditions mutually acceptable to the municipality and land bank;

(ii) shall otherwise confer upon the land bank the rights, privileges and remedies of an assignee as stated in section 33 of the Municipal Claim and Tax Lien Law; and

(iii) for tax liens assigned to the land bank under this section, the land bank shall adopt policies providing for plans and agreements by which low-income, owner-occupant households may pay their delinquent taxes. Such plans and agreements shall take into account the household's ability to pay and shall be designed to promote the continued occupancy by that household whenever feasible.

(2) All of the following apply to upset sales:

Table of Contents | Part I Ch. 1–3 Ethics, Records, Open Meetings | Part II Ch. 4–10 Taxation | Part III Ch. 11–18 Torts, Contracts & Civil Rules | Part IV Ch. 19–24 Zoning & Planning | Part V Ch. 25–30 Construction and Emergency Codes | Part VI Ch. 31–39 Municipal Codes | Index

(i) The land bank and the plaintiff in the claim may enter into an agreement for the land bank to purchase the property at the minimum amount described in section 29 of the Municipal Claim and Tax Lien Law in the event there is no bid tendered for a higher amount than the minimum amount.

(ii) If there is an agreement under subparagraph (i) and no one bids a higher price than the minimum amount described in section 29 of the Municipal Claim and Tax Lien Law, the property shall be sold to the land bank upon payment by the land bank for the upset sale costs and liens, claims and subordinate encumbrances shall be discharged by the sale.

(3) All of the following apply to judicial sales:

(i) Notwithstanding section 31 of the Municipal Claim and Tax Lien Law, the form, substance and timing of the land bank's payment of the sales price may be according to the agreement mutually acceptable to the plaintiff and the land bank if all of the following apply:

(A) A judicial sale is ordered pursuant to a judgment on a tax or municipal claim.

(B) The purchaser of the property is the land bank.

(C) The sales price is an amount agreed to by the land bank and the plaintiff.

(ii) The obligation of the land bank to perform in accordance with the agreement under subparagraph (i) shall be deemed to be in full satisfaction of the municipal claim which was the basis for the judgment.

(iii) The land bank, as purchaser at the sale, shall have an absolute title to the property sold, free and discharged of tax and municipal claims, liens, mortgages, ground rents, charges and estates.

(4) Notwithstanding sections 31.1 and 31.2 of the Municipal Claim and Tax Lien Law and sections 4 and 6 of the act of March 1, 1956 (1955 P.L.1196, No.372), entitled "An act authorizing the sale of vacant land located in areas certified as conservation areas in counties of the first class, under a judgment obtained on a tax claim, by the sheriff of the county; providing for the discharge of all liens, mortgages, ground rents, estates and claims against the property by sale; and limiting the right of redemption," all of the following apply:

(i) The land bank may tender a bid at the sale in an amount equal to the total amount of all municipal claims and liens which were the basis for the judgment. Upon tender under this subparagraph, the property shall be deemed sold to the land bank regardless of bids by other parties.

(ii) The bid of the land bank shall be paid as to its form, substance and timing according to an agreement that is mutually acceptable to the plaintiff and the land bank. The obligation of the land bank to perform in accordance with the agreement shall be deemed to be in full satisfaction of the tax or municipal claim which was the basis for the judgment.

(iii) The land bank, as purchaser at the sale, shall have an absolute title to the property sold, free and discharged of tax and municipal claims, liens, mortgages, ground rents, charges and estates.

(iv) The deed to the land bank shall be executed, acknowledged and delivered within 30 days of the sale.

(5) All of the following apply to judicial sales for multiple tracts:

(i) In a petition for a judicial sale, a municipality or a land bank, if it is the holder of municipal tax liens, may combine in a petition multiple tracts of real property if the petition and accompanying affidavits provide all of the following:

(A) Identification of each tract of real property.

(B) The identities of each party having an interest in a tract of real property.

(C) The amount of the taxes then due and owing.

(D) The nature of the notice of the proposed sale provided to the interested parties.

(ii) The court may authorize in a single final judgment that all or part of the real properties identified in the petition be sold free and clear of tax and municipal claims, mortgages, liens, ground rents, charges and estates.

(e) Procedure relating to Second Class City Treasurer's Sale and Collection Act.—For a land bank located in a municipality which follows the act of October 11, 1984 (P.L.876, No.171), known as the Second Class City Treasurer's Sale and Collection Act, all of the following apply:

(1) Regardless of the time of filing, a municipality:

(i) may assign and transfer a tax or municipal claim to the land bank under the Second Class City Treasurer's Sale and Collection Act upon terms and conditions mutually acceptable to the municipality and the land bank; and

(ii) shall otherwise confer upon the land bank the rights, privileges and remedies of the municipality under the Second Class City Treasurer's Sale and Collection Act.

(iii) For tax liens assigned to the land bank under this section, the land bank shall adopt policies providing for plans and agreements by which low-income, owner-occupant households may pay their delinquent taxes. Such plans and agreements shall take into account the household's ability to pay and shall be designed to promote the continued occupancy by that household whenever feasible.

(2) All of the following apply to upset sales:

(i) The land bank and the plaintiff in the claim may enter into an agreement for the land bank to purchase the property for the minimum amount of the upset sale price described in section 301 of the Second Class City Treasurer's Sale and Collection Act in the event there is no bid tendered for a higher amount than the minimum amount.

(ii) The land bank may tender a bid for the mutually agreed upset sale price.

(iii) Notwithstanding section 301 of the Second Class City Treasurer's Sale and Collection Act, the bid of the land bank shall be paid as to its form, substance and timing according to an agreement between the municipality and land bank. The obligation of the land bank to perform in accordance with the agreement shall be deemed to be in full satisfaction of the tax or claim which was the basis for the sale.

(3) The notice and advertisement under sections 203 and 204 of the Second Class City Treasurer's Sale and Collection Act must contain reference to a potential bid by the land bank.

(4) Subject to redemption under section 304 of the Second Class City Treasurer's Sale and Collection Act and confirmation under section 305 of the Second Class City Treasurer's Sale and Collection Act, the land bank, as purchaser at the sale, shall have an absolute title to the property sold, free and discharged of tax and municipal claims, liens, mortgages, ground rents, charges and estates.

(5) The deed to the land bank under section 307 of the Second Class City Treasurer's Sale and Collection Act shall be delivered, acknowledged and recorded within 30 days of the date of confirmation.

Table of Contents | Part I Ch. 1–3 Ethics, Records, Open Meetings | Part II Ch. 4–10 Taxation | Part III Ch. 11–18 Torts, Contracts & Civil Rules | Part IV Ch. 19–24 Zoning & Planning | Part V Ch. 25–30 Construction and Emergency Codes | Part VI Ch. 31–39 Municipal Codes | Index

(e.1) Land bank.—Notwithstanding subsections (d) and (e), in counties of the second class containing a city of the second class, a land bank may not engage in any of the following absent an agreement with a county, city, borough, incorporated town, township, school district or body politic and corporate created as a municipal authority pursuant to law whose claims comprise the upset sales price:

(1) Purchase property for less than the upset sales price described in section 29 of the Municipal Claim and Tax Lien Law or section 301 of the Second Class City Treasurer's Sale and Collection Act.

(2) Alter the form, substance or timing of the payment of the sales price by the land bank.

(f) Involuntary transfers.—A land bank which acquires real property under this section shall be deemed to have acquired the real property as an involuntary transfer within the meaning of section 701(b)(1)(vi)(B) of the act of October 18, 1988 (P.L.756, No.108), known as the Hazardous Sites Cleanup Act.

(g) Expiration.—This section shall expire upon publication of the notice under section 2120 (relating to determination on procedural revision).

§ 2118. Expedited quiet title proceedings.

(a) Authorization.—

(1) A land bank may file an action to quiet title to real property in which the land bank has an interest.

(2) A land bank may join in a single complaint to quiet title to one or more parcels of real property.

(3) For purposes of an action under this section, the land bank shall be deemed to be the holder of sufficient legal and equitable interests and possessory rights so as to qualify the land bank as an adequate complainant in the action.

(b) Procedural requirements.—

(1) Prior to the filing of an action to quiet title the land bank must conduct an examination of title to determine the identity of any person possessing a claim or interest in or to the real property.

(2) Service of the complaint to quiet title shall be provided to interested parties as follows:

(i) By first class mail to the identity and address reasonably ascertainable by an inspection of public records.

(ii) In the case of occupied real property, by first class mail, addressed to "Occupant."

(iii) By posting a copy of the notice on the real property.

(iv) By publication.

(v) As ordered by the court.

(3) As part of the complaint to quiet title, the land bank must file an affidavit identifying:

(i) persons discovered under paragraph (1); and

(ii) the form of service under paragraph (2).

(c) Hearing.—

(1) The court shall schedule a hearing on the complaint within 90 days following filing of the complaint and as to all matters upon which an answer was not filed by an interested party.

(2) The court shall issue its final judgment within 120 days of the filing of the complaint.

§ 2119. Annual audit and report.

The following shall apply:

(1) The land bank shall annually, within 120 days after the end of the fiscal year, submit an audit of income and expenditures, together with a report of its activities for the preceding year, to the department.

(2) A duplicate of the audit and the report shall be filed with the governing body of:

(i) the land bank jurisdiction which created the land bank; and

(ii) each political subdivision which opted to participate in the land bank pursuant to an intergovernmental agreement.

§ 2120. Determination on procedural revision.

If the department determines that comprehensive reform legislation on property-tax foreclosure has been enacted revising procedure under the statutory provisions referred to in section 2117 (relating to delinquent property tax enforcement), the department shall transmit notice of the determination to the Legislative Reference Bureau for publication in the Pennsylvania Bulletin.

§ 2121. Exemption from realty transfer tax.

A transfer of real property to or from a land bank shall be exempt from both the State and local realty transfer tax under Articles XI-C and XI-D of the act of March 4, 1971 (P.L.6, No.2), known as the Tax Reform Code of 1971, and section 301.1 of the act of December 31, 1965 (P.L.1257, No.511), known as The Local Tax Enabling Act.

CHAPTER 23

CONSERVATION AND PRESERVATION EASEMENTS ACT

32 P.S. §§ 5051–5059

TABLE OF CONTENTS

§ 5051. Short title.

This act shall be known and may be cited as the Conservation and Preservation Easements Act.

§ 5052. Purpose of act.

The General Assembly recognizes the importance and significant public and economic benefit of conservation and preservation easements in its ongoing efforts to protect, conserve or manage the use of the natural, historic, agricultural, open space and scenic resources of this Commonwealth.

§ 5053. Definitions.

The following words and phrases when used in this act shall have the meanings given to them in this section unless the context clearly indicates otherwise:

"Conservation easement." A nonpossessory interest of a holder in real property, whether appurtenant or in gross, imposing limitations or affirmative obligations, the purposes of which include, but are not limited to, retaining or protecting for the public and economic benefit the natural, scenic or open space values of real property; assuring its availability for agricultural, forest, recreational or open space use; protecting, conserving or managing the use of natural resources; protecting wildlife; maintaining or enhancing land, air or water quality or preserving the historical, architectural, archaeological or cultural aspects of real property.

"Holder." The term means the following:

(1) A governmental body empowered to hold an interest in real property under the laws of the United States or this Commonwealth.

(2) A charitable corporation, charitable association or charitable trust registered with the Bureau of Charitable Organizations of the Department of State and exempt from taxation pursuant to section 501(c)(3) of the Internal Revenue Code of 1986 (Public Law 99-514, 26 U.S.C. § 501(c)(3)) or other Federal or Commonwealth statutes or regulations, the purposes or powers of which include retaining or protecting the natural, scenic, agricultural or open space values of real property; assuring the availability of real property for

agricultural, forest, recreational or open space use; protecting, conserving or managing the use of natural resources; protecting wildlife; maintaining or enhancing land, air or water quality or preserving the historical, architectural, archaeological or cultural aspects of real property.

"Preservation easement." A nonpossessory interest in a historical building.

"Successive holder." A holder who is not the original holder and who acquired its interest in a conservation or preservation easement by assignment or transfer.

"Third-party right of enforcement." A right provided in a conservation easement to enforce any of its terms, granted to a governmental body, charitable corporation, charitable association or charitable trust, which, although eligible to be a holder, is not a holder.

§ 5054. Creation, transfer and duration.

(a) Creating an easement.—Except as otherwise provided in this act, a conservation or preservation easement may be created, conveyed, recorded, assigned, released, modified, terminated or otherwise altered or affected in the same manner as other easements.

(b) Scope.—A conservation easement may encompass an entire fee simple interest in a parcel of real property as described in the deed to the property or any portion thereof or estate therein. Except when referencing an easement's boundary using setback descriptions from existing deed boundaries or natural or artificial features such as streams, rivers or railroad rights-of-way, a metes and bounds description of the portion of property subject to the easement shall be provided in the easement document.

(c) Acceptance.—No right or duty of a holder, successive holder named in the conservation or preservation easement or person having a third-party right of enforcement may arise under a conservation or preservation easement before the acceptance of the easement by the holder, successive holder or third party with right of enforcement and recordation of the acceptance.

(d) Duration.—Except as provided in section 5(c), a conservation or preservation easement created after the effective date of this act may be perpetual in duration but in no event shall be for a duration of less than 25 years. To the extent the easement is in gross, the easement shall be transferred to a willing successive holder, should the original holder or successive holder be dissolved or otherwise cease to exist, in order to accomplish the goal of the easement. If a willing successive holder cannot be identified, the municipality in which the easement is located shall automatically become the successive holder for perpetuity or the remaining term of the easement. Upon expiration of the easement, the holder shall terminate the easement by recording a written document in the same office of recorder of deeds where the easement was first recorded.

(e) Existing interests.—An interest in real property in existence at the time a conservation or preservation easement is created, including easements intended to provide services of a public utility nature and operating rights and easements appurtenant to real property contiguous to real property burdened by the easement which are of record or which arise by operation of law, may not be impaired unless the owner of the interest is a party to the easement or consents in writing to comply with the restrictions of such easement.

§ 5055. Judicial and related actions.

(a) Persons who have standing.—A legal or equitable action affecting a conservation or preservation easement may only be brought by any of the following:

(1) An owner of the real property burdened by the easement.

(2) A person that holds an estate in the real property burdened by the easement.

(3) A person that has any interest or right in the real property burdened by the easement.

(4) A holder of the easement.

(5) A person having a third-party right of enforcement.

(6) A person otherwise authorized by Federal or State law.

(7) The owner of a coal interest in property contiguous to the property burdened by the easement or of coal interests which have been severed from the ownership of the property burdened by the easement.

(b) Limitation on actions.—No action may be brought for activities occurring outside the boundaries of a conservation or preservation easement except in circumstances where such activities have or pose a substantial threat of direct, physically identifiable harm within the boundaries of the easement.

(c) Authority of courts.—

(1) This act shall not affect the power of a court to modify or terminate a conservation or preservation easement in accordance with the principles of law and equity consistent with the public policy of this act as stated under when the easement is broadly construed to effect that policy.

(2) Any general rule of construction to the contrary notwithstanding, conservation or preservation easements shall be liberally construed in favor of the grants contained therein to effect the purposes of those easements and the policy and purpose of this act.

(d) Eminent domain right preserved.—

(1) Nothing in this act shall be construed either:

(i) to limit the lawful exercise of the right of eminent domain or the power of condemnation by any person or entity having such power over real property subject to a conservation or preservation easement by any person or entity having legal authority to do so or in lieu thereof; or

(ii) to limit the right of such person or entity to purchase rights for its public purposes over real property subject to a conservation or preservation easement without resort to condemnation.

(2) In the event of exercise of eminent domain, nothing in this act shall be construed so as to restrict any right to compensation a holder of a conservation or preservation easement may have under applicable law.

(e) Just compensation.—A court order issued under subsection (d) shall provide for the holder of the easement to be compensated in accordance with the applicable provisions of the conservation or preservation easement which specify a particular allocation of damages and, in the absence of such a provision, for the fair market value of the easement. Nothing in this act shall be construed to prevent a purchase agreement in lieu of condemnation as a means of settling such claims by providing either the specifically allocated damages or the fair market value to the holder of the easement. The net proceeds of the condemnation received by the holder shall be applied in furtherance of the public benefit in accordance with its charter or articles of incorporation. The court in adjudicating damages to a conservation or preservation easement shall be guided by principles generally applicable to condemnation proceedings.

§ 5056. Validity.

A conservation or preservation easement is valid even though:

(1) it is not appurtenant to an interest in real property;

(2) it can be or has been assigned to another holder;

(3) it is not of a character that has been recognized traditionally at common law;

(4) it imposes a negative burden;

(5) it imposes affirmative obligations upon the owner of an interest in the burdened property or upon the holder;

(6) the benefit does not touch or concern real property;

(7) there is no privity of estate or of contract; or

(8) the holder is or becomes the owner in fee of the subject property.

§ 5057. Applicability.

(a) Interests created after effective date.—This act shall apply to any interest created after the effective date of this act which complies with this act, whether designated as a conservation or preservation easement or as a covenant, equitable servitude, restriction, easement or otherwise.

(b) Interests created before effective date.—This act shall apply to any interest created before the effective date of this act when the interest would have been enforceable had it been created after the effective date of this act and has been recorded or, if not previously recorded, is recorded or otherwise placed of record within 180 days of the effective date of this act unless retroactive application contravenes the Constitution of the United States or laws of the United States or of this Commonwealth.

(c) Enforceable interests not invalidated.—This act does not invalidate any interest, whether designated as a conservation or preservation easement or as a covenant, equitable servitude, restriction, easement or otherwise, enforceable under another law of this Commonwealth or the common law.

(d) Agricultural Area Security Law.—Notwithstanding any other provision of this act, nothing contained in this act shall be construed as altering, modifying or superseding either the method of creating agricultural conservation easements or the rights, duties, powers and obligations appurtenant to these easements under the act of June 30, 1981 (P.L. 128, No. 43),[1] known as the Agricultural Area Security Law.

§ 5058. Uniformity of application and construction.

This act shall be applied and construed to effectuate its general purpose to make uniform the laws with respect to the subject of this act among states enacting similar laws. Except as expressly otherwise provided in this act, nothing in this act is intended to be construed to alter or supersede applicable law pertaining to the creation, perfection, priority or enforceability of instruments affecting real estate, including conservation or preservation easements. The owner of real property which is subject to a conservation or preservation easement retains the right to transfer, encumber or otherwise alienate the real property, subject to applicable limitations, including any provision requiring notice to the holder, contained in the conservation or preservation easement.

§ 5059. Coal interests not affected and notice of mineral interests required.

(a) Coal rights preserved.—Nothing in this act limits, expands, modifies or preempts the rights, powers, duties and liabilities of operators or other persons under the act of May 31, 1945 (P.L. 1198, No. 418),[2] known as the Surface Mining Conservation and Reclamation Act, or the act of April 27, 1966 (1st Sp.Sess., P.L. 31, No. 1),[3] known as The Bituminous Mine Subsidence and Land Conservation Act. This act does not limit or restrict any coal mining activity which was permitted or for which an application for permit was filed prior to the recording of a conservation easement under this act.

---

1. 3 P.S. §§ 901 et seq.
2. 52 P.S. §§ 1396.1 et seq.
3. 52 P.S. §§ 1406.1 et seq.

(b) Prohibited action.—The existence of a conservation easement on contiguous property may not serve as the sole grounds for designation of areas unsuitable for mining pursuant to section 4.5[4] of the Surface Mining Conservation and Reclamation Act.

(c) Easements of necessity.—Nothing in this act shall be construed to limit the exercise of rights created by easements of necessity or inherent in the ownership of property contiguous to the property burdened by the easement or of coal interests which have been severed from the ownership of the property burdened by the easement.

(d) Notice of coal interests.—A conservation easement affecting real property containing workable coal seams or from which an interest in coal has been severed may not be recorded or effective unless the grantor or donor of the easement signs a statement printed on the instrument creating the conservation easement stating that the easement may impair the development of such coal interest. This statement must be printed in no less than 12-point type and must be preceded by the word "Notice" printed in no less than 24-point type.

4. 52 P.S. § 1396.4e.

CHAPTER 24
RELIGIOUS ISSUES

Chapter 24.1

RELIGIOUS LAND USE AND INSTITUTIONALIZED PERSONS ACT OF 2000

42 U.S.C. §§ 2000cc et seq. (Federal Law)

TABLE OF CONTENTS

Practitioners may wish to consult three recent cases construing the Constitutionality of this Act.

Lighthouse Institute for Evangelism, Inc. v. City of Long Branch, 510 F.3d 253, 255× (3rd Cir. (N.J.) Nov. 27, 2007) (NO. 06-1319); *Lovelace v. Lee,* 472 F.3d 174, 175× (4th Cir. (Va.) Dec. 29, 2006) (NO. 04-7797); and *Elsinore Christian Center v. City of Lake Elsinore,* 197 Fed. Appx. 718, 718 (9th Cir. (Cal.) Aug. 22, 2006) (NO. 04-55320).

§ 1. Short Title.

This act may be cited as the 'Religious Land Use and Institutionalized Persons Act of 2000'.

§ 2. Protection of Land Use as Religious Exercise.

(a) Substantial Burdens—

(1) General Rule—No government shall impose or implement a land use regulation in a manner that imposes a substantial burden on the religious exercise of a person, including a religious assembly or institution, unless the government demonstrates that imposition of the burden on that person, assembly, or institution—

(A) is in furtherance of a compelling government interest; and

(B) is the least restrictive means of furthering that compelling government interest.

(2) Scope of Application—This subsection applies in any case in which—

(A) the substantial burden is imposed in a program or activity that receives Federal financial assistance, even if the burden results from a rule of general applicability.

(B) the substantial burden affects, or removal of that substantial burden would affect, commerce with foreign nations, among the several States, or with Indian tribes, even if the burden results from a rule of general applicability; or

Table of Contents
Part I Ch. 1–3 Ethics, Records, Open Meetings
Part II Ch. 4–10 Taxation
Part III Ch. 11–18 Torts, Contracts & Civil Rules
Part IV Ch. 19–24 Zoning & Planning
Part V Ch. 25–30 Construction and Emergency Codes
Part VI Ch. 31–39 Municipal Codes
Index

Chapter 24 Religious Land Use
Chapter 23 Conservation Easements
Chapter 22.1 Land Banks
Chapter 22 Open Space Lands
Chapter 21-B Regulation of Local Agriculture
Chapter 21-A Gas and Oil
Chapter 20 Bluff Recession and Setback Act
Chapter 19.2 Development Permit Extension Act
Chapter 19.1 Wireless Broadband Collocation Act
Chapter 19 Municipalities Planning Code

(C) the substantial burden is imposed in the implementation of a land use regulation or system of land use regulations, under which a government makes, or has in place formal or informal procedures or practices that permit the government to make, individualized assessments of the proposed uses for the property involved.

(b) Discrimination and Exclusion—

(1) EQUAL TERMS—No government shall impose or implement a land use regulation in a manner that treats a religious assembly or institution on less than equal terms with a nonreligious assembly or institution.

(2) NONDISCRIMINATION—No government shall impose or implement a land use regulation that discriminates against any assembly or institution on the basis of religion or religious denomination.

(3) EXCLUSIONS AND LIMITS—No government shall impose or implement a land use regulation that—

(A) totally excludes religious assemblies from a jurisdiction; or

(B) unreasonably limits religious assemblies, institutions, or structures within a jurisdiction.

§ 3. Protection of Religious Exercise of Institutionalized Persons.

(a) General Rule—No government shall impose a substantial burden on the religious exercise of a person residing in or confined to an institution, as defined in section 2 of the Civil Rights of Institutionalized Persons Act (42 U.S.C. 1997), even if the burden results from a rule of general applicability, unless the government demonstrates that imposition of the burden on that person—

(1) is in furtherance of a compelling government interest; and

(2) is the least restrictive means of furthering that compelling government interest.

(b) Scope of Application—This section applies in any case in which—

(1) the substantial burden is imposed in a program or activity that receives Federal financial assistance; or

(2) the substantial burden affects, or removal of that substantial burden would affect, commerce with foreign nations, among the several States, or with Indian tribes.

§ 4. Judicial Relief.

(a) Cause of Action—A person may assert a violation of this Act as a claim or defense in a judicial proceeding and obtain appropriate relief against a government. Standing to assert a claim or defense under this section shall be governed by the general rules of standing under article III of the Constitution.

(b) Burden of Persuasion—If a plaintiff produces prima facie evidence to support a claim alleging a violation of the Free Exercise Clause or a violation of section 2, the government shall bear the burden of persuasion on any element of the claim, except that the plaintiff shall bear the burden of persuasion on whether the law (including a regulation) or government practice that is challenged by the claim substantially burdens the plaintiff's exercise of religion.

(c) Full Faith and Credit—Adjudication of a claim of a violation of section 2 in a non-Federal forum shall not be entitled to full faith and credit in a Federal court unless the claimant had a full and fair adjudication of that claim in the non-Federal forum.

(d) Attorney's Fees—Section 722(b) of the Revised Statutes (42 U.S.C. 1988(b)) is amended—

(1) by inserting 'the Religious Land Use and Institutionalized Persons Act of 2000,' after 'Religious Freedom Restoration Act of 1993'; and

(2) by striking the comma that follows a comma.

(e) Prisoners—Nothing in this Act shall be construed to amend or repeal the Prison Litigation Reform Act of 1995 (including provisions of law amended by that Act).

(f) Authority of United States to Enforce This Act—The United States may bring an action for injunctive or declaratory relief to enforce compliance with this Act. Nothing in this subsection shall be construed to deny, impair, or otherwise affect any right or authority of the Attorney General, the United States, or any agency, officer, or employee of the United States, acting under any law other than this subsection, to institute or intervene in any proceeding.

(g) Limitation—If the only jurisdictional basis for applying a provision of this Act is a claim that a substantial burden by a government on religious exercise affects, or that removal of that substantial burden would affect, commerce with foreign nations, among the several States, or with Indian tribes, the provision shall not apply if the government demonstrates that all substantial burdens on, or the removal of all substantial burdens from, similar religious exercise throughout the Nation would not lead in the aggregate to a substantial effect on commerce with foreign nations, among the several States, or with Indian tribes.

§ 5. Rules of Construction.

(a) Religious Belief Unaffected—Nothing in this Act shall be construed to authorize any government to burden any religious belief.

(b) Religious Exercise not Regulated—Nothing in this Act shall create any basis for restricting or burdening religious exercise or for claims against a religious organization including any religiously affiliated school or university, not acting under color of law.

(c) Claims to Funding Unaffected—Nothing in this Act shall create or preclude a right of any religious organization to receive funding or other assistance from a government, or of any person to receive government funding for a religious activity, but this Act may require a government to incur expenses in its own operations to avoid imposing a substantial burden on religious exercise.

(d) Other Authority to Impose Conditions on Funding Unaffected—Nothing in this Act shall—

(1) authorize a government to regulate or affect, directly or indirectly, the activities or policies of a person other than a government as a condition of receiving funding or other assistance; or

(2) restrict any authority that may exist under other law to so regulate or affect, except as provided in this Act.

(e) Governmental Discretion in Alleviating Burdens on Religious Exercise—A government may avoid the preemptive force of any provision of this Act by changing the policy or practice that results in a substantial burden on religious exercise, by retaining the policy or practice and exempting the substantially burdened religious exercise, by providing exemptions from the policy or practice for applications that substantially burden religious exercise, or by any other means that eliminates the substantial burden.

(f) Effect on Other Law—With respect to a claim brought under this Act, proof that a substantial burden on a person's religious exercise affects, or removal of that burden would affect, commerce with foreign nations, among the several States, or with Indian tribes, shall not establish any inference or presumption that Congress intends that any religious exercise is, or is not, subject to any law other than this Act.

(g) Broad Construction—This Act shall be construed in favor of a broad protection of religious exercise, to the maximum extent permitted by the terms of this Act and the Constitution.

(h) No Preemption or Repeal—Nothing in this Act shall be construed to preempt State law, or repeal Federal law, that is equally as protective of religious exercise as, or more protective of religious exercise than, this Act.

(i) Severability—If any provision of this Act or of an amendment made by this Act, or any application of such provision to any person or circumstance, is held to be unconstitutional, the remainder of this Act, the amendments made by this Act, and the application of the provision to any other person or circumstance shall not be affected.

§ 6. Establishment Clause Unaffected.

Nothing in this Act shall be construed to affect, interpret, or in any way address that portion of the first amendment to the Constitution prohibiting laws respecting an establishment of religion (referred to in this section as the 'Establishment Clause'). Granting government funding, benefits, or exemptions, to the extent permissible under the Establishment Clause, shall not consitute a violation of this Act. In this section, the term 'granting', used with respect to government funding, benefits, or exemptions, does not include the denial of government funding, benefits, or exemptions.

§ 7. Amendments to Religious Freedom Restoration Act.

(a) Definitions—Section 5 of the Religious Freedom Restoration Act of 1993 (42 U.S.C. 2000bb-2) is amended—

(1) in paragraph (1), by striking 'a State, or a subdivision of a State' and inserting 'or of a covered entity';

(2) in paragraph (2), by striking 'term' and all that follows through 'includes' and inserting 'term 'covered entity' means'; and

(3) in paragraph (4), by striking all after 'means' and inserting 'religious exercise, as defined in section 8 of the Religious Land Use and Institutionalized Persons Act of 2000'.

(b) Conforming Amendment—Section 6(a) of the Religious Freedom Restoration Act of 1993 (42 U.S.C. 2000bb-3(a)) is amended by striking 'and State'.

§ 8. Definitions.

In this Act:

(1) CLAIMANT—The term 'claimant' means a person raising a claim or defense under this Act.

(2) DEMONSTRATES—The term 'demonstrates' means meets the burdens of going forward with the evidence and of persuasion.

(3) FREE EXERCISE CLAUSE—The term 'Free Exercise Clause' means that portion of the first amendment to the Constitution that proscribes laws prohibiting the free exercise of religion.

(4) GOVERNMENT—The term 'government'—

(A) means—

(i) a State, county, municipality, or other governmental entity created under the authority of a State;

(ii) any branch, department, agency, instrumentality, or official of an entity listed in clause (i); and

(iii) any other person acting under color of State law; and

(B) for the purposes of sections 4(b) and 5, includes the United States, a branch, department, agency, instrumentality, or official of the United States, and any other person acting under color of Federal law.

(5) LAND USE REGULATION—The term 'land use regulation' means a zoning or landmarking law, or the application of such a law, that limits or restricts a claimant's use or development of land (including a structure affixed to land), if the claimant has an ownership, leasehold, easement, servitude, or other property interest in the regulated land or a contract or option to acquire such an interest.

(6) PROGRAM OR ACTIVITY—The term 'program or activity' means all of the operations of any entity as described in paragraph (1) or (2) of section 606 of the Civil Rights Act of 1964 (42 U.S.C. 2000d-4a).

(7) RELIGIOUS EXERCISE—

(A) IN GENERAL—The term 'religious exercise' includes any exercise of religion, whether or not compelled by, or central to, a system of religious belief.

(B) RULE—The use, building, or conversion of real property for the purpose of religious exercise shall be considered to be religious exercise of the person or entity that uses or intends to use the property for that purpose.

Chapter 24.2

PENNSYLVANIA RELIGIOUS FREEDOM PROTECTION ACT

ACT NO. 2002–214

71 P.S. §§ 2401–2408

TABLE OF CONTENTS

Sec.

AN ACT Protecting the free exercise of religion; and prescribing the conditions under which government may substantially burden a person's free exercise of religion.

The General Assembly of the Commonwealth of Pennsylvania hereby enacts as follows:

Section 1. Short Title[1]

This act shall be known and may be cited as the Religious Freedom Protection Act.

Section 2. Legislative findings[2]

The General Assembly finds and declares as follows:

(1) Laws and governmental actions which are facially neutral toward religion, as well as laws and governmental actions intended to interfere with religious exercise, may have the effect of substantially burdening the free exercise of religion. However, neither State nor local government should substantially burden the free exercise of religion without compelling justification.

(2) The General Assembly intends that all laws which it has heretofore enacted or will hereafter enact and all ordinances and regulations which have been or will be adopted by political subdivisions or executive agencies shall be construed so as to avoid the imposition of substantial burdens upon the free exercise of religion without compelling justification.

Section 3. Definitions[3]

The following words and phrases when used in this act shall have the meanings given to them in this section unless the context clearly indicates otherwise:

"Agency." A Commonwealth agency or a non-Commonwealth agency. The term shall not include the courts of this Commonwealth or a grand jury acting pursuant to 42 Pa.C.S. § 4548 (relating to powers of investigating grand jury).

---

1. 71 P.S. § 2401.
2. 71 P.S. § 2402.
3. 71 P.S. § 2403.

"Commonwealth agency." The Commonwealth, including the Executive Department and its boards and commissions; an independent administrative department, board and commission; or a public official thereof, acting under color of State law.

"Correctional employee." A public official, employee, agent, contractor or volunteer working for or providing services relating to a correctional facility or its inmates.

"Free exercise of religion." The practice or observance of religion under section 3 or Article I of the Constitution of Pennsylvania.

"Non-Commonwealth agency." A political subdivision, municipal authority or any other local government instrumentality authorized by law, or a public official thereof, acting under the color of State law.

"Person." An individual or a church, association of churches or other religious order, body or institution which qualifies for exemption from taxation under section 501(c)(3) or (d) of the Internal Revenue Code of 1986 (Public Law 99–514, 26 U.S.C. § 501).

"Substantially burden." An agency action which does any of the following:

(1) Significantly constrains or inhibits conduct or expression mandated by a person's sincerely held religious beliefs.

(2) Significantly curtails a person's ability to express adherence to the person's religious faith.

(3) Denies a person a reasonable opportunity to engage in activities which are fundamental to the person's religion.

(4) Compels conduct or expression which violates a specific tenet of a person's religious faith.

Section 4. Free exercise of religion protected[4]

(a) General rule.—Except as provided in subsection (b), an agency shall not substantially burden a person's free exercise of religion, including any burden which results from a rule of general applicability.

(b) Exceptions.—An agency may substantially burden a person's free exercise of religion if the agency proves, by a preponderance of the evidence, that the burden is all of the following:

(1) In furtherance of a compelling interest of the agency.

(2) The least restrictive means of furthering the compelling interest.

Section 5. Actions[5]

(a) Claim or defense.—A person whose free exercise of religion has been burdened or likely will be burdened in violation of section 4 may assert that violation against an agency as a claim or defense in any judicial or administrative proceeding.

(b) Notice.—Notwithstanding subsection (a) and except as provided in subsection (c), a person may not bring an action in court to assert a claim under this act unless, at least 30 days prior to bringing the action, the person gives written notice to the agency by certified mail, return receipt requested, informing the agency of all of the following:

(1) The person's free exercise of religion has been or is about to be substantially burdened by an exercise of the agency's governmental authority.

4. 71 P.S. § 2404.
5. 71 P.S. § 2405.

(2) A description of the act or refusal to act which has burdened or will burden the person's free exercise of religion.

(3) The manner in which the exercise of the governmental authority burdens the person's free exercise of religion.

(c) Exception.—A person may bring an action in court without providing the notice required by subsection (b) if any of the following occur:

(1) The exercise of governmental authority which threatens to substantially burden the person's free exercise of religion is imminent.

(2) The person was not informed and did not otherwise have knowledge of the exercise of the governmental authority in time to reasonably provide notice.

(3) The provision of the notice would delay an action to the extent that the action would be dismissed as untimely.

(4) The claim or defense is asserted as a counterclaim in a pending proceeding.

(d) Limitation.—Prior to the expiration of the 30-day period referred to in subsection (b), an agency which receives notice in accordance with subsection (b) may remedy the substantial burden on the person's free exercise of religion.

(e) Jurisdiction.—A person alleging a violation of section 4 by a Commonwealth agency may bring an action in Commonwealth Court in accordance with this section and the applicable rules of court. In accordance with this section and applicable rules of court, a person alleging a violation of section 4 by a non-Commonwealth agency may bring an action in the court of common pleas for the county where the non-Commonwealth agency's office is located.

(f) Remedies.—If a person asserts a claim or defense in accordance with this section and proves, by clear and convincing evidence, that the person's free exercise of religion has been burdened or likely will be burdened in violation of section 4, a court may award the person such declaratory or injunctive relief as may be appropriate. No court shall award monetary damages for a violation of this act. Unless the court finds that the actions of the agency were dilatory, obdurate or vexatious, no court shall award attorney fees for a violation of this act.

(g) Inmate claims.—To the extent permitted under the Federal law, an agency shall be deemed not to have violated the provisions of this act if a rule, policy, action, omission or regulation of a correctional facility or its correctional employees is reasonably related to legitimate penological interests, including the deterrence of crime, the prudent use of institutional resources, the rehabilitation of prisoners or institutional security.

Section 6. Applicability[6]

(a) General rule.—This act shall apply to any State or local law or ordinance and the implementation of that law or ordinance, whether statutory or otherwise and whether adopted or effective prior to or after the effective date of this act. Any law enacted by the General Assembly after the effective date of this act shall be subject to this act unless the General Assembly expressly excludes that law from this act by specific reference to this act. This act shall not apply to actions of the courts of this Commonwealth or to any rules of procedure or to common law adopted by the courts of this Commonwealth.

(b) Exceptions.—Notwithstanding subsection (a) and subject to existing religious exceptions, this act shall not apply to any of the following:

6. 71 P.S. § 2406.

(1) Any criminal offense under 18 Pa.C.S. (relating to crimes and offenses) or under the act of April 14, 1972 (P.L. 233, No. 64),[7] known as The Controlled Substance, Drug, Device and Cosmetic Act, which is graded as a felony or a misdemeanor.

(2) Any provision of 75 Pa.C.S. (relating to vehicles) which does any of the following:

(i) Requires the licensing of motor vehicle operators.

(ii) Requires the registration of motor vehicles.

(iii) Requires financial responsibility for motor vehicle accidents.

(iv) Protects the public from the unsafe operation of motor vehicles or from dangerous conditions on the highways.

(3) Any provision of law which requires physicians or professional nurses to be properly licensed in order to practice their profession.

(4) Any provision of the act of June 13, 1967 (P.L.31, No.21),[8] known as the Public Welfare Code, which prevents the endangerment of the health or safety of individuals in facilities which are licensed or supervised under the Public Welfare Code.

(5) Any provision of the act of July 19, 1979 (P.L.130, No.48),[9] known as the Health Care Facilities Act, which requires the safe construction or operation of licensed health care facilities.

(6) Any provision of the act of November 10, 1999 (P.L.491, No.45),[10] known as the Pennsylvania Construction Code Act, which prevents the endangerment of health and safety.

(7) Any provision of law which requires the reporting of abuse.

Section 7. Construction[11]

Nothing in this act shall be construed to authorize any government to prohibit or penalize the holding of any religious belief or to take any action contrary to the Constitution of the United States or the Constitution of Pennsylvania. Nothing in this act shall be construed to require a religiously affiliated health care facility to provide, allow, participate in or refer for health care services which are contrary to the religious beliefs or practices of the facility, provided that the facility shall provide notice to its patients of its policies regarding those health care services.

Section 8. Effective date

This act shall take effect immediately.

Approved December 9, 2002.

7. 35 P.S. § 780–101 et seq.
8. 62 P.S. § 101 et seq.
9. 35 P.S. § 448.101 et seq.
10. 35 P.S. § 7210.101 et seq.
11. 71 P.S. § 2407.

Table of Contents
Part I Ch. 1–3 Ethics, Records, Open Meetings
Part II Ch. 4–10 Taxation
Part III Ch. 11–18 Torts, Contracts & Civil Rules
Part IV Ch. 19–24 Zoning & Planning
Part V Ch. 25–30 Construction and Emergency Codes
Part VI Ch. 31–39 Municipal Codes
Index

PART V

CONSTRUCTION AND EMERGENCY CODES

CHAPTER 25

CONSTRUCTION CODE ACT

TABLE OF CONTENTS

35 P.S. §§ 7210.101–7210.1103

CHAPTER 1
PRELIMINARY PROVISIONS

CHAPTER 3
UNIFORM CONSTRUCTION CODE

CHAPTER 5
ADOPTION AND ENFORCEMENT BY MUNICIPALITIES

Chapter 30 Emergency Management
Chapter 29 Counterterrorism Planning
Chapter 28 Social Security Number Privacy Act
Chapter 27 Municipal Code Compliance & Blight
Chapter 26 Construction Code Regulations
Chapter 25 Construction Code Act

CHAPTER 7
TRAINING AND CERTIFICATION OF INSPECTORS

CHAPTER 9
EXEMPTIONS, APPLICABILITY AND PENALTIES

CHAPTER 11
MISCELLANEOUS PROVISIONS

CHAPTER 1
PRELIMINARY PROVISIONS

§ 101. Short title[1]

This act shall be known and may be cited as the Pennsylvania Construction Code Act.

§ 102. Legislative findings and purpose[2]

(a) Findings.—The General Assembly finds as follows:

(1) Many municipalities within this Commonwealth have no construction codes to provide for the protection of life, health, property and the environment and for the safety and welfare of the consumer, general public and the owners and occupants of buildings and structures. Consumers and occupants may be at risk from substandard construction.

(2) Likewise, in some regions of this Commonwealth a multiplicity of construction codes currently exist and some of these codes may contain cumulatively needless requirements which limit the use of certain materials, techniques or products and lack benefits to the public. Moreover, the variation of construction standards caused by the multiplicity of codes may slow the process of construction and increase the costs of construction.

(3) The way to insure uniform, modern construction standards and regulations throughout this Commonwealth is to adopt a Uniform Construction Code.

(4) The model code of the Building Officials and Code Administrators International, Inc. (BOCA), is a construction code which has been widely adopted in this Commonwealth and in the geographical region of the United States of which this Commonwealth is a part. Adoption of a nationally recognized code will insure that this Commonwealth has a uniform, modern construction code which will insure safety, health and sanitary construction.

(b) Intent and purpose.—It is the intent of the General Assembly and the purpose of this act:

---

1. 35 P.S. § 7210.101.
2. 35 P.S. § 7210.102.

(1) To provide standards for the protection of life, health, property and environment and for the safety and welfare of the consumer, general public and the owners and occupants of buildings and structures.

(2) To encourage standardization and economy in construction by providing requirements for construction and construction materials consistent with nationally recognized standards.

(3) To permit to the fullest extent feasible the use of state-of-the-art technical methods, devices and improvements consistent with reasonable requirements for the health, safety and welfare of occupants or users of buildings and structures.

(4) To eliminate existing codes to the extent that these codes are restrictive, obsolete, conflicting and contain duplicative construction regulations that tend to unnecessarily increase costs or retard the use of new materials, products or methods of construction or provide preferential treatment to certain types or classes of materials or methods of construction.

(5) To eliminate unnecessary duplication of effort and fees related to the review of construction plans and the inspection of construction projects.

(6) To assure that officials charged with the administration and enforcement of the technical provisions of this act are adequately trained and supervised.

(7) To insure that existing Commonwealth laws and regulations, including those which would be repealed or rescinded by this act, would be fully enforced during the transition to Statewide administration and enforcement of a Uniform Construction Code. Further, it is the intent of this act that the Uniform Construction Code requirements for making buildings accessible to and usable by persons with disabilities to not diminish from those requirements previously in effect under the former provisions of the act of September 1, 1965 (P.L. 459, No. 235),[3] entitled, as amended, "An act requiring that certain buildings and facilities adhere to certain principles, standards and specifications to make the same accessible to and usable by persons with physical handicaps, and providing for enforcement."

(8) To start a process leading to the design, construction and alteration of buildings under a uniform standard.

§ 103. Definitions[4]

The following words and phrases when used in this act shall have the meanings given to them in this section unless the context clearly indicates otherwise:

"Addition." An extension or increase in floor area or height of a building or structure.

"Advisory board." The Accessibility Advisory Board created in section 106.[5]

"Agricultural building." A structure utilized to store farm implements, hay, feed, grain or other agricultural or horticultural products or to house poultry, livestock or other farm animals, a milk house and a structure used to grow mushrooms, agricultural or horticultural products. The term includes a carriage house owned and used by members of a recognized religious sect for the purposes of housing horses and storing buggies. The term includes a structure that is less than 1,000 square feet in size which is utilized to process maple sap. The term shall not include habitable space or spaces in which agricultural products are processed, treated or packaged and shall not be construed to mean a place of occupancy by the general public.

"Agricultural commodity." Any of the following, transported or intended to be transported in commerce:

---

3. 71 P.S. § 1455.1 et seq.

4. 35 P.S. § 7210.103.

5. 35 P.S. § 7210.106.

(1) Agricultural, aquacultural, horticultural, floricultural, viticultural or dairy products.

(2) Livestock and the products of livestock.

(3) Ranch-raised fur-bearing animals and the products of ranch-raised fur-bearing animals.

(4) The products of poultry or bee raising.

(5) Forestry and forestry products.

(6) Products raised or produced on farms intended for human consumption and the processed or manufactured products of such products intended for human consumption.

"Alteration." Any construction or renovation to an existing structure other than repair or addition.

"Board of appeals." The body created by a municipality or more than one municipality to hear appeals from decisions of the code administrator as provided for by regulations promulgated by the department.

"BOCA." Building Officials and Code Administrators International, Inc.

"Code administrator." A municipal code official, a construction code official, a third-party agency or the Department of Labor and Industry.

"Collective codes." The term includes:

(1) Provisions of the ICC codes specified in 34 Pa. Code § 403.21 (relating to Uniform Construction Code).

(2) Any other sections of the ICC codes which were previously subject to review by the council whether or not those sections were incorporated into the Uniform Construction Code or specified in 34 Pa. Code § 403.21.

"Construction code official." An individual certified by the Department of Labor and Industry in an appropriate category established pursuant to section 701(b)[6] of this act to perform plan review of construction documents, inspect construction or administer and enforce codes and regulations in such code category under this act or related acts.

"Council." The Uniform Construction Code Review and Advisory Council established under this act.

"Department." The Department of Labor and Industry of the Commonwealth.

"Existing sections." All sections of the collective codes that have been incorporated into the Uniform Construction Code that are currently in effect at the time of review by the council pursuant to section 108.[7]

"Habitable space." Space in a structure for living, sleeping, eating or cooking. Bathrooms, toilet compartments, closets, halls, storage or utility spaces and similar areas shall not be construed as habitable spaces.

"Health care facility." As defined in section 802.1 of the act of July 19, 1979 (P.L. 130, No. 48),[8] known as the Health Care Facilities act.

"ICC." the International Code Council.

"Industrial Board." The Industrial Board under sections 445 and 2214 of the act of April 9, 1929 (P.L. 177, No. 175), known as The Administrative Code of 1929, which hears requests for variances and extensions of time and appeals of decisions of the Department of Labor and Industry under the Uniform Construction Code.

"Industrialized housing." The term shall have the meaning ascribed to it in the act of May 11, 1972 (P.L. 286, No. 70),[9] known as the Industrialized Housing Act.

---

6. 35 P.S. § 7210.701.
7. 35 P.S. § 7210.108.
8. 35 P.S. § 448.802a.
9. 35 P.S. § 1651.1 et seq.

"Manufactured housing." Housing which bears a label, as required by and referred to in the act of November 17, 1982 (P.L. 676, No. 192),[10] known as the Manufactured Housing Construction and Safety Standards Authorization Act, certifying that it conforms to Federal construction and safety standards adopted under the Housing and Community Development Act of 1974 (Public Law 93–383, 88 Stat. 633).

"Municipal code official." An individual employed by a municipality or more than one municipality and certified by the Department of Labor and Industry under this act to perform plan review of construction documents, inspect construction or administer and enforce codes and regulations under this act or related acts.

"Municipality." A city, borough, incorporated town, township or home rule municipality.

"NCSBCS." The National Conference of State Building Codes and Standards.

"Occupancy." The purpose for which a building, or portion thereof, is used.

"Producer." A person engaged within this Commonwealth or a production area within this Commonwealth in the business of producing agricultural commodities or causing agricultural commodities to be produced.

"Recreational cabin." A structure which is:

(1) utilized principally for recreational activity;

(2) not utilized as a domicile or residence for any individual for any time period;

(3) not utilized for commercial purposes;

(4) not greater than two stories in height, excluding basement;

(5) not utilized by the owner or any other person as a place of employment;

(6) not a mailing address for bills and correspondence; and

(7) not listed as an individual's place of residence on a tax return, driver's license, car registration or voter registration.

"Repair." The reconstruction or renewal of any part of an existing building for the purpose of its maintenance.

"Residential building." Detached one-family and two-family dwellings and multiple single-family dwellings which are not more than three stories in height with a separate means of egress which includes accessory structures.

"Secretary." The Secretary of Labor and Industry of the Commonwealth.

"State institutions." As defined in section 901 of the act of June 13, 1967 (P.L. 31, No. 21),[11] known as the Public Welfare Code.

"Technically infeasible." An alteration of a building or a facility that has little likelihood of being accomplished because the existing structural conditions require the removal or alteration of a load-bearing member that is an essential part of the structural frame or because other existing physical or site constraints prohibit modification or addition of elements, spaces or features which are in full and strict compliance with the minimum requirements for new construction and which are necessary to provide accessibility.

"Third-party agency." A person, firm or corporation certified by the Department of Labor and Industry as a construction code official and contracted to perform plan review of construction documents, inspect construction or administer and enforce codes and regulations under this act.

"Uncertified building." An existing building which, prior to April 9, 2004, was not approved for use and occupancy by the Department of Labor and Industry or

10. 35 P.S. § 1656.1 et seq.

11. 62 P.S. § 901.

a municipality which was enforcing a building code. The term does not include a residential building.

"Uniform Construction Code." The code established in section 301.[12]

"Unopposed sections." Any and all updated sections that:

(1) Do not receive a public comment recommending modification or rejection pursuant to section 108(a)(3)(ii).

(2) Are not selected for further review by a technical advisory committee pursuant to section 108(a)(3)(v).

(3) Are not selected for further review by the council pursuant to section 108(a)(3)(ix)(A).

"Updated sections." Any and all sections of the newest editions of the ICC codes subject to review by the council under section 108(a)(1) that are different from, added to or deleted from the immediately preceding editions of the ICC codes. Each updated section shall be referenced by the section number assigned to such section by the ICC codes.

"Utility and miscellaneous use structures." Buildings or structures of an accessory character and miscellaneous structures not classified by the Building Officials and Code Administrators International, Inc., in any specific use group. The term includes carports, detached private garages, greenhouses and sheds having a building area less than 1,000 square feet. The term does not include swimming pools or spas.

§ 104. Application[13]

(a) General rule.—This act shall apply to the construction, alteration, repair and occupancy of all buildings in this Commonwealth.

(b) Exclusions.—This act shall not apply to any of the following:

(1) New buildings or renovations to existing buildings for which an application for a building permit has been made to the municipality prior to the effective date of the regulations promulgated under this act.

(2) New buildings or renovations to existing buildings on which a contract for design or construction has been signed prior to the effective date of the regulations promulgated under this act on projects requiring department approval.

(3) Utility and miscellaneous use structures that are accessory to detached one-family dwellings.

(4) Any agricultural building.

(5) Alterations to residential buildings which do not make structural changes or changes to means of egress, except as might be required by ordinances in effect pursuant to section 303(b)(1) or adopted pursuant to section 503. For purposes of this paragraph, a structural change does not include a minor framing change needed to replace existing windows or doors.

(6) Repairs to residential buildings, except as might be required by ordinances in effect pursuant to section 303(b)(1) or adopted pursuant to section 503.

(6.1) The installation of aluminum siding or vinyl siding onto an existing residential or an existing commercial building, except as might be required by ordinances in effect pursuant to section 301 or adopted pursuant to section 503.

(7) Any recreational cabin if:

12. 35 P.S. § 7210.301.

13. 35 P.S. § 7210.104.

(i) the cabin is equipped with at least one smoke detector, one fire extinguisher and one carbon monoxide detector in both the kitchen and sleeping quarters;

(ii) the owner of the cabin files with the municipality either:

(A) an affidavit on a form prescribed by the department attesting to the fact that the cabin meets the definition of a "recreational cabin" in section 103; or

(B) a valid proof of insurance for the recreational cabin, written and issued by an insurer authorized to do business in this Commonwealth, stating that the structure meets the definition of a "recreational cabin" as defined in section 103.

(8) Temporary structures which are:

(i) Erected for the purpose of participation in a fair, flea market, arts and crafts festival or other public celebration.

(ii) Less than 1,600 square feet in size.

(iii) Erected for a period of less than 30 days.

(iv) Not a swimming pool, spa or hot tub.

(v) Subject to section 503(a)(2).

(9) No more than one structure per parcel of land which meets all of the following requirements:

(i) The structure is used for the direct, seasonal sale of agricultural commodities.

(ii) The structure is open on at least 25% of the perimeter of the structure when in operation.

(iii) The structure is operated by a producer whose products make up not less than 50% of the agricultural commodities being sold.

(iv) If not located on the producer's property, the structure is erected for less than 180 days of a calendar year.

(v) The structure has an area of not more than 1,000 square feet.

(10) Structures used to load, unload or sort livestock at livestock auction facilities.

(b.1) Continuity of exclusion.—

(1) If a recreational cabin is subject to exclusion under subsection (b)(7), upon transfer of ownership of the recreational cabin, written notice must be provided in the sales agreement and the deed that the recreational cabin:

(i) is exempt from this act;

(ii) may not be in conformance with the Uniform Construction Code; and

(iii) is not subject to municipal regulation.

(2) Failure to comply with the notice requirement under paragraph (1) shall render the sale voidable at the option of the purchaser.

(c) Prior permits and construction.—

(1) Subject to paragraph (2), a construction permit issued under valid construction regulations prior to the effective date of the regulations issued under this act shall remain valid, and the construction of any building or structure may be completed pursuant to and in accordance with the permit.

(2) If the requirements of the permit have not been actively prosecuted within two years of the effective date of the regulations or the period specified by a municipal ordinance, whichever is less, the former permit holder shall be required to acquire a new permit. Where construction of a building or

structure commenced before the effective date of the regulations promulgated under this act and a permit was not required at that time, construction may be completed without a permit.

(d) Preemption.—

(1) Except as otherwise provided in this act, construction standards provided by any statute or local ordinance or regulation promulgated or adopted by a board, department, commission, agency of State government or agency of local government shall continue in effect only until the effective date of regulations promulgated under this act, at which time they shall be preempted by regulations promulgated under this act and deemed thereafter to be rescinded.

(2)(i) Except as otherwise provided in this act and as specifically excepted in subparagraph (ii), a homeowners' association or community association shall be preempted from imposing building construction standards or building codes for buildings to be constructed, renovated, altered or modified.

(ii) In municipalities which have not adopted an ordinance for the administration and enforcement of this act, a homeowners' association or community association may adopt by board regulations the Uniform Construction Code or the ICC International One and Two Family Dwelling Code, 1998 Edition. The applicable building code shall constitute the standard governing building structures in the association's community.

(3) Nothing in this act shall preempt any licensure or Federal certification requirements for health care facilities, intermediate care facilities for the mentally retarded or for persons with related conditions or State institutions. This paragraph includes building and life safety code standards set forth in applicable regulations.

(4) Nothing in this act shall limit the ability of the Department of Aging, the Department of Health or the Department of Public Welfare to promulgate or enforce regulations which exceed the requirements of this act.

(e) Municipal regulation.—Nothing in this act shall prohibit a municipality from licensing any persons engaged in construction activities or from establishing work rules or qualifications for such persons.

(f) Application to swimming pools and spas.—

(1) The provisions of this act as they relate to swimming pools and spas shall not be applicable to those constructed or installed prior to the effective date of this act.

(2) All swimming pools and spas constructed or installed after the effective date of this act shall be governed by the requirements of this act including section 503.[14]

§ 105. Department of Labor and Industry[15]

(a) Review.—

(1) The department shall with reasonable cause review municipalities, municipal code officials, third-party agencies, construction code officials and code administrators concerning the enforcement and administration of this act, including specifically complaints concerning accessibility requirements.

(2) The department shall make a report to the governing body of the municipality that was the subject of the review. The report shall include recommendations to address any deficiency observed by the department.

(3) The department may require compliance with this act through proceedings in Commonwealth Court.

14. 35 P.S. § 7210.503.
15. 35 P.S. § 7210.105.

(b) State-owned buildings.—

(1) The department shall maintain plan and specification review and inspection authority over all State-owned buildings. State-owned buildings shall be subject to regulations promulgated under this act. The department shall notify municipalities of all inspections of State-owned buildings and give municipalities the opportunity to observe the department inspection of such buildings.

(2) Municipalities shall notify the department of all inspection of buildings owned by political subdivisions and give the department the opportunity to observe municipal inspection of such buildings.

(3) The department shall make available to municipalities, upon request, copies of all building plans and plan review documents in the custody of the department for State-owned buildings.

(4) A municipality shall make available to the department, upon request, copies of all building plans and plan review documents in the custody of the municipality for buildings owned by political subdivisions.

(c) Elevators and conveying systems.—

(1) The department shall maintain Statewide administration and inspection authority over ski lifts, inclined passenger lifts and related devices, and elevators, conveying systems and related equipment as defined in section 3002.0 (definitions) of Chapter 30 of the 1999 BOCA National Building Code, Fourteenth Edition.

(2) Notwithstanding Chapters 3 and 5, the department may, subject to the act of June 25, 1982 (P.L. 633, No. 181),[16] known as the Regulatory Review Act, by regulation modify the 1999 BOCA National Building Code, Fourteenth Edition, Referenced Standards for elevator construction, repair, maintenance and inspection. The department shall not require reshackling more than once every two years.

(3) Nothing in this section shall be construed to disallow third-party elevator inspections.

(d) Department of Health.—

(1) Health care facilities, intermediate care facilities for the mentally retarded or for persons with related conditions and State institutions shall continue to comply with building codes and standards set forth in the applicable licensure laws and regulations. This paragraph includes the applicable edition of the National Fire Protection Association's Life Safety Code, NFPA No. 101, and the applicable edition of the Guidelines for Construction and Equipment of Hospital and Medical Facilities.

(2) The department may delegate its responsibility for conducting plan reviews and inspections for health care facilities to the Department of Health.

(e) Limitation.—Nothing in this act, the regulations under this act or the administration of the act or the regulations by the department shall contravene the rights of builders to freely compete for and perform contracts for construction of commercial buildings in this Commonwealth.

§ 106. Accessibility Advisory Board[17]

(a) Creation and composition.—

(1) There is hereby created an Accessibility Advisory Board which shall be composed of 11 members appointed by the secretary. At least six members of the advisory board shall be public members, three of whom shall be persons with

16. 71 P.S. § 745.1 et seq.
17. 35 P.S. § 7210.106.

physical disabilities, one shall be an architect registered in Pennsylvania, one shall be a member of the business community, and one shall be a representative of the multifamily housing industry. One member shall be a municipal official. The chairman and minority chairman of the Labor and Industry Committee of the Senate and the chairman and minority chairman of the Labor Relations Committee of the House of Representatives, or their designees, shall be members. All members of the advisory board, except the members of the General Assembly, shall serve for a term of two years and until their successors are appointed.

(2) The members of the advisory board shall be paid traveling expenses and other necessary expenses and may receive a per diem compensation at a rate to be determined by the secretary for each day of actual service in the performance of their duties under this act.

(3) Meetings of the advisory board shall be called by the secretary. A quorum of the advisory board shall consist of four members.

(4) The initial advisory board shall be the body constituted under the former provisions of section 3.1 of the act of September 1, 1965 (P.L. 459, No. 235),[18] entitled, as amended, "An act requiring that certain buildings and facilities adhere to certain principles, standards and specifications to make the same accessible to and usable by persons with physical handicaps, and providing for enforcement."

(b) Advice on regulation.—The advisory board shall review all proposed regulations under this act and shall offer comment and advice to the secretary on all issues relating to accessibility by persons with physical disabilities, including those which relate to the enforcement of the accessibility requirements.

(c) Recommendations for modifications.—The advisory board shall review all applications from individual projects for modifications of the provisions of Chapter 11 (Accessibility) of the Uniform Construction Code and any other accessibility requirements contained in or referenced by the Uniform Construction Code and shall advise the secretary regarding whether modification should be granted or whether compliance by existing facilities with provisions of Chapter 11 (Accessibility) of the Uniform Construction Code and any other accessibility requirements contained in or referenced by the Uniform Construction Code is technically infeasible.

§ 107. Uniform Construction Code Review and Advisory Council[19]

(a) Establishment.—The Uniform Construction Code Review and Advisory Council is hereby established.

(b) Duties.—The council shall do the following:

(1) Gather information from municipal officers, building code officials, construction code officials, licensed design professionals, builders, property owners, construction trades and consumer representatives concerning issues with the Uniform Construction Code raised by council members or changes proposed by members of the General Assembly.

(2) Evaluate the information compiled under paragraph (1) and make recommendations to the following:

(i) The Governor.

(ii) The Secretary of Labor and Industry.

(iii) The members of any legislative committee considering amendments to this act.

---

18. 71 P.S. § 1455.3a.
19. 35 P.S. § 7210.107.

(iv) The President pro tempore of the Senate.

(v) The Speaker of the House of Representatives.

(vi) The International Code Council.

(3) With the exception of the accessibility provisions of the most recently published editions of ICC codes, or any other accessibility requirements specified in regulation, contained in or referenced by the Uniform Construction Code relating to persons with physical disabilities, review the updated sections, as provided under section 108 or other sections of the collective codes, as provided under section 108(a)(1)(iii).

(c) **Composition.**—The council shall be comprised of members who are legal residents of this Commonwealth selected as follows:

(1) One member, appointed by the President pro tempore of the Senate, who must be a general contractor from an association representing the residential construction industry and have a recognized ability and experience in the construction of new residential dwellings.

(2) One member, appointed by the Minority Leader of the Senate, who must be a second or third class city official and have recognized ability and experience in the construction of buildings.

(3) One member, appointed by the Speaker of the House of Representatives, who must be a general contractor from an association representing the nonresidential construction industry and have recognized ability and experience in the construction of nonresidential buildings.

(4) One member, appointed by the Minority Leader of the House of Representatives, who must have recognized ability and experience in construction trades so as to represent employees in the industry.

(5) Seventeen members appointed by the Governor to include the following:

(i) One member who must be a Uniform Construction Code-certified residential building inspector, possess all five residential certifications from an association representing building code officials and have experience administering and enforcing residential codes.

(ii) One member who must be a Uniform Construction Code-certified building inspector, who possesses all nonresidential inspection certifications but does not need to possess a fire inspector certification, or a certified plans examiner, who holds an accessibility certification from an association representing building code officials and has experience administering and enforcing nonresidential codes.

(iii) One member who must be a Uniform Construction Code-certified fire inspector from an association representing fire code officials.

(iv) One member who must be a Uniform Construction Code-certified building code official from an association representing building code officials with building code official certification.

(v) One member who must be a residential contractor from an association representing contractors engaged in remodeling residential buildings and have recognized ability and experience in remodeling residential and nonresidential buildings.

(vi) One member who must be a licensed architect from an association representing architects and have recognized ability and experience in the design and construction of nonresidential buildings.

(vii) One member who must be a licensed architect from an association representing architects and have recognized ability and experience in the design and construction of residential buildings.

Chapter 30 Emergency Management
Chapter 29 Counterterrorism Planning
Chapter 28 Social Security Number Privacy Act
Chapter 27 Municipal Code Compliance & Blight
Chapter 26 Construction Code Regulations
Chapter 25 Construction Code Act

(viii) One member who must be a licensed structural engineer from an association representing professional engineers and have recognized ability and experience in the design and construction of buildings.

(ix) One member who must be a licensed mechanical engineer specializing in HVAC systems from an association representing professional engineers and have recognized ability and experience in the design and construction of buildings.

(x) One member who must be a licensed mechanical engineer specializing in plumbing and fire protection from an association representing professional engineers and have recognized ability and experience in the design and construction of buildings.

(xi) One member who must be a licensed electrical engineer from an association representing professional engineers and have recognized ability and experience in the design and construction of buildings.

(xii) One member who must be a public official of a borough and have recognized ability and experience in the construction of buildings.

(xiii) One member from an association representing manufactured housing who must be knowledgeable, licensed or certified to sell and install manufactured housing.

(xiv) One member who must be a first class city official and have recognized ability and experience in the administration and enforcement of this act.

(xv) One member from an association representing modular housing manufacturers who must be knowledgeable, licensed or certified under the act of May 11, 1972 (P.L. 286, No. 70),[20] known as the Industrialized Housing Act, to manufacture and sell modular homes in this Commonwealth.

(xvi) One member who is a public official of a township of the second class and has recognized ability and experience in the construction of buildings.

(xvii) One member from an association representing commercial building owners who has recognized ability and experience in the construction and renovation of nonresidential buildings.

At least one of the inspectors appointed to the council shall be a municipal employee, and at least one inspector shall be a third-party private sector inspector. All members shall present documentation to the secretary that they meet the qualifications of the member's appointment and the secretary shall maintain the documentation for public inspection.

(d) Vacancies.—Vacancies on the council shall be filled in the manner provided under subsection (c) within 90 business days of the vacancy. If the appointing authority fails to act within 90 business days, the council chairperson shall appoint an individual to fill the vacancy.

(e) Removal.—Council members who miss three or more consecutive meetings or who miss three or more meetings of a technical advisory committee to which they have been appointed may be removed from the council and any technical advisory committees to which they have been appointed and a new council member shall be appointed in accordance with this section. Notwithstanding any other provision to the contrary, the council chair shall appoint a council member to serve on a technical advisory committee and replace a council member removed from that technical advisory committee pursuant to this subsection. A council member may also be removed for just cause by the Governor. A council member who does not meet the qualifications of their appointment shall be removed.

(f) Terms.—

20. 35 P.S. § 1651.1 et seq.

(1) Except as otherwise provided under this subsection, a member of the council shall serve terms of three years and until his successor is appointed.

(2) The term of a member appointed under subsection (c)(1), (2), (3), (4) or (5)(xvii) shall commence immediately upon appointment and shall expire June 30, 2020, and the member shall serve until a successor is appointed.

(3) A member appointed to the council before the effective date of this section[21] shall serve on the council according to the following:

(i) If the member meets the qualifications as specified under subsection (c)(5)(x) or (xiv), the member shall fill the appointment under subsection (c)(5)(x) or (xiv) until June 30, 2017, and until a successor is appointed.

(ii) If the member meets the qualifications as specified under subsection (c)(5)(i), (ii), (iv), (vi), (viii), (ix) or (xv), the member shall fill the appointment under subsection (c)(5)(i), (ii), (iv), (vi), (viii), (ix) or (xv) until June 30, 2018, and until a successor is appointed.

(iii) If the member meets the qualifications as specified under subsection (c)(5)(iii), (v), (vii), (xi),(xii), (xiii) or (xvi), the member shall fill the appointment under subsection (c)(5)(iii), (v), (vii)(xi), (xii), (xiii) or (xvi) until June 30, 2019, and until a successor is appointed.

(4) If a member serving the council under paragraph (3)(i), (ii) or (iii) resigns or is removed in accordance with subsection (e), the member's successor shall serve for the remainder of the member's term and until a successor is appointed.

(g) Chairperson and vice chairperson.—The members shall elect, by a majority vote, a chairperson and vice chairperson of the council.

(h) Quorum.—Eleven members shall constitute a quorum.

(i) Meetings.—Meetings shall be conducted as required under 65 Pa.C.S. Ch. 7 (relating to open meetings) as follows:

(1) The council shall meet at least once every six months. Meeting dates shall be set by majority vote of the council members or by the call of the chair along with at least seven business days' notice to all members.

(2) All meetings of the council shall be publicly advertised and shall be open to the public. Members of the general public shall be given reasonable opportunity to address the council.

(3) The council shall publish a schedule of its meetings in the Pennsylvania Bulletin and in at least one newspaper of general circulation. The notice shall be published at least five business days in advance of each meeting. The notice shall specify the date, time and place of the meeting and shall state that the meetings of the council are open to the general public.

(4) Council members may participate in council meetings in person, via telephone conference or via video conference. Council members may submit votes in person, telephonically or by electronic mail to the chair of the council. The department may approve similar methods of communication for participation and voting by council members.

(j) Administrative support.—The department shall provide a facility for council meetings under this act, stenographic services, secretarial services, legal representation and required notice of the council's meetings. The department shall provide staff support in drafting any reports required under this act.

---

21. This section was added by Act of Oct. 25, 2017, P.L. 356, No. 36, § 2, immediately effective.

Table of Contents
Part I Ch. 1–3 Ethics, Records, Open Meetings
Part II Ch. 4–10 Taxation
Part III Ch. 11–18 Torts, Contracts & Civil Rules
Part IV Ch. 19–24 Zoning & Planning
Part V Ch. 25–30 Construction and Emergency Codes
Part VI Ch. 31–39 Municipal Codes
Index

(k) Technical support.—The council may solicit and retain, with or without compensation, individuals who are qualified by training or experience to provide expert input to the council. At the discretion of the council:

(1) Except as set forth in paragraph (2), such individuals may be compensated for their services or reimbursed for reasonable travel expenses at a reasonable rate established by the secretary, or both.

(2) Paragraph (1) does not apply to a member of a technical advisory committee appointed under subsection (m)(1)(v).

(l) Compensation and expenses.—Members of the council shall not receive a salary or per diem allowance for their service but shall be reimbursed in amounts and as determined by the department for reasonable travel, lodging and other necessary expenses incurred in performing their duties.

(m) Technical advisory committees.—

(1) The council shall establish a process by which technical advisory committees will assist the council in the review of the updated sections. The technical advisory committee process shall comply with the following requirements:

(i) There shall be a technical advisory committee for each of the codes included in the Uniform Construction Code and specified in 34 Pa. Code § 403.21 (relating to Uniform Construction Code), and such other technical advisory committees as the council deems necessary to facilitate its review. Members of industry and interest groups associated with code development and enforcement shall be permitted to participate in the technical advisory committee.

(ii) Each technical advisory committee shall be limited to a maximum of 12 members. The chair of the council shall appoint a council member to chair each technical advisory committee. Any other council member may seek appointment to a technical advisory committee and, if no more than four additional council members seek appointment to a specified technical advisory committee, those council members shall also be appointed to the technical advisory committee. If more than four council members seek appointment to a technical advisory committee, the chair of the council shall appoint four of the council members seeking appointment to serve and the remaining council members seeking appointment shall serve only if additional positions on the technical advisory committee remain after selection of the technical advisory committee members pursuant to subparagraph (v).

(iii) The department shall publish a notice seeking participation in the technical advisory committees in the Pennsylvania Bulletin and on the department's publicly accessible Internet website or, in the absence of an Internet website, in such other manner as the secretary determines will provide substantially similar public notice.

(iv) Interested persons shall submit to the chair of the council the following information within 30 days following the publication of the notice:

(A) name;

(B) the name or subject matter area of the technical advisory committee to which the individual seeks to be appointed;

(C) contact information;

(D) industry sector, interest group or area of construction industry expertise, if applicable; and

(E) summary of experience and expertise.

(v) The chair of the council shall seek to ensure diversity of interests on each technical advisory committee. Technical advisory committee members shall be selected by the chair of the council from among the interested persons identified in subparagraph (iv) so as to ensure that the technical advisory committee as a whole has, at minimum, representation from affected contractor associations, affected building trade organizations, the code enforcement community, the design professional community and other relevant industries.

(vi) Meetings of the technical advisory committees may be in person, via telephone conference or via video conference. The department may approve similar methods of communication for participation and voting by technical advisory committee members.

(vii) Technical advisory committee members may submit votes in person, telephonically or by electronic mail to the chair of the technical advisory committee. Recommendations of a technical advisory committee shall be by majority of the votes received from council members on the technical advisory committee and shall be nonbinding.

§ 108. Review of updated sections and adoption of updated sections into Uniform Construction Code[22]

(a) Code review process.—

(1)(i) Except as specifically provided in this act with respect:

(A) to the 2015 changes to the Uniform Construction Code adopted by the council; and

(B) to the procedure outlined in subparagraph (iii),

the council shall commence its review of the updated sections 21 months following the publication of a new edition of the ICC codes in accordance with paragraph (3). Notwithstanding any other provision of this act to the contrary, the council shall initiate a new review of the updated sections contained in the 2015 edition of the ICC codes within 30 days of the effective date of this section, and this review shall be referred to as the 2015 Code Review. The decisions by the council with respect to the 2015 edition of the ICC codes previously provided to the department on May 29, 2015, and the regulations promulgated by the department as a result shall remain in full force and effect until September 30, 2018. As of October 1, 2018, the decisions of the council as a result of the 2015 Code Review and the regulations promulgated by the department as a result shall supersede any previous inconsistent council decisions or departmental regulations.

(ii) The 2015 code review shall be conducted in accordance with provisions of this act, except that:

(A) the public comment period under paragraph (3)(i) shall be 30 days;

(B) notwithstanding the requirements under paragraph (3)(viii), the council shall only be required to conduct one public hearing which shall be held within 30 days after the end of the public comment period and shall be held in Harrisburg;

(C) the council shall not be required to establish technical subcommittees as required by section 107(m) and may establish a committee composition based on past practices of the council provided that the committees shall follow the process as specified under this act to the furthest extent practicable; and

(D) the council may rely on the technical analysis of the 2015 edition of the triennial codes performed by the council during the council's previous review.

22. 35 P.S. § 7210.107.

(iii) The council shall also review, in accordance with the procedures outlined in this act, any section of the collective codes that do not otherwise constitute updated sections but only if two-thirds of the council membership so determine. The sections selected for review shall be referred to as "additional sections." The additional sections shall be treated for purposes of review and approval or disapproval by the council as updated sections. The selection of additional sections shall occur prior to commencement of the review process.

(2) Each updated section subject to review under paragraph (3)(v) shall be examined by applying all of the following criteria:

(i) The impact that the section may have upon the health, safety and welfare of the public.

(ii) The economic and financial impact of the section, including impact on the end consumer.

(iii) The technical feasibility of the section.

(3) The council shall review the updated sections as follows:

(i) A 120-day period to receive comments from council members and the general public regarding the updated sections shall commence 30 days following the start of the council's review pursuant to paragraph (1). The public comment period shall be announced in the Pennsylvania Bulletin and on the department's publicly accessible Internet website or, in the absence of an Internet website, in such other manner as the secretary determines will provide substantially similar public notice.

(ii) All public comments shall be submitted on a form created by the council. Each comment shall relate to a single updated section. The comment shall, at a minimum, specify the updated section to which the comment relates, state whether the updated section should be adopted, rejected or modified and specify the rationale for the recommended action based on the criteria set forth in paragraph (2). A proposed modification shall meet or exceed the standards of the section in effect or being reviewed and the proposed modification shall be within the standards under review.

(iii) All public comments submitted in accordance with subparagraph (ii) shall be provided to all council members, posted on the department's publicly accessible Internet website or, in the absence of an Internet website, in such other manner as the secretary determines will provide substantially similar public notice. All public comments submitted in accordance with subparagraph (ii) shall be reviewed individually by a technical advisory committee.

(iv) After the expiration of the public comment period, the chair shall assign each updated section, regardless of whether a public comment has been received, to the technical advisory committee for the code that contains the updated section.

(v) The technical advisory committee shall review all of the updated sections it has been assigned as provided in this section. The technical advisory committee may also review any related updated section, any existing section or any related collective code section as needed to ensure consistency and effectiveness of the Uniform Construction Code. Even if an updated section has not received a public comment in accordance with subparagraph (ii), a technical advisory committee member may select one or more of the updated sections assigned to the technical advisory committee for individual consideration by the council pursuant to subparagraph (ix)(B).

(vi) For each updated section that:

(A) receives a comment recommending modification or rejection in accordance with subparagraph (ii); or

(B) a member of the technical advisory committee to which it has been assigned has separately selected for individual review by the council;

the technical advisory committee shall submit to the chair of the council a recommendation that the section and any related section identified in subparagraph (v) be adopted, rejected or modified. The technical advisory committee shall submit the rationale for its recommendations. Notwithstanding any other provision of this subparagraph, updated sections that do not receive a comment recommending modification or rejection in accordance with subparagraph (ii) and that a member of the technical advisory committee has not separately selected for individual review by the council shall be noted in the report as unopposed.

(vii) The technical advisory committee's recommendations shall be posted on the department's publicly accessible Internet website or, in the absence of an Internet website, in such other manner as the secretary determines will provide substantially similar public notice. The technical advisory committee's recommendations shall be posted at least 10 business days prior to holding the first hearing pursuant to this section.

(viii) After submission of all recommendations of the technical advisory committees, the council shall hold at least three public hearings. One of the public hearings shall be held in Harrisburg, one shall be held in the eastern region of this Commonwealth and one shall be held in the western region of this Commonwealth.

(ix) Upon completion of the hearings, the council shall hold one or more official meetings of the council to decide whether to adopt, reject or modify the updated sections and any related section identified in subparagraph (v). The following shall apply:

(A) The council shall consider and vote on the unopposed sections as a group. Prior to a vote on the unopposed sections as a group, the council shall first consider any motion made by a council member to exclude a section from the unopposed group. A motion to exclude shall only be in order if it is supported by written explanation, made available to the council, describing new information not considered by the technical advisory committees and the underlying rationale for the motion. If the motion is supported by a two-thirds majority of the council membership, that section shall be removed from the unopposed group. Unopposed sections that remain as part of the group, after consideration of motions to exclude sections, shall be adopted by a majority vote of the council members. If the unopposed sections fail to be adopted by a majority vote, the council shall conduct a subsequent vote to reject the unopposed sections by a two-thirds majority vote of the council members. If the council fails to reject the unopposed sections by a two-thirds majority vote, the unopposed sections shall be adopted. All unopposed sections that are rejected as a group or successfully excluded from the group shall be subject to the procedure specified in clause (B).

(B) Except for the unopposed sections, a two-thirds majority of the council members is required for adoption or modification of the updated sections. The council may vote on the updated sections individually or in groups. A modification shall meet or exceed the standards of the section in effect or being reviewed and shall be within the standards under review.

(b) **Submission of report.**—With the exception of the council's review of the 2015 ICC codes, the council shall submit a report to the secretary within the 24-month period following the commencement of the review process by the council with sections of the updated codes and additional codes that are specified for adoption or modification. The sections of the codes that are specified for adoption or modification shall be separately designated in the report. For the council's review of the 2015 ICC codes only, the council shall submit a report to the secretary on or before May 1, 2018.

CHAPTER 3
UNIFORM CONSTRUCTION CODE

§ 301. Adoption by regulations[23]

(a) Regulations.—

(1) The department shall, within 180 days of the effective date of this section, promulgate regulations adopting the 1999 BOCA National Building Code, Fourteenth Edition, as a Uniform Construction Code, except as provided in section 105(c)(2)[24] and this section. The department shall promulgate separate regulations which may make changes to Chapter 1 of the 1999 BOCA National Building Code, Fourteenth Edition, relating to administration that are necessary for the department's implementation of this act.

(2) The regulations shall include a provision that all detached one-family and two-family dwellings and one-family townhouses that are not more than three stories in height and their accessory structures shall be designed and constructed either in accordance with the ICC International One and Two Family Dwelling Code, 1998 Edition, or in accordance with the requirements of the Uniform Construction Code at the option of the building permit applicant. The provision shall require that an irrevocable election be made at the time plans are submitted for review and approval. If the building permit applicant does not indicate a code, the design and construction shall be in accordance with the Uniform Construction Code.

(3) The regulations shall include a provision that the secretary shall have the exclusive power to grant modifications and decide issues of technical infeasibility under Chapter 11 (Accessibility) of the Uniform Construction Code and any other accessibility requirements contained in or referenced by the Uniform Construction Code for individual projects.

(4) The secretary shall consider the recommendations of the advisory board as provided in section 106(c).[25] The department shall consider the comments of the advisory board with respect to accessibility issues in any proposed regulations.

(5) The regulations shall provide for a system of periodic compliance reviews conducted by the department and for enforcement procedures conducted by the department to ensure that code administrators are adequately administering and enforcing Chapter 11 (Accessibility) of the Uniform Construction Code and any other accessibility requirements contained in or referenced by the Uniform Construction Code.

(6) The regulations shall include the provisions of exception 8 to section 1014.6 (relative to stairway treads and risers) of the 1993 BOCA National Building Code, Twelfth Edition, and the provisions of section R–213.1 (relative to stairways) of the CABO One and Two Family Dwelling Code, 1992 Edition, and such provisions shall be applicable notwithstanding section 303(b),[26] which shall not apply to the provisions of any municipal building code ordinance which equals or exceeds these provisions.

23. 35 P.S. § 7210.301.
24. 35 P.S. § 7210.105.
25. 35 P.S. § 7210.106.
26. 35 P.S. § 7210.303.

(7) The department shall consult with the Department of Health in the development of regulations relating to health care facilities, intermediate care facilities for the mentally retarded or for persons with related conditions and State institutions.

(8) The regulations shall exclude section R313.1.1 of the 2003 International Residential Code for One- and Two-Family Dwellings or its successor code from applying to existing one-family and two-family unit dwellings undergoing alterations, repairs or additions but shall include provisions requiring non-interconnected battery-operated smoke alarms in one-family and two-family dwellings in accordance with section R813.1.1 of the 2003 International Residential Code for One- and Two-Family Dwellings.

(9) Regulations under this subsection shall include the adoption of section 110.3 (temporary occupancy) of the International Building Code.

(10) (i) Section R404.1 and Tables R404.1(1), R404.1(2) and R404.1(3) of the 2006 International Residential Code and its successor codes are not part of the Uniform Construction Code. In lieu of section R404.1 of the 2006 International Residential Code, the provisions of subparagraph (ii) shall apply and are part of the Uniform Construction Code.

(ii) Concrete and masonry foundation walls shall be selected and constructed in accordance with:

(A) all provisions of section R404 of the 2006 International Residential Code and its successor codes except those excluded by subparagraph (i);

(B) ACI 318, ACI 332, NCMA TR68-A or ACI 530/ASCE 5/TMS 402; or

(C) other approved structural standards.

(b) International Fuel Gas Code.—The department shall, within 180 days of the effective date of this section, promulgate regulations adopting the International Fuel Gas Code for the installation of fuel gas piping systems, fuel gas utilization equipment and related accessories as the standard for the installation of piping, equipment and accessories in this Commonwealth.

(c) Prescriptive methods for energy-related standards.—The department shall, within 180 days of the effective date of this section, by regulation promulgate prescriptive methods to implement the energy-related standards of the Uniform Construction Code which take into account the various climatic conditions through this Commonwealth. In deriving these standards the department shall seek to balance energy savings with initial construction costs.

(d) Scope of regulations.—

(1) The regulations adopted by the department implementing these codes shall supersede and preempt all local building codes regulating any aspect of the construction, alteration and repair of buildings adopted or enforced by any municipality or authority or pursuant to any deed restriction, rule, regulation, ordinance, resolution, tariff or order of any public utility or any State or local board, agency, commission or homeowners' association except as may be otherwise specifically provided in this act.

(2) The department may establish by regulation plan review and inspection fees where the department is responsible for administration and enforcement and requirements for municipal notification to the department of ordinance adoption and repeal under Chapter 5. The department shall consult with the Department of Aging, the Department of Health or the Department of Public Welfare, as appropriate, to determine fees for health care facilities, intermediate care facilities for the mentally retarded or for persons with related conditions and State institutions.

(3) The department shall establish by regulation standards for the retention and sharing of building plans and other documents, for other than one-fam-

Table of Contents
Part I Ch. 1–3 Ethics, Records, Open Meetings
Part II Ch. 4–10 Taxation
Part III Ch. 11–18 Torts, Contracts & Civil Rules
Part IV Ch. 19–24 Zoning & Planning
Part V Ch. 25–30 Construction and Emergency Codes
Part VI Ch. 31–39 Municipal Codes
Index

ily or two-family dwelling units and utility and miscellaneous use structures, by the department, municipalities and third-party agencies.

§ 302. Referenced standards[27]

(a) General rule.—(1) Subject to paragraph (2), the standards referenced in Chapters 30 and 35 relating to elevators and conveying systems and referenced standards, respectively, or the applicable chapter, of the 1999 BOCA National Building Code, Fourteenth Edition, and the American National Standards for Passenger Tramways, Aerial Tramways, Aerial Lifts, Surface Lifts and Tows, ASME/ANSI B77.1, shall be considered part of the requirements of the Uniform Construction Code to the prescribed extent of each such reference except that BNPMC-96 BOCA National Property Maintenance Code and ASME/ANSI A17.3 (safety code for existing elevators and escalators) shall be excluded.

(2) The standards under paragraph (1) shall include the latest ANSI standards applicable to the operation of ski lifts.

(b) No preemption.—Nothing contained in this act shall be construed to preempt the ability of a municipality to adopt or enforce the codes referred to in this section to the extent not referenced, in whole or in part, in Chapter 35 relating to referenced standards or applicable chapter of the 1999 BOCA National Building Code, Fourteenth Edition.

§ 303. Existing municipal building codes[28]

(a) Failure to meet minimum requirements.—

(1) Except as provided in paragraph (2), the provisions of municipal building code ordinances in effect on the effective date of this act that do not equal or exceed the minimum requirements of the regulations promulgated under this act shall be amended by the effective date of the regulations promulgated under this act to provide for the minimum requirements.

(2) A municipal building code ordinance provision in effect in or adopted by a city of the first class on or before January 1, 1998, shall remain in effect until December 31, 2003, by which time those provisions of the ordinance which do not comply with the minimum requirements of the regulations promulgated under this act shall be amended to provide for the minimum requirements of regulations promulgated under this act.

(b) Provisions which equal or exceed the Uniform Construction Code.—

(1) Municipal building code ordinances in effect on July 1, 1999, or reenactments of provisions of simultaneously repealed ordinances which were originally adopted prior to July 1, 1999, which contain provisions which equal or exceed the specific requirements of the regulations promulgated under this act shall remain in effect until such time as any such provisions fail to equal or exceed the minimum requirements of the regulations promulgated under this act, at which time the provisions of such ordinances shall be amended to provide for the minimum requirements of the regulations promulgated under this act.

(2) Municipal building code ordinances adopted or effective after July 1, 1999, except reenactments of provisions of simultaneously repealed ordinances which were originally adopted prior to July 1, 1999, shall continue in effect only until the effective date of the regulations promulgated under this act, at which time the municipal building code ordinance shall be preempted by the regulations promulgated under this act and shall be deemed thereafter to be rescinded.

---

27. 35 P.S. § 7210.302.

28. 35 P.S. § 7210.303.

§ 304. Revised or successor codes

(a) Duties of department.—

(1) Subject to sections 105(c) and (d), 301(a)(3), (4), (5), (6) and (7), (c) and (d) and 302, within nine months of the receipt of the report under section 108(b), the department shall promulgate final-omitted regulations under the act of June 25, 1982 (P.L. 633, No. 181),[29] known as the Regulatory Review Act, to adopt the council's decisions contained in the report without change. The regulations shall take effect as follows:

(i) Except as provided in subparagraph (ii), regulations adopted under this act shall become effective 33 months after the commencement of council review as provided for in section 108(a)(1)(i).

(ii) Regulations promulgated by the department as a result of the 2015 Code Review shall take effect October 1, 2018.

(2) Regulations promulgated under this subsection are exempt from:

(i) section 205 of the act of July 31, 1968 (P.L. 769, No. 240),[30] referred to as the Commonwealth Documents Law; and

(ii) sections 204(b) and 301(10) of the act of October 15, 1980 (P.L. 950, No. 164),[31] known as the Commonwealth Attorneys Act.

(3) The department shall promulgate regulations updating accessibility standards under Chapter 3 by adopting by December 31 of the year of issuance of the accessibility provisions of the most recently published edition of the ICC codes and any other accessibility requirements which shall be specified in the regulations, or contained in or referenced by the Uniform Construction Code relating to persons with disabilities.

(4) The department may contract with the ICC to establish and publish code manuals that contain the standards of the Uniform Construction Code. The department shall require in any contract under this paragraph that the documentation be made available on the department's publicly accessible Internet website.

(a.1) Continuity.—If an updated section is not adopted or modified under section 108, the relevant provisions of the existing sections shall remain in effect.

(b) Deleted by 2011, April 25, P.L. 1, No. 1, § 2, imd. effective.

(c) Prior permits, contracts and construction.—

(1) A construction permit issued under valid construction regulations prior to the effective date of regulations for a subsequent Uniform Construction Code or International Fuel Gas Code issued under this act shall remain valid, and the construction of any building or structure may be completed pursuant to and in accordance with the permit.

(2) If the permit has not been actively prosecuted within two years of the effective date of the regulation or the period specified by a municipal ordinance, whichever is less, the former permitholder shall be required to acquire a new permit.

(3) Where construction of a building or structure commenced before the effective date of the regulations for a subsequent Uniform Construction Code or International Fuel Gas Code issued under this act and a permit was not required at that time, construction may be completed without a permit.

---

29. 71 P.S. § 745.1 et seq.

30. 45 P.S. § 1205.

31. 71 P.S. §§ 732-204, 732-301.

(4) Where a design or construction contract was signed before the effective date of regulations for a subsequent Uniform Construction Code or International Fuel Gas Code issued under this act, the permit may be issued under the Uniform Construction Code or International Fuel Gas Code in effect at the time the design or construction contract was signed if the permit is applied for within six months of the effective date of the regulation or the period specified by a municipal ordinance, whichever is less.

CHAPTER 5
ADOPTION AND ENFORCEMENT BY MUNICIPALITIES

§ 501. Administration and enforcement[32]

(a) Adoption of ordinance.—

(1) In order to administer and enforce the provisions of this act, municipalities shall enact an ordinance concurrently adopting the current Uniform Construction Code as their municipal building code and the current International Fuel Gas Code[33] for the purposes described in section 102. Municipalities may adopt the Uniform Construction Code and incorporated codes and the International Fuel Gas Code by reference.

(2) Municipalities shall have 90 days after the promulgation of regulations under section 301 to adopt such an ordinance. Municipalities shall notify the department of the adoption of such an ordinance within 30 days. A municipality may adopt such an ordinance at any time thereafter, upon giving the department 180 days' notice of its intention to adopt such ordinance.

(a.1) Counties of the second class.—Notwithstanding the provisions of subsection (a), a municipality located within a county of the second class shall not administer and enforce plumbing code provisions of an ordinance adopting the Uniform Construction Code and incorporated codes for the purposes of section 102. A county of the second class that has adopted a plumbing code and accompanying rules and regulations pursuant to the act of August 24, 1951 (P.L. 1304, No. 815),[34] known as the Local Health Administration Law, shall retain the authority to promulgate and enforce such plumbing code and to make such changes as it deems necessary, provided that such changes meet the minimum requirements as defined in the Uniform Construction Code.

(b) Municipal administration and enforcement.—This act may be administered and enforced by municipalities in any of the following ways:

(1) By the designation of an employee to serve as the municipal code official to act on behalf of the municipality for administration and enforcement of this act.

(2) By the retention of one or more construction code officials or third-party agencies to act on behalf of the municipality for administration and enforcement of this act.

(3) Two or more municipalities may provide for the joint administration and enforcement of this act through an intermunicipal agreement under 53 Pa.C.S. Ch. 23 Subch. A (relating to intergovernmental cooperation).

(4) By entering into a contract with the proper authorities of another municipality for the administration and enforcement of this act. When such a contract has been entered into, the municipal code official shall have all

32. 35 P.S. § 7210.501.

33. 35 P.S. § 7210.302.

34. 16 P.S. § 12001 et seq.

the powers and authority conferred by law in the municipality which has contracted to secure such services.

(5) By entering into an agreement with the department for plan reviews, inspections and enforcement of structures other than one-family or two-family dwelling units and utility and miscellaneous use structures.

(c) Board of appeals.—

(1) A municipality which has adopted an ordinance for the administration and enforcement of this act or municipalities which are parties to an agreement for the joint administration and enforcement of this act shall establish or designate a board of appeals as provided by regulations promulgated by the department to hear appeals from decisions of the code administrator. Members of the municipality's governing body may not serve as members of the board of appeals. A municipality may establish a board of appeals or may establish or designate a joint board of appeals in accordance with 53 Pa.C.S. Ch. 23 Subch. A (relating to intergovernmental cooperation).

(2) An application for appeal shall be based on a claim that the true intent of this act or regulations legally adopted under this act have been incorrectly interpreted, the provisions of this act do not fully apply or an equivalent form of construction is to be used.

(3) When a municipality cannot find persons to serve on a board of appeals who meet the minimum qualifications established by the department, the municipality may fill a position on the board with a qualified person who resides outside of the municipality.

(4) The fee for an appeal to the Board of Appeals for a municipality that is administering and enforcing this act shall not exceed actual costs of the public notice of the hearing, appearance fee for the court reporter and administrative fees as necessary.

(5) In the case of an appeal or request for variance or extension of time involving the construction of a one-family or two-family residential building, the board of appeals shall convene a hearing within 30 days of the appeal. The Board of Appeals shall render a written decision to the parties within five business days, or within ten business days in cities of the first class, of the last hearing. If the board of appeals fails to act within the time period under this paragraph, the appeal shall be deemed granted.

(d) Registration.—Nothing in this act shall allow a municipality to prohibit a construction code official who meets the requirements of Chapter 7 and remains in good standing from performing inspections in the municipality. This section does not alter the power and duties given to municipalities under subsection (b) (1), (3) and (4).

(e) Nonmunicipal administration.—

(1) In municipalities which have not adopted an ordinance for the administration and enforcement of this act, it shall be the duty of the municipality to notify an applicant for a construction permit that it shall be the responsibility of the permit applicant of one-family or two-family dwelling units and utility and miscellaneous use structures to obtain the services of a construction code official or third-party agency with appropriate categories of certification to conduct the plan review and inspections. For one-family and two-family dwelling units and utility and miscellaneous use structures, all of the following five inspections shall be required:

(i) Foundation inspection.

(ii) Plumbing, mechanical and electrical inspection.

(iii) Frame and masonry inspection.

(iv) Wallboard inspection.

Table of Contents | Part I Ch. 1–3 Ethics, Records, Open Meetings | Part II Ch. 4–10 Taxation | Part III Ch. 11–18 Torts, Contracts & Civil Rules | Part IV Ch. 19–24 Zoning & Planning | Part V Ch. 25–30 Construction and Emergency Codes | Part VI Ch. 31–39 Municipal Codes | Index

(v) Final inspection. The final inspection shall not be deemed approved until all previous inspections have been successfully completed and passed.

(2) In municipalities which have not adopted an ordinance for the administration and enforcement of this act, it shall be the duty of the municipality to notify the department and an applicant for a construction permit that it shall be the responsibility of the owner of structures other than one-family or two-family dwelling units and utility and miscellaneous use structures to obtain the services of the department or a third-party agency with appropriate categories of certification under contract to the department to conduct the plan review and inspections required by this act.

(3) A copy of the final inspection report shall be sent to the property owner and to the builder and to a lender designated by the builder.

(4) In municipalities which require a building permit or a certificate of occupancy but do not conduct inspections, the code administrator shall also be required to submit a copy of the report to the municipality. No certificate of occupancy shall be issued for a building unless it meets all of the applicable accessibility provisions of the Uniform Construction Code or has been granted a variance for the requirements it does not meet. A certificate of partial occupancy may be issued if the space to be occupied complies with the accessibility requirements contained in the Uniform Construction Code unless a variance for the space has been obtained in accordance with this act.

(f) Private right of action.—

(1) In relation to complaints arising out of Chapter 11 (Accessibility) of the Uniform Construction Code, any individual, partnership, agency, association or corporation who reasonably believes there is a violation of the accessibility provisions of this act and its regulations by a governmental entity or private owner may file a complaint with the body responsible for enforcement of the Uniform Construction Code. The complaint shall be in writing, shall be verified and shall set forth the grounds for the complaint. Within 60 days after the receipt of the complaint, the code enforcement body shall respond to the complaint by acknowledging receipt of the complaint in writing. The enforcement body shall investigate the complaint and respond to the complainant in writing with its findings, determinations and any enforcement measures initiated or contemplated within 120 days after the receipt of the complaint. For the purpose of investigating a complaint, an employee of the enforcement organization may inspect at reasonable times the building or building site which is the subject of the complaint and may make any additional investigation deemed necessary for the full and effective determination of compliance with this act and regulations promulgated pursuant to it.

(2) Any individual, partnership, agency, association or corporation aggrieved by a final determination of the enforcement agency of a complaint filed pursuant to paragraph (1) hereof may file a petition for review within 30 days of the final determination in the Commonwealth Court pursuant to 42 Pa.C.S. § 763(a) (relating to direct appeals from government agencies). The decision of the enforcement agency shall not be reversed unless it is found to be arbitrary, capricious, illegal or not supported by substantial evidence.

(3) (i) Any individual, partnership, agency, association or corporation who filed a complaint pursuant to paragraph (1) and received no written response from the enforcement agency acknowledging receipt of its complaint within 60 days or received a response from the enforcement agency indicating that a violation was found but enforcement measures were not contemplated or enforcement measures were contemplated but such measures were not initiated after a period of 60 days from said response may bring a civil action

in the appropriate court of common pleas against the agency for failure to enforce the provisions of this act and the regulations promulgated thereto or a building owner or owner's agent for a violation of any provisions of this act or regulations promulgated pursuant to it.

(ii) If the court finds a violation of this act or of regulations adopted pursuant to it, the court may enjoin construction or remodeling of the building, direct the correction of violations within a reasonable and specified time period or order such other relief deemed appropriate. The court, in issuing any final orders in any action brought pursuant to this section, may award costs of litigation, attorney and expert witness fees to any party whenever the court determines such an award is appropriate. The court may, if a temporary restraining order or preliminary injunction is sought, require the filing of a bond or equivalent security in accordance with the rules of civil procedures.

(iii) An architect or licensed design professional who has complied with the provisions of this act and its regulations and prepared construction documents in accordance with accepted professional standards shall have no further liability pursuant to litigation commenced under this section.

(g) Technical assistance to municipalities.—The Governor's Center for Local Government Services in the Department of Community and Economic Development shall be the principal agency for developing and providing technical assistance to municipalities for implementing, administrating and enforcing the provisions of this act.

(h) Interpretation of Uniform Construction Code.—In interpreting a provision of a code adopted by regulation of the department as part of the Uniform Construction Code, a construction code official, a board of appeal and a court shall consider and may rely upon relevant written interpretations of the ICC or any organization whose referenced standard is relevant and listed in the Uniform Construction Code, or the regulations promulgated under this act or any municipal construction code ordinance.

§ 502. Consideration of applications and inspections[35]

(a) Applications for construction permits.—

(1) Every application for a construction permit for one-family and two-family dwelling units and utility and miscellaneous use structures shall be granted or denied, in whole or in part, within 15 business days of the filing date. or, if the drawings have been prepared by design professionals who are licensed or registered under the laws and regulations of this Commonwealth and the application contains a certification by the licensed or registered design professional that the plans meet the applicable standards of the Uniform Construction Code and ordinance as appropriate, within five business days of the filing date. Every application for a certificate of occupancy for one-family and two-family dwelling units and miscellaneous use structures shall be granted or denied, in whole or in part, within five business days, or within ten business days in cities of the first class, after receipt of a final inspection report indicates compliance with the Uniform Construction Code and ordinance as appropriate. All other construction permits shall be granted or denied, in whole or in part, within 30 business days of the filing date. Municipalities may establish different time limits to consider applications for construction permits in historic districts. A code administrator shall review a construction plan of a building permit application upon submission and shall issue a notice of construction plan approval on a building permit application within the periods set forth in this section if the construction plans comply with the Construction Code Act and any

35. 35 P.S. § 7210.502.

Table of Contents
Part I Ch. 1–3 Ethics, Records, Open Meetings
Part II Ch. 4–10 Taxation
Part III Ch. 11–18 Torts, Contracts & Civil Rules
Part IV Ch. 19–24 Zoning & Planning
Part V Ch. 25–30 Construction and Emergency Codes
Part VI Ch. 31–39 Municipal Codes
Index

other applicable municipal construction code ordinance. The municipality shall also provide a list of all other required permits necessary prior to issuance of the building permit. The municipality will not be liable for the completeness of any list. When a construction plan h–as been approved, a code administrator shall issue a building permit immediately upon receipt of all other required permits or approvals related to the construction. All revisions or changes to construction plans so approved under this subsection shall necessitate an additional plan review prior to the issuing of the building permit.

(2) If an application is denied in whole or in part, the code administrator shall set forth the reasons in writing., identifying the elements of the application which are not in compliance with the relevant provisions of the Uniform Construction Code and ordinance as appropriate and providing a citation to the relevant provisions of the Uniform Construction Code and ordinance as appropriate.

(3) If the code administrator fails to act on an application for a construction permit for one-family and two-family dwelling units and utility and miscellaneous use structures within the time prescribed, the application shall be deemed approved. The time limits established in this section for permit applications other than one-family and two-family dwellings may be extended upon agreement in writing between the applicant and the municipality for a specific number of additional days.

(a.1) Exceptions.—A permit is not required for the installation, alteration or repair of generation, transmission, distribution, metering or other related equipment under the ownership or control of public service agencies.

(b) Highway occupancy permit.—

(1) No building permit shall be issued for any property which will require access to a highway under the jurisdiction of the Department of Transportation, unless the permit contains a notice that a highway occupancy permit is required pursuant to section 420 of the act of June 1, 1945 (P.L. 1242, No. 428),[36] known as the State Highway Law, before driveway access to a State highway is permitted.

(2) The Department of Transportation shall, within 60 days of the date of receipt of an application for a highway occupancy permit:

(i) approve the permit;

(ii) deny the permit;

(iii) return the application for additional information or correction to conform with regulations of the Department of Transportation; or

(iv) determine that no permit is required, in which case the Department of Transportation shall notify the municipality and applicant in writing.

(3) (i) If the Department of Transportation fails to take any action within the 60-day period, the permit shall be deemed to be issued. The permit shall be marked to indicate that access to the State highway shall be only as authorized by a highway occupancy permit.

(ii) Notwithstanding the provisions of subparagraph (i), if the highway occupancy permit requires a determination by the United States Department of Transportation, the Pennsylvania Department of Transportation shall have 60 days from the receipt of the determination to take action on the permit or the permit shall be deemed to be issued.

(4) (i) Neither the Department of Transportation nor any municipality to which permit-issuing authority has been delegated under section 420 of the State Highway Law shall be liable in damages for any injury to persons

36. 36 P.S. § 670–420.

or property arising out of the issuance or denial of a driveway permit or for failure to regulate any driveway.

(ii) The municipality from which the building permit approval has been requested shall not be held liable for damages to persons or property arising out of the issuance or denial of a driveway permit by the Department of Transportation.

(c) **Financial interest prohibited.**—A code administrator shall not review or approve any plans for or construction of any building or structure in which the code administrator has any financial interest.

§ 503. Changes in Uniform Construction Code[37]

(a) **Administration.**—

(1) Municipalities may enact ordinances which equal or exceed the minimum requirements of Chapter 1 of the 1999 BOCA National Building Code, Fourteenth Edition, or successor codes, relating to administration consistent with the provisions of section 501(c)[38].

(2) An ordinance under this subsection applicable to the exception under section 104(b)(8)[39] may require compliance with any of the following standards:

(i) Flame propagation criteria of the applicable edition of NFPA No. 701.

(ii) The ICC Electrical Code.

(iii) International Fire Code criteria as to number of portable fire extinguishers.

(b) **Minimum requirement.**—Subject to the provisions of this act, no municipality may propose or enact any ordinance which is less than the minimum requirement of the Uniform Construction Code, except as provided in subsection (b.1).

(b.1) **Cities of the first class.**—

(1) A city of the first class may enact an ordinance that adopts provisions of the 2018 ICC triennial codes for the purpose of regulating the construction, alteration, repair and use of buildings that do not meet the definition of "residential building" under section 103.

(2) The scope of the provisions that may be adopted under paragraph (1) shall be limited to the scope of what the council is authorized to review and adopt under section 108(a)(1).

(3) The adoption of an ordinance under this subsection shall be in accordance with subsections (d), (e), (f), (g) and (h).

(4) If an ordinance is adopted under this subsection, the provisions adopted in the ordinance shall remain in effect until the effective date of the regulations promulgated under section 304(a)(1) implementing the findings of the 2021 triennial code review.

(5) All statutory exclusions and exemptions shall remain in effect.

(c) **Modification of minimum requirement.**—Subject to the provisions of this act, the municipal governing body may propose and enact an ordinance to equal or exceed the minimum requirements of the Uniform Construction Code under the law governing the adoption of ordinances in that jurisdiction. An ordinance under this subsection shall not be effective nor enforceable unless subsections (d), (e), (f), (g), (h) and (i) have been satisfied. Municipalities may enact ordinances

37. 35 P.S. § 7210.503.

38. 35 P.S. § 7210.501.

39. 35 P.S. § 7210.104.

Table of Contents | Part I Ch. 1–3 Ethics, Records, Open Meetings | Part II Ch. 4–10 Taxation | Part III Ch. 11–18 Torts, Contracts & Civil Rules | Part IV Ch. 19–24 Zoning & Planning | Part V Ch. 25–30 Construction and Emergency Codes | Part VI Ch. 31–39 Municipal Codes | Index

pursuant to this section which adopt additional code requirements for alterations or repairs to residential buildings. Municipalities may enact ordinances pursuant to this section which adopt stricter code requirements than required by this act for the regulation of utility and miscellaneous use structures.

(d) Public hearing.—The municipality shall hold at least one public hearing prior to adoption of the ordinance.

(e) Notice of public hearing.—The municipality shall place notice in a newspaper of general circulation in the municipality at least seven days, but not more than 60 days, in advance of a public hearing to consider the proposed ordinance.

(f) Filing of proposed notice and ordinance with department.—The municipality shall provide notice and file a copy of the proposed ordinance with the department at least 30 days prior to public hearing. The notice shall contain the time and place of the public hearing and a summary of the changes proposed by the ordinance, including code sections affected by the changes. The department shall make proposed ordinances available for public inspection and shall post the notice on its Internet website within seven business days after receipt.

(g) Municipal action.—Following the public hearing, the municipal governing body may enact the ordinance under the law governing the adoption of ordinance in that jurisdiction.

(h) Amendment of proposed ordinance.—If the municipality proposes any substantive amendment to a proposed ordinance, the municipal governing body shall be required to meet the advertising, filing, notice and public hearing requirements of this section before enacting the proposed ordinance.

(i) Department review.—The department shall review all proposed ordinances required to be filed with the department under subsection (f) for compliance with subsection (b). If the proposed ordinance does not comply with subsection (b), the department shall advise the municipality of its finding setting forth the reasons in writing. The municipality shall then withdraw the proposed ordinance or revise the proposed ordinance to meet the minimum requirements of the Uniform Construction Code.

(j) Challenge of ordinance.—

(1) Aggrieved parties shall have 30 days from date of enactment of the ordinance to file a written challenge with the department and shall serve a copy of the challenge upon the municipality. The challenge shall state the reason or reasons for the challenge. A municipal ordinance may not take effect for a period of 35 days following its enactment. If a challenge is filed in writing with the department within 30 days, the department has five business days from the end of the 30-day filing period to notify a municipality of the challenge. There may be no enforcement of the ordinance until a ruling is issued by the secretary or 45 days after the filing date of the last challenge to the ordinance, whichever occurs first.

(2) The department shall review any ordinance which would equal or exceed the minimum requirements of the Uniform Construction Code based on the following standards:

(i) that certain clear and convincing local climatic, geologic, topographic or public health and safety circumstances or conditions justify the exception;

(ii) the exception shall be adequate for the purpose intended and shall meet a standard of performance equal to or greater than that prescribed by the Uniform Construction Code;

(iii) the exception would not diminish or threaten the health, safety and welfare of the public; and

(iv) the exception would not be inconsistent with the legislative findings and purpose described in section 102.[40]

The department shall take into consideration, in rendering the determination, the provision, code development process history, purpose and intent of relevant provisions of the 1999 BOCA National Building Code, Fourteenth Edition, ICC International One and Two Family Dwelling Code, 1998 Edition, or their successor codes.

(k) Ruling by secretary.—A ruling on a challenge by an aggrieved party shall be issued by the secretary within 45 days of receipt of the filing of the last challenge to the ordinance or within 30 days of the hearing on the challenge which must be held by the department upon the request of the municipality in the municipality wherein the ordinance is proposed, whichever last occurs. If the secretary approves the ordinance, the municipality may begin to administer and enforce the ordinance. If the secretary disapproves the ordinance, the ordinance shall be null and void. The secretary shall state the reasons for the disapproval in writing to the municipality.

§ 504. Appeals[41]

(a) Ruling of secretary.—An appeal of the secretary's ruling may be taken to the appropriate court of common pleas within 30 days of the date of the ruling.

(b) Application for enforcement of ordinance.—Any person aggrieved by the application or enforcement of any provision of an ordinance adopted pursuant to section 503[42] shall have the right to challenge the validity of the ordinance in the appropriate court of common pleas. In order to be aggrieved, a person must have a direct, immediate and substantial interest in the application or enforcement of the ordinance. The appropriate court of common pleas shall determine the validity of the ordinance.

CHAPTER 7
TRAINING AND CERTIFICATION OF INSPECTORS

§ 701. Training of inspectors[43]

(a) Training program.—The department, in consultation with the advisory board, ICC, NCSBCS and other interested parties, shall by regulation adopt a program of required training and certification for all categories of code administrators. This education program shall include accessibility requirements contained in and referenced by the Uniform Construction Code. The department may contract with third parties to provide the code training and testing programs.

(b) Categories of inspectors.—

(1) The department, in consultation with the ICC and other interested parties, shall establish appropriate categories of code administrators.

(2) A code administrator may act in place of a lumber grading or inspection agency to satisfy the requirement set forth under section 2303.1.1 of the 2003 International Building Code or its successor code or section R404.2.1, R502.1, R602.1 or R802.1 of the 2003 International Residential Code for One-and Two-Family Dwellings or its successor code.

(c) Certification.—Upon determination of qualification, the department shall issue a certificate to the code administrator stating that he is so certified.

---

40. 35 P.S. § 7210.102.
41. 35 P.S. § 7210.504.
42. 35 P.S. § 7210.503.
43. 35 P.S. § 7210.701.

(d) Waiver.—The department shall by regulation establish a procedure for the consideration of requests for waivers of the initial training and certification requirements for individuals who present documentation that they have previously satisfied substantially similar training, testing and certification requirements. The department may also consider past work experience as an inspector when deciding a request for a waiver. Any waiver shall not apply to continuing education requirements.

(e) Current officials.—

(1) The department shall by regulation determine the time period for current code administrators to meet the training and certification requirements of this act. This time period shall not be less than three years and not exceed seven years from the effective date of this act for individuals conducting plan review and inspections of one-family or two-family residential property or not be less than five years and not exceed ten years for individuals conducting plan reviews and inspections on all other buildings and structures.

(2) Notwithstanding the provisions of this subsection, the department shall adopt regulations specifically providing for the department's administration and enforcement of the provisions of Chapter 11 (Accessibility) of the Uniform Construction Code and any other accessibility requirements contained in or referenced by the Uniform Construction Code until code administrators have been certified regarding accessibility provisions. The department shall maintain jurisdiction over the provisions of Chapter 11 (Accessibility) of the Uniform Construction Code and any other accessibility requirements contained in or referenced by the Uniform Construction Code until such time as municipal code administrators meet the requirements for certification.

(f) Continuing education.—The department shall by regulation adopt and implement the continuing education program, and all code administrators shall participate in the department's continuing education programs.

(g) Remedial education.—The department is empowered to require code administrators to participate in remedial education programs for just cause.

(h) Decertification.—The department is empowered to decertify code administrators for just cause. The department shall by regulation establish a procedure for the notification of code administrators of decertification and the right of the individual to receive a hearing before the department on decertification.

(i) List of code administrators.—The department shall maintain a list of code administrators, indicating the categories of certifications, which shall be made available to municipalities and, upon request, the public.

(j) Fees.—The department shall determine and approve reasonable fees for educational programs, testing and certification of code administrators. The department shall consult with the Department of Aging, the Department of Health or the Department of Public Welfare, as appropriate, to determine fees for health care facilities, intermediate care facilities for the mentally retarded or for persons with related conditions and State institutions.

(k) Insurance.—The department shall promulgate regulations requiring code administrators in third-party agencies to carry minimum levels of liability insurance.

§ 702. Reciprocity[44]

The department may develop reciprocity agreements with other states or jurisdictions which have established accreditations and certification requirements

44. 35 P.S. § 7210.702.

which the department determines to be substantially similar to those set forth in this act.

§ 703. Education and training programs[45]

(a) Fee.—Municipalities administering and enforcing this act under section 501(a) and third-party agencies providing services under section 501(e) shall assess a fee of $4.50 on each construction or building permit issued under the authority of this act. The fee shall be in addition to any other fee imposed for the permit.

(b) Accounts.—There are hereby established within the State Treasury three restricted accounts which shall be known as the Municipal Code Official Training Account, the Review and Advisory Council Administration Account and the Construction Contractor Training Account.

(c) Deposit.—

(1) The fee collected as authorized under subsection (a) shall be transmitted quarterly to the State Treasury and shall be divided and deposited in the accounts established in subsection (b) as follows:

(i) Forty-three and one-half percent of the fee shall be deposited in the Municipal Code Official Training Account for the purpose of education and training programs for municipal code officials and individuals employed by third-party agencies under contract with a municipality.

(ii) Forty-three and one-half percent of the fee shall be deposited in the Construction Contractor Training Account for a Pennsylvania-based housing research center located at a land grant university for the construction industry. To assure the programs meet the needs of the construction industry, the education, training and other activities provided by the housing research center must be approved by its industry advisory committee.

(iii) Thirteen percent of the fee shall be deposited in the Review and Advisory Council Administration Account for expenses of the council as authorized under section 107(l), for technical assistance as provided for under section 107(k), for administrative assistance as provided under section 107(j), for fees associated with the ICC to establish and publish code manuals which contain the standards of the Uniform Construction Code as provided under section 304(a)(4) and as otherwise determined necessary by the department as funds are available.

(2) Money deposited under paragraph (1)(i) and (ii) is hereby appropriated on approval of the Governor to the Department of Community and Economic Development. The Department of Community and Economic Development may utilize up to 3% of the funds allocated to the account under paragraph (1)(i) and up to 3% of the funds allocated to the account under paragraph (1)(ii) for administrative and program expenses. Notwithstanding any other provision of this paragraph to the contrary, the Department of Community and Economic Development may continue to abide by the provisions of an agreement permitting the retention or collection of a greater percentage for administrative and program expenses, but only for a period of one year from the effective date of this paragraph.[46]

(3) All money deposited under paragraph (1)(iii) shall be transmitted quarterly to the department. The department shall not be required to utilize other sources of funding to carry out activities under this act if the funds provided under this section are insufficient.

45. 35 P.S. § 7210.703.

46. This section was amended by Act of Oct. 25, 2017, P.L. 356, No. 36, § 6, immediately effective.

(d) Reports.—

(1) No later than November 1 of each calendar year, the Department of Community and Economic Development shall provide a report to the chairperson and minority chairperson of the Labor and Industry Committee of the Senate and the chairperson and minority chairperson of the Labor and Industry Committee of the House of Representatives. The report shall detail expenditures for the most recent fiscal year. The report shall include:

(i) The number of construction and building permits issued and the total fees collected.

(ii) A separate accounting of revenue and expenditures for each account under subsection (c)(1)(i) and (ii). The separate accounting shall include, to the extent available, revenue and expenditures by a contractor, vendor or other party engaged to perform the services under subsection (c)(1)(i) and (ii). All contracts entered into after the effective date of this paragraph by the Department of Community and Economic Development with a contractor, vendor or other party shall require the contractor, vendor or other party to provide the information required under this paragraph.

(iii) The amount utilized by the Department of Community and Economic Development for personnel, including the position title, hours charged, amount paid and description of the duties and responsibilities of each individual paid in whole or in part from the account.

(iv) The amount utilized by the Department of Community and Economic Development for operational costs and a description of each expenditure.

(v) The amount utilized by the Department of Community and Economic Development for other program purposes and a description of each expenditure.

(2) No later than November 1 of each calendar year, the department shall provide a report to the chairperson and minority chairperson of the Labor and Industry Committee of the Senate and the chairperson and minority chairperson of the Labor and Industry Committee of the House of Representatives. The report shall detail expenditures for the most recent fiscal year. The report shall include:

(i) A separate accounting of revenue and expenditures for the account under subsection (c)(1)(iii). The separate accounting provided under this paragraph shall include, to the extent available, revenue and expenditures by a contractor, vendor or other party engaged to perform the services under subsection (c)(1)(iii). All contracts entered into after the effective date of this paragraph[47] by the department with a contractor, vendor or other party shall require the contractor, vendor or other party to provide the information required under this paragraph.

(ii) The amount utilized by the Uniform Construction Code Review and Advisory Council for reimbursement of travel expenses.

(iii) The amount utilized by the Uniform Construction Code Review and Advisory Council for other purposes and a description of each expenditure.

(iv) The amount utilized by the department for personnel, including the position title, hours charged, amount and description of the duties and responsibilities of each individual paid in whole or in part from the account.

(v) The amount utilized by the department for operational costs and a description of each expenditure.

(vi) The amount utilized by the department for other program purposes and a description of each expenditure.

---

47. This section was added by Act of Oct. 25, 2017, P.L. 356, No. 36, § 6, immediately effective.

CHAPTER 9
EXEMPTIONS, APPLICABILITY AND PENALTIES

§ 901. Exemptions[48]

(a) Manufactured housing.—This act shall not apply to manufactured housing which bears a label, as required by and referred to in the act of November 17, 1982 (P.L. 676, No. 192),[49] known as the Manufactured Housing Construction and Safety Standards Authorization Act, which certifies that it conforms to Federal construction and safety standards adopted under the Housing and Community Development Act of 1974 (Public Law 93–383, 88 Stat. 633), nor shall it apply to industrialized housing, as defined in the act of May 11, 1972 (P.L. 286, No. 70),[50] known as the Industrialized Housing Act, with the exception that any model code enacted pursuant to the Industrialized Housing Act shall not include code provisions specifically omitted from adoption pursuant to this act.

(b) Religious beliefs.—

(1) An applicant for a construction permit for a dwelling unit or one-room schoolhouse utilized by a member or members of a recognized religious sect may file an application with a code administrator to be exempted from the Uniform Construction Code, as provided in this subsection, which conflicts with the applicant's religious beliefs. The application shall state the manner in which the provision conflicts with the applicant's religious beliefs and shall include an affidavit by the applicant stating that:

(i) the applicant is a member of a recognized religious sect;

(ii) the religious sect has established tenets or teachings which conflict with:

(A) an electrical provision of the Uniform Construction Code;

(B) a lumber or wood provision, not relating to pressure treatment, of the Uniform Construction Code.; or

(C) a plumbing provision of the Uniform Construction Code.

(iii) the applicant adheres to the established tenets or teachings of the sect;

(iv) in the case of a dwelling unit, the dwelling unit will be used solely as a residence for the applicant and the applicant's household; and

(v) in the case of a one-room schoolhouse, the one-room schoolhouse will be used solely by members of the religious sect.

(c) Natural cut trees.—Section 804.1.1 (relating to natural cut trees) of the International Fire Code (2003) and any successor provision is excluded from this act. A municipality that elects to adopt an ordinance for the administration and enforcement of this act may, by ordinance, restrict the placement of natural cut trees in an occupancy group. The ordinance restricting the placement shall not be subject to section 503(b) through (k).

(d) Coal-fired boilers in residential buildings.—Coal-fired boilers installed in residential buildings shall be designed, constructed and tested in accordance with the requirements of Chapter 20, Section M2001.1.1 of the International Residential Code of 2003, or its successor provisions, except that these boilers shall not be subject to the stamping requirements of Section M2001.1.1.

(e) Pole barns at agricultural fairs.—Neither this act nor any adoption of the International Fire Code by a Commonwealth agency, a political subdivision or a local agency shall apply to a pole barn that is constructed on agricultural fairgrounds

48. 35 P.S. § 7210.901.

49. 35 P.S. § 1656.1 et seq.

50. 35 P.S. § 1651.1 et seq.

and is only used for agricultural purposes and animal display. This section shall not apply to inspections required pursuant to the ICC Electrical Code or its successor codes.

(f) Log walls.—Log walls with a minimum average wall thickness of five inches or greater which comply with the International Code Council, Standard on the Design and Construction of Log Structures, ICC 400-2007, or other successor standard which the department may specify by regulation, shall be permitted in residential buildings if:

(1) the area weighted average U-factor for fenestration products in the log walls is a maximum of 0.31; and

(2)(i) the building heating equipment meets or exceeds the following Department of Energy ratings:

(A) Gas furnace—90 annual fuel utilization efficiency (AFUE).

(B) Oil furnace—85 annual fuel utilization efficiency (AFUE).

(C) Boilers—85 annual fuel utilization efficiency (AFUE).

(D) Air source heat pumps—8.2 heating seasonal performance factor (HSPF) split systems.

(E) For water-to-air geothermal heat pumps:

(I) Closed loop water-to-air, an energy efficiency rating of 14.1 and coefficient of performance of 3.3.

(II) Open loop water-to-air, an energy efficiency rating of 16.2 and coefficient of performance of 3.6.

[compiler's note: this section (f) applies retroactively to January 1, 2010.]

(g) Automatic fire sprinkler systems in one-family and two-family dwellings.—

(1) Section R313.2 (relating to one- and two-family dwellings automatic fire sprinkler systems) of the International Residential Code (2009 edition), and any successor triennial revisions, is excluded from this act and shall not be part of Chapter 3.

(2) A builder of a one-family or two-family dwelling subject to the International Residential Code shall, at or before the time of entering into the purchase contract, do all of the following:

(i) Offer to a buyer the option to install or equip, at the buyer's expense, an automatic fire sprinkler system in the building or dwelling unit designed and installed in accordance with the provisions of section R313.2.1 (relating to design and installation) of the International Residential Code (2009 edition).

(ii) Provide the buyer with information which explains the initial and ongoing cost of installing and equipping an automatic fire sprinkler system in the building or dwelling unit.

(iii) Provide the buyer with information, as made available by the State Fire Commissioner on the agency's Internet website, on the possible benefits of installing an automatic sprinkler system.

[compiler's note: this section (g) applies retroactively to January 1, 2011]

(h) Fire protection of floors.—

(1) Except as set forth in paragraph (2), a floor assembly not required in the International Residential Code, or its successor building code, to be fire-resistance rated shall be provided with a 1/2 -inch gypsum wallboard membrane, 5/8 -inch wood structural panel membrane, or equivalent, on the underside of the floor framing member.

(2) Paragraph (1) shall not apply to any of the following:

(i) A floor assembly located directly over a space protected by an automatic sprinkler system in accordance with section P2904, NFPA13D or other equivalent sprinkler system approved by a municipal code official.

(ii) A floor assembly located directly over a crawl space not intended for storage or fuel fired appliances.

(iii) A portion of a floor assembly which complies with all of the following:

(A) The aggregate area of the unprotected portions shall not exceed 80 square feet per story.

(B) Fire blocking in accordance with section R302.11.1 shall be installed along the perimeter of the unprotected portion to separate the unprotected portion from the remainder of the floor assembly.

(iv) A wood floor assembly using dimension lumber or structural composite lumber equal to or greater than two inch by ten inch nominal dimension or a floor assembly approved by a municipal code official demonstrating equivalent fire performance.

(i) **Wall bracing requirements.**—Sections R602.10 through R602.12.1.6 of the 2009 International Residential Code, or its successor provisions, are excluded from the Uniform Construction Code. The wall bracing requirements of sections R602.10 through R602.11.3 of the 2006 International Residential Code shall be part of the Uniform Construction Code.

(j) **Refrigerants.**—

(1) If a provision of the Uniform Construction Code or related technical standards prohibit the use of a refrigerant that is authorized in accordance with section 612 of the Clean Air Act (69 Stat. 322, 42 U.S.C. § 7671k), the refrigerant may be used if:

(i) the refrigerant is permitted for the applicable use conditions by the United States Environmental Protection Agency; and

(ii) the equipment containing the refrigerant is listed and installed in accordance with the applicable use conditions imposed in accordance with section 612 of the Clean Air Act.

(2) This subsection shall expire upon the effective date of the final-omitted regulation promulgated by the department under section 304(a)(1) to adopt the council's report following its review of the 2024 model codes developed by the International Code Council.

§ 902. Applicability to certain buildings[51]

(a) **Historic buildings, structures and sites.**—The provisions of the 1999 BOCA National Building Code, Fourteenth Edition, relating to the construction, repair, alteration, addition, restoration and movement of structures shall not apply to existing buildings and structures, or new buildings and structures not intended for residential use on historic sites, that are identified and classified by the Federal, State or local government authority as historic buildings or sites where such buildings and structures are judged by the code official to be safe and in the interest of public health, safety and welfare.

(b) **Uncertified buildings under department's jurisdiction.**—Subject to subsection (d), all of the following apply to a building subject to the jurisdiction of the department:

(1) The department shall issue a certificate of occupancy to an uncertified building if that building meets the requirements of this subsection, unless the department deems the building to be unsafe because of inadequate means

51. 35 P.S. § 7210.902.

Table of Contents
Part I Ch. 1–3 Ethics, Records, Open Meetings
Part II Ch. 4–10 Taxation
Part III Ch. 11–18 Torts, Contracts & Civil Rules
Part IV Ch. 19–24 Zoning & Planning
Part V Ch. 25–30 Construction and Emergency Codes
Part VI Ch. 31–39 Municipal Codes
Index

of egress, inadequate light and ventilation, fire hazards or other dangers to human life or to public welfare.

(2) An uncertified building shall comply with the following:

(i) Maximum story height, minimum allowable construction type based on floor area, vertical opening and shaft protection, means of egress requirements of the International Building Code pertaining to minimum number of exits, maximum travel distances to exits, means of egress illumination, minimum egress widths and heights for exit doors, exit stairs, exit ramps and exit corridors. Waivers shall be as follows:

(A) The department may waive requirements for minimum egress widths and heights for exits, exit access doors, exit ramps and exit corridors if the department determines that any nonconforming openings provide sufficient width and height for building occupants to pass through or egress the building.

(B) The department may waive any requirements under this subparagraph if:

(I) the department determines a requirement to be technically infeasible; or

(II) the building owner demonstrates that the building met the applicable egress requirements which existed under the act of April 27, 1927 (P.L. 465, No. 299), referred to as the Fire and Panic Act.

(C) A waiver shall be documented on the certificate of occupancy.

(ii) Fire safety requirements of the International Building Code with respect to fire alarms, fire extinguishers, heat and smoke detectors, automatic sprinkler systems and occupancy and incidental use separations. If the code requires that a building have automatic sprinkler systems, the only buildings required to install automatic sprinkler systems shall be those buildings classified in use groups E (educational), H (high-hazard), I (institutional), R-1 or R-2 (residential) and those buildings which have occupied floors more than 75 feet above lowest level of fire department access. Buildings in use groups R-1 and R-2 which do not have occupied floors more than 75 feet above lowest level of fire department access may, instead of installing automatic sprinkler systems, install hard-wired interconnected heat and smoke detectors located in all lobbies, corridors, equipment rooms, storage rooms and other spaces that are not normally occupied. If construction began on a building prior to May 19, 1984, there is no requirement for the installation of automatic sprinkler systems under this subparagraph. If construction of a building began after May 18, 1984, automatic sprinkler installation required under this subparagraph shall be completed within five years of the effective date of this subsection, or an occupancy permit issued under this subsection shall be invalid. Waivers shall be as follows:

(A) The department may waive any requirements under this subparagraph if:

(I) the department determines a requirement to be technically infeasible; or

(II) the building owner demonstrates that the building met the applicable fire safety requirements which existed under the Fire and Panic Act.

(B) A waiver shall be documented on the certificate of occupancy.

(iii) Accessibility requirements as follows:

(A) If construction of a building began before September 1, 1965, no accessibility requirements shall be imposed.

(B) If construction of a building began after August 31, 1965, and before February 18, 1989, and if the building was subject to the requirements of the former act of September 1, 1965 (P.L. 459, No. 235, 35 P.S. § 1221) entitled "An act requiring that certain buildings and facilities adhere to certain principles, standards and specifications to make the same accessible to and usable by persons with physical handicaps, and providing for enforcement," it shall have:

(I) at least one accessible entrance;

(II) an accessible route from the accessible entrance to any public spaces on the same level as the accessible entrance; and

(III) if toilet rooms are provided, at least one accessible toilet room for each sex or a unisex toilet room, complying with the accessibility requirements of the International Building Code.

(C) If construction of the building began after February 17, 1989, all accessibility requirements of the International Building Code shall be met.

(3) Structural requirements shall not be imposed unless the department determines that the building or a portion of the building has defects which are dangerous as defined in the International Existing Building Code. The department may impose only those requirements minimally necessary to remove any danger to the building's occupants.

(4) A building owner may file an application for a variance from this subsection concerning accessibility with the advisory board under section 106. A building owner may file an application for a variance from this subsection concerning other standards. The application must be filed with the Industrial Board if any of the following apply:

(i) The building is located in a municipality where the department has jurisdiction.

(ii) The building is a State-owned building. As used in this subparagraph, the term "State-owned building" means a building owned or constructed for Commonwealth entities consisting of the General Assembly, the Unified Judicial System, the Pennsylvania Higher Education Assistance Agency, an executive agency, an independent agency, and a State-affiliated entity or State-related institution, as defined in 62 Pa.C.S. § 103 (relating to definitions).

(5) A building subject to this subsection shall be permitted to maintain its current occupancy as long as the owner demonstrates reasonable efforts to comply with this subsection.

(6) An uncertified building which was built before April 27, 1927, shall be deemed a certified building for purposes of this act.

(c) Uncertified buildings over which the department does not have jurisdiction.—

(1) A construction code official shall issue a certificate of occupancy to an uncertified building if it meets the requirements of subsection (b) or the latest adopted version of the International Existing Building Code. The construction code official shall utilize the code that, in his professional judgment, he deems to best apply.

(2) A construction code official may deny the issuance of a certificate of occupancy if the official deems that a building is unsafe because of inadequate means of egress, inadequate lighting and ventilation, fire hazards or other dangers to human life or to public welfare.

(d) Applicability of Uniform Construction Code.—Nothing in subsection (b) shall be construed as to affect applicability of Chapter 3 if a building is subject to renovation, additions, alterations or a change in use or occupancy.

§ 903. Penalties[52]

(a) Violation of act.—

(1) Any individual, firm or corporation that violates any provision of this act commits a summary offense and shall, upon conviction, be sentenced to pay a fine of not more than $1,000 and costs.

(2) Each day that a violation of this act continues shall be considered a separate violation.

(b) Disposition of penalties.—The amount of the penalty shall be forwarded to the entity with enforcement jurisdiction.

CHAPTER 11
MISCELLANEOUS PROVISIONS

§ 1101. Savings[53]

This act shall not repeal or in any way affect:

Sections 1, 3.3, 3.4, 3.5, 3.6(f)(1)(i), (f.1) and (g), 10.1, 13, 14 and 15 of the act of April 27, 1927 (P.L. 465, No. 299),[54] **referred to as the Fire and Panic Act.**

Section 2203-A of the act of April 9, 1929 (P.L. 177, No. 175),[55] **known as The Administrative Code of 1929.**

Act of May 2, 1929 (P.L. 1513, No. 451),[56] **referred to as the Boiler Regulation Law.**

Act of August 24, 1951 (P.L. 1304, No. 315),[57] **known as the Local Health Administration Law, insofar as it applies to counties of the first class and of the second class, and rules and regulations adopted by counties of the first class and of the second class under the act. Any construction standard adopted after October 31, 1996, by counties of the first class and of the second class under the authority of the Local Health Administration Law shall comply with Chapters 3 and 5 of this act.**

Act of December 27, 1951 (P.L. 1793, No. 475),[58] **referred to as the Liquefied Petroleum Gas act.**

Act of October 27, 1955 (P.L. 744, No. 222),[59] **known as the Pennsylvania Human Relations Act, and regulations promulgated under the act.**

Act of January 24, 1966 (1965 P.L. 1535, No. 537),[60] **known as the Pennsylvania Sewage Facilities Act, and regulations promulgated under the act.**

Act of June 13, 1967 (P.L. 31, No. 21),[61] **known as the Public Welfare Code.**

Act of October 4, 1978 (P.L. 851, No. 166),[62] **known as the Flood Plain Management Act, and regulations and ordinances promulgated under the act.**

Act of July 19, 1979 (P.L. 130, No. 48),[63] **known as the Health Care Facilities Act.**

---

52. 35 P.S. § 7210.903.
53. 35 P.S. § 7210.1101.
54. 35 P.S. §§ 1221, 1223.3 to 1223.5, 1223.6(f)(1), (f.1), (g), 1230.1, 1233 to 1235.
55. 71 P.S. § 581–3.
56. 35 P.S. § 1301 et seq.
57. 16 P.S. § 12001 et seq.
58. 35 P.S. § 1321 et seq.
59. 43 P.S. § 951 et seq.
60. 35 P.S. § 750.1 et seq.
61. 62 P.S. § 101 et seq.
62. 32 P.S. § 679.101 et seq.
63. 35 P.S. § 448.101 et seq.

Table of Contents
Part I Ch. 1–3 Ethics, Records, Open Meetings
Part II Ch. 4–10 Taxation
Part III Ch. 11–18 Torts, Contracts & Civil Rules
Part IV Ch. 19–24 Zoning & Planning
Part V Ch. 25–30 Construction and Emergency Codes
Part VI Ch. 31–39 Municipal Codes
Index

Act of July 11, 1990 (P.L. 499, No. 118),[64] known as the Older Adult Daily Living Centers Licensing Act.

§ 1102. Repeals[65]

(a) Absolute.—The following acts and parts of acts are repealed:

Sections 2, 3, 3.1, 3.2, 3.6(a), (b), (c), (d), (e), (f)(1)(ii), (iii) and (2), 4, 4.1, 4.2, 5, 6, 7, 8, 9, 10, 11, 12 and 15.1 of the act of April 27, 1927 (P.L. 465, No. 299),[66] referred to as the Fire and Panic Act.

Act of May 2, 1929 (P.L. 1518, No. 452),[67] referred to as the Elevator Regulation Law.

Act of September 1, 1965 (P.L. 459, No. 235),[68] entitled, as amended, "An act requiring that certain buildings and facilities adhere to certain principles, standards and specifications to make the same accessible to and usable by persons with physical handicaps, and providing for enforcement."

Act of July 9, 1976 (P.L. 919, No. 170),[69] entitled "An act providing for the approval or disapproval of applications for a permit relating to the construction or maintenance of improvements to real estate."

Act of December 15, 1980 (P.L. 1203, No. 222),[70] known as the Building Energy Conservation Act, and regulations promulgated thereunder.

Act of December 17, 1990 (P.L. 742, No. 185),[71] entitled "An act providing for restrooms in facilities where the public congregates; and requiring that restroom facilities be provided for women on an equitable basis."

Act of December 19, 1990 (P.L. 1387, No. 214),[72] known as the Dry Cleaning Law.

(b) General.—All other acts and parts of acts are repealed insofar as they are inconsistent with this act.

§ 1103. Effective date[73]

This act shall take effect as follows:

(1) Sections 104(d)(3) and (4), 301, 302, 701[74] and this section shall take effect immediately.

(2) The remainder of this act shall take effect 90 days following publication of notice in the Pennsylvania Bulletin that the regulations required by this act have been finally adopted.

Approved November 10, 1999.

---

64. 62 P.S. § 1511.1 et seq.
65. 35 P.S. § 7210.1102.
66. 35 P.S. §§ 1222 to 1223.2, 1223.6, 1224 to 1224.2, 1225 to 1232, 1235.1.
67. 35 P.S. §§ 1341 to 1356.
68. 71 P.S. §§ 1455.1 to 1455.3b.
69. 53 P.S. § 4104.
70. 35 P.S. §§ 7201.101 to 7201.103, 7201.201 to 7201.240, 7201.301 to 7201.311, 7201.313 to 7201.315, 7201.401, 7201.501 to 7201.505, 7201.601, 7201.602.
71. 35 P.S. §§ 5820.1 to 5820.6.
72. 35 P.S. §§ 1270.1 to 1270.14.
73. 35 P.S. § 7210.1103.
74. 35 P.S. §§ 7210.104, 7210.301, 7210.302, 7210.701.

CHAPTER 26

UNIFORM CONSTRUCTION CODE REGULATIONS

TITLE 34: THE PENNSYLVANIA CODE

CHAPTER 401

TRAINING AND CERTIFICATION OF CODE ADMINISTRATORS

CHAPTER 403

ADMINISTRATION

GENERALLY

STANDARDS

PERMIT AND INSPECTION PROCESS FOR COMMERCIAL CONSTRUCTION

PERMIT AND INSPECTION PROCESS FOR RESIDENTIAL BUILDINGS

DEPARTMENT, MUNICIPAL AND THIRD-PARTY ENFORCEMENT FOR NONCOMPLIANCE

MUNICIPAL ELECTION

BOARD OF APPEALS

DEPARTMENT ENFORCEMENT

CHAPTER 405
ELEVATORS AND OTHER LIFTING DEVICES

STAGE, ORCHESTRA AND ORGAN CONSOLE ELEVATORS

CHAPTER 401
TRAINING AND CERTIFICATION OF CODE ADMINISTRATORS

The provisions of this Chapter 401 adopted April 12, 2002, effective July 12, 2002, 32 Pa.B. 1849, unless otherwise noted.

§ 401.1. Definitions.

The following words and terms, when used in this part, have the following meanings, unless the context clearly indicates otherwise:

ALI—The Automatic Lift Institute, Post Office Box 33116, Indialantic, Florida, 32903-3116.

ANSI—American National Standards Institute, 11 West 42nd Street, New York, New York 10036.

APSP—The Association of Pool and Spa Professionals, 2111 Eisenhower Avenue, Alexandria, Virginia 22314-4695.

ASME—The American Society of Mechanical Engineers, Three Park Avenue, New York, New York 10016-5990.

ASTM—The American Society of Testing and Materials, 100 Barr Harbor Drive, P.O. Box C700, West Conshohocken, Pennsylvania 19428-2959.

Chapter 30 Emergency Management
Chapter 29 Counterterrorism Planning
Chapter 28 Social Security Number Privacy Act
Chapter 27 Municipal Code Compliance & Blight
Chapter 26 Construction Code Regulations
Chapter 25 Construction Code Act

Accessibility Advisory Board—The Department's Accessibility Advisory Board created under section 106 of the act (35 P.S. § 7210.106).

Accredited academic institution—A high school, technical or vocational school, private school licensed or registered with the Department of Education, junior college, community college or university.

Act—The Pennsylvania Construction Code Act (35 P. S. § § 7210.101—7210.1103).

Addition—An extension or increase in floor area or height of a building or structure.

Agricultural building—

(i) A structure utilized to store farm implements, hay, feed, grain or other agricultural or horticultural products or to house poultry, livestock or other farm animals, a milk house and a structure used to grow mushrooms.

(ii) The term includes a carriage house owned and used by members of a recognized religious sect for the purposes of housing horses and storing buggies.

(iii) The term does not include habitable space or spaces in which agricultural products are processed, treated or packaged and will not be construed to mean a place of occupancy by the general public.

Alteration—Any construction or renovation to an existing structure other than repair or addition.

Board of appeals—A body established by a municipality or municipalities which are parties to an agreement for the joint administration and enforcement of the act to hear requests for variances or extensions of time, and appeals from code administrator decisions.

Building—A structure used or intended for supporting or sheltering any occupancy.

Building code official—A construction code official, or the building code official's designee, who manages, supervises and administers building code enforcement activities under § 401.7(a)(18) (relating to certification category specifications). Duties include, but are not limited to: management of building code enforcement activities; supervision of building inspectors or plan examiners; authorizing issuance of certificates of occupancy; issuance of building permits, violation notices and orders to vacate; and the initiation of prosecutions.

Certificate of occupancy—A certificate issued by a building code official allowing occupancy of a building or structure under the Uniform Construction Code.

Certified building official—A classification administered by the International Code Council or its predecessor organization.

Chapter 11—Chapter 11 of the International Building Code relating to accessibility requirements adopted as part of the Uniform Construction Code.

Code administrator—A municipal code official, construction code official or third-party agency certified with the Department under the act or the Department under section 103 of the act (35 P. S. § 7210.103). The term includes an individual certified in a category established under this chapter to perform plan review of construction documents or administer and enforce codes and regulations in that category under the act or related acts.

Commercial construction—A building, structure or facility that is not a residential building.

Construction code official—An individual certified by the Department in an appropriate category established under section 701(b) of the act (35 P.S. § 7210.701(b)) to perform plan review of construction documents, inspect construction or administer and enforce codes and regulations in that category under the act or related acts under section 103 of the act.

Conveyor—A horizontal, inclined or vertical device for moving or transporting bulk material, packages or objects in a path predetermined by the design of the device and having points of loading and discharge, fixed or selected, and related equipment and devices described in and governed by the ASME standards adopted in this chapter.

Current code administrator—An individual who performed plan review of construction documents, inspections of one-family or two-family residential property or other buildings, structures and equipment or administered and enforced a construction code program, and who was employed by or under contract with the Commonwealth or a municipality prior to the effective date of adoption of the final-form regulations for the Uniform Construction Code. The term includes an individual who performed these duties as an employee, contractor or agent of a person employed by or under contract with the Commonwealth or a municipality of this Commonwealth prior to April 9, 2004.

Department—The Department of Labor and Industry of the Commonwealth.

Elevator—Hoisting and lowering devices governed by ASME standards adopted by the Department under the Uniform Construction Code and other lifting devices subject to the requirements of the Uniform Construction Code.

Facility—All or any portion of buildings, structures, site improvements, elements and pedestrian or vehicular routes located on sites where the buildings or structures are located.

Filing date—The date that the Department or building code official receives the completed permit application.

Fire and Panic Act—The act of April 27, 1927 (P.L. 465, No. 299) (35 P.S. § § 1221—1235), known as the Fire and Panic Act.

Health care facility—A facility licensed under the Health Care Facilities Act.

Health Care Facilities Act—The Health Care Facilities Act (35 P.S. § § 448.101—448.904b).

ICC—International Code Council, 5203 Leesburg Pike, Suite 600, Falls Church, Virginia 22041-3401.

ICC Evaluation Services, Inc.—The ICC Evaluation Services, Inc., 5360 Workman Mill Road, Whittier, California 90601.

ISO—The International Organization for Standardization, 1, Rue de Varembé, Case Postale 56 CH 1211, Geneva 20, Switzerland.

Industrial Board—The Department's Industrial Board established under sections 445 and 2214 of The Administrative Code of 1929 (71 P.S. § § 155 and 574), which hears requests for variances and extensions of time and appeals of decisions of the Department under the Uniform Construction Code.

Industrialized housing—Under section 3 of the Industrialized Housing Act (35 P.S. § 1651.3), a structure designed primarily for residential occupancy which is wholly or in substantial part made, fabricated, formed or assembled in manufacturing facilities for installation, or assembly and installation, on the building site. The term does not include housing units defined as mobile homes.

International Accreditation Service, Inc.—The International Accreditation Service, Inc., 5360 Workman Mill Road, Whittier, California 90601.

International Building Code—An International Building Code issued by the ICC. Chapter 11 and Appendix E of the "International Building Code 2021" issued by the ICC. The term includes all errata issued by the ICC.

International Energy Conservation Code—An International Energy Conservation Code issued by the ICC. The term includes all errata issued by the ICC.

International Existing Building Code—An International Existing Building Code for Buildings and Facilities issued by the ICC. The accessibility provisions in the ''International Existing Building Code for Buildings 2021'' issued by the ICC. The term includes all errata issued by the ICC.

International Fire Code—An International Fire Code issued by the ICC. The term includes all errata issued by the ICC.

International Fuel Gas Code—An International Fuel Gas Code issued by the ICC. The term includes all errata issued by the ICC.

International Mechanical Code—An International Mechanical Code issued by the ICC. The term includes all errata issued by the ICC.

International Performance Code—An International Performance Code for Buildings and Facilities issued by the ICC. The term includes all errata issued by the ICC.

International Plumbing Code—An International Plumbing Code issued by the ICC. The term includes all errata issued by the ICC.

International Residential Code—An International Residential Code for One- and Two-Family Dwellings issued by the ICC. The term includes all errata issued by the ICC.

International Swimming Pool and Spa Code—An International Swimming Pool and Spa Code issued by the ICC. The term includes all errata issued by the ICC.

International Wildland-Urban Interface Code—An International Wildland-Urban Interface Code issued by the ICC. The term includes all errata issued by the ICC.

Legally occupied—Use or habitation of a building or facility that was occupied in accordance with all valid construction statutes and ordinances in effect before April 9, 2004.

Manufactured housing—Under section 901(a) of the act (35 P.S. § 7210.901(a)), housing which bears a label as required by and referenced in the Manufactured Housing Act (35 P.S. § § 656.1—1656.9), certifying that it conforms to Federal construction and safety standards adopted under the National Manufactured Housing Construction and Safety Standards Act of 1974 (42 U.S.C.A. § § 5401—5426).

NEC—NFPA-70, a National Electrical Code issued by the NFPA. The term includes all errata issued by the NFPA.

NFPA—The National Fire Protection Association, One Batterymarch Park, Quincy, MA 02169.

Occupancy—Approved use of a building or a structure under the Uniform Construction Code.

PHRC—The Pennsylvania Housing Research Center, 219 Sackett Building, University Park, Pennsylvania 16802.

Passenger ropeway—An aerial tramway, aerial lift, surface lift, tow, conveyor or other lifting device which carries, pulls or pushes passengers along a level or inclined path by means of a haul rope or other flexible element which is driven by a power unit remaining essentially at a single location.

Pennsylvania's Alternative Residential Energy Provisions—The ''Pennsylvania Alternative Residential Energy Provisions'' issued in 2009 by the PHRC. This term includes all errata issued by the PHRC.

Permit—A document issued by a building code official authorizing the construction, alteration, repair, demolition, location, maintenance or installation relating to a building, structure, elevator or equipment under the Uniform Construction Code.

Person—Includes a corporation, partnership, business trust, other association, estate, trust, foundation or natural person. The term also includes the governing authority for a county or municipality, and a government entity other than the Commonwealth.

Personal delivery—The date that the appeal or request for a variance or extension of time under § § 403.122 and 403.142 (relating to appeals, variances and extensions of time; and Accessibility Advisory Board) was delivered to a common carrier, or was received by facsimile transmission or hand-delivery at the office of the building code official.

Postmark—The date of the official United States Postal Service postmark on the envelope containing an appeal or request for variance or extension of time under § § 403.122 and 403.142 or the date of a private postage meter mark on the envelope containing the appeal or request.

Recreational cabin—A structure where all of the following apply:

(i) The cabin is utilized principally for recreational activity.

(ii) The cabin is not utilized as a domicile or residence for any individual for any time period.

(iii) The cabin is not utilized for commercial purposes.

(iv) The cabin is not greater than two stories in height, excluding basement.

(v) The cabin is not utilized by the owner or any other person as a place of employment.

(vi) The cabin is not a mailing address for bills and correspondence.

(vii) The cabin is not listed as an individual's place of residence on a tax return, driver's license, car registration or voter registration.

Repair—Reconstruction or renewal of any part of an existing building for the purpose of its maintenance.

Residential building—Detached one-family and two-family dwellings and townhouses which are not more than three stories above grade plane in height with a separate means of egress and their accessory structures.

Secretary—The Secretary of the Department.

State-owned building—A building owned by or to be constructed for Commonwealth entities consisting of the General Assembly, the Unified Judicial System, the Pennsylvania Higher Education Assistance Agency, an executive agency, independent agency, and a State-affiliated entity or State-related institution as defined in 62 Pa.C.S. § 103 (relating to definitions).

Structure—A combination of materials that are built or constructed with a permanent location or attached to something that has a permanent location.

Third-party agency—A person, firm or corporation certified by the Department as a construction code official and contracted to perform plan review of construction documents, inspect construction or administer and enforce codes and regulations under the act.

Uncertified building—

(i) An existing building which was not approved for use and occupancy by the Department or a municipality which was enforcing a building code before April 9, 2004.

(ii) The term does not include a residential building.

Uniform Construction Code—This part, An International Building Code and the International Residential Code for One- and Two-Family Dwellings, available from the International Code Council, Inc., 4051 W. Flossmoor Road, Country Club Hills, Illinois 60478-5795, (888) 422-7233; and any standards adopted by the Department in this part under sections 301 and 304 of the act (35 P.S. § § 7210.301 and 7210.304).

Utility and miscellaneous use structures—

(i) Buildings or structures of an accessory character and miscellaneous structures not classified by the ICC in any specific use group.

(ii) The term includes carports, detached private garages, greenhouses and sheds having a building area less than 1,000 square feet.

(iii) The term does not include swimming pools or spas.

Variance—A modification of a Uniform Construction Code standard approved by a board of appeals or the Industrial Board and by the Secretary for accessibility requirements.

§ 401.2. Department fees.

(a) The following fees apply to the certification of code officials. The Department will charge one fee per certification application. An individual may apply for certification for multiple categories on a single application form. Fees are nonrefundable.

(1) Initial certification and registration—$50.

(2) Certification renewal—$50.

(3) Third-party agency certification and renewal—$250.

(4) Identification card replacement—$10.

(b) The following fees shall apply to the Department's issuance of a permit for the construction, alteration or demolition of a building or structure:

(1) New construction	
(i) New buildings and additions	$100 plus 20¢ per square foot of floor area or each fraction of floor area.
(ii) New structures and facilities other than buildings	$300
(2) Alterations, renovations or modifications of existing buildings or structures	$100 plus $20 for each $1,000 of estimated cost of alterations, renovations or modification certified by the permit applicant
(3) Revisions of approved plans and accelerated approval	$300
(4) Department accessibility plan review and inspection under § 403.141(b) (relating to enforcement by the Department)	$200
(5) Building or structure demolition	$100
(6) Annual permit	$100

(c) The following fees apply to plan review and application for a permit for installation:

(1) Passenger, freight and combination passenger/freight elevators (not hydraulic elevators):	
(i) 1–7 floors	$363
(ii) 8–20 floors	$436
(iii) More than 20 floors	$508

(2)	Hydraulic passenger, freight, combination passenger/freight elevators and other lifting devices	$290
(3)	Ski lifts	$508
(4)	Escalator and moving walks	$290
(5)	Wheelchair lift and inclined stairway chairlift	$150
(6)	Orchestra lift, belt manlift, stage lift, organ lift and other lifting devices	$300
(7)	Permit for alterations and major repairs	$145
(8)	Reinspection following failed major repair inspection (per inspection) reinspection	$100 paid before
(9)	Reinspection following failed acceptance inspection (to a maximum of $300 per inspection)	50% of initial permit fee paid before reinspection
(10)	Revision of plans	50% of initial permit fee

(d) The following fees apply to periodic elevator and other lifting device inspections under § 405.7 (relating to periodic inspections):

(1)	Passenger, freight and combination passenger/freight elevators (not hydraulic):	
	(i) 1–7 floors	$94
	(ii) 8–20 floors	$116
	(iii) More than 20 floors	$145
(2)	Hydraulic passenger, freight, combination passenger/freight elevators and other lifting devices	$73
(3)	Ski lifts	$145
(4)	Wheelchair lift and inclined stairway chairlift	$75
(5)	Escalator and moving walk	$94
(6)	Orchestra lift, belt manlift, stage lift, organ lift and other lifting devices	$75

(e) The following fees apply to witnessing periodic tests under § 405.8 (relating to periodic testing):

(1)	Electric elevators with one to ten openings	$125
(2)	Electric elevators with 11-20 openings	$150
(3)	Electric elevators with more than 20 openings	$175
(4)	Roped hydraulic elevator and roped/chained vertical reciprocal conveyor	$110
(5)	Hydraulic elevator, limited use/limited application elevator and direct hydraulic vertical reciprocating conveyor	$85

(6) Escalator and moving walks	$85
(7) Wheelchair lift and inclined stairway chairlift	$75
(8) Orchestra lift, stage lift and organ lift	$125
(9) Other equipment	$85

(f) The following fees apply to the witnessing of periodic dynamic testing required under § 405.9 (relating to periodic dynamic testing):

(1) Aerial tramways	$300
(2) Detachable aerial grips	$300
(3) Fixed grip aerial lifts	$200

(g) The following fees apply to a certificate of operation:

(1) Annual renewal	$36
(2) Duplicate	$25

(h) The following fees shall apply to a variance request:

(1) Industrial Board variance request appeal or extension of time	$100
(2) Accessibility Advisory Board variance request application	$100

§ 401.2a. Municipal and third-party agency fees.

(a) A municipality or third-party agency that enforces the Uniform Construction Code may establish fees for its administration and enforcement and time periods for payment of the fees. The municipality or third-party agency may establish a required time period for payment of the fees and fees for plan review, inspections and other activities related to the Uniform Construction Code.

(b) The building code official for the municipality and a third-party agency shall make the fee schedule available to the public.

(c) A municipality or third-party agency may establish a fee refund policy.

(d) A municipality or third-party agency may withhold issuance of a certificate or permit until a required fee is paid.

(e) A municipality may establish other fees authorized by law.

§ 401.3. Certification required.

(a) A person may not perform a plan review of construction documents, inspect construction or equipment, or administer and enforce the Uniform Construction Code without being currently certified or registered by the Department in the category applicable to the work that is to be performed.

(b) A person may not approve plans or perform inspections relating to accessibility requirements without being certified by the Department as an accessibility inspector/plans examiner.

§ 401.4. Application and identification.

(a) An applicant for certification shall submit a Department-provided application, pay the required fee and submit verification of meeting the requirements of this chapter and passing all of the certification examinations for a specific certification category in § 401.6 (relating to certification categories and testing) on or after July 12, 1996.

(b) The Department will issue an identification card to an applicant who meets the certification requirements.

(c) A certification holder shall notify the Department in writing if the identification card is lost or destroyed. The Department will charge a required fee for issuance of a new identification card.

(d) Certification and certification renewal will not be valid until the Department receives the required fee.

(e) The period of certification shall be 3 years from the issuance date of a certification under § 401.8(a) (relating to certification renewal).

(f) The Department may refuse to issue certification for just cause in accordance with § 401.14 (relating to decertification or refusal). The Department will provide written notification of the reasons for the refusal to issue certification.

§ 401.5. Waivers.

(a) The Department may grant a request for waiver of the testing requirements of § 401.6 (relating to certification categories and testing) if the applicant meets any of the following criteria:

(1) Passed a test substantially similar to the testing categories in § 401.6 within the 6 years prior to July 12, 2002.

(2) Passed a test substantially similar to the testing categories in § 401.6 before July 12, 1996, so long as the applicant submits any of the following to the Department:

(i) Evidence of continued employment as a code administrator in the related field.

(ii) Current certification issued by a model code organization.

(iii) Evidence of completion of 30 hours of continuing education or a college degree program in associated fields.

(3) Passed a certified building official examination. An applicant who passed the examination may be eligible to receive certification in the following categories:

(i) Residential building inspector.

(ii) Building inspector.

(iii) Building plans examiner.

(b) An applicant for waiver shall complete a Department-provided application form and pay the required initial certification fee under § 401.2 (relating to Department fees). If the Department approves the waiver, the applicant shall comply with § 401.4 (relating to application and identification).

(c) A code administrator may act in place of a lumber grading or inspection agency to satisfy the requirement under section 2303.1.1 of the International Building Code or its successor code or sections R404.2.1, R502.1, R602.1, R802.1 of the "International Residential Code" or its successor code under section 701(b)(2) of the act (35 P. S. § 7210.701(b)(2)).

§ 401.6. Certification categories and testing.

The Department will issue a certification for a specific category to an applicant who receives a passing grade in all of the examinations required for that category. The Department will accept the following category examinations or successor examinations administered by the Department, the National Certification Program for Construction Code Inspectors, Assessment Services, Incorporated, the National Association of Elevator Safety Authorities or other Nationally-recognized testing program approved by the Department. The Department will list the approved providers on its Internet website.

Certification Categories	Examination Number and Name
Residential building inspector	1A Building 1 & 2 family dwelling
Residential electrical inspector	2A Electrical 1 & 2 family dwelling
Residential mechanical inspector	4A Mechanical 1 & 2 family dwelling

Certification Categories	Examination Number and Name
Residential plumbing inspector	5A Plumbing 1 & 2 family dwelling
Residential energy inspector	E1 Residential energy plan review & inspection
Building inspector	1B Building general 3B Fire protection general
Fire inspector	F1 Fire prevention inspection general I
Electrical inspector	2B Electrical general
Mechanical inspector	4B Mechanical general
Plumbing inspector	5B Plumbing general
Energy inspector	E2 Commercial energy inspection
Accessibility inspector/plan examiner	A1 accessibility inspector/plan examiner
Building plans examiner	1B Building general 1C Building plan review 3B Fire protection general 3C Fire protection plan review
Electrical plans examiner	2B Electrical general 2C Electrical plan review
Mechanical plans examiner	4B Mechanical general 4C Mechanical plan review
Plumbing plans examiner	5B Plumbing general 5C Plumbing plan review
Energy plans examiner	E3 Commercial energy plan review
Building code official (code administrator)	Department-administered test on State law and application
Elevator inspector	Qualified elevator inspector test or its equivalent
Passenger ropeway inspector	Department administered test on ANSI B77.1-1999 edition

§ 401.7. Certification category specifications.

An individual certified by the Department in the following categories may perform the duties described in the specific category as a construction code official:

(1) ***Residential building inspector.***

(i) Inspects one-family and two-family dwellings and jurisdictional accessory structures to ensure that these structures are free from hazardous structural conditions and comply with the Uniform Construction Code.

(ii) Duties include inspection of footings and foundations, concrete slabs, wood decay and termite protection, floor and ceiling framing, wall framing, roof framing, masonry walls, sheathing, roof covering, interior and exterior wall coverings, means of egress system and safety glazing.

(2) ***Residential electrical inspector.***

(i) Inspects one-family and two-family dwellings and jurisdictional accessory structures to ensure that these structures are free from hazardous electrical installations and comply with the Uniform Construction Code.

(ii) Duties include determining compliance of electrical service, electrical distribution systems, wiring methods, panel boards, control devices, conductors and electrical fixture installation.

(3) *Residential mechanical inspector.*

(i) Inspects one-family and two-family dwellings and jurisdictional accessory structures to ensure that these structures are free from hazardous mechanical installations and comply with the Uniform Construction Code.

(ii) Duties include determining compliance of mechanical equipment, gas fuel supply systems, venting of appliances, air ducts, combustion air and comfort cooling.

(4) *Residential plumbing inspector.*

(i) Inspects one-family and two-family dwellings and jurisdictional accessory structures to ensure that these structures are free from hazardous plumbing installations and comply with the Uniform Construction Code.

(ii) Duties include determining compliance of water service, building sewer, water distribution, drainage, waste and vents and fixtures.

(5) *Residential energy inspector.*

(i) Inspects one-family and two-family dwellings and jurisdictional accessory structures to ensure that energy installations are made in the manner specified in the Uniform Construction Code.

(ii) Duties include determining compliance of conditioned or unconditioned spaces, R-values for roof/ceiling, floor and wall assemblies and insulation placement, installation of materials for the building envelope and its components, moisture control methods such as caulking, sealing and weather-stripping, duct and dipping insulation and sealing criteria, thermostats for each heating and cooling system, electrical metering, lighting installation and controls and piping insulation, circulation pump controls, heat traps, shower heads and pool cover installations.

(6) *Building inspector.*

(i) Ensures that buildings and structures are constructed in accordance with the Uniform Construction Code.

(ii) Duties include inspection of construction site and building location, footings and foundations, wood and steel framing and connections, masonry construction, precast and cast-in-place concrete, exterior weather boarding, fire-stopping and draft-stopping, building components related to life safety and fire protection systems and building components related to size, installation and workmanship.

(iii) May perform residential inspector duties listed in paragraph (1).

(7) *Electrical inspector.*

(i) Ensures that electrical installations are made in accordance with the Uniform Construction Code regardless of the size or components used in the installation.

(ii) Duties include determining compliance of raceways (installations, size), cables, panel boards and boxes, conductors, control devices, motors and generators, electrical equipment and special occupancies.

(iii) May perform residential electrical inspector duties listed in paragraph (2).

(8) *Mechanical inspector.*

(i) Ensures that mechanical installations are made in the manner specified in the Uniform Construction Code.

Table of Contents
Part I Ch. 1–3 Ethics, Records, Open Meetings
Part II Ch. 4–10 Taxation
Part III Ch. 11–18 Torts, Contracts & Civil Rules
Part IV Ch. 19–24 Zoning & Planning
Part V Ch. 25–30 Construction and Emergency Codes
Part VI Ch. 31–39 Municipal Codes
Index

(ii) Duties include determining compliance of fuel piping systems, heating, cooling and ventilation, fuel-fired equipment venting, steam and hot water heating systems and piping and energy conservation.

(iii) May perform residential mechanical inspector duties listed in paragraph (3).

(9) *Plumbing inspector.*

(i) Ensures that plumbing installations are made in accordance with the Uniform Construction Code.

(ii) Duties include determining compliance of underground piping installation, rough-in inspections, drain-waste-venting (DWV) systems, pressure testing, water distribution systems, observation and elimination of cross connections, system pumps, tanks and pressure vessels and fixtures, traps and valves and their connections.

(iii) May perform residential plumbing inspector duties listed in paragraph (4).

(10) *Energy inspector.*

(i) Ensures that the building envelope, mechanical systems, electrical power and lighting systems and building service systems and equipment comply with the approved construction documents and the Uniform Construction Code.

(ii) Duties include verifying that building envelope and components meet minimum requirements for installation of materials and that building envelope penetrations are caulked, sealed and weather-stripped, determining compliance of moisture control methods, installation of and types of mechanical equipment and efficiencies, heating, ventilation and air conditioning (HVAC) equipment, ducts and piping, insulation and sealing, lighting installation and lighting controls for building interiors and exteriors, permanently wired poly-phase motors and their efficiencies, piping insulation, circulation pump controls, heat traps, point-of-use controls and pool cover installations.

(iii) May perform residential energy inspector duties listed in paragraph (5).

(11) *Accessibility inspector/plans examiner.*

(i) Ensures that buildings and structures are constructed in accordance with the accessibility provisions of the Uniform Construction Code and that construction documents submitted as part of a permit application comply with the accessibility provisions of the Uniform Construction Code.

(ii) Duties include inspection of building sites and all interior building components to verify compliance with the accessibility standards or review of construction documents to verify that the design of building sites and all interior components comply with the accessibility standards.

(12) *Building plans examiner.*

(i) Determines that the construction documents submitted as part of a permit application comply with the Uniform Construction Code.

(ii) Duties include determining the degree of compliance necessary for new construction projects, alterations or repairs, proper use group/type of construction classification, determining height and area requirements, minimum means of egress requirements, minimum light and ventilation requirements, minimum design structural loads, adequacy of soils investigations, adequacy of footing and foundation designs, minimum fire-resistance requirements, adequacy of barrier-free designs, minimum energy conservation requirements and adequacy of fire-protection systems.

(13) *Fire inspector.*

(i) Conducts basic fire prevention inspections and has a general knowledge of applicable codes and standards.

(ii) Duties include field inspections, preparation of correspondence and inspection reports, handling complaints, and maintaining files related to inspections that were conducted.

(14) *Electrical plans examiner.*

(i) Determines that the construction documents submitted as part of a permit application comply with the Uniform Construction Code.

(ii) Duties include determining proper number of services, proper location of services, adequacy of emergency systems, proper service size, proper over-current protection, special use applications and proper conductor size and application.

(15) *Mechanical plans examiner.*

(i) Determines that the construction documents submitted as part of a permit application comply with the Uniform Construction Code.

(ii) Duties include determining compliance of fuel piping systems, fuel-burning appliances, mechanical refrigeration systems, incinerators, energy conservation equipment and controls, boilers and pressure vessels, venting systems, hydronic and steam-piping systems and ventilation air systems.

(16) *Plumbing plans examiner.*

(i) Determines that the construction documents submitted as part of a permit application comply with the Uniform Construction Code.

(ii) Duties include determining that water service, building sewer/storm sewer and other underground piping are properly sized and located, determining that proper drainage fixture units, fixture locations and clearances are used, determining the adequacy of drain-waste-venting (DWV) riser diagrams and water distribution systems and determining the proper number of fixtures and proper materials as proposed.

(17) *Energy plans examiner.*

(i) Ensures that the design criteria specified for a building are correct and in accordance with the Uniform Construction Code and that alterations, additions and change of use or occupancy are in compliance with the Uniform Construction Code.

(ii) Duties include determining compliance of the design conditions specified, conditioned or unconditioned spaces, R values for roof/ceiling, floor and wall assemblies and insulation placement, insulation of materials for the building envelope and its components, moisture control methods such as caulking, sealing and weather-stripping, duct and dipping insulation and sealing criteria, thermostats for each heating and cooling system, electrical metering, lighting installation and controls, piping insulation, circulation pump controls, heat raps, shower heads and pool cover installations.

(18) *Building code official.*

(i) Manages, supervises and administers building code enforcement activities. The Department, municipality or a third-party agency that operates an enforcement program under the act will employ at least one person certified or registered as a building code official.

(ii) Duties include management of building code enforcement activities, supervision of building inspectors or plans examiners, issuing building permits, occupancy permits, notice of violations and orders to vacate, and initiation of prosecutions.

(19) *Elevator inspector.*

(i) Inspects electric and hydraulic elevators, conveying systems and other lifting devices to ensure that these installations are free from conditions that would present a life safety or fire hazard to persons using the installations.

(ii) Duties include determining compliance with the Uniform Construction Code regarding door closers, interlocks, car safeties, over-speed governors, safety tests, reshackling, ropes, fireman's recall, brakes and other related elevator equipment and the investigation of accidents.

(20) *Passenger ropeway inspector.*

(i) Inspects passenger ropeways to ensure that the installation is free from conditions that would present a life safety or fire hazard to a person using the installation.

(ii) Duties include investigation of accidents and determining compliances of power units, auxiliary power units, carriers, cabins, cars, location, vertical and horizontal clearances, haul rope sleeves, guides, haul rope condition and splice, structures and foundations, capacity, speed, acceleration/deceleration, loading and unloading areas, required stopping devices, brakes and rollback devices, tension systems, manual and automatic control devices, haul rope grips, operation and maintenance of equipment, electrical components, emergency shut down circuits, bypass circuits, speed regulating devices, and other related ropeway equipment with the Uniform Construction Code.

§ 401.8. Certification renewal.

(a) A certification holder shall renew a certification every 3 years from date of issuance to continue to act as a code administrator. If a certification holder receives certification in an additional category, the expiration date of all his certifications shall be the date of expiration of the certification that was last issued to the certification holder.

(b) To renew a certification, an applicant shall submit a completed Department-provided renewal form, acceptable proof of completion of continuing education and the required certification fee under § 401.2 (relating to Department fees). The Department will post this form on its Internet website (www.dli.state.pa.us) and provide it upon request.

(c) An applicant for renewal shall obtain identification in accordance with § 401.4 (relating to application and identification).

(d) The Department will not renew a certification that is expired for more than 1 year unless the applicant submits a certification application under § 401.4 and passes the required examinations under § 401.6 (relating to certification categories and testing).

(e) An applicant for certification renewal shall submit proof of completion of each continuing education course. The proof of completion shall be completed by the course provider and contain the following information:

(1) The name and address of the training provider.

(2) The dates attended.

(3) The credit hours claimed.

(4) The title of the course.

(5) The subject matter of the course.

(f) The Department will not renew the certification of a person who was decertified in accordance with § 401.14 (relating to decertification or refusal to certify) during the period that the Department ordered the decertification.

§ 401.9. Continuing education.

(a) Prior to certification renewal, an applicant shall complete 15 credit hours of continuing education in courses relating to the professional competency of code administrators. An applicant with multiple certification areas shall complete 15 credit hours of continuing education for each category after the issuance of the certification or most recent renewal of certification. The applicant is not required to complete more than 45 credit hours for renewal. At least 1/3 of the applicant's continuing education requirement shall be in approved courses relating to the applicant's certification categories.

(b) The Department will approve credit as follows:

(1) One credit hour for each 60 minutes actually spent at one course except as otherwise listed in this subsection.

(2) One credit hour for each 60-minutes of completion time for a self-study course calculated by the sponsor. The Department may modify credit hours for a self-study course to comply with this section.

(3) Five credit hours for successful completion of an examination for an additional certification category under subsection (c)(5).

(4) One credit hour for each 60 minutes actually spent in attendance at a model code organization code change hearing under subsection (c)(6).

(c) The Department approves the following as acceptable courses of study for continuing education credits:

(1) Attendance at a seminar or technical presentation by an approved provider.

(2) Completion of a self-study course offered by an approved provider.

(3) Completion of a classroom course offered by an accredited academic institution.

(4) Instruction at a continuing education seminar or technical presentation for an approved provider.

(5) Successful completion of an examination for an additional certification category listed in § 401.6 (relating to certification categories and testing).

(6) Attendance at a model code organization code change hearing.

§ 401.10. Department-approved providers.

(a) The following providers are approved to offer instruction for continuing education credit hours:

(1) The National Conference of States on Building Codes and Standards.

(2) A Federal, Commonwealth or state agency.

(3) An accredited academic institution.

(4) A model code organization or its accredited local chapter.

(5) A trade association representing design professionals or the construction industry.

(6) A National standards writing organization.

(7) An association serving or representing Commonwealth municipalities.

(8) Approved testing providers under § 401.6 (relating to certification categories and testing) for credit hours under § 401.9(c)(5) (relating to continuing education).

(b) The Department will approve additional providers who demonstrate the competency to provide approved continuing education programs. An applicant for approval as a provider shall submit a completed Department-provided application and appropriate documentation that it meets the requirements of § 401.9. The Department will post a list of approved providers on its Internet website (www.dli.state.pa.us) and provide the list upon request.

(c) The Department may revoke approval of any provider that does not comply with § 401.9 or this section. Actions will be taken subject to the right of notice, hearing and adjudication in accordance with 2 Pa.C.S. (relating to administrative law and procedure).

§ 401.11. Certification of third-party agency.

(a) Current certification as a third-party agency is required to act as a construction code official, perform plan review of construction documents, inspect construction or administer and enforce codes and regulations in accordance with the act under contract with a person, firm, corporation or the Commonwealth.

(b) An applicant for certification as a third-party agency shall submit a completed Department-provided application to the Department and pay the required fee.

(c) An applicant for certification as a third-party agency shall submit documentation that its employees or agents who act as construction code officials and perform plan review of construction documents, inspect construction or administer or enforce codes and regulations under the act are currently registered or certified in the specific categories applicable to the work performed.

(d) An applicant for certification under this section shall submit acceptable documentation of insurance coverage required under § 401.12 (relating to liability insurance).

(e) A third-party agency shall provide written notification to the Department within 60 days of the hiring or change of employment status of an employee or agent who acts as a construction code official and performs plan review of construction documents, inspects construction or administers or enforces codes and regulations under the act.

(f) A certification expires 3 years after date of issuance. The Department will renew a third-party agency certification when the applicant meets all of the following:

(1) Submits a completed Department-provided renewal form.

(2) Pays the required fee under § 401.2 (relating to Department fees).

(3) Submits proof of liability insurance coverage under § 401.12.

(4) Not decertified under § 401.14 (relating to decertification or refusal to certify).

§ 401.12. Liability insurance.

(a) A third-party agency shall carry errors and omissions liability insurance in at least the amount of $1 million for each person and each occurrence to satisfy claims or judgments for property damage or personal injury, or both.

(b) As a condition for obtaining and renewing certification, a third-party agency shall submit to the Department satisfactory evidence that it has obtained errors and omissions liability insurance as required by this section. A certification or renewal will not be issued unless the third-party agency provides proof of insurance which shall consist of a certificate of insurance or copy of the declaration page from the insurance policy setting forth the effective date, expiration date and policy coverage in the amounts required.

(c) A third-party agency shall notify the Department immediately of the cancellation of its errors and omissions liability insurance, the failure or refusal to renew its errors and omissions liability insurance, change of insurance carrier, change of policy dates or changes of coverage amounts. Upon notice of loss or cancellation of insurance coverage, the Department will immediately initiate action to decertify the third party agency under § 401.14 (relating to decertification or refusal to certify).

§ 401.13. List of code administrators.

The Department will maintain a list of code administrators indicating their categories of certifications on its Internet website (www.dli.state.pa.us). The Department will also make the list available to municipalities and, upon request, the public.

§ 401.14. Decertification or refusal to certify.

(a) *Decertification or refusal to certify.* The Department may initiate action against a code administrator or refuse to issue certification for just cause. Just cause includes the following:

(1) Failure to remedy an error or omission specified in a formal warning or to comply with an order issued by the Department under this section.

(2) Fraud or deceit or making untrue representations in obtaining a certification.

(3) Failure to remit the required certification fee.

(4) Violation of the act or this chapter.

(5) Incompetence or gross negligence.

(6) Acting in a manner presenting a danger to the public health and safety.

(7) Pleading guilty, entering a plea of nolo contendere, being found guilty, receiving probation without verdict, disposition in lieu of trial or an Accelerated Rehabilitative Disposition to a felony or any crime relating to the business of code administrator in the courts of this Commonwealth, a Federal court or a court of any other state, territory or insular possession of the United States.

(8) Having a certification or any authorization to engage in the business of code administrator revoked or suspended or having other disciplinary action taken, or an application for certification or authorization to engage in the business of code administrator refused or denied by the proper authority of another state or Federal district, territory or insular possession of the United States, the Federal government or Canada.

(9) Failing to complete continuing education requirements of the act or engaging in deceit or misrepresentation in the reporting of continuing education requirements.

(10) Engaging in fraud, deceit or an act of moral turpitude while acting as code administrator.

(11) Failing to enforce the act or Uniform Construction Code.

(12) Knowingly aiding and abetting a person engaging in code administrator activity who is not currently certified or registered.

(13) Being a third-party agency that does not comply with § 401.12 (relating to liability insurance).

(14) Engaging in the activities of a code administrator or advertising as a code administrator without a current certification required for the work performed, or registration issued by the Department.

(b) *Notice and hearing.* Actions of the Department relating to decertification under this section will be taken subject to the right of notice, hearing and adjudication in accordance with 2 Pa.C.S. (relating to administrative law and procedure). Decertification proceedings shall be con-ducted under 1 Pa. Code Part II (relating to the General Rules of Administrative Practice and Procedure).

(c) *Procedure for decertification.*

(1) The Department will serve the code administrator with an order to show cause under 1 Pa. Code § 35.14 (relating to orders to show cause). The order to show cause shall contain notification that the certification may be subject to action and the grounds for the action. The order to show cause shall contain notification that the code administrator is to respond in writing within 30 days after the date of service of the order. The Department will also serve a copy of the order to show cause upon the supervising official in the municipality where the alleged incidents occurred and upon the code administrator's current employer.

(2) The code administrator may respond in writing to the allegations in the order to show cause in accordance with 1 Pa. Code § 35.37 (relating to answers to orders to show cause). If made, the answer shall be filed with the Department within 30 days after the date of service of the order to show cause.

(3) At the request of the code administrator, the Department will hold a hearing on the matter. The Secretary will designate a presiding officer to conduct the hearing and to issue a proposed report under 1 Pa. Code §§ 35.201–35.207 (relating to proposed reports generally).

(4) The presiding officer shall have the power to conduct hearings under 1 Pa. Code §§ 35.185–35.190 (relating to presiding officers). The presiding officer shall issue a proposed report that shall be served upon counsel of record or to the parties in the hearing. The presiding officer shall transmit the proposed report and the certified record to the Secretary within 15-days after issuance of the proposed report.

(5) A participant desiring to appeal to the Secretary shall, within 30 days after the service of a copy of the proposed report, file exceptions to the proposed report under 1 Pa. Code § 35.211 (relating to procedure to except to proposed report). A response may be filed within 20 days to the exceptions.

(6) The Secretary or a designee will issue a final order under 1 Pa. Code § 35.226 (relating to final orders).

(d) *Types of corrective action*. When the Department is authorized to take action against a code administrator, the Department may:

(1) Administer a formal warning.

(2) Require the code administrator to take remedial educational courses.

(3) Decertify the code administrator for a period set by the Department. The Department will order the code administrator to surrender his certificate after decertification.

(4) Deny the application for certification.

(e) *Conditions for reinstatement*. Unless ordered to do so by a court of competent jurisdiction, the Department will not reinstate certification to a person who was decertified until the following conditions are met:

(1) The full period of decertification ordered by the Department has elapsed.

(2) The person has complied with conditions imposed by the Department's order of decertification and recertification would not be detrimental to the public health and safety.

(3) The person complies with § 401.4 (relating to application and identification).

(f) Subsection (c) supplements 1 Pa. Code §§ 35.14, 35.37, 35.201–35.207, 35.185–35.190, 35.211 and 35.226.

§ 401.15. Registration of current code administrators.

(a) A current code administrator engaged in plan review or inspection of one-family or two-family residential property may continue to engage in these activities without meeting the training and certification requirements of this chapter until 3 years from effective date of the adoption of the final-form regulations for the Uniform Construction Code. To engage in plan review or inspection of one-family or two-family dwelling units after 3 years from effective date of adoption of the final-form regulations for the Uniform Construction Code, a current code administrator shall meet the certification and training requirements of this chapter.

(b) A current code administrator engaged in plan review or inspection of other buildings and structures that are not one-family or two-family residential structures may continue to engage in these activities without meeting the training and certification requirements of this chapter until 5 years from effective date of adoption of the final-form regulations for the Uniform Construction Code. To engage in plan review and inspection of other buildings and structures after 5 years from the effective date of adoption of the final-form regulations for the Uniform Construction Code, a current code administrator shall meet the training and certification requirements of this chapter.

(c) A current code administrator shall register with the Department by submitting a completed Department-provided form and furnishing required documentation. Documentation is to consist of an affidavit completed by the employer responsible for oversight of the current code administrator's activities and an affidavit completed by the current code administrator containing a description of the current code administrator's duties, employment and length of employment.

(d) The Department will issue an identification card to a current code administrator who meets the requirements of this section, completes a Department-provided form and pays the required fee under § 401.2 (relating to Department fees).

(e) The identification card will expire as registration on the date that the current code administrator must meet the training and certification requirements of this chapter.

(f) A current code administrator shall notify the Department in writing if the identification card is lost or destroyed. The Department will charge a required fee for issuance of a new identification card under § 401.2.

(g) A current code administrator is not required to obtain a new registration for a change of employer.

(h) A current code administrator may not approve plans or perform inspections relating to accessibility requirements without being currently certified by the Department as an accessibility inspector/plans examiner.

§ 401.16. Change of address or employer.

A certification or registration holder shall notify the Department of any change of mailing address or employer within 30 days.

CHAPTER 403
ADMINISTRATION

GENERALLY

§ 403.1. Scope.

(a) *Application.*

(1) The Uniform Construction Code applies to the construction, alteration, repair, movement, equipment, removal, demolition, location, maintenance, occupancy or change of occupancy of every building or structure which occurs on or after April 9, 2004, and all existing structures that are not legally occupied.

(2) The Department will promulgate regulations adopting the new triennial BOCA National Building Code, or its successor building code as the Uniform Construction Code by December 31 of the year of the issuance under section 304(a)(1) of the act (35 P. S. § 7210.304(a)(1)). This deadline will not apply if the Uniform Construction Code Review and Advisory Council established under section 107 of the act (35 P. S. § 7210.107) informs the Department that it should exclude any provisions of the triennial codes from the Uniform Construction Code. New buildings or renovations to existing buildings for which a design or construction contract was executed before the effective date of the regulatory amendment adopting the latest triennial versions of the construc-

Table of Contents | Part I Ch. 1–3 Ethics, Records, Open Meetings | Part II Ch. 4–10 Taxation | Part III Ch. 11–18 Torts, Contracts & Civil Rules | Part IV Ch. 19–24 Zoning & Planning | Part V Ch. 25–30 Construction and Emergency Codes | Part VI Ch. 31–39 Municipal Codes | Index

tion codes and standards shall comply with the codes and standards in effect at the time that the design or construction contract was executed.

(b) *Exclusions and exemptions.* The Uniform Construction Code does not apply to:

(1) New buildings or renovations to existing buildings for which an application for a permit was made to the Department or a municipality before April 9, 2004.

(2) New buildings or renovations to existing buildings on which a contract for design or construction was signed before April 9, 2004.

(3) The following structures if the structure has a building area less than 1,000 square feet and is accessory to a detached one-family dwelling except as might be required by an ordinance adopted under section 503 of the act (35 P. S. § 7210.503):

(i) Carports.

(ii) Detached private garages.

(iii) Greenhouses.

(iv) Sheds.

(4) An agricultural building.

(5) Manufactured or industrialized housing shipped from the factory under section 901(a) of the act (35 P. S. § 7210.901(a)) as provided in § 403.25 (relating to manufactured and industrialized housing).

(6) Installation of tubing, piping, propane gas burning appliances, equipment or fixtures related to liquefied petroleum gas under the Propane and Liquefied Petroleum Gas Act (35 P. S. § § 1329.1—1329.19).

(7) Construction of individual sewage disposal systems under 25 Pa. Code Chapter 73 (relating to onlot sewage treatment facilities).

(8) Alterations to residential buildings which do not make structural changes or changes to means of egress, except as required by ordinances in effect under sections 303(b)(1) or 503 of the act (35 P. S. § § 7210.303(b)(1) and 7210.503). Under this subsection, a structural change does not include a minor framing change needed to replace existing windows or doors.

(9) Repairs to residential buildings, except as required by ordinances in effect under sections 303(b)(1) and 503 of the act.

(10) Installation of aluminum or vinyl siding onto an existing residential or an existing commercial building, except as might be required by ordinances in effect under section 303(b)(1) (35 P. S. § § 7210.303(b)(1)) or section 503 of the act.

(11) A recreational cabin if the following conditions are met:

(i) The cabin is equipped with at least one smoke detector, one fire extinguisher and one carbon monoxide detector in both the kitchen and sleeping quarters.

(ii) The owner of the cabin files one of the following with the municipality:

(A) A Department form UCC-13 attesting to the fact that the cabin meets the definition of a "recreational cabin" in § 401.1 (relating to definitions).

(B) A valid proof of insurance for the recreational cabin, written and issued by an insurer authorized to do business in this Commonwealth, stating that the structure meets the definition of a "recreational cabin."

(12) Structures which are:

(i) Erected for the purpose of participation in a fair, flea market, arts and crafts festival or other public celebration.

(ii) Less than 1,600 square feet in size.

(iii) Erected for a period of less than 30 days.

(iv) Not a swimming pool, spa or hot tub.

(13) A pole barn that is constructed on agricultural fairgrounds and is only used for agricultural purposes and animal display. If an exempted pole barn has electrical service, a permit and inspections to determine compliance with the electrical provisions of the Uniform Construction Code are required.

(c) *Continuity of recreational cabin exclusion.*

(1) Upon the transfer of ownership of a recreational cabin subject to the recreational cabin exclusion, written notice of the following shall be provided in the sales agreement and the deed:

(i) The recreational cabin is exempt from the act.

(ii) The recreational cabin may not be in conformance with the Uniform Construction Code.

(iii) The recreational cabin is not subject to municipal regulation.

(2) Failure to comply with the notice requirement under paragraph (1) renders the sale void at the purchaser's option.

(d) *Prior permits and construction.*

(1) A permit issued under construction regulations before April 9, 2004, remains valid and the construction of the building or structure may be completed in accordance with the approved permit. The permit is invalid unless the construction commenced within 2 years of permit issuance or a time period specified by municipal ordinance, whichever is less. The permit holder shall acquire a new permit under section 104(c) of the act (35 P.S. § 7210.104(c)) if the permit was not actively prosecuted during this time period.

(2) Construction may be completed without a permit under section 104(c)(2) of the act when construction of a building or structure commenced before April 9, 2004, and a permit was not required at that time.

(3) The legal occupancy of a structure existing on April 9, 2004, may continue without change except where the Uniform Construction Code provides otherwise.

(e) The Uniform Construction Code applies to the construction of a residential building or structure governed by a homeowner's or community association under section 104(d)(2)(ii) of the act.

(f) The electrical, plumbing and lumber and wood provisions, except for the wood provisions related to pressure treatment, of the Uniform Construction Code do not apply to a dwelling unit or one-room school house utilized by a member or members of a recognized religious sect if a code administrator grants an exemption under section 901(b) of the act (35 P.S. § 7210.901(b)) as follows:

(1) The permit applicant shall file an application with the code administrator stating the manner in which an electrical provision, a plumbing provision or a lumber and wood provision of the Uniform Construction Code conflicts with the applicant's religious beliefs. The application must also contain an affidavit by the applicant stating:

(i) The permit applicant is a member of a religious sect.

(ii) The religious sect has established tenets or teachings which conflict with an electrical, a plumbing or a lumber and wood provision of the Uniform Construction Code.

(iii) The permit applicant adheres to the established tenets or teachings of the sect.

(A) For a dwelling unit, the dwelling will be used solely as a residence for the permit applicant and the applicant's household.

(B) For a one-room school house, the school house will be used solely by members of the religious sect.

(2) The code administrator shall grant the application for the exemption if made in accordance with paragraph (1).

(3) If the permit applicant receives an exemption for a building under section 901(b) of the act and the applicant subsequently sells or leases the building, the applicant shall bring the building into compliance with the provision of the Uniform Construction Code from which it was exempted prior to the sale or lease of the building unless the prospective subsequent owner or lessee files an affidavit in compliance with paragraph (1).

(g) Coal-fired boilers installed in residential buildings must be designed, constructed and tested in accordance with the requirements of Chapter 20, section M2001.1.1 of the ''International Residential Code of 2018,'' except for the ASME stamping requirement.

CROSS REFERENCES

This section cited in 34 Pa. Code § 403.42 (relating to permit requirements and exemptions); and 34 Pa. Code § 403.62 (relating to permit requirements and exemptions); and 34 Pa. Code § 102 (relating to municipalities electing to enforce the Uniform Construction Code).

§ 403.2. Other statutes or ordinances.

(a) Under section 104(d)(1) of the act (35 P. S. § 7210.104(d)(1)), the provisions of the Uniform Construction Code listed in § 403.21 (relating to Uniform Construction Code) preempt and rescind construction standards provided by a statute, local ordinance or regulation. The recission or preemption does not apply to ordinances in effect on July 1, 1999, or reenactments of simultaneously repealed ordinances which were originally adopted before July 1, 1999, which contain provisions which meet or exceed the Uniform Construction Code under section 303(b)(1) of the act (35 P. S. § 7210.303(b)(1)).

(b) Under section 303(a)(2) of the act, a municipal building code ordinance provision in effect in or adopted by a city of the first class on or before January 1, 1998, shall remain in effect until December 31, 2003. The provisions of the ordinance which do not comply with the Uniform Construction Code on December 31, 2003, will be amended to provide for the minimum requirements of the Uniform Construction Code.

§ 403.3. Building code official delegation.

(a) The Department, a municipality or third-party agency shall employ or contract with a building code official to enforce the act.

(b) A building code official may delegate his duties to a construction code official or current code administrator.

STANDARDS

§ 403.21. Uniform Construction Code.

(a) The Department adopts and incorporates by reference the following codes as the Uniform Construction Code:

(1) The provisions of Chapters 2—10, 12—29 and 31—35 of the ''International Building Code of 2018,'' except:

(i) In occupancies in Use Group R-3 and within dwelling units in occupancies in Use Group R-2 the maximum riser height shall be 8 1/4 inches (210 mm) and the minimum tread depth shall be 9 inches (229 mm). A 1-inch (25 mm) nosing shall be provided on stairways with solid risers.

(ii) The following provisions of Chapter 30 are adopted:

(A) Section 3002.1 (relating to hoistway enclosure protection).

(B) Section 3002.2 (relating to number of elevator cars in a hoistway).

(C) Section 3002.4 (relating to elevator car to accommodate ambulance stretcher).

(D) Section 3002.7 (relating to common enclosure with stairway).

(E) Section 3004.2.1 (relating to enclosure).

(F) Section 3004.3.1 (relating to enclosure).

(G) Section 3005.4 (relating to machine rooms, control rooms, machinery spaces, and control spaces).

(H) Section 3006 (relating to elevator lobbies and hoistway opening protection).

(I) Section 3007 (relating to fire service access elevators).

(J) Section 3008 (relating to occupant evacuation elevators).

(iii) Section 803.3 (relating to heavy-timber exemption) is modified to add the phrase: "In buildings equipped throughout with an automatic sprinkler system installed in accordance with section 903.3" before the word exposed.

(iv) The following provisions are excluded:

(A) Section 704.2 (relating to column protection).

(B) Section 704.4.1 (relating to light frame construction).

(v) The following provisions of the "International Building Code of 2015" are adopted:

(A) Section 704.2 (related to column protection).

(B) Section 704.4.1 (relating to light-frame construction).

(2) Chapter 11 of the "International Building Code of 2021."

(3) The "International Mechanical Code of 2018."

(4) The "International Fuel Gas Code of 2018."

(5) The "International Performance Code for Buildings and Facilities of 2018."

(6) The "International Plumbing Code of 2018" except:

(i) A municipality within a county of the second class may not administer and enforce the "International Plumbing Code" adopted under this chapter.

(ii) A municipality within a county of the second class that has adopted a plumbing code and accompanying rules and regulations under the Local Health Administration Law (16 P.S. § § 12001—12028), shall retain the authority to promulgate and enforce this plumbing code and to make any changes it deems necessary if the changes meet the Uniform Construction Code's minimum requirements.

(iii) The accessibility provisions contained in the following sections of the "International Plumbing Code of 2021" are adopted:

(A) Section 403.4 (relating to signage).

(B) Section 403.5 (relating to drinking fountain location).

(C) Section 404 (relating to accessible plumbing facilities).

(D) Section 405.3.1 (relating to water closets, urinals, lavatories and bidets).

(7) The "International Residential Code of 2018," except that:

(i) The provisions of R314.4 requiring interconnected smoke alarms do not apply to one-family and two-family dwellings undergoing alterations, repairs or additions. Noninterconnected battery operated smoke alarms shall be installed in these dwellings.

(ii) The following specifications apply to residential stairway treads and risers.

(A) The maximum riser height is 8 1/4 inches. There may be no more than a 3/8 inch variation in riser height within a flight of stairs. The riser height is to be measured vertically between leading edges of the adjacent treads.

(B) The minimum tread depth is 9 inches measured from tread nosing to tread nosing.

(C) The greatest tread depth within any flight of stairs may not exceed the smallest by more than 3/8 inch.

(D) Treads may have a uniform projection of not more than 1 1/2 inches when solid risers are used.

(E) Stairways may not be less than 3 feet in clear width and clear headroom of 6 feet 8 inches shall be maintained for the entire run of the stair.

(F) Handrails may project from each side of a stairway a distance of 3 1/2 inches into the required width of the stair.

(iii) The following provisions are excluded:

(A) Section R302.5.1 (relating to opening protection).

(B) Section R322.2.1 (relating to elevation requirements for flood hazard areas).

(C) Section R322.3.2 (relating to elevation requirements for coastal high hazard areas).

(D) Exception 2 of section R325.5 (relating to openness).

(E) Section R703.7.1 (relating to lath).

(F) Section R703.7.2 (relating to plaster).

(G) Section R703.7.3 (relating to water-resistive barriers).

(H) Section R806.2 (relating to minimum vent area).

(I) Section R1005.8 (relating to insulation shield).

(J) Section N1101.4 (relating to above code programs).

(K) Section N1103.3.5 (relating to building cavities).

(L) Section N1105.4.2 (relating to compliance report).

(M) Section N1106.3 (relating to energy rating index).

(N) Section N1106.6.1 (relating to compliance software tools).

(O) Section N1106.6.4 (relating to specific approval).

(P) Section N1106.6.5 (relating to input values).

(Q) Section N1108.1.1.2 (relating to heating and cooling systems).

(R) Section N1109.1.2 (relating to heating and cooling systems).

(S) Section M1305.1.3.2 (relating to pit locations).

(T) Section M1502.3.1 (relating to exhaust termination outlet and passageway size).

(U) Section P2503.5.1 (relating to rough plumbing).

(V) Section P2903.5 (relating to water hammer).

(W) Section P2906.6.1 (relating to saddle tap fittings).

(iv) The following provisions are modified:

(A) Section R311.7.4 (relating to walkline) is amended by adding figure R311.7.4 (relating to winder tread and landing detail).

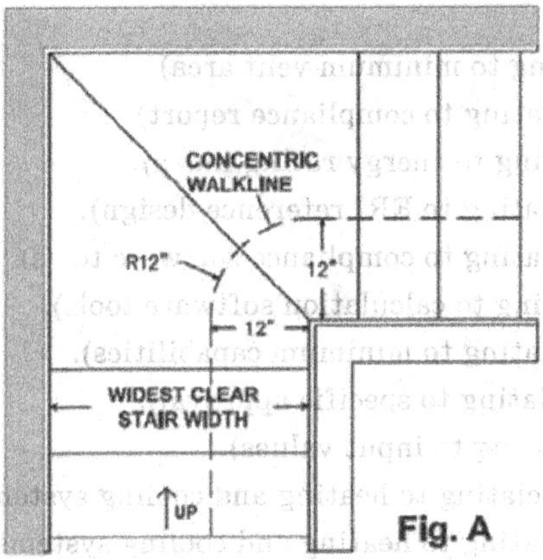

Fig. A

(B) Section R325.6 (relating to habitable attic) is amended by removing subsection 4.

(C) Subsection 2.4 of section R408.3 (relating to unvented crawl space) is amended to read as follows: "Dehumidification sized in accordance with manufacturer's specifications."

(D) Section R702.7.3 (relating to minimum clear airspaces and vented openings for vented cladding) is amended by adding a comma after the word "vinyl" in subsection 1.

(E) Section R703.7 (relating to exterior plaster (stucco)) is amended by requiring compliance with ASTM standards C926-2018B and C1063-2018B.

(F) The last sentence of section R806.1 (relating to ventilation required) is amended to read as follows: "Required ventilation openings shall open directly to the outside air."

(G) The first sentence of section R806.3 (relating to vent and insulation clearance) is amended to read as follows: "Where eave or cornice vents are installed, nothing shall block the free flow of air."

(H) The Fenestration U-Factor in Climate Zone 3 for Table N1102.1.2 (relating to insulation and fenestration requirements by Component) is amended to 0.35.

(I) Section N1105.2 (relating to mandatory requirements) is amended to require compliance with the mandatory provisions of section N1102.4.1.2 (relating to testing).

(J) Section E3901.11 (relating to foyers) is amended by replacing 3 feet (914 mm) with 6 feet (1829 mm) and a minimum of one receptacle.

(v) The following provisions of the International Residential Code of 2009 are adopted:

(A) Section R302.5.1 (relating to opening protection).

(B) Section R322.2.1 (relating to elevation requirements for flood hazard areas).

(C) Section R322.3.2 (relating to elevation requirements for coastal high hazard areas).

(D) Section N1101.8 (relating to above code programs).

(E) Section N1103.2.3 (relating to building cavities).

(F) Section P2503.5.1 (relating to rough plumbing).

(G) [Reserved].

(vi) The following provisions of the ''International Residential Code of 2015'' are adopted:

(A) Section R806.2 (relating to minimum vent area).

(B) Section N1105.4.2 (relating to compliance report).

(C) Section N1106.3 (relating to energy rating index).

(D) Section N1106.3.1 (relating to ERI reference design).

(E) Section N1106.6.1 (relating to compliance software tools).

(F) Section N1106.7 (relating to calculation software tools).

(G) Section N1106.7.1 (relating to minimum capabilities).

(H) Section N1106.7.2 (relating to specific approval).

(I) Section N1106.7.3 (relating to input values).

(J) Section N1108.1.1.2 (relating to heating and cooling systems).

(K) Section N1109.1.2 (relating to heating and cooling systems).

(L) Section M1305.1.4.2 (relating to excavations).

(M) Section P2903.5 (relating to water hammer).

(vii) The following provisions of the ''International Residential Code of 2021'' are adopted:

(A) Section R703.7.1 (relating to lath).

(B) Section R703.7.1.1 (relating to furring).

(C) Section R703.7.2 (relating to plaster).

(D) Section R703.7.3 (relating to water-resistive barriers).

(E) Section R703.7.3.1 (relating to dry climates).

(F) Section R703.7.3.2 (relating moist or marine climates).

(G) Section M1411.6.1 (relating to refrigerant line insulation protection).

(8) The ''International Fire Code of 2018'' to the extent it is referenced by other ICC codes adopted in this chapter.

(9) The ''International Energy Conservation Code of 2018'' except that:

(i) The following provisions are excluded:

(A) Section R102.1.1 (relating to above code programs)

(B) Section C105.2.6 (relating to final inspection).

(C) Section R403.3.5 (relating to building cavities (mandatory)).

(D) Section C402.2.1 (relating to roof assembly).

(E) Section R405.4.2 (relating to compliance report).

(F) Section R406.3 (relating to energy rating index).

(G) Section R406.6.1 (relating to compliance software tools).

(H) Section R406.6.4 (relating to specific approval).

(I) Section R406.6.5 (relating to input values).

(J) Section R502.1.1.2 (relating to heating and cooling systems).

(K) Section R503.1.2 (relating to heating and cooling systems).

(ii) The following provisions are modified:

(A) Chapter RE 2 is amended by adding the definition of "framing factor" as the fraction of the total building component area that is structural framing.

(B) Table R402.1.2 (relating to insulation and fenestration requirements by component) is amended by modifying the Fenestration U-Factor in Climate Zone 3 to 0.35.

(C) Section R405.2 (relating to mandatory requirements) is amended to require compliance with the mandatory provisions of section R402.4.1.2 (relating to testing).

(D) [Reserved].

(E) [Reserved].

(iii) The following provisions of the "International Energy Conservation Code of 2009" are adopted:

(A) Section 102.1.1 (relating to above code programs).

(B) Section 104.3 (relating to final inspection).

(C) Section 403.2.3 (relating to building cavities).

(iv) The following provisions of the "International Energy Conservation Code of 2015" are adopted:

(A) Section C402.2.2 (relating to roof assembly).

(B) Exception 1 of section C402.5.3 (relating to rooms containing fuel-burning appliances).

(C) Section R405.4.2 (relating to compliance report).

(D) Section R406.3 (relating to energy rating index).

(E) Section R406.3.1 (relating to ERI reference design).

(F) Section R406.6.1 (relating to compliance software tools).

(G) Section R406.7 (relating to calculation software tools).

(H) Section R406.7.1 (relating to minimum capabilities).

(I) Section R406.7.2 (relating to specific approval).

(J) Section R406.7.3 (relating to input values).

(K) Section R502.1.1.2 (relating to heating and cooling systems).

(L) Section R503.1.2 (relating to heating and cooling systems).

(10) The "International Existing Building Code of 2018" except:

(i) The accessibility provisions contained in the following sections of the "International Existing Building Code of 2021" are adopted:

(A) Section 301.5 (relating to compliance with accessibility).

(B) Section 305 (relating to accessibility for existing buildings).

(C) Section 1101.2 (relating to creation or extension of nonconformity).

(D) Appendix B (relating to supplementary accessibility requirements for existing buildings and facilities).

(ii) Section 1106 (relating to storm shelters) is excluded.

(iii) The second sentence in section 106.2.5 is modified to read as follows: "The manufacturer's installation instructions shall be available to the code official during inspection as a deferred submittal."

(11) The "International Wildland-Urban Interface Code of 2018."

(12) Appendix E of the "International Building Code of 2021."

(13) Appendix H of the "International Building Code of 2009."

(14) The "International Swimming Pool and Spa Code of 2018."

(b) The code adopted under subsection (a)(8) is part of the Uniform Construction Code to the extent that it is referenced in Chapter 35 of the "International Building Code of 2018" under section 302(a)(1) of the act (35 P.S. § 7210.302(a)(1)). The provisions of the Uniform Construction Code apply if there is a difference between the Uniform Construction Code and the codes or standards adopted in subsection (a). This chapter's administrative provisions govern under § 403.27(e) (relating to applicability and use of standards) if there is a conflict with the provisions of the codes relating to administration incorporated under subsection (a).

(c) Appendices to a code or standard listed in subsection (a) are not adopted in the Uniform Construction Code except for the appendices and resource information found in the "International Existing Building Code of 2018" and the appendices found in subsection (a)(12) and (13).

(d) A permit applicant may utilize one of the following prescriptive methods to demonstrate compliance with the energy conservation requirements of the Uniform Construction Code. The standards are those listed for the climatic zone of this Commonwealth where the building or structure is located:

(1) The prescriptive methods for detached residential buildings contained in the "International Energy Conservation Code of 2018" compliance guide containing State maps, prescriptive energy packages and related software published by the United States Department of Energy, Building Standards and Guidelines Program (REScheckTM) or "Pennsylvania's Alternative Residential Energy Provisions."

(2) The prescriptive methods for all other buildings or structures contained in the "International Energy Conservation Code of 2018" compliance guide containing State maps, prescriptive packages and related software published by the United States Department of Energy, Building Standards and Guidelines Program (COMcheckTM).

(e) Construction of individual sewage disposal systems is governed under 25 Pa. Code Chapter 73 (relating to standards for onlot sewage treatment facilities).

(f) The repair, alteration, change of occupancy, addition and relocation of existing buildings must comply with Chapter 34 of the "International Building Code of 2018" or with the "International Existing Building Code of 2018."

CROSS REFERENCES

This section cited in 34 Pa. Code § 403.2 (relating to other statutes or ordinances); 34 Pa. Code § 403.27 (relating to applicability and use of standards); 34 Pa. Code § 403.44 (relating to alternative construction materials and methods); and 34 Pa. Code § 403.102 (relating to municipalities electing to enforce the Uniform Construction Code).

§ 403.22. Health care facilities.

(a) A health care facility shall comply with all of the following under sections 104(d)(3) and 105(d)(1) of the act (35 P. S. §§ 7210.104(d)(3) and 7210.105(d)(1)):

(1) The Health Care Facilities Act.

(2) Regulations of the Department of Health in 28 Pa. Code Part IV (relating to health facilities).

(3) Building codes and regulations set forth in the applicable licensure laws and regulations under section 105(d) of the act (35 P. S. § 7210.105(d)).

(4) This chapter.

(b) Chapter 405 (relating to elevators and other lifting devices) always applies to health care facilities.

(c) In addition to the requirements of this chapter, a permit applicant for a health care facility shall obtain a license from the Department of Health under the Health Care Facilities Act and its regulations and comply with the Department of Health's license application procedures and its licensing regulations.

(d) A permit applicant for construction or alteration of a health care facility shall do all of the following:

(1) Submit construction or alteration plans to the Department of Health and obtain Department of Health approval before commencing construction or performing the alteration.

(2) Obtain approval from the Department of Health before occupancy of a new health care facility under 28 Pa. Code § 51.5 (relating to building occupancy).

(3) Obtain approval from the Department of Health before occupancy of an altered portion of an existing health care facility.

(e) A Department of Health inspector may inspect a health care facility site before, during and after construction to monitor compliance with Department of Health's health facility regulations.

(f) A building code official may not approve plans for a health care facility under this chapter unless the Department of Health has approved the plans.

(g) A building code official may not issue a certificate of occupancy for the health care facility under this chapter unless the Department of Health approved occupancy under 28 Pa. Code § 51.5.

(h) This section applies to construction or alteration of all health care facilities that the Department or a building code official review and approve under this chapter.

§ 403.23. Child day care facilities.

(a) A dwelling unit where child day care services are provided for less than 24 hours for 4 to 12 children is an R-3 occupancy if the dwelling unit is used primarily as a private residence and the provision of day care services is accessory to the principal use of the dwelling unit as a residence.

(b) A day care facility that is an R-3 occupancy under subsection (a) which provides day care services to 4—6 children shall comply with all of the following:

(1) Have a smoke detector on each floor and in the basement. The smoke detector may be powered by a nonreplacable, lithium battery listed by Underwriters Laboratories® that is warranted for 10 years and should sound an alarm when activated that is audible to persons in the unit's indoor child care space with all intervening doors closed. Where this type of detector is utilized, the unit owner of this detector shall keep the proof and date of purchase of the detector in the unit's fire drill logs.

(2) Have a portable fire extinguisher rated for Class B Fires in the kitchen and other cooking areas.

(3) Meet the exiting requirements for an R-3 occupancy and licensure under 55 Pa. Code Chapter 3290 (relating to family child day care homes).

(c) A day care facility that is an R-3 occupancy under subsection (a) which provides day care services to 7—12 children shall comply with all of the following:

(1) Have an interconnected smoke detector system.

Table of Contents | Part I Ch. 1–3 Ethics, Records, Open Meetings | Part II Ch. 4–10 Taxation | Part III Ch. 11–18 Torts, Contracts & Civil Rules | Part IV Ch. 19–24 Zoning & Planning | Part V Ch. 25–30 Construction and Emergency Codes | Part VI Ch. 31–39 Municipal Codes | Index

(2) Have a fire extinguisher rated for Class B fires in the kitchen and other cooking areas.

(3) Meet the exiting requirements for an R-3 occupancy and licensure under 55 Pa. Code Chapter 3280 (relating to group child day care homes).

(d) All other child day care facilities shall be classified under Chapter 3 of the "International Building Code of 2018." The facilities shall meet all Uniform Construction Code standards for these occupancy classifications.

§ 403.24. Historic buildings, structures and sites.

A building code official may exclude an entire historic building or structure or part of the building or structure from compliance with the Uniform Construction Code if it meets all of the following conditions under section 902 of the act (35 P. S. § 7210.902):

(1) The building or structure is an existing building or structure, or a new building or structure that is not intended for residential use on an historic site.

(2) The building or structure is identified and classified by Federal or local government authority or the Historical and Museum Commission as an historic building or site.

(3) A building code official judges the building or structure or parts of the building and structure as safe and the exclusion is in the interest of public health, safety or welfare. The building code official shall apply the Uniform Construction Code to parts of the building or structure where its exclusion is not within the interest of the public health, safety and welfare. A building code official may not waive the Uniform Construction Code's accessibility requirements under this section.

§ 403.25. Manufactured and industrialized housing.

(a) Manufactured housing is governed by the following under section 901(a) of the act (35 P. S. § 7210.901(a)):

(1) Except as provided in paragraph (2), the Uniform Construction Code does not apply to new manufactured housing assembled by and shipped from the manufacturer and which bears a label which certifies that it conforms to Federal construction and safety standards adopted under the Housing and Community Development Act of 1974 (42 U.S.C.A. §§ 5401–5426) and installation of new manufactured housing in conformity with the manufacturer's approved design applicable to the particular home.

(2) Construction activities or processes including utility connections and grading not addressed by the manufacturer's approved design must comply with the Uniform Construction Code.

(3) The Uniform Construction Code applies to the following:

(i) Alteration or repair to the unit that does not fall within 24 CFR 3280.1–3280.904 (relating to manufactured home construction and safety standards) and the manufacturer's installation instructions after assembly and shipment by the manufacturer.

(ii) Additions to the unit after delivery to the site.

(iii) Construction, alteration, repair or change of occupancy if the manufactured housing is resold to a subsequent purchaser.

(iv) Construction, alteration, repair or change of occupancy if the original purchaser relocates the manufactured housing.

(b) Industrialized housing is governed by the following under section 901(a) of the act:

(1) Except as provided in subsection (b)(2), the Uniform Construction Code does not apply to industrialized housing assembled by and shipped from the manufacturer.

(2) The Uniform Construction Code applies to all of the following:

(i) Site preparation.

(ii) Foundation construction.

(iii) Utilities connection.

(iv) Construction, alteration or repair to the industrialized housing unit after installation.

(v) Construction, alteration, repair or occupancy if industrialized housing is resold to a subsequent purchaser.

(vi) Construction, alteration, repair or occupancy if industrialized housing is relocated.

(c) The Department of Community and Economic Development may enforce and take action under the Industrialized Housing Act (35 P. S. §§ 1651.1–1651.12) and the Manufactured Housing Construction and Safety Standards Authorization Act (35 P. S. §§ 1656.1–1656.9).

§ 403.26. Swimming pools.

(a) A swimming pool, hot tub and spa which is accessory to a one-family or two-family dwelling must comply with the "International Swimming Pool and Spa Code of 2018."

(b) A swimming pool, hot tub or spa that is not accessory to a one-family or two-family dwelling must comply with the Public Bathing Law (35 P.S. § § 672—680d) and the "International Swimming Pool and Spa Code of 2018." The accessibility provisions contained in section 307.1.4 (relating to general design requirements) of the "International Swimming Pool and Spa Code of 2021" are adopted.

§ 403.27. Applicability and use of standards.

(a) Portions of this chapter designate and incorporate portions of the following ICC copyrighted works:

(1) The "International Building Code of 2018."

(2) The "International Residential Code of 2018."

(3) The "International Plumbing Code of 2018."

(4) The "International Mechanical Code of 2018."

(b) The "International Residential Code of 2018" and the "International Existing Building Code of 2018" apply to the construction, alteration, movement, enlargement, replacement, repair, equipment, use and occupancy, location, removal and demolition of detached one-family and two-family dwellings and multiple single-family dwellings no more than three stories in height with a separate means of egress and their accessory structures.

(c) The ICC owns the copyrighted works in subsection (a). Reproduced with permission. All rights reserved.

(d) If different sections of this chapter specify different materials, method of construction or other requirements, the most restrictive material, method of construction or other requirement shall govern. The specific requirement of this part applies if there is a conflict between a general requirement and a specific requirement.

(e) This chapter governs if there is a conflict between this chapter and the provisions of the codes relating to administration incorporated under § 403.21(a) (relating to Uniform Construction Code).

(f) A provision of the "International Mechanical Code of 2018" does not apply if the provision conflicts with the Boiler and Unfired Pressure Vessel Law (35 P.S. § § 1331.1—1331.18).

CROSS REFERENCES

This section cited in 34 Pa. Code § 403.21 (relating to Uniform Construction Code).

§ 403.28. Uncertified buildings.

(a) Under section 902(b)(6) of the act (35 P.S. § 7210.902(b)(6)), an uncertified building that was built before April 27, 1927, is deemed to be legally occupied until the owner proposes to renovate, add an addition, alter or change the occupancy of the building. The renovation, addition, alteration or change in occupancy must comply with the Uniform Construction Code.

(b) Under section 902(b) of the act, uncertified buildings within the Department's jurisdiction must meet the following requirements which do not apply to uncertified buildings under subsection (a):

(1) Maximum story height, minimum allowable construction type based on floor area, vertical opening and shaft protection requirements, means of egress requirements pertaining to minimum number of exits, maximum travel distances to exits, means of egress illumination, minimum egress widths and heights for exit doors, exit stairs, exit ramps and exit corridors requirements under the "International Building Code of 2018."

(2) Fire safety requirements in the "International Building Code of 2018" for fire alarms, fire extinguishers, heat and smoke detectors, automatic sprinkler systems and occupancy and incidental use separations. The following also apply:

(i) If construction began on a building before May 19, 1984, the installation of automatic sprinkler systems is not required.

(ii) If construction began on a building after May 19, 1984, automatic sprinklers are only required if the building is classified in use groups E (educational), H (high-hazard), I (institutional), or R-1 or R-2 (residential) or if the building has occupied floors more than 75 feet above lowest level of fire department access. Buildings in use groups R-1 and R-2 which do not have occupied floors more than 75 feet above lowest level of fire department access may, instead of installing automatic sprinkler systems, install hard-wired interconnected heat and smoke detectors in all rooms or spaces, whether they are occupied or unoccupied.

(iii) If construction of a building began after May 18, 1984, automatic sprinkler installation shall be completed by December 22, 2010, or any certificate of occupancy issued shall be invalid.

(3) Accessibility requirements are applicable as follows:

(i) If construction of an uncertified building began before September 1, 1965, accessibility requirements will not be imposed by the Department.

(ii) If construction of a building began after August 31, 1965, and before February 18, 1989, and if the building is a State-owned building, a restaurant or a retail commercial establishment, the building must have at least one accessible main entrance, an accessible route from the accessible entrance to any public spaces on the same level as the accessible entrance and, if toilet rooms are provided, the building must have at least one toilet room for each sex or a unisex toilet room complying with the accessibility requirements of the "International Building Code of 2021."

(iii) If construction of the building began after February 17, 1989, all accessibility requirements of the "International Building Code of 2018" shall be met.

(4) Structural requirements will not be imposed unless the Department determines that the building or a portion of the building has defects that are defined as dangerous in section 202 of the "International Existing Building Code of 2018." If the building is dangerous, the Department may impose only those requirements minimally necessary to remove danger to the building's occupants.

(5) A construction code official may deny the issuance of a certificate of occupancy if the official deems that a building is unsafe because of inadequate means of egress, inadequate lighting and ventilation, fire hazards or other dangers to human life or to public welfare.

(c) The following apply to uncertified buildings where the Department does not have jurisdiction and which are not governed under subsection (a):

(1) A construction code official shall issue a certificate of occupancy to an uncertified building if it meets the requirements of the latest version of the "International Existing Building Code of 2018" or Chapter 34 of the "International Building Code of 2018." The construction code official shall utilize the code for the municipality which best applies, in the official's professional judgment.

(2) A construction code official may deny the issuance of a certificate of occupancy if the official deems that a building is unsafe because of inadequate means of egress, inadequate lighting and ventilation, fire hazards or other dangers to human life or to public welfare.

(3) A municipality governed under this subsection may utilize the standards of subsection (b) for the issuance of certificates of occupancy to uncertified buildings if the municipality adopts an ordinance.

PERMIT AND INSPECTION PROCESS FOR COMMERCIAL CONSTRUCTION

§ 403.41. Commercial construction.

This section and §§ 403.42–403.48 apply to the Department and municipalities electing to enforce the Uniform Construction Code under § 403.102 (relating to municipalities electing to enforce the Uniform Construction Code).

§ 403.42. Permit requirements and exemptions.

(a) An owner or authorized agent who intends to construct, enlarge, alter, repair, move, demolish or change the occupancy of a commercial building, structure and facility or to erect, install, enlarge, alter, repair, remove, convert or replace any electrical, gas, mechanical, or plumbing system regulated by the Uniform Construction Code shall first apply to the building code official and obtain the required permit under § 403.42a (relating to permit application).

(b) Emergency repairs or replacement of equipment may be made without first applying for a permit if a permit application is submitted to the building code official within 3 business days of the repair or replacement.

(c) A permit is not required for the exceptions listed in § 403.1(b) (relating to scope) and the following construction as long as the work does not violate a law or ordinance:

Table of Contents | Part I Ch. 1–3 Ethics, Records, Open Meetings | Part II Ch. 4–10 Taxation | Part III Ch. 11–18 Torts, Contracts & Civil Rules | Part IV Ch. 19–24 Zoning & Planning | Part V Ch. 25–30 Construction and Emergency Codes | Part VI Ch. 31–39 Municipal Codes | Index

(1) Building construction for the following:

(i) Fences that are not over 6 feet high.

(ii) Oil derricks.

(iii) Retaining walls, which are not over 4 feet in height measured from the lowest level of grade to the top of the wall, unless it is supporting a surcharge or impounding Class I, II or III-A liquids.

(iv) Water tanks supported directly upon grade if the capacity does not exceed 5,000 gallons and the ratio of height to diameter or width does not exceed 2 to 1.

(v) Sidewalks and driveways not more than 30 inches above grade and that are not located over a basement or story below it and which are not part of an accessible route.

(vi) Painting, papering, tiling, carpeting, cabinets, counter tops and similar finishing work.

(vii) Temporary motion picture, television, and theater stage sets and scenery.

(viii) Prefabricated swimming pools accessory to a Group R-3 occupancy which are less than 24 inches deep, do not exceed 5,000 gallons and are installed entirely aboveground.

(ix) Shade cloth structures constructed for nursery or agricultural purposes that do not include service systems.

(x) Swings and other playground equipment accessory to one- or two-family dwellings.

(xi) Window awnings supported by an exterior wall which do not project more than 54 inches from the exterior wall and do not require additional support of group R-3 as applicable in the "International Building Code of 2018," and Group U occupancies.

(xii) Movable cases, counters and partitions that are not over 5 feet 9 inches in height.

(xiii) Window replacement without structural change.

(2) Electrical work for the following:

(i) Minor repair and maintenance work that includes the replacement of lamps or the connection of approved portable electrical equipment to approved permanently installed receptacles.

(ii) Electrical equipment used for radio and television transmissions. The provisions of the Uniform Construction Code apply to equipment and wiring for power supply and the installation of towers and antennas.

(iii) The installation of a temporary system for the testing or servicing of electrical equipment or apparatus.

(3) The following gas work:

(i) A portable heating appliance.

(ii) Replacement of a minor part that does not alter approval of equipment or make the equipment unsafe.

(4) The following mechanical work or equipment:

(i) A portable heating appliance.

(ii) Portable ventilation equipment.

(iii) A portable cooling unit.

(iv) Steam, hot or chilled water piping within any heating or cooling equipment governed under the Uniform Construction Code.

(v) Replacement of any part that does not alter its approval or make it unsafe.

(vi) A portable evaporative cooler.

(vii) A self-contained refrigeration system containing 10 pounds or less of refrigerant and placed into action by motors that are not more than 1 horsepower.

(5) The following plumbing repairs:

(i) Stopping leaks in a drain and a water, soil, waste or vent pipe. The Uniform Construction Code applies if a concealed trap, drainpipe, water, soil, waste or vent pipe becomes defective and is removed and replaced with new material.

(ii) Clearing stoppages or repairing leaks in pipes, valves or fixtures, and the removal and installation of water closets, faucets and lavatories if the valves or pipes are not replaced or rearranged.

(d) An ordinary repair does not require a permit. The following are not ordinary repairs:

(1) Cutting away a wall, partition or portion of a wall.

(2) The removal or cutting of any structural beam or load-bearing support.

(3) The removal or change of any required means of egress, or rearrangement of parts of a structure affecting the egress requirements.

(4) The addition to, alteration of, replacement or relocation of any standpipe, water supply, sewer, drainage, drain leader, gas, soil, waste, vent or similar piping, electric wiring or mechanical.

(e) A permit is not required for the installation, alteration or repair of generation, transmission, distribution, metering or other related equipment under the ownership and control of public service agencies.

(f) A building code official may issue an annual permit instead of an individual permit for each alteration to an already approved electrical, gas, mechanical or plumbing installation. All of the following are required:

(1) The applicant shall regularly employ at least one qualified trades person in the building or structure owned or operated by the applicant.

(2) The applicant shall submit an application in accordance with § 403.42a(m).

(3) An annual permit holder shall keep detailed records of alterations made in accordance with the annual permit. The permit holder shall provide access to these records to the building code official.

CROSS REFERENCES

This section cited in 34 Pa. Code § 403.41 (relatiing to commercial construction); 34 Pa. Code § 403.42a (relating to permit application); and 34 Pa. Code § 403.102 (relating to municipalities electing to enforce the Uniform Construction Code).

§ 403.42a. Permit application.

(a) Applications for a permit required under § 403.42 (relating to permit requirements and exemptions) shall be submitted to the building code official in accordance with this section.

(b) A permit applicant shall submit an application to the building code official and attach construction documents, including plans and specifications, and information concerning special inspection and structural observation programs, Department of Transportation highway access permits, all other permits or approvals related to the construction required under § 403.102(n) (relating to municipalities electing to enforce the Uniform Construction Code) and other data required by the building code official with the permit application. The applicant shall submit three sets of documents when the Department conducts the review.

(c) A licensed architect or licensed professional engineer shall prepare the construction documents under the Architects Licensure Law (63 P. S. § § 34.1—34.22), or the Engineer, Land Surveyor and Geologist Registration Law (63 P. S. § § 148—158.2). An unlicensed person may prepare design documents for the remodeling or alteration of a building if there is no compensation and the remodeling or alteration does not relate to additions to the building or changes to the building's structure or means of egress.

(d) A building code official may require submission of additional construction documents in special circumstances.

(e) The permit applicant shall submit construction documents in a format approved by the building code official. Construction documents shall be clear, indicate the location, nature and extent of the work proposed, and show in detail that the work will conform to the Uniform Construction Code.

(f) All of the following fire egress and occupancy requirements apply to construction documents:

(1) The permit applicant shall submit construction documents that show in sufficient detail the location, construction, size and character of all portions of the means of egress in compliance with the Uniform Construction Code.

(2) The construction documents for occupancies other than Groups R-2 and R-3 shall contain designation of the number of occupants to be accommodated on every floor and in all rooms and spaces.

(3) The permit applicant shall submit shop drawings for a fire protection system that indicates conformance with the Uniform Construction Code in accordance with the following:

(i) The shop drawings shall be approved by the building code official before the start of the system installation.

(ii) The shop drawings must contain the information required by the referenced installation standards contained in Chapter 9 of the "International Building Code of 2018."

(g) Construction documents shall contain the following information related to the exterior wall envelope:

(1) Description of the exterior wall envelope indicating compliance with the Uniform Construction Code.

(2) Flashing details.

(3) Details relating to intersections with dissimilar materials, corners, end details, control joints, intersections at roof, eaves, or parapets, means of drainage, water-resistive membrane and details around openings.

(h) Construction documents shall contain a site plan that is drawn to scale. The building code official may waive or modify the following site plan requirements if the permit application is for an alteration or repair or if waiver or modification is warranted. Site plan requirements include all of the following:

(1) The size and location of new construction and existing structures on the site.

(2) Accurate boundary lines.

(3) Distances from lot lines.

(4) The established street grades and the proposed finished grades.

(5) If the construction involves demolition, the site plan shall indicate construction that is to be demolished and the size and location of existing structures and construction that will remain on the site or plot.

(6) Location of parking spaces, accessible routes, public transportation stops and other required accessibility features.

(i) A permit applicant shall submit certifications required in the "International Building Code of 2018" for construction in a flood hazard area to the building code official.

(j) A permit applicant shall identify, on the application, the name and address of the licensed architect or engineer in responsible charge. The permit applicant shall notify the building code official in writing if another licensed architect or engineer assumes responsible charge.

(k) The permit applicant shall describe an inspection program, identify a person or firm who will perform special inspections and structural observations if section 1704 and 1705 of the "International Building Code of 2018" requires special inspections or structural observations for the construction.

(l) A building code official may waive or modify the submission of construction documents, that are not required to be prepared by a licensed architect or engineer, or other data if the nature of the work applied for does not require review of construction documents or other data to obtain compliance with the Uniform Construction Code. The building code official may not waive the submission of site plans that relate to accessibility requirements.

(m) An applicant for an annual permit under § 403.42(f) shall complete an application and provide information regarding the system that may be altered and the date that approval was previously provided for the approved electrical, gas, mechanical or plumbing installation.

(n) A permit applicant shall comply with the permit, certification or licensure requirements of the following laws applicable to the construction:

(1) The Boiler and Unfired Pressure Vessel Law (35 P. S. § § 1331.1—1331.19).

(2) The Propane and Liquefied Petroleum Gas Act (35 P. S. § § 1329.1—1329.19).

(3) The Health Care Facilities Act.

(4) The Older Adult Daily Living Centers Licensing Act (62 P. S. § § 1511.1—1511.22).

§ 403.43. Grant, denial and effect of permits.

(a) A building code official shall grant or deny a permit application, in whole or in part, within 30 business days of the filing date. Reasons for the denial shall be in writing and sent to the applicant. The building code official and the permit applicant may agree in writing to extend the deadline by a specific number of days. A building code official may establish a different deadline to consider applications for a permit in an historic district.

(b) A building code official shall examine the construction documents and shall determine whether the construction indicated and described is in accordance with the Uniform Construction Code and other pertinent laws or ordinances as part of the application process.

(c) A building code official shall stamp or place a notation on each page of the set of reviewed construction documents that the documents were reviewed and approved for Uniform Construction Code compliance before the permit is issued. The building code official shall clearly mark any required nondesign changes on the construction documents. The building code official shall return a set of the

construction documents with this notation and any required changes to the applicant. The permit holder shall keep a copy of the construction documents at the work site open to inspection by the construction code official or an authorized representative.

(d) A building code official may not issue a permit for any property requiring access to a highway under the Department of Transportation's jurisdiction unless the permit contains notice that a highway occupancy permit is required under section 420 of the State Highway Law (36 P. S. § 670-420) before driveway access to a Commonwealth highway is permitted.

(e) A building code official may issue a permit for the construction of the foundations or other parts of a building or structure before the construction documents for the whole building or structure are submitted if the permit applicant previously filed adequate information and detailed statements for the building or structure under the Uniform Construction Code. Approval under this section is not assurance that the building code official will issue a permit for the entire building or structure.

(f) Issuance of a permit does not bar prosecution or other legal action for violations of the act, the Uniform Construction Code or a construction ordinance. A building code official may suspend or revoke a permit issued under the Uniform Construction Code when the permit holder does not make the required changes directed by the building code official under subsection (c), when the permit is issued in error, on the basis of inaccurate or incomplete information or in violation of any act, regulation, ordinance or the Uniform Construction Code.

(g) A permit becomes invalid unless the authorized construction work begins within 180 days after the permit's issuance or if the authorized construction work permit is suspended or abandoned for 180 days after the work has commenced. A permit holder may submit a written request for an extension of time to commence construction for just cause. The building code official may grant extensions of time to commence construction in writing. A permit may be valid for no more than 5 years from its issue date.

(h) The permit holder shall keep a copy of the permit on the work site until the completion of the construction.

(i) A permit applicant may request extensions of time or variances or appeal a building code official's action on the permit application to a board of appeals under § 403.122 (relating to appeals, variances and extensions of time).

(j) A board of appeals may not rule on requests for extensions of time, variances or appeals relating to this chapter's accessibility requirements. The Secretary has the exclusive power to grant modifications and extensions of time and decide issues of technical infeasibility under § 403.142 (relating to Accessibility Advisory Board)

(k) A building code official may allow deferred submittals of portions of the design of the building and structure from the time of the application until a specified time set by the building code official. All of the following apply to deferred submittals:

(1) The building code official shall provide prior approval of the deferral of any submittal items.

(2) A licensed architect or professional engineer in responsible charge shall list the deferred submittals on the construction documents for review by the building code official.

(3) A licensed architect or professional engineer shall first review submittal documents for deferred submittal items and place a notation on the documents

that the architect or engineer reviewed the documents and that the documents are in general conformance with the design of the building or structure.

(4) Deferred submittal items may not be installed until the building code official approves the design and submittal documents for the deferred submittal items.

(l) Work shall be installed in accordance with the approved construction documents. The permit holder shall submit a revised set of construction documents for approval for changes made during construction that are not in accordance with the approved construction documents.

(m) A permit is not valid until the required fees are collected under §§ 401.2 and 401.2a (relating to Department fees; and municipal and third-party agency fees).

CROSS REFERENCES

This section cited in 34 Pa. Code § 403.102 (relating to municipalities electing to enforce the Uniform Construction Code).

§ 403.44. Alternative construction materials and methods.

(a) Materials, products and methods of construction that were evaluated as meeting codes enumerated in § 403.21 (relating to Uniform Construction Code) by the ICC Evaluation Service, Inc. or an evaluation service accredited under the ''General Requirements for Bodies Operating Product Certification Systems'' issued by the ISO (ISO Guide 65) are approved for use. The use shall conform with the evaluation.

(b) Materials, equipment and devices bearing the label or listed by a testing laboratory or quality assurance agency accredited by the International Accreditation Service, Inc. or another agency accredited under the ''Calibration and Testing Laboratory Accreditation Systems-General Requirements for Operation and Recognition'' issued by ISO (ISO Guide 58) are approved for use if:

(1) The testing laboratory or quality assurance agency deemed the material as meeting Uniform Construction Code-required standards.

(2) The scope of accreditation is applicable to Uniform Construction Code-required standards.

(c) A new building or remodeling, alteration, addition or change of use and occupancy of an existing building which complies with the ''International Performance Code of 2018'' shall also be in compliance with the Uniform Construction Code.

CROSS REFERENCES

This section cited in 34 Pa. Code § 403.41 (relating to commercial construction); and 34 Pa. Code § 403.102 (relating to municipalities electing to enforce the Uniform Construction Code).

§ 403.45. Inspections.

(a) A construction code official shall perform inspections to insure that the construction complies with the approved permit and the Uniform Construction Code.

(b) Before issuing a permit, a building code official may examine, or cause to be examined, buildings, structures, facilities or sites related to the permit application.

(c) The permit holder or an authorized agent shall notify the construction code official when work is ready for inspection and provide access for the inspec-

Table of Contents
Part I Ch. 1–3 Ethics, Records, Open Meetings
Part II Ch. 4–10 Taxation
Part III Ch. 11–18 Torts, Contracts & Civil Rules
Part IV Ch. 19–24 Zoning & Planning
Part V Ch. 25–30 Construction and Emergency Codes
Part VI Ch. 31–39 Municipal Codes
Index

tion. The work shall remain accessible and exposed for inspection. A construction code official may inspect the construction and equipment only during normal hours at the construction site unless the permit holder or agent requests or agrees to another time. Inspections may be conducted under § 403.86 (relating to right of entry to inspect).

(d) A construction code official shall notify a permit holder if construction complies with the Uniform Construction Code or fails to comply with the Uniform Construction Code.

(e) A construction code official shall conduct a final inspection of the completed construction work and file a final inspection report, which indicates that all of the following areas met Uniform Construction Code requirements after a final inspection of the completed construction work:

(1) General building under § 401.7(6) (relating to certification category specification).

(2) Electrical under § 401.7(7).

(3) Plumbing under § 401.7(9).

(4) Accessibility under § 401.7(11).

(5) Fire protection under § 401.7(6).

(6) Mechanical under § 401.7(8).

(7) Energy conservation under § 401.7(10)

(f) A code administrator may act in place of a lumber grading or inspection agency to satisfy the requirements under section 2303.1.1 of the ''International Building Code of 2018'' or its successor code.

CROSS REFERENCES

This section cited in 34 Pa. Code § 403.102 (relating to municipalities electing to enforce the Uniform Construction Code).

§ 403.46. Certificate of occupancy.

(a) A building, structure or facility may not be used or occupied without a certificate of occupancy issued by a building code official.

(b) A building code official shall issue a certificate of occupancy within 5 business days after receipt of a final inspection report that indicates compliance with the Uniform Construction Code. The certificate of occupancy shall contain the following information:

(1) The permit number and address of the building, structure or facility.

(2) The permit holder's name and address.

(3) A description of the portion of the building, structure or facility covered by the occupancy permit.

(4) The name of the building code official who issued the occupancy permit.

(5) The applicable construction code edition applicable to the occupancy permit.

(6) The use and occupancy classification under Chapter 3 (Use and Occupancy Classification) of the ''International Building Code of 2018,'' when designated.

(7) The type of construction defined in Chapter 6 (Types of Construction) of the ''International Building Code of 2018,'' when designated.

(8) Special stipulations and conditions relating to the permit and board of appeals' decisions and variances for accessibility requirements granted by the Secretary.

(9) The date of the final inspection.

(c) A building code official may issue a certificate of occupancy for a portion of a building, structure or facility if the portion independently meets the Uniform Construction Code.

(d) A building code official may suspend or revoke a certificate of occupancy when the certificate was issued in error, on the basis of incorrect information supplied by the permit applicant or in violation of the Uniform Construction Code. Before a certificate of occupancy is revoked, a building owner may request a hearing before the board of appeals under § 403.122 (relating to appeals, variances and extensions of time).

(e) A building code official may issue a temporary certificate of occupancy for a portion or portions of the building or structure before the completion of the entire work covered by the permit if the portion or portions may be occupied safely. The building code official shall set a time period during which the temporary certificate of occupancy is valid.

CROSS REFERENCES

This section cited in 34 Pa. Code § 403.102 (relating to municipalities electing to enforce the Uniform Construction Code).

§ 403.47. Public utility connections.

(a) A building code official may authorize the temporary connection of a building or system under construction to a utility source of energy, fuel or power.

(b) Connection to a public electric or gas utility for the completed construction may not occur unless the permit holder provides written proof to the utility company that the building or structure passed inspections under this chapter.

CROSS REFERENCES

This section cited in 34 Pa. Code § 403.102 (relating to municipalities electing not to enforce the Uniform Construction Code).

§ 403.48. Boilers.

(a) The Boiler and Unfired Pressure Law (35 P. S. §§ 1331.1–1331.19) and Chapter 3 (relating to boilers and unfired pressure vessels) govern the new installation, repair or replacement of a boiler or other pressure vessel.

(b) A permit under this chapter is not required for the installation, repair or replacement of a boiler or unfired pressure vessel under subsection (a). The building or structure containing the boiler or unfired pressure vessel shall comply with the Uniform Construction Code or the regulation or ordinance in effect at the time of its legal occupancy.

PERMIT AND INSPECTION PROCESS FOR RESIDENTIAL BUILDINGS

§ 403.61. Residential buildings.

This subchapter and §§ 403.62–403.66 apply to municipalities electing to enforce the Uniform Construction Code under § 403.102 (relating to municipalities electing to enforce the Uniform Construction Code) and third-party agencies.

CROSS REFERENCES

This section cited in 34 Pa. Code § 403.103 (relating to municipalities electing not to enforce the Uniform Construction Code).

§ 403.62. Permit requirements and exemptions.

(a) An owner or authorized agent who intends to construct, enlarge, alter, repair, move, demolish or change the occupancy of a residential building or erect, install, enlarge, alter, repair, remove, convert or replace an electrical, gas, mechanical or plumbing system regulated by the Uniform Construction Code shall first apply to the building code official and obtain the required permit under § 403.62a (relating to permit application).

(b) An emergency repair or replacement of equipment may be made without first applying for a permit if a permit application is submitted to the building code official within 3 business days of the repair or replacement.

(c) A permit is not required for the exceptions listed in § 403.1(b) (relating to scope) and the following, if the work does not violate a law or ordinance:

(1) Fences that are no more than 6 feet high.

(2) Retaining walls that are not over 4 feet in height measured from the lowest level of grade to the top of the wall unless the wall supports a surcharge.

(3) Water tanks supported directly upon grade if the capacity does not exceed 5,000 gallons and the ratio of height to diameter or width does not exceed 2 to 1.

(4) Sidewalks and driveways that are 30 inches or less above adjacent grade and not placed over a basement or story below it.

(5) Prefabricated swimming pools that are less than 24 inches deep.

(6) Swings and other playground equipment accessory to a one- or two-family dwelling.

(7) Window awnings supported by an exterior wall which do not 'project more than 54 inches from the exterior wall and do not require additional support.

(8) Installation of an uncovered deck where the floor of the deck is no more than 30 inches above grade.

(9) Installation or rearrangement of communications wiring.

(d) An ordinary repair does not require a permit. The following are not ordinary repairs:

(1) Cutting away a load-bearing wall, partition or portion of a wall.

(2) The removal or cutting of any structural beam or load-bearing support.

(3) The removal or change of any required means of egress, or rearrangement of parts of a structure affecting the egress requirements.

(4) The addition to, or relocation of any standpipe, water supply, sewer, drainage, drain leader, gas, soil, waste, vent or similar piping, electric wiring or mechanical.

(e) A permit is not required for the installation, alteration or repair of generation, transmission, distribution, metering or other related equipment under the ownership and control of public service agencies.

CROSS REFERENCES

This section cited in 34 Pa. Code § 403.61 (relating to residential buildings); 34 Pa. Code § 403.62a (relating to permit application); 34 Pa. Code § 403.102 (relating to municipalities electing to enforce the Uniform Construction Code); and 34 Pa. Code § 403.103 (relating to municipalities electing not to enforce the Uniform Construction Code).

§ 403.62a. Permit application.

(a) Applications for a permit required under § 403.62 (relating to permit requirements and exemptions) shall be submitted to the building code official in accordance with this section.

(b) A permit applicant shall submit an application to the building code official and attach construction documents with plans and specifications.

(c) A building code official may waive the submission of construction documents if the nature of the construction does not require the review of the construction documents to determine compliance with the Uniform Construction Code.

(d) A permit applicant for a building or structure located in a flood hazard area under the National Flood Insurance Program shall submit the following information with the construction documents:

(1) Delineation of flood hazard areas, floodway boundaries and flood zones and the design flood elevation, as appropriate.

(2) The elevation of the proposed lowest floor including basement and the height of the proposed lowest floor including basement above the highest adjacent grade is to be included in the documents if the building or structure is located in areas of shallow flooding (Zone AO).

(3) Design flood elevations contained on the municipality's Flood Insurance Rate Map produced by the Federal Emergency Management Agency. The building code official and the applicant shall obtain and reasonably utilize design flood elevation and floodway data available from other sources if this information is not contained on the municipality's Flood Insurance Rate Map.

(e) The application must contain a site plan showing the size and location of the new construction and existing structures on the site and the structure's distance from lot lines. If the construction involves demolition, the site plan shall indicate construction that is to be demolished and the size and location of existing structures and construction that will remain on the site or plot. A building code official may waive or modify the site plan requirement when the permit application is for an alteration or a repair or if the waiver is warranted for other reasons.

CROSS REFERENCES

This section cited in 34 Pa. Code § 403.61 (relating to residential buildings); 34 Pa. Code § 403.62 (relating to permit requirements and exemptions); and 34 Pa. Code § 403.103 (relating to municipalities electing not to enforce the Uniform Construction Code).

§ 403.63. Grant, denial and effect of permits.

(a) A building code official shall grant or deny a permit application, in whole or in part, within 15 business days of the filing date or the application is deemed approved. If the drawings were prepared by a design professional who is licensed or registered under the laws and regulations of the Commonwealth and the application contains a certification by the licensed or registered design professional that the plans meet the applicable standards of the Uniform Construction Code and ordinance as appropriate, a building code official shall grant or deny a permit application, in whole or in part, within 5 business days of the filing date or the application is deemed approved. Reasons for denial must be in writing, identifying the elements of the application which are not in compliance with the relevant provisions of the Uniform Construction Code and ordinance as appropriate and providing a citation to the relevant provisions of the Uniform Construction Code and ordinance as appropriate, and sent to the permit applicant. The building code official and the applicant may agree in writing to extend the deadline by a specific number of days.

(b) A building code official shall examine the construction documents and shall determine whether the construction indicated and described is in accordance with the Uniform Construction Code and other pertinent laws or ordinances as part of the application process.

(c) A building code official shall stamp or place a notation on each page of the set of reviewed construction documents that the documents were reviewed and approved for Uniform Construction Code compliance before the permit is issued. The building code official shall clearly mark any required nondesign changes on the construction documents. The building code official shall return a set of the construction documents with this notation and any required changes to the applicant. The applicant shall keep a copy of the construction documents at the work site open to inspection by the construction code official or an authorized representative.

(d) A building code official may not issue a permit for any property requiring access to a highway under the Department of Transportation's jurisdiction unless the permit contains notice that a highway occupancy permit is required under section 420 of the State Highway Law (36 P. S. § 670-420) before driveway access to a Commonwealth highway is permitted.

(e) A building code official may issue a permit for the construction of the foundations or other parts of a building or structure before the construction documents for the whole building or structure are submitted if the permit applicant previously filed adequate information and detailed statements for the building or structure under the Uniform Construction Code. Approval under this section is not assurance that the building code official will issue a permit for the entire building or structure.

(f) Issuance of a permit does not bar prosecution or other legal action for violations of the act, the Uniform Construction Code or a construction ordinance. A building code official may suspend or revoke a permit issued under the Uniform Construction Code when the owner does not make the required changes directed by the building code official under subsection (c), when the permit is issued in error, on the basis of inaccurate or incomplete information or in violation of any act, regulation, ordinance or the Uniform Construction Code.

(g) A permit becomes invalid unless the authorized construction work begins within 180 days after the permit's issuance or if the authorized construction work permit is suspended or abandoned for 180 days after the work has commenced. A permit holder may submit a written request for an extension of time to commence construction for just cause. The building code official may grant extensions of time to commence construction in writing. A permit may be valid for no more than 5 years from its issue date.

(h) The permit holder shall keep a copy of the permit on the work site until the completion of the construction.

(i) A permit applicant may request extensions of time or variances or appeal a building code official's action on the permit application to a board of appeals under § 403.122 (relating to appeals, variances and extensions of time) in a municipality which has adopted an ordinance for the administration and enforcement of the act or municipalities which are parties to an agreement for the joint administration and enforcement of the act.

(j) Work shall be installed in accordance with the approved construction documents. The permit holder shall submit a revised set of construction documents for approval for changes made during construction that are not in accordance with the approved construction documents.

(k) A permit is not valid until the required fees are collected under § 401.2a (relating to municipal and third-party agency fees).

CROSS REFERENCES

This section cited in 34 Pa. Code § 403.61 (relating to residential buildings); and 34 Pa. Code § 403.103 (relating to municipalities electing not to enforce the Uniform Construction Code).

§ 403.64. Inspections.

(a) A construction code official shall inspect all construction for which a permit was issued. The permit holder shall insure that the construction is accessible for inspection. An inspection does not bar prosecution or other legal action for violation of the Uniform Construction Code.

(b) The permit holder or an authorized agent shall notify the construction code official when work is ready for inspection and provide access for the inspection.

(c) The construction code official shall notify a permit holder if construction complies with the Uniform Construction Code or fails to comply with the Uniform Construction Code.

(d) A construction code official shall make the following inspections and file inspection reports relating to Uniform Construction Code compliance in all of the following areas:

(1) Foundation inspection.

(2) Plumbing, mechanical and electrical system inspection.

(3) Frame and masonry inspection.

(4) Wallboard inspection.

(e) The construction code official may conduct other inspections to ascertain compliance with the Uniform Construction Code or municipal ordinances.

(f) A construction code official shall conduct a final inspection of the completed construction work and file a final inspection report that indicates compliance with the Uniform Construction Code.

(g) A third-party agency under contract with a permit holder shall submit a copy of the final inspection report to the property owner, builder and the lender designated by the builder.

CROSS REFERENCES

This section cited in 34 Pa. Code § 403.61 (relating to residential buildings); 34 Pa. Code § 403.102 (relating to municipalities electing to enforce the Uniform Construction Code); and 34 Pa. Code § 403.103 (relating to municipalities electing not to enforce the Uniform Construction Code).

§ 403.65. Certificate of occupancy.

(a) A residential building may not be used or occupied without a certificate of occupancy issued by a building code official.

(b) A building code official shall issue a certificate of occupancy after receipt of a final inspection report that indicates compliance with the Uniform Construction Code and ordinance within 5 business days or within 10 business days in cities of the first class. The certificate of occupancy must contain the following information:

(1) The permit number and address of the residential building.

(2) The name and address of the owner of the residential building.

(3) A description of the portion of the residential building covered by the occupancy permit.

(4) A statement that the described portion of the residential building was inspected for compliance with the Uniform Construction Code.

(5) The name of the building code official who issued the occupancy permit.

(6) The construction code edition applicable to the occupancy permit.

(7) If an automatic sprinkler system is provided.

(8) Any special stipulations and conditions relating to the building permit.

(c) A building code official may issue a certificate of occupancy for a portion of a residential building if the portion independently meets the Uniform Construction Code.

(d) A building code official may suspend or revoke a certificate of occupancy when the certificate was issued in error, on the basis of incorrect information supplied by the permit applicant, or in violation of the Uniform Construction Code. Before a certificate of occupancy is revoked, a building owner may request a hearing before the board of appeals in accordance with § 403.122 (relating to appeals, variances and extensions of time).

(e) A third-party agency under contract with a building permit holder shall submit a copy of the certificate of occupancy to the municipality.

(f) A building code official may issue a temporary certificate of occupancy for a portion or portions of the building or structure before the completion of the entire work covered by the permit if the portion or portions may be occupied safely. The building code official shall set a time period during which the temporary certificate of occupancy is valid.

CROSS REFERENCES

This section cited in 34 Pa. Code § 403.61 (relating to residential buildiings); 34 Pa. Code § 403.102 (relating to municipalities electing to enforce the Uniform Construction Code); and 34 Pa. Code § 403.103 (relating to municipalities electing not to enforce the Uniform Construction Code).

§ 403.66. Public utility connections.

(a) A building code official may authorize the temporary connection of a building or system under construction to a utility source of energy, fuel or power.

(b) Connection to a public electric or gas utility for the completed construction may not occur unless the permit holder provides written proof to the utility company that the building or structure passed inspections under this chapter.

CROSS REFERENCES

This section cited in 34 Pa. Code § 403.61 (relating to residential buildings); 34 Pa. Code § 403.102 (relating to municipalities electing to enforce the Uniform Construction Code); and 34 Pa. Code § 403.103 (relating to municipalities electing not to enforce the Uniform Construction Code).

DEPARTMENT, MUNICIPAL AND THIRD-PARTY ENFORCEMENT FOR NONCOMPLIANCE

§ 403.81. Stop work order.

(a) A building code official may issue a written stop work order when the official determines that construction violates the Uniform Construction Code or is being performed in a dangerous or unsafe manner. The stop work order is to contain the reasons for the order and list the required conditions for construction to resume.

(b) The building code official shall serve the stop work order on the permit owner or the owner's agent by certified mail or personal service.

(c) A person who continues construction after service of a stop work order, except for construction work that is necessary to remove a violation or an unsafe condition, may be subject to the penalties under section 903 of the act (35 P. S. § 7210.903). A building code official may seek enforcement of a stop work order in a court of competent jurisdiction.

CROSS REFERENCES

This section cited in 34 Pa. Code § 403.102 (relating to municipalities electing to enforce the Uniform Construction Code).

§ 403.82. Notice of violations.

A building code official shall follow the following procedures if an inspection reveals a violation of the Uniform Construction Code:

(1) A construction code official shall discuss the inspection results with the permit holder at the completion of the inspection.

(2) The building code official may issue a written notice of violations to the permit holder. The notice is to contain a description of the violations and an order requiring correction of the violations within a reasonable period determined by the building code official. When a violation relates to an unsafe building, structure or equipment, a building code official shall act in accordance with § 403.84 (relating to unsafe building, structure or equipment).

(3) After the compliance date contained in the order, the building code official shall inspect the building, structure or equipment to determine whether the violation was corrected. The building code official shall close the order if the violation was corrected. The building code official may issue an order to show cause under § 403.83 (relating to order to show cause/order to vacate) to the owner for a violation that was not corrected.

CROSS REFERENCES

This section cited in 34 Pa. Code § 403.102 (relating to municipalities electing to enforce the Uniform Construction Code).

§ 403.83. Order to show cause/order to vacate.

(a) A building code official may initiate action to vacate or close a building, structure or equipment for violations of the Uniform Construction Code by issuing an order to show cause to the owner or owner's agent of a building or structure.

(b) The order to show cause shall contain a statement of the grounds for the action, the alleged violations of the Uniform Construction Code and notification that the building, structure or equipment may be closed or vacated. The order to show cause shall contain notification that the owner or owner's agent shall submit a written answer within 30 days. The building code official shall serve the order to show cause upon the owner or owner's agent by certified mail or personal service.

(c) The owner or owner's agent may file a written answer to the order to show cause with the building code official within 30 days following service of the order to show cause. The answer shall contain specific admissions or denials of the allegations contained in the order to show cause and set forth the specific facts, matters of law or Uniform Construction Code interpretation relied upon by the owner. The answer may contain a request for a variance or an extension of time for compliance. The building code official shall forward all requests for variances, extensions of time or appeals regarding interpretations of the Uniform Construction Code to the board of appeals within 5 business days. The building code official shall send a request for variance, extension of time or appeals regarding interpretation of the Uniform Construction Code's accessibility requirements to the Department within 5 business days.

(d) If the owner or owner's agent files an appeal, the board of appeals or Department will assume jurisdiction and consolidate the answer with any pending request for variance, extension of time or appeal filed by the owner with the board of appeals.

(e) The building code official shall consider the pending request for variance or extension of time or appeal as a stay to an enforcement action.

(f) After receipt of the answer, the building code official may take the following actions if the owner or owner's agent did not previously file an appeal or request for variance or extension of time:

(1) Issue a stop work order.

(2) Vacate or close the building or structure or place equipment out of operation.

(3) Abate or modify the alleged violation.

(4) Order other action to protect persons or property.

(g) A construction code official shall inspect the construction at the expiration of an extension of time or other time period granted for compliance under this section. If the building, structure or equipment violates the Uniform Construction Code following inspection, the building code official may issue an order vacating or closing the building or structure or placing equipment out of operation. The building code official shall serve this order upon the owner or owner's agent by certified mail or personal service.

(h) Where an unsafe condition exists, a building code official shall act in accordance with § 403.84 (relating to unsafe building, structure or equipment).

CROSS REFERENCES

This section cited in 34 Pa. Code § 403.102 (relating to municipalities electing to enforce the Uniform Construction Code).

§ 403.84. Unsafe building, structure or equipment.

(a) A building code official may determine that a building, structure or equipment is unsafe because of inadequate means of egress, inadequate light and ventilation, fire hazard, other dangers to human life or the public welfare, illegal or improper occupancy or inadequate maintenance. A vacant building or structure that is not secured against entry is unsafe under this section.

(b) When a building code official determines the existence of an unsafe condition, the building code official shall order the vacating of the building or structure.

(c) A building code official shall serve a written notice on the owner or owner's agent of the building, structure or equipment that is unsafe under this section. The notice shall contain the order to vacate the building, structure or seal the equipment out of service and state the unsafe conditions, required repairs or improvements. The order shall be served by certified mail or personal service to the owner or to the owner's agent's last known address or on the owner, agent or person in control of the building, structure or equipment. A building code official shall post the written notice at the entrance of the structure or on the equipment if service cannot be accomplished by certified mail or personal service.

(d) When a building or structure is ordered vacated under this section, the building code official shall post a notice at each entrance stating that the structure is unsafe and its occupancy is prohibited.

(e) A building code official may not rescind the order to vacate until the owner abates or corrects the unsafe condition.

(f) The Department may seal an elevator for an unsafe condition under section 105(c)(1) of the act (35 P. S. § 7210.105(c)(1)). The Department is the only entity that may remove or authorize the removal of a seal if an owner abates or corrects the unsafe condition.

CROSS REFERENCES

This section cited in 34 Pa. Code § 403.82 (relating to notice of violations); 34 Pa. Code § 403.83 (relating to order to show cause/order to vacate); 34 Pa. Code § 403.102 (relating to municipalities electing to enforce the Uniform Construction Code); 34 Pa. Code § 403.122 (relating to appeals, variances and extensions of time); 34 Pa. Code § 403.142 (relating to Accessibility Advisory Board); and 34 Pa. Code § 405.11 (relating to accident report).

§ 403.85. Release, retention and sharing of commercial construction records.

(a) A building code official shall keep records of all applications received, permits issued, reviewed building plans and specifications, certificates issued, fees collected, reports of inspections, notices and orders issued for all commercial buildings and structures under the Uniform Construction Code. A building code official shall retain these records as long as the related building, structure or equipment remains in existence.

(b) A building code official shall reproduce records kept in an electronic format to a hard-copy format upon request. A building code official may charge for the reproduction costs.

(c) A municipality that discontinues enforcing the Uniform Construction Code shall keep records of previous Uniform Construction Code enforcement. A municipality shall make these records available to the Department.

(d) The Department will make its records available to a municipality that elects to enforce the Uniform Construction Code under section 501 of the act (35 P. S. § 7210.501).

(e) The Department, a municipality and a third-party agency acting on behalf of a municipality may prohibit release of applications received, building plans and specifications, inspection reports and similar documents to the public under the act of June 21, 1957 (P. L. 390, No. 212) known as the Right-to-Know Law (65 P. S. §§ 66.1–66.9). The Department, the municipality or the third-party agency may release these documents to the building owner of record, the permit holder, the design professional of record or a third party authorized by the building owner in writing to receive the documents upon presentation of valid identification.

(f) The Department, a municipality and a third-party agency acting on behalf of a municipality may release any document obtained under this chapter to the following:

(1) The Department.

(2) The Department of General Services.

(3) Law enforcement or emergency response entities.

(4) Federal, State or local health entities.

CROSS REFERENCES

This section cited in 34 Pa. Code § 403.102 (relating to municipalities electing to enforce the Uniform Construction Code).

§ 403.86. Right of entry to inspect.

(a) A construction code official may enter a building, structure or premises during normal business hours or at a time agreed to by the owner or owner's agent to perform inspections under the Uniform Construction Code, to enforce Uniform Construction Code provisions or if there is reasonable cause to believe a condition on the building, structure or premises violates the Uniform Construction Code or which constitutes an unsafe condition.

(b) A construction code official may enter a building, structure or premises when the official presents credentials to the occupant and receives permission to enter.

(c) A construction code official may not enter a building, structure or premises that is unoccupied or after normal business hours without obtaining permission to enter from the owner or the owner's agent.

(d) A construction code official may seek the assistance of a law enforcement agency to gain entry to enforce the Uniform Construction Code when the construction code official has reasonable cause to believe that the building, structure or premises is unsafe.

(e) This section shall be used in conjunction with the Fire and Panic Act.

CROSS REFERENCES

This section cited in 34 Pa. Code § 403.45 (relating to inspections).

MUNICIPAL ELECTION

§ 403.101. Effective date.

(a) The Fire and Panic Act, the act of September 1, 1965 (P. L. No. 235) (71 P. S. §§ 1455.1–1455.3b), known as the Universal Accessibility Act and a locally-enacted building code shall remain in effect until the date that one of the following has transpired:

(1) A municipality enacts an ordinance adopting the Uniform Construction Code and the municipality provides written notification to the Department of the adopted ordinance before August 7, 2004.

(2) The initial election and notification period ended on August 7, 2004, and the municipality has not provided written notification to the Department.

(3) The municipality elects not to adopt an ordinance enforcing the Uniform Construction Code and provides written notification to the Department.

(b) After the expiration of the initial election period, a municipality may elect to administer and enforce the Uniform Construction Code. The municipality shall provide 180 days notice to the Department of its intention to pass an ordinance adopting the Uniform Construction Code.

(c) The Fire and Panic Act, the Universal Accessibility Act and a locally-enacted building code shall remain in effect for the following construction:

(1) New buildings or renovations to existing buildings for which an application for a building permit was made to the municipality before April 9, 2004.

(2) New buildings or renovations to existing buildings on which a contract for design or construction was signed before April 9, 2004.

§ 403.102. Municipalities electing to enforce the Uniform Construction Code.

(a) A municipality which elects to enforce the Uniform Construction Code shall enact an ordinance adopting the Uniform Construction Code as its municipal building code under section 501(a) of the act (35 P. S. § 7210.501(a)).

(b) The initial election period is from April 9, 2004, through July 8, 2004. A municipality shall enact an ordinance adopting the Uniform Construction Code by July 8, 2004.

(c) A municipality shall submit written notification to the Department of adoption of the ordinance and the following information within 30 days of its adoption:

(1) The number and date of adoption of the ordinance.

(2) The name of building code official.

(3) The business address of building code official.

(4) The business phone number of building code official.

(5) The electronic mail address of building code official, if available.

(d) A municipality may retain ordinances in effect on July 1, 1999, that contain standards that equal or exceed the Uniform Construction Code under section 303(b) of the act (35 P. S. § 7210.303(b)).

(e) A municipality that administers and enforces the Uniform Construction Code may cease administration and enforcement if it provides 180 days notice to the Department of its intention to adopt an ordinance ceasing administration and enforcement.

(f) A municipality shall notify the Department in writing within 30 days of any changes to the information it provided under subsections (b) and (e).

(g) A municipality that elects to administer and enforce the Uniform Construction Code shall utilize any of the following ways under section 501(b) of the act:

(1) Employ at least one construction code official and designating an employee to serve as a building code official.

(2) Retaining one or more third-party agencies.

(3) Utilizing an intermunicipal agreement under 53 Pa.C.S. §§ 2301–2315 (relating to intergovernmental cooperation).

(4) Contracting with another municipality.

(5) Contracting with the Department for plan reviews, inspection and enforcement of structures other than one-family and two-family dwelling units and utility and miscellaneous use structures.

(h) A municipality may charge fees under § 401.2a (relating to municipal and third-party agency fees).

(i) A municipality may enact an ordinance containing standards that equal or exceed the Uniform Construction Code as adopted by § 403.21 (relating to the Uniform Construction Code) under section 503 of the act (35 P. S. § 7210.503) after Department review and approval. A municipality may enact ordinances under this section which adopt additional code requirements for alterations or repairs to residential buildings. A municipality may enact ordinances under this section which adopt stricter code requirements than required by the act for the regulation of utility and miscellaneous use structures. The municipality shall notify the Department of the proposed ordinance and submit the following to the Department for its review:

(1) The complete ordinance.

(2) The information required in subsection (c).

(3) A detailed statement containing the differences between the proposed ordinance and the Uniform Construction Code including code sections affected by the changes and how the ordinance will equal or exceed the Uniform Construction Code.

(4) The time and place of public hearing.

(j) The Department will review all proposed ordinances that are filed with the Department in accordance with section 503(f) and (i) of the act (35 P. S. § 7210.503(f) and (i)). The Department will provide written notification of its findings to the municipality including the Department's finding on the municipality's compliance with section 503(b) of the act.

(k) A written challenge of an ordinance is governed by the following:

(1) An aggrieved party may file a written challenge of an ordinance within 30 days of its enactment with the Department and shall serve a copy of the challenge upon the municipality under section 503(j) of the act.

(2) The Secretary will issue a ruling on the challenge within 45 days of receipt of the filing of the last challenge to the ordinance or within 30 days of the Department hearing on the challenge, whichever occurs last, under section 503(k) of the act.

(l) A municipality may enact an ordinance relating to the administration and enforcement of the Uniform Construction Code that meets or exceeds the requirements of the following sections:

(1) Section 403.42(b) and (c) (relating to permit requirements and exemptions).

(2) Section 403.42a(a)–(e) and (g)–(n) (relating to permit application).

(3) Section 403.43(b), (c), (g), (h) and (k) (relating to grant, denial and effect of permits).

(4) Section 403.44 (relating to alternative construction material and methods).

(5) Section 403.45 (relating to inspections).

(6) Section 403.46 (relating to certificate of occupancy).

(7) Section 403.47 (relating to public utility connections).

(8) Section 403.62(a)–(e) (relating to permit requirements and exemptions).

(9) Section 403.64 (relating to inspections).

(10) Section 403.65 (relating to certificates of occupancy).

(11) Section 403.66 (relating to public utility connections).

(12) Section 403.81(a) and (b) (relating to stop work order).

(13) Section 403.82 (relating to notice of violations).

(14) Section 403.83 (relating to order to show cause/order to vacate).

(15) Section 403.84(a)–(e) (relating to unsafe building structure or equipment).

(16) Section 403.85(a)–(c) (relating to release, retention and sharing of commercial construction records).

(m) A municipality may utilize forms provided by the Department of Community and Economic Development as the permit application under §§ 403.42a and 403.62a.

(n) A municipality will provide a list of all other required permits necessary before issuance of the building permit. A municipality will not be liable for the completeness of any list.

(o) The Department will enforce Chapter 11 (Accessibility) of the Uniform Construction Code and other accessibility requirements contained in or referenced by the Uniform Construction Code until a municipality employs or contracts with a code administrator certified as an accessibility inspector/plans examiner under this part.

(p) A municipality may observe Department inspections of State-owned buildings in its jurisdiction under section 105(b)(1) of the act (35 P. S. § 7210.105(b)(1)). A municipality may review all building plans and plan review documents for State-owned buildings in the Department's custody.

(q) A municipality may enact an ordinance imposing the code requirements spelled out in section 503(a)(2) of the act (35 P. S. § 7210.503(a)(2)) on the structures exempted under § 403.1(b)(12) (relating to scope).

CROSS REFERENCES

This section cited in 34 Pa. Code § 403.41 (relating to commercial construction); and 34 Pa. Code § 403.61 (relating to residential buildings).

§ 403.103. Municipalities electing not to enforce the Uniform Construction Code.

(a) A municipality shall provide written notification to the Department before August 7, 2004, if it elects not to administer and enforce the Uniform Construction Code.

(b) An applicant for a residential building permit shall obtain the services of a third-party agency certified in the appropriate categories to conduct the plan review and inspections under § § 403.61—403.66 (relating to permit and inspection process for residential buildings).

(c) A building code official shall approve an alternative material, design or method of construction if the proposed design is satisfactory and complies with the intent of the Uniform Construction Code and the offered material, method or work is equivalent to Uniform Construction Code requirements for its intended purpose. The building code official shall accept compliance with the "International Performance Code of 2018" as an alternative to compliance with the Uniform Construction Code.

(d) A building code official shall determine the climatic and geographic design criteria contained in Table R301.2(1) of the "International Residential Code of 2018" for residential construction.

(e) A third-party agency which conducts plan review and inspection of residential buildings and utility and miscellaneous use structures shall retain copies of all final inspection reports relating to Uniform Construction Code compliance.

(f) A third-party agency shall send a copy of the final inspection report to the property owner, builder, and a lender designated by the builder.

(g) A municipality shall provide written notification to a permit applicant for buildings and structures other than residential buildings that the applicant shall obtain the Department's services for plan review and inspection. The municipality shall send a copy of the notice to the Department. The notice shall contain the following information:

(1) The name of the applicant.

(2) The address of the applicant.

(3) The name of the building or structure.

(4) The address of the building or structure.

(5) Proposed occupancy or use of building or structure under the Uniform Construction Code.

§ 403.104. Department review.

(a) The Department will investigate written and signed complaints concerning the enforcement and administration of the Uniform Construction Code under section 105(a) of the act (35 P. S. § 7210.105(a)). The Department will make a report to the governing body of the municipality or third-party agency that was the subject of the review and provide recommendations to address any deficiencies found by the Department.

(b) The Department will review each municipal enforcement program at least once every 5 years unless a complaint is received under section 105(a) of the act to ensure that code administrators are adequately administering and enforcing the provisions of Chapter 11 (Accessibility) of the Uniform Construction Code and any other accessibility requirements contained in or referenced by the Uniform Construction Code. The Department will submit a written report to the municipality of its findings. The municipality may submit a written response to the Department.

(c) The Department may take any of the following actions for violations of the act or to obtain compliance with the act:

(1) Initiate proceedings in Commonwealth Court under section 105(a)(3) of the act.

(2) Initiate proceedings against code administrators under section 701 of the act (35 P. S. § 7210.701) and § 401.14 (relating to decertification or refusal to certify).

(3) Initiate prosecutions under section 903 of the act (35 P. S. § 7210.903).

BOARD OF APPEALS

§ 403.121. Board of appeals.

(a) A municipality which has adopted an ordinance for the administration and enforcement of the Uniform Construction Code or is a party to an agreement for the joint administration and enforcement of the Uniform Construction Code shall establish and appoint members to serve on a board of appeals under section 501(c) of the act (35 P. S. § 7210.501(c)).

(b) The board of appeals shall hear and rule on appeals, requests for variances and requests for extensions of time. An application for appeal shall be based on a claim that the true intent of the act or Uniform Construction Code has been incorrectly interpreted, the provisions of the act or Uniform Construction Code do not fully apply or an equivalent form of construction is to be used.

(c) The composition of a board of appeals is governed by all of the following:

(1) A member of the board of appeals shall be qualified by training and experience to pass on matters pertaining to building construction. Training and experience may consist of licensure as an architect or engineer, experience in the construction industry, and training or experience as an inspector or plan reviewer.

(2) A member of the board of appeals holds office at the pleasure of the municipality's governing body.

(3) Members of a municipality's governing body and its code administrators may not serve on a board of appeals.

(4) A municipality may fill a position on the board of appeals with a qualified person who resides outside of the municipality when it cannot find a person within the municipality who satisfies the requirements of this section.

(d) Two or more municipalities may establish a joint board of appeals through an intermunicipal agreement under 53 Pa.C.S. §§ 2301–2315 (relating to intergovernmental cooperation).

(e) A board of appeals member may not cast a vote or participate in a hearing in any appeal, request for variance or request for extension of time in which the member has a personal, professional or financial interest.

(f) A board of appeals shall schedule meetings and provide public notice of meetings in accordance with 65 Pa.C.S. §§ 701–716 (relating to Sunshine Act).

(g) A board of appeals may not act upon appeals, requests for variance or requests for extension of time relating to accessibility under the act.

(h) The fee for an appeal in a municipality which has adopted an ordinance for the administration and enforcement of the Uniform Construction Code or is a party to an agreement for the joint administration and enforcement of the Uniform Construction Code will not exceed the actual costs of publishing the hearing notice, court reporter services and other necessary administrative services under section 501(c) of the act (35 P. S. § 7210.501(c)(4)).

§ 403.122. Appeals, variances and extensions of time.

(a) An owner or owner's agent may seek a variance or extension of time or appeal a building code official's decision by filing a petition with the building code official or other person designated by the board of appeals on a form provided by the municipality.

(b) The postmark date or the date of personal service will establish the filing date of the appeal and request for variance or extension of time.

(c) An appeal or request for variance or extension of time to a board of appeals will automatically suspend an action to enforce an order to correct until the matter is resolved. An action under § 403.84 (relating to unsafe building, structure or equipment) may not be stayed.

(d) A board of appeals shall decide an appeal, variance request or request for extension of time by reviewing documents and written brief or argument unless the owner or owner's agent requests a hearing.

(e) A board of appeals shall hold a hearing within 60 days from the date of an applicant's request unless the applicant agreed in writing to an extension of time. A board of appeals shall convene a hearing within 30 days of receipt of an appeal or request for variance or extension of time involving the construction of a one- or two-family residential building.

(f) A board of appeals shall only consider the following factors when deciding an appeal under section 501(c)(2) of the act:

(1) The true intent of the act or Uniform Construction Code was incorrectly interpreted.

(2) The provisions of the act do not apply.

(3) An equivalent form of construction is to be used.

(g) A board of appeals may consider the following factors when ruling upon a request for extension of time or the request for variance:

(1) The reasonableness of the Uniform Construction Code's application in a particular case.

(2) The extent to which the granting of a variance or an extension of time will pose a violation of the Uniform Construction Code or an unsafe condition.

(3) The availability of professional or technical personnel needed to come into compliance.

(4) The availability of materials and equipment needed to come into compliance.

(5) The efforts being made to come into compliance as quickly as possible.

(6) Compensatory features that will provide an equivalent degree of protection to the Uniform Construction Code.

(h) If the owner or owner's agent requests a hearing, the board of appeals shall schedule a hearing and notify the owner or owner's agent and building code official of the date, time and place of the hearing.

(i) The board of appeals may:

(1) Deny the request in whole or in part.

(2) Grant the request in whole or in part.

(3) Grant the request upon certain conditions being satisfied.

(j) The board of appeals shall provide a written notice of its decision to the owner and to the building code official. A board of appeals shall render a written decision regarding an appeal or request for variance or extension of time involving the construction of a one- or two-family residential building within 5 business days, or within 10 business days in cities of the first class, of the latest hearing. The appeal shall be deemed granted if a board of appeals fails to act within this time period.

(k) An owner shall file an appeal, request for variances and request for extension of time relating to accessibility with the Accessibility Advisory Board under § 403.142 (relating to Accessibility Advisory Board).

CROSS REFERENCES

This section cited in 34 Pa. Code § 401.1 (relating to definitions); 34 Pa. Code § 403.43 (relating to grant, denial and effects of permits); 34 Pa. Code § 403.46 (relating to certificate of occupancy); 34 Pa. Code § 403.63 (relating to grant, denial and effect of permits); 34 Pa. Code § 403.122 (relating to appeals, variances and extensions of time); 34 Pa. Code § 403.141 (relating to enforcement by the Department); and 34 Pa. Code § 405.3 (relating to permit application).

DEPARTMENT ENFORCEMENT

§ 403.141. Enforcement by the Department.

(a) The Department will conduct plan and specification review and inspections for all State-owned buildings under section 105(b) of the act (35 P. S. § 7210.105(b)). The Department will notify municipalities of all inspections of State-owned buildings and provide municipalities the opportunity to observe inspection of the buildings.

(b) The Department will retain jurisdiction over the provisions of Chapter 11 (Accessibility), and any other accessibility requirements contained in or referenced by the Uniform Construction Code, until a municipality administering and enforcing the Uniform Construction Code obtains the services of a code administrator certified as an accessibility specialist.

(c) The Department will enforce the Uniform Construction Code for all buildings and structures except for residential buildings and utility and miscellaneous use structures in municipalities that have not adopted an ordinance to enforce the act under section 501(a)(1) of the act (35 P. S. § 7210.501(a)(1)).

(d) The Industrial Board will decide petitions for variances and extensions of time and appeals of Department decisions under the Uniform Construction Code. The Industrial Board will hold the first hearing on a petition within 45 days of receipt of the petition.

(e) An owner or owner's agent may file a petition for variance or extension of time or an appeal with the Industrial Board under § 403.122 (relating to appeals, variances and extensions of time). An owner or owner's agent may file an appeal concerning technical infeasibility under Chapter 11 (Accessibility) of the Uniform Construction Code and other accessibility requirements contained in or referenced by the Uniform Construction Code with the Accessibility Advisory Board under § 403.142 (relating to Accessibility Advisory Board).

CROSS REFERENCES

This section cited in 34 Pa. Code § 401.2 (relating to Department fees).

§ 403.142. Accessibility Advisory Board.

(a) The Secretary has the exclusive power to grant modifications and extensions of time and decide issues of technical infeasibility under Chapter 11 (Accessibility) of the Uniform Construction Code and other accessibility requirements contained in or referenced by the Uniform Construction Code for individual projects under section 301(a)(3) of the act (35 P. S. § 7210.301(a)(3)).

(b) The Accessibility Advisory Board is created with the following powers and duties under section 106 of the act (35 P. S. § 7210.106):

(1) Review all proposed regulations under the act and offer comment and advice to the Secretary on all issues related to accessibility by persons with physical disabilities and enforcement of accessibility requirements.

(2) Review all applications for modifications or variances of Chapter 11 (Accessibility) of the Uniform Construction Code and any other accessibility requirements contained in or referenced by the Uniform Construction Code. The Accessibility Advisory Board will advise the Secretary whether modification or variance should be granted or whether compliance is technically feasible.

(3) Hear appeals from decisions of building code officials and recommend modifications, variances or extensions of time. An appeal of a decision of a building code official shall be based on a claim that the true intent of the act or the Uniform Construction Code was incorrectly interpreted, the act does not apply or an equivalent form of construction is to be used.

(c) The Accessibility Advisory Board will schedule meetings and provide public notice of meetings in accordance with 65 Pa.C.S. §§ 701–716 (relating to the Sunshine Act).

(d) The Accessibility Advisory Board will hear requests for variances or modification, requests for extensions of time and appeals in accordance with the following procedure:

(1) An owner or owner's agent shall file an appeal with the Accessibility Advisory Board on a Department-provided form.

(2) The postmark date or the date of personal service will establish the filing date of the appeal.

(3) An appeal to the Accessibility Advisory Board will automatically suspend an action to enforce an order to correct except where there is an unsafe

building, structure or equipment under § 403.84 (relating to unsafe building, structure or equipment).

(4) The Accessibility Advisory Board will make recommendations based upon documents and written brief unless the owner requests a hearing.

(5) If the owner or owner's agent requests a hearing, the Accessibility Advisory Board will schedule a hearing and will provide written notification to the owner or owner's agent and the building code official of the date, time and place of the hearing. The notification will be made no less than 5 days prior to the hearing unless the owner waives this period.

(6) The Accessibility Advisory Board may consider the following factors when a request for an extension of time or a variance or other appropriate relief is reviewed:

(i) The reasonableness of the regulations or Uniform Construction Code as applied in the specific case.

(ii) The extent to which an extension of time or a variance will subject occupants of the building or structure to conditions which do not comply with the Uniform Construction Code.

(iii) The availability of professional or technical personnel needed to comply with the Uniform Construction Code.

(iv) The availability of materials and equipment needed to comply with the Uniform Construction Code.

(v) The efforts made to safeguard occupants.

(vi) The efforts made to comply with the Uniform Construction Code.

(vii) Compensatory features that will provide an equivalent degree of compliance with the intent of the Uniform Construction Code.

(7) The Accessibility Advisory Board will recommend that the Secretary take one of the following actions:

(i) Deny the request in whole or in part.

(ii) Grant the request in whole or in part.

(iii) Grant the request upon certain conditions being satisfied.

(iv) Grant other appropriate relief.

(8) The Secretary will make a final decision on the request and will issue written notice of the decision to the owner or the owner's agent and the building code official.

(e) An individual, partnership, agency, association or corporation who reasonably believes there is a violation of the accessibility provisions of the act or the Uniform Construction Code by a governmental entity or private owner may file a complaint with the body responsible for enforcement of the Uniform Construction Code under section 501(f) of the act (35 P. S. § 7210.501(f)).

CROSS REFERENCES

This section cited in 34 Pa. Code § 401.1 (relating to definitions); 34 Pa. Code § 403.43 (relating to grant, denial and effects of permits); 34 Pa. Code § 403.122 (relating to appeals, variances and extensions of time); and 34 Pa. Code § 403.141 (relating to enforcement by the Department).

ELEVATORS AND OTHER LIFTING DEVICES

§ 405.1. Scope.

(a) *Application of chapter.* This chapter constitutes the Uniform Construction Code technical requirements for elevators and other lifting devices. This chapter applies to the construction, alteration, addition, repair, movement, equipment, removal, maintenance, use and change in use of every elevator and lifting device after April 9, 2004.

(b) *Exceptions.* The Uniform Construction Code does not apply to:

(1) New elevators and lifting devices or renovations to existing elevators and lifting devices for which a permit application was made to the Department before April 9, 2004.

(2) New elevators and lifting devices or renovations to existing elevators and lifting devices for which a contract for design or construction was signed before April 9, 2004.

(3) Elevators and lifting devices solely in residential buildings used by the occupants of a dwelling unit except where the lifting device is used or accessible by the occupants of more than 1 dwelling unit.

(c) Prior permits and construction.

(1) A permit issued under valid regulations before April 9, 2004, remains valid and the construction of the elevator or lifting device may be completed in accordance with the approved permit if construction commences by April 9, 2006.

(2) If construction of the elevator or lifting device has not commenced within the time period allowed under paragraph (1), the permit becomes rescinded. The permit holder shall acquire a new permit under section 304(c)(2) of the act (35 P. S. § 7210.304(c)(2)) before construction.

(3) An elevator or lifting device that was issued a certificate of operation by the Department before April 9, 2004, may remain in use if the owner maintains the elevator or lifting device in accordance with a previous Department permit or approval, the owner complied with the regulations in effect when the certificate of operation was issued and the owner complies with the applicable requirements of §§ 405.7–405.9 (relating to periodic inspections; periodic testing; and periodic dynamic testing).

§ 405.2. Standards.

(a) The following standards are adopted as part of the Uniform Construction Code and apply to the listed type of elevator or other lifting device. Other authorities referenced in the standards are adopted if the authority is not excluded in subsection (b):

(1) "ASME A17.1-2000" with "A17.1a-2002" addenda:

(i) Part 1 (General).

(ii) Part 2 (Electric elevators).

(iii) Part 3 (Hydraulic elevators).

(iv) Part 4 (Elevators with other types of driving machines).

(v) Part 5 (Special application elevators).

(vi) Part 6 (Escalators and moving walks).

(vii) Part 7 (Dumbwaiters and material lifts).

(viii) Part 8 (General requirements).

(ix) Part 9 (Standard codes and specifications).

(2) "ASME B20.1-2000" for vertical and inclined reciprocating conveyors without automatic transfer devices.

(3) "ASME A90.1-1997" including "A90.1a-1999" and "A90.1b-2001" addenda for belt man-lifts.

(4) "ANSI B77.1-2017" for passenger ropeways, aerial tramways, aerial lifts, surface lifts, tows and conveyors.

(5) "ASME A18.1-1999" including "A.18.1a-2001" addenda for vertical and inclined wheelchair lifts and stairway lifts. Testing under sections 10.3.2 and 10.3.3 shall comply with § 405.8 (relating to periodic test results).

(6) Electric wiring and apparatus shall comply with the "ICC Electrical Code."

(b) The following sections of "ASME A17.1-2000" with "A17.1b-2002" addenda are not adopted as the Uniform Construction Code:

(1) Section 5.3 (Private residence elevators).

(2) Section 5.4 (Private residence inclined elevators).

(3) Section 5.8 (Shipboard elevators).

(4) Section 5.9 (Mine elevators).

(5) Section 7.7 (Automatic transfer devices).

(6) Section 7.8 (Power dumbwaiter with automatic transfer devices).

(7) Section 7.9 (Electric material lifts with automatic transfer devices).

(8) Section 7.10 (Hydraulic material lifts with automatic transfer devices).

(9) Section 7.11 (Material lifts with obscured transfer devices).

(10) Section 8.6.7.3 (Private residence elevator).

(11) Section 8.6.7.4 (Private residence inclined elevators).

(12) Section 8.6.7.8 (Shipboard elevators).

(13) Section 8.6.7.9 (Mine elevators).

(14) Section 8.6.9.2 (Material lifts and dumbwaiters with automatic transfer devices).

(15) Section 8.7.5.3 (Private residence elevators).

(16) Section 8.7.5.4 (Private residence inclined elevators).

(17) Section 8.7.5.8 (Shipboard elevators).

(18) Section 8.7.5.9 (Mine elevators).

(19) Section 8.7.7.3 (Material lifts and dumbwaiters with automatic transfer devices).

(20) Section 8.10.5.2 (Private residence elevators and lifts).

(21) Section 8.10.5.5 (Material lifts and dumbwaiters with automatic transfer devices).

(22) Section 8.10.5.8 (Shipboard elevators).

(23) Section 8.11.5.2 (Private residence elevators and lifts).

(24) Section 8.11.5.5 (Material lifts and dumbwaiters with automatic transfer devices).

(25) Section 8.11.5.8 (Shipboard elevators).

(c) The following portions of "ASME B20.1-2000" are not adopted as the Uniform Construction Code:

(1) Section 3 (Intent).

(2) Section 5.14 (Hoppers and chutes).

(3) Section 6.1 (Belt conveyors—fixed in place).

(4) Section 6.2 (Bucket conveyors).

(5) Section 6.3 (Chain conveyors).

(6) Section 6.4 (En masse conveyors).

(7) Section 6.5 (Flight and apron conveyors—bulk material).

(8) Section 6.7 (Live roller conveyors—belt or chain driven).

(9) Section 6.8 (Mobile conveyors).

(10) Section 6.9 (Portable conveyors, extendible belt conveyors and car unloaders).

(11) Section 6.10 (Pusher bar conveyors).

(12) Section 6.11 (Roller and wheel conveyors).

(13) Section 6.12 (Screw conveyors).

(14) Section 6.13 (Shuttle conveyors, belt trippers and transfer cars).

(15) Section 6.14 (Skip hoists—bulk materials).

(16) Section 6.15 (Slat conveyors and roller slat conveyors).

(17) Section 6.16 (Suspended vertical tray conveyors).

(18) Section 6.17 (Tow conveyors—in the floor).

(19) Section 6.18 (Trolley conveyors and power and free conveyors).

(20) Section 6.19 (Vertical articulated conveyors).

(21) Section 6.20 (Vertical chain opposed shelf type conveyors).

(d) The following portions of ''ASME A18.1-1999'' with ''A18.1a-2001'' addenda are not adopted as the Uniform Construction Code:

(1) Part V (Private residence vertical platform lifts).

(2) Part VI (Private residence inclined platform lifts).

(3) Part VII (Private residence incline stairway chairlifts).

(e) This chapter applies when there is a conflict with a code or standard related to elevators or lifting devices.

§ 405.3. Permit application.

(a) An owner of an elevator or lifting device or an authorized agent shall apply to the Department for a permit before the construction, alteration, replacement or repair of an elevator or lifting device.

(b) An owner or owner's agent shall submit four copies of a permit application and supporting documents to the Department for review. The application and supporting construction documents shall be submitted in Department-approved media and clearly detail the location, nature and extent of the proposed construction and its compliance with the Uniform Construction Code.

(c) The Department may suspend or revoke a permit when the permit was issued erroneously, on inaccurate, incorrect or incomplete information or issued in violation of the Uniform Construction Code. The Department may charge an applicant a new application and inspection fee when a previous permit was suspended or revoked based upon inaccurate, incomplete or incorrect information provided by the permit applicant.

(d) A permit becomes invalid unless construction work is commenced within 180 days after its issuance or if the work is suspended or abandoned for a period of 180 days after it is commenced. The Department may grant written extensions of time for periods of 180 days each. A permit remains valid for no more than 5 years.

(e) The Department will grant or deny a permit in whole or in part within 30 business days of the filing date of a complete application. The Department will provide written notification to the applicant for applications denied in whole or in part.

(f) The Department will place the written or stamped notation "Reviewed and Approved for Code Compliance'' on the documents accompanying the permit application. The Department will keep three sets of the construction documents and send one set of construction documents to the permit applicant.

(g) An owner or owner's agent may request a variance or appeal the code administrator's decision to the Industrial Board under § 403.122 (relating to appeals, variances and extensions of time). The appeal shall be based on a claim that the true intent of the act or the Uniform Construction Code were incorrectly interpreted, the act does not fully apply or an equivalent form of construction is to be used.

(h) A permit is not valid until the Department collects the required fees under § 401.2 (relating to Department fees).

§ 405.4. Approved designs, equipment and devices.

A platform, car, cabin or chair safety device may be installed after it receives a Department-issued certificate of acceptance. An applicant for a certificate of acceptance shall meet the following requirements:

(1) The manufacturer, designer or engineer of the platform, car, cabin or chair safety device shall submit the design to the Department.

(2) The Department will observe the operation of the device for compliance with the Uniform Construction Code before use of the device in this Commonwealth.

(3) The Department will issue a certificate of acceptance after it observes successful testing of the device.

§ 405.5. Acceptance inspection.

The Department will conduct an acceptance inspection to confirm compliance with the Uniform Construction Code before a new elevator or lifting device or an elevator or lifting device under repair is put into service.

§ 405.6. Certificate of operation.

(a) An elevator or lifting device may not be operated unless the Department issues a certificate of operation for the elevator or other lifting device. The Department will issue a certificate of operation for the elevator or other lifting device if it passes inspection.

(b) A certificate of operation is valid for 24 months from the issue date for equipment that requires a 6-month periodic inspection under § 405.7 (relating to periodic inspections). A certificate of operation is valid for 48 months from the issue date for equipment requiring a 12-month periodic inspection cycle under § 405.7.

(c) A certificate of operation may remain valid for an additional 30 days after its expiration date if a periodic inspection is conducted within 30 days of the certificate's expiration date. A certificate of operation is not valid until the Department collects the required fee under § 401.2 (relating to Department fees).

(d) The certificate of operation or a copy of the certificate of operation for equipment with a machine room shall be posted in the elevator car or other lifting device enclosure, or attached to the controller in the machine room. The certificate of operation for escalators, moving walks and other equipment without a machine room shall be made available to a construction code official during a periodic inspection.

§ 405.7. Periodic inspections.

(a) A construction code official of the Department or a third-party agency shall conduct periodic inspections and document compliance with the Uniform Construction Code at intervals that do not exceed 6 months for the following equipment:

(1) Electric elevator.

(2) Hydraulic elevator.

(3) Escalator.

(4) Belt man-lift.

(5) Lumber elevator.

(6) Moving walk.

(7) Orchestra elevator.

(8) Organ elevator.

(9) Limited use/limited application elevator.

(10) Special purpose personnel elevator.

(11) Stage elevator.

(12) Power sidewalk elevator.

(13) Elevators used for construction.

(14) Inclined elevator.

(15) Rooftop elevator.

(b) A construction code official shall perform periodic inspections of all other lifting devices at intervals that do not exceed 12 months. A construction code official shall inspect a lifting device that is used on a seasonal basis before the beginning of the season of operation.

(c) A construction code official who performed a periodic inspection shall complete an inspection report containing all of the following information:

(1) The inspection results.

(2) The day, month and year of the inspection.

(3) The beginning and conclusion times of the inspection.

(4) The construction code official's certification number.

(5) The construction code official's signature. An electronic signature may be used.

(d) A construction code official who performed a periodic inspection shall insure that the following information is completed on the certificate of operation:

(1) The day, month and year of inspection.

(2) The construction code official's certification number.

(3) The construction code official's signature.

(e) A construction code official shall submit the results of routine inspections to the Department within 15 days of the inspection in a format acceptable to the Department.

(f) A construction code official shall notify the Department if a lifting device failed a periodic inspection within 1 business day from the inspection.

§ 405.8. Periodic testing.

(a) The following periodic testing under "ASME A17.1-2000" with "A17.1a-2002" addenda is required. A construction code official shall witness all of the testing:

(1) Category One under section 8.11.2.2 at 5-year intervals.

(2) Category Five under section 8.11.2.3 at 5-year intervals.

(3) Category One under section 8.11.3.2 at 3-year intervals. Periodic inspection and testing shall be phased in over a 3-year period as follows:

(i) Elevators installed before 1973 shall receive periodic inspection and testing on or before April 9, 2005.

(ii) Elevators installed between 1973 and 1992 shall receive periodic inspection by April 9, 2006.

(iii) Elevators installed after 1992 shall receive periodic inspection and testing by April 9, 2007.

(4) Category Three under section 8.11.3.3 at 5-year intervals.

(5) Category Five under section 8.11.3.4 at 5-year intervals.

(6) Category One under section 8.11.4.2 at 3-year intervals.

(7) Other equipment under section 8.11.5 at 5-year intervals as follows:

(i) Sidewalk elevators under section 8.11.5.1.

(ii) Hand elevators under section 8.11.5.3.

(iii) Dumbwaiters under section 8.11.5.4.

(iv) Special purpose personnel elevators under section 8.11.5.6.

(v) Inclined elevators under section 8.11.5.7.

(vi) Screw column elevators under section 8.11.5.9.

(vii) Rooftop elevators under section 8.11.5.10.

(viii) Rack and pinion elevators under section 8.11.5.11.

(ix) Limited use and limited application elevators under section 8.11.5.12.

(x) Elevators used for construction under section 8.11.5.13.

(b) A construction code official shall witness each test enumerated in this section.

(c) Inspection and testing under "ASME A.18.1-1999'' with "A18.1a-2001'' addenda are required at the following intervals:

(1) Testing under section 10.3.1 shall be conducted at 5-year intervals.

(2) Testing under section 10.3.2 shall be conducted at 5-year intervals.

(3) Testing under section 10.3.3 shall be conducted at 5-year intervals.

(d) A lumber elevator equipped with platform safety devices shall be tested with rated load at intervals that may not exceed 5 years.

(e) Stage, orchestra and organ lifts equipped with a platform safety device shall be tested with rated loads at intervals that may not exceed 5 years.

(f) Vertical reciprocating conveyers with a platform safety device shall be tested at intervals that do not exceed 5 years.

(g) A construction code official shall complete a test report after the official witnesses a periodic test in a format acceptable to the Department. The construction code official shall submit the report to the Department within 15 days of witnessing the tests. All of the following information is required in the report:

(1) The test results.

(2) The day, month and year of the test.

(3) The beginning and concluding times of the test.

(4) The construction code official's signature. The construction code official may use an electronic signature.

(h) A metal tag shall be permanently attached on an elevator that successfully passes the test under this section in accordance with all of the following:

(1) The metal tag shall be furnished by the company that performed the testing.

(2) The metal tag shall be attached to the elevator safety-releasing carrier for safety tests or to the controller for all other tests.

(3) The tag shall contain all of the following:

(i) The day, month and year of the test.

(ii) The name of the company that performed the test.

(iii) The type of test performed.

Table of Contents
Part I Ch. 1–3 Ethics, Records, Open Meetings
Part II Ch. 4–10 Taxation
Part III Ch. 11–18 Torts, Contracts & Civil Rules
Part IV Ch. 19–24 Zoning & Planning
Part V Ch. 25–30 Construction and Emergency Codes
Part VI Ch. 31–39 Municipal Codes
Index

§ 405.9. Periodic dynamic testing.

(a) The following periodic dynamic testing shall be conducted under "ANSI B77.1-1999":

(1) Aerial tramways dynamic testing under section 2.3.3.1.2.

(2) Detachable grip aerial lifts dynamic testing under section 3.3.3.1.2.

(3) Fixed grip aerial lifts dynamic testing under section 4.3.3.1.2.

(b) A construction code official shall witness all periodic dynamic testing under this section.

(c) A construction code official shall complete and submit a test report to the Department within 15 days of witnessing a periodic dynamic test. The report shall be in a format acceptable to the Department and contain all of the following information:

(1) The test results.

(2) The day, month and year of test.

(3) The beginning and concluding times of test.

(4) The construction code official's signature. The construction code official may use an electronic signature.

§ 405.10. Major repairs, replacements and alterations.

(a) Repairs, replacement and alterations of elevators or other lifting devices shall comply with the following sections of "ASME A17.1-2000" with "A17.1a-2002" addenda:

(1) Section 8.6.2 (Repairs).

(2) Section 8.6.3 (Replacements)

(3) Section 8.7 (Alterations).

(b) The requirements of subsection (a) apply to major repairs, replacements and alterations performed on other types of lifting devices that are not referenced in "ASME A17.1-2000" with "A17.1a-2002" addenda.

(c) An elevator or lifting device shall be taken out of service when a major repair, replacement or alteration is performed upon it. The owner or owner's agent shall provide written notification to the Department when the major repair, replacement or alteration is completed. The elevator or lifting device may be returned to service when it passes a Department inspection.

§ 405.11. Accident report.

(a) An owner of an elevator or lifting device or an authorized agent shall submit an accident report to the Department if the elevator or lifting device is involved in an accident resulting in any of the following:

(1) Fatal injury or hospitalization to a person.

(2) Damage to the elevator or lifting device rendering it unsafe under § 403.84 (relating to unsafe building, structure or equipment).

(b) The owner or authorized representative shall submit the accident report on a Department-prescribed form, which must be received by the Department within 24 hours of the accident.

(c) The Department may order an investigation of the accident.

(d) An elevator or lifting device that was involved in a fatal accident may not return to operation until the Department provides approval.

(e) An elevator or lifting device involved in a nonfatal accident resulting from mechanical or electrical failure may not return to operation until the Department provides approval. This requirement does not apply to ski lifts.

§ 405.12. Lumber elevators.

(a) A lumber elevator is a platform that is used to raise or lower stacked lumber under the requirements of this section. An individual may not ride a lumber elevator.

(b) The shaftway is enclosed on all sides that are not used for loading or unloading with flush partitions that are at least 6 feet high. Movable bars or railings are required to protect all points of loading and unloading, unless gates are provided. Flaring is at an angle of at least 75° from the horizontal and shall protect all shearing points in the shaftway excluding each loading and unloading landing.

(c) Gates are required to protect all points of loading and unloading when the platform's vertical travel exceeds 6 feet or when there are two or more landings. The following types of automatic and semiautomatic gates may be used:

(1) Semiautomatic vertical-rising gates.

(2) Fully automatic vertical-rising gates only at terminal landings.

(3) Manually operated swinging or horizontal gates with locking devices and electric brakes.

(4) Department-approved, power-operated horizontal gates.

(d) A locking device shall comply with the following requirements:

(1) An automatic locking device shall be placed on, or attached to a manually operated gate. The locking device shall prevent the normal operation of the platform when the gate is open and unsecured. The locking device shall prevent the opening of the gate when the car is away from the landing.

(2) A shield shall be installed on openwork gates and shall be of sufficient size to prevent access to the lock from the outside of the shaftway.

(e) The shaftway shall have a pit with a depth of at least 2 feet from the lowest point of the underside of the platform framing to the pit floor or highest projection when the platform is at its lowest limit of travel. Toe guards, guide shoes or rollers attached to the platform and buffers or bumpers may extend into this space.

(f) Substantial guides of either wood or steel are required for installation on lumber elevators.

(g) Lifting capacity shall equal a live load of at least 50 pounds per square foot of platform floor area. The gross weight of the movable platform shall include railings, aprons, wirings, conduits, outlets and every item that is permanently attached to the platform and its rated lifting capacity.

(h) The lifting speed of a lumber elevator may not exceed 15 feet per minute.

(i) A lumber elevator shall be equipped with operating switches that meet the following requirements:

(1) An operating switch shall be located where the entire shaftway is visible when gates are not installed.

(2) An operating switch shall be a continuous pressure switch.

(3) A manually operated emergency stop switch shall be placed adjacent to the elevator's operating switches, driving machines, pit entrances, machine controller and landings. An emergency stop switch shall be a manually reset switch and cannot be dependent upon springs for proper operation.

(4) An emergency stop switch shall be red. No other switch may be red.

(5) Operating switches shall be labeled by function.

(j) Reverse phase protection is required when alternating current is used.

(k) Elevator screws shall be directly connecting with worm or beveled gears. Gears shall be enclosed in a housing.

(l) A lumber elevator that is not supported or operated by screws, plungers or similar means shall have approved platform safeties capable of stopping and holding the platform at any point of its travel and its rated lifting capacity.

(m) The motor, controller and brake shall be located in a lighted room outside of the shaftway, unless the devices are located in the pit. The lumber elevator shall be equipped with stone or masonry piers or columns capable of absorbing the impact of a full-loaded platform when the motor and controller are located in the pit.

(n) A lumber elevator shall be equipped with normal terminal limit switches located in the shaftway or stop motion devices on the operating machine and arranged to automatically bring the platform to rest at either terminal landing.

(o) Final terminal limit switches shall be installed and connected so the switch will function if a lumber elevator runs by the normal terminal limit switch. Final terminal limit switches will automatically shut off the power, apply the brake and prevent the operation of the lumber elevator in either direction until adjustments are made to return the lumber elevator to normal operation. Final terminal limit switches shall be located in the shaftway.

(p) A slack cable or slack chain device shall be installed on all winding drum or sprocket power-driven lumber elevator machinery. The device shall automatically shut off the power, apply the brake and stop the machinery when the platform is obstructed in its descent.

(q) A lumber elevator shall be equipped with an approved and enclosed fused main line switch or an approved and enclosed circuit breaker switch. The switch shall be located adjacent to the entrance door in the machine room when the motor and controller are located in a machine room. The switch shall be located outside of the shaftway and adjacent to the pit access door when the motor and controller are located in the pit.

(r) A motor or controller shall be equipped with a second device for disconnection when the motor or controller is not visible from the disconnection equipment required in subsection (q). The second disconnection device shall be equipped to accept a padlock that can lock the device in an "open" and "off" position.

(s) Lighting shall be provided in all machine spaces and pits within the shaftway and landings. The light switch shall be mounted at the entryway to a machine space and pit.

(t) A lumber elevator shall be equipped with a door that allows access to the pit when the motor or controller is located in the pit. A pit access door is to meet all of the following requirements:

(1) A pit access door shall be located below the bottom of the platform when the platform is at its lowest limit of travel.

(2) A pit access door shall be at least 30 inches by 30 inches in size, self-closing and self-locking.

(3) A pit access door shall have a switch to prevent operation of the elevator while the pit access door is open.

(4) An emergency stop switch shall be installed on the strike side of each pit access door.

(5) A switch for operating the pit lights shall be installed on the strike side of all pit access doors.

(6) A sign shall be located on the exterior strike side of each pit access door with the notation, "CAUTION-Elevator Pit Access Door-Authorized Personnel Only." The sign lettering shall be a minimum of ¼ inch in width and 1½

inches in height. The color of the lettering shall contrast with the color of the access door.

(7) An owner or owner's agent shall have sole possession of keys to each pit access door.

(u) A lumber elevator platform shall have a steel frame designed with a minimum safety factor of six based on the highest rating of either the rated lifting load or the rated static load, uniformly distributed.

(v) A platform shall be equipped with an apron on all its sides. When the travel distance of a lumber elevator extends above the top of the surrounding floor level, the apron shall have sufficient depth to enclose the space between the floor level and the under side of the platform when the platform is at its travel limit.

(w) As part of the initial inspection, the elevator shall be loaded to rated lifting capacity and operated throughout its entire travel. Platform safeties are to be tested with the maximum rated lifting capacity.

STAGE, ORCHESTRA AND ORGAN CONSOLE ELEVATORS

§ 405.31. Applicability.

The following types of elevators shall meet the requirements of this section and § § 405.32—405.41:

(1) A stage elevator consisting of a section of the stage arranged to be raised and lowered above and below the stage in a vertical direction.

(2) An orchestra elevator consisting of a platform arranged to be raised and lowered in a vertical direction.

(3) An organ console elevator used for raising and lowering an organ console, including the organist in a vertical direction.

§ 405.32. Platforms.

(a) A stage, orchestra or organ console elevator platform shall be comprised of steel frame construction and designed with a safety factor of at least six based on the highest rating of either the rated lifting load or the rated static load uniformly distributed.

(b) When the travel of a stage, orchestra or organ console elevator extends above the top of the shaftway enclosure, the platform shall be equipped with an apron at least as deep as the space between the top of the shaftway enclosure and the underside of the platform when the platform is at its limit of travel.

CROSS REFERENCES

This section cited in 34 Pa. Code § 405.31 (relating to applicability).

§ 405.33. Shaftway requirements.

(a) The inside surface of a shaftway shall have a smooth finish within the limits of travel without any projections or recesses except for landing entrances, guides and guide brackets, vertical slots required for concealed guides, junction boxes and conduits for wiring, seating cart storage areas, orchestra areas and piano storage areas.

(b) Shaftway guide rails shall be made of steel.

(c) Adjacent lift sides shall be equipped with aprons, railings and toeboards and pressure-sensing strips that are necessary to avoid shearing and fall hazards when elevators or other lifts under this section are installed in the same shaftway.

CROSS REFERENCES

This section cited in 34 Pa. Code § 405.31 (relating to applicability).

§ 405.34. Projections and recesses.

Projections or recesses for landing entrances, junction boxes and conduits for wiring, seating cart storage areas, orchestra areas and piano storage areas shall have the following protection:

(1) Metal bevel plates shall protect the underside and topside of projections and the underside of all recesses. The plates shall extend from the edge of the projection or recess to the wall. The beveled angle may not be less than 75° relative to a horizontal position. Instead of plates, the bevel surfaces may be made of concrete and troweled to a smooth finish. Pressure sensing strips meeting the requirements in paragraph (2) may be used instead of beveled plates.

(2) Pressure sensing strips shall be placed on the underside of the platform on sides where there is a projection or recessed opening and on an apron attached to the platform. Pressure sensing strips shall meet the following requirements:

(i) A strip shall be interconnected to the operating and controlling circuit of the elevator.

(ii) A strip shall detect an obstruction that exerts a force of 5 pounds or greater per square inch.

(iii) The elevator shall immediately stop and automatically reverse direction for travel of 2—4 inches when a strip detects an obstruction. The pressure strips may automatically reset once the elevator has stopped its reverse travel.

CROSS REFERENCES

This section cited in 34 Pa. Code § 405.31 (relating to applicability).

§ 405.35. Landing doors.

(a) Swinging doors installed at the bottom landing of the shaftway shall open outward.

(b) Shaftway landing doors shall be equipped with a Department-approved interlock. The interlock shall:

(1) Secure the platform in the stop position or place the power of controlling the elevator beyond the operator's control while any landing door is open.

(2) Operate in conjunction with a normally closed electrical valve operating system when used for maintained pressure hydraulic elevators.

(c) A landing door may unlock only when the platform is stopped at the level where the landing doors are located.

(d) Landing doors shall open manually from inside the shaftway regardless of the platform's position.

CROSS REFERENCES

This section cited in 34 Pa. Code § 405.31 (relating to applicability).

§ 405.36. Lifting capacity.

(a) The lifting capacity of an orchestra or organ console elevator shall equal a live load of at least 25 pounds per square foot of floor area of the platform.

(b) The lifting capacity of a stage elevator shall equal a live load of at least 75 pounds per square foot of floor area of the platform.

Chapter 30 Emergency Management
Chapter 29 Counterterrorism Planning
Chapter 28 Social Security Number Privacy Act
Chapter 27 Municipal Code Compliance & Blight
Chapter 26 Construction Code Regulations
Chapter 25 Construction Code Act

CROSS REFERENCES

This section cited in 34 Pa. Code § 405.31 (relating to applicability).

§ 405.37. Operating speed.

Operating speed of an orchestra or organ console elevator may not exceed 30 feet per minute.

CROSS REFERENCES

This section cited in 34 Pa. Code § 405.31 (relating to applicability).

§ 405.38. Operating controls.

Operating controls shall be located so that the operator may view the platform and load throughout their entire travel. Operating controls are governed by the following:

(1) Operating controls shall be continuous pressure switches.

(2) Detachable pendent switches that plug into the platform or at an area other than the platform may be installed as operating controls if the operator can view the platform and load throughout their entire travel.

(3) Emergency stop switches that comply with all of the following:

(i) Manually operated emergency stop switches shall be located adjacent to the operating controls, driving machines, pit entrances, machine controller, orchestra areas and recessed storage areas located within the shaftway.

(ii) Emergency stop switches shall be manually reset and not depend upon springs for proper operation.

(iii) Emergency stop switches shall be red. No other switch may be red.

(iv) An emergency stop switch shall be installed on an organ console elevator in a location accessible to the organist.

(4) Operating controls shall be labeled by function.

(5) A key is required for use of the operating controls other than emergency stop switches.

(6) A stage, orchestra or organ console elevator that intersects with other stage, orchestra, organ console elevators, storage areas or orchestra areas below the stage level shall be equipped with a constant pressure pushbutton switch which meets the following requirements:

(i) The additional switch shall be located to permit an unobstructed view of the intersecting area.

(ii) The switch shall be held in the closed or ''run'' position to complete the operating circuit and permit the operator's controls to function.

(iii) Release of the switch will stop the elevator immediately.

(iv) An additional switch is not required for elevators that are completely enclosed in an operating shaftway.

CROSS REFERENCES

This section cited in 34 Pa. Code § 405.31 (relating to applicability).

§ 405.39. Switches.

(a) An elevator shall be equipped with normal terminal limit switches located in the shaft way or a stop motion device on the operating machine. The switches or device shall automatically bring the platform to rest at either terminal landing.

(b) Final terminal limit switches shall be installed in the shaftway and meet the following requirements:

(1) The switches shall be connected so that the functioning of the switch will occur if the elevator runs by the normal terminal limit switch.

(2) A final terminal limit switch is to automatically shut off power, apply the brake and prevent the operation of the elevator in either direction until adjustments are made to return the elevator to normal operation.

(c) An approved and enclosed fused main line switch or an approved circuit breaker switch shall be installed to disconnect the elevator and meet the following requirements:

(1) The switch shall be located adjacent to the entrance door in a machine room containing the motor and controller.

(2) The switch shall be located outside the shaftway and adjacent to the pit access door when the motor and controller are located in the pit.

CROSS REFENENCES

This section cited in 34 Pa. Code § 405.31 (relating to applicability).

§ 405.40. Pit and pit access.

(a) The pit shall be equipped with stone or masonry piers or columns or buffers capable of absorbing the impact of a fully loaded platform while maintaining a minimum refuge space of 2 feet throughout the pit area.

(b) A pit access door has to meet all of the following requirements:

(1) A pit access door shall be a minimum of 30 inches by 30 inches in size, self-closing and self-locking.

(2) Have a switch to prevent the operation of the elevator while the pit access door is open.

(3) An emergency stop switch shall be installed on the strike side of each pit access door.

(4) A switch for operating the pit lights shall be installed on the strike side of each pit access door.

(5) Contain a sign located on the exterior strike side of all pit access doors with the notation, "CAUTION—Elevator Pit Access Door—Authorized Personnel Only." The sign lettering is to be a minimum of 1/4 inch in width and 1 1/2 inches in height. The color of the lettering shall contrast with the color of the access door.

(6) An owner or owner's agent shall have sole possession of keys to each access door.

(c) A shaftway shall have a pit that meets all of the following requirements:

(1) Pit depth shall be at least 2 feet from the lowest point of the underside of the platform framing to the pit floor or highest floor projection when the platform is at its lowest limit of travel. Toe guards, guide shoes or rollers attached to the platform and buffers or bumpers may extend into this space.

(2) Clearance between the lowest point of an apron, guide shoe or rollers on the underside of the platform and any portion of the pit floor shall be at least 6 inches when the platform has reached its lowest limit of travel.

(3) Pit floor area directly beneath any apron area of the platform shall be marked with paint of at least two contrasting colors to a minimum width of 12 inches past the inside edge of the apron, guide shoe or rollers

(d) A door shall be installed to provide access to a pit when the motor or controller for a stage, orchestra or organ console elevator is located in the pit by one of the following means:

(1) A door below the bottom of the platform when the platform is at its lowest limit of travel.

(2) A door that opens outward in the platform.

(3) The pit shall be equipped with a ladder for gaining access to the pit through this access door.

(4) The ladder and access door shall be arranged to secure the ladder to the platform during access to the pit.

(5) The ladder shall extend from the platform to the pit floor regardless of the location of the platform in the shaftway.

CROSS REFERENCES

This section cited in 34 Pa. Code § 405.31 (relating to applicability).

§ 405.41. Single operator requirement.

A single operator is required to control operation of a stage, orchestra or organ console elevator under all of the following conditions:

(1) The operator and designated material handlers are the only persons that may ride on a stage or orchestra elevator.

(2) The operator and organist are the only persons that may ride on an organ console elevator. An organist may be the operator of the elevator if he receives adequate training on the operation of the elevator and all its controls.

(3) An operator is required to work with an assistant when using a stage, orchestra or organ console elevator that intersects with another stage, orchestra, organ console elevator, storage areas or orchestra areas below the stage level. The assistant shall insure that there are no obstructions in the path of the elevator being operated. The assistant shall always use a two-way communication device with the operator.

CROSS REFERENCES

This section cited in 34 Pa. Code § 405.31 (relating to applicability).

§ 405.42. Additional requirements.

(a) Railings and toeboards shall be provided at floor levels when the elevator is not at floor level. The railing and toeboard are to be interconnected to the operating circuit so that if any portion of the rail and toeboard is not in its proper placement, the elevator cannot operate.

(b) A key shall be located at the lowest floor in a container with a glass surface. This key shall open a landing door regardless of the location of the platform.

(c) A plate attached to the equipment controller shall contain the manufacturer's listed rated lifting capacity and maximum static load.

(d) The gross weight of the movable platform shall be posted on the controller and will include railings, aprons, wiring, conduits, outlets or an item that is permanently attached to the platform and related lifting capacity.

(e) Reverse phase protection shall be provided when alternating current is used.

(f) Elevator screws are to be directly connecting with worm or beveled gears. Gears shall be enclosed in a housing.

(g) A stage, orchestra or organ console elevator that is not supported or operated by screws, plungers or similar means shall have platform safeties capable of stopping and holding the platform with a full-rated load at any point of its travel.

(h) The motor controller and brake shall be located in a lighted room outside the shaftway, unless the devices are located in the pit.

(i) A slack cable or slack chain device shall be installed on all winding drum or sprocket power-driven stage, orchestra or organ console elevator machinery. The device shall automatically shut off the power, apply the brake and stop the machinery when the platform is obstructed in its descent.

(j) A motor or controller shall be equipped with a second device for disconnection when the motor or controller is not visible from the mainline disconnect switch.

(k) Lighting shall be provided in all machine spaces, pits, storage areas, orchestra areas and landings within the shaftway. A light switch shall be mounted at the entryway to each area.

CHAPTER 27.1

MUNICIPAL CODE AND ORDINANCE COMPLIANCE ACT AND BLIGHT

68 P.S. §§ 1081–1083

TABLE OF CONTENTS

---

§ 1. Short title.[1]

This act shall be known and may be cited as the Municipal Code and Ordinance Compliance Act.

§ 2. Definitions.[2]

The following words and phrases when used in this act shall have the meanings given to them in this section unless the context clearly indicates otherwise:

"Constructive knowledge." (Deleted by amendment)

"Date of purchase." The date on which title and right to possess the property transfers to the purchaser or, in cases where the property is sold pursuant to the act of May 16, 1923 (P.L.207, No.153), referred to as the Municipal Claim and Tax Lien Law, the first day following the right of redemption period authorized under the Municipal Claim and Tax Lien Law.

"Known to have." (Deleted by amendment)

"Municipality." Any of the following:

(1) Any city, borough, incorporated town, township, home rule municipality, optional plan municipality, optional charter municipality or any similar general purpose unit of government which may be created or authorized by statute.

(2) An authority or instrumentality of a unit of government specified under paragraph (1).

"Substantial violation." A violation of an adopted building, housing, property maintenance or fire code or maintenance, health or safety nuisance ordinance that makes a building, structure or any part thereof unfit for human habitation and is discovered during the course of a municipal inspection of a property and disclosed to the record owner or prospective purchaser of the property through issuance of a municipal report.

"Temporary access certificate." A certificate issued by a municipality as a result of the municipal inspection of a property incident to the resale of the property that identifies at least one substantial violation, and the purpose of the certificate is to authorize the purchaser to access the property for the purpose of correcting substantial violations pursuant to the maintenance and repair provi-

---

1. 68 P.S. § 1081.
2. 68 P.S. § 1082.

sions of this act. No new occupant who has not previously occupied a property may occupy a property during the term of a temporary access certificate, but tenants, in the case of a tenant-occupied property, already occupying the property may remain in the property at the discretion of code enforcement based on human habitability. The owner shall be permitted to store personalty that is related to the proposed use or occupancy of the property or is needed to repair the substantial violations during the time of the temporary access certificate.

"Temporary use and occupancy certificate." A certificate issued by a municipality as a result of the municipal inspection of a property incident to the resale of the property that reveals a violation but no substantial violation, and the purpose of the certificate is to authorize the purchaser to fully utilize or reside in the property while correcting violations pursuant to the maintenance and repair provisions of this act.

"Unfit for human habitation." A condition which renders a building or structure, or any part thereof, dangerous or injurious to the health, safety or physical welfare of an occupant or the occupants of neighboring dwellings. The condition may include substantial violations of a property that show evidence of: a significant increase to the hazards of fire or accident; inadequate sanitary facilities; vermin infestation; or a condition of disrepair, dilapidation or structural defects such that the cost of rehabilitation and repair would exceed one-half of the agreed-upon purchase price of the property.

"Use and occupancy certificate." A certificate issued by a municipality stipulating that the property meets ordinances and codes and may be used or occupied as intended.

"Violation." A violation of a properly adopted building, housing, property maintenance or fire code or maintenance, health or safety nuisance ordinance that does not rise to the level of a substantial violation and is discovered during the course of a municipal inspection of a property and disclosed to the record owner or prospective purchaser of the property through issuance of a municipal report.

§ 2.1. Issuance of use and occupancy certificate.[3]

(a) General rule.—A municipality requiring a use and occupancy certificate shall issue the certificate in the following manner:

(1) If the municipal inspection reveals no violations.

(2) If the municipal inspection reveals at least one violation, but no substantial violations, the municipality shall issue a temporary use and occupancy certificate.

(3) If the municipal inspection reveals at least one substantial violation, the municipality shall specifically note those items on the inspection report and shall issue a temporary access certificate.

(b) Escrows and bonds prohibited.—A municipality may not require the escrowing of funds or posting of a bond, or impose any similar financial security as a condition of issuing a certificate.

(c) Construction.—Subsection (b) shall not be construed to prohibit a municipality from requiring an owner, prior to accessing the property, to acquire the necessary permits and meet all other related obligations in other statutes that pertain to building, property maintenance, fire codes or other health or safety codes.

§ 2.2. Applicability.[4]

(a) Applicability.—Except as set forth in subsection (b), this act shall not apply to, and a municipality may not require, a certificate of occupancy, a temporary use and occupancy certificate or a temporary access certificate for a real estate

3. 68 P.S. § 1082.1.
4. 68 P.S. § 1082.2.

transfer, including a residential or nonresidential transfer, as provided under 68 Pa.C.S. § 7103(b)(2) (relating to application of part), to any of the following which take title to property for the purpose of holding the property for sale to offset losses incurred on a loan or other obligation in default secured by a mortgage, deed of trust or other lien on the property:

(1) Bank.

(2) Savings association.

(3) Credit union.

(4) Mortgage lender.

(5) Financial institution similar to an institution listed in paragraphs (1) through (4).

(6) Subsidiary of a financial institution listed in paragraphs (1) through (5).

(b) Exception.—A financial institution not subject to this act under subsection (a) may be required by a municipality to correct a substantial violation.

§ 3. Compliance requirement.[5]

(a) General rule.—Within 12 months of the date of purchase, the purchaser of a property known to be in violation or substantial violation of a municipal code or ordinance shall, at his option, either:

(1) bring the property into compliance with municipal codes or ordinances; or

(2) demolish the building or structure in accordance with law.

(a.1) Negotiation of longer time periods.—At the request of the property owner, the municipality may negotiate, at its discretion, longer time periods for maintenance and repair of the structure under a temporary certificate, but the time periods stated in subsection (a) may not be shortened.

(a.2) Reinspection of property.—

(1) At the expiration of the time period set forth in subsection (a) or before that time, if requested by the property owner, the municipality shall reinspect the property for the purpose of determining compliance with the cited violations.

(2) If a temporary access certificate has been issued and reinspection indicates that the noted substantial violations have been corrected and no other substantial violations that make the property unfit for human habitation are noticed but other cited violations have not yet been corrected, the municipality shall issue a temporary use and occupancy certificate to be valid for the time remaining on the original temporary access certificate.

(3) If the reinspection indicates that all noted violations have been corrected, the municipality shall issue a use and occupancy certificate for the property.

(b) Penalty.—

(1) Failure to comply with the requirements of subsection (a) shall result in:

(i) Revocation of the temporary certificate.

(ii) The purchaser being subject to any existing municipal ordinances or codes relating to the occupation of a property without a use and occupancy certificate.

(iii) The purchaser being personally liable for the costs of maintenance, repairs or demolition sufficient to correct the cited violations, and a fine of not less than $1,000 and not more than $10,000.

(2) Fines shall be remitted to the municipality in which the building, structure or part of a building or structure is located.

---

5. 68 P.S. § 1083.

(3) In municipalities with low-income housing, not less than one-third of the fine imposed specifically for code violations shall be used by the municipality for low-income housing in a manner determined by the municipality.

(c) Nuisance ordinances.—(Deleted by amendment)

(d) Enforcement.—(Deleted by amendment)

(e) Coordination with other requirements.—(Deleted by amendment)

(f) Exception.—A violation of a municipal code or ordinance, for which a fine, other penalty or a judgment to abate or correct was imposed by a magisterial district judge or municipal court, or a judgment at law or in equity was imposed by a court of common pleas prior to purchase, shall not be subject to the requirements of this section.

(g) Nonapplicability.—This section shall not apply where the municipality denies the certificate or permit pursuant to 53 Pa.C.S. Ch. 61 (relating to neighborhood blight reclamation and revitalization).

CHAPTER 27.2

MUNICIPALITY CONDEMNATION ORDER ACT

53 P.S. §§ 4271–4277

AN ACT Providing for filing and recording by municipalities of condemnation orders and for statements of vacated condemnation orders.

§ 1. Short title.

This act shall be known and may be cited as the Municipality Condemnation Order Act.

§ 2. Definitions.

The following words and phrases when used in this act shall have the meanings given to them in this section unless the context clearly indicates otherwise:

"Condemnation order." A declaration by an authorized official of a municipality that a dwelling, building, structure or premises is unfit for human habitation or other use or conditions exist that are dangerous or injurious to the health or safety of the occupants of the dwelling, building, structure or premises, the occupants of neighboring dwellings or other residents of the municipality and which declaration includes a demand for the owner to take corrective action to the dwelling, building, structure or premises.

"Municipality." A city, borough, incorporated town, township, home rule municipality, optional plan municipality, optional charter municipality or similar general purpose unit of government that may be created or authorized by statute.

§ 3. Filing and recording of condemnation orders.

(a) General rule.—A municipality that issues a condemnation order on a property may record the condemnation order with the office of recorder of deeds of the county in which the property is located.

(b) Constructive notice.—If recorded, the condemnation order shall be constructive notice to all purchasers and other persons who are responsible for the property.

§ 4. Cost of recording.

A municipality may recover the cost of recording a condemnation order on a property from the tax sale proceeds or directly from the purchaser of the property.

§ 5. Validity of condemnation order.

Notwithstanding section 612(a) of the act of July 7, 1947 (P.L.1368, No.542), known as the Real Estate Tax Sale Law, a properly recorded condemnation order shall be a lien on the property and shall not be affected by an upset sale, a judicial sale or a repository sale of the property.

§ 6. Statement of vacated condemnation order.

After a condemnation order on a property has been recorded under this section, if the municipality vacates the condemnation order, the municipality shall, within 15 days of the condemnation order being vacated, record with the office of recorder of deeds a statement indicating that the condemnation order has been vacated.

§ 7. Effective date.

This act shall take effect in 60 days.

Note: Approved by the Governor October 29, 2020
Effective date: December 28, 2020

CHAPTER 27.3

FAILURE TO COMPLY WITH A CODE REQUIREMENT

53 Pa.C.S. § 6115

§ 6115. Failure to comply with a code requirement.

(a) Offense defined.—The owner of real property commits the offense of failure to comply with a code requirement if all of the following apply:

(1) The owner of real property has been convicted of a second or subsequent serious violation of the same provision of a municipal code for the same property.

(2) The violation poses a threat to the public's health, safety or property and the owner has not taken a substantial step to correct the violation.

(3) The violation is considered a public nuisance and the owner has not made a reasonable attempt to correct the violation.

(b) Grading.—Failure to comply with a code requirement shall constitute a:

(1) Misdemeanor of the second degree if the offense is a second conviction of a serious violation of the same provision of a municipal code relating to the same property.

(2) Misdemeanor of the first degree if the offense is based on three or more convictions of serious violations of the same provision of a municipal code relating to the same property.

(c) Definition.—As used in this section, "code requirement" shall mean a building, housing or property maintenance code or ordinance of a municipality.

CHAPTER 27.4

NEIGHBORHOOD BLIGHT RECLAMATION AND REVITALIZATION ACT

53 Pa.C.S. § 6101-6145

TABLE OF CONTENTS

NEIGHBORHOOD BLIGHT RECLAMATION AND REVITALIZATION

SUBCHAPTER A. PRELIMINARY PROVISIONS

§ 6101. Short title of chapter.

This chapter shall be known and may be cited as the Neighborhood Blight Reclamation and Revitalization Act.

§ 6102. Legislative findings and purpose.

The General Assembly finds and declares as follows:

(1) There are deteriorated properties located in all municipalities of this Commonwealth as a result of neglect by their owners in violation of applicable State and municipal codes.

(2) These deteriorated properties create public nuisances which have an impact on crime and the quality of life of our residents and require significant expenditures of public funds in order to abate and correct the nuisances.

(3) In order to address these situations, it is appropriate to deny certain governmental permits and approvals in order:

Table of Contents
Part I Ch. 1–3 Ethics, Records, Open Meetings
Part II Ch. 4–10 Taxation
Part III Ch. 11–18 Torts, Contracts & Civil Rules
Part IV Ch. 19–24 Zoning & Planning
Part V Ch. 25–30 Construction and Emergency Codes
Part VI Ch. 31–39 Municipal Codes
Index

(i) To prohibit property owners from further extending their financial commitments so as to render themselves unable to abate or correct the code, statutory and regulatory violations or tax delinquencies.

(ii) To reduce the likelihood that other municipalities will have to address the owners' neglect and resulting deteriorated properties.

(iii) To sanction the owners for not adhering to their legal obligations to the Commonwealth and its municipalities, as well as to tenants, adjoining property owners and neighborhoods.

§ 6103. Definitions.

The following words and phrases when used in this chapter shall have the meanings given to them in this section unless the context clearly indicates otherwise:

"Agent." Any director, officer, servant, employee or other person authorized to act in behalf of a corporation or association and, in the case of an unincorporated association, a member of such association.

"Building." A residential, commercial or industrial building or structure and the land appurtenant to it.

"Corporation." The term does not include a municipal authority.

"Court." The appropriate court of common pleas.

"Mortgage lender." A business association defined as a "banking institution" or "mortgage lender" under 7 Pa.C.S. Ch. 61 (relating to mortgage loan industry licensing and consumer protection) that is in possession of or holds title to real property pursuant to, in enforcement of or to protect rights arising under a mortgage, mortgage note, deed of trust or other transaction that created a security interest in the real property.

"Municipal code" or "code." A building, housing, property maintenance, fire, health or other public safety ordinance, related to the use or maintenance of real property, enacted by a municipality. The term does not include a subdivision and land development ordinance or a zoning ordinance enacted by a municipality.

"Municipality." A city, borough, incorporated town, township or home rule, optional plan or optional charter municipality or municipal authority in this Commonwealth and any entity formed pursuant to Subchapter A of Chapter 23 (relating to intergovernmental cooperation).

"Municipal permits." Privileges relating to real property granted by a municipality, including, but not limited to, building permits, exceptions to zoning ordinances and occupancy permits. The term includes approvals pursuant to land use ordinances other than decisions on the substantive validity of a zoning ordinance or map or the acceptance of a curative amendment.

"Owner." A holder of the title to residential, commercial or industrial real estate, a mortgage lender, who possesses and controls the real estate. The term includes, but is not limited to, heirs, assigns, beneficiaries and lessees, provided this ownership interest is a matter of public record.

"Public nuisance." Property which, because of its physical condition or use, is regarded as a public nuisance at common law or has been declared by the appropriate official a public nuisance in accordance with a municipal code.

"Serious violation." A violation of a State law or a code that poses an imminent threat to the health and safety of a dwelling occupant, occupants in surrounding structures or a passersby.

"State law." A statute of the Commonwealth or a regulation of an agency charged with the administration and enforcement of Commonwealth law.

"Substantial step." An affirmative action as determined by a property code official or officer of the court on the part of a property owner or managing agent to remedy a serious violation of a State law or municipal code, including, but not limited to, physical improvements or repairs to the property, which affirmative action is subject to appeal in accordance with applicable law.

"Tax delinquent property." Tax delinquent real property as defined under:

(1) the act of July 7, 1947 (P.L.1368, No.542), known as the Real Estate Tax Sale Law;[1]

(2) the act of May 16, 1923 (P.L.207, No. 153), referred to as the Municipal Claim and Tax Lien Law;[2] or

(3) the act of October 11, 1984 (P.L.876, No.171), known as the Second Class City Treasurer's Sale and Collection Act, located in any municipality in this Commonwealth.[3]

SUBCHAPTER B. ACTIONS AGAINST OWNER OF PROPERTY WITH SERIOUS CODE VIOLATIONS

§ 6111. Actions.

In addition to any other remedy available at law or in equity, a municipality may institute the following actions against the owner of any real property that is in serious violation of a code or for failure to correct a condition which causes the property to be regarded as a public nuisance:

(1)(i) An in personam action may be initiated for a continuing violation for which the owner takes no substantial step to correct within six months following receipt of an order to correct the violation, unless the order is subject to a pending appeal before the administrative agency or court.

(ii) Notwithstanding any law limiting the form of action for the recovery of penalties by a municipality for the violation of a code, the municipality may recover, in a single action under this section, an amount equal to any penalties imposed against the owner and any costs of remediation lawfully incurred by or on behalf of the municipality to remedy any code violation.

(2) A proceeding in equity.

§ 6112. Asset attachment.

(a) General rule.—A lien may be placed against the assets of an owner of real property that is in serious violation of a code or is regarded as a public nuisance after a judgment, decree or order is entered by a court of competent jurisdiction against the owner of the property for an adjudication under section 6111 (relating to actions).

(b) Construction.—Nothing in this section shall be construed to authorize, in the case of an owner that is a corporation, association or trust, a lien on the individual assets of the general partner, agent or trustee, except as otherwise allowed by law, limited partner, shareholder, member or beneficiary of the association or trust.

§ 6113. Duty of out-of-state owners of property in this commonwealth.

A person or other responsible party who lives or has a principal place of residence outside this Commonwealth, who owns or is responsible for property in this Commonwealth against which code violations have been cited and the person is charged under 18 Pa.C.S. (relating to crimes and offenses), and who has been properly notified of the violations may be extradited to this Commonwealth to face criminal prosecution to the full extent allowed and in the manner authorized by 42 Pa.C.S. Ch. 91 (relating to detainers and extradition).

---

1. 72 P.S. § 5860.101 et seq.
2. 53 P.S. § 7101 et seq.
3. 53 P.S. § 27101 et seq.

§ 6114. Duty of corporation, association and trust owners.

Where, after reasonable efforts, service of process for a notice or citation for any code violation for any real property owned by a corporation, association or trust cannot be accomplished by handing a copy of the notice or citation to an agent, executive officer, partner or trustee of the corporation, association or trust or to the manager, trustee or clerk in charge of the property, the delivery of the notice or citation may occur by registered, certified or United States Express mail, accompanied by a delivery confirmation:

(1) To the registered office of the corporation, association or trust.

(2) Where the corporation, association or trust does not have a registered office, to the mailing address used for real estate tax collection purposes, if accompanied by the posting of a conspicuous notice to the property and by handing a copy of the notice or citation to the person in charge of the property at that time.

(3) In the case of a corporation, notice shall be sent to the registered office on file with the Department of State.

§ 6115. Failure to comply with a code requirement.

(a) Offense defined.—The owner of real property commits the offense of failure to comply with a code requirement if all of the following apply:

(1) The owner of real property has been convicted of a second or subsequent serious violation of the same provision of a municipal code for the same property.

(2) The violation poses a threat to the public's health, safety or property and the owner has not taken a substantial step to correct the violation.

(3) The violation is considered a public nuisance and the owner has not made a reasonable attempt to correct the violation.

(b) Grading.—Failure to comply with a code requirement shall constitute a:

(1) Misdemeanor of the second degree if the offense is a second conviction of a serious violation of the same provision of a municipal code relating to the same property.

(2) Misdemeanor of the first degree if the offense is based on three or more convictions of serious violations of the same provision of a municipal code relating to the same property.

(c) Definition.—As used in this section, "code requirement" shall mean a building, housing or property maintenance code or ordinance of a municipality.

SUBCHAPTER C. PERMIT DENIALS BY MUNICIPALITIES

§ 6131. Municipal permit denial.

(a) Denial.—

(1) A municipality or a board under subsection (c) may deny issuing to an applicant a municipal permit if the applicant owns real property in any municipality for which there exists on the real property:

(i) a final and unappealable tax, water, sewer or refuse collection delinquency on account of the actions of the owner; or

(ii) a serious violation of State law or a code and the owner has taken no substantial steps to correct the violation within six months following notification of the violation and for which fines or other penalties or a judgment to abate or correct were imposed by a magisterial district judge or municipal

Chapter 30 Emergency Management
Chapter 29 Counterterrorism Planning
Chapter 28 Social Security Number Privacy Act
Chapter 27 Municipal Code Compliance & Blight
Chapter 26 Construction Code Regulations
Chapter 25 Construction Code Act

court, or a judgment at law or in equity was imposed by a court of common pleas. However, no denial shall be permitted on the basis of a property for which the judgment, order or decree is subject to a stay or supersedeas by an order of a court of competent jurisdiction or automatically allowed by statute or rule of court until the stay or supersedeas is lifted by the court or a higher court or the stay or supersedeas expires as otherwise provided by law. Where a stay or supersedeas is in effect, the property owner shall so advise the municipality seeking to deny a municipal permit.

(2) A municipality or board shall not deny a municipal permit to an applicant if the municipal permit is necessary to correct a violation of State law or a code.

(3) The municipal permit denial shall not apply to an applicant's delinquency on taxes, water, sewer or refuse collection charges that are under appeal or otherwise contested through a court or administrative process.

(4) In issuing a denial of a permit based on an applicant's delinquency in real property taxes or municipal charges or for failure to abate a serious violation of State law or a code on real property that the applicant owns in this Commonwealth, the municipality or board shall indicate the street address, municipal corporation and county in which the property is located and the court and docket number for each parcel cited as a basis for the denial. The denial shall also state that the applicant may request a letter of compliance from the appropriate State agency, municipality or school district, in a form specified by such entity as provided in this section.

(b) Proof of compliance.—

(1) All municipal permits denied in accordance with this subsection may be withheld until an applicant obtains a letter from the appropriate State agency, municipality or school district indicating the following:

(i) the property in question has no final and unappealable tax, water, sewer or refuse delinquencies;

(ii) the property in question is now in State law and code compliance; or

(iii) the owner of the property has presented and the appropriate State agency or municipality has accepted a plan to begin remediation of a serious violation of State law or a code. Acceptance of the plan may be contingent on:

(A) Beginning the remediation plan within no fewer than 30 days following acceptance of the plan or sooner, if mutually agreeable to both the property owner and the municipality.

(B) Completing the remediation plan within no fewer than 90 days following commencement of the plan or sooner, if mutually agreeable to both the property owner and the municipality.

(2) In the event that the appropriate State agency, municipality or school district fails to issue a letter indicating tax, water, sewer, refuse, State law or code compliance or noncompliance, as the case may be, within 45 days of the request, the property in question shall be deemed to be in compliance for the purpose of this section. The appropriate State agency, municipality or school district shall specify the form in which the request for a compliance letter shall be made.

(3) Letters required under this section shall be verified by the appropriate municipal officials before issuing to the applicant a municipal permit.

(4)(i) Municipal permits may be denied by a board in accordance with the requirements of this section to the extent that approval of the municipal permit is within the jurisdiction of the board. For purposes of this section, "board"

Table of Contents
Part I Ch. 1–3 Ethics, Records, Open Meetings
Part II Ch. 4–10 Taxation
Part III Ch. 11–18 Torts, Contracts & Civil Rules
Part IV Ch. 19–24 Zoning & Planning
Part V Ch. 25–30 Construction and Emergency Codes
Part VI Ch. 31–39 Municipal Codes
Index

shall mean a zoning hearing board or other body granted jurisdiction to render decisions in accordance with the act of July 31, 1968 (P.L. 805, No. 247),[1] known as the Pennsylvania Municipalities Planning Code, or a similar board in municipalities not subject to that act.

(ii) In any proceeding before a board other than the governing body of the municipality, the municipality may appear to present evidence that the applicant is subject to a denial by the board in accordance with this section.

(iii) For purposes of this subsection, a municipal permit may only be denied to an applicant other than an owner if:

(A) the applicant is acting under the direction or with the permission of an owner; and

(B) the owner owns real property satisfying the conditions of subsection (a).

(c) Applicability of other law.—A denial of a permit shall be subject to the provisions of 2 Pa.C.S. Chs. 5 Subch. B[2] (relating to practice and procedure of local agencies) and 7 Subch. B[3] (relating to judicial review of local agency action) or the Pennsylvania Municipalities Planning Code, for denials subject to the act.

SUBCHAPTER D. MISCELLANEOUS PROVISIONS

§ 6141. (Reserved)

§ 6142. (Reserved)

§ 6143. Conflict with other law.

In the event of a conflict between the requirements of this chapter and Federal requirements applicable to demolition, disposition or redevelopment of buildings, structures or land owned by or held in trust for the Government of the United States and regulated pursuant to the United States Housing Act of 1937 (50 Stat. 888, 42 U.S.C. § 1437 et seq.) and the regulations promulgated thereunder, the Federal requirements shall prevail.

§ 6144. Relief for inherited property.

Where property is inherited by will or intestacy, the devisee or heir shall be given the opportunity to make payments on reasonable terms to correct code violations or to enter into a remediation agreement under section 6131(b)(1)(iii) (relating to municipal permit denial) with a municipality to avoid subjecting the devisee's or heir's other properties to asset attachment or denial of permits and approvals on other properties owned by the devisee or heir.

§ 6145. Construction.

Nothing in this chapter shall be construed to abridge or alter the remedies now existing at common law or by statute, but the provisions of this chapter are in addition to such remedies.

1. 53 P.S. § 10101 et seq
2. 2Pa.C.S.A. § 551 et seq.
3. 2 Pa.C.S.A. § 751 et seq.

CHAPTER 27.5

ABANDONED AND BLIGHTED PROPERTY CONSERVATORSHIP ACT

68 P.S. §§ 1101–1111

---

§ 1101. Short title

This act shall be known and may be cited as the Abandoned and Blighted Property Conservatorship Act.

§ 1102. Legislative findings and purpose

The General Assembly finds and declares that:

(1) Pennsylvania's older communities are important to the Commonwealth's economic health by providing a focal point for businesses and services and to this Commonwealth's quality of life with its rich history and diverse communities. However, many older communities suffer from blighted properties that have been abandoned by their owners.

(2) Many citizens of this Commonwealth are adversely affected by abandoned and blighted residential, commercial and industrial properties, including those citizens who live in proximity to such substandard buildings, as well as those who own property in the vicinity of such buildings.

(3) Substandard, deteriorating and abandoned residential, commercial and industrial structures are a public safety threat and nuisance and their blighting effect diminishes property values in the communities in which these properties are located.

(4) If these buildings are not rehabilitated, they are likely to remain abandoned and further deteriorate, resulting in increased costs to the Commonwealth, municipality and taxpayers to secure and ultimately demolish them.

(5) Providing a mechanism to transform abandoned and blighted buildings into productive reuse is an opportunity for communities to modernize, revitalize grow, and to improve the quality of life for neighbors who are already there.

(6) If the owner of a residential, commercial or industrial building fails to maintain the property in accordance with applicable municipal codes or standards of public welfare or safety, it is in the best interest of the Commonwealth, the municipality and the community for the court, pursuant to the provisions of this act, to appoint a conservator to make the necessary improvements before the building deteriorates further and necessitates demolition, resulting in the

removal of the building from the housing supply or prohibiting future productive economic use.

§ 1103. Definitions

The following words and phrases when used in this act shall have the meanings given to them in this section unless the context clearly indicates otherwise:

"Abandoned property." Any property that meets the requirements of conditions for conservatorship as provided in section 5(d).[1]

"Actively marketed." A "for sale" sign has been placed on the property with accurate contact information and the owner has done at least one of the following:

(1) engaged the services of a licensee under the act of February 19, 1980 (P.L. 15, No. 9),[2] known as the Real Estate Licensing and Registration Act, to place the property in a Multiple Listing Service or otherwise market the property;

(2) placed weekly or more frequent advertisements in print or electronic media; or

(3) distributed printed advertisements.

"Building." A residential, commercial or industrial building or structure and the land appurtenant thereto, including a vacant lot on which a building has been demolished.

"Code." A building, housing, property maintenance, fire, health or other public safety ordinance enacted by a municipality.

"Competent entity." A person or entity, including a governmental unit with experience in the rehabilitation of residential, commercial or industrial buildings and the ability to provide or obtain the necessary financing for such rehabilitation.

"Conservator's or developer's fee." A fee equal to the greatest of the following:

(1) an amount equal to $2,500, adjusted upward by 2% each year;

(2) a 20% markup of the costs and expenses for construction, stabilization, rehabilitation, maintenance and operation or demolition as described in the proposed conservator's plan and any subsequent plan approved by the court; or

(3) twenty percent of the sale price of the property.

"Costs of rehabilitation." Costs and expenses for construction, stabilization, rehabilitation, maintenance and operation or demolition, including reasonable nonconstruction costs associated with the project, including, but not limited to, environmental remediation, architectural, engineering and legal fees and costs, permits, financing fees and a conservator's or developer's fee.

"Court." The appropriate court of common pleas.

"Historic property." A property which is listed on the National Register of Historic Places or is a contributing property in a national register historic district or is located in a local government ordinance historic district.

"Immediate family." A parent, spouse, child, brother or sister.

"Nonprofit corporation." A nonprofit corporation that has, as one of its purposes, remediation of blight, community development activities, including economic development, historic preservation or the promotion or enhancement of affordable housing opportunities.

"Owner." The holder or holders of title to, or of a legal or equitable interest in, a residential, commercial or industrial building. The term shall include an

---

1. 68 P.S. § 1105(d).
2. 63 P.S. § 455.101 et seq.

heir, assignee, trustee, beneficiary and lessee provided the ownership interest is a matter of public record.

"Party in interest." A person or entity who has a direct and immediate interest in a residential, commercial or industrial building, including:

(1) The owner.

(2) A lienholder and other secured creditor of the owner.

(3) A resident or business owner within 2,000 feet of the building.

(4) A nonprofit corporation, including a redevelopment authority, which:

(i) except as set forth in subparagraph (ii), is located in the municipality where the building is located; and

(ii) for a building located in a city of the first class, is located in the city and has participated in a project within a five-mile radius of the location of the building.

(5) A municipality or school district in which the building is located.

(6) A land bank as defined under 68 Pa.C.S. § 2103 (relating to definitions).

"Public nuisance." A property that, because of physical condition or use, has been declared by the appropriate official a public nuisance in accordance with the local housing, building, health, fire or related code or is determined to be a public nuisance by the court.

"Substantial rehabilitation." Repairs to the building where:

(1) the cost of repairs, replacements and improvements exceeds 15% of the property's value after completion of all repairs, replacements and improvements; or

(2) more than one major building component is being replaced. Major building components include:

(i) roof structures;

(ii) ceilings;

(iii) wall or floor structures;

(iv) foundations;

(v) plumbing systems;

(vi) heating and air conditioning systems; and

(vii) electrical systems.

§ 1104. Initiation of action

(a) Filing of petition.—A petition for the appointment of a conservator to take possession and to undertake the rehabilitation of a building may be filed by a party in interest in a court in the county in which the building is located. The proceeding on the petition shall constitute an action in rem.

(b) Contents.—The petition submitted to the court shall include a sworn statement that, to the best of the petitioner's knowledge, the property meets the conditions for conservatorship set forth in section 5(d)[3] and to the extent available to the petitioner after reasonable efforts to obtain such information:

(1) A copy of any citation charging the owner with being in violation of municipal code requirements or declaring the building to be a public nuisance.

(2) A recommendation as to which person or entity should be appointed conservator.

---

3. 68 P.S. § 1105.

(3) A preliminary plan with initial cost estimates for rehabilitation of the building to bring it into compliance with all municipal codes and duly adopted plans for the area in which the building is located and anticipated funding sources.

(4) A schedule of mortgages, liens and other encumbrances on the property.

(c) Notice of lis pendens.—The petitioner shall file a notice of lis pendens in the office of the recorder of deeds for the county in which the property is located.

(d) Notification of owner, political subdivisions and lienholders.—

(1) Upon filing the petition with the court, the petitioner shall notify the current owner of the property, all political subdivisions in which the property is located, all municipal authorities known to have provided service to the property and all lienholders of the filing by registered or certified mail to the last known address of each and by posting a copy of the notice on the building.

(2) In the event the registered or certified mail is returned with notation by the postal authorities that the recipient refused to accept the mail, the petitioner may mail a copy to the recipient at the same address by ordinary mail with the return address of the petitioner appearing thereon.

(3) Service by ordinary mail shall be presumed complete if the mail is not returned to the petitioner within 30 days after mailing.

(4) In the event that the registered or certified mail is returned with the notation by the postal authorities that it was unclaimed, the notice shall be personally served.

(5) In the event that the personal service is not able to be made after two such attempts, then the petitioner shall mail the petition to the recipient at the same address by ordinary mail with the return address of the petitioner appearing thereon with service by ordinary mail deemed complete if the mail is not returned to the petitioner within 15 days after the mailing.

(6) The petitioner shall also notify the owner and each lienholder of the hearing date and provide notice that the owner and lienholders may petition to intervene in the action.

(e) Adjacent properties.—The petition may include one or more adjacent properties in a single action if:

(1) the property that is the primary subject of the action is owned by the same owner as the adjacent property; and

(2) the properties are or were used for a single or interrelated function.

§ 1105. Appointment of conservator

(a) General rule.—The court shall act upon a petition submitted by holding a hearing within 60 days of receipt of the petition and by rendering a decision no later than 30 days after completion of the hearing.

(b) Intervention.—A party in interest may intervene in the proceeding and be heard with respect to the petition, the requested relief or any other matter which may come before the court in connection with the proceeding.

(c) Hearing.—At the hearing, any party in interest shall be permitted to present evidence to support or contest the petition, including, but not limited to, the schedule of encumbrances.

(d) Conditions for conservatorship.—If a petition is filed under section 4,[4] the court may appoint a conservator if all of the following apply as of the date of filing:

4. 68 P.S. § 1104.

(1) The building has not been legally occupied for at least the previous 12 months.

(2) The owner fails to present compelling evidence that he has actively marketed the property during the preceding 60-day period and made a good faith effort to sell the property at a price which reflects the circumstances and market conditions.

(3) The property is not subject to a pending foreclosure action by an individual or nongovernmental entity.

(4) The current owner fails to present sufficient evidence that he has acquired the property within the preceding six months. The evidence shall not include instances where the prior owner is a member of the immediate family of the current owner, unless the transfer of title results from the death of the prior owner, or where the current or prior owner is a corporation, partnership or other entity in which either owner or the immediate family of either owner has an interest in excess of 5%.

(5) The court finds at least three of the following:

(i) The building or physical structure is a public nuisance.

(ii) The building is in need of substantial rehabilitation and no rehabilitation has taken place during the previous 12 months.

(iii) The building is unfit for human habitation, occupancy or use.

(iv) The condition and vacancy of the building materially increase the risk of fire to the building and to adjacent properties.

(v) The building is subject to unauthorized entry leading to potential health and safety hazards and one of the following applies:

(A) The owner has failed to take reasonable and necessary measures to secure the building.

(B) The municipality has secured the building in order to prevent such hazards after the owner has failed to do so.

(vi) The property is an attractive nuisance to children, including, but not limited to, the presence of abandoned wells, shafts, basements, excavations and unsafe structures.

(vii) The presence of vermin or the accumulation of debris, uncut vegetation or physical deterioration of the structure or grounds has created potential health and safety hazards and the owner has failed to take reasonable and necessary measures to remove the hazards.

(viii) The dilapidated appearance or other condition of the building negatively affects the economic well-being of residents and businesses in close proximity to the building, including decreases in property value and loss of business, and the owner has failed to take reasonable and necessary measures to remedy appearance or the condition.

(ix) The property is an attractive nuisance for illicit purposes, including prostitution, drug use and vagrancy.

(e) Appointment.—

(1) If the court determines after a hearing that the property has met the conditions of subsection (d), the court may appoint a conservator, certify the schedule of encumbrances and grant such other relief as may be just and appropriate. The certification shall be binding with respect to all mortgages, liens and encumbrances, including municipal liens, arising or attaching to the property prior to the date of the petition.

(2) The court shall give first consideration for appointment as conservator to the most senior nongovernmental lienholder on the property.

Table of Contents
Part I Ch. 1–3 Ethics, Records, Open Meetings
Part II Ch. 4–10 Taxation
Part III Ch. 11–18 Torts, Contracts & Civil Rules
Part IV Ch. 19–24 Zoning & Planning
Part V Ch. 25–30 Construction and Emergency Codes
Part VI Ch. 31–39 Municipal Codes
Index

(3) In the event the senior lienholder is found to be not competent or declines the appointment, the court may appoint a nonprofit corporation or other competent entity. If the property is located in a city of the first class, the nonprofit corporation or entity must be located in the city and must have participated in a project within a five-mile radius of the location of the property. In appointing a conservator, the court shall:

(i) consider any recommendations contained in the petition or otherwise presented by a party in interest; and

(ii) give preference to the appointment of a nonprofit corporation or governmental unit over an individual.

(f) Conditional relief.—

(1) If the court finds after a hearing that the conditions for conservatorship set forth in subsection (d) have been established, but the owner represents that the conditions, violations or nuisance or emergency condition will be abated in a reasonable period, the court may allow the owner to proceed to remedy the conditions.

(2) If the conditions set forth in paragraph (1) have been satisfied, the court shall enter an order providing that, in the event that the violations or nuisance or emergency conditions are not abated by the owner by a specific date or that other specified remedial activities have not occurred by a specific date or dates, an order granting the relief requested in the petition shall be entered.

(3) The court shall also require the owner to post a bond in the amount of the repair costs estimated in the petition as a condition to retaining possession of the building.

(4) Upon a finding that:

(i) the petition states conditions for conservatorship; or

(ii) the owner elects to either:

(A) remedy all violations and nuisance or emergency conditions; or

(B) sell the property subject to the conservatorship, the owner shall reimburse the petitioner for all costs incurred by the petitioner in preparing and filing the petition in accordance with the requirements of section 4 and the conservator's or developer's fee.

(g) Conservator's lien.—The conservator may file a lien against the property in an amount based on the costs incurred during the conservatorship, including, but not limited to, costs of rehabilitation, attorney fees and court costs. The lien amount may be adjusted from time to time.

(h) Immediate possession.—The conservator shall promptly take possession of the building and other property subject to the conservatorship and shall immediately be authorized to exercise all powers of this act.

(i) Removal by court.—A conservator may be removed by the court at any time upon the request of the conservator or upon a showing by a party to the action that the conservator is not carrying out its responsibilities under this act.

§ 1106. Powers and duties of conservator

(a) Full powers and duties.—The conservator shall have all powers and duties necessary or desirable, from time to time, for the efficient operation, management and improvement of the building in order to bring it into compliance with all municipal building and housing code requirements and to fulfill the conservator's responsibilities under this act. Such powers and duties shall include, but not be limited to, the power to:

(1) Take possession and control of the building, appurtenant land and any personal property of the owner used with respect to the building, including any bank or operating account for the building.

(2) Collect outstanding accounts receivable.

(3) Pursue all claims or causes of action of the owner with respect to the building and all other property subject to the conservator.

(4) Contract for the repair and maintenance of the building. The contracts shall be appropriately documented and included in the reports and accounting which the conservator is required to submit or file under the provisions of this act. The conservator shall make a reasonable effort to solicit three bids for contracts valued at more than $25,000, except when the contractor or developer provides or obtains financing for the conservatorship.

(5) Borrow money and incur credit in accordance with section 8.[5]

(6) Contract and pay for the maintenance and restoration of utilities to the building.

(7) Purchase materials, goods and supplies to accomplish repairs and operate the building.

(8) With the court's approval, enter into new rental contracts and leases for a period not to exceed one year.

(9) Affirm, renew or enter into contracts providing for insurance coverage on the building.

(10) Engage and pay legal, accounting, appraisal and other professionals to aid the conservator in the conduct of the conservatorship.

(11) When the building has been designated a historic property, consult with the municipality's historical commission or board of historical and architectural review, a local historic preservation organization or, in the absence thereof, the Pennsylvania Historical and Museum Commission for recommendations on preserving the property's historic character.

(12) Apply for and receive public grants or loans.

(13) Sell the building in accordance with section 9.[6]

(14) Exercise all authority that an owner of the building would have to improve, maintain and otherwise manage the building, including the extent to which rehabilitation will satisfy the goals of the conservatorship.

(b) **Affirmative duty.**—While in possession of the building, the conservator shall:

(1) Maintain, safeguard and insure the building.

(2) Apply all revenue generated from the building consistent with the provisions of this act.

(3)(i) Develop a final plan for abatement of the conditions which caused the petition to be granted or, if no such feasible final plan can be developed, to develop alternatives, including the closing, sealing or demolition of all or part of the building.

(ii) When the building has been designated a historic property, rehabilitate architectural features that define the property's historic character.

(iii) When demolition of a property in a historic district is necessary, design any replacement construction on the site to comply with applicable standards under current law.

(4) Implement the final plan referred to in paragraph (3) upon approval by the court.

---

5. 68 P.S. § 1108.
6. 68 P.S. § 1109.

Table of Contents | Part I Ch. 1–3 Ethics, Records, Open Meetings | Part II Ch. 4–10 Taxation | Part III Ch. 11–18 Torts, Contracts & Civil Rules | Part IV Ch. 19–24 Zoning & Planning | Part V Ch. 25–30 Construction and Emergency Codes | Part VI Ch. 31–39 Municipal Codes | Index

(5) Submit a status report to the court and parties to the action annually or more frequently as the court may deem appropriate. The status report shall include:

(i) A copy of any contract entered into by the conservator regarding the improvement of the building.

(ii) An account of the disposition of all revenue generated from the building.

(iii) An account of all expenses and improvements.

(iv) The status of developing and implementing the final plan pursuant to this subsection.

(v) A description of any proposed actions to be taken in the next six months to improve the building.

(c) Hearing on conservator's final plan for abatement.—

(1) At the time the court appoints a conservator, the conservator may present and the court may approve the final plan for abatement. If no plan is presented at that hearing, a hearing date on the conservator's final plan for abatement shall be set within 120 days of the appointment.

(2) Thirty days prior to the date of the hearing, the conservator shall submit the plan to the court and to all parties to the action.

(3) The plan shall include a cost estimate, a financing plan and either a description of the work to be done for the rehabilitation of the building or, if rehabilitation is not feasible, a proposal for the closing, sealing or demolition of the building.

(4) The plan shall conform with all existing municipal codes, duly adopted plans for the area and historic preservation requirements.

(5) At the time of the hearing, all parties shall be allowed to comment on the plan, and the court shall take all comments into consideration when assessing the feasibility of the plan and the proposed financing. In making its assessment, the court shall give reasonable regard to the conservator's determination of the scope and necessity of work to be done for the rehabilitation or demolition of the building in approving the final plan and in approving the costs of conservatorship and sale of the property.

(6) Within 15 days of the hearing, the court shall issue a decision approving the plan or requiring that the plan be amended.

(7) If the court decision requires that the plan be amended, a hearing date shall be set within 60 days from the date of the decision.

(d) Accounting.—Upon the implementation of the final plan approved by the court, the conservator shall file with the court a full accounting of all income and expenditures during the period of time it took to implement the final plan.

§ 1107. Ownership of property

(a) Ownership interest of conservator.—A conservator appointed under section 5[7] shall be deemed to have an ownership interest in and legal control of the property for the purposes of filing plans with public agencies and boards, seeking and obtaining construction permits and other approvals and submitting applications for financing or other assistance to public or private entities.

(b) Liability of owner.—Notwithstanding the appointment of a conservator under section 5, nothing in this act shall be construed to relieve the owner of any civil or criminal liability or of any obligation to pay taxes, municipal liens

7. 68 P.S. § 1105.

and charges, mortgages, private liens or other fees or charges, whether incurred before or after the appointment of the conservator and no such liability shall transfer to the conservator.

(c) Limitation of conservator's environmental liability.—

(1) Notwithstanding any law to the contrary, the conservator shall not be held liable for any environmental damage to the building or the real property upon which the building is located that existed prior to the appointment by the court of the conservator.

(2) Paragraph (1) does not apply to the owner or any other person or entity regarding the building and its real property that is subject to an appointed conservator under this act.

§ 1108. Incurring indebtedness

(a) Borrowing.—From time to time, a conservator may borrow money or incur indebtedness in order to cover the costs of rehabilitation or to otherwise fulfill the conservator's obligations under this act.

(b) Liens.—In order to facilitate the borrowing of funds for the costs of rehabilitation, the court may grant priority status to a lien given to secure payment on a debt incurred for purposes authorized under this chapter, provided that:

(1) the conservator sought to obtain the necessary financing from the senior, nongovernmental lienholder, but the lienholder declined to provide financing for reasonable improvements or other costs of rehabilitation on reasonable terms; and

(2) lien priority is necessary in order to induce another lender to provide financing on reasonable terms

(c) Lien status of rehabilitation expenses.—Should the senior lienholder agree to provide financing for the costs of rehabilitation, any funds lent to cover the costs shall be deemed to be added to the senior lienholder's preexisting first lien.

(d) Approval of financing.—The court may approve financing for the costs of rehabilitation, the terms of which may include deferred repayment and use restrictions. The terms of the financing may remain with the property after the conservatorship has ended and be assumed by any of the following:

(1) The owner, if the owner regains possession of the property under section 10(2).[8]

(2) The buyer who takes title under section 9.[9]

§ 1109. Sale of property

(a) Sale by owner or lienholder.—If a property subject to conservatorship is sold by the owner or foreclosed upon by a lienholder or if any interest therein is transferred, such sale, foreclosure or transfer shall be subject to the conservatorship.

(b) Sale by conservator.—Upon application of the conservator, the court may order the sale of the property if the court finds that:

(1) Notice and an opportunity to provide comment to the court was given to each record owner of the property and each lienholder.

(2) The conservator has been in control of the building for more than three months and the owner has not successfully petitioned to terminate the conservatorship under section 10.[10]

8. 68 P.S. § 1110.

9. 68 P.S. § 1109.

10. 68 P.S. § 1110.

(3) The terms and conditions of the sale are acceptable to the court, and the buyer has a reasonable likelihood of maintaining the property.

(c) **Sale free and clear.—**

(1) The court may authorize the conservator to sell the building free and clear of all liens, claims and encumbrances, provided that the proceeds of the sale are distributed pursuant to subsection (d) at settlement.

(2) In the event that the proceeds of the sale are insufficient to pay all existing liens, claims and encumbrances, the proceeds shall be distributed according to the priorities set forth in subsection (d) and all unpaid liens, claims or encumbrances which have not been assumed under section 8(d)[11] shall be extinguished.

(d) **Distribution.**—The proceeds of the sale shall be applied in accordance with the following priorities to:

(1) All court costs.

(2) Liens of the Commonwealth, liens for unpaid property taxes and properly recorded municipal liens.

(3) Costs and expenses of sale.

(4) Principal and interest on any borrowing or incurrence of indebtedness granted priority over existing liens and security interest under section 8(b).

(4.1) Costs incurred by the petitioner in preparing and filing the petition in accordance with the requirements of section 4.[12]

(5) Costs of rehabilitation and any fees and expenses incurred by the conservator in connection with the sale or the safeguarding of the property for which the lien authorized under section (5)(g)[13] was filed.

(6) Valid liens and security interests in accordance with their priority.

(7) Any unpaid obligations of the conservator.

(8) Deleted by 2014, Oct. 22, P.L. 2557, No. 157, § 5, effective Dec. 22, 2014.

(9) The owner.

(e) **Owner's proceeds as unclaimed property.**—In the event the owner cannot be located, any proceeds from the sale which belong to the owner shall be presumed to be abandoned and unclaimed and shall be subject to the custody and control of the Commonwealth pursuant to Article XIII.1 of the act of April 9, 1929 (P.L. 343, No. 176),[14] known as The Fiscal Code.

§ 1110. Termination of conservatorship

Upon request of a party in interest or the conservator, the court may order the termination of the conservatorship if it determines:

(1) the conditions that were the grounds for the petition and all other code violations have been abated or corrected, the obligations, expenses and improvements of the conservatorship, including all fees and expenses of the conservator, have been fully paid or provided for and the purposes of the conservatorship have been fulfilled;

(2) the owner, mortgagee or lienholder has requested the conservatorship be terminated and has provided adequate assurances to the court that the conditions that constituted grounds for the petition will be promptly abated, all

11. 68 P.S. § 1108.
12. 68 P.S. § 1104.
13. 68 P.S. § 1105.
14. 72 P.S. § 1301.1 *et seq.*

obligations, expenses and improvements of the conservatorship, including all fees and expenses of the conservator, have been fully paid or provided for and the purposes of the conservatorship have been fulfilled;

(3) the building has been sold by the conservator and the proceeds distributed in accordance with section 9(d);[15] or

(4) the conservator has been unable, after diligent effort, to present a plan that could be approved under section 6(b)(3)[16] or to implement a previously approved plan or, for any reason, the purposes of the conservatorship cannot be fulfilled.

§ 1111. Applicability

(a) General inapplicability.—This act shall not apply to commercial and residential buildings, structures or land owned by or held in trust for the Federal Government and regulated under the United States Housing Act of 1937 (50 Stat. 888, 42 U.S.C. § 1437 et seq.) and regulations promulgated under that act.

(b) Inapplicability to service members.—This act shall not apply if the property owner has vacated the property in order to perform military service in time of war, armed conflict or in order to assist with relief efforts during a declared Federal or State emergency as a member of the United States Armed Forces or its reserve component.

15. 68 P.S. § 1109.

16. 68 P.S. § 1106.

CHAPTER 27.6

BLIGHTED PROPERTY—DEFINITION

1 Pa.C.S. § 1991. Definitions

The following words and phrases, when used in any statute finally enacted on or after September 1, 1937, unless the context clearly indicates otherwise, shall have the meanings given to them in this section.

* * *

"Blighted property." The term includes:

(1) A premises:

(i) ascertained to be a public nuisance due to physical condition or use and regarded as such at common law and deemed to be a danger to public health, safety and welfare or public nuisance as regulated by a locally adopted property maintenance code or, if no such code exists, any compatible code enacted by the act of November 10, 1999 (P.L.491, No.45), known as the Pennsylvania Construction Code Act; or

(ii) the condition of which contains an attractive nuisance created by physical condition, use or occupancy, including abandoned water wells, shafts, basements, excavations and unsafe fences or other structures, or which contains an unauthorized entry, unsafe equipment or other safety risk.

(2) A dwelling that has been condemned or otherwise deemed unfit for occupancy or use by the local authority having jurisdiction due to dilapidated, unsanitary, unsafe or vermin-infested condition or that is lacking in the facilities and equipment as required by the Pennsylvania Construction Code Act.

(3) A structure determined by the local authority having jurisdiction to be a fire hazard or otherwise that could easily catch fire or cause a fire and endanger public health, safety and welfare.

(4) A vacant or unimproved lot or parcel of ground located in a predominantly developed neighborhood that has become a place for the accumulation of trash and debris or a haven for rodents and other vermin by reason of neglect or lack of maintenance.

(5) A property that is vacant and has not been rehabilitated within one year from receipt of notice for corrective action as issued by the local authority having jurisdiction, except a property where a valid construction permit is in place.

(6) A vacant or unimproved lot or parcel of ground that is subject to a municipal lien for the cost of demolition of a structure previously located on the property and for which no payments on the lien have been made for a period of 12 months.

(7) A vacant or unimproved lot or parcel of ground on which the total municipal liens for delinquent real estate and property tax or any other type of municipal claim are greater than 150% of the fair market value of the property as established by the board of assessment appeals or other body with legal authority to determine the taxable value of the property.

(8) A property that has been declared abandoned in writing by the owner, including an estate that is in possession of the property.

Table of Contents
Part I Ch. 1–3 Ethics, Records, Open Meetings
Part II Ch. 4–10 Taxation
Part III Ch. 11–18 Torts, Contracts & Civil Rules
Part IV Ch. 19–24 Zoning & Planning
Part V Ch. 25–30 Construction and Emergency Codes
Part VI Ch. 31–39 Municipal Codes
Index

CHAPTER 28
SOCIAL SECURITY NUMBER PRIVACY ACT

71 P.S. §§ 2601–2608

TABLE OF CONTENTS

§ 1. Short title.

This act shall be known and may be cited as the Social Security Number Privacy Act.

§ 2. Definitions.

The following words and phrases when used in this act shall have the meanings given to them in this section unless the context clearly indicates otherwise:

"Commonwealth agency." As defined in 42 Pa.C.S. § 102 (relating to definitions).

"Department." The Department of Transportation of the Commonwealth.

"Health insurer." An entity licensed in this Commonwealth which issues any individual or group health, sickness and accident insurance policy, group health insurance plans or policies and all other forms of managed or capitated care plans or policies or subscriber contracts or certificates subject to the act of May 17, 1921 (P.L. 682, No. 284),[1] known as The Insurance Company Law of 1921, the act of December 29, 1972 (P.L. 1701, No.364),[2] known as the Health Maintenance Organization Act, the act of May 18, 1976 (P.L. 123, No. 54),[3] known as the Individual Accident and Sickness Insurance Minimum Standards Act, or 40 Pa.C.S. Ch. 61 (relating to hospital plan corporations) or 63 (relating to professional health services plan corporations).

"SSN." Social Security number.

§ 3. Use of Social Security numbers alternatives.

(a) General rule.—Except as provided in section 7 and notwithstanding any other law to the contrary, individuals applying for or renewing a professional license or certification, occupational license or certification or recreational license required by a Commonwealth agency or municipality shall be permitted to provide an alternative to disclosing their SSNs if the SSNs are collected by the agency or municipality solely for the purpose of complying with 23 Pa.C.S.

1. 40 P.S. § 341 et seq.
2. 40 P.S. § 1551 et seq.
3. 40 P.S. § 776.1 et seq.

§ 4304.1(a)(2) (relating to cooperation of government and nongovernment agencies). Alternate forms of identification shall include the individual's department-issued driver's license number or department issued nondriver identification card number.

(b) Effect of alternatives.—Any individual who provides an alternative under subsection (a) shall not be required to supply a Social Security number.

(c) Licensing agencies and municipalities.—Commonwealth agencies and municipalities issuing or renewing a professional license or certification, occupational license or certification or recreational license and collecting the individual's SSN for the purpose of complying with 23 Pa.C.S. § 4304.1(a)(2) shall develop application and renewal forms containing all of the following:

(1) Space for the individual's department-issued driver's license number as an alternative to the individual's SSN.

(2) Space for the individual's department-issued nondriver identification card number as an alternative to the individual's SSN.

(3) A statement to read as follows:

By affixing my driver's license number or nondriver's identification number issued by the Pennsylvania Department of Transportation, I authorize the Pennsylvania Department of Transportation to release my Social Security number to (insert Commonwealth agency or municipality) for the limited purpose of complying with 23 Pa.C.S. § 4304.1(a)(2).

§ 4. Duties of department.

The department shall, in a secure fashion, provide an individual's SSN to a Commonwealth agency or municipality when the Commonwealth agency or municipality provides the department with an alternative number pursuant to section 3(a) in a manner prescribed by the department, and provided the Commonwealth agency or municipality states the individual's Social Security number will not be further released, except as required pursuant to Federal or State law.

§ 5. Use of Social Security number prohibited.

No health insurer shall place an insured's SSN on a health insurance identification card.

§ 6. Exemption.

(a) Application.—The Department of Public Welfare shall apply for an exemption under section 666(d) of the Social Security Act (49 Stat. 620, 42 U.S.C. § 666(d)).

(b) Publication.—The Secretary of the Commonwealth shall transmit to the Legislative Reference Bureau, for publication in the **Pennsylvania** Bulletin, notice of the granting of an exemption under subsection (a).

§ 7. Nonapplicability.

This act shall not apply to forms required by the department for the purposes of driver licensing and nondriver identification.

§ 8. Construction.

Nothing in this act shall be construed to prevent any Commonwealth agency, municipality or other entity which is required to obtain a Social Security number on behalf of a Commonwealth agency or municipality from collecting, using or releasing a Social Security number as required by Federal or State law for child support enforcement purposes pending approval of an exemption under section 6.

§ 20. Effective date.

This act shall take effect as follows:

(1) Sections 3, 4 and 7 of the act shall take effect one year after the publication of the notice under section 6(b).

(2) The remainder of this act shall take effect immediately.

Approved November 29, 2006.

CHAPTER 29

EMERGENCY MANAGEMENT—COUNTERTERRORISM PLANNING, PREPAREDNESS AND RESPONSE ACT[1]

35 P.S. §§ 2140.101–103

ACT NO. 2002–227

S.B. No. 1569

AN ACT Providing for counterterrorism planning, preparedness and response; imposing powers and duties on the Pennsylvania Emergency Management Agency, the Department of Health, counties and municipalities; and providing for the organization of various response teams.

TABLE OF CONTENTS

CHAPTER 1

GENERAL PROVISIONS

Section 101. Short title[2]

This act shall be known and may be cited as the Counterterrorism Planning, Preparedness and Response Act.

Section 102. Definitions[3]

The following words and phrases when used in this act shall have the meanings given to them in this section unless the context clearly indicates otherwise:

"Agency." The Pennsylvania Emergency Management Agency.

"Department." The Department of Health of the Commonwealth.

1. *See* 2024 Act 113 and Title 35 of the Pennsylvania Consolidated Statutes, Chapter 72, which will repeal in part, continue in part, and amend in part the Counterterrorism Planning, Preparedness and Response Act, effective 60 days from October 29, 2024.

2. 35 P.S. § 2140.101.

3. 35 P.S. § 2140.202.

"Disaster medical assistance teams." A complement of individuals organized in accordance with standards developed by the Pennsylvania Emergency Management Agency and applicable Federal agencies to provide medical service at the scene of natural and manmade disasters and mass casualty incidents.

"Disaster mortuary teams." A complement of individuals organized in accordance with standards developed by the Pennsylvania Emergency Management Agency and applicable Federal agencies to provide mortuary service at the scene of natural and manmade disasters and mass casualty incidents.

"FEMA." The Federal Emergency Management Agency.

"Letter of agreement." A written agreement between a regional counterterrorism task force and a public, semipublic, private or nonprofit corporation, business, association, partnership, authority, individual or other entity that agrees to provide personnel, equipment, supplies, training facilities or other resources either directly to or in support of the task force's specialized regional counterterrorism response team. All letters of agreement entered into under the provisions of this act must, at a minimum, address all of the following:

(1) Workers' compensation and death benefits.

(2) Use of county 911 communications centers, county emergency management agencies or the State Emergency Operations Center.

(3) Member participation in training exercises, drills and actual activation and deployment.

"Local health department." A county department of health under the act of August 24, 1951 (P.L. 1304, No. 315),[4] known as the Local Health Administration Law, or a department of health in a municipality approved for a Commonwealth grant to provide local health services under section 25 of the Local Health Administration Law.

"Manmade disaster." Any biological, chemical, nuclear, radiological, industrial, commercial or transportation accident, attack, explosion, conflagration, contamination, power failure, computer or communications failure, natural resource shortage or other condition, including enemy or terrorist act, which threatens or causes substantial property damage, human suffering and hardship or loss of life.

"Municipal or municipality." A city, borough, incorporated town, township or home rule municipality of this Commonwealth.

"Mutual aid." A county's, municipality's or volunteer service organization's affirmative act of sending its personnel, equipment or resources to the scene of an actual or potential natural or manmade disaster, whether inside or outside the boundaries of this Commonwealth, in response to an official dispatch request from a county 911 communications center, county emergency management agency or the State emergency operations center.

"Mutual aid agreement." A written agreement between a regional counterterrorism task force and a county, municipality or volunteer service organization whereby the county, municipality or volunteer service organization agrees to provide personnel, equipment or other resources in response to an actual or potential natural or manmade disaster. All mutual aid agreements entered into under the provisions of this act must, at a minimum, address all of the following:

(1) Workers' compensation and death benefits.

(2) Use of county 911 communications centers, county emergency management agencies or the State Emergency Operations Center.

4. 16 P.S. § 12001 et seq.

(3) Member participation in training exercises, drills and actual activation and deployment.

"Natural disaster." Any hurricane, tornado, storm, flood, high water, earthquake, landslide, mudslide, snowstorm, drought, insect infestation, fire, explosion or other natural catastrophe which results in substantial property damage, human suffering and hardship or loss of life.

"Regional counterterrorism task force." A complement of Federal, State, county and municipal emergency management, health, law enforcement, public safety and other officials and representatives from volunteer service organizations, private business and industry, hospitals and medical care facilities and other entities within a multicounty area as determined by the agency that is responsible for conducting counterterrorism planning, training preparedness and response activities.

"Specialized regional counterterrorism response team." A complement of individuals established by a regional counterterrorism task force and organized in accordance with standards developed by the Pennsylvania Emergency Management Agency and applicable Federal agencies to respond to emergencies involving an actual or potential natural or manmade disaster. Such teams may include disaster medical assistance teams and disaster mortuary response teams.

"Specialized Statewide response team." A complement of individuals organized by the Commonwealth to provide specialized personnel, equipment and other support capabilities in response to an actual or potential natural or manmade disaster in this Commonwealth. Such teams may include disaster medical assistance teams and disaster mortuary response teams.

"Terrorism." The unlawful use of force or violence committed by a group or individual against persons or property to intimidate or coerce a government, the civilian population or any segment thereof in furtherance of political or social objectives.

"Urban search and rescue task force." A complement of individuals organized by the agency in accordance with standards developed by the agency and the Federal Emergency Management Agency to provide emergency response and search and rescue capabilities and resources at the scene of a natural or manmade disaster.

"Volunteer service organization." A volunteer fire company, volunteer ambulance or medical company, volunteer rescue squad or any other volunteer entity organized and chartered or incorporated in this Commonwealth or chartered by Congress for the primary purpose of providing emergency services as defined in 35 Pa.C.S. § 7102 (relating to definitions).

CHAPTER 2

COUNTERTERRORISM PLANNING, PREPAREDNESS AND RESPONSE

Section 201. Counterterrorism planning, preparedness and response program[5]

(a) Program.—The Pennsylvania Emergency Management Agency shall coordinate and consult with other State agencies, departments and offices, including the Office of Homeland Security of the Commonwealth, to establish, develop and maintain a counterterrorism planning, preparedness and response program

5. 35 P.S. § 2140.201.

to promote and protect the health, safety and welfare of emergency responders, public officials and the general public from actual or potential natural or man-made disasters in this Commonwealth.

(b) Agency responsibilities.—The agency shall:

(1) Define the necessary components and composition of regional counterterrorism task forces and specialized regional counterterrorism response teams and the respective regional counterterrorism zones for each. The agency shall not be responsible for appointing individual members to the regional counterterrorism task forces or the specialized regional counterterrorism response teams.

(2) Provide training and technical assistance for counterterrorism planning, preparedness and response.

(3) Establish guidelines and policies to coordinate emergency response activities with Federal, State, county and municipal emergency management, health, law enforcement, public safety and other officials and representatives from volunteer service organizations, private business and industry, hospitals and medical care facilities and other entities responsible for the health, safety and welfare of the citizens of this Commonwealth. The agency shall consult with representatives of the regional counterterrorism task forces to develop such policies and guidelines and those necessary to carry out the provisions of this chapter.

(4) Require the counterterrorism task force to prepare counterterrorism emergency response plans or protocols, readiness evaluation reports or other documents deemed necessary by the agency.

(5) Provide grants and other funding assistance as required by the provisions of this chapter.

(6) Conduct terrorist incident exercises.

(7) Provide technical assistance to regional counterterrorism task forces in developing and entering into mutual aid agreements and letters of agreement.

(8) Establish a certification program for specialized regional counterterrorism response teams which may include standards for the administration, composition, training and equipping of the teams.

Section 202. Regional counterterrorism task forces[6]

(a) Establishment.—The agency, in coordination with State, county and municipal emergency management, health, law enforcement, public safety and other officials and representatives from volunteer service organizations, private business and industry, hospitals and medical care facilities and other entities responsible for the health, safety and welfare of the citizens of this Commonwealth, shall establish regional counterterrorism task forces throughout this Commonwealth.

(b) Response plans.—Each regional counterterrorism task force shall prepare a counterterrorism preparedness and response plan in accordance with guidelines developed by the agency. The plan shall be submitted to the agency within 180 days of the effective date of this act. The agency shall review and approve each plan in a timely manner, but no later than 90 days after its submission to the agency. The task force shall review and update the plan on an annual basis.

(c) Meetings.—Regional counterterrorism task force meetings that are called to discuss sensitive or classified law enforcement, terrorist threat assessment or other confidential public and/or private facility safety information shall not be

6. 35 P.S. § 2140.202.

subject to the provisions of 65 Pa.C.S. Ch. 7 (relating to open meetings).

Section 203. Regional counterterrorism response and preparedness[7]

(a) Specialized regional counterterrorism response teams.—A regional counterterrorism task force shall establish specialized regional counterterrorism response teams.

(b) Regional counterterrorism response zones.—The agency shall establish primary and secondary regional response zones within this Commonwealth for specialized regional counterterrorism response teams. The regional response zones may consist of multiple counties or portions of several adjoining counties as determined by the agency.

(c) Activation and deployment.—A specialized regional counterterrorism response team may be activated and deployed by the Governor, his designee or an official designated by the appropriate regional counterterrorism task force.

Section 204. Urban search and rescue task force[8]

(a) Establishment of task forces.—The agency shall establish urban search and rescue task forces. The task forces shall also provide professional, logistical, material and other forms of support to regional counterterrorism task forces and specialized regional counterterrorism response teams.

(b) Organization.—An urban search and rescue task force shall be organized in accordance with guidelines developed by the agency in coordination with FEMA and members of the task force.

(c) Responsibilities.—An urban search and rescue task force shall respond to actual or potential natural or manmade disasters in this Commonwealth and shall also perform search and rescue functions as delineated in The Robert T. Stafford Disaster Relief and Emergency Assistance Act (Public Law 93-288, 42 U.S.C. § 5121 et seq.), the Federal Response Plan or its successor and the counterterrorism preparedness and response plans created in accordance with the provisions of this chapter.

(d) Activation and deployment.—An urban search and rescue task force or any of its components, subgroups or regional elements may only be activated and deployed to the scene of a disaster by either the Governor or his designee, the President of the United States or a FEMA-designated official. During an activation and deployment by the Governor, the administrative and operational costs of the task force, its individual members and their employers, State agencies and other parties shall be paid under the provisions of the Governor's declaration of disaster emergency, including paying or reimbursing any parties for workers' compensation and death benefits in the event of injury or death of a task force member.

(e) Workers' compensation and death benefits.—A member of an urban search and rescue task force shall be eligible to receive workers' compensation and death benefits in the event of injury or death that occurs during the period of activation or deployment.

(f) Funding, grants and donations.—In addition to any funds that are provided to a task force under section 206 or the authority of 35 Pa.C.S. § 7307 (relating to use and appropriation of unused Commonwealth funds), the urban search and rescue task force may be eligible to receive grants, donations of equipment and supplies and other funds from any source. As an agent of the Commonwealth, a task force is entitled to tax-exempt status from the Federal Government.

7. 35 P.S. § 2140.203.

8. 35 P.S. § 2140.204.

Section 205. Specialized Statewide response teams[9]

(a) Establishment.—The Commonwealth may establish one or more specialized Statewide response teams. These teams shall also provide professional, logistical, material and other forms of support to the regional counterterrorism task forces and specialized regional counterterrorism response teams organized in this Commonwealth. The Commonwealth may enter into an agreement with a One Call System as defined in the act of December 10, 1974 (P.L. 852, No. 287),[10] referred to as the Underground Utility Line Protection Law, for the provision of specialized communications services.

(b) Organization and responsibilities.—Specialized Statewide response teams shall be organized in accordance with guidelines developed by the Commonwealth in consultation with applicable Federal or State agencies.

(c) Activation.—Specialized Statewide response teams may only be activated and deployed to the scene of a disaster by the Governor or his designee.

Section 206. Grant program[11]

(a) Authorization.—The agency shall have the authority to make grants to regional counterterrorism task forces, specialized regional counterterrorism response teams, specialized Statewide response teams and urban search and rescue task forces to assist them in carrying out the provisions of this act, including, but not limited to, entering into letters of agreement or mutual aid agreements or providing mutual aid.

(b) Grants and funding.—Regional counterterrorism task forces, specialized regional counterterrorism response teams, specialized Statewide response teams and urban search and rescue task forces may receive grants and funding from the Federal Government and the Commonwealth through application to the agency or another entity providing grants or funding for the purposes of this act.

(c) Limitation.—Grants shall only be made by the agency to the extent that funding is available.

Section 207. Miscellaneous provisions[12]

(a) Immunity from liability.—The provisions of 42 Pa.C.S. § 8331 (relating to medical good Samaritan civil immunity), 8332 (relating to nonmedical good Samaritan civil immunity) or 8332.4 (relating to volunteer-in-public-service negligence standard) shall apply to members of a specialized regional counterterrorism response team, an urban search and rescue task force or a specialized Statewide response team and individuals who provide logistical, material or other forms of emergency response support to such a team or task force during activation or deployment of a team or task force to a potential or actual manmade or natural disaster or while engaged in a task force or team drill or training exercise.

(b) Effect on workers' compensation premiums.—Nothing in this act shall be construed to permit an insurer to raise workers' compensation premiums due to the participation or membership of a county, municipality, volunteer service organization, individual or employer on a regional counterterrorism task force, specialized regional counterterrorism response team, specialized Statewide response team or urban search and rescue task force.

---

9. 35 P.S. § 2140.205.
10. 73 P.S. § 176 et seq.
11. 35 P.S. § 2140.206.
12. 35 P.S. § 2140.207.

Section 208. Commonwealth indemnification[13]

The Commonwealth shall indemnify a county or municipality for any costs related to damaged county or municipal property which results from participation in a regional counterterrorism task force, specialized regional counterterrorism response team or specialized Statewide response team response only when all of the following are met:

(1) the county or municipality is responding upon activation or deployment by the Governor;

(2) the damage to county or municipal property occurs outside of the primary regional counterterrorism response zone;

(3) the county or municipality's insurance does not cover the property damage; and

(4) the property damage was not caused by the willful misconduct of the county or municipality or any of its employees or agents.

CHAPTER 3
PUBLIC HEALTH EMERGENCY MEASURES

Section 301. Temporary isolation and quarantine without notice[14]

(a) Temporary isolation or quarantine.—In the case of an actual or suspected outbreak of a contagious disease or epidemic due to an actual or suspected bioterrorist or biohazardous event, the Governor, in consultation with the Secretary of Health, may temporarily isolate or quarantine an individual or groups of individuals through a written order if delay in imposing the isolation or quarantine through judicial proceedings currently available to the department and local health departments would significantly jeopardize the department's ability to prevent or limit the transmission of a contagious or potentially contagious disease to others. This subsection shall not require a declaration of disaster emergency by the Governor in order to be effective.

(b) Judicial review.—

(1) After issuing the written order, the department or local health department shall promptly file a petition with the court within 24 hours or the next court business day after the issuance of the order for a hearing to authorize the continued isolation or quarantine.

(2) The court shall hold a hearing on the petition not more than 72 hours after the filing of the petition to determine whether continued isolation or quarantine is warranted.

(3) Reasonable notice, either oral or written, stating the time, place and purpose of the hearing shall be given to the isolated or quarantined individual. The court may determine the manner in which the hearing shall occur, including through the use of closed-circuit television.

(4) An isolated or quarantined individual is entitled to representation by legal counsel at all stages of any proceedings under this section and, if the individual is without financial resources or otherwise unable to employ counsel, the court shall provide counsel for him.

(5) If the court determines continued isolation or quarantine is warranted, the court shall so order the continued isolation or quarantine and shall fix the time and duration of the isolation or quarantine, which in no case shall exceed 30 days except as set forth in paragraph (6).

13. 35 P.S. § 2140.208.
14. 35 P.S. § 2140.301.

(6) Where an individual has been isolated or quarantined for a period of 30 days, the department shall ask the court to review the order to determine if further isolation or quarantine is warranted.

(7) The department or local health department shall provide the court with ongoing reports on the isolated or quarantined individual during the period of isolation or quarantine.

(c) **Relation to other laws.**—Nothing in this section shall be construed to limit the existing authority of the Secretary of Health or the department or a local health department.

Section 302. Immunity from liability[15]

The provisions of 42 Pa.C.S. § 8331 (relating to medical good Samaritan civil immunity), 8332 (relating to nonmedical good Samaritan civil immunity) or 8332.4 (relating to volunteer-in-public-service negligence standard) shall apply to any person who provides assistance in carrying out the provisions of this chapter.

Section 303. Effective date[16]

This act shall take effect in 30 days.

Approved December 16, 2002.

15. 35 P.S. § 2140.302.
16. 35 P.S. § 2140.303.

CHAPTER 30

EMERGENCY MANAGEMENT SERVICES CODE

35 Pa. C.S. §§ 7101–7111

35 Pa. C.S. §§ 7501–7515

TABLE OF CONTENTS

GENERAL PROVISIONS

§ 7101. Short title of part.

This part shall be known and may be cited as the "Emergency Management Services Code."

§ 7102. Definitions.

The following words and phrases when used in this part shall have, unless the context clearly indicates otherwise, the meanings given to them in this section:

"Agency." The Pennsylvania Emergency Management Agency.

"Council." The Pennsylvania Emergency Management Council.

"Custodial child care facility." A child day care center as defined under section 1001 of the act of June 13, 1967 (P.L. 31, No. 21), [62 P.S. § 1001] known as the Public Welfare Code, or nursery school licensed or regulated by the Commonwealth.

"Disaster." A man-made disaster, natural disaster or war-caused disaster.

"Disaster emergency." Those conditions which may by investigation made, be found, actually or likely, to:

(1) affect seriously the safety, health or welfare of a substantial number of citizens of this Commonwealth or preclude the operation or use of essential public facilities;

(2) be of such magnitude or severity as to render essential State supplementation of county and local efforts or resources exerted or utilized in alleviating the danger, damage, suffering or hardship faced; and

Table of Contents
Part I Ch. 1–3 Ethics, Records, Open Meetings
Part II Ch. 4–10 Taxation
Part III Ch. 11–18 Torts, Contracts & Civil Rules
Part IV Ch. 19–24 Zoning & Planning
Part V Ch. 25–30 Construction and Emergency Codes
Part VI Ch. 31–39 Municipal Codes
Index

(3) have been caused by forces beyond the control of man, by reason of civil disorder, riot or disturbance, or by factors not foreseen and not known to exist when appropriation bills were enacted.

"Emergency management." The judicious planning, assignment and coordination of all available resources in an integrated program of prevention, mitigation, preparedness, response and recovery for emergencies of any kind, whether from attack, man-made or natural sources.

"Emergency services." The preparation for and the carrying out of functions, other than functions for which military forces are primarily responsible, to prevent, minimize and provide emergency repair of injury and damage resulting from disasters, together with all other activities necessary or incidental to the preparation for and carrying out of those functions. The functions include, without limitation, fire-fighting services, police services, medical and health services, rescue, engineering, disaster warning services, communications, radiological, shelter, chemical and other special weapons defense, evacuation of persons from stricken areas, emergency welfare services, emergency transportation, emergency resources management, existing or properly assigned functions of plant protection, temporary restoration of public utility services and other functions related to civilian protection.

"Local emergency." The condition declared by the local governing body when in their judgment the threat or actual occurrence of a disaster is or threatens to be of sufficient severity and magnitude to warrant coordinated local government action to prevent or alleviate the damage, loss, hardship or suffering threatened or caused thereby. A local emergency arising wholly or substantially out of a resource shortage may be declared only by the Governor, upon petition of the local governing body, when he deems the threat or actual occurrence of a disaster to be of sufficient severity and magnitude to warrant coordinated local government action to prevent or alleviate the damage, loss, hardship or suffering threatened or caused thereby.

"Local organization." A local emergency management organization.

"Man-made disaster." Any industrial, nuclear or transportation accident, explosion, conflagration, power failure, natural resource shortage or other condition, except enemy action, resulting from man-made causes, such as oil spills and other injurious environmental contamination, which threatens or causes substantial damage to property, human suffering, hardship or loss of life.

"Natural disaster." Any hurricane, tornado, storm, flood, high water, wind-driven water, tidal wave, earthquake, landslide, mudslide, snowstorm, drought, fire, explosion or other catastrophe which results in substantial damage to property, hardship, suffering or possible loss of life.

"Person." An individual, corporation, association, partnership, limited liability company, business trust, government entity, including the Commonwealth, foundation, public utility, trust or estate.

"Political subdivision." Any county, city, borough, incorporated town or township.

"Resource shortage." The absence, unavailability or reduced supply of any raw or processed natural resource, or any commodities, goods or services of any kind which bear a substantial relationship to the health, safety, welfare and economic well-being of the citizens of this Commonwealth.

"War-caused disaster." Any condition following an attack upon the United States resulting in substantial damage to property or injury to persons in the United States caused by use of bombs, missiles, shellfire, nuclear, radiological, chemical or biological means, or other weapons or overt paramilitary actions, or other conditions such as sabotage.

§ 7103. Purposes of part.

The purposes of this part are to:

(1) Reduce vulnerability of people and communities of this Commonwealth to damage, injury and loss of life and property resulting from disasters.

(2) Prepare for prompt and efficient rescue, care and treatment of persons victimized or threatened by disaster.

(3) Provide a setting conducive to the rapid and orderly start of restoration and rehabilitation of persons and property affected by disasters.

(4) Clarify and strengthen the roles of the Governor, Commonwealth agencies and local government in prevention of, preparation for, response to and recovery from disasters.

(5) Authorize and provide for cooperation in disaster prevention, preparedness, response and recovery.

(6) Authorize and provide for coordination of activities relating to disaster prevention, preparedness, response and recovery by agencies and officers of this Commonwealth, and similar State-local and Federal-State activities in which the Commonwealth and its political subdivisions participate.

(7) Provide a disaster management system embodying all aspects of predisaster preparedness and postdisaster response.

(8) Assist in prevention of disaster caused or aggravated by inadequate planning for and regulation of public and private facilities and land use.

(9) Supplement, without in any way limiting, authority conferred by previous statutes of this Commonwealth and increase the capability of the Commonwealth and local agencies having responsibilities for civil defense to perform both civil defense and disaster services.

(10) Further the operational capacities of Commonwealth agencies to deal with disaster situations.

(11) Further programs of education and training.

(12) Establish integrated communications capabilities and warning systems.

§ 7104. Limitations.

This part is not intended to:

(1) Interfere with the course or conduct of a labor dispute, except that actions otherwise authorized by this part or other laws may be taken when necessary to forestall or mitigate imminent or existing danger to public health or safety.

(2) Affect the jurisdiction or responsibilities of police forces, firefighting forces, units of the armed forces of the United States or of any personnel thereof when on active duty except that Commonwealth and local disaster emergency plans shall place reliance upon the forces available for performance of functions related to disaster emergencies.

(3) Limit, modify or abridge the authority of the Governor to proclaim martial law or exercise any other powers vested in him under the Constitution, statutes or common law of this Commonwealth independent of, or in conjunction with, any provisions of this part.

§ 7111. Interstate civil defense and disaster compact enacted.

The Interstate Civil Defense and Disaster Compact is hereby enacted into law and entered into with all jurisdictions legally joining therein in the form substantially as follows:

ARTICLE 1

The purpose of this compact is to provide mutual aid among the States in meeting any emergency or disaster from enemy attack or other cause (natural or otherwise), including sabotage and subversive acts and direct attacks by bombs, shellfire and atomic, radiological, chemical, bacteriological means and other weapons. The prompt, full and effective utilization of the resources of the respective States, including such resources as may be available from the United States Government or any other source are essential to the safety, care and welfare of the people thereof in the event of enemy action or other emergency, and any other resources, including personnel, equipment or supplies, shall be incorporated into a plan or plans of mutual aid to be developed among the civil defense agencies or similar bodies of the States that are parties hereto. The directors of civil defense of all party States shall constitute a committee to formulate plans and to take all necessary steps for the implementation of this compact.

ARTICLE 2

It shall be the duty of each party State to formulate civil defense plans and programs for application within such State. There shall be frequent consultation between the representatives of the States and with the United States Government and the free exchange of information and plans, including inventories of any materials and equipment available for civil defense. In carrying out such civil defense plans and programs, the party States shall, so far as possible, provide and follow uniform standards, practices and rules and regulations including:

(a) Insignia, arm bands and any other distinctive articles to designate and distinguish the different civil defense services.

(b) Blackouts and practice blackouts, air raid drills, mobilization of civil defense forces, and other tests and exercises.

(c) Warnings and signals for drills or attacks and the mechanical devices to be used in connection therewith.

(d) The effective screening or extinguishing of all lights and lighting devices and appliances.

(e) Shutting off water mains, gas mains, electric power connections, and the suspension of all other utility services.

(f) All materials or equipment used or to be used for civil defense purposes in order to assure that such materials and equipment will be easily and freely interchangeable when used in or by any other party State.

(g) The conduct of civilians and the movement and cessation of movement of pedestrians and vehicular traffic prior, during and subsequent to drills or attacks.

(h) The safety of public meetings or gatherings.

(i) Mobile support units.

ARTICLE 3

Any party State requested to render mutual aid shall take such action as is necessary to provide and make available the resources covered by this compact in accordance with the terms hereof: Provided, That it is understood that the State rendering aid may withhold resources to the extent necessary to provide reasonable protection for such State. Each party State shall extend to the civil defense forces of any other party State while operating within its State limits under the terms and conditions of this compact, the same powers (except that of arrest, unless specifically authorized by the receiving State), duties, rights, privileges and immunities as if they were performing their duties in the State in which normally employed or rendering services. Civil defense forces will continue under the command and control of their regular leaders but the organizational units will come under the operational control of the civil defense authorities of the State receiving assistance.

ARTICLE 4

Whenever any person holds a license, certificate or other permit issued by any State evidencing the meeting of qualifications for professional, mechanical or other skills, such person may render aid involving such skill in any party State to meet an emergency or disaster and such State shall give due recognition to such license, certificate or other permit as if issued in the State in which aid is rendered.

ARTICLE 5

No party State or its officers or employees rendering aid in another State pursuant to this compact shall be liable on account of any act or omission in good faith on the part of such forces while so engaged or on account of the maintenance or use of any equipment or supplies in connection therewith.

ARTICLE 6

Inasmuch as it is probable that the pattern and detail of the machinery for mutual aid among two or more States may differ from that appropriate among other States party hereto, this instrument contains elements of a broad base common to all States and nothing herein contained shall preclude any State from entering into supplementary agreements with another State or States. Such supplementary agreements may comprehend but shall not be limited to provisions for evacuation and reception of injured and other persons and the exchange of medical, fire, police, public utility, reconnaissance, welfare, transportation and communications personnel, equipment and supplies.

ARTICLE 7

Each party State shall provide for the payment of compensation and death benefits to injured members of the civil defense forces of that State and the representatives of deceased members of such forces in case such members sustain injuries or are killed while rendering aid pursuant to this compact in the same manner and on the same terms as if the injury or death were sustained within such State.

ARTICLE 8

Any party State rendering aid in another State pursuant to this compact shall be reimbursed by the party State receiving such aid for any loss or damage to or expense incurred in the operation of any equipment answering a request for aid and for the cost incurred in connection with such requests: Provided, That any aiding party State may assume in whole or in part such loss, damage, expense or other cost, or may loan such equipment or donate such services to the receiving party State without charge or cost: And, provided further, That any two or more party States may enter into supplementary agreements establishing a different allocation of costs as among those States. The United States Government may relieve the party State receiving aid from any liability and reimburse the party State supplying civil defense forces for the compensation paid to and the transportation, subsistence and maintenance expenses of such forces during the time of the rendition of such aid or assistance outside the State and may also pay fair and reasonable compensation for the use or utilization of the supplies, materials, equipment or facilities so utilized or consumed.

ARTICLE 9

Plans for the orderly evacuation and reception of the civilian population as the result of an emergency or disaster shall be worked out from time to time between representatives of the party States and the various local civil defense areas thereof. Such plans shall include the manner of transporting such evacuees, the number of evacuees to be received in different areas, the manner in which food, clothing, housing, and medical care will be provided, the registration of the evacuees, the providing of facilities for the notification of relatives or friends and the forwarding of such evacuees to other areas, or the bringing in of additional materials, supplies and all other relevant factors. Such plans shall provide that the party State receiving evacuees shall be reimbursed generally for the out-of-pocket expenses incurred in receiving and caring for such evacuees, for expenditures for transportation, food, clothing, medicines and medical care and like items. Such expenditures shall be reimbursed by the party State of which the evacuees are residents or by the United States Government under plans approved by it. After the termination of the emergency or disaster the party State of which the evacuees are resident shall assume the responsibility for the ultimate support or repatriation of such evacuees.

ARTICLE 10

This compact shall be available to any State, territory or possession of the United States and the District of Columbia. The term "State" may also include any neighboring foreign country or province or state thereof.

ARTICLE 11

The committee established pursuant to Article 1 of this compact may request the Civil Defense Agency of the United States Government to act as an informational and coordinating body under this compact and representatives of such agency of the United States Government may attend meetings of such committee.

ARTICLE 12

This compact shall become operative immediately upon its ratification by any State as between it and any other State or States so ratifying, and shall be subject to approval by Congress unless prior Congressional approval has been given. Duly authenticated copies of this compact and of such supplementary agreements as may be entered into shall, at the time of their approval, be deposited with each of the party States and with the Civil Defense Agency and other appropriate agencies of the United States Government.

ARTICLE 13

This compact shall continue in force and remain binding on each party State until the Legislature or the Governor of such party State takes action to withdraw therefrom. Such action shall not be effective until 30 days after notice thereof has been sent by the Governor of the party State desiring to withdraw to the Governors of all other party States.

ARTICLE 14

This compact shall be construed to effectuate the purposes stated in Article 1. If any provision of this compact is declared unconstitutional or the applicability thereof to any person or circumstance is held invalid, the constitutionality of the remainder of this compact and the applicability thereof to other persons and circumstances shall not be affected thereby.

LOCAL ORGANIZATIONS AND SERVICES

§ 7501. General authority of political subdivisions.

(a) Establishing emergency management organization.—Each political subdivision of this Commonwealth is directed and authorized to establish a local emergency management organization in accordance with the plan and program of the Pennsylvania Emergency Management Agency. Each local organization shall have responsibility for emergency management, response and recovery within the territorial limits of the political subdivision within which it is organized and, in addition, shall conduct such services outside of its jurisdictional limits as may be required under this part.

(b) Declaration of disaster emergency.—A local disaster emergency may be declared by the governing body of a political subdivision upon finding a disaster has occurred or is imminent. The governing body of a political subdivision may authorize the mayor or other chief executive officer to declare a local disaster emergency subject to ratification by the governing body. The declaration shall not be continued or renewed for a period in excess of seven days except by or with the consent of the governing body of the political subdivision. Any order or proclamation declaring, continuing or terminating a local disaster emergency shall be given prompt and general publicity and shall be filed promptly with the agency. The effect of a declaration of a local disaster emergency is to activate the response and recovery aspects of any and all applicable local emergency management plans and to authorize the furnishing of aid and assistance thereunder.

(c) Contracts and obligations.—In carrying out the provisions of this part, each political subdivision shall have the power to enter into contracts and incur obligations necessary to disaster emergency management, response and recovery.

(d) Temporary suspension of formal requirements.—Each political subdivision included in a declaration of disaster emergency declared by either the Governor or the governing body of the political subdivision affected by the disaster emergency is authorized to exercise the powers vested under this section in the light of the exigencies of the emergency situation without regard to time-consuming procedures and formalities prescribed by law (excepting mandatory constitutional requirements) pertaining to the performance of public work, entering into contracts, the incurring of obligations, the employment of temporary workers, the rental of equipment, the purchase of supplies and materials, the levying of taxes and the appropriation and expenditure of public funds. Notwithstanding any other provision of law, the governing body of a political subdivision shall not be required to have a quorum physically present at any one location in order to conduct business if a quorum is otherwise established by the participating members through an authorized telecommunication device.

(e) Employment of personnel.—In order to meet prescribed requirements for eligibility to receive Federal contributions authorized under the provisions of the Federal Civil Defense Act of 1950 (64 Stat. 1245, 50 U.S.C.App. § 2251 et seq.) or any amendment or reenactment thereof, political subdivisions are authorized to avail themselves of services offered by the State Civil Service Commission under the provisions of the act of August 5, 1941 (P.L. 752, No. 286), known as the "Civil Service Act," [71 P.S. § 741.1 et seq.] in connection with the employment of personnel in local organizations established pursuant to the provisions of this part.

§ 7502. Local coordinator of emergency management.

(a) General rule.—Each local organization of emergency management shall have a coordinator who shall be responsible for the planning, administration and operation of the local organization subject to the direction and control of the executive officer or governing body.

(b) County coordinator.—A coordinator shall be appointed in all counties with approval of the director of the agency. The executive officer or governing body of the county shall recommend a coordinator whose recommendation must be endorsed by the director of the agency prior to appointment by the Governor. Upon failure of the executive officer or governing body of the county to make a recommendation of a person for coordinator within the time fixed by the agency, the Governor is authorized to appoint a coordinator based upon the recommendation of the director of the agency. The coordinator of the county organization shall not be assigned any duties that will conflict with his duty as coordinator.

(c) Local level.—At the local level, the coordinator shall be appointed by the Governor upon the recommendation of the executive officer or governing body of the political subdivision. Upon the failure of the executive officer or governing body of a political subdivision to make a recommendation to the Governor of a candidate for coordinator within the time fixed by the agency, the Governor is authorized to appoint a coordinator without any recommendation. A candidate for coordinator for two or more political subdivisions may be recommended to the Governor for appointment upon agreement by resolution of the governing bodies of such political subdivisions. Any other law notwithstanding, a local government official may be recommended for appointment.

(d) Qualifications.—The coordinator shall be professionally competent and capable of planning, effecting coordination among operating agencies of government and controlling coordinated operations by local emergency preparedness forces.

(e) In-service training.—Each appointed coordinator shall:

(1) Attend and successfully complete the first phase of the career development program as prescribed by the agency within one year after appointment.

(2) Attend and successfully complete the second phase of the career development program as prescribed by the agency within three years after appointment.

(3) Attend basic and advanced seminars, workshops and training conferences called by the State director and/or official having responsibility for providing the coordinator with in-service training.

Failure to attend the instruction described in this subsection or failure to attend a prescribed training conference for a period of two consecutive years shall be cause for replacement. The State director of emergency management may grant credit toward meeting the requirements of this subsection to appointed local coordinators on the basis of prior experience and training.

(f) Responsibility for training.—Responsibility for the professional in-service training of each coordinator rests with each successive higher political subdivision than the one in which the coordinator is functioning.

(g) Expenses.—Each appointed coordinator shall be reimbursed for actual expenses incurred in the performance of his duties and attendance at scheduled meetings.

§ 7503. Powers and duties of political subdivisions.

Each political subdivision shall, either individually or pursuant to the provisions of the act of July 12, 1972 (P.L. 762, No. 180), referred to as the Intergovernmental Cooperation Law, [53 Pa.C.S.A. § 2301 et seq.] adopt an Intergovernmental Cooperation agreement with other political subdivisions to:

(1) Prepare, maintain and keep current a disaster emergency management plan for the prevention and minimization of injury and damage caused by disaster, prompt and effective response to disaster and disaster emergency relief and recovery in consonance with the Pennsylvania Emergency Management Plan.

(2) Establish, equip and staff an emergency operations center, consolidated with warning and communication systems to support government operations in

emergencies and provide other essential facilities and equipment for agencies and activities assigned emergency functions.

(3) Provide individual and organizational training programs to insure prompt, efficient and effective disaster emergency services.

(4) Organize, prepare and coordinate all locally available manpower, materials, supplies, equipment, facilities and services necessary for disaster emergency readiness, response and recovery.

(5) Adopt and implement precautionary measures to mitigate the anticipated effects of disaster.

(6) Execute and enforce such rules and orders as the agency shall adopt and promulgate under the authority of this part.

(7) Cooperate and coordinate with any public and private agency or entity in achieving any purpose of this part.

(8) Have available for inspection at its emergency operations center all emergency management plans, rules and orders of the Governor and the agency.

(9) Provide prompt and accurate information regarding local disaster emergencies to appropriate Commonwealth and local officials and agencies and the general public.

(10) Participate in all tests, drills and exercises, including remedial drills and exercises, scheduled by the agency or by the Federal Government.

(11) Participate in the program of integrated flood warning systems under section 7313(6) (relating to powers and duties).

§ 7504. Coordination, assistance and mutual aid.

(a) Responsibility for direction and coordination.—Direction of disaster emergency management services is the responsibility of the lowest level of government affected. When two or more political subdivisions within a county are affected, the county organization shall exercise responsibility for coordination and support to the area of operations. When two or more counties are involved, coordination shall be provided by the agency or by area organizations established by the agency.

(b) Assistance from higher government unit.—When all appropriate locally available forces and resources are fully committed by the affected political subdivision, assistance from a higher level of government shall be provided.

(c) Municipal mutual aid agreements.—County and local coordinators of emergency management shall develop mutual aid agreements with adjacent political subdivisions for reciprocal emergency assistance. The agreements shall be consistent with the plans and programs of the agency. In disaster emergencies, requests for mutual aid assistance shall be referred to the organization having responsibility for coordination as specified in subsection (a) and in time of emergency it shall be the duty of each local organization to render assistance in accordance with the provisions of the mutual aid agreements.

(d) Interstate mutual aid arrangements.—The coordinator of each local organization may, subject to approval of the Governor, enter into mutual aid arrangements with similar agencies or organizations in other states for reciprocal disaster emergency services.

(e) Ratification of agreements.—Mutual aid agreements shall be ratified by the governing bodies of the political subdivisions involved.

(f) Control of outside support forces.—Support forces furnished political subdivisions from outside its jurisdiction shall be under the operational control of the department, agency or office furnishing the force.

§ 7511. Appropriations by political subdivisions.

(a) General rule.—Every political subdivision shall have the power to make appropriations for the payment of expenses of the local organization in the manner provided by law for making appropriations for the ordinary expenses of the political subdivision. In making appropriations, the political subdivision shall specify the amounts and purposes for which the moneys appropriated may be used by the organization to or for which such appropriation may be made.

(b) Two or more local organizations.—Nothing in this subchapter or any other provision of this part shall be deemed to limit the power of any political subdivision to appropriate money for the purpose of paying the expenses of a local organization having jurisdiction both within and without the political subdivision even though an appropriation has been or is to be made to another local organization coterminous with or having jurisdiction within the political subdivision. Payments on account of an appropriation under this subsection shall be made pursuant to an agreement under section 7513 (relating to agreements among political subdivisions) or in the form of a gift or grant to the political subdivision responsible in the first instance for the payment of bills and claims against the local organization for the payment of the expenses for which the appropriation was made.

§ 7512. Law applicable to local organizations.

(a) General rule.—Where the jurisdiction of the local organization is coterminous with the political subdivision making an appropriation for the payment of the expenses, the local organization shall be deemed an agency, board or commission of the political subdivision, subject to all of the laws governing the making of contracts or purchases, the employment of persons or otherwise incurring financial obligations which apply to the political subdivision.

(b) Second class townships.—No purchase or purchases shall be made, no contract entered into and no expenses incurred by any local organization which involves the payment of more than $25 out of the treasury of any second class township unless the proposed expenditure has been approved in writing by the township supervisors. If any purchase or contract is made or other expenses incurred contrary to the provisions of this subsection, the township shall not be responsible for the payment thereof but the person acting for the local organization in the transaction shall be personally liable for the payment.

§ 7513. Agreements among political subdivisions.

(a) General rule.—Where a local organization has jurisdiction in an area including all or parts of more than one political subdivision which does not include the whole area of any county, the political subdivisions, all or part of which lie within the jurisdiction of the organization, shall, before paying any expenses of the organization, enter into an agreement designating one of the political subdivisions as the agent of each of them for the purpose of paying the expenses of the local organization. The agreement shall also set forth the proportionate share of the expenses of the organization to be paid by each political subdivision party to the agreement and an estimate of the amount required to be appropriated by each of them for the purpose of paying the expenses. The agreement shall be effective when approved by the corporate authorities of each of the political subdivisions by a majority vote and each of the subdivisions shall thereupon make an appropriation pursuant to section 7511 (relating to appropriations by political subdivisions) sufficient to pay its share of the expenses of the organization.

(b) Counties.—Where the local organization has jurisdiction in an area including the whole area of one or more counties which is not coterminous with any one county, before paying any expenses of the organization, the counties, all or part of which lie within the jurisdiction of the organization, shall enter into an agreement in the manner and form provided in subsection (a) and with like effect, and no other political subdivision lying within the jurisdiction of the organization shall be a party to the agreement.

§ 7514. Payments involving one political subdivision.

(a) General rule.—All bills or claims to be paid from any appropriation made by a political subdivision coterminous with the local organization, after first being approved by the local organization or an appropriate officer thereof designated for that purpose, shall be paid from the treasury of the political subdivision only upon the warrant or order of the officer or officers of the political subdivision designated by law to approve or countersign warrants or orders for the payment of the ordinary expenses of the political subdivision, and shall be subject to audit in the same manner as other financial transactions of the political subdivision. In each case, the officer or officers shall have the same power to approve or disapprove as they have in case of warrants for ordinary expenses of the political subdivision, and no warrant or order for the payment thereof shall be issued without the approval.

(b) Gift or grant of money.—Any gift or grant of money made to the local organization or to the political subdivision for the payment of expenses incurred or to be incurred by or for the organization shall be deposited in the treasury of the political subdivision and shall be appropriated by the political subdivision for the purpose for which the gift or grant was made, and any bills or claims to be paid from the gift or grant shall be paid in the manner provided in this subchapter for the payment of other bills and claims against the political subdivision.

§ 7515. Payments involving two or more political subdivisions.

(a) General rule.—Where two or more political subdivisions have entered into an agreement as provided by section 7513 (relating to agreements among political subdivisions), all bills and claims for expenses incurred by or for the local organization shall thereafter be paid in the first instance by the political subdivision named as agent in the agreement in the manner provided in section 7514 (relating to payments involving one political subdivision) as though the organization were coterminous with the political subdivision, and the organization shall be subject to all of the laws governing the making of contracts or purchases, the employment of persons or otherwise incurring financial obligations which apply to the political subdivision.

(b) Accounting by agent.—The political subdivision designated as agent shall, not later than the fifteenth day of each month, submit an itemized account of the expenses of the organization paid by it during the preceding calendar month to each of the other political subdivisions party to the agreement, together with a request for reimbursement of the proportionate share of expenses agreed to be paid by each of the other political subdivisions.

(c) Reimbursement of agent.—Each political subdivision requested to make reimbursement shall do so within 30 days after the request from the appropriation made for the payment of the expenses of the organization and, in the event of failure to do so, mandamus shall lie to compel the officers of the political subdivision to pay the agreed-upon proportionate share of the proper expenses of the organization out of the first moneys thereafter in the treasury of the political subdivision and not previously pledged to any other purpose. No political subdivision may be compelled to pay for any one year an amount greater than the amount estimated in the agreement as its proportionate share. Any payment made by any political subdivision to the political subdivision named as agent in the agreement for reimbursement for the payment of the expenses of the organization shall be credited by the agent political subdivision to the appropriation made by it for the payment of the expenses of the organization and shall be available for the payment of future expenses of the organization without further appropriation or action by the agent political subdivision.

(d) Gift or grant of money.—Any gift or grant of money made to or for the local organization, if made to a political subdivision, shall be deposited in its treasury and be appropriated by it for the purpose for which the gift or grant was made and the political subdivision shall notify the political subdivision named as agent in the agreement of the appropriation and the purpose for which it is available. If the gift or grant of money is made to the organization, it shall be deposited in the treasury of the political subdivision named as agent in the agreement and shall be appropriated by the political subdivision for the purpose for which the gift or grant was made. Any expenditure made by the agent political subdivision from any gift or grant deposited in its treasury or reimbursed from any gift or grant deposited in the treasury of any other political subdivision shall not be included in computing the reimbursement requested from any other political subdivision under the agreement.

PART VI
MUNICIPAL CODES

CHAPTER 31
MUNICIPALITY AUTHORITIES ACT
53 Pa.C.S. §§ 5601–5623

TABLE OF CONTENTS

Sec.

---

§ 5601. Short title of chapter.

This chapter shall be known and may be cited as the Municipality Authorities Act.

§ 5602. Definitions.

The following words and phrases when used in this chapter shall have the meanings given to them in this section unless the context clearly indicates otherwise:

"Administrative service." In the case of authorities created for the purpose of making business improvements or providing administrative services, the term means those services which improve the ability of the commercial establishments of a district to serve the consumers, such as free or reduced-fee parking for customers, transportation repayments, public relations programs, group advertising, and district maintenance and security services.

"Authority." A body politic and corporate created under this chapter; under the former act of June 28, 1935 (P.L. 463, No. 191), known as the Municipality Authorities Act of one thousand nine hundred and thirty-five; or under the act of May 2, 1945 (P.L. 382, No. 164), known as the Municipality Authorities Act of 1945.

"Board." The governing body of an authority.

"Bonds." Notes, bonds and other evidence of indebtedness or obligations which each authority is authorized to issue pursuant to section 5608 (relating to bonds).

"Business improvement." In the case of authorities created for the purpose of making business improvements or providing administrative services, the term means those improvements designated by an authority to be needed by a district in general or by specific areas or individual properties within or near the district, including, but not limited to, sidewalks, retaining walls, street paving, street lighting, parking lots, parking garages, trees and shrubbery, pedestrian walks, sewers, water lines, rest areas and acquisition and remodeling or demolition of blighted buildings or structures. Improvements shall not be made to property not acquired by purchase or lease other than those improvements made within a right-of-way.

"Construction." Acquisition and construction. The term "to construct" shall mean and include to acquire and to construct, all in such manner as may be deemed desirable.

"Eligible educational institution." An independent institution of higher education located in and chartered by the Commonwealth or a private secondary school located in this Commonwealth and approved by the Department of Education which is not a State-owned institution, which is operated not for profit, which is determined by the authority not to be a theological seminary or school of theology or a sectarian and denominational institution and which is approved as eligible by the authority pursuant to regulations approved by it.

"Federal agency." The United States of America, the President of the United States of America and any department of or corporation, agency or instrumentality created, designated or established by the United States of America.

"Financing," "to finance" or "financed." The lending or providing of funds to or on behalf of a person for payment of the costs of a project or for refinancing such costs, repayment of loans previously incurred to pay the cost of a project or otherwise.

"Health center." A facility which:

(1) is operated by a nonprofit corporation and:

(i) provides health care services to the public;

(ii) provides health care-related services or assistance to one or more organizations in aid of the provision of health care services to the public, including, without limitation, such facilities as blood banks, laboratories, research and testing facilities, medical and administrative office buildings and ancillary facilities;

(iii) constitutes an integrated facility which provides substantial health care services on a nonsectarian basis and other reasonably related services, including, without limitation, life care or continuing care communities and nursing, personal care or assisted living facilities for the elderly, handicapped or disabled; or

(iv) provides educational and counseling services regarding the prevention, diagnosis and treatment of health care problems; and

(2) if required by law to be licensed to provide such services by the Department of Health, the Department of Public Welfare or the Insurance Department, is so licensed or, in the case of a facility to be constructed, renovated or expanded, is designed to comply with applicable standards for such licensure.

"Improvement." Extension, enlargement and improvement. The term "to improve" shall mean and include to extend, to enlarge and to improve all in such manner as may be deemed desirable.

"Local government unit." This term shall have the same meaning as provided under section 8002 (relating to definitions).

"Municipal authority." The body or board authorized by law to enact ordinances or adopt resolutions for the particular municipality.

"Municipality." A county, city, town, borough, township or school district of the Commonwealth.

"Project." Equipment leased by an authority to the municipality or municipalities that organized it or to any municipality or school district located wholly or partially within the boundaries of the municipality or municipalities that organized it, or any structure, facility or undertaking which an authority is authorized to acquire, construct, finance, improve, maintain or operate, or provide financing for insurance reserves under the provisions of this chapter, or any working capital which an authority is authorized to finance under the provisions of this chapter.

"Provide financing for insurance reserves." Financing, on behalf of one or more local government units or authorities, all or any portion of a reserve or a contribution toward a combined reserve, pool or other arrangement relating to self-insurance which has been established by one or more local government units pursuant to 42 Pa.C.S. § 8564 (relating to liability insurance and self-insurance) up to, but not exceeding, the amount provided in section 8007 (relating to cost of project).

"Working capital." Shall include, but not be limited to, funds for supplies, materials, services, salaries, pensions and any other proper operating expenses, provided that the term shall be limited solely to hospitals and health centers, and private, nonprofit, nonsectarian colleges and universities, State-related universities and community colleges, which are determined by the authority to be eligible educational institutions. Nothing in this chapter shall prohibit the borrowing of working capital as may be necessary or incidental to the undertaking or placing in operation of any project undertaken in whole or in part pursuant to this chapter.

§ 5603. Method of incorporation.

(a) Resolution of intent.—Whenever the municipal authorities of any municipality singly or of two or more municipalities jointly desire to organize an authority under this chapter, they shall adopt a resolution or ordinance signifying their intention to do so. No such resolution or ordinance shall be adopted until after a public hearing has been held, the notice of which shall be given at least 30 days before the hearing and in the same manner as provided in subsection (b) for the giving of notice of the adoption of the resolution or ordinance.

(b) General notice of adopted resolution.—If the resolution or ordinance is adopted, the municipal authorities of such municipality or municipalities shall cause a notice of such resolution or ordinance to be published at least one time in the legal periodical of the county or counties in which the authority is to be organized and at least one time in a newspaper published and in general circula-

Table of Contents | Part I Ch. 1–3 Ethics, Records, Open Meetings | Part II Ch. 4–10 Taxation | Part III Ch. 11–18 Torts, Contracts & Civil Rules | Part IV Ch. 19–24 Zoning & Planning | Part V Ch. 25–30 Construction and Emergency Codes | Part VI Ch. 31–39 Municipal Codes | Index

tion in such county or counties. The notice shall contain a brief statement of the substance of the resolution or ordinance, including the substance of the articles making reference to this chapter. In the case of authorities created for the purpose of making business improvements or providing administrative services, if appropriate, the notice shall specifically provide that the municipality or municipalities have retained the right which exists under this chapter to approve any plan of the authority. The notice shall state that on a day certain, not less than three days after publication of the notice, articles of incorporation of the proposed authority shall be filed with the Secretary of the Commonwealth. No municipality shall be required to make any other publication of the resolution or ordinance under the provisions of existing law.

(c) Filing articles of incorporation.—On or before the day specified in the notice required under subsection (b), the municipal authorities shall file with the Secretary of the Commonwealth articles of incorporation together with proof of publication of the notice required under subsection (b). The articles of incorporation shall set forth:

(1) The name of the authority.

(2) A statement that the authority is formed under this chapter.

(3) A statement whether any other authority has been organized under this chapter or under the former act of June 28, 1935 (P.L. 463, No. 191), entitled "An act providing for the incorporation, as bodies corporate and politic, of "Authorities" for municipalities, counties, and townships; defining the same; prescribing the rights, powers, and duties of such Authorities; authorizing such Authorities to acquire, construct, improve, maintain, and operate projects, and to borrow money and issue bonds therefor; providing for the payment of such bonds, and prescribing the rights of the holders thereof; conferring the right of eminent domain on such Authorities; authorizing such Authorities to enter into contracts with and to accept grants from the Federal Government or any agency thereof; and for other purposes," or the act of May 2, 1945 (P.L. 382, No. 164), known as the Municipality Authorities Act of 1945, and is in existence in or for the incorporating municipality or municipalities. If any one or more of the municipalities have already joined with other municipalities not composing the same group in organizing a joint authority, the application shall set forth the name of that authority, together with the names of the municipalities joining in it.

(4) The name of the incorporating municipality or municipalities, together with the names and addresses of its municipal authorities.

(5) The names, addresses and term of office of the first members of the board of the authority.

(6) In the case of authorities created for the purpose of making business improvements or providing administrative services, if appropriate, a statement that the municipality or municipalities have retained the right which exists under this chapter to approve any plan of the authority.

(7) Any other matter which shall be determined in accordance with the provisions of this chapter.

(d) Execution of articles.—The articles of incorporation shall be executed by each incorporating municipality by its proper officers and under its municipal seal.

(e) Certification of incorporation.—If the Secretary of the Commonwealth finds that the articles of incorporation conform to law, he shall, but not prior to the day specified in the notice published in accordance with subsection (b), endorse his approval of them and, when all proper fees and charges have been paid, shall file the articles and issue a certificate of incorporation to which shall be attached a copy of the approved articles. Upon the issuance of a certificate of incorporation by the Secretary of the Commonwealth, the corporate existence of the authority shall begin. The certificate of incorporation shall be conclusive evidence of the fact that the authority has been incorporated, but proceedings may be instituted by the Commonwealth to dissolve an authority which was formed without substantial compliance with the provisions of this section.

(f) Certification of officers.—When an authority has been organized and its officers elected, its secretary shall certify to the Secretary of the Commonwealth the names and addresses of its officers as well as the principal office of the authority. Any change in the location of the principal office shall likewise be certified to the Secretary of the Commonwealth within ten days after such change. An authority created under the laws of the Commonwealth and existing at the time this chapter is enacted, in addition to powers granted or conferred upon the authority, shall possess all the powers provided under this chapter.

§ 5604. Municipalities withdrawing from and joining in joint authorities.

(a) Power to withdraw.—When an authority has been incorporated by two or more municipalities, any one or more of such municipalities may withdraw from it, but no municipality shall be permitted to withdraw from an authority after an obligation has been incurred by that authority.

(b) Power to join.—When an authority has been incorporated by one or more municipalities, a municipality not having joined in the original incorporation may subsequently join in the authority.

(c) Procedure.—Any municipality wishing to withdraw from or to become a member of an existing authority shall signify its desire by resolution or ordinance. If the authority shall by resolution express its consent to such withdrawal or joining, the municipal authorities of the withdrawing or joining municipality shall cause a notice of its resolution or ordinance to be published at least one time in the legal periodical of the county or counties in which the authority is organized and at least one time in a newspaper published and in general circulation in such county or counties. This notice shall contain a brief statement of the substance of the resolution or ordinance, making reference to this chapter, and shall state that on a day certain, not less than three days after publication of the notice, an application to withdraw from or to become a member of the authority, as the case may be, will be filed with the Secretary of the Commonwealth.

(d) Filing an application to withdraw or join.—On or before the day specified in the notice, the municipal authorities shall file an application with the Secretary of the Commonwealth together with proof of publication of the notice required under subsection (c). In the case of a municipality seeking to become a member of the authority, the application shall set forth all of the information required in the case of original incorporation insofar as it applies to the incoming municipality, including the name and address and term of office of the first member or members of the board of the authority from the incoming municipality and, if there is to be a reapportionment of representation or revision of the terms of office of the members of the board, the names, addresses and terms of office of all the members of the board as so reapportioned or revised. The application in all cases shall be executed by the proper officers of the withdrawing or incoming municipality under its municipal seal and shall be joined in by the proper officers of the governing body of the authority and, in the case of a municipality seeking to become a member of the authority, also by the proper officers of each of the municipalities that are then members of the authority, pursuant to resolutions by the municipal authorities of the participating municipalities.

(e) Certification of withdrawal or joinder.—If the Secretary of the Commonwealth finds that the application conforms to law, he shall, but not prior to the day specified in the notice, endorse his approval of it, and, when all proper fees and charges have been paid, shall file the same and issue a certificate of withdrawal or a certificate of joinder, as the case may be, to which shall be attached a copy of the approved application. The withdrawal or joining shall become effective upon the issuing of the certificate.

§ 5605. Amendment of articles.

(a) **Purpose.**—An authority may amend its articles for the following reasons:

(1) To adopt a new name.

(2) To modify or add a provision to increase its term of existence to a date not exceeding 50 years from the date of approval of the articles of amendment.

(3) To change, add to or diminish its powers or purposes or to set forth different or additional powers or purposes.

(4) To increase or decrease the number of members of the board of the authority, to reapportion the representation on the board of the authority and to revise the terms of office of members, all in a manner consistent with the provisions of section 5610 (relating to governing body).

(b) **Procedure.**—Every amendment to the articles shall first be proposed by the board by the adoption of a resolution setting forth the proposed amendment and directing that it be submitted to the governing authorities of the municipality or municipalities composing the authority. The resolution shall contain the language of the proposed amendment to the articles by providing that the articles shall be amended so as to read as set forth in full in the resolution, that any provision of the articles be amended so as to read as set forth in full in the resolution, or that the matter stated in the resolution be added to or stricken from the articles. After the amendments have been submitted to the municipality or municipalities, such municipality or municipalities shall adopt or reject such amendment by resolution or ordinance.

(c) **Execution and verification.**—After an amendment has been adopted by the municipality or municipalities, articles of amendment shall be executed under the seal of the authority and verified by two duly authorized officers of the corporation and shall set forth:

(1) The name and location of the registered office of the authority.

(2) The act under which the authority was formed and the date when the original articles were approved and filed.

(3) The resolution or ordinance of the municipality or municipalities adopting the amendment.

(4) The amendment adopted by the municipality or municipalities which shall be set forth in full.

(d) **Advertisement.**—The authority shall advertise its intention to file articles of amendment with the Secretary of the Commonwealth as provided under section 5603 (relating to method of incorporation) for forming an authority. Advertisements shall appear at least three days prior to the day upon which the articles of amendment are presented to the Secretary of the Commonwealth and shall set forth briefly:

(1) The name and location of the registered office of the authority.

(2) A statement that the articles of amendment are to be filed under the provisions of this chapter.

(3) The nature and character of the proposed amendment.

(4) The time when the articles of amendment will be filed with the Secretary of the Commonwealth.

(e) **Filing the amendment.**—The articles of amendment and proof of the required advertisement shall be delivered by the authority or its representative to the Secretary of the Commonwealth. If the Secretary of the Commonwealth finds that the articles conform to law, he shall forthwith, but not prior to the day specified in the advertisement required in subsection (d), endorse his approval of it and, when all fees and charges have been paid, shall file the articles and issue to the authority or its representative a certificate of amendment to which shall be attached a copy of the approved articles.

§ 5606. School district projects.

(a) Merger and consolidation authorized.—Any two or more existing authorities, all the projects of all of which are leased to the same school district, may be merged into one authority, hereinafter designated as the surviving authority, or consolidated into a new authority.

(b) Articles of merger or consolidation.—Articles of merger or articles of consolidation, as the case may be, shall first be proposed by the board of school directors of the school district leasing the projects. The governing body of the school district and of any other municipality or municipalities incorporating one or more of the existing authorities shall each adopt a resolution which shall contain the language of the proposed merger or consolidation. The articles of merger or consolidation shall be signed by the proper officers of the respective school districts and other municipalities, if any, and under their respective municipal seals and shall set forth the following:

(1) The name of the surviving or new authority.

(2) The location of the registered office of the surviving or new authority.

(3) The names and addresses and term of office of the members of the board of the surviving or new authority as specified in the plan of merger or consolidation, and the initial terms of office shall be staggered as provided in this chapter with respect to the incorporation of an authority.

(4) A statement indicating the date on which each existing authority was formed and the purpose for which it was formed, taken from the articles of incorporation, the name of the original incorporating school district or districts or other incorporating municipality or municipalities and the name of any successor to any thereof.

(5) The time and place of the meetings of the governing bodies of the school district and other municipalities parties to the plan of merger or consolidation.

(6) A statement of the plan of merger.

(7) Any changes in the articles of incorporation of the surviving authority in the case of a merger and a statement of the articles of incorporation in full in the case of the new authority to be formed, in each case in conformity with the provisions of this chapter relating to the incorporation of authorities, except that any item required to be stated which is covered elsewhere in the articles of merger or consolidation need not be repeated.

(c) Publication of resolution.—The reorganized school district and each other municipality party to the plan of merger or consolidation shall cause a notice of the resolution setting forth the merger or consolidation to be published at least one time in the legal periodical of the county or counties in which the surviving authority is to be organized and at least one time in a newspaper published and in general circulation in such county or counties. The notice shall contain a brief statement of the substance of the resolution, including the substance of the articles of merger making reference to this chapter, and shall state that on a day certain, not less than three days after publication of the notice, articles of merger or consolidation, shall be filed with the Secretary of the Commonwealth. The publication shall be sufficient compliance with the laws of this Commonwealth or any existing laws dealing with publication for municipalities.

(d) Documentation.—The articles of merger or consolidation shall be filed on or before the day specified in the advertisement with the Secretary of the Commonwealth, together with the proof of publication of the notice required under subsection (c).

(e) Certification of merger or consolidation.—The Secretary of the Commonwealth shall file the articles of merger or consolidation and the proof of advertisement required in subsection (c) but not prior to the day specified in the advertisement, certify the date of such filing when all fees and charges have been paid and issue to the surviving or new authority or its representative a certificate of merger or consolidation to which shall be attached a copy of the filed articles of merger or consolidation.

(f) Filing the articles of merger or consolidation.—Upon the filing of the articles of merger or the articles of consolidation by the Secretary of the Commonwealth, the merger or consolidation shall be effective, and in the case of a consolidation the new authority shall come into existence, and, in either case, the articles of merger and consolidation shall constitute the articles of incorporation of the surviving or new authority, and the reorganized school district, lessee of the projects, shall be deemed to be the incorporating municipality of the authority.

(g) Creation of surviving or new authority.—Upon the merger or consolidation becoming effective, the several existing authorities to the plan of merger or consolidation shall become a single authority, which in the case of a merger shall be that authority designated in the articles of merger as the surviving authority and in the case of a consolidation shall be a new authority as provided in the articles of consolidation. The separate existence of all existing authorities named in the articles of merger or consolidation shall cease, except that of the surviving authority in the case of a merger.

(h) Disposition of property and accounts.—All of the property, real, personal and mixed, and all interests therein of each of the existing authorities named in the plan of merger or consolidation, all debts due and whatever amount due to any of them, including their respective right, title and interest in and to all lease rentals, sinking funds on deposit, all funds deposited under lease or trust instruments shall be taken and deemed to be transferred to and vested in the surviving or new authority as the case may be without further act or deed.

(i) Continuation of contracts.—The surviving authority or the new authority shall be responsible for the liabilities and obligations of each of the existing authorities so merged or consolidated but shall be subject to the same limitations, pledges, assignments, liens, charges, terms and conditions as to revenues and restrictions as to and leases of properties as were applicable to each existing authority. The liabilities of the merging or consolidating authorities of the members of their boards or officers shall not be affected nor shall the rights of creditors thereof or any persons dealing with such authorities or any liens upon the property of such authorities or any outstanding bonds be impaired by the merger or consolidation, and any claim existing or action or proceeding pending by or against any such authorities shall be prosecuted to judgment as if such merger or consolidation had not taken place, or the surviving authority or the new authority may be proceeded against or substituted in its place.

§ 5607. Purposes and powers.

(a) Scope of projects permitted.—Every authority incorporated under this chapter shall be a body corporate and politic and shall be for the purposes of financing working capital; acquiring, holding, constructing, financing, improving, maintaining and operating, owning or leasing, either in the capacity of lessor or lessee, projects of the following kind and character and providing financing for insurance reserves:

(1) Equipment to be leased by an authority to the municipality or municipalities that organized it or to any municipality or school district located wholly or partially within the boundaries of the municipality or municipalities that organized it.

(2) Buildings to be devoted wholly or partially for public uses, including public school buildings, and facilities for the conduct of judicial proceedings and for revenue-producing purposes.

(3) Transportation, marketing, shopping, terminals, bridges, tunnels, flood control projects, highways, parkways, traffic distribution centers, parking spaces, airports and all facilities necessary or incident thereto.

(4) Parks, recreation grounds and facilities.

(5) Sewers, sewer systems or parts thereof.

(6) Sewage treatment works, including works for treating and disposing of industrial waste.

(7) Facilities and equipment for the collection, removal or disposal of ashes, garbage, rubbish and other refuse materials by incineration, landfill or other methods.

(8) Steam heating plants and distribution systems.

(9) Incinerator plants.

(10) Waterworks, water supply works, water distribution systems.

(11) Facilities to produce steam which is used by the authority or is sold on a contract basis for industrial or similar use or on a sale-for-resale basis to one or more entities authorized to sell steam to the public, provided that such facilities have been approved by resolution or ordinance adopted by the governing body of the municipality or municipalities organizing such authority and that the approval does not obligate the taxing power of the municipality in any way.

(12) Facilities for generating surplus electric power which are related to incinerator plants, dams, water supply works, water distribution systems or sewage treatment plants pursuant, where applicable, to section 3 of the Federal Power Act (41 Stat. 1063, 16 U.S.C. § 796) and section 210 of the Public Utility Regulatory Policies Act of 1978 (Public Law 95-617, 16 U.S.C. § 824a-3) or Title IV of the Public Utility Regulatory Policies Act of 1978 (Public Law 95-617, 16 U.S.C. §§ 2701 to 2708), if:

(i) electric power generated from the facilities is sold or distributed only on a sale-for-resale basis to one or more entities authorized to sell electric power to the public;

(ii) the facilities have been approved by resolution or ordinance adopted by the governing body of the municipality or municipalities organizing the authority and the approval does not obligate the taxing power of the municipality in any way; and

(iii) the incinerator plants, dams, water supply works, water distribution systems or sewage treatment plants are or will be located within or contiguous with a county in which at least one of the municipalities organizing the authority is located, except that this subparagraph shall not apply to incinerator plants, dams, water supply works, water distribution systems or sewage treatment plants located in any county which have been or will be constructed by or acquired by the authority to perform functions, the primary purposes of which are other than that of generation of electric power for which the authority has been organized.

(13) Swimming pools, playgrounds, lakes and low-head dams.

(14) Hospitals and health centers.

(15) Buildings and facilities for private, nonprofit, nonsectarian secondary schools, colleges and universities, State-related universities and community colleges, which are determined by the authority to be eligible educational institutions, provided that such buildings and facilities shall have been approved by resolution or ordinance adopted by the governing body of the municipality or municipalities organizing the authority and that the approval does not obligate the taxing power of the governing body in any way.

(16) Motor buses for public use, when such motor buses are to be used within any municipality, and subways.

Chap. 39 Res. During Mil. Service
Chap. 38 Intergov. Coop.
Chap. 37 3rd Class City Code
Chap. 36 Bor. Code
Chap. 35 2nd Class Twp. Code
Chap. 34 1st Class Twp. Code
Chap. 33 Home Rule Chart. Opt. Plans Law
Chap. 32 Water Serv. Act
Chap. 31 Munic. Auth. Act

(17) Industrial development projects, including, but not limited to, projects to retain or develop existing industries and the development of new industries, the development and administration of business improvements and administrative services related thereto.

(18) Storm water planning, management and implementation as defined in the articles of incorporation by the governing body. Authorities, existing as of the effective date of this paragraph, already operating storm water controls as part of a combined sewer system, sanitary sewer system or flood control project may continue to operate those projects.

(b) Limitations.—This section is subject to the following limitations:

(1) An authority created by a school district or school districts shall have the power only to acquire, hold, construct, improve, maintain, operate and lease public school buildings and other school projects acquired, constructed or improved for public school purposes.

(2) The purpose and intent of this chapter being to benefit the people of the Commonwealth by, among other things, increasing their commerce, health, safety and prosperity, and not to unnecessarily burden or interfere with existing business by the establishment of competitive enterprises; none of the powers granted by this chapter shall be exercised in the construction, financing, improvement, maintenance, extension or operation of any project or projects or providing financing for insurance reserves which in whole or in part shall duplicate or compete with existing enterprises serving substantially the same purposes. This limitation shall not apply to the exercise of the powers granted under this section:

(i) for facilities and equipment for the collection, removal or disposal of ashes, garbage, rubbish and other refuse materials by incineration, landfill or other methods if each municipality organizing or intending to use the facilities of an authority having such powers shall declare by resolution or ordinance that it is desirable for the health and safety of the people of such municipality that it use the facilities of the authority and state if any contract between such municipality and any other person, firm or corporation for the collection, removal or disposal of ashes, garbage, rubbish and other refuse material has by its terms expired or is terminable at the option of the municipality or will expire within six months from the date such ordinance becomes effective;

(ii) for industrial development projects if the authority does not develop industrial projects which will compete with existing industries;

(iii) for authorities created for the purpose of providing business improvements and administrative services if each municipality organizing an authority for such a project shall declare by resolution or ordinance that it is desirable for the entire local government unit to improve the business district;

(iv) to hospital projects or health centers to be leased to or financed with loans to public hospitals, nonprofit corporation health centers or nonprofit hospital corporations serving the public or to school building projects and facilities to be leased to or financed with loans to private, nonprofit, nonsectarian secondary schools, colleges and universities, State-related universities and community colleges, or to facilities, as limited under the provisions of this section, to produce steam or to generate electric power if each municipality organizing an authority for such a project shall declare by resolution or ordinance that it is desirable for the health, safety and welfare of the people in the area served by such facilities to have such facilities provided by or financed through an authority;

(v) to provide financing for insurance reserves if each municipality or authority intending to use any proceeds thereof shall declare by resolution or ordinance that it is desirable for the health, safety and welfare of the people in such local government unit or served by such authority; or

(vi) to projects for financing working capital.

(3) It is the intent of this chapter in specifying and defining the authorized purposes and projects of an authority to permit the authority to benefit the people of this Commonwealth by, among other things, increasing their commerce, health, safety and prosperity while not unnecessarily burdening or interfering with any municipality which has not incorporated or joined that authority. Therefore, notwithstanding any other provisions of this chapter, an authority shall not have as its purpose and shall not undertake as a project solely for revenue-producing purposes the acquiring of buildings, facilities or tracts of land which, in the case of an authority incorporated or joined by a county or counties are located either within or outside the boundaries of the county or counties and in the case of all other authorities are located outside the boundaries of the municipality or municipalities that incorporated or joined the authority, unless either:

(i) the governing body of each municipality in which the project will be undertaken has by resolution evidenced its approval; or

(ii) in cases where the property acquired is not subject to tax abatement, the authority covenants and agrees with each municipality in which the authority will acquire real property as part of the project either to make annual payments in lieu of real estate taxes and special assessments for amounts and time periods specified in the agreement or to pay annually the amount of real estate taxes and special assessments which would be payable if the real property so acquired were fully taxable and subject to special assessments.

(c) Effect of specificity.—The municipality or municipalities organizing such an authority may, in the resolution or ordinance signifying their intention so to do or from time to time by subsequent resolution or ordinance, specify the project or projects to be undertaken by the authority, and no other projects shall be undertaken by the authority than those so specified. If the municipal authorities organizing an authority fail to specify the project or projects to be undertaken, then the authority shall be deemed to have all the powers granted by this chapter.

(d) Powers.—Every authority may exercise all powers necessary or convenient for the carrying out of the purposes set forth in this section, including, but without limiting the generality of the foregoing, the following rights and powers:

(1) To have existence for a term of 50 years and for such further period or periods as may be provided in articles of amendment approved under section 5605(e) (relating to amendment of articles).

(2) To sue and be sued, implead and be impleaded, complain and defend in all courts.

(3) To adopt, use and alter at will a corporate seal.

(4) To acquire, purchase, hold, lease as lessee and use any franchise, property, real, personal or mixed, tangible or intangible, or any interest therein necessary or desirable for carrying out the purposes of the authority, and to sell, lease as lessor, transfer and dispose of any property or interest therein at any time acquired by it.

(5) To acquire by purchase, lease or otherwise and to construct, improve, maintain, repair and operate projects.

(6) To finance projects by making loans, which may be evidenced by and secured as may be provided in loan agreements, mortgages, security agreements or any other contracts, instruments or agreements, which contracts, instruments or agreements may contain such provisions as the authority shall deem necessary or desirable for the security or protection of the authority or its bondholders.

(7) To make bylaws for the management and regulation of its affairs.

(8) To appoint officers, agents, employees and servants, to prescribe their duties and to fix their compensation.

Table of Contents
Part I Ch. 1–3 Ethics, Records, Open Meetings
Part II Ch. 4–10 Taxation
Part III Ch. 11–18 Torts, Contracts & Civil Rules
Part IV Ch. 19–24 Zoning & Planning
Part V Ch. 25–30 Construction and Emergency Codes
Part VI Ch. 31–39 Municipal Codes
Index

Chap. 39 Res. During Mil. Service
Chap. 38 Intergov. Coop.
Chap. 37 3rd Class City Code
Chap. 36 Bor. Code
Chap. 35 2nd Class Twp. Code
Chap. 34 1st Class Twp. Code
Chap. 33 Home Rule Chart. Opt. Plans Law
Chap. 32 Water Serv. Act
Chap. 31 Munic. Auth. Act

(9) To fix, alter, charge and collect rates and other charges in the area served by its facilities at reasonable and uniform rates to be determined exclusively by it for the purpose of providing for the payment of the expenses of the authority, the construction, improvement, repair, maintenance and operation of its facilities and properties and, in the case of an authority created for the purpose of making business improvements or providing administrative services, a charge for such services which is to be based on actual benefits and which may be measured on, among other things, gross sales or gross or net profits, the payment of the principal of and interest on its obligations and to fulfill the terms and provisions of any agreements made with the purchasers or holders of any such obligations, or with a municipality and to determine by itself exclusively the services and improvements required to provide adequate, safe and reasonable service, including extensions thereof, in the areas served. If the service area includes more than one municipality, the revenues from any project shall not be expended directly or indirectly on any other project unless such expenditures are made for the benefit of the entire service area. Any person questioning the reasonableness or uniformity of a rate fixed by an authority or the adequacy, safety and reasonableness of the authority's services, including extensions thereof, may bring suit against the authority in the court of common pleas of the county where the project is located or, if the project is located in more than one county, in the court of common pleas of the county where the principal office of the project is located. The court of common pleas shall have exclusive jurisdiction to determine questions involving rates or service. Except in municipal corporations having a population density of 300 persons or more per square mile, all owners of real property in eighth class counties may decline in writing the services of a solid waste authority. The owner of multiple residential units that are served by a single water meter may periodically request the authority to adjust the amount billed by showing a minimum of five consecutive years of actual usage data to determine if the amount billed exceeds the actual usage by 30% or more. If the usage data shows that an adjustment is needed, the authority shall appropriately adjust the billing and use the adjusted amount going forward. When calculating the new amount, the authority may include up to 10% over the amount used. After an initial adjustment, the owner may not request another adjustment for five years after the adjustment is completed.

(10) In the case of an authority which has agreed to provide water service through a separate meter and separate service line to a residential dwelling unit in which the owner does not reside, to impose and enforce the owner's duty to pay a tenant's bill for service rendered to the tenant by the authority only if the authority notifies the owner and the tenant within 30 days after the bill first becomes overdue. Notification shall be provided by first class mail to the address of the owner provided to the authority by the owner and to the billing address of the tenant, respectively. Nothing in this paragraph shall be construed to require an authority to terminate service to a tenant, and the owner shall not be liable for any service which the authority provides to the tenant 90 or more days after the tenant's bill first becomes due unless the authority has been prevented by court order from terminating service to that tenant.

(11) In the case of an authority which has agreed to provide sewer service to a residential dwelling unit in which the owner does not reside, to impose and enforce the owner's duty to pay a tenant's bill for service rendered by the authority to the tenant. The authority shall notify the owner and the tenant within 30 days after the tenant's bill for that service first becomes overdue. Notification shall be provided by first class mail to the address of the owner provided to the authority by the owner and to the billing address of the tenant, respectively. Nothing in this paragraph shall be construed to relieve the owner of liability for such service unless the authority fails to provide the notice required in this paragraph.

(12) To borrow money, make and issue negotiable notes, bonds, refunding bonds and other evidences of indebtedness or obligations, hereinafter called bonds, of the authority. Bonds shall have a maturity date not longer than 40 years from the date of issue, except that no refunding bonds shall have a maturity date later than the life of the authority; also, to secure the payment of the bonds or any part thereof by pledge or deed of trust of all or any of its revenues and receipts; to make agreements with the purchasers or holders of the bonds or with others in connection with any bonds, whether issued or to be issued, as the authority shall deem advisable; and in general to provide for the security for the bonds and the rights of the bondholders. In respect to any project constructed and operated under agreement with any authority or any public authority of any adjoining state, to borrow money and issue notes, bonds and other evidences of indebtedness and obligations jointly with that authority. Notwithstanding any of the foregoing, no authority shall borrow money on obligations to be paid primarily out of lease rentals or other current revenues other than charges made to the public for the use of the capital projects financed if the net debt of the lessee municipality or municipalities shall exceed any limit provided by any law of the Commonwealth.

(13) To make contracts of every name and nature and to execute all instruments necessary or convenient for the carrying on of its business.

(14) Without limitation of the foregoing, to borrow money and accept grants from and to enter into contracts, leases or other transactions with any Federal agency, the Commonwealth or a municipality, school district, corporation or authority.

(15) To have the power of eminent domain.

(16) To pledge, hypothecate or otherwise encumber all or any of the revenues or receipts of the authority as security for all or any of the obligations of the authority.

(17) To do all acts and things necessary or convenient for the promotion of its business and the general welfare of the authority to carry out the powers granted to it by this chapter or other law, including, but not limited to, the adoption of reasonable rules and regulations that apply to water and sewer lines located on a property owned or leased by a customer and to refer for prosecution as a summary offense any violation dealing with rules and regulations relating to water and sewer lines located on a property owned or leased by a customer. Under this paragraph, an authority established by a county of the second class A which is not a home rule county shall have powers for the inspection and repair of sewer facilities comparable to the powers of health officials under section 3007 of the act of May 1, 1933 (P.L. 103, No. 69),[1] known as The Second Class Township Code.

(18) To contract with any municipality, corporation or a public authority of this and an adjoining state on terms as the authority shall deem proper for the construction and operation of any project which is partly in this Commonwealth and partly in the adjoining state.

(19) To enter into contracts to supply water and other services to and for municipalities that are not members of the authority or to and for the Commonwealth, municipalities, school districts, persons or authorities and fix the amount to be paid therefor.

(20) (i) To make contracts of insurance with an insurance company, association or exchange authorized to transact business in this Commonwealth, insuring its employees and appointed officers and officials under a policy or policies of insurance covering life, accidental death and dismemberment and disability income. Statutory requirements for such insurance, including, but

1. 53 P.S. § 68007.

Table of Contents
Part I Ch. 1–3 Ethics, Records, Open Meetings
Part II Ch. 4–10 Taxation
Part III Ch. 11–18 Torts, Contracts & Civil Rules
Part IV Ch. 19–24 Zoning & Planning
Part V Ch. 25–30 Construction and Emergency Codes
Part VI Ch. 31–39 Municipal Codes
Index

not limited to, requisite number of eligible employees, appointed officers and officials, as provided for in section 621.2 of the act of May 17, 1921 (P.L. 682, No. 284), known as The Insurance Company Law of 1921, and sections 1, 2, 6, 7 and 9 of the act of May 11, 1949 (P.L. 1210, No. 367), known as the Group Life Insurance Policy Law, shall be met.

(ii) To make contracts with an insurance company, association or exchange or any hospital plan corporation or professional health service corporation authorized to transact business in this Commonwealth insuring or covering its employees and their dependents but not its appointed officers and officials nor their dependents for hospital and medical benefits and to contract for its employees but not its appointed officers and officials with an insurance company, association or exchange authorized to transact business in this Commonwealth granting annuities or to establish, maintain, operate and administer its own pension plan covering its employees, but not its appointed officers and officials.

(iii) For the purposes set forth under this paragraph, to agree to pay part or all of the cost of this insurance, including the premiums or charges for carrying these contracts, and to appropriate out of its treasury any money necessary to pay such costs, premiums or charges. The proper officers of the authority who are authorized to enter into such contracts are authorized, enabled and permitted to deduct from the officers' or employees' pay, salary or compensation that part of the premium or cost which is payable by the officer or employee and as may be so authorized by the officer or employee in writing.

(21) To charge the cost of construction of any sewer or water main constructed by the authority against the properties benefited, improved or accommodated thereby to the extent of such benefits. These benefits shall be assessed in the manner provided under this chapter for the exercise of the right of eminent domain.

(22) To charge the cost of construction of a sewer or water main constructed by the authority against the properties benefited, improved or accommodated by the construction according to the foot front rule. Charges shall be based upon the foot frontage of the properties benefited and shall be a lien against such properties. Charges may be assessed and collected and liens may be enforced in the manner provided by law for the assessment and collection of charges and the enforcement of liens of the municipality in which such authority is located. No charge shall be assessed unless prior to the construction of a sewer or water main the authority submitted the plan of construction and estimated cost to the municipality in which the project is to be undertaken and the municipality approved it. The properties benefited, improved or accommodated by the construction may not be charged an aggregate amount in excess of the approved estimated cost.

(23) To require the posting of financial security to insure the completion in accordance with the approved plat and with the rules and regulations of the authority of any water mains or sanitary sewer lines, or both, and related apparatus and facilities, required to be installed by or on behalf of a developer under an approved land development or subdivision plat as these terms are defined under the act of July 31, 1968 (P.L. 805, No. 247), known as the Pennsylvania Municipalities Planning Code. If financial security is required by the authority and without limitation as to other types of financial security which the authority may approve, which approval shall not be unreasonably withheld, federally chartered or Commonwealth-chartered lending institution irrevocable letters of credit and restrictive or escrow accounts in these lending institutions shall be deemed acceptable financial security. Financial security shall be posted with a bonding company or federally chartered or Commonwealth-chartered lending institution chosen by the party posting the financial security if the bonding

company or lending institution is authorized to conduct business within this Commonwealth. The bond or other security shall provide for and secure to the authority the completion of required improvements within one year from the date of posting of the security. The amount of financial security shall be equal to 110% of the cost of the required improvements for which financial security is to be posted. The cost of required improvements shall be established by submitting to the authority a bona fide bid from a contractor chosen by the party posting the financial security. In the absence of a bona fide bid, the cost shall be established by an estimate prepared by the authority's engineer. If the party posting the financial security requires more than one year from the date of posting the financial security to complete the required improvements, the amount of financial security may be increased by an additional 10% for each one-year period beyond the first anniversary date from the initial posting date or to 110% of the cost of completing the required improvements as reestablished on or about the expiration of the preceding one-year period by using the above bidding procedure. As the work of installing the required improvements proceeds, the party posting the financial security may request the authority to release or authorize the release of, from time to time, portions of the financial security necessary to pay the contractor performing the work. Release requests shall be in writing addressed to the authority, and the authority shall have 45 days after receiving a request to ascertain from the authority engineer, certified in writing, that the portion of the work has been completed in accordance with the approved plat. Upon receiving written certification, the authority shall authorize release by the bonding company or lending institution of an amount estimated by the authority engineer to fairly represent the value of the improvements completed. If the authority fails to act within the 45-day period, it shall be deemed to have approved the requested release of funds. The authority may, prior to final release at the time of completion and certification by its engineer, retain 10% of the original amount of the posted financial security for the improvements. If the authority accepts dedication of all or some of the required improvements following completion, it may require the posting of financial security to secure structural integrity of the dedicated improvements as well as the functioning of the improvements in accordance with the design and specifications as depicted on the final plat and the authority's rules and regulations. This financial security shall expire not later than 18 months from the date of acceptance of dedication and shall be of the same type as set forth in this paragraph with regard to that which is required for installation of the improvements, except that it shall not exceed 15% of the actual cost of installation of the improvements. Any inconsistent ordinance, resolution or statute is null and void.

(24) To charge enumerated fees to property owners who desire to or are required to connect to the authority's sewer or water system. Fees shall be based upon the duly adopted fee schedule which is in effect at the time of payment and shall be payable at the time of application for connection or at a time to which the property owner and the authority agree. In the case of projects to serve existing development, fees shall be payable at a time to be determined by the authority. An authority may require that no capacity be guaranteed for a property owner until the tapping fees have been paid or secured by other financial security. The fees shall be in addition to any charges assessed against the property in the construction of a sewer or water main by the authority under paragraphs (21) and (22) as well as any other user charges imposed by the authority under paragraph (9) except that no reservation of capacity fee or other similar charge shall be imposed or collected from a property owner who has applied for service unless the charge is based on debt and fixed operating expenses. A reservation of capacity fee or other similar charge may not exceed 60% of the average sanitary sewer bill for a residential customer in the same

sewer service area for the same billing period. Any authority opting to collect a reservation of capacity fee or other similar charge may not collect the tapping fee until the time as the building permit fee is due. Tapping fees shall not include costs included in the calculation of any other fees, assessments, rates or other charges imposed under this act.

(i) The fees may include any of the following if they are separately set forth in a resolution adopted by the authority:

(A) Connection fee. A connection fee shall not exceed an amount based upon the actual cost of the connection of the property extending from the authority's main to the property line or curb stop of the property connected. The authority may also base the connection fee upon an average cost for previously installed connections of similar type and size. Such average cost may be trended to current cost using published cost indexes. In lieu of payment of the fee, an authority may require the construction of those facilities by the property owner who requested the connection.

(B) Customer facilities fee. A customer facilities fee shall not exceed an amount based upon the actual cost of facilities serving the connected property from the property line or curb stop to the proposed dwelling or building to be served. The fee shall be chargeable only if the authority installs the customer facilities. In lieu of payment of the customer facilities fee, an authority may require the construction of those facilities by the property owner who requests customer facilities. In the case of water service, the fee may include the cost of a water meter and installation if the authority provides or installs the water meter. If the property connected or to be connected with the sewer system of the authority is not equipped with a water meter, the authority may install a meter at its own cost and expense. If the property is supplied with water from the facilities of a public water supply agency, the authority shall not install a meter without the consent and approval of the public water supply agency.

(C) Tapping fee. A tapping fee shall not exceed an amount based upon some or all of the following parts which shall be separately set forth in the resolution adopted by the authority to establish these fees. In lieu of payment of this fee, an authority may require the construction and dedication of only such capacity, distribution-collection or special purpose facilities necessary to supply service to the property owner or owners.

(I) Capacity part. The capacity part shall not exceed an amount that is based upon the cost of capacity-related facilities, including, but not limited to, source of supply, treatment, pumping, transmission, trunk, interceptor and outfall mains, storage, sludge treatment or disposal, interconnection or other general system facilities. Except as specifically provided in this paragraph, such facilities may include only those that provide existing service. The cost of capacity-related facilities, excluding facilities contributed to the authority by any person, government or agency, or portions of facilities paid for with contributions or grants other than tapping fees, shall be based upon their historical cost trended to current cost using published cost indexes, or upon the historical cost plus interest and other financing fees paid on debt financing such facilities. To the extent that historical cost is not ascertainable, tapping fees may be based upon an engineer"s reasonable written estimate of current replacement cost. Such written estimate shall be based upon and include an itemized listing of those components of the actual facilities for which historical cost is not ascertainable. Outstanding debt related to the facilities shall be subtracted from the cost except when calculating the initial tapping fee imposed for connection to facilities exclusively serving new customers. The outstanding debt shall be subtracted for all subsequent revisions of the initial tapping fee where the historical cost has been updated to reflect current cost except as specifically provided in this section. For tapping fees or components related to facilities initially serving exclusively new customers, an authority may, no more frequently than annually and without updating the historical cost of or subtracting the outstanding debt related to such facilities, increase such tapping fee by an amount calculated by multiplying the tapping fee by the weighted average interest rate on the debt related to such facilities applicable for the period since the fee was initially established or the last increase of the tapping fee for such facilities. The capacity part of the tapping fee per unit of design capacity of said facilities required by the new customer shall not exceed the total cost of the facilities as described herein divided by the system design capacity of all such facilities. Where the cost of facilities to be constructed or acquired in the future are included in the calculation of the capacity part as permitted herein, the total cost of the facilities shall be divided by the system design capacity plus the additional capacity to be provided by the facilities to be constructed or acquired in the future. An authority may allocate its capacity-related facilities to different sections or districts of its system and may impose additional capacity-related tapping fees on specific groups of existing customers such as commercial and industrial customers in conjunction with additional capacity requirements of those customers. The cost of facilities to be constructed or acquired in the future that will increase the system design capacity may be included in the calculation of the capacity part, subject to the provisions of clause (VI). The cost of such facilities shall not exceed their reasonable estimated cost set forth in a duly adopted annual budget or a five-year capital improvement plan. The authority shall have taken at least two of the following actions toward construction of the facilities:

(a) obtained financing for the facilities;

(b) entered into a contract obligating the authority to construct or pay for the cost of construction of the facilities or its portion thereof in the event that multiple parties are constructing the facilities;

(c) obtained a permit for the facilities;

(d) obtained title to or condemned additional real estate upon which the facilities will be constructed;

(e) entered into a contract obligating the authority to purchase or acquire facilities owned by another;

(f) prepared an engineering feasibility study specifically related to the facilities, which study recommends the construction of the facilities within a five-year period;

(g) entered into a contract for the design or construction of the facilities or adopted a budget which includes the use of in-house resources for the design or construction of the facilities.

(II) Distribution or collection part. The distribution or collection part may not exceed an amount based upon the cost of distribution or collection facilities required to provide service, such as mains, hydrants and pumping stations. Facilities may only include those that provide existing service. The cost of distribution or collections facilities, excluding facilities contributed to the authority by any person, government or agency, or portions of facilities paid for with contributions or grants other than tapping fees, shall be based upon historical cost trended to current cost using published cost indexes or upon the historical cost plus interest and other financing fees paid on debt financing such facilities.

Chap. 39 Res. During Mil. Service
Chap. 38 Intergov. Coop.
Chap. 37 3rd Class City Code
Chap. 36 Bor. Code
Chap. 35 2nd Class Twp. Code
Chap. 34 1st Class Twp. Code
Chap. 33 Home Rule Chart. Opt. Plans Law
Chap. 32 Water Serv. Act
Chap. 31 Munic. Auth. Act

To the extent that historical cost is not ascertainable, tapping fees may be based upon an engineer's reasonable written estimate of replacement cost. Such written estimate shall be based upon and include an itemized listing of those components of the actual facilities for which historical cost is not ascertainable. Outstanding debt related to the facilities shall be subtracted from the cost except when calculating the initial tapping fee imposed for connection to facilities exclusively serving new customers. The outstanding debt shall be subtracted for all subsequent revisions of the initial tapping fee where the historical cost has been updated to reflect current cost except as specifically provided in this section. For tapping fees or components related to facilities initially serving exclusively new customers, an authority may, no more frequently than annually and without updating the historical cost of or subtracting the outstanding debt related to such facilities, increase such tapping fee by an amount calculated by multiplying the tapping fee by the weighted average interest rate on the debt related to such facilities applicable for the period since the fee was initially established or the last increase of the tapping fee for such facilities. The distribution or collection part of the tapping fee per unit of design capacity of said facilities required by the new customer shall not exceed the cost of the facilities divided by the design capacity. An authority may allocate its distribution-related or collection-related facilities to different sections or districts of its system and may impose additional distribution-related or collection-related tapping fees on specific groups of existing customers such as commercial and industrial customers in conjunction with additional capacity requirements of those customers.

(III) Special purpose part. A part for special purpose facilities shall be applicable only to a particular group of customers or for serving a particular purpose or a specific area, based upon the cost of the facilities, including, but not limited to, booster pump stations, fire service facilities, water or sewer mains, pumping stations and industrial wastewater treatment facilities. Such facilities may include only those that provide existing service. The cost of special purpose facilities, excluding facilities contributed to the authority by any person, government or agency, or portions of facilities paid for with contributions or grants other than tapping fees, shall be based upon historical cost trended to current cost using published cost indexes or upon the historical cost plus interest and other financing fees paid on debt financing such facilities. To the extent that historical cost is not ascertainable, tapping fees may be based upon an engineer's reasonable written estimate of current replacement cost. Such written estimate shall be based upon and include an itemized listing of those components of the actual facilities for which historical cost is not ascertainable. Outstanding debt related to the facilities shall be subtracted from the cost except when calculating the initial tapping fee imposed for connection to facilities exclusively serving new customers. The outstanding debt shall be subtracted for all subsequent revisions of the initial tapping fee where the historical cost has been updated to reflect current cost except as specifically provided in this section. For tapping fees or components related to facilities initially serving exclusively new customers, an authority may, no more frequently than annually and without updating the historical cost of or subtracting the outstanding debt related to such facilities, increase such tapping fee by an amount calculated by multiplying the tapping fee by the weighted average interest rate on the debt related to such facilities applicable for the period since the fee was initially established or the last increase of the tapping fee for such facilities. The special purpose part of the tapping fee per unit of design capacity of such special purpose facilities required by the new customer shall not exceed the cost of the facilities as described herein divided by the design capacity of the facilities. Where an authority constructs special purpose facilities at its own expense, the design capacity for the facilities may be expressed in terms of the number of equivalent dwelling units to be served by the facilities. In no event shall an authority continue to collect any tapping fee which includes a special purpose part after special purpose part fees have been imposed on the total number of design capacity units used in the original calculation of the special purpose part. An authority may allocate its special purpose facilities to different sections or districts of its system and may impose additional special purpose tapping fees on specific groups of existing customers such as commercial and industrial customers in conjunction with additional capacity requirements of those customers.

(IV) Reimbursement part. The reimbursement part shall only be applicable to the users of certain specific facilities when a fee required to be collected from such users will be reimbursed to the person at whose expense the facilities were constructed as set forth in a written agreement between the authority and such person at whose expense such facilities were constructed.

(V) Calculation of tapping fee.

(a) In arriving at the cost to be included in the tapping fee, the same cost shall not be included in more than one part of the tapping fee.

(b) No tapping fee may be based upon or include the cost of expanding, replacing, updating or upgrading facilities serving only existing customers in order to meet stricter efficiency, environmental, regulatory or safety standards or to provide better service to or meet the needs of existing customers.

(c) The cost used in calculating tapping fees shall not include maintenance and operation expenses.

(d) As used in this subclause, "maintenance and operation expenses" are those expenditures made during the useful life of a sewer or water system for labor, materials, utilities, equipment accessories, appurtenances and other items which are necessary to manage and maintain the system capacity and performance and to provide the service for which the system was constructed. Costs or expenses to reduce or eliminate groundwater infiltration or inflow may not be included in the cost of facilities used to calculate tapping fees unless these costs or expenses result in an increase in system design capacity.

(e) Except as otherwise provided for the calculation of a special purpose part, the design capacity required by a new residential customer used in calculating sewer or water tapping fees shall not exceed an amount established by multiplying 65 gallons per capita per day for water capacity, 90 gallons per capita per day for sewer capacity times the average number of persons per household as established by the most recent census data provided by the United States Census Bureau. If an authority service area is entirely within a municipal boundary for which there is corresponding census data specifying the average number of persons per household, issued by the United States Census Bureau, the average shall be used. If an authority service area is not entirely within a municipal boundary but is entirely within a county or other geographic area within Pennsylvania for which the United States Census Bureau has provided the average number of persons per household, then that average for the county or geographic area shall be used. If an authority service area is not entirely within a municipal, county or other geographic area within Pennsylvania for which the United States Census Bureau has calculated an average number of persons per household, then the

Chap. 39 Res. During Mil. Service
Chap. 38 Intergov. Coop.
Chap. 37 3rd Class City Code
Chap. 36 Bor. Code
Chap. 35 2nd Class Twp. Code
Chap. 34 1st Class Twp. Code
Chap. 33 Home Rule Chart. Opt. Plans Law
Chap. 32 Water Serv. Act
Chap. 31 Munic. Auth. Act

Pennsylvania average number of persons per household shall be used as published by the United States Census Bureau. Alternatively, the design capacity required for a new residential customer shall be determined by a study but shall not exceed:

(i) for water capacity, the average residential water consumption per residential customer, or, for sewage capacity, the average residential water consumption per residential customer plus ten percent. The average residential water consumption shall be determined by dividing the total water consumption for all metered residential customers in the authority's service area over at least a 12-consecutive-month period within the most recent five years by the average number of customers during the period; or

(ii) for sewer capacity, the average sewage flow per residential customer determined by a measured sewage flow study. Such study shall be completed in accordance with sound engineering practices within the most recent five years for the lesser of three or all residential subdivisions of more than ten lots which have collection systems in good repair and which connected to the authority's facilities within the most recent five years. The study shall calculate the average sewage flow per residential customer in such developments by measuring actual sewage flows over at least 12 consecutive months at the points where such developments connected to the authority's sewer main.

(iii) All data and other information considered or obtained by an authority in connection with determining capacity under this subsection shall be made available to the public upon request.

(iv) If any person required to pay a tapping fee submits to the authority an opinion from a professional engineer that challenges the validity of the results of the calculation of design capacity required to serve new residential customers prepared under subparagraph (i) or (ii), the authority shall within 30 days obtain a written certification from another professional engineer, who is not an employee of the authority, verifying that the results and the calculations, methodology and measurement were performed in accordance with this title[2] and generally accepted engineering practices. If an authority does not obtain a certification required under this subsection within 30 days of receiving such challenge, the authority may not impose or collect tapping fees based on any such challenged calculations or study until such engineering certification is obtained.

(f) An authority may use lower design capacity requirements and impose lower tapping fees for multifamily residential dwellings than imposed on other types of residential customers.

(VI) Separate accounting for future facility costs. Any portion of tapping fees collected which, based on facilities to be constructed or acquired in the future in accordance with this section, shall be separately accounted for and shall be expended only for that particular facility or a substitute facility accomplishing the same purpose which is commenced within the same period. Such accounting shall include, but not be limited to, the total fees collected as a result of including facilities to be constructed in the future, the source of the fees collected and the amount of fees expended on specific facilities. The proportionate share of tapping fees based upon facilities to be constructed or acquired in the future under this section shall be refunded to the payor of such fees within 90 days of the occurrence of the following:

(a) the authority abandons its plan or a part thereof to construct or acquire a facility or facilities which are the basis for such fee; or

2. "act" in enrolled bill.

(b) the facilities have not been placed into service within seven years, or, for an authority which provides service to five or more municipalities, the facilities have not been placed into service within 20 years, after adoption of a resolution which imposes tapping fees which are based upon facilities to be constructed or acquired in the future. Any refund of fees held for 20 years shall include interest for the period the money was held.

(VII) Definitions. As used in this clause, the following words and phrases shall have the meanings given to them in this subclause:

"BOD5." The five-day biochemical-oxygen demand.

"Design capacity." For residential customers, the permitted or rated capacity of facilities expressed in million gallons per day. For nonresidential customers, design capacity may also be expressed in pounds of BOD5 per day, pounds of suspended solids per day or any other capacity-defining parameter that is separately and specifically set forth in the permit governing the operation of the system and based upon its original design as modified by those regulatory agencies having jurisdiction over these facilities. Additionally, for separate fire service customers, the permitted or rated capacity of fire service facilities may be expressed in peak flows. The units of measurement used to express design capacity shall be the same units of measurement used to express the system design capacity. Except as otherwise provided for special purpose facilities, design capacity may not be expressed in terms of equivalent dwelling units.

"Outstanding debt." The principal amount outstanding of any bonds, notes, loans or other form of indebtedness used to finance or refinance facilities included in the tapping fee.

"Service line." A water or sewer line that directly connects a single building or structure to a distribution or collection facility.

"System design capacity." The design capacity of the system for which the tapping fee is being calculated which represents the total design capacity of the treatment facility or water sources.

(ii) Every authority charging a tapping, customer facilities or connection fee shall do so only pursuant to a resolution adopted at a public meeting of the authority. The authority shall have available for public inspection a detailed itemization of all calculations, clearly showing the maximum fees allowable for each part of the tapping fee and the manner in which the fees were determined, which shall be made a part of any resolution imposing such fees. A tapping, customer facilities or connection fee may be revised and imposed upon those who subsequently connect to the system, subject to the provisions and limitations of the act.

(iii) No authority shall have the power to impose a connection fee, customer facilities fee, tapping fee or similar fee except as provided specifically under this section.

(iv) A municipality or municipal authority with available excess sewage capacity, wishing to sell a portion of that capacity to another municipality or municipal authority, may not charge a higher cost for the capacity portion of the tapping fee as the selling entity charges to its customers for the capacity portion of the tapping fee. In turn, the municipality or municipal authority buying this excess capacity may not charge a higher cost for the capacity portion of the tapping fee to its residential customers than that charged to them by the selling entity.

(v) As used in this paragraph, the term "residential customer" shall also include those developing property for residential dwellings that require multiple tapping fee permits. This paragraph shall not be applicable to intermunicipal or interauthority agreements relative to the purchase of excess capacity by an authority or municipality in effect prior to February 20, 2001.

(25) To construct tunnels, bridges, viaducts, underpasses or other structures and relocate the facilities of public service companies to effect or permit the abolition of a grade crossing or grade crossings subject to approval of and in accordance with a duly issued order of the Pennsylvania Public Utility Commission. A commission order shall provide that costs payable by a public utility, political subdivision, the Commonwealth or others shall be payable to the authority. Before proceedings are instituted before the commission, the authority and the public utilities or the political subdivisions shall enter an agreement to provide for the conveyance to the authority of title to the land, structure or improvement involved, as security for bonds issued to finance the improvement and the leasing of the improvement to the utility or utilities or the political subdivision or subdivisions involved on such terms as will provide for interest and sinking fund charges on the bonds issued for the improvement.

(26) To appoint police officers who shall have the same rights as other peace officers in this Commonwealth with respect to the property of the authority.

(27)(i) In the case of an authority created to provide business improvements and administrative services, to impose an assessment on each benefited property within a business improvement district. This assessment shall be based upon the estimated cost of the improvements and services in the district stated in the planning or feasibility study and shall be determined by one of the following methods:

(A) The authority may determine an assessment determined by multiplying the total improvement and service cost by the ratio of the assessed value for real estate tax purposes of the benefited property to the total assessed value of all benefited properties in the district.

(B) The authority may determine assessments upon the several properties in the district in proportion to benefits as ascertained by viewers appointed in accordance with municipal law.

(C) If the district served by the authority contains single-family residential properties, including those that are part of a planned unit development, residential cooperative properties or condominium properties formed under 68 Pa.C.S. Pt. II Subpt. B (relating to condominiums) and other properties, the authority may elect to calculate assessments based on all of the following:

(I) The business improvement district assessed value of each benefited single-family or residential cooperative property shall be one-half of the assessed value of the property for real estate tax purposes.

(II) In the case of a condominium, the unit owners' association formed under 68 Pa.C.S. Pt. II Subpt. B shall be assessed. Individual units may not be assessed. The business improvement district assessed value of the unit owners' association shall be the sum of the assessed value for real estate tax purposes of any real estate owned by the association and such assessed value of all units, including their undivided interests in the common elements and any limited common elements, except that the value of any single-family residential unit shall be one-half of such assessed value of the unit for real estate tax purposes. The authority shall provide to the unit owners' association the calculation of the business improvement district assessed value of the unit owners' association, itemizing the assessed value of each unit as provided in this clause. The unit owners' association shall add to the condominium fee charged to a unit owner the amount of the district assessment attributable to the unit which amount shall be separately itemized on any assessment, invoice, bill or other document presented to the unit owner for payment of the condominium fee.

Chap. 39 Res. During Mil. Service
Chap. 38 Intergov. Coop.
Chap. 37 3rd Class City Code
Chap. 36 Bor. Code
Chap. 35 2nd Class Twp. Code
Chap. 34 1st Class Twp. Code
Chap. 33 Home Rule Chart. Opt. Plans Law
Chap. 32 Water Serv. Act
Chap. 31 Munic. Auth. Act

(III) The district assessment shall be calculated on each benefited single-family residential property, benefited residential cooperative property and benefited unit owners' association by multiplying in each case the total improvement and services cost by the ratio of the district assessed value of the benefited single-family residential property, benefited residential cooperative property or benefited unit owners' association to the sum of the district assessed value of all benefited single-family residential properties, the district assessed value of all residential cooperative properties, the district assessed value of all benefited unit owners' associations and the assessed value of all remaining benefited properties in the business improvement district.

(IV) The remaining benefited properties shall be assessed by multiplying in each case the total improvement and services cost by the ratio of the assessed value of the remaining benefited property to the sum of the district assessed value of all benefited single-family residential properties, the district assessed value of all residential cooperative properties, the district assessed value of all benefited unit owners' associations and the assessed value of all remaining benefited properties in the business improvement district.

(V) An election by an authority under this clause shall not be revoked except through the procedures stated in subparagraph (ii) and subsection (g).

(ii) An assessment or charge may not be made unless:

(A) An authority submits a plan for business improvements and administrative services, together with estimated costs and the proposed method of assessments for business improvements and charges for administrative services, to the municipality in which the project is to be undertaken.

(B) The municipality approves the plan, the estimated costs and the proposed method of assessment and charges.

(iii) An authority may not assess charges against the improved properties in an aggregate amount in excess of the estimated cost.

(iv) An authority may by resolution authorize payment of an assessment or charge in equal, annual or more frequent installments over a fixed period of time and bearing interest of 6% or less. If bonds, notes or guarantees are used to raise revenue to provide for the cost of improvements or services, the installments shall not be payable beyond the term for which the bonds, notes or guarantees are payable.

(v) Claims to secure the payment of assessments shall be entered in the prothonotary's office of the county at the same time and in the same form and shall be collected in the same manner as municipal claims are filed and collected notwithstanding the provisions of this section as to installment payments.

(vi) In case of default of 60 days or more after an installment is due, the entire assessment and interest shall be due.

(vii) An owner of property against whom an assessment has been made may pay the assessment in full at any time along with accrued interest and costs. Upon proof of payment the lien shall be discharged.

(viii) For purposes of determining assessments in accordance with subparagraph (i)(A) and (C), the assessed value of a benefited property shall be without reduction for any value attributable to improvements for which an exemption or abatement has been granted under law.

(ix) Any claim entered to secure the payment of an assessment against a unit owners' association shall be enforceable as a judgment for money against the unit owners' association within the meaning of and under the provisions of 68 Pa.C.S. § 3319 (relating to other liens affecting the condominium), provided that if an assessment against a unit owners' association is paid in part and the unit owners' association specifies in writing to the authority the units with respect to which full payment was made, the claim shall not be enforceable against units with respect to which full payment was made or against the unit owners' association. An authority shall discharge a lien against a unit owners' association to the extent that it constitutes a lien on a particular unit upon proof of payment, either to the unit owners' association or to the authority, by the owner of the particular unit of his itemized share of the assessment on the unit owners' association.

(x) An authority that has made an election under subparagraph (i)(C) may further elect to calculate, for the assessment years included in a plan and budget, the assessments on single-family residential properties, including those that are part of a planned unit development, residential cooperative properties and residential condominium properties, at the lower of the amount determined under subparagraph (i)(C) or that aggregate value of assessments that will not exceed 5% of the authority's total annual assessments, subject to the following:

(A) Any aggregate reduction in assessments on residential properties shall increase the assessments on the remaining properties in proportion to the assessments of the remaining properties calculated under subparagraph (i)(C)(IV).

(B) Any further election shall be made for all assessment years included in a plan and budget, except that, for a current plan and budget, the further election shall be made for the years remaining in the plan and budget. Once made, the further election shall remain in effect for all such assessment years included in the plan and budget.

(C) An authority making the further election shall hold a hearing on the proposed method of calculation. Written notice of the hearing shall be given to all owners of properties assessed by the district at least 30 days prior to the hearing. The notice shall state the proposed method of calculation.

(D) The authority shall take no action on the proposed method of calculation if objection is made in writing by owners of properties representing one-third of the amount of all assessments in the district. In the case of a condominium formed under 68 Pa.C.S. Pt. II Subpt. B, the condominium association and all condominium units shall be treated as one property, valued in the manner described in subparagraph (i)(C)(II). Any objection must be made within 30 days of the hearing in writing signed by the property owner and filed in the registered office of the authority.

(E) No further hearing shall be required, no amendment of the authority's plan and budget shall be required and no action on the part of the municipality shall be required.

(28) To adopt rules and regulations to provide for the safety of persons using facilities of an airport authority pertaining to vehicular traffic control. Police officers appointed under paragraph (26) shall enforce them.

(29) To provide financing for insurance reserves by making loans evidenced and secured by loan agreements, security agreements or other instruments or agreements. These instruments or agreements may contain provisions the authority deems necessary or desirable for the security or protection of the authority or its bondholders.

(30) Where a sewer or water system of an authority is to be extended at the expense of the owner of properties or where the authority otherwise would construct customer facilities referred to in paragraph (24), other than water meter installation, a property owner shall have the right to construct the extension or install the customer facilities himself or through a subcontractor approved by the authority, which approval shall not be unreasonably withheld. The authority shall have the right, at its option, to perform the construction itself only if

the authority provides the extension or customer facilities at a lower cost and within the same timetable specified or proposed by the property owner or his approved subcontractor. Construction by the property owner shall be in accordance with an agreement for the extension of the authority's system and plans and specifications approved by the authority and shall be undertaken only pursuant to the existing regulations, requirements, rules and standards of the authority applicable to such construction. Construction shall be subject to inspection by an inspector authorized to approve similar construction and employed by the authority during construction. When a main is to be extended at the expense of the owner of properties, the property owner may be required to deposit with the authority, in advance of construction, the authority's estimated reasonable and necessary cost of reviewing plans, construction inspections, administrative, legal and engineering services. The authority may require that construction shall not commence until the property owner has posted appropriate financial security in accordance with paragraph (23). The authority may require the property owner to reimburse it for reasonable and necessary expenses it incurred as a result of the extension. If an independent firm is employed for engineering review of the plans and the inspection of improvements, reimbursement for its services shall be reasonable and in accordance with the ordinary and customary fees charged by the independent firm for work performed for similar services in the community. The fees shall not exceed the rate or cost charged by the independent firm to the authority when fees are not reimbursed or otherwise imposed on applicants. Upon completion of construction, the property owner shall dedicate and the authority shall accept the extension of the authority's system if dedication of facilities and the installation complies with the plans, specification regulations of the authority and the agreement. An authority may provide in its regulations those facilities which, having been constructed at the expense of the owner of properties, the authority will require to be dedicated and which facility or facilities the authority will accept as a part of its system.

(i) In the event the property owner disputes the amount of any billing in connection with the review of plans, construction inspections, administrative, legal and engineering services, the property owner shall, within 60 days of the date of billing, notify the authority that the billing is disputed as excessive, unreasonable or unnecessary, in which case the authority shall not delay or disapprove any application or any approval or permit related to the extension or facilities due to the property owner's dispute over the disputed billings unless the property owner has failed to make payment in accordance with the decision rendered under clause (iii) within 60 days after the mailing date of such decision.

(ii) If, within 60 days from the date of billing, the authority and the property owner cannot agree on the amount of billings which are reasonable and necessary, the property owner shall have the right to request the appointment of another professional consultant to serve as arbitrator. The property owner and the authority whose fees are being challenged shall, by mutual agreement, appoint a professional of the same profession or discipline licensed in Pennsylvania to review the billings and make a determination as to the amount of billings which is reasonable and necessary.

(iii) The professional appointed as arbitrator under clause (ii) shall hear evidence and review the documentation as the professional in his or her sole opinion deems necessary and shall render a decision within 50 days of the date of appointment. Based upon the decision of the arbitrator, the property owner or authority shall be required to pay any amounts necessary to implement the decision within 60 days. In the event the property owner has paid the authority or retained professional consultant an amount in excess of the amount determined to be reasonable and necessary, the authority or retained professional consultant shall within 60 days reimburse the excess payment.

(iv) In the event that the authority and property owner cannot agree upon the professional to be appointed within 20 days of the request for appointment of an arbitrator, the president judge of the court of common pleas of the judicial district in which the municipality is located, or if at the time there is no president judge, the senior active judge then sitting upon application of either party shall appoint a professional, who shall be neither the authority engineer nor any professional who has been retained by or performed services for the authority or the property owner within the preceding five years.

(v) The fee of the arbitrator shall be paid by the property owner if the disputed fee is upheld by the arbitrator. The fee of the arbitrator shall be paid by the authority if the disputed fee is $2,500 or greater than the payment decided by the arbitrator. The fee of the arbitrator shall be paid in an equal amount by the property owner and the authority if the disputed fee is less than $2,500 of the payment decided by the arbitrator.

(vi) In the event that the disputed fees have been paid and the arbitrator finds that the disputed fees are unreasonable or excessive by more than $10,000, the arbitrator shall:

(A) award the amount of the fees found to be unreasonable or excessive to the party that paid the disputed fee; and

(B) impose a surcharge of 4% of the amount found as unreasonable or excessive to be paid to the party that paid the disputed fee.

(vi) An authority or property owner shall have 100 days after paying a fee to dispute any fee charged as being unreasonable or excessive.

(31) Where a property owner constructs or causes to be constructed at his expense any extension of a sewer or water system of an authority, the authority shall provide for the reimbursement to the property owner when the owner of another property not in the development for which the extension was constructed connects a service line directly to the extension within ten years of the date of the dedication of the extension to the authority in accordance with the following provisions:

(i) Reimbursement shall be equal to the distribution or collection part of each tapping fee collected as a result of subsequent connections. An authority may deduct from each reimbursement payment an amount equal to 5% of it for administrative expenses and services rendered in calculating, collecting, monitoring and disbursing the reimbursement payments to the property owner.

(ii) Reimbursement shall be limited to those lines which have not previously been paid for by the authority.

(iii) The authority shall, in preparing necessary reimbursement agreements with a property owner for whose benefit reimbursement will be provided, attach as an exhibit an itemized listing of all sewer and water facilities for which reimbursement shall be provided.

(iv) The total reimbursement which a property owner may receive may not exceed the cost of labor and material, engineering design charges, the cost of performance and maintenance bonds, authority review and inspection charges as well as flushing and televising charges and any and all charges involved in the acceptance and dedication of such facilities by the authority, less the amount which would be chargeable to the property owner based upon the authority's collection and distribution tapping fees which would be applicable to all lands of the property owner directly or indirectly served through extensions if the property owner did not fund the extension.

(v) An authority shall notify by certified mail, to the last known address, the property owner for whose benefit a reimbursement shall apply. This shall be done within 30 days of the authority's receipt of the reimbursement payment. If a property owner does not claim a reimbursement payment within 120 days after the mailing of the notice, the payment shall become the sole property of the authority with no further obligation on the part of the authority to refund the payment to the property owner.

(32) [Deleted by Act No. 2003-57]

(33) Provisions of paragraphs (30) and (31) shall apply to residential customers in a municipality where the sewer service is being purchased by the municipality or sewer authority from another municipality or sewer authority having excess sewage capacity.

(34) In the case of an authority that performs storm water planning, management and implementation, reasonable and uniform rates may be based in whole or in part on property characteristics, which may include installation and maintenance of best management practices approved and inspected by the authority.

(e) **Prohibition.**—

(1) An authority may not pledge the credit or taxing power of the Commonwealth or its political subdivision.

(2) The obligations of an authority are not obligations of the Commonwealth or its political subdivision.

(3) Neither the Commonwealth nor a political subdivision shall be liable for the payment of principal of or interest on obligations of an authority.

(f) **Authorization to control airports.**—Nothing in this chapter shall be construed to prevent an authority which owns or operates an airport as a proj-ect from leasing airport land on a short-term or long-term basis for commercial, industrial or residential purposes when the land is not immediately needed for aviation or aeronautical purposes in the judgment of the authority.

(g) **Authorization to make business improvements and provide administrative services.**—An authority may be established to make business improvements or provide administrative services in districts designated by a municipality or by municipalities acting jointly and zoned commercial or used for general commercial purposes or in contiguous areas if the inclusion of a contiguous area is directly related to the improvements and services proposed by the authority. The authority shall make planning or feasibility studies to determine needed improvements or administrative services. The following shall also apply:

(1) The authority shall be required to hold a public hearing on the proposed improvement or service, the estimated costs thereof and the proposed method of assessment and charges. Notice of the hearing shall be advertised at least ten days before it occurs in a newspaper whose circulation is within the municipality where the authority is established. At the public hearing any interested party may be heard.

(2) Written notice of the proposed improvement or service, its estimated cost, the proposed method of assessment and charges and project cost to individual property owners shall be given to each property owner and commercial lessee in benefited properties in the district at least 30 days prior to the public hearing.

(3) Except as otherwise provided in paragraph (4), the authority shall take no action on proposed improvement or service if objection is made in writing by:

(i) persons representing the ownership of one-third of the benefited properties in the district; or

(ii) property owners of the proposed district whose property valuation as assessed for taxable purposes shall amount to more than one-third of the total property valuation of the district.

(4) In the case of an authority that has elected to make assessments under subsection (d)(27)(i)(C), the objections in writing must be made by either:

(i) one-third of the owners of benefited commercial properties; or

(ii) owners of properties representing one-third of the amount of all business improvement district assessments for the first year of the proposed plan and budget after the reduction in district assessments under subsection (d)(27)(i)(C).

For purposes of calculating one-third of the benefited commercial properties, the term benefited commercial properties shall include all nonresidential property, each condominium association formed under 68 Pa.C.S. Pt. II Subpt. B as one property and may not include any individual condominium so formed nor any single-family residential property.

(5) Objection must be made within 45 days after the conclusion of the public hearing. Objections must be in writing, signed and filed in the office of the governing body of the municipality in which the district is located and in the registered office of the authority.

§ 5608. Bonds.

(a) Authorization.—

(1) A bond must be authorized by resolution of the board. The resolution may specify all of the following:

(i) Series.

(ii) Date of maturity not exceeding 40 years from date of issue.

(iii) Denomination.

(iv) Form, either coupon or fully registered without coupons.

(v) Registration, exchangeability and interchangeability privileges.

(vi) Medium of payment and place of payment.

(vii) Terms of redemption not exceeding 105% of the principal amount of the bond.

(viii) Priorities in the revenues or receipts of the authority.

(2) A bond must be signed by or shall bear the facsimile signature of such officers as the authority determines. Coupon bonds must have attached interest coupons bearing the facsimile signature of the treasurer of the authority as prescribed in the authorizing resolution. A bond may be issued and delivered notwithstanding that one or more of the signing officers or the treasurer has ceased to be an officer when the bond is actually delivered. A bond must be authenticated by an authenticating agent, a fiscal agent or a trustee, if required by the authorizing resolution.

(3) A bond may be sold at public or private sale for a price determined by the authority.

(4) Pending the preparation of a definitive bond, interim receipts or temporary bonds with or without coupons, may be issued to the purchaser and may contain terms and conditions as the authority determines.

(b) Provisions.—A resolution authorizing a bond may contain provisions which shall be part of the contract with the bond holder as to the following:

(1) Pledging the full faith and credit of the authority but not of the Commonwealth or any political subdivision for the bond or restricting the obligation of the authority on the bond to all or any of the revenue of the authority from all or any projects or properties.

(2) The construction, financing, improvement, operation, extension, enlargement, maintenance and repair of the project, the financing for insurance reserves and the duties of the authority with reference to these matters.

(3) Terms and provisions of the bond.

(4) Limitations on the purposes to which the proceeds of the bond or of a loan or grant by the United States may be applied.

(5) Rate of tolls and other charges for use of the facilities of or for the services rendered by the authority.

(6) The setting aside, regulation and disposition of reserves and sinking funds.

(7) Limitations on the issuance of additional bonds.

(8) Terms and provisions of any deed of trust or indenture securing the bond or under which any deed of trust or indenture may be issued.

(9) Other additional agreements with the holder of the bond.

(c) Deeds of trust.—An authority may enter into any deed of trust, indenture or other agreement with any bank or trust company or other person in the United States having power to enter into such an arrangement, including any Federal agency, as security for a bond and may assign and pledge all or any of the revenues or receipts of the authority under such deed, indenture or agreement. The deed of trust, indenture or other agreement may contain provisions as may be customary in such instruments or as the authority may authorize, including provisions as to all of the following:

(1) Construction, financing, improvement, operation, maintenance and repair of a project; financing for insurance reserves; and the duties of the authority with reference to these matters;

(2) Application of funds and the safeguarding of funds on hand or on deposit;

(3) Rights and remedies of trustee and bondholder, including restrictions upon the individual right of action of a bondholder;

(4) Terms and provisions of the bond or the resolution authorizing the issuance of the bond.

(d) Negotiability.—A bond shall have all the qualities of negotiable instruments under 13 Pa.C.S. Div. 3 (relating to negotiable instruments).

§ 5609. Bondholders.

(a) Rights and remedies.—The rights and the remedies conferred upon bondholders under this section shall be in addition to and not in limitation of rights and remedies lawfully granted them by the resolution for the bond issue or by any deed of trust, indenture or other agreement under which the bond is issued.

(b) Trustee.—

(1) The holders of 25% of the aggregate principal amount of outstanding bonds may appoint a trustee to represent the bondholders for purposes of this chapter if any of the following apply:

(i) The authority defaults in the payment of principal or interest on a bond, at maturity or upon call for redemption; and the default continues for 30 days.

(ii) The authority fails to comply with this chapter.

(iii) The authority defaults in an agreement made with the bondholders.

(2) The trustee must be appointed by instrument:

(i) filed in the office of the recorder of deeds of the county where the authority is located; and

(ii) proved or acknowledged in the same manner as a deed to be recorded.

(3) A trustee under this subsection and a trustee under any deed of trust, indenture or other agreement may and, upon written request of the holders

of 25% of the aggregate principal amount of outstanding bonds or such other percentage specified in the deed of trust, indenture or other agreement, shall in the trustee's name do any of the following:

(i) By action at law or in equity enforce rights of the bondholders. This subparagraph includes the right to require the authority to:

(A) collect rates, rentals or other charges adequate to carry out any agreement as to or pledge of revenues or receipts of the authority;

(B) carry out any other agreements with or for the benefit of bondholders; and

(C) perform its and their duties under this chapter.

(ii) Bring suit upon the bond.

(iii) By action in equity require the authority to account as if it were the trustee of an express trust for the bondholders.

(iv) Enjoin an action which may be unlawful or in violation of the rights of the bondholders.

(v) By notice in writing to the authority, declare all bonds due and payable and, if all defaults are made good, with the consent of the bondholders of 25% of the principal amount of outstanding bonds, or such other percentage specified in the deed of trust, indenture or other agreement, to annul such declaration and its consequences.

(4) A trustee under this subsection or a trustee under any deed of trust, indenture or other agreement, whether or not all bonds have been declared due and payable, shall be entitled to the appointment of a receiver.

(5) A receiver under paragraph (4):

(i) may enter and take possession of a facility of the authority or any part of a facility the revenues or receipts from which are or may be applicable to the payment of the bonds in default;

(ii) may operate and maintain the facility or part of the facility;

(iii) may collect and receive all rentals and other revenues arising from the facility after entry and possession in the same manner as the authority or the board might do; and

(iv) shall deposit money collected under subparagraph (iii) in a separate account and apply the money as the court directs.

(6) Nothing in this chapter authorizes a receiver appointed under paragraph (4) to sell, assign, mortgage or otherwise dispose of assets of whatever kind and character belonging to the authority. It is the intention of this chapter to limit the powers of the receiver to the operation and maintenance of the facilities of the authority as the court directs. No bondholder or trustee shall have the right in an action at law or in equity to compel a receiver, nor shall a receiver be authorized or a court empowered to direct the receiver, to sell, assign, mortgage or otherwise dispose of assets of whatever kind or character belonging to the authority.

(7) The trustee has all powers necessary or appropriate for the exercise of functions specifically set forth in this subsection or incident to the general representation of the bondholders in the enforcement or protection of their rights.

(c) Jurisdiction.—The court of common pleas of the judicial district in which the authority is located shall have jurisdiction of an action by the trustee on behalf of the bondholders.

(d) Costs and fees.—In an action by the trustee the court costs, attorney fees and expenses of the trustee and of the receiver and all costs and disbursements alloted by the court shall be a first charge on revenue and receipts derived from the facilities of the authority, the revenue or receipts from which are or may be applicable to the payment of the bonds so in default.

(e) deleted 2001, Dec. 17, P.L. 926, No. 110 § 3

§ 5610. Governing body.

(a) **Board.**—Except as set forth in subsection (a.1), the powers of each authority shall be exercised by a board composed as follows:

(1) If the authority is incorporated by one municipality, the board shall consist of a number of members, not less than five, as enumerated in the articles of incorporation. The governing body of the municipality shall appoint the members of the board, whose terms of office shall commence on the effective date of their appointment. One member shall serve for one year, one for two years, one for three years, one for four years and one for five years commencing with the first Monday in January next succeeding the date of incorporation or amendment. If there are more than five members of the board, their terms shall be staggered in a similar manner for terms of one to five years from the first Monday in January next succeeding. Thereafter, whenever a vacancy has occurred by reason of the expiration of the term of any member, the governing body shall appoint a member of the board for a term of five years from the date of expiration of the prior term to succeed the member whose term has expired.

(2) If the authority is incorporated by two or more municipalities, the board shall consist of a number of members at least equal to the number of municipalities incorporating the authority, but in no event less than five. When one or more additional municipalities join an existing authority, each of the joining municipalities shall have similar membership on the board as the municipalities then members of the authority and the joining municipalities may determine by appropriate resolutions. The members of the board of a joint authority shall each be appointed by the governing body of the incorporating or joining municipality he represents, and their terms of office shall commence on the effective date of their appointment. One member shall serve for one year, one for two years, one for three years, one for four years and one for five years from the first Monday in January next succeeding the date of incorporation, amendment or joinder, and if there are more than five members of the board, their terms shall be staggered in a similar manner for terms of from one to five years commencing with the first Monday in January next succeeding. Thereafter, whenever a vacancy has occurred by reason of the expiration of the term of any member, the governing body of the municipality which has the power of appointment shall appoint a member of the board for a term of five years from the date of expiration of the prior term.

(a.1) **Water authorities and sewer authorities.**—If a water or sewer authority incorporated by one municipality provides water or sewer services to residents in at least two counties and has water or sewer projects in more than two counties where the combined population of the served municipalities, excluding the incorporating municipality, is at least five times the population of the incorporating municipality, all of the following apply:

(1) Ninety days after the effective date of this subsection,[1] the governing body in existence on the effective date of this subsection shall be replaced by a governing body comprised of the following:

(i) Three members appointed by the governing body from each county in which the services to residents are provided. A member under this subparagraph must reside in a town, township or borough, which receives services from the authority.

(ii) Three members appointed by the governing body of the incorporating municipality.

(2) A member serving under paragraph (1) shall serve for a term of five years.

(b) Residency.—

(1) Except as provided for in subsection (c), the members of the board, each of whom shall be a taxpayer in, maintain a business in or be a citizen of the municipality by which he is appointed or be a taxpayer in, maintain a business in or be a citizen of a municipality into which one or more of the projects of the authority extends or is to extend or to which one or more projects has been or is to be leased, shall be appointed, their terms fixed and staggered and vacancies filled pursuant to the articles of incorporation or the application of membership under section 5604 (relating to municipalities withdrawing from and joining in joint authorities). Where two or more municipalities are members of the authority, they shall be apportioned pursuant to the articles of incorporation or the application for membership under section 5604. Except for special service districts located in whole or in part in cities of the first class or as provided in paragraph (2), a majority of an authority's board members shall be citizens residing in the incorporating municipality or incorporating municipalities of the authority.

(2) Each member of the board of a business improvement district authority that was estabished by a borough pursuant to the act of May 2, 1945 (P.L. 382, No. 164), known as the Municipality Authorities Act of 1945, on or before the effective date of this paragraph shall be a taxpayer in, maintain a business in or be a citizen of the borough by which that member is appointed.

NOTE ON CONSTITUTIONALITY: Sections 5610(b)(1) and (2) as contained in the law prior to December 30, 2002, are set forth above. By Act 2002-230, [Act 2002, Dec. 30, P.L. 2001, No. 230], the following modifications to the sections were enacted by the state legislature. An additional sentence was added to the end of § 5610 (b)(1), after "incorporating municipalities of the authority." The added sentence reads "In the case of a municipality which is a town, the requirement of maintaining a business is satisfied if the individual at any time has maintained a business."

In addition, § 5610(b)(2) as set forth above was deleted by Act 2002-230, and replaced with the following:

(2) Each member of the board of a business improvement district authority established by a municipality pursuant to the act of May 2, 1945 (P.L.382, No.164), [now 53 Pa.C.S.A. § 5601] known as the Municipality Authorities Act of 1945, or pursuant to this title, or each member of the board of a neighborhood improvement district management association (NIDMA) authority established by a municipality pursuant to the act of December 20, 2000 (P.L.949, No.130), [73 P.S. § 831] known as the Neighborhood Improvement District Act, shall be a taxpayer in, maintain a business in or be a citizen of the municipality by which that member is appointed.

However, Act 2002, Dec. 30, P.L. 2001, No. 230 was declared unconstitutional by the Pennsylvania Supreme Court in the case of City of Philadelphia v. Com. 575 Pa. 542, 838 A.2d 566 (Pa. 2003) due to violation of the "single subject rule" of the Pennsylvania Constitution in the process of enactment.

(c) Grade crossings.—If the authority is created for the purpose of eliminating grade crossings, the members of the board, the majority of whom shall be citizens of the municipality by which they are appointed or of a municipality into which one or more of the projects of the authority extends or is to extend or to which one or more of the projects has been or is to be leased, shall be appointed, their terms fixed and staggered and vacancies filled pursuant to the articles of incorporation or the application of membership under section 5604. Where two or more municipalities are members of the authority, they shall be apportioned pursuant to the articles of incorporation or the application for membership under section 5604.

(d) Successor.—Members shall hold office until their successors have been appointed and may succeed themselves and, except members of the boards of authorities organized or created by a school district, shall receive such salaries as may be determined by the governing body of the municipality, but no salaries shall be increased or diminished by a governing body during the term for which the member shall have been appointed. Members of the board of any authority organized or created by a school district shall receive no compensation for their services. A member may be removed for cause by the court of common pleas of the county in which the authority is located after having been provided with a copy of the charges against him for at least ten days and after having been provided a full hearing by the court. If a vacancy shall occur by reason of the death, disqualification, resignation or removal of a member, the municipal authorities shall appoint a successor to fill his unexpired term. In joint authorities, such vacancies shall be filled by the municipal authorities of the municipality in the representation of which the vacancy occurs. If any municipality withdraws from a joint authority, the term of any member appointed from the municipality shall immediately terminate.

(e) Quorum.—A majority of the members shall constitute a quorum of the board for the purpose of organizing and conducting the business of the authority and for all other purposes, and all action may be taken by vote of a majority of the members present unless the bylaws shall require a larger number. The board shall have full authority to manage the properties and business of the authority and to prescribe, amend and repeal bylaws, rules and regulations governing the manner in which the business of the authority may be conducted and the powers granted to it may be exercised and embodied. The board shall fix and determine the number of officers, agents and employees of the authority and their respective powers, duties and compensation and may appoint to such office or offices any member of the board with such powers, duties and compensation as the board may deem proper. The treasurer of the board of any authority organized or created by a school district shall give bond in such sums as may be fixed by the bylaws, which bond shall be subject to the approval of the board and the premiums for which shall be paid by the authority.

(f) Removal.—Unless excused by the board, a member of a board who fails to attend three consecutive meetings of the board may be removed by the appointing municipality up to 60 days after the date of the third meeting of the board which the member failed to attend.

(g) Definitions.—As used in this section, the following words and phrases shall have the meanings given to them in this subsection unless the context clearly indicates otherwise:

"Water or sewer authority." An authority incorporated by a city of the third class, a borough, a town or a township to provide water or sewer services.

"Water or sewer project." Any pumping station, filtering plant, impoundment facility, dam, spillway or reservoir.

§ 5611. Investment of authority funds.

(a) Powers.—The board shall have the power to:

(1) Invest authority sinking funds in the manner provided for local government units by Subpart B of Part VII (relating to indebtedness and borrowing).

(2) Invest moneys in the General Fund and in special funds of the authority other than the sinking funds as authorized by this section.

(3) Liquidate any such investment in whole or in part by disposing of securities or withdrawing funds on deposit. Any action taken to make or to liquidate any investment shall be made by the officers designated by action of the board.

(b) Investment.—The board shall invest authority funds consistent with sound business practice and the standard of prudence applicable to the State Employees' Retirement System set forth in 71 Pa.C.S. § 5931(a) (relating to management of fund and accounts).

(c) Program.—The board shall provide for an investment program subject to restrictions contained in this chapter and in any other applicable statute and any rules and regulations adopted by the board.

(d) Types.—Authorized types of investments for authority funds shall be:

(1) United States Treasury bills.

(2) Short-term obligations of the United States Government or its agencies or instrumentalities.

(3) Deposits in savings accounts or time deposits or share accounts of institutions insured by the Federal Deposit Insurance Corporation or the Federal Savings and Loan Insurance Corporation or the National Credit Union Share Insurance Fund to the extent that such accounts are so insured and for any amounts above the insured maximum if the approved collateral as provided by law shall be pledged by the depository.

(4) Obligations of the United States of America or any of its agencies or instrumentalities backed by the full faith and credit of the United States of America, the Commonwealth or any of its agencies or instrumentalities backed by the full faith and credit of the Commonwealth or of any political subdivision of the Commonwealth or any of its agencies or instrumentalities backed by the full faith and credit of the political subdivision.

(5) Shares of an investment company registered under the Investment Company Act of 1940 (54 Stat. 789, 15 U.S.C. § 80a-1 et seq.) whose shares are registered under the Securities Act of 1933 (48 Stat. 74, 15 U.S.C. § 77a et seq.) if the only investments of that company are in the authorized investments for authority funds listed in paragraphs (1) through (4).

(6) Sovereign debt if the instruments are dollar denominated and backed by the full faith and credit of the sovereign government and if the investments do not exceed more than 2% of the market value of the authority's assets at the time of investment and if the maturity of the instruments does not exceed 15 years and if the obligations are permitted investments of the State Employees' Retirement System and it is established that the issuer had issued such sovereign debt over a period of at least 30 years and has not defaulted on the payment either of principal or interest on its obligations. This paragraph shall only apply to a board in a county of the first class, second class or second class A or in a city of the first class, second class, second class A or third class.

(e) Authority.—In making investments of authority funds, the board shall have authority to:

(1) Permit assets pledged as collateral under subsection (d)(3), to be pooled in accordance with the act of August 6, 1971 (P.L. 281, No. 72), entitled "An act standardizing the procedures for pledges of assets to secure deposits of public funds with banking institutions pursuant to other laws; establishing a standard rule for the types, amounts and valuations of assets eligible to be used as collateral for deposits of public funds; permitting assets to be pledged against deposits on a pooled basis; and authorizing the appointment of custodians to act as pledgees of assets."

(2) Combine moneys from more than one fund under authority control for the purchase of a single investment if lack of the funds combined for the purpose shall be accounted for separately in all respects and if earnings from the investment are separately and individually computed, recorded and credited to the accounts from which the investment was purchased.

(3) Join with one or more other political subdivisions and municipal authorities in accordance with Subchapter A of Chapter 23 (relating to intergovernmental cooperation) in the purchase of a single investment pursuant to the requirements of paragraph (2).

§ 5612. Money of authority.

(a) Treasurer.—The treasurer of an authority, or other designated recipient, shall receive the money due the authority and deposit the money in an account with a designated depository. The money shall be remitted in the name of the authority or designated recipient and may not include the name of an individual.

(a.1) Prohibition.—

(1) Money of the authority may not be used for any grant, loan or other expenditure for any purpose other than a service or project directly related to the mission or purpose of the authority as set forth in the articles of incorporation or in the resolution or ordinance establishing the authority under section 5603 (relating to method of incorporation).

(2) A ratepayer to an authority shall have a cause of action in the court of common pleas where the authority is located to seek the return of money expended in violation of paragraph (1) from the recipient.

(3) Paragraph (1) shall not apply to the following:

(i) A monetary contribution to a nonprofit community organization or activity that does not exceed $1,000.

(ii) An in-kind service, including the provision of water or other resources to a nonprofit community organization or activity, the value of which does not exceed $1,000.

(iii) An agreement for the joint purchase and use of equipment.

(iv) An agreement for the sharing of equipment during emergency situations.

(a.2) Fiscal procedures.—

(1) An authority shall establish, according to generally accepted accounting principles, procedures to bill customers, collect payments, issue receipts, handle funds received and deposit money in an account or accounts managed by a designated depository. All bill payments shall be made in the name of the authority or designated public or contracted entity collecting revenue and shall not include the name of an individual.

(2) The required annual audit and financial report of the authority shall be presented at a meeting of the authority board, discussed publicly and require an official vote of acceptance.

(3) Nothing in this subsection shall be construed to preclude an authority from adopting rules and regulations regarding fiscal controls that are more stringent than required by this section.

(b) Report.—A required annual report shall be published in accordance with the following:

(1) Every authority shall file, on or before 180 days following the end of its fiscal year, an annual report of its fiscal affairs covering the preceding fiscal year with the Department of Community and Economic Development and with the municipality or municipalities creating the authority on forms prepared and distributed by the Department of Community and Economic Development. The reports shall also be provided, and may be provided electronically, to any other municipality that has residents served by the authority.

(2) Every authority shall have its books, accounts and records audited annually by a certified public accountant, and a copy of the audit report shall be filed in the same manner and within the same time period as the annual report. The audit shall comply with the following, if applicable:

Chap. 39 Res. During Mil. Service
Chap. 38 Intergov. Coop.
Chap. 37 3rd Class City Code
Chap. 36 Bor. Code
Chap. 35 2nd Class Twp. Code
Chap. 34 1st Class Twp. Code
Chap. 33 Home Rule Chart. Opt. Plans Law
Chap. 32 Water Serv. Act
Chap. 31 Munic. Auth. Act

(i) The generally accepted government auditing standards, including the standards published by the Government Accountability Office.

(ii) The Single Audit Act of 1984 (31 U.S.C. § 7501 et seq.).

(iii) 2 CFR Pt. 200 (relating to uniform administrative requirements, cost principles, and audit requirements for Federal awards).

(iv) Any other Federal or State requirements for an audit relating to the finances of an authority.

(3) A concise financial statement shall be published annually at least once in a newspaper of general circulation in the municipality where the principal office of the authority is located. If the publication is not made by the authority, the municipality shall publish such statement at the expense of the authority.

(4) If the authority fails to make such an audit or if the municipality determines that there is a need for a review, then the controller, auditor or accountant designated by the municipality is hereby authorized and empowered from time to time to examine the accounts and books of it, including its receipts, billing systems, disbursements, transparency of contracts and how the contracts are awarded, leases, sinking funds, investments, compliance with relevant Federal and State statutes, conflicts of interest by the authority and its board members, staff and contractors and any other matters relating to its finances, operation and affairs. The review by the municipality shall be conducted within one year of an authority's annual audit required under paragraph (2), the review shall be done at the expense of the municipality and the authority shall be exempt the following fiscal year from conducting an audit. If the review by the municipality is being done due to the failure of the authority to make an annual audit, the review shall be at the expense of the authority.

(c) Attorney General.—The Attorney General of the Commonwealth shall have the right to examine the books, accounts and records of any authority.

Note on Constitutionality: Act 230 of 2002 was declared unconstitutional by *City of Philadelphia v. Commonwealth*, 575 Pa. 542, 838 A.2d 566 (Pa. 2003).

§ 5613. Transfer of existing facilities to authority.

(a) Authorization.—Any municipality, school district or owner may sell, lease, lend, grant, convey, transfer or pay over to any authority with or without consideration any project or any part of it, any interest in real or personal property, any funds available for building construction or improvement purposes, including the proceeds of bonds previously or hereafter issued for building construction or improvement purposes, which may be used by the authority in the construction, improvement, maintenance or operation of any project. Any municipality or school district may transfer, assign and set over to any authority any contracts which may have been awarded by the municipality or school district for the construction of projects not initiated or completed. The territory being served by any project or the territory within which a project is authorized to render service at the time of the acquisition of a project by an authority shall include the area served by the project and the area in which the project is authorized to serve at the time of acquisition and any other area into which the service may be extended, subject to the limitations of section 5607(a) (relating to purposes and powers).

(b) Acquisition.—

(1) An authority may not acquire by any device or means, including a consolidation, merger, purchase or lease, or through the purchase of stock, bonds or other securities, title to or possession or use of all or a substantial portion of any existing facilities constituting a project as defined under this chapter if the project is subject to the jurisdiction of the Pennsylvania Public Utility Commission without first reporting to and advising the municipality which created or which are members of the authority of the agreement to acquire, including all its terms and conditions.

(2) The proposed action of the authority and the proposed agreement to acquire shall be approved by the governing body of the municipality which cre-

ated or which are members of the authority and to which the report is made. Where there are one or two member municipalities of the authority, such approval shall be by two-thirds vote of all of the members of the governing body or of each of the governing bodies. If there are more than two member municipalities of the authority, approval shall be by majority vote of all the members of each governing body of two-thirds of the member municipalities.

(c) **Complete provision.**—Notwithstanding any other provision of law, this section, without reference to any other law, shall be deemed complete for the acquisition by agreement of projects as defined in this chapter located wholly within or partially without the municipality causing such authority to be incorporated, and no proceedings or other action shall be required except as provided for in this section.

§ 5614. Competition in award of contracts.

(a) **Services.**—

(1) Except as set forth in paragraph (2), all construction, reconstruction, repair or work of any nature made by an authority if the entire cost, value or amount, including labor and materials, exceeds a base amount of $18,500, subject to adjustment under subsection (c.1), shall be done only under contract to be entered into by the authority with the lowest responsible bidder upon proper terms after public notice asking for competitive bids as provided in this section.

(2) Paragraph (1) does not apply to construction, reconstruction, repair or work done by employees of the authority or by labor supplied under agreement with a Federal or State agency with supplies and materials purchased as provided in this section.

(3) No contract shall be entered into for construction or improvement or repair of a project or portion thereof unless the contractor gives an undertaking with a sufficient surety approved by the authority and in an amount fixed by the authority for the faithful performance of the contract.

(4) The contract must provide among other things that the person or corporation entering into the contract with the authority will pay for all materials furnished and services rendered for the performance of the contract and that any person or corporation furnishing materials or rendering services may maintain an action to recover for them against the obligor in the undertaking as though such person or corporation was named in the contract if the action is brought within one year after the time the cause of action accrued.

(5) Nothing in this section shall be construed to limit the power of the authority to construct, repair or improve a project or portion thereof or any addition, betterment or extension thereto directed by the officers, agents and employees of the authority or otherwise than by contract.

(b) **Supplies and materials.**—All supplies and materials with a base price costing at least $18,500, subject to adjustment under subsection (c.1), shall be purchased only after advertisement as provided in this section. The authority shall accept the lowest bid, kind, quality and material being equal, but the authority shall have the right to reject any or all bids or select a single item from any bid. The provisions as to bidding shall not apply to the purchase of patented and manufactured products offered for sale in a noncompetitive market or solely by a manufacturer's authorized dealer.

(c) **Quotations.**—Written or telephonic price quotations from at least three qualified and responsible contractors shall be requested for a contract in excess of the base amount of $10,000, subject to adjustment under subsection (c.1), but is less than the amount requiring advertisement and competitive bidding. In lieu of price quotations, a memorandum shall be kept on file showing that fewer than three qualified contractors exist in the market area within which it is practicable to obtain quotations. A written record of telephonic price quotations shall be made and shall contain at least the date of the quotation; the name of the contractor and the contractor's representative; the construction, reconstruction, repair, maintenance or work which was the subject of the quotation; and the price. Written price quotations, written records of telephonic price quotations and memoranda shall be retained for a period of three years.

(c.1) Adjustments.—Adjustments to the base amounts specified under subsections (a)(1), (b) and (c) shall be made as follows:

(1) The Department of Labor and Industry shall determine the percentage change in the Consumer Price Index for All Urban Consumers: All Items (CPI-U) for the United States City Average as published by the United States Department of Labor, Bureau of Labor Statistics, for the 12-month period ending September 30, 2012, and for each successive 12-month period thereafter. [*Ed. Note: see footnote 1 below for Notice effective for 2016*]

(2) If the department determines that there is no positive percentage change, then no adjustment to the base amounts shall occur for the relevant time period provided for in this subsection.

(3)(i) If the department determines that there is a positive percentage change in the first year that the determination is made under paragraph (1), the positive percentage change shall be multiplied by each base amount, and the products shall be added to the base amounts, respectively, and the sums shall be preliminary adjusted amounts.

(ii) The preliminary adjusted amounts shall be rounded to the nearest $100 to determine the final adjusted base amounts for purposes of subsections (a)(1), (b) and (c).

(4) In each successive year in which there is a positive percentage change in the CPI-U for the United States City Average, the positive percentage change shall be multiplied by the most recent preliminary adjusted amounts, and the products shall be added to the preliminary adjusted amount of the prior year to calculate the preliminary adjusted amounts for the current year. The sums thereof shall be rounded to the nearest $100 to determine the new final adjusted base amounts for purposes of subsections (a)(1), (b) and (c).

(5) The determinations and adjustments required under this subsection shall be made in the period between October 1 and November 15 of the year following the effective date of this subsection1 and annually between October 1 and November 15 of each year thereafter.

(6) The final adjusted base amounts and new final adjusted base amounts obtained under paragraphs (3) and (4) shall become effective January 1 for the calendar year following the year in which the determination required under paragraph (1) is made.

(7) The department shall publish notice in the Pennsylvania Bulletin prior to January 1 of each calendar year of the annual percentage change determined under paragraph (1) and the unadjusted or final adjusted base amounts determined under paragraphs (3) and (4) at which competitive bidding is required under subsection (a)(1) and (b) and written or telephonic price quotations are required under subsection (c), for the calendar year beginning the first day of January after publication of the notice. The notice shall include a written and illustrative explanation of the calculations performed by the department in establishing the unadjusted or final adjusted base amounts under this subsection for the ensuing calendar year. (8) The annual increase in the preliminary adjusted base amounts obtained under paragraphs (3) and (4) shall not exceed 3%.

(d) Notice.—The term "advertisement" or "public notice," wherever used in this section, shall mean a notice published at least ten days before the award of a contract in a newspaper of general circulation published in the municipality where the authority has its principal office or, if no newspaper of general circulation is published therein, in a newspaper of general circulation in the county where the authority has its principal office. Notice may be waived if the authority determines that an emergency exists which requires the authority to purchase the supplies and materials immediately.

(e) Conflict of interest.—No member of the authority or officer or employee of the authority may directly or indirectly be a party to or be interested in any contract or agreement with the authority if the contract or agreement establishes liability against or indebtedness of the authority. Any contract or agreement made in violation of this subsection is void, and no action may be maintained on the agreement against the authority.

(f) Entry into contracts.—

(1) Subject to subsection (e), an authority may enter into and carry out contracts or establish or comply with rules and regulations concerning labor and materials and other related matters in connection with a project or portion thereof as the authority deems desirable or as may be requested by a Federal agency to assist in the financing of the project or any part thereof. This paragraph shall not apply to any of the following:

(i) A case in which the authority has taken over by transfer or assignment a contract authorized to be assigned to it under section 5613 (relating to transfer of existing facilities to authority).

(ii) A contract in connection with the construction of a project which the authority may have had transferred to it by any person or private corporation.

(2) This subsection is not intended to limit the powers of an authority.

(g) Compliance.—A contract for the construction, reconstruction, alteration, repair, improvement or maintenance of public works shall comply with the provisions of the act of March 3, 1978 (P.L. 6, No. 3), known as the Steel Products Procurement Act.

(h) Evasion.—

(1) An authority may not evade the provisions of this section as to bids or purchasing materials or contracting for services piecemeal for the purpose of obtaining prices under the amount required by this section upon transactions which should, in the exercise of reasonable discretion and prudence, be conducted as one transaction amounting to more than the amount required by this section.

(2) This subsection is intended to make unlawful the practice of evading advertising requirements by making a series of purchases or contracts each for less than the advertising requirement price or by making several simultaneous purchases or contracts each below that price when in either case the transaction involved should have been made as one transaction for one price.

(3) An authority member who votes to unlawfully evade the provisions of this section and who knows that the transaction upon which the member votes is or ought to be a part of a larger transaction and that it is being divided in order to evade the requirements as to advertising for bids commits a misdemeanor of the third degree for each contract entered into as a direct result of that vote.

---

1. [See section (c.1) above].

DEPARTMENT OF LABOR AND INDUSTRY
Consumer Price Index Adjustment of Base Amounts on Bids Effective January 1, 2016 [44 Pa.B. 7797]
[Saturday, December 12, 2015]

Each year the Department of Labor and Industry (Department) is required by the following statutes to publish changes to the base amounts triggering the requirement for public bids, telephonic bids or separate bids, or both, for certain contracts. The Department is required to announce the percentage change in the Consumer Price Index for All Urban Consumers (CPI-U): all items CPI-U for the United States city average for the 12-month period ending September 30 of each year. The Department utilizes the most current nonseasonally adjusted series, as published by the United States Bureau of Labor Statistics (BLS), which at present uses 1982-1984 as the index base period (set equal to 100). The percentage change for the 12-month period ending September 30, 2015, is 0.0%.

The change to the base rate is determined as follows:

1) Calculate the percentage change in CPI-U (I) from September 2014 to September 2015. This is derived as $I = (CPI_{15} - CPI_{14})/CPI_{14}$, where the subscripts refer to September 2015 and 2014 values of CPI-U. As reported by the BLS these values are (237.945 − 238.031)/238.031 = -0.086/238.031 = -0.0361%,1 which when rounded to 1 decimal place = 0.0%. (This was also reported as 0.0% in Table A of the BLS news release on the Consumer Price Index Summary for September 2015.)

2) The legislation puts a floor of 0 and a cap of 3% on the percentage change to be utilized in the calculations (technically these restrictions are on the Preliminary Adjusted Base (PAB), defined in step 4, however this is mathematically equivalent). The truncated value of the percentage change to be used in the adjustment formula is denoted as PC, resulting in:

a) PC = I, for 0<=I<=3%,

b) PC = 0, for I<0 and

c) PC = 3% for I>3%.

3) The base value (either original for new legislation or the prior year's PAB) is designated as B and the product of B and PC (determined previously) is P. (There are different values of the base depending on the entity and the type of bid, so technically B could be designated with 2 subscripts. For illustration purposes, the subscripts are omitted.) Then P = B*PC. A common value for the base amount in 2015 for a public bid is $19,421.08. (The other two prior PABs, which are this year's bases for a variety of bid types, were $10,497.88 and $26,244.7.) For example, using B = $19,421.08, results in P = $19,421.08 *0.0% = $0.00.

4) Then the Preliminary Adjusted Base, PAB = P + B, which reduces to $0.00 + $19,421.08 = $19,421.08

5) The Final Adjusted Base Amount, FAA (which is used as the limit for the next year that is 2016) is the PAB rounded to the nearest 100. Therefore the FAA = $19,400.00.

	Final Adjusted Base Amount for use in 2016			
Entity and Legislation	**Public Bid**	**Written/ Telephonic Bid**	**Separate Bids**	**Concessions**
The County Code (16 P.S. §§ 1801—1803 and 2317)	**19,400.00**	**10,500.00**	**19,400.00**	
Second Class County Code (16 P.S. §§ 3112, 5001, 5511-A and 5517)	**19,400.00**	**10,500.00**	**19,400.00**	
Public School Code (24 P.S. §§ 1-120, 7-751 and 8-807.1)	**19,400.00**	**10,500.00**	**19,400.00**	
Public School Code, Thaddeus Stevens College of Technology (24 P.S. § 19-1913.1-B)	**19,400.00**			
Public School Code, State System of Higher Education (24 P.S. §§ 20-2003-A.1 and 20-2010-A)	**19,400.00**			
Prevention and Control of Floods, Flood Control Districts (32 P.S. §§ 662 and 662.1)	**19,400.00**			
Housing Authorities (35 P.S. § 1551)	**19,400.00**	**10,500.00**		
Intergovernmental Cooperation (53 Pa.C.S. §§ 2308, 2311 and 2312)	**19,400.00**	**10,500.00**		
General Municipal Law, Flood Control (53 P.S. § 2863)	**19,400.00**	**10,500.00**		
Political Subdivisions Joint Purchases Law (53 P.S. § 5432)	**19,400.00**	**10,500.00**		
Parking Authorities (53 Pa.C.S. § 5511)	**26,200.00**	**10,500.00**		

Entity and Legislation	Public Bid	Written/ Telephonic Bid	Separate Bids	Concessions
Municipal Authorities (53 Pa.C.S. § 5614)	19,400.00	10,500.00		
Public Auditorium Authorities Law (53 P.S. § 23851)	19,400.00	10,500.00		
Third Class City Code (53 P.S. §§ 36901.1, 36901.2, 36901.4, 36902, 36903.1 and 36909)	19,400.00		19,400.00	
The Borough Code (53 P.S. §§ 1402, 1403 and 1405)	19,400.00	10,500.00	19,400.00	
Incorporated Towns (53 P.S. §§ 53202, 53202.1, 53203, 53203.1 and 53205)	19,400.00	10,500.00	19,400.00	
First Class Township Code (53 P.S. §§ 56802, 56803 and 56805)	19,400.00	10,500.00	19,400.00	
Second Class Township Code (53 P.S. §§ 68102 and 68107)	19,400.00	10,500.00	19,400.00	
Economic Development Financing Law (73 P.S. § 382)	19,400.00	10,500.00		
Metropolitan Transportation Authorities (74 Pa.C.S. § 1750)	26,200.00			19,400.00

§ 5615. Acquisition of lands, water and water rights.

(a) Authorization.—

(1) Except as provided in paragraph (2), the authority shall have the power to acquire by purchase or eminent domain proceedings either the fee or the rights, title, interest or easement in such lands, water and water rights as the authority deems necessary for any of the purposes of this chapter. Water and water rights may not be acquired unless approval is obtained from the Department of Environmental Protection.

(2) The right of eminent domain does not apply to:

(i) Property owned or used by the United States, the Commonwealth or any of its political subdivisions or an agency of any of them, or any body politic and corporate organized as an authority under any law of the commonwealth or by any agency.

(ii) Property of a public service company.

(iii) Property used for burial purposes.

(iv) Places of public worship.

(b) Exercise.—The right of eminent domain shall be exercised by the authority in the manner provided by law for the exercise of such right by municipalities of the same class, as the municipality which organized the authority. Eminent domain shall be exercised by a joint authority in the same manner as is provided by law for the exercise of such right by municipalities of the same class as the municipality in which the right of eminent domain is to be exercised. The right of eminent domain herein conferred by this section may be exercised either within or without the municipality.

§ 5616. Acquisition of capital stock.

(a) Acquisition.—In the event that the authority shall own 90% or more of all the outstanding capital stock entitled to vote upon liquidation and dissolution and

Chap. 39 Res. During Mil. Service
Chap. 38 Intergov. Coop.
Chap. 37 3rd Class City Code
Chap. 36 Bor. Code
Chap. 35 2nd Class Twp. Code
Chap. 34 1st Class Twp. Code
Chap. 33 Home Rule Chart. Opt. Plans Law
Chap. 32 Water Serv. Act
Chap. 31 Munic. Auth. Act

which is not subject by its terms to be called for redemption of any corporation owning a project and organized and existing under the laws of this Commonwealth, the authority shall have the power to acquire the remainder of the stock by eminent domain as a part of a plan for the liquidation of the corporation.

(b) Exercise.—The right of eminent domain with respect to the remainder of capital stock shall be exercised by the authority pursuant to this subsection. In the event that the authority has not agreed with an owner of any of the capital stock as to the value of the stock, the authority shall file with the court of common pleas of the county in which the corporation's principal place of business is located its bond for the benefit of the owner and for any other persons who may be found entitled to receive damages for the taking of the capital stock, of which the owner shall be obligee, the condition of which bond shall be that the authority shall pay or cause to be paid to the owner of the stock or to such other persons as may be found entitled to receive damages for the taking of the capital stock, an amount as the owner or such other persons shall be entitled to receive for the taking of the stock, after the amount shall have been agreed upon by the parties or assessed in the manner provided by subsection (d). The bond shall be accompanied by proof that notice of the proposed filing was mailed by registered mail not less than ten days prior to the proposed filing to the owner of the stock at his address as shown by the records of the corporation. Upon approval by the court of the bond, the authority shall be vested with all the right, title and interest in and to the stock, and the owner and all other persons shall cease to have any rights or interest with regard to the stock other than the right to compensation for the taking of it under the procedure set forth in subsection (d). The word "owner," as used in this subsection, shall mean the person in whose name the stock is registered on the books of the corporation.

(c) Approval.—In the event that the authority shall have contracted in writing to purchase 90% or more of any outstanding capital stock, it shall have the right to obtain the approval of the court to the bond required by the provisions of subsection (b), but the approval shall not be effective for the purposes of this section unless and until there is also filed with the prothonotary of the court within ten days after the approval a sworn statement by the chairman of the board of the authority, duly attested by the secretary of the authority, that the authority has become the owner of 90% or more of the capital stock.

(d) Appraisal.—

(1) If the authority and the former owner of the stock fail to agree as to the amount which the former owner is entitled to receive as compensation for the taking of the stock within 30 days after the approval of the bond by the court under the provisions of subsection (b) or the filing of the required statement under the provisions of subsection (c), either party may apply by petition to the court for the appointment by the court of three disinterested persons to appraise the fair value of the stock immediately prior to its acquisition by the authority, without regard to any depreciation or appreciation in consequence of the acquisition.

(2) The appraisers or a majority of them shall file their award, which shall include the costs of the appraisal, with the court and shall mail a copy to each party with the date of filing stated thereon. When the award is filed with the court, the prothonotary shall mark the same "confirmed nisi" and, if no exceptions are filed within ten days, he shall enter a decree that the award is confirmed absolutely. If exceptions to the award are filed by either party before the award is confirmed, the court shall hear the same and shall have the power to confirm, modify, change or otherwise correct the award or refer the same back to the same or new appraisers with similar power as to their award.

§ 5617. Use of projects.

The use of the facilities of the authority and the operation of its business shall be subject to the rules and regulations as adopted by the authority. The authority shall not be authorized to do anything which will impair the security of the holders of the obligations of the authority or violate any agreements with them or for their benefit.

§ 5618. Pledge by Commonwealth.

(a) Power of authorities.—The Commonwealth pledges to and agrees with any person, firm or corporation or Federal agency subscribing to or acquiring the bonds to be issued by the authority for the construction, extension, improvement or enlargement of a project or part thereof that the Commonwealth will not limit or alter the rights vested by this chapter in the authority until all bonds and the interest on them are fully met and discharged.

(b) Federal matters.—The Commonwealth pledges to and agrees with the United States and all Federal agencies that, if a Federal agency constructs or contributes funds for the construction, extension, improvement or enlargement of a project or any portion thereof:

(1) the Commonwealth will not alter or limit the rights and powers of the authority in any manner which would be inconsistent with the continued maintenance and operation of the project or the improvement thereof or which would be inconsistent with the due performance of agreements between the authority and any federal agency; and

(2) the authority shall continue to have and may exercise all powers granted in this chapter as long as the powers are necessary or desirable for carrying out the purposes of this chapter and the purposes of the United States in the construction or improvement or enlargement of the project or portion thereof.

§ 5619. Termination of authority.

(a) Conveyance of projects.—When an authority has finally paid and discharged all bonds, with interest due, which have been secured by a pledge of any of the revenues or receipts of a project, the authority may, subject to agreements concerning the operation or disposition of the project, convey the project to the municipality creating the authority or, if the project is a public school project, to the school district to which the project is leased.

(b) Conveyance of property.—When an authority has finally paid and discharged all bonds issued and outstanding and the interest due on them, and settled all other outstanding claims against it, the authority may convey all its property to the municipality or municipalities or, if the property is public school property, then to the school district for which the property was financed, and terminate its existence.

(c) Certificate.—An authority requesting to terminate its existence must submit a certificate requesting termination to the municipality which created it. If the certificate is approved by the municipality by its ordinance, or resolution, the certificate shall be filed in the office of the Secretary of the Commonwealth; and the secretary shall note the termination of existence on the record of incorporation and return the certificate with approval to the board. The board shall cause the certificate to be recorded in the office of the recorder of deeds of the county. Upon recording, the property of the authority shall pass to the municipality, or municipalities or, if the property is public school property, then to the school district for which the property was financed; and the authority shall cease to exist.

§ 5620. Exemption from taxation and payments in lieu of taxes.

The effectuation of the authorized purposes of authorities created under this chapter shall be for the benefit of the people of this Commonwealth, for the increase of their commerce and prosperity and for the improvement of their health and living conditions. Since authorities will be performing essential governmental functions in effectuating these purposes, authorities shall not be required

Chap. 39 Res. During Mil. Service
Chap. 38 Intergov. Coop.
Chap. 37 3rd Class City Code
Chap. 36 Bor. Code
Chap. 35 2nd Class Twp. Code
Chap. 34 1st Class Twp. Code
Chap. 33 Home Rule Chart. Opt. Plans Law
Chap. 32 Water Serv. Act
Chap. 31 Munic. Auth. Act

to pay taxes or assessments upon property acquired or used by them for such purposes. Whenever in excess of 10% of the land area of any political subdivision in a sixth, seventh or eighth class county has been taken for a waterworks, water supply works or water distribution system having a source of water within a political subdivision which is not provided with water service by the authority, in lieu of such taxes or special assessments the authority may agree to make payments in the county to the taxing authorities of any or all of the political subdivisions where any land has been taken. The bonds issued by any authority, their transfer and the income from the bonds, including any profits made on their sale, shall be free from taxation within the Commonwealth.

§ 5621. Constitutional construction.

The provisions of this chapter shall be severable, and if any of the provisions are held to be unconstitutional, it shall not affect the validity of any of the remaining provisions of this chapter. It is hereby declared as the legislative intent that this chapter would have been adopted had such unconstitutional provisions not been included.

§ 5622. Conveyance by authorities to municipalities or school districts of established projects.

(a) Project.—If a project established under this chapter by a board appointed by a municipality is of a character which the municipality has power to establish, maintain or operate, and the municipality desires to acquire the project it may, by appropriate resolution or ordinance adopted by the proper authorities signify its desire to do so, and the authorities shall convey by appropriate instrument the project to the municipality upon the assumption by the municipality of all the obligations incurred by the authorities with respect to that project.

(b) Public school project.—A public school project undertaken under this chapter may be acquired by a school district to which the project was leased if the school district by appropriate resolution signifies a desire to do so. An authority shall convey the public school project to the school district by appropriate instrument upon the assumption by the school district of all the obligations incurred by the authority with respect to that project.

(c) Conveyance.—An authority formed by any county for the purpose of acquiring, constructing, improving, maintaining or operating any project for the benefit of any one or more but not all of the cities, boroughs, towns and townships of the county may, with the approval of the board of county commissioners of the county, convey the project to the cities, boroughs, towns or townships of the county for the benefit of which the project was acquired, constructed, improved, maintained or operated or to any authority organized by such cities, boroughs, towns or townships for the purpose of taking over such project. All such conveyances shall be made subject to any and all obligations incurred by the authority with respect to the project conveyed.

(d) Reserves.—Following transfer of a project pursuant to this section, the municipality, including an incorporated town or home rule municipality, which has acquired the project shall retain the reserves received from the authority which have been derived from operations in a separate fund, and the reserves shall only be used for the purposes of operating, maintaining, repairing, improving and extending the project. Money received from the authority which represents the proceeds of financing shall be retained by the municipality in a separate fund which shall only be used for improving or extending the project or other capital purposes related to it.

Section 2. The provisions of 53 Pa.C.S. Ch. 56 shall apply to all authorities now existing that were incorporated under the provisions of the former act of June 28, 1935 (P.L. 463, No. 191) entitled "An act providing, for a limited period of time, for the incorporation, as bodies corporate and politic, of "Authorities" for municipalities; defining the same; prescribing the rights, powers, and duties of such Authorities; authorizing such Authorities to acquire, construct, improve, maintain, and operate projects, and to borrow money and issue bonds therefor; providing for the payment of such bonds, and prescribing the rights of the holders thereof; conferring the right of eminent domain on such Authorities; authorizing such Authorities to enter into contracts with and to accept grants from the Federal Government or any agency thereof; and for other purposes," and the act of May 2, 1945 (P.L. 382, No. 164), known as the Municipality Authorities Act of 1945. The provisions of 53 Pa.C.S. Ch. 56, so far as they are the same as those of existing laws, are intended as a continuation of such laws and not as new enactments. The repeal by this act of any act or part of any act shall not affect the existence of any authority previously incorporated. The provisions of this act shall not affect any act done, liability incurred or right accrued or vested or affect any suit pending or to be instituted to enforce any right or penalty under the authority of such repealed laws. All rules and regulations made pursuant to any act or part of any act repealed by 53 Pa.C.S. Ch. 56 shall continue with the same force and effect as if such act had not been repealed.

Repealer. The following acts are repealed:

Act of May 2, 1945 (P.L. 382, No. 164), known as the Municipality Authorities Act of 1945.

Act of June 5, 1947 (P.L. 458, No. 208), known as the Parking Authority Law.

Section 4. The addition of 53 Pa.C.S. Ch. 56 is a continuation of the act of May 2, 1945 (P.L. 382, No. 164), known as the Municipality Authorities Act of 1945. The following apply:

(1) Except as otherwise provided in 53 Pa.C.S. Ch. 56, all activities initiated under the municipality authorities act of 1945 shall continue and remain in full force and effect and may be completed under 53 Pa.C.S. Ch. 56. Orders, regulations, rules and decisions which were made under the Municipality Authorities Act of 1945 and which are in effect on the effective date of section 3 of this act shall remain in full force and effect until revoked, vacated or modified under 53 Pa.C.S. Ch. 56. Contracts, obligations and collective bargaining agreements entered into under the Municipality Authorities Act of 1945 are not affected nor impaired by the repeal of the Municipality Authorities Act of 1945.

(2) Except as set forth in paragraph (3), any difference in language between 53 Pa.C.S. Ch. 56 and the Municipality Authorities Act of 1945 is intended only to conform to the style of the Pennsylvania Consolidated Statutes and is not intended to change or affect the legislative intent, judicial construction or administration and implementation of the Municipality Authorities Act of 1945.

(3) Paragraph (2) does not apply to any of the following provisions:

(i) The addition of the last sentence of 53 Pa.C.S. § 5610(b).

(ii) The addition of 53 Pa.C.S. § 5610(f).

Section 5. The addition of 53 Pa.C.S. Ch. 55 is a continuation of the act of June 5, 1947 (P.L. 458, No. 208), known as the Parking Authority Law. The following apply:

(1) Except as otherwise provided in 53 Pa.C.S. Ch. 55, all activities initiated under the Parking Authority Law shall continue and remain in full force and effect and may be completed under 53 Pa.C.S. Ch. 55. Orders, regulations, rules and decisions which were made under the Parking Authority Law and which are in effect on the effective date of section 3 of this act shall remain in full force and effect until revoked, vacated or modified under 53 Pa.C.S. Ch. 55. Contracts, obligations and collective bargaining agreements entered

into under the Parking Authority Law are not affected nor impaired by the repeal of the Parking Authority Law.

(2) Except as set forth in paragraph (3), any difference in language between 53 Pa.C.S. Ch. 55 and the Parking Authority Law is intended only to conform to the style of the Pennsylvania Consolidated Statutes and is not intended to change or affect the legislative intent, judicial construction or administration and implementation of the Parking Authority Law.

(3) Paragraph (2) does not apply to the addition of 53 Pa.C.S. §§ 5508(a) and 5508.1.

Section 6. This act shall take effect immediately.

§ 5623. Revival of an expired authority

(a) Retroactive revival.—Upon the filing of the required municipal statements of revival with the Secretary of the Commonwealth and issuance of a certificate of revival, an expired authority shall become a retroactively revived authority.

(b) Municipal statement of revival.—A municipal statement of revival shall be executed in the name of each municipality that incorporated or subsequently joined in and had not withdrawn from the expired authority and shall set forth:

(1) The name of the expired authority and of each municipality that incorporated or subsequently joined in and had not withdrawn from the expired authority.

(2) The date on which the authority's term of existence expired.

(3) The address, including street and number of the expired authority.

(4) A statement that the municipality desires the revival of the authority as a body politic and corporate for an additional term not exceeding 50 years.

(5) A statement that the filing of the municipal statement of revival has been authorized and approved by the municipal authorities of the municipality by resolution.

(c) Expiration interval.—An expired authority may not become a retroactively revived authority if its term of expiration exceeds five years.

(d) Certificate of revival.—The Secretary of the Commonwealth shall issue a certificate of revival after verifying that required municipal statements of revival have been filed in proper form.

(e) Definitions.—The following words and phrases when used in this section shall have the meanings given to them in this subsection unless the context clearly indicates otherwise:

"Certificate of revival." A certification issued by the Secretary of the Commonwealth that, as a result of required municipal statements of revival having been filed in proper form, the expired authority which is the subject of the municipal statements of revival is certified as having been retroactively revived for the term specified.

"Expired authority." An authority whose term of existence has expired in accordance with this chapter.

"Municipal statement of revival." A written statement prepared in accordance with subsection (b) and filed with the Secretary of the Commonwealth by the municipal authorities of each municipality that incorporated or subsequently joined in and had not withdrawn from an expired authority indicating that approval has been given for the retroactive revival of the expired authority by municipal authorities by resolution.

"Retroactively revived authority." An expired authority whose existence has been revived retroactively so that the authority is restored to its previous legal position in the same manner and to the same extent as if its term of existence had never expired. Retroactive revival shall have the effect of validating the business and affairs of the authority during its term of expiration, including all contracts and other transactions made and effected within the scope of the articles of the authority by its representatives and any rights, privileges, liabilities and obligations that the authority would have had if its term of existence had not expired.

"Term of expiration." The period of time that commences when an authority becomes an expired authority and that ends when the expired authority is retroactively revived in accordance with this section.

NOTES TO ACT 2003–57

H.B. No. 51 Approved December 30, 2003:

Notwithstanding section 5(1) of this act, this act shall apply immediately to any connection, customer facilities, tapping or similar fees which are increased or initially imposed subsequent to the effective date of this section.

Notwithstanding section 5(1) of this act, the mandatory refund provisions of 53 Pa.C.S. § 5607(d)(24)(i)(C)(VI) applicable to tapping fees based upon facilities to be constructed or acquired in the future shall apply to tapping fees collected subsequent to the effective date of this section regardless of when the resolution adopting such tapping fees was adopted.

The following shall apply:

(1) The provisions of 53 Pa.C.S. § 5607(d)(24)(i)(C)(I) and (V)(e) shall not apply for a period of 15 years after the effective date of this section to sewer tapping fees imposed by a joint authority having six or more municipal members which is prohibited from implementing any increase in sewer user fees pursuant to the terms of a contract executed prior to January 1, 2003.

(2) The provisions of 53 Pa.C.S. § 5607(d)(24)(i)(C)(V)(e) shall not apply for a period of five years after the date of closing of original financing when an authority, in order to support the construction of new facilities, used original financing which closed on or before July 1, 2003, which has a term of at least 15 years and in which tapping fees were relied upon to support the debt service on the financing.

This act shall take effect as follows:

(1) The amendment of 53 Pa.C.S. § 5607(d)(24), (30), (32) and (33) shall take effect in 18 months.

(2) The remainder of this act [53 Pa.C.S. § 5607(d)(17)-ed.] shall take effect immediately.

Approved December 30, 2003.

CHAPTER 32

WATER SERVICES ACT

53 P.S. §§ 3102.101 et seq.

TABLE OF CONTENTS

Sec.

CHAPTER 1

PRELIMINARY PROVISIONS

§ 101. Short title.

This act shall be known and may be cited as the Water Services Act.

§ 102. Definitions.

The following words and phrases when used in this act shall have the meanings given to them in this section unless the context clearly indicates otherwise:

"Act 1949-98." The act of April 14, 1949 (P.L. 482, No. 98)[1] entitled, as amended, "An act authorizing and requiring cities, boroughs, townships, municipal authorities and public utility companies engaged in the supplying of water, to shut off the supply of water for nonpayment of sewer, sewerage, or sewage treatment rentals, rates, or charges imposed by municipal authorities organized by counties of the second class, by cities of the second class, by cities of the second class A, by cities of the third class, by boroughs or by townships of the first or second class; authorizing and requiring them to supply to such authorities lists of metered water readings and flat-rate water bills and other data; authorizing them to act as billing and collecting agents for such authorities; and conferring certain powers upon the Pennsylvania Public Utility Commission in connection therewith."

"Commission." The Pennsylvania Public Utility Commission.

1. 53 P.S. §§ 2261 et seq.

Table of Contents | Part I Ch. 1–3 Ethics, Records, Open Meetings | Part II Ch. 4–10 Taxation | Part III Ch. 11–18 Torts, Contracts & Civil Rules | Part IV Ch. 19–24 Zoning & Planning | Part V Ch. 25–30 Construction and Emergency Codes | Part VI Ch. 31–39 Municipal Codes | Index

Chap. 39 Res. During Mil. Service
Chap. 38 Intergov. Coop.
Chap. 37 3rd Class City Code
Chap. 36 Bor. Code
Chap. 35 2nd Class Twp. Code
Chap. 34 1st Class Twp. Code
Chap. 33 Home Rule Chart. Opt. Plans Law
Chap. 32 Water Serv. Act
Chap. 31 Munic. Auth. Act

CHAPTER 3

MUNICIPAL AUTHORITY APPROVAL OF ACTIONS

§ 301. Definitions.

The following words and phrases when used in this chapter shall have the meanings given to them in this section unless the context clearly indicates otherwise:

"Authority." A body politic and corporate which meets all of the following:

(1) Is established by a city and incorporated under any of the following:

(i) The former act of June 28, 1935 (P.L. 463, No. 191),[2] entitled, "An act providing, for a limited period of time, for the incorporation, as bodies corporate and politic, of 'Authorities' for municipalities; defining the same; prescribing the rights, powers, and duties of such Authorities; authorizing such Authorities to acquire, construct, improve, maintain, and operate projects, and to borrow money and issue bonds therefor; providing for the payment of such bonds, and prescribing the rights of the holders thereof; conferring the right of eminent domain on such Authorities; authorizing such Authorities to enter into contracts with and to accept grants from the Federal Government or any agency thereof; and for other purposes."

(ii) The former act of May 2, 1945 (P.L. 382, No. 164)[3] known as the Municipality Authorities Act of 1945.

(iii) 53 Pa.C.S. Ch. 56 (relating to municipal authorities).

(2) Provides water and sewer services in accordance with all of the following:

(i) The water or sewer services, or both, are provided, either by an agreement with a municipality or directly, to users who are residents of one or more municipalities outside the boundaries of the city.

(ii) The total number of residents of municipalities which are outside the boundaries of the city and in which water or sewer services, or both, are offered or provided exceeds by at least 50% the number of residents who reside within the boundaries of the city.

(3) Owns:

(i) a sewer, sewer system or parts of a sewer or sewer system or sewage treatment works; and

(ii) a waterworks, water supply works or water distribution system.

"City." A city of the third class which has adopted a home rule charter and has a population of not more than 30,000.

"Project." As defined in 53 Pa.C.S. § 5602 (relating to definitions).

§ 302. Approvals.

(a) Commission.—If a city intends to continue the water and sewer service previously provided by the authority to municipalities outside the city, the city must obtain approval of the commission prior to:

(1) termination of an authority;

(2) conveyance of a project of the authority to the city under 53 Pa.C.S. § 5622 (relating to conveyance by authorities to municipalities or school districts of established projects); or

(3) transfer of reserves, assets or funds from an authority to the city.

---

2. See now 53 P.S. §§ 5601 et seq.

3. See now 53 P.S. §§ 5601 et seq.

Table of Contents
Part I Ch. 1–3 Ethics, Records, Open Meetings
Part II Ch. 4–10 Taxation
Part III Ch. 11–18 Torts, Contracts & Civil Rules
Part IV Ch. 19–24 Zoning & Planning
Part V Ch. 25–30 Construction and Emergency Codes
Part VI Ch. 31–39 Municipal Codes
Index

(b) Other municipalities.—

(1) A city must obtain approval from 75% of the municipalities which have service agreements with or whose residents previously received water or sewer services, or both, from the authority prior to:

(i) termination of the authority;

(ii) conveyance of a project of the authority under 53 Pa.C.S. § 5622; or

(iii) transfer of reserves, assets or funds from the authority to the city.

(2) Approval under paragraph (1) is as follows:

(i) The approval must be in the form of a resolution.

(ii) The resolution must be adopted at a public meeting by an affirmative vote of a majority of the members of the governing body of the municipality.

(iii) The result of an affirmative vote under subparagraph (ii) must be transmitted to the city within 48 hours of the vote.

§ 303. Applicability.

(a) General rule.—This chapter shall apply to any action by an authority or city to terminate, convey or transfer a water or sewer system under 53 Pa.C.S. Ch. 56 (relating to municipal authorities) which are initiated after November 1, 2005.

(b) Exception.—

(1) This chapter shall not apply to the merger of two or more authorities when the merger, including the conveyance of all projects, obligations and reserves, has been approved by each of the member municipalities and the merging authorities.

(2) For purposes of this subsection, the term "authority" shall have the same meaning as provided in 53 Pa.C.S. § 5602 (relating to definitions).

CHAPTER 5
WATER UTILITIES

§ 501. Definitions.

The following words and phrases when used in this chapter shall have the meanings given to them in this section unless the context clearly indicates otherwise:

"Water utility." The term includes a city, borough, township, municipal authority and public utility engaged in supplying water or water service.

§ 502. Termination of service.

(a) General rule.—Except as set forth in subsection (c), all of the following apply:

(1) If the owner or occupant of a premises served by a water utility neglects or fails to pay, for a period of 30 days from the due date, a rental, rate or charge for sewer, sewerage or sewage treatment service imposed by a municipality or municipal authority, the water utility shall, at the request and direction of the municipality, the authority or a city, borough or township to which the authority has assigned its claim or lien, shut off the supply of water to the premises until all overdue rentals, rates, charges and associated penalties and interest are paid.

Chap. 39 Res. During Mil. Service
Chap. 38 Intergov. Coop.
Chap. 37 3rd Class City Code
Chap. 36 Bor. Code
Chap. 35 2nd Class Twp. Code
Chap. 34 1st Class Twp. Code
Chap. 33 Home Rule Chart. Opt. Plans Law
Chap. 32 Water Serv. Act
Chap. 31 Munic. Auth. Act

(2) If the authority, city, borough or township also supplies water to premises, the authority, city, borough or township is authorized to shut off the supply of water to the premises.

(3) If the rental rate or charge for sewer, sewerage or sewage treatment service is imposed by a municipality as lessee of an authority and the lessee also supplies water to the premises, the municipality is authorized to shut off the supply of water to the premises without prior request from the authority or without prior assignment of its claim or lien for the service.

(b) Written notice.—Except as set forth in subsection (c), all of the following apply:

(1) In no case shall the water supply to premises be shut off until ten days after a written notice of intention to do so has been posted at a main entrance and mailed to the person liable for payment of the rentals and charges and the owner of the property or property manager.

(2) If during the ten-day period the person liable for payment of the rentals and charges delivers to the water utility authority or municipality supplying water to the premises a written statement under oath or affirmation averring that there is a just defense to all or part of the claim and that the statement was not executed for the purpose of delay, the water supply shall not be shut off until the claim has been judicially determined.

(c) Exception.—Prior to discontinuing service in a residential building as defined under the act of November 26, 1978 (P.L. 1255, No. 299)[4] known as the Utility Service Tenants Rights Act, a water utility shall comply with the provisions of that act.

(d) Failure of previous lessee to pay bill.—Nothing in this section shall be construed to authorize an authority or privately owned sewer or water company to shut off or deny water service to a lessee for failure of a previous lessee to pay a water or sewer service rate, rental or charge.

§ 503. Submission of water meter readings and flat-rate water bills.

A water utility shall, at the request of an authority, supply to the authority, on or before the 15th day of the month following the month during which water bills are issued, a list of all water meter readings and flat-rate water bills issued during the preceding calendar month and the basis of each flat-rate customer's water charge for use by the authority in calculating or computing its rentals, rates or charges for furnishing sewer, sewerage or sewage treatment service to the water customers.

§ 504. Billing and collecting agent.

(a) General rule.—A water utility may act as billing and collecting agents of a municipal authority which imposes rentals, rates or charges for use of a sewer, sewerage system or sewage treatment works upon owners or occupants of premises served by the water utility. Upon request of an authority, the water utility may include with its own bills for water or water service the rentals, rates and charges for sewer, sewerage and sewage treatment service. If the water utility agrees to do so, the added rentals, rates and charges shall be set forth separately from the charges for water or water service, but both shall be payable to and collected by the water utility and payment of either may be refused unless both are paid.

(b) Accounting.—The water utility shall, at least once each calendar quarter, account for and turn over the moneys it has collected to the authority imposing the rentals, rates and charges.

4. 68 P.S. §§ 399.1 et seq.

§ 505. Payment for billing and collecting services.

(a) General rule.—An authority imposing sewer, sewerage or sewage treatment rentals, rates or charges shall pay to a water utility the reasonable additional clerical and other expenses incurred in providing billing and collecting services.

(b) Shut-off service.—An authority, city, borough or township requesting and directing the shutoff of water shall also pay to the water utility the cost of the shut-off service and the estimated loss of water revenues resulting from such shutoff.

(c) Long-term agreements.—A water utility may enter into a long-term agreement with an authority for performing billing and collecting services and with an authority, city, borough or township for shut-off services. The agreement shall be binding on the utility, its successors and assigns.

(d) Disputes.—If a dispute arises between the utility and an authority, city, borough or township as to the cost of such services, the amount of revenues lost or the provisions of an agreement under this subsection, the dispute may be submitted by either party to the commission, whose decision, unless reversed on appeal, shall be final. This subsection shall not be construed to grant to the commission any other regulatory power or jurisdiction over counties, cities, boroughs, townships or authorities.

§ 506. Severability.

The provisions of this chapter are severable. If any provision is held to be unconstitutional, the decision shall not affect the validity of the remaining provisions, and it is declared as the intent of the General Assembly that this chapter would have been adopted had the unconstitutional provision not been included.

§ 507. Inconsistent repeals.

All acts and parts of acts are repealed to the extent that they are inconsistent with the provisions of this chapter.

CHAPTER 40
MISCELLANEOUS PROVISIONS

§ 4001. Repeals.

Repeals are as follows:

(1) The General Assembly declares that the repeal under paragraph (2) is necessary to effectuate Chapter 5.

(2) Act 1949-98 is repealed.[5]

§ 4002. Continuation.

Chapter 5 is a continuation of Act 1949-98. Except as otherwise provided in Chapter 5, all activities initiated under Act 1949-98 shall continue and remain in full force and effect and may be completed under Chapter 5. Orders, regulations, rules and decisions which were made under Act 1949-98 and which are in effect on the effective date of section 4001 shall remain in full force and effect until revoked, vacated or modified under Chapter 5.

5. 53 P.S. §§ 2261–2265 repealed.

CHAPTER 33

HOME RULE AND OPTIONAL PLANS GOVERNMENT

53 Pa.C.S. §§ 2901–3171

Chapter of Home Rule Charter and Optional Plans Law

GENERAL PROVISIONS

Subchapter

SUBCHAPTER A
PRELIMINARY PROVISIONS

53 Pa.C.S. §§ 2901–2902

Sec.

§ 2901. Short title and scope of subpart.

(a) Short title of subpart.—This subpart shall be known and may be cited as the Home Rule Charter and Optional Plans Law.

(b) Scope of subpart.—This subpart applies to all municipalities except cities of the first class and counties of the first class.

§ 2902. Definitions.

Subject to additional definitions contained in subsequent provisions of this subpart which are applicable to specific provisions of this subpart, the following words and phrases when used in this subpart shall have the meanings given to them in this section unless the context clearly indicates otherwise:

"Council" County commissioner, city council, borough council, town council, township commissioner in a township of the first class and supervisor in a township of the second class.

"Election officials." The county boards of elections.

"Electors." The registered voters of any municipality involved in proceedings relating to the adoption and repeal of optional forms of government.

"Governing body." Board of county commissioners, city council, borough or incorporated town council, commissioners of a township of the first class and supervisors of a township of the second class or their successor forms of government.

"Government study commission" or "commission." The body elected under the provisions of Subchapter B (relating to procedure for adoption of home rule charter or optional plan of government).

"Home rule charter." A written document defining the powers, structure, privileges, rights and duties of the municipal government and limitations thereon. The charter shall also provide for the composition and election of the governing body which in all cases shall be chosen by popular elections.

"Local municipality." Municipal corporation except a city of the first class.

"Nonresident." Any person or entity not a resident within the meaning of this subpart.

"Optional forms." Includes home rule charters and optional plans.

"Optional plans." Optional municipal powers, procedures and administrative structures as provided by this subpart.

"Rate of taxation." The amount of tax levied by a municipality on a permissible subject of taxation.

"Resident." Any person or other entity living in or maintaining a permanent or fixed place of abode in a municipality or conducting or engaging in a business for profit within a municipality.

"Subject of taxation." Any person, business, corporation, partnership, entity, real property, tangible or intangible personal property, property interest, transaction, occurrence, privilege, transfer, occupation or any other levy which is determined to be taxable by the General Assembly. The term shall not be construed to mean the rate of tax which may be imposed on a permissible subject of taxation.

SUBCHAPTER B
PROCEDURE FOR ADOPTION OF HOME RULE CHARTER OR OPTIONAL PLAN OF GOVERNMENT

53 Pa.C.S. §§ 2911–2930

Sec.

§ 2911. Submission of question for election of government study commission.

(a) General rule.—Whenever authorized by ordinance of the governing body or upon petition of the electors to the county board of electors of the county wherein the municipality is located, an election shall be held upon one of the following questions:

Shall a government study commission of (seven, nine or eleven) members be elected to study the existing form of government of the municipality, to consider the advisability of the adoption of an optional form of government and to recommend whether or not an optional plan of government should be adopted?

Shall a government study commission of (seven, nine or eleven) members be elected to study the existing form of government of the municipality, to consider the advisability of the adoption of a home rule charter and, if advisable, to draft and to recommend a home rule charter?

Shall a government study commission of (seven, nine or eleven) members be elected to study the existing form of government of the municipality, to consider the advisability of the adoption of an optional form of government or a home rule charter, to recommend the adoption of an optional form of government or to draft and recommend a home rule charter?

(b) Petition for election.—The petition calling for the election shall be in the form required by subsection (e) and shall be signed by electors comprising 5% of the number of electors voting for the office of Governor in the last gubernatorial general election.

(c) Ordinance authorizing election.—Within five days after the final enactment of an ordinance authorizing the election, the municipal clerk or secretary shall file a certified copy of the ordinance with the county board of elections, together with a copy of the question to be submitted to the electors.

(d) Duty of election board.—At the next general or municipal or primary election occurring not less than the 13th Tuesday after the filing of the ordinance or the petition with the county board of elections, it shall cause the appropriate question to be submitted to the electors as other questions are submitted under the act of June 3, 1937 (P.L. 1333, No. 320), known as the Pennsylvania Election Code.

(e) Requirements for petitions.—A referendum petition under this section shall be filed not later than the 13th Tuesday prior to the election, and the petition and the proceeding therein shall be in the manner and subject to the provisions of the election laws which relate to the signing, filing and adjudication of nomination petitions insofar as those provisions are applicable. No referendum petition may be signed or circulated prior to the 20th Tuesday before the election nor later than the 13th Tuesday before the election. No candidate's nomination petition may be signed or circulated prior to the 13th Tuesday before the election nor later than the tenth Tuesday before the election. Any petition under this section shall be filed on or before the tenth Tuesday before the election.

§ 2912. Election of members of commission.

(a) General rule.—A governmental study commission of seven, nine or eleven members, as designated in the question, shall be elected by the qualified voters at the same election the question is submitted to the electors.

(b) Nomination of candidates.—Each candidate for the office of member of the commission shall be nominated and placed upon the ballot containing the question in the manner provided by and subject to the provisions of the act of

June 3, 1937 (P.L. 1333, No. 320), known as the Pennsylvania Election Code, which relate to the nomination of a candidate nominated by nomination papers filed for other offices elective by the voters. Each candidate shall be nominated and listed without any political designation or slogan, and no nomination paper shall be signed or circulated prior to the 13th Tuesday before the election nor later than the tenth Tuesday before the election. No signature shall be counted unless it bears a date within this period.

(c) Instructions to electors.—Each elector shall be instructed to vote on the question and, regardless of the manner of his vote on the question, to vote for the designated number of members of a government study commission who shall serve if the question is or has been determined in the affirmative.

(d) Insufficient number of candidates or members.—If an insufficient number of nominating papers is filed to fill all of the designated positions on the study commission, the question of establishing a commission shall be placed on the ballot, and, unless a sufficient number of study commission members are elected by receiving at least as many votes as signatures are required to file a nominating position, then the question of creating a study commission shall be deemed to have been rejected.

§ 2913. Nomination of candidates.

(a) General rule.—All candidates for the government study commission shall be electors. Each candidate shall be nominated by nomination papers signed by a number of electors equal at least to 2% of the number of electors voting for the office of Governor in the last gubernatorial general election or 200 electors, whichever is less, and filed with the county board of elections not later than the tenth Tuesday prior to the date of the election.

(b) Content and signing of nomination papers.—Each nomination paper shall set forth the name, place of residence and post office address of the candidate thereby nominated, that the nomination is for the office of government study commissioner and that the signers are legally qualified to vote for the candidate. An elector may not sign nomination papers for more candidates for the commission than he could vote for at the election. Every elector signing a nomination paper shall write his place of residence, post office address and street number, if any, on the petition.

(c) Acceptance by candidate.—Each nomination paper shall, before it may be filed with the county board of elections, contain under oath of the candidate an acceptance of the nomination in writing, signed by the candidate therein nominated, upon or annexed to the paper, or, if the same person be named in more than one paper, upon or annexed to one of the papers. The acceptance shall certify that the candidate is an elector, that the nominee consents to run as a candidate at the election and that, if elected, the candidate agrees to take office and serve.

(d) Verification of nomination papers.—Each nomination paper shall be verified by an oath of one or more of the signers, taken and subscribed before a person qualified under the laws of this Commonwealth to administer an oath, to the effect that the paper was signed by each of the signers in his proper handwriting, that the signers are, to the best knowledge and belief of the affiant, electors and that the nomination paper is prepared and filed in good faith for the sole purpose of endorsing the person named therein for election as stated in the paper.

§ 2914. Results of election.

The result of the votes cast for and against the question as to the election of a government study commission shall be returned by the election officers, and a canvas of the election had, as is provided by law in the case of other public questions put to the electors. The votes cast for members of the commission shall be counted and the result returned by the county board of electors, and a canvas of the election had, as is provided by law in the case of election of members of municipal councils or boards. The designated number of candidates receiving the greatest number of votes shall be elected and shall constitute the commission. If a majority of those voting on the question vote against the election of a commission, none of the candidates shall be elected. If two or more candidates for the last seat shall be equal in number of votes, they shall draw lots to determine which one shall be elected.

§ 2915. Oath of office of members of commission.

(a) Members elected on country wide basis.—As soon as possible and in any event no later than ten days after its certification of election, the members of a government sudy commission elected on a countywide basis shall, before a judge of a court of common pleas, make oath to support the Constitution of the United States and the Constitution of Pennsylvania and to perform the duties of the office with fidelity.

(b) Other members.—As soon as possible and in any event no later than ten days after its certification of election, the members of a government study commission elected on other than a countywide basis shall, before a magisterial district judge, make oath to support the Constitution of the United States and the Constitution of Pennsylvania and to perform the duties of the office with fidelity.

§ 2916. First meeting of commission.

(a) Procedure.—As soon as possible and in any event no later than 15 days after its certification of election, the government study commission shall organize and hold its first meeting and elect one of its members chairman and another member vice chairman, fix its hours and place of meeting and adopt rules for the conduct of its business it deems necessary and advisable.

(b) Quorum.—A majority of the members of the commission shall constitute a quorum for the transaction of business, but no recommendation of the commission shall have any legal effect unless adopted by a majority of the whole number of the members of the commission.

§ 2917. Vacancies.

In case of a vacancy in the government study commission, the remaining members of the commission shall fill it by appointing thereto some other properly qualified elector.

§ 2918. Function and duty of commission.

The government study commission shall study the form of government of the municipality to compare it with other available forms under the laws of this Commonwealth and determine whether or not in its judgment the government could be strengthened or made more clearly responsible or accountable to the people or whether its operation could become more economical or efficient under a changed form of government.

§ 2919. Compensation and personnel.

(a) Compensation and expenses of members.—Members of the government study commission shall serve without compensation, but shall be reimbursed by the municipality for their necessary expenses incurred in the performance of their duties. Council shall appropriate moneys necessary for this purpose.

(b) Appointment and compensation of personnel.—Within the limits of the appropriations and other public and privately contributed funds and services made available to it, the commission may appoint one or more consultants and clerical and other assistants to serve at the pleasure of the commission and may fix reasonable therefor to be paid the consultants and clerical and other assistants.

Table of Contents
Part I Ch. 1–3 Ethics, Records, Open Meetings
Part II Ch. 4–10 Taxation
Part III Ch. 11–18 Torts, Contracts & Civil Rules
Part IV Ch. 19–24 Zoning & Planning
Part V Ch. 25–30 Construction and Emergency Codes
Part VI Ch. 31–39 Municipal Codes
Index

§ 2920. Hearings and public forums.

The government study commission shall hold one or more public hearings, may hold private hearings and sponsor public forums and generally shall provide for the widest possible public information and discussion respecting the purposes and progress of its work.

§ 2921. Report of findings and recommendations.

(a) General rule.—The government study commission shall report its findings and recommendations to the citizens of the municipality within nine months from the date of its election except that it shall be permitted an additional nine months if it elects to prepare and submit a proposed home rule charter and an additional two months if it chooses to elect its municipal council by districts. It shall publish or cause to be published sufficient copies of its final report for public study and information and shall deliver to the municipal clerk or secretary sufficient copies of the report to supply it to any interested citizen upon request. If the commission recommends the adoption of a home rule charter or any of the optional plans of government as authorized in this subpart, the report shall contain the complete plans as recommended.

(b) List of resources used.—There shall be attached to each copy of the report of the commission, as a part thereof, a statement sworn to by the members of the commission listing in detail the funds, goods, materials and services, both public and private, used by the commission in the performance of its work and the preparation and filing of the report. In addition, the list shall identify specifically the supplier of each item thereon.

(c) Filing copy with Department of Community and Economic Development.—A copy of the final report of the commission with its findings and recommendations shall be filed with the Department of Community and Economic Development.

(d) Disposition of records.—All the records, reports, tapes, minutes of meetings and written discussions of the commission shall, upon its discharge, be turned over to the municipal clerk or secretary for permanent safekeeping and made available for public inspection at any time during regular business hours.

§ 2922. Discharge of petition and amended reports.

(a) General rule.—The government study commission shall be discharged upon the filing of its report, but, if the commission's recommendations require further procedure in the form of a referendum on the part of the electors, the commission shall not be discharged until the procedure has been finally concluded. At any time prior to 60 days before the date of the referendum, the commission may modify or change any recommendation set forth in the final report by publishing an amended report.

(b) Effect of amended report.—Whenever a commission issues an amended report pursuant to subsection(a), the amended report shall supersede the final report and the final report shall cease to have any legal effect.

(c) Procedure under amended report.—The procedure to be taken under the amended report shall be governed by the provisions of this subpart applicable to the final report of a commission submitted pursuant to section 2921 (relating to report of findings and recommendations).

§ 2923. Types of action recommended.

The government study commission shall report and recommend in accordance with the question presented to the electorate as provided in section 2911 (relating to submission of question for election of government study commission):

(1) That a referendum shall be held to submit to the electors the question of adopting one of the optional plans of government authorized by this subpart to be specified by the commission.

(2) That a referendum shall be held to submit to the electors the question of adopting a home rule charter as prepared by the commission and as authorized by this subpart.

(3) That the form of government shall remain unchanged.

(4) Such other action as it deems advisable consistent with its functions as set forth in this subpart.

§ 2924. Specificity of recommendations.

(a) Optional plan of government.—

(1) If the government study commission report recommends the adoption or the amendment of any of the optional plans of government set forth in this subpart, except the optional county plan, the report of the commission may specify the following:

(i) That the municipal council shall consist of three, five, seven or nine members, except that under the small municipality plan and under the optional county plan the number of council members shall be as provided in sections 3073 (relating to election of council members) and 3092 (relating to county officers).

(ii) That the office of treasurer shall be omitted or that it shall be filled by election by the electors rather than by appointment.

(iii) That the office of controller shall be omitted or that it shall be filled by election by the electors rather than by appointment.

(2) If a commission report, initiative petition or ordinance shall recommend any optional plan, except for the optional county plan, it may specify that the then existing basis for electing council members shall be changed to an at-large or district or combination at-large and district basis.

(3) If a commission report, initiative petition or ordinance recommends the adoption of the council-manager form of government, it may specify that the mayor or president of council or chairman be elected directly by the electors rather than by council.

(4) If a commission report, initiative petition or ordinance for a county recommends that adoption of any of the optional plans, except the optional county plan, it may specify that the sheriff be elected directly by the voters of the county as provided in section 3094 (relating to additional options for election of county sheriff).

(5) In all cases, except for the council-manager plan, the commission report, initiative petition or ordinance shall specify whether the executive (mayor) shall be called "executive" or "mayor."

(b) Home rule charter.—If the commission recommends the adoption of a home rule charter, it shall specify the number to be on the municipal council, all offices to be filled by election and whether elections shall be on an at-large, district or combination district and at-large basis.

(c) Elections in new or revised districts.—Notwithstanding any other provisions of this subpart, if an approved home rule charter or optional plan of government or other form of government adopted pursuant to the provisions of this subpart specifies that the election of the municipal council shall be on an at-large or district or combination district and at-large basis and the basis recommended differs from the existing basis and therefore requires eliminating districts or establishing revised or new districts, then election of municipal officials shall not take place on the new basis until the municipal election following the next primary election taking place more than 180 days after the election at which the referendum on the question of a new form of government has been approved by the electorate. The new form of government shall not go into effect until the first Monday in January following the election of municipal officials on the new basis.

New or revised districts shall be established by the government study commission and included in the proposed charter.

§ 2925. Form of question on form of government.

The question to be submitted to the voters for the adoption of a home rule charter or any of the optional plans of government authorized by this subpart shall be submitted in one of the following forms or such part of them as shall be applicable.

Shall the Home Rule Charter contained in the report, dated (insert date), of the government study commission, prepared in accordance with the Home Rule Charter and Optional Plans Law, be adopted by the (insert type and name of municipality)?

Shall (insert name of plan), including recommendations pertaining to optional provisions contained in the report of the government study commission, dated (insert date), as authorized by the Home Rule Charter and Optional Plans Law, be adopted by the (insert type and name of municipality)?

Shall the (Home Rule Charter) (Optional Plan) of the (insert type and name of municipality) be repealed and the form of government recommended in the report of the government study commission, dated (insert date), be adopted as authorized by the Home Rule Charter and Optional Plans Law?

Shall an Optional Plan for the (insert type and name of municipality) be amended as specified in the report of the government study commission filed with the election officials of the County of (insert name of county), on (insert date), as authorized by the Home Rule Charter and Optional Plans Law?

§ 2926. Submission of question on form of government.

If the government study commission recommends that the question of adopting a home rule charter or one of the optional plans of government authorized by this subpart shall be submitted to the electors, the municipal clerk or secretary shall, within five days thereafter, certify a copy of the commission's report to the county board of elections, which shall cause the question of adoption or rejection to be placed upon the ballot or voting machines at the time as the commission specifies in its report. The commission may cause the question to be submitted to the electors at the next primary, municipal or general election occurring not less than 60 days following the filing of a copy of the commission's report with the county board of elections, at the time the commission's report directs. At the election, the question of adopting that form of government recommended by the commission shall be submitted to the electors by the county board of elections in the same manner as other questions are submitted to the electors under the act of June 3, 1937 (P.L. 1333, No. 320), known as the Pennsylvania Election Code. The commission shall frame the question to be placed upon the ballot as provided for in section 2925 (relating to form of question on form of government) and, if it deems appropriate, an interpretative statement to accompany the question.

§ 2927. Limitation on enactment of ordinance or filing of petition.

(a) General rule.—An ordinance may not be passed and a petition may not be filed for the election of a government study commission pursuant to section 2911 (relating to submission of question for election of government study commission) while proceedings are pending under any other petition or ordinance filed or passed under the authority of this subpart nor on the same question if it has been defeated within four years after an election has been held pursuant to any such ordinance or petition passed or filed.

(b) Time for commencement of proceedings.—For the purpose of this section, proceedings shall be considered as having started:

(1) In the case of an ordinance, upon the final vote of council in favor of

the ordinance, notwithstanding the fact that the ordinance cannot take effect until a certain number of days thereafter.

(2) In the case of a petition, as soon as it is properly signed by one-third of the number of registered voters required for the petition and written notice thereof filed in the office of the county board of elections and in the office of the municipal clerk or secretary, who shall cause the notice to be immediately posted in a conspicuous place in the office, open to public inspection.

§ 2928. Time when change of form of government takes effect.

Whenever the electors by a majority of those voting on the question vote in favor of adopting a change in their form of government pursuant to this subpart, the proposed form shall take effect according to its terms and the provisions of this subpart.

§ 2929. Limitation on changing new form of government.

The voters of any municipality which has adopted a home rule charter or an optional plan of government pursuant to this subpart may not vote on the question of changing the form of government until five years after the home rule charter or optional plan became effective.

§ 2930. Status of forms of government provided in subpart.

For the purposes of this subpart, each of the optional forms of government provided by this subpart and each of those optional forms as modified by any available provisions concerning size of council, election of municipal officials and the basis for electing councilmen is hereby declared to be a complete and separate form of government provided by the General Assembly for submission to the electors.

SUBCHAPTER C
AMENDMENT OF EXISTING CHARTER OR OPTIONAL PLAN
53 Pa.C.S. §§ 2941–2944

---

§ 2941. Procedure for amendment of charter or optional plan.

(a) Procedure.—The procedure for amending a home rule charter or optional plan of government shall be through the initiative procedure and referendum or ordinance of the governing body as provided for in this subpart.

(b) Changes in method of election.—Changes in the method of election of a municipal governing body from at-large elections to elections by district, maintain at-large elections or a combination of at-large elections and elections by district may be implemented by amending a home rule charter or optional plan without creation of a government study commission.

(c) Conflict in the question.—If two or more questions appear on the ballot at the same election and such questions are in conflict and more than one receives the approval of the voters, the question which receives the largest number of affirmative votes shall prevail over the others.

(d) Initial apportionment.—If the referendum on the question results in the approval by the voters to amend the home rule charter or optional plan to provide for the election of the governing body either by districts or partially by districts

Chap. 39 Res. During Mil. Service
Chap. 38 Intergov. Coop.
Chap. 37 3rd Class City Code
Chap. 36 Bor. Code
Chap. 35 2nd Class Twp. Code
Chap. 34 1st Class Twp. Code
Chap. 33 Home Rule Chart. Opt. Plans Law
Chap. 32 Water Serv. Act
Chap. 31 Munic. Auth. Act

and partially at large or in a change in the number of members of the governing body, the initial apportionment of the districts shall be made as follows:

(1) Except as provided in paragraph (2), by an apportionment commission consisting of seven members, all of whom shall reside in the municipality. Two members of the apportionment commission shall be appointed by the mayor. Two members of the apportionment commission shall be appointed by the governing body, one shall be appointed by the mayor from a list of at least three qualified persons recommended by the municipal committee of the political party whose mayoral candidate received the highest number of votes cast in the most recent mayoral election and one shall be appointed by the mayor from a list of at least three qualified persons recommended by the municipal committee of the political party whose mayoral candidate received the second highest votes in the most recent mayoral election. The seventh member of the commission shall be elected at large by a majority vote of the other six members and shall serve as chairperson of the commission.

(2) At the option of a municipality with a mayor, or for a municipality without a mayor, the initial apportionment shall be made by the members of the governing body of the municipality consistent with section 903 (relating to reapportionment by governing body).

(e) Subsequent apportionment.—For any municipality, including a municipality with a mayor, a subsequent apportionment shall be under Chapter 9 (relating to municipal reapportionment).

§ 2942. Initiation of amendment by electors or council.

A referendum on the question of amendment of a home rule charter or an optional plan of government may be initiated by petition of the electors or such a referendum may be initiated by an ordinance of the governing body. A proposal for amendment of an optional plan shall be limited to the additional options provided for in section 2924 (relating to specificity of recommendations).

§ 2943. Petition for referendum or ordinance proposing amendment.

(a) Filing.—A petition containing a proposal for referendum on the question of amending a home rule charter or an optional plan of government signed by electors comprising 10% of the number of electors voting for the office of Governor in the last gubernatorial general election in the municipality or an ordinance of the municipal governing body proposing amendment of a home rule charter or an optional plan shall be filed with the election officials not later than the 13th Tuesday prior to the next primary, municipal or general election. The petition and the proceedings therein shall be in the manner and subject to the provisions of the election laws which relate to the signing, filing and adjudication of nomination petitions insofar as such provisions are applicable, except that no referendum petition shall be signed or circulated prior to the 20th Tuesday before the election nor later than the 13th Tuesday before the election. The name and address of the person filing the petition shall be clearly stated on the petition.

(b) Review and disposition of petition.—The election officials shall review the initiative petition as to the number and qualifications of signers. If the petition appears to be defective, the election officials shall immediately notify the persons filing the petition of the defect. When the election officials find that the petition as submitted is in proper order, they shall send copies of the initiative petition without signatures thereon to the governing body and to the Department of Community and Economic Development. The initiative petition as submitted to the election officials, along with a list of signatories, shall be open to inspection in the office of the election officials.

§ 2944. Time and manner of submission of question.

A referendum on the question of the amendment of a home rule charter or an optional plan of government shall be held when the election officials find that the initiative petition or ordinance of the governing body is in proper order. The referendum shall be governed by the provisions of the act of June 3, 1937 (P.L. 1333, No. 320), known as the Pennsylvania Election Code. The election officials shall cause the question to be submitted to the electors at the next primary, general or municipal election occurring not less than the 13th Tuesday following the filing of the initiative petition or ordinance with county board of elections. At the election, the question shall be submitted to the voters in the same manner as other questions are submitted under the Pennsylvania Election Code. The county board of elections shall frame the question to be placed upon the ballot.

SUBCHAPTER D
CONDUCT OF ELECTION
53 Pa.C.S. §§ 2951–2952

§ 2951. Conduct and results of election.

All elections provided for in this subpart shall be conducted by the election officials for such municipality in accordance with the act of June 3, 1937 (P.L. 1333, No. 320), known as the Pennsylvania Election Code. The election officials shall count the votes cast and make return thereof to the county board of elections. The results of the election shall be computed by the county board of elections in the same manner as is provided by law for the computation of similar returns. Certificates of the results of the election shall be filed by the county board of elections with the municipal council or board, the Department of State and the Department of Community and Economic Development.

§ 2952. Notice of election.

At least 30 days' notice of each election provided for under this subpart shall be given by the clerk or secretary of the municipality. A copy of the notice shall be posted at each polling place on the day of the election and shall be published in at least one newspaper of general circulation in the municipality once a week for three consecutive weeks during the period of 30 days prior to the election.

SUBCHAPTER E
GENERAL POWERS AND LIMITATIONS OF HOME RULE CHARTER MUNICIPALITIES
53 Pa.C.S. §§ 2961–2967

§ 2961. Scope of powers of home rule.

A municipality which has adopted a home rule charter may exercise any powers and perform any function not denied by the Constitution of Pennsylvania, by statute or by its home rule charter. All grants of municipal power to municipalities governed by a home rule charter under this subchapter, whether in the form of specific enumeration or general terms, shall be liberally construed in favor of the municipality.

§ 2962. Limitation on municipal powers.

(a) Powers granted by statute.—With respect to the following subjects, the home rule charter shall not give any power or authority to the municipality contrary to or in limitation or enlargement of powers granted by statutes which are applicable to a class or classes of municipalities:

(1) The filing and collection of municipal tax claims or liens and the sale of real or personal property in satisfaction of them.

(2) The proceudres in the exercise of the powers of eminent domain and the assessment of damages and benefits for property taken, injured or destroyed.

(3) Boundary changes.

(4) Regulation of public schools.

(5) The registration of electors and the conduct of elections.

(6) The fixing of subjects of taxation.

(7) The fixing of the rates of nonproperty or personal taxes levied upon nonresidents.

(8) The assessment of real or personal property and persons for taxation purposes.

(9) Defining or providing for the punishment of any felony or misdemeanor.

(10) Municipal planning under the act of July 31, 1968 (P.L.805, No.247), known as the Pennsylvania Municipalities Planning Code.

(11) The procedure for the filling of vacancies in the office of district attorney.[1]

(b) Taxing powers.—Unless prohibited by the Constitution of Pennsylvania, the provisions of this subpart or any other statute or its home rule charter, a municipality which has adopted a home rule charter shall have the power and authority to enact and enforce local tax ordinances upon any subject of taxation granted by statute to the class of municipality of which it would be a member but for the adoption of a home rule charter at any rate of taxation determined by the governing body. No home rule municipality shall establish or levy a rate of taxation upon nonresidents which is greater than the rate which a municipality would have been authorized to levy on nonresidents but for the adoption of a home rule charter. The governing body shall not be subject to any limitation on the rates of taxation imposed upon residents.

(c) Prohibited powers.—A municipality shall not:

(1) Engage in any proprietary or private business except as authorized by statute.

(2) Exercise powers contrary to or in limitation or enlargement of powers granted by statutes which are applicable in every part of this Commonwealth.

(3) Be authorized to diminish the rights or privileges of any former municipal employee entitled to benefits or any present municipal employee in his pension or retirement system.

---

1. Section 2 of Act of Mar. 23, 2021, P.L. 35, No. 9 provides: "The addition of 53 Pa.C.S. § 2962(a)(11) is intended to preempt and supersede any contrary provision in a county home rule charter, ordinance or local administrative code."

(4) Enact or promulgate any ordinance or regulation with respect to definitions, sanitation, safety, health, standards of identity or labeling pertaining to the manufacture, processing, storage, distribution and sale of any foods, goods or services subject to any Commonwealth statutes and regulations unless the municipal ordinance or regulation is uniform in all respects with the Commonwealth statutes and regulations thereunder. This paragraph does not affect the power of any municipality to enact and enforce ordinances relating to building codes or any other safety, sanitation or health regulation pertaining thereto.

(5) Enact any provision inconsistent with any statute heretofore enacted prior to April 13, 1972, affecting the rights, benefits or working conditions of any employee of a political subdivision of this Commonwealth.

(d) Reduction of police force.—Notwithstanding any provision of this subpart or any other statute to the contrary, any municipality that is or was a city of the second class A may reduce its police force or its firefighting force for economic reasons, as determined by ordinance.

(e) Statutes of general application.—Statutes that are uniform and applicable in every part of this Commonwealth shall remain in effect and shall not be changed or modified by this subpart. Such statutes shall supersede any municipal ordinance or resolution on the same subject.

(f) Regulation of business and employment.—A municipality which adopts a home rule charter shall not determine duties, responsibilities or requirements placed upon businesses, occupations and employers, including the duty to withhold, remit or report taxed or penalties levied or imposed upon them or upon persons in their employment, except as expressly provided by statutes which are applicable in every part of this Commonwealth or which are applicable to all municipalities or to a class or classes of municipalities. This subsection shall not be construed as a limitation in fixing rates of taxation on permissible subjects of taxation.

(g) Regulation of firearms.—A municipality shall not enact any ordinance or take any other action dealing with the regulation of the transfer, ownership, transportation or possession of firearms.

(h) Levying taxes.—This section does not limit or take away any right of a municipality which adopts a home rule charter from levying any tax which it had the power to levy had it not adopted a home rule charter.

(i) Establishment of rates of taxation.—No provision of this subpart or any other statute shall limit a municipality which adopts a home rule charter from establishing its own rates of taxation upon all authorized subjects of taxation except those specified in subsection (a)(7).

(j) Retroactive fee increase prohibited.—A municipality which adopts a home rule charter may not retroactively increase any fee or charge for any municipal service which has been provided.

§ 2963. Exercise of municipal powers by home rule county.

A county which has adopted a home rule charter shall not at any time thereafter exercise within any municipality in the county a power or function being exercise by that municipality, except under all of the following conditions:

(1) The exercise of such powers or function by the county shall be authorized by ordinance of the governing body of the county, which ordinance, in addition to such other filings as may be required by law, shall be filed with the clerk or secretary of each local municipality within the county within 30 days of its enactment.

(2) The tranfer of a power or function to the county from any local municipality within the county, as authorized by the ordinance, shall not become effective for at least 15 months from the date of adoption of the ordinance.

(3) Within 120 days from the adoption of the ordinance, the governing body of any local municipality, exercising on the date of the adoption of the ordinance any power or function authorized by ordinance of the county to be exercised by

Table of Contents
Part I Ch. 1–3 Ethics, Records, Open Meetings
Part II Ch. 4–10 Taxation
Part III Ch. 11–18 Torts, Contracts & Civil Rules
Part IV Ch. 19–24 Zoning & Planning
Part V Ch. 25–30 Construction and Emergency Codes
Part VI Ch. 31–39 Municipal Codes
Index

the county, may elect by ordinance to be excluded from the county's exercise of the power or function. Within 60 days after the date of adoption by the governing body of a local municipality of an ordinance excluding the local municipality from the exercise by the county of a power or function or in the absence of any action of the governing body, the qualified electors of the local municipality may initiate a petition requiring that the question of inclusion or exclusion from the exercise of the power or function by the county be submitted to a referendum of the electorate at the election held on the date of the next ensuing primary, municipal or general election not less than 60 days after the filing of the initiative petition with the county board of elections. The initiative and referendum procedures set forth in this subchapter or Subchapter F (relating to general provisions and limitations for optional plan municipalities) shall be followed, except where the same may be inconsistent with any of the provisions of this section. In the event the county determines there is insufficient interest or that it is not feasible to establish the proposed municipal function or power as provided for in the ordinance passed by the county, the county may repeal the county ordinance prior to the effective date of the ordinance.

(4) The governing body of any local municipality may by ordinance, subsequent to the time limit for action as set forth in paragraph (3), request the county to be included in a municipal power or function being exercised by the county. However, the county may specify the terms and conditions for acceptance or denial of the power or function requested by the local municipality to be exercised by the county, which shall be subject to court review if the local municipality determines that the terms and conditions as set forth by the county are unreasonable.

(5) No assessment, tax, fee or levy in the nature thereof made by the governing body of a county in support of the exercise of a power or function as authorized by ordinance of the county shall be applicable in any local municipality within the county which is providing the same municipal power or function.

(6) If the electors of a local municipality by referendum vote to exclude the local municipality from the exercise of a power or function by the county, a petition may not be initiated nor may a referendum be held on the same question more often than every five years thereafter.

(7) A local municipality may, by action of the governing body or by initiative and referendum, withdraw from a power or function which it was exercising at the date of the adoption of the county home rule charter which it transferred to a county, provided it again assumes and exercises the power or function, but may not vote on the question of withdrawing sooner than four years from the time the county assumed the power or function of the local municipality.

§ 2964. General powers of municipalities.

Municipalities adopting a home rule charter shall have the power to:

(1) Sue and be sued.

(2) Have a corporate seal.

(3) Contract and be contracted with.

(4) Buy, sell, lease, hold and dispose of real and personal property.

(5) Appropriate and expend moneys.

(6) Adopt, amend and repeal any ordinances and resolutions as may be required.

§ 2965. Recording and filing of charter.

The municipal clerk or secretary shall have the new charter as approved by the qualified electors recorded in the ordinance books and shall also file a certified copy of the charter with the Department of State, the Department of Community and Economic Development and the county board of elections.

§ 2966. Continuation of office of existing elective officials.

All elective officials in office at the time of the adoption of a home rule charter shall continue in office until their terms expire.

§ 2967. Repeal of home rule charter.

(a) General rule.—The procedure for repeal of a home rule charter shall be the same as for adoption of a home rule charter. Whenever the electors, by a majority vote of those voting on the question, vote in favor of repeal of a home rule charter and the establisment of a particular form of government, the municipality shall be governed under the form of government selected by the electors from the first Monday of January following the municipal election at which the elective officials of the form of government selected by the electors shall have been elected. The government study commission shall provide in its report for the new form of government to be established.

(b) Election of new officials.—The elective officials under a new form of government selected by the electors shall be elected at the first municipal election held after the referendum on the repeal of a home rule charter or at a late date as may be specified by the commission in its report.

SUBCHAPTER F
GENERAL PROVISIONS AND LIMITATIONS FOR OPTIONAL PLAN MUNICIPALITIES
53 Pa.C.S. §§ 2971–2974

Sec.

---

§ 2971. Law applicable to optional plan.

Upon the adoption by the electors of any of the optional plans of government as set forth in this subpart, the municipality shall thereafter be governed by the plan adopted and by the provisions of general law applicable to that class or classes of municipality except as otherwise provided in this subpart. Until the municipality adopts another form of government, the plan adopted and the provisions of general law applicable to that class or classes of municipality shall be law. All statutes affecting the organization, government and powers of the municipality which are not inconsistent or in conflict with this subpart shall remain in full force until modified or repealed.

§ 2972. Recording and filing of plan.

The municipal clerk or secretary shall immediately cause the new plan of government as adopted to be recorded in the ordinance book of the municipality and shall also file a certified copy thereof with the Department of State, the Secretary of Community and Economic Development and the county board of elections.

§ 2973. Scope of powers of optional plan.

The general grant of municipal power under this subpart is intended to confer the greatest power of self government consistent with the Constitution of Pennsylvania and with the provisions of and the limitations prescribed by this subpart. Any specific enumeration of municipal powers contained in this subpart

Table of Contents
Part I Ch. 1–3 Ethics, Records, Open Meetings
Part II Ch. 4–10 Taxation
Part III Ch. 11–18 Torts, Contracts & Civil Rules
Part IV Ch. 19–24 Zoning & Planning
Part V Ch. 25–30 Construction and Emergency Codes
Part VI Ch. 31–39 Municipal Codes
Index

or in other statutes does not limit the general description of power contained in this subpart. Any specifically enumerated municipal powers are in addition and supplementary to the powers conferred in general terms by this subchapter. All grants of municipal power to municipalities governed by an optional plan under this subpart, whether in the form of specific enumeration or general terms, shall be liberally construed in favor of the municipality.

§ 2974. Limitation on powers of optional plan.

The optional plan of any municipality adopted in accordance with this subpart shall not give any power or authority to diminish any rights or privileges of any present municipal employee in his pension or retirement system. No municipality shall exercise any powers or authority beyond the municipal limits except those conferred by statute, and no municipality shall engage in any proprietary or private business except as authorized by the General Assembly.

SUBCHAPTER G
MISCELLANEOUS PROVISIONS
53 Pa. C.S. § 2981–2983

Sec.

---

§ 2981. Limitation on local municipality.

No local municipality within a county shall supersede or exercise any power, function or service presently exercised by the county.

§ 2982. Retention of existing form of government.

Each municipality which does not adopt a home rule charter or an optional plan under this subpart shall retain its existing form of government as otherwise provided by law.

§ 2983. Retention of existing form of government when electors disapprove proposal.

In case the electors of any municipality disapprove a proposal to adopt a home rule charter or an optional plan of government, the municipality shall retain its existing form of government.

§ 2984. Assumption of functions previously assumed by other municipality.

(a) Assumption of indebtedness.—A municipality assuming a function previously performed by another municipality under the terms of this subchapter shall also assume all the indebtedness and obligations of the municipality relating to the function. If property, indebtedness or obligations of another municipality not within the boundaries of the municipality assuming the function is involved, the governing bodies of the respective municipalities shall make an adjustment and apportionment of all public property involved.

(b) Procedure for adjustment and apportionment.—The adjustment and apportionment shall be reduced to a written agreement which shall be filed with the court of common pleas of the county and the Department of Community and Economic Development.

(c) Petition for adjustment and apportionment.—In case the municipalities cannot make an amicable adjustment and apportionment of the property, obligations and indebtedness within six months after the function is assumed, any of the municipalities may present a petition to the court of common pleas. The court shall then appoint three disinterested commissioners, all residents and taxpayers of the county, but none residing in or owners of real property in any of the municipalities. After hearing, notice of which shall be given to the municipalities as the court shall direct, the commissioners shall file a report with the court making an adjustment and apportionment of all the property as well as the obligations or indebtedness. The report shall state the amount that shall be due and payable from each municipality, the forms of payment and the amount of obligations and indebtedness that shall be assumed by each.

(d) Notice to municipalities.—The commissioners shall give the municipalities at least five days' written notice of the filing of their report. Unless exceptions are filed to the report within 30 days after the date of the filing, the report shall be confirmed by the court absolutely. Any sum awarded by the report shall be a legal and valid claim in its favor against the municipality charged. Any real or personal property given to a municipality shall become its property. Any claim or indebtedness charged against the municipality may be collected from it.

(e) Exceptions to report.—If exceptions are filed to the report of the commissioners, the court shall dispose of them, taking testimony if it deems advisable. The court shall enter its decree confirming the award of the commissioners or modifying the same as appears just and proper.

(f) Compensation to commissioners.—The commissioners shall be allowed any compensation and expenses for their services as the court shall fix. The costs of the proceedings, including the compensation and expenses of the commissioners, shall be apportioned by the court between the municipalities as it deems proper.

(g) Jurisdiction of court.—If a municipality or part of a municipality is located in two or more counties, the court of common pleas of the county where the larger part of the municipality assuming the function is located shall have exclusive jurisdiction over the proceedings.

CHAPTER 30
TYPES OF OPTIONAL PLANS OF GOVERNMENT

53 Pa.C.S. §§ 3001–3018

Subchapter
A. Executive (Mayor)—Council Plan A
B. Executive (Mayor)—Council Plan B
C. Executive (Mayor)—Council Plan C
D. Council—Manager Plan
E. Small Municipality Plan
F. Optional County Plan

SUBCHAPTER A
EXECUTIVE (MAYOR)—COUNCIL PLAN A

53 Pa.C.S. §§ 3001–3018

Sec.
3001. Designation and applicability of plan.
3002. Officers and employees.
3003. Election and term of office of officials.
3004. Election and term of office of council members.
3005. First election of council members.
3006. Legislative power vested in council.
3007. Organization of council.

Table of Contents | Part I Ch. 1–3 Ethics, Records, Open Meetings | Part II Ch. 4–10 Taxation | Part III Ch. 11–18 Torts, Contracts & Civil Rules | Part IV Ch. 19–24 Zoning & Planning | Part V Ch. 25–30 Construction and Emergency Codes | Part VI Ch. 31–39 Municipal Codes | Index

§ 3001. Designation and applicability of plan.

The form of government provided in this subchapter shall be known as the "Executive (Mayor)—Council Plan A" and shall, together with the laws applicable to that class of municipality and Subchapter F of Chapter 29 (relating to general provisions and limitations for optional plan municipalities) and Chapter 31 (relating to general provisions common to optional plans), govern any municipality the electors of which adopted it under this subpart.

§ 3002. Officers and employees.

Each municipality under this subchapter shall be governed by an elected council, an elected executive who may be called mayor, as determined by the government study commission, an elected district attorney in the case of counties and, when recommended by the commission and adopted by the voters, an elected treasurer, an elected controller and by such other officers and employees as may be duly appointed pursuant to this subchapter or other applicable law.

§ 3003. Election and term of office of officials.

The executive (mayor), the treasurer, if elected, the district attorney in the case of counties and the controller, if elected, shall be elected by the electors at a regular municipal election and shall serve for a term of four years beginning on the first Monday of January next following his election.

§ 3004. Election and term of office of council members.

The council shall consist of five members unless, under the authority granted under section 2924 (relating to specificity of recommendations), the municipality shall be governed by a council of three, seven or nine members. Members of the council shall be elected at large by the electors unless, under the authority granted pursuant to section 2924, members shall be elected on a district basis in which each district is as equal in population as is feasible, or on a combination at-large and district basis as determined by the government study commission, or as specified in an initiative petition or ordinance of the governing body under the provisions of sections 2942 (relating to initiation of amendment by electors or council), 2943 (relating to petition for referendum or ordinance proposing amendment) and 2944 (relating to time and manner of submission of question) at a regular municipal election and shall serve for a term of four years, except as otherwise provided in this subchapter, beginning on the first Monday of January next following their elections.

§ 3005. First election of council members.

At the first municipal election following the adoption of this plan, council members shall be elected and shall serve for the terms as provided in section 3162 (relating to status and term of office of officials).

§ 3006. Legislative power vested in council.

The legislative power of the municipality as provided by laws applicable to that class of municipality shall be exercised by the municipal council, except as may otherwise be provided for under this subpart.

§ 3007. Organization of council.

On the first Monday of January following the regular municipal election, the members of council shall assemble at the usual place of meeting, organize and elect a president from among its members who shall preside at its meetings and perform such other duties as council may prescribe and a vice president who shall preside in the absence of the president. If the first Monday is a legal holiday, the meeting shall be held on the next day.

§ 3008. Powers of council concerning officers and agencies.

The council, in addition to other powers and duties as may be conferred upon it by general law, may require any municipal officer to prepare and submit sworn statements regarding the performance of the officer's official duties and may otherwise investigate the conduct of any department, office or agency of the municipal government.

§ 3009. Appointment and duties of municipal clerk or secretary.

A municipal clerk or secretary shall be appointed in the manner set forth in the adminstrative ordinance as provided pursuant to section 3146 (relating to passage of administrative ordinance). The municipal clerk or secretary shall serve as clerk of the council, keep its minutes and records of its proceedings, maintain and compile its ordinances and resolutions as this subpart requires and perform such functions as may be required by law or by local ordinance. The municipal clerk shall, prior to the appointment, have been qualified by training or experience to perform the duties of the office.

§ 3010. Executive power vested in executive.

The executive power of the municipality shall be exercised by the executive (mayor).

§ 3011. Powers and duties of executive.

The executive (mayor) shall enforce the plan and ordinances of the municipality and all general laws applicable to them. The executive shall, annually, report to the council and the public on the work of the previous year and on the condition and requirements of the municipal government and shall from time to time make these recommendations for action by the council as he deems in the public interest. He shall supervise the departments of the municipal government and shall require each department to make annual and other reports of its work as he deems desirable.

§ 3012. Approval or veto of ordinances.

(a) General rule.—Ordinances adopted by the council shall be submitted to the executive (mayor) who shall, within ten days after receiving any ordinance, either approve the ordinance by affixing his signature thereto or veto the ordinance by delivering it to the municipal clerk together with a statement setting forth his objections. The clerk shall immediately notify the council of the veto. No ordinance or any item or part thereof shall take effect without the executive's (mayor's) approval unless the executive (mayor) fails to return an ordinance to the clerk within ten days after it has been presented to him or unless council upon reconsideration of the veto on or after the third day following its return by the executive (mayor) shall override the executive's (mayor's) veto by a vote of a majority plus one of the members.

(b) Attendance at meetings of council.—The executive (mayor) may attend meetings of council and may take part in discussions of council but shall have no

Chap. 39 Res. During Mil. Service
Chap. 38 Intergov. Coop.
Chap. 37 3rd Class City Code
Chap. 36 Bor. Code
Chap. 35 2nd Class Twp. Code
Chap. 34 1st Class Twp. Code
Chap. 33 Home Rule Chart. Opt. Plans Law
Chap. 32 Water Serv. Act
Chap. 31 Munic. Auth. Act

vote except in the case of a tie on the question of filling a vacancy in the council, in which case he may cast the deciding vote.

§ 3013. Mayor, departments and department heads.

(a) Inability of executive to perform duties.—The executive (mayor) shall designate any department head to act as executive (mayor) whenever the executive (mayor) shall be prevented, by absence from the municipality, disability or other cause, from attending to the duties of his office. During such time, the person so designated by the executive (mayor) shall possess all the rights, powers and duties of the executive (mayor). Whenever the executive (mayor) had been unable to attend to the duties of his office for a period of 60 consecutive days for any of the reasons stated in this subsection, a member of council shall be appointed by the council as acting executive (mayor), who shall succeed to all the rights, powers and duties of the executive (mayor) or the then acting executive (mayor), until he shall return or his disability ceases.

(b) Establisment and exercise of functions of department.—The municipality may have a department of administration and shall have such other departments as council may establish by ordinance. All of the administrative functions, powers and duties of the municipality, other than those vested in the office of the clerk, treasurer, if elected, and controller, shall be assigned among and within the departments.

(c) Appointment and term of department heads and solicitors.—Each department shall be headed by a director who shall be appointed by the executive (mayor) with the advice and consent of the council. Each municipality shall also have a solicitor who shall be appointed by the executive (mayor) with the advice and consent of the council. Each department head and the solicitor shall serve during the term of office of the executive (mayor) appointing him and until the appointment and qualification of his successor. No member of municipal council shall head a department.

(d) Removal of department head.—The executive (mayor) may remove any department head after notice and an opportunity to be heard. Prior to removing a department head, the executive (mayor) shall first file written notice of his intention with the council. The removal shall become effective 20 days after the filing of the notice.

(e) Department officers and employees.—Department heads shall appoint subordinate officers and employees within their departments under procedures established in section 3122 (relating to appointment of subordinate officers and employees).

§ 3014. Department of administration.

(a) Department heads.—Where a department of administration is established, it shall be headed by a director. The director shall be chosen solely on the basis of his executive and administrative qualifications with special reference to his actual experience in or his knowledge of accepted practice in respect to the duties of his office. At the time of appointment, the director need not be a resident of the municipality or this Commonwealth. He shall have, exercise and discharge the functions, powers and duties of the department.

(b) Department functions.—The department, under the direction and supervision of the executive (mayor), shall have the following powers and duties:

(1) To assist in the preparation of the budget.

(2) To administer a centralized purchasing system.

(3) To establish and administer a centralized personnel system.

(4) To establish and maintain a centralized accounting system which shall be so designed as to accurately reflect the assets, liabilities, receipts and expenditures of the municipality.

(5) To perform any other duties as council may prescribe through the administrative ordinance or as the executive (mayor) may direct.

§ 3015. Budget.

The municipal budget shall be prepared by the executive (mayor) with the assistance of the director of the department of administration or other officer designated by the executive (mayor).

§ 3016. Form and adoption of budget.

The budget shall be in the form required by council and shall have appended to it a detailed analysis of the various items of expenditure and revenue. The budget as submitted and adopted shall be balanced. Council may reduce any item or items in the executive's (mayor's) budget by a vote of a majority of the council, but an increase in any item or items therein shall become effective only upon an affirmative vote of a majority plus one of the members of council. Council shall, upon the introduction of the proposed budget, fix a date for adoption which shall except as otherwise provided be not later than December 31 immediately following.

§ 3017. Amended budget.

During January next following any municipal election, the executive (mayor) may submit an amended budget to council. Council shall consider it in the same manner as provided in section 3016 (relating to form and adoption of budget), but final consideration of the amended budget shall be completed by February 15 of the same year.

§ 3018. Council amendments to budget.

Council may amend the budget during January next following any municipal election. Final adoption of the amended budget shall be completed by February 15 of the same year.

SUBCHAPTER B
EXECUTIVE (MAYOR)—COUNCIL PLAN B

53 Pa.C.S. §§ 3031–3033

---

§ 3031. Designation and applicability of plan.

The form of government provided in this subchapter shall be known as the "Executive (Mayor)—Council Plan B" and shall, together with Subchapter F of Chapter 29 (relating to general provisions and limitations for optional plan municipalities). Subchapter A of Chapter 30 (relating to executive (mayor)—council plan A) and Subchapter A of Chapter 31 (relating to officers and employees), with the exception of section 3013(b) (relating to mayor, departments and department heads), govern any municipality the voters of which have adopted it pursuant to this subpart.

§ 3032. Departments.

The municipality shall have a department of administration and shall have such other departments as council may establish by ordinance. The adminstrative functions, powers and duties of the municipality, other than those vested in the office of the clerk, treasurer and controller, if provided for, shall be allocated and assigned among and within the departments except that the functions specified in section 3014 (relating to department of administration) shall be assigned to the department of administration.

§ 3033. Mandatory department of administration.

Under Executive (Mayor)—Council Plan B a department of administration shall be established.

SUBCHAPTER C
EXECUTIVE (MAYOR)—COUNCIL PLAN C
53 Pa.C.S. §§ 3041–3043

Sec.

§ 3041. Designation and applicability of plan.

The form of government provided in this subpart shall be known as the "Executive (Mayor) - Council Plan C" and shall, together with Subchapter F of Chapter 29 (relating to general provisions and limitations for optional plan municipalities), Subchpter A of Chapter 30 (relating to executive (mayor) Council plan A) and Subchapter A of Chapter 31 (relating to officers and employees), with the exception of section 3011 (relating to powers and duties of executive), govern any municipality the voters of which have adopted it pursuant to this subpart.

§ 3042. Powers and duties of exective.

The executive (mayor) shall enforce the plan and ordinances of the municipality and all general laws applicable thereto. The executive shall, annually, report to the council and the public on the work of the previous year and on the condition and requirements of the municipal government and shall from time to time make those recommendations for action by the council he deems in the public interest.

§ 3043. Appointment and duties of managing director.

(a) General rule.—The executive (mayor) shall appoint, with the advice and consent of the council, a managing director who shall supervise the departments of government and who shall be the contact officer between the mayor and the departments. The managing director shall make periodic report with those recommendations as he deems appropriate to the executive (mayor) concerning the affairs of municipal government and particularly of the departments.

(b) Removal.—The executive (mayor) may remove a managing director after notice and an opportunity to be heard. Prior to removing a managing director, the executive (mayor) shall first file written notice of his intention with the council. The removal shall become effective 20 days after the filing of the notice.

SUBCHAPTER D
COUNCIL—MANAGER PLAN
53 Pa.C.S. §§ 3051–3064

Sec.

---

§ 3051. Designation and applicability of plan.

The form of government provided in this subchapter shall be known as the "Council-Manager Plan" and shall, together with Subchapter F of Chapter 29 (relating to provisions and limitations for optional plan municipalities) and Subchapter A of Chapter 31 (relating to officers and employees), govern any municipality the voters of which have adopted this plan pursuant to this subpart.

§ 3052. Officers and employees.

Each municipality under this subchapter shall be governed by an elected council, one member of which shall be the mayor or president of council or chairman chosen under section 2924 (relating to specificity of recommendations) and 3056 (relating to selection of mayor, council president or chairman), an elected district attorney in the case of counties and an appointed municipal manager, and, if so provided under the plan, an elected treasurer, an elected controller and by those other officers and employees as may be duly appointed pursuant to this subchapter, general law or ordinance.

§ 3053. Election and term of office of elected officials.

The district attorney in the case of counties and the teasurer and controller, if provided for and if elected, shall be elected by the electors at a regular municipal election and shall serve for a term of four years beginning the first Monday of January next following the election.

§ 3054. Election and term of office of council members.

The municipal council shall consist of five members unless, under the authority granted pursuant to section 2924 (relating to specificity of recommendations), the municipality shall be governed by a council of three, seven or nine members. Members of the municipal council shall be elected at large by the electors unless, pursuant to the authority granted under section 2924, members shall be elected on a district basis in which each district is as equal in population as is feasible, or on a combination at-large and district basis as determined by the charter study commission or as specified in an initiative petition or ordinance of the governing body under the provisions of sections 2942 (relating to initiation of amendment by electors or council), 2943 (relating to petition for referendum or ordinance proposing amendment) and 2944 (relating to time and manner of submission of question), at a regular municipal election. The members shall serve for a term of four years, except as provided in this subchapter, beginning on the first Monday of January next following their election.

§ 3055. First election of council members.

At the first municipal election following the adoption by a municipality of this charter plan, council members shall be elected and shall serve for the terms as provided in section 3162 (relating to status and term of office of officials).

Table of Contents
Part I Ch. 1–3 Ethics, Records, Open Meetings
Part II Ch. 4–10 Taxation
Part III Ch. 11–18 Torts, Contracts & Civil Rules
Part IV Ch. 19–24 Zoning & Planning
Part V Ch. 25–30 Construction and Emergency Codes
Part VI Ch. 31–39 Municipal Codes
Index

§ 3056. Selection of mayor, council president or chairman.

(a) General rule.—On the first Monday of January following the municipal election, the members of the municipal council shall assemble at the usual place of meeting, organize and elect one of their number as mayor or president of council or chairman unless otherwise provided. The mayor or president of council or chairman shall be chosen by ballot by majority vote of all members of the municipal council. If the members shall be unable, within five ballots to be taken within two days of the organization meeting, to elect a mayor or president of council or chairman, then the member who in the election for members of the municipal council received the greatest number of votes shall be the mayor, president of council or chairman. If that person declines to accept the office, then the person receiving the next highest vote shall be the mayor, president of council or chairman and so on until the office is filled. The mayor or president of council or chairman shall preside at all meetings of the municipal council and shall have a voice and vote in its proceedings.

(b) Election of mayor.—On the recommendation of the government study commission as provided under section 2924 (relating to specificity of recommendations) or as specified in an initiative petition or ordinance of the governing body as authorized by sections 2942 (relating to initiation of amendment by electors or council), 2943 (relating to petition for referendum or ordinance proposing amendment) and 2944 (relating to time and manner of submission of question), the mayor shall be elected directly by the electors at the regular municipal election in lieu of being chosen as provided in subsection (a).

§ 3057. Appointment and duties of municipal clerk or secretary.

A municipal clerk or secretary shall be appointed in the manner set forth in the administrative ordinance as provided in section 3146 (relating to passage of administrative ordinance). The municipal clerk or secretary shall serve as clerk of the council, keep its minutes and records of its proceedings, maintain and compile its ordinances and resolutions as this subpart requires and perform any functions as may be required by law or ordinance. The municipal clerk shall, prior to his appointment, have been qualified by training or experience to perform the duties of the office.

§ 3058. Powers and duties of council.

(a) General rule.—All powers as provided by laws applicable to that class of municipality shall be vested in the municipal council, except as otherwise provided by this subchapter, and the council shall provide for the exercise thereof and for the performance of all duties imposed on the municipality by law.

(b) Adoption of administrative ordinance.—The council shall by ordinance adopt an administrative ordinance defining the responsibilities of the municipal departments and agencies as it deems necessary and proper for the efficient conduct of municipal affairs.

(c) Appointment of municipal manager.—The municipal council shall appoint a municipal manger. The office of municipal manager and municipal clerk or secretary may be held by the same person.

(d) Investigations.—The council may make investigations into the affairs of the municipality and the conduct of any municipal department, office or agency.

(e) Administrative departments, boards and offices.—The municipal council shall continue or create and determine and define the powers and duties of any executive and administrative departments, boards and offices, in addition to those provided for in this subpart, as it deems necessary for the proper and efficient conduct of the affairs of the municipality, including the office of deputy manager. Any department, board or office so continued or created may be abolished by the municipal council. No member of municipal council shall head an administrative department.

(f) Additional powers and limitations.—It is the intention of this subchapter that the municipal council shall act in all matters as a body, and it is contrary to the spirit of this subchapter for any of its members to seek individually to influence the official acts of the municipal manager or any other officer, or for the council or any of its members to direct or request the appointment of any person to or his removal from office, or to interfere in any way with the performance by the officers of their duties. The council and its members shall deal with the administrative service solely through the municipal manager and shall not give orders to any subordinates of the municipal manager, either publicly or privately. This subchapter does not prevent the municipal council from appointing committees of its own members or of citizens to conduct investigations into the conduct of any officer or department, or any matter relating to the welfare of the municipality, and delegating to those committees such powers of inquiry as the municipal council deems necessary.

§ 3059. Qualifications of municipal manager.

The municipal manager shall be chosen by the council on the basis of his executive and administrative qualifications. At the time of his appointment, he need not be a resident of the municipality or this Commonwealth. The municipal manager shall not hold any elective governmental office.

§ 3060. Removal of municipal manager from office.

The municipal manager shall be appointed for an indefinite term and may be removed by a majority vote of the council. At least 30 days before the removal becomes effective, the council shall notify the municipal manager of its decision to remove him from office, by a majority vote of its members, stating the reasons for his removal. The municipal manager may reply in writing and may request a public hearing which shall be held not earlier than 20 days nor later than 30 days after filing of the request. After the public hearing, if one is requested, and after full consideration, the council by majority vote of its members may adopt a final resolution of removal. By the preliminary resolution, the council may suspend the municipal manager from duty but may in any case cause to be paid immediately any unpaid balance of his salary and his salary for the next three calendar months.

§ 3061. Inability of municipal manager to perform duties.

The municipal manager may designate a qualified administrative officer of the municipality to perform his duties during his temporary absence or disability. In the event of his failure to make a designation or if the absence or disability continues more than 30 days, the council may appoint an officer of the municipality to perform the duties of the manager during the absence or disability until the manager returns or his disability ceases.

§ 3062. Powers and duties of municipal manager.

The municipal manager shall have the following powers and duties:

(1) To be the chief executive and administrative official of the municipality.

(2) To execute all laws and ordinances.

(3) To appoint and remove department heads and the deputy manager, if one is authorized by council, and appoint subordinate officers and employees under procedures established in section 3122 (relating to appointment of subordinate officers and employees).

(4) To negotiate contracts for the municipality, subject to the approval of the municipal council, make recommendations concerning the nature and location of municipal improvements and execute municipal improvements as determined by the municipal council.

(5) To assure that all terms and conditions imposed in favor of the municipality or its inhabitants in any statute, public utility franchise or other con-

tract are faithfully kept and performed and, upon knowledge of any violation, to call the same to the attention of the municipal council.

(6) To prepare the agenda for and attend all meetings of the municipal council with the right to take part in the discussions, but without the right to vote.

(7) To make such recommendations to the council concerning policy formulation as he deems desirable and keep the council and the public informed as to the conduct of municipal affairs.

(8) To prepare and submit the annual budget to the council together with such explanatory comment as he deems desirable and to administer the municipal budget.

(9) To perform such other duties as may be required of the municipal manager by ordinance or resolution of the municipal council.

(10) To be responsible to the council for carrying out all policies established by it and for the proper administration of all affairs of the municipality within the jurisdiction of the council.

§ 3063. Preparation and adoption of budget.

The municipal manager shall submit to council his recommended budget, together with any explanatory comment or statement he deems desirable. The budget shall be in such form as is required by council for municipal budgets and shall in addition have appended thereto a detailed analysis of the various items of expenditure and revenue. The budget as submitted and adopted shall be balanced. Council shall upon introduction of the proposed budget fix a date for adoption thereof which shall be not later than December 31 immediately following submission.

§ 3064. Amended budget.

During January next following any municipal election, council may request the manager to submit an amended budget to council which shall consider it in the same manner as provided in section 3063 (relating to preparation and adoption of budget), except that final adoption of the amended budget shall not be later than February 15 of the same year.

SUBCHAPTER E
SMALL MUNICIPALITY PLAN

53 Pa.C.S. §§ 3071–3080

Sec.

§ 3071. Designation and applicability of plan.

The form of government provided in this subchapter shall be known as the "Small Municipality Plan." It may be adopted by any municipality having a population of less than 7,500 inhabitants by the last Federal census. The plan, together with Subchapter F of Chapter 29 (relating to general provisions and limitations for optional plan municipalities) and Subchapter A of Chapter 31 (relating to officers and employees), shall govern any municipality the voters of which have adopted it pursuant to this subpart.

§ 3072. Officers.

Each municipality shall be governed by an elected executive (mayor) and council member, an elected district attorney in the case of counties and, if so provided under the plan, an elected treasurer or elected controller and any other officers as shall be appointed pursuant to this subchapter, general law or ordinance.

§ 3073. Election of council members.

The council shall consist of the executive (mayor), who shall by elected at large, and two council members unless pursuant to the authority granted under section 2924 (relating to specificity of recommendations) the municipality is governed by an executive (mayor) and four council members, an executive (mayor) and six council members or an executive (mayor) and eight council members. Members of the council shall be elected at large unless the plan provides that members shall be elected on a distict basis in which each district is as equal in population as is feasible or on a combination at-large and district basis as determined by the government study commission or as specified in an initiative petition or ordinance of the coverning body under the provisions of sections 2942 (relating to initiation of amendment by electors or council). 2943 (relating to petition for referendum or ordinance proposing amendment) and 2944 (relating to time and manner of submission of question) at a regular municipal election by the voters of the municipality. The members of the council shall serve a term of four years beginning on the first Monday in January next following their election, except as provided in this subpart.

§ 3074. Organization of council.

On the first Monday of January following the regular municipal election, the members of the council shall assemble at the usual place of meeting and organize. The executive (mayor) shall preside at all meetings of the council and shall have a voice and vote on its proceedings. The council shall select from among its members a president of the council who shall serve in place of the executive (mayor) in the event of his absence or disability.

§ 3075. Powers and duties of council.

The legislative power of the municipality shall be exercised by the council, except as may be otherwise provided by general law. A majority of the whole number of the council shall constitute a quorum for the transaction of business, but a smaller number may meet and adjourn from time to time.

§ 3076. Municipal clerk or secretary, solicitor and agencies.

(a) Municipal clerk or secretary.—A municipal clerk or secretary shall by appointed in the manner set forth in the administrative ordinance, as provided pursuant to section 3146 (relating to passage of administrative ordinance). The municipal clerk or secretary shall serve as clerk of the council, keep its minutes and records of its proceedings, maintain and compile its ordinances and resolutions as this subpart requires and perform any functions as may be required by law. The clerk shall, prior to his appointment, have been qualified by training or experience to perform the duties of the office.

(b) Solicitor and agencies.—The council may, consistent with statutes applicable to that class of municipality, provide for the manner of appointment of a solicitor, any planning board, zoning board of adjustment, zoning hearing board or personnel board in the municipality and may create commissions and other bodies with advisory powers.

§ 3077. Powers and duties of executive.

The executive power of the municipality shall be exercised by the executive (mayor). The executive shall see that all laws and ordinances in force and effect within the municipality are observed. He shall address the council and report to the residents, annually and at any other times as he deems desirable, on the condition of the municipality and upon its problems of government. The executive (mayor) shall also appoint a finance committee of the council, which shall consist of one or more council members, and may appoint and designate other committees of council of similar composition.

§ 3078. Appointment of officers and employees by executive.

The executive (mayor) shall appoint subordinate officers and employees with the advice and consent of council under procedures established in section 3122 (relating to appointment of subordinate officers and employees), except that, in counties, the office of prothonotary and clerk of courts, register of wills and clerk of orphans court shall be filled by appointment by the president judge of the appropriate court with advice and consent of a majority of the council.

§ 3079. Preparation and adoption of budget.

The municipal budget shall be prepared by the executive (mayor) and shall be submitted to council in the form required by council. The budget as submitted and adopted shall be balanced. Council shall, upon introduction of the proposed budget, fix a date for adoption thereof which shall be not later than December 31 immediately following.

§ 3080. Amended Budget.

During the month of January next following any municipal elections, the executive (mayor), upon his own initiative or at the request of council, may submit an amended budget to council which shall consider it in the same manner as provided in section 3079 (relating to preparation and adoption of budget), except that final adoption of the amended budget shall not be later than February 15 of the same year.

SUBCHAPTER F
OPTIONAL COUNTY PLAN
53 Pa.C.S §§ 3091–3095

Sec.

§ 3091. Designation and applicability of plan.

The form of government provided in this subpart shall be known as the "Optional County Plan" and shall, together with Subchapter F of Chapter 29 (relating to general provisions and limitations for optional plan municipalities) and Subchapter A of Chapter 31 (relating to officers and employees), govern any county the voters of which have adopted this plan pursuant to this subpart. This option shall be available only to counties.

§ 3092. County officers.

(a) Enumeration.—The county officers shall be as follows:

(1) County commissioner.

(2) Controller or auditor.

(3) District attorney.

(4) Public defender.

(5) Treasurer.

(6) Sheriff.

(7) Register of wills.

(8) Recorder of deeds.

(9) Prothonotary.

(10) Clerk of the courts.

(b) Election and term of office.—County officers, except for public defenders, who shall be appointed as provided by law shall be elected at the municipal election and shall hold their offices for the term of four years, beginning on the first Monday of January next after their election, and until their successors are duly qualified. Vacancies shall be filled in the manner provided by law.

(c) Salaries and fees.—County officers shall be paid only by salary as provided by law for services performed for the county or any other governmental unit. Fees incidental to the conduct of county office shall be payable directly to the county or the Commonwealth or as otherwise provided by law.

(d) County commissioners.—Three county commissioners shall be elected in each county. In the election of these officers, each qualified elector shall vote for not more than two persons, and the three persons receiving the highest number of votes shall be elected.

(e) Coroner or medical examiner.—The coroner or medical examiner shall be a statutory office elected at the municipal election and shall hold the office for the term of four years, beginning on the first Monday of January next after election, and until his successor is duly qualified. He shall be paid only by salary as provided by law. Vacancies shall be filled in the manner provided by law.

(f) Jury commissioner.—Jury commissioners shall be statutory officers and shall be elected at the municipal election and shall hold their office for the term of four years, beginning on the first Monday of January next after election, and until their successors are duly qualified. The salary board shall fix the salary of the jury commissioners. Vacancies in the office of jury commissioner shall be filled by the president judge of the court of common pleas.

§ 3093. Powers.

All county officers may exercise those powers granted by general law to county offices of the class of county to which it belongs.

§ 3094. Additional options for election of county sheriff.

A government study commission created and constituted as provided in Subchapter B of Chapter 29 (relating to procedure for adoption of home rule charter or optional plan of government) for counties or an initiative petition or ordinance of the governing body as authorized by sections 2942 (relating to initiation of amendment by electors or council). 2943 (relating to petition for referendum or ordinance proposing amendment) and 2944 (relating to time and manner of submission of question) may recommend and cause to be placed on the ballot, as a part of the question submitted to the voters for approval, additional options as part of the optional plans as set forth in this chapter providing for the election of the county sheriff.

§ 3095. Approval of plan.

If the optional plan, including an additional option or options as provided in section 3091 (relating to designation and applicability of plan), is approved by the

Table of Contents
Part I Ch. 1–3 Ethics, Records, Open Meetings
Part II Ch. 4–10 Taxation
Part III Ch. 11–18 Torts, Contracts & Civil Rules
Part IV Ch. 19–24 Zoning & Planning
Part V Ch. 25–30 Construction and Emergency Codes
Part VI Ch. 31–39 Municipal Codes
Index

voters, the county shall be governed by the provisions of the subchapter providing the basic optional plan and by the provisions of Subchapter F of Chapter 29 (relating to general provisions and limitations for optional plan municipalities) and Subchapter A of Chapter 31 (relating to officers and employees), except that the elected sheriff shall be subject to the provisions pertaining to that office as provided in this subchapter.

CHAPTER 31
GENERAL PROVISIONS COMMON TO OPTIONAL PLANS
53 Pa.C.S. §§ 3101–3171

SUBCHAPTER A
OFFICERS AND EMPLOYEES
53 Pa.C.S. § 3101–3104

---

§ 3101. Adverse interest in contracts for purchase or services.

(a) General rule.—If a municipal officer or official elected or appointed knows or by the exercise of reasonable diligence should know that he is interested to any appreciable degree, either directly or indirectly, in any contract for the sale or furnishing of any personal property for the use of the municipality or for any services to be rendered for the municipality involving the expenditure of more than $300 in any year, he shall notify council. Any such contract shall not be passed and approved by council except by an affirmative vote of at least three-fourths of the members. If the interested officer is a member of council, he shall refrain from voting upon the contract.

(b) Exception.—This section does not apply to cases where the officer or official is an employee of the person, firm or corporation to which money is to be paid in a capacity with no possible influence on the transaction and in which he cannot possibly be benefited either financially or in any other material manner.

(c) Penalties.—Any officer or official who knowingly violates this section shall be liable to the municipality upon his bond, if any, or personally, to the extent of the damage to be sustained by the municipality, and to ouster from office and commits a misdemeanor of the third degree and shall, upon conviction, be sentenced to pay a fine not exceeding $500, or imprisonment not exceeding one year, or both.

§ 3102. Acceptance of services at more favorable terms.

An officer or employee shall not accept or receive, directly or indirectly, from any person operating within the territorial limits of a municipality any

Chap. 39 Res. During Mil. Service
Chap. 38 Intergov. Coop.
Chap. 37 3rd Class City Code
Chap. 36 Bor. Code
Chap. 35 2nd Class Twp. Code
Chap. 34 1st Class Twp. Code
Chap. 33 Home Rule Chart. Opt. Plans Law
Chap. 32 Water Serv. Act
Chap. 31 Munic. Auth. Act

interurban railway, bus line, street railway, gas works, waterworks, electric light or power plant, heating plant, telegraph line, telephone exchange or other business using or operating under a public franchise, any frank, free pass, free ticket or free service or accept or receive, directly or indirectly, from any person any other service upon terms more favorable than is granted to the public generally, except that the prohibition of free transportation shall not apply to police officers or firefighters in uniform. Free service to the municipal officials provided by any franchise or ordinance shall not be affected by this section.

§ 3103. Gift or promise of thing of value to influence political support.

(a) General rule.—A candidate for office, appointment or employment or an officer, appointee or employee in any municipality shall not, directly or indirectly, give or promise to any person any office, position, employment, benefit or anything of value for the purpose of influencing or obtaining the political support, aid or vote of any person.

(b) Penalty—Any person who violates subsection (a) shall be disqualified to hold the office or employment to which he may be or may have been elected or appointed.

§ 3104. Refusal or failure to appear or testify before court.

Any person elected or appointed to any office or position in a municipality govered under this subpart who, after lawful notice or process, willfully refuses or fails to appear before any court, any legislative committee or the Governor, or having appeared refuses to testify or to answer any question regarding the property, government or affairs of the municipality or regarding his nomination, election, appointment or official conduct on the ground that his answer would tend to incriminate him, or refuses to waive immunity from prosecution on account of any matter in relation to which he may be asked to testify, may be removed from office by the council of the municipality.

SUBCHAPTER B
TREASURER

53 Pa. C.S. §§ 3111

Sec.

---

§ 3111. Selection and duties of municipal treasurer.

(a) General rule.—Under any of the optional plans as set forth in this subpart, except for the plan set forth in Subchapter F or Chapter 30 (relating to optional county plan), the office of municipal treasurer may be omitted or may be filled by appointment or by election, as provided in the plan. If the office of municipal treasurer is to be filled by appointment, the appointment shall be made in accordance with the appointment procedures for other department heads.

(b) Powers and duties of elected treasurer.—The municipal treasurer, if elected, shall perform the functions and duties and have the powers relating to the collection, receiving, safekeeping and payment over of public moneys, including municipal, county, institution district and school district taxes, as provided by law and shall have any other functions, powers and duties assigned to him by the executive of the municipality.

SUBCHAPTER C
APPOINTMENT POWER AND PERSONNEL

53 Pa. C.S. §§ 3121–3122

---

§ 3121. Appointment of members of boards and commissions.

The appointment power of the chief executive of the municipality under any of the plans authorized by this subpart shall include the appointment of members of boards and commissions authorized by this subpart, by law or by action of municipal council. All such appointments shall be with the advise and consent of a majority of municipal council.

§ 3122. Appointment of subordinate officers and employees.

(a) General rule.—Appointments and promotions of subordinate officers and employees within departments shall be made by the department head on the basis of a personnel system which shall include written procedures for appointment and promotion based on merit and fitness as demonstrated by examination or other evidence of competence for the position.

(b) Personnel rules.—The personnel system shall be governed by personnel rules which shall be prepared by the executive (mayor) or manager and submitted to the municipal council which shall adopt them with or without amendments unless otherwise provided for or arrived at by collective bargaining. The personnel rules may provide for:

(1) The classification of all municipal positions, based on the duties, authority and responsibility of each position, with adequate provision for reclassification of any position whenever warranted to change of circumstances.

(2) A pay plan for all municipal positions.

(3) Methods for determining the merit and fitness of candidates for appointment or promotion.

(4) The policies and procedures regulating reduction in force and disciplinary action, including suspension and removal of employees.

(5) The hours of work and provisions for sick and vacation leave and holidays and overtime compensation.

(6) Grievance procedures, including procedures for the hearing of grievances.

(7) Other practices and procedures necessary to the administration of the municipal personnel system.

SUBCHAPTER D
FILLING VACANCIES IN ELECTED OFFICE

53 Pa.C.S. §§ 3131–3132

---

§ 3131. Applicability of subchapter.

This subchapter shall apply to the filling of vacancies in elected office in all optional plans and options except those set forth in Subchapter F of Chapter 30 (relating to optional county plan).

§ 3132. Manner of filling vacancies in office.

(1) Members of council.—

(1) If a vacancy exists in the municipal council, the municipal council shall, by a majority of its remaining members, fill the vacancy within 30 days thereafter by electing a qualified person to serve until that first Monday of January when his successor is duly sworn into office for the remainder of the term of the person originally elected to the office. The successor shall be elected at the next municipal election occurring at least 50 days after the vacancy begins.

(2) In case vacancies should exist whereby the offices of a majority or more members of the municipal council becomes vacant, the remaining members shall fill the vacancies, one at a time, giving each new appointee reasonable notice of his appointment as will enable him to meet and act with the then qualified member or members of the municipal council in making further appointments until a bare majority of members of municipal council members have been qualified. At that time these members shall appoint persons to fill the remaining vacancies at a meeting attended by the majority members of municipal council, such appointees to receive a majority of the votes of the members present at the meeting. Each person seleted to fill the vacancy or vacancies shall hold his office as provided in this subsection.

(3) If, by reason of a tie vote or otherwise, the vacancy shall not have been filled by the remaining members of municipal council within the time as limited in this subsection, the court of common pleas upon the petiion of ten or more qualified electors shall fill the vacancy by the appointment of a qualified person for the portion of the unexpired term as provided in this subsection.

(b) Others Officers.—

(1) If a vacancy occurs in the office of executive (mayor), municipal treasurer, if elected, municipal controller, if elected, county district attorney or county sheriff, if elected, the municipal council shall fill the vacancy within 30 days thereafter by choosing an executive (mayor), a municipal treasurer, a municipal controller, a county district attorney or a county sheriff, as the case may be, to serve until his successor is elected by the qualified electors at the next municipal election occurring at least 50 days after the vacancy occurs and is duly sworn into office. The person so elected shall serve from the first Monday of January next succeeding his election for the remainder of the term of the person originally elected to the office.

(2) If, by reason of a tie vote or otherwise, a vacancy in the office of executive (mayor), treasurer, controller, county district attorney or county sheriff has not been filled by council within the time as limited in this subsection, the court of common pleas, upon petition of ten or more qualified electors, shall fit the vacancy by the appointment of a qualified person for the portion of the unexpired term as provided in this subsection.

SUBCHAPTER E
LEGISLATION BY COUNCIL

53 Pa. C.S. §§ 3141–3146

Sec.

---

§ 3141. Regular and special meetings of council.

The council shall, by ordinance or resolution, designate the time of holding regular meetings which shall be at least monthly. The executive (mayor) or the president of council may and, upon written request of a majority of the members of the council, shall call a special meeting of the council. In the call, he shall designate the purpose of the special meeting and no other business shall be considered. All meetings of the council shall be open to the public. The municipal clerk or secretary shall keep a journal of its proceedings and record the minutes of every meeting.

§ 3142. Procedure and functions of council.

(a) Rules of procedure.—Council shall determine its own rules of procedure, not inconsistent with ordinance or statute. A majority of the whole number of members of the council shall constitute a quorum, and no ordinance shall be adopted by the council without the affirmative vote of a majority of all the members of the council.

(b) Adoption of ordinances and resolutions.—Each ordinance or resolution shall be presented and considered as determined by council rules of procedure. The vote upon every motion, resolution or ordinance shall be taken by roll call, and the yeas and nays shall be entered on the minutes. The minutes of each meeting shall be signed by the officer presiding at the meeting and by the municipal clerk or secretary.

(c) Administrative ordinance.—Council shall adopt by ordinance an administrative ordinance which shall provide for the establishment and filling of additional administrative offices which it deems necessary and shall provide for administrative procedures not otherwise provided for in this subpart or by general law.

(d) Compensation of controller and treasurer.—The compensation of the controller and treasurer shall be fixed by the council.

§ 3143. Adoption of ordinances.

(a) General rule.—Except as may otherwise be provided in this subpart, all ordinances shall be adopted and published as provided by law. Any ordinance may incorporate by reference any standard technical regulation or code, official or unofficial, which need not be so published whenever ten copies of the regulations or code have been placed on file in the office of the municipal clerk or secretary and in the office of the body or department charged with the enforcement of the ordinance.

(b) Effective date.—No ordinance, other than the local budget ordinance, shall take effect less than ten days after its final passage by council and approval by the executive (mayor) where that approval is required, unless the council adopts a resolution declaring an emergency and at least a majority plus one of all the members of the council vote in favor of the resolution.

§ 3144. Recording and compilation of ordinances and resolutions.

The municipal clerk or secretary shall record all ordinances and resolutions adopted by council and, at the close of each year, with the advice and assistance of the municipal solicitor, shall bind, compile or codify all the ordinances and resolutions or true copies thereof which then remain in force and effect. He shall also properly index, the record books, compilation or codification of ordinances and resolutions.

§ 3145. Filing and publication of rules and regulations.

No rule or regulation made by any department, officer, agency or authority of the municipality, except as it relates to the organization or internal management of the municipal government or a part thereof, shall take effect until it is filed either with the municipal clerk or secretary or in any other manner provided by ordinance. The council shall provide for the prompt publication of such rules and regulations.

§ 3146. Passage of administrative ordinance.

The council shall prepare and pass an administrative ordinance which shall provide for the manner of appointment of a solicitor, clerk or secretary, may create commissions and other bodies with advisory powers and may include additional provisions relating to the internal structure of the municipality as long as the provisions of the administrative ordinance are not in conflict with this subpart.

SUBCHAPTER F
AUDIT AND CONTROL

53 Pa.C.S. §§ 3151–3153

§ 3151. Exercise of financial management control functions.

The council shall provide by separate ordinance or in the administrative ordinance for the exercise of a control function in the management of the finances of the municipality by the municipal controller or an independent auditor or, in the case of the optional plan set forth in Subchapter F of Chapter 30 (relating to optional county plan), by the controller or auditors.

§ 3152. Post audits by independent auditor.

The council may provide for annual post audits of all accounts by an independent auditor who shall be a ceritified public accountant registered in this Commonwealth or a firm of certified public accountants registered in this Commonwealth.

§ 3153. Selection of controller.

Under any of the optional plans as set forth in this subpart, except for the plans set forth in Subchapter F of Chapter 30 (relating to optional county plan), the office of controller may be omitted or it may be filled by election by the electors rather than by appointment when recommended by the government study commission and adopted by the electors. If the office of controller is to be filled by appointment, a controller shall be appointed for an indefinite term by a majority of the members of the governing body.

SUBCHAPTER G
TRANSITION TO OPTIONAL PLAN GOVERNMENT

53 Pa. C.S. §§ 3161–3166

Sec.

---

§ 3161. Applicability of plan.

Whenever the electors of a municipality adopt any of the optional plans provided by this subpart at any election for that purpose, the municipality shall be governed under the provisions of that plan, the provisions of law applicable to that class of municipality and this subpart from the first Monday in January following the municipal election occuring after the next succeeding primary election, except as provided in section 2924 (c) (relating to specificity of recommendations).

§ 3162. Status and term of office of officials.

(a) Existing elected official.—Any elected municipal official in office at the time of the adoption of any optional plan provided by this subpart shall continue in office only until the new plan of government goes into effect as provided in section 3161 (relating to applicability of plan), except as otherwise provided in subsections (c) and (d).

(b) Members of council.—At the municipal election next succeeding the adoption of one of the optional plans provided for in this subpart, if four or fewer council members are elected, they shall serve for terms of four years. If five are elected, the four successful candidates receiving the highest percentage of the votes cast for the office to which they are elected shall serve for terms of four years, and the candidate receiving the next highest percentage of votes shall serve for a term of two years. If six or more council members are elected, the five candidates receiving the highest percentage of the votes cast for the office to which they are elected shall serve for terms of four years, and the remaining successful candidates receiving the next highest percentage of votes shall serve for terms of two years. Thereafter, all council members shall be elected for terms of four years. Where the term of office for council members under the adopted plan is different from the term of office for council members under an existing form of government, the terms of office for council members so elected shall be established so that, at each subsequent municipal election at which council members are elected, the number of council members to be elected shall be as nearly equal as possible to the number of council members to be elected at every other regular municipal election at which council members are elected.

(c) Treasurer, controller, district attorney and sheriff.—If an elected municipal treasurer or elected municipal controller, elected county district attorney or elected county sheriff is in office at the time of the adoption of an optional plan under the provisions of this subpart, a treasurer, controller, district attorney or sheriff, as the case may be, shall not be elected or appointed to take office until after the resignation, death, removal or expiration of the term of the incumbent in the office. At the expiration of the term of the incumbent, a treasurer, controller, district attorney or sheriff, as the case may be, shall be elected or appointed for the full term for the office as provided by the optional plan adopted.

(d) Continuation of existing members of council in office.—Any member of a municipal governing body in office at the time of the adoption of an optional plan shall remain in office, continuing as an at-large or district council member, as the case may be, until the expiration of this term in office and shall receive the compensation provided by law at that time:

(1) If that council member was elected on an at-large basis, the newly adopted optional plan provides for a total number of at-large council members equal to or exceeding the total number of at-large council members under the existing form of government.

(2) If that council member was elected on a district basis, the district from which that council member was elected remains unchanged and continues to encompass the exact same georgraphical area under the newly adopted optional plan as under the existing form of government and the number of council members to be elected from that district under the newly adopted optional plan is equal to or exceeds the number elected from that district under the existing form of government.

Any council member may, by writing filed with the municipal treasurer, direct that any portion of his annual compensation for serving in office be returned to the municipal treasury. For the purpose of this section, an executive or mayor who is also a member of the council under an existing plan shall be considered as a member of the council, and, after the new plan goes into effect, his duties shall be only those of a member of council as prescribed by the new plan.

(e) Number of members of council to be elected.—At the municipal election next succeeding the adoption of one of the optional plans provided for in this subpart, the number of council members prescribed by the terms in the plan less the number of council members then in office whose terms do not expire on the first Monday of January next following, as may be determined by subsection (d), shall be elected.

(f) Filling vacancies on council existing prior to election.—If there are vacancies in council occurring by reason of resignation, death or removal 90 days or more before the election, they shall be filled for the remainder of the term of the person originally elected to that office.

§ 3163. Compensation of elected officials.

(a) Officials elected prior to transition year.—The annual compensation of the executive (mayor) and council members elected to their offices in the year prior to the transition year under any of the optional plans, except the plan set forth in Subchapter F of Chapter 30 (relating to optional county plan), adopted pursuant to this subpart shall be established by the commission as part of its recommendations or by the initiative petition or ordinance of the governing body authorized by sections 2942 (relating to initiation of amendment by electors or council), 2943 (relating to petition for referendum or ordinance proposing amendment) and 2944 (relating to time and manner of submission of question).

(b) Officials elected subsequent to transition.—The compensation of the executive (mayor), council members, controller and treasurer elected to their offices subsequent to the transition to any of the optional plans set forth in this subpart, except for the plan set forth in Subchapter F of Chapter 30, shall be fixed by ordinance of council adopted at least two days prior to the last day fixed by law for candidates to withdraw their names from nomination previous to the municipal election. After the compensation is fixed by ordinance, only an increase or decrease thereof need to be fixed by the ordinance.

Chap. 39 Res. During Mil. Service
Chap. 38 Intergov. Coop.
Chap. 37 3rd Class City Code
Chap. 36 Bor. Code
Chap. 35 2nd Class Twp. Code
Chap. 34 1st Class Twp. Code
Chap. 33 Home Rule Chart. Opt. Plans Law
Chap. 32 Water Serv. Act
Chap. 31 Munic. Auth. Act

§ 3164. Status of existing ordinances and resolutions.

On the effective date of an optional plan adopted pursuant to this subpart, all ordinances and resolutions of the municipality to the extent that they are not inconsistent with the provisions of this subpart shall remain in full force and effect.

§ 3165. Abolishment of existing appointive offices.

(a) General rule.—On the effective date of an optional plan adopted pursuant to this subpart, all appointive offices then existing in such municipality shall be abolished and the terms of all appointed officers shall immediately cease and terminate. This section does not abolish the office or terminate the terms of office of any alderman or constable or of any official or employee now protected by any tenure of office or civil service law or of any police officer or firefighter whether or not protectrd by a tenure of office law.

(b) Use of resolution to govern interim proceedings.—Provisions for officers and for the organization and administration of the municipal government under the optional plan may be made by resolution pending the adoption of ordinances, but any such resolution shall expire not later than 60 days after the effective date of the optional plan.

§ 3166. Pending actions and proceedings.

All actions and proceedings of a legislative, executive or judicial character, pending upon the effective date of an optional plan, may continue. The appropriate officer or employee under the optional plan shall be substituted for the officer or employee exercising or discharging the function, power or duty involved in the action or proceeding before the effective date.

SUBCHAPTER H
REPEAL OF OPTIONAL PLAN
53 Pa C.S. §§ 3171

Sec.

§ 3171. Repeal of optional plan and establishment of new form of government.

(a) General rule.—The procedure for repeal of an optional plan shall be the same as for adoption of an optional plan as provided in Subchapter B of Chapter 29 (relating to procedure for adoption of home rule charter or optional plan of government), excluding the procedure provided in sections 2942 (relating to initiation of amendment by electors or council), 2943 (relating to petition for referendum or ordinance proposing amendment) and 2944 (relating to time and manner of submission of question). Whenever the electors, by a majority vote of those voting on the question, vote in favor of repeal of an optional plan and the establishment of a particular form of government, the municipality shall be governed under the form of government selected by the electors. The form of government so approved shall take effect on the first Monday of January following the municipal election at which the elective officials of the form of government selected by the electors shall have been elected. The government study commission shall provide in its report for the new form of government to be established.

(b) Amendment procedure.—This section does not prohibit or limit the procedure provided in sections 2942, 2943 and 2944 to amend an optional plan.

CHAPTER 34

FIRST CLASS TOWNSHIP CODE

53 P.S. §§ 55101 to 58502

Act of Jun. 24, 1931, P.L. 1206, No. 331 Cl. 73
(Reenacted and amended May 27, 1949, P.L.1955, No.569)

Concerning townships of the first class; amending, revising, consolidating, and changing the law relating thereto.

Compiler's Note: Section 2 of Act 209 of 1990 provided that Act 331 is repealed insofar as it is inconsistent with Act 209.

Compiler's Note: Section 1 of Act 165 of 1970 provided that the limits heretofore imposed by Act 331 upon the rates of interest for such bonds, obligations or indebtedness. and interest costs permitted to be paid upon bonds, obligations and indebtedness issued by the Commonwealth or its agencies or instrumentalities or authorities, and by local political subdivisions or their agencies or authorities, are hereby removed for such bonds, obligations or indebtedness.

Compiler's Note: Section 31 of Act 708 of 1961 provided that Act 331 is repealed insofar as it relates to the licensing and regulation of auctioneers.

TABLE OF CONTENTS

FIRST CLASS TOWNSHIP CODE

Table of Contents
Part I Ch. 1–3 Ethics, Records, Open Meetings
Part II Ch. 4–10 Taxation
Part III Ch. 11–18 Torts, Contracts & Civil Rules
Part IV Ch. 19–24 Zoning & Planning
Part V Ch. 25–30 Construction and Emergency Codes
Part VI Ch. 31–39 Municipal Codes
Index

Chap. 39 Res. During Mil. Service
Chap. 38 Intergov. Coop.
Chap. 37 3rd Class City Code
Chap. 36 Bor. Code
Chap. 35 2nd Class Twp. Code
Chap. 34 1st Class Twp. Code
Chap. 33 Home Rule Chart. Opt. Plans Law
Chap. 32 Water Serv. Act
Chap. 31 Munic. Auth. Act

The General Assembly of the Commonwealth of Pennsylvania hereby enacts as follows:

ARTICLE XXXI-A
UNIFORM CONSTRUCTION CODE, PROPERTY MAINTENANCE CODE AND RESERVED POWERS

(Art. XXXI-A added Oct. 30, 2015, P.L.207, No.51)

Compiler's Note: Section 3 of Act 51 of 2015, which added Article XXXI-A, provided that nothing in Act 51 shall be construed to repeal or modify any township ordinance in effect on the effective date of Act 51 or affect any proceeding or enforcement of any township ordinance instituted prior to the effective date of Act 51.

ARTICLE I
PRELIMINARY PROVISIONS

53 P.S. §§ 55101–55110

§ 101. Short Title; Effective Date.—This act shall be known, and may be cited, as "The First Class Township Code." This reenactment, revision, amendment and consolidation of the laws relating to townships of the first class shall become effective the first day of January, 1950.

§ 102. Definitions.—The following words, terms and phrases, as used in this act, shall have the following meanings unless the context clearly indicates otherwise:

"Board of commissioners." The board of township commissioners of a township of the first class.

"Highway." A road or highway of the State highway system.

"Individual." A natural person.

"Municipal authority" or **"municipality authority."** A body politic and corporate created under 53 Pa.C.S. Ch. 56 (relating to municipal authorities).

"Municipal corporation." A city, borough, incorporated town, township of the first or second class or any home rule municipality other than a county.

"Municipality." A county, city, borough, incorporated town, township of the first or second class or any home rule municipality.

"Pennsylvania Municipalities Planning Code." The act of July 31, 1968 (P.L.805, No.247), known as the "Pennsylvania Municipalities Planning Code."

"Person." Includes a natural person, corporation, partnership, limited liability company, business trust, other association, government entity other than the Commonwealth, estate, trust or foundation.

"Street." Includes a street, road, lane, alley, court or public square.

"Township." A township of the first class.

(a) (Deleted by amendment).

(b) (Deleted by amendment).

(c) (Deleted by amendment).

(102 amended Oct. 29, 2020, P.L.782, No.96)

§ 103. Excluded Provisions.—This act does not include any provisions, and shall not be construed to repeal any act, relating to:

(a) The assessment and valuation of property and persons for the purposes of taxation and collection of taxes, except as provided herein;

(a.1) The collection of municipal claims by liens;

(b) The method of incurring or increasing bonded indebtedness;

(c) Conduct of elections;

(d) Public schools and school districts;

(e) The powers and duties of constables;

(f) Magisterial district judges;

(g) State highways and private roads;

(g.1) Any of the provisions of 75 Pa.C.S. (relating to vehicles);

(h) Validation of elections, bonds, ordinances, and acts of corporate officers;

(i) Any of the provisions of 24 Pa.C.S. Ch. 93 (relating to public library code);

(j) Crimes and offenses provided for in 18 Pa.C.S. (relating to crimes and offenses);

(k) Any law relating to the giving of municipal consent to public utilities.

(103 amended Oct. 29, 2020, P.L.782, No.96)

Compiler's Note: Section 28 of Act 207 of 2004 provided that any and all references in any other law to a "district justice" or "justice of the peace" shall be deemed to be references to a magisterial district judge.

§ 104. Construction of Act Generally.—(a) The provisions of this act so far as they are the same as those of laws in effect prior to June 24, 1931, are intended as a continuation of laws in effect prior to June 24, 1931, and not as new enactments. The repeal by this act of any act of Assembly, or part thereof, shall not revive any act, or part thereof, repealed or superseded prior to June 24, 1931, nor affect the existence of class of any township created prior to June 24, 1931. The provisions of this act shall not affect any act done, liability incurred, or right accrued or vested, or affect any suit or prosecution, pending or to be instituted, to enforce any right or penalty or punish any offense under the authority of the repealed laws. All ordinances, resolutions, regulations, and rules, made pursuant to any act of Assembly repealed by this act, shall continue with the same force and effect as if the act had not been repealed. Any person, holding office under any act of Assembly repealed by this act, shall continue to hold office until the expiration of the term thereof, subject to the conditions attached to the office prior to June 24, 1931.

(b) The board of commissioners shall have the corporate powers and duties and township officials shall have the powers and duties not only as set forth in this act but also as provided in other laws to the extent that the powers and duties are not repealed by this act.

(104 amended Oct. 29, 2020, P.L.782, No.96)

§ 105. Constitutional Construction.—The provisions of this act shall be severable, and if any of the provisions shall be held to be unconstitutional, such decision shall not affect the validity of any of the remaining provisions of this act. It is hereby declared as the legislative intent that this act would have been adopted had such unconstitutional provision not been included therein.

§ 106. Construction of References.—Whenever, in this act, reference is made to any act by title or otherwise, such reference shall also apply to and include any codification wherein the provisions of the act referred to are substantially reenacted.

(106 amended Oct. 29, 2020, P.L.782, No.96)

§ 107. How Act Applies.—This act shall apply to all townships of the first class within the Commonwealth existing on June 24, 1931, or created thereafter.

(107 amended Oct. 29, 2020, P.L.782, No.96)

§ 108. Saving Clauses Where Class of Township Changed.—If a township of the second class is designated a township of the first class, or if a township of the first class is reestablished as a township of the second class, all liabilities incurred, rights accrued or vested, obligations issued or contracted, and all suits and prosecutions pending or to be instituted to enforce any right or penalty accrued or to punish any offense committed before the change of class, and all ordinances, resolutions, rules and regulations shall continue with the same force and effect as if no change had been made.

(108 amended Oct. 29, 2020, P.L.782, No.96)

§ 109. Exception as to Taxation.—(109 repealed Oct. 29, 2020, P.L.782, No.96)

§ 110. Legal Advertising.—(a) Whenever, under the provisions of this act, notice is required to be published in one or more newspapers, the publication shall be made in a newspaper of general circulation, as defined in 45 Pa.C.S. § 101 (relating to definitions), printed in the township, if there is such a newspaper, and, if not, then in a newspaper circulating generally in the township.

(b) Unless dispensed with by special order of court, if the notice relates to any proceeding or matter in any court, or the holding of an election for the increase of indebtedness, or the issue and sale of bonds to be paid by taxation, the notice shall also, in counties of the second, third, fourth and fifth classes, be published in the legal newspaper of the county, if any, designated by the rules of court. Ordinances, auditors' statements, summaries of auditors' statements, advertisements inviting proposals for public contracts and for bids for materials and supplies, or lists of delinquent taxpayers, shall be published only in newspapers of general circulation.

(110 amended Oct. 29, 2020, P.L.782, No.96)

Compiler's Note: The act of May 16, 1929 (P.L.1784, No.587), referred to as the Newspaper Advertising Act, was repealed by the act of July 9, 1976 (P.L.877, No.160). The subject matter is now contained in 45 Pa.C.S. Ch.3 (relating to legal advertising).

ARTICLE II
CLASSIFICATION, CREATION, REESTABLISHMENT AND CHANGE OF NAME OF TOWNSHIPS

53 P.S. §§ 55201–55240

(Art. hdg. amended Oct. 29, 2020, P.L.782, No.96)

(a) Classification

§ 201. Classification of Townships.—The townships now in existence and those to be created are divided into two classes: townships of the first class and townships of the second class. A township of the first class shall be a township having a population of at least 300 inhabitants to the square mile and is functioning as a township of the first class on June 24, 1931, or that were created after June 24, 1931, as a township of the first class in the manner provided in this act. A township that is not a township of the first class or a home rule municipality shall be classified as a township of the second class. A change from one class to the other shall be made only as provided by this act or the laws relating to townships of the second class.

(201 amended Oct. 29, 2020, P.L.782, No.96)

(b) Creation of Townships of the First Class from Townships of the Second Class

§ 205. Enrollment to Ascertain Population.—(205 repealed Oct. 29, 2020, P.L.782, No.96)

§ 205.1. Creation of Townships of the First Class from Townships of the Second Class.—At any time, a township of the second class may be established as a township of the first class as follows:

(1) A township of the second class may only become a township of the first class if the township of the second class has a population density of three hundred or more inhabitants to the square mile. The population density shall be determined from the most recent census data as made available by the United States Census Bureau, whether it is from the decennial census, special census or from the Population Estimates Program.

(2) The board of supervisors of the township of the second class on its own initiative may, or within fifteen days after the receipt of a petition signed by at least five percent of the electors of the township of the second class shall, pass a resolution and record it on its minutes, submitting the question of whether the township of the second class shall be established as a township of the first class to the electors of the township of the second class. The petition and resolution shall include the population density of the township of the second class.

(3) At the next primary, general or municipal election occurring at least ninety days after the passage of the resolution, the question under paragraph (2) shall be submitted to the electors of the township. The county board of elections shall place the question of establishing a township of the first class on the ballot in accordance with the act of June 3, 1937 (P.L.1333, No.320), known as the "Pennsylvania Election Code."

(4) The election officers shall compute the votes cast at the election and certify the votes to the county board of elections. The county board of elections shall compute the votes cast and certify the result to the county commissioners, the board of supervisors of the township of the second class and the clerk of the court of common pleas. If a majority of the votes cast at the election are in favor of becoming a township of the first class, the government of the township of the first class shall be organized and become effective on the first Monday of January after the election. When the township of the first class is organized and becomes effective, the terms of the officers of the township of the second class shall cease and the officers appointed by the court for the township under section 225 shall take office. If a majority of the votes cast at the election are in favor of remaining a township of the second class, no further proceedings may be initiated for a period of two years from the date of the election.

(205.1 added Oct. 29, 2020, P.L.782, No.96)

§ 206. Proclamations by County Commissioners.—(206 repealed Oct. 29, 2020, P.L.782, No.96)

§ 207. Submission of Question to Voters.—(207 repealed Oct. 29, 2020, P.L.782, No.96)

§ 208. Returns of Election and Effect Thereof.—(208 repealed Oct. 29, 2020, P.L.782, No.96)

(bb) Reestablishment of Townships of the Second Class

§ 209. Ascertainment of Population.—(209 repealed Oct. 29, 2020, P.L.782, No.96)

§ 209.1. Reestablishment of Townships of the Second Class.—A township of the first class may, no sooner than five years after becoming a township of the first class, be reestablished as a township of the second class as provided in the act of May 1, 1933 (P.L.103, No.69), known as "The Second Class Township Code."

(209.1 added Oct. 29, 2020, P.L.782, No.96)

§ 209a. Submission of Question to Voters; Returns of Election, and Effect Thereof.—(209a repealed Oct. 29, 2020, P.L.782, No.96)

(c) Creation of Townships of the First Class by Merger or Consolidation

(Subdiv. hdg. amended Oct. 29, 2020, P.L.782, No.96)

Compiler's Note: Section 2 of Act 90 of 1994 repealed provisions relating to the consolidation of townships. Provisions for merger and consolidation of municipalities are now found in 53 Pa.C.S. Ch. 7 Subch. C (relating to consolidation and merger).

§ 210. Manner in Which Townships of the First Class May Be Created.—(210 repealed Oct. 13, 1994, P.L.596, No.90)

§ 211. Petitions.—(211 repealed Oct. 13, 1994, P.L.596, No.90)

§ 212. Confirmation Nisi of Petition; Notice of Filing.—(212 repealed Oct. 13, 1994, P.L.596, No.90)

§ 213. Exceptions; Confirmation Absolute of Petition.—(212 repealed Oct. 13, 1994, P.L.596, No.90)

§ 214. Elections.—(214 repealed Oct. 13, 1994, P.L.596, No.90)

§ 216. Return of Election; Decree.—(216 repealed Oct. 13, 1994, P.L.596, No.90)

§ 217. Boundary Monuments.—(217 repealed Oct. 13, 1994, P.L.596, No.90)

§ 218. Classification of New Townships.—(218 repealed Oct. 13, 1994, P.L.596, No.90)

§ 219. Costs.—(219 repealed Oct. 13, 1994, P.L.596, No.90)

§ 220. Consolidation or Merger.—A township may be merged or consolidated into a new or existing municipal corporation in accordance with 53 Pa.C.S. Ch. 7 Subch. C (relating to consolidation and merger).

(220 added Oct. 29, 2020, P.L.782, No.96)

(d) Officers of Newly Created Townships

§ 225. Officers for New Townships.—(a) If a new township of the first class is created from a township of the second class pursuant to this article, the court of common pleas shall appoint the elective officers for the new township and determine the polling place or places in the new township. The appointed officers shall hold office until the first Monday of January after the next municipal election as provided in this act.

(b) At the first municipal election following the creation of a township as provided in section 205.1, if the township has not been divided into wards, five township commissioners shall be elected at large. Three of the commissioners shall be elected for terms of four years each, and two for terms of two years each, from the first Monday of January next following the election. The ballots at the election shall designate the term for which each commissioner is elected. Their successors shall be elected for terms of four years in accordance with this act. If the township has been divided into wards, the township commissioners shall be elected as provided in section 407.

(c) At the first municipal election, a tax collector shall be elected for a two or four year term so that the term shall expire at the same time as the terms of tax collectors of other townships of the first class under the provisions of this act. Thereafter the term of tax collector of the township shall be four years from the first Monday of January next following the tax collector's election.

(225 amended Oct. 29, 2020, P.L.782, No.96)

§ 226. Election of Commissioners in New Townships.—(226 repealed Oct. 29, 2020, P.L.782, No.96)

§ 227. Election of Tax Collector in New Townships.—(227 repealed Oct. 29, 2020, P.L.782, No.96)

Compiler's Note: See sections 14 and 15 of Act 188 of 2012 in the appendix to this act for special provisions relating to applicability of law and municipal officers affected by Act 188.

§ 228. Election of Township Assessor and Assistant Township Assessor in New Townships.—(228 repealed Feb. 2, 2012, P.L.62, No.7)

Compiler's Note: Section 8832(d) of the Consolidated County Assessment Law (53 Pa.C.S. Ch. 88) provides that the office of local elected assessor is abolished.

(e) Certificate of Creation of Townships to Be Furnished State Departments

§ 235. Certificate of Creation of Township.—If a township of the first class is created, the clerk of the court shall certify to the Department of State, the Department of Transportation, the Department of Community and Economic Development and the county planning commission a copy of the record constituting the charter of the township. The clerk of the court may charge a fee of three dollars and fifty cents ($3.50), to be paid as part of the costs of the proceedings.

(235 amended Oct. 29, 2020, P.L.782, No.96)

Compiler's Note: Section 301(a)(16) of Act 58 of 1996, which created the Department of Community and Economic Development and abolished the Department of Community Affairs, provided that all other powers and duties delegated to the Department of Community Affairs not otherwise expressly transferrred elsewhere by Act 58 and currently performed by the Department of Community Affairs under section 235 are transferred to the Department of Community and Economic Development.

(f) Change of Name of Township of First Class

(Subdiv. hdg. added Oct. 29, 2020, P.L.782, No.96)

§ 240. Change of Name of Township.—(a) Upon petition to the court of common pleas of at least 10% of the electors of a township, or upon passage of a resolution by the board of commissioners, seeking a change of the name of the township, the court shall order a referendum on the question.

(b) If the court determines that the petition or resolution for change of name of the township is in proper form and properly executed, the original petition or resolution shall be filed with the clerk of the court. A copy of the petition or resolution and order of the court shall be filed with the county board of elections which shall frame the question to be submitted to the electors at the next general or municipal election which occurs at least 60 days after the court order.

(c) The election officers shall compute the votes cast on the question and certify the votes to the clerk of the court of common pleas who shall tabulate the votes and certify the result. If a majority of the votes cast at the election are in favor of the change of township name, the court shall so order and shall order the record of the proceedings to be permanently recorded. If a majority of the votes are against the change, there shall be no further proceedings on the petition or resolution.

(240 added Oct. 29, 2020, P.L.782, No.96)

ARTICLE II.I

CHANGE OF NAME OF TOWNSHIP OF FIRST CLASS

53 P.S. §§ 55251–55253

(Art. repealed Oct. 29, 2020, P.L.782, No.96)

§ 2.201. Petition of Electors.—(2.201 repealed Oct. 29, 2020, P.L.782, No.96)

§ 2.202. Filing and Advertisement of Petition.—(2.202 repealed Oct. 29, 2020, P.L.782, No.96)

§ 2.203. Returns and Effect of Election.—(2.203 repealed Oct. 29, 2020, P.L.782, No.96)

ARTICLE III

TOWNSHIP LINES AND BOUNDARIES [REPEALED]

53 P.S. §§ 55301–55307

§ 55301. Repealed by 2022, July 7, P.L. 455, NO. 41—§ 4(2)(IV), Effective in 60 Days [Sept. 6, 2022]

§ 55302. Repealed by 2022, July 7, P.L. 455, NO. 41—§ 4(2)(IV), Effective in 60 Days [Sept. 6, 2022]

§ 55303. Repealed by 2022, July 7, P.L. 455, NO. 41—§ 4(2)(IV), Effective in 60 Days [Sept. 6, 2022]

§ 55304. Repealed by 2022, July 7, P.L. 455, NO. 41—§ 4(2)(IV), Effective in 60 Days [Sept. 6, 2022]

§ 55305. Repealed by 2022, July 7, P.L. 455, NO. 41—§ 4(2)(IV), Effective in 60 Days [Sept. 6, 2022]

§ 55306. Repealed by 2022, July 7, P.L. 455, NO. 41—§ 4(2)(IV), Effective in 60 Days [Sept. 6, 2022]

§ 55307. Repealed by 2022, July 7, P.L. 455, NO. 41—§ 4(2)(IV), Effective in 60 Days [Sept. 6, 2022]

ARTICLE IV

WARDS

53 P.S. §§ 55401–55409

§ 401. Creation and Alteration of Wards.—(a) In addition to reapportionment initiated in accordance with 53 Pa.C.S. Ch. 9 (relating to municipal reapportionment) and section 11 of Article IX of the Constitution of Pennsylvania, the board of commissioners may, by ordinance, do any of the following:

(1) Divide townships into wards.

(2) Create new wards out of two or more adjoining wards or parts of wards.

(3) Consolidate two or more wards into one ward.

(4) Divide any ward already erected into two or more wards.

(5) Alter the lines of two or more adjoining wards.

(6) Cause the lines or boundaries of wards to be ascertained or established.

(7) Abolish all wards.

(b) The following shall apply:

(1) No township may be divided or redivided into more than 15 wards.

(2) No ward shall be created containing less than 300 registered electors.

(3) At the discretion of the board of commissioners, any ward which contains less than 350 registered electors may be abolished, and the territory of the ward may be merged into a contiguous existing ward or wards. If two or more contiguous wards have respective populations not meeting the population threshold of 350 registered electors, the commissioners may consolidate those contiguous wards into one ward. All other wards shall remain as established until altered or divided as provided in this article. The composition of the wards shall be subject to subsection (d).

(c) If a ward is abolished under this section and the number of wards in the township is reduced to less than five, then the commissioner or commissioners in the abolished ward or wards shall continue in office for the term for which elected, and shall become a commissioner or commissioners at large from the township.

(d) All wards in the township shall be numbered and composed of compact and contiguous territory as nearly equal in population as practicable as officially and finally reported in the latest official census.

(401 amended Oct. 29, 2020, P.L.782, No.96)

Compiler's Note: Section 9 of Act 312 of 1974 provided that section 401 is repealed insofar as it is inconsistent. Act 312 of 1974, in turn, was repealed by the act of December 19, 1996 (P.L.1158, No.177). The subject matter is now contained in 53 Pa.C.S. Ch. 9 (relating to municipal reapportionment).

§ 402. Signing Petition; Appointment and Powers of Commissioners.—(402 repealed Oct. 4, 1978, P.L.946, No.186)

§ 402.1. Petition of Electors.—(a) At least 5% of registered electors of the township or, for a proposal affecting only a portion of the township, at least 5% of the registered electors of the ward which would be affected by the proposal, may petition the board of commissioners to initiate proceedings under section 401 and may present to the board of commissioners a plot showing the boundaries of the proposed wards of the township. The board of commissioners shall, by motion approved by a majority of the commissioners and within 90 days of presentment of the petition, determine whether to initiate proceedings under section 401.

(b) If the board of commissioners has not approved a motion within 90 days after the presentment of a petition under subsection (a), 10 registered electors may petition the court of common pleas and contest the existing apportionment as violating section 401(b) or (d). The proceedings before the court shall be conducted in accordance with 53 Pa.C.S. §§ 906 (relating to contest of reapportionment by governing body) and 907 (relating to costs and expenses of contest).

(402.1 added Oct. 29, 2020, P.L.782, No.96)

§ 403. Filing and Confirmation of Report; Exceptions.—(403 repealed Oct. 29, 2020, P.L.782, No.96)

Compiler's Note: Section 9 of Act 312 of 1974 provided that section 403 is repealed insofar as it is inconsistent. Act 312 of 1974, in turn, was repealed by the act of December 19, 1996 (P.L.1158, No.177). The subject matter is now contained in 53 Pa.C.S. Ch. 9 (relating to municipal reapportionment).

§ 403.1. County Board of Elections.—A copy of the ordinance enacted pursuant to section 401, along with a plot showing the boundaries of the wards established, shall be forwarded to the county board of elections.

(403.1 added Oct. 29, 2020, P.L.782, No.96)

§ 404. Compensation of Commissioners.—(404 repealed Oct. 29, 2020, P.L.782, No.96)

Compiler's Note: Section 9 of Act 312 of 1974 provided that section 404 is repealed insofar as it is inconsistent. Act 312 of 1974, in turn, was repealed by the act of December 19, 1996 (P.L.1158, No.177). The subject matter is now contained in 53 Pa.C.S. Ch. 9 (relating to municipal reapportionment).

§ 405. Election Districts.—(405 repealed Oct. 29, 2020, P.L.782, No.96)

Compiler's Note: Section 9 of Act 312 of 1974 provided that section 405 is repealed insofar as it is inconsistent. Act 312 of 1974, in turn, was repealed by the act of December 19, 1996 (P.L.1158, No.177). The subject matter is now contained in 53 Pa.C.S. Ch. 9 (relating to municipal reapportionment).

§ 406. Numbering of Wards.—(406 repealed Oct. 29, 2020, P.L.782, No.96)

Compiler's Note: Section 9 of Act 312 of 1974 provided that section 406 is repealed insofar as it is inconsistent. Act 312 of 1974, in turn, was repealed by the act of December 19, 1996 (P.L.1158, No.177). The subject matter is now contained in 53 Pa.C.S. Ch. 9 (relating to municipal reapportionment).

§ 407. Schedule for Election of Commissioners in Townships First Divided into Wards.—When a township is first divided into wards, the township commissioners then in office shall continue in office until the expiration of their respective terms.

At the first municipal election occurring at least 90 days after the division into wards, there shall be elected, by the registered electors of each ward of the township, one township commissioner, who shall reside in the ward for which the commissioner is elected. At the election, the township commissioners elected in even-numbered wards shall be elected for terms of two years each, and those in odd-numbered wards for terms of four years each, or vice versa, as the case may be, in order that the expiration of the terms will harmonize with the expiration of terms of township commissioners elected for the even or odd numbered wards under the provisions of this act. Thereafter, successors to the commissioners shall be elected for terms of four years each at the municipal election immediately preceding the expiration of the terms of ward commissioners.

If the number of wards into which the township has been divided is less than five, then, at the municipal election preceding the expiration of the terms of any commissioner or commissioners elected at large, if the expiration of terms will leave the township with less than five township commissioners, there shall be elected at large a sufficient number of township commissioners so that the total number of commissioners elected by wards and at large in the township shall thereafter be five. If one township commissioner is elected at large, the commissioner shall be elected for a term of four years. If two township commissioners are elected at large, one shall be elected for a term of two years, and one for a term of four years. If three township commissioners are elected at large, two shall be elected for terms of four years each, and one for a term of two years. Successors to the township commissioners elected at large shall be elected for terms of four years each.

All terms of office of township commissioners, elected at large or by wards, shall commence on the first Monday of January next following their election.

(407 amended Oct. 29, 2020, P.L.782, No.96)

Compiler's Note: Section 9 of Act 312 of 1974 provided that section 407 is repealed insofar as it is inconsistent. Act 312 of 1974, in turn, was repealed by the act of December 19, 1996 (P.L.1158, No.177). The subject matter is now contained in 53 Pa.C.S. Ch. 9 (relating to municipal reapportionment).

§ 408. Schedule of Election of Commissioners in Newly Created Wards.—If a new ward is created in a township previously divided into wards and the number of wards in the township, including the new ward, is less than five, then, at the next municipal election following the expiration of the term of the commissioner or commissioners elected at large whose terms shall first expire after the creation of the new ward, there shall be elected, by the registered electors of the new ward, one township commissioner, who shall reside in the ward for which the commissioner is elected, for a term of two or four years, so that the expiration of the commissioner's term will harmonize with the expiration of terms of commissioners for the even or odd numbered wards under the provisions of this act. Successors to the township commissioners shall be elected for terms of four years. The number of commissioners thereafter elected at large in the township shall be the difference between the number of wards and five, and a sufficient number of commissioners shall be elected at large at each municipal election preceding the expiration of terms of commissioners at large so that the total number of commissioners in the township will at all times be five.

If a new ward is created in any township previously divided into wards and the number of wards thereafter in the township is five, then, at the municipal election preceding the expiration of the term of office of any commissioner or commissioners elected at large, a township commissioner shall be elected for the ward, who shall reside in the ward. The election shall be for a two or four year term so that the expiration of the commissioner's term will harmonize with the expiration of terms of commissioners for the even or odd numbered wards under the provisions of this act. The successor to the ward commissioner shall be elected for a four-year term. No township commissioner shall thereafter be elected at large in the township.

If the number of wards in the township, including the new ward, will be more than five, the court of common pleas shall appoint a township commissioner for the new ward, who shall hold office until the first Monday in January succeeding the first municipal election at which township commissioners are elected in the even or odd numbered wards under the provisions of this act, at which election, and every four years thereafter, a township commissioner, who shall reside in the ward, shall be elected by the qualified electors of the ward for a term of four years.

All township commissioners elected under this section shall take office on the first Monday of January next succeeding their election.

(408 amended Oct. 29, 2020, P.L.782, No.96)

> **Compiler's Note:** Section 9 of Act 312 of 1974 provided that section 408 is repealed insofar as it is inconsistent. Act 312 of 1974, in turn, was repealed by the act of December 19, 1996 (P.L.1158, No.177). The subject matter is now contained in 53 Pa.C.S. Ch. 9 (relating to municipal reapportionment).

§ 409. Pennsylvania Election Code.—Nothing in this article shall be construed as affecting the powers and duties of the court of common pleas, the county board of elections or restrictions on alteration of election districts as provided in Article V of the act of June 3, 1937 (P.L.1333, No.320), known as the "Pennsylvania Election Code."

(409 added Oct. 29, 2020, P.L.782, No.96)

ARTICLE V
ELECTION OF OFFICERS; VACANCIES IN OFFICE

53 P.S. §§55501–55533

(a) General Provisions

Compiler's Note: Act 54 of 2017 added 53 Pa.C.S. § 1142, which provides that "active military duty" shall not disqualify a person from fulfilling residency requirements for municipal elective office and that one who is a resident of a municipality for at least one year immediately prior to the person's absence due to active military duty shall be deemed to be an ongoing resident of the municipality for purposes of any residency requirement of office unless and until the person demonstrates an intent to establish a new domicile outside the municipality.

§ 501. Eligibility.—(a) Only a registered elector of a township may be eligible to an elective office in the township. Before being sworn into office, each elected township officer, or, except as provided under section 530, each appointed township officer in case of a vacancy in an elective office, shall present a signed affidavit to the township secretary stating that the officer resides in the township, or within the ward in the case of a ward office, from which elected or appointed and has resided in the township or ward continuously for at least one year immediately prior to the officer's election or appointment. In the case of a newly created ward in existence for less than one year at the time of a township officer's election or appointment, the affidavit shall state that the officer has resided within the township continuously for at least one year immediately prior to the officer's election or appointment and within the ward from the date of the ward's creation continuously until the officer's election or appointment.

(b) If an individual elected to office, or appointed to an elective office, fails to give the required bond, take the required oath or provide a signed affidavit, a vacancy is created in the office for which the individual was elected or appointed and the vacancy shall be filled as provided in section 530.

(c) No individual may hold more than one elective township office at the same time.

(501 amended Oct. 29, 2020, P.L.782, No.96)

§ 502. Term of Office.—Except if a vacancy in office occurs pursuant to section 530, officers shall hold office for the term for which the individual was elected. Officers shall not serve longer than the first Monday of January succeeding the municipal election at which a successor was elected.

(502 amended Oct. 29, 2020, P.L.782, No.96)

§ 503. Elected Officers.—(a) The electors of each township shall elect:

(1) At least five township commissioners. The following shall apply:

(i) In townships divided into wards but having less than five wards, the number of commissioners shall be five. One commissioner shall be elected from each ward, and the remaining number of commissioners, to which the township is entitled, shall be elected at large. In townships having five or more wards, one commissioner shall be elected from each ward. Township commissioners shall be elected at municipal elections, preceding the expiration of the terms of commissioners then in office, for terms of four years each. Commissioners from odd-numbered wards shall be elected at alternate municipal elections than the municipal elections at which commissioners from even-numbered wards are elected. Elections at large shall be held at the municipal election preceding the expiration of the term of any commissioner elected at large.

(ii) In townships not divided into wards, there shall be five township commissioners, who shall be elected at large by the voters of the township. At each municipal election, two or three township commissioners, as the case may be, shall be elected for terms of four years each to take the place of the commissioners whose terms then expire.

(2) One township tax collector, and the following shall apply:

(i) The township tax collector shall be elected at municipal elections every four years. An individual must be a qualified tax collector or, in the case of an individual appointed to fill a vacancy in the office of tax collector, become a qualified tax collector, in accordance with the act of May 25, 1945 (P.L.1050, No.394), known as the Local Tax Collection Law.

(ii) If no individual is elected to the position of tax collector in the municipal election, or if the position of tax collector becomes vacant, the board of commissioners may, by resolution, appoint an individual or person to collect taxes. If a person other than an individual is appointed, the person shall post bonds to the same extent as would an individual appointed to fill the vacancy and as further provided by terms and conditions as set forth by the board of commissioners. Notwithstanding the Local Tax Collection Law, if a person other than an individual is appointed as a tax collector, no individual employed by the appointed tax collector or any of the appointed tax collector's officers shall be required to be or become a qualified tax collector or to file criminal history record information.

(3) Three elected auditors, and the following shall apply:

(i) At each municipal election, one auditor shall be elected for a term of six years. No auditor shall at the same time hold any other elective or appointive office.

(ii) The board of commissioners may provide by ordinance for the appointment of an independent auditor, in lieu of providing for the election of three auditors, as provided in subparagraph (i) or one controller as provided in paragraph (4). After enactment of the ordinance, an independent auditor shall be appointed annually by resolution at least thirty days prior to the close of the fiscal year. The office of elected auditor is abolished upon the appointment of an independent auditor.

(iii) The board of commissioners shall have the right at any time to repeal the ordinance providing for the appointed independent auditor, whereupon three auditors shall be elected at the next municipal election following the repeal of the ordinance, to whom the following shall apply:

(A) One elected auditor shall serve a term of two years.

(B) One elected auditor shall serve a term of four years.

(C) One elected auditor shall serve a term of six years.

(D) The three elected auditors shall have all the powers and perform all the duties as provided in this act for elected auditors.

(4) One elected controller in lieu of three elected auditors, and the following shall apply:

(i) The provisions of this act relating to the controller shall not become operative or effective until the board of commissioners shall, by ordinance, accept the provisions of this act relating to the office of controller.

(ii) When a township has provided by ordinance for the office of an elected controller, the board of commissioners shall petition the court of common pleas to appoint a controller to hold office until the first Monday of January next succeeding the next municipal election when a controller shall be elected. When a controller is appointed or elected as provided within this paragraph, the office of elected auditor is abolished.

(iii) One controller, who shall be a competent accountant, shall be elected at municipal elections every four years.

(iv) The office of controller shall be continued until the ordinance is repealed, when the office of controller shall terminate. The township shall either appoint an independent auditor or, at the next municipal election following the repeal of the ordinance, provide for the election of three auditors, to whom the following shall apply:

(A) One elected auditor shall serve a term of two years.

(B) One elected auditor shall serve a term of four years.

(C) One elected auditor shall serve a term of six years.

(D) The three elected auditors shall have all the powers and perform all the duties as provided in this act for elected auditors.

(b) The terms of each elected officer under this section shall begin the first Monday of January next succeeding the individual's election.

(503 amended Oct. 29, 2020, P.L.782, No.96)

Compiler's Note: See sections 14 and 15 of Act 188 of 2012 in the appendix to this act for special provisions relating to applicability of law and municipal officers affected by Act 188.

(b) Commissioners
(Subdiv. repealed Oct. 29, 2020, P.L.782, No.96)

§ 504. Number and Election of Commissioners in Townships Having Wards.—(504 repealed Oct. 29, 2020, P.L.782, No.96)

§ 505. Number and Election of Commissioners in Townships Not Divided into Wards.—(505 repealed Oct. 29, 2020, P.L.782, No.96)

(c) Tax Collector
(Subdiv. repealed Oct. 29, 2020, P.L.782, No.96)

§ 510. Election of Tax Collector.—(510 repealed Oct. 29, 2020, P.L.782, No.96)

§ 511. Eligibility.—(511 repealed Oct. 24, 2012, P.L.1478, No.188)

(d) Assessors
(Subdiv. repealed Oct. 29, 2020, P.L.782, No.96)

§ 515. Election of Township Assessor and Assistant Township Assessor.—(515 repealed Feb. 2, 2012, P.L.62, No.7)

Compiler's Note: Section 8832(d) of the Consolidated County Assessment Law (53 Pa.C.S. Ch. 88) provides that the office of local elected assessor is abolished.

(e) Auditors
(Subdiv. repealed Oct. 29, 2020, P.L.782, No.96)

§ 520. Election of Auditors.—(520 repealed Oct. 29, 2020, P.L.782, No.96)

(f) Controller
(Subdiv. repealed Oct. 29, 2020, P.L.782, No.96)

§ 525. Election of Controller.—(525 repealed Oct. 29, 2020, P.L.782, No.96)

§ 526. Acceptance of Controller; Provisions by Ordinance.—(526 repealed Oct. 29, 2020, P.L.782, No.96)

(g) Vacancies in Office

§ 530. Vacancies in General.—(a) If a vacancy occurs in the office of township commissioner, auditor, controller, or tax collector by death, resignation, removal provided in section 604, termination of residency from the township or ward in the case of a ward office, or by failure to take the required oath, give required bond or provide the affidavit required under section 501, or otherwise, the board of commissioners shall fill the vacancy within thirty (30) days by appointing by resolution a registered elector of the township or ward in the case of a ward office, in which the vacancy occurs. If a person other than an individual is appointed to fill a vacancy in the office of tax collector under section 503(a)(2)(ii), the person shall not be required to file the affidavit required under section 501. An individual appointed as a tax collector under section 4.2 or 4.4 of the act of May 25, 1945 (P.L.1050, No.394), known as the Local Tax Collection Law, shall not be required to file an affidavit required under section 501.

(a.1) Except as provided under subsection (b.2), the following shall apply:

(1) A vacancy shall not be created by a resignation until the date that the resignation is accepted by a majority vote of a quorum of the board of commissioners at a public meeting or the effective date of the tendered resignation, whichever is later. The board of commissioners must accept a resignation no later than forty-five (45) days after it has been tendered in writing to the board of commissioners, unless it is withdrawn in writing prior to acceptance.

(2) A resignation that is not accepted as provided under paragraph (1) shall be deemed accepted after forty-five (45) days.

(b) The following apply:

(1) A vacancy board shall be convened to fill a vacancy within fifteen (15) days if the board of commissioners of a township, for any reason, fails to fill a vacancy after thirty (30) days. The board of commissioners may vote to convene the vacancy board within thirty (30) days of a vacancy if the board of commissioners is unable, for any reason, to fill the vacancy and shall provide a justification at a public meeting.

(2) The vacancy board shall consist of the board of commissioners and one registered elector of the township, who shall be appointed by the board of commissioners at the board's first meeting each calendar year or as soon thereafter as practical.

(3) The registered elector shall act as chairperson of the vacancy board and shall serve as the chairperson until the chairperson's successor is appointed. The chairperson of the vacancy board may not vote for themselves to fill a vacancy in any office.

(b.1) The vacancy board chairperson shall, or in the case of a vacancy in the chairpersonship the remaining members of the vacancy board shall, petition the court of common pleas to fill the vacancy by appointing a registered elector of the township or ward, in which the vacancy occurs if one of the following occur:

(1) the vacancy board fails to fill the position within fifteen (15) days; or

(2) the position of vacancy board chairperson is vacant and the remaining members of the vacancy board provide justification for the reason the vacancy board is not able to fill the position sooner than fifteen (15) days and vote publicly to disband.

(b.2) Notwithstanding any other subsections in this section, if there are vacancies in a majority of the offices of commissioners, the court of common pleas shall fill the vacancies upon presentation of a petition signed by the remaining commissioners or at least fifteen (15) registered electors of the township. A resignation that precludes a majority of commissioners from accepting the resignation shall create a vacancy on the date specified in the tendered resignation or, if no date is specified, the second business day after the day the resignation is tendered, unless sooner withdrawn in writing.

(b.3) The registered elector appointed to fill a vacancy shall hold the office until the first Monday in January after the first municipal election occurring more than sixty (60) days after the vacancy occurs, at which election an eligible person shall be elected to the office for the remainder of the term. The appointed registered elector shall have been a resident of the township or ward continuously for at least one (1) year immediately prior to the appointment.

(530 amended Oct. 29, 2020, P.L.782, No.96)

Compiler's Note: See sections 14 and 15 of Act 188 of 2012 in the appendix to this act for special provisions relating to applicability of law and municipal officers affected by Act 188.

§ 531. Auditors.—(531 repealed June 15, 1978, P.L.475, No.69)

§ 532. Township Treasurer and Controller.—(532 repealed June 15, 1978, P.L.475, No.69)

§ 533. Assessors.—(533 repealed June 15, 1978, P.L.475, No.69)

ARTICLE VI
GENERAL PROVISIONS RELATING TO TOWNSHIP OFFICERS
53 P.S. §§ 55601–55650

(a) General Provisions

§ 601. Oath.—Every person elected or appointed to any township office in any township shall, before entering upon the duties of office, take and subscribe an oath or affirmation of office under 53 Pa.C.S. § 1141 (relating to form of oaths of office), before any judge or magisterial district judge of the county or a notary public. A copy of the oath or affirmation shall, within ten days thereafter, be filed with the township secretary.

(601 amended Oct. 29, 2020, P.L.782, No.96)

Compiler's Note: Section 3(3) of Act 76 of 2008 provided that all acts and parts of acts are repealed insofar as they are inconsistent with Act 76. Section 1 of Act 76 amended 53 Pa.C.S. Ch. 11 (relating to general provisions) by adding section 1141 (relating to form of oaths of office), which provides the form of oaths of office for elected or appointed officials of municipalities.

§ 602. Bonds.—(a) Except as provided for in subsection (b), when any officer or employe of any township is required by law or action of the board of commissioners to give bond for the faithful performance of the officer's or employe's duties, the bond shall be with a surety company or other company authorized by law to act as surety. The township shall pay the premium on the bond, except that the premium on the bond of the township tax collector shall be paid by the respective taxing districts, as provided by the act of May 25, 1945 (P.L.1050, No.394), known as the "Local Tax Collection Law."

(b) When any officer or employe of a township, other than a tax collector, is required to give a bond for the faithful performance of the officer's or employe's duties, the board of commissioners may purchase insurance in lieu of a bond if the insurance covers the same events of loss and insures the township against the same misconduct as the bond.

(602 amended Oct. 29, 2020, P.L.782, No.96)

Compiler's Note: See sections 14 and 15 of Act 188 of 2012 in the appendix to this act for special provisions relating to applicability of law and municipal officers affected by Act 188.

§ 603. Compensation.—(a) Elected officers of townships other than tax collector shall receive a salary, compensation or emoluments of office as may from time to time be fixed by ordinance of the township in accordance with this act.

(a.1) Notwithstanding section 34 of the act of May 25, 1945 (P.L.1050, No.394), known as the "Local Tax Collection Law," a township treasurer who is the elected tax collector of the township may receive a salary, compensation or emoluments of office in accordance with subsection (a) for the township treasurer's work as the township treasurer.

(b) Tax collectors shall receive a salary, compensation or emoluments of office as may from time to time be fixed by ordinance of the township in accordance with the "Local Tax Collection Law."

(c) Any change in salary, compensation or emoluments of office of an elected officer shall become effective at the beginning of the next term of the elected officer.

(d) Appointed officers and employes of the township shall receive compensation for their services as the board of commissioners shall prescribe.

(603 amended Oct. 29, 2020, P.L.782, No.96)

Compiler's Note: See sections 14 and 15 of Act 188 of 2012 in the appendix to this act for special provisions relating to applicability of law and municipal officers affected by Act 188.

§ 604. Removal of Township Officers and Appointees.—Whether elected or duly appointed to fill a vacancy in elective office, a township officer shall be removable from office only by impeachment, or by the Governor for reasonable cause after due notice and full hearing on the advice of two-thirds of the Senate, or upon conviction of misbehavior in office or of an infamous crime in accordance with the Constitution of Pennsylvania, but the officer's title to office may be tried by proceedings of quo warranto as provided by law.

(604 carried without amendment Oct. 29, 2020, P.L.782, No.96)

§ 605. Annuities in Lieu of Joining Pension or Retirement System.—(a) A township may provide, by ordinance, to employes of not less than ten years of satisfactory service and who are not less than sixty years of age upon termination of active employment with the township a proportion of the compensation last paid to them but not in excess of 50% of the compensation.

(b) Any arrangement to provide post retirement compensation to retired appointees and employes pursuant to this section shall be a pension plan within the meaning of that term pursuant to the act of December 18, 1984 (P.L.1005, No.205), known as the "Municipal Pension Plan Funding Standard and Recovery Act," and the township establishing that plan shall provide funding of that pension plan in an amount sufficient to meet the minimum obligation of the municipality with respect to the pension plan pursuant to the "Municipal Pension Plan Funding Standard and Recovery Act."

(c) Nothing in this section shall be construed to preclude any employe of the township from joining any pension system or municipal retirement system that the township may establish or adopt.

(d) Upon the effective date of this subsection, a township may not provide for an annuity in lieu of employes joining a pension or retirement system. Nothing in this subsection shall be construed to affect the rights of any current or retired employes or appointees of a township entitled to payments granted in accordance with any annuity entered into prior to the effective date of this subsection.

(605 amended Oct. 29, 2020, P.L.782, No.96)

(b) County Associations of Township Officers
(Subdiv. repealed Oct. 29, 2020, P.L.782, No.96)

§ 610. Formation of County Associations; Meetings.—(610 repealed Oct. 29, 2020, P.L.782, No.96)

§ 611. Membership of Associations; Expenses of Members.—(611 repealed Oct. 29, 2020, P.L.782, No.96)

§ 612. Officers of Association; Ex-Officio Membership.—(612 repealed Oct. 29, 2020, P.L.782, No.96)

(c) State Association of Township Officers

§ 620. State Association of Township Commissioners.—(a) The formation of a State association of township commissioners is authorized.

(b) The association shall hold annual meetings and educational conferences at a designated time and place within the Commonwealth for the purpose of addressing the interests of the townships. The expenses of the annual meetings and educational conferences may be paid, in full or in part, by the townships joining the association.

(c) The association, at its annual meeting and educational conference, by majority vote of all the voting delegates attending, shall have power to adopt and amend bylaws to govern the association. The bylaws shall govern the qualifications of delegates, election of officers, their designation, qualifications and duties, payment of dues and other organizational details. The association shall function under these bylaws for advancing the interest of and betterment of township government in townships of the first class.

(d) The dues adopted in the bylaws shall be paid by each township upon becoming a member of the association and shall be used for association purposes and activities authorized or ratified by the association or incurred on behalf of the association by its officers and executive committee.

(620 amended Oct. 29, 2020, P.L.782, No.96)

§ 621. Delegates from Townships.—(621 repealed Oct. 29, 2020, P.L.782, No.96)

§ 621.1. Authorization to Attend Annual Meetings and Educational Conferences.—(a) Township commissioners may attend each annual meeting and educational conference of the State association of township commissioners. The board of commissioners shall, by motion, designate at least one township officer as a delegate to each annual meeting and educational conference. The delegate shall be a township commissioner or other township officer. The board of commissioners may, by motion, designate no more than two township officers, other than the township commissioners or the delegate, to attend each annual meeting and educational conference as nondelegates and authorize township employees to attend each annual meeting and educational conference.

(b) In addition to each annual meeting and educational conference as specified under subsection (a), the board of commissioners may authorize township officers and employes of the township to attend other conferences or educational training of the association.

(621.1 added Oct. 29, 2020, P.L.782, No.96)

§ 622. Expenses Paid by Townships.—(a) The board of commissioners shall, for each delegate and other officer or employe attending the annual meeting or other conference or educational training of the State association of township commissioners, pay expenses upon receipt of an itemized account of expenses, which shall be limited to the registration fee, mileage for use of personal vehicle or reimbursement of actual transportation expense going to and returning from

Chap. 39 Res. During Mil. Service
Chap. 38 Intergov. Coop.
Chap. 37 3rd Class City Code
Chap. 36 Bor. Code
Chap. 35 2nd Class Twp. Code
Chap. 34 1st Class Twp. Code
Chap. 33 Home Rule Chart. Opt. Plans Law
Chap. 32 Water Serv. Act
Chap. 31 Munic. Auth. Act

the meeting, conference or educational training plus all other actual expenses that the board of commissioners may have agreed to pay.

(b) The board of commissioners may authorize township employes to be compensated at their regular employe rate during their attendance at the annual meeting or other conference or educational training. The board of commissioners may authorize a commissioner to receive total or partial reimbursement for lost wages or salary while attending the annual meeting or other conference or educational training if sufficient documentation is presented to the board of commissioners to justify the reimbursement. The maximum time for which a delegate, township employe or commissioner shall be reimbursed for lost wages or salary while attending the annual meeting or other conference or educational training shall not be more than four days, including the time spent traveling to and from the event.

(622 amended Oct. 29, 2020, P.L.782, No.96)

§ 623. Expenses of Annual Meeting.—(623 repealed Oct. 29, 2020, P.L.782, No.96)

Section 624. Conferences, Institutes and Schools.—(624 repealed Oct. 29, 2020, P.L.782, No.96)

(c.1) County Associations of Township Officers
(Subdiv. added Oct. 29, 2020, P.L.782, No.96)

§ 624.1. Formation of County Associations; Meetings.—County associations of township officers may be formed in the respective counties, or the township officers of two or more counties may form a joint county or regional association. The associations, when formed, shall hold annual, semiannual or quarterly conferences or educational training at the county seats of the respective counties, or some other suitable place within the Commonwealth, for the purpose of advancing the interests of the townships in the association and the inhabitants of the townships.

(624.1 added Oct. 29, 2020, P.L.782, No.96)

§ 624.2. Membership of Associations; Expenses of Members.—

(a) The board of commissioners, newly elected township commissioners prior to officially taking office and other township officers designated by the board shall attend the conferences or educational training whenever possible. A township officer attending a conference or educational training shall receive a certificate, signed by the presiding officer and secretary or acting secretary of the association, attesting to the township officer's presence at the conference or educational training.

(b) The certificate shall authorize an officer to collect from the township treasurer expenses which shall be limited to the registration fee, mileage for use of personal vehicle or reimbursement of actual transportation expense going to and returning from a conference or educational training, plus all other actual expenses that the board of commissioners may have agreed to pay. Each officer attending a conference or educational training shall submit to the board of commissioners an itemized account of expenses incurred.

(c) The board of commissioners may authorize township employes to be compensated at their regular employe rate during their attendance at a conference or educational training. The board of commissioners may authorize a commissioner to receive total or partial reimbursement for lost wages or salary while attending the conference or educational training if sufficient documentation of the wages or salary is presented to the board of commissioners to justify the reimbursement.

(624.2 added Oct. 29, 2020, P.L.782, No.96)

§ 624.3. Officers of Association; Ex-Officio Membership.—(a) The officers of the association shall consist of a president and other officers as determined by the association's bylaws. All of the officers, except any secretary, shall be members

Chap. 39 Res. During Mil. Service
Chap. 38 Intergov. Coop.
Chap. 37 3rd Class City Code
Chap. 36 Bor. Code
Chap. 35 2nd Class Twp. Code
Chap. 34 1st Class Twp. Code
Chap. 33 Home Rule Chart. Opt. Plans Law
Chap. 32 Water Serv. Act
Chap. 31 Munic. Auth. Act

of the association and shall hold office as determined by the association's bylaws or until their successors are chosen.

(b) Every township shall have one vote in a conference. A county association of townships may admit to membership of the association representatives of political subdivisions other than townships of the first class within the county, the judges of the court of common pleas in the county and engineers or other personnel from the Department of Transportation of the Commonwealth. Representatives of political subdivisions other than townships of the first class within the county, the judges of the court of common pleas in the county and engineers or other personnel from the Department of Transportation shall not be entitled to vote at the conference or hold office in the association.

(624.3 added Oct. 29, 2020, P.L.782, No.96)

(d) Civil Service for Police and Firefighters
(Subdiv. hdg. amended Oct. 29, 2020, P.L.782, No.96)

§ 625. Appointments of Police and Firefighters.—(a) This subdivision shall not apply to any township having a police force of less than three members or to volunteer fire departments or companies employing their own firefighters or to townships having less than three salaried firefighters.

(b) This subdivision shall be subject to the power of the board of commissioners to determine compensation.

(c) An appointment to and promotion in the township's police force or fire department paid directly by the township shall be made only according to qualifications and fitness to be ascertained by an examination. An examination for qualifications and fitness shall be competitive as provided under this subdivision.

(d) No individual shall be suspended, removed or demoted as a paid employe in any police force or as a paid firefighter of any township, except in accordance with the provisions of this subdivision.

(e) Nothing in this subdivision shall apply to retirement or be construed to prevent a township from adopting a compulsory retirement age for the township's employes or any class of employes or to prevent the township from retiring the township employes automatically when they attain the compulsory retirement age.

(625 amended Oct. 29, 2020, P.L.782, No.96)

§ 626. Civil Service Commission Created; Appointments; Vacancies.—(a) Subject to section 625(a), a civil service commission is established in each township where a police force or paid firefighters force is maintained.

(b) The commission shall consist of three civil service commissioners who shall be qualified electors of the township and shall be appointed by the board of commissioners initially to serve for the terms of two, four and six years. Upon the expiration of the term of a civil service commissioner, the successor shall be appointed for a term of six years.

(c) A vacancy occurring in the commission for any reason shall be filled by the board of commissioners for the remainder of the unexpired term no later than 30 days after the vacancy occurs.

(d) Before entering upon the discharge of the duties of office, a civil service commissioner shall take an oath or affirmation of office in accordance with 53 Pa.C.S. § 1141 (relating to form of oaths of office).

(e) The board of commissioners may appoint no more than three qualified electors of the township to serve as alternate members of the commission. The term of office of the alternate members shall be six years. If seated pursuant to section 628, an alternate shall be entitled to participate in all proceedings and discussions of the commission to the same and full extent as provided by law for

commission members, including specifically the right to cast a vote as a voting member during the proceedings, and shall have all the powers and duties set forth in this act and as otherwise provided by law. Alternates shall hold no other office in the township. An alternate may participate in any proceeding or discussion of the commission but shall not be entitled to vote as a member of the commission unless designated as a voting alternate member pursuant to section 628.

(f) The civil service commissioners shall receive no compensation.

(626 amended Oct. 29, 2020, P.L.782, No.96)

Compiler's Note: Section 3(3) of Act 76 of 2008 provided that all acts and parts of acts are repealed insofar as they are inconsistent with Act 76. Section 1 of Act 76 amended 53 Pa.C.S. Ch. 11 (relating to general provisions) by adding section 1141 (relating to form of oaths of office), which provides the form of oaths of office for elected or appointed officials of municipalities.

§ 627. Offices Incompatible With Civil Service Commissioner.—No civil service commissioner shall at the same time hold an elective or appointed office under the United States government, the Commonwealth of Pennsylvania, or any political subdivision of the Commonwealth, except that one member of the commission may be a member of the board of commissioners.

(627 amended Oct. 29, 2020, P.L.782, No.96)

§ 628. Organization of Commission; Quorum.—(a) The first commission appointed shall organize within ten days of its appointment and shall elect one of its members as the chairperson and one as the secretary. The commission shall thereafter meet and organize within 30 days of the first Monday of each even-numbered year. Each civil service commissioner shall be notified in writing of each and every meeting.

(b) Three members of the commission shall constitute a quorum. If, by reason of absence or disqualification of a member, a quorum is not reached, the chairperson shall designate as many alternate members of the commission to sit on the commission as may be needed to provide a quorum.

(c) An alternate member of the commission shall continue to serve on the commission in all proceedings involving the matter or case for which the alternate was initially designated until the commission has made a final determination of the matter or case. Designation of an alternate member pursuant to this section shall be made on a case-by-case basis in rotation according to declining seniority among all alternates.

(d) An action by the commission shall only be valid if the commission has the concurrence of a majority of the quorum.

(628 amended Oct. 29, 2020, P.L.782, No.96)

§ 629. Clerks and Supplies; Solicitor.—The township shall provide to the commission, on its requisition, clerical assistance that may be necessary for the work of the commission. The township shall provide a suitable and convenient room for the use of the commission. The commission shall order from the township the necessary stationery, postage, printing or supplies. The commission may appoint a solicitor. The township shall pay for the solicitor's services to the commission. The township may place a reasonable limit on the amount of compensation authorized each year for the services of the solicitor. The elected and appointed officials of the township shall aid the commission in carrying out the provisions of this subdivision.

(629 amended Oct. 29, 2020, P.L.782, No.96)

§ 630. Rules and Regulations.—(a) The commission shall have power to prescribe, amend and enforce rules and regulations for carrying into effect the provisions of this subdivision and shall be governed by the commission's rules and regulations. The board of commissioners may not promulgate rules and regulations, or amendments to them, for carrying into effect the provisions of this subdivision. The board of commissioners may make suggestions regarding proposed rules and regulations or amendments to the rules and regulations to members of the commission for their consideration. Regardless of whether the board of commissioners makes suggestions regarding proposed rules and regulations or amendments to the rules and regulations, rules and regulations or amendments shall be approved by the board of commissioners before the effective date of the rules and regulations or amendments. When the rules and regulations or amendments have been approved by the board of commissioners, the rules and regulations or amendments shall not be abrogated, amended or added to without the approval of the board of commissioners.

(b) The rules and regulations of the civil service commission shall reflect any minimum qualifications for police officers and paid firefighters pertaining to age, educational background, years of experience and areas of desired special expertise or certifications adopted by resolution of the board of commissioners.

(c) All rules and regulations or amendments to the rules and regulations shall be made available for public distribution or open to public inspection in accordance with the act of February 14, 2008 (P.L.6, No.3), known as the Right-to-Know Law.

(630 amended Oct. 29, 2020, P.L.782, No.96)

§ 631. **Minutes and Records.**—The commission shall keep minutes of its proceedings and records of examinations and other official actions. All recommendations of applicants for appointment received by the commission shall be kept and preserved for a period of five years, and all records and all written causes of removal filed with the commission, except as otherwise provided in section 645, shall be subject to reasonable regulation and open to public inspection in accordance with the act of February 14, 2008 (P.L.6, No.3), known as the Right-to-Know Law.

(631 amended Oct. 29, 2020, P.L.782, No.96)

§ 632. **Investigations.**—The commission may conduct investigations concerning all matters regarding the administration and enforcement of this subdivision and rules and regulations promulgated under this subdivision. The chairperson of the commission may administer oaths and affirmations in relation to the investigations.

(632 amended Oct. 29, 2020, P.L.782, No.96)

§ 633. **Subpoenas.**—(a) The commission may issue subpoenas over the signature of the chairperson to require the attendance of witnesses and the production of records and papers pertaining to any investigation or inquiry. The fees of witnesses for attendance and travel shall be the same as for witnesses appearing in the courts and shall be paid from appropriations for the incidental expenses of the commission.

(b) All officers in public service and employes shall attend and testify if required to do so by the commission.

(c) If an individual refuses or neglects to obey a subpoena issued by the commission, the individual shall, upon conviction, be sentenced to pay a fine of no less than $250 and no more than $500. If the individual is in default of the payment of the fine under this subsection, the individual shall be imprisoned for a period not to exceed 30 days.

(d) If an individual refuses or neglects to obey a subpoena issued by the commission, the commission may petition the court of common pleas of the county to order the individual to appear before the commission or the court to testify and produce records and papers as the commission deems necessary. If the indi-

Chap. 39 Res. During Mil. Service
Chap. 38 Intergov. Coop.
Chap. 37 3rd Class City Code
Chap. 36 Bor. Code
Chap. 35 2nd Class Twp. Code
Chap. 34 1st Class Twp. Code
Chap. 33 Home Rule Chart. Opt. Plans Law
Chap. 32 Water Serv. Act
Chap. 31 Munic. Auth. Act

vidual refuses to comply with the court's order, the individual shall be held in contempt of court.

(633 amended Oct. 29, 2020, P.L.782, No.96)

§ 634. Annual Report.—The commission shall make an annual report to the board of commissioners containing a brief summary of its work during the year, which shall be available for public inspection in accordance with the act of February 14, 2008 (P.L.6, No.3), known as the Right-to-Know Law.

(634 amended Oct. 29, 2020, P.L.782, No.96)

§ 635. General Provisions Relating to Examinations.—(a) The commission shall make rules and regulations to be approved as provided in section 630, providing for the examination of applicants for positions in the police force and as paid firefighters and for promotions, which rules and regulations shall prescribe the minimum qualifications of all applicants to be examined and the passing grades. All examinations for positions or promotions shall be practical in character and shall relate to matters and include inquiries as will fairly test the merit and fitness of the individuals examined to discharge the duties of the employment sought by them. All examinations shall be open to all applicants who have the minimum qualifications required by the rules and regulations. Each applicant for examination for an original position shall:

(1) be subject to the regulations adopted by the commission;

(2) either before or after the written examination, submit to a physical fitness or agility examination that is job-related and consistent with business necessity;

(3) if made a conditional offer of employment, be given a physical and psychological medical examination in accordance with section 643; and

(4) be subject to a background investigation. Background investigations may be restricted to those candidates on an eligibility list or those to be certified to the board of commissioners for appointment in accordance with section 638.

(a.1) An applicant for promotion shall be subject to the regulations adopted by the commission and to examination and selection in accordance with section 642. A physical fitness or agility examination that is job related and consistent with business necessity and physical and psychological medical examinations may, but need not, be required for promotions.

(b) Public notice of the time and place of every examination, together with the information as to the kind of position to be filled, shall be given by publication once in a newspaper of general circulation at least two weeks prior to each examination, and a copy of the notice shall be prominently posted in the office of the commission or other public place.

(c) The commission shall post in its office the eligibility list containing the names and grades of those who have passed the examination.

(635 amended Oct. 29, 2020, P.L.782, No.96)

Compiler's Note: Section 2 of Act 100 of 2011, which amended section 635, provided that the amendment shall apply to promotions made on or after October 19, 2010.

Compiler's Note: Section 7 of Act 75 of 2010, which amended section 635, provided that nothing contained in the amendment shall affect the validity of any civil services appointments or promotions made prior to the effective date of section 7.

§ 636. Application for Examination.—An individual who desires to apply for examination must file with the commission a formal application in which the applicant shall provide under oath or affirmation information required by the commission's rules and regulations showing the applicant's qualifications for the position for which the applicant is being examined.

(636 amended Oct. 29, 2020, P.L.782, No.96)

§ 637. Rejection of Applicant; Hearing.—(a) The commission may refuse to examine or, if examined, may refuse to certify after examination as eligible, any applicant who:

(1) is found to lack any of the minimum qualifications for examination prescribed in the rules and regulations adopted for the position or employment for which the applicant has applied;

(2) is physically unfit for the performance of the duties of the position or employment for which the applicant has applied;

(3) is illegally using a controlled substance as defined in the Controlled Substances Act (Public Law 91-513, 21 U.S.C. § 802);

(4) has been found guilty of any crime involving moral turpitude or of infamous or notoriously disgraceful conduct;

(5) has been dismissed from public service for delinquency or misconduct in office; or

(6) is affiliated with any group which have policies or engage in activities that are subversive to the form of government established in Federal or State law.

(b) If an applicant is aggrieved by the commission's refusal to certify the applicant as eligible after an examination or an individual is aggrieved by the commission's refusal to examine the individual, the commission shall, at the request of the applicant or individual aggrieved, set a date, time and place for a public hearing within 10 days after the receipt of the request for a public hearing. At the public hearing, the applicant or individual aggrieved may appear with or without counsel and the commission shall take testimony and review the commission's refusal to provide the examination or certification. The deliberations of the commission regarding the matter, including interim rulings on evidentiary or procedural issues, may be held in the nature of a closed executive session. The commission's disposition of the matter shall constitute official action which shall occur at a public meeting held pursuant to 65 Pa.C.S. Ch. 7 (relating to open meetings) and the commission's decision on the matter shall be final.

(637 amended Oct. 29, 2020, P.L.782, No.96)

Compiler's Note: Section 7 of Act 75 of 2010, which amended section 637, provided that nothing contained in the amendment shall affect the validity of any civil services appointments or promotions made prior to the effective date of section 7.

§ 638. Eligibility List and Manner of Filling Appointments.—(a) At the completion of the testing process, including a physical agility or other examination, with the exception of a background investigation to be conducted after the establishment of an eligibility list and physical and psychological medical examination under section 643, the commission shall rank the candidates who have satisfied the minimum requirements for appointment on an eligibility list. The eligibility list shall contain the names of individuals eligible for appointment listed from highest to lowest based on their scores on the examinations administered by the commission and any points for which the applicant was entitled by virtue of 51 Pa.C.S. Ch. 71 (relating to veterans' preference). The eligibility list will be valid for one year from the date the commission formally adopts the eligibility list. Prior to expiration of the one-year period, the commission may extend the validity of the eligibility list for up to an additional twelve (12) months by a majority vote of the commission at a duly authorized commission meeting. In the absence of a lawful extension by the commission, the list shall expire.

(b) Except as provided under subsection (c), an original position or employment in the police force or as a paid firefighter, except for the chief of police or chief of the fire department or an equivalent official, shall be filled only in the following manner:

(1) The board of commissioners shall notify the commission of a vacancy which is to be filled and shall request the certification of an eligibility list.

(2) For each vacancy, the commission shall certify three individuals from the eligibility list, or a fewer number of individuals if three individuals are not available, who have received the highest average for the vacancy.

(3) The board of commissioners shall make a conditional appointment from the certified individuals by the commission based solely on the merits and fitness of the certified individuals, unless the board of commissioners objects to the commission regarding one or more of the certified individuals for a cause specified under section 637.

(4) If any objections are sustained by the commission under paragraph (3), or if the conditional appointee is determined to be unqualified in accordance with the procedures set forth under section 643, the commission shall strike the name of the individual from the eligibility list and certify the next highest individual from names stricken from the eligibility list.

(b.1) The procedure under subsection (b) shall be used to fill each subsequent vacancy that occurs in the same or another position.

(c) A vacancy in an existing position in the police force or as a paid firefighter which occurs as a result of retirement, resignation, disability or death may be filled by the board of commissioners by the reappointment or reinstatement of a former employe of the police force or fire department who had previously complied with this section. No examination, other than a physical examination as directed by the civil service commission, shall be required in a case of reappointment or reinstatement to the force or department with which the employe previously served, except at the discretion of the board of commissioners or as otherwise required by law.

(d) In the case of a vacancy in the office of chief of police or chief of the fire department or equivalent official, the board of commissioners may nominate an individual to the commission. The commission shall subject the nominee to a noncompetitive examination. If the nominee is certified by the commission as qualified, the nominee may be appointed to the position and shall be subject to the provisions of this subdivision.

(638 amended Oct. 29, 2020, P.L.782, No.96)

Compiler's Note: Section 2 of Act 100 of 2011, which amended section 638, provided that the amendment shall apply to promotions made on or after October 19, 2010.

Compiler's Note: Section 7 of Act 75 of 2010, which amended section 638, provided that nothing contained in the amendment shall affect the validity of any civil services appointments or promotions made prior to the effective date of section 7.

§ 639. Age; Applicant's Residence.—No individual shall be eligible to apply for examination unless the individual is at least 18 years of age at the date of application. The board of commissioners may accept applications from nonresidents of the township and may require nonresident police officers and nonresident paid firefighters to become residents of the township after appointment to the positions. The rules and regulations of the civil service commission shall reflect the residency requirements of the board of commissioners or a collective bargaining agreement or award.

(639 amended Oct. 29, 2020, P.L.782, No.96)

Table of Contents
Part I Ch. 1–3 Ethics, Records, Open Meetings
Part II Ch. 4–10 Taxation
Part III Ch. 11–18 Torts, Contracts & Civil Rules
Part IV Ch. 19–24 Zoning & Planning
Part V Ch. 25–30 Construction and Emergency Codes
Part VI Ch. 31–39 Municipal Codes
Index

§ 640. Probationary Period.—(a) An original appointment to a position in the police force or as a paid firefighter shall be for a probationary period of not less than six months and not more than one year, but during the probationary period an appointee may be dismissed only for a cause specified in section 637 or because of incapacity for duty due to the use of alcohol or drugs.

(b) If, at the close of a probationary period, the conduct or fitness of the probationer has not been satisfactory to the board of commissioners, the probationer shall be notified in writing that the probationer will not receive a permanent appointment and the appointment shall cease. If the probationer is not notified or dismissed in accordance with this section, the probationer's retention shall be equivalent to a permanent appointment.

(c) The decision of a township to suspend or discharge a probationer shall be final and shall not be subject to the hearing provisions under section 645. The decision of a township to suspend or discharge a probationer shall be rendered in accordance with 65 Pa.C.S. Ch. 7 (relating to open meetings).

(640 amended Oct. 29, 2020, P.L.782, No.96)

Compiler's Note: Section 7 of Act 75 of 2010, which amended section 640, provided that nothing contained in the amendment shall affect the validity of any civil services appointments or promotions made prior to the effective date of section 7.

§ 641. Provisional Appointments.—(a) If there are urgent reasons for the filling of a vacancy in a position in the police force and there are no names on the eligibility list for the appointment, the board of commissioners may nominate an individual to the commission for a noncompetitive examination. If the nominee is certified by the commission as qualified after the noncompetitive examination, the nominee may be provisionally appointed to fill the vacancy.

(b) Within 90 days of the provisional appointment under subsection (a), the commission shall hold a competitive examination, certify an eligibility list and make a regular appointment to the position in accordance with section 638 from the names submitted by the commission. Nothing in this section shall be construed to prevent the appointment without an examination of individuals temporarily as police officers in cases of riot or other emergencies or firefighters in emergency cases.

(641 amended Oct. 29, 2020, P.L.782, No.96)

§ 642. Promotions.—(a) A promotion shall be based on merit to be ascertained by an examination to be prescribed by the commission. All questions relative to a promotion shall be practical in character and fairly test the merit and fitness of individuals seeking promotion.

(b) The board of commissioners shall notify the commission of a vacancy on the police force or fire department which is to be filled by promotion and shall request the certification of an eligibility list.

(c) The commission shall certify for each vacancy the names of three individuals on the eligibility list who have received the highest average in the last promotion examination held within a period of two years preceding the date of the request for the eligibility list. If three names are not available, the commission shall certify the names remaining on the eligibility list. The board of commissioners shall make an appointment from the names certified, based solely on the merits and fitness of the candidate, unless the board of commissioners make objections to the commission regarding any individual on the eligibility list for any reason provided under section 637.

(d) The board of commissioners may determine in each instance whether an increase in salary constitutes a promotion.

(642 amended Oct. 29, 2020, P.L.782, No.96)

Compiler's Note: Section 7 of Act 75 of 2010, which amended section 642, provided that nothing contained in the amendment shall affect the validity of any civil services appointments or promotions made prior to the effective date of section 7.

§ 643. Physical and Psychological Medical Examinations.—(a) An applicant selected from the eligibility list shall receive a conditional offer of employment. The offer of employment shall be conditioned upon the conditional employee undergoing a physical and psychological medical examination and a determination that the conditional employee is capable of performing all the essential functions of the position. Physical medical examinations shall be conducted under the direction of a physician or other qualified medical professional. Psychological medical examinations shall be conducted under the direction of a psychiatrist or psychologist.

(b) The physician, other qualified medical professional, psychiatrist or psychologist shall be appointed by the board of commissioners and shall render an opinion as to whether the conditional appointee has a physical or mental condition which calls into question the individual's ability to perform all of the essential functions of the position for which the individual was conditionally appointed.

(c) If the opinion rendered by the physician, other qualified medical professional, psychiatrist or psychologist calls into question the conditional appointee's ability to perform all essential functions of a position, an individual designated by the board of commissioners shall meet with the conditional appointee for the purpose of having one or more interactive discussions on whether the conditional appointee can, with or without reasonable accommodation, perform all the essential functions of the position.

(d) If, at the conclusion of the interactive discussion conducted under subsection (c), the board of commissioners determine that the conditional appointee is not qualified, the board of commissioners shall give written notice to the conditional appointee and the commission.

(e) Nothing in this subdivision shall be construed to authorize physical or psychological medical examinations prior to conditional appointment.

(f) As used in this section, the following words and phrases shall have the meanings given to them in this subsection unless the context clearly indicates otherwise:

"Medical examination" shall mean any examination, procedure, inquiry or test designed to obtain information about medical history or a physical or mental condition which might disqualify an applicant if it would prevent the applicant from performing, with or without a reasonable accommodation, all of the essential functions of the position.

"Physician" (Deleted by amendment).

"Qualified medical professional" shall mean an individual, in collaboration with or under the supervision or direction of a physician, as may be required by law, who is licensed:

(1) as a physician assistant pursuant to the act of December 20, 1985 (P.L.457, No.112), known as the "Medical Practice Act of 1985," or the act of October 5, 1978 (P.L.1109, No.261), known as the "Osteopathic Medical Practice Act"; or

(2) as a certified registered nurse practitioner pursuant to the act of May 22, 1951 (P.L.317, No.69), known as "The Professional Nursing Law."

(643 amended Oct. 29, 2020, P.L.782, No.96)

Compiler's Note: Section 7 of Act 75 of 2010, which amended section 643, provided that nothing contained in the amendment shall affect the

Table of Contents
Part I Ch. 1–3 Ethics, Records, Open Meetings
Part II Ch. 4–10 Taxation
Part III Ch. 11–18 Torts, Contracts & Civil Rules
Part IV Ch. 19–24 Zoning & Planning
Part V Ch. 25–30 Construction and Emergency Codes
Part VI Ch. 31–39 Municipal Codes
Index

Chap. 39 Res. During Mil. Service
Chap. 38 Intergov. Coop.
Chap. 37 3rd Class City Code
Chap. 36 Bor. Code
Chap. 35 2nd Class Twp. Code
Chap. 34 1st Class Twp. Code
Chap. 33 Home Rule Chart. Opt. Plans Law
Chap. 32 Water Serv. Act
Chap. 31 Munic. Auth. Act

validity of any civil services appointments or promotions made prior to the effective date of section 7.

§ 644. Removals.—(a) An individual employed in a police or fire force of a township may not be suspended without pay, removed or demoted except for the following reasons:

(1) Physical or mental disability affecting the individual's ability to continue in service, in which case the individual shall receive an honorable discharge from service.

(2) Neglect or violation of any official duty.

(3) Violation of any law of this Commonwealth, if the violation constitutes a misdemeanor or felony.

(4) Inefficiency, neglect, intemperance, disobedience of orders or conduct unbecoming an officer.

(5) Intoxication while on duty.

(6) Engaging or participating in the conduct of a political or election campaign otherwise than to exercise the individual's own right of suffrage, except that this clause shall only apply to a police officer while on duty or in uniform or while using township property.

(7) Engaging or participating in the conduct of a political or election campaign for an incompatible office under section 1401.

(a.1) An individual employed by a police or fire force may not be removed for religious, racial or political reasons.

(a.2) A written statement of charges made against an individual employed shall be furnished to the individual within five days after the same statement of charges are filed with the commission. The individual shall have 10 days from the date of receiving the notice to submit a written request for a hearing to the commission under section 645.

(b) If, for reasons of economy or other reasons, it shall be deemed necessary by a township to reduce the number of paid employes of the police or fire force, the township shall furlough the individual, including a probationer, last appointed to the respective force. The removal shall be accomplished by furloughing in numerical order commencing with the individual last appointed until the reduction shall have been accomplished. If the police or fire force shall again be increased, the employes furloughed shall be reinstated in the order of their seniority in the respective service. This subsection, as to reductions in force, is not applicable to a chief of police or fire chief.

(644 amended Oct. 29, 2020, P.L.782, No.96)

§ 645. Hearings on Dismissals and Demotions.—(a) An individual suspended, removed or demoted may make written answers to charges filed against the individual not later than the day scheduled for the hearing. The commission shall grant the individual a hearing which shall be held within a period of ten days from the filing of written charges, unless continued by the commission for cause at the request of the board of commissioners or the accused. The failure of the commission to hold a hearing within ten days from the filing of the written charges shall not result in the dismissal of the charges filed.

(b) At a hearing, the individual against whom the charges are made may be present in person and by counsel. The board of commissioners, or the chief of police or fire chief, as applicable, when the board of commissioners is not in session, may suspend the individual without pay pending the determination of the charges against the individual, but if the commission fails to uphold the charges, the individual sought to be suspended, removed or demoted shall be reinstated with full pay for the period during which the individual was suspended, removed or demoted, and no charges shall be officially recorded against the individual's record.

A stenographic record of all testimony taken at the hearings shall be filed with and preserved by the commission, which record shall be sealed and not be available for public inspection if the charges are dismissed.

(c) All parties shall have immediate right of appeal to the court of common pleas of the county, and the case shall there be determined as the court deems proper. No order of suspension made by the commission shall be for a longer period than one year. The appeal shall be taken within 30 days from the date of entry by the commission of its final order and shall be by petition. Upon the appeal being taken and docketed, the court of common pleas shall schedule a day for a hearing and shall proceed to hear the appeal on the original record and additional proof or testimony as the parties concerned may desire to offer in evidence. The decision of the court affirming or reversing the decision of the commission shall be final and the employe shall be suspended, discharged, demoted or reinstated in accordance with the order of the court.

(d) The board of commissioners and the individual sought to be suspended, removed or demoted shall at all times have the right to employ counsel before the commission and upon appeal to the court of common pleas. Unless the board of commissioners or the individual sought to be suspended, removed or demoted requests that the proceedings before the commission be open to the public, the proceedings before the commission under this section shall be held in the nature of a closed executive session that shall not be open to the public. The request shall be presented to the commission before the civil service hearing commences. The deliberations of the commission, including interim rulings on evidentiary or procedural issues, may be held in private and shall not be subject to a request for being open to the public by the board of commissioners or the individual sought to be suspended, removed or demoted. The commission's disposition of the disciplinary action shall constitute official action which shall occur at a public meeting held under 65 Pa.C.S. Ch. 7 (relating to open meetings).

(e) In any case in which a police officer or firefighter who is a member of a bargaining unit is subject to suspension, discharge or discipline, the police officer or firefighter shall have the option of challenging the suspension, discharge or discipline imposed by using the procedures provided in this section or by a proceeding in grievance arbitration. A choice to proceed either by the procedures provided for in this section or by grievance arbitration shall foreclose the opportunity to proceed in the alternative method.

(645 amended Oct. 29, 2020, P.L.782, No.96)

§ 646. Present Employes Exempted.—All appointments in the police or fire forces of townships, including the chief of police or equivalent official, prior to the creation of a commission, shall continue to hold their positions and shall not be required to take any examination under the provisions of this act except that which may be required for promotion. This section shall not be construed to apply to individuals employed temporarily in emergency cases.

(646 amended Oct. 29, 2020, P.L.782, No.96)

§ 647. Discrimination Prohibited.—(a) No question in a form of application for examination or in an examination or inquiry shall be so framed as to elicit information from an applicant in violation of Federal or State antidiscrimination laws, such as the Civil Rights Act of 1964 (Public Law 88-352, 78 Stat. 241) or the act of October 27, 1955 (P.L.744, No.222), known as the Pennsylvania Human Relations Act. All disclosures by an applicant of information protected by antidiscrimination laws shall be ignored.

(b) No discrimination shall be exercised, threatened or promised by a person against or in favor of an applicant or employe in violation of Federal or State antidiscrimination laws, such as the Civil Rights Act of 1964 or the Pennsylvania Human Relations Act, and no offer or promise of reward, favor or benefit, directly or indirectly, shall be made to or received by an individual for an act done or duty omitted or to be done under this subdivision.

(647 amended Oct. 29, 2020, P.L.782, No.96)

§ 648. Penalty.—A township commissioner who, by vote, appoints an individual to the police force or as a firefighter contrary to the provisions of this subdivision, or a township commissioner or member of the commission who willfully refuses to comply with or conform to the provisions of this subdivision, commits a misdemeanor and, upon conviction, shall be sentenced to pay a fine not exceeding five hundred dollars ($500) or to imprisonment not exceeding ninety days, or both.

(648 amended Oct. 29, 2020, P.L.782, No.96)

§ 649. Salaries of Civil Service Commission.—(649 repealed Oct. 29, 2020, P.L.782, No.96)

§ 650. Police Force and Firefighters Defined.—(a) Police force as used in this subdivision shall mean a police force organized and operating as prescribed by law, the members of which devote their normal working hours to police duty or duty in connection with the bureau, agencies and services connected with police protection work and who are paid a stated salary or compensation for the work by the township.

(b) Firefighter as used in this subdivision shall mean an individual who operates fire apparatus and devotes the individual's normal working hours to operating a piece of fire apparatus or other services connected with fire protection work and who is paid a stated salary or compensation for the work done by the township.

(650 amended Oct. 29, 2020, P.L.782, No.96)

ARTICLE VII

TOWNSHIP COMMISSIONERS

53 P.S. §§ 55701–55704

§ 701. Organization; Failure to Organize.—(a) The board of commissioners shall organize on the first Monday of January of each even-numbered year. If the first Monday is a legal holiday the meeting shall be held the following day. The board of commissioners shall assemble for the organization meeting at their place of meeting at a time convenient to the governing body.

(b) At the organization meeting, the board shall elect one member as president and one as vice-president, who, as long as they continue to be commissioners, shall hold office until their successors are elected and qualified. The president, or, in the president's absence, the vice-president, shall preside at all meetings of the board, and perform other duties as are specified in this act or which may be prescribed by ordinance.

If a majority of the board of commissioners do not attend the organization meeting, those present may adjourn the meeting from day to day until a majority attend.

(c) If the board of commissioners of a township fails to organize within ten days from the time prescribed by this section, the court of common pleas, upon the petition of at least ten registered electors, verified by the affidavit of one of the petitioners, shall issue a rule upon the delinquent commissioners to show cause why their seats should not be declared vacant. The rule shall be returnable not less than five days from the time of its issue, and after hearing, the court may declare the seats of the members of the board responsible for the failure to

Chap. 39 Res. During Mil. Service | Chap. 38 Intergov. Coop. | Chap. 37 3rd Class City Code | Chap. 36 Bor. Code | Chap. 35 2nd Class Twp. Code | Chap. 34 1st Class Twp. Code | Chap. 33 Home Rule Chart. Opt. Plans Law | Chap. 32 Water Serv. Act | Chap. 31 Munic. Auth. Act organize vacant, and shall appoint others in their place to hold office for the respective unexpired terms.

(d) The organization meeting under this section may be considered a regular monthly meeting for the transaction of business that may come before the board of commissioners. The first order of business at this meeting shall be organization of the board. The board of commissioners may, at the organization meeting, appoint other officers as may be provided for by law or ordinance, or as may be deemed necessary for the conduct of affairs of the township.

(701 amended Oct. 29, 2020, P.L.782, No.96)

§ 702. Monthly Meetings, Quorum, Voting.—(a) The board of commissioners shall meet at least once a month, at a time and place designated by ordinance.

(b) A majority of the members of the board of commissioners shall constitute a quorum. Except as provided in subsection (b.1)(1)(i), only members of the board of commissioners physically present at a meeting place within the township shall be counted in establishing a quorum.

(b.1) Telecommunication.—

(1) The board of commissioners may, pursuant to an established telecommunications policy and as provided in paragraph (2), provide for the participation of members of the board in township meetings by means of telecommunication devices, such as telephones or computer terminals, which permit, at a minimum, audio communication between locations, if the following apply:

(i) A majority of the members of the board is physically present at the advertised meeting place within the township and a quorum is established at the convening or reconvening of the meeting. If, after the convening or reconvening of a meeting, a member of the board has been disqualified from voting as a matter of law, but is still physically present, members of the board participating by telecommunication device in accordance with this section shall be counted to maintain a quorum.

(ii) The telecommunication device used permits the member or members of the board not physically present at the meeting to:

(A) speak to and hear the comments and votes, if any, of the members of the board who are physically present, as well as other members of the board who may not be physically present and are also using a telecommunication device to participate in the meeting; and

(B) speak to and hear the comments of the public who are physically present at the meeting.

(iii) The telecommunication device used permits the members of the board and the members of the public who are physically present at the meeting to speak to and hear the comments and the vote, if any, of the member or members of the board who are not physically present at the meeting.

(2) Any changes to the board of commissioner's established telecommunications policy shall become effective no sooner than thirty days following the vote to change the policy.

(3) Nothing in this subsection shall be construed to limit the protections and prohibitions contained in any law or regulation relating to the rights of the disabled.

(c) A member of the board shall not be disqualified from voting on any issue before the board solely because the member had previously expressed an opinion on the issue in either an official or unofficial capacity.

(702 amended Oct. 29, 2020, P.L.782, No.96)

§ 703. Compensation.—(a) Each township commissioner may receive a salary, established by ordinance, as follows:

Table of Contents
Part I Ch. 1–3 Ethics, Records, Open Meetings
Part II Ch. 4–10 Taxation
Part III Ch. 11–18 Torts, Contracts & Civil Rules
Part IV Ch. 19–24 Zoning & Planning
Part V Ch. 25–30 Construction and Emergency Codes
Part VI Ch. 31–39 Municipal Codes
Index

(1) In townships with a population of less than 5,000, a maximum of $3,145 per year.

(2) In townships with a population of 5,000 or more but less than 10,000, a maximum of $4,190 per year.

(3) In townships with a population of 10,000 or more but less than 15,000, a maximum of $5,450 per year.

(4) In townships with a population of 15,000 or more but less than 25,000, a maximum of $6,915 per year.

(5) In townships with a population of 25,000 or more but less than 35,000, a maximum of $7,335 per year.

(6) In townships with a population of 35,000 or more but less than 45,000, a maximum of $8,385 per year.

(7) In townships with a population of 45,000 or more, a maximum of $210 per year per 1,000 residents or fraction of 1,000.

The salaries shall be payable monthly or quarterly for the duties imposed by this act. Benefits provided to the commissioners under section 1502.39 shall not be considered pay, salary or compensation, but payment for all or a part of the premiums or charges for the benefits shall be in accordance with section 1502.39.

(a.1) Notwithstanding subsection (a), the board of commissioners may provide for a member of the board of commissioners to receive compensation on a per-meeting basis based on attendance of board members. Total annual compensation may not exceed the amounts specified in subsection (a). Compensation shall only be payable for duly advertised public meetings in which a member of the board of commissioners participated. If the board of commissioners has provided that board members shall receive compensation on a per-meeting basis, the board of commissioners may provide for the forfeiture of up to one-twelfth (1/12) of the annual compensation of a board member or impose another appropriate penalty for each unexcused absence from a regularly scheduled meeting.

(b) The population shall be determined by the latest available official census figures. No township shall be required to reduce the salary of a commissioner as a result of a decrease in population. Any change in salary, compensation or emoluments of the elected office shall become effective at the beginning of the next term of the township commissioner.

(703 amended Oct. 29, 2020, P.L.782, No.96)

§ 704. **Reports to Auditors.**—The board of commissioners shall annually, on or before the first day of February, furnish to the township auditors information concerning the construction, reconstruction, maintenance and repair of streets or other matters that may be required by a department of the Commonwealth to be included in the annual township report.

(704 amended Oct. 29, 2020, P.L.782, No.96)

ARTICLE VIII
TOWNSHIP TREASURER
53 P.S. §§ 55801–55809

(Hdg. repealed Oct. 24, 2012, P.L.1478, No.188)

§ 801. Fidelity Bond.—(801 repealed Oct. 24, 2012, P.L.1478, No.188)

§ 802. Compensation.—(802 repealed May 25, 1945, P.L.1050, No.394)

§ 803. Accounts to Be Kept by Treasurer.—(803 repealed Oct. 24, 2012, P.L.1478, No.188)

§ 804. Payment of Moneys on Orders.—(804 repealed Oct. 24, 2012, P.L.1478, No.188)

§ 805. Powers as Tax Collector.—(805 repealed Oct. 24, 2012, P.L.1478, No.188)

§ 806. Oath.—(806 repealed Oct. 24, 2012, P.L.1478, No.188)

§ 807. Special Funds; Penalty.—(807 repealed Oct. 24, 2012, P.L.1478, No.188)

§ 808. Depositories of Township Funds; Selection; Bonds.—(808 repealed Oct. 24, 2012, P.L.1478, No.188)

ARTICLE VIII-A
APPOINTED TOWNSHIP TREASURER
53 P.S. §§55801-A–55806-A

(Art. added Oct. 24, 2012, P.L.1478, No.188)

§ 801-A. Township treasurer.

(a) Appointment.—The board of commissioners shall appoint a township treasurer, who may be the elected tax collector or an employee of the township, to serve at the pleasure of the board of commissioners. The township treasurer shall not be a member of the board of commissioners.

(b) Compensation.—The board of commissioners shall determine the compensation of the township treasurer. Notwithstanding section 34 of the act of May 25, 1945 (P.L.1050, No.394), known as the "Local Tax Collection Law," a township treasurer who is the elected tax collector of the township may receive a salary, compensation or emoluments of office for the treasurer's work.

(c) Deputy.—

(1) The township treasurer shall, within 60 days of the treasurer's appointment, nominate to the board of commissioners a person to be appointed by the board as the deputy treasurer. The board may, subject to the nominated person meeting the bonding qualifications in paragraph (3), appoint the nominated person as the deputy treasurer.

(2) The deputy treasurer shall have the rights and powers and shall perform the duties of the township treasurer if the township treasurer is unable to perform the duties of office due to sickness, absence or inability to act. If the township treasurer is unable to perform the duties of office and has failed to nominate a person for appointment as the deputy treasurer, the board of commissioners may appoint a deputy treasurer. The deputy treasurer shall serve until the township treasurer is again able to perform the duties of the office.

(3) The deputy treasurer shall be bonded for the same amount, and in the same manner pursuant to section 802-A, as the township treasurer when acting in the capacity of township treasurer. The board of commissioners shall determine the compensation of the deputy treasurer.

(801-A amended Oct. 29, 2020, P.L.782, No.96)

§ 802-A. Treasurer's and deputy treasurer's bond.

(a) **Requirements for bond.**—The township treasurer shall, before entering upon the duties of office, give a fidelity bond to the township in an amount established by ordinance or resolution and at least equal to 50% of the amount of township funds estimated by the board of commissioners to be available to the township treasurer at any time during the current year. The bond shall be provided by a surety company or companies duly authorized to do business in this Commonwealth. The bond given by the treasurer shall be conditioned on the faithful performance of the duties as stated in section 803-A. The treasurer shall not, in any event, be required to give bond or bonds aggregating an amount in excess of the taxes to be paid over to the treasurer by the tax collector. The bonding requirements of this section shall also apply to the deputy treasurer.

(b) **Insurance in lieu of bond.**—In lieu of the bond required for the faithful performance by the township treasurer or deputy treasurer of official duties other than those of tax collector, the board of commissioners may purchase insurance as provided in section 602(b).

(802-A amended Oct. 29, 2020, P.L.782, No.96)

§ 803-A. Treasurer's duties.

The township treasurer shall:

(1) Receive all money due the township and promptly deposit the money in a designated depository in the name of the township.

(2) Keep distinct and accurate accounts of all sums received from taxes and other sources, which accounts shall be open to the inspection of the board of commissioners, township auditor or controller.

(3) Annually submit the accounts to the township auditors or controller for audit.

(4) Pay out all money of the township only on direction by the board of commissioners, upon an order signed by the president or vice president and attested by the secretary or assistant secretary of the board and designating the appropriation out of which the order shall be paid. The order shall not be executed unless there is money available in the treasury. The following apply:

(i) Nothing in this act shall be construed to preclude the use of electronic signatures and transactions to the extent authorized by the act of December 16, 1999 (P.L.971, No.69), known as the "Electronic Transactions Act," or any other law.

(ii) When a treasurer pays out money except upon orders or pays money in excess of the appropriation, the treasurer shall receive no credit in the settlement of the treasurer's accounts for those amounts, nor shall the treasurer have any claim or right of action against the township.

(5) Preserve the account books, papers, documents and other records of the office and turn them over to the successor in office.

(6) Pay over to the successor any balance in money remaining in the treasurer's accounts or charged against the treasurer in the settlement of the treasurer's accounts.

(803-A amended Oct. 29, 2020, P.L.782, No.96)

§ 804-A. Penalty for failure to perform duties.

A township treasurer or deputy treasurer who fails to perform any duties of the office other than those for which specific penalties are provided commits a summary offense and, in addition to the fine or penalty which may be imposed upon conviction, is required to pay to the township an amount equal to the amount of the financial loss that occurred, if any, for not performing the duties of the office. That person is disqualified from holding the office of township treasurer or deputy treasurer.

(804-A added Oct. 24, 2012, P.L.1478, No.188)

§ 805-A. Use of special funds; penalty.

When money is collected for a special purpose, a township treasurer or township commissioner may not apply that money to any purpose other than that for which it was collected. Every misapplication shall be a misdemeanor of the third degree, and, in addition to the fine or penalty which may be imposed upon conviction, the defendant shall be required to pay restitution in the amount of money improperly spent.

(805-A amended Oct. 29, 2020, P.L.782, No.96)

§ 806-A. Depositories of township funds.

The following shall apply:

(1) The board of commissioners shall designate by resolution a depository or depositories for township funds. Funds deposited with a banking institution of this Commonwealth shall be insured with the Federal Deposit Insurance Corporation or the National Credit Union Share Insurance Fund or their successor agencies, to the extent that accounts are so insured. The designation is valid for a period of one year or until another depository or other depositories are designated by similar action of the board of commissioners.

(2) The depository or depositories shall be banks, banking institutions or trust companies located in this Commonwealth.

(3) The depository or depositories shall not be required to furnish bond or collateral security to cover the amount of any deposit to the extent that the same is insured as provided in paragraph (1).

(4) The township treasurer or deputy treasurer shall, upon the designation of the depository or depositories by the board of commissioners, immediately transfer to the depository or depositories the township funds and after that make deposits solely in the depository or depositories in the name of the township.

(5) The township treasurer or deputy treasurer, acting in accordance with law, shall not be liable for the loss of township funds caused solely by the insolvency or negligence of the depository or depositories.

(6) The following apply:

(i) The designated depositories shall, upon receipt of notice of their selection as a depository of township funds, collateralize deposits of public funds in accordance with the act of August 6, 1971 (P.L.281, No.72), entitled, "An act standardizing the procedures for pledges of assets to secure deposits of public funds with banking institutions pursuant to other laws; establishing a standard rule for the types, amounts and valuations of assets eligible to be used as collateral for deposits of public funds; permitting assets to be pledged against deposits on a pooled basis; and authorizing the appointment of custodians to act as pledgees of assets," which authorizes financial institutions to pledge collateral in an account in the name of the township or utilize a letter of credit from the Federal Home Loan Bank, to secure public deposits in excess of Federal Deposit Insurance Corporation insurance limits. The depository shall provide a monthly report within 15 days after the end of each month to the board of commissioners in accordance with the reporting requirements in the act of August 6, 1971 (P.L.281, No.72), including the composition of the collateral and related market value.

(ii) Townships may elect to require that depositories must pledge collateral in an account in the name of the township to collateralize deposits above the Federal Deposit Insurance Corporation limit. These accounts may be custodied with the depository's trust department or at a third-party financial institution. The arrangement with the depository may be governed by a written agreement, approved by the board of directors or loan committee of the depository, with approval reflected in the minutes of the board or com-

Chap. 39 Res. During Mil. Service
Chap. 38 Intergov. Coop.
Chap. 37 3rd Class City Code
Chap. 36 Bor. Code
Chap. 35 2nd Class Twp. Code
Chap. 34 1st Class Twp. Code
Chap. 33 Home Rule Chart. Opt. Plans Law
Chap. 32 Water Serv. Act
Chap. 31 Munic. Auth. Act

mittee, which are kept continuously as an official record of the depository, and include the following if collateral is pledged instead of a Federal Home Loan Bank Letter of Credit:

(A) Collateral shall be marked to market no less frequently than weekly.

(B) Collateral shall be in investments as prescribed in the investment program provided by the board of investment or board of commissioners.

(C) If the financial institution serves as the custodian, the pledged collateral shall be held in a separate account established under the act of August 6, 1971 (P.L.281, No.72), in the depository's trust department.

(D) The market value of the pledged collateral shall be at least 102% of the township's deposits in excess of federally insured limits.

(E) A monthly report shall be provided as specified in subparagraph (i).

(806-A amended Oct. 29, 2020, P.L.782, No.96)

ARTICLE VIII-B
TAX COLLECTOR

53 P.S. § 55801-B

(Art. added Oct. 24, 2012, P.L.1478, No.188)

§ 801-B. Powers and duties of tax collector.

(a) Collection of taxes required.—The township tax collector shall collect all county, institution district, township, school and other taxes levied within the townships by authorities authorized to levy taxes.

(b) Collection of taxes permitted.—

(1) The tax collector may also be designated in the tax-levying ordinance or resolution or be employed by the tax-levying authority to collect taxes levied under the act of December 31, 1965 (P.L.1257, No.511), known as The Local Tax Enabling Act.

(2) No such ordinance or resolution may authorize the collection of income taxes in a manner other than as provided in Chapter 5 of The Local Tax Enabling Act.

(c) Other powers and duties.—In addition to the powers, duties and responsibilities under this act, the tax collector shall exercise all the powers and perform all the duties and be subject to all the obligations and responsibilities for the collection of taxes as are conferred upon tax collectors by law.

(801-B amended Oct. 29, 2020, P.L.782, No.96)

ARTICLE IX
TOWNSHIP SECRETARY

53 P.S. §§ 55901–55903

§ 901. Appointment of Secretary and Salary.—The board of commissioners shall appoint a secretary to serve at the pleasure of the board and who shall not be a member of the board. The secretary shall act as secretary of the board. The secretary's salary shall be fixed by ordinance or resolution.

(901 amended Oct. 29, 2020, P.L.782, No.96)

§ 901.1. Assistant Secretary.—The board of commissioners may, by resolution, appoint an assistant secretary. The assistant secretary shall assist the secretary in the performance of the secretary's duties and, in the absence or disability of the secretary, perform the duties and exercise the powers of the secretary. The compensation of an assistant secretary shall be determined by the board of commissioners, and the assistant secretary shall be required to give bond in an amount as required by the board of commissioners. The assistant secretary may be appointed from the membership of the board of commissioners but shall not be any other officer of the board. If a member of the board of commissioners is appointed as the assistant secretary, the appointed member shall not receive compensation for the services and shall be bonded.

(901.1 amended Oct. 29, 2020, P.L.782, No.96)

§ 902. Duties and Penalty.—(a) The secretary of a township shall:

(1) Record the proceedings of the board of commissioners.

(2) Preserve the minutes and other records and documents of the township and turn them over to the successor in office.

(3) Record appropriations made by the board of commissioners and the amounts charged to each appropriation.

(4) Perform other duties as required by law or the board of commissioners.

(b) The township shall furnish the secretary with the necessary equipment and supplies as are necessary for the conduct of the office, which shall be and remain the property of the township.

(902 amended Oct. 29, 2020, P.L.782, No.96)

§ 903. Records Open to Inspection.—The minutes and other records and documents of every township shall be open in accordance with the act of February 14, 2008 (P.L.6, No.3), known as the Right-to-Know Law.

(903 amended Oct. 29, 2020, P.L.782, No.96)

ARTICLE X
AUDITORS

53 P.S. §§ 56001–56052

(a) Elected Auditors
(Subart. hdg. added Oct. 29, 2020, P.L.782, No.96)

§ 1001. Meetings; General Duties.—(a) The township auditors shall meet annually, on the day following the day which is fixed by this act for the organization of the township commissioners. The auditors shall organize by the election of a chair and secretary. Two auditors shall constitute a quorum.

(b) The auditors shall:

(1) Audit, settle, and adjust the accounts of the township commissioners, township treasurer, tax collector, secretary, and other officers and persons receiving and disbursing or authorizing the disbursement of the moneys of the township during the preceding fiscal year.

(2) Audit the dockets, transcripts, and other official records of the offices of the magisterial district judge of the township to determine the amounts of fines and costs paid or due to the township. A magisterial district judge of the township shall open and make available to the auditors their dockets, transcripts, records, and all other official books or papers for the purpose of the audit. If a magisterial district judge charges a fine contrary to ordinances, or to any act which makes the fine payable to the township, the auditors have the power to surcharge the magisterial district judge in the amount undercharged.

(3) As directed by the board of commissioners, audit and report to the board of commissioners on the accounts of every officer of the township, upon the death, resignation, removal or expiration of the term of the officer.

Chap. 39 Res. During Mil. Service
Chap. 38 Intergov. Coop.
Chap. 37 3rd Class City Code
Chap. 36 Bor. Code
Chap. 35 2nd Class Twp. Code
Chap. 34 1st Class Twp. Code
Chap. 33 Home Rule Chart. Opt. Plans Law
Chap. 32 Water Serv. Act
Chap. 31 Munic. Auth. Act

(c) Unless otherwise agreed to by the auditors and the person being audited, the audit shall be conducted at the place the records of the person are normally kept.

(1001 amended Oct. 29, 2020, P.L.782, No.96)

Compiler's Note: Section 28 of Act 207 of 2004 provided that any and all references in any other law to a "district justice" or "justice of the peace" shall be deemed to be references to a magisterial district judge.

§ 1001.1. Compensation.—(a) Subject to the limitations set forth in subsection (b), each auditor shall receive twenty dollars ($20) per diem, to be paid by the township, for each day necessarily employed in the discharge of the auditor's duties. A day shall consist of not less than five hours in the aggregate.

(b) A township auditor shall not be entitled to receive compensation for more than the following number of days:

(1) In townships with a population of less than three thousand, a maximum of twenty days.

(2) In townships with a population of three thousand or more but less than ten thousand, a maximum of thirty days.

(3) In townships with a population of ten thousand or more, a maximum of forty days.

(1001.1 added Oct. 29, 2020, P.L.782, No.96)

§ 1002. Subpoenas, oaths and perjury.—(a) The auditors of each township may:

(1) Issue subpoenas to obtain the attendance of:

(i) the officers and persons whose accounts the auditors are required to adjust;

(ii) executors and administrators of an office under subparagraph (i); and

(iii) any persons whom it may be necessary to examine as a witness.

(2) Compel the production of documents, including financial records, relative to township accounts. If any person refuses or neglects to appear, to produce documents or to testify, the auditors shall petition the court of common pleas of the county to issue a subpoena to the person and to require the person to produce documents or to appear and to testify before the court. The court shall issue the subpoena if it deems the documents or testimony relevant to the issue.

(b) The auditors may administer oaths and affirmations to all persons brought or appearing before them, whether accountants, witnesses, or otherwise. A person swearing or affirming falsely upon examination is guilty of perjury.

(1002 amended Oct. 29, 2020, P.L.782, No.96)

Compiler's Note: Section 28 of Act 207 of 2004 provided that any and all references in any other law to a "district justice" or "justice of the peace" shall be deemed to be references to a magisterial district judge.

§ 1003. Completion, Filing and Publication of Auditor's Report and Financial Statement.—(a) The auditors shall complete the annual audit, settlement, and adjustment as soon as possible after the end of the fiscal year.

(b) The auditors shall, within ten days after the completion of the report under subsection (c), publish, by advertisement in at least one newspaper of general circulation in accordance with the provisions of section 110, concise financial information prepared or approved by the auditors and consistent with the audited financial statements for total assets, total liabilities and total net position at the end of the fiscal year and total revenue, total expenses and changes in total net position for that fiscal year and a reference to a place within the township where copies of the financial statements and accompanying auditors' report may be examined. If the full financial statements and accompanying auditors' report

are not published, copies shall be supplied to the publishing newspaper when the request for publication is submitted.

(c) The annual auditors' report and annual financial statement shall be presented on a uniform form prepared and furnished as provided in section 1701a.

(d) The auditors' report and financial statement shall be signed by all of the auditors and the auditors' report shall be duly verified by the oath of one of the auditors. A secretary of the auditors shall file a copy of the report with the secretary of the township, the clerk of the court or the prothonotary, as may be provided by local rules of court, the Department of Community and Economic Development and the Department of Transportation not later than ninety days after the close of the fiscal year. Any secretary of the auditors refusing or wilfully neglecting to file the report commits a summary offense. If the failure to file the report within the period specified is due to the failure of any or all of the auditors to prepare the statement upon which the report is to be based, the auditor commits a summary offense.

(1003 amended Oct. 29, 2020, P.L.782, No.96)

Compiler's Note: Section 301(a)(16) of Act 58 of 1996, which created the Department of Community and Economic Development and abolished the Department of Community Affairs, provided that all other powers and duties delegated to the Department of Community Affairs not otherwise expressly transferrred elsewhere by Act 58 and currently performed by the Department of Community Affairs under section 1003 are transferred to the Department of Community and Economic Development.

§ 1004. Canceling Orders.—The auditors shall cancel all orders and vouchers that the auditors find have been paid by writing the word "audited" on the face of the orders or vouchers.

(1004 amended Oct. 29, 2020, P.L.782, No.96)

§ 1005. Penalty for Failure to Perform Duty.—Any auditor who fails to comply with the provisions of this subdivision commits a summary offense.

(1005 amended Oct. 29, 2020, P.L.782, No.96)

§ 1006. Attorney to Auditors.—(a) The auditors may employ an attorney if a disagreement occurs between the auditors and any official or board of officials whose accounts the auditors are required to audit. The attorney shall not be employed until reasonable effort to reach an agreement has been made, and only after notice of the auditors' intention to hire the attorney has been given to the official or board of officials.

(b) The auditors, with the agreement of the board of commissioners, shall determine the compensation to be paid to the attorney. If the auditors and board of commissioners cannot agree on the compensation, upon petition of the auditors, the court of common pleas shall establish the compensation for the attorney employed by the auditors. The compensation for the attorney shall be paid out of the township general fund.

(1006 amended Oct. 29, 2020, P.L.782, No.96)

§ 1006.1. Surcharge by Auditors.—(a) The amount of a balance or shortage or of an expenditure of a kind or made in a manner prohibited or not authorized by statute that causes a financial loss to the township shall be a surcharge against an officer or person responsible for the balance or shortage, or who by vote, act or neglect has permitted or approved the expenditure.

(b) The following shall apply:

(1) An elected or appointed officer of a township or person may not be surcharged for an act, error or omission in excess of the actual financial loss sustained by the township.

Chap. 39 Res. During Mil. Service
Chap. 38 Intergov. Coop.
Chap. 37 3rd Class City Code
Chap. 36 Bor. Code
Chap. 35 2nd Class Twp. Code
Chap. 34 1st Class Twp. Code
Chap. 33 Home Rule Chart. Opt. Plans Law
Chap. 32 Water Serv. Act
Chap. 31 Munic. Auth. Act

(2) A surcharge shall take into consideration as the surcharge's basis the results of the act, error or omission and the results had the procedure been strictly in accordance with law. The surcharge imposed shall be limited to the difference between the costs actually incurred by the township and the costs that would have been incurred had legal means and authorized procedures been employed.

(3) Paragraph (1) shall not apply to a case involving fraud or collusion on the part of officers nor to any penalty enuring to the benefit of or payable to the Commonwealth. Notwithstanding this section, the procedures in the act of May 25, 1945 (P.L.1050, No.394), known as the "Local Tax Collection Law," shall apply to balances and shortages in the tax accounts of the tax collector.

(4) An elected or appointed officer of a township may not be surcharged if the official acted in good faith reliance on a written, nonconfidential opinion of the solicitor of the township or on an opinion of the solicitor of the township publicly stated at an open meeting of the township and recorded in the official minutes of the meeting. This paragraph shall not apply if a solicitor's opinion has been rendered under duress or if the parties seeking and rendering the solicitor's opinion have colluded to purposefully commit a violation of law. As used in this paragraph, the term "solicitor" shall include a special counsel appointed by the township for a specific matter.

(c) In any matter involving a financial transaction, an officer knowingly and wilfully acting contrary to law commits a misdemeanor and, upon conviction, may be sentenced to pay a fine not exceeding one hundred dollars.

(1006.1 added Oct. 29, 2020, P.L.782, No.96)

§ 1007. Balances Due to Be Entered as Judgments.—Any balance, in any report of the auditors, against any officer of the township shall constitute a surcharge against such officer as fully as if expressly stated in the report to be a surcharge. The amount of a balance and of any express surcharge shall, if no appeal is taken or after an appeal has been finally determined in favor of the township, be entered by the prothonotary as a judgment against the officer. The clerk of the court of common pleas shall certify the amount of every balance or surcharge contained in a report from which no appeal has been taken within the time provided under this subarticle to the court of common pleas for entry by the prothonotary as a judgment.

(1007 amended Oct. 29, 2020, P.L.782, No.96)

§ 1008. Collection of Surcharges.—Any auditor, registered elector or taxpayer of the township may enforce the collection of a judgment entered for a surcharge for the benefit of the township, by any appropriate action or execution, upon filing in the court of common pleas a bond, with one or more sureties (in the case of a registered elector or taxpayer), conditioned to indemnify the township from all costs of the proceedings undertaken by the registered elector or taxpayer, subject, however, to all rights of appeal from the report of the auditors granted by this subarticle.

(1008 amended Oct. 29, 2020, P.L.782, No.96)

§ 1009. Appeals from Report.—The township, or any registered elector or taxpayer of the township on its behalf, or any officer or person whose account is settled or audited by the township auditors, may appeal from the settlement or audit to the court of common pleas within forty-five days from the date of the filing of the auditors' report with the clerk of the court of common pleas.

(1009 amended Oct. 29, 2020, P.L.782, No.96)

§ 1010. Appeal Bond.—No appeal by a registered elector or taxpayer or officer shall be allowed unless the appellant secures a bond with sufficient surety to prosecute the appeal and to pay all costs of appeal in case, if the appellant is a registered elector or taxpayer, the appellant fails to obtain a final decision more favorable to the township than that awarded by the auditors, or in case the appellant is an accounting officer, the appellant fails to obtain a final decision more favorable to the officer than that awarded by the auditors.

(1010 amended Oct. 29, 2020, P.L.782, No.96)

§ 1011. Intervention by Taxpayers.—(1011 repealed Apr. 28, 1978, P.L.202, No.53)

§ 1012. Procedure on Appeals.—(a) In any proceeding upon an appeal from a report of the auditors, the accounts of the officer or the person in question may be investigated de novo, and the burden shall be upon each officer or person whose accounts are involved in the appeal of establishing the right to credits claimed by the officer or person, but the opposing party in the appeal may use any facts, figures or findings of the report of the auditors as prima facie evidence against any officer or person.

(b) If more than one appeal from the report of the auditors is taken, the court may on its own motion and shall, upon petition of any interested party, direct the several appeals be consolidated.

(1012 amended Oct. 29, 2020, P.L.782, No.96)

§ 1013. Testimony and Argument.—(1013 repealed Oct. 29, 2020, P.L.782, No.96)

§ 1014. Framed Issues.—(1014 repealed Oct. 29, 2020, P.L.782, No.96)

§ 1015. Prima Facie Evidence.—(1015 repealed Oct. 29, 2020, P.L.782, No.96)

§ 1016. Findings of Facts and Law, Judgment and Appeals.—After hearing, the court shall file its findings of fact and law and enter judgment accordingly, and the judgment entered may be enforced by the prevailing party by any appropriate proceedings. An appeal from the court's ruling may be taken in accordance with law.

(1016 amended Oct. 29, 2020, P.L.782, No.96)

§ 1017. Cost.—In all cases of appeal from the report or audit of the township auditors to the court of common pleas, the costs shall be determined by the court.

(1017 amended Oct. 29, 2020, P.L.782, No.96)

§ 1018. Appeals.—(1018 repealed Oct. 29, 2020, P.L.782, No.96)

§ 1019. Attorney Fees.—(a) Upon final determination of an appeal taken under section 1009 from any report, audit or settlement of the account of any township officer, attorney fees shall be awarded as follows:

(1) If, in the opinion of the court, the final determination is more favorable to the township officer involved than that awarded by the auditors, the township shall pay reasonable attorney fees or, under paragraph (3), a portion of reasonable attorney fees incurred by the officer in connection with the surcharge proceeding.

(2) If, in the opinion of the court, the final determination is more favorable to the township than that awarded by the auditors in the case of an appeal taken by the township or a taxpayer, the township officer who is the subject of the surcharge proceeding shall pay reasonable attorney fees or, under paragraph (3), a portion of reasonable attorney fees incurred by the township, elector or taxpayer in connection with the surcharge proceeding.

(3) If, in the opinion of the court, the final determination is in part more favorable to the township and in part more favorable to the township officer involved in the surcharge proceeding than that awarded by the auditors, the court may order:

Table of Contents
Part I Ch. 1–3 Ethics, Records, Open Meetings
Part II Ch. 4–10 Taxation
Part III Ch. 11–18 Torts, Contracts & Civil Rules
Part IV Ch. 19–24 Zoning & Planning
Part V Ch. 25–30 Construction and Emergency Codes
Part VI Ch. 31–39 Municipal Codes
Index

(i) the township to pay a portion of reasonable attorney fees incurred by the officer in connection with the surcharge proceeding; or

(ii) the township officer who is the subject of the surcharge proceeding to pay a portion of reasonable attorney fees incurred by the township or taxpayer in connection with the surcharge proceeding.

(b) The attorney fees in cases of appeals involving accounts other than those of township officers shall be allocated in the court's discretion.

(1019 amended Oct. 29, 2020, P.L.782, No.96)

(b) Appointed Independent Auditor
(Subart. added Oct. 29, 2020, P.L.782, No.96)

§ 1050. Appointment of independent auditor.

If an ordinance has been enacted for the appointment of an independent auditor in lieu of elected auditors under section 503(a)(3), the board of commissioners shall appoint an independent auditor by resolution and the provisions of this subarticle shall apply. The independent auditor shall be a certified public accountant or a firm of certified public accountants.

(1050 added Oct. 29, 2020, P.L.782, No.96)

§ 1051. Audits.

(a) **Annual audit.**—The independent auditor shall conduct an annual audit of the finances of the township, as presented in the annual audit and financial report, which shall include each account in which the township is concerned and the accounts of township officers, departments and offices which collect, receive and disburse public money or are authorized with the management, control or custody of public money on which the independent auditor is required to report under this subarticle. Nothing under this subarticle shall prohibit the board of commissioners from requiring the independent auditor to conduct a more complete or comprehensive audit than is required under this subarticle.

(b) **Interim audits.**—The following shall apply:

(1) The board of commissioners may require advisory interim reports from the independent auditor.

(2) The board of commissioners may direct the independent auditor to audit the accounts of a township officer upon the death, resignation, removal or expiration of the term of the officer.

(c) **Standards.**—An annual or interim audit shall consist of an examination in accordance with United States generally accepted auditing standards. Errors or irregularities detected in the course of an audit shall be communicated in accordance with the standards under this subsection.

(d) **Definition.**—As used in this subarticle, the term "annual audit and financial report" means the report that is presented on the uniform form as provided in section 1052(d).

(1051 added Oct. 29, 2020, P.L.782, No.96)

§ 1052. Completion, filing and publication of annual audit and financial report.

(a) **Completion.**—The independent auditor shall complete the annual audit as soon as practical after the end of the fiscal year as directed by the board of commissioners.

(b) **Filing.**—A copy of the audited annual audit and financial report shall be filed with the following:

(1) The secretary of the township, in accordance with applicable rules and regulations of the township.

Chap. 39 Res. During Mil. Service | Chap. 38 Intergov. Coop. | Chap. 37 3rd Class City Code | Chap. 36 Bor. Code | Chap. 35 2nd Class Twp. Code | Chap. 34 1st Class Twp. Code | Chap. 33 Home Rule Chart. Opt. Plans Law | Chap. 32 Water Serv. Act | Chap. 31 Munic. Auth. Act

(2) The clerk of the court or the prothonotary, as may be provided by local rules of court.

(3) The Department of Community and Economic Development, in accordance with the department's rules and regulations.

(c) **Publication.**—Notice that the audited annual audit and financial report is available for public inspection shall be published by the township secretary once in at least one newspaper of general circulation in accordance with section 110. Public inspection shall be in accordance with the act of February 14, 2008 (P.L.6, No.3), known as the Right-to-Know Law. A copy, which may be in electronic format, of the complete annual audit and financial report, including the accompanying independent auditor's report, shall be supplied to the publishing newspaper when the request for publication is submitted. Nothing in this section shall preclude the township from providing its audited annual audit and financial report on the township's website.

(d) **Presentation.**—The annual audit report and annual financial statements shall be presented on a uniform form prepared and furnished as provided in section 1701a.

(e) **Appeal.**—Nothing in this subarticle shall prohibit a registered elector or taxpayer from appealing an annual audit and financial report of the independent auditor in accordance with and subject to the procedures in sections 1009, 1010, 1012, 1016, 1017 and 1019 if the registered elector or taxpayer believes a surcharge as described in section 1006.1 should exist against an officer or person. The appeal shall be initiated within 45 days of the filing specified in subsection (b).

(1052 added Oct. 29, 2020, P.L.782, No.96)

ARTICLE XI
CONTROLLER

53 P.S. §§ 56101–56110

§ 1101. Oath and Bond of Controller.—(a) The township controller, if the office has been created, shall, before entering upon the duties of office, take the required oath or affirmation of office under 53 Pa.C.S. § 1141 (relating to form of oaths of office).

(b) Pursuant to section 602, the controller shall give bond to the township, with a surety company or other company authorized by law to act as surety, to be approved by the board of commissioners, in a sum as the board of commissioners may direct by ordinance, conditioned for the faithful discharge of the controller's duties. The amount of the bond shall be sufficient to adequately protect the township from any illegal or unfaithful action by the controller. The cost of the bond shall be paid by the township.

(c) In lieu of the bond required for the faithful performance by the township controller of official duties, the board of commissioners may purchase insurance as provided in section 602(b).

(1101 amended Oct. 29, 2020, P.L.782, No.96)

> **Compiler's Note:** Section 3(3) of Act 76 of 2008 provided that all acts and parts of acts are repealed insofar as they are inconsistent with Act 76. Section 1 of Act 76 amended 53 Pa.C.S. Ch. 11 (relating to general provisions) by adding section 1141 (relating to form of oaths of office), which provides the form of oaths of office for elected or appointed officials of municipalities.

§ 1102. Salary of Controller.—The annual salary of the controller shall be fixed by ordinance, passed at least thirty days before the controller's election. Any change in salary, compensation or emoluments of the elected office shall become

Table of Contents
Part I Ch. 1–3 Ethics, Records, Open Meetings
Part II Ch. 4–10 Taxation
Part III Ch. 11–18 Torts, Contracts & Civil Rules
Part IV Ch. 19–24 Zoning & Planning
Part V Ch. 25–30 Construction and Emergency Codes
Part VI Ch. 31–39 Municipal Codes
Index

effective at the beginning of the next term of the controller.

(1102 amended Oct. 29, 2020, P.L.782, No.96)

§ 1103. General Powers and Duties of Controller.—(a) The township controller shall manage the fiscal affairs of the township. The controller shall examine, audit, and settle all accounts in which the township is concerned, either as debtor or creditor, if provisions for the settlement are made by law. If no provisions, or an insufficient provision, has been made, the controller shall examine the accounts and report to the board of commissioners the relevant facts and opinions on the accounts.

(b) In the examination, audit and settlement of accounts the controller shall have all of the powers and perform all of the duties vested in and imposed on the auditors by this act. In the authentication of any account or claim or demand against the township, the controller shall have the same power and authority as the elected township auditors to obtain the attendance of parties and witnesses and the production of documents and to administer oaths and affirmations. An individual guilty of swearing or affirming falsely before the controller commits perjury. The controller shall make and file an annual report of the audit and make and publish the annual financial statement in the same form and manner and at the same time as is required of the elected township auditors by this act.

(c) The township controller shall:

(1) have supervision and control of the accounts of all departments, bureaus, and officers of the township, authorized to collect, receive, or disburse the public money, or who are charged with the management or custody of the accounts;

(2) audit their respective accounts and may at any time require from any of them a statement in writing of any money or property of the township in their possession or under their control, showing the amount of cash on hand and the amount deposited in banks and banking institutions, together with the names of the institutions;

(3) have power to examine every account of a township officer in any bank or banking institution to verify the accuracy of the statement of the township, department, bureau, or officer, and it shall be the duty of every bank and banking institution, and its officers and agents, to furnish full information to the controller in relation to the account. No banker or banking institution, its officers or agents, shall be subject to prosecution under other laws of this Commonwealth for disclosing any such information with respect to an account;

(4) immediately upon the discovery of any default, irregularity or delinquency, report the same to the board of commissioners; and

(5) audit and report upon the account of an officer upon the death, resignation, removal, or expiration of the term of the officer.

(1103 amended Oct. 29, 2020, P.L.782, No.96)

§ 1104. Countersigned Warrants.—The township controller shall countersign all warrants upon the township treasurer, with the form of the warrant to be prescribed by the board of commissioners, but no warrant shall be countersigned unless there is sufficient unencumbered money in the respective appropriation item to pay the same. Whenever a warrant on the treasurer shall be presented to the controller to be countersigned, the person presenting the warrant shall, if the controller requires, produce evidence that:

(1) the amount expressed in the warrant is due to the person in whose favor it is drawn; and

(2) the supplies or services for payment of which the warrant is drawn have been furnished or performed according to law and the terms of the contract.

(1104 amended Oct. 29, 2020, P.L.782, No.96)

§ 1105. Prevention of Appropriation Overdrafts.—The township controller shall not permit any appropriation made by the board of commissioners to be overdrawn. If an appropriation is exhausted, the object of which is not complete, the commissioner shall immediately report the fact to the board of commissioners, and accompany the report with a statement of the money which has been drawn on the appropriation and the particular purpose for which it was drawn.

(1105 amended Oct. 29, 2020, P.L.782, No.96)

§ 1106. Amount of Contracts to Be Charged Against Appropriations.—(a) Every contract involving appropriation of money shall designate the item of appropriation on which it is founded, and the estimated amount of the expenditure which shall be charged against the item and certified by the township controller on the contract, before it shall take effect as a contract. Payment required by the contract shall be made from the fund for which the contract is appropriated.

(b) If the controller certifies a contract in excess of the appropriation made, the township shall not be liable for the excess, but the controller and the controller's sureties shall be liable for the excess amount, which may be recovered in an action at law by the aggrieved contracting party.

(c) The controller shall certify contracts for the payment of which sufficient appropriations have been made.

(1106 amended Oct. 29, 2020, P.L.782, No.96)

§ 1107. Management and Improvement of Township Finances.—The township controller shall, as often as the controller may deem expedient or the board of commissioners shall direct, suggest plans to the board of commissioners for the management and improvement of the township finances.

(1107 amended Oct. 29, 2020, P.L.782, No.96)

§ 1108. Financial Records to Be Kept by Controller.—The township controller shall maintain financial records and maintain as many accounts, under appropriate titles, as may be necessary to show separately and distinctly all the estates and property, real and personal, vested in the township, all trusts in the care of the township, all debts due and owing the township, all receipts and expenditures of the various departments of the township government, and all appropriations made by the board of commissioners and the sums under the same, respectively.

(1108 amended Oct. 29, 2020, P.L.782, No.96)

§ 1109. Appeals from Controller's Report.—Appeals may be taken from the settlement and audit of the controller as shown in the controller's report to the court of common pleas of the county, by the same persons, in the same manner, within the same time, subject to the same conditions and procedure, and with like effect in every respect as provided in this act in the cases of appeals from the settlement and audit of the auditors as shown in their report.

(1109 amended Oct. 29, 2020, P.L.782, No.96)

§ 1110. Controller to Retain Financial Records, Pending Appeals.—Every township controller shall retain possession, during the forty-five days' period elapsing between the date of filing the report and the expiration of the time for filing the appeal from the report, all financial records and other papers that were submitted to the controller for audit of the accounts of township officers. If an appeal is taken, the controller shall continue to hold the financial records and papers for production in the proceeding to determine the appeal.

(1110 amended Oct. 29, 2020, P.L.782, No.96)

ARTICLE XII
TOWNSHIP SOLICITOR

53 P.S. §§ 56201–56204

§ 1201. Township Solicitor.—The board of commissioners may appoint and determine the compensation of a township solicitor and, as needed, special counsel. The township solicitor or special counsel must be licensed to practice law in this Commonwealth and may be an individual or a law firm, partnership, association or professional corporation. The township solicitor or special counsel shall serve at the pleasure of the board of commissioners.

(1201 amended Oct. 29, 2020, P.L.782, No.96)

§ 1202. Bond.—(1202 repealed Oct. 29, 2020, P.L.782, No.96)

§ 1203. Control of Legal Matters.—

(a) Except where the board of commissioners has appointed special counsel for a specific matter, the township solicitor shall advise on the legal matters of the township.

(b) No department or officer of the township, except as otherwise provided by law, shall employ or retain an additional counsel without the consent or ratification of the board of commissioners.

(1203 amended Oct. 29, 2020, P.L.782, No.96)

§ 1204. Duties of Solicitor.—The township solicitor or special counsel, as applicable, shall:

(1) Prepare or approve, if directed or requested to do so by the board of commissioners, bonds, obligations, contracts, leases, conveyances, ordinances and assurances to which the township, or any department of the township, may be a party.

(2) Commence and prosecute all actions brought by the township for or on account of any of the estates, rights, trusts, privileges, claims or demands of the township and defend the township or any township officer against all actions or suits brought against the township or township officer in which any of the estates, rights, privileges, trusts, ordinances or accounts of the township may be brought in question before a court in this Commonwealth.

(3) Furnish the board of commissioners and the township committees, upon request, with an opinion in writing upon a question of law, which may be submitted by any of them in their official capacities.

(4) Perform every other professional act incident to the office which the township solicitor or special counsel may be authorized or required to perform by the board of commissioners or by any ordinance or resolution.

(1204 amended Oct. 29, 2020, P.L.782, No.96)

ARTICLE XIII
TOWNSHIP ENGINEER
53 P.S. §§ 56301–56316

(a) General Provisions

§ 1301. Township Engineer.—

(a) The board of commissioners may appoint and determine the compensation of a township engineer who must be a registered professional engineer. The township engineer serves at the pleasure of the board of commissioners.

(b) As used in this article, the term "engineer" means one or more registered professional engineers or a firm of registered professional engineers.

(1301 amended Oct. 29, 2020, P.L.782, No.96)

§ 1302. Bond.—(1302 repealed Oct. 29, 2020, P.L.782, No.96)

§ 1303. Control of Engineering Matters.—

(a) Except where the board of commissioners has appointed an engineer for a specific matter, the township engineer shall direct and control the engineering matters of the township.

(b) No department or officer of the township, except as otherwise provided by law, may employ or retain an additional engineer without the consent or ratification of the board of commissioners.

(1303 amended Oct. 29, 2020, P.L.782, No.96)

§ 1304. Duties; Preparation of Plans.—The township engineer shall perform duties and provide reports as the board of commissioners may direct for the construction, reconstruction, maintenance and repair of streets, bridges, culverts and other engineering work. The township engineer may prepare plans, specifications and estimates of the work undertaken by the township and shall furnish the board of commissioners and the committees of the township with reports, information or estimates on any township engineering work or on questions submitted by the board of commissioners.

(1304 amended Oct. 29, 2020, P.L.782, No.96)

§ 1305. Certificate of Commencement and of Completion of Municipal Improvements.—

(a) The township engineer shall certify to the township secretary the date of commencement and date of completion of all municipal improvements, the cost of which, in whole or in part, is to be paid by the owners of the abutting property. The certification shall be made a part of the permanent records of the township. The certified date of commencement and certified date of completion shall be conclusive on all parties.

(b) As used in this section, the phrase "certified date of completion" means the date of the completion of the whole contract for the improvement.

(1305 amended Oct. 29, 2020, P.L.782, No.96)

§ 1306. Surveys.—The township engineer shall have the charge and direction of all surveys and regulations authorized by any act of Assembly or ordinance of the township.

(1306 amended Oct. 29, 2020, P.L.782, No.96)

(b) Real Estate Registry

(Subdiv. repealed Oct. 29, 2020, P.L.782, No.96)

Compiler's Note: Section 9 of Act 110 of 2008, known as the Uniform Municipal Deed Registration Act, provided that Subarticle (b) is repealed insofar as it is inconsistent with Act 110.

§ 1310. Provisions for Registration of Real Estate.—(1310 repealed Oct. 29, 2020, P.L.782, No.96)

§ 1311. Preparation of Books, Plans and Maps.—(1311 repealed Oct. 29, 2020, P.L.782, No.96)

§ 1312. Preservation of Records.—(1312 repealed Oct. 29, 2020, P.L.782, No.96)

Compiler's Note: Section 1 of Act 264 of 1945 provided that the recorder of deeds of every county except counties of the second class, upon written request, is required to furnish each township within the county, a monthly record of all transfers of property located within the township.

§ 1313. Certified Copies of Entries Admissible as Evidence.—(1313 repealed Oct. 29, 2020, P.L.782, No.96)

§ 1314. Duties Imposed on Owners of Real Estate When Registry Established; Penalty.—(1314 repealed Oct. 29, 2020, P.L.782, No.96)

§ 1315. Registry of Properties; Duty of County Officers.—(1315 repealed Oct. 29, 2020, P.L.782, No.96)

§ 1316. Conservation District.—(1316 repealed Oct. 29, 2020, P.L.782, No.96)

ARTICLE XIII-A

TOWNSHIP MANAGER

53 P.S. §§ 56301-A–56304-A

(Art. added Oct. 29, 2020, P.L.782, No.96)

§ 1301-A. Township manager.

(a) Authorization.—The board of commissioners may create by ordinance the office of township manager and, in like manner, abolish the office. While the office exists, the board of commissioners may appoint one individual, a partnership, a limited partnership, an association or a professional corporation as the township manager.

(b) Nature of office.—The township manager shall serve at the pleasure of the board of commissioners, subject to contractual rights that may arise under an employment agreement or professional services agreement that may be entered in accordance with section 1302-A.

(1301-A added Oct. 29, 2020, P.L.782, No.96)

§ 1302-A. Powers and duties; agreement.

(a) General rule.—The powers and duties of the township manager shall be regulated by ordinance. The board of commissioners may delegate, subject to recall, any of their nonlegislative and nonjudicial powers and duties to the township manager.

(b) Scope of agreement and validity.—

(1) The board of commissioners may enter into an employment agreement or professional services agreement with the township manager that specifies the terms and conditions of the appointment.

(2) The agreement may remain in effect for a specified period terminating no later than the date of the board of commissioners' organizational meeting following the next municipal election.

(3) An agreement with a township manager executed on or after a municipal election but before the first meeting in January the year after the municipal election shall be void.

(4) An agreement entered into under this section may specify conditions under which a township manager who is an individual would be entitled to severance compensation, or, in the case of a partnership, limited partnership, association or a professional corporation, payments for the termination of the

appointment. In no event may the agreement guarantee retention or employment through the term of the agreement or confer upon the township manager a legal remedy based on specific performance.

(c) Status as public official.—The township manager, if an individual, and, in the case of a partnership, limited partnership, association or a professional corporation appointed as the township manager, all officers and those employees directly providing services as required or authorized by the agreement, shall be considered a public official for purposes of the provisions of 65 Pa.C.S. § 1103 (relating to restricted activities).

(1302-A added Oct. 29, 2020, P.L.782, No.96)

§ 1303-A. Bond.

(a) General rule.—The township manager shall, if required by the board of commissioners, give a bond to the township, with a surety company or other company authorized by law to act as surety, to be approved by the board of commissioners, in such sum as the board of commissioners, by ordinance or resolution, directs, conditioned for the faithful performance of the township manager's duties.

(b) Insurance in lieu of bond.—In lieu of the bond required for the faithful performance by the township manager of official duties, the board of commissioners may purchase insurance as provided in section 602(b).

(1303-A added Oct. 29, 2020, P.L.782, No.96)

§ 1304-A. Incompatibility.

(a) General rule.—No township manager may be eligible to hold the office of township commissioner.

(b) Applicability.—In the case of a partnership, limited partnership, association or a professional corporation appointed as the township manager, the restriction in subsection (a) applies to all officers and employees who directly provide services as required or authorized by the agreement.

(1304-A added Oct. 29, 2020, P.L.782, No.96)

ARTICLE XIII-B
VETERANS' AFFAIRS

53 P.S. §§ 56301-B–56314-B

(Art. added Oct. 29, 2020, P.L.782, No.96)

(a) Pennsylvania National Guard

(Subart. added Oct. 29, 2020, P.L.782, No.96)

§ 1301-B. Eminent domain for National Guard purposes.

(a) General rule.—Except as provided in subsection (b), the board of commissioners may take, by the right of eminent domain for the purpose of appropriating to the township for the use of the Pennsylvania National Guard, public lands, easements and public property in the township's possession or control and used or held by the township for any other purpose notwithstanding any limitation of the use by the township whether by donation, dedication, appropriation, statute or otherwise.

(b) Limitation.—Eminent domain may not be exercised as to a street, highway or wharf.

(1301-B added Oct. 29, 2020, P.L.782, No.96)

§ 1302-B. Land for armory purposes.

(a) General rule.—Except as provided in subsection (b), the board of commissioners may acquire, by purchase, gift or eminent domain, land for the use of the

Table of Contents | Part I Ch. 1–3 Ethics, Records, Open Meetings | Part II Ch. 4–10 Taxation | Part III Ch. 11–18 Torts, Contracts & Civil Rules | Part IV Ch. 19–24 Zoning & Planning | Part V Ch. 25–30 Construction and Emergency Codes | Part VI Ch. 31–39 Municipal Codes | Index

Pennsylvania National Guard, to be conveyed to the Commonwealth in order to assist the State Armory Board in the erection of armories.

(b) Limitation.—The power conferred by subsection (a) may not be exercised to take church property or other actual place of regularly stated religious worship, graveyard, cemetery or a dwelling house or the curtilage of any of them in the actual occupancy of the owner.

(1302-B added Oct. 29, 2020, P.L.782, No.96)

§ 1303-B. Assistance to armories.

(a) Appropriation or conveyance.—The board of commissioners may appropriate money or convey land, either independently or in conjunction with any other municipality, to the Commonwealth for the following purposes:

(1) To assist the State Armory Board in the erection of armories for the use of the Pennsylvania National Guard.

(2) To furnish reasonable utilities free of cost to the Commonwealth for use in an armory of the Pennsylvania National Guard.

(b) Authority.—The board of commissioners may do all things necessary to accomplish the purposes specified in this section.

(1303-B added Oct. 29, 2020, P.L.782, No.96)

§ 1304-B. Support of Pennsylvania National Guard units.

(a) Annual appropriation.—The board of commissioners may appropriate annually a sum not to exceed $1,500 for the support, maintenance, discipline and training of a unit of the Pennsylvania National Guard. If the units are organized as a battalion, regiment or similar organization, the total amount due may be paid to the commanding officer of the battalion, regiment or similar organization.

(b) Condition.—Money appropriated under this section shall be paid by warrant drawn to the order of the commanding officer of the unit conditioned upon certification by the Adjutant General of the Commonwealth to the township that the unit has satisfactorily passed the annual inspection provided by law.

(c) Use of funds.—Money appropriated under this section shall be used and expended solely and exclusively for the support, maintenance, discipline and training of the company, battalion, regiment or similar organization.

(d) Accounting required.—

(1) The commanding officer shall account, by proper vouchers to the township each year, for the expenditure of money appropriated under this section.

(2) No appropriation may be made for any subsequent year until the expenditure of the previous year is duly and satisfactorily accounted for.

(3) The accounts of the expenditures shall be subject to the inspection of the Department of Military and Veterans Affairs and shall be audited by the Auditor General in accordance with law.

(1304-B added Oct. 29, 2020, P.L.782, No.96)

(b) Support of Veterans' Organizations and Memorials

(Subart. added Oct. 29, 2020, P.L.782, No.96)

§ 1311-B. Appropriations to veterans' home associations.

The board of commissioners may make an annual appropriation not to exceed $300 for the support of any Veterans' Home Association that provides a home or meeting facility within the township for the use of United States war veterans, and which is not maintained in whole or in part by the United States or any governmental agency other than the township.

(1311-B added Oct. 29, 2020, P.L.782, No.96)

§ 1312-B. Memorial Day or Veterans' Day appropriations.

The board of commissioners may appropriate money for the expenses of services for Memorial Day, Veterans' Day or a similar day provided for by Federal or State law.

(1312-B added Oct. 29, 2020, P.L.782, No.96)

§ 1313-B. Care of memorials.

(a) **Maintenance and repair.**—The board of commissioners may maintain and keep in good order and repair, at the expense of the township, a soldiers' monument, gun or carriage or similar memorial if the memorial is not in the charge or care of an individual, body or organization and the memorial was not erected by the Federal Government, the Commonwealth or the commissioners of the county or by the direction or authority of any other state.

(b) **Donations.**—The board of commissioners may receive money from an individual or organization and may expend the money for the benefit of memorials.

(1313-B added Oct. 29, 2020, P.L.782, No.96)

§ 1314-B. Purchase of burial grounds for deceased service persons.

The board of commissioners may appropriate money and purchase plots of ground in a cemetery or burial ground for the interment of deceased service persons:

(1) Who die within the township or die beyond the township limits but had a legal residence within the township at the time of death.

(2) Whose bodies are entitled to be buried by the county under the provisions of existing law.

(1314-B added Oct. 29, 2020, P.L.782, No.96)

ARTICLE XIV

POLICE

53 P.S. §§ 56401–56416

§ 1401. Appointment, Compensation and Training of Police Officers.—(a) The board of commissioners may, subject to the civil service provisions of this act, appoint and fix the number, rank and compensation of the members of the township police force.

(b) Subject to the requirements of 53 Pa.C.S. Ch. 23 Subch. A (relating to intergovernmental cooperation), the board of commissioners may provide for police services as follows:

(1) by municipal police officers under a contract;

(2) through the purchase of police services; or

(3) by joining or developing a consolidated regional police service.

(c) The board of commissioners may remove, suspend or demote a police officer:

(1) in accordance with the act of June 15, 1951 (P.L.586, No.144), entitled "An act regulating the suspension, removal, furloughing and reinstatement of police officers in boroughs and townships of the first class having police forces of less than three members, and in townships of the second class"; or

(2) subject to subdivision (d) of Article VI.

(d) The following shall apply:

(1) No police officer shall at the same time hold any public office other than constable, health officer or school director of a school district situated within a county of the second class.

(2) A police officer who holds the office of school director in a school district situated within a county of the second class pursuant to paragraph (1), whether contracted or otherwise employed by the school district, shall not be permitted to serve as a school police officer, as provided for in section 1302-C of the act of March 10, 1949 (P.L.30, No.14), known as the Public School Code of 1949.

(e) No police officer may participate in a political or election campaign while on duty or in uniform or while using township property other than to exercise the officer's right of suffrage.

(f) Except as provided in section 630, the board of commissioners shall promulgate rules and regulations for the organization of the police force.

(g) The board of commissioners may assign the chief of police or any other member of the police force to attend training classes offered by the Federal Government, State or county government, and may pay a member's expenses while attending the training classes.

(1401 amended Oct. 29, 2020, P.L.782, No.96)

§ 1401.1. Special Fire Police.—The president of the board of commissioners may confirm any member of a volunteer fire company nominated to serve as special fire police under 35 Pa.C.S. Ch. 74 Subch. D (relating to special fire police). The president of the board of commissioners may swear in or affirm special fire police officers.

(1401.1 added Oct. 29, 2020, P.L.782, No.96)

§ 1402. Chief of Police and Other Officers.—The board of commissioners may designate the superintendent or the chief of police and other officers who shall serve until their successors are duly designated and qualified.

(1402 amended Oct. 29, 2020, P.L.782, No.96)

§ 1403. Powers of Police Officers.—A township police officer shall have those powers and duties as are granted to police officers under the laws of this Commonwealth, the rules of the Supreme Court or the ordinances of the township, for the violation of which a fine or penalty may be imposed.

(1403 amended Oct. 29, 2020, P.L.782, No.96)

§ 1404. Service of Process; Fees.—Police officers may serve and execute criminal process or processes issued for the violation of township ordinances and shall charge the same fees and costs as pertain by law to constables of the township for similar services, but the fees and costs shall be paid to the township treasurer for the use of the township.

(1404 amended Oct. 29, 2020, P.L.782, No.96)

> **Compiler's Note:** Section 28 of Act 207 of 2004 provided that any and all references in any other law to a "district justice" or "justice of the peace" shall be deemed to be references to a magisterial district judge.

§ 1405. Supervision of Police.—The chief of police and police officers shall obey the orders of the board of commissioners or any other person or committee as designated by ordinance or resolution of the board for that purpose.

(1405 amended Oct. 29, 2020, P.L.782, No.96)

§ 1406. Keepers to Receive Prisoners.—(1406 repealed Oct. 29, 2020, P.L.782, No.96)

§ 1407. Badge.—Township police officers, when on duty, shall wear a badge or shield with the words "Township Police" and the name of the township inscribed on the badge or shield.

(1407 amended Oct. 29, 2020, P.L.782, No.96)

§ 1408. Compensation.—

(a) A township that employs police officers shall pay to all the police officers a fixed or stipulated salary.

(b) No police officer may charge or accept a fee or other compensation in addition to the salary paid by the township for a service rendered or performed by the police officer, except public rewards and the expenses incurred in the discharge of the police officer's duties.

(1408 amended Oct. 29, 2020, P.L.782, No.96)

§ 1409. Police Pension Fund.—

(a) If a police force of less than three full-time members is maintained, the township shall, unless there is a private organization or association constituting and managing an existing pension fund for the members of the police force in the township, by ordinance, establish a police pension fund to be maintained by member contributions of an equal percentage charge against each member of the police force. The member contributions, except to the extent that subsection (c) of section 607 of the act of December 18, 1984 (P.L.1005, No.205), known as the "Municipal Pension Plan Funding Standard and Recovery Act," applies, shall not exceed annually four percent of the pay of the member.

(b) In lieu of establishing a pension fund in accordance with subsection (a), the township may, by ordinance, provide investment or insurance instruments for the purpose of the payment of pensions or annuities to the members of the police force who receive honorable discharge by reason of age or disability and the families of police officers injured or killed in service.

(c) (1) All pension funds or investment or insurance instruments established under this section shall be under the direction of the board of commissioners, or a committee as the board of commissioners may designate, and shall be applied under regulations as the board of commissioners may, by ordinance, prescribe for the benefit of the members of the police force who receive honorable discharge by reason of age or disability and the families of police officers injured or killed in the service.

(2) The board of commissioners shall appoint by resolution a chief administrative officer who shall have the primary responsibility for the execution of the administrative affairs of the pension plan, subject to the direction of the board of commissioners.

(3) An allowance made to an individual who retires by reason of disability or age shall be in conformity with a uniform scale.

(d) The ordinance establishing the police pension fund may prescribe a minimum period of continuous service of not less than 20 years and an age limit after which members of the police force may be retired from active duty and may be entitled to benefits of the fund.

(e) Payments made on account of police pensions shall not be a charge on any fund in the treasury of the township or under the control of the township, except the police pension fund.

(f) A township that establishes a police pension fund under this section shall make contributions to the police pension fund in an amount sufficient to meet the minimum obligation of the municipality with respect to the pension plan under the "Municipal Pension Plan Funding Standard and Recovery Act."

(g) A township may take, by gift, grant, devise or bequest, any money or property, real, personal or mixed, in trust for the benefit of the police pension fund. The care, management, investment and disposal of the trust funds or property, real, personal or mixed, shall be vested in the officers as the board of commissioners shall direct by ordinance and shall be governed by the officers, subject to any directions not inconsistent with the ordinance as the donors of the funds and property may prescribe.

(h) (1) The basis of the apportionment of the pension benefit shall be determined by the rate of monthly pay of the member at the date of death, honorable discharge or retirement, and shall not exceed in any year one-half the annual pay of the member, computed at the member's monthly rate.

(2) No person who participates in the police pension fund and becomes entitled to receive a benefit from the fund may be deprived of the person's right to an equal and proportionate share of the fund upon the basis upon which the person first became entitled to the benefit.

(i) (Reserved).

(j) The act of May 29, 1956 (1955 P.L.1804, No.600), referred to as the Municipal Police Pension Law, or the act of February 1, 1974 (P.L.34, No.15), known as the Pennsylvania Municipal Retirement Law, shall govern any township police pension fund not established under the provisions of this section.

(1409 amended Oct. 29, 2020, P.L.782, No.96)

Compiler's Note: Section 12 of Act 600 of 1955 provided that section 1409 is repealed insofar as it applies to townships maintaining a police force of three or more members, except that the benefits that have accrued under this Code shall continue.

§ 1409.1. Private Police Pension Funds; Optional Transfers.—(a) If there is a private organization or association constituting and managing an existing pension fund for the members of the police force in any township, the township shall establish a police pension fund for the purpose of paying pensions to the members of the police force if the membership of the organization or association, by a two-thirds vote, elects to transfer its funds with all its assets and liabilities into a township police pension fund as required to be established by this act.

(b) The transfer under subsection (a) may be made by the transfer of securities. After the transfer, the township police pension fund shall assume the liability of continuing the payment of pensions to members of the police force retired prior to the transfer in accordance with the laws and regulations under which the members were retired.

(1409.1 amended Oct. 29, 2020, P.L.782, No.96)

Compiler's Note: Section 12 of Act 600 of 1955 provided that section 1409.1 is repealed insofar as it applies to townships maintaining a police force of three or more members, except that the benefits that have accrued under this Code shall continue.

§ 1410. Minimum Service for Retirement.—(1410 repealed Oct. 29, 2020, P.L.782, No.96)

Compiler's Note: Section 4 of Act 600 of 1955 provides that time spent in military service of the United States shall be credited to such member's employment record for pension or retirement benefits. Section 12 of Act 600 of 1955 provided that section 1410 is repealed insofar as it applies to townships maintaining a police force of three or more members, except that the benefits that have accrued under this Code shall continue.

§ 1411. Retirement Allowance.—(1411 repealed Oct. 29, 2020, P.L.782, No.96)

Compiler's Note: Section 12 of Act 600 of 1955 provided that section 1411 is repealed insofar as it applies to townships maintaining a police force of three or more members, except that the benefits that have accrued under this Code shall continue.

§ 1412. General Funds of Township not Liable.—(1412 repealed Oct. 29, 2020, P.L.782, No.96)

Compiler's Note: Section 12 of Act 600 of 1955 provided that section 1412 is repealed insofar as it applies to townships maintaining a police force of three or more members, except that the benefits that have accrued under this Code shall continue.

§ 1413. Township Appropriations; Gifts; Management.—(1413 repealed Oct. 29, 2020, P.L.782, No.96)

Compiler's Note: Section 12 of Act 600 of 1955 provided that section 1413 is repealed insofar as it applies to townships maintaining a police force of three or more members, except that the benefits that have accrued under this Code shall continue.

Compiler's Note: Section 1 of Act 444 of 1949 provided that townships are authorized to appropriate moneys to police pension funds.

§ 1414. Reasons for Denying Retirement Allowance.—(1414 repealed Oct. 29, 2020, P.L.782, No.96)

Compiler's Note: Section 12 of Act 600 of 1955 provided that section 1414 is repealed insofar as it applies to townships maintaining a police force of three or more members, except that the benefits that have accrued under this Code shall continue.

§ 1415. Annuity Contracts in Lieu of Police Pension Fund.—(1415 repealed Oct. 29, 2020, P.L.782, No.96)

Compiler's Note: Section 12 of Act 600 of 1955 provided that section 1415 is repealed insofar as it applies to townships maintaining a police force of three or more members, except that the benefits that have accrued under this Code shall continue.

§ 1416. School Crossing Guards.—(a) (1) The board of commissioners, by resolution, may appoint school crossing guards who shall be authorized only to manage traffic and pedestrians at or near schools while the school crossing guards are in uniform.

(2) School crossing guards shall serve at the pleasure of the board of commissioners, except as provided in subsection (b), shall not be subject to the civil service provisions of this act and shall not be eligible to join any township pension fund.

(3) The compensation of the school crossing guards, if any, shall be fixed by the board of commissioners and shall be paid by the board of commissioners, or jointly by the board of commissioners and the board of school directors, in a ratio to be determined by the boards. If the board of commissioners and board of school directors are unable to determine the ratio of compensation of the school crossing guards to be paid by each board, each board shall pay one-half of the compensation of the school crossing guards.

(b) (1) The board of commissioners may adopt a resolution allowing a board of school directors to assume hiring and oversight of school crossing guards. Before the board of commissioners adopts the resolution, the board of directors of the school district must adopt a resolution requesting authority from the board of commissioners to assume the hiring and oversight of school crossing guards.

(2) The resolution adopted by the board of commissioners shall outline the manner in which the police department will provide necessary training and assistance of the school crossing guards while on duty.

(3) The school crossing guards shall be authorized only to manage traffic and pedestrians in and around areas identified by the police department and the school district superintendent or the superintendent's designees.

(4) The school crossing guards shall not:

(i) Be subject to the civil service provisions of this act.

(ii) Be considered part of the bargaining unit of the school district.

(iii) Be considered an employe as defined under section 1101-A of the act of March 10, 1949 (P.L.30, No.14), known as the "Public School Code of 1949," or a school employe as defined under 24 Pa.C.S. § 8102 (relating to definitions) or an employe under any township or school district pension or benefit plan.

(5) After the resolution is adopted by the board of commissioners, the school district shall assume the cost of compensation, including fixing compensation, if any, of the school crossing guards.

(6) Notwithstanding any other provision of law, auxiliary police officers appointed as prescribed by law may be hired by the school district to serve as school crossing guards.

(7) The board of school directors shall notify the board of commissioners of the individuals hired to serve as school crossing guards and request that the necessary training or assistance be provided as specified in the resolution adopted by the board of commissioners.

(1416 amended Oct. 29, 2020, P.L.782, No.96)

ARTICLE XV
CORPORATE POWERS

53 P.S. §§ 56501–56590

§ 1501. Suits; Property.—Townships of the first class may:

(1) Sue and be sued.

(2) Have and use a corporate seal and alter the seal.

(3) Purchase, exchange, acquire by gift or otherwise, hold, lease, let and convey, by sale or lease, real and personal property deemed to be to the best interest of the township subject to the restrictions, limitations or exceptions as set forth in this act.

(1501 amended Oct. 29, 2020, P.L.782, No.96)

Compiler's Note: The act of May 2, 1945 (P.L.382, No.164), referred to as the Municipality Authorities Act of 1945, referred to in clause II, was repealed by the act of June 19, 2001 (P.L.287, No.22). The subject matter is now contained in 53 Pa.C.S. Ch. 56 (relating to municipal authorities).

§ 1501.1. Real Property.—(a) No real estate owned by the township may be sold for a consideration in excess of six thousand dollars except to the highest bidder after due notice by advertisement for bids or advertisement of a public auction.

(b) The advertisement shall be published once in one newspaper of general circulation not less than ten days prior to the date scheduled for the opening of bids or public auction. The date for opening bids or public auction shall be announced in the advertisement.

(c) The award of contracts shall be made only by public announcement at a regular or special meeting of the board of commissioners or at the public auction. A bid shall be accepted on the condition that payment of the purchase price in full shall be made within sixty days of the acceptance of a bid unless otherwise specified in the bid advertisement. If no compliant bids are received after advertisement, the applicable procedures in the act of October 27, 1979 (P.L.241, No.78), entitled "An act authorizing political subdivisions, municipality authorities and transportation authorities to enter into contracts for the purchase of goods and the sale of real and personal property where no bids are received," shall be followed.

(d) The board of commissioners shall have the authority to reject all bids if the bids are deemed to be less than the fair market value of the real property. In the case of a public auction, the board of commissioners may establish a minimum bid based on the fair market value of the real property.

(e) Real estate owned by a township may be sold for a consideration of six thousand dollars or less without advertisement or competitive bidding only after the board of commissioners estimates the value of the property upon receipt of an appraisal by a qualified real estate appraiser. Prior to selling real estate valued at six thousand dollars or less without advertisement or competitive bidding, the board of commissioners shall make a public announcement of the board's intention to sell the real estate at a regular or special meeting of the board at least thirty days prior to the sale.

(f) (1) Notwithstanding this section, the board of commissioners shall have the authority to exchange real property for real property of equal or greater value without complying with this section if the property being acquired by the township is to be used for municipal purposes. Municipal purposes as used in this subsection include a subsequent sale or lease of the property to any of the entities listed in section 1501.3.

(2) A conveyance of real property acquired in an exchange to an entity listed in section 1501.3 may contain a clause under which the lands and buildings will revert to the township if they are no longer being used for the purposes of the entity.

(3) If the board of commissioners chooses to exercise its power of real property exchange under this section, it shall be by resolution adopted by the board of commissioners. Notice of the resolution, including a description of the properties to be exchanged, shall be published once in one newspaper of general circulation not more than sixty days nor fewer than seven days prior to adoption.

(4) Participation in a real property exchange may not prohibit the application of the requirements of the act of October 4, 1978 (P.L.851, No.166), known as the Flood Plain Management Act.

(1501.1 added Oct. 29, 2020, P.L.782, No.96)

§ 1501.2. Personal Property.—(a) Except as provided in subsection (d), no township personal property may be disposed of, by sale or otherwise, except upon approval of the board of commissioners. In cases when the board of commissioners approves a sale of the property, the board of commissioners shall estimate the fair market value of the entire lot to be disposed of. If the board of commissioners estimates the fair market value to be two thousand dollars or more, the entire lot shall be advertised for sale once, in at least one newspaper of general circulation, not less than ten days prior to the date fixed for the opening of bids or public auction. The date of opening of bids or public auction shall be announced in the advertisement, and sale of the property advertised shall be made to the highest bidder.

(b) A public auction of personal property may be conducted by means of an online or electronic auction sale. During an electronic auction sale, bids shall be accepted electronically at the time and in the manner designated in the advertisement. During the electronic auction, each bidder shall have the capability to view the bidder's bid rank or the high bid price. A bidder may increase his bid price during the electronic auction. The record of the electronic auction shall be accessible for public inspection. The purchase price shall be paid by the highest bidder immediately or at a reasonable time after the conclusion of the electronic auction as determined by the board of commissioners. In the event that shipping costs are incurred, they shall be paid by the highest bidder. A

Chap. 39 Res. During Mil. Service
Chap. 38 Intergov. Coop.
Chap. 37 3rd Class City Code
Chap. 36 Bor. Code
Chap. 35 2nd Class Twp. Code
Chap. 34 1st Class Twp. Code
Chap. 33 Home Rule Chart. Opt. Plans Law
Chap. 32 Water Serv. Act
Chap. 31 Munic. Auth. Act

township that has complied with the advertising requirements of this section may provide additional public notice of the sale by bids or public auction in any manner deemed appropriate by the board of commissioners. The advertisement for electronic auction sales authorized in this section shall include the Internet address or means of accessing the electronic auction and the date, time and duration of the electronic auction.

(c) The board of commissioners may reject any bids received if the bids are believed to be less than the fair market value of the property. If no compliant bids are received after advertisement, the applicable procedures in the act of October 27, 1979 (P.L.241, No.78), entitled "An act authorizing political subdivisions, municipality authorities and transportation authorities to enter into contracts for the purchase of goods and the sale of real and personal property where no bids are received," shall be followed.

(d) The board of commissioners shall, by resolution, adopt a procedure for the sale of surplus personal property, either individual items or lots of items, of an estimated fair market value of less than two thousand dollars. The approval of the board of commissioners shall not be required for an individual sale that shall be made in conformity to the procedure.

(e) The provisions of this section shall not be mandatory where township personal property is to be traded in or exchanged for new or used personal property being acquired by the township, except that the trade or exchange shall be by resolution.

(1501.2 added Oct. 29, 2020, P.L.782, No.96)

§ 1501.3. Exceptions.—(a) Nothing under this article requiring advertising for bids or sale at public auction and sale to the highest bidder shall apply if township real or personal property is to be sold to any of the following:

(1) A county, city, borough, town, township, institution district, school district, volunteer fire company, volunteer ambulance service or volunteer rescue squad located within the township.

(2) A council of government, consortium, cooperative or other similar entity created under 53 Pa.C.S. Ch. 23 Subch. A (relating to intergovernmental cooperation).

(3) An authority as defined in 53 Pa.C.S. § 5602 (relating to definitions) or an authority or industrial and commercial development authority as defined under section 3 of the act of August 23, 1967 (P.L.251, No.102), known as the Economic Development Financing Law.

(4) A nonprofit corporation engaged in community, industrial, commercial or affordable housing development or reuse.

(5) A person for the person's exclusive use in an industrial development program.

(6) A nonprofit corporation organized as a public library.

(7) A nonprofit medical service corporation as authorized by section 1502.46.

(8) A nonprofit housing corporation as authorized under section 1502.47.

(b) If real property is to be sold to a nonprofit corporation organized as a public library or to a nonprofit medical service corporation or to a nonprofit housing corporation, the board of commissioners may elect to accept nominal consideration for the sale as the board deems appropriate.

(c) Real property sold under this section to a volunteer fire company, volunteer ambulance service or volunteer rescue squad, nonprofit medical service corporation or to a nonprofit housing corporation shall be subject to the condi-

tion that when the property is not used for the purposes of the company, service, squad or corporation the property shall revert to the township.

(1501.3 added Oct. 29, 2020, P.L.782, No.96)

§ 1501.4. Surcharge from Sale or Lease.—A commissioner who votes in favor of or knowingly participates in the sale or lease of township real or personal property in violation of this article is subject to a surcharge to the extent of any loss or injury to the township as a result of the sale or lease.

(1501.4 added Oct. 29, 2020, P.L.782, No.96)

§ 1501.5. General Powers.—The board of commissioners may make and adopt any ordinances, bylaws, rules and regulations not inconsistent with or restrained by the Constitution and laws of this Commonwealth as may be expedient or necessary for the proper management, care and control of the township and its finances, and the maintenance of peace, good government and welfare of the township and its trade, commerce and manufactures.

(1501.5 added Oct. 29, 2020, P.L.782, No.96)

§ 1502. Specific Powers.—The corporate power of a township of the first class shall be vested in a board of commissioners. In the exercise of any specific powers involving the enactment of an ordinance, passage of a resolution or the making of any regulation, restriction or prohibition, the township may provide for enforcement and penalties for violations. The specific powers of the township shall include the powers provided under this article.

(1502 amended Oct. 29, 2020, P.L.782, No.96)

Compiler's Note: Section 3 of Act 51 of 2015, which amended clause XIX, provided that nothing in Act 51 shall be construed to repeal or modify any township ordinance in effect on the effective date of Act 51 or affect any proceeding or enforcement of any township ordinance instituted prior to the effective date of Act 51.

Compiler's Note: See sections 14 and 15 of Act 188 of 2012 in the appendix to this act for special provisions relating to applicability of law and municipal officers affected by Act 188.

Compiler's Note: Section 28 of Act 207 of 2004 provided that any and all references in any other law to a "district justice" or "justice of the peace" shall be deemed to be references to a magisterial district judge.

Compiler's Note: Section 302(d) of Act 177 of 1988, known as the General Association Act of 1988, provided that clause LVII is repealed insofar as it is inconsistent with 15 Pa.C.S. § 1511, (relating to additional powers of certain public utility corporations).

Compiler's Note: The act of April 28, 1961 (P.L.111, No.5), known as the "Tourist Promotion Law," referred to in this section, was repealed by the act of July 4, 2008 (P.L.621, No.50), known as the Tourist Promotion Act.

Compiler's Note: Section 1 of Act 21 of 1947 provided that townships are authorized to regulate parking lots within their boundaries and to collect license or permit fees from the operators.

Compiler's Note: The act of May 2, 1945 (P.L.382, No.164), referred to as the Municipality Authorities Act of 1945, referred to in clause LXXVII, was repealed by the act of June 19, 2001 (P.L.2877, No.22). The subject matter is now contained in 53 Pa.C.S. Ch. 56 (relating to municipal authorities).

Compiler's Note: The Municipal Borrowing Law, referred to in clause LXI, has been repealed, renamed and codified over time. The subject matter is now contained in 53 Pa.C.S. Pt. VII Subpt. B (relating to indebtedness and borrowing.)

§ 1502.1. Officers, Positions and Departments.—(a) The board of commissioners may create any office, position or department which the board may deem necessary for the good of government and interests of the township and may fix the compensation of appointed individuals.

(b) The board of commissioners may provide for and regulate the manner of hiring and discharging employes and the fixing of salaries or compensation, consistent with applicable Federal and State law.

(1502.1 added Oct. 29, 2020, P.L.782, No.96)

§ 1502.2. Police Force.—The board of commissioners may establish, equip, maintain and define the duties of a police force.

(1502.2 added Oct. 29, 2020, P.L.782, No.96)

§ 1502.3. Lockup facilities.—The board of commissioners may provide for lockup facilities in the township for the temporary detention and confinement of individuals.

(1502.3 added Oct. 29, 2020, P.L.782, No.96)

§ 1502.4. Rewards.—The board of commissioners may offer rewards for information leading to the arrest and conviction of an individual guilty of a crime within the township.

(1502.4 added Oct. 29, 2020, P.L.782, No.96)

§ 1502.5. Disorderly Conduct.—The board of commissioners may, by ordinance, prohibit disorderly conduct within the limits of the township and provide for the imposition of penalties for the conduct in accordance with this act. If an ordinance is enacted, it shall define disorderly conduct in a manner substantially similar to the provisions of 18 Pa.C.S. § 5503 (relating to disorderly conduct).

(1502.5 added Oct. 29, 2020, P.L.782, No.96)

§ 1502.6. Public Safety.—The board of commissioners may take all necessary means to secure the safety of persons or property within the township.

(1502.6 added Oct. 29, 2020, P.L.782, No.96)

§ 1502.7. Fire Protection.—The board of commissioners may:

(1) Appropriate money for the use of the township or to fire companies providing fire protection to the township for the purchase, operation and maintenance of fire engines and fire apparatus and for the construction, repair and maintenance of fire stations.

(2) Contract with or make grants to near or adjacent municipal corporations or volunteer fire companies for fire protection in the township.

(3) By ordinance or resolution, make rules and regulations for the government of fire companies providing fire protection to the township and their officers.

(1502.7 added Oct. 29, 2020, P.L.782, No.96)

§ 1502.8. Building and Housing Regulations.—In addition to other remedies provided by law, the board of commissioners may enact and enforce suitable ordinances relating to building and housing regulations in accordance with Article XXXI-A.

(1502.8 added Oct. 29, 2020, P.L.782, No.96)

§ 1502.9. Numbering Buildings.—The board of commissioners may, by ordinance, require and regulate the numbering of buildings and lots.

(1502.9 added Oct. 29, 2020, P.L.782, No.96)

§ 1502.10. Regulation of Business.—To provide for the prohibition, licensing and regulation of business, a board of commissioners may:

(1) In addition to licensing in accordance with Article XXIX, prohibit, license and regulate by ordinance the following:

(i) The carrying on of any manufacture, art or business which may be noxious or offensive and prejudicial to the public health or safety of the inhabitants.

(ii) The establishment and maintenance of junk yards, salvage yards and other places used and maintained for the collection, storage and disposal of used or second-hand goods and materials.

(iii) With respect to marketplaces:

(A) regulate markets whether for individual use or for resale;

(B) purchase and own ground;

(C) erect, establish and maintain marketplaces for which parts of a street or sidewalk may be temporarily used;

(D) contract with a person for the erection, maintenance and regulation of marketplaces, on terms and conditions and in a manner as the board of commissioners may prescribe;

(E) provide and enforce suitable regulations respecting marketplaces;

(F) provide for the payment of the cost or expense of marketplaces, either in whole or in part, out of the funds of the township; and

(G) levy and collect a suitable license fee from each person who may be authorized by the board of commissioners to occupy any portion of a marketplace or any portion of a street or sidewalk for temporary market purposes.

(2) Notwithstanding paragraph (1), prohibit, license and regulate businesses unless prohibited by law.

(3) Issue licenses under the act of July 31, 1963 (P.L.410, No.217), entitled "An act regulating and licensing all sales at retail when such sales are advertised as 'Closing Out Sale,' 'Fire, Smoke or Water Damage Sale,' or 'Defunct Business Sale,' with exceptions; requiring filing of inventory and bond; and providing for appeals and penalties."

(1502.10 added Oct. 29, 2020, P.L.782, No.96)

§ 1502.11. Nuisances and Dangerous Structures.—(a) A board of commissioners may prohibit and remove any nuisance or dangerous structure on public or private grounds, including, but not limited to weeds, accumulations of municipal waste, the storage of abandoned or junked automobiles and obstructions or nuisances in the streets of the township.

(b) The board of commissioners may:

(1) require the removal of any nuisance or dangerous structure by the owner or occupier of the grounds; or

(2) in default of the removal by the owner or occupier of grounds under paragraph (1), remove the nuisance or dangerous structure itself and collect the cost of removal, together with a penalty of 10% of the cost, in the manner provided by law for the collection of municipal claims, or by action of assumpsit without the filing of a claim, or the township may seek relief by bill in equity.

(1502.11 added Oct. 29, 2020, P.L.782, No.96)

§ 1502.12. Municipal Waste.—(a) A board of commissioners, in the manner authorized by the act of July 7, 1980 (P.L.380, No.97), known as the Solid Waste Management Act, and the act of July 28, 1988 (P.L.556, No.101), known as the

Municipal Waste Planning, Recycling and Waste Reduction Act, may prohibit accumulations of municipal waste on public and private property, including the imposition and collection of reasonable fees and charges for the collection, removal and disposal of the municipal waste. As used in this act, "municipal waste" shall have the same meaning as given to the term in the Municipal Waste Planning, Recycling and Waste Reduction Act.

(b) (1) The board of commissioners may collect and remove, by contract or otherwise, municipal waste and recyclable materials and prescribe penalties for the enforcement of the collection and removal.

(2) A contract with refuse haulers may be made for an initial period not exceeding five years with optional renewal periods of up to five years.

(3) Paragraph (2) shall not apply to a contract with any other political subdivision or with any municipality authority.

(c) (1) The board of commissioners may dispose of, by contract or otherwise, municipal waste.

(2) A contract with the owner of a private facility for the disposal or incineration of municipal waste may be made for a period not to exceed 20 years.

(3) Paragraph (2) shall not apply to a contract with any other political subdivision or with any municipality authority.

(d) The board of commissioners may:

(1) Acquire any real property and erect, maintain, improve, operate and lease, either as lessor or lessee, facilities for incineration, landfill or other methods of disposal, either inside or outside the limits of the township, including equipment, either separately or jointly, with any other political subdivision or with any municipality authority in order to provide for the:

(i) collection, removal, disposal and destruction of municipal waste;

(ii) collection and storage of recyclable materials; or

(iii) composting of leaf and yard waste.

(2) Provide for the payment of the cost, either in whole or part, out of the funds of the township.

(3) Acquire land for landfill purposes and may maintain lands and places for the dumping of municipal waste.

(e) The board of commissioners may establish, alter, charge and collect rates and other charges for the:

(1) collection, removal and disposal of municipal waste and recyclable materials;

(2) cost of including the payment of any indebtedness incurred for the construction, purchase, improvement, repair, maintenance and operation of any facilities for collection, removal and disposal; and

(3) amount due under a contract with any other political subdivision or with any municipal authority furnishing the services or facilities.

(f) The board of commissioners may make appropriations to any other political subdivision or any municipality authority out of the township's general funds, or out of any other available funds, for the construction, purchase, improvement, repair, maintenance and operation of a facility for the collection, removal, disposal or marketing of municipal waste, recyclable materials or composted leaf and yard waste.

(g) A township shall not be subject to requirements otherwise imposed by law for the sale of personal property owned by the township when selling recyclable materials or materials separated, collected, recovered or created by recycling, as provided in the act of April 9, 1992 (P.L.70, No.21) entitled "An act excluding the sale of recyclable material from political subdivision personal property sale restrictions relating to advertising and bidding."

(1502.12 added Oct. 29, 2020, P.L.782, No.96)

§ 1502.13. Fireworks and Inflammable Articles.—In conformity with Federal and State laws and regulations, the board of commissioners may provide for fireworks and inflammable articles as follows:

(1) Regulate and prohibit, by ordinance, the manufacture of fireworks or inflammable or dangerous articles.

(2) Grant permits for display fireworks and adopt rules and regulations governing the displays.

(3) Adopt, by ordinance, rules and regulations relating to the storage of inflammable articles.

(4) Impose, by ordinance, other safeguards concerning fireworks and inflammable articles as may be necessary for the health, safety and welfare of the public.

(1502.13 added Oct. 29, 2020, P.L.782, No.96)

§ 1502.14. Smoke Regulations.—The board of commissioners may regulate the emission of smoke from chimneys, smokestacks and other sources, except locomotive smokestacks, to the extent that the regulation is not otherwise prohibited by applicable Federal or State law.

(1502.14 added Oct. 29, 2020, P.L.782, No.96)

§ 1502.15. Prohibition of Fire-Producing Devices and Smoking.—The board of commissioners may prohibit and regulate the smoking or carrying of lighted cigarettes, cigars, pipes or matches and the use of matches or fire-producing devices. An ordinance enacted or regulation or resolution adopted under this section shall not regulate smoking in a manner that conflicts with the act of June 13, 2008 (P.L.182, No.27), known as the Clean Indoor Air Act.

(1502.15 added Oct. 29, 2020, P.L.782, No.96)

§ 1502.16. Animals.—The board of commissioners may prohibit or regulate, by ordinance, the following:

(1) The running at large of dogs and direct the seizure, detention or euthanization of dogs running at large, including reasonable associated charges, and provide for the sale of the dogs for the benefit of the township.

(2) The running at large of other animals and authorize their seizure and detention, including reasonable associated charges, and provide for sale of the animals for the benefit of the township.

(1502.16 added Oct. 29, 2020, P.L.782, No.96)

§ 1502.17. Regulation of Foundations, Party Walls and Partition Fences.—(a) Subject to the provisions of and regulations adopted pursuant to the act of November 10, 1999 (P.L.491, No.45), known as the Pennsylvania Construction Code Act, and other applicable law, the board of commissioners may provide regulations for foundations, party walls and partition fences.

(b) The board of commissioners may prescribe and enforce reasonable fees for the services of its officers and agents in the adjustment of party walls, partition fences and similar items.

(1502.17 added Oct. 29, 2020, P.L.782, No.96)

§ 1502.18. Ambulances and Rescue and Lifesaving Services.—The board of commissioners may:

(1) Acquire, operate and maintain motor vehicles for the purposes of transporting sick and injured individuals to and from hospitals.

(2) Appropriate funds toward ambulance and rescue and lifesaving services.

(3) Enter into contracts relating to rescue and lifesaving services.

(1502.18 added Oct. 29, 2020, P.L.782, No.96)

§ 1502.19. Display of Flags.—The board of commissioners may display the flag of the United States, the Commonwealth, the official POW/MIA flag or the flag of any county or municipal corporation in this Commonwealth on any public building or grounds of the township.

(1502.19 added Oct. 29, 2020, P.L.782, No.96)

§ 1502.20. Health and Cleanliness Regulations.—The board of commissioners may make regulations as necessary for the health, safety, morals, general welfare, cleanliness, beauty, convenience and comfort of the township and its inhabitants.

(1502.20 added Oct. 29, 2020, P.L.782, No.96)

§ 1502.21. Public Facilities.—The board of commissioners may acquire property for the purposes of providing, maintaining and operating public facilities, such as comfort and waiting stations, drinking fountains and watering troughs.

(1502.21 added Oct. 29, 2020, P.L.782, No.96)

§ 1502.22. Hospital Appropriations.—The board of commissioners may, in townships having a population of two thousand inhabitants or more, appropriate money for the support of any incorporated hospital that is engaged in charitable work and extends treatment and medical attention to the residents of the township.

(1502.22 added Oct. 29, 2020, P.L.782, No.96)

§ 1502.23. Community Nursing Services.—The board of commissioners may appropriate money annually to any nonprofit associations or corporations that provide for:

(1) community nursing services for the elderly and other needy persons;

(2) the control of communicable disease;

(3) the immunization of children;

(4) the operation of child health centers; or

(5) instructive visits to parents of new babies beginning in the prenatal period and family health guidance, including nutrition, detection and correction of defects.

(1502.23 added Oct. 29, 2020, P.L.782, No.96)

§ 1502.24. Parking and Parking Lots.—(a) The board of commissioners may:

(1) regulate parking and parking lots and provide parking accommodations to promote the convenience and protection of the public;

(2) establish or designate, at the board's discretion, areas exclusively reserved for parking by handicapped individuals and post signs regulating the areas;

(3) erect parking meters and regulate parking meter charges;

(4) acquire by gift, purchase, lease or eminent domain, lands that the board may deem necessary or desirable for the purpose of establishing and maintaining parking lots; and

(5) plan, design, locate, hold, construct, improve, maintain, operate, own or lease, either in the capacity of lessor or lessee, and install facilities and equipment on any land to be devoted to the parking of vehicles.

(b) Consistent with 75 Pa.C.S. (relating to vehicles), the right to regulate the use of the lots shall include the right to impose fines and fees for violation of any law or ordinance regulating parking.

(c) Nothing in this section may be construed to limit statutory and regulatory protections and prohibitions relating to the rights of disabled individuals.

(1502.24 added Oct. 29, 2020, P.L.782, No.96)

§ 1502.25. Appropriations for Certain Streets.—The board of commissioners may appropriate money annually for improvements to any street, as defined in section 102, located wholly or partially within the township which has been adversely affected by parking availability as determined by the board.

(1502.25 added Oct. 29, 2020, P.L.782, No.96)

§ 1502.26. Airports.—(a) A township is authorized and empowered to acquire by grant, lease, purchase or condemnation proceedings, subject to the limitations in 26 Pa.C.S. § 206 (relating to extraterritorial takings), any land lying either within or without the limits of the township which, in the judgment of the board of commissioners, may be necessary and desirable for the purpose of establishing and maintaining a municipal airport, landing field, intermediate landing field, aviation easement or other airport facility.

(b) A township acquiring land under this section is authorized to establish, equip, condition, operate and maintain the land as a municipal airport, landing field, intermediate landing field, aviation easement or other airport facility and may lease the land, or any part, to any individual or corporation desiring to use the land for aviation purposes. A township may enter into a contract in the form of a lease providing for the use of the land, or any part, by the Federal Government for the Federal Government's use of the land for aviation purposes upon nominal rental or without consideration.

(c) In accordance with this section, a township may acquire land jointly with another municipality for aviation purposes and may jointly operate and maintain a municipal airport, landing field, intermediate landing field, aviation easement or other airport facility on the jointly acquired land in accordance with 53 Pa.C.S. Ch. 23 Subch. A (relating to intergovernmental cooperation).

(1502.26 added Oct. 29, 2020, P.L.782, No.96)

§ 1502.27. Appropriations for Airports.—The board of commissioners may appropriate funds to assist a municipality or municipal airport authority to acquire, establish, operate and maintain air navigation facilities lying either within or without the limits of the township.

(1502.27 added Oct. 29, 2020, P.L.782, No.96)

§ 1502.28. Purchase and Planting of Trees.—The board of commissioners may accept, purchase and plant, or contribute to the purchase and planting of, shade trees and shrubs along the streets, highways and sidewalks of the township and have the care, custody and control of shade trees pursuant to Article XXX.

(1502.28 added Oct. 29, 2020, P.L.782, No.96)

§ 1502.29. Intergovernmental Cooperation.—The board of commissioners may enter into agreements under 53 Pa.C.S. Ch. 23 Subch. A (relating to intergovernmental cooperation) with the following:

(1) Other political subdivisions, in accordance with existing laws, to:

(i) make joint purchases of materials, supplies or equipment; and

(ii) perform governmental powers, duties and functions.

(2) The proper authorities of municipal corporations, regional police or fire forces or other public safety or governmental entities created by two or more municipal corporations under 53 Pa.C.S. Ch. 23 Subch. A, for:

(i) mutual aid or assistance in police and fire protection or any other public safety services or for the furnishing to or receiving from the municipal

Table of Contents
Part I Ch. 1–3 Ethics, Records, Open Meetings
Part II Ch. 4–10 Taxation
Part III Ch. 11–18 Torts, Contracts & Civil Rules
Part IV Ch. 19–24 Zoning & Planning
Part V Ch. 25–30 Construction and Emergency Codes
Part VI Ch. 31–39 Municipal Codes
Index

corporations or governmental entities police and fire protection or any other public safety service; and

(ii) making appropriations for public safety services.

(3) In connection with an agreement under paragraph (2) for police or fire protection or any other public safety service, the township shall not be required to advertise for bids or receive bonds as required for contracts under existing law. When an agreement has been entered into, the police, firefighters, fire police or any other public safety services of the employing municipal corporation or governmental entity shall have the powers and authority conferred by law on police, firefighters, fire police or any other public safety services in the territory of the municipal corporation which has contracted to secure the service.

(1502.29 added Oct. 29, 2020, P.L.782, No.96)

§ 1502.30. Widening and Deepening of Watercourses.—(a) After permits have been secured from all applicable agencies, the board of commissioners or an agent or employe of the board may widen and deepen a watercourse running through the township and erect dykes, retaining walls and embankments along the watercourse as necessary to prevent water from overflowing the watercourse's banks.

(b) For the purposes under subsection (a), a township may enter and condemn property as may be necessary. A township may enter land lying near the watercourse and secure materials as may be necessary in connection with the work. Damages for property taken, injured or destroyed as the result of the work shall be fixed and determined as provided under 26 Pa.C.S. (relating to eminent domain). Townships may appropriate money to effectuate the provisions of this section.

(1502.30 added Oct. 29, 2020, P.L.782, No.96)

§ 1502.31. Regulation of Charges.—The board of commissioners may make and regulate charges for the use of township facilities.

(1502.31 added Oct. 29, 2020, P.L.782, No.96)

§ 1502.32. Street, Sewer, Sidewalk, Etc., Regulations.—(a) The board of commissioners may:

(1) regulate the streets, sewers, public squares, common grounds, sidewalks, curbs, gutters, culverts and drains within a township;

(2) regulate the heights, grades, widths, slopes and construction of any item listed under paragraph (1); and

(3) grant rights for the installation and maintenance of public utilities in the streets, including pipes, wires, fibers, cables or any other utility or service medium.

(b) The power granted under subsection (a) shall be exercised in compliance with Federal and State law and shall be subject to the power of the Pennsylvania Public Utility Commission under 66 Pa.C.S. Pt. I (relating to public utility code) to regulate the business, facilities and service of public utilities, including determining the location and installation of utility facilities.

(1502.32 added Oct. 29, 2020, P.L.782, No.96)

§ 1502.33. Capital Reserve Fund.—The board of commissioners may create and maintain a separate capital reserve fund for anticipated legal capital expenditures and the following shall apply:

(1) The fund shall be designated for a specific purpose or purposes when created.

(2) The money in the fund shall be used for the construction, purchase or replacement of or addition to municipal buildings, equipment, machinery, mo-

tor vehicles or other capital assets of the township as specified at the time of the creation of the fund and for no other purpose unless the commissioners by a four-fifths vote declare that the original purpose or purposes have become impracticable, inadvisable or impossible, or that conditions in the township make other capital expenditures more urgent than those for which the fund was created.

(3) The board of commissioners may appropriate money from the general township fund to be paid into the capital reserve fund, or place in the fund any money received from the sale, lease or other disposition of any township property or from any other source unless received or acquired for a particular purpose.

(4) The fund shall be controlled, invested, reinvested and administered and the money and any income derived from it expended for any of the purposes for which the fund is created in a manner determined by the board of commissioners.

(5) The money in the fund, when invested, shall be invested in securities designated by 53 Pa.C.S. Pt. VII Subpt. B (relating to indebtedness and borrowing) as legal investments for sinking funds of municipalities.

(1502.33 added Oct. 29, 2020, P.L.782, No.96)

§ 1502.34. Operating Reserve Fund.—(a) The board of commissioners may create and maintain a separate operating reserve fund in order to:

(1) minimize future revenue shortfalls and deficits;

(2) provide greater continuity and predictability in the funding of vital government services;

(3) minimize the need to increase taxes to balance the budget in times of fiscal distress; and

(4) provide the capacity to undertake long-range financial planning and to develop fiscal resources to meet long-term needs.

(b) The board of commissioners may annually make appropriations from the general township fund to the operating reserve fund, but no appropriation may be made to the operating reserve fund if the effect of the appropriation would cause the fund to exceed 25% of the estimated revenues of the township's general fund in the current fiscal year.

(c) The board of commissioners may, at any time by resolution, make appropriations from the operating reserve fund for the following purposes only:

(1) meet emergencies involving the health, safety and welfare of the residents of the township;

(2) counterbalance potential budget deficits resulting from shortfalls in anticipated revenues or program receipts from any source;

(3) counterbalance potential budget deficits resulting from increases in anticipated costs for goods or services; or

(4) provide anticipated operating expenditures related either to the planned growth of existing projects or programs or to establish new projects or programs if, for a project or program, appropriations have been made and allocated to a separate restricted account established within the operating reserve fund.

(d) The operating reserve fund shall be invested, reinvested and administered in a manner consistent with the provisions of section 1705.1.

(1502.34 added Oct. 29, 2020, P.L.782, No.96)

§ 1502.35. Surplus Foods.—The board of commissioners may make an appropriation for the handling, storage and distribution of surplus foods obtained through a Federal, State or local agency.

(1502.35 added Oct. 29, 2020, P.L.782, No.96)

§ 1502.36. Industrial Promotions.—The board of commissioners may make appropriations to an industrial development agency.

(1502.36 added Oct. 29, 2020, P.L.782, No.96)

§ 1502.37. Nondebt Revenue Bonds.—(a) The board of commissioners may issue nondebt revenue bonds pursuant to provisions of 53 Pa.C.S. Pt. VII Subpt. B (relating to indebtedness and borrowing) to provide sufficient money for and toward the acquisition, construction, reconstruction, extension or improvement of:

(1) municipal facilities, including water systems or facilities;

(2) sewers, sewer systems and sewage disposal systems or facilities;

(3) systems for the treatment or disposal of garbage and refuse;

(4) aeronautical facilities, including, but not limited to, airports, terminals and hangars; and

(5) park and recreational facilities, including parking lots.

(b) Any nondebt revenue bonds issued under subsection (a) shall be secured solely by the pledge of the whole or part of the rent, toll or charge for the use or services of the facilities.

(c) Included in the cost of the issue may be any costs and expenses incident to constructing and financing the facilities and selling and distributing the bonds.

(1502.37 added Oct. 29, 2020, P.L.782, No.96)

§ 1502.38. Historical Properties.—The board of commissioners may appropriate money to nonprofit associations or corporations organized for the purpose of acquiring and maintaining historical properties. The appropriations shall only be used by the association or corporation for the acquisition, restoration and maintenance of the historical properties.

(1502.38 added Oct. 29, 2020, P.L.782, No.96)

§ 1502.39. Insurance.—(a) The board of commissioners may secure insurance or compensation in accordance with Article VI of the act of June 2, 1915 (P.L.736, No.338), known as the Workers' Compensation Act, for:

(1) volunteer firefighters of companies duly recognized by the township, by motion or resolution, killed or injured while going to, returning from or attending fires, or while performing any other duties authorized by the township; and

(2) township employes, as defined in section 601 of the Workers' Compensation Act.

(b) The board of commissioners may enter into contracts for insurance with any insurance company, association or exchange, authorized by law to transact business in this Commonwealth, to insure any building or property owned or leased by the township.

(c) The board of commissioners may enter into contracts for insurance with any insurance company, association or exchange authorized by law to transact business in this Commonwealth to insure any public liability of the township.

(d) (1) The board of commissioners may enter into contracts for insurance with any insurance company, nonprofit hospitalization corporation, nonprofit medical service corporation, association or exchange authorized by law to transact business in this Commonwealth to insure its employes or commissioners, or any class or classes of the employes or commissioners or dependents of the em-

ployes or commissioners, under a policy or policies of group insurance covering life, health, hospitalization, medical and surgical service, or accident insurance.

(2) Any life, health, hospitalization, medical service or accident insurance coverage contract entered into by a township between January 1, 1959, and December 31, 1984, that includes or provides coverage for commissioners shall not be void or unlawful solely because the inclusion of commissioners was subsequently found to be without lawful authority. No penalty, assessment, surcharge, forfeiture or disciplinary action of any kind may occur as a result of participation by those commissioners. Insurance benefits payable to insureds or their beneficiaries arising out of or on account of deaths, injuries, accidents or illnesses occurring before November 29, 1985, remain the property of the insureds or beneficiaries of the insureds.

(e) (1) The board of commissioners may contract with any insurance company, granting annuities or pensions for the pensioning of employes or any class or classes of employes and pay part or all of the premiums or charges for carrying the contracts.

(2) Any pension or annuity contract entered into by a township between January 1, 1959, and December 31, 1984, that includes or provides for benefits for commissioners at township expense shall not be void or unlawful solely because the inclusion of commissioners was subsequently found to be without lawful authority. No penalty, assessment, surcharge or disciplinary action of any kind may occur as a result of participation by those commissioners provided that anyone entitled to benefit coverage under a pension paid for, in whole or in part, by a township without lawful authority shall deliver, surrender and assign to the township all benefits paid under the contract after December 31, 1984.

(3) If any official personally contributed toward a pension plan or a purchase of an annuity under paragraph (2), the official shall be refunded the official's total contributions, plus any accumulated interest, less any amount already paid to the official under the annuity or pension plan, when the annuity or pension benefits are delivered, surrendered or assigned to the township, or when the annuity becomes the property of the township by operation of this section. In lieu of a refund of total contributions plus accumulated interest, an official who personally contributed toward the pension plan or toward the purchase of the annuity may elect to purchase from the township the township's interest in that pension plan or annuity program. The election option shall be exercised within sixty days of November 29, 1985. The value of the interest of the township in the pension plan or annuity program with respect to the official shall be determined by the actuary who prepared the 1983 municipal pension report for the township pension plan or annuity program pursuant to the act of December 6, 1972 (P.L.1383, No.293), entitled "An act requiring municipal pension systems to have an actuarial investigation of the fund made by an actuary who shall report his findings to the Department of Community Affairs," using the same applicable actuarial assumptions as used in that report or, if no actuary was retained for the 1983 report or no 1983 report was filed, by an actuary retained for the purpose of valuing the township interest. The cost of the actuarial valuation of the township interest and any future administrative costs of the pension plan or the annuity program attributable to the official shall be payable by the official in a manner to be established by agreement with the township auditors.

(4) No elected or appointed township official included in a township-paid pension or annuity plan entered into prior to December 31, 1984, shall be subject to any penalty, assessment, surcharge or disciplinary action of any kind as a result of the participation. Any residual interest, value, refund of premium or benefits payable on or after December 31, 1984, arising out of

the township-paid interest of the elected or appointed township officials shall become the exclusive property of the township.

(f) The board of commissioners may appropriate money from the general township fund for the purposes of this section.

(g) Nothing in this section shall affect any contract, right or coverage of insurance vested or existing on the effective date of this subsection. Contract, as used in this section, includes an annuity contract if the option to renew continues to provide the same rights to the annuitant that existed on the effective date of this subsection.

(h) The commissioners are hereby authorized, enabled and permitted to deduct from the employe's or commissioner's pay, salary or compensation the part of the premium or charge, as is payable by the employe or commissioner, and as may be authorized by the employe or commissioner in writing. The insurance shall be uniformly applicable to each employe or commissioner covered and shall not give eligibility preference to, or improperly discriminate in favor of, commissioners. As used in this section, the terms "employe" and "employes" exclude independent contractors and all township engineers and solicitors.

(1502.39 added Oct. 29, 2020, P.L.782, No.96)

§ 1502.40. Appropriations for Urban Common Carrier Mass Transportation.—The board of commissioners may:

(1) appropriate funds for urban common carrier mass transportation purposes from current revenues;

(2) make annual contributions to county departments of transportation or urban common carrier mass transportation authorities to assist the departments or the authorities to meet the costs of operation, maintenance, capital improvements and debt service; and

(3) enter into long-term agreements providing for the payment of the contributions.

(1502.40 added Oct. 29, 2020, P.L.782, No.96)

§ 1502.41. Open Burning.—The board of commissioners may regulate open burning, including the prohibition of the open burning of combustible material.

(1502.41 added Oct. 29, 2020, P.L.782, No.96)

§ 1502.42. Community Development.—The board of commissioners may undertake community development programs, including, but not limited to, urban renewal, public housing, model cities programs and neighborhood development projects.

(1502.42 added Oct. 29, 2020, P.L.782, No.96)

§ 1502.43. Observances and Celebrations.—The board of commissioners may appropriate funds annually for the observance of holidays, centennials or other anniversaries or for township celebrations or civic projects or programs.

(1502.43 added Oct. 29, 2020, P.L.782, No.96)

§ 1502.44. Building Hospitals.—The board of commissioners may appropriate funds toward the purchase, erection, maintenance or support of any medical center or hospital building facilities. Approval by the appropriate health planning agency is required if the total cost of the purchase or erection exceeds $100,000.

(1502.44 added Oct. 29, 2020, P.L.782, No.96)

§ 1502.45. Tourist Promotion Agencies.—The board of commissioners may appropriate funds annually to any tourist promotion agency to assist the agencies in carrying out tourist promotional activities. "Tourist promotion agency" shall have the same meaning given to it under section 2 of the act of July 4, 2008 (P.L.621, No.50), known as the Tourism Promotion Act.

(1502.45 added Oct. 29, 2020, P.L.782, No.96)

§ 1502.46. Sale of Real or Personal Property to Nonprofit Medical Service Corporation.—The board of commissioners may sell to a nonprofit medical service corporation any township-owned:

(1) real property for its exclusive use as a site for a medical service facility; and

(2) personal property for its use at the medical service facility.

(1502.46 added Oct. 29, 2020, P.L.782, No.96)

§ 1502.47. Sale of Real or Personal Property to Nonprofit Housing Corporation.—The board of commissioners may sell to a nonprofit housing corporation any township-owned:

(1) real property for its exclusive use for housing for the elderly; and

(2) personal property for its use at the nonprofit housing corporation.

(1502.47 added Oct. 29, 2020, P.L.782, No.96)

§ 1502.48. Nonprofit Art Corporations.—(a) The board of commissioners may appropriate funds annually, of an amount not more than equal to one mill of the real estate tax, to any nonprofit art corporation for the conduct of the corporation's artistic and cultural activities.

(b) As used in this section, the following words and phrases shall have the meanings given to them in this subsection:

"Artistic and cultural activities." The term shall include the display or production of theater, music, dance, painting, architecture, sculpture, arts and crafts, photography, film, graphic arts and design and creative writing.

"Nonprofit art corporation." A local arts council, commission or coordinating agency or any other nonprofit corporation engaged in the production or display of works of art, including the visual, written or performing arts.

(1502.48 added Oct. 29, 2020, P.L.782, No.96)

§ 1502.49. Neighborhood Crime Watch Programs.—The board of commissioners may appropriate annually an amount toward a neighborhood crime watch program. Notwithstanding any other provision of law, no township or official of a township shall become subject to contractual, tort or other liability as a result of having made an appropriation pursuant to this section.

(1502.49 added Oct. 29, 2020, P.L.782, No.96)

§ 1502.50. Drug and Alcohol Abuse Programs.—The board of commissioners may appropriate annually, out of the general funds of the township, a sum to be divided in amounts as the commissioners may determine and to be used for education and development of programs within the community dealing with drug and alcohol abuse. The funds may also be contributed to existing programs available to the township's residents in adjacent communities or in the county where the township is situate at the discretion of the board of commissioners.

(1502.50 added Oct. 29, 2020, P.L.782, No.96)

§ 1502.51. Watershed Associations.—The board of commissioners may make appropriations to nonprofit watershed associations for watersheds serving the township. Appropriations may not be used to undertake litigation against any municipality or to seek redress against any individual landowner.

(1502.51 added Oct. 29, 2020, P.L.782, No.96)

§ 1502.52. Emergency Services.—(a) The township shall be responsible for ensuring that fire and emergency medical services are provided within the township by the means and to the extent determined by the township, including the

Table of Contents
Part I Ch. 1–3 Ethics, Records, Open Meetings
Part II Ch. 4–10 Taxation
Part III Ch. 11–18 Torts, Contracts & Civil Rules
Part IV Ch. 19–24 Zoning & Planning
Part V Ch. 25–30 Construction and Emergency Codes
Part VI Ch. 31–39 Municipal Codes
Index

appropriate financial and administrative assistance for these services.

(b) The township shall consult with fire and emergency medical services providers to discuss the emergency services needs of the township.

(c) The township shall require each emergency services organization receiving township funds to provide to the township an annual itemized listing of all expenditures of these funds before the township may consider budgeting additional funding to the organization.

(1502.52 added Oct. 29, 2020, P.L.782, No.96)

§ 1502.53. Mines and Quarries.—(a) The owner, operator or superintendent of each mine, colliery or quarry located wholly or partially within the limits of the township shall furnish maps, plans and drawings of workings, excavations and surface support to the township as the board of commissioners may require, and the following shall apply:

(1) In the case of a coal mine or colliery, the map or plan shall exhibit the workings or excavations in every seam of coal on a separate sheet and the tunnels and passages connecting with the workings or excavations.

(2) The map or plan under paragraph (1) shall show:

(i) in degrees the general inclination of the strata, with any material deflection in the strata in the workings or excavations, and shall also show the tidal elevations of the bottom of every shaft, slope, tunnel and gangway and of any other point in the mine or on the surface where the elevation shall be deemed necessary by the township;

(ii) the number of the last survey on the gangways or the most advanced workings.

(3) Each owner, operator or superintendent of a mine, colliery or quarry shall update, at least once every three months, the pertinent maps, plans and drawings to reflect any extensions made in any mine, colliery or quarry during the three preceding months, except those made within thirty days immediately preceding the time of placing the extensions upon the map or drawing.

(4) A township engineer, assistant or other person authorized by the board of commissioners may enter and survey any mine, colliery or quarry within the limits of the township, at all reasonable times, but not so as to impede or obstruct the workings of the mine, colliery or quarry.

(5) The owner, operator or superintendent of the mine, colliery or quarry shall furnish the means necessary for the entry, survey and exit.

(b) (Reserved).

(1502.53 added Oct. 29, 2020, P.L.782, No.96)

§ 1502.54. Conservation District.—The board of commissioners may make appropriations to a conservation district, as the term is defined under section 3 of the act of May 15, 1945 (P.L.547, No.217), known as the Conservation District Law, in which the township is located.

(1502.54 added Oct. 29, 2020, P.L.782, No.96)

§ 1502.55. Electricity.—The board of commissioners may manufacture and sell electricity and regulate its use and prices pursuant to Article XXVII-A.

(1502.55 added Oct. 29, 2020, P.L.782, No.96)

§ 1502.56. Storm Water.—A township may, by ordinance, after obtaining any required permit from the Department of Environmental Protection or other Federal or State entity, acquire, operate and maintain areas for the infiltration, detention or retention of storm water and for other methods of storm water management authorized by the Department of Environmental Protection.

(1502.56 added Oct. 29, 2020, P.L.782, No.96)

§ 1503. Typewritten, printed, photocopied, microfilmed and electronically or digitally stored records valid and recording or transcribing records.—(a) All township records required to be recorded or transcribed shall be deemed valid if typewritten, printed, photocopied, microfilmed or electronically or digitally stored or retained by any other process that accurately reproduces the original and forms a durable medium for recording, storing and reproducing in accordance with the act of May 9, 1949 (P.L.908, No.250), entitled "An act relating to public records of political subdivisions other than cities and counties of the first class; authorizing the recording and copying of documents, plats, papers and instruments of writing by digital, photostatic, photographic, microfilm or other process, and the admissibility thereof and enlargements thereof in evidence; providing for the storage of duplicates and sale of microfilm and digital copies of official records and for the destruction of other records deemed valueless; and providing for the services of the Pennsylvania Historical and Museum Commission to political subdivisions."

(b) If recording or transcribing in a specified book of record is required, including minutes of the proceedings of the board of commissioners, the records shall be recorded or transcribed as follows:

(1) in a mechanical post binder book capable of being permanently sealed with consecutively numbered pages with a security code printed on it and a permanent locking device with the township seal being impressed upon each page; or

(2) in a bound book with pages being consecutively numbered by transcribing directly upon the pages of the book of record or by permanently attaching the records or copies to the book of record with the township seal being impressed upon each page to which the record is attached, with each impression covering both a portion of the attached record and a portion of the page of the book of record to which the record is attached.

(c) All records previously recorded or transcribed in any manner authorized by this act at the time the records were recorded or transcribed are validated.

(1503 amended Oct. 29, 2020, P.L.782, No.96)

ARTICLE XV-A

REAL ESTATE REGISTRY

53 P.S. §§ 56501-A

(Art. added Oct. 29, 2020, P.L.782, No.96)

§ 1501-A. Real Estate Registry.

(a) General rule.—For the purpose of procuring accurate information on the ownership of all real estate, the board of commissioners may provide, by ordinance, for a real estate registry in a manner not inconsistent with the act of October 9, 2008 (P.L.1400, No.110), known as the Uniform Municipal Deed Registration Act.

(b) Registry.—The board of commissioners shall designate a person to have charge of the registry who shall cause to be made and shall carefully preserve all necessary books, maps and plans as may show the location and ownership of every lot, piece of real estate and subdivision of real estate. For purposes of establishing or maintaining the registry, the person in charge of the registry shall have access to public records without charge.

(c) Validity of certain claims.—Information contained within a real estate registry shall not affect the validity of any municipal claim or tax claim of the township.

(d) Additional information as may be required.—Nothing in this section shall prohibit a township from requiring owners to provide information relevant to the enforcement of any township ordinance in accordance with law.

(1501-A added Oct. 29, 2020, P.L.782, No.96)

ARTICLE XVI
PUBLIC HEALTH

53 P.S. §§ 56601–56627

(a) Boards of Health
(Subdiv. hdg. repealed Oct. 29, 2020, P.L.782, No.96)

§ 1601. Appointment of Boards of Health and Health Officers.—(a) The board of commissioners may, by ordinance, establish a board of health or the office of health officer to administer and enforce the health ordinances and related ordinances of the township. A health officer must, whether appointed by the board of commissioners or by the board of health, have experience or training in public health work and must, within six months of taking the oath of office, be certified for the office of health officer by the State Department of Health.

(b) Expenses incurred by the board of health or a health officer shall be paid by the township.

(c) A township may, by ordinance, dissolve a board of health or the office of health officer and decide to become subject to the jurisdiction of a county department of health or joint county department of health under the act of August 24, 1951 (P.L.1304, No.315), known as the Local Health Administration Law.

(1601 amended Oct. 29, 2020, P.L.782, No.96)

§ 1602. Members of Board; Terms; Secretary.—(a) A board of health appointed by the board of commissioners shall be composed of three or five members, at the discretion of the board, and the following shall apply:

(1) At least one of the board members shall be a reputable professional health care provider of not less than two years' experience in the practice of the respective profession.

(2) If no professional health care provider can be identified to serve on the board, the board of commissioners may appoint an individual at a public meeting who has experience in, or is knowledgeable of, public health issues.

(b) At the first appointment for a board:

(1) With three members:

(i) one member shall be appointed to serve for one year;

(ii) one member shall be appointed to serve for two years; and

(iii) one member shall be appointed to serve for three years.

(2) With five members:

(i) one member shall be appointed to serve for one year;

(ii) one member shall be appointed to serve for two years;

(iii) one member shall be appointed to serve for three years;

(iv) one member shall be appointed to serve for four years; and

(v) one member shall be appointed to serve for five years.

(3) Subsequent terms for board members shall be staggered, and, for a three-member board, a subsequent term shall be three years, and, for a five-member board, a subsequent term shall be five years.

(c) The members of the board of health shall serve without compensation, but if any member of the board shall be elected to the office of secretary, the member shall be entitled to receive a salary fixed by the board for that office.

(d) Definitions.—As used in this section, the following words and phrases shall have the meanings given to them in this subsection:

"Professional health care provider." An individual who is licensed, certified or registered to practice or operate in the health care field under the laws of this Commonwealth. The term shall include the following:

(1) A physician.

(2) A dentist.

(3) A podiatrist.

(4) A chiropractor.

(5) An optometrist.

(6) A psychologist.

(7) A pharmacist.

(8) A registered or practical nurse.

(9) A physical therapist.

(10) A physician's assistant.

(11) A paramedic.

(12) An administrator of any hospital, nursing or convalescent home or other health care facility.

(13) A veterinarian.

(1602 amended Oct. 29, 2020, P.L.782, No.96)

§ 1603. Organization of Board; Salary of Secretary; Bonds; Fees and Penalties; Power to Administer Oaths.—(a) The members of the board shall each take the oath or affirmation prescribed for township officers.

(b) The board shall annually organize by electing a president from among the members of the board, a secretary, who may or may not be a member of the board, and a health officer, who shall not be a member of the board. The secretary and the health officer shall receive salaries fixed by the board and ratified by the board of commissioners, and shall serve for a period of one year or until a successor is elected and qualified.

(c) The board of commissioners may require the secretary and health officer to furnish a bond to the township, in an amount fixed by ordinance, for the faithful discharge of the secretary's or health officer's duties and shall also take and subscribe to the oath or affirmation required of members of the board.

(d) All fees collected or received by the board, or by any officer in the officer's official capacity, shall be paid over into the township treasury monthly, together with all penalties which shall be recovered for the violation of any regulation of the board. The president and secretary shall have full power to administer oaths or affirmations in any proceeding or investigation regarding the regulations of the board, but shall not be entitled to receive any fee for the administration of oaths and affirmations.

(1603 amended Oct. 29, 2020, P.L.782, No.96)

Compiler's Note: Section 3(3) of Act 76 of 2008 provided that all acts and parts of acts are repealed insofar as they are inconsistent with Act 76. Section 1 of Act 76 amended 53 Pa.C.S. Ch. 11 (relating to general provisions) by adding section 1141 (relating to form of oaths of office), which provides the form of oaths of office for elected or appointed officials of municipalities.

Table of Contents
Part I Ch. 1–3 Ethics, Records, Open Meetings
Part II Ch. 4–10 Taxation
Part III Ch. 11–18 Torts, Contracts & Civil Rules
Part IV Ch. 19–24 Zoning & Planning
Part V Ch. 25–30 Construction and Emergency Codes
Part VI Ch. 31–39 Municipal Codes
Index

Chap. 39 Res. During Mil. Service
Chap. 38 Intergov. Coop.
Chap. 37 3rd Class City Code
Chap. 36 Bor. Code
Chap. 35 2nd Class Twp. Code
Chap. 34 1st Class Twp. Code
Chap. 33 Home Rule Chart. Opt. Plans Law
Chap. 32 Water Serv. Act
Chap. 31 Munic. Auth. Act

§ 1604. Duties of Secretary.—The secretary of the board has the following duties:

(1) Maintain, under 53 Pa.C.S. Ch. 13 Subch. F (relating to records), the minutes of the proceedings of the board and keep accurate accounts of the expenditures of the board.

(2) Transmit all bills to the board of commissioners for payment in the same manner as other bills of the township are paid.

(3) Draw requisitions for the payment of money on account of the board of health and present the requisitions to the president of the board for the president's approval.

(4) Render statements of the expenditures to the board at each stated meeting or as frequently as the board requires.

(5) Prepare, under the direction of the board, the annual report to the board of commissioners and the estimate of appropriation needed for the ensuing year.

(6) Report to the State Department of Health at statutory or regulatory required intervals the cases of communicable disease reported to the board of health on the form provided by the State Department of Health and make an annual report to the State Department of Health.

(7) Perform other duties as may be required by the board of health.

(1604 amended Oct. 29, 2020, P.L.782, No.96)

§ 1605. Powers and Duties of Health Officer.—(a) A health officer may issue a citation for the violation of a health ordinance or related law.

(b) A health officer has the following duties:

(1) Administer and enforce the health ordinances of the township and related laws.

(2) Perform the duties as are vested in local health officers by statute or regulation.

(3) Make sanitary inspections.

(4) Execute the orders of the board of health.

(5) Attend all regular and special meetings of the board of health.

(1605 amended Oct. 29, 2020, P.L.782, No.96)

§ 1606. Powers and Duties of Board of Health.—(a) A board of health has the following powers:

(1) Recommend to the board of commissioners rules and regulations necessary for the preservation of the public health and for carrying into effect the functions of the board.

(2) Appoint a health officer.

(3) Abate and remove nuisances the board of health deems detrimental to the public health.

(4) Mark infected premises.

(b) A board of health has the duty to enforce all of the following related to the promotion of public health and prevention of the introduction and spread of infectious or contagious disease:

(1) A statute.

(2) A regulation of the State Department of Health.

(3) An ordinance of the township.

(1606 amended Oct. 29, 2020, P.L.782, No.96)

§ 1607. Entry of Premises.—(a) A member of the board of health, a health officer, an employee of a board or a health officer or an agent of a board or a health officer may, upon order of the board or upon order of a health officer if there is no board, enter a premises in the township where an infectious or contagious disease or a nuisance detrimental to the public health is suspected and examine and abate the disease or nuisance.

(b) If entry to the premises under subsection (a) is prevented, the board of health or health officer may obtain an administrative search warrant from a magisterial district judge with jurisdiction over the premises upon a showing of any of the following:

(1) Reasonable standards and an administrative plan for conducting inspections.

(2) The condition of the premises or general area and the passage of time since the last inspection.

(3) Probable cause of a violation of a law specified in section 1606(b).

(1607 amended Oct. 29, 2020, P.L.782, No.96)

§ 1608. Abatement of Nuisances.—(a) If the board of health, or health officer if there is no board, finds a condition or premises to be a nuisance to the health of the residents of the township, it shall issue a written order of abatement directed to the owner, agent of the owner or the occupant of the premises. The order, which shall be a public record, shall state that the conditions specified in the order constitute a nuisance and order an abatement of the nuisance within a specified reasonable time.

(b) Upon noncompliance of the order under subsection (a), the board shall issue a written order to the health officer directing removal or abatement of the nuisance. An order shall be executed by the health officer or an agent of the health officer. The expense of the execution of the order shall be recoverable as a nuisance claim from the owner of the premises with a ten percent penalty.

(c) In lieu of or in addition to the procedure under subsections (a) and (b), the board of commissioners may seek relief from a nuisance or threatened nuisance by an action at law or in equity. The board of commissioners may seek guidance of the board or the health officer in determining the nature of the relief requested.

(1608 amended Oct. 29, 2020, P.L.782, No.96)

§ 1609. Expenditures.—(a) The board of health or the health officer shall submit to the board of commissioners, before commencement of the township's fiscal year, an estimate of the probable expenditures of the board of health or the health officer during the ensuing fiscal year.

(b) The board of commissioners shall make appropriations based on the estimate as deemed necessary.

(c) The board of health or the health officer shall, each January, submit a report to the board of commissioners on the appropriation and expenditures for the preceding fiscal year and information on subjects relative to the sanitary conditions or requirements of the township.

(1609 amended Oct. 29, 2020, P.L.782, No.96)

§ 1610. Cooperation in Health Work.—A township may cooperate with any political subdivision and with the State Department of Health in the administration and enforcement of health laws.

(1610 amended Oct. 29, 2020, P.L.782, No.96)

§ 1611. Powers of State Department of Health.—(a) Nothing in this act may be construed to limit the powers and duties of the State Department of Health, including the powers and duties under Article XXI of the act of April 9, 1929 (P.L.177, No.175), known as "The Administrative Code of 1929."

(b) (1) The expenses of the State Department of Health for which the township is liable shall be paid by the township where the expenses have been incurred.

(2) If expenses under paragraph (1) are unpaid for a period of more than three months after a statement of the expenses has been rendered to the township and demand for payment is made, the Secretary of Health shall, with the approval of the Governor, institute an action against the township for the collection of the expenses. The reasonableness of the expenditures made by the secretary shall be submitted to the jury for its determination.

(3) Upon payment, the State Department of Health shall return the money to the State Treasurer, who shall credit the amount to the appropriation made to the State Department of Health.

(1611 amended Oct. 29, 2020, P.L.782, No.96)

§ 1612. Expenses Incurred by Board or Secretary of Health.—(1612 repealed Oct. 29, 2020, P.L.782, No.96)

§ 1613. Suits by State Secretary of Health to Recover Expenses.—(1613 repealed Oct. 29, 2020, P.L.782, No.96)

§ 1614. Payment of Expenses Recovered Into State Treasury.—(1614 repealed Oct. 29, 2020, P.L.782, No.96)

(b) Vacation of Streets Declared Nuisances by Board of Health

(Subdiv. repealed Oct. 29, 2020, P.L.782, No.96)

§ 1620. Petitions to Vacate Nuisances.—(1620 repealed Oct. 29, 2020, P.L.782, No.96)

§ 1621. Jury of View.—(1621 repealed Oct. 29, 2020, P.L.782, No.96)

§ 1622. Hearings and Report.—(1622 repealed Oct. 29, 2020, P.L.782, No.96)

§ 1623. Notice of Filing Report.—(1623 repealed Oct. 29, 2020, P.L.782, No.96)

§ 1624. Exceptions to Report.—(1624 repealed Oct. 29, 2020, P.L.782, No.96)

§ 1625. Appeals from Report.—(1625 repealed Oct. 29, 2020, P.L.782, No.96)

§ 1626. Confirmation of Report.—(1626 repealed Oct. 29, 2020, P.L.782, No.96)

§ 1627. When Vacation Proceedings not to Be Had.—(1627 repealed Oct. 29, 2020, P.L.782, No.96)

ARTICLE XVII
FINANCE AND TAXATION

53 P.S. §§ 56701–56721

§ 1701. Fiscal Year; Annual Budget; Regulation of Appropriations.—(a) The fiscal year in townships of the first class shall begin on January 1 and end on December 31.

(b) The board of commissioners shall annually prepare a proposed budget for all funds for the ensuing fiscal year. The proposed budget shall reflect as nearly as possible the estimated revenues and expenditures of the township for the year for which the budget is prepared.

(b.1) Notice that the proposed budget is available for inspection and copying shall be published by the township in a newspaper of general circulation in accordance with the provisions of section 110. The proposed budget shall be kept on file with the township secretary and be made available for public inspection and copying by the township secretary for a period of twenty days. The notice shall state the date fixed by the board of commissioners for adoption of the proposed budget and notice shall be published at least twenty days prior to the time fixed by the board of commissioners for adoption of the proposed budget. A township shall not prepare and advertise notice of a proposed budget when it is knowingly inaccurate.

(b.2) After the proposed budget has been available for public inspection for at least twenty days, the board of commissioners shall, after making revisions as appropriate, adopt the final budget not later than December 31.

(b.3) Upon any revision of the proposed budget, if the estimated revenues or expenses in the budget will be increased more than ten percent in the aggregate, or more than twenty-five percent on any individual item, over the proposed budget, it shall be presumed that the tentative budget was inaccurate, and the proposed budget may not be legally adopted with the increases unless the proposed budget is again advertised once, at least ten days before adoption, and an opportunity given to taxpayers to examine the amended proposed budget.

(b.4) The tax levied by the board of commissioners shall be fixed within the limit allowed by law that together with other sources of revenue will meet and cover appropriations. The total appropriation shall not exceed the revenues estimated as available for the fiscal year. If the funds available from taxation and other sources shall be estimated to be in excess of the requirements of the ensuing fiscal year, an appropriation may be made for the payment of township orders or indebtedness of the previous years. A budget adopted in the December prior to the fiscal year to which the budget applies may be amended.

(c) The board of commissioners may at any time by resolution make supplemental appropriations for any lawful purpose from any funds on hand or estimated to be received within the fiscal year and not appropriated to any other purpose, including the proceeds of any borrowing as authorized by law. Supplemental appropriations may be made whether or not an appropriation for that purpose was included in the original budget as adopted.

(d) The board of commissioners may, by resolution, transfer unencumbered money from one township account to another, but no money may be transferred from the fund allocated for the payment of debts or from any fund raised by a special tax levy or assessment for a particular purpose. Transfers may not be made during the first three months of the fiscal year. No funds shall be paid out of the township treasury except upon appropriation made according to law.

(1701 amended Oct. 29, 2020, P.L.782, No.96)

§ 1701.1. Amending Budget; Notice.—(a) During the month of January next, following any municipal election, the board of commissioners may amend the budget and the levy and tax rate to conform with its amended budget. A period of ten days' public inspection at the office of township secretary of the proposed amended budget after notice by the township secretary to that effect is published once in a newspaper of general circulation, as provided in section 110, shall intervene between the proposed amended budget and its adoption. An amended budget must be adopted by the board of commissioners on or before the fifteenth day of February.

(b) No proposed amended budget shall be revised upward in excess of ten percent in the aggregate or in excess of twenty-five percent of the amount of an individual item in the proposed amended budget.

(1701.1 amended Oct. 29, 2020, P.L.782, No.96)

§ 1701a. Uniform Financial Report and Forms.—(a) The uniform forms for the annual financial report required to be made by the township auditors or controller to the Department of Community and Economic Development shall be prepared by a committee consisting of four representatives from the Pennsylvania State Association of Township Commissioners and the Secretary of Community and Economic Development, or the secretary's agent or designee who shall be a person trained in the field of municipal finance.

(b) The representatives of townships shall be appointed by the president of the Pennsylvania State Association of Township Commissioners. The representatives shall be chosen from among the finance officers or other officers of townships who have knowledge of fiscal procedures. As far as possible, the representatives shall be chosen to represent townships in the various population groups within the range of townships of the first class. The president of the organization shall supply to the Department of Community and Economic Development the names and addresses of the representatives immediately upon their appointment.

(c) The representatives shall serve without compensation but shall be reimbursed by the Commonwealth for the necessary expenses incurred in attending meetings of the committee. The committee shall meet at the call of the Secretary of Community and Economic Development, or the secretary's agent or designee, who shall serve as chairperson of the committee.

(d) It shall be the duty of the Secretary of Community and Economic Development, or the secretary's agent or designee, to ensure that the forms required by this act are prepared in cooperation with the committee. In the event that the committee should for any reason fail to cooperate, the Secretary of Community and Economic Development, or the secretary's agent or designee, shall prepare the forms. After the forms are prepared, the Secretary of Community and Economic Development, or the secretary's agent or designee, shall issue the forms and distribute them annually, as needed, to the designated officers of each township.

(1701a amended Oct. 29, 2020, P.L.782, No.96)

§ 1702. Appropriations Not to Be Exceeded; Changes in Appropriations.—The township may not hire employees, purchase materials, execute contracts or issue orders for the payment of any money if it would result in the total expenditure of money for a specific purpose to exceed the amount appropriated for that purpose.

(1702 amended Oct. 29, 2020, P.L.782, No.96)

§ 1703. Certain Contracts Invalid.—(1703 repealed Oct. 29, 2020, P.L.782, No.96)

Compiler's Note: Section 1307 of Act 185 of 1972 provided that section 1703 is repealed insofar as it relates to the authorization, issue and sale of tax anticipation notes. The act of July 12, 1972 (P.L.781, No.185), known as the Local Government Unit Debt Act, was repealed by the act of December 19, 1996 (P.L.1158, No.177). The subject matter is now contained in 53 Pa.C.S. Pt. VII Subpt. B (relating to indebtedness and borrowing).

§ 1704. Power to Create Indebtedness; Sinking Fund; Temporary Indebtedness.—(1704 repealed Oct. 29, 2020, P.L.782, No.96)

§ 1705. Sinking Fund; Regulations and Investments.—(1705 repealed Oct. 29, 2020, P.L.782, No.96)

Compiler's Note: The act of July 12, 1972 (P.L.781, No.185), known as the Local Government Unit Debt Act, was repealed by the act of December 19, 1996 (P.L.1158, No.177). The subject matter is now contained in 53 Pa.C.S. Pt. VII Subpt. B (relating to indebtedness and borrowing).

§ 1705.1. Investment of Township Funds.—(a) The board of commissioners shall have power to provide for the investment of money, in the general township fund or in special funds.

(a.1) The board of commissioners shall have power to invest township sinking funds as authorized by 53 Pa.C.S. Pt. VII Subpt. B (relating to indebtedness and borrowing).

(b) The board of commissioners shall invest township funds consistent with sound business practice.

(c) The board of commissioners shall provide for an investment program subject to restrictions contained in this act and in any other applicable statute and any rules and regulations adopted by the board of commissioners.

(d) Authorized types of investments for township funds, in addition to those authorized under the act of July 25, 1973 (P.L.217, No.53), entitled "An act authorizing cities of the first class and second class to invest all funds received and deposited with the city treasurer in certain commercial paper under certain terms and conditions; and providing for investment of public corporation or municipal authority funds," are:

(i) United States Treasury bills.

(ii) Short-term obligations of the United States Government or its agencies or instrumentalities.

(iii) Deposits in savings accounts or time deposits, other than certificates of deposit, or share accounts of institutions insured by the Federal Deposit Insurance Corporation or the National Credit Union Share Insurance Fund to the extent that the accounts are so insured, and, for any amounts above the insured maximum, provided that approved collateral as provided by law therefore shall be pledged by the depository. Such deposits are differentiated from savings or demand deposits as authorized by the act of July 25, 1973 (P.L.217, No.53).

(iv) Obligations of the United States of America or any of its agencies or instrumentalities backed by the full faith and credit of the United States of America, the Commonwealth of Pennsylvania or any of its agencies or instrumentalities backed by the full faith and credit of the Commonwealth, or of any political subdivision of the Commonwealth of Pennsylvania or any of its agencies or instrumentalities backed by the full faith and credit of the political subdivision.

(v) Shares of an investment company registered under the Investment Company Act of 1940 (54 Stat. 789, 15 U.S.C. § 80a-1 et seq.), whose shares are registered under the Securities Act of 1933 (48 Stat. 74, 15 U.S.C. § 77a et seq.), provided that the only investments of that company are in the authorized investments for township funds listed in (i) through (iv), and both of the following conditions are met:

(A) The investment company is managed in accordance with 17 CFR 270.2a-7 (relating to money market funds).

(B) The investment company is rated in the highest category by a nationally recognized rating agency.

(vi) Certificates of deposit purchased from institutions insured by the Federal Deposit Insurance Corporation or the National Credit Union Share Insurance Fund to the extent that the accounts are so insured, and, for any amounts above the insured maximum, provided that approved collateral as provided by law therefore shall be pledged by the depository. Certificates of deposit purchased from commercial banks shall be limited to an amount equal to twenty percent of a bank's total capital and surplus. Certificates of deposit purchased

from savings and loan associations or savings banks shall be limited to an amount equal to twenty percent of an institution's assets minus liabilities.

(vii) Any investment authorized by 20 Pa.C.S. Ch. 73 (relating to municipalities investments) shall be an authorized investment for any pension or retirement fund.

(e) In making investments of township funds, the board of commissioners shall have authority to:

(i) Permit assets pledged as collateral under subsection (d)(iii), to be pooled in accordance with the act of August 6, 1971 (P.L.281, No.72), entitled "An act standardizing the procedures for pledges of assets to secure deposits of public funds with banking institutions pursuant to other laws; establishing a standard rule for the types, amounts and valuations of assets eligible to be used as collateral for deposits of public funds; permitting assets to be pledged against deposits on a pooled basis; and authorizing the appointment of custodians to act as pledgees of assets."

(ii) Combine money from more than one fund under township control for the purchase of a single investment, if each of the funds combined for the purpose shall be accounted for separately in all respects and that the earnings from the investment are separately and individually computed and recorded and credited to the accounts from which the investment was purchased.

(iii) Join with one or more other political subdivisions and municipal authorities in accordance with 53 Pa.C.S. Ch. 23 Subch. A (relating to intergovernmental cooperation) in the purchase of a single investment, provided that the requirements of subclause (ii) are adhered to.

(1705.1 amended Oct. 29, 2020, P.L.782, No.96)

Compiler's Note: The act of July 12, 1972 (P.L.762, No.180), referred to as the Intergovernmental Cooperation Law, referred to in subsec. (e)(iii), was repealed by the act of December 19, 1996 (P.L.1158, No.177). The subject matter is now contained in 53 Pa.C.S. Ch. 23 Subch. A (relating to intergovernmental cooperation).

§ 1706. Indebtedness and Orders of Previous Years.—No orders or indebtedness of any previous years shall be paid out of the funds of any fiscal year, unless the funds available from taxation and other sources shall be estimated to be in excess of requirements for the current fiscal year. If the available funds are in excess of the current fiscal year requirements, an appropriation may be made for this purpose to the extent of the excess, or unless, after the close of the fiscal year, it shall be ascertained that the funds appropriated and available therefor are in excess of the amount required, in which case the surplus may be applied to the former orders of indebtedness.

(1706 amended Oct. 29, 2020, P.L.782, No.96)

§ 1707. Sale of Securities.—(1707 repealed June 25, 1941, P.L.159, No.87)

§ 1708. Disbursements to Pay Indebtedness.—All disbursements in discharge of township indebtedness duly incurred shall be made by the township treasurer or the treasurer's deputy, by virtue of warrants or orders drawn on the treasurer by the order of the board of commissioners, signed by the president or vice president and attested to by the secretary or assistant secretary of the board. The board shall prescribe, by ordinance, the manner in which bills for township indebtedness shall be approved for payment.

(1708 amended Oct. 29, 2020, P.L.782, No.96)

§ 1709. Tax Levies.—(a) The board of commissioners may levy taxes by resolution for taxes levied at the same rate as or a rate lower than the previous fiscal year, and by ordinance if the tax rate increases from the previous fiscal year, upon all property and upon all occupations within the township made taxable for township purposes and subject to valuation and assessment by the county assessment office, for the following purposes and at the following rates:

(1) An annual tax for general township purposes, not exceeding thirty mills, unless the board of commissioners by majority action shall, upon due cause shown by resolution, petition the court of common pleas for the right to levy additional millage for general revenue purposes. The court, after public notice as it may direct and after hearing, may order a greater rate than thirty mills but not exceeding five additional mills to be levied.

(2) (i) An annual tax not exceeding three mills for the purpose of:

(A) building and maintaining suitable places for the housing of fire apparatus;

(B) purchasing, maintaining and operating fire apparatus;

(C) making of appropriations to fire companies located inside or outside the township;

(D) contracting with adjacent municipalities or volunteer fire companies therein for fire protection;

(E) the training of fire personnel and payments to fire training schools and centers;

(F) the purchase of land upon which to erect a fire house; and

(G) the erection and maintenance of a fire house or fire training school and center.

(ii) The township may appropriate up to one-half, but not to exceed one mill, of the revenue generated from a tax under this clause for the purpose of paying salaries, benefits or other compensation of fire suppression employes of the township or a fire company serving the township. For any calendar year, the board of commissioners may waive the appropriation limitation under this subparagraph by resolution.

(iii) If an annual tax for the purposes specified in this clause is proposed to be set at a level higher than three mills the question shall be submitted to the voters of the township, and the county board of elections shall frame the question in accordance with the election laws of the Commonwealth for submission to the voters of the township.

(3) An annual tax, not exceeding one-tenth of one mill, for the purpose of caring for trees planted under the supervision of the shade tree commission, and for the purpose of publishing notices of meetings to consider the planting, removing, or changing of trees. In lieu of the tax provided for in this clause, the board of commissioners may, by specific appropriation, provide for the maintenance of shade trees by appropriation from the general funds of the township.

(4) An annual tax so long as necessary, for the purpose of procuring a lot and/or erecting a building thereon for a municipal building, and for the payment of indebtedness incurred in connection therewith.

(5) An annual tax sufficient to pay interest and principal on any indebtedness incurred pursuant to 53 Pa.C.S. Pt. VII Subpt. B (relating to indebtedness and borrowing) or any prior or subsequent act governing the incurrence of indebtedness of the township.

(6) An annual tax not exceeding one-half (1/2) mill to provide for pensions, retirement, or the purchase of annuity contracts for township employes. This

Chap. 39 Res. During Mil. Service
Chap. 38 Intergov. Coop.
Chap. 37 3rd Class City Code
Chap. 36 Bor. Code
Chap. 35 2nd Class Twp. Code
Chap. 34 1st Class Twp. Code
Chap. 33 Home Rule Chart. Opt. Plans Law
Chap. 32 Water Serv. Act
Chap. 31 Munic. Auth. Act

tax shall be kept in a separate fund and used only for the purposes provided in this clause.

(7) (i) An annual tax not exceeding one-half mill for the purpose of supporting ambulance, rescue and other emergency services serving the township, except as provided in subsection (c).

(ii) The township may appropriate up to one-half of the revenue generated from a tax under this clause for the purpose of paying salaries, benefits or other compensation of employes of an ambulance, rescue or other emergency service serving the township. For any calendar year, the board of commissioners may waive the appropriation limitation under this subparagraph by resolution.

(8) An annual tax not exceeding five mills to create and maintain a revolving fund to be used in making permanent street, sidewalk, water supply or sewer improvements before the collection of all or part of the cost from property owners as otherwise authorized by this act. A revolving fund may also be used for the deposit of funds raised through the issuance of general obligation bonds of the township for the making of permanent street, sidewalk, water supply or sewer improvements. When all or part of the cost of the construction of any permanent street, sidewalk, water supply or sewer improvement is paid from the revolving fund and is later assessed and collected from property owners as otherwise authorized by this act, the collections shall be applied to the credit of the revolving fund to the extent of the withdrawal from the revolving fund for that purpose.

(9) An annual tax sufficient for the purpose of constructing, maintaining and operating parks, recreation areas, facilities and programs or for paying the township's share of a joint action with one or more political subdivisions, in accordance with section 3013.

(b) This section does not include the levy of any taxes upon particular districts, or parts of any township, for particular purposes, nor special levies otherwise provided for in this act.

(c) The tax for supporting ambulance and rescue squads serving the township shall not exceed the rate specified in subsection (a)(7) except when the question is submitted to the voters of the township in the form of a referendum which will appear on the ballot in accordance with the election laws of the Commonwealth, in which case the rate shall not exceed three mills. The county board of elections shall frame the question to be submitted to the voters of the township in accordance with the election laws of the Commonwealth.

(1709 amended Oct. 29, 2020, P.L.782, No.96)

Compiler's Note: The act of July 12, 1972 (P.L.781, No.185), known as the Local Government Unit Debt Act, referred to in subsec. (a) Five, was repealed by the act of December 19, 1996 (P.L.1158, No.177). The subject matter is now contained in 53 Pa.C.S. Pt. VII Subpt. B (relating to indebtedness and borrowing).

§ 1709.1. Additions and Revisions to Duplicates.—If in any township there is any construction of a building or buildings not otherwise exempt as a dwelling after January first of any year and the building is not included in the tax duplicate of the township, the county assessment office shall, upon the request of the board of commissioners, direct the assessor in the county assessment office to inspect and reassess, subject to the right of appeal and adjustment by statute, all taxable property in the township to which major improvements have been made after January first of any year and to give notice of the reassessments within ten days to the authority responsible for assessments, the township and the property owner. The real property shall be added to the duplicate and shall be taxable for township purposes at the reassessed valuation for that proportionate part of the fiscal year of the township remaining after the property was improved. Any improvement made during the month shall be computed as having been made on the first day of the month. A certified copy of the additions or revisions to the duplicate shall be furnished by the board of township commissioners to the township tax collector, together with the board's warrant for collection of the same, and within ten days the township tax collector shall notify the owner of the property of the taxes due the township.

(1709.1 amended Oct. 29, 2020, P.L.782, No.96)

Compiler's Note: See sections 14 and 15 of Act 188 of 2012 in the appendix to this act for special provisions relating to applicability of law and municipal officers affected by Act 188.

§ 1709.2. Authority to Levy, Assess and Collect Mercantile and Business Privilege Taxes on Gross Receipts.—Notwithstanding section 533(b) of the act of December 13, 1988 (P.L.1121, No.145), known as the "Local Tax Reform Act," a township of the first class or a home rule municipality that previously had been a township of the first class and that has a population exceeding 70,000 which before December 1, 1988, has levied, assessed or collected or provided for the levying, assessment or collection of a mercantile tax on gross receipts or parts of gross receipts may levy, assess and collect or provide for the levying, assessment or collection of mercantile and business privilege taxes on gross receipts or parts of gross receipts. This authority shall apply to the tax year beginning January 1, 1998, and to each tax year thereafter.

(1709.2 added Dec. 19, 1997, P.L.618, No.64)

§ 1710. Tax Rates to Be Expressed in Dollars and Cents.—Whenever the board of commissioners shall, by ordinance or resolution, fix the rate of taxation for any year at a mill rate, the ordinance or resolution shall also include a statement expressing the rate of taxation in dollars and cents on each one hundred dollars of assessed valuation of taxable property.

(1710 amended Oct. 29, 2020, P.L.782, No.96)

§ 1711. Special Levies to Pay Indebtedness.—In addition to the levies provided for in section 1709, when it is shown to the court that the debts due by any township exceed the amount which the board of commissioners may collect in any year by taxation, the court, after ascertaining the amount of indebtedness of the township, may, in an action of mandamus, direct the board of commissioners, by special taxation, to collect an amount sufficient to pay the debts. If the amount of the indebtedness is so large as to render it unadvisable to collect the entire amount in any one year, taking into consideration other necessary taxation, the court may direct the special taxes to be levied and collected during successive years as may be required for payment of the debt.

(1711 amended Oct. 29, 2020, P.L.782, No.96)

§ 1712. Delivery of Duplicates.—The board of commissioners shall within thirty days after adoption of the budget or within thirty days after receipt of the assessment roll from the county, whichever is later, deliver a duplicate of the assessment of township taxes to the township tax collector, together with the board's warrant for collection of the taxes.

(1712 amended Oct. 29, 2020, P.L.782, No.96)

Compiler's Note: See sections 14 and 15 of Act 188 of 2012 in the appendix to this act for special provisions relating to applicability of law and municipal officers affected by Act 188.

ARTICLE XVIII
CONTRACTS

53 P.S. §§ 56801–56811

§ 1801. Power to Make Contracts.—(a) A township may make contracts for lawful purposes and for the purposes of carrying into execution the provisions of this act and the laws of the Commonwealth.

(b) Except as otherwise specifically provided in this act, all contracts and purchases must be made with and from the lowest responsible bidder. For purposes of this article, the lowest responsible bidder need not be the bidder submitting the lowest dollar amount bid. A township may also consider the quality of goods or services supplied, ease of repair, compatibility with other township equipment or services, responsiveness, past performance of the bidder and any other reasonable factors specified in the advertisement for bids.

(c) A township may permit the electronic submission of bids and may receive bids electronically for competitive bid purchases and contracts pursuant to 62 Pa.C.S. Ch. 46 (relating to electronic bidding by local government units).

(1801 amended Oct. 29, 2020, P.L.782, No.96)

§ 1802. Regulation of Contracts.—(a) All contracts or purchases in excess of the base amount of eighteen thousand five hundred dollars, subject to adjustment under subsection (a.2), except those mentioned in this section and except as provided by the act of October 27, 1979 (P.L.241, No.78), entitled "An act authorizing political subdivisions, municipality authorities and transportation authorities to enter into contracts for the purchase of goods and the sale of real and personal property where no bids are received," shall be in writing, and shall be made only after notice by the secretary, published once in one newspaper of general circulation, published or circulating in the county in which the township is situated. The advertisement shall be published not less than ten days prior to the date fixed for the opening of bids and shall also be posted in a conspicuous place within the township. The advertisement for contracts or purchases shall contain the date, time and location for opening of bids and shall state the amount of the performance bond determined under subsection (c). The advertisement shall also contain full plans and specifications, or refer to the places where copies thereof can be obtained. All plans and specifications shall be on file not less than ten days in advance of opening bids. The amount of the contract shall in all cases, whether of straight sale price, conditional sale, lease, lease purchase or otherwise, be the entire amount which the township pays to the successful bidder or the bidder's assigns in order to obtain the services or property, or both, and shall not be construed to mean only the amount that is paid to acquire title or to receive any other particular benefit or benefits of the whole bargain.

(a.1) Written or telephonic price quotations from at least three qualified and responsible contractors shall be requested for all contracts in excess of the base amount of ten thousand dollars, subject to adjustment under subsection (a.2) but less than the amount requiring advertisement and competitive bidding or, in lieu of price quotations, a memorandum shall be kept on file showing that fewer than three qualified contractors exist in the market area within which it is practicable to obtain quotations. A written record of telephonic price quotations shall be made and shall contain at least the date of the quotation, the name of the contractor and the contractor's representative, the construction, reconstruction, repair, maintenance or work that was the subject of the quotation and the price. Written price quotations, written records of telephonic price quotations and memoranda shall be retained for a period of three years. Written price quotations as used throughout this section include electronic mail.

(a.2) Adjustments to the base amounts specified under subsections (a) and (a.1) shall be made as follows:

(1) The Department of Labor and Industry shall determine the percentage change in the Consumer Price Index for All Urban Consumers: All Items (CPI-U) for the United States City Average as published by the United States Department of Labor, Bureau of Labor Statistics, for the twelve-month period ending September 30, 2012, and for each successive twelve-month period.

(2) If the department determines that there is no positive percentage change, then no adjustment to the base amounts shall occur for the relevant time period provided for in this subsection.

(3) (i) If the department determines that there is a positive percentage change in the first year that the determination is made under paragraph (1), the positive percentage change shall be multiplied by each base amount, and the products shall be added to the base amounts, respectively, and the sums shall be preliminary adjusted amounts.

(ii) The preliminary adjusted amounts shall be rounded to the nearest one hundred dollars, to determine the final adjusted base amounts for purposes of subsections (a) and (a.1).

(4) In each successive year in which there is a positive percentage change in the CPI-U for the United States City Average, the positive percentage change shall be multiplied by the most recent preliminary adjusted amounts, and the products shall be added to the preliminary adjusted amount of the prior year to calculate the preliminary adjusted amounts for the current year. The sums shall be rounded to the nearest one hundred dollars to determine the new final adjusted base amounts for purposes of subsections (a) and (a.1).

(5) The determinations and adjustments required under this subsection shall be made in the period between October 1 and November 15 of each year.

(6) The final adjusted base amounts and new final adjusted base amounts obtained under paragraphs (3) and (4) shall become effective January 1 for the calendar year following the year in which the determination required under paragraph (1) is made.

(7) The department shall transmit notice to the Legislative Reference Bureau for publication in the Pennsylvania Bulletin prior to January 1 of each calendar year of the annual percentage change determined under paragraph (1) and the unadjusted or final adjusted base amounts determined under paragraphs (3) and (4) at which competitive bidding is required under subsection (a) and written or telephone price quotations are required under subsection (a.1), respectively, for the calendar year beginning the first day of January after publication of the notice. The notice shall include a written and illustrative explanation of the calculations performed by the department in establishing the unadjusted or final adjusted base amounts under this subsection for the ensuing calendar year.

(8) The annual increase in the preliminary adjusted base amounts obtained under paragraphs (3) and (4) shall not exceed three percent.

(b) (1) (i) If advertisement and bidding are required, the advertisement shall specify the date, time and place bids will be received and the date, time and place for the opening of bids.

(ii) At the board of commissioners' request, the bids advertised for must be accompanied by cash, money order, a certified or cashier's good faith check or other irrevocable letter of credit drawn upon a bank authorized to do business in this Commonwealth or by a bond with corporate surety in the amount as the board of commissioners determine, and, when requested, no bid may be considered unless so accompanied.

(iii) Bids received pursuant to an advertisement shall be opened publicly by the board of commissioners or the board's agent or employees. The amount of each bid and any other relevant information as may be specified by the board, together with the name of each bidder, shall be disclosed and recorded, and the record shall be open to public inspection and copying.

(iv) At a public meeting of the board of commissioners, the board shall either award the contract or reject all bids.

(2) Any contract executed in violation of the provisions of this section shall be void. Nothing in this section shall prevent the making of contracts for governmental services for a period exceeding one year, but any contract shall be executed only for the amounts agreed to be paid for the services to be rendered in succeeding fiscal years.

(c) The successful bidder, when advertising is required, shall be required to furnish bond or irrevocable letter of credit or other security with suitable reasonable requirements guaranteeing the performance of the contract, with sufficient surety, in an amount as determined by the board of commissioners which shall be not less than ten percent nor more than one hundred percent of the amount of the liability under the contract within twenty days after the contract has been awarded, unless the board of commissioners shall prescribe a shorter period of not less than ten days. Upon failure to furnish the security within the prescribed time, the previous award shall be void. Deliveries, accomplishment and guarantees may be required in all cases of expenditures including exceptions herein.

(d) The contracts or purchases made by the board of commissioners which shall not require advertising, bidding or price quotations, as provided in this article, are as follows:

(1) Those for maintenance, repairs or replacements for water, electricity, or other public works of the township, provided they do not constitute new additions, extensions or enlargements of existing facilities and equipment but security may be required by the board of commissioners as in other cases of work done.

(2) Those made for improvements, repairs and maintenance of any kind made or provided by a township through its own employes if the materials used for street improvement or construction in excess of the amount specified or adjusted under subsection (a.1) are subject to the relevant price quotation or advertising requirements contained in this section.

(3) Those where particular types, models or pieces of new equipment, articles, apparatus, appliances, computer software, vehicles or parts thereof are desired by the board of commissioners which are patented or copyrighted products or are needed to ensure compatibility with existing systems, facilities or equipment.

(3.1) Those for used personal property, such as equipment, articles, apparatus, appliances, vehicles or parts thereof being purchased from a public utility, municipal corporation, county, school district, municipal authority, council of government, volunteer fire company, volunteer ambulance service, volunteer rescue squad or Federal or State Government.

(4) Those involving a policy of insurance or a surety bond.

(4.1) Those made for public utility service and electricity, natural gas or telecommunications services.

(4.2) Those made with another political subdivision or a county, or council of governments, consortium, cooperative or other similar entity created under 53 Pa.C.S. Ch. 23 Subch. A (relating to intergovernmental cooperation) or the Federal Government, the Commonwealth, any agency of the Federal Government or the Commonwealth or any municipal authority, including the sale, leasing or loan of any supplies or materials by the Federal Government or the Commonwealth or their agencies. The price may not be in excess of that fixed by the Federal Government or the Commonwealth, or their agencies.

(5) Those involving personal or professional services.

Chap. 39 Res. During Mil. Service
Chap. 38 Intergov. Coop.
Chap. 37 3rd Class City Code
Chap. 36 Bor. Code
Chap. 35 2nd Class Twp. Code
Chap. 34 1st Class Twp. Code
Chap. 33 Home Rule Chart. Opt. Plans Law
Chap. 32 Water Serv. Act
Chap. 31 Munic. Auth. Act

(6) Those made for materials and supplies or equipment rental under emergency conditions under 35 Pa.C.S. Pt. V (relating to emergency management services).

(7) Those involving equipment rental with operators if more than fifty percent of the total labor personnel hours required for the completion of the contract is supplied by the township through its own employees.

(8) Those for the purchase of repair parts or materials for use in existing township equipment or facilities if the item or material to be purchased is the sole item of its kind on the market or is manufactured as a replacement for the original item or equipment being repaired.

(9) Those for emergency maintenance, repairs or replacements for water, electricity or public works of the township, if they do not constitute new additions, extensions or enlargements of existing facilities and equipment, but security may be required by the board of commissioners, as in other cases of work done. The actual emergency and the nature of the procurement shall be stated in a resolution by the board of commissioners and adopted at the next public meeting.

(10) Those for the mitigation of a real or potential emergency involving a clear and present danger to the health, safety and welfare of the residents of the township. For those contracts or purchases made in cases of emergencies, the actual emergency and the nature of the procurement shall be stated in a resolution by the board of commissioners and adopted at the next public meeting.

Nothing in this subsection prohibits the board of commissioners from engaging in advertising, bidding or price quotations if the board of commissioners determines that the advertising, bidding or price quotations are in the public interest.

(e) The board of commissioners shall award contracts subject to the requirements of and may exercise any powers granted by the following acts to the extent applicable:

(1) The act of August 15, 1961 (P.L.987, No.442), known as the "Pennsylvania Prevailing Wage Act."

(2) The act of December 20, 1967 (P.L.869, No.385), known as the "Public Works Contractors' Bond Law of 1967."

(3) The act of January 17, 1968 (P.L.11, No.5), known as "The Minimum Wage Act of 1968."

(4) The act of January 23, 1974 (P.L.9, No.4), referred to as the Public Contract Bid Withdrawal Law.

(5) The act of March 3, 1978 (P.L.6, No.3), known as the "Steel Products Procurement Act."

(6) The act of February 17, 1994 (P.L.73, No.7), known as the "Contractor and Subcontractor Payment Act."

(7) 62 Pa.C.S. Pt. II (relating to general procurement provisions).

(f) No person, consultant, firm or corporation contracting with a township for purposes of rendering personal or professional services to the township shall share with any township officer or employe, and no township officer or employe shall accept, any portion of the compensation or fees paid by the township for the contracted services provided to the township except under the following terms or conditions:

(1) Full disclosure of all relevant information regarding the sharing of the compensation or fees shall be made to the board of commissioners.

(2) The board of commissioners must approve the sharing of any fee or compensation for personal or professional services prior to the performance of the services.

Chap. 39 Res. During Mil. Service
Chap. 38 Intergov. Coop.
Chap. 37 3rd Class City Code
Chap. 36 Bor. Code
Chap. 35 2nd Class Twp. Code
Chap. 34 1st Class Twp. Code
Chap. 33 Home Rule Chart. Opt. Plans Law
Chap. 32 Water Serv. Act
Chap. 31 Munic. Auth. Act

(3) No fee or compensation for personal or professional services may be shared except for work actually performed.

(4) No shared fee or compensation for personal or professional services may be paid at a rate in excess of that commensurate for similar personal or professional services.

(1802 amended Oct. 29, 2020, P.L.782, No.96)

Compiler's Note: Section 3 of Act 85 of 2011, which amended subsecs. (a), (a.1) and (d)(2) and added subsec. (a.2), provided that Act 85 shall apply to contracts and purchases advertised on or after January 1 of the year following the effective date of section 3.

§ 1802.1. Evasion of Advertising Requirements.—(a) (1) No commissioner or commissioners shall evade the provisions of section 1802 as to advertising for bids by purchasing or contracting for services and personal properties piecemeal for the purpose of obtaining prices under eighteen thousand five hundred dollars, subject to adjustment under section 1802(a.2), upon transactions, which transactions should, in the exercise of reasonable discretion and prudence, be conducted as one transaction amounting to more than eighteen thousand five hundred dollars, subject to adjustment under section 1802(a.2).

(2) This subsection is intended to make unlawful the evading of advertising requirements by making a series of purchases or contracts, each for less than the advertising requirement price, or by making several simultaneous purchases or contracts, each below the price, when in either case, the transactions involved should have been made as one transaction for one price.

(3) Any commissioners who vote in violation of this subsection and know that the transaction upon which they so vote is or should be a part of a larger transaction and is being divided in order to evade the requirements as to advertising for bids, shall be jointly and severally subject to surcharge for ten percent of the full amount of the contract or purchase.

(4) If it appears that a commissioner may have voted in violation of this section, but the purchase or contract on which the commissioner voted was not approved by the board of commissioners, this section shall not apply.

(b) Any commissioner who votes to unlawfully evade the provisions of section 1802 and who knows that the transaction upon which the member votes is or should be a part of a larger transaction and is being divided in order to evade the requirements as to advertising for bids commits a misdemeanor of the third degree for each contract entered into as a direct result of that vote. The penalty under this subsection shall be in addition to a surcharge that may be assessed under subsection (a).

(1802.1 amended Oct. 29, 2020, P.L.782, No.96)

Compiler's Note: Section 3 of Act 85 of 2011, which amended section 1802.1, provided that Act 85 shall apply to contracts and purchases advertised on or after January 1 of the year following the effective date of section 3.

§ 1804. Bonds for Protection of Labor and Materials.—Before a contract exceeding ten thousand dollars is awarded to a prime contractor or construction manager for the construction, erection, installation, completion, alteration, repair of or addition to a public work or improvement of any kind, the contractor shall furnish to the township a payment bond for the protection of claimants supplying labor or materials to the prime contractor to whom the contract is awarded, at no less than one hundred percent of the contract amount, conditioned for the prompt payment of the materials furnished or labor supplied or performed in the prosecution of the contract under the act of December 20, 1967 (P.L.869, No.385), known as the "Public Works Contractors' Bond Law of 1967." The bond requirement is in addition to any other bond requirement required by law to be given in connection with the contract.

(1804 amended Oct. 29, 2020, P.L.782, No.96)

Compiler's Note: Section 10 of Act 385 of 1967 provided that section 1803 is repealed insofar as it is inconsistent with Act 385.

§ 1804.1. Purchase Contracts for Petroleum Products; Fire Company, Etc., Participation.—The board of commissioners of each township shall have power to permit, subject to terms and conditions as it may, and as specifically provided, shall, prescribe a paid or volunteer fire company, paid or volunteer rescue company and paid or volunteer ambulance company in the township to participate in purchase contracts for petroleum products entered into by the township. A company desiring to participate in purchase contracts shall file with the township secretary a request to authorize it to participate in contracts for the purchase of petroleum products of the township and agreeing that it will be bound by the terms and conditions as the township may, and as specifically provided, shall, prescribe and that it will be responsible for payment directly to the vendor under each purchase contract. Among the terms and conditions, the township shall prescribe that all prices shall be F.O.B. destination.

(1804.1 amended Oct. 29, 2020, P.L.782, No.96)

§ 1805. Separate Specifications for Branches of Work.—In the preparation of specifications for the erection or alteration of any public building, when the entire cost of the work exceeds the base amount of eighteen thousand five hundred dollars ($18,500), subject to annual adjustment under section 1802(a.2), the architect, engineer, or person preparing the specifications shall prepare separate specifications for the plumbing, heating, ventilating, and electrical work, and the township shall receive separate bids upon each of the branches of work, and award the contract for the same to the lowest responsible bidder for each of the branches.

(1805 amended Oct. 29, 2020, P.L.782, No.96)

Compiler's Note: Section 3 of Act 85 of 2011, which amended section 1805, provided that Act 85 shall apply to contracts and purchases advertised on or after January 1 of the year following the effective date of section 3.

§ 1806. Workers' Compensation Insurance.—(a) A contract executed by a township or an officer of a township, which involves the construction or doing of work involving the employment of labor, shall contain a provision that the contractor shall accept, insofar as the work covered by the contract is concerned, the provisions of the act of June 2, 1915 (P.L.736, No.338), known as the "Workers' Compensation Act," and any supplements or amendments to the act, and that the contractor will insure the contractor's liability under the act and will file with the township with which the contract is made a certificate of exemption from insurance from the Bureau of Workers' Compensation of the Department of Labor and Industry. The certificate of exemption from insurance may be issued on the basis of either individual self-insurance or group self-insurance. Additionally, a contractor shall file with the township with which the contract is made any applications to be excepted by the provisions of the "Workers' Compensation Act" in respect to certain employees on religious grounds if the applications have been accepted by the Department of Labor and Industry.

(b) A contract executed in violation of subsection (a) is void.

(1806 amended Oct. 29, 2020, P.L.782, No.96)

§ 1807. Engineers and Architects Not to Be Interested in Contracts.—(1807 repealed Oct. 29, 2020, P.L.782, No.96)

§ 1808. Minimum Wages under Contracts.—(1808 repealed Oct. 29, 2020, P.L.782, No.96)

§ 1809. Discrimination Between Employes.—(1809 repealed May 15, 1998, P.L.358, No.57)

§ 1810. Publication of Contract Notices.—(1810 repealed July 9, 1976, P.L.877, No.160)

§ 1811. Personal Interest in Contracts and Purchases.—Elected and appointed township officials and township employees are restricted from an interest in township contracts and purchases to the extent provided in 65 Pa.C.S. Ch. 11 (relating to ethics standards and financial disclosure).

(1811 amended Oct. 29, 2020, P.L.782, No.96)

ARTICLE XIX
EMINENT DOMAIN; ASSESSMENT OF DAMAGES AND BENEFITS
53 P.S. §§ 56901–56953

(a) General Provisions Relating to Eminent Domain
(Subdiv. hdg. repealed Oct. 29, 2020, P.L.782, No.96)

§ 1901. Exercise of Eminent Domain.—(a) A township may acquire property by eminent domain, including entering upon, appropriating, taking, using and occupying private lands and property for any of the following public purposes:

(1) The laying out, opening, widening, extending, vacating, grading or changing the grades or lines of streets or highways.

(2) The construction of bridges and the piers and abutments for bridges.

(3) The construction of slopes, embankments and storm water sewers and storm water facilities, the changing of watercourses, and the construction of sanitary sewer mains, drains or treatment works.

(4) The erection and extension of water systems, wharves and docks, public buildings, public works or land for a public works related function, municipal waste processing and disposal facilities, including municipal waste landfills, libraries, and the establishing of parks, playgrounds and recreation places.

(5) For all other purposes authorized by this act.

(b) Eminent domain proceedings shall be subject to and conform with the provisions of 26 Pa.C.S. (relating to eminent domain).

(1901 amended Oct. 29, 2020, P.L.782, No.96)

§ 1902. Restrictions As to Certain Property.—(a) In addition to the restrictions made by other provisions of this act in particular cases or by any other provision of law, no township shall exercise the right of eminent domain against:

(1) land now occupied by any building that was used during the Colonial or Revolutionary period as a place of Assembly by the Council of the Colony of Pennsylvania, the Supreme Executive Council of the Commonwealth of Pennsylvania, or the Congress of the United States;

(2) the land occupied by any fort, redoubt, or blockhouse erected during the Colonial or Revolutionary period or any building used as headquarters by the Commander-in-Chief of the Continental Army; or

(3) the site of any building, fort, redoubt, blockhouse, or headquarters that is preserved for the site's historic associations and not for private profit.

(b) For the purposes of subsection (a), the Colonial and Revolutionary period shall be deemed to have ended on September 3, 1783.

(1902 amended Oct. 29, 2020, P.L.782, No.96)

§ 1902.1. Declaration of Intention.—A township shall declare its intention to acquire, enter upon, take, use and appropriate any private property or land for any of the purposes authorized by this act by ordinance or resolution.

(1902.1 added Oct. 29, 2020, P.L.782, No.96)

§ 1903. Possession of Property upon Tender of Bond.—(1903 repealed Apr. 28, 1978, P.L.202, No.53)

§ 1904. Notice to Quit; Possession; Procedure.—(1904 repealed Apr. 28, 1978, P.L.202, No.53)

§ 1905. Bond of Township Without Surety Sufficient.—(1905 repealed Apr. 28, 1978, P.L.202, No.53)

§ 1906. Value of Land or Property Not to Be Assessed as Benefits; Exceptions.—In the appropriation of land or property for public use, other than for streets, it shall not be lawful to assess any portion of the damage done to or value of the appropriated land or property against the other property adjoining or in the vicinity of the appropriated land or property.

(1906 amended Oct. 29, 2020, P.L.782, No.96)

§ 1907. Right to Damages.—(1907 repealed Apr. 28, 1978, P.L.202, No.53)

§ 1908. Viewers' Report.—(1908 repealed Apr. 28, 1978, P.L.202, No.53)

§ 1909. Plans of Properties Condemned to Be Furnished to Viewers.—(1909 repealed Apr. 28, 1978, P.L.202, No.53)

§ 1910. Condemnation Petition to Specify Liens; Exception.—(1910 repealed Apr. 28, 1978, P.L.202, No.53)

§ 1911. Findings of Facts as to Liens.—(1911 repealed Apr. 28, 1978, P.L.202, No.53)

§ 1912. Reports of Viewers as to Liens; Appeals; Distribution to Lien Creditors; Discharge of Liens.—(1912 repealed Apr. 28, 1978, P.L.202, No.53)

§ 1913. Vesting Title.—(1913 repealed Apr. 28, 1978, P.L.202, No.53)

§ 1914. Competency of Evidence as to Market Value of Land or Property.—(1914 repealed Apr. 28, 1978, P.L.202, No.53)

§ 1915. Proceedings Where Assessments by Viewers Waived.—(1915 repealed Apr. 28, 1978, P.L.202, No.53)

§ 1916. Appeals in Eminent Domain Proceedings; Payment of Money Into Court.—(1916 repealed Apr. 28, 1978, P.L.202, No.53)

§ 1917. Title Acquired.—Except as otherwise provided by law, if land or other real or personal property is acquired by a township in eminent domain proceedings other than for street or highway or easement purposes, or is acquired by gift, purchase or otherwise, the title obtained by the township shall be in fee simple absolute or like absolute ownership unless the parties agree otherwise in writing and the agreement expressly appears in a recorded deed affecting any real property acquired by the township or in the notice of condemnation.

(1917 amended Oct. 29, 2020, P.L.782, No.96)

§ 1918. Land Transferable.—(1918 repealed Apr. 18, 1978, P.L.202, No.53)

(b) Procedure for the Exercise of Eminent Domain and for the Assessment of Damages and Benefits
(Subdiv. repealed Oct. 29, 2020, P.L.782, No.96)

§ 1920. Petition for Viewers; Time of Meeting.—(1920 repealed Apr. 28, 1978, P.L.202, No.53)

§ 1921. When Viewers May Be Appointed.—(1921 repealed Apr. 28, 1978, P.L.202, No.53)

§ 1922. Notice of Meeting of Viewers.—(1922 repealed Apr. 28, 1978, P.L.202, No.53)

§ 1923. Swearing Viewers; Hearings; Schedules of Damages and Benefits.—(1923 repealed Apr. 28, 1978, P.L.202, No.53)

§ 1924. Assessment of Damages and Benefits.—(1924 repealed Oct. 29, 2020, P.L.782, No.96)

§ 1925. Assessment Awards.—(1925 repealed Oct. 29, 2020, P.L.782, No.96)

§ 1926. Separate Reports of Damages and Benefits.—(1926 repealed Apr. 28, 1978, P.L.202, No.53)

§ 1927. Notice When Schedules Will Be Exhibited.—(1927 repealed Apr. 28, 1978, P.L.202, No.53)

§ 1928. Service of Notices.—(1928 repealed Apr. 28, 1978, P.L.202, No.53)

§ 1929. Report of Viewers; Plan of Improvements.—(1929 repealed Apr. 28, 1978, P.L.202, No.53)

§ 1930. Notice of Filing of Report.—(1930 repealed Apr. 28, 1978, P.L.202, No.53)

§ 1931. Townships to Pay Costs of Proceedings.—(1931 repealed Apr. 28, 1978, P.L.202, No.53)

§ 1932. Bond of Township.—(1932 repealed Apr. 28, 1978, P.L.202, No.53)

§ 1933. Condition of Bond; Notice of Filing in Court.—(1933 repealed Apr. 28, 1978, P.L.202, No.53)

§ 1934. Filing Bond; Recovery Thereon.—(1934 repealed Apr. 28, 1978, P.L.202, No.53)

§ 1935. Exceptions to Report of Viewers.—(1935 repealed Apr. 28, 1978, P.L.202, No.53)

§ 1936. Confirmation of Report of Viewers.—(1936 repealed Apr. 28, 1978, P.L.202, No.53)

§ 1937. Effect of Exceptions on Confirmation of Report.—(1937 repealed Apr. 28, 1978, P.L.202, No.53)

§ 1938. Appeals from Confirmations after Exceptions.—(1938 repealed June 3, 1971, P.L.118, No.6 and Apr. 28, 1978, P.L.202, No.53)

§ 1939. Effect of Appeals.—(1939 repealed Apr. 28, 1978, P.L.202, No.53)

§ 1940. Filing Assignments of Error, Et Cetera.—(1940 repealed Apr. 28, 1978, P.L.202, No.53)

§ 1941. Certificate of Judge of the Court Below.—(1941 repealed Apr. 28, 1978, P.L.202, No.53)

§ 1942. Effect of Affirmation of Decree of Court Below.—(1942 repealed Apr. 28, 1978, P.L.202, No.53)

§ 1943. Consolidation of Appeals.—(1943 repealed June 3, 1971, P.L.118, No.6 and Apr. 28, 1978, P.L.202, No.53)

§ 1944. Appellants May Unite in Appeals; Effect Thereof.—(1944 repealed June 3, 1971, P.L.118, No.6 and Apr. 28, 1978, P.L.202, No.53)

§ 1945. Appeals from Reports of Viewers for Jury Trial.—(1945 repealed Apr. 28, 1978, P.L.202, No.53)

§ 1946. Reason for Appeals to Be Stated.—(1946 repealed Apr. 28, 1978, P.L.202, No.53)

§ 1947. Costs.—(1947 repealed Apr. 28, 1978, P.L.202, No.53)

§ 1948. Notices; Appeals from the Court Below.—(1948 repealed Apr. 28, 1978, P.L.202, No.53)

§ 1949. Appeals to the Wrong Court.—(1949 repealed June 3, 1971, P.L.118, No.6 and repealed Apr. 28, 1978, P.L.202, No.53)

§ 1950. Appeals Not to Prevent Filing Liens.—(1950 repealed Apr. 28, 1978, P.L.202, No.53)

§ 1951. Discontinuance of Proceedings.—(1951 repealed Apr. 28, 1978, P.L.202, No.53)

§ 1952. Assessments to Bear Interest.—(1952 repealed Oct. 29, 2020, P.L.782, No.96)

§ 1953. Damages to Bear Interest.—(1953 repealed Apr. 28, 1978, P.L.202, No.53)

ARTICLE XX
STREETS AND HIGHWAYS
53 P.S. §§ 57001–57099.1

(Hdg. amended May 27, 1953, P.L.220, No.30)

(a) Plans of Streets and Highways

(Subdiv. hdg. repealed Oct. 29, 2020, P.L.782, No.96)

§ 2001. (2001 repealed July 31, 1968, P.L.805, No.247)

§ 2002. Definitions.—The following words and phrases when used in this article shall have the meanings given to them in this section unless the context clearly indicates otherwise:

"Improving a street" or "improvement." The term includes work on a street or portion thereof done or proposed to be done in order to open the street if the street has not previously been opened or, if previously opened, to make the street more usable or more suitable for use by the traveling public or safer for use. The term includes, but is not limited to, grading, paving and curbing. The term shall not include maintenance or repaving.

"Laying out." The term includes the plotting of:

(1) An unopened street or portion of the street on a township plan or official map adopted in accordance with the act of July 31, 1968 (P.L.805, No.247), known as the "Pennsylvania Municipalities Planning Code," on a subdivision or land development plan or by the enactment of an ordinance adopted in accordance with this article.

(2) An unopened street in a case where any of the lines of the street are proposed to be revised or in a case where the street was never previously laid out although the street may have been opened and used.

"Opened streets." The term includes the streets within the township used as public passageways.

"Opening a street." The term includes the construction and grading of a street or portion thereof and the act of physically taking possession of an area or laid-out street for the purpose of making the same usable to the traveling public.

"Portion." The term includes a portion either of the width or length of a street. Opening a portion of a street may mean extending or widening a street, and vacating a portion of a street may mean closing or narrowing a street.

"Street." The term includes a street, road, lane, alley, court or public square, either for or intended for public use and shall include the cartway, sidewalk, gutter, curb or the right-of-way area, whether or not the street, or any portion of the street, is owned in fee by others than the township. Streets are of two classes, opened and unopened.

"Unopened streets." The term includes the streets within the township neither used as a public passageway nor accepted or maintained, but plotted in one of the following:

(1) a township plan or official map adopted in accordance with the Pennsylvania Municipalities Planning Code;

(2) an ordinance laying out the street in accordance with this article;

(3) a subdivision or land development plan; or

(4) an individual deed.

(2002 added Oct. 29, 2020, P.L.782, No.96)

§ 2003. Township Street Plan.—(a) A township that has not maintained an accurate plan of township streets adopted in accordance with this article prior to the effective date of this section may only adopt a plan of streets under the act of July 31, 1968 (P.L.805, No.247), known as the "Pennsylvania Municipalities Planning Code."

(b) If a township maintains a plan of streets adopted prior to the effective date of this section, or maintains an official map containing opened and unopened streets, a street laid out in accordance with this article by ordinance or by final approval of a subdivision or land development plan must be deemed an amendment to the plan. Notwithstanding any other provision of law, a deemed amendment as provided in this section and a subsequent placement of the street on a plan may not be subject to public notice or public hearing if the street has been laid out in accordance with the requirements of this article.

(c) The maintenance of a plan of streets or official map shall not be required in order for a township to lay out streets in accordance with sections 2005 and 2007.

(2003 added Oct. 29, 2020, P.L.782, No.96)

§ 2004. Certain Streets Declared Public Streets.—(a) Every street which has been used for public travel and maintained and kept in repair continuously by the township for a period of at least twenty-one years, pursuant to authorization by the board of commissioners, is a public street having a right-of-way of not less than twenty-four feet, even though there is no public record of the laying out or dedication for public use of the street.

(b) In any proceeding pursuant to this section, any relevant oral or documentary evidence of public travel or maintenance and repairs by the township shall, if presented, be considered, including, but not limited to:

(1) Maps or surveys which are either generated by any governmental unit or are created pursuant to any judicial proceeding of the courts of this Commonwealth.

(2) Evidence concerning the distribution of government funds to the township pursuant to the act of June 1, 1956 (1955 P.L.1944, No.655), referred to as the Liquid Fuels Tax Municipal Allocation Law.

(3) Approved subdivision plans, deeds or other documents containing a designation of the street as either a township street or otherwise.

(4) Evidence that the street is an extension from a public street or public cul-de-sac or a throughway between other municipal or State streets or provides the only access to a municipal boundary line.

(5) Court orders, decisions, findings of fact or other matters of judicial record relating to public or private rights in the street.

(c) For purposes of this section:

(1) The frequency of use of a street may be considered relevant in any proceeding pursuant to this section, but, in the absence of additional findings on the purpose of such use, shall not alone be sufficient to establish that the street has been used for public travel.

(2) The condition or sufficiency of the street surface for public travel may be considered relevant in any proceeding pursuant to this section, but, absent additional findings of actual public maintenance and repair, shall not alone be sufficient to establish maintenance and repair by the township.

(d) Nothing in this section shall be construed as affecting the weight or persuasiveness of any evidence presented in accordance with subsection (b) or the relevance of any evidence presented except as otherwise provided in this section.

(e) In any proceeding in which this section is relied upon to allege the existence of a public street, the proponent of the public status of the street shall present evidence first, and the burden shall then shift to the opponent to present evidence to refute the public status of the street.

(2004 added Oct. 29, 2020, P.L.782, No.96)

(b) Laying Out, Opening, Widening, Straightening, Vacating and Relaying Streets, Highways, Et Cetera; Repairs and Detours

(Subdiv. hdg. repealed Oct. 29, 2020, P.L.782, No.96)

§ 2005. Power to Lay Out, Open, Vacate and Alter Streets.—With regard to any street or portion of a street within township limits, a township may, with or without petition of abutting property owners, do any of the following:

(1) Lay out, open, widen, straighten, alter, extend, relocate and improve.

(2) Establish or reestablish the grades.

(3) Keep in order and repair and in safe passable condition.

(4) Vacate and discontinue when deemed expedient for the public good.

(5) With the approval of the Department of Transportation, vacate highways laid out by the Commonwealth within the township limits which have remained unopened for thirty years.

(2005 amended Oct. 29, 2020, P.L.782, No.96)

§ 2006. Prohibition.—No street shall be laid out and opened through any burial ground or cemetery, nor through any grounds occupied by a building used as a place for public worship, or as a public or parochial school or educational or charitable institution or seminary, unless the consent of the owner of the premises is first secured.

(2006 amended Oct. 29, 2020, P.L.782, No.96)

§ 2007. Procedures for Laying Out, Opening, Changing, Improving or Vacating Streets.—(a) Before the enactment of any ordinance for the laying out, opening, widening, straightening, extending, altering, improving, relocating or vacating of any street or highway or portion of any street or highway, the board of commissioners shall give ten days' written notice to the owners of property

Table of Contents
Part I Ch. 1–3 Ethics, Records, Open Meetings
Part II Ch. 4–10 Taxation
Part III Ch. 11–18 Torts, Contracts & Civil Rules
Part IV Ch. 19–24 Zoning & Planning
Part V Ch. 25–30 Construction and Emergency Codes
Part VI Ch. 31–39 Municipal Codes
Index

adjacent to the street or highway or portions of the street or highway affected thereby of the time and place set for a hearing on the proposed matter. Witnesses may be summoned and examined by the board of commissioners and by the parties interested at the hearing.

(b) After the hearing and a consideration of the matter under subsection (a), if the board of commissioners votes in favor of exercising the power so conferred, the board shall make written report, together with a draft or survey of the street or highway, which shall include:

(1) the width of the street or highway;

(2) the improvements along the street or highway; and

(3) the names of the owners of property which the street or highway shall pass through or abut.

(c) The report and draft shall be filed in the recorder of deeds office of the county.

(d) Any resident or property owner affected by the report may, within thirty days after the filing of the report of the board of commissioners, upon entering in the court sufficient surety to indemnify the board of commissioners for all costs incurred in the proceedings, file exceptions to the report, together with a petition for a review.

(e) The following shall apply after the expiration of the term allowed for filing exceptions or upon an order of the court upon disposition of any exceptions:

(1) If the board of commissioners desires to lay out, open, widen, straighten, alter, extend, improve, relocate or vacate the street or highway or portion thereof, the board of commissioners shall enact an ordinance for the same.

(2) The court of common pleas, on application by petition by the board of commissioners or any person interested, shall appoint three viewers from the county board of viewers to assess the damages and benefits occasioned by the proceeding unless the damages and benefits are otherwise agreed upon.

(2007 amended Oct. 29, 2020, P.L.782, No.96)

§ 2008. Draft; Report.—(2008 repealed Oct. 29, 2020, P.L.782, No.96)

§ 2009. Exceptions to Report.—(2009 repealed Oct. 29, 2020, P.L.782, No.96)

§ 2010. Appointment of Viewers.—(2010 repealed Oct. 29, 2020, P.L.782, No.96)

§ 2011. Notices to Be Posted Along Improvement.—(2011 repealed Oct. 29, 2020, P.L.782, No.96)

§ 2011.1. Petition for Opening, Etc.—(a) A petition may be presented to the board of commissioners for the opening, widening, straightening, extending, altering, improving, relocating, vacating or establishing or reestablishing the grade of any street.

(b) A petition made pursuant to this section must be:

(1) Signed by a majority, in number and interest, of the owners of property abutting on the line of the proposed improvement or vacation as fixed at the time of presentation of the petition.

(2) Verified by affidavit of one or more of the petitioners.

(3) Accompanied by payment of reasonable and necessary fees established by resolution in a form acceptable to the township. Fees may include those reasonable and necessary costs and expenses anticipated to be incurred by the township in responding to the petition, such as advertising, engineering, hearing, legal and similar costs.

(c) The majority in interest of owners of undivided interests in any piece of property shall be deemed as one person for the purposes of the petition.

(2011.1 added Oct. 29, 2020, P.L.782, No.96)

§ 2011.2. Notice of Petition.—(a) After a petition has been presented in accordance with section 2011.1 and the board of commissioners has determined the adequacy of the petition, but before final enactment of any ordinance enacted pursuant to the petition, notice shall be published once in a newspaper of general circulation pursuant to section 110, and handbills shall be posted in conspicuous places along the line of the proposed improvement.

(b) The notice and handbills shall include the following:

(1) Statement that the petition for the improvement was signed by a majority, in interest and number, of the owners of property abutting the line of the proposed improvement.

(2) Any person interested may provide comments at a public hearing to be held at a date, time and place as stated in the published notice and handbills.

(c) If, after a hearing, the board of commissioners determines to proceed with the consideration of an ordinance pursuant to the petition, it shall publish notice of the proposed ordinance and incorporate reference to any maps or drawing in accordance with Article XXXIII-A.

(2011.2 added Oct. 29, 2020, P.L.782, No.96)

§ 2012. Width of Public Streets.—(a) The width of a street in townships shall not be less than twenty-four feet nor more than one hundred and twenty feet. The minimum required width shall be in addition to any width required for necessary slopes in cuts or fills.

(b) The width of an alley shall be subject to the discretion of the board of commissioners.

(2012 amended Oct. 29, 2020, P.L.782, No.96)

§ 2013. Opening and Repairing Streets.—(a) Laid out public streets in townships shall, as soon as practicable, be effectually opened and constantly kept in repair. All streets shall, at all seasons, be kept reasonably clear of all impediments to easy and convenient traveling, at the expense of the township.

(b) When proceedings have been initiated under this act for the opening and laying out of any public street in any township, the street shall be physically opened for use by the public within a period of five years after the completion of the proceedings. If the street is not opened or if no proceedings have been commenced to compel the opening in five years, then the proceedings are void and the land proposed to be taken shall revert to the owners of the land free of any easement or right of the public to use the land.

(2013 amended Oct. 29, 2020, P.L.782, No.96)

§ 2014. Street Closings and Detours.—(a) The following shall apply to the closing of a street to vehicular traffic:

(1) No street shall be closed to vehicular traffic, except upon order of the board of commissioners or, in cases of emergency, when immediate action is necessary to protect public safety, by order of the police, an authorized fire official or other authorized public employee.

(2) A street may not remain closed for a longer period than is necessary for the purpose for which the order to close was issued.

(3) Except in cases of emergency, when immediate action is necessary to protect public safety, no street shall be closed to vehicular traffic when the street has been designated as a detour by the Department of Transportation, unless the Secretary of Transportation has provided written consent or the

Chap. 39 Res. During Mil. Service
Chap. 38 Intergov. Coop.
Chap. 37 3rd Class City Code
Chap. 36 Bor. Code
Chap. 35 2nd Class Twp. Code
Chap. 34 1st Class Twp. Code
Chap. 33 Home Rule Chart. Opt. Plans Law
Chap. 32 Water Serv. Act
Chap. 31 Munic. Auth. Act

board of commissioners has, by resolution duly recorded on its minutes, declared the closing necessary for the safety of the public.

(4) When any street which forms a part or section of a State highway or has been designated as a detour by the Department of Transportation is closed to vehicular traffic, the township shall at once notify the Department of Transportation of the creation of a detour under this section. The Department of Transportation shall be notified immediately after the detour is removed.

(5) When any street is to be closed, it shall be the duty of the board of commissioners or official authorizing the closing to immediately designate or lay out a detour.

(6) While the detour is in use, legible signs shall be erected and maintained at reasonable intervals indicating the proper direction and the detour shall be maintained in a safe and passable condition, except in the case of State or county highways.

(7) When the street that had been closed is opened for traffic, all detour signs shall be removed.

(8) Except in the case of State or county highways, the board of commissioners shall, as soon as possible, repair the street designated as a detour and place the street in a condition at least equal to its condition when designated as a detour.

(b) The board of commissioners may enter into agreement with the owners of private lands, covering the acquisition of right of way privileges for a detour over private property for the period when the street shall be closed to traffic. If the parties cannot reach an agreement, the township may proceed with the construction of the detour with the owner of the property taken for the detour entitled to seek damages, if any, in the same manner as damages are now ascertained for the opening of streets in the township.

(c) In the exercise of the rights conferred by this section relating to detours, the board of commissioners is empowered to pay for the necessary maintenance, subsequent repair, and land rental out of the money available for the construction and maintenance of township streets.

(d) Any person who willfully removes, defaces, destroys or disregards any barricade, light, danger sign, detour sign, or warning of any other type legally erected or placed or who drives on, over or across any street which has been closed by proper authority commits a summary offense punishable upon conviction in accordance with section 3321-A.

(e) A person who has no outlet due to the closing of a street may drive on, over or across the street, subject to reasonable conditions as may be prescribed by the township without being subject to the penalties imposed by this section.

(f) In addition to the penalties provided in subsection (d), the township or the township's agents or contractors may, in an action at law, recover damages, including costs of labor, materials and prosecution from any person who damages a street when it is closed to vehicular traffic.

(g) All money collected under the provisions of this section shall be paid over to the township treasurer.

(h) The board of commissioners may temporarily close any street when it determines that excessive or unusual conditions have rendered the street unfit or unsafe for travel, and immediate repair, because of the time of year or other conditions, is impracticable. The street or portion of the street closed shall be properly marked at the street's extremities and a means of passage for the customary users of the street shall, whenever possible, be provided.

(2014 amended Oct. 29, 2020, P.L.782, No.96)

Compiler's Note: Section 28 of Act 207 of 2004 provided that any and all references in any other law to a "district justice" or "justice of the peace" shall be deemed to be references to a magisterial district judge.

§ 2015. Laying out Roads under the General Road Law.—(2015 repealed Oct. 29, 2020, P.L.782, No.96)

§ 2016. Street Connecting with Street of Another Municipal Corporation.—(a) All streets partly within a township of the first class shall be laid out, opened, widened, straightened, altered, extended, vacated, improved, relocated or have grades established or reestablished pursuant to this article to the extent the street or portion of the street is within the township.

(b) (1) The procedures applicable to any portion of the street outside the township shall be pursuant to the code applicable to the classification of the other municipal corporation with which the street is shared.

(2) Notwithstanding paragraph (1), no action may be taken under this article that would result in the change of location or grade or the vacation of a street or portion of the street that connects with a street of another municipal corporation without approval of the court of common pleas of the county in which the other municipal corporation is located, unless the municipal corporation first files with the township secretary the municipal corporation's approval of the proposed action.

(2016 added Oct. 29, 2020, P.L.782, No.96)

(c) Dedicated Streets and Drainage Facilities
(Subdiv. hdg. repealed Oct. 29, 2020, P.L.782, No.96)

§ 2019. Scope of Subdivison.—(2019 repealed Oct. 29, 2020, P.L.782, No.96)

§ 2020. Acceptance of Land for Street Purposes.—(a) The board of commissioners may, by ordinance or resolution, accept in the name of the township any land dedicated by deed to the township to be used in any manner for street purposes.

(b) No person shall construct, open, or dedicate any street or any drainage facilities in connection with the street for public use or travel in any township without first submitting plans to the board of commissioners for their approval. The plans shall be prepared in accordance with rules and regulations as may be prescribed by the commissioners and shall show the profiles of the streets, the course, structure, and capacity of any drainage facilities and the method of drainage of the adjacent or contiguous territory and any other details required under the rules and regulations adopted by the board of commissioners.

(c) The act of July 31, 1968 (P.L.805, No.247), known as the Pennsylvania Municipalities Planning Code, shall apply to the construction, security requirements and dedication of streets and connected drainage facilities if the streets proposed to be constructed are part of a plan required by an ordinance adopted under the Pennsylvania Municipalities Planning Code.

(d) (1) Before acting upon plans not subject to review under subsection (c), the board of commissioners may, in the board's discretion, arrange for a public hearing, after giving notice as they may deem desirable in each case. The board of commissioners may alter the plans and specify changes or modifications of any kind and may make its approval of the plans subject to alterations, changes or modifications. Plans, when so approved, shall be signed on behalf of the township by an officer as the commissioners may designate, and an approved copy shall be filed in the township engineer's office or other proper office, where the same shall be available to public inspection.

Table of Contents
Part I Ch. 1–3 Ethics, Records, Open Meetings
Part II Ch. 4–10 Taxation
Part III Ch. 11–18 Torts, Contracts & Civil Rules
Part IV Ch. 19–24 Zoning & Planning
Part V Ch. 25–30 Construction and Emergency Codes
Part VI Ch. 31–39 Municipal Codes
Index

(2) No street or any drainage facilities in connection with the street shall be opened, constructed, or dedicated for public use or travel except in compliance with plans approved by the board of commissioners and until the approved plan is recorded as required in this article.

(e) If the board of commissioners refuses to approve any plans submitted to the board under this section, any person aggrieved by the action of the board of commissioners may within thirty days after the action appeal from the action by petition to the court of common pleas and the court shall hear the matter de novo. The following shall apply:

(1) After a hearing, the court may enter a decree affirming, reversing or modifying the action of the board of commissioners as may appear just.

(2) The court shall designate the manner in which notices of the hearing of any appeal shall be given to all parties interested.

(3) The decision of the court shall be final.

(4) A plan approved by the action of the board of commissioners or by the court on appeal shall be recorded by the person applying for approval in the office of the recorder of deeds of the county.

(f) If any street or any drainage facilities in connection with a street is opened, constructed or dedicated for public use or travel, except in compliance with plans approved and recorded, neither the board of commissioners nor any public authority shall be required to place, construct or operate any sewer, drain, water pipe or other facilities or do any work of any kind in or upon the street. Neither the board of commissioners nor any other public authority shall have any responsibility of any kind with respect to the street or drainage facilities even if the street or drainage facilities are in use by the public, unless the street or drainage facilities is accepted by ordinance or by deed of dedication. Nothing in this act shall prevent the laying of trunk sewers, drains or water or gas mains if required by engineering necessity for the accommodation of other territory.

(g) If a person opens a street or drainage facility in connection with the street without submitting and obtaining approval of plans as provided in this section, and if the board of commissioners shall have no information that the street or drainage facility is intended for public use or travel, the board of commissioners may, in their discretion, file with the recorder of deeds of the county a certificate containing a description of the land served by the street or drainage facility in connection with the street. The board of commissioners shall include a statement that, as the board of commissioners have not approved the plans, neither the board of commissioners nor any other public authority shall have any responsibility to furnish any facilities or services with respect to the land or have any responsibility of any kind with respect to the street or drainage facility. The owner of the land shall be designated and indexed as grantor in the records of the office of the recorder of deeds, and the township shall be designated and indexed as grantee. It shall not be necessary for the certificate to be executed by any party other than the board of commissioners filing the same.

(h) The following shall apply:

(1) Nothing in this section shall be deemed to prevent the board of commissioners from enforcing the provisions of this act in which any street or any drainage facility in connection with the street is intended for public use or travel.

Chap. 39 Res. During Mil. Service
Chap. 38 Intergov. Coop.
Chap. 37 3rd Class City Code
Chap. 36 Bor. Code
Chap. 35 2nd Class Twp. Code
Chap. 34 1st Class Twp. Code
Chap. 33 Home Rule Chart. Opt. Plans Law
Chap. 32 Water Serv. Act
Chap. 31 Munic. Auth. Act

(2) If a township fails to file a certificate under subsection (g), nothing in this section shall be interpreted to create a deemed approval of the plans nor create any responsibility of the township with respect to the land, street or drainage facility.

(i) Any person who constructs, opens or dedicates any street or drainage facilities for public use or travel in any township without having first complied with the provisions of this section and of any ordinances or resolutions of the board of commissioners commits a misdemeanor of the third degree and is subject to suit for all costs and damages incurred by the township or property owners in the course of correcting substantive violations of State or municipal law or regulations resulting from or arising out of the unlawfully constructed street or facility. All money recovered shall be paid to the township treasurer.

(j) No approval of plans by the board of commissioners shall obligate or require the township to construct, reconstruct, maintain, repair or grade the streets.

(2020 amended Oct. 29, 2020, P.L.782, No.96)

§ 2021. Appeals where Commissioners Refuse Approval.—(2021 repealed Oct. 29, 2020, P.L.782, No.96)

§ 2022. No Responsibility on Township Where Plans Not Approved.—(2022 repealed Oct. 29, 2020, P.L.782, No.96)

§ 2023. Entry of Lands.—(2023 repealed Oct. 29, 2020, P.L.782, No.96)

§ 2024. Penalty.—(2024 repealed Oct. 29, 2020, P.L.782, No.96)

§ 2025. Powers of State and Counties Preserved.—(2025 repealed Oct. 29, 2020, P.L.782, No.96)

§ 2025.1. Powers of State and Counties Preserved.—Nothing contained in this article shall be held to restrict or limit the Department of Transportation or any county in the exercise of any of its duties, powers and functions under the provisions of any State law.

(2025.1 added Oct. 29, 2020, P.L.782, No.96)

§ 2026. Exclusive Nature of Provisions.—No street may be dedicated, accepted, acquired, laid out, opened or vacated by a township except under this article.

(2026 added Oct. 29, 2020, P.L.782, No.96)

§ 2027. Failure of Board of Commissioners to Hold Hearing.—If, after the filing of a petition under this article, the board of commissioners fails to hold a required hearing, an aggrieved party may file a mandamus action in the court of common pleas requesting that a hearing be held.

(2027 added Oct. 29, 2020, P.L.782, No.96)

§ 2028. Entry on Land to Maintain Marks and Monuments.—The board of commissioners and the board of commissioners' agents and employees may enter upon any land or property to maintain marks and monuments as the board of commissioners deems necessary in carrying out the board of commissioners' powers and duties under this article.

(2028 added Oct. 29, 2020, P.L.782, No.96)

§ 2029. Bike Paths.—The board of commissioners may provide for the construction and maintenance of bike paths for the protection or convenience of the traveling public.

(2029 added Oct. 29, 2020, P.L.782, No.96)

Table of Contents
Part I Ch. 1–3 Ethics, Records, Open Meetings
Part II Ch. 4–10 Taxation
Part III Ch. 11–18 Torts, Contracts & Civil Rules
Part IV Ch. 19–24 Zoning & Planning
Part V Ch. 25–30 Construction and Emergency Codes
Part VI Ch. 31–39 Municipal Codes
Index

(d) Relocation, Alteration, and Vacation of Streets in or near State Parks

(Subdiv. hdg. repealed Oct. 29, 2020, P.L.782, No.96)

§ 2030. Streets in or near Public Parks.—(a) The board of commissioners may contract with the Commonwealth, a county or a municipal corporation owning and operating parks inside the township to establish, relocate, alter or vacate public streets inside or contiguous to those parks. The board of commissioners shall take no action with respect to the public streets without the written consent and agreement of the Commonwealth, county or municipal corporation owning and operating the parks. Any street when altered or relocated under this section shall be maintained and repaired the same as other township streets.

(b) The agreement shall be adopted by ordinance and within thirty days the street shall be a public street of the township.

(c) The owner of any land through which any public street may be located or relocated may apply by petition to the court of common pleas, setting forth the injury that has been sustained by reason of the relocation of the public street. The proceedings relative to the assessment and payment of damages of the landowner shall be pursuant to 26 Pa.C.S. (relating to eminent domain).

(2030 amended Oct. 29, 2020, P.L.782, No.96)

§ 2031. Agreement to Be Filed in Court; Effect of Filing.—(2031 repealed Oct. 29, 2020, P.L.782, No.96)

§ 2032. Altered and Relocated Streets Declared Township Streets.—(2032 repealed Oct. 29, 2020, P.L.782, No.96)

§ 2033. Assessment of Damages.—(2033 repealed Oct. 29, 2020, P.L.782, No.96)

(e) Elimination of Curves

(Subdiv. repealed Oct. 29, 2020, P.L.782, No.96)

§ 2035. (2035 repealed Oct. 29, 2020, P.L.782, No.96)

(f) Acquisition of Unobstructed Views at Curves and Intersections

(Subdiv. hdg. repealed Oct. 29, 2020, P.L.782, No.96)

§ 2040. Elimination of Curves and Acquisition of Views.—(a) Any township may, singly or jointly with another municipality, acquire, by purchase or by the right of eminent domain, lands or easements along or adjacent to any township street that may be necessary to eliminate dangerous curves, widen streets or provide a free and unobstructed view down and across lands located at or near the intersection of any two streets or highways, or a street or highway and a railroad or railway or at a curve in any street or highway, for the better protection and safety to the traveling public.

(b) After condemnation, the township may abate or remove, or cause to be abated or removed, any obstruction to the view over and across the lands.

(c) The proceedings for the condemnation of lands and for the assessment of damages for property, or portions of property, taken, injured or destroyed, agreed to be paid by the township if the taking is jointly with another municipality, shall be taken in the manner provided under the law governing eminent domain.

(d) Upon the purchase or condemnation of lands or easements for a free and unobstructed view, the owner of the lands may make every use of the lands as will not interfere with a free and unobstructed view at the dangerous crossing or curve.

(2040 amended Oct. 29, 2020, P.L.782, No.96)

(g) Changing or Altering Streets by Agreement with Property Owners

(Subdiv. hdg. repealed Oct. 29, 2020, P.L.782, No.96)

§ 2045. Improving or Vacating Streets by Agreement.— (a) When the board of commissioners constructs, changes, widens, relocates, vacates or alters any portion of any public street under their supervision, and can agree with the property owners affected by the change as to damages, the board of commissioners may, upon payment of damages agreed upon, construct, change, widen, relocate, vacate or alter the portion of the street as contemplated in the agreement without the formality of a view.

(b) A copy of the agreement setting forth the facts regarding the construction, change, widening, relocation, vacation or alteration, accompanied by a map or draft of the street agreed to be constructed, changed, widened, relocated, vacated or altered, shall be presented and recorded in the office of the recorder of deeds or similar office in home rule counties after which the new location is the public street or the old location is vacated.

(c) Nothing contained in this section shall be construed to prohibit a township from paying for curbs, gutters, sidewalks, retaining walls and incidental work necessitated by such construction, change, alteration, relocation, vacation or widening in cases where the necessary land is dedicated to the township for public use.

(2045 amended Oct. 29, 2020, P.L.782, No.96)

(h) Grading, Draining, Curbing, Paving, Macadamizing Streets or Highways on Petition, and Assessment of Benefits by Viewers

(Subdiv. hdg. repealed Oct. 29, 2020, P.L.782, No.96)

§ 2050. Proceedings With or Without Petition.—Townships may improve streets, portions of streets or a particular width or additional widths of streets, with or without the assistance or contribution of the Federal Government, the Commonwealth, the county or a corporation occupying the thoroughfare, and may assess and collect the following from the owners of real estate abutting on the improvement in accordance with Article XXV-A:

(1) The whole cost of improvement.

(2) The whole cost of improvement not aided or contributed to by the Federal Government, the Commonwealth, the county or a corporation.

(3) Any part of the cost.

(2050 amended Oct. 29, 2020, P.L.782, No.96)

§ 2051. Grading Restrictions.—(2051 repealed Oct. 29, 2020, P.L.782, No.96)

§ 2052. Notice.—(2052 repealed Oct. 29, 2020, P.L.782, No.96)

§ 2053. Contents of Notice.—(2053 repealed Oct. 29, 2020, P.L.782, No.96)

§ 2054. Appeals from Ordinance.—(2054 repealed Oct. 29, 2020, P.L.782, No.96)

§ 2055. Assessment of Damages and Benefits by Viewers.—(2055 repealed Oct. 29, 2020, P.L.782, No.96)

Chap. 39 Res. During Mil. Service
Chap. 38 Intergov. Coop.
Chap. 37 3rd Class City Code
Chap. 36 Bor. Code
Chap. 35 2nd Class Twp. Code
Chap. 34 1st Class Twp. Code
Chap. 33 Home Rule Chart. Opt. Plans Law
Chap. 32 Water Serv. Act
Chap. 31 Munic. Auth. Act

§ 2056. Assessments to Bear Interest; Collection.—(2056 repealed Oct. 29, 2020, P.L.782, No.96)

(i) Grading, Draining, Curbing, Paving or Macadamizing Streets or Highways, and Collection of Cost by Foot Front Rule

(Subdiv. repealed Oct. 29, 2020, P.L.782, No.96)

§ 2060. Proceedings With or Without Petition.—(2060 repealed Oct. 29, 2020, P.L.782, No.96)

§ 2061. Grading Restrictions.—(2061 repealed Oct. 29, 2020, P.L.782, No.96)

§ 2062. Notice of Assessments.—(2062 repealed Oct. 29, 2020, P.L.782, No.96)

§ 2063. Collection of Assessments.—(2063 repealed Oct. 29, 2020, P.L.782, No.96)

(j) Road Material, Ditches, Drains and Watercourses

(Subdiv. repealed Oct. 29, 2020, P.L.782, No.96)

§ 2065. Power to Enter Lands.—(2065 repealed Oct. 29, 2020, P.L.782, No.96)

§ 2066. Viewers to Fix Damages.—(2066 repealed Oct. 29, 2020, P.L.782, No.96)

§ 2067. Ditches, Drains, and Watercourses; Approval of Plans.—(2067 repealed Oct. 29, 2020, P.L.782, No.96)

§ 2068. Power to Open Drains and Ditches.—(a) The board of commissioners or its agents and employees may enter any lands or enclosures and cut, open, maintain and repair drains or ditches through the property when necessary to carry the water from the streets.

(b) Any person who damages or diverts any drain or ditch without the authority of the board of commissioners commits a summary offense and is liable for the cost of restoring the drain or ditch. All money recovered under this subsection shall be paid to the township treasurer.

(2068 added Oct. 29, 2020, P.L.782, No.96)

(k) Trees, Shrubbery, and Obstructions within Limits of Streets or Highways

(Subdiv. hdg. repealed Oct. 29, 2020, P.L.782, No.96)

§ 2070. Trees and Shrubbery Within Right-of-Way.—(a) In order to provide for easy and convenient traveling upon the public streets or highways, the board of commissioners may cut, alter or remove any trees, shrubbery, underbrush, refuse or obstructions within the legal width of any public street or highway, or any portion thereof.

(b) All logs, cordwood, branch wood or other forms of wood derived from the destruction or removal of any trees growing along streets or highways shall be surrendered to and remain the property of the abutting owners, provided that the abutting owners shall, within ten days after notice from the township, remove the logs, cordwood, branch wood or other forms of wood from the legal width of the street or highway. In the event of the abutting owners' failure to do so, they shall forfeit all interest therein, and the same may be disposed of as the board of commissioners deems proper.

(2070 amended Oct. 29, 2020, P.L.782, No.96)

(l) Protection of Streets or Highways from Snowdrifts
(Subdiv. hdg. repealed Oct. 29, 2020, P.L.782, No.96)

§ 2078. Protection of Streets or Highways from Snowdrifts.—(a) A township may enter upon private property adjacent to any public street or highway and place thereon a snow fence to within a limit of one hundred (100) feet from the right of way line of the public street or highway in order to eliminate snow drifting on the traveled portion of the street.

(b) A snow fence may not be placed before the first day of November or remain in place after the first day of April of the succeeding year unless the written consent of the owner of the adjacent property is obtained agreeing to an extension of time for the removal of the snow fence.

(c) If the board of commissioners and the owner of the property upon which a snow fence is placed and removed under this section cannot agree to the amount of compensation, if any, to be paid to the owner for placing the fence, including the amount of damages, if any, to be paid for injury to the property resulting from placing and removing the fence, the owner may petition the court of common pleas of the county for the appointment of viewers to ascertain the amount of damage incurred in the manner provided in this act for eminent domain proceedings. Damages, if any, when ascertained, shall be paid by the township from the general township fund.

(2078 amended Oct. 29, 2020, P.L.782, No.96)

(m) Guideposts and Index Boards
(Subdiv. hdg. repealed Oct. 29, 2020, P.L.782, No.96)

§ 2080. Duty to Erect.—(2080 repealed Oct. 29, 2020, P.L.782, No.96)

§ 2080.1. Naming of Streets.—The board of commissioners may provide for and regulate the naming of streets and highways. When the naming of a street or highway will affect signing maintained by the Department of Transportation, the board of commissioners shall notify the department.

(2080.1 added Oct. 29, 2020, P.L.782, No.96)

§ 2080.2. Street Lighting, Ornamental Lighting and Traffic Control Signals and Devices.—The board of commissioners may provide street lights and ornamental lighting and make regulations for the protection of lighting. The board may assess the costs of street lighting and ornamental lighting in accordance with Article XXV-A. The board may provide for the erection, maintenance and operation of traffic control signals and devices in accordance with 75 Pa.C.S. (relating to vehicles).

(2080.2 added Oct. 29, 2020, P.L.782, No.96)

§ 2081. Penalty for Destroying Signs.—(a) It shall be unlawful for any person to wilfully destroy, remove, injure, or deface any sign legally erected upon or near any public street, highway or bridge by the board of commissioners, or legally erected with the consent of the board of commissioners over any public street, highway or bridge, by any club, association, or other organized body, for the direction, guidance or safety of travelers. It shall also be unlawful for any person to wilfully destroy, remove, injure or deface any temporary traffic-control device legally erected to enhance traffic or worker safety in a construction or maintenance work zone, including, but not limited to, cones, batons, barrels, barricades, signs, sign trucks, arrow boards or other devices specified in a traffic safety plan approved by the township or the Department of Transportation.

Table of Contents
Part I Ch. 1–3 Ethics, Records, Open Meetings
Part II Ch. 4–10 Taxation
Part III Ch. 11–18 Torts, Contracts & Civil Rules
Part IV Ch. 19–24 Zoning & Planning
Part V Ch. 25–30 Construction and Emergency Codes
Part VI Ch. 31–39 Municipal Codes
Index

(b) Any person who violates this section commits a summary offense punishable upon conviction in accordance with section 3321-A, which may include the costs of labor, materials and prosecution. Money collected shall be paid to the township treasurer.

(2081 amended Oct. 29, 2020, P.L.782, No.96)

(n) Streets Crossing Railroad; Special Uses of Streets
(Subdiv. hdg. repealed Oct. 29, 2020, P.L.782, No.96)

§ 2083. Railroad Crossings.—(a) Every township constructing a street across a railroad shall construct the same above or below the grade of the railroad, unless permitted by the Pennsylvania Public Utility Commission to construct the street at grade.

(b) Any new construction of a street crossing a railroad or any vacation of any street crossing a railroad shall be constructed or vacated only in the manner consistent with the rules and regulations and under the jurisdiction of the Pennsylvania Public Utility Commission.

(c) Compensation for damages to the owners of adjacent property taken, injured or destroyed by the construction of a street crossing a railroad or any vacation of any street crossing a railroad shall be ascertained, fixed and paid under 66 Pa.C.S. Pt. I (relating to public utility code).

(2083 amended Oct. 29, 2020, P.L.782, No.96)

§ 2084. Street Permits.—No railroad or street railway shall be constructed upon any township street, nor shall any railroad or street railway crossings, driveway connections, gas pipe, water pipe, electric conduits, or other piping be laid upon or in, nor shall any telephone, telegraph or electric light or power poles, or any coal tipples or any other obstructions or facilities of nonpublic utility communication providers be erected upon or in, any portion of a township street, except under conditions, restrictions and regulations, and subject to the payment of fees for permits as may be prescribed and required by the board of commissioners, not exceeding the reasonable cost of issuing the permit and expense of inspecting the work authorized by the permit upon completion thereof. All fees collected for permits shall be paid into the township treasury.

(2084 amended Oct. 29, 2020, P.L.782, No.96)

Compiler's Note: Section 302(d) of Act 177 of 1988, known as the General Association Act of 1988, provided that section 2084 is repealed insofar as it is inconsistent with 15 Pa.C.S. § 1511 (relating to additional powers of certain public utility corporations).

(o) County-aid in the Improvement of Township Streets
(Subdiv. hdg. repealed Oct. 29, 2020, P.L.782, No.96)

§ 2086. County Aid in the Improvement of Township Streets.—(a) Whenever the owners of the majority of the assessed valuation of real property within any township desire any principal street within the township to be improved and maintained at the joint expense of the county and township, they may petition the board of commissioners of the township for the improvement and require the board of commissioners to make application to the county commissioners for the improvement and maintenance in accordance with the provisions of existing law

(b) If the board of commissioners refuse to act upon, or unduly delay action on, any petition for the improvement and maintenance of any street, any citizen taxpayer of the township or county may, by petition, present the facts of the matter to the court of common pleas, requesting the court to order such action thereon as the case may require. If after due hearing had before the court it shall appear that the truth of the matters alleged in the petition are sustained, the court shall make an order directing the board of commissioners to forthwith act upon the application or applications, and that the application or petition for the improvement be forthwith forwarded to the county commissioners.

(2086 amended Oct. 29, 2020, P.L.782, No.96)

(p) Penal Provisions

(Subdiv. repealed Oct. 29, 2020, P.L.782, No.96)

§ 2088. (2088 repealed Oct. 29, 2020, P.L.782, No.96)

(q) Opening, Making, Amending, and Repairing Streets and Bridges by Contracts with Taxpayers

(Subdiv. repealed Oct. 29, 2020, P.L.782, No.96)

§ 2090. Taxpayers' Rights.—(2090 repealed Oct. 29, 2020, P.L.782, No.96)

§ 2091. Petition to Court.—(2091 repealed Oct. 29, 2020, P.L.782, No.96)

§ 2092. Bond of Petitioner.—(2092 repealed Oct. 29, 2020, P.L.782, No.96)

§ 2093. Notice to Commissioners and Auditors.—(2093 repealed Oct. 29, 2020, P.L.782, No.96)

§ 2094. Contracts; Stipulations.—(2094 repealed Oct. 29, 2020, P.L.782, No.96)

§ 2095. No Street Tax to Be Levied.—(2095 repealed Oct. 29, 2020, P.L.782, No.96)

§ 2096. Inspection.—(2096 repealed Oct. 29, 2020, P.L.782, No.96)

§ 2097. Boundary Streets.—(a) When any street, other than a State or county road, is created or located along, on or over boundaries between a township and any other municipal corporation, the creation, location, construction, maintenance and repair of the street shall be the joint responsibility of the township and the municipal corporation with which the common boundary is shared.

(b) The board of commissioners may make agreements with the governing body of the municipal corporation with which the common boundary is shared to provide for the apportionment of the cost of construction, maintenance and repair of boundary streets.

(c) If an amicable agreement on the proportionate share of costs of construction, maintenance and repair of boundary streets cannot be executed, the board of commissioners or the governing body of the other municipal corporation involved may petition the court of common pleas of the county for a determination of the rights and responsibilities of the respective municipal corporations involved.

(d) The court, after hearing of which notice shall be given to all parties interested as the court may direct, shall make an order directing the manner of the opening and maintenance and the division of the costs between the township and the other municipal corporation.

(2097 added Oct. 29, 2020, P.L.782, No.96)

§ 2098. Streets, the Center Line of Which is the Boundary Between a Township and Another Municipal Corporation.—(a) A township may enter into a contract with a municipal corporation to provide for the grading, curbing, draining, and paving of any street that constitutes the dividing line between the township and the municipal corporation.

(b) The alterations and improvements shall be made under the supervision of the township or municipal corporation, or by contract let by the township or the municipal corporation, as may be provided for in the contract between the township and the municipal corporation.

(2098 added Oct. 29, 2020, P.L.782, No.96)

Table of Contents
Part I Ch. 1–3 Ethics, Records, Open Meetings
Part II Ch. 4–10 Taxation
Part III Ch. 11–18 Torts, Contracts & Civil Rules
Part IV Ch. 19–24 Zoning & Planning
Part V Ch. 25–30 Construction and Emergency Codes
Part VI Ch. 31–39 Municipal Codes
Index

§ 2099. Streets Having More Than Half of Their Width Within Township.— (a) If any street, more than one-half the width of which is within the limits of the township, shall divide the township from any other municipal corporation, the street may be improved by the township in the same manner as if the street were entirely located within the limits of the township.

(b) The property, within or outside the township, that abuts the street and benefits from the improvements may, for a depth of one hundred fifty feet plus one-half the width of the street measured from its center line, be assessed for any and all municipal improvements to or on the street in the same manner as the property would be assessed under the provisions of this article if it were entirely located within the limits of the township.

(2099 added Oct. 29, 2020, P.L.782, No.96)

§ 2099.1. Assessment for Improvements on Property Outside Limits Where Street Entirely Within Township.—Whenever any street, entirely within the limits of any township, shall divide the township from any other municipal corporation, the property on the side of the street, within or outside the township, that abuts the street and benefits from the improvement may, for a depth of one hundred fifty feet from its center line, be assessed for any and all municipal improvements to or on the streets on which the property abuts in the same manner as the property would be assessed under the provisions of this act if it were entirely located within the limits of the township.

(2099.1 added Oct. 29, 2020, P.L.782, No.96)

ARTICLE XXI
BOUNDARY ROADS AND STREETS
53 P.S. §§ 57101–57130

(Art. repealed Oct. 29, 2020, P.L.782, No.96)

(a) Opening, Repairing and Improving Streets on Division Line of Townships

(Subdiv. repealed Oct. 29, 2020, P.L.782, No.96)

§ 2101. (2101 repealed Oct. 29, 2020, P.L.782, No.96)

(b) Maintenance of Streets between Township and Cities or Boroughs

(Subdiv. repealed Oct. 29, 2020, P.L.782, No.96)

§ 2105. (2105 repealed Oct. 29, 2020, P.L.782, No.96)

(c) Street, the Centre Line of which is the Dividing Line between Townships and Boroughs or Cities in the Same County

(Subdiv. repealed Oct. 29, 2020, P.L.782, No.96)

§ 2110. (2110 repealed Oct. 29, 2020, P.L.782, No.96)

(d) Street, the Centre Line of which is the Dividing Line between Townships and Cities in an Adjacent County

(Subdiv. repealed Oct. 29, 2020, P.L.782, No.96)

§ 2115. (2115 repealed Oct. 29, 2020, P.L.782, No.96)

(e) Improvement of Street where more than One-Half of Width is in Township; Assessment of Property outside Limits

(Subdiv. repealed Oct. 29, 2020, P.L.782, No.96)

§ 2120. (2120 repealed Oct. 29, 2020, P.L.782, No.96)

(f) Assessment of Property outside Limits of Township for Street Improvements

(Subdiv. repealed Oct. 29, 2020, P.L.782, No.96)

§ 2125. (2125 repealed Oct. 29, 2020, P.L.782, No.96)

(g) Grading, Curbing, Paving, Macadamizing Boundary Street or Highway, Et Cetera

(Subdiv. repealed Oct. 29, 2020, P.L.782, No.96)

§ 2130. (2130 repealed Oct. 29, 2020, P.L.782, No.96)

ARTICLE XXII
BRIDGES
53 P.S. §§ 57201–57255

(Art. hdg. amended Oct. 29, 2020, P.L.782, No.96)

(a) As Part of Street

(Subdiv. hdg. repealed Oct. 29, 2020, P.L.782, No.96)

§ 2201. Construction and Acquisition of Bridges.—(a) Any township may erect and construct, or acquire by purchase, condemnation or otherwise, any bridge and the piers, abutments and approaches for the bridge, to be used and thereafter improved and maintained as a street whether the bridge is wholly or partly within the township limits.

(b) The proceedings for laying out and opening a bridge shall be the same as provided by this act for the laying out and opening of streets, and the bridge or portion of the bridge may thereafter be vacated under the same procedure as provided in this act for the relocation or vacation of streets or portions of streets.

(c) Nothing in this article shall affect the powers or duties of the Pennsylvania Public Utility Commission to the extent otherwise provided by law.

(d) Bridges over railroads shall not obstruct the railroad over which it is built. Nothing in this section shall release railroad or other companies or the Commonwealth from the requirements of existing laws.

(e) As used in this article, the term "bridge" shall mean a structure built to span and provide passage over a valley, street, railroad track, private property, gully, river, creek, stream or any other body of water or physical obstacle and shall include viaducts constructed from a series of spans or arches.

(2201 amended Oct. 29, 2020, P.L.782, No.96)

(b) Over Railroads

(Subdiv. hdg. repealed Oct. 29, 2020, P.L.782, No.96)

§ 2205. Power to Construct.—(2205 repealed Oct. 29, 2020, P.L.782, No.96)

§ 2206. Maintenance.—(a) A bridge shall be maintained as a township structure, and the township may contract with any party interested, except the county, for the maintenance of the bridge.

(b) Whenever a bridge, or part thereof, has been built by the county, or the whole or part of the money necessary to build it has been furnished by the county, and the bridge has not been entered on record as a county bridge, the bridge shall be maintained, kept in repair, and rebuilt, when necessary, by the township or municipal corporation in which, or on the boundary line of which it is located, without rendering the county liable for the same.

(2206 amended Oct. 29, 2020, P.L.782, No.96)

(c) Over Marshy or Swampy Grounds, Creeks, Rivulets, Gullies, Canals and Railroads

(Subdiv. repealed Oct. 29, 2020, P.L.782, No.96)

§ 2210. Power to Make and Maintain.—(2210 repealed Oct. 29, 2020, P.L.782, No.96)

§ 2211. Damages.—(2211 repealed Oct. 29, 2020, P.L.782, No.96)

(d) Over Streams, Railroads and Canals on Township Boundaries

(Subdiv. hdg. repealed Oct. 29, 2020, P.L.782, No.96)

§ 2220. Boundary Bridges.—(a) If a bridge crosses the boundary line of a township and another municipal corporation, the township may enter into an intergovernmental cooperation agreement in accordance with 53 Pa.C.S. Ch. 23 Subch. A (relating to intergovernmental cooperation) with the municipal corporation for the construction and maintenance of the bridge and for apportionment of the costs.

(b) If an amicable agreement on the proportionate share of costs of construction, maintenance and repair of boundary bridges cannot be executed, the board of commissioners or the governing body of the other municipal corporation involved may petition the court of common pleas of the county or counties for a determination of the rights and responsibilities of the respective municipal corporations involved.

(2220 amended Oct. 29, 2020, P.L.782, No.96)

§ 2221. Bridges between Townships and Municipalities.—(2221 repealed Oct. 29, 2020, P.L.782, No.96)

§ 2222. Bridges over Railroad or Canal.—(2222 repealed Oct. 29, 2020, P.L.782, No.96)

(e) Maintenance, Repair, and Rebuilding of Bridges Built by County

(Subdiv. repealed Oct. 29, 2020, P.L.782, No.96)

§ 2225. (2225 repealed Oct. 29, 2020, P.L.782, No.96)

ARTICLE XXIII
SIDEWALKS

53 P.S. §§ 57301–57305

§ 2301. Power to Lay Out and Establish Grades.—Townships may, by ordinance, lay out and establish sidewalks, curbs, gutters and surface water drains along any street and, with the consent of the Secretary of Transportation, along any State highway, and with the consent of the county commissioners, along any county road. Townships may establish grades for the sidewalks, which grades may be separate and apart from the grade established for the street or highway. For the purposes of this section, any township may acquire land by purchase, gift, or by the right of eminent domain.

(2301 amended Oct. 29, 2020, P.L.782, No.96)

§ 2302. Width.—The width of any sidewalk shall be fixed by the board of commissioners either by ordinance or resolution.

(2302 amended Oct. 29, 2020, P.L.782, No.96)

§ 2303. Paving and Curbing Sidewalks.—(a) Townships may, upon notice as provided by ordinance, require owners of property abutting on any street, including State highways and county roads, to construct, grade, pave, curb, repave and recurb the sidewalks along the property under regulations and specifications prescribed by ordinance. All reconstruction, repaving and recurbing may be provided for in the ordinance providing for the original construction, paving and curbing, without the necessity for adopting a new ordinance providing for the reconstruction, repaving and recurbing.

(b) Upon the failure of any property owner to comply with the notice under subsection (a), a township may cause the construction, grading, paving, curbing, repaving and recurbing to be done by the township itself, or by contract, and to levy and collect the cost of the work from the property owner abutting the sidewalk.

(c) The cost of any work incurred by the township pursuant to subsection (b) may be levied against and collected from the owner who failed to complete the work pursuant to notice to do so, together with a penalty of ten percent of the costs and all charges and expenses. The costs, penalties, charges and expenses provided for shall be a lien upon the property for which the notice to do the work was given. The lien shall exist from the time of the commencement of the work, which date shall be fixed by the township engineer and certified to the township secretary in accordance with section 1305. Any lien may be collected by action in assumpsit or by lien filed in the manner provided by law for the filing and collection of municipal claims or the cost of any construction, grading, paving, curbing, repaving and recurbing may be borne in whole or in part by the township. If the township pays in part, the remaining cost shall be collected as provided by this section.

(d) The following shall apply:

(1) Each notice shall be served upon the owner of the premises to which the notice refers, if the owner is a resident of the township. If the owner is not a resident, the notice may be served upon the agent or tenant of the owner or upon the occupant of the premises. If the owner has no agent or tenant or there is no occupier of the premises, service shall be by notice posted upon the premises.

(2) The notice required by this section shall specify a period of time of not less than sixty days for the owner to complete the specified work. If the work has not been completed after the specified time has elapsed, the owner shall be deemed to have failed to comply.

(2303 amended Oct. 29, 2020, P.L.782, No.96)

§ 2304. Repair of Sidewalks.—(a) An abutting property owner shall keep the sidewalk, together with any portion of the property paved and used as a sidewalk or public walk immediately in front of the property, in good order and repair, and, at all times, free and clear of all obstruction to safe and convenient passage.

(b) If the property owner neglects to perform the duty imposed in subsection (a), the board of commissioners may serve written notice upon the property owner pursuant to section 2303(d)(1) to do what is necessary. If the property owner fails to comply with the requirements of the notice within thirty days from the date of its service, the township may make the necessary repairs or remove any obstruction. The cost of the same, together with a penalty of ten percent, shall be paid by the delinquent property owner, and may be collected by action of assumpsit, or the township may file a municipal lien against the property.

(2304 amended Oct. 29, 2020, P.L.782, No.96)

§ 2305. Emergency Repairs.—(a) A township may make emergency repairs to sidewalks, within its corporate limits, if an officer or designated individual representing the department or committee in charge of repairs to sidewalks upon inspection determines that a substantial and immediate danger exists to public health, safety and welfare.

(b) The officer or individual shall prepare a written report of those conditions which shall be conclusive evidence of the existence of the emergency justifying the repair.

(c) This section is intended to provide an additional remedy for townships in connection with emergency repairs of sidewalks.

(d) The following shall apply:

(1) A copy of the written report shall be served upon the abutting property owner, along with a notice to make emergency repairs to the sidewalk within forty-eight hours of service of the notice and report.

(2) The notice and copy of the report shall be served pursuant to section 2303(d)(1).

(3) The report shall expressly state that emergency repairs are required.

(4) If the owner fails to make the emergency repairs within the prescribed time, the township may make the emergency repairs to the sidewalk.

(e) Upon the completion of any emergency repairs, the cost of the repairs shall be a charge against the owner of the abutting property and shall be a lien, until paid, upon the abutting property, provided that a claim is filed for the lien in accordance with the law providing for the filing and collection of municipal claims.

(f) The amount of the claim against the owner of the abutting property may also be collected from the owner by an action in assumpsit.

(2305 added Oct. 29, 2020, P.L.782, No.96)

ARTICLE XXIV
SANITARY SEWERS AND DRAINS
53 P.S. §§ 57401–57445

(Art. hdg. amended Oct. 29, 2020, P.L.782, No.96)

Compiler's Note: Section 2 of Act 209 of 1990 provided that the provisions of this Code relating to the charging of a tapping fee for connection to a municipally owned water or sewer system are repealed insofar as they are inconsistent with Act 209, which amends the act of July 31, 1968 (P.L.805, No.247), known as the Pennsylvania Municipalities Planning Code (MPC). Section 507-A of the MPC prohibits the imposition of a tapping fee or similar fee unless such fee is calculated as provided in the applicable provisions of the act of May 2, 1945 (P.L.382, No.164), known as the Municipality Authorities Act of 1945. The Municipality Authorities Act of 1945 was repealed by the act of June 19, 2001 (P.L.287, No.22). The subject matter is now contained in 53 Pa.C.S. Ch. 56 (relating to municipal authorities).

(a) Establishing and Constructing Sewer and Drainage Systems; Sewer Connections and Rates; Disposal of Sewage; Assessment of Cost of Construction

§ 2401. Power to Establish and Construct Sewers and Drains; Require Connections; Sewer Rentals.—(a) Townships may establish and construct a system of sanitary sewers and drainage, locating the system, as far as practicable, in the right-of-way of the street in any street and may be for the service and use of properties on both sides of the street or on only one side of the street in which they are laid, as seems advisable to the township commissioners.

(b) The board of commissioners may, in accordance with section 2401.1(a), permit, and, if necessary for the public health by ordinance, require any owner of property benefited, improved or accommodated by sanitary sewers, to make connections with the sanitary sewer system in the manner specified by the board of commissioners. All connections required shall be uniform.

(c) The board of commissioners may, by ordinance, make regulations relating to the use and maintenance of the sanitary sewer system and treatment works. Violations of the ordinance may be enforced by penalties. The regulations may do all of the following:

(1) Specify materials and substances which may or may not enter the public sewer or sewer system.

(2) Require that certain types or classes of waste be subjected to treatment or to grinding or other reduction in size before entering into the sewer.

(3) Restrict the quantity of waste material that may enter a sanitary sewer from any premises within any time interval.

(d) (1) Each person whose property is connected to a sanitary sewer system shall pay a monthly, quarterly, semiannual or annual rate to the township, in addition to the cost of making connections to the sanitary sewer system.

(2) The initial imposition of the rate under paragraph (1) shall be established by ordinance. Any subsequent rate adjustments may be by resolution provided that the ordinance establishing the rate allows for future rate adjustments by resolution adopted at a public meeting. This paragraph shall not be construed to invalidate or void any rate imposed or adjusted prior to the effective date of this paragraph.

(3) The rate under this subsection shall constitute a lien, until paid, against the property connected to the sanitary sewer system, and the amount thereof may be recovered by due process of law through an action in assumpsit in the name of the township against the owner of the property charged or by a lien filed in the nature of a municipal lien.

(e) All water utilities supplying water to users within the boundaries of any township shall, at the request of the board of commissioners, furnish to the township, on or before the fifteenth day of the month following the month during which bills are issued, a list of all water meter readings and flat-rate water bills and the basis for each flat-rate water charge, so that the data may be used in calculating sewer rates. The township may reimburse utilities reasonable amounts for necessary clerical and other expenses incurred in the preparation of the lists.

(f) The term "sanitary sewer," as used in this article, shall mean and include a sewer used for receiving and collecting sewage matter and liquid waste from the inside of buildings and structures, and, in those townships where there shall be what is known as "combined sewers," receiving, in addition to such sewage and liquid waste from the inside of buildings and structures, storm, roof or surface drainage or any of them, the term "sanitary sewer," as used in this article, shall include such combined sewers.

(g) Nothing in this section shall be construed to repeal or modify any of the provisions of 66 Pa.C.S. (relating to public utilities).

(h) If required by other law, a township shall obtain the consent and permit of the Department of Environmental Protection or other Federal, State or county entity, including the Pennsylvania Turnpike Commission, for the laying out and construction of a sanitary sewer and treatment works.

(2401 amended Oct. 29, 2020, P.L.782, No.96)

Compiler's Note: The act of May 28, 1937 (P.L.1053, No.286), known as the Public Utility Law, was repealed by the act of July 1, 1978 (P.L.598, No.116). The subject matter is now contained in 66 Pa.C.S. (relating to public utilities).

§ 2401.1. Required Connection and Fees.—(a) A township may, by ordinance, require a property owner to connect with and use a sanitary sewer system established or constructed by the township, joint sanitary sewer board or a municipal authority serving the township if the property abuts on or adjoins any street or highway along which the sewer system is located or whose principal building is within one hundred fifty feet from the sanitary sewer.

(b) (1) If an owner of property abutting on or adjoining or whose principal building is within one hundred fifty feet from the sanitary sewer fails to connect with and use the sanitary sewer under subsection (a) for a period of sixty days after notice to do so has been served by the board of commissioners, either by personal service or by registered mail, the board of commissioners or their agents may enter the property and construct the connection.

(2) The board of commissioners shall send an itemized bill of the cost of construction under paragraph (1) to the owner of the property to which connection has been made, which shall be payable immediately.

(3) If the owner fails to pay the bill under paragraph (2), the board of commissioners shall file a municipal lien for the cost of the construction. The township may also by ordinance impose penalties to enforce regulations or orders in regards to sewer connections.

(c) As a condition of connection to a sanitary sewer collection, treatment or disposal facility, owned or operated by a township, a township may impose and charge the following to property owners who desire or are required to connect to the sanitary sewer system or who desire to increase their usages of the system:

(1) A connection fee.

(2) A customer facilities fee.

(3) A tapping fee.

(4) Similar fees, as enumerated and defined by 53 Pa.C.S. § 5607(d)(24) (relating to purposes and powers).

(2401.1 amended Oct. 29, 2020, P.L.782, No.96)

§ 2401.2. Notice of Contemplated Construction.—No sanitary sewer system shall be constructed under this article unless an ordinance of the board of commissioners authorizing the construction is published once in a newspaper of general circulation pursuant to section 110.

(2401.2 added Oct. 29, 2020, P.L.782, No.96)

§ 2402. Location of Sanitary Sewers on Private Property.—Where it is reasonably impracticable, in the judgment of the board of commissioners, in any part of the sanitary sewer system, to carry sanitary sewers along the lines of public streets or highways, the board of commissioners may locate and construct so much of the sanitary sewers as is necessary through private lands and may acquire the necessary land or right of way for this purpose by gift, purchase or by the exercise of the right of eminent domain.

(2402 amended Oct. 29, 2020, P.L.782, No.96)

§ 2403. Treatment Works and Facilities.—The board of commissioners may acquire by eminent domain or enter into contracts with other municipal corporations, corporations or persons for the acquisition of lands or facilities for the location, construction, maintenance, use and operation of sanitary sewer systems and treatment facilities. Acquisitions may be made for the purpose of future additions to and enlargements of existing systems. The acquired land may be located either inside or outside the boundaries of the township. Any extension shall be in conformity with 26 Pa.C.S. § 206 (relating to extraterritorial takings) and any other applicable requirement of 26 Pa.C.S. (relating to eminent domain).

(2403 amended Oct. 29, 2020, P.L.782, No.96)

§ 2404. Entry on Lands to Mark Sewer Routes; Damages.—(2404 repealed Oct. 29, 2020, P.L.782, No.96)

§ 2405. Enforcement of Judgment for Damages.—(2405 repealed Oct. 29, 2020, P.L.782, No.96)

§ 2406. Cost of Construction and Payment.—The cost of construction of any system of sanitary sewers or drains, constructed by the authority of this subdivision of this article, may be charged upon the properties benefited, improved or accommodated thereby to the extent of the benefits, or may be paid for wholly or partially by general taxation. Any amount not legally chargeable upon properties benefited, improved or accommodated shall be paid out of the general township fund.

(2406 amended Oct. 29, 2020, P.L.782, No.96)

§ 2407. Sewer Districts.—(a) When a sanitary sewer system is constructed by a township for the accommodation of a certain portion of the township, the board of commissioners may designate the territory accommodated into a sewer district or divide the portion into several sewer districts.

(b) The board of commissioners shall estimate the proportion of the cost of the sanitary sewer system to be charged on each of the districts and declare and establish the apportionment by resolution and the following shall apply:

(1) No district shall be charged more than the district's due proportion of the cost of a sanitary sewer system, or any part of the system, used jointly by more than one district.

(2) The aggregate amount charged on a property in any district shall not exceed the amount of the estimate.

(3) Where the whole of the township is accommodated by the sanitary sewer system, the township may be treated as a single district or divided into districts, and be subject to the provisions of this section.

(2407 amended Oct. 29, 2020, P.L.782, No.96)

§ 2408. Assessments.—Assessments, whether based according to benefits conferred or by the front foot basis, and assessment awards, if any, shall be calculated pursuant to Article XXV-A.

(2408 amended Oct. 29, 2020, P.L.782, No.96)

§ 2409. Procedure for Assessment of Benefits.—(2409 repealed Oct. 29, 2020, P.L.782, No.96)

§ 2410. Lien for Assessments; Costs of Proceedings.—(2410 repealed Oct. 29, 2020, P.L.782, No.96)

§ 2411. Assessment of Property Outside Limits of Townships for Sewers.—(2411 repealed Oct. 29, 2020, P.L.782, No.96)

(b) Acquisition of Sewer System from Private Interests; Distribution of Costs

§ 2415. Power to Acquire Community Sewage Collection or Disposal Systems.— (a) A township may, by ordinance, acquire ownership of a community sewage collection or disposal system by purchase, the exercise of eminent domain pursuant to 26 Pa.C.S. (relating to eminent domain) or by gift from the owner or owners.

(b) In eminent domain proceedings, the viewers shall assess the costs and expenses of the community sewage collection or disposal system acquired by the township upon the property or properties benefited according to benefits. Any deficiency that is not assessed upon the benefited property or properties shall be paid by the township.

(c) After a community sewage collection or disposal system has been acquired under this section by the township, the board of commissioners shall have the power to enlarge the system if they deem it advisable. The cost and expenses of the enlargement may be distributed or assessed in the same manner as if the enlargement was a regular sewer constructed by the township under other provisions of this act.

(d) If a community sewage collection or disposal system is established or constructed within a township by a private owner or owners, and the board of commissioners are empowered by ordinance to acquire the ownership of the sewage disposal system, or when the system has been enlarged by the township, the acquisition and ownership shall be subject to the following provisions:

(1) An agreement shall be considered a valid agreement by the owners of the sewage collection or disposal system and shall be a transfer of ownership to the township when any of the following enter into an agreement with the township for the acquisition of the system by the township:

(i) The person or persons having established or constructed a community sewage collection or disposal system.

(ii) More than one-half of the number of owners of properties which are connected with, have a right to use and are using a community sewage collection or disposal system.

(2) The township shall operate and maintain any community sewage collection or disposal system acquired or enlargement or addition to a system for the use of the following:

(i) Persons having acquired from the township or from the former owner or owners the right to use the system.

(ii) Other owners of property accessible to the system up to the capacity of the community sewage collection or disposal system.

(3) All persons whose property connects with the community sewage collection or disposal system acquired or constructed by the township shall pay to the township treasurer, a monthly, quarterly, semiannual or annual charge prescribed by a resolution of the board of commissioners. The amount of the charges shall not be in excess of the estimated amount necessary to maintain and operate the system and to establish a reserve fund sufficient for its future replacement.

(4) All sewer rentals or charges imposed by the board of commissioners against properties connected with a community sewage collection or disposal system under this section shall constitute liens against the properties and may be collected in the same manner as other sewer charges.

(5) All money received from the sewer charges shall be deposited as a special reserve fund and shall be used only for the payment of the cost of operating

and maintaining the community sewage collection or disposal system and the replacement, if necessary and economically desirable. If, at any time after the acquisition or enlargement of the community sewage system, a regular sewer system is made available by the township for connection with the properties using the community sewage collection or disposal system, the owners of the properties shall be subject to the other provisions of this act relating to sewers, and all money at that time in the reserve fund which was received from charges for the use of that particular community sewage collection or disposal system and which is over and above the amount expended for the operation and maintenance of that particular sewage collection or disposal system shall be used towards the payment of any sewer assessments charged against the properties under other sections of this act.

(e) The following words and phrases when used in this section shall have the meanings given to them in this subsection unless the context clearly indicates otherwise:

"Community sewage collection or disposal system." All or part of a device or devices installed on any privately or publicly owned parcel of land intended to treat or dispose of the sewage or equivalent volume of domestic sewage from two or more residences, buildings or occupied parcels of land, or any system of piping used in collection and conveyance of sewage on private or public property.

(f) Nothing in this section may be construed to supersede the requirements of the act of January 24, 1966 (1965 P.L.1535, No.537), known as the "Pennsylvania Sewage Facilities Act."

(2415 amended Oct. 29, 2020, P.L.782, No.96)

(c) Contracts with Individuals or Corporations for Construction and Maintenance of Sewer and Drainage Systems

§ 2420. Contracts for Sewer and Drainage Systems.—(a) In a case where, under the authority of section 2401, a system of sewage and drainage covering a township in whole or in part shall have been approved and authorized by ordinance, the board of commissioners may enter into a contract with any responsible individual or corporation for the construction of a system of sewage or drainage at the expense of the individual or corporation and the following shall apply:

(1) The individual or corporation shall be entitled under the contract to exercise all the powers of the township in the construction, maintenance and operation of the system of sewage or drainage, with the right to collect fees connected to the construction, maintenance and operation as the board of commissioners prescribes, in as full manner as the fees might have been collected by the township or the commissioners.

(2) In the contract the board of commissioners shall reserve to the township the right at any time, after a prescribed time, to take possession of the system of sewage and drainage, and the system's appurtenances, at a price and upon terms to be fixed in the contract.

(b) Nothing in this section shall be construed to repeal or modify any of 66 Pa.C.S. (relating to public utilities).

(2420 amended Oct. 29, 2020, P.L.782, No.96)

Compiler's Note: The act of May 28, 1937 (P.L.1053, No.286), known as the Public Utility Law, was repealed by the act of July 1, 1978 (P.L.598, No.116). The subject matter is now contained in 66 Pa.C.S. (relating to public utilities).

(d) Sewers and Drains in Streets or Highways, or over Private Property; Assessment of Cost of Construction According to Benefits

(d) amended May 27, 1953, P.L.220, No.30)

§ 2425. Cost of Construction.—Townships may construct sanitary sewers and drains in any street or highway, or through or on or over private property. The costs, damages, and expenses of the construction of any sanitary sewers or drains may be paid for wholly or partially by general taxation, or may be assessed upon the properties accommodated or benefited pursuant to Article XXV-A.

(2425 amended Oct. 29, 2020, P.L.782, No.96)

(e) Sewers under State and County Highways

§ 2430. State and County Highways and Consent Required.—(a) A township may construct a sanitary sewer and drain in or under any State or county highway within the township boundaries.

(b) (1) For the construction of a sanitary sewer in or under a county highway, the consent of the county commissioners of the county shall be obtained.

(2) For the construction of a sanitary sewer in or under a State highway, the consent of the Department of Transportation shall be obtained.

(2430 amended Oct. 29, 2020, P.L.782, No.96)

§ 2431. Assessment of Cost.—(2431 repealed Oct. 29, 2020, P.L.782, No.96)

(f) Connecting with Adjoining Sewer

(Subdiv. hdg. amended Oct. 29, 2020, P.L.782, No.96)

§ 2435. Connection by Agreement or Petition and Appointment of Viewers.—(a) If a township desires to connect with the existing sanitary sewer of an adjacent municipal corporation or municipal authority for either sewage collection or treatment purposes, the entities may enter into an agreement for this purpose. If no agreement has been reached between the township and the adjacent municipal corporation or municipal authority, the township shall proceed as provided under subsection (b).

(b) An application shall be made by the board of commissioners to the court of common pleas of the county where the proposed connection is to be located, setting forth the desire of the township to connect with the existing sanitary sewer of the municipal corporation or municipal authority. If the court determines that the connection can be made without impairing the usefulness of the existing sanitary sewer, it shall appoint three viewers who shall:

(1) View the premises and investigate the facts of the case.

(2) Assess the proportionate part of the expense of building the original sanitary sewer upon the petitioning township.

(3) Fix the proportion of the expense for repairs which the municipal corporation or municipal authority and the township shall thereafter bear.

(4) Determine all other questions which are likely to arise in connection with the sanitary sewer.

(c) The viewers shall report the results of their investigation under subsection (b) to the court, and the court shall confirm the report within thirty days of the report's submission unless exceptions are filed. Any interested party may appeal the disposition of filed exceptions.

(2435 amended Oct. 29, 2020, P.L.782, No.96)

§ 2436. Notice of Contemplated Construction; Protests by Property Owners.—(2436 repealed Oct. 29, 2020, P.L.782, No.96)

(g) Joint Sanitary Sewers and Drains
(Subdiv. hdg. amended Oct. 29, 2020, P.L.782, No.96)

§ 2440. Building Joint Sewers.—(a) Pursuant to 53 Pa.C.S. Ch. 23 Subch. A (relating to intergovernmental cooperation), a township may contract with another municipal corporation providing for the joint construction or maintenance of sanitary sewer systems and for joint construction onto existing sanitary sewer systems, and the following shall apply:

(1) The agreement shall provide for the apportionment of costs among the municipal corporations.

(2) The board of commissioners may assess the township's respective portion of the costs, as may be legally assessable, upon property benefited by the facilities pursuant to Article XXV-A.

(3) Any portion of the cost not assessed or assessable shall be paid by the respective municipal corporations under the agreement.

(4) In addition to or in lieu of contracting with other municipal corporations, townships may contract with municipal authorities for the purposes of this section.

(b) (1) The municipal corporations joining or contemplating joining in any improvement, in order to facilitate the building of the sanitary sewer system and in securing preliminary surveys and estimates, may by ordinance provide for the appointment of a joint sanitary sewer board composed of one representative from each of the municipal corporations joining. The board shall act as the advisory and administrative agency in the construction of the improvement and its subsequent operation and maintenance.

(2) Members of the joint sanitary sewer board established under paragraph (1) shall serve for terms of six years each, from the date of the member's appointment until the member's successor is appointed. The joint sanitary sewer board shall organize by the election of a chairperson, secretary, and treasurer.

(3) The municipal corporations may, in the ordinances creating the joint sanitary sewer board, authorize the board to appoint an engineer, a solicitor and other assistants as deemed necessary and agree to the share of the compensation of those persons each municipal corporation is to pay.

(4) The members of the joint sanitary sewer board shall receive compensation for attending board meetings as established in the budget that is prepared by the joint sanitary sewer board and submitted to and adopted by the municipal corporations. The members shall be entitled to actual expenses to be paid by the respective municipal corporations the members represent.

(c) (1) A joint sanitary sewer board may adopt rules and regulations consistent with the requirements of this article to govern its proceedings and shall prepare and suggest any practical measures and plans by means of which the joint improvement may be carried to successful completion and plan the future development of the system, so as to conform to a general plan.

(2) The joint sanitary sewer board may prepare a joint agreement or agreements for submission to and adoption by the municipal corporations defining the advisory and administrative powers of the joint sanitary sewer board and setting forth the following:

(i) consent of the municipal corporations to the proposed improvement;

(ii) the manner in which preliminary and final plans, specifications and estimates for the proposed improvement shall be prepared and adopted;

Table of Contents | Part I Ch. 1–3 Ethics, Records, Open Meetings | Part II Ch. 4–10 Taxation | Part III Ch. 11–18 Torts, Contracts & Civil Rules | Part IV Ch. 19–24 Zoning & Planning | Part V Ch. 25–30 Construction and Emergency Codes | Part VI Ch. 31–39 Municipal Codes | Index

Chap. 39 Res. During Mil. Service
Chap. 38 Intergov. Coop.
Chap. 37 3rd Class City Code
Chap. 36 Bor. Code
Chap. 35 2nd Class Twp. Code
Chap. 34 1st Class Twp. Code
Chap. 33 Home Rule Chart. Opt. Plans Law
Chap. 32 Water Serv. Act
Chap. 31 Munic. Auth. Act

(iii) how proposals for bids shall be advertised and contracts awarded;

(iv) the manner in which the costs of the improvement and other incidental and preliminary expenses in connection with the improvement and the future cost of operation and maintenance shall be equitably shared, apportioned and paid; and

(v) all other matters, including the preparation and submission of annual and other budgets, as may be deemed necessary or required by law to complete the proposed improvement and to assure future maintenance and operation thereof.

(3) The joint sanitary sewer board may not make any improvement or expend any public money which has not first been authorized by all of the municipal corporations proceeding with the improvement.

(d) (1) When it is necessary to acquire, appropriate, injure or destroy private property to build a joint sanitary sewer system or improvement and the property cannot be acquired by purchase or gift, the right of eminent domain shall vest in the municipal corporation where the property is located.

(2) When it is necessary to acquire, injure or destroy property in any territory not within the limits of any of the municipal corporations joining in the improvement, the right of eminent domain shall be vested in a municipal corporation adjacent to the territory where the property is located subject to 26 Pa.C.S. § 206 (relating to extraterritorial takings).

(3) Damages for any property taken, injured or destroyed shall be assessed as provided by the laws relating to the municipal corporation exercising the right of eminent domain and shall be paid by the municipal corporations joining in the same proportion as other costs of the improvement.

(e) Each township joining in an improvement shall have power to incur or increase the township's indebtedness, not exceeding constitutional limits, for the purpose of paying the township's share or portion of the cost of the improvement in the manner now provided by law for the incurring of indebtedness.

(2440 amended Oct. 29, 2020, P.L.782, No.96)

§ 2441. State Permit.—(2441 repealed Oct. 29, 2020, P.L.782, No.96)

(h) Non-debt Revenue Sewer Bonds

(Subdiv. hdg. repealed Oct. 29, 2020, P.L.782, No.96)

§ 2445. Sewer Bonds.—(2445 repealed June 8, 1965, P.L.98, No.67)

§ 2446. Issuance and Sale of Bonds; Maturity; Negotiability.—(2446 repealed June 25, 1941, P.L.159, No.87)

§ 2447. Remedies of Bondholders.—(2447 repealed June 25, 1941, P.L.159, No.87)

ARTICLE XXV
COLLECTION BY INSTALMENT OF THE COST OF STREET, CURB, SIDEWALK AND SEWER IMPROVEMENTS
53 P.S. §§ 57501–57507

(Art. repealed Oct. 29, 2020, P.L.782, No.96)

Compiler's Note: Section 2 of Act 209 of 1990 provided that the provisions of this Code relating to the charging of a tapping fee for connection to a municipally owned water or sewer system are repealed insofar as they are inconsistent with Act 209, which amends the act of July 31, 1968 (P.L.805, No.247), known as the Pennsylvania Municipalities Planning Code (MPC). Section 507-A of the MPC prohibits the imposition of a tapping fee or similar fee unless such fee is calculated as provided in the applicable provisions of the act of May 2, 1945 (P.L.382, No.164), known as the Municipality Authorities Act of 1945. The Municipality Authorities Act of 1945 was repealed by the act of June 19, 2001 (P.L.287, No.22). The subject matter is now contained in 53 Pa.C.S. Ch. 56 (relating to municipal authorities).

§ 2501. Ordinances for Instalment Payments.—(2501 repealed Oct. 29, 2020, P.L.782, No.96)

§ 2502. Issue of Bonds.—(2502 repealed Oct. 29, 2020, P.L.782, No.96)

§ 2503. Sale of Bonds; Interest.—(2503 repealed Oct. 29, 2020, P.L.782, No.96)

§ 2504. Entry of Liens.—(2504 repealed Oct. 29, 2020, P.L.782, No.96)

§ 2505. Assessments, Where Payable.—(2505 repealed Oct. 29, 2020, P.L.782, No.96)

§ 2506. Default in Payment of Instalment.—(2506 repealed Oct. 29, 2020, P.L.782, No.96)

§ 2507. Payments in Full; Subdivisions of Property.—(2507 repealed Oct. 29, 2020, P.L.782, No.96)

ARTICLE XXV-A
ASSESSMENTS FOR PUBLIC IMPROVEMENTS
53 P.S. §§ 57501-A–57509-A

(Art. added Oct. 29, 2020, P.L.782, No.96)

§ 2501-A. Definitions.

The following words and phrases when used in this article shall have the meanings given to them in this section unless the context clearly indicates otherwise:

"Front foot." The term includes, but is not limited to, front linear foot, lot, parcel, dwelling unit or square foot.

"Public improvement." The term includes, but is not limited to, the following:

(1) The building, paving, grading, rebuilding, repaving and regrading of streets, sidewalks, curbs and gutters.

(2) The creation, extension and renovation of water treatment, transmission, distribution and disposal systems.

(3) The creation, extension and renovation of sewage collection, transmission, distribution, treatment and disposal systems.

(4) The creation, extension and renovation of storm, surface and subsurface drainage systems.

(5) The construction, reconstruction and repair of wharves and docks.

(6) The installation, maintenance or operation of lighting that services the streets, sidewalks and other public places within the township.

(7) The planting, transplanting, removal and protection of shade trees.

(2501-A added Oct. 29, 2020, P.L.782, No.96)

§ 2502-A. Authority to assess.

(a) Authority.—Unless otherwise provided for in this article, a township is authorized to assess all or any portion of the costs of a public improvement against any properties that are benefited by the public improvement.

(b) Payment of costs.—Unless otherwise provided in this article, in addition to the authority to assess the cost of public improvements against properties benefited either on the front foot method or benefit conferred method of assessment, a township may pay for the cost of public improvements, in whole or in

Table of Contents | Part I Ch. 1–3 Ethics, Records, Open Meetings | Part II Ch. 4–10 Taxation | Part III Ch. 11–18 Torts, Contracts & Civil Rules | Part IV Ch. 19–24 Zoning & Planning | Part V Ch. 25–30 Construction and Emergency Codes | Part VI Ch. 31–39 Municipal Codes | Index

part, from the township general fund or from a special township fund dedicated to that purpose.

(c) Indebtedness.—If a township incurs indebtedness pursuant to 53 Pa.C.S. Pt. VII Subpt. B (relating to indebtedness and borrowing) for the purposes of funding the cost and expense of making public improvements for which assessments are made in accordance with this article, payments made on the assessments must be applied to pay the debt service for the indebtedness incurred for funding the cost and expense of making the public improvements.

(d) Assessment outside of township.—Property benefited, improved or accommodated that is located outside the limits of the township that constructed the public improvement may, if located no more than 150 feet from the public improvement, be assessed for the cost of the public improvement in the same manner as the property would be assessed under the laws of this Commonwealth if it were entirely located within the limits of the township.

(2502-A added Oct. 29, 2020, P.L.782, No.96)

§ 2503-A. Method of assessment.

(a) Ordinance.—If the board of commissioners elects to exercise the power to make assessments for a given public improvement as authorized in section 2502-A, the board of commissioners shall, by ordinance and in conformity with this article, establish the method and procedure pursuant to which assessments shall be made.

(b) Allocation of costs and expenses.—The following shall apply:

(1) The board of commissioners may, by ordinance, make the assessment by any means that results in fairly allocating all or a portion of the costs and expenses of the public improvement among all properties benefited by the improvement in reasonable proportion to the benefits conferred upon each property. The methods that may be used to make assessments in accordance with this subsection may include, but are not limited to:

(i) An equal assessment per front foot.

(ii) An assessment made by benefits conferred.

(2) Only one assessment method may be used in allocating the costs for a particular public improvement unless a township is divided into districts for sanitary sewer or water, in which case the assessment in each district may be by different methods so long as the same assessment method is used within a particular district.

(c) Front foot method.—If the front foot method is used:

(1) The cost to be collected shall be divided by the total number of linear feet of street frontage of all properties benefited.

(2) The assessment against each property shall be that portion of the cost which is determined by multiplying the dividend under paragraph (1) by the number of linear feet for street frontage of that property.

(3) In the case of corner or irregularly shaped lots or where special conditions exist, the board of commissioners shall have the power and its duty shall be to provide for an equitable adjustment, as necessary, to prevent an unjust or excessive assessment.

(4) If the front foot method is used but is comprised of other than linear feet, such as lots, parcels, dwelling units or square feet, the formula in paragraphs (1) and (2) shall be adapted to comport with the unit of lots, parcels, dwelling units or square feet as applicable.

(d) Assessment of benefits conferred method.—In lieu of the front foot method, the board of commissioners may elect to have the benefits of public improvements assessed, in whole or in part, upon property benefited, improved or accommodated by assessing an equal assessment on the properties benefited, improved or accommodated in proportion to the total cost of construction of the improvement. The amount of the charge on each property shall be determined by the board of commissioners.

(e) Certificate of assessment.—The board of commissioners shall issue a certificate of assessment when either assessing on the front foot method or on the basis of benefits conferred upon property benefited, improved or accommodated, duly certified under the seal of the township and attested by the president of the board of commissioners and secretary. The certificate of assessment shall state the method of assessment used. The certificate of assessment shall be prima facie evidence in any suit for recovery of the same of the correctness and validity of the assessment.

(2503-A added Oct. 29, 2020, P.L.782, No.96)

§ 2504-A. Petition for viewers by board of commissioners.

The board of commissioners may petition the court of common pleas for the appointment of viewers to assess the total cost of an improvement as set forth in this article. The viewers shall assess the total cost of the improvement, or so much of the cost as may be just and reasonable, upon the lands or properties peculiarly benefited.

(2504-A added Oct. 29, 2020, P.L.782, No.96)

§ 2505-A. Petition for viewers by taxpayers.

(a) Petition.—Taxpayers of the township whose property is being assessed for benefits for a public improvement may present a petition to the court of common pleas stating that the assessment insufficiently represents the benefits accruing to abutting, benefited or accommodated properties. The petition may include a request for the appointment of viewers to assess benefits if at least 50% of the taxpayers whose parcels are abutting, benefited or accommodated by the public improvement in question join the petition or if taxpayers whose property valuation as assessed for taxable purposes within the township amounts to at least 50% of the total property valuation of the properties being assessed for the public improvement join the petition. The petition must be presented within 90 days of the issuance of the certificate of assessment.

(b) Viewers.—The court shall appoint three disinterested viewers, none of whom shall be a resident of that portion of the township that is benefited or accommodated by the public improvement in question. The viewers shall proceed under this article and 26 Pa.C.S. (relating to eminent domain) for the assessment of damages and benefits by viewers. Upon the filing of the petition by taxpayers for the appointment of viewers, any assessment made by the board of commissioners and any proceedings shall be stayed pending the disposition of the petition by the court.

(2505-A added Oct. 29, 2020, P.L.782, No.96)

§ 2506-A. Notice of assessment.

(a) Personal notice.—After the amounts to be assessed against the properties to be benefited by the public improvement have been calculated pursuant to the method and procedures as prescribed by ordinance, the township shall give personal notice of the assessment to the owner of each property that is being assessed. The notice shall also state that the owner has 30 days from receipt of the notice to appeal the assessment. If a certificate is required to be filed with the board of commissioners relating to the public improvement as otherwise provided in this act, a copy of the certificate shall accompany the notice.

(b) **Assessment effective.**—An assessment made pursuant to this article shall become effective 30 days after personal notice is given by any of the following means:

(1) Personal service on the owner or the owner's agent.

(2) Certified mail, addressee only, return receipt requested, to the owner at the owner's last known address.

(3) Posting notice at or upon the property after reasonable attempts to give personal notice pursuant to paragraphs (1) and (2) have failed.

(2506-A added Oct. 29, 2020, P.L.782, No.96)

§ 2507-A. Benefits and damages.

In any proceeding in which damages to property are being sought as a result of a public improvement for which an assessment of benefits has been made, the excess of damages over benefits, the excess of benefits over damages or nothing in case the benefits and damages are equal, shall be awarded to or assessed against the owner of land and property affected by the public improvement. Damages shall be calculated pursuant to 26 Pa.C.S. (relating to eminent domain).

(2507-A added Oct. 29, 2020, P.L.782, No.96)

§ 2508-A. Payment of assessments in installments.

(a) **Authorization.**—An ordinance providing for a public improvement, the expense of which is to be defrayed by an assessment against properties benefited by the public improvement, may authorize payment of the assessment in installments. The ordinance shall:

(1) Set a time when the installment payments shall commence.

(2) Specify the length of time over which the installments may be extended. The period during which installments may be paid shall not exceed the lesser of 10 years or the number of years equal to the period of maturity of the bonds issued to fund the public improvement.

(3) Specify whether payments are to be made by equal annual or more frequent installments.

(b) **Interest rate.**—The ordinance shall set forth the rate of interest for the installments, which shall not be more than 6% per year unless a bond is issued for the improvement, in which case the maximum interest rate on the installment payments shall be in accordance with section 9 of the act of May 16, 1923 (P.L.207, No.153), referred to as the Municipal Claim and Tax Lien Law.

(c) **Written agreement.**—The township shall enter into a written installment agreement with each property owner that will pay the assessment in installments, subject to the requirements of the ordinance pertaining to the agreements and this article.

(d) **Installments not paid.**—If any of the installments remain unpaid for 60 days after the installments have become due and payable:

(1) The entire unpaid assessment, plus unpaid accrued interest and any costs, shall be due and payable.

(2) The township may proceed to collect the installments by filing a lien in the same manner as municipal claims are filed under the Municipal Claim and Tax Lien Law or by instituting a civil action.

(e) **Advance payments.**—A property owner upon whom an assessment has been made may pay all or as many of the installments before they are due, with interest and costs to the due date of the next installment.

(2508-A added Oct. 29, 2020, P.L.782, No.96)

§ 2509-A. Collection of assessments.

(a) Authority.—The board of commissioners shall have the power to authorize the township treasurer or other township official to collect assessments.

(b) Procedure.—The following shall apply to the collection of assessments:

(1) A township may collect an assessment that remains unpaid for 60 days after personal notice was given pursuant to section 2506-A unless an installment agreement has been entered into pursuant to section 2508-A.

(2) An assessment made under this article may be collected in the same manner as municipal claims under the act of May 16, 1923 (P.L.207, No.153), referred to as the Municipal Claim and Tax Lien Law, or by instituting a civil action against the owner of the benefited property.

(3) Interest on an unpaid assessment shall begin to accrue from the time of completion of the improvement at a rate not to exceed 6% per year unless a bond is issued for the improvement, in which case the maximum interest rate shall be pursuant to section 9 of the Municipal Claim and Tax Lien Law.

(4) If a property owner has two or more lots against which there is an assessment for the same improvement, all of the lots may be embraced in one claim.

(5) Assessments, whether paid one time or by installments, shall be payable at the office of the township treasurer or any other place designated by ordinance.

(2509-A added Oct. 29, 2020, P.L.782, No.96)

ARTICLE XXVI
REVOLVING FUND FOR STREET AND SEWER IMPROVEMENTS

53 P.S. §§ 57601–57602

(Art. repealed Oct. 29, 2020, P.L.782, No.96)

§ 2601. Special Tax; Bond Issue.—(2601 repealed Oct. 29, 2020, P.L.782, No.96)

§ 2602. Repayments into Revolving Fund.—(2602 repealed Oct. 29, 2020, P.L.782, No.96)

ARTICLE XXVII
WATER SUPPLY

53 P.S. §§ 57701–57712

(Art. hdg. amended Oct. 29, 2020, P.L.782, No.96)

Compiler's Note: Section 2 of Act 209 of 1990 provided that the provisions of this Code relating to the charging of a tapping fee for connection to a municipally owned water or sewer system are repealed insofar as they are inconsistent with Act 209, which amends the act of July 31, 1968 (P.L.805, No.247), known as the Pennsylvania Municipalities Planning Code (MPC). Section 507-A of the MPC prohibits the imposition of a tapping fee or similar fee unless such fee is calculated as provided in the applicable provisions of the act of May 2, 1945 (P.L.382, No.164), known as the Municipality Authorities Act of 1945. The Municipality Authorities Act of 1945 was repealed by the act of June 19, 2001 (P.L.287, No.22). The subject matter is now contained in 53 Pa.C.S. Ch. 56 (relating to municipal authorities).

(a) Acquisition, Construction and Maintenance

§ 2701. Contracts for Water Supply; Development of Own Water Supply.—(a) Townships may contract with any adjoining municipal corporation owning

Table of Contents
Part I Ch. 1–3 Ethics, Records, Open Meetings
Part II Ch. 4–10 Taxation
Part III Ch. 11–18 Torts, Contracts & Civil Rules
Part IV Ch. 19–24 Zoning & Planning
Part V Ch. 25–30 Construction and Emergency Codes
Part VI Ch. 31–39 Municipal Codes
Index

a water system, or with a municipal authority or a private company, for a supply of water for public and private uses to be delivered into the lines of the township at or near or within the boundaries of the township.

(b) This section does not prohibit a contract between a township and a municipal corporation, or a private company, for the supply of water in territory being supplied by any other private company.

(c) A township may construct, maintain and operate its own water system and shall have full power by contract to develop an independent supply of water at any time, and it is not required to purchase a water supply needed by the township from either an adjoining municipal corporation or from a private company.

(2701 amended Oct. 29, 2020, P.L.782, No.96)

§ 2701.1. Public Utility Law Saved.—Nothing contained in this article shall be construed to repeal or to supersede any of the provisions of 66 Pa.C.S. (relating to public utilities).

(2701.1 added Oct. 29, 2020, P.L.782, No.96)

§ 2701.2. Rates.—(a) For water supplied by the township, the board of commissioners shall fix the rates charged to users of water or to owners whose properties are connected to the water system. The board of commissioners shall provide for the collection of the water rates. The rates shall be in addition to the cost of making any connections under section 2707. In the case of users outside the township, the fixing of rates shall be subject to, and in accordance with, applicable law and the rules and regulations of the Pennsylvania Public Utility Commission.

(b) The initial imposition of the rate imposed under subsection (a) shall be established by ordinance. Any subsequent rate adjustments may be by resolution provided that the ordinance establishing the rate allows for future rate adjustments by resolution adopted at a public meeting. This subsection shall not be construed to invalidate or void any rate imposed or adjusted prior to the effective date of this section.

(2701.2 added Oct. 29, 2020, P.L.782, No.96)

§ 2702. Distribution System; State Permit.—A township entering into a contract for the supply of water may, by ordinance, provide, regulate and protect a system of water distribution after filing a certified copy of the plans and surveys for the system, with a description of the sources from which it is proposed to derive the supply, with the Department of Environmental Protection and, if required by law, other Federal or State entities, and written permits for the construction of the system are issued in accordance with existing law.

(2702 amended Oct. 29, 2020, P.L.782, No.96)

§ 2703. Occupation of Highways.—(a) In providing for, regulating, protecting and extending its system of distribution of water, a township may occupy streets, roads or highways, and may take, injure or destroy private property as provided in this article. No highway under the jurisdiction of the Department of Transportation shall be occupied until a permit has been obtained from the Department of Transportation.

(b) Property belonging to or used as a cemetery, a place of public worship, or any public or parochial school, or other educational or charitable institution or seminary, shall not be taken, injured or destroyed by virtue of this section.

(2703 amended Oct. 29, 2020, P.L.782, No.96)

§ 2704. Property Damages.—If the compensation and damages arising from the taking, injury or destruction of private property cannot be agreed upon, the township shall proceed pursuant to 26 Pa.C.S. (relating to eminent domain).

(2704 amended Oct. 29, 2020, P.L.782, No.96)

§ 2705. Appointment of Viewers.—(2705 repealed Oct. 29, 2020, P.L.782, No.96)

§ 2706. Water Districts.—The board of commissioners may designate, define and create one or more water districts within the township, and the board of commissioners shall determine the proportion of the cost of the water system which shall be equitably charged on each district and declare and establish the apportionment by resolution. No district shall be charged with more than its due proportion of the cost of the main pipe lines, pumping stations or other parts of the water system used jointly by more than one district.

(2706 amended Oct. 29, 2020, P.L.782, No.96)

§ 2707. Connection to Water System.—(a) The board of commissioners may, by ordinance, require that a property owner connect with and use a water system of the township or municipal authority or a joint water system in either of the following cases:

(1) Except as provided in subsection (b), if the nearest property line is located within one hundred fifty feet of a water system or any part or extension of the system.

(2) If the property has no supply of water which is safe for human consumption.

(b) With respect to water supplied for human consumption, a property owner who, after the effective date of this subsection, is subject to mandatory connection pursuant to subsection (a)(1), shall not be required to connect to the water system pursuant to that subsection if all of the following conditions exist:

(1) The water system or part or extension of the system that is within one hundred fifty feet of the nearest property line was in existence on the effective date of this subsection.

(2) The property has its own supply of water which is safe for human consumption.

(3) Prior to the effective date of this subsection, the property owner was not required to connect to the existing system.

(c) Those industries and farms which have their own supply of water for uses other than human consumption through installed and operating wells existing prior to the effective date of this subsection may continue to use their preexisting wells for that purpose but are required to use the water system of the township or municipal authority to provide water for human consumption.

(d) A township may require any owner of property to install and maintain a backflow prevention device based on the degree of potential hazard of the connected property in accordance with other applicable law.

(e) A township may assess penalties for the violation of ordinances pertaining to water connections or backflow prevention devices.

(f) (1) A township may, by ordinance, impose and charge certain fees to property owners who desire or are required to connect to the water system owned or operated by the township, a municipal authority or a joint water board or who desire to increase their usage of the water system.

(2) The fees in paragraph (1) may be a connection fee, a customer facilities fee, a tapping fee and other similar fees as enumerated and calculated under 53 Pa.C.S. § 5607(d)(24) (relating to purposes and powers).

(3) The tapping fee may include a reimbursement part as provided in 53 Pa.C.S. § 5607(d)(24)(i)(C)(IV) to be refunded to the private person or corporation who paid for the construction of the water system or any part or extension thereof.

(g) (1) If any property owner required under subsection (a) to connect with and use the system fails to do so within ninety days after notice to do so has been served by the board of commissioners, either by personal service or registered mail, the board of commissioners or their agents may enter the property and construct the connection.

(2) The board of commissioners shall send an itemized bill of the cost of construction of the connection to the owner of the property to which connection has been made, which bill is payable immediately, or the board of commissioners may authorize the payment of the cost of construction of connections in equal monthly installments and the installments shall bear interest at a rate not to exceed six percent.

(2707 amended Oct. 29, 2020, P.L.782, No.96)

§ 2708. Connection to Water Supply System of Municipality Authorities.—(2708 repealed Oct. 29, 2020, P.L.782, No.96)

§ 2709. Cost of Connection; Where Payable.—The cost of construction of connections shall be payable immediately at the office designated by the board of commissioners, or if authorized by the board of commissioners, in monthly installments, with interest from the date of completion of the construction of the connection.

(2709 amended Oct. 29, 2020, P.L.782, No.96)

§ 2709.1. Default in Payment of Installment.—In case of default in the payment of any installment and interest for a period of sixty days after the same has become due, the entire cost of construction of the connection and accrued interest shall become due and the township may collect the unpaid cost of construction of the connection and accrued interest from the owner by a municipal claim or in an action of assumpsit.

(2709.1 amended Oct. 29, 2020, P.L.782, No.96)

§ 2709.2. Entry of Liens.—(2709.2 repealed Oct. 29, 2020, P.L.782, No.96)

(b) Joint Water System

(Subdiv. hdg. amended Oct. 29, 2020, P.L.782, No.96)

§ 2710. Joint Construction, Acquisition or Maintenance.—Any township may join with one or more municipal corporations in the construction or acquisition and maintenance of a water system.

(2710 amended Oct. 29, 2020, P.L.782, No.96)

§ 2711. Permits.—The construction of a water system shall be commenced only after plans for the water system have been filed with the Department of Environmental Protection and, if required by law, other Federal or State entities and permits issued in accordance with law.

(2711 amended Oct. 29, 2020, P.L.782, No.96)

§ 2712. Joint Commission.—(a) The municipal corporations joining in the construction or acquisition and maintenance of a water system may, by ordinance, provide for the appointment of a joint commission of a water system in order to facilitate the construction, operation and maintenance of the water system and to secure preliminary surveys and estimates.

(b) The joint commission shall act generally as the advisory and administrative agency in the construction of the improvement and its subsequent operation and maintenance.

(c) The joint commission shall be composed of one representative, or alternatively an equal number of representatives, from each of the joining municipal corporations. The members of the joint commission shall serve for terms of six years each from the dates of their respective appointments and until their successors are appointed.

(d) The joint commission shall organize by the election of a chairperson, secretary and treasurer. The secretary and treasurer may be the same person.

(e) The municipal corporations may, in the ordinances creating the joint commission, authorize the joint commission to appoint an engineer, a solicitor and other assistants as are deemed necessary, and agree to share the compensation costs for members who attend its meetings as shall be fixed in the budget prepared by the joint commission and submitted to and adopted by the joining municipal corporations. In addition to the agreed upon compensation that a member receives for each attendance at a meeting, members shall be entitled to actual expenses to be paid by the respective municipal corporations that the members represent.

(2712 amended Oct. 29, 2020, P.L.782, No.96)

ARTICLE XXVII-A

MANUFACTURE AND SALE OF ELECTRICITY

53 P.S. §§ 57751–57756

(Art. added Feb. 20, 1982, P.L.90, No.33)

§ 2701-A. Manufacture and Sale of Electricity.—Any township may manufacture electricity by means of a hydroelectric generating facility owned or operated by the township for the use of the inhabitants of the township. Any township owning or operating a hydroelectric generating facility may make contracts for the sale of electricity to persons engaged in the business of the manufacture or sale of electricity.

(2701-A amended Oct. 29, 2020, P.L.782, No.96)

§ 2702-A. Regulation of Use and Prices.—Any township furnishing electricity pursuant to this article may regulate the use of electricity in dwellings, business places and other places in the township and the rate to be charged for the electricity.

(2702-A amended Oct. 29, 2020, P.L.782, No.96)

§ 2703-A. Sale of Hydroelectric Generating Facilities.—A township may sell, by ordinance, all or part of its hydroelectric generating facilities to a purchaser for the sale price as the parties may agree upon.

(2703-A amended Oct. 29, 2020, P.L.782, No.96)

§ 2704-A. Construction or Purchase of Hydroelectric Generating Facilities.—Any township may construct or purchase facilities to manufacture electricity by hydroelectric generation. Any township may purchase a hydroelectric generating facility at the price agreed upon by the township and the person, partnership or a majority of the stockholders of a corporation that owns the facilities.

(2704-A amended Oct. 29, 2020, P.L.782, No.96)

§ 2705-A. Submission to Electors.—Before any township constructs or purchases a hydroelectric generating facility, the question of the increase of the debt of the township shall first be submitted to the qualified voters of the township in the manner provided by law for the increase of indebtedness of municipal corporations.

(2705-A amended Oct. 29, 2020, P.L.782, No.96)

§ 2706-A. Limitation on Indebtedness.—No township which constructs or purchases a hydroelectric generating facility shall incur any indebtedness for the construction or enlargement of a new or existing dam or impoundment structure but may incur indebtedness for repairs or reconstruction of an existing dam or impoundment in connection with the hydroelectric project.

(2706-A added Feb. 20, 1982, P.L.90, No.33)

ARTICLE XXVIII
PUBLIC BUILDINGS

53 P.S. §§ 57801–57806

§ 2801. Township Buildings.—The board of commissioners may procure by purchase, gift, exchange or the exercise of eminent domain a lot or lots of ground located within the township, and erect or use buildings thereon for township purposes.

(2801 amended Oct. 29, 2020, P.L.782, No.96)

§ 2802. Garages and Warehouses.—The board of commissioners may purchase or lease land inside or outside the limits of the township, and erect garages, warehouses or other buildings as may be necessary for handling and storing equipment, materials and supplies.

(2802 amended Oct. 29, 2020, P.L.782, No.96)

§ 2803. Appropriation of Property.—(a) Townships may enter upon and appropriate private property and also land previously granted or dedicated to public or other use within the limits of the township, and which is no longer used for the purpose for which the same was granted or dedicated, for the erection thereon of a municipal building, fire house, lockup, and other public buildings as are necessary for public purposes.

(b) Notwithstanding subsection (a), no land or property used for any cemetery, burying ground, public or parochial school, educational or charitable institution, seminary, or place of public worship shall be taken or appropriated.

(2803 amended Oct. 29, 2020, P.L.782, No.96)

§ 2804. Ordinance of Commissioners.—Whenever the board of commissioners desires to acquire, enter upon, take, use, and appropriate private property or lands for public buildings, they shall declare their intention by ordinance.

(2804 amended Oct. 29, 2020, P.L.782, No.96)

§ 2805. Assessment of Damages.—The compensation and damages arising from taking, using and appropriating of private or public property for township purposes shall be pursuant to 26 Pa.C.S. (relating to eminent domain).

(2805 amended Oct. 29, 2020, P.L.782, No.96)

§ 2806. Use of Public Lands Acquired for other Purposes.—Whenever the board of commissioners desires to take any public lands previously granted or dedicated to a use or purpose for which they are no longer used, the board of commissioners shall pass an ordinance declaring its intention, and shall petition the court of common pleas for leave to file the bond of the township to secure any person or persons who may be entitled to compensation for the taking. The court shall direct notice to be given by publication in at least one newspaper of general circulation pursuant to section 110. If no exceptions are filed to the bond on or before the day fixed in the notice, the court shall approve the same. The court may increase the amount of the bond, shall hear and determine all exceptions that are filed against the petition and the sufficiency of the bond and may grant or deny the request of the petition. Upon the granting of the petition and the approval of the bond, the board of commissioners may enter upon and take the lands for the purposes of erecting public buildings. The bond, which shall be in the name of the Commonwealth for the use of any person or persons who are entitled to damages by reason of the taking of the lands, shall remain on file for their use and benefit.

(2806 amended Oct. 29, 2020, P.L.782, No.96)

ARTICLE XXIX
LICENSES AND LICENSE FEES
53 P.S. §§ 57901–57912

(a) Transient Retail Merchants

§ 2901. Licensing Transient Retail Business.—(a) A township may, by ordinance, regulate and license transient retail merchants engaged in any transient retail business within the township. The ordinance may prohibit the commencement or doing of any transient retail business until or unless the license required by the ordinance has been obtained from the township by the person, firm or corporation desiring to commence the transient retail business. The ordinance may be enforced by penalties, not exceeding three hundred dollars, for a violation of its provisions and may provide for other means of enforcement.

(b) The board of commissioners may establish license fees for businesses regulated under this section. The license fees shall bear a reasonable relationship to the cost of administering the ordinance and regulating, inspecting and supervising each business.

(c) Nothing contained in this section shall be construed to apply to any of the following:

(1) farmers selling their own produce;

(2) any person selling personal property, donated by the owners, if the proceeds of the sale are to be applied to a charitable or philanthropic purpose; or

(3) any manufacturer or producer in the sale of bread and bakery products, meat and meat products, or milk and milk products.

(2901 amended Oct. 29, 2020, P.L.782, No.96)

(b) Restrictions

§ 2910. Persons Taking Orders by Samples.—A township may not impose, levy or collect a license fee or mercantile tax upon a person that takes, by sample, from a dealer or merchant an order for merchandise on behalf of an individual or company that pays a license fee or mercantile tax at the individual's or company's chief place of business. Nothing in this section shall authorize a person to sell by retail to a person other than a dealer or merchant without payment of a license or permit fee.

(2910 amended Oct. 29, 2020, P.L.782, No.96)

§ 2911. Insurance Business.—A township may not impose or collect a license fee upon an insurance company, including an agent, or an insurance broker, authorized to transact business under the act of May 17, 1921 (P.L.682, No.284), known as "The Insurance Company Law of 1921."

(2911 amended Oct. 29, 2020, P.L.782, No.96)

§ 2912. License Fees on Residents not to Exceed those on Nonresidents.—A township may not enact an ordinance imposing a license fee upon a manufacturer, including an agent, representative, or employe of any manufacturer, who is a resident of the Commonwealth and solicits orders for or sells personal property manufactured within this Commonwealth if the township could not legally impose the same license fee upon a manufacturer, including an agent, representative or employee, that is a nonresident of the Commonwealth and solicits orders for or sells personal property manufactured outside this Commonwealth.

(2912 amended Oct. 29, 2020, P.L.782, No.96)

ARTICLE XXX
PARKS, RECREATION CENTERS, SHADE TREES AND FORESTS

53 P.S. §§ 58001–58048

(a) Public Parks, Playgrounds, and Recreation Centers

§ 3001. Acquisition of Lands and Buildings.—(a) Townships may, separately or jointly, by ordinance dedicate and set apart lands not dedicated to other public uses or purposes, and may enter upon, appropriate, and acquire by gift, devise, purchase, lease or otherwise, private property for the purpose of making, enlarging, and maintaining public parks, recreation areas and facilities.

(b) Townships may construct and equip new facilities upon such lands and may levy and collect general taxes, or special taxes pursuant to section 1709(a)(9), as necessary to pay for the same and may make appropriations for the construction, improvement, maintenance, care, regulation and government of the same.

(c) No township, acting individually or jointly, may acquire private property within the limits of another municipal corporation for the purposes designated in this section without the consent of the governing body of the municipal corporation in which the property is located.

(3001 amended Oct. 29, 2020, P.L.782, No.96)

§ 3002. Limitation of Expenditures.—(3002 repealed July 2, 1953, P.L.321, No.69)

§ 3003. Submission of Question to Voters.—(3003 repealed July 2, 1953, P.L.321, No.69)

§ 3004. Notice of Election.—(3004 repealed July 2, 1953, P.L.321, No.69)

§ 3005. Form of Ballot.—(3005 repealed July 2, 1953, P.L.321, No.69)

§ 3006. Result of Election; Resubmission of Question Limited.—(3006 repealed July 2, 1953, P.L.321, No.69)

§ 3007. Liability of Township for Property Taken.—(3007 repealed July 2, 1953, P.L.321, No.69)

§ 3008. Appointment of Viewers.—(3008 repealed July 2, 1953, P.L.321, No.69)

§ 3009. Creation of Recreation Board.—(a) Townships may improve, maintain, and regulate public parks, recreation areas, and facilities and conduct recreation programs.

(b) The authority to supervise, maintain and regulate parks, recreation areas and facilities may be vested in any existing body or board or in a park board or recreation board, as the board of commissioners may determine. The board of commissioners may equip, operate and maintain the parks, recreation areas and facilities as authorized by this act and shall, for the purpose of carrying out the provisions of this act, employ any officers or employees as they deem proper.

(c) If the board of commissioners determines that the power to equip, operate and maintain parks, recreation areas and facilities shall be exercised by a recreation board, the board of commissioners may, by ordinance, establish in the township a recreation board which shall possess those powers and duties as may be delegated to it by ordinance.

(3009 amended Oct. 29, 2020, P.L.782, No.96)

§ 3010. Composition of Park or Recreation Boards.—(a) Park or recreation boards, when established, shall consist of five or seven persons who are residents of or property owners in the township and shall be appointed by the board of commissioners.

(b) The members of the park or recreation board shall serve for terms of five years or until their successors are appointed, except that the members of the board first appointed shall be appointed for staggered terms so that the terms of no more than two members shall expire annually thereafter.

(c) Members of the board shall serve without pay.

(d) All persons appointed to the board shall serve their full terms unless they shall voluntarily resign or be removed by the board of commissioners for malfeasance or nonfeasance of duty. Vacancies in the board, occurring other than by expiration of term, shall be filled for the unexpired term, in the same manner as original appointments.

(3010 amended Oct. 29, 2020, P.L.782, No.96)

§ 3011. Organization of Park or Recreation Boards; Delegated Powers and Duties.—The members of a park board or recreation board established pursuant to this article shall elect their own chairperson and secretary and select all other necessary officers to serve for a period of one year. The park or recreation board may, if delegated, select, employ or discharge persons as may be needed as authorized by this article. The board shall have power to adopt rules and regulations for the conduct of all business within its jurisdiction unless otherwise provided by the ordinance establishing the board. The board shall submit an annual report to the board of commissioners, including an analysis of the community recreation areas, facilities and leadership, with particular reference to the extent and adequacy of the program and its effectiveness in view of the public expenditure involved and the public needs to be met.

(3011 amended Oct. 29, 2020, P.L.782, No.96)

§ 3012. Maintenance and Tax Levy.—(a) All expenses incurred in the maintenance and operation of parks, recreation areas and facilities established under this article shall be payable from the treasury of the township or from the treasury of the applicable political subdivisions pursuant to an intergovernmental cooperation agreement.

(b) The board of commissioners may annually appropriate and raise by general or special taxation an amount necessary for the purpose of maintaining and operating the parks, recreation areas and facilities and programs.

(3012 amended Oct. 29, 2020, P.L.782, No.96)

§ 3013. Joint Ownership and Maintenance.—(a) Any township may join or create, with one or more municipalities, a joint recreation board in accordance with 53 Pa.C.S. Ch. 23 Subch. A (relating to intergovernmental cooperation). The joint recreation board may acquire property for and operate and maintain any parks, public recreation areas and facilities. Any school district may join with the township in equipping, operating and maintaining parks, public recreation areas and facilities and may appropriate money therefor.

(b) All the costs and expenses of the joint recreation board, including those relative to property jointly acquired, shall be paid for by the respective municipalities as specified in the intergovernmental cooperation agreement.

(3013 amended Oct. 29, 2020, P.L.782, No.96)

§ 3014. Issue of Bonds.—The township may incur indebtedness and may issue general obligation bonds for the purpose of acquiring lands or buildings for parks and recreation areas and the equipment thereof in accordance with 53 Pa.C.S. Pt. VII Subpt. B (relating to indebtedness and borrowing).

(3014 amended Oct. 29, 2020, P.L.782, No.96)

Chap. 39 Res. During Mil. Service
Chap. 38 Intergov. Coop.
Chap. 37 3rd Class City Code
Chap. 36 Bor. Code
Chap. 35 2nd Class Twp. Code
Chap. 34 1st Class Twp. Code
Chap. 33 Home Rule Chart. Opt. Plans Law
Chap. 32 Water Serv. Act
Chap. 31 Munic. Auth. Act

§ 3015. Plan of Parks, Recreation Areas and Facilities.—(3015 repealed July 31, 1968, P.L.805, No.247)

§ 3016. Lands for Planned Parks and Recreation Areas to be Appropriated Within Three Years.—(3016 repealed July 31, 1968, P.L.805, No.247)

(b) Shade Tree Commission

§ 3020. Right of Establishment.—Townships may, by ordinance, establish a shade tree commission. In townships where the township commissioners shall not elect to create by ordinance a shade tree commission, the board of commissioners may exercise all the rights and perform the duties and obligations imposed by this article upon the shade tree commission.

(3020 amended Oct. 29, 2020, P.L.782, No.96)

§ 3021. Appointment; Terms; Vacancies.—(a) A shade tree commission shall be composed of three or five residents of the township who shall be appointed by the board of commissioners and shall serve without compensation.

(b) If a shade tree commission of three members is established by any township, the board of commissioners shall appoint one member for a term of three years, one for a term of four years, and one for a term of five years. If a shade tree commission of five members is established by any township, the board of commissioners shall appoint members to staggered terms so that one term expires every year. On the expiration of the term of any shade tree commissioner, a successor shall be appointed by the board of commissioners to serve for a term of five years.

(c) Vacancies in the office of shade tree commissioner shall be filled by the board of commissioners for the unexpired term.

(3021 amended Oct. 29, 2020, P.L.782, No.96)

§ 3022. Powers may be Vested in Park Commission.—If in any township there exists a commission for the care of public parks, the board of commissioners may, by ordinance, confer on the park commission all the powers and all the duties prescribed by this article for the shade tree commission.

(3022 amended Oct. 29, 2020, P.L.782, No.96)

§ 3023. General Powers of Shade Tree Commission.—Except as provided in section 2070, the shade tree commission shall have exclusive custody and control of the shade trees in the township, and is authorized to plant, remove, maintain and protect shade trees on the public streets and highways in the township.

(3023 amended Oct. 29, 2020, P.L.782, No.96)

§ 3024. Hiring of Employes; Regulations.—The shade tree commission may, with the approval of the board of commissioners, select, employ and discharge and pay persons to perform the duties and directions of the shade tree commission and make, publish and enforce regulations for the care and protection of the shade trees of the township. No regulations shall be in force until approved by the board of commissioners and until published at least once in a newspaper of general circulation in accordance with the provisions of section 110.

(3024 amended Oct. 29, 2020, P.L.782, No.96)

§ 3025. Report of Shade Tree Commission.—The shade tree commission shall annually report in full to the board of commissioners its transactions and expenses for the preceding fiscal year of the township. The park commission may incorporate the transactions and expenses in its regular report to the board of commissioners.

(3025 amended Oct. 29, 2020, P.L.782, No.96)

§ 3026. Notice of Work.—If a shade tree commission proposes to plant, transplant or remove shade trees on any street or highway, notice of the time and place of the meeting at which the work is to be considered shall be given once in one newspaper of general circulation immediately preceding the time of the meeting. The notice shall specify in detail the streets or highways, or portions thereof, upon which trees are proposed to be planted, transplanted or removed.

(3026 amended Oct. 29, 2020, P.L.782, No.96)

§ 3027. Payment by Owners; Assessment.—(a) The cost of planting, transplanting or removing any shade trees in the streets or highways of the township, of the necessary and suitable guards, curbing or grading for protection of the shade trees and of the replacing of any pavement or sidewalk necessarily disturbed in the execution of the work shall be paid by the owner of the real estate abutting the location of the work.

(b) In the event that the township undertakes the work described in this section, costs shall be assessed in accordance with Article XXV-A and if the benefit conferred method of assessment is used, the benefit conferred shall be no greater than actual costs.

(3027 amended Oct. 29, 2020, P.L.782, No.96)

§ 3027.1. Removal of Diseased or Dangerous Trees.—The shade tree commission may, by regulation and upon notice provided by ordinance, require owners of property to cut and remove trees afflicted with any disease which threatens to injure or destroy shade trees in the township. Upon failure of any owner to comply with the notice, the township may cause the work to be done by the township and assess and collect the cost against the owner of the property in accordance with section 3027.

(3027.1 amended Oct. 29, 2020, P.L.782, No.96)

§ 3028. Assessments Liens.—(3028 repealed Oct. 29, 2020, P.L.782, No.96)

§ 3029. Maintenance by Township; Funds For.—(a) The cost and expenses of caring for shade trees after planting, and the expense of publishing the notice required by this article shall be paid by the township.

(b) The shade tree commission shall annually certify the amount needed under this article to the board of commissioners.

(c) Instead of levying the tax authorized under the general tax levying powers of this act, the board of commissioners may provide for the expenses of caring for trees previously planted and publishing the notice, by appropriations equal to the amount certified to be required by the shade tree commission.

(3029 amended Oct. 29, 2020, P.L.782, No.96)

§ 3030. Penalties.—(a) As provided by ordinance of the township, the shade tree commission may assess penalties for the violation of its regulations and this article relating to shade trees. Any penalty assessed shall be a lien upon the real estate of the offender and may be collected as a municipal claim.

(b) All penalties or assessments imposed under this article shall be paid to the township treasurer to be kept in a separate fund and utilized only for the purposes authorized by this article.

(3030 amended Oct. 29, 2020, P.L.782, No.96)

§ 3031. Disposition of Penalties.—(3031 repealed Oct. 29, 2020, P.L.782, No.96)

(c) Forests

Compiler's Note: Section 302(h) of Act 18 of 1995, which created the Department of Conservation and Natural Resources and renamed the Department of Environmental Resources as the Department of Environmental

Table of Contents
Part I Ch. 1–3 Ethics, Records, Open Meetings
Part II Ch. 4–10 Taxation
Part III Ch. 11–18 Torts, Contracts & Civil Rules
Part IV Ch. 19–24 Zoning & Planning
Part V Ch. 25–30 Construction and Emergency Codes
Part VI Ch. 31–39 Municipal Codes
Index

Protection, provided that the Department of Conservation and Natural Resources shall exercise the powers of duties conferred upon the Department of Forests and Waters by subarticle (c).

§ 3040. Right of Acquisition of Forest Lands.—A township may acquire by purchase, gift or lease tracts of land covered with forest or tree growth or suitable for the growth of trees for the benefit of the township, and administer the tracts in accordance with the practices and principles of scientific forestry. The tracts may be of any size suitable for the purpose and may be located within or without the township limits.

(3040 amended Oct. 29, 2020, P.L.782, No.96)

§ 3041. Approval of Department of Forests and Waters.—(3041 repealed Oct. 29, 2020, P.L.782, No.96)

§ 3042. Ordinance and Notice.—If the board of commissioners deems it expedient to acquire land for forests, it shall enact an ordinance setting forth the facts and conditions relating to the proposed action.

(3042 amended Oct. 29, 2020, P.L.782, No.96)

§ 3043. Appropriation for Acquisition.—Money necessary for the purchase of the tracts shall be appropriated in the same manner as appropriations for township purposes. Money may be provided from the current revenue or by the proceeds of a sale of general obligation bonds.

(3043 amended Oct. 29, 2020, P.L.782, No.96)

§ 3044. Regulations.—Upon the acquisition of any forests or lands suitable for forests, the board of commissioners may promulgate regulations governing the proper administration of the acquired forestry as necessary to produce continuing township revenue by the sale of forest products. The regulations may provide for the administration, maintenance, protection and development of the forests or lands suitable for forests as necessary or expedient.

(3044 amended Oct. 29, 2020, P.L.782, No.96)

§ 3045. Appropriation for Maintenance; Revenue.—Money necessary for the administration, maintenance, protection and development of forests shall be appropriated and applied for township purposes. The revenue and the return on the revenue arising from the forests shall be paid into the township treasury to be used for general township purposes.

(3045 amended Oct. 29, 2020, P.L.782, No.96)

§ 3046. Use of Township Forests.—Township forests may be used by the public as general outing or recreation grounds subject to the regulations under section 3044.

(3046 amended Oct. 29, 2020, P.L.782, No.96)

§ 3047. Ordinance of Sale.—(a) If the board of commissioners deem it expedient to sell or lease a township forest, a part of a township forest or a product from a township forest, the board shall enact an ordinance setting forth the facts and conditions relating to the proposed action.

(b) To enact an ordinance under this section, the board shall comply with the advertising and bidding requirements of section 1501.1.

(3047 amended Oct. 29, 2020, P.L.782, No.96)

§ 3048. Appropriation of Money to Forestry Organizations.—The board of commissioners may appropriate money from the township treasury to a forest protection association cooperating in forest work with the Department of Conservation and Natural Resources or to be expended in direct cooperation with the Department of Conservation and Natural Resources in forest work.

(3048 amended Oct. 29, 2020, P.L.782, No.96)

ARTICLE XXX-A
LAND SUBDIVISION

53 P.S. §§ 58601–58068

(Art. hdg. repealed Oct. 29, 2020, P.L.782, No.96)

§ 3061. Grant of Power.—(3061 repealed July 31, 1968, P.L.805, No.247)

§ 3062. Public Hearing.—(3062 repealed July 31, 1968, P.L.805, No.247)

§ 3063. Subdivision Control.—(3063 repealed July 31, 1968, P.L.805, No.247)

§ 3064. Definition of Subdivision.—(3064 repealed July 31, 1968, P.L.805, No.247)

§ 3065. Subdivisions Wherein Lots Abut Existing Improved Streets or Highways of Sufficient Width.—(3065 repealed July 31, 1968, P.L.805, No.247)

§ 3066. Subdivisions Wherein Lots Abut Existing Streets or Highways of Insufficient Width or Proposed Streets.—(3066 repealed July 31, 1968, P.L.805, No.247)

§ 3067. Sale of Lots; Issuance of Building Permit or Erection of Building.—(3067 repealed July 31, 1968, P.L.805, No.247)

§ 3068. Penalty.—(3068 repealed July 31, 1968, P.L.805, No.247)

ARTICLE XXXI
ZONING

53 P.S. §§ 58101–58111

(Art. hdg. repealed Oct. 29, 2020, P.L.782, No.96)

§ 3101. Grant of Power.—(3101 repealed July 31, 1968, P.L.805, No.247)

§ 3102. Districts.—(3102 repealed July 31, 1968, P.L.805, No.247)

§ 3103. Purpose in View.—(3103 repealed July 31, 1968, P.L.805, No.247)

§ 3104. Methods of Procedure.—(3104 repealed July 31, 1968, P.L.805, No.247)

§ 3105. Changes.—(3105 repealed July 31, 1968, P.L.805, No.247)

§ 3106. Zoning Commission.—(3106 repealed July 31, 1968, P.L.805, No.247)

§ 3107. Board of Adjustment.—(3107 repealed July 31, 1968, P.L.805, No.247)

§ 3107.1. Salary of Members of Board of Adjustment.—(3107.1 repealed July 31, 1968, P.L.805, No.247)

§ 3107.2. Counsel for Board of Adjustment.—(3107.2 repealed July 31, 1968, P.L.805, No.247)

§ 3108. Remedies.—(3108 repealed July 31, 1968, P.L.805, No.247)

§ 3109. Conflict with Other Laws.—(3109 repealed July 31, 1968, P.L.805, No.247)

§ 3110. Act not to Apply to Certain Buildings of Public Service Corporations.—(3110 repealed July 31, 1968, P.L.805, No.247)

§ 3111. Finances.—(3111 repealed July 31, 1968, P.L.805, No.247)

ARTICLE XXXI-A
UNIFORM CONSTRUCTION CODE, PROPERTY MAINTENANCE CODE AND RESERVED POWERS

53 P.S. §§ 58101-A–58106-A

(Art. XXXI-A added Oct. 30, 2015, P.L.207, No.51)

Compiler's Note: Section 3 of Act 51 of 2015, which added Article XXXI-A, provided that nothing in Act 51 shall be construed to repeal or modify any township ordinance in effect on the effective date of Act 51 or affect any proceeding or enforcement of any township ordinance instituted prior to the effective date of Act 51.

§ 3101-A. Definitions.

The following words and phrases when used in this article shall have the meanings given to them in this section unless the context clearly indicates otherwise:

"Pennsylvania Construction Code Act." The act of November 10, 1999 (P.L.491, No.45), known as the Pennsylvania Construction Code Act.

"Uniform Construction Code." The Uniform Construction Code adopted under section 301 of the Pennsylvania Construction Code Act.

(3101-A added Oct. 30, 2015, P.L.207, No.51)

§ 3102-A. Primacy of Uniform Construction Code.

(a) General rule.—The Pennsylvania Construction Code Act and the Uniform Construction Code shall apply to the construction, alteration, repair and occupancy of the buildings and structures within a township.

(b) Primacy.—This section and an ordinance, rule or regulation adopted under this section shall not supersede or abrogate the Pennsylvania Construction Code Act or the Uniform Construction Code and shall be construed and read in pari materia with both.

(3102-A added Oct. 30, 2015, P.L.207, No.51)

§ 3103-A. Changes in Uniform Construction Code.

The board of commissioners may propose and enact an ordinance to equal or exceed the minimum requirements of the Uniform Construction Code in accordance with and subject to the requirements of section 503 of the Pennsylvania Construction Code Act. An ordinance exceeding the provisions of the Uniform Construction Code shall be required to meet the standards provided in section 503(j)(2) of the Pennsylvania Construction Code Act.

(3103-A amended Oct. 29, 2020, P.L.782, No.96)

§ 3104-A. Public nuisance.

A building, housing or property, or part of a building, housing or property erected, altered, extended, reconstructed, removed or maintained, contrary to the provisions of an ordinance passed for a purpose specified in this article may be declared, by a court of law, a public nuisance, and may be abatable as such. However, a violation of the Uniform Construction Code or an ordinance that equals or exceeds the Uniform Construction Code shall be subject to the provisions of the Pennsylvania Construction Code Act and the regulations adopted thereunder by the Department of Labor and Industry relating to enforcement for noncompliance.

(3104-A added Oct. 30, 2015, P.L.207, No.51)

§ 3105-A. Property maintenance code.

(a) Property maintenance code.—Notwithstanding the primacy of the Uniform Construction Code, the board of commissioners may enact a property maintenance ordinance, and they may incorporate a standard or nationally recognized property maintenance code, or a variation or change or part of the code, published and printed in book form, without incorporating the text of the code in the ordinance, or the board of commissioners may enact a standard or nationally recognized property maintenance code or a change or variation or part, as the ordinance. In either event, the ordinance, or a change or variation or part, need not be advertised after passage, but notice of its consideration, in reasonable detail, shall be published as will give adequate notice of its contents and a reference to the place or places within the township where copies of the proposed property maintenance code may be examined or obtained. The notice required by this subsection shall be published once in one newspaper of general circulation at least one week and not more than three weeks prior to the presentation of the proposed property maintenance code to the board of commissioners. No fewer than three copies of the ordinance adopted by the board of commissioners shall be made available for public inspection and use during business hours or be made available to an interested party at the cost of the copies or may be furnished or lent without charge. A property maintenance code adopted by reference need not be recorded in or attached to the ordinance book but shall be deemed to have been legally recorded if the ordinance by which the code was adopted by reference shall have been recorded, with an accompanying notation stating where the full text of the code shall have been filed. The ordinance may provide for reasonable property fines and penalties for violations of the ordinance. The procedure under this section relating to the adoption of the ordinance may likewise be utilized in amending, supplementing or repealing a provision of the ordinance.

(b) Property maintenance inspectors.—The board of commissioners may appoint property maintenance inspectors who shall have the right to enter upon and inspect any premises, subject to constitutional standards, at reasonable hours and in a reasonable manner for the administration and enforcement of the township's property maintenance code or ordinance incorporating a standard or nationally recognized property maintenance code. A fee payable to property maintenance inspectors under the ordinance shall be promptly paid by them to the township treasurer for the use of the township.

(c) Legal actions.—In addition to the penalties provided by the property maintenance ordinance, the township may institute appropriate actions or proceedings at law or in equity to prevent or restrain property maintenance violations.

(d) Construction.—The powers of a township as provided in this section shall be in addition to, but not limited to, the powers provided in the act of November 26, 2008 (P.L.1672, No.135), known as the Abandoned and Blighted Property Conservatorship Act, 53 Pa.C.S. Ch. 61 (relating to neighborhood blight reclamation and revitalization) and 68 Pa.C.S. Ch. 21 (relating to land banks).

(3105-A amended Oct. 29, 2020, P.L.782, No.96)

§ 3106-A. Reserved powers.

If, as a result of legislative action or final order of court for which the time for appeal has expired and no appeal has been taken or from which there is no pending appeal, the Uniform Construction Code or a replacement code is no longer applicable in townships, the board of commissioners may:

(1) Enact and enforce ordinances to govern and regulate the construction, reconstruction, alteration, extension, repair, conversion, maintenance, occupation, sanitation, ventilation, heating, egress, lighting, electrical wiring, wa-

Table of Contents
Part I Ch. 1–3 Ethics, Records, Open Meetings
Part II Ch. 4–10 Taxation
Part III Ch. 11–18 Torts, Contracts & Civil Rules
Part IV Ch. 19–24 Zoning & Planning
Part V Ch. 25–30 Construction and Emergency Codes
Part VI Ch. 31–39 Municipal Codes
Index

Chap. 39 Res. During Mil. Service
Chap. 38 Intergov. Coop.
Chap. 37 3rd Class City Code
Chap. 36 Bor. Code
Chap. 35 2nd Class Twp. Code
Chap. 34 1st Class Twp. Code
Chap. 33 Home Rule Chart. Opt. Plans Law
Chap. 32 Water Serv. Act
Chap. 31 Munic. Auth. Act

ter supply, toilet facilities, drainage, plumbing, fire prevention, fireproofing, including prescribing limitations wherein only buildings of noncombustible material and fireproofed roofs are used in construction, erection or substantial reconstruction, use and inspection of all buildings and housing or parts of buildings and housing and the roofs, walls and foundations of buildings and housing, and all facilities and services in or about the buildings or housing constructed, erected, altered, designed or used, in whole or in part, for use or occupancy, and the sanitation and inspection of land appurtenant to the buildings or housing. The codes may be combined or separately enacted or combined with the property maintenance code. The board of commissioners may adopt, amend or incorporate by reference a standard or nationally recognized code or a variation or change or part of the code as its ordinance in the manner provided in section 3105-A. The ordinance may provide for reasonable fines and penalties for violations of the ordinance.

(2) Require that, before work of construction, reconstruction, alteration, extension, repair or conversion of a building has begun, approval of the plans and specifications be secured.

(3) Appoint building inspectors, housing inspectors, property maintenance inspectors, fire prevention inspectors, electrical inspectors and plumbing inspectors and fix their compensation. The inspectors shall have the right to enter upon, subject to constitutional standards, and inspect a premises at reasonable hours and in a reasonable manner, for the administration and enforcement of the township's adopted codes or ordinances incorporating standard or nationally recognized codes. A fee payable to inspectors under the ordinances shall be paid by them to the township treasurer for the use of the township as promptly as may be.

(4) In addition to the penalties provided by ordinances, institute appropriate actions or proceedings at law or in equity to prevent or restrain the unlawful construction, reconstruction, alteration, extension, repair, conversion, maintenance, use or occupation of property located within the township, to restrain, correct or abate the violation and to prevent the use or occupancy of the building, housing or structure.

(3106-A amended Oct. 29, 2020, P.L.782, No.96)

ARTICLE XXXII
TOWNSHIP PLANNING COMMISSION

53 P.S. §§ 58201–58203

(Art. hdg. repealed Oct. 29, 2020, P.L.782, No.96)

§ 3201. Power to Create Planning Commission; Residence of Commissioners; Employes; Rules and Regulations.—(3201 repealed July 31, 1968, P.L.805, No.247)

§ 3202. Maps and Plans; Recommendations of Planning Commission.—(3202 repealed July 31, 1968, P.L.805, No.247)

§ 3203. Reference of Proposals to Planning Commission.—(3203 repealed July 31, 1968, P.L.805, No.247)

ARTICLE XXXIII
ENFORCEMENT OF ORDINANCES

53 P.S. §§ 58301–58305

(Art. repealed Oct. 29, 2020, P.L.782, No.96)

§ 3301. Proceedings for Violation of Township Ordinances.—(3301 repealed Oct. 29, 2020, P.L.782, No.96)

Compiler's Note: Section 28 of Act 207 of 2004 provided that any and all references in any other law to a "district justice" or "justice of the peace" shall be deemed to be references to a magisterial district judge.

§ 3302. Arrests on View; Complaints.—(3302 repealed Oct. 29, 2020, P.L.782, No.96)

§ 3303. Disposition of Fines and Penalties.—(3303 repealed Apr. 28, 1978, P.L.202, No.53)

§ 3304. Incarceration of Violators of Township Ordinances; Collection of Fines and Penalties.—(3304 repealed Oct. 29, 2020, P.L.782, No.96)

§ 3305. Township's Liability for Costs of Prisoners to County.—(3305 repealed Oct. 29, 2020, P.L.782, No.96)

ARTICLE XXXIII-A

ORDINANCES

53 P.S. §§ 58301-A–58323-A

(Art. added Oct. 29, 2020, P.L.782, No.96)

(a) General Provisions

(Subart. added Oct. 29, 2020, P.L.782, No.96)

§ 3301-A. Ordinances and resolutions.

(a) General rule.—The board of commissioners shall enact ordinances in accordance with this article and the laws of this Commonwealth in which the powers of the township shall be exercised as deemed beneficial to the township and to provide for the enforcement of the powers of the township. The board of commissioners may amend, repeal or revise existing ordinances by the enactment of subsequent ordinances.

(b) Ordinances.—Every legislative act of the board of commissioners shall be by ordinance. Legislative acts shall include, but not be limited to:

(1) Legislation doing any of the following:

(i) Exercising the police power of the township.

(ii) Regulating land use, development and subdivision.

(iii) Imposing building, plumbing, electrical, property maintenance, housing and similar standards.

(iv) Regulating the conduct of a person or entity within the township and imposing penalties for violation of the regulated conduct.

(2) Imposing assessments on benefited property for public improvements in accordance with Article XXV-A.

(3) Increasing the rate of taxation from the previous fiscal year.

(c) Resolutions.—The board of commissioners shall adopt resolutions in accordance with this article and the laws of this Commonwealth. Resolutions may be adopted for any purpose, including, but not limited to, the following:

(1) Ceremonial or congratulatory expressions of the good will of the board of commissioners.

(2) Statements of public policy of the board of commissioners.

(3) Approval of formal agreements of the township, except for agreements arising under an established purchasing system of the township.

(4) Approval, if required, of administrative rules, regulations and bylaws arising under State statutes or township ordinances.

Table of Contents
Part I Ch. 1–3 Ethics, Records, Open Meetings
Part II Ch. 4–10 Taxation
Part III Ch. 11–18 Torts, Contracts & Civil Rules
Part IV Ch. 19–24 Zoning & Planning
Part V Ch. 25–30 Construction and Emergency Codes
Part VI Ch. 31–39 Municipal Codes
Index

(5) Levying taxes at the same rate as or a rate lower than the previous fiscal year.

(3301-A added Oct. 29, 2020, P.L.782, No.96)

§ 3302-A. Publication.

(a) **Requirements.**—Except as provided under this article or other law, the board of commissioners shall publish every proposed ordinance once in one newspaper of general circulation at least seven days and not more than 60 days prior to enactment. Publication of any proposed ordinance shall include all of the following:

(1) The full text or the subject matter and a brief summary prepared by the township solicitor setting forth all the provisions in reasonable detail.

(2) A reference to the township office or other place where township records are kept where copies of the proposed ordinance may be examined.

(b) **Summary.**—If the full text is not included in the publication of the proposed ordinance, the following shall apply:

(1) The newspaper in which the proposed ordinance is published shall, upon request, be furnished a copy of the full text without charge.

(2) The following shall apply:

(i) In addition to copies of the full text of the proposed ordinance retained where township records are kept in accordance with subsection (a), an attested copy of the full text shall be filed within 30 days after enactment in the county law library or other county office designated by the county commissioners.

(ii) The county commissioners may impose a fee not greater than the actual costs of storing the proposed ordinance.

(iii) Filing with the county may be completed by the submission of an electronic copy of the ordinance through a method available, in the sole discretion of the county, to permit receipt by the office storing municipal ordinances. No fee pursuant to clause (ii) shall be imposed for storing an electronic copy of an ordinance.

(iv) Upon request by the township, the county shall notify the township of the method by which electronic copies may be submitted.

(v) The county may store the ordinance electronically if the public is able to access the electronically stored township ordinances during regular business hours at the office or at a remote location.

(vi) The township shall retain a printed copy of the email and ordinance as transmitted.

(3) The date of the filing with the county under paragraph (2) shall not affect the effective date of the ordinance and shall not be deemed a defect in the process of the enactment of the ordinance.

(c) **Notice of amendments.**—If substantial amendments are made in the proposed ordinance, before voting upon enactment, the board of commissioners shall within at least ten days before enactment readvertise in one newspaper of general circulation the subject matter and a brief summary setting forth all the provisions in reasonable detail together with a summary of the amendments. A copy of the full text of the amended proposed ordinance shall be retained where township records are kept.

(d) **Maps.**—When maps, plans or drawings of any kind are adopted as part of an ordinance, instead of publishing them as part of the proposed ordinance, the board of commissioners may refer in publishing the proposed ordinance to the place where the maps, plans or drawings are on file and may be examined.

(3302-A added Oct. 29, 2020, P.L.782, No.96)

§ 3303-A. Recording and proof.

(a) Recording.—All township ordinances and all township resolutions pertaining to tax levies shall, within thirty days after enactment, be recorded by the township secretary in an ordinance book. A failure to record within the time provided shall not be deemed a defect in the process of enactment of the ordinance or resolution pertaining to a tax levy. The ordinance book shall be open to the inspection of citizens during normal business hours.

(b) Proof.—All ordinances may be proved by the certificate of the township secretary under the corporate seal. If an ordinance is printed or published in book or pamphlet form by the authority of the township, the ordinance shall be accepted as evidence without further proof. The entry of the township ordinance in the ordinance book shall be sufficient without the signature of the president of the board of commissioners or other person.

(c) Prior ordinances.—The text of a township ordinance or a portion of an ordinance which was attached to the ordinance book before July 31, 1963, shall be considered in force as if the ordinances or portions of ordinances had been recorded directly upon the pages of the ordinance book if all other requirements of this act applicable to the enactment, approval, advertising and recording of the ordinances or portions of ordinances were complied with within the time limits prescribed under this act.

(3303-A added Oct. 29, 2020, P.L.782, No.96)

§ 3304-A. Codification of ordinances.

(a) Consolidation, codification and revision.—The board of commissioners may prepare or have prepared a consolidation, codification or revision of the general body of township ordinances or the ordinances on a particular subject. The board of commissioners may enact the consolidation, codification or revision as an ordinance of the township except the required advertised notice of the proposed enactment of the consolidation, codification or revision shall specify its general nature and shall include a listing of its table of contents. The procedure for the consolidation, codification or revision of township ordinances as a single ordinance may also be followed in enacting a complete group or body of ordinances, repealing or amending existing ordinances as may be necessary, in the course of preparing a consolidation, codification or revision of the township ordinances, except that the advertisement giving notice of the proposed enactment shall list, in lieu of a table of contents, the titles only of each of the ordinances in the complete group or body of ordinances.

(b) Enactment.—For a consolidation, codification or revision under subsection (a), the ordinance shall be introduced by the board of commissioners at least 30 days before its final enactment and, at least 15 days before final enactment, notice of the introduction of the ordinance shall be given by advertisement in a newspaper of general circulation.

(c) Subsequent notice.—When any consolidation, codification or revision under subsection (a) has been enacted as an ordinance, it shall not be necessary to advertise the entire text, but it shall be sufficient to publish a notice stating that the consolidation, codification or revision, which had previously been given, was finally enacted.

(3304-A added Oct. 29, 2020, P.L.782, No.96)

§ 3305-A. Appeals from ordinances.

Complaint as to the legality of any ordinance or resolution shall be made to the court of common pleas pursuant to 42 Pa.C.S. § 5571.1 (relating to appeals from ordinances, resolutions, maps, etc.). In cases of ordinances laying out streets over private lands, the court shall have jurisdiction to review the propriety as well as the legality of the ordinance.

(3305-A added Oct. 29, 2020, P.L.782, No.96)

Chap. 39 Res. During Mil. Service
Chap. 38 Intergov. Coop.
Chap. 37 3rd Class City Code
Chap. 36 Bor. Code
Chap. 35 2nd Class Twp. Code
Chap. 34 1st Class Twp. Code
Chap. 33 Home Rule Chart. Opt. Plans Law
Chap. 32 Water Serv. Act
Chap. 31 Munic. Auth. Act

§ 3306-A. Standard or nationally recognized codes.

(a) **Authority to enact.**—In the same manner as other ordinances, and except as otherwise provided in this article or the act of November 10, 1999 (P.L.491, No.45), known as the Pennsylvania Construction Code Act, the board of commissioners may enact, by reference to a standard or nationally recognized code, all or a portion of the standard or nationally recognized code as an ordinance of the township. No portion of any code which limits the work to be performed to any type of construction contractor or labor or mechanic classification shall be enacted. Three copies of the proposed standard or nationally recognized code, portion of the code or amendment to the code shall be filed with the secretary of the township at least 10 days before the board of commissioners considers the proposed ordinance. Upon enactment, a copy shall be kept with the ordinance book and available for public use, inspection, examination and copying.

(b) **Time frame.**—

(1) Except as otherwise provided by the Pennsylvania Construction Code Act and regulations adopted pursuant to the act, an ordinance adopting, by reference, a standard or nationally recognized code shall be enacted within 60 days after it is filed with the secretary of the township and shall encompass the provisions of the code effective as of the code date stated in the ordinance.

(2) A township that has adopted any standard or nationally recognized code by reference may adopt subsequent ordinances which incorporate by reference any subsequent changes thereof, properly identified as to date and source, as may be adopted by the agency or association which promulgated the code.

(3) An ordinance which incorporates standard or nationally recognized code amendments by reference shall become effective after the same procedure and in the same manner as is specified in this section for original adoption of the code.

(c) **Technical regulations or code.**—An ordinance that incorporates, by reference, standard technical regulations or code shall be subject to the provisions of the Pennsylvania Construction Code Act, if applicable.

(3306-A added Oct. 29, 2020, P.L.782, No.96)

(b) Enforcement
(Subart. added Oct. 29, 2020, P.L.782, No.96)

§ 3321-A. Fines and penalties.

(a) **Prescription.**—

(1) A township ordinance shall prescribe fines and penalties for violation.

(i) A civil penalty may not exceed $600 per violation.

(ii) The board of commissioners may prescribe a criminal fine not to exceed $1,000 per violation and may prescribe imprisonment to the extent allowed by law for the punishment of a summary offense.

(2) An ordinance under this subsection may provide that a separate violation under paragraph (1)(i) or (ii) shall arise for:

(i) each day of violation; and

(ii) each applicable section of the ordinance.

(3) An ordinance may provide for assessment of court costs and reasonable attorney fees incurred by the township in the enforcement proceedings.

(4) The board of commissioners may delegate the initial determination of ordinance violation and the service of notice of violation to a qualified officer or agent.

(b) **Enforcement at law.**—Unless otherwise provided by statute, a township ordinance shall set forth the method of its enforcement in accordance with the following:

(1) Except as provided in paragraph (2), if the penalty is not paid, the township shall initiate a civil action for collection in accordance with the Pennsylvania Rules of Civil Procedure. A township shall be exempt from the payment of costs in an action under this paragraph.

(2) For an ordinance regulating building, housing, property maintenance, health, fire, public safety, parking, solicitation, curfew, water or air or noise pollution, enforcement shall be by a criminal action in the same manner provided for the enforcement of summary offenses under the Pennsylvania Rules of Criminal Procedure. The municipal solicitor may assume charge of the prosecution without the consent of the district attorney as required under Pa.R.Crim.P. No. 454 (relating to trial in summary cases). Violations of the property maintenance code or ordinance may also be enforced under section 3105-A(c).

(3) Except for an ordinance subject to paragraph (2), an ordinance enacted prior to the effective date of this section shall be deemed automatically amended so that it shall be enforced under paragraph (1).

(4) If a civil claim under this subsection, exclusive of interest, costs or fees, exceeds the monetary jurisdiction of a magisterial district judge under 42 Pa.C.S. § 1515(a) (relating to jurisdiction and venue), the township may:

(i) bring the action in a court of common pleas; or

(ii) make a waiver under 42 Pa.C.S. § 1515(a)(3).

(c) Enforcement in equity.—In addition to or in lieu of enforcement under subsection (b), a township may enforce an ordinance in equity in a court of common pleas of the county where the township is situate.

(d) Payment.—Money collected under subsection (b) shall be paid to the township treasurer.

(3321-A added Oct. 29, 2020, P.L.782, No.96)

§ 3322-A. Commitment pending trial.

An individual arrested for the violation of a township ordinance may, pending hearing or trial, be committed to the township lockup, or if there is no suitable township lockup, a county correctional facility.

(3322-A added Oct. 29, 2020, P.L.782, No.96)

§ 3323-A. Township's liability for costs of prisoners to county.

If a prisoner is committed to a county correctional facility under section 3322-A, the expenses of maintaining the prisoner during confinement shall be paid by the township and the county shall not be liable for the maintenance.

(3323-A added Oct. 29, 2020, P.L.782, No.96)

ARTICLE XXXIV

ACTIONS BY AND AGAINST TOWNSHIPS

53 P.S. §§ 58401–58406

§ 3401. Commissioners to Bring and Defend Suits.—(3401 repealed Apr. 28, 1978, P.L.202, No.53)

§ 3402. Rights of Taxpayers to Inquire into Judgments.—(3402 repealed Apr. 28, 1978, P.L.202, No.53)

§ 3403. Appeals by Taxpayers.—(3403 repealed Apr. 28, 1978, P.L.202, No.53)

§ 3404. Affidavit and Bail by Taxpayers.—(3404 repealed Apr. 28, 1978, P.L.202, No.53)

§ 3405. Taxpayers Parties to Suits.—(3405 repealed Apr. 28, 1978, P.L.202, No.53)

Chap. 39 Res. During Mil. Service
Chap. 38 Intergov. Coop.
Chap. 37 3rd Class City Code
Chap. 36 Bor. Code
Chap. 35 2nd Class Twp. Code
Chap. 34 1st Class Twp. Code
Chap. 33 Home Rule Chart. Opt. Plans Law
Chap. 32 Water Serv. Act
Chap. 31 Munic. Auth. Act

§ 3406. Collection of Municipal Claims.—(a) In addition to the remedies provided by law for the filing of liens for the collection of municipal claims, including, but not limited to, water rates, sewer rates and the removal of nuisances, townships may proceed for the recovery and collection of municipal claims by action of assumpsit against the person or persons who were the owner or owners of the property at the time of the completion of the improvement or at the time the water or sewer rates or the cost of the removal of nuisances first became payable, notwithstanding the fact that there was a failure on the part of the township or its agents to enter the municipal claim as a lien against the property assessed for the improvement or for the furnishing of water or sewer services and for the removal of nuisances, and for the recovery of which the action of assumpsit was brought.

(b) The action in assumpsit shall be commenced either within six years after the completion of the improvement from which the claim arises or within six years after the applicable rates or the cost of abating a nuisance first became payable.

(3406 amended Oct. 29, 2020, P.L.782, No.96)

ARTICLE XXXV
REPEALS

53 P.S. §§ 58501–58502

§ 3501. Repeals.—(a) Nothing contained in this amendment, revision and reenactment shall be construed to revive any act or part of an act heretofore repealed.

(b) The following additional acts and parts of acts are hereby repealed as respectively indicated:

(1) The act, approved the twenty-second day of June, one thousand nine hundred thirty-one (Pamphlet Laws 844), entitled, as amended, "An act authorizing the Commonwealth of Pennsylvania, or any department or division thereof, and counties, cities, boroughs, incorporated towns, townships, school districts, vocational school districts, and institution districts to make contracts of life, health, hospitalization, medical services, and accident policies for the benefit of employes thereof, and contracts for pensions for such employes; and providing for the payment of the cost thereof," so far as it relates to townships of the first class.

(2) The act, approved the twenty-second day of June, one thousand nine hundred thirty-one (Pamphlet Laws 845), entitled "An act authorizing the publication of advertisements for bids for public works, supplies or equipment in certain publications and journals devoted to information about construction work," so far as it relates to townships of the first class.

(3) The act, approved the first day of May, one thousand nine hundred thirty-five (Pamphlet Laws 124), entitled "An act authorizing the insurance of deposits of funds, of this Commonwealth and of the political subdivisions thereof, with the Federal Deposit Insurance Corporation or other similar agency; and prohibiting requiring further security for amounts so insured," so far as it relates to townships of the first class.

(4) The act, approved the eighteenth day of July, one thousand nine hundred thirty-five (Pamphlet Laws 1173), entitled "An act to prohibit discrimination on account of race, creed or color in employment under contracts for public buildings or public works," so far as it relates to townships of the first class.

(5) The act, approved the sixteenth day of March, one thousand nine hundred thirty-seven (Pamphlet Laws 98), entitled "An act authorizing po-

litical subdivisions to stipulate in specifications, upon which contracts for the construction, alteration or repairs of any public work or improvement are entered into, the minimum wages to be paid to laborers and mechanics, and providing for the stipulation of penalties in such contracts where such minimum wage stipulations are violated, and for the recovery of such penalties, and their return in certain cases," so far as it relates to townships of the first class.

(6) The act, approved the fifth day of June, one thousand nine hundred forty-one (Pamphlet Laws 84), entitled "An act providing for and regulating the appointment, promotion and reduction in rank, suspension and removal of paid members of the police force in boroughs, incorporated towns and townships of the first class maintaining a police force of not less than three members; creating a civil service commission in each borough, incorporated town and township of the first class; defining the duties of such civil service commission; imposing certain duties and expense on boroughs, incorporated towns and townships of the first class; imposing penalties, and repealing inconsistent laws," so far as it relates to townships of the first class.

(7) The act, approved the first day of June, one thousand nine hundred forty-five (Pamphlet Laws 1232), entitled "An act providing for and regulating the appointment, promotion and reduction in rank, suspension and removal of paid operators of fire apparatus in boroughs, incorporated towns and townships of the first class; creating a civil service commission in each borough, incorporated town and township of the first class; defining the duties of such civil service commission; imposing certain duties and expenses on boroughs, incorporated towns and townships of the first class; imposing penalties; and repealing inconsistent laws," so far as it relates to townships of the first class.

(8) The act of April 9, 1931 (P.L.22, No.20), entitled "An act to validate and confirm tax levies made for general township purposes, in excess of ten mills, by boards of township commissioners of townships of the first class, when such excess was for the purpose of the payment of interest on indebtedness and sinking fund charges," absolutely.

(9) The act of July 2, 1937 (P.L.2803, No.588), entitled "An act providing a method of annexation of townships of the first class, and parts thereof, to cities and boroughs, and regulating the proceedings pertaining thereto," absolutely.

(10) The act of July 18, 1935 (P.L.1172, No.381), entitled "An act requiring tax collectors of townships of the first class to secure from banks, banking institutions or trust companies a bond to secure payment of deposits of all township tax money deposited therein by such tax collector, secured by a surety company authorized to transact business within the Commonwealth of Pennsylvania, or a depository agreement secured by the deposit of bonds or interest bearing securities of the United States, the Commonwealth of Pennsylvania, or any city, borough, township or school district in the Commonwealth of Pennsylvania," absolutely.

(c) All other acts and parts of acts inconsistent with, supplied by, or appertaining to the subject matter covered by this act are repealed. It is the intention that this act shall furnish a complete and exclusive system for the government and regulation of townships of the first class, except as to the several matters enumerated in section 103 of this act.

(d) This act shall not repeal or modify any of the provisions of the following:

(1) 66 Pa.C.S. Pt. I (relating to Public Utility Code).

(2) A law, the enforcement of which is vested in the Department of Health.

(3) A law, the enforcement of which is vested in the Department of Environmental Protection.

(4) A law, the enforcement of which is vested in the Department of Conservation and Natural Resources.

(3501 amended Oct. 29, 2020, P.L.782, No.96)

§ 3502. (3502 repealed Oct. 29, 2020, P.L.782, No.96)

Compiler's Note: The act of May 28, 1937 (P.L.1053, No.286), known as the Public Utility Law, was repealed by the act of July 1, 1978 (P.L.598, No.116). The subject matter is now contained in 66 Pa.C.S. (relating to public utilities).

APPENDIX

Supplementary Provisions of Amendatory Statutes

2012, OCTOBER 24, P.L.1478, NO.188

§ 14. Notwithstanding any other provision of law to the contrary, the following shall apply:

(1) The term of the person who holds the office of elected treasurer in a first class township shall end on the first Monday in January immediately following the municipal election of 2013.

(2) After the effective date of this section, if the elected township treasurer is unable to perform the duties of his office and fails or refuses to appoint a deputy, the court of common pleas, on petition of the board of township commissioners, shall appoint a deputy treasurer to serve until the treasurer is again able to perform the duties of his office, or until such deputy is removed by the court, but in no instance shall such deputy serve beyond the term of the treasurer in whose office he is serving as deputy treasurer. The court shall also fix the compensation of such deputy treasurer at a rate not to exceed that paid to the elected township treasurer. For the time such deputy shall serve, such compensation shall be deducted from the compensation otherwise payable to the township treasurer. Such deputy shall furnish bond in the same manner as the bond of the treasurer.

Compiler's Note: Act 188 added, amended or repealed sections 227 and 503, Article V, subdivision (c) heading, sections 510, 511, 530, 602 and 603, Article VIII heading, sections 801, 803, 804, 805, 806, 807, and 808, Articles VIII-A and VIII-B and sections 1502, 1709.1 and 1712 of Act 331.

§ 15. Municipal officers affected by this act shall transfer all necessary records to effectuate this act.

CHAPTER 35

SECOND CLASS TOWNSHIP CODE

53 P.S. §§ 65101–68701

Concerning townships of the second class; and amending, revising, consolidating and changing the law relating thereto.

The General Assembly of the Commonwealth of Pennsylvania hereby enacts as follows:

TABLE OF CONTENTS

ARTICLE I
PRELIMINARY PROVISIONS

53 P.S. §§ 65101–65109

§ 101. Short Title.—This act shall be known and may be cited as "The Second Class Township Code."

§ 102. Definitions.—The following words, terms and phrases, as used in this act, shall have the following meanings, unless the context clearly indicates otherwise:

"Census" or "official census," the latest United States Census Bureau population count resulting from a decennial or special census conducted by the United States Census Bureau.

"Highway" or "State highway," any highway, road or street which qualifies as a State highway or a portion of the rural State highway system as provided in section 102 of the act of June 1, 1945 (P.L. 1242, No. 428), known as the "State Highway Law."

"Municipal corporation," any city, borough, incorporated town, township of the second class, township of the first class or home rule municipality, except home rule counties.

"Road" or "public road," the entire width between the boundary lines of every way, street, lane, alley, court or public square maintained by the township which is open to the use of the public for purposes of vehicular travel.

"Township," a township of the second class.

§ 103. Excluded Provisions.—(a) This act does not repeal any acts relating to:

(1) The assessment and valuation of property and persons for the purposes of taxation and collection of taxes and the collection of municipal claims by liens.

(2) The method of incurring or increasing indebtedness.

(3) Election officers and conduct of elections.

(4) Public schools and school districts.

(5) Constables.

(6) District justices.

(7) State highways and private roads.

(8) Validations of elections, bonds, ordinances and acts of corporate officers.

(9) Free nonsectarian libraries.

(10) Intergovernmental cooperation.

(11) Planning and land use.

(12) Public meetings.

(13) Inspection of records.

(14) Ethics of elected officers and employes.

(15) The levy or collection of taxes under general law.

(b) It is the intention that this act shall furnish a complete and exclusive system for the government and regulation of townships except as to the several matters enumerated in subsection (a).

§ 104. Construction of act Generally.—The provisions of this act, insofar as they are the same as those of existing laws, are intended as a continuation of those laws and not as new enactments. The repeal by this act of any State law or part thereof does not revive any act or part thereof previously repealed or superseded. The provisions of this act do not affect any act done, liability incurred or right accrued or vested or affect any suit or prosecution pending or to be instituted to enforce any right or penalty or punish any offense under the authority of any repealed laws.

§ 105. Constitutional Construction.—The provisions of this act are severable, and, if any of the provisions are held to be unconstitutional, that decision shall not affect the validity of any of the remaining provisions of this act. It is the legislative intent that this act would have been adopted had the unconstitutional provision not been included.

§ 106. Construction of References.—When, in this act, reference is made to any act by title, it includes any codification in which the provisions of the act referred to are substantially reenacted.

§ 107. How act Applies.—This act shall apply to all townships of the second class as now exist and those created, established or reestablished after this act takes effect.

Chap. 39 Res. During Mil. Service
Chap. 38 Intergov. Coop.
Chap. 37 3rd Class City Code
Chap. 36 Bor. Code
Chap. 35 2nd Class Twp. Code
Chap. 34 1st Class Twp. Code
Chap. 33 Home Rule Chart. Opt. Plans Law
Chap. 32 Water Serv. Act
Chap. 31 Munic. Auth. Act

§ 108. Saving Clauses When Class of Township Changed.—When any township of the second class is reestablished as a township of the first class or when any township of the first class is reestablished as a township of the second class, all liabilities incurred, rights accrued or vested, obligations issued or contracted and all suits and prosecutions pending or to be instituted to enforce any right or penalty accrued or punish any offense committed before the change of class and all resolutions, rules and regulations shall continue with the same force and effect as if no change had been made.

§ 109. Legal Advertising.—When notice is required to be published by a township in one or more newspapers, unless otherwise specified, publication shall be made in the legal notice section in a newspaper of general circulation in the township, as defined by 45 Pa.C.S. (relating to legal notices). When the notice relates to any proceeding or matter in any court or the holding of an election for the increase of indebtedness or the issue and sale of bonds to be paid by taxation, the notice shall also be published in the legal newspaper of the county, if any, so designated by the rules of court. Auditors' statements, summaries of auditors' statements, notices of public meetings and hearings, notices of budget proposals, ordinances, lists of delinquent taxpayers and advertisements inviting proposals for public contracts and for bids for materials and supplies shall be published only in newspapers of general circulation.

ARTICLE II
CLASSIFICATION, CREATION, REESTABLISHMENT AND CHANGE OF NAME OF TOWNSHIPS

53 P.S. §§ 65201–65207

§ 201. Classification of Townships.—The townships now in existence and those to be created after this act takes effect are divided into two classes, townships of the first class and townships of the second class. Townships of the first class are those having a population of at least three hundred inhabitants to the square mile, which are now established as townships of the first class, or which may be created townships of the first class under laws relating to townships of the first class. All townships that are not townships of the first class or home rule townships are townships of the second class. A change from one class to the other shall be made only under this act or the laws relating to townships of the first class.

§ 202. Reestablishment of Townships.—A township of the first class may, irrespective of population, be reestablished a township of the second class in the following manner:

(1) The board of commissioners of the township of the first class on its own initiative may, or within fifteen days after the receipt of a petition signed by at least five percent of the electors of the township of the first class shall, pass a resolution and record it on its minutes, submitting the question of whether the township of the first class shall be reestablished as a township of the second class to the electors of the township of the first class.

(2) At the next primary, general or municipal election occurring at least ninety days after the passage of the resolution, the question, whether the township of the first class shall be reestablished as a township of the second class, shall be submitted to the voters of the township; and the county board of elections shall place the question of reestablishment as a township of the second class on the ballot under the election laws of this Commonwealth.

(3) The election officers shall compute the votes cast at the election and certify them to the county board of elections, which shall compute them and certify the result to the county commissioners and the board of commissioners of the township of the first class and to the clerk of the court of common pleas. If a majority of the votes cast at the election are in favor of the reestablishment

of the township of the first class as a township of the second class, the government of the township of the second class shall be organized and become effective on the first Monday of January after the election, when the terms of the officers of the township of the first class shall cease, and the officers appointed by the court for the township under section 205 shall take office. If a majority of the votes cast at the election are in favor of remaining a township of the first class, no further proceedings may be initiated for a period of two years from the date of the election.

§ 203. Creation of Townships by Annulment of Charter of Borough.—Townships of the second class may be created by the annulment of a charter of a borough under laws governing boroughs.

§ 204. Classification of New Townships.—When a new township is created either by consolidation of two or more townships or reestablishment of a township of the first class as a township or by annulment of a charter of a borough, the new township shall be classified as a township of the second class.

§ 205. Appointment and Election of Officers of New Townships.—When a new township results from the consolidation of townships or is created as a result of the annulment of a charter of a borough or when a township of the first class is reestablished as a township of the second class, the court of common pleas shall appoint the elective officers for the new township and determine the polling place or places in the new township. The appointed officers shall hold their offices until the first Monday of January after the next municipal election which occurs at least ninety days after the appointments. At the municipal election, a tax collector shall be elected for a regular four-year term if the election occurs in the year when such officer is elected for a regular term, and, if not, he shall be elected for a term of two years and his successor shall be elected for a four-year term. At the first municipal election, one supervisor and one auditor shall be elected for terms of six years each, one supervisor and one auditor for terms of four years each and one supervisor and one auditor for terms of two years each. All officers shall take office on the first Monday of January after their election.

§ 206. Certificates of Clerk of Court; Fee; Penalty.—(a) When a township of the second class results from the consolidation of two or more townships or is created or reestablished, the clerk of the court of common pleas within thirty days shall certify the action to the Department of Community Affairs and the Department of Transportation. The clerk may charge a fee of three dollars and fifty cents ($3.50) to be paid as part of the costs of the proceedings.

(b) A clerk who fails to furnish the certifications, or either of them, shall, upon conviction thereof, in a summary proceeding, be sentenced to pay a fine of not more than fifty dollars ($50) and, in default of the payment of the fine and costs, undergo imprisonment of not more than ten days.

§ 207. Change of Name of Township.—(a) Upon petition to the court of common pleas of at least ten percent of the electors of a township or upon passage of a resolution by the board of supervisors seeking a change of the name of the township, the court shall order a referendum on the question.

(b) If the court determines that the petition or resolution for change of name of the township is in proper form and properly executed, the original petition or resolution shall be filed with the clerk of the court. A copy of the petition or resolution and order of the court shall be filed with the county board of elections, which shall frame the question to be submitted to the electors at the next general or municipal election which occurs at least sixty days after the court order.

(c) The election officers shall compute the votes cast on the question and certify them to the clerk of the court of common pleas, who shall tabulate them and certify the result. If a majority of the votes cast at the election are in favor of the change of township name, the court shall so order and shall order the

record of the proceedings to be permanently recorded. If a majority of the votes are against the change, there shall be no further proceedings on the petition or resolution.

ARTICLE III
TOWNSHIP LINES AND BOUNDARIES [REPEALED]

53 P.S. §§ 65301–65307

§ 65301. Repealed by 2022, July 7, P.L. 455, NO. 41—§ 4(2)(V), Effective in 60 Days [Sept. 6, 2022]

§ 65302. Repealed by 2022, July 7, P.L. 455, NO. 41—§ 4(2)(V), Effective in 60 Days [Sept. 6, 2022]

§ 65303. Repealed by 2022, July 7, P.L. 455, NO. 41—§ 4(2)(V), Effective in 60 Days [Sept. 6, 2022]

§ 65304. Repealed by 2022, July 7, P.L. 455, NO. 41—§ 4(2)(V), Effective in 60 Days [Sept. 6, 2022]

§ 65305. Repealed by 2022, July 7, P.L. 455, NO. 41—§ 4(2)(V), Effective in 60 Days [Sept. 6, 2022]

§ 65306. Repealed by 2022, July 7, P.L. 455, NO. 41—§ 4(2)(V), Effective in 60 Days [Sept. 6, 2022]

§ 65307. Repealed by 2022, July 7, P.L. 455, NO. 41—§ 4(2)(V), Effective in 60 Days [Sept. 6, 2022]

§ 65308. Deleted by 1995, Nov. 9, P.L. 350, NO. 60—§ 1, Effective in 180 Days

ARTICLE IV
ELECTION OF OFFICERS; VACANCIES IN OFFICE

53 P.S. §§ 65401–65407

§ 401. Township Officers to Be Electors.—No person is eligible for the office of supervisor, auditor or tax collector in any township unless that person is an elector of the township.

§ 402. Officers to be Elected.—(a) Except as provided in subsection (b), the electors of each township shall elect three supervisors, three auditors and one tax collector. No person shall at the same time hold more than one elective township office.

(b) Upon petition of at least five percent of the electors of the township or under a resolution of the board of supervisors and upon approval by a majority of those electors voting at the next municipal or general election, there shall be elected two additional supervisors. The referendum petition or resolution of the board of supervisors certified by the township secretary shall be filed with the county board of elections not later than the thirteenth Tuesday before the next municipal or general election. The county board of elections shall place the question before the electors as provided under the act of June 3, 1937 (P.L. 1333, No. 320), known as the "Pennsylvania Election Code." The form of the question shall be as follows:

Should two additional supervisors be	**Yes**
elected to serve in this township	**No**

The county board of elections shall tabulate and publish the results of the referendum within thirty days of the election. The total number of supervisors shall

not exceed five. In no event shall the question of additional supervisors be voted on more than once in any three-year period.

(c) At the first municipal election following approval at a general election of the question providing for the election of two additional supervisors, one of the additional supervisors shall be elected for a term of four years and one for a term of six years, each to serve from the first Monday of January after the election. At the first general election following approval at a municipal election of the question providing for the election of two additional supervisors, one of the additional supervisors shall be elected for a term of three years and one for a term of five years, each to serve from the first Monday of January after the election. After that time, the additional supervisors shall be elected for terms of six years each to serve from the first Monday of January after the election.

(d) In townships in which the electorate has opted for a five-member board, the township shall return to a three-member board of supervisors upon petition of at least five percent of the electors of the township, or under a resolution of the board of supervisors, and upon approval by a majority of electors voting at the next municipal or general election. The referendum petition shall be filed with the county board of elections not later than the thirteenth Tuesday before the next municipal or general election. The county board of elections shall place the question before the electors as provided under the "Pennsylvania Election Code." The form of the question shall be as follows:

Should this township return to a	Yes
three-member board of supervisors	No

The county board of elections shall tabulate and publish the results of the referendum within thirty days of the election. In no event shall the question of reducing the five-member board of supervisors be voted on more than once in any five-year period.

(e) At the first municipal election following approval of the question providing for a return to a three-member board, three supervisors shall be elected to serve from the first Monday of January after the election, when the terms of the officers of the five-member board of supervisors shall cease. The three candidates receiving the highest number of votes for the office of supervisor shall be elected. The candidate receiving the highest number of votes shall serve for a term of six years. The candidate receiving the second highest number of votes shall serve for a term of four years. The candidate receiving the third highest number of votes shall serve for a term of two years. After that, supervisors shall be elected under section 403.

§ 403. Supervisors.—(a) Except as provided under section 402(b) for the election of additional supervisors or under section 402(e) for a return to a three-member board, or when vacancies create shorter terms, at each municipal election, the electors of each township shall elect one supervisor to serve for a term of six years from the first Monday of January after the election.

(b) A supervisor may not at the same time hold any other elective township office.

(b.1) A supervisor may hold an appointed position within the township as long as the appointed position is not prohibited under this act or any other statute. Nothing under this subsection shall prohibit a supervisor from being a member of a township planning commission created under the act of July 31, 1968 (P.L. 805, No. 247), known as the "Pennsylvania Municipalities Planning Code."

(c) Supervisors shall reside in the township from which elected and shall have resided in that township continuously for at least one year before their election.

§ 404. Auditors.—(a) Except when vacancies create shorter terms, at each municipal election, the electors of each township shall elect one auditor to serve for a term of six years from the first Monday of January after the election. Auditors shall reside in the township from which elected and shall have resided in that township continuously for at least one year immediately preceding their election.

(b) No auditor shall at the same time hold any other elective or appointive township office or position or be an employe of the township for which he has been elected or appointed. ((b) amended Dec. 18, 1996, P.L., No. 172)

(c) In the event that there concurrently exists two or more vacancies for the position of township auditor, a person shall be ineligible to seek nomination or election to fill more than one such vacancy.

Note: Act 166 of 2006 eliminated the office of Assessor. Elected assessors in office in townships of the second class as November 29, 2006 shall serve the remainder of their unexpired terms. Thereafter, assessors shall neither be elected nor appointed.

§ 405. Assessor.—[Repealed].

§ 406. Tax Collector.—(a) At the municipal election in the year 1993 and at the municipal election every four years after that, the electors of each township shall elect one tax collector to serve for a term of four years, except when vacancies create shorter terms, from the first Monday of January after the election. Tax collectors shall reside in the township from which elected and shall have resided in that township continuously for at least one year immediately preceding their election.

(b) If the electors of any township fail to choose a tax collector or if any person elected to the office fails to give the required bond or to take the required oath, the vacancy shall be filled under section 407.

§ 407. Vacancies in General.—(a) If the electors of any township fail to choose a supervisor, tax collector or auditor, or if any person elected to any office fails to serve in the office, or if a vacancy occurs in the office by death, resignation under subsection (b), removal from the township or otherwise, the board of supervisors may appoint a successor who is a registered elector of the township and has resided in that township continuously for at least one year prior to their appointment.

(b) A resignation:

(1) Shall not create a vacancy until the date that the resignation is accepted by a majority vote of the board of supervisors at a public meeting or the effective date of the tendered resignation, whichever is later. The board of supervisors must accept a tendered resignation no later than forty-five days after the resignation has been tendered to the board of supervisors, unless the resignation is withdrawn in writing prior to acceptance.

(2) That is not accepted as under paragraph (1) shall be deemed accepted forty-five days after the resignation has been tendered to the board of supervisors.

(c) If, for any reason, the board of supervisors refuses, fails, neglects or is unable to fill a vacancy within thirty days after the vacancy occurs, as under this section, the vacancy shall be filled within fifteen additional days by the vacancy board. The vacancy board shall consist of the board of supervisors and one registered elector of the township, who shall be appointed by the board of supervisors at the board's first meeting each calendar year or as soon thereafter as is practical. The appointed elector shall act as the chairperson of the vacancy board.

(d) If the vacancy board fails to fill the position within fifteen days, the chairperson, or if the position of the chairperson is vacant, the remaining members of the vacancy board shall petition the court of common pleas to fill the vacancy.

(e) If two or more vacancies in the office of supervisor occur on a three-member board, or three or more vacancies occur on a five-member board, the court of common pleas shall fill the vacancies upon presentation of a petition signed by at least fifteen registered electors of the township.

(f) A successor appointed under this section shall hold office until the first Monday in January after the first municipal election which occurs at least sixty days after the vacancy occurs, at which election an eligible person shall be elected for the unexpired term.

ARTICLE V
TOWNSHIP OFFICERS GENERALLY
53 P.S. §§ 65501–65503

§ 501. Oath of Office.—Every person elected or appointed to any township office shall before assuming the duties of the office take and subscribe an oath or affirmation before a notary public, district justice or judge to support the Constitutions of the United States and of the Commonwealth and to perform the duties of the office with fidelity. A copy of the oath or affirmation shall be filed with the township secretary before assuming the duties of the office.

§ 502. Bonds.—When any officer or employe of any township is required to give bond for the faithful performance of the duties of the office, the bond shall be with a surety company or other company authorized by law to act as surety, and the township may pay the premium on the bond.

§ 503. Removal of Township Officers and Appointees.—Whether elected or duly appointed to fill a vacancy in elective office, a township officer shall be removable from office only by impeachment, or by the Governor for reasonable cause after due notice and full hearing on the advice of two-thirds of the Senate, or upon conviction of misbehavior in office, or of an infamous crime in accordance with the Constitution of Pennsylvania, but the officer's title to office may be tried by proceedings of quo warranto as provided by law.

ARTICLE VI
TOWNSHIP SUPERVISORS
53 P.S. §§ 65601–65607

§ 601. Supervisors and Government of Townships.—Townships shall be governed and supervised by boards of supervisors. Boards of supervisors shall consist of three members or, if approved by the electors under section 402(b), five members.

§ 602. Organization Meeting; Appointment of Secretary and Treasurer.—(a) The board of supervisors shall meet at a convenient time and place on the first Monday in January of each year. If the first Monday is a legal holiday, the meeting shall be held the following day. The board of supervisors shall elect one member as chairman and another as vice-chairman, and it shall appoint a treasurer and a secretary. The secretary shall be an individual; however, the board of supervisors may select either a trust company, a banking institution or an individual to serve as treasurer, or the board of supervisors may appoint one individual to serve as both secretary and treasurer. Members of the board of supervisors may be appointed as secretary-treasurer, secretary or treasurer. With regard to boards of supervisors which are designated as three-member boards, any supervisor who is to be considered by the board for any appointed township position or for employment by the township as authorized by law shall not be excluded from voting on the issue of such appointment or employment. Action taken by a supervisor shall be deemed to be within the scope of authority as a

Table of Contents
Part I Ch. 1–3 Ethics, Records, Open Meetings
Part II Ch. 4–10 Taxation
Part III Ch. 11–18 Torts, Contracts & Civil Rules
Part IV Ch. 19–24 Zoning & Planning
Part V Ch. 25–30 Construction and Emergency Codes
Part VI Ch. 31–39 Municipal Codes
Index

Chap. 39 Res. During Mil. Service
Chap. 38 Intergov. Coop.
Chap. 37 3rd Class City Code
Chap. 36 Bor. Code
Chap. 35 2nd Class Twp. Code
Chap. 34 1st Class Twp. Code
Chap. 33 Home Rule Chart. Opt. Plans Law
Chap. 32 Water Serv. Act
Chap. 31 Munic. Auth. Act

supervisor and shall not be deemed to constitute an illegal or an improper conflict of interest. ((a) amended Dec. 18, 1996, P.L., No. 172)

(b) The meeting under this section may be considered a regular monthly meeting of the board of supervisors. The first order of business at this meeting shall be organization of the board of supervisors.

(c) The board of supervisors may appoint a supervisor to be employed as roadmaster, laborer, secretary, treasurer, assistant secretary, assistant treasurer or in any employe capacity not otherwise prohibited by this or any other act.

(d) The board of supervisors may authorize a supervisor who is employed by the township to be compensated at the supervisor's regular employe rate and a supervisor who is not employed by the township to receive total or partial reimbursement for lost wages or salary if the supervisor's presence is required in a court of law concerning a township-related matter or the supervisor's attendance is required at any meeting of a board, council of government, commission, authority or county government-sponsored committee to which the supervisor has been appointed by the board of supervisors, board of county commissioners or county council of the county in which the supervisor resides. The compensation may be granted at the discretion of the board of supervisors, and any rate may be granted to the supervisor up to the supervisor's normal pay rate or lost wages or salary. This subsection shall be subject to the following conditions:

(1) The court must be in session or other meeting must occur during the supervisor's normal working hours.

(2) The supervisor must not receive any compensation from the other board, council of government, commission, authority or county government committees for the particular meeting the supervisor attends.

(3) No supervisor may be compensated for attending more than 120 hours of court sessions, other board, council of government, commission, authority or county government committee meetings within a calendar year. The secretary or manager of the township shall keep an accurate and timely accounting of the number of hours that a supervisor has accrued.

§ 603. **Monthly Meetings; Quorum and Voting.**—The board of supervisors shall meet for the transaction of business at least once each month at a time and place determined by the board of supervisors. A quorum is two members of a three-member board of supervisors or three members of a five-member board of supervisors. An affirmative vote of a majority of the entire board of supervisors at a public meeting is necessary in order to transact any business. A member of the board shall not be disqualified from voting on any issue before the board solely because the member has previously expressed an opinion on the issue in either an official or unofficial capacity.

§ 604. **Special Meetings.**—Upon call of the chairman or by agreement of a majority of its members, the board of supervisors may schedule special meetings of the board of supervisors after notice required under the act of July 3, 1986 (P.L. 388, No. 84), known as the "Sunshine Act." Notice of a special meeting shall state the nature of the business to be conducted at the meeting.

§ 605. **Minutes and Records.**—(a) The board of supervisors shall provide for the recording of minutes of its proceedings and other books it may find necessary in the performance of its duties. The records shall be made available to the board of auditors during the annual audit. Unless the custodian of the records agrees otherwise, the records shall be audited or inspected at the place where they are normally maintained. Supervisors who leave office shall deliver all township records in their possession to their successors or to the township secretary.

(b) All township records required to be recorded or transcribed are valid if typewritten, printed, photostated or microfilmed, and, where recording in a specified book of record is required, including minutes of the proceedings of the board of supervisors, the records may be recorded or transcribed in a mechanical post binder book capable of being permanently sealed, with consecutively numbered pages with a security code printed thereon and a permanent locking device with the township seal being impressed upon each page, or bound book with pages being consecutively numbered by transcribing directly upon the pages of the book of record, or may be attached to the book of record by stapling or by glue or any other adhesive substance or material, and all records previously recorded or transcribed in any manner authorized by this section are validated. When any record is recorded or transcribed by attaching the record or a copy of it to the book of record, the township seal shall be impressed upon each page to which the record is attached, each impression covering both a portion of the attached record and a portion of the page of the book of record to which the record is attached.

(c) Original or certified copies of ordinances may also be stored in a locking or mechanical post binder book, capable of being permanently sealed, without being fastened onto pages in the binder.

§ 606. Compensation of Supervisors.—(a) Supervisors may receive as compensation an amount established by ordinance not in excess of the following:

Township Population	Annual Maximum Compensation
not more than 4,999	$3,145
5,000 to 9,999	$4,190
10,000 to 14,999	$5,450
15,000 to 24,999	$6,915
25,000 to 34,999	$7,335
35,000 or more	$8,385

Salaries are payable monthly or quarterly for the duties imposed by this act. The population is determined by the latest official census figures, except that no township shall be required to reduce the salary of a supervisor as a result of a decrease in population. The compensation of supervisors, when employed as roadmasters, laborers, secretary, treasurer, assistant secretary, assistant treasurer or in any employe capacity not otherwise prohibited by this or any other act, shall be determined by the board of auditors, at an hourly, daily, weekly, semi-monthly or monthly basis, which shall be comparable to compensation paid in the locality for similar services. The board of supervisors may establish a mileage allowance, under the act of July 20, 1979 (P.L.156, No.51), referred to as the Uniform Mileage Fee Law, to be paid to officers and employes for the use of a personal vehicle when required and actually used for authorized township business. No supervisor may receive compensation as an employe for attending a meeting of the board of supervisors. Supervisors may continue to be compensated under prior law until such time as an ordinance is enacted under this act. Any change in salary, compensation or emoluments of the elected office becomes effective at the beginning of the next term of the supervisor. A decision by the township to pay, in whole or in part, to include supervisors not employed by the township in insurance plans, as authorized in subsection (c), shall not be implemented with regard to any nonemploye supervisor until the beginning of the next term of that supervisor.

(a.1) Notwithstanding subsection (a), the board of supervisors may provide that a supervisor shall receive compensation on a per-meeting basis based on attendance of supervisors. Total annual compensation may not exceed the amounts specified in subsection (a). Compensation shall only be payable for duly advertised public meetings in which a supervisor participated, except compensation is not payable if a supervisor is absent from a meeting and the absence is not excused. Excused absence from a meeting shall be determined by the board of supervisors and shall include, but not be limited to, an emergency or illness of the supervisor or the supervisor's immediate family as well as family or business travel. The board of supervisors may require documentation to support an excused absence.

(a.2) If the board of supervisors determines that a supervisor shall receive compensation on a per-meeting basis under subsection (a.1), the determination must be made by ordinance.

(b) Any benefit provided to or for the benefit of a supervisor employed by the township in any employe capacity under this act in the form of inclusion in a pension plan paid for in whole or in part by the township is compensation within the meaning of this act to the extent that benefit is paid for by the township and is determined by the board of auditors; however:

(1) Supervisors are eligible for inclusion in township pension plans only if they are employed by the township in any employe capacity under this act. In order to be eligible for inclusion in the plans, supervisor-employes must meet the same requirements as other employes of the township who are eligible to participate in a pension plan. Pension plans shall not improperly discriminate in favor of a supervisor-employe.

(2) Once given, auditor approval for inclusion of supervisor-employes shall not be rescinded in any subsequent years as long as the pension plan remains in effect and the supervisors remain employed by the township and continue to meet the same requirements as other employes of the township who are eligible to participate in a pension plan; nor shall the auditors act in any way that disqualifies the pension plan under Federal law.

(3) No change in the nature or rate of the contributions of a defined contribution plan and no change in the benefit formula of a defined benefit plan shall be initiated by the board of supervisors with respect to a supervisor-employe without auditor approval.

(4) A pension or annuity contract made by a township between January 1, 1959, and March 31, 1985, that includes or provides for benefits for supervisor-employes or retired supervisor-employes at township expense is not void or unlawful solely because the inclusion of supervisor-employes or retired supervisor-employes was not previously approved by the township auditors. No penalty, assessment, surcharge, forfeiture or disciplinary action of any kind may occur as a result of that participation by supervisor-employes.

(5) All premium, contribution or similar payments made by a township on pension or annuity contracts on behalf of supervisor-employes between January 1, 1959, and March 31, 1985, which would have been proper but for the absence of auditor approval are hereby approved. Any benefits payable to any supervisor-employe or his beneficiaries on account of any premium, contribution or similar payments made by a township during that period shall continue. Any premium, contribution or similar payments made by a township after March 31, 1985, requires auditor approval under this subsection.

(6) If a supervisor-employe personally contributed toward a township-sponsored pension plan or annuity that is not approved by the township auditors or not approved by this act, he shall receive a refund of his total contributions thereto plus any interest accumulated thereon. In lieu of a refund of contributions plus accumulated interest, a supervisor-employe who personally contributed toward a pension or annuity plan in which he participated may elect to purchase that portion of his pension or annuity funded by the township. A qualified actuary, who shall report his determination under the act of December 18, 1984 (P.L. 1005, No. 205), known as the "Municipal Pension Plan Funding Standard and Recovery Act," shall determine the amount the supervisor-employe shall pay to purchase the township-funded portion of the annuity or pension.

(7) Supervisors who are not employes of the township are not eligible for participation in any pension or annuity contract paid in whole or in part by the township. No supervisor who was not an employe of the township but was included in a township-paid pension or annuity plan made by a township between January 1, 1959, and March 31, 1985, is subject to any penalty, assessment, surcharge, forfeiture or disciplinary action. Any residual interest, value, refund of premium or benefits payable on or after March 31, 1985, arising out of the township-paid interest of a supervisor who was not an employe is the exclusive property of the township.

(c) In addition to the compensation authorized under this section, supervisors while in office or while in the employ of the township may be eligible for inclusion in township-paid insurance plans, as follows:

(1) Supervisors, whether or not they are employed by the township, and their dependents are eligible for inclusion in group life, health, hospitalization, medical service and accident insurance plans paid in whole or in part by the township. Supervisors and their dependents who are over sixty-five years of age are eligible for inclusion in supplemental Medicare insurance coverage paid in whole or in part by the township. Their inclusion in those plans does not require auditor approval, but does require submission of a letter requesting participation at a regularly scheduled meeting of the board of supervisors before commencing participation. The insurance shall be uniformly applicable to those covered and shall not give eligibility preference to or improperly discriminate in favor of supervisors. No policy of group life insurance shall contain any provision for a cash surrender value, loan value or any other benefit beyond the face amount of insurance. The policy may contain a provision that when the insurance ceases because of termination of employment or term of office, the person is entitled to have issued to him by the insurer, without evidence of insurability, an individual policy of insurance on any form customarily issued by the insurer at the age and for the amount applied for if the amount is not in excess of the amount of life insurance which ceases because of the termination and the application for the individual policy is made and first premium is paid to the insurer within thirty-one days after termination.

(2) Any life, health, hospitalization, medical service or accident insurance coverage contract made by a township between January 1, 1959, and March 31, 1985, that includes or provides coverage for supervisors not employed by the township is not void or unlawful because inclusion of those supervisors was subsequently found to be without lawful authority. No penalty, assessment, surcharge, forfeiture or disciplinary action may occur as a result of participation by those supervisors. Insurance benefits paid or payable to insureds or their beneficiaries arising out of or on account of deaths, injuries, accidents or illnesses occurring before March 30, 1988, are the property of the insureds or their beneficiaries.

(3) All payments made by a township on any group life, health, hospitalization, medical service or accident insurance coverage contracts on behalf of supervisors who were not employes between January 1, 1959, and March 31, 1985, which would have been proper but for the absence of auditor approval are hereby approved. Any benefits payable to any supervisor or his beneficiaries on account of those payments during that time shall continue.

(4) The township may deduct from any compensation payable to a supervisor such part of any insurance premium or charge which is payable by the supervisor within the terms of the particular township's insurance plan.

(5) The township may pay the cost, in whole or in part, of supplemental Medicare insurance coverage for supervisors and employes who are over sixty-five years of age.

Chap. 39 Res. During Mil. Service
Chap. 38 Intergov. Coop.
Chap. 37 3rd Class City Code
Chap. 36 Bor. Code
Chap. 35 2nd Class Twp. Code
Chap. 34 1st Class Twp. Code
Chap. 33 Home Rule Chart. Opt. Plans Law
Chap. 32 Water Serv. Act
Chap. 31 Munic. Auth. Act

§ 607. Duties of Supervisors.—The board of supervisors shall:

(1) Be charged with the general governance of the township and the execution of legislative, executive and administrative powers in order to ensure sound fiscal management and to secure the health, safety and welfare of the citizens of the township.

(2) Have the responsibility for maintenance of township-owned equipment and facilities.

(3) Employ persons as may be necessary for the general conduct of the business of the township and provide for the compensation, organization and supervision of the persons so employed. Records shall be kept and reports made and filed giving the names of all persons employed, dates on which work was done and the number of hours worked with compensation paid to each person and the capacity in which employed.

(4) Authorize attendance at conferences, institutes, schools and conventions. Any supervisor or newly elected supervisor prior to officially taking office, elected or appointed officer or township employe may if directed by the board of supervisors attend any conference, institute, school or convention dealing with the duties and functions of elected or appointed officers or employes. The expenses for attending the meetings may be paid by the township and are limited to the registration fee, mileage for the use of a personal vehicle or reimbursement of actual transportation expense going to and returning from the meeting plus all other actual expenses that the board of supervisors agrees to pay. Every attendee shall submit to the board of supervisors an itemized account of expenses incurred at the meeting. The board of supervisors may authorize employes to be compensated at their regular employe rate, and auditors to be compensated at the rate of ten dollars ($10) for each hour up to a maximum of eight hours per day, during their attendance at the meeting.

(5) Annually, on or before the first day of February, furnish to the board of auditors information on the construction or maintenance of roads or other matters that may be required by any department of the Commonwealth to be included in the annual township report.

(6) Provide for the annual tax duplicate to be prepared and presented to the tax collector.

(7) Perform duties and exercise powers as may be imposed or conferred by law or the rules and regulations of any agency of the Commonwealth.

ARTICLE VII

TOWNSHIP TREASURER

53 P.S. §§ 65701–65708

§ 701. Township Treasurer.—The board of supervisors shall appoint a township treasurer to serve at the pleasure of the board of supervisors.

§ 702. Treasurer's Bond.—The township treasurer, if an individual, shall give bond with a surety company in an amount established by the board of supervisors for the faithful performance of the duties of the office. The amount of the bond shall equal the highest amount of township funds estimated by the board of supervisors to be available to the township treasurer at any time during the current year. The bond shall be filed with the board of auditors of the township.

§ 703. Treasurer's Compensation.—The board of supervisors shall determine the compensation of the township treasurer. When a supervisor is appointed as township treasurer, the board of auditors shall determine the compensation. A person may not receive hourly compensation for work as a superintendent, roadmaster or laborer for time spent in the performance of the duties of township treasurer.

§ 704. Treasurer's Duties.—The township treasurer shall:

(1) Receive all moneys due the township and deposit them promptly in a designated depository in the name of the township.

(2) Keep distinct and accurate accounts of all sums received from taxes and other sources, which accounts shall be open to the inspection of the board of supervisors and any citizen of this Commonwealth.

(3) Pay out all moneys of the township only on direction by the board of supervisors.

(4) Annually state the accounts and make them available to the board of auditors for settlement.

(5) Preserve the account books, papers, documents and other records of the office and turn them over to the successor in office.

§ 705. Assistant Treasurer.—The board of supervisors may appoint an assistant treasurer who shall assist the township treasurer or, in the absence or disability of the township treasurer, perform the duties of the township treasurer. The assistant treasurer may be appointed from the membership of the board of supervisors. The assistant treasurer shall be bonded for the same amount as the township treasurer when acting in the capacity of township treasurer. The board of supervisors shall determine the compensation of the assistant treasurer. When a supervisor is appointed assistant treasurer, the board of auditors shall determine the compensation.

§ 706. Use of Special Funds; Penalty.—When any moneys are collected for any special purpose, no township treasurer or board of supervisors may apply those moneys to any purpose other than that for which they were collected. Every misapplication shall be a misdemeanor of the third degree, and, in addition to the fine or penalty which may be imposed upon conviction, the defendant shall be required to pay restitution in the amount of moneys improperly spent.

§ 707. Penalty for Failure to Perform Duties.—A township treasurer or assistant treasurer who fails to perform any duties of the office other than those for which specific penalties are provided commits a summary offense and, in addition to the fine or penalty which may be imposed upon conviction, is required to pay to the township an amount equal to the amount of the financial loss that occurred, if any, for not performing the duties of the office. That person is disqualified from holding the office of township treasurer or assistant treasurer.

§ 708. Depositories of Township Funds.—(a) The board of supervisors shall designate by resolution a depository or depositories for township funds. Any funds deposited with any banking institution of this Commonwealth shall be insured with the Federal Deposit Insurance Corporation or the National Credit Union Share Insurance Fund or their successor agencies, to the extent that accounts are so insured. The board of supervisors shall require each banking institution to furnish additional bond, insurance or security to cover the amount of any deposits in excess of the insured limits. The designation is valid for a period of one year or until another depository or other depositories are designated by similar action of the board of supervisors.

(b) The depository or depositories shall be banks, banking institutions or trust companies located in this Commonwealth.

(c) The township treasurer or assistant treasurer shall, upon the designation of the depository or depositories by the board of supervisors, immediately transfer thereto the township funds and after that make deposits solely in the depository or depositories in the name of the township.

(d) No township treasurer or assistant treasurer complying with the provisions of this section, nor his surety or sureties, shall be chargeable with losses of township funds caused solely by the failure or negligence of the depository or depositories.

ARTICLE VIII

TOWNSHIP SECRETARY

53 P.S. § 65801–65804

§ 801. Township Secretary.—The board of supervisors shall appoint a township secretary to serve at the pleasure of the board of supervisors.

§ 802. Secretary's Duties.—The township secretary is a clerk to the board of supervisors. The township secretary shall:

(1) Record the proceedings of the board of supervisors and all court orders relative to the laying out, opening and vacating of roads in a minute book.

(2) Preserve the minute book and other records and turn them over to the successor in office.

(3) With the consent of the board of supervisors and in conformity with other laws governing the retention and disposition of municipal records, have the authority to destroy records and papers of the township other than the minute book and account book after the lapse of six years from the date of the records.

(4) Inform supervisors of all township meetings, including special meetings of the board of supervisors.

§ 803. Secretary's Compensation.—The board of supervisors shall determine the compensation of the township secretary. When a supervisor is appointed township secretary, the board of auditors shall determine the compensation. A person may not receive hourly compensation for work as a superintendent, roadmaster or laborer for time spent in the performance of the duties of township secretary.

§ 804. Assistant Secretary.—The board of supervisors may appoint an assistant secretary who shall assist the township secretary or, in the absence or disability of the township secretary, perform the duties of the township secretary. The assistant secretary may be appointed from the membership of the board of supervisors. The board of supervisors shall determine the compensation of the assistant secretary. When a supervisor is appointed assistant secretary, the board of auditors shall determine the compensation.

ARTICLE IX

AUDITORS; ACCOUNTANTS

53 P.S. §§ 65901–65917

§ 901. Township Auditors; Meetings; Duties; Quorum.—(a) The board of auditors shall meet annually at the place of meeting of the board of supervisors on the day following the day designated by this act for organization of the board of supervisors, and they shall organize by the election of a chairman and secretary. The board of auditors shall audit, settle and adjust the accounts of all elected or appointed officials of the township and its boards or agencies that received or disbursed funds of or owing to the township during the immediately preceding calendar year. The board of auditors shall determine the compensations for the current year authorized in section 606 for supervisors employed by the township. Two auditors shall constitute a quorum. The auditors may also make an audit of the dockets, transcripts and other official records of the district justices to determine the amount of fines and costs paid over or due the township, and the dockets and records of the district justices shall be open to inspection by the auditors for that purpose. Unless otherwise agreed to by the board of auditors and the officer being audited, the audit shall be conducted at the place the records of the officer are normally kept.

Chap. 39 Res. During Mil. Service
Chap. 38 Intergov. Coop.
Chap. 37 3rd Class City Code
Chap. 36 Bor. Code
Chap. 35 2nd Class Twp. Code
Chap. 34 1st Class Twp. Code
Chap. 33 Home Rule Chart. Opt. Plans Law
Chap. 32 Water Serv. Act
Chap. 31 Munic. Auth. Act

(b) Upon the death or resignation of any of the officials designated in this section to be audited, the board of auditors, upon call of the chairman, shall meet and audit the accounts of the former incumbent and determine the compensation of the successor if so authorized by this act.

§ 902. Auditor's Compensation.—(a) Each auditor shall receive ten dollars ($10) for each hour necessarily employed in the duties of the office upon presentation to the board of supervisors of an itemized listing of the dates, times, places and hours worked to perform the audit. No auditor in a township having a population of ten thousand or less is entitled to receive more than one thousand eight hundred dollars ($1,800) for completing the annual audit, settlement and adjustment. No auditor in a township having a population in excess of ten thousand is entitled to receive more than three thousand five hundred dollars ($3,500) for completing the annual audit, settlement and adjustment.

(a.1) The board of supervisors may, by adoption of a resolution, increase the rate of compensation for each auditor under subsection (a) to an amount not greater than eighteen dollars ($18) for each hour necessarily employed in the duties of the office upon presentation to the board of supervisors of an itemized listing of the dates, times, places and hours worked to perform the audit.

(b) In addition to the time actually used by the board of auditors to complete the audit, settlement and adjustment, each auditor may be compensated at the rate of ten dollars ($10) each hour for not more than fifty hours to audit the accounts of any public official who handles public funds when a vacancy occurs in the office of the public official.

(b.1) The board of supervisors may, by adoption of a resolution, increase the rate of compensation for each auditor under subsection (b) to an amount not greater than eighteen dollars ($18) per hour for not more than fifty hours to audit the accounts of any public official who handles public funds when a vacancy occurs in the office of the public official.

(c) Each auditor shall be reimbursed for travel costs incurred in the performance of the auditing duties at the rate established by the board of supervisors under the act of July 20, 1979 (P.L. 156, No. 51), referred to as the Uniform Mileage Fee Law, and for other expenses, including postage, notary fees or publication costs, incurred during the audit.

§ 903. Subpoenas; Oaths; Perjury.—The board of auditors may issue subpoenas to obtain the attendance of the officers whose accounts they are required to audit or adjust, of their executors and administrators and of any person whom it may be necessary to examine as a witness and to compel their attendance, by attachment, the same as any court of common pleas may in cases pending before them and may also compel the production of all books, vouchers and papers relative to township accounts. The subpoena and attachment shall be issued by a district justice. The board of auditors may administer oaths and affirmations to all persons brought or appearing before them, whether accountants, witnesses or otherwise. All persons swearing or affirming falsely upon examination are guilty of perjury.

§ 904. Completion, Filing and Publication of Annual Township Report and Financial Statement.—(a) The board of auditors shall complete their audit, settlement and adjustment before the first day of April of each year.

(b) The board of auditors shall make a report of the affairs of the township, executed copies of which report shall be filed not later than ninety days after the close of the fiscal year by the secretary of the board of auditors with the township secretary, the clerk of the court of the county or the prothonotary under local rules of court, the Department of Community Affairs and the Department of Transportation. Each copy of the report shall be signed by at least a majority of the board of auditors and duly verified by the oath of the secretary of the board of auditors. Any secretary of the board of auditors who fails to file the township report or to publish the required financial statement commits a summary offense.

(c) The township report shall be presented on a uniform form prepared and furnished under section 3203.

(d) The township report shall contain the names and addresses of the chairman and members of the board of supervisors, the township secretary and the township treasurer, a statement of the receipts of the township from all sources and of all accounts and revenue which may be due and uncollected at the close of the fiscal year, a statement of the disbursements of the township during the fiscal year, a statement of the balance in the township treasury at the beginning of the fiscal year, a statement of the resources and liabilities of the township at the end of the fiscal year, a detailed statement of the indebtedness of the township at the close of the fiscal year and the provisions made for the payment thereof together with the purposes for which it was incurred, a statement of the cost of ownership and operation of each public service industry owned, maintained or operated by the township and other information as may be required in this act.

(e) On or before the fifteenth day of April of each year, the secretary of the township shall publish, once in one newspaper of general circulation in the township, concise financial information prepared or approved by the auditors and consistent with the audited financial statements, for total assets, total liabilities and total net position at year end and total revenue, expenses and changes in net position for the year just ended and a reference to a place within the township where copies of the financial statements and accompanying auditor's report may be examined. If the full financial statements and accompanying auditor's report are not published, copies shall be supplied to the publishing newspaper when the request for publication is submitted.

(f) If any township has a population of less than two hundred, as shown by the latest official census, the board of auditors may post five copies of the financial statement in public places in the township in lieu of publication in a newspaper.

§ 905. Penalty for Failure to Perform Duty.—Any auditor who fails to comply with this article commits a summary offense.

§ 906. Employment and Compensation of Attorney.—If a disagreement occurs with the board of auditors and any official it is required to audit, the board of auditors may petition the court of common pleas to appoint an attorney to represent or advise the board of auditors on the matter. The court shall not appoint an attorney unless reasonable effort to reach an agreement has been made and only after the board of auditors has given notice to the official or the board of supervisors of its intent to petition the court for the appointment. The board of auditors, with the agreement of the board of supervisors, shall determine the compensation of the attorney. If the dispute results in litigation or if the board of auditors and the board of supervisors cannot agree upon the compensation to be paid to the attorney, the court shall establish the compensation for the attorney appointed for the board of auditors. The compensation for the attorney shall be paid out of the general township fund.

§ 907. Surcharge by Auditors.—(a) The board of auditors shall surcharge any elected or appointed officer for the amount of any loss to the township caused in whole or in part by the officer's act or omission in violation of law or beyond the scope of the officer's authority. If the auditors find an absence of intent to violate the law or exceed the scope of authority and find the result of the officer's act could have been achieved by legal means and authorized procedures, the surcharge imposed shall be limited to the difference between the costs actually incurred by the township and the costs that would have been incurred had legal means and authorized procedures been employed. Provisions of this section which limit the amount of surcharge do not apply to cases involving fraud or collusion on the part of the officers or to any penalty ensuing to the benefit of or payable to the Commonwealth.

(b) Any balance in any report of the board of auditors against any officer of the township constitutes a surcharge against the officer as fully as if expressly stated in the report to be a surcharge. The board of auditors shall direct the clerk of court of common pleas to certify the amount of every balance or surcharge from which no appeal has been taken under sections 909 and 910 to the court of common pleas, and the prothonotary shall enter the balance or surcharge as a judgment against the officer in favor of the township.

§ 908. Collection of Surcharge; Bond.—Any auditor, elector or taxpayer of the township may enforce the collection of a judgment entered for a surcharge for the benefit of the township, by any appropriate action or execution, upon filing in the court of common pleas a bond (in the case of an elector or taxpayer), with one or more sureties, conditioned to indemnify the township for all costs which may accrue in the proceedings undertaken, subject, however, to all rights of appeal from the report of the board of auditors.

§ 909. Appeals from Report.—The board of supervisors or any elector or taxpayer of the township or any officer whose account is settled or audited by the board of auditors may appeal from any settlement or audit of the board of auditors to the court of common pleas within forty-five days after the settlement has been filed in the court of common pleas.

§ 910. Taxpayer's Appeal; Bond.—No appeal by an elector, taxpayer or officer shall be allowed unless the appellant enters into recognizance to prosecute the appeal with effect, and to pay all costs accruing thereon, in case, if the appellant is an elector or taxpayer, he fails to obtain a final decision more favorable to the township than that awarded by the board of auditors or, if the appellant is an officer, he fails to obtain a final decision more favorable to the officer than that awarded by the board of auditors.

§ 911. Consolidation of Appeals.—When more than one appeal from the report of the board of auditors is taken, whether by the board of supervisors, by an officer thereof or by an elector or taxpayer, the court may direct that the several appeals be consolidated.

§ 912. Report; Prima Facie Evidence; Burden of Proof.—The accounts of the officer in question may be investigated de novo. The figures and facts found and stated by the auditors in their report of audit shall be taken as prima facie correct as against any officer, and the burden shall be upon each officer whose accounts are in question to establish the validity of the credits which he claims.

§ 913. Findings; Judgment.—After hearing, the court shall file findings of fact and law and enter judgment, and the judgment so entered may be enforced by appropriate proceedings by any auditor, officer, elector or taxpayer of the township.

§ 914. Costs.—In all cases of appeal from the report or audit of the board of auditors to the court of common pleas, the costs shall be determined by the court.

§ 915. Attorney Fees.—Upon final determination of an appeal taken under section 909 from any report, audit or settlement of the account of any township officer, attorney fees shall be awarded as follows:

(1) If in the opinion of the court the final determination is more favorable to the township officer involved than that awarded by the board of auditors, the township shall pay reasonable attorney fees, or under paragraph (3) a portion of reasonable attorney fees, incurred by the officer in connection with the surcharge proceeding.

(2) In the case of an appeal taken by the township, an elector or a taxpayer, if in the opinion of the court the final determination is more favorable to the township than that awarded by the board of auditors, the township officer who is the subject of the surcharge proceeding shall pay reasonable attorney fees, or under paragraph (3) a portion of reasonable attorney fees, incurred by the township, elector or taxpayer in connection with the surcharge proceeding.

Chap. 39 Res. During Mil. Service
Chap. 38 Intergov. Coop.
Chap. 37 3rd Class City Code
Chap. 36 Bor. Code
Chap. 35 2nd Class Twp. Code
Chap. 34 1st Class Twp. Code
Chap. 33 Home Rule Chart. Opt. Plans Law
Chap. 32 Water Serv. Act
Chap. 31 Munic. Auth. Act

(3) If in the opinion of the court the final determination is in part more favorable to the township and in part more favorable to the township officer involved in the surcharge proceeding than that awarded by the board of auditors, the court may order the township to pay a portion of reasonable attorney fees incurred by the officer in connection with the surcharge proceeding, or it may order the township officer who is the subject of the surcharge proceeding to pay a portion of reasonable attorney fees incurred by the township, elector or taxpayer in connection with the surcharge proceeding.

§ 916. Interest in Township Transactions.—Any auditor who is financially interested, directly or indirectly, in any township transaction commits a summary offense. The auditor shall forfeit the office and forfeit to the township any financial benefit derived from the transaction.

§ 917. Appointment of Accountant.—(a) The board of supervisors may contract with a certified or competent public accountant or a firm of certified or competent public accountants, either of which shall be registered in this Commonwealth, to be appointed by the court of common pleas at least thirty days before the close of the fiscal year to audit the accounts of the township and the township officers if a petition has been presented to the supervisors by at least twenty-five taxpayers of the township asking for the appointment. The amount paid to the accountant or firm in any year shall not exceed the maximum allowed by law to be paid to the board of auditors in any year unless the payment of an additional amount is approved by the court.

(b) (1) At its annual organization meeting, or anytime thereafter, the board of supervisors may by resolution appoint a certified or competent public accountant or a firm of certified or competent public accountants, either of which shall be registered in this Commonwealth, to make an examination of all the accounts of the township for the fiscal year stated in the resolution. The board of supervisors shall determine the compensation of the appointed accountant.

(2) At least thirty days prior to the initial vote to appoint a certified or competent public accountant or a firm of certified or competent public accountants to replace the elected auditors, the board of supervisors shall advertise in a newspaper of general circulation the intent to appoint a certified or competent public accountant or a firm of certified or competent public accountants to replace the elected auditors.

(3) At least thirty days prior to the replacement, by resolution, of an appointed certified or competent public accountant or a firm of certified or competent public accountants with the elected auditors for purposes of the audit, settlement and adjustment of the accounts audited by the appointee, the board of supervisors shall advertise in a newspaper of general circulation the intent to return all powers and duties of the elected auditors.

(c) When an accountant or firm is appointed under subsection (a) or (b), the board of auditors shall not audit, settle or adjust the accounts audited by an appointee in any year after an appointment under this section, but shall perform the other duties of the office until auditing duties are returned to the board in accordance with subsection (b)(3). The accountant or firm has the powers given to the board of auditors under this act, except the audit shall be made in accordance with generally accepted auditing standards, and further provide that the accountant or firm appointed under subsection (a) or (b) shall not have the power to determine compensations, and they are subject to the same penalties as the elected auditors under this act. The report of the accountant or firm is subject to appeals the same as reports of the board of auditors under this act.

(d) For the purposes of meeting Federal or State requirements, the board of supervisors may contract with an independent certified or competent public accountant to audit the fiscal affairs of the township, independent of that conducted by the elected or appointed auditors.

ARTICLE X
TAX COLLECTOR; ASSESSOR
53 P.A. §§ 66001–66002

§ 1001. Tax Collector; Powers, Duties and Liabilities.—The tax collector shall collect all county, township, school, institution district and other taxes levied within townships by authorities authorized to levy taxes. The tax collector may also be designated in the tax-levying ordinance or resolution or be employed by the tax-levying authority to collect taxes levied under the act of December 31, 1965 (P.L. 1257, No. 511), known as "The Local Tax Enabling Act." In addition to the powers, duties and responsibilities under this act, the tax collector shall exercise all the powers and perform all the duties and be subject to all the obligations and responsibilities for the collection of taxes as are conferred upon tax collectors by law.

§ 1002. Assessor; Powers and Duties.—[Repealed].

ARTICLE XI
TOWNSHIP SOLICITOR
53 P.S. §§ 66101–66103

§ 1101. Township Solicitor.—The board of supervisors may appoint and determine the compensation of a township solicitor. The township solicitor shall be licensed to practice law in this Commonwealth and may be one person or a law firm, partnership, association or professional corporation. The township solicitor serves at the pleasure of the board of supervisors.

§ 1102. Solicitor to Have Control of Legal Matters.—The township solicitor shall direct and control the legal matters of the township, and no official or official body of the township, except as otherwise provided under law, shall employ an additional attorney without the assent or ratification of the board of supervisors.

§ 1103. Duties of Solicitor.—The township solicitor, when directed or requested so to do, shall prepare or approve any bonds, obligations, contracts, leases, conveyances, ordinances and assurances to which the township may be a party. The township solicitor shall commence and prosecute all actions brought by the township for or on account of any of the estates, rights, trusts, privileges, claims or demands, as well as defend the township or any township officer against all actions or suits brought against the township or township officer in which any of the estates, rights, privileges, trusts, ordinances or accounts of the township may be brought in question before any court in this Commonwealth and do every professional act incident to the office which the township solicitor may be authorized or required to do by the board of supervisors or by any resolution. The township solicitor shall furnish the board of supervisors, upon request, with an opinion in writing upon any question of law.

ARTICLE XII
TOWNSHIP ENGINEER
53 P.S. § 66201–66203

§ 1201. Township Engineer.—The board of supervisors may appoint and determine the compensation of a township engineer who shall be a registered professional engineer. The township engineer serves at the pleasure of the board of supervisors.

§ 1202. Engineer's Duties; Preparation of Plans.—The township engineer shall perform duties as the board of supervisors may direct for the construction, reconstruction, maintenance and repair of streets, roads, pavements, sanitary sewers, bridges, culverts and other engineering work. The township engineer shall prepare plans, specifications and estimates of the work undertaken by the township and furnish the board of supervisors with reports, information or estimates on any township engineering work or on questions submitted by the board of supervisors.

§ 1203. Certificate of Commencement and of Completion of Municipal Improvements.—The township engineer shall certify to the township secretary the date of commencement and of completion of all municipal improvements, the cost of which, in whole or in part, is to be paid by the owners of the abutting property. The certification shall be made a part of the permanent records of the township. The certified time of commencement and completion is conclusive on all parties. The term "certified time of completion" means the time of the completion of the whole contract for the improvement.

ARTICLE XIII
TOWNSHIP MANAGER
53 P.S. § 66301

§ 1301. Township Manager; Appointment, Removal, Powers and Duties; Compensation; Bond.—(a) The board of supervisors may by ordinance at any time create the office of township manager and may in like manner abolish the office. While the office exists, the board of supervisors shall appoint one person to fill the office. The township manager shall serve at the pleasure of the board of supervisors, subject to contractual rights that may arise under an employment agreement that may be entered into in accordance with subsection (a.1).

(a.1) The board of supervisors may enter into an employment agreement with the township manager. The employment agreement may set forth the terms and conditions of employment, and the agreement may provide that it shall remain in effect for a specified period terminating no later than two years after the effective date of the agreement or the date of the board of supervisors' organizational meeting following the next municipal election, whichever shall first occur. An employment agreement entered into pursuant to this subsection may specify conditions under which a township manager would be entitled to severance compensation, but in no event shall an employment agreement guarantee employment through the term of the agreement or confer upon the township manager any legal remedy based on specific performance.

(b) The powers and duties of the township manager shall be established by ordinance. The compensation shall be set by resolution and paid out of the general fund of the township. The board of supervisors may delegate, subject to recall, any of their nonlegislative powers and duties to the township manager. The township manager shall give bond to the township, with sufficient surety, in the amount directed by the board of supervisors, conditioned for the faithful performance of the duties of the office.

(c) The office of township manager is not incompatible with the office of township secretary, township treasurer or any other township office or employment, except that of supervisor, auditor or township police officer.

Chap. 39 Res. During Mil. Service
Chap. 38 Intergov. Coop.
Chap. 37 3rd Class City Code
Chap. 36 Bor. Code
Chap. 35 2nd Class Twp. Code
Chap. 34 1st Class Twp. Code
Chap. 33 Home Rule Chart. Opt. Plans Law
Chap. 32 Water Serv. Act
Chap. 31 Munic. Auth. Act

ARTICLE XIV
COUNTY AND STATE ASSOCIATIONS OF TOWNSHIPS
53 P.S. § 66401–66402

§ 1401. County Associations.—(a) County associations of township officials may be formed. County associations shall hold annual or semi-annual conventions at places determined by the association to consider and discuss questions and subjects pertaining to improvement of township government, assessment of property, collection of taxes and construction, improvement and maintenance of roads. Associations of two or more adjacent counties may arrange to meet in joint sessions.

(b) The supervisors, auditors, tax collectors, managers, solicitors, engineers, treasurer and secretary of the board of supervisors shall attend the conventions when possible.

(c) (1) Each supervisor, auditor, tax collector, manager, solicitor, engineer, treasurer and secretary attending the convention shall receive a certificate, signed by the secretary of the county association, attesting their presence at the convention. The certificate entitles the official to collect from the township treasurer the sum of fifty dollars ($50) for each day's attendance, expenses which are limited to the registration fee, mileage for use of a personal vehicle or reimbursement of actual transportation expense going to and returning from the meeting plus all other actual expenses that the board of supervisors agrees to pay. Every delegate attending the meeting shall submit to the board of supervisors an itemized account of expenses incurred at the meeting.

(c) (2) If the meeting is held during township employes' normal work schedule, the board of supervisors may authorize township employes, including supervisors employed by the township, to be compensated at their regular employe rate during their attendance at the meeting, in which case the employe is not entitled to the fifty dollars ($50) mentioned in this section.

(3) The board of supervisors may authorize a supervisor who is not employed by the township to receive total or partial reimbursement for lost wages or salary while attending the annual meeting, in which case the supervisor is not entitled to the fifty dollars ($50) mentioned in this section, provided that sufficient documentation of such wages or salary is presented to the board of supervisors to justify the reimbursement.

(4) No supervisor, auditor, tax collector, manager, solicitor, engineer, treasurer or secretary shall be paid for more than two days' attendance in any one year.

(d) The officers of the association shall consist of a president, one or two vice-presidents, a secretary and a treasurer, all of whom, except the secretary, shall be members of the association and shall hold office for one year or until their successors are chosen. The secretary of the association may be compensated for services an amount determined by the members of the association. Every supervisor, tax collector, manager, secretary, treasurer and auditor attending the convention may vote on policy matters and in the election of officers of the association.

(d.1) If a meeting of the officers and members of the executive board of the county association is held during the township employes' normal work schedule, the board of supervisors may authorize a supervisor who is employed by the township to be compensated at the supervisor's regular employe rate and a supervisor who is not employed by the township to receive total or partial reimbursement for lost wages or salary during the supervisor's attendance at the meeting, for up to six days total in a year. A supervisor may not be compensated by the township under this subsection if the supervisor receives any other compensation from the county association for attending the meeting.

(e) Expenses of each county association convention shall be paid from dues assessed by the association on each member township or from other funds as the members of the county association determine.

(f) Each county association of township officials may elect one township supervisor, township manager, township treasurer or township secretary for each ten townships, or fraction thereof, within the county, as a voting delegate to each annual meeting of the State association, but each county association is entitled to a minimum of two delegates at each meeting. These delegates' expenses may be paid by the respective county association.

§ 1402. State Association of Township Supervisors Authorized.—(a) The formation of a State Association of Township Supervisors is authorized.

(b) The State association shall hold annual meetings, at a time and place within this Commonwealth as it may designate, to discuss questions and subjects pertaining to the duties of elected and appointed township officials and the improvement of township government.

(c) The State association, at its annual meeting, by majority vote of all qualified voting delegates present, may adopt and amend bylaws to govern the State association. The bylaws shall govern the qualification of delegates, election of officers, their designation, qualifications and duties, payment of dues and other organizational matters. The State association shall function under the bylaws to advance the interest of township government.

(d) The board of supervisors may designate one or more of the following elected or appointed officials of the township to attend the annual meeting of the State association: supervisors, secretary, treasurer and manager. The convention shall be held in this Commonwealth under the procedures adopted by the State association.

(e) Each township with dues paid in the State association shall elect one of those delegates designated in subsection (d) to be the voting delegate at the convention.

(f) Each township shall certify the name and address of its delegate or delegates and the designated voting delegate to the State association at least thirty days before the opening of the State convention.

(g) (1) The expenses allowed to the delegates attending the annual meeting are limited to the registration fee, mileage for use of a personal vehicle or reimbursement of actual transportation expense going to and returning from the meeting plus all other actual expenses that the board of supervisors agrees to pay. Every delegate attending the annual meeting shall submit to the board of supervisors an itemized account of expenses incurred at the meeting.

(2) The board of supervisors may authorize township employes, including supervisors employed by the township, to be compensated at their regular employe rate during their attendance at the annual meeting.

(3) The board of supervisors may authorize a supervisor who is not employed by the township to receive total or partial reimbursement for lost wages or salary while attending the annual meeting, provided that sufficient documentation is presented to the board of supervisors to justify the reimbursement.

(4) No delegate shall receive expenses for attending more than four days each year.

(h) Membership dues of the State association are legal expenses of the townships and shall be used for the payment of expenses incurred, including, but not limited to, the rental or acquisition of real estate to be used for State association purposes and activities, cost of publications, salaries, cost of services provided to or for townships and other expenses incurred on behalf of the State association.

(i) The State association may purchase, receive, lease as lessee, accept by gift or devise or otherwise acquire and own, use and otherwise deal with any real estate in its own name for association purposes and mortgage, sell and convey, lease as lessor and otherwise dispose of all or part of the real estate.

(j) The board of supervisors may authorize a supervisor who is employed by the township to be compensated at the supervisor's regular employe rate and a supervisor who is not employed by the township to receive total or partial reimbursement for lost wages or salary if the supervisor attends a meeting for which the supervisor is a member of the executive committee, a standing committee or a trustee of the State Association of Township Supervisors subject to the following limitations:

(1) A supervisor on a standing committee of the State Association of Township Supervisors shall be limited to two days per year of regular employe rate compensation or lost wages or salary, as applicable.

(2) A supervisor on the Board of Trustees Insurance Fund of the State Association of Township Supervisors shall be limited to four days per year of regular employe rate compensation or lost wages or salary, as applicable.

(3) Any supervisor on the executive board or committee of the State Association of Township Supervisors shall be limited to fifteen days per year of regular employe rate compensation or lost wages or salary, as applicable.

(4) A supervisor on any of the committees, funds or boards identified under paragraph (1), (2) or (3) may not be compensated by the township under this section if the supervisor receives any compensation from the committee, fund or board for attending that meeting.

ARTICLE XV
CORPORATE POWERS
53 P.S. § 66501–66549

§ 1501. Suits.—Any township may sue and be sued.

§ 1502. Property; Penalty for Violation.—(a) The board of supervisors may purchase, acquire by gift or otherwise, hold, lease, let and convey, by sale or lease, any real and personal property it judges to be to the best interest of the township.

(b) Any supervisor who votes in favor of or knowingly participates in the sale or lease of township real or personal property in violation of this article is subject to surcharge to the extent of any loss or injury to the township as a result of the sale or lease.

§ 1503. Real Property.—(a) No real estate owned by the township having a value in excess of six thousand dollars ($6,000) may be sold except to the highest bidder after due notice by advertisement for bids or advertisement of a public auction in one newspaper of general circulation in the township. The advertisement shall be published once not less than ten days before the date set for the opening of bids or public auction, and the date for opening bids or public auction shall be announced in the advertisement. The award of contracts shall be made only by public announcement at a regular or special meeting of the board of supervisors or at the public auction. All bids shall be accepted on the condition that payment of the purchase price in full shall be made within sixty days of the acceptance of bids. Real estate owned by the township may be sold at a consideration of six thousand dollars ($6,000) or less without advertisement or competitive bidding only after the board of supervisors estimates the value of the real estate upon receipt of an appraisal by a qualified real estate appraiser. Prior to selling real estate valued at six thousand dollars ($6,000) or less without advertisement or competitive bidding, the board of supervisors shall make a public announcement of the board of supervisors' intention to sell the real estate at a regular or special meeting of the board of supervisors at least thirty days prior to the sale.

(b) The board of supervisors may reject all bids if the bids are deemed to be less than the fair market value of the property. In the case of a public auction, the board of supervisors may establish a minimum bid based on the fair market value of the real property.

(b.1) The board of supervisors may sell real property under the act of October 27, 1979 (P.L. 241, No. 78), (73 P.S. § 1641 et seq.) entitled, as amended, "An act authorizing political subdivisions, municipality authorities and transportation authorities to enter into contracts for the purchase of goods and the sale of real and personal property where no bids are received," if no bids are received on real property after proper notices.

(c) The requirements of this section do not apply to conveyances or leases of real property by a township to any of the following

(1) A municipal corporation.

(2) The Federal Government

(3) The Commonwealth

(4) An institution district.

(5) A school district.

(6) A municipality authority.

(7) A county.

(8) A public utility.

(9) A volunteer fire company.

(10) A nonprofit corporation engaged in community industrial, commercial or affordable housing development.

(11) A volunteer ambulance service or volunteer rescue squad located within the township.

(12) A nonprofit corporation organized as a public library.

(13) A nonprofit medical service corporation.

(14) A nonprofit housing corporation.

(15) A nonprofit organization providing community service or development activities.

(16) A nonprofit corporation established for the preservation of historical, architectural or aesthetic sites or artifacts.

(17) A nonprofit association or nonprofit corporation organized to acquire and maintain real property for the preservation, conservation and stewardship of open space.

(18) A council of government, consortium, cooperative or other similar entity created pursuant to 53 Pa.C.S. Ch. 23 Subch. A (relating to intergovernmental cooperation).

Such conveyances or leases shall be at the sole discretion of the township.

(d) When real property is sold to a nonprofit corporation organized as a public library or to a nonprofit medical service corporation, nonprofit housing corporation, volunteer fire company, volunteer ambulance service, volunteer rescue squad or a council of government, consortium, cooperative or other similar entity created pursuant to 53 Pa.C.S. Ch. 23 Subch. A involving one or more of the entities listed in this subsection, the board of supervisors may elect to accept any nominal consideration for the property as it believes appropriate. Real property sold under this subsection is subject to the condition that when the property is not used for the purposes of the corporation or volunteer fire company, the property reverts to the township.

(e) No real estate may be purchased by a township unless the board of supervisors obtains at least one appraisal on the real property in question by a person authorized to perform an appraisal on the subject property under the act of July 10, 1990 (P.L. 404, No. 98), known as the "Real Estate Appraisers Certification Act," and the township supervisors may require that an environmental impact statement be prepared, indicating the potential liability of the township for any environmental problems associated with the real estate to be purchased. The person making the appraisal shall not be interested directly or indirectly in any aspect of the sale of the real estate. The price paid by the board of supervisors for the purchase of the real estate shall not exceed the price established by the appraisal: Provided, however, That if more than one appraisal is obtained, the price paid by the board of supervisors shall not exceed the average of the appraisals.

(f) When real property has been dedicated, deeded or devised to a township to be used for a designated purpose and the real property is accepted and used for that purpose, or the real property is not used for the purpose designated for a period of ten years or more, and the township supervisors determine that it is not possible or not desirable for the best interest of the township to use the real property for the purpose designated, the township supervisors, with the prior approval of the court of common pleas, may by ordinance reconvey to the original owners or their successors, heirs or assigns, or otherwise dispose of, the real property free and clear of any public right.

§ 1504. Personal Property.—(a) No personal property of the township shall be sold or disposed of without the approval of the board of supervisors. No personal property owned by the township, the estimated fair market value of which is two thousand dollars ($2,000) or more, shall be sold except to the highest bidder after due notice by advertisement for bids or for public auction in one newspaper of general circulation in the township. The advertisement shall be published once not less than ten days before the date set for the opening of bids or public auction, and the date for opening bids or public auction shall be announced in the advertisement. The advertisement for electronic auction sales authorized in subsection (d) shall include the Internet address or means of accessing the electronic auction and the date, time and duration of the electronic auction. If after attempting twice to receive bids or if at a public auction no bid was received, the board of supervisors may by resolution adopt a procedure by which the personal property may be sold without further action of the board of supervisors. A procedure adopted pursuant to this authorization shall be subject to and shall conform with the requirements of any law governing the sale of property by municipal corporations generally when no bids have been received. The award of contracts shall be made only by public announcement at a regular or special meeting of the board of supervisors or at the public auction. Except as provided in subsection (d), all bids shall be accepted on the condition that payment of the purchase price in full is made immediately upon acceptance of the successful bid. The board of supervisors may reject any bids received if the bids are believed to be less than the fair market value of the property.

(b) With respect to personal property, either individual items or lots of items, the fair market value of which is estimated to be less than two thousand dollars ($2,000), the board of supervisors shall by resolution adopt a procedure by which the property may be sold without further action by the board of supervisors. The board of supervisors may arrange for the sale of the item or items at public auction.

(b.1) The board of supervisors may sell personal property under the act of October 27, 1979 (P.L. 241, No. 78), [73 P.S. § 1641 et seq.] entitled, as amended, "An act authorizing political subdivisions, municipality authorities and transportation authorities to enter into contracts for the purchase of goods and the sale of real and personal property where no bids are received," if no bids are received on personal property after proper notices.

(c) The bidding and advertising requirements of this section do not apply to the following transactions:

(1) If personal property of the township is being traded in or exchanged for other personal property.

(2) The sale or lease of personal property by the township to any of the following:

(i) A municipal corporation.

(ii) The Federal Government.

Table of Contents
Part I Ch. 1–3 Ethics, Records, Open Meetings
Part II Ch. 4–10 Taxation
Part III Ch. 11–18 Torts, Contracts & Civil Rules
Part IV Ch. 19–24 Zoning & Planning
Part V Ch. 25–30 Construction and Emergency Codes
Part VI Ch. 31–39 Municipal Codes
Index

(iii) The Commonwealth.

(iv) An institution district.

(v) A school district.

(vi) A municipality authority.

(vii) A county.

(viii) A public utility.

(ix) A volunteer fire company.

(x) A nonprofit corporation engaged in community industrial, commercial or affordable housing development.

(xi) A volunteer ambulance service or volunteer rescue squad located within the township.

(xii) A nonprofit corporation organized as a public library.

(xiii) A nonprofit medical service corporation.

(xiv) A nonprofit housing corporation.

(xv) A nonprofit organization providing community service or development activities.

(xvi) A nonprofit corporation established for the preservation of historical architectural or aesthetic sites or artifacts.

(xvii) A council of government, consortium, cooperative or other similar entity created pursuant to 53 Pa.C.S. Ch. 23 Subch. A (relating to intergovernmental cooperation).

(d) A "public auction" shall include an online or electronic auction sale. During an electronic auction sale, bids shall be accepted electronically at the time and in the manner designated in the advertisement. During the electronic auction, each bidder shall have the capability to view the bidder's bid rank or the high bid price. Bidders may increase their bid prices during the electronic auction. The record of the electronic auction shall be accessible for public inspection. The purchase price shall be paid by the high bidder immediately or at a reasonable time after the conclusion of the electronic auction as determined by the township. In the event that shipping costs are incurred, they shall be paid by the high bidder.

(e) A township that has complied with the advertising requirements of subsection (a) may provide additional public notice of the sale by bids or public auction in any manner deemed appropriate by the township.

§ 1505. Boards of Supervisors to Exercise Powers.—The corporate powers of townships shall be exercised by the board of supervisors. If no specific authority is given for the payment of costs incurred in the exercise of any power contained in this act, the expenses may be paid from the general township fund.

§ 1506. General Powers.—The board of supervisors may make and adopt any ordinances, bylaws, rules and regulations not inconsistent with or restrained by the Constitution and laws of this Commonwealth necessary for the proper management, care and control of the township and its finances and the maintenance of peace, good government, health and welfare of the township and its citizens, trade, commerce and manufacturers.

§ 1507. Intergovernmental Cooperation.—The board of supervisors may make agreements with other municipal corporations in performing governmental powers, duties and functions and in carrying into effect provisions of 53 Pa.C.S. Ch. 23 Subch. A (relating to intergovernmental cooperation).

§ 1508. Capital Reserve Fund.—(a) The board of supervisors may create and maintain a separate capital reserve fund for any anticipated capital expenses, which fund shall be designated for a specific purpose or purposes when created. The moneys in the fund shall be used for no other purpose unless the board of supervisors declares that conditions in the township make other expenses more urgent than those for which the fund was created.

(b) The board of supervisors may appropriate moneys from the general township funds to be paid into the capital reserve fund or place in the fund any moneys received from the sale, lease or other disposition of any township property or from any other source.

§ 1508.1. Operating Reserve Fund.—(a) The board of supervisors shall have the power to create and maintain a separate operating reserve fund in order to minimize future revenue shortfalls and deficits, provide greater continuity and predictability in the funding of vital government services, minimize the need to increase taxes to balance the budget in times of fiscal distress, provide the capacity to undertake long-range financial planning and develop fiscal resources to meet long-term needs.

(b) The board of supervisors may annually make appropriations from the general township fund to the operating reserve fund, but no appropriation shall be made to the operating reserve fund if the effect of the appropriation would cause the fund to exceed twenty-five per centum of the estimated revenues of the township's general fund in the current fiscal year.

(c) The board of supervisors may at any time by resolution make appropriations from the operating reserve fund for the following purposes only:

(1) to meet emergencies involving the health, safety or welfare of the residents of the township;

(2) to counterbalance potential budget deficits resulting from shortfalls in anticipated revenues or program receipts from whatever source;

(2.1) to counterbalance potential budget deficits resulting from increases in anticipated costs for goods or services; or

(3) to provide for anticipated operating expenditures related either to the planned growth of existing projects or programs or to the establishment of new projects or programs if for each such project or program appropriations have been made and allocated to a separate restricted account established within the operating reserve fund.

(d) The operating reserve fund shall be invested, reinvested and administered in a manner consistent with the provisions of section 3204 relating to the investment of township funds generally.

§ 1509. Indebtedness.—The board of supervisors may incur indebtedness and issues notes, bonds or other evidence of indebtedness under the act of July 12, 1972 (P.L. 781, No. 185), known as the "Local Government Unit Debt Act," to provide sufficient moneys for any expense of the township.

§ 1510. Display of Flags.—The board of supervisors may display the flag of the United States or the Commonwealth, the official POW/MIA flag or the flag of any county or municipal corporation on any public building or grounds of the township.

§ 1511. Township Seals.—The board of supervisors may adopt a seal which contains the name of the township and the word "seal" and which shall be in the custody of the township secretary or manager. The official acts of the board of supervisors may be authenticated by use of the seal. The seal has the same effect as the seal of a notary public.

§ 1512. Insurance.—(a) The board of supervisors shall secure workers' compensation insurance for its employes, including volunteer firemen and volunteer ambulance and rescue personnel of companies duly recognized by the township by resolution, killed or injured in the course of their appointed functions or while performing any other duties expressly authorized by the board of supervisors.

(b) The board of supervisors may contract with any insurance company to insure property owned by the township.

(c) The board of supervisors may contract with any insurance company to insure any public liability of the township, including insurance on every township officer, official and employe for liability arising from errors and omissions in the performance of their duties in the course of their employment, except that liability of elected or appointed officials or officers for surcharge under law shall not be affected hereby.

(d) The board of supervisors may contract with any insurance company, nonprofit hospitalization corporation or nonprofit medical service corporation to insure its supervisors under section 606, employes and their dependents under a policy or policies of group insurance covering life, health, hospitalization, medical service or accident insurance. This provision is subject to the following qualifications:

(1) Elected officials, except supervisors under section 606, and appointed officials who are not employes of the township are not eligible for participation in any life, health, hospitalization, medical service or accident insurance coverage contract paid in whole or in part by the township.

(2) Any insurance coverage contract made by a township between January 1, 1959, and March 31, 1985, that includes or provides coverage for elected officials, except under section 606, or appointed township officials who are not employes of the township are not void or unlawful solely because the inclusion of those officials was subsequently found to be without lawful authority. No penalty, assessment, surcharge, forfeiture or disciplinary action of any kind may occur as a result of participation by those officials. Insurance benefits payable to insureds or their beneficiaries arising out of or on account of deaths, injuries, accidents or illnesses occurring before March 30, 1988, remain the property of the insureds or their beneficiaries.

(2.1) to counterbalance potential budget deficits resulting from increases in anticipated costs for goods or services; or

(e) The board of supervisors may contract with any insurance company for the pensioning of employes and may pay part or all of the premiums or charges for group pension or annuity plans. This provision is subject to the following qualifications:

(1) The benefit coverage may be provided to supervisor-employes under section 606.

(2) The board of supervisors may deduct from the employe's pay, salary or compensation the part of the premium or charge that is payable by the employee.

(3) Elected officials, except township supervisors under section 606, and appointed township officials who are not employes of the township are not eligible for participation in any pension or annuity contract paid in whole or in part by the township. No elected official, except under section 606, or appointed township official who is not an employe of the township included in a township-paid pension or annuity plan made by a township between January 1, 1959, and March 31, 1985, is subject to any penalty, assessment, surcharge, forfeiture or disciplinary action of any kind as a result of that participation. Any residual interest, value, refund of premium or benefits payable on or after March 31, 1985, arising out of the township-paid interest of the elected or appointed township officials is the exclusive property of the township.

(4) If an elected official, except supervisors under section 606, or an appointed official who is not an employe of the township personally contributed toward a township-sponsored pension plan or annuity, he shall receive a refund of his total contributions thereto plus any interest accumulated thereon. In lieu of a refund of contributions plus accumulated interest, a township official who personally contributed toward a pension or annuity plan in which he participated may elect to purchase that portion of his pension or annuity funded by the township. A qualified actuary, who shall report his determination under

the act of December 18, 1984 (P.L. 1005, No. 205), known as the "Municipal Pension Plan Funding Standard and Recovery Act," shall determine the amount the official shall pay to the township to purchase the township-funded portion of the annuity or pension.

§ 1513. Widening and Deepening Watercourses.—After permits have been secured from the Department of Environmental Protection and the Pennsylvania Fish and Boat Commission, the board of supervisors or its agents or employes may widen and deepen watercourses running through the township and erect dikes, retaining walls and embankments along the watercourses as are necessary to prevent water from overflowing the banks. For these purposes, townships may enter and condemn property as may be necessary. Townships may enter land lying near the watercourses and secure materials as may be necessary in connection with the work. Damages for property taken, injured or destroyed as the result of the work shall be determined under this act.

§ 1514. Airports.—(a) The board of supervisors may acquire by grant, lease, purchase or, where appropriate, eminent domain any property located inside or outside the boundaries of the township which in the judgment of the board of supervisors may be necessary to establish and maintain municipal airport facilities. Any township having acquired land for those purposes may establish, equip, condition, operate and maintain the property as a municipal airport, may lease all or part of the property to any individual or corporation desiring to use the property for aviation purposes and may contract in the form of a lease of all or part of the property by the Federal Government for aviation purposes upon nominal rental or without consideration.

(b) The board of supervisors may acquire by lease or purchase land for aviation purposes jointly with any county or municipal corporation of this Commonwealth and operate and maintain the municipal airport jointly with any county or municipal corporation of this Commonwealth upon terms and conditions as may be agreed upon between the proper authorities of the county or municipal corporation.

§ 1515. Urban Common Carrier Mass Transportation.—The board of supervisors may appropriate funds for urban common carrier mass transportation purposes, make contributions to county departments of transportation or urban common carrier mass transportation authorities to assist the departments or the authorities to meet costs of planning, operation, maintenance, capital improvements and debt service and make long-term agreements providing for the payment of contributions.

§ 1516. Land Use Regulations.—The board of supervisors may plan for the development of the township through zoning, subdivision and land development regulations under the act of July 31, 1968 (P.L. 805, No. 247), known as the "Pennsylvania Municipalities Planning Code."

§ 1517. Building and Housing Regulations.—The board of supervisors may enact and enforce codes and ordinances to govern and regulate the construction, alteration, repair, occupation, maintenance, sanitation, lighting, ventilation, water supply, toilet facilities, drainage, use and inspection of all buildings and housing constructed, erected, altered, designed or used for any use or occupancy and the sanitation and inspection of land in accordance with Article XVII-A..

§ 1518. [Repealed by Act 69 of 2015].

§ 1519. Building Lines.—The board of supervisors may by ordinance establish and maintain uniform building lines upon any or all public streets or highways of the township.

§ 1520. Numbering of Buildings.—The board of supervisors may by ordinance require and regulate the numbering of buildings.

§ 1521. Insect, Pest and Vector Programs.—The board of supervisors may appropriate moneys toward insect, pest and vector programs.

Chap. 39 Res. During Mil. Service
Chap. 38 Intergov. Coop.
Chap. 37 3rd Class City Code
Chap. 36 Bor. Code
Chap. 35 2nd Class Twp. Code
Chap. 34 1st Class Twp. Code
Chap. 33 Home Rule Chart. Opt. Plans Law
Chap. 32 Water Serv. Act
Chap. 31 Munic. Auth. Act

§ 1522. Sewage Treatment Facilities Regulations.—The board of supervisors may by ordinance make regulations respecting the installation of individual or community sewage treatment facilities under the act of January 24, 1966 (1965 P.L. 1535, No. 537), known as the "Pennsylvania Sewage Facilities Act."

§ 1523. Surplus Foods.—The board of supervisors may appropriate moneys for the handling, storage and distribution of surplus foods obtained through a Federal, State or local agency.

§ 1524. Community Nursing Services.—The board of supervisors may appropriate moneys to nonprofit associations or corporations which provide community nursing services.

§ 1525. Mental Health Centers.—The board of supervisors may appropriate moneys toward any nonprofit association or corporation which operates or conducts a mental health center.

§ 1526. Hospitals.—The board of supervisors may appropriate not exceeding one dollar ($1) for each township resident each year toward the erection, maintenance or support of any medical center or hospital building facilities. If the total cost of the purchase or erection exceeds one hundred thousand dollars ($100,000), approval by the appropriate health planning agency is required. The number of residents is determined from the latest official census.

§ 1527. Public Safety.—The board of supervisors may adopt ordinances to secure the safety of persons or property within the township and to define disturbing the peace within the limits of the township.

§ 1528. Ambulances and Rescue and Life Saving Services.—The board of supervisors may acquire, operate and maintain motor vehicles for the purposes of conveying persons to and from hospitals, and it may appropriate moneys toward ambulance and rescue and life saving services and make contracts relating thereto.

§ 1529. Nuisances.—The board of supervisors may by ordinance prohibit nuisances, including, but not limited to, the storage of abandoned or junked automobiles, on private and public property and the carrying on of any offensive manufacture or business.

§ 1530. Regulation of Dogs.—The board of supervisors may by ordinance prohibit and regulate the running at large of dogs.

§ 1531. Animal Shelters.—The board of supervisors may appropriate moneys to foster, encourage or assist the operation of humane societies, animal shelters or animal control centers or programs.

§ 1532. Regulation of Business.—(a) The board of supervisors may license and regulate by ordinance the following business activities within the township:

(1) Transient merchants conducting business within the township, except farmers selling their own produce, or to any sale of goods, wares or merchandise donated by the owners thereof, the proceeds of which are to be applied to any charitable or philanthropic purpose or the imposition or collection of any license fee upon insurance companies or their agents or insurance brokers authorized to transact business under the insurance laws of this Commonwealth.

(2) Cable television companies operating within the township to the extent allowed by Federal and State law and regulation.

(3) Restaurants operating within the township. This power includes the power to inspect these establishments.

(4) Junk dealers and the establishment and maintenance of junk yards and scrap yards, including, but not limited to, automobile junk yards or automobile grave yards.

(b) The board of supervisors may establish license fees for regulated businesses enumerated in subsection (a). These fees shall bear a reasonable relationship to the cost of administering the ordinance and regulating, inspecting and supervising each business. Licenses may be issued on an annual or monthly basis and any fee charged to transient merchants shall not exceed three hundred dollars ($300) per year or twenty-five dollars ($25) for each month or part of a month. ((b) amended Dec. 18, 1996, P.L., No. 172)

§ 1533. Dangerous Structures.—The board of supervisors may by ordinance require the owner to remove any nuisance or dangerous structure on public or private grounds after notice to the owner to do so. In the owner's default, the board of supervisors may remove the nuisance or structure and collect the cost of the removal, together with the penalty imposed by the ordinance, from the owner by summary proceedings or under law for the collection of municipal liens.

§ 1534. Fireworks and Inflammable Articles.—The board of supervisors may:

(1) By ordinance regulate and prohibit the manufacture of fireworks or inflammable or dangerous articles.

(2) Grant permits for supervised public displays of fireworks and adopt rules and regulations governing the displays.

(3) By ordinance adopt rules and regulations not inconsistent with State regulations relating to the storage of inflammable articles.

(4) By ordinance impose other safeguards concerning inflammable articles as may be necessary.

§ 1535. Human Services.—The board of supervisors may, under the provisions of the act of December 10, 1974 (P.L. 865, No. 292), entitled "An act authorizing municipalities to expend Federal general revenue sharing or general funds for social service programs for the poor, the disabled and the aging, and to jointly cooperate in the sponsorship, establishment, administration, maintenance and operation of such programs," by ordinance or resolution appropriate moneys for social service programs for the poor, the disabled and the aging.

§ 1536. Cemeteries.—(a) The board of supervisors may by ordinance make rules and regulations regarding the location, operation and maintenance of cemeteries in the township.

(b) When any cemetery or burial ground is abandoned or is being neglected, the board of supervisors may give notice to the owner directing the removal of weeds, refuse and debris from the cemetery within thirty days. If the removal is not completed within thirty days after the notice, the board of supervisors shall provide for the removal to be done by employes of the township or persons hired for that purpose at the expense of the township. All costs of removal shall be assessed against the owner of the cemetery, if known, and collected under section 3302(b).

(c) The cemetery shall remain open to the public under the regulation and control of the board of supervisors.

§ 1537. Burial Plots of Service Persons.—The board of supervisors may purchase plots of ground in any cemetery or burial ground for the interment of deceased or former service men and women who at the time of their death maintained legal residence within the township.

§ 1538. Care of Memorials.—The board of supervisors may maintain and repair any soldiers' monument or memorial existing or erected within the township and may receive funds from persons or organizations for those purposes.

§ 1539. Libraries.—The board of supervisors may, in accordance with the act of June 14, 1961 (P.L. 324, No. 188), known as "The Library Code," appropriate moneys toward any nonprofit association or corporation which operates or conducts a library or contract with or make grants to counties or municipal corporations for the furnishing of library service to the township.

Chap. 39 Res. During Mil. Service
Chap. 38 Intergov. Coop.
Chap. 37 3rd Class City Code
Chap. 36 Bor. Code
Chap. 35 2nd Class Twp. Code
Chap. 34 1st Class Twp. Code
Chap. 33 Home Rule Chart. Opt. Plans Law
Chap. 32 Water Serv. Act
Chap. 31 Munic. Auth. Act

§ 1540. Observances and Celebrations.—The board of supervisors may appropriate moneys for the observance of holidays, centennials or other anniversaries or for township celebrations or civic projects or programs.

§ 1541. Historical Property.—The board of supervisors may acquire by purchase or by gift, repair, supervise, operate and maintain ancient landmarks and other property of historical or antiquarian interest and make appropriations to nonprofit associations or corporations organized to acquire and maintain historical properties.

§ 1542. Community Development.—The board of supervisors may undertake community development programs, including, but not limited to, urban renewal, public housing, model cities programs and neighborhood development projects.

§ 1543. Industrial Promotion.—The board of supervisors may make appropriations to an industrial development agency.

§ 1544. Tourist Promotion Agencies.—The board of supervisors may appropriate moneys not in excess of ten cents (10¢) for each resident of the township, as determined by the latest official census, to any tourist promotion agency, as defined in the act of April 28, 1961 (P.L. 111, No. 50), known as the "Tourist Promotion Law," to assist the agencies in carrying out tourist promotional activities.

§ 1545. Nonprofit Art Corporations.—The board of supervisors may appropriate moneys, not exceeding an amount equal to one mill of the real estate tax, to any nonprofit art corporation for the conduct of its artistic and cultural activities. For the purposes of this section, the term "nonprofit art corporation" means a local arts council, commission or coordinating agency or any other nonprofit corporation engaged in the production or display of works of art, including the visual, written or performing arts and the term "artistic and cultural activities" includes the display or production of theater, music, dance, painting, architecture, sculpture, arts and crafts, photography, film, graphic arts and design and creative writing.

§ 1546. Neighborhood Crime Watch Programs.—The board of supervisors may appropriate moneys toward a neighborhood crime watch program. No township or township official is subject to contractual, tort or other liability as a result of making an appropriation under this section.

§ 1547. Public Rewards.—The board of supervisors may offer rewards for information leading to the arrest and conviction of persons who commit capital or other crimes within the township or for the violation of any township ordinance.

§ 1548. Municipality Authorities.—The board of supervisors may by ordinance or resolution individually or in cooperation with other municipal corporations form municipality authorities as authorized by the act of May 2, 1945 (P.L. 382, No. 164), known as the "Municipality Authorities Act of 1945," specify the project or projects to be undertaken by the authorities, appoint members and establish their compensation.

§ 1549. Racetracks.—(a) In addition to the powers and duties imposed upon the township supervisors by this act or any other provision of law, the township supervisors shall have the power and duty to secure the health, safety and welfare of persons and property by adopting an ordinance prohibiting the conducting of live horse race meets by a licensed corporation at a racetrack located within the area of fifty air miles from the center of an existing, currently licensed racetrack, notwithstanding the provisions of the act of December 17, 1981 (P.L. 435, No. 135), known as the "Race Horse Industry Reform Act," provided that a majority of electors of the township approve a referendum pursuant to subsection (b) prohibiting the conducting of such horse race meets within the township.

(b) The township supervisors may, or upon the petition of a number of electors of the township equal to at least twenty-five percent of the highest number of votes for a public office of the township at the last preceding municipal election shall, adopt a resolution directing the county board of elections to place a referendum question on the ballot for the primary or general election, with respect to the conducting of live horse race meets by licensed corporations within the township. The question shall be in the following form:

Shall live horse race meets conducted by licensed corporations be prohibited within the area of fifty air miles from the center of an existing, currently licensed racetrack?

(c) The definitions provided for in the "Race Horse Industry Reform Act" shall apply to this section.

§ 1550. Conservation District.—The board of supervisors may make appropriations to a conservation district as defined in the act of May 15, 1945 (P.L. 547, No. 217), known as the "Conservation District Law."

§ 1551. Watershed Associations.—The board of supervisors may make appropriations to nonprofit watershed associations for watersheds serving the township. Such appropriations may not be used to undertake litigation against any municipal corporation or to seek redress against any individual landowner.

§ 1552. Counties.—The board of supervisors may make appropriations to the county in which the township is situated for land acquisition related to community and economic development projects located within the township.

§ 1553. Emergency Services.—(a) The township shall be responsible for ensuring that fire and emergency medical services are provided within the township by the means and to the extent determined by the township, including the appropriate financial and administrative assistance for these services.

(b) The township shall consult with fire and emergency medical services providers to discuss the emergency services needs of the township.

(c) The township shall require any emergency services organizations receiving township funds to provide to the township an annual itemized listing of all expenditures of these funds before the township may consider budgeting additional funding to the organization.

ARTICLE XVI
ORDINANCES

53 P.S. § 66601

§ 1601. Ordinances.—(a) The board of supervisors may adopt ordinances in which general or specific powers of the township may be exercised, and, by the enactment of subsequent ordinances, the board of supervisors may amend, repeal or revise existing ordinances. All proposed ordinances, whether original, amended, repealed, revised, consolidated or codified, shall be published not more than sixty days nor less than seven days before passage at least once in one newspaper circulating generally in the township. Public notices shall include either the full text or a brief summary of the proposed ordinance which lists the provisions in reasonable detail and a reference to a place within the township where copies of the proposed ordinance may be examined.

(a.1) If the full text is not included, a copy shall be supplied to the publishing newspaper when the notice is published, and an attested copy shall be filed within thirty days after enactment in the county law library or other county office designated by the county commissioners, who may impose a fee no greater than that necessary to cover the actual costs of storing the ordinances. Filing with the county may be completed by the submission of an electronic copy of the ordinance through a method available, in the sole discretion of the county, to permit receipt by the office storing municipal ordinances. Upon request by the township, the county shall notify the township of the method by which electronic copies may be submitted. The county may store the ordinance electronically, provided that the public is able to access the electronically stored township ordinances during regular business hours at the office or at a remote location. The township shall

Table of Contents
Part I Ch. 1–3 Ethics, Records, Open Meetings
Part II Ch. 4–10 Taxation
Part III Ch. 11–18 Torts, Contracts & Civil Rules
Part IV Ch. 19–24 Zoning & Planning
Part V Ch. 25–30 Construction and Emergency Codes
Part VI Ch. 31–39 Municipal Codes
Index

Chap. 39 Res. During Mil. Service
Chap. 38 Intergov. Coop.
Chap. 37 3rd Class City Code
Chap. 36 Bor. Code
Chap. 35 2nd Class Twp. Code
Chap. 34 1st Class Twp. Code
Chap. 33 Home Rule Chart. Opt. Plans Law
Chap. 32 Water Serv. Act
Chap. 31 Munic. Auth. Act

retain a printed copy of the e-mail and ordinance as transmitted. The date of such filing shall not affect the effective date of the ordinance, the validity of the process of the enactment or adoption of the ordinance; nor shall a failure to record within the time provided be deemed a defect in the process of the enactment or adoption of such ordinance. If substantial amendments are made in the proposed ordinance, before voting upon enactment, the board of supervisors shall at least ten days before enactment readvertise in one newspaper of general circulation in the township a brief summary setting forth all the provisions in reasonable detail, together with a summary of the amendments. Ordinances shall be recorded in the ordinance book of the township and are effective five days after adoption unless a date later than five days after adoption is stated in the ordinance.

(b) When maps, plans or drawings of any kind are adopted as part of an ordinance, instead of publishing them as part of the ordinance, the board of supervisors may refer in publishing the ordinance to the place where the maps, plans or drawings are on file and may be examined.

(c) Deleted

(c.1) An ordinance enacted by the board of supervisors pursuant to this act shall prescribe the fines and penalties which may be imposed for its violation and shall, unless otherwise specified in another statute, designate the method of its enforcement in accordance with the following:

(1) Civil enforcement. Except as provided in paragraph (2), when the penalty imposed for the violation of an ordinance enacted pursuant to the provisions of this act is not voluntarily paid to the township, the township shall initiate a civil enforcement proceeding before a district justice. The civil enforcement proceeding shall be initiated by complaint or by such other means as may be provided by the Pennsylvania Rules of Civil Procedure. An ordinance which is to be enforced through a civil enforcement proceeding may prescribe civil penalties not to exceed six hundred dollars ($600) per violation. In addition to or in lieu of civil actions before a district justice, townships may enforce ordinances in equity. In any case where a penalty for a violation of a township ordinance has not been timely paid and the person upon whom the penalty was imposed is found to have been liable therefor in civil proceedings, the violator shall be liable for the penalty imposed, including additional daily penalties for continuing violations, plus court costs and reasonable attorney fees incurred by the township in the enforcement proceedings. A township shall be exempt from the payment of costs in any civil case brought to enforce an ordinance in accordance with this paragraph.

(2) Enforcement as summary offenses. For an ordinance regulating building, housing, property maintenance, health, fire, public safety, parking, solicitation, curfew, water, air or noise pollution, the board of supervisors shall provide that its enforcement shall be by action brought before a district justice in the same manner provided for the enforcement of summary offenses under the Pennsylvania Rules of Criminal Procedure. The municipal solicitor may assume charge of the prosecution without the consent of the District Attorney as required under Pa.R.Crim.P. No. 83(c) (relating to trial in summary cases). The board of supervisors may prescribe criminal fines not to exceed one thousand dollars ($1,000) per violation and may prescribe imprisonment to the extent allowed by law for the punishment of summary offenses.

(3) Existing ordinances. With regard to ordinances enacted prior to May 7, 1996, those regulating building, housing, property maintenance, health, fire, public safety, parking, solicitation, curfew, water, air or noise pollution shall be deemed automatically amended so that they shall be enforced by an action brought before a district justice in the same manner provided for the enforcement of summary offenses in accordance with paragraph (2). All other ordinances enacted prior to May 7, 1996, shall be deemed automatically

amended so that they shall be enforced through a civil enforcement proceeding in accordance with paragraph (1).

(4) Enforcement in equity. Ordinances may be enforced by a township through an action in equity brought in the court of common pleas of the county where the township is situate.

(5) Separate offenses. Ordinances may provide that a separate offense shall arise for each day or portion thereof in which a violation is found to exist or for each section of the ordinance which is found to have been violated.

(6) Payment to treasurer. All fines and penalties collected for the violation of any township ordinance shall be paid to the township treasurer.

(7) Enforcement officers or agents. The board of supervisors may delegate the initial determination of ordinance violation and the service of notice of violation to such officers or agents as the township shall deem qualified for that purpose.

(d) The board of supervisors may prepare or have prepared a consolidation or codification of the general body of township ordinances or the ordinances on a particular subject. The board of supervisors may adopt the consolidation or codification as an ordinance of the township, except the required advertised notice of the proposed adoption of the consolidation or codification shall include a listing of its table of contents. The procedure for the consolidation or codification of township ordinances as a single ordinance may also be followed in enacting a complete group or body of ordinances repealing or amending existing ordinances as may be necessary in the course of preparing a consolidation or codification of the township ordinances, except that the advertisement giving notice of the proposed adoption shall list, in lieu of a table of contents, the titles only of each of the ordinances in the complete group or body of ordinances.

(e) In the same manner as other ordinances, the board of supervisors may adopt, by reference to a standard or nationally recognized code in a township ordinance, all or any portion of the code as an ordinance of the township. No portion of any code which limits the work to be performed to any type of construction contractor or labor or mechanic classification shall be adopted. Copies of the proposed code or portion or amendment shall be filed with the township secretary at least ten days before the board of supervisors considers the proposed ordinance and upon enactment kept with the ordinance book and available for public use, inspection and examination.

(f) Any person aggrieved by the adoption of any ordinance may make complaint as to the legality of the ordinance to the court of common pleas.

(1601 amended Dec. 18, 1996, P.L., No.172)

ARTICLE XVII
PUBLIC BUILDINGS
53 P.S. § 66701–66704

§ 1701. Township Buildings.—(a) The board of supervisors may procure by purchase, gift, devise or the exercise of eminent domain a lot or lots of ground located within the township and erect or use buildings thereon for township purposes. No land or property used for any cemetery, burying ground, public or parochial school, educational or charitable institution, seminary or place of public worship shall be taken or appropriated under this section.

(b) Subject to the restrictions contained in section 3402, townships in counties of the second class A may enter upon and appropriate historic land and structures which are privately owned, provided the sole purpose of the taking is the preservation and maintenance of the property for its historic value and

Table of Contents | Part I Ch. 1–3 Ethics, Records, Open Meetings | Part II Ch. 4–10 Taxation | Part III Ch. 11–18 Torts, Contracts & Civil Rules | Part IV Ch. 19–24 Zoning & Planning | Part V Ch. 25–30 Construction and Emergency Codes | Part VI Ch. 31–39 Municipal Codes | Index

Chap. 39 Res. During Mil. Service
Chap. 38 Intergov. Coop.
Chap. 37 3rd Class City Code
Chap. 36 Bor. Code
Chap. 35 2nd Class Twp. Code
Chap. 34 1st Class Twp. Code
Chap. 33 Home Rule Chart. Opt. Plans Law
Chap. 32 Water Serv. Act
Chap. 31 Munic. Auth. Act

the Pennsylvania Historical and Museum Commission or the county historical society has certified both the historic value of the property and that it is not being maintained in an appropriate manner.

§ 1702. Use of Public Land Acquired for Other Purposes.—When the board of supervisors desires to take any public lands previously granted or dedicated to a use or purpose for which they are no longer used, it shall pass an ordinance declaring its intention and shall petition the court of common pleas for leave to file the bond of the township to secure any person or persons who may be entitled to compensation for the taking. The court shall direct notice to be given by publication in at least one newspaper circulating generally in the township. The court may increase the amount of the bond, shall hear all exceptions that are filed against the petition and the sufficiency of the bond and may grant or deny the request of the petition. Upon the granting of the petition and the approval of the bond, the board of supervisors may enter lands for the purposes of erecting public buildings. The bond, which shall be in the name of the Commonwealth for the use of any person or persons who are entitled to damages by reason of the taking of the lands, shall remain on file for their use and benefit.

§ 1703. How Damages Are Assessed.—The compensation and damages arising from taking, using and appropriating private or public property for township purposes shall be ascertained, determined, awarded and paid under this act for eminent domain proceedings.

§ 1704. Garages and Warehouses.—The board of supervisors may purchase or lease land inside or outside the limits of the township and erect garages, warehouses or other buildings as may be necessary for handling and storing equipment, materials and supplies.

ARTICLE XVII-A
UNIFORM CONSTRUCTION CODE, PROPERTY MAINTENANCE CODE AND RESERVED POWERS

§ 1701-A. Definitions.

The following words and phrases when used in this article shall have the meanings given to them in this section unless the context clearly indicates otherwise:

"Uniform Construction Code." The Uniform Construction Code adopted in accordance with the act of November 10, 1999 (P.L.491, No.45), known as the Pennsylvania Construction Code Act.

§ 1702-A. Primacy of Uniform Construction Code.

(a) General rule.—The Uniform Construction Code shall apply to the construction, alteration, repair and occupancy of all buildings and structures within a township.

(b) Primacy.—This section and an ordinance, rule or regulation adopted under this section, including an ordinance exceeding the requirements of the Uniform Construction Code, shall not supersede or abrogate the act of November 10, 1999 (P.L.491, No.45), known as the Pennsylvania Construction Code Act, and shall conform to, and be construed and read in *pari materia* with the provisions of that act.

§ 1703-A. Public Nuisance.

A building, housing or property, or part of a building, housing or property erected, altered, extended, reconstructed, removed or maintained, contrary to a provision of an ordinance passed for a purpose specified in this article may be declared, by a court of law, a public nuisance, and may be abatable as such. However, a violation of the Uniform Construction Code or an ordinance that equals or exceeds the Uniform Construction Code shall be subject to the provisions of the act of November 10, 1999 (P.L.491, No.45), known as the Pennsylvania Construction Code Act, and the regulations adopted thereunder by the Department of Labor and Industry relating to enforcement for noncompliance.

§ 1704-A. Property Maintenance Code.

(a) Property maintenance code.—Notwithstanding the primacy of the Uniform Construction Code, the township supervisors may enact a property maintenance ordinance, and they may incorporate a standard or nationally recognized property maintenance code, or a variation or change or part of the code, published and printed in book form, without incorporating the text of the code in the ordinance, or the supervisors may enact a standard or nationally recognized property maintenance code or a change or variation or part, as the ordinance. In either event, the proposed ordinance, or a brief summary of the proposed ordinance, shall be published not more than 60 days nor less than seven days before passage at least once in one newspaper circulating generally in the township. The notice shall state the time and place of the meeting and the particular nature of the ordinance to be considered. The notice shall also state where copies of the proposed ordinance and property maintenance code can be examined or obtained at cost. A property maintenance code adopted by reference need not be recorded in or attached to the ordinance book, but shall be deemed to have been legally recorded if the ordinance by which the code was adopted by reference shall have been recorded, with an accompanying notation stating where the full text of the code has been filed. The ordinance may provide for reasonable property fines and penalties for violations of the ordinance. The procedure under this section relating to the adoption of the ordinance may likewise be utilized in amending, supplementing or repealing a provision of the ordinance.

(b) Code enforcement officers—The township supervisors may appoint code enforcement officers who shall have the right to enter upon and inspect any premises, subject to constitutional standards, at reasonable hours and in a reasonable manner for the administration and enforcement of the township's property maintenance code. A fee payable to code enforcement officers under the ordinance shall be promptly paid by the township supervisors to the township treasurer for the use of the township.

(c) Legal actions.—In addition to the penalties provided by the property maintenance ordinance, the township may institute appropriate actions or proceedings at law or in equity to prevent or restrain property maintenance violations.

(d) Construction.—The powers of a township as provided in this section shall be in addition to, but not limited to, the powers provided in the act of November 26, 2008 (P.L.1672, No.135), known as the Abandoned and Blighted Property Conservatorship Act, 53 Pa.C.S. Ch. 61 (relating to neighborhood blight reclamation and revitalization) and 68 Pa.C.S. Ch. 21 (relating to land banks).

§ 1705-A. Reserved Powers.

If, as a result of legislative action or final order of court for which the time for appeal has expired and no appeal has been taken or from which there is no pending appeal, the Uniform Construction Code or a replacement code is no longer applicable in townships, the township supervisors may:

(1) Enact and enforce ordinances to govern and regulate the construction, reconstruction, alteration, extension, repair, conversion, maintenance, use or occupation, and provide for the approval, inspection and enforcement of the ordinance as it relates to the property. The codes may be combined or separately enacted or combined with the property maintenance code. The township supervisors may adopt, amend or incorporate by reference any standard or nationally recognized code or any variations or changes or parts of the code as its ordinance in the manner provided in section 1704-A. The ordinance may provide for reasonable fines and penalties for violations of the ordinance.

(2) Require that before construction, reconstruction, alteration, extension, repair or conversion of a building has begun, approval of the plans and specifications shall be secured.

(3) Appoint building inspectors, housing inspectors, code enforcement officers, fire prevention inspectors, electrical inspectors and plumbing inspectors and fix their compensation. The inspectors shall have the right to enter upon, subject to constitutional standards, and inspect any premises at reasonable hours and in a reasonable manner, for the administration and enforcement of the township's adopted codes or ordinances incorporating standard or nationally recognized codes. A fee payable to an inspector under the ordinance shall be promptly paid by the township supervisors to the township treasurer for the use of the township.

(4) In addition to the penalties provided by ordinances, institute appropriate actions or proceedings at law or in equity to prevent or restrain the unlawful construction, reconstruction, alteration, extension, repair, conversion, maintenance, use or occupation of property located within the township, to restrain, correct or abate the violation and to prevent the use or occupancy of the building, housing or structure.

[Ed. Note: per §4 of Act 69 of 2015, this Article XXVII-A shall not be construed to repeal or modify any township ordinance in effect on the effective date of this act or affect any proceeding or enforcement of any township ordinance instituted prior to the effective date of this act. (Jan. 24, 2016)].

ARTICLE XVIII

FIRE PREVENTION AND PROTECTION

53 P.S. § 66801–66806

§ 1801. Authority of Board of Supervisors.—The board of supervisors may provide for fire protection within the township.

§ 1802. Fire Hydrants and Water Supply.—(a) The board of supervisors may place, replace, operate, maintain and repair or contract with water companies or municipal authorities for the placing, replacing, operating, maintaining and repairing of fire hydrants to water mains, maintaining pressures approved by fire insurance underwriters along highways, streets, roads and alleys within the township or provide for or acquire a water supply system equipped to supply sufficient water for the protection of property from fire. The moneys necessary for providing or acquiring these fire protection services may be obtained by one of the following methods:

(1) The board of supervisors may annually assess the cost of fire protection by an equal assessment upon all property, whether or not exempt from taxation by existing law, within seven hundred and eighty feet of any fire hydrant based upon the assessment of property for county tax purposes.

(2) The board of supervisors may annually assess the cost of fire protection by an equal assessment on all property, whether or not exempt from taxation under existing law, abutting upon highways, streets, roads and alleys within seven hundred and eighty feet of any fire hydrant in proportion to the number of feet the property abuts any water main or within seven hundred and eighty feet of any fire hydrant on the water main. The board of supervisors may provide for an equitable reduction from the frontage of lots at intersections or where, due to the irregular shape of lots, an assessment of the full frontage would be inequitable.

(3) The board of supervisors may pay the cost for fire protection out of the general township fund. If the board of supervisors elects to pay the cost of fire protection services out of the general fund, any special fire protection districts

and annual assessments shall be abolished. All moneys in the separate accounts for the special fire protection districts shall be paid into the general fund.

(b) When assessments are made under this section, no assessment shall be made against any farmland or an airport which is privately owned and which is not open nor intended to be open to the public; but vacant lots between built-up sections, either tilled or not tilled, are not farmland.

(c) All assessments for fire protection shall be collected by the tax collector under section 3301(a).

(d) The assessment may be billed on the annual real estate tax bill for township purposes if authorized by the board of supervisors.

§ 1803. Fire Companies, Facilities and Training.—(a) The board of supervisors may appropriate moneys for the use of the township or to fire companies located in the township for the operation and maintenance of fire companies, for the purchase and maintenance of fire apparatus, for the construction, repair and maintenance of fire company houses, for training of fire company personnel and, as set forth in this section, for fire training schools or centers in order to secure fire protection for the inhabitants of the township. The fire companies shall submit to the board of supervisors an annual report of the use of the appropriated moneys for each completed year of the township before any further payments may be made to the fire companies for the current year.

(b) The board of supervisors may by ordinance make rules and regulations for the government of fire companies which are located within the township and their officers.

(c) The board of supervisors may contract with or make grants to near or adjacent municipal corporations or volunteer fire companies therein for fire protection in the township.

(d) No volunteer fire company not in existence in the township before the effective date of this act may organize or operate unless the establishment or organization is approved by resolution of the board of supervisors.

(e) The board of supervisors may annually appropriate funds to fire companies located within the township for the training of its personnel and to lawfully organized or incorporated county or regional firemen's associations or an entity created pursuant to the act of July 12, 1972 (P.L. 762, No. 180), referred to as the Intergovernmental Cooperation Law, to establish, equip, maintain and operate fire training schools or centers for the purpose of giving instruction and practical training in the prevention, control and fighting of fire and related fire department emergencies to the members of fire departments and volunteer fire companies in any city, borough, town or township within this Commonwealth.

(1803 amended Dec. 18, 1996, P.L., No. 175)

Compiler's Note: The act of July 12, 1972 (P.L. 762, No. 180), referred to as the Intergovernmental Cooperation Law, referred to in subsec. (e), was repealed by the act of December 19, 1996, P.L., No. 177. The subject matter is now contained in 53 Pa.C.S. Ch. 23 Subch. A (relating to intergovernmental cooperation).

§ 1804. Ponds, Dams or Impoundments for Fire Protection.—The board of supervisors may construct or contribute moneys for or participate in the construction of ponds, dams or other impoundments to provide water for fire protection for the township.

§ 1805. Fire Prevention Code.—The board of supervisors may adopt any standard fire prevention code published and printed in book form as provided under this act for adopting standard codes.

§ 1806. Prohibition of Fire-Producing Devices in Certain Retail Stores.—The board of supervisors may by ordinance prohibit the smoking or carrying of lighted

Table of Contents
Part I Ch. 1–3 Ethics, Records, Open Meetings
Part II Ch. 4–10 Taxation
Part III Ch. 11–18 Torts, Contracts & Civil Rules
Part IV Ch. 19–24 Zoning & Planning
Part V Ch. 25–30 Construction and Emergency Codes
Part VI Ch. 31–39 Municipal Codes
Index

cigarettes, cigars, pipes or matches and the use of matches or fire-producing devices in retail stores arranged to accommodate one hundred persons or more or which employ ten or more employes. Any ordinance passed under this section may not prohibit smoking in any restaurant room, rest room, beauty parlor, executive office or any shopping center area designated for smoking.

ARTICLE XIX

TOWNSHIP POLICE

53 P.S. § 66901–66915

§ 1901. Creating or Disbanding Police Force.—The board of supervisors may by resolution create or disband a police force within the township or, upon the petition of not less than twenty-five registered electors or taxpayers of the township, appoint police officers.

§ 1902. Appointment of Police.—The board of supervisors shall provide for the organization and supervision and determine the number and the compensation of the police officers. The position of police officer is incompatible with the office of supervisor, auditor, tax collector and manager. The chairman of the board of supervisors may swear in police officers. The board of supervisors may assign any police officer to undergo a course of training at any training school for police officers established or made available by the Federal or State Government and provide for payment of the officer's expenses while in attendance at the training school.

§ 1903. Contracts to Secure Police Service.—Any township may contract with any municipal corporation to secure the services within the township of the police of the municipal corporation. When any contract is made, the police officers of the employing municipal corporation have all the powers and authority conferred by law on police officers in the township which has contracted to secure police service.

§ 1904. Contract to Provide Police Service.—Any township may contract with any municipal corporation to provide police services within the other municipal corporation. When a contract is made, the township police have all the powers and authority conferred by law on police in the municipal corporation which has contracted to secure police service.

§ 1905. Powers.—Each township police officer has those powers and abilities as are granted to police officers under the laws of this Commonwealth or the rules of the Supreme Court or the ordinances of the township for which a fine or penalty is imposed unless otherwise excepted in this act.

§ 1906. Shield.—Each police officer when on duty shall wear a shield or badge with the words "township police" and the name of the township inscribed thereon.

§ 1907. Equipment.—The board of supervisors may provide each police officer with a uniform, equipment and means of transportation and the maintenance thereof.

§ 1908. Lockups.—The board of supervisors may provide lockup facilities.

§ 1909. Certain Compensation Prohibited.—No police officer may charge or accept any fee or other compensation in addition to the salary paid by the township for any service rendered or performed by the police officer, except public rewards.

§ 1910. Police Pension Fund.—(a) In those townships maintaining police forces of less than three full-time police officers, the board of supervisors may by ordinance or resolution establish a police pension fund or pension annuity into which each member of the police force may be required to pay a member contribution of an equal and proportionate charge which, except to the extent that section 607(c) of the act of December 18, 1984 (P.L. 1005, No. 205), known as the "Municipal Pension Plan Funding Standard and Recovery Act," applies, shall not exceed annually three percent of the pay of the member.

(b) The fund shall be under the direction of the board of supervisors for the benefit of members of the police force who receive honorable discharge therefrom by reason of age or disability and the families of members who may be injured or killed in the service. Any allowances made to those who are retired by reason of disability or age shall be in conformity with a uniform scale.

(c) The ordinance or resolution establishing the police pension fund shall prescribe a minimum period of continuous service of not less than twenty years, after which the members of the force may be retired from active duty. Township police officers so retired may be subject to service as police reserves until unfit for service by reason of age or disability, when they may be finally discharged.

(d) The basis of the apportionment of the pension is determined by the rate of monthly pay of the member at the date of death, honorable discharge or retirement.

(e) Payments made on account of police pensions are a charge on no fund of the township other than the police pension fund.

(f) Townships shall make contributions to the police pension fund in an amount sufficient to meet the minimum obligation of the municipality with respect to the pension plan pursuant to the "Municipal Pension Plan Funding Standard and Recovery Act," and may take by gift, grant, devise or bequest any money or property in trust for the benefit of the police pension fund. The care, management, investment and disposal of trust funds or property is vested in the board of supervisors subject, whenever possible or practical, to any directions for administration which the donors of the funds and property may prescribe.

(g) A person participating in the police pension fund and entitled to receive a benefit therefrom may not be deprived of his right to an equal and proportionate share therein except for the following causes: conviction of a crime or misdemeanor or failing to comply with some general regulation relating to the management of the fund, which may be made by ordinance or resolution and which provides that a failure to comply therewith terminates the right to participate in the pension fund after notice and hearing as it prescribes.

(h) Police pension funds of townships with a police force of three or more full-time officers are governed by the act of May 29, 1956 (1955 P.L. 1804, No. 600), referred to as the Municipal Police Pension Law.

§ 1911. Police Protection Districts.—On petition of a majority of the property owners of any territory within the township, the board of supervisors may designate the territory as a district for the purpose of providing police protection. The board of supervisors may annually assess the cost of the maintenance of the police protection by an equal assessment on all property benefited by the protection in proportion to the number of feet the property fronts on the street or highway or portion thereof to be protected. The board of supervisors may provide for an equitable reduction from the frontage of lots at intersections or where, due to the irregular shape of lots, an assessment of the full frontage would be inequitable. No assessment shall be made against any farmland, but vacant lots between built-up sections, whether tilled or not tilled, are not farmland. The assessment for each foot front against vacant lots shall be only twenty-five percent of the assessment for each foot front against property with improvements. All assessments for police protection shall be filed with the township tax collector under section 3301(a).

§ 1912. Removal of Police Officers.—No person employed as a regular full-time police officer in any police department, except officers appointed for a probationary period of one year or less, shall be suspended, removed or reduced in rank except under the act of June 15, 1951 (P.L. 586, No. 144), entitled "An act regulating the suspension, removal, furloughing and reinstatement of police officers in boroughs and townships of the first class having police forces of less than three members, and in townships of the second class."

§ 1913. Auxiliary Police.—The board of supervisors may confirm persons to serve as auxiliary police officers under the act of January 14, 1952 (1951 P.L. 2016, No. 561), entitled "An act providing for supplementing the police forces of cities, boroughs, towns and townships, for the appointment, powers and control of auxiliary police therein, and for the transfer during disasters and emergencies of such auxiliary police, members of the regular police forces, and police equipment thereof."

§ 1914. Special Fire Police.—The board of supervisors may confirm any members of a volunteer fire company to serve as special fire police under the act of June 18, 1941 (P.L. 137, No. 74), entitled, as amended, "An act providing for the appointment, powers and control of members of volunteer fire companies as special fire police, and conferring powers on them at fires attended by their fire companies in any city, borough, town, township or home rule municipality." The chairman of the board of supervisors may swear in special fire police officers.

(1914 amended Dec. 18, 1996, P.L., No. 172)

§ 1915. School Crossing Guards.—(a) Upon request of the board of school directors of a school district located wholly or partially within the township, the board of supervisors by resolution may appoint school crossing guards to control and direct traffic at or near schools. The school crossing guards shall be in uniform and shall be authorized only in the management of traffic and pedestrians. School crossing guards serve at the pleasure of the board of supervisors, except as provided in subsection (c) and are not eligible to join any police township pension fund. The board of supervisors shall determine the compensation of school crossing guards, to be paid by the township or jointly by the township and the school district in a ratio to be determined by the two boards. If the township and school district cannot determine the ratio of compensation to be paid by each board, each board shall pay one-half of the compensation of the school crossing guards.

(b) The board of supervisors may create an educational service agency under section 402.1 of the act of December 5, 1936 (2nd Sp.Sess., 1937 P.L. 2897, No. 1), known as the "Unemployment Compensation Law," to provide school crossing guards to one or more educational institutions in conjunction with the school district. The educational service agency shall serve as the agency for management and control of the school crossing guards.

(c) The board of supervisors may approve an ordinance allowing a board of school directors to assume hiring and oversight of school crossing guards. Before the board of supervisors may approve such an ordinance, the board of directors of the school district shall approve a resolution requesting the authority to assume the hiring and oversight of school crossing guards. The ordinance shall outline how the police department will provide any necessary training and assistance of the school crossing guards while on duty. Such school crossing guards will be authorized only in the management of traffic and pedestrians in and around areas identified by the police department and the school district superintendent or his or her designees. The school crossing guards shall not come within the civil service provision of this act, nor shall they fall under the bargaining unit of the school district nor be considered an employee as defined under section 1101-A of the act of March 10, 1949 (P.L. 30, No. 14), known as the "Public School Code of 1949," or a "School employee" as defined under 24 Pa. C.S. § 8102 (relating to definitions), or under any plans hereafter effective. Once the ordinance receives approval by the board of supervisors, the school district shall assume the cost of compensation, including fixing such compensation, if any, of the school crossing guards. Auxiliary policemen, appointed as prescribed by general law, may be hired by the school district to serve as school crossing guards. The board of school directors shall notify the board of supervisors of those hired to serve as school crossing guards and request the necessary training or assistance be provided as outlined by the ordinance.

ARTICLE XX
STREET LIGHTS
53 P.S. § 67001–67003

§ 2001. Lighting.—The board of supervisors may light and illuminate the highways, roads and other public places of the township and remove, alter or improve lighting as may be appropriate and in the best interests of the township and make contracts for securing and maintaining a supply of light.

§ 2002. Street Light Districts.—(a) The board of supervisors may provide street lights and make regulations therefor within the township or within any district of the township established by the board of supervisors for that purpose.

(b) Upon receipt of a petition signed by seventy percent of the property owners within any defined area of the township, the board of supervisors shall establish the defined area as a lighting district or include the defined area within an existing lighting district and shall provide public lighting within the area.

(c) The board of supervisors may contract with electric, gas or other lighting companies to light and illuminate roads and highways and other public places with electric light, gas light or other illuminating substances.

§ 2003. Costs.—(a) The board of supervisors may pay for the cost of public lighting by any one or a combination of the following means, whether the installation of the lighting was initiated by action of the board of supervisors or by petition:

(1) From the general fund.

(2) Through uniform annual assessments made upon benefited properties on the foot-front basis.

(3) By uniform annual assessment upon each property benefited.

(4) By an equal assessment upon each property benefited, based upon the assessment for county tax purposes.

(5) By any combination of the above methods or other equitable means of assessment as the board of supervisors may determine.

(b) If public street lighting is currently in existence and is being paid for by a certain means or method, the board of supervisors may alter or amend the means of assessing the cost of the lighting.

(c) Properties are subject to assessment for this purpose, whether or not the property is exempt from taxation by existing law.

(d) If the foot-front method of assessment is used, the assessment shall be by equal assessment on all property in proportion to the number of feet the property fronts on the street or highway or portion thereof to be lighted. The board of supervisors may provide for an equitable reduction from the frontage of lots at intersections or where, due to the irregular shape of lots, an assessment of the full frontage would be inequitable. No assessment shall be made against any farmland, but vacant lots between built-up sections, whether tilled or not tilled, are not farmland. The assessment for each foot front against vacant lots shall be only twenty-five percent of the assessment for each foot front against property with improvements.

(e) All annual assessments for street lights shall be filed with the township tax collector under section 3301(a). The assessment may be billed on the annual real estate tax bill for general township purposes if authorized by the board of supervisors.

Chap. 39 Res. During Mil. Service
Chap. 38 Intergov. Coop.
Chap. 37 3rd Class City Code
Chap. 36 Bor. Code
Chap. 35 2nd Class Twp. Code
Chap. 34 1st Class Twp. Code
Chap. 33 Home Rule Chart. Opt. Plans Law
Chap. 32 Water Serv. Act
Chap. 31 Munic. Auth. Act

ARTICLE XXI
SOLID WASTE COLLECTION AND DISPOSITION

53 P.S. § 67101–67108

§ 2101. Accumulation of Ashes, Garbage, Solid Waste and Refuse Materials.—The board of supervisors in the manner authorized by the act of July 7, 1980 (P.L. 380, No. 97), known as the "Solid Waste Management Act," and the act of July 28, 1988 (P.L. 556, No. 101), known as the "Municipal Waste Planning, Recycling and Waste Reduction Act," may prohibit accumulations of ashes, garbage, solid waste and other refuse materials upon private property, including the imposition and collection of reasonable fees and charges for the collection, removal and disposal thereof.

§ 2102. Collection.—The board of supervisors may collect and remove, by contract or otherwise, ashes, garbage, solid waste and other refuse materials and recyclables and prescribe penalties for the enforcement thereof. Any contract with refuse haulers may be made for a period not exceeding five years. This limitation does not apply to contracts with any other county or municipal corporation.

§ 2103. Disposal.—The board of supervisors may dispose of, by contract or otherwise, ashes, garbage, solid waste and other refuse materials. Any contract with the owner of a private facility for the disposal or incineration of ashes, garbage, solid waste and other refuse materials may be made for a period not exceeding twenty years. This limitation does not apply to contracts with any county or municipal corporation.

§ 2104. Acquisition of Land.—The board of supervisors may acquire any real property and erect, maintain, improve, operate and lease, either as lessor or lessee, facilities for incineration, landfill or other methods of disposal, either inside or outside the limits of the township, including equipment, either separately or jointly, with any county or municipal corporation in order to provide for the destruction, collection, removal and disposal of ashes, garbage, solid waste or other refuse materials, for the collection and storage of recyclable materials or for the composting of leaf and yard waste. The board of supervisors may provide for the payment of the cost thereof out of the funds of the township. The board of supervisors may acquire land for landfill purposes, either amicably or by exercising the power of eminent domain, and maintain lands and places for the dumping of ashes, garbage, solid waste and other refuse materials.

§ 2105. Charge for Services.—The board of supervisors may establish, alter, charge and collect rates and other charges for the collection, removal and disposal of ashes, garbage, solid waste, other refuse materials and recyclable materials, and the costs of including the payment of any indebtedness incurred for the construction, purchase, improvement, repair, maintenance and operation of any facilities therefor, and the amount due under any contract with any county or municipal corporation furnishing the services or facilities.

§ 2106. Appropriations.—The board of supervisors may make appropriations to any county or municipal corporation for the construction, purchase, improvement, repair, maintenance and operation of any facilities for the collection, removal, disposal or marketing of ashes, garbage, solid waste, other refuse materials, recyclable materials or composted leaf and yard waste.

§ 2107. Refuse Collection District.—On petition of a majority of the owners, occupants or tenants of any territory inside the township which is definitely defined, set apart and limited by the board of supervisors as a refuse collection district, either with township employes and facilities or with independent contractors, the board of supervisors may provide for the removal from the refuse collection district of ashes, garbage, solid waste or other refuse materials and for the disposal thereof, including the collection and marketing of recyclable materials. The board of supervisors may levy an assessment upon all owners, occupants or tenants of the district sufficient to defray the cost of the removal, disposal or marketing under section 3301(b).

§ 2108. Exclusion from Bidding Requirements.—A township shall not be subject to requirements otherwise imposed by law for the sale of personal property owned by the township when selling recyclable materials or materials separated, collected, recovered or created by recycling, as provided in the act of April 9, 1992 (P.L. 70, No. 21), entitled "An act excluding the sale of recyclable material from political subdivision personal property sale restrictions relating to advertising and bidding."

ARTICLE XXII
PARKS, RECREATION CENTERS AND FORESTS
53 P.S. § 67201–67207

§ 2201. Acquisition of Lands and Buildings.—The board of supervisors may designate lands or buildings owned, leased or controlled by the township for use as parks, playgrounds, playfields, gymnasiums, swimming pools, indoor recreation centers, public parks and other recreation areas and facilities and acquire lands or buildings by lease, gift, devise, purchase or by the exercise of the right of eminent domain for recreational purposes and construct and equip facilities for recreational purposes.

§ 2202. Recreation Facilities Employes.—The board of supervisors may employ persons to maintain the recreation facilities or supervise the use of the recreation facilities.

§ 2203. Regulation of Parks and Public Amusements.—(a) The board of supervisors may by ordinance regulate the use and enjoyment by the public of any park or recreation grounds owned and operated by the township or charitable organizations for the use of the public.

(b) The board of supervisors may prescribe rules for the use by the public of parks and recreation grounds and the facilities and amusements connected therewith and post the rules at conspicuous places in the parks or recreation grounds. Any person who violates the rules commits a summary offense.

(c) The board of supervisors may by ordinance not inconsistent with State law and regulations regulate the time of opening and closing and the conduct of places of public entertainment, amusement and recreation.

(d) The board of supervisors may by ordinance or resolution appropriate funds for recreation programs not directly sponsored by the township.

§ 2204. Creation of Recreation Boards.—(a) The board of supervisors may by ordinance create a recreation board to supervise, regulate, equip and maintain township-funded recreation programs and facilities. The recreation board has only those powers specifically delegated to it by the board of supervisors.

(b) Recreation boards, when established, shall consist of five, seven or nine persons. The members shall be appointed by the board of supervisors and shall serve for terms of five years or until their successors are appointed, except that the members first appointed shall be appointed so that the terms of not more than two members expire annually. Members shall serve without pay but may be reimbursed by the township for all expenses incurred in performing their duties. All persons appointed shall serve their full terms unless voluntarily resigned or removed by the board of supervisors for dereliction or neglect of duty. Vacancies occurring other than by expiration of term shall be for the unexpired term and shall be filled in the same manner as original appointments.

(c) The members of a recreation board shall elect a chairman and secretary and select all other necessary officers to serve for a period of one year. The recreation board may adopt rules and regulations for the conduct of all business within its jurisdiction and exercise powers and functions concerning parks and recreation facilities as may be delegated to it by the board of supervisors. The recreation board shall submit an annual report to the board of supervisors, including an analysis of the adequacy and effectiveness of community recreation areas, facilities and leadership.

§ 2205. Joint Ownership and Maintenance.—The board of supervisors may join with any one or more municipal corporations, counties or school districts to acquire, create, equip, maintain and operate any park or recreation area to serve residents of the township under the act of July 12, 1972 (P.L. 762, No. 180), referred to as the Intergovernmental Cooperation Law.

§ 2206. Expenses for Maintenance.—All expenses incurred in the operation of parks, recreation areas and facilities are payable from the general township fund or from the treasury of the municipal corporations, counties or school districts under the agreement of the corporate authorities.

§ 2207. Forest Lands.—(a) Townships may acquire, by purchase, gift or lease, and hold tracts of land covered with forest or tree growth, or suitable for the growth of trees, and administer the tracts under the direction of the Department of Conservation and Natural Resources. The tracts may be of any size suitable for the purpose and may be located inside or outside the township limits.

(b) When the board of supervisors intends to acquire any lands for forests, it shall so declare by an ordinance, setting forth all facts and conditions relating to the proposed action.

(c) Upon the acquisition of any forests or lands suitable for forests, the board of supervisors shall notify the Department of Conservation and Natural Resources which may make rules for the government and proper administration of the lands as may be necessary. The Department of Conservation and Natural Resources shall publish the rules, declare the uses of the forest under the intent of this article and make provision for its administration, maintenance, protection and development as necessary. The rules governing the administration of the forests shall have for their main purpose the producing of a continuing township revenue by the sale of forest products.

(d) All revenue and emoluments arising from the forests shall be paid into the general township fund.

(e) Township forests may be used by the public as general outing or recreation grounds, subject to the rules of the Department of Conservation and Natural Resources governing their administration and rules adopted by the board of supervisors not inconsistent with law and the rules of the Department of Conservation and Natural Resources.

(f) When the board of supervisors decides to sell or lease any township forest, or part thereof, it shall so declare by an ordinance, setting forth all the facts and conditions relating to the proposed action. No ordinance shall be effective until it has been approved by a majority vote of the electorate at the next ensuing municipal or general election. Nothing in this subsection shall prohibit the board of supervisors, at its discretion, by resolution, from allowing the selective harvesting of forest products for the purpose of properly caring for and maintaining a township forest.

(g) The board of supervisors may, on behalf of the township, accept the title to lands which may be donated to the township for any of the purposes mentioned in this article.

ARTICLE XXIII
ROADS, STREETS, BRIDGES AND HIGHWAYS
53 P.S. § 67301–67332

§ 2301. Road and Bridge Maintenance, Repair and Construction.—(a) The board of supervisors may purchase or hire materials, equipment, machinery and implements necessary for the construction, repair and maintenance of roads and bridges and make and maintain bridges over streams, gullies, canals and railroads where bridges are necessary for the ease and safety of travelers. The bridges shall be deemed to be a part of the road.

(b) The board of supervisors may for adequate consideration construct, reconstruct, improve or maintain driveways on lands owned or occupied by school districts in the township.

(c) The board of supervisors may construct, reconstruct and improve and contract for the construction, reconstruction and improvement of roads in the township.

(d) The board of supervisors may for adequate consideration contract with the Commonwealth, a county or a municipal corporation to construct, reconstruct, improve or maintain public roads or highways under the jurisdiction of the Commonwealth, a county or a municipal corporation. Contracts executed under this subsection need not be submitted to the Local Government Commission for review under the act of July 12, 1972 (P.L. 762, No. 180), referred to as the Intergovernmental Cooperation Law.

(e) The board of supervisors may employ one or more roadmasters. The roadmasters are subject to removal by the board of supervisors.

§ 2302. Duties of Roadmasters.—The roadmasters shall:

(1) Report to the board of supervisors any information that may be required by the board of supervisors and by the Department of Transportation.

(2) Inspect all roads and bridges as directed by the board of supervisors.

(3) Do or direct to be done all work necessary to carry out the responsibilities imposed by the board of supervisors with respect to the maintenance, repair and construction of township roads.

§ 2303. Road Complaints.—If any complaint alleges that the public roads and highways of any township are not maintained in accordance with law, the court may appoint three persons who shall examine the highways and report the findings to the court. In these cases, the complainants shall first enter security, in a sum as the court may fix, to pay all costs.

§ 2304. Power to Lay Out, Open, Widen, Vacate, Et Cetera.—(a) The board of supervisors may by ordinance enact, ordain, survey, lay out, open, widen, straighten, vacate and relay all roads and bridges and parts thereof which are located wholly or partially within the township.

(b) The board of supervisors may by ordinance provide for the widening, straightening or improvement of a State highway, with the consent of the Department of Transportation, and may spend township funds in connection therewith.

(c) When any petition is presented to the board of supervisors requesting the board of supervisors to open or vacate a specific road in the township and the board of supervisors fails to act on the petition within sixty days, the petitioners may present their petition to the court of common pleas which shall proceed thereon under the act of June 13, 1836 (P.L. 551, No. 169), referred to as the General Road Law. If the board of supervisors acts on the petition but denies the request of the petition, the board of supervisors shall notify the person designated in the petition of its denial. If the request of the petition is denied, the petitioners, or a majority of them, may within thirty days after receipt of the notice petition the court of common pleas for the appointment of viewers and proceedings shall be taken thereon under the General Road Law.

(d) No road shall be laid out and opened through any burial ground or cemetery, nor through any grounds occupied by a building used as a place for public worship or as a public or parochial school, educational or charitable institution or seminary, unless the consent of the owner of the premises is first secured. If the owner is unknown, this prohibition does not apply.

§ 2305. Hearing; Report; Exceptions Thereto; View and Notice.—(a) Before the passage of any ordinance for the laying out, opening, changing or vacating of any road or highway or section thereof, the board of supervisors shall give ten days' written notice to the owners of property adjacent to the road or portions thereof involved of the time and place set for a hearing on the proposed ordinance.

(b) If the board of supervisors votes in favor of exercising the power, it shall enact the necessary ordinance and file a copy of the ordinance, together with a draft or survey of the road showing the location and width thereof, in the office of the clerk of the court of common pleas.

(c) Any resident or property owner affected by the ordinance may within thirty days after the enactment of the ordinance of the board of supervisors, upon entering in the court sufficient surety to indemnify the board of supervisors for all costs incurred in the proceedings, file exceptions to the ordinance together with a petition for a review. Upon receipt of the exception and surety, the court of common pleas shall appoint viewers from the county board of viewers for the purpose of reviewing the ordinance and exceptions thereto.

(d) After the expiration of the term allowed for filing exceptions or upon the order of the court upon disposition of any exceptions, the court of common pleas, on application by petition by the board of supervisors or any person interested, shall appoint three viewers from the county board of viewers to assess the damages and benefits occasioned by the proceeding unless the damages and benefits are otherwise agreed upon.

§ 2306. Width of Public Roads.—The width of the right-of-way of a public road in townships shall not be less than thirty-three feet or more than one hundred and twenty feet, and the width of the right-of-way of alleys opened by the township as public roads shall not be less than fifteen feet. The minimum required width shall be in addition to any width required for necessary slopes in cuts or fills.

§ 2307. Certain roads declared public roads

(a) Every road which has been used for public travel and maintained and kept in repair by the township for a period of at least twenty-one years is a public road having a right-of-way of thirty-three feet even though there is no public record of the laying out or dedication for public use of the road.

(b) In any proceeding pursuant to this section, any relevant oral or documentary evidence of public travel or maintenance and repairs by the township shall, if presented, be considered, including, but not limited to:

(i) Maps or surveys which are either generated by any governmental unit or are created pursuant to any judicial proceeding of the courts of this Commonwealth.

(ii) Evidence concerning the distribution of government funds to the township pursuant to the act of June 1, 1956 (1955 P.L. 1944, No. 655),[1] referred to as the "Liquid Fuels Tax Municipal Allocation Law."

(iii) Approved subdivision plans, deeds or other documents containing a designation of the road as either a township road or otherwise.

(iv) Evidence that the road is an extension from a public road or public cul-de-sac, a throughway between other municipal or State roads or provides the only access to a municipal boundary line.

(v) Court orders, decisions, findings of fact or other matters of judicial record relating to public or private rights in the road.

(c) For purposes of this section:

(i) The frequency of use of a road may be considered relevant in any proceeding pursuant to this section, but, in the absence of additional findings on the purpose of such use, shall not alone be sufficient to establish that the road has been used for public travel.

(ii) The condition or sufficiency of the road surface for public travel may be considered relevant in any proceeding pursuant to this section, but, absent additional findings of actual public maintenance and repair, shall not alone be sufficient to establish maintenance and repair by the township.

(d) Nothing in this section shall be construed as affecting the weight or persuasiveness of any evidence presented in accordance with subsection (b) or the relevance of any evidence presented except as otherwise provided in this section.

(e) In any proceeding in which this section is relied upon to allege the existence of a public road, the proponent of the public status of the road shall present evidence first, and the burden shall then shift to the opponent to present evidence to refute the public status of the road.

§ 2308. Opening, Repairing and Closing Roads.—(a) Public roads in townships shall, as soon as practicable, be effectually opened. All public roads shall at all seasons be kept in repair and reasonably clear of all impediments to easy and convenient traveling at the expense of the township.

(b) The board of supervisors may temporarily close any township road when it determines that conditions have rendered that road unfit or unsafe for travel and immediate repair or maintenance, because of the time of year or other conditions, is impracticable. The road or portion of road closed shall be properly marked at its extremities, and a means of passage for the customary users of the road shall, when possible, be provided.

(c) Anyone using the road or portion thereof after the road has been properly closed and marked, without a permit from the board of supervisors, commits a summary offense. All fines recovered are payable to the general township fund. Persons who have no outlet due to the closing of a road may drive on, over or across the road with the written consent of, and subject to conditions imposed by, the board of supervisors or their agents or contractors without being subject to the penalties imposed by this section.

§ 2309. Time Within Which Roads to be Opened.—When proceedings have been initiated under this act for the opening and laying out of any public road in the township, the road shall be physically opened for use by the public within a period of five years after completion of the proceeding. If the road is not opened or if no proceedings have been commenced to compel the opening in five years, then the proceedings are void and the land proposed to be taken shall revert to the owners of the land free of any easement or right of the public to use the land.

1. 72 P.S. § 2615.1 et seq.

Table of Contents
Part I Ch. 1–3 Ethics, Records, Open Meetings
Part II Ch. 4–10 Taxation
Part III Ch. 11–18 Torts, Contracts & Civil Rules
Part IV Ch. 19–24 Zoning & Planning
Part V Ch. 25–30 Construction and Emergency Codes
Part VI Ch. 31–39 Municipal Codes
Index

§ 2310. Detours.—(a) Except for emergencies, no public road shall be closed to traffic except upon order of the board of supervisors, and no public road shall be closed to traffic when it has been designated as a detour by the Department of Transportation unless the written consent of the Department of Transportation is first obtained or unless the board of supervisors by resolution declares the closing necessary for the protection of the public safety.

(b) When any public road is closed, the board of supervisors shall designate a detour on which shall be erected and maintained while the detour is in use legible direction signs at each public road intersection through the length of the detour. When the detour is in use, the board of supervisors shall maintain the detour in safe and passable condition, except for State and county highways. The board of supervisors shall immediately remove all detour signs when the road that was originally closed is open for traffic. Except for State and county highways, the board of supervisors may acquire, by agreement or right of eminent domain, right-of-way privileges over private property for the period when the road is closed to traffic. In the exercise of the rights conferred by this section, the board of supervisors may pay for the necessary maintenance, subsequent repair and land rental.

(c) Any person who removes, defaces, destroys or disregards any barricade, light, danger sign, detour sign or warning of any other character whatsoever erected or placed under authority of this section or who drives on, over or across any road which has been properly closed commits a summary offense.

(d) In addition to the penalties imposed by this section, the board of supervisors may in an action at law recover damages from any person or persons who have damaged a road by driving on the road when it is closed to vehicular traffic under this act.

(e) All fines and moneys collected under this section shall be paid to the township treasurer.

§ 2311. Relocating or Vacating Roads by Agreement.—(a) When the board of supervisors relocates or vacates any part of any public road under its supervision and can agree with the property owners affected by the relocation or vacation, it may relocate or vacate the public road without the formality of a view.

(b) A copy of the agreement setting forth the facts regarding the relocation or vacation, accompanied by a map or draft of the road agreed to be relocated or vacated, shall be presented and recorded in the office of the recorder of deeds or similar office in home rule counties after which the new location is the public road or the old location is vacated.

§ 2312. Elimination of Curves; Acquisition of Views.—(a) Any township may acquire, by purchase or by the right of eminent domain, any property and lands along or adjacent to any township road that may be necessary to eliminate dangerous curves and widen roads and provide a free and unobstructed view over lands located at or near the intersection of any two roads or highways, or a road and a railroad or railway, or at any curve in any road, for the better protection and safety to the traveling public.

(b) The proceedings for the condemnation of the property or land and for the assessment of damages for property or land taken, injured or destroyed shall be taken under Article XXXIV.

§ 2313. Roads in or near Public Parks.—(a) The board of supervisors may contract with the Commonwealth, a county or a municipal corporation owning and operating parks inside the township to establish, relocate, alter or vacate public roads inside or contiguous to those parks. The board of supervisors shall take no action with respect to the public roads without the written consent and agreement of the Commonwealth, county or municipal corporation owning and operating the parks. Any road when altered or relocated under this section shall be maintained and repaired the same as other township roads.

(b) The agreement shall be adopted by ordinance, and, within thirty days, the road shall be a public road of the township.

(c) The owner of any land through which any public road may be located or relocated may apply by petition to the court of common pleas, setting forth the injury which has been sustained by reason of the relocation of the public road, and the proceedings relative to the assessment and payment of damages of the landowner shall be under this act for eminent domain.

§ 2314. Petition of Property Owners for Improvements.—(a) Any township may improve any public street in the township upon the petition of property owners representing a majority in number of feet front of the properties abutting on the street proposed to be improved at the expense of the property owners.

(b) The cost of the improvement may be collected from the owners of the real estate abutting on the street or highway, or part thereof, by an equal assessment on the foot-front basis.

(c) The assessments for improvement shall be filed with the township treasurer under section 3302(a).

(d) The term "owner," as used in this section, means all individuals and public or private corporations, copartnerships and associations having title in the assessed property. If the owner is a nonresident of the township and the place of residence is unknown or if the ownership of the property cannot be ascertained, the notice shall be posted on the premises and a copy shall be left with the occupant, if any.

§ 2315. Improvements Without Petition.—(a) The board of supervisors may by ordinance provide for the construction, reconstruction, repair or other improvements to any public street in the township.

(b) The cost of improvements may be collected from the owners of the real estate abutting on the street or highway, or part thereof, by an equal assessment on the foot-front basis; but in no instance shall any abutting property owner be liable for the cost of improvements in an amount greater than fifteen percent of the assessed valuation of the abutting property: Provided, further, with respect to any property used exclusively for forestry purposes, for agricultural purposes, or for both as of the time of the assessment, That the assessment shall be based upon the actual foot frontage of such property or one hundred and fifty feet, whichever is less. Any expense above the maximum liability of abutting property owners shall be paid by the township.

(c) All assessments for improvements shall be filed with the township treasurer under section 3302(a).

(d) If abutting property owners fail to pay the expenses of the improvements for which they are liable, the board of supervisors may recover the amount by action of assumpsit or may file municipal liens therefor against the abutting properties under law for the filing and collection of municipal liens.

§ 2316. Acceptance of Land for Road Purposes.—(a) The board of supervisors may by resolution accept any land dedicated by deed to the township to be used as a road, street or alley. A copy of the resolution, together with a draft or survey of the road, street or alley, showing location and width thereof, shall be filed with the clerk of the court of common pleas.

(b) When plans of dedicated roads, streets or alleys located in townships have been approved and recorded under this article, the board of supervisors may by resolution accept any roads, streets or alleys as public roads if shown in the plans as dedicated to that use and if the roads or streets are not less than thirty-three feet in width and the alleys are not less than fifteen feet in width.

Table of Contents
Part I Ch. 1–3 Ethics, Records, Open Meetings
Part II Ch. 4–10 Taxation
Part III Ch. 11–18 Torts, Contracts & Civil Rules
Part IV Ch. 19–24 Zoning & Planning
Part V Ch. 25–30 Construction and Emergency Codes
Part VI Ch. 31–39 Municipal Codes
Index

(c) Upon the filing with the clerk of court of common pleas of the county a certified and attested copy of the resolution, the roads, streets or alleys become a part of the public road system of the township and shall be so recorded in the court.

§ 2317. Approval of Plans.—(a) No person shall construct, open or dedicate any road or any drainage facilities for public use or travel without first submitting plans thereof to the board of supervisors for its approval. The plans shall be prepared under rules and regulations adopted by the board of supervisors and shall show the profiles of the roads, the course, structure and capacity of any drainage facilities, the method of drainage of the adjacent or contiguous territory and any other details that may be required under the rules or regulations adopted by the board of supervisors. The board of supervisors may alter the plans and specify any changes or modifications of any kind and may make its approval of the plans subject to those alterations, changes or modifications. The plans when so approved shall be signed by the board of supervisors, and a copy shall be filed with the secretary of the township. No road or drainage facilities shall be opened, constructed or dedicated for public use or travel except in compliance with plans approved by the board of supervisors and until the approved plan is recorded as required in this section.

(b) If the board of supervisors refuses to approve any plans submitted to it under this section, any person aggrieved by the action of the board of supervisors may within thirty days appeal to the court of common pleas. The court shall hear the matter de novo and, after hearing, may enter a decree affirming, reversing or modifying the action of the board of supervisors.

(c) The action of the board of supervisors, or of the court on appeal, in approving any plans shall be recorded by the person applying for the approval in the office of the recorder of deeds of the county.

(d) No person shall present to the recorder of deeds any plan which has not been approved by the board of supervisors. Approval shall be so indicated on the plan presented for recording.

(e) If any road or any drainage facilities are opened, constructed or dedicated for public use or travel, except in compliance with plans approved and recorded, neither the board of supervisors nor any public authorities shall be required to place, construct or operate any sewer, drain, water pipe or other facilities or do any work of any kind in or upon that road; and neither the board of supervisors nor any other public authorities have any responsibility of any kind with respect to the road or drainage facilities even if they are in use by the public. Nothing in this act shall prevent the laying of trunk sewers, drains or water or gas mains if required by engineering necessity for the accommodation of other territory.

(f) Any person who constructs, opens or dedicates any road or any drainage facilities in connection therewith for public use or travel in any township without having first complied with this section and any resolutions of the board of supervisors commits a misdemeanor of the third degree and is subject to a suit for all costs and damages incurred by the township or property owners in the course of correcting all substantive violations of State or municipal law or regulations resulting from or arising out of the unlawfully recorded plan. All fines and moneys so recovered shall be paid to the township treasurer.

(g) No approval of plans by the board of supervisors shall obligate or require the township to construct, reconstruct, maintain, repair or grade the roads.

§ 2318. Markers and Monuments.—The board of supervisors and its agents may enter any land and property and maintain marks and monuments in carrying out its powers and duties under this article.

§ 2319. Powers of State and Counties Preserved.—Nothing contained in this article shall be held to restrict or limit the Department of Transportation or any county in the exercise of any of its duties, powers and functions under any State law.

§ 2320. Power to Open Drains and Ditches.—(a) The board of supervisors or its agents may enter any lands or enclosures and cut, open, maintain and repair drains or ditches through the property when necessary to carry the water from the roads.

(b) Any person who damages or diverts any drain or ditch without the authority of the board of supervisors commits a summary offense and is liable for the cost of restoring the drain or ditch. All fines and moneys so recovered shall be paid to the township treasurer.

§ 2321. Railroad Crossings.—(a) Every township constructing a road across a railroad shall construct the road above or below the grade thereof unless permitted by the Pennsylvania Public Utility Commission to construct the road at grade.

(b) Any crossing of a railroad by a road or any vacation of any road crossing a railroad shall be made only under the jurisdiction of the Pennsylvania Public Utility Commission. Compensation for damages to the owners of adjacent property taken, injured or destroyed shall be determined under 66 Pa.C.S. (relating to public utilities).

§ 2322. Permits.—No railroad or street railway shall be constructed upon any township road, nor shall any railroad or street railway crossings, driveway connections, gas pipe, water pipe, electric conduits or other piping be laid upon or in, nor shall any telephone, telegraph or electric light or power poles or any coal tipples or any other obstructions be erected upon or in, any portion of a township road except under conditions, restrictions and regulations specified in permits granted by the township for that purpose. Each application shall be submitted to the township in duplicate. The township shall collect a fee as determined by the Department of Transportation for processing the application and another fee for making the inspection. Each application shall be accompanied by both fees. When the township grants the permit, the board of supervisors or its agents shall inspect the work authorized by the permit upon the completion thereof and, when necessary, enforce compliance with the conditions, restrictions and regulations specified by the township. In addition to that inspection, the board of supervisors or its agents may reinspect the work not more than two years after its completion, and, if any settlement of the road surface or other defect appears in the work contrary to the conditions, restrictions and regulations of the township, it may enforce compliance therewith. If the applicant fails to rectify a defect which presents an immediate or imminent safety or health problem within forty-eight hours or any other defect within sixty days after written notice from the board of supervisors to do so, the board of supervisors or its agents may do the work and impose upon the applicant the cost thereof, together with an additional twenty percent of the cost, which may be recovered by an action in assumpsit in the court of common pleas of the county. All fees received by the township shall be paid into the township treasury. Nothing in this section shall be construed to require a permit in advance for emergency repairs necessary for the safety of the public or the restoration or continuance of public utility service or other public service, but application for the permit and the fees shall be submitted within five days after completion of the work, after which time the remaining provisions of this section apply. Nothing in this section authorizes a township to regulate or control the operations of any permittee except under this section.

§ 2323. Penalty for Destroying Signs.—A person shall not destroy, remove, injure or deface any sign legally erected upon or near any public street, road or bridge by the board of supervisors, or by any club, association or other organized body, for the direction, guidance or safety of travelers. A person shall not

Table of Contents
Part I Ch. 1–3 Ethics, Records, Open Meetings
Part II Ch. 4–10 Taxation
Part III Ch. 11–18 Torts, Contracts & Civil Rules
Part IV Ch. 19–24 Zoning & Planning
Part V Ch. 25–30 Construction and Emergency Codes
Part VI Ch. 31–39 Municipal Codes
Index

destroy, remove, injure or deface any temporary traffic-control device legally erected to enhance traffic or worker safety in a construction or maintenance work zone, including, but not limited to, cones, batons, barrels, barricades, signs, sign trucks, arrow boards or other devices specified in a traffic safety plan approved by the township or the Department of Transportation. Any person who violates this section commits a summary offense and shall, upon conviction, be sentenced to pay a fine of not less than two hundred dollars ($200) nor more than five hundred dollars ($500) for the first offense and a mandatory fine of five hundred dollars ($500) for the second or any subsequent offense, with costs of prosecution, together with the value of the destroyed, removed or defaced sign. All fines and moneys imposed and collected shall be paid to the township treasurer.

§ 2324. Protection of Highways from Snowdrifts.—(a) The board of supervisors may enter private property adjacent to any public road or highway and place thereon a snow fence to within a limit of one hundred feet from the right-of-way line of the public road in order to eliminate snow drifting on the traveled portion of the public road.

(b) A snow fence may not be placed before the first day of November or remain in place after the first day of April of the succeeding year unless the written consent of the owner is obtained, agreeing to an extension of time for the removal of the snow fence.

(c) If the board of supervisors and the owner of the property upon which a snow fence is placed and removed under this section cannot agree to the amount of compensation, if any, to be paid to the owner for placing the fence, including the amount of damages, if any, to be paid for injury to the property resulting from placing and removing the fence, the owner may petition the court of common pleas of the county for the appointment of viewers to ascertain the amount of damage incurred in the manner provided in this act for eminent domain proceedings. Damages, if any, when ascertained shall be paid by the township from the general township fund.

§ 2325. Saving Trees and Shrubbery.—(a) The board of supervisors or its agents shall not remove any shrub or tree growing within the right-of-way of any township road or street except those shrubs and trees the board of supervisors finds to constitute a hazardous or dangerous condition to the use of the highway or those which impair the use or maintenance of the public road or street. No tree having a trunk diameter in excess of six inches shall be removed without notice of the proposed removal having first been given to the abutting property owner. The township supervisors shall determine by resolution the form of notice to property owners.

(b) All logs, cordwood, branch wood or other forms of wood derived from the destruction or removal of any trees growing along the highways shall be surrendered to and remain the property of the abutting owners.

(c) The board of supervisors may clear out brush and other refuse along the sides of the road to the legal width thereof. All clearing and removal of brush and refuse shall be confined to growth that is within the right-of-way and to the removal of branches that in any way interfere with public travel. No other injury by fire, cutting, abrasion or otherwise shall be done to the standing timber.

(d) By person who violates the provisions of this section commits a summary offense. All fines shall be paid into the general township fund.

(e) Nothing in this section prevents the board of supervisors or roadmasters or other persons in their employ from removing roadside trees which may be thrown down by wind or lodged in a position as to be a menace to public travel or which, by reason of any other cause, may become a source of danger to the public.

§ 2326. Obstructions and Nuisances.—Any person who obstructs any public road or commits any nuisance thereon by felling trees, making fences, turning the road, diverting water onto or in any other way and who does not, on notice given by the board of supervisors, immediately remove the obstruction or nuisance and repair the damages done to the road commits a summary offense. Nothing in this section shall debar a prosecution for any nuisance as in case of misdemeanor at common law.

§ 2327. Traffic Lights and Signals.—The board of supervisors may provide for the erection, maintenance and operation of traffic lights and traffic signals in accordance with 75 Pa.C.S. (relating to vehicles).

§ 2328. Regulation of Parking.—(a) The board of supervisors may by ordinance regulate parking, provide parking accommodations to promote the convenience and protection of the public, post signs regulating parking in areas established or designated for handicapped or severely disabled veteran parking and impose penalties for the violation of those regulations.

(b) The board of supervisors may provide for the erection, maintenance and regulation of parking meters, and it may by ordinance establish parking meter charges and impose penalties for the violation of those regulations.

§ 2329. Naming of Streets.—The board of supervisors may provide for and regulate the naming of streets, roads and highways. When the naming of a street, road or highway will affect signing maintained by the Department of Transportation, the board of supervisors shall notify the department.

§ 2330. Bike Paths.—The board of supervisors may provide for the construction and maintenance of bike paths for the protection or convenience of the traveling public.

§ 2331. County Bridges.—When the cost of construction or maintenance of a bridge located within the township is paid in whole or in part by the county, the board of supervisors may make agreements for the maintenance and repair of the bridge.

§ 2332. Boundary Roads and Bridges.—(a) When any road or bridge, other than a State or county road or bridge, is created or located along, on or over boundaries between townships and any other municipal corporation, the creation, location, construction, maintenance and repair of the road or bridge shall be the joint responsibility of the township and the municipal corporation with which the common boundary is shared.

(b) The board of supervisors may make agreements with any adjacent municipal corporation to provide for the apportionment of the cost of construction, repair and maintenance of boundary roads or bridges.

(c) If an amicable agreement on the proportionate share of costs of construction, repair and maintenance of boundary roads or bridges cannot be executed, the board of supervisors or the governing body of the other municipal corporation involved may petition the court of common pleas of the county or counties for a determination of the rights and responsibilities of the respective municipal corporations involved.

ARTICLE XXIV
SIDEWALKS, FOOTPATHS AND CURBS

53 P.S. § 67401

§ 2401. Location, Lines, Grades and Width of Curbs, Sidewalks or Footpaths; Costs.—(a) The board of supervisors may by ordinance regulate the line, grade

Table of Contents
Part I Ch. 1–3 Ethics, Records, Open Meetings
Part II Ch. 4–10 Taxation
Part III Ch. 11–18 Torts, Contracts & Civil Rules
Part IV Ch. 19–24 Zoning & Planning
Part V Ch. 25–30 Construction and Emergency Codes
Part VI Ch. 31–39 Municipal Codes
Index

and width of curbs, sidewalks or footpaths constructed along the roads or highways in the township, shall have general supervision over them and may establish a grade or grades for curbs, sidewalks or footpaths, which grade or grades may be separate and apart from the grade or grades established for the cartway or roadway.

(b) If the highway is a State or county highway, the written consent of the Department of Transportation or the county commissioners shall first be obtained.

(c) The costs of construction of sidewalks, footpaths or curbs may be paid by one of the following methods:

(1) The board of supervisors, upon the request of any landowner whose land fronts upon a public road or highway within the township, may establish a sidewalk or curbs along one or both sides of the road or highway along the lands of the owner. When the sidewalks or curbs are established, the landowner shall pay for the construction of the sidewalks or curbs and keep them in repair.

(2) The board of supervisors may construct sidewalks or curbs along the roads or highways, upon the petition of property owners representing a majority in number of feet front of the properties abutting on the roads or highways where the sidewalks or curbs are to be constructed. When a petition is filed with the board of supervisors, the property owner shall be given notice by the board of supervisors to construct the sidewalk or curb. If the owner fails to complete the sidewalk or curb within a period of sixty days after the receipt of the notice, the board of supervisors may construct the sidewalk or curb. When any sidewalk or curb is constructed by the board of supervisors, the expense of the construction of the sidewalk or curb shall be paid by the abutting property owners in proportion to their frontage. If the owners fail to pay the expenses of the construction of the sidewalk or curb, the board of supervisors may recover the amount by action of assumpsit or may file municipal liens therefor against the abutting properties under law for the filing and collection of municipal liens.

(3) The board of supervisors may by ordinance in absence of a petition, provide for the construction, reconstruction and repair of sidewalks and curbs within the township. When any sidewalks or curbs are constructed, reconstructed or repaired by the board of supervisors under the ordinance, the expense of the construction of the sidewalks or curbs shall be paid by the abutting property owners in proportion to their frontage, but no owner shall be liable for the cost of construction of the sidewalk or curb in an amount greater than fifteen percent of the assessed valuation of the abutting property. Any expense above the maximum liability of abutting property owners shall be paid by the township. If abutting property owners fail to pay the expenses of the construction of the sidewalks or curbs for which they are liable, the board of supervisors may recover the amount by action of assumpsit or may file municipal liens therefor against the abutting properties under law for the filing and collection of municipal liens.

(4) When the board of supervisors establishes that any part of any road or highway is dangerous to the traveling public and the danger could be materially reduced or lessened by the construction of a sidewalk, curb or footpath, the board of supervisors may lay out and construct a sidewalk, curb or footpath along the dangerous portion of the road or highway at township expense.

(d) All assessments for costs levied under this article shall be filed with the township treasurer and collected under section 3302(a).

ARTICLE XXV
SANITARY SEWERS
53 P.S. § 67501–67517

§ 2501. Sanitary Sewers.—The board of supervisors may establish and construct sanitary sewer systems which shall if possible be constructed along and within the lines of the rights-of-way of public roads. If the board of supervisors determines that the systems shall be located on or through private property, the board of supervisors may acquire the land by gift, purchase or eminent domain.

§ 2502. Sanitary Sewer Connections.—(a) The board of supervisors may by ordinance require adjoining and adjacent property owners to connect with and use the sanitary sewer system, whether constructed by the township or a municipality authority or a joint sanitary sewer board. In the case of a sanitary sewer system constructed by the township pursuant to either section 2501 or 2516, the board of supervisors may impose and charge to property owners who desire to or are required to connect to the township's sewer system a connection fee, a customer facilities fee, a tapping fee and other similar fees, as enumerated and defined by clause (t) of subsection B of section 4 of the act of May 2, 1945 (P.L. 382, No. 164), known as the "Municipality Authorities Act of 1945," as a condition of connection to a township-owned sewer collection, treatment or disposal facility. If any owner of property adjoining or adjacent to or whose principal building is within one hundred and fifty feet from the sanitary sewer fails to connect with and use the sanitary sewer for a period of sixty days after notice to do so has been served by the board of supervisors, either by personal service or by registered mail, the board of supervisors or their agents may enter the property and construct the connection. The board of supervisors shall send an itemized bill of the cost of construction to the owner of the property to which connection has been made, which bill is payable immediately. If the owner fails to pay the bill, the board of supervisors shall file a municipal lien for the cost of the construction within six months of the date of completion of the connection.

(b) When an existing sanitary sewer system owned by or leased to a township is extended or altered at the expense of a developer or other private person or corporation under the supervision of the township or a municipality authority of the township, the board of supervisors may by ordinance or resolution take over the extension or alteration and compel all owners of property which is not already connected to an existing public sanitary sewer system and which is accessible to and whose principal building is within one hundred and fifty feet from the sanitary sewer extension to make connection therewith and use the sanitary sewer system as the board of supervisors may order.

(c) Whenever a sewer system or any part or extension thereof owned by a township has been constructed by the township at the expense of a private person or corporation or has been constructed by a private person or corporation under the supervision of the township at the expense of the private person or corporation, the board of supervisors shall have the right to charge a tapping fee, including a reimbursement component, and refund said reimbursement component to the person or corporation who has paid for the construction of said sewer system or any part or extension thereof.

(d) The board of supervisors shall not require any commercial or industrial business to connect to the township sanitary sewer system when the commercial or industrial business is operating a private sanitary sewage treatment plant under mandate of any agency of the Federal or State Government. This exemption shall last as long as the private sanitary sewage treatment plant continues to meet the specifications and standards mandated by the Federal or State agency and for forty-five days after that. If, during the days immediately after the day a business' private sanitary sewage treatment plant is determined to be below Federal or State mandates, repairs cannot be made to bring the private sewage treatment system back up to satisfactory condition, the board of supervisors may require the business to connect to the township sanitary sewer system. The full costs of connection to and any necessary refurbishing of the township sanitary sewer system shall be paid by the business.

(e) The exemption in subsection (d) is not available in any situation where the business seeking to use it had notice, either actual or constructive, before construction of its sewage treatment plant, of the township's intention to construct a sanitary sewer system and to require that business to connect with its system.

(f) The Department of Environmental Protection shall not issue any permit to allow a commercial or industrial business to construct its own private sewage treatment plant without the written consent of the board of supervisors of the township in which the private sewage treatment plant is proposed to be located.

§ 2503. Notice of Contemplated Construction.—No sanitary sewer system shall be constructed under this article unless a resolution of the board of supervisors authorizing the construction is published in a newspaper of general circulation in the township once a week for three successive weeks.

§ 2504. Entering Lands to Mark Sanitary Sewer Routes; Damages.—In the absence of an agreement with the owners of land required for sanitary sewer systems or for the marking of the route of the systems, the board of supervisors or its agents have the right to enter the lands for that purpose. For all damage done by entering the land under this section, the general fund of the township shall be pledged as security. Damages shall be determined by viewers under this act for eminent domain proceedings.

§ 2505. Sanitary Sewer Systems; Acquisition of Land and Facilities; Damages.—The board of supervisors may acquire by eminent domain or make contracts with other municipal corporations, corporations or persons for the acquisition of lands or facilities for the location, construction, maintenance, reconstruction and enlargement of sanitary sewer systems and treatment facilities. Acquisitions may be made for the purpose of future construction or additions to existing systems. The acquired land may be located either inside or outside the boundaries of the township. For all damage done to owners of land by reason of the taking of the land, the general fund of the township shall be pledged as security. Damages shall be determined by viewers under this act for eminent domain proceedings.

§ 2506. Cost of Construction; How Paid.—All or part of the cost of construction of a sanitary sewer system constructed under this article may be charged upon the properties accommodated or benefited by the construction.

§ 2507. Sanitary Sewer Districts.—(a) When a sanitary sewer system is constructed by a township for the accommodation of a certain portion of the township, the board of supervisors may before or after the construction designate the territory accommodated as one sanitary sewer district or divide it into several sanitary sewer districts. The board of supervisors shall estimate the proportion of the cost of the sanitary sewer system to be charged on each of the districts and declare and establish the apportionment by resolution.

(b) When a sanitary sewer system is constructed by a township for the benefit only of a certain portion of the township and the cost of main sanitary sewers, pumping stations, pressure lines, et cetera, is charged against the sanitary sewer district or sanitary sewer districts, all or part of the amount charged to each district may be assessed to the district by an assessment upon each lot or piece of land in the district, in proportion to its frontage abutting on the sanitary sewer, or by an assessment upon the several properties abutting on the sanitary sewer, in proportion to benefits, or upon the properties connected with and using the sanitary sewers as rental fees, or each lot or piece of ground abutting upon the sanitary sewer may be assessed, in proportion to its frontage or according to benefits, the cost of a local sanitary sewer, and the balance of the amount charged against the district may be assessed upon the properties connected with and using the sanitary sewer, as rental fees. No district shall be charged with more than its due proportion of the cost of the main sanitary sewers, pumping stations, et cetera, used jointly by more than one district. If the whole of the township is accommodated by the sanitary sewer system, it may be treated as a single district.

§ 2508. Manner of Assessment.—When a township is divided into sanitary sewer districts, the assessment in each district may be by different methods. The assessment, if any, for sanitary sewer system construction shall be charged upon the properties accommodated or benefited by one of the following methods:

(1) By an assessment, under a resolution or ordinance of the board of supervisors, of each lot or piece of land in proportion to its frontage abutting on the sanitary sewer system, allowing an equitable reduction in the case of corner properties and unusually shaped properties or those properties abutting on more than one collector line of the sanitary sewer as the resolution or ordinance may specify. When the lot or piece of land is on a corner, it shall be assessed for its entire frontage abutting on any sanitary sewer system.

(2) By an equal assessment on all properties abutting on the sanitary sewer system in proportion to the total cost of construction of the sanitary sewer system. The amount of the charge on each property shall be determined by the board of supervisors.

§ 2509. Procedure for Assessments.—If taxpayers of the district whose property valuation as assessed for taxable purposes within the district amounts to fifty percent of the total property valuation so assessed or if taxpayers representing fifty percent of the parcels within the district present a petition within three months of the adoption of a resolution or ordinance levying an assessment under section 2508 to the court of common pleas stating that the assessment insufficiently represents the benefits accruing to abutting properties, they may include in the petition a request for the appointment of viewers to assess benefits. The court shall appoint three disinterested viewers, none of whom shall be a resident of that portion of the township which is accommodated by the sanitary sewer system in question, and the viewers shall proceed under this act for the assessment of damages and benefits by viewers. Upon the filing of a petition by taxpayers for appointment of viewers, any assessment made by the board of supervisors and any proceedings shall be stayed pending the disposition of the petition by the court.

§ 2510. Liens for Assessments; Costs of Proceedings.—After the amount of the assessment charged upon the several properties has been established by resolution making assessments according to section 2508 or by confirmation of any report of viewers, in whole or in part, the amounts of all assessments are payable to the township treasurer for the use of the sanitary sewer district or districts or the township in which they are assessed. The board of supervisors shall make out bills for the amounts charged against each property, which shall be sent to all property owners whose property will be served by the sanitary sewer system. If the assessment is not paid within ninety days after the mailing of a bill therefor, the board of supervisors shall collect it by action of assumpsit or under law for the filing and recovery of municipal claims.

(2510 amended Dec. 18, 1996, P.L., No. 172)

Chap. 39 Res. During Mil. Service
Chap. 38 Intergov. Coop.
Chap. 37 3rd Class City Code
Chap. 36 Bor. Code
Chap. 35 2nd Class Twp. Code
Chap. 34 1st Class Twp. Code
Chap. 33 Home Rule Chart. Opt. Plans Law
Chap. 32 Water Serv. Act
Chap. 31 Munic. Auth. Act

§ 2511. Rental Fees.—(a) All persons whose property is connected to a sanitary sewer system shall pay to the township treasurer, in addition to the cost of making the connection, a monthly, quarterly, semi-annual or annual charge adopted by a resolution of the board of supervisors. The charges constitute a lien until paid against the property connected to the sanitary sewer system, and the amount thereof may be recovered by due process of law. All water utilities supplying water to users within the boundaries of any township shall at the request of the board of supervisors furnish to the township, on or before the fifteenth day of the month following the month during which bills are issued, a list of all water meter readings and flat-rate water bills and the basis for each flat-rate water charge so that the data may be used in calculating rental fees. The township may pay to the utilities clerical and other expenses incurred in the preparation of the lists.

(b) Nothing in this section shall be construed to repeal or modify any of the provisions of 66 Pa.C.S. (relating to public utilities).

(c) All sewer rentals received shall be deposited in a special fund to be used only for the payment of the cost of construction, reconstruction, repair, operation and maintenance of the sanitary sewer system.

§ 2512. State and County Highways; Consents Necessary.—Sanitary sewers may be constructed in or under any State or county highway. If the construction of sanitary sewers is in or under county highways, the consent of the county commissioners of the county shall first be obtained and, if the construction of sanitary sewers is in or under any State highway, the consent of the Department of Transportation shall first be obtained.

§ 2513. Municipal Corporation; Municipality Authority; Agreements for Connections; Appointment of Viewers.—(a) Any township may by agreement connect with an existing sanitary sewer owned by any municipal corporation or municipality authority for either sewage collection or treatment purposes.

(b) When any township desires to connect with the existing sewer of any municipal corporation or municipality authority, a petition shall be presented by the board of supervisors to the court of common pleas setting forth the facts. The court shall fix a day for hearing upon the petition and direct public notice be given to all interested parties. If the court is of the opinion that the connection can be made without impairing the usefulness of the existing sanitary sewer system, it shall appoint three viewers to view the premises, investigate the facts of the case, assess the necessary costs and expenses of making the connection and the proportionate part of the expense of building the original sanitary sewer system upon the township, determine the proportion of the expense for repairs which the municipal corporation or municipality authority and the township shall bear and determine all other questions liable to arise in connection therewith.

§ 2514. Report of Viewers.—The viewers shall report the results of their investigation to the court, and the court shall confirm the report within thirty days of its submission unless exceptions are filed. Any interested party may appeal the disposition of filed exceptions.

§ 2515. Acquisition of Existing Sanitary Sewer Systems.—(a) The board of supervisors of the township in which the facilities are located may acquire all or part of an existing sanitary sewer system or community subsurface sewage collection and treatment system.

(b) Acquisition may be by either purchase, when the board of supervisors and the owner can agree on a price not exceeding the actual value of the sanitary sewer system or part thereof to be transferred, or by deed of dedication to the township by the owners of the sanitary sewer system or part thereof or by the exercise of eminent domain.

(c) If any sanitary sewer system or community subsurface disposal collection and treatment system is acquired by purchase or taking under this section, the cost of acquisition may be distributed or assessed under this act as when a sanitary sewer system is constructed by the township.

(d) The rights, powers and duties of the board of supervisors with respect to acquired systems are the same as exist with respect to sanitary sewer systems constructed by the township.

§ 2516. Joint Sanitary Sewer Systems.—(a) Townships may contract with other municipal corporations and municipal authorities providing for the joint construction or maintenance of sanitary sewer systems and for the connection onto existing sanitary sewer systems. The agreements shall provide for the apportionment of costs among the municipal corporations. The board of supervisors may assess the township's respective portions of the costs, as may be legally assessable, upon property benefited by the facilities. Any portion of the cost not assessed or assessable shall be paid by the respective municipal corporations under the agreement.

(b) The municipal corporations joining or contemplating joining in the project in order to facilitate the building of the sanitary sewer system and in securing preliminary surveys and estimates may by ordinance provide for the appointment of a joint sanitary sewer board composed of one representative from each of the municipal corporations joining which shall act generally as the advisory and administrative agency in the construction of the improvement and its subsequent operation and maintenance. Members of the joint sanitary sewer board shall serve for terms of six years each from the dates of their respective appointments and until their successors are appointed. The joint sanitary sewer board shall organize by the election of a chairman, vice-chairman, secretary and treasurer. The municipal corporations may in the ordinances creating the joint sanitary sewer board authorize it to appoint an engineer, a solicitor and other necessary assistants and agree to the share of the compensation of those persons each municipal corporation is to pay. The members of the joint sanitary sewer board shall receive compensation for attending board meetings as established in the budget that is prepared by the joint sanitary sewer board and submitted to and adopted by the municipal corporations. The budget item providing for the compensation to members for attending meetings shall not exceed a total of two hundred and fifty dollars ($250) for each member in each year, but the members shall be entitled to actual expenses to be paid by the respective municipal corporations the members represent.

(c) The joint sanitary sewer board may adopt rules and regulations to govern its proceedings and prepare and suggest measures and plans under which the joint improvement may be completed and for the future development of the system. It may prepare a joint agreement or agreements for submission to and adoption by the municipal corporations defining the advisory and administrative powers of the joint sanitary sewer board and setting forth: the consents of the municipal corporations to the proposed improvement; the manner in which preliminary and final plans, specifications and estimates for the proposed improvement shall be prepared and adopted and in which proposals for bids shall be advertised and contracts let; the manner in which the costs of the improvement and other incidental and preliminary expenses in connection therewith, and the future cost of operation and maintenance, shall be equitably shared, apportioned and paid; and all other matters, including the preparation and submission of annual and other budgets, that are necessary or required by law to complete the proposed improvement and to assure future maintenance and operation thereof. The board may not make any improvement or spend any public moneys which have not first been authorized by all of the municipal corporations proceeding with the improvement.

Chap. 39 Res. During Mil. Service
Chap. 38 Intergov. Coop.
Chap. 37 3rd Class City Code
Chap. 36 Bor. Code
Chap. 35 2nd Class Twp. Code
Chap. 34 1st Class Twp. Code
Chap. 33 Home Rule Chart. Opt. Plans Law
Chap. 32 Water Serv. Act
Chap. 31 Munic. Auth. Act

(d) When it is necessary to acquire, appropriate, damage or destroy private property to build any joint sanitary sewer system or improvement and the property cannot be acquired by purchase or gift, the right of eminent domain shall vest in the municipal corporation where the property is located. When it is necessary to acquire, damage or destroy property in any territory not within the limits of any of the municipal corporations joining in the improvement, the right of eminent domain shall be vested in the municipal corporation adjacent to the territory where the property is located. Damages for any property that is taken, damaged or destroyed shall be assessed under laws relating to the municipal corporations exercising the right of eminent domain and shall be paid by the municipal corporations joining in the same proportion as other costs of the improvements.

§ 2517. State Permit.—No sanitary sewer or plant may be constructed until plans and specifications are submitted to the Department of Environmental Protection and approved.

ARTICLE XXVI
WATER SUPPLY
53 P.S. § 67601–67614

§ 2601. Contracts With Water Companies and Municipal Corporations and Acquisition of Water Systems.—(a) The board of supervisors may by contract with any private corporation or any adjacent municipal corporation owning a waterworks system provide water for public and private uses, to be delivered through lines owned by that company or municipal corporation within the township. The contract shall provide the manner by which the cost of the water service shall be paid by the consumers.

(b) The board of supervisors may purchase or acquire a privately owned water system to provide water for public and private uses. If a privately owned water company fails to render service as required by the Pennsylvania Public Utility Commission, the board of supervisors may with the approval of the Pennsylvania Public Utility Commission exercise the right of eminent domain to acquire the water system of the water company to provide water for public and private uses.

(c) Any township may by agreement connect with an existing water system owned by any adjacent municipal corporation. When any township desires to connect with the existing water system of any adjacent municipal corporation and no agreement has been reached between the township and the adjacent municipal corporation, a petition seeking approval of the connection shall be presented by the board of supervisors to the court of common pleas. The court shall set a day for hearing upon the petition and shall direct public notice be given to all interested parties. If the court is of the opinion that the connection can be made without impairing the usefulness of the existing water system, it shall appoint three viewers to view the premises, investigate the facts of the case, assess the necessary costs and expenses of making the connection and the proportionate part of the expense of building the original water system upon the township, determine the proportion of the expense for repairs which the municipal corporation and the township shall bear and determine all other questions likely to arise in connection therewith.

§ 2602. Water Lines and Connections.—The board of supervisors may contract with any private corporation or any adjacent municipal corporation owning a water system to provide water for public and private uses to be delivered into the lines of the township at or near the boundary thereof. The board of supervisors may by contract lay water lines and extensions and regulate the making of connections therewith.

§ 2603. Connection to water system.—(a) the board of supervisors may by ordinance require that a property owner connect with and use a water system of the township or municipality authority or a joint water board in either of the following cases:

(1) if, except as provided in subsection (b), the property owner's principal building is located within one hundred fifty feet of a water system or any part or extension of the system.

(2) if the property owner's principal building has no supply of water which is safe for human consumption.

(b) a property owner who, after the effective date of this subsection, is subject to mandatory connection pursuant to subsection (a)(1), shall not be required to connect to the water system pursuant to that subsection if all of the following conditions exist:

(1) the water system or part or extension of the system that is within one hundred fifty feet of the principal building was in existence on the effective date of this subsection.

(2) the principal building has its own supply of water which is safe for human consumption.

(3) Prior to the effective date of this subsection, the property owner was not required to connect to the existing system.

(c) Those industries and farms which have their own supply of water for uses other than human consumption may continue to use their own water for that purpose but are required to use the township water system to provide water for human consumption.

(d) in the case of a water system provided by the township or a municipality authority or a joint water board, the board of supervisors may impose and charge to property owners who desire to or are required to connect to the water system a connection fee, a customer facilities fee, a tapping fee and other similar fees as enumerated under 53 pa.c.s. § 5607(d)(24) (relating to purposes and powers).

(e) whenever a water system or any part or extension thereof owned by a township has been constructed by the township at the expense of a private person or corporation or has been constructed by a private person or corporation under the supervision of the township at the expense of the private person or corporation, the board of supervisors shall have the right to charge a tapping fee, including a reimbursement component, and refund said reimbursement component to the person or corporation who has paid for the construction of said water system or any part or extension thereof.

(f)(1) if any property owner required under subsection (a) to connect with and use the system fails to do so within ninety days after notice to do so has been served by the board of supervisors, the board of supervisors or their agents may enter the property and construct the connection.

(2) the board of supervisors shall send an itemized bill of the cost of construction of connection to the owner of the property to which connection has been made, which bill is payable immediately, or the board of supervisors may authorize the payment of the cost of construction of connections in equal installments under article XXXIII.

§ 2604. Water Rents.—The board of supervisors may provide for the collection of water rents from users of water supplied by the township.

§ 2605. Distribution System; State Permit.—The board of supervisors may by ordinance provide, acquire, establish, regulate and protect any system of distribution of water for private and public use after a certified copy of the plans and surveys for the system, with a description of the sources from which it is proposed to derive the supply, are filed with the Department of Environmental Protection and a written permit for the construction of the system is obtained from the Department of Environmental Protection.

§ 2606. Occupation of Highways.—In regulating, protecting and extending its system of distribution of water, the township may occupy public highways, but no highway under the jurisdiction of the Department of Transportation shall be occupied until a permit therefor has been obtained from the department nor any highway under the jurisdiction of the county until a permit therefor has been obtained from the county commissioners.

§ 2607. Joint Construction, Acquisition or Maintenance of Water Systems.—Any township may join with any other municipal corporation in the construction or acquisition and maintenance of water systems. The construction of water systems shall be commenced only after plans for the systems have been filed with the Department of Environmental Protection and permits have been issued.

§ 2608. Joint Water Board.—The municipal corporations joining in the improvement, in order to facilitate the building of the water system and in securing preliminary surveys and estimates, may by ordinance provide for the appointment of a joint water board composed of one representative from each of the municipal corporations joining to act generally as the advisory and administrative agency in the construction of the improvement and its subsequent operation and maintenance. Members of the joint water board shall serve for terms of six years each from the dates of their respective appointments and until their successors are appointed. The joint water board shall organize by the election of a chairman, vice-chairman, secretary and treasurer. The municipal corporations may in the ordinances creating the joint water board authorize it to appoint an engineer, a solicitor and other necessary assistants and agree to the share of the compensation of those persons each municipal corporation is to pay. The members of the joint water board shall receive compensation for attending board meetings as established in the budget that is prepared by the joint water board and submitted to and adopted by the municipal corporations. The compensation to members for attending meetings shall not exceed a total of two hundred and fifty dollars ($250) for each member in each year, but the members shall be entitled to actual expenses to be paid by the respective municipal corporations the members represent.

§ 2609. Public Utility Law Saved.—Nothing contained in this article shall be construed to repeal or to supersede any of the provisions of 66 Pa.C.S. (relating to public utilities).

§ 2610. Cost of Construction; How Paid.—All or part of the cost of construction of any water system constructed by the authority of this article may be charged upon the properties accommodated or benefited thereby.

§ 2611. Water Districts.—The board of supervisors may designate, define and create one or more water districts within the township, and the board of supervisors shall determine the proportion of the cost of the water system which shall be equitably charged on each district and declare and establish the apportionment by resolution. No district shall be charged with more than its due proportion of the cost of the main pipe lines, pumping stations, et cetera, used jointly by more than one district.

§ 2612. Assessment.—The board of supervisors may provide for the payment of the cost of water lines or water systems in the township or in districts thereof by an assessment upon the properties accommodated or benefited by one of the following methods:

(1) By an assessment under a resolution or ordinance of the board of supervisors of each lot or piece of land in proportion to its frontage abutting on the water mains, allowing an equitable reduction in the case of corner properties and unusually shaped properties or in the case of properties abutting on more than one main as the resolution or ordinance may specify.

(2) By an equal assessment on all properties abutting on the mains in proportion to the total cost of construction. The amount of the charge on each property shall be determined by the board of supervisors.

§ 2613. Procedure for Assessment.—If taxpayers of the district whose property valuation as assessed for taxable purposes within the district amounts to fifty percent of the total property valuation so assessed or if taxpayers representing fifty percent of the parcels within the district present a petition within three months of the adoption of a resolution or ordinance levying an assessment under section 2612 to the court of common pleas stating that the assessment insufficiently represents the benefits accruing to abutting properties, they may include in the petition a request for the appointment of viewers to assess benefits. The court shall appoint three disinterested viewers, none of whom shall be a resident of that portion of the township which is accommodated by the water system in question, and the viewers shall proceed under this act for the assessment of damages and benefits by viewers. Upon the filing of the petition by taxpayers for appointment of viewers, any assessment made by the board of supervisors and any proceedings shall be stayed pending the disposition of the petition by the court.

§ 2614. Liens for Assessments; Costs of Proceedings.—After the amount of the assessment charged upon the several properties has been established by resolution making assessments according to section 2612 or by confirmation of any report of viewers, in whole or in part, the amounts of all assessments are payable to the township treasurer for the use of the township in which they are assessed. The board of supervisors shall make out bills for the amounts charged against each property, which shall be sent to all property owners whose property will be served by the water system. If the assessment is not paid within sixty days after the mailing of a bill therefor, the board of supervisors shall collect it by action of assumpsit or under law for the filing and recovery of municipal claims.

(2614 amended Dec. 18, 1996, P.L., No. 172)

ARTICLE XXVII
STORM WATER MANAGEMENT PLANS AND FACILITIES
53 P.S. § 67701–67704

§ 2701. Storm Water Management Systems Authorized.—The board of supervisors may plan, design, construct, assemble, install and alter facilities, including, but not limited to, inlets, outlets, systems of piping, diversion terraces, grass waterways, energy dissipaters, storm water retention devices and natural or artificial infiltration areas, to manage surface water runoff.

§ 2702. Construction of Storm Water Management Facilities.—(a) The board of supervisors may acquire by purchase, deed of dedication or eminent domain proceedings all or part of any existing system or facility for the management of surface water runoff which may have been established or constructed by any property owner in the township or establish, construct and maintain systems or facilities in the best interest of the township.

(b) If the board of supervisors and the owners of systems can agree upon a price to be paid by the township, the purchase may be consummated if the amount to be paid does not exceed the actual value of the facilities to be transferred.

(c) If the board of supervisors acquires the system by the exercise of eminent domain, the damages shall be determined by viewers under this act for eminent domain proceedings.

§ 2703. System Management.—(a) When exercising the powers under this article, the board of supervisors shall manage storm water originating in or passing through the township in a manner which is consistent with the requirements of the act of October 4, 1978 (P.L. 864, No. 167), known as the "Storm Water Management Act," and the storm water management guidelines and any regulations which may be adopted by the Department of Environmental Protection.

(b) All storm water management activities undertaken must be consistent with any watershed storm water management plan when the plan has been approved by the Department of Environmental Protection.

(c) When storm water management activities are undertaken in watersheds for which there is no approved storm water management plan, all drawings, documents, profiles and designs and descriptions of the proposed activities to be undertaken by the township shall be submitted to the county conservation district for review and comment before the initiation of earthmoving activities. The conservation district shall have thirty days to review and respond with comments to the board of supervisors. Failure to respond within that time constitutes favorable comment by the conservation district.

§ 2704. Ordinances.—(a) The board of supervisors may enact storm water management ordinances and require persons conducting earthmoving activities to obtain approval from the board of supervisors for those activities. Ordinances must be consistent with watershed storm water management plans where they exist and in all cases must be consistent with the act of October 4, 1978 (P.L.864, No.167), known as the "Storm Water Management Act."

(b) The board of supervisors may enact and enforce ordinances to govern and regulate the planning, management, implementation, construction and maintenance of storm water facilities.

§ 2705. Fees.—(a) For the purposes of funding the construction, maintenance and operation of storm water management facilities, systems and management plans authorized under this article, a township may assess reasonable and uniform fees based in whole or in part on the characteristics of the property benefited by the facilities, systems and management plans. The fees assessed may not exceed the amount necessary to meet the minimum requirements of the Federal Water Pollution Control Act (62 Stat. 1155, 33 U.S.C. § 1251 et seq.), and Federal or State laws governing the implementation of the Federal Water Pollution Control Act, for the construction, maintenance and operation of storm water management facilities, systems and management plans, as specified in 40 CFR 122.26 (relating to storm water discharges (applicable to State NPDES programs, see § 123.25)). In establishing the fees, the township shall consider and provide appropriate exemptions or credits for properties which have installed and are maintaining storm water facilities that meet best management practices and are approved or inspected by the township.

(b) Any fee levied by the township can be assessed in one of the following methods:

(1) On all properties in the township.

(2) On all properties benefited by a specific storm water project.

(3) By establishing a storm water management district and assessing the fee on all property owners in the district.

(c) Any fee collected for the purposes of storm water management may only be used for the purposes authorized by this article

(d) The assessments shall be filed with the township treasurer.

(e) An ordinance shall specify whether payments are to be made by annual or more frequent installments.

ARTICLE XXVIII
MANUFACTURE AND SALE OF ELECTRICITY

53 P.S. § 67801–67806

§ 2801. Manufacture and Sale of Electricity.—Any township may manufacture electricity by means of a hydroelectric generating facility owned or operated by the township for the use of the inhabitants of the township. Any township owning or operating a hydroelectric generating facility may make contracts for the sale of electricity to persons engaged in the business of the manufacture or sale of electricity.

§ 2802. Regulation of Use and Prices.—Any township furnishing electricity under this article may regulate the use of electricity in dwellings, business places and other places in the township and the rate to be charged for the electricity.

§ 2803. Sale of Hydroelectric Generating Facilities.—A township may by ordinance sell all or part of its hydroelectric generating facilities to a purchaser for that sale price as the parties may agree upon.

§ 2804. Construction or Purchase of Hydroelectric Generating Facilities.—Any township may construct or purchase facilities to manufacture electricity by hydroelectric generation. Any township may purchase a hydroelectric generating facility at that price as may be agreed upon by the township and the person, partnership or a majority of the stockholders of a corporation that owns the facilities.

§ 2805. Submission to Electors.—Before any township constructs or purchases a hydroelectric generating facility, the question of the increase of the debt of the township shall first be submitted to the qualified voters of the township in the manner provided by law for the increase in indebtedness of municipal corporations.

§ 2806. Limitation on Indebtedness.—No township which constructs or purchases a hydroelectric generating facility shall incur any indebtedness for the construction or enlargement of a new or existing dam or impoundment structure but may incur indebtedness for repairs or reconstruction of an existing dam or impoundment in connection with the hydroelectric project.

ARTICLE XXIX
SHADE TREE COMMISSION

53 P.S. § 67901–67910

§ 2901. Right of Establishment.—The board of supervisors may regulate the planting, maintenance and removal of shade trees in the township, or it may appoint a shade tree commission to administer regulations for shade trees.

§ 2902. Commission Members; Appointment; Terms; Vacancies.—(a) Except as provided in subsection (b), a shade tree commission shall be composed of three members who shall be residents of the township.

(b) The board of supervisors may, by ordinance, provide that the commission be composed of five members who shall be residents of the township.

(c) Whenever a shade tree commission of three members is established by any township, the initial terms of members shall be for periods of three years, four years and five years respectively. On the expiration of the term of any shade tree commissioner, a successor shall be appointed by the board to serve for a term of five years.

(d) Whenever a shade tree commission of five members is established by any township, the board of supervisors shall appoint members to staggered terms so that one term expires every year. On the expiration of the term of any shade tree commissioner, a successor shall be appointed by the board to serve for a term of five years.

(e) Members of the commission shall serve without compensation but shall be reimbursed for actual and necessary expenses incurred in the performance of their duties.

(f) Vacancies in the office of shade tree commissioner shall be filled by the board of supervisors for the unexpired term.

[Ed. Note: This section 2902 effective May 24, 2004]

§ 2903. Powers May be Vested in Recreation Board.—When there exists a board for the care of public parks, the board of supervisors may by ordinance confer on the recreation board all the powers and duties under this article for a shade tree commission.

§ 2904. General Powers of Commission.—The shade tree commission has exclusive control of the shade trees in the township and is authorized to plant, remove, maintain and protect shade trees on the public streets and highways in the township, excluding State highways.

§ 2905. Hiring of Employes.—The shade tree commission may with the approval of the board of supervisors employ persons to perform the duties and directions of the commission and make, publish and enforce regulations for the care and protection of the shade trees of the township. No regulations shall be in force until approved by the board of supervisors and until published at least once in a newspaper of general circulation in the township.

§ 2906. Report of Commission.—The shade tree commission shall annually report to the board of supervisors its transactions and expenses for the preceding fiscal year of the township.

§ 2907. Removal of Diseased or Dangerous Trees.—(a) The shade tree commission or, if no commission exists, the board of supervisors may by ordinance require owners of property to cut and remove trees located on the property if the condition of the trees, through disease or otherwise, unreasonably affects or interferes with the health, safety or welfare of the public or the right of the public to the unobstructed use of public roads or property.

(b) If within thirty days after the date of notice by certified mail, return receipt requested, to remove the trees, the property owner has not complied with that order, the commission or the board of supervisors may enter the premises and remove the trees.

(c) The cost of cutting and removal of trees by the township shall be charged to the property owner. The charge shall be a lien against the real estate of the property owner and shall be collected in the same manner as other municipal liens.

§ 2908. Maintenance by Township Funds.—The shade tree commission shall annually certify the costs incurred under this article to the board of supervisors. The costs shall be paid from the general township fund.

§ 2909. Penalties.—The shade tree commission, to the extent provided by ordinance of the township, may assess penalties for the violation of its regulations and of this article as far as it relates to shade trees. Any penalty so assessed shall be a lien upon the real estate of the offender and may be collected as municipal claims are collected.

§ 2910. Disposition of Penalties.—All penalties or assessments imposed under this article shall be paid to the township.

ARTICLE XXX
BOARD OF HEALTH

53 P.S. § 68001–68010

§ 3001. Establishment of Board of Health.—The board of supervisors may appoint a township board of health and township health officer to administer and enforce the health and sanitation laws of the township. If a board of health is appointed, the board of health may appoint a health officer or inspector whose duties shall be to implement and enforce the health and sanitation laws of the township and actions of the board of health. The health officer or inspector, whether appointed by the board of supervisors or by the board of health, shall not assume the performance of the duties of office until certified as a qualified health officer or inspector by the Department of Environmental Protection, the Department of Agriculture and the Department of Health.

§ 3002. Members of Board of Health.—A board of health appointed under this article shall be composed of five members, at least one of whom shall be a licensed physician with not less than two years' experience in the practice of his profession. The members of the board of health shall be appointed by the board of supervisors. Upon the creation of a board of health, one member shall be appointed to serve for one year, one for two years, one for three years, one for four years and one for five years, and after that one member shall be appointed each year to serve for five years. Upon the creation of a board of health in a township which has an existing sanitary board, the board of supervisors may continue the incumbent members of the sanitary board as members of the board of health. The members of the board of health shall serve without compensation but shall be reimbursed for actual and necessary expenses incurred in the performance of their duties.

§ 3003. Organization, Secretary, Health Officer and Inspectors.—The members of the board of health shall annually organize by electing a chairman from among the members of the board of health, a secretary who may be a member of the board of health and a health officer and inspectors who shall not be members of the board of health. The secretary, health officer and inspectors shall each receive a salary as determined by the board of supervisors and shall serve for a period of one year or until their successors may be appointed and qualified.

§ 3004. Duties of Secretary.—The secretary of the board of health shall keep the minutes of the proceedings of the board of health, keep accurate accounts of the expenses of the board of health, draw all requisitions for the payment of moneys on account of the board of health from appropriations made by the board of supervisors to the board of health and present them to the board of health for approval, render statements of the expenses to the board of health at each stated meeting or as frequently as the board of health may require, prepare under the direction of the board of health the annual report to the board of supervisors, together with the estimate of appropriation needed for the ensuing year, and make other reports and perform other duties as the board of health may require.

§ 3005. Powers and Duties of Health Officer and Inspectors.—The health officer and inspectors shall attend all stated and special meetings of the board of health and at all times be ready and available for the prompt performance of their official duties. They shall make inspections and execute the orders of the board of health.

§ 3006. Powers of Board of Health.—(a) The board of health shall enforce the health and sanitation laws of this Commonwealth and any regulations adopted under those laws and the health and sanitation laws and regulations of the township.

(b) Regulations, when authorized by ordinance of the township, shall have the force of ordinances of the township. All penalties prescribed for violation of the regulations, as well as the expenses actually and necessarily incurred in enforcing ordinances and regulations, are recoverable in enforcement proceedings and shall be paid into the general township fund. Townships may establish and revise fees for licenses or permits issued by the township as necessary.

§ 3007. Entering Premises.—The board of health, health officer or inspectors may enter at any time any premises within the township where there is reasonably suspected to exist any health hazard or violation of health or sanitation laws or regulations or which are of a type that may give rise to a health hazard.

§ 3008. Written Order for Violation.—When the board of health, health officer or inspectors determine that a health or sanitation hazard or violation exists, a written order shall be directed to the owner or occupant of the premises involved, ordering an abatement of the hazard or violation and the taking of corrective action as the board of health, health officer or inspectors may deem necessary under the circumstances. The order shall set forth a specific time in which the abatement and corrective action shall be accomplished. If the order is not complied with within the time provided, the board of health, health officer or inspectors may enter the premises and issue orders for the immediate termination of activities creating the violation, the potential violation and all acts of commerce conducted in, on or at the premises in question. In addition, the board of health, health officer or inspectors may proceed to enforce the law or regulation being violated the same as ordinances of the township.

§ 3009. Appropriations and Annual Report.—The board of supervisors shall make an annual appropriation to the board of health as the board of supervisors determines. The board of health or health officer shall before the preparation of the annual budget of the township submit to the board of supervisors the estimated expenses of the board of health or health officer for the ensuing year. The board of health or health officer shall by the first day of February of each year prepare and submit to the board of supervisors and the regional office of the Department of Environmental Protection, the Department of Agriculture and the Department of Health an annual report in writing, setting forth the activities and expenditures of the board of health or health officer during the prior calendar year.

§ 3010. Cooperation With Other Municipal Corporations.—(a) Any township may cooperate and contract with any other municipal corporation in the administration and enforcement of health and sanitation laws.

(b) If the board of supervisors abolishes the board of health or positions of health officers or inspectors and discontinues services under this article, the Department of Environmental Protection, the Department of Agriculture and the Department of Health shall be notified. An official copy of the action of the board of supervisors shall be transmitted to the regional office of the Department of Environmental Protection, the Department of Agriculture and the regional office of the Department of Health.

(c) The board of supervisors, the board of health or the health officer may request assistance from the Department of Environmental Protection, the Department of Agriculture or the Department of Health if the assistance is deemed necessary for the health and safety of township citizens.

ARTICLE XXXI
CONTRACTS
53 P.S. § 68101–68109

§ 3101. Power to Make Contracts.—The board of supervisors may make contracts for purchases under this act and the laws of this Commonwealth.

§ 3102. Letting Contracts.—(a) All contracts or purchases in excess of the required advertising base amount of eighteen thousand five hundred dollars ($18,500), subject to adjustment under subsection (b.1), except those specifically excluded, shall not be made except with and from the lowest responsible bidder after due notice in one newspaper of general circulation in the township. The notice for bids shall be published at least two times at intervals of not less than three days in daily newspapers or once a week for two successive weeks in weekly newspapers. The first advertisement shall be published not more than forty-five days, and the second advertisement not less than ten days, before the date set for the opening of bids. Notice of proposed contracts or purchases shall also be posted where the board of supervisors normally meets or in a conspicuous place within the township. Any published notice for bids shall contain full plans and specifications, or refer to the places where copies thereof can be obtained, state the amount of the performance bond determined under subsection (g) and give the date, time and place of a meeting at which an individual or committee appointed by the board of supervisors or the board of supervisors will open and read the bids.

(b) Written or telephonic price quotations from at least three qualified and responsible contractors shall be requested for all contracts in excess of the base amount of ten thousand dollars ($10,000), subject to adjustment under subsection (b.1), but are less than the amount requiring advertisement and competitive bidding, or, in lieu of price quotations, a memorandum shall be kept on file showing that fewer than three qualified contractors exist in the market area within which it is practicable to obtain quotations. A written record of telephonic price quotations shall be made and shall contain at least the date of the quotation, the name of the contractor and the contractor's representative, the construction, reconstruction, repair, maintenance or work which was the subject of the quotation and the price. Written price quotations, written records of telephonic price quotations and memoranda shall be retained for a period of three years.

(b.1) Adjustments to the base amounts specified under subsections (a) and (b) shall be made as follows:

(1) The Department of Labor and Industry shall determine the percentage change in the All Items Consumer Price Index for All Urban Consumers (CPI-U) for the United States City Average as published by the United States Department of Labor, Bureau of Labor Statistics for the twelve-month period ending September 30, 2012, and for each successive twelve-month period thereafter.

(2) If the department determines that there is no positive percentage change, then no adjustment to the base amounts shall occur for the relevant time period provided for in this subsection.

(3)(i) If the department determines that there is a positive percentage change in the first year that the determination is made under paragraph (1), the positive percentage change shall be multiplied by each base amount and the products shall be added to the base amounts, respectively, and the sums shall be preliminary adjusted amounts.

(ii) The preliminary adjusted amounts shall be rounded to the nearest one hundred dollars ($100), to determine the final adjusted base amounts for purposes of subsections (a) and (b).

Chap. 39 Res. During Mil. Service
Chap. 38 Intergov. Coop.
Chap. 37 3rd Class City Code
Chap. 36 Bor. Code
Chap. 35 2nd Class Twp. Code
Chap. 34 1st Class Twp. Code
Chap. 33 Home Rule Chart. Opt. Plans Law
Chap. 32 Water Serv. Act
Chap. 31 Munic. Auth. Act

(4) In each successive year in which there is a positive percentage change in the CPI-U for the United States City Average, the positive percentage change shall be multiplied by the most recent preliminary adjusted amounts and the products shall be added to the preliminary adjusted amount of the prior year to calculate the preliminary adjusted amounts for the current year. The sums thereof shall be rounded to the nearest one hundred dollars ($100) to determine the new final adjusted base amounts for purposes of subsections (a) and (b).

(5) The determinations and adjustments required under this subsection shall be made in the period between October 1 and November 15 of the year following the effective date of this subsection, and annually between October 1 and November 15 of each year thereafter.

(6) The final adjusted base amounts and new final adjusted base amounts obtained under paragraphs (3) and (4) shall become effective January 1 for the calendar year following the year in which the determination required under paragraph (1) is made.

(7) The department shall publish notice in the Pennsylvania Bulletin prior to January 1 of each calendar year of the annual percentage change determined under paragraph (1) and the unadjusted or final adjusted base amounts determined under paragraphs (3) and (4) at which competitive bidding is required under subsection (a) and written or telephonic price quotations are required under subsection (b), respectively, for the calendar year beginning the first day of January after publication of the notice. The notice shall include a written and illustrative explanation of the calculations performed by the department in establishing the unadjusted or final adjusted base amounts under this subsection for the ensuing calendar year.

(8) The annual increase in the preliminary adjusted base amounts obtained under paragraphs (3) and (4) shall not exceed three percent.

(c) The board of supervisors may purchase or make contracts under the act of October 27, 1979 (P.L. 241, No. 78), entitled "An act authorizing political subdivisions, municipality authorities and transportation authorities to enter into contracts for the purchase of goods where no bids are received," if no bids are received on an item after proper notices.

(d) The amount of the contract, whether of straight sale price, conditional sale, lease, lease purchase or otherwise, is the entire amount the township pays to the successful bidder in order to obtain the services or property, or both, and does not mean only the amount which is paid to acquire title or to receive any other particular benefit or benefits.

(e) The award of contracts shall only be made by public announcement at the meeting at which bids are opened by the board of supervisors, or received from the individual or committee appointed by the board of supervisors to open and read bids, or at a subsequent meeting of the board of supervisors, the time and place of which shall be publicly announced when bids are received. If for any reason one or both of the meetings are not held, the same business may be transacted at a subsequent meeting if at least five days' notice of the meeting is published in the same newspaper as the notice of bids. Bidders shall be notified and other interested parties, upon request, shall be notified of the date, time and location of the opening of bids and may be present when the bids are opened.

(f) The board of supervisors may reject all bids received if it is believed to be in the best interest of the township, and at a public meeting the reasons for the rejection of all bids shall be announced and be noted in the minutes.

(g) Unless covered under the bonding requirements of the act of December 20, 1967 (P.L. 869, No. 385), known as the "Public Works Contractors' Bond Law of 1967," the successful bidder shall furnish a bond guaranteeing performance of the contract, in an amount as determined by the supervisors at the time of advertising for bids which shall be not less than ten percent nor more than one hundred percent of the amount of the contract, within twenty days after the contract is awarded. If the bidder fails to furnish the bond within twenty days, unless delivery is made or the entire contract is fulfilled during that time, the contract is void. Delivery, accomplishment and guarantees may be required in all cases, including the exceptions contained in this section.

(h) The contracts or purchases made by the board of supervisors involving payments in excess of the required advertising amount, which do not require advertising, bidding or price quotations are as follows:

(1) Those made for emergency or routine maintenance, repairs or replacements for water, electric light and other public works of the township if they do not constitute new additions, extensions or enlargements of existing facilities and equipment.

(2) Those made for improvements, repairs or maintenance of any kind made or provided by any township through its own employes. All contracts or purchases of materials used for improvement, maintenance or construction are subject to the provisions contained in subsection (a) and (b).

(3) Those involving any policies of insurance or surety company bonds, those made for public utility service, those made for electricity, natural gas or telecommunications service either directly or with an association authorized under Article XIV (§1401, 53 P.S. 66401 et seq.) in which the township is a member and those made with another municipal corporation, county, school district or municipality authority, a council of government, consortium, cooperative or other similar entity created pursuant to 53 Pa.C.S. Ch. 23 Subch. A (relating to intergovernmental cooperation) or Federal or State Government, including the sale, leasing or loan of any supplies or materials by the Federal or State Government or their agencies.

(4) Those involving personal or professional services.

(5) Those made for materials and supplies or equipment rental under emergency conditions under 35 Pa.C.S. Pt. V (relating to emergency management services).

(6) Those contracts involving equipment rental with operators if more than fifty percent of the total labor personnel hours required for the completion of the contract is supplied by the township through its own employes.

(7) Those contracts for the purchase of repair parts or materials for use in existing township equipment or facilities if the item or material to be purchased is the sole item of its kind on the market or is manufactured as a replacement for the original item or equipment being repaired.

(8) Those for used personal property, such as equipment, articles, apparatus, appliances, vehicles or parts thereof being purchased from a public utility, municipal corporation, county, school district, municipality authority, council of government, volunteer fire company, volunteer ambulance service, volunteer rescue squad or Federal or State Government.

(9) Those where particular types, models or pieces of equipment, articles, apparatus, appliances, vehicles or parts thereof which are patented and manufactured products.

(i) No township official, either elected or appointed, or township employe who knows, or who by the exercise of reasonable diligence could know, shall be interested to any appreciable degree, either directly or indirectly, in any contract for the sale or furnishing of any supplies or materials for the use of the township or for any work to be done for the township involving the payment by the township of more than five hundred dollars ($500) in any year unless the contract is awarded through the public bid process. This limitation does not apply if the

Table of Contents
Part I Ch. 1–3 Ethics, Records, Open Meetings
Part II Ch. 4–10 Taxation
Part III Ch. 11–18 Torts, Contracts & Civil Rules
Part IV Ch. 19–24 Zoning & Planning
Part V Ch. 25–30 Construction and Emergency Codes
Part VI Ch. 31–39 Municipal Codes
Index

officer or appointee of the township is an employe of the person, firm or corporation to which the money is to be paid in a capacity with no possible influence on the transaction and the officer cannot possibly be benefited thereby, either financially or otherwise. If a supervisor is within this exception, the supervisor shall so inform the board of supervisors and refrain from voting on the payments and shall in no manner participate in the contract. Any official or appointee who knowingly violates this provision is subject to surcharge to the extent of the damage shown to be sustained by the township, is ousted from office or employment and commits a misdemeanor of the third degree.

(j) Contracts for the purchase of materials or rental of equipment for the construction, reconstruction, maintenance and improvement of roads and bridges shall be in writing and let only on standard specifications of the Department of Transportation.

(k) Contracts for the purchase of materials or supplies may be bid on a per-unit basis.

(l) Every contract for the construction, reconstruction, alteration, repair, improvement or maintenance of public works shall comply with the act of March 3, 1978 (P.L. 6, No. 3), known as the "Steel Products Procurement Act."

(m) No person, consultant, firm or corporation contracting with a township for purposes of rendering personal or professional services to the township shall share with any township officer or employe, and no township officer or employe shall accept, any portion of the compensation or fees paid by the township for the contracted services provided to the township except under the following terms or conditions:

(1) Full disclosure of all relevant information regarding the sharing of the compensation or fees shall be made to the board of supervisors.

(2) The board of supervisors must approve the sharing of any fee or compensation for personal or professional services before the performance of the services.

(3) No fee or compensation for personal or professional services may be shared except for work actually performed.

(4) No shared fee or compensation for personal or professional services may be paid at a rate in excess of the commensurate for similar personal or professional services.

§ 3103. Road Contracts.—The board of supervisors may make a contract for the improvement and keeping in repair of township roads. No contract shall extend over a period of more than four years. Every contractor for road work shall give bond for the amount of the contract and sign specifications furnished by the board of supervisors for the building and care of the contract roads.

§ 3104. Evasion of Advertising Requirements.—(a) No supervisor shall evade the provisions of section 3101 as to advertising for bids by purchasing or contracting for services and personal properties piecemeal to obtain prices under the required advertising price. This provision is intended to make unlawful the evading of advertising requirements by making a series of purchases or contracts each for less than the advertising requirement price, or by making several simultaneous purchases or contracts each below the required advertising price, when the transactions involved should have been made as one transaction for one price. Any supervisors who vote in violation of this provision and who know that the transaction upon which they vote is or ought to be part of a larger transaction and that it is being divided in order to evade the requirements as to advertising for bids are jointly and severally subject to surcharge for ten percent of the full amount of the contract or purchase.

(b) Any supervisor who votes to unlawfully evade the provisions of this article and who knows that the transaction upon which he so votes is or ought to be a part of a larger transaction and that it is being divided in order to evade the requirements as to advertising for bids commits a misdemeanor of the third degree for each contract entered into as a direct result of that vote. This penalty shall be in addition to any surcharge which may be assessed pursuant to subsection (a).

§ 3105. Bonds for Protection of Labor and Material Suppliers.—Before any contract exceeding five thousand dollars ($5,000) is awarded to any prime contractor or construction manager for the construction, reconstruction, alteration or repair of any building or other public work or public improvement of the township, the contractor shall furnish to the township a payment bond for the protection of claimants supplying labor or materials to the prime contractor to whom the contract is awarded, at one hundred percent of the contract amount, conditioned for the prompt payment of all materials furnished or labor supplied or performed in the prosecution of the contract under the act of December 20, 1967 (P.L. 869, No. 385), known as the "Public Works Contractors' Bond Law of 1967."

§ 3106. Purchase Contracts for Supplies and Equipment; Fire Company, Et Cetera; Participation.—The board of supervisors may permit any paid or volunteer fire company, paid or volunteer rescue company and paid or volunteer ambulance company in the township to participate in purchase contracts for supplies and equipment of the township and agreeing that it will be bound by any terms and conditions the township prescribes.

§ 3107. Separate Specifications for Branches of Work.—In the preparation of specifications for the erection or alteration of any public building, when the entire cost of the work exceeds the advertising requirement price, the architect, engineer or person preparing the specifications shall prepare separate specifications for the plumbing, heating, ventilating and electrical work, and the township shall receive separate bids upon each of those branches of work and award the contract to the lowest bidder.

§ 3108. Workers' Compensation Insurance.—(a) All contracts executed by any township which involve the construction or performance of any work involving the employment of labor shall contain a provision that the contractor shall accept, and file with the township proof of compliance with or exemption from, insofar as the work covered by the contract is concerned, the act of June 2, 1915 (P.L.736, No. 338), known as the "Workers' Compensation Act."

(b) Any contract executed in violation of this section is void.

§ 3109. Engineers and Architects Not to be Interested in Contracts.—(a) No architect or engineer in the employ of a township and engaged in the preparation of plans, specifications or estimates may bid on any public work at any letting of the work in the township.

(b) An officer of a township who is charged with letting any public work may not award a contract to any architect or engineer in the employ of the township.

(c) An architect or engineer in the employ of a township may not be interested in any contract for public work in the township or receive any remuneration or gratuity from any person interested in any contract except under section 3102(l).

(d) Any person who violates this section commits a misdemeanor of the third degree.

ARTICLE XXXII
TAXATION AND FINANCE
53 P.S. § 68201–68210

§ 3201. Fiscal Year.—The fiscal year in townships commences on the first day of January in each year. All receipts, disbursements, contracts and purchases shall be entered as of record in the fiscal year in which made.

§ 3202. Annual Budget.—(a) The board of supervisors shall annually prepare a proposed budget for all funds for the ensuing fiscal year. The proposed budget shall reflect as nearly as possible the estimated revenues and expenses of the township for the year for which the budget is prepared. A township shall not prepare and advertise notice of a proposed budget when it is knowingly inaccurate. Upon any revision of the proposed budget, if the estimated revenues or expenses in the final budget are increased more than ten percent in the aggregate or more than twenty-five percent in any major category over the proposed budget, it may not be legally adopted with those increases unless it is again advertised once at least ten days before adoption and an opportunity given to taxpayers to examine the amended proposed budget. A major category is a group of related revenue or expense items, the combined total of which is listed as a line item. The estimates in the budget shall specify the amount of money necessary for each governmental activity of the township for which a special tax levy may or may not be authorized and the amount of money necessary for the payment of debts and other miscellaneous purposes.

(b) Upon the preparation of the proposed budget, the board of supervisors shall give public notice by advertisement once in one newspaper of general circulation in the township that the proposed budget is available for public inspection at a designated place in the township. After the proposed budget has been available for public inspection for twenty days, the board of supervisors shall, after making revisions as are appropriate, adopt the final budget not later then the thirty-first day of December and the necessary appropriation measures required to put it into effect.

(c) The total appropriation shall not exceed the revenues estimated as available for the fiscal year.

(d) During the month of January next following any municipal election, the board of supervisors may amend the budget and the levy and tax rate to conform with its amended budget. A period of ten days'0 public inspection at the office of the township secretary of the proposed amended budget, after notice by the township secretary to that effect is published once in a newspaper of general circulation in the township, shall intervene between the adoption of the proposed amended budget and the final adoption of the amended budget. Any amended budget must be adopted by the board of supervisors on or before the fifteenth day of February. No proposed amended budget shall before final adoption be revised upward in excess of ten percent in the aggregate or in excess of twenty-five percent of the amount of any major category in the proposed amended budget. A major category is a group of related revenue or expense items, the combined total of which is listed as a line item.

(e) The board of supervisors may by resolution make supplemental appropriations for any purpose from any funds on hand or estimated to be received within the fiscal year and not otherwise appropriated, including the proceeds of any borrowing authorized by law. Supplemental appropriations may be made whether or not an appropriation for that purpose was included in the original budget as adopted.

(f) The board of supervisors may by resolution transfer unencumbered moneys from one township account to another, but no moneys may be transferred from the fund allocated for the payment of debts or from any fund raised by a special tax levy or assessment for a particular purpose. Transfers shall not be made during the first three months of the fiscal year. No moneys shall be paid out of the township treasury except upon appropriation made according to law.

§ 3203. Uniform Report Forms.—(a) The uniform forms for the annual financial report required to be made by the auditors shall be prepared by a committee consisting of four representatives of the State Association of Township Supervisors and one representative each from the Department of Transportation and the Department of Community and Economic Development.

(b) Representatives of the State Association of Township Supervisors shall be appointed by the president of that organization. The representatives may be township supervisors, auditors or secretaries and should represent townships in the various population groups. The president of the State Association of Township Supervisors shall supply to the Department of Community and Economic Development the names and addresses of the representatives immediately upon their appointment.

(c) Representatives of the townships shall serve without compensation but shall be reimbursed by the Commonwealth for all necessary expenses incurred in attending meetings of the committee from appropriations made to the Department of Community and Economic Development. The committee shall meet at the call of the Secretary of Community and Economic Development, or an agent of the secretary, who shall chair the committee.

(d) Repealed.

(e) The Department of Community and Economic Development shall prepare and furnish the forms required by this act in cooperation with the committee. If the committee fails to cooperate, the Department of Community and Economic Development shall issue the forms and distribute them annually, as needed, to the proper township officers.

§ 3204. Investment of Township Funds.—(a) The board of supervisors may:

(1) Make investment of township sinking funds as authorized by the act of July 12, 1972 (P.L. 781, No. 185), known as the "Local Government Unit Debt Act."

(2) Make investment of moneys in the general fund and in special funds of the township.

(3) Liquidate any investment, in whole or in part, by disposing of securities or withdrawing funds on deposit. Any action taken to make or to liquidate any investment shall be made by the officers designated by action of the board of supervisors.

(b) The board of supervisors shall invest township funds consistent with sound business practice.

(c) The board of supervisors shall provide for an investment program subject to restrictions contained in this act and in any other applicable statute and any rules and regulations adopted by the board of supervisors.

(d) Authorized types of investments of township funds are:

(1) United States Treasury bills.

(2) Short-term obligations of the Federal Government or its agencies or instrumentalities.

(3) Deposits in savings accounts or time deposits, other than certificates of deposit, or share accounts of institutions insured by the Federal Deposit Insurance Corporation, the National Credit Union Share Insurance Fund, the Pennsylvania Deposit Insurance Corporation or the Pennsylvania Savings Association Insurance Corporation, or their successor agencies, to the extent that the accounts are so insured and, for any amounts above the insured maximum, if approved collateral therefor is pledged by the depository.

(4) Obligations of the United States of America or any of its agencies or instrumentalities backed by the full faith and credit of the United States of America, of the Commonwealth of Pennsylvania or any of its agencies or instrumentalities backed by the full faith and credit of the Commonwealth or of any political subdivision of the Commonwealth of Pennsylvania or any of its

Table of Contents
Part I Ch. 1–3 Ethics, Records, Open Meetings
Part II Ch. 4–10 Taxation
Part III Ch. 11–18 Torts, Contracts & Civil Rules
Part IV Ch. 19–24 Zoning & Planning
Part V Ch. 25–30 Construction and Emergency Codes
Part VI Ch. 31–39 Municipal Codes
Index

agencies or instrumentalities backed by the full faith and credit of the political subdivision.

(5) Shares of an investment company registered under the Investment Company Act of 1940 (54 Stat. 789, 15 U.S.C. § 80a-1 et seq.), whose shares are registered under the Securities Act of 1933 (48 Stat. 74, 15 U.S.C. § 77a et seq.), if the only investments of that company are in the authorized investments for township funds listed in paragraphs (1) through (4).

(6) Certificates of deposit purchased from institutions insured by the Federal Deposit Insurance Corporation, the National Credit Union Share Insurance Fund, the Pennsylvania Deposit Insurance Corporation or the Pennsylvania Savings Association Insurance Corporation, or their successor agencies, to the extent that the accounts are so insured. However, for any amounts above the insured maximum, the certificates of deposit shall be secured by a pledge or assignment of assets of the institution, and the collateral may include loans, including interest in pools of loans, secured by first mortgage liens on real property. Certificates of deposit purchased from commercial banks shall be limited to an amount equal to twenty percent of a bank's total capital and surplus. Certificates of deposit purchased from savings and loan associations or savings banks shall be limited to an amount equal to twenty percent of an institution's assets minus liabilities.

(7) Any investment authorized by 20 Pa.C.S. Ch. 73 (relating to fiduciaries investments). This paragraph is limited to investments for any pension or retirement fund.

(e) In making investments of township funds, the board of supervisors may:

(1) Permit assets pledged as collateral under subsection (d)(3) to be pooled under the act of August 6, 1971 (P.L. 281, No. 72), entitled "An act standardizing the procedures for pledges of assets to secure deposits of public funds with banking institutions pursuant to other laws; establishing a standard rule for the types, amounts and valuations of assets eligible to be used as collateral for deposits of public funds; permitting assets to be pledged against deposits on a pooled basis; and authorizing the appointment of custodians to act as pledgees of assets."

(2) Combine moneys from more than one fund under township control for the purchase of a single investment if each of the funds combined for the purpose is accounted for separately in all respects and the earnings from the investment are separately and individually computed and recorded and credited to the accounts from which the investment was purchased.

(3) Join with one or more other municipal corporations, municipality authorities or school districts under the act of July 12, 1972 (P.L. 762, No. 180), referred to as the Intergovernmental Cooperation Law, in the purchase of a single investment if the requirements of paragraph (2) on separate accounting of individual funds and separate computation, recording and crediting of the earnings therefrom are adhered to.

§ 3205. Township and Special Tax Levies.—(a) The board of supervisors may by resolution levy taxes upon all real property within the township made taxable for township purposes, as ascertained by the last adjusted valuation for county purposes, for the purposes and at the rates specified in this section. All taxes shall be collected in cash.

(1) An annual tax not exceeding fourteen mills for general township purposes. If the board of supervisors petitions the court of common pleas for the right to levy additional millage, the court may order a greater rate than fourteen mills, but not exceeding five additional mills, to be levied.

(2) An annual tax not exceeding five mills to light the highways, roads and other public places in the township.

(3) An annual tax not exceeding fifty percent of the rate of assessment for the general township tax to procure land and erect public buildings thereon and for the payment of indebtedness incurred in connection therewith.

(4) An annual tax not exceeding three mills to purchase and maintain fire apparatus and a suitable place to house fire apparatus, to make appropriations to fire companies located inside and outside the township, to make appropriations for the training of fire company personnel and for fire training schools or centers and to contract with adjacent municipal corporations or volunteer fire companies therein for fire protection.

(i) The township may appropriate up to one-half, but not to exceed one mill, of the revenue generated from a tax under this clause for the purpose of paying salaries, benefits or other compensation of fire suppression employes of the township or a fire company serving the township. For any calendar year, the board of supervisors may waive the appropriation limitation under this subparagraph by resolution.

(ii) If an annual tax is proposed to be set at a level higher than three mills, the question shall be submitted to the voters of the township.

(5) A tax not exceeding two mills to establish and maintain fire hydrants and fire hydrant water service.

(6) A tax to acquire, maintain and operate parks, playgrounds, playfields, gymnasiums, swimming pools and recreation centers.

(7) An annual tax sufficient to pay interest and principal on any indebtedness incurred under 53 Pa.C.S. Pt. VII Subpt. B 53 Pa.C.S. [§ 8001 et. Seq.] (relating to indebtedness and borrowing).

(8) An annual tax not exceeding one-half mill to support ambulance, rescue and other emergency services serving the township.

(i) The township may appropriate up to one-half of the revenue generated from a tax under this clause for the purpose of paying salaries, benefits or other compensation of employes of the ambulance, rescue or other emergency service. For any calendar year, the board of supervisors may waive the appropriation limitation under this subparagraph by resolution.

(ii) If an annual tax is proposed to be set higher than one-half mill, the question shall be submitted to the voters of the township.

(9) An annual tax not exceeding five mills to create and maintain a revolving fund to be used in making permanent street, sidewalk, water supply or sewer improvements before the collection of all or part of the cost from the property owners. A revolving fund may also be used for the deposit of funds raised through the issuance of general obligation bonds of the township for the making of permanent street, sidewalk, water supply or sewer improvements. When all or part of the cost of the construction of any permanent street, sidewalk, water supply or sewer improvement is paid from the revolving fund and is later assessed and collected from the owners of the property adjoining or abutting upon the improvement, the collections shall be applied to the credit of the revolving fund to the extent of the withdrawal therefrom for that purpose.

(10) An annual special tax not exceeding two mills to create and accumulate moneys in a road equipment fund to be used exclusively for purchasing road equipment.

(b) When it is shown to the court that the debts due by any township exceed the amount which the board of supervisors may collect in any year by taxation, the court, after ascertaining the amount of indebtedness of the township, may in an action of mandamus direct the board of supervisors, by special taxation, to collect an amount sufficient to pay the debts. If the amount of indebtedness is so large as to render it inadvisable to collect the entire amount in any one year, the court may direct the special taxes to be levied and collected during successive years as may be required for payment of the debt.

§ 3206. Procedure for Referendum on Tax Questions.—When the assent of the electors is required under this article for special tax levies, the county board of elections shall frame the question under the election laws of this Commonwealth for submission to the voters of the township at the first municipal or general election occurring not less than sixty days after submission of the question.

§ 3207. Taxes for Special Districts.—This article does not include the levy of any taxes upon particular districts or parts of any township for particular purposes.

§ 3208. Tax Rate to be Expressed in Dollars and Cents.—When the board of supervisors by resolution establishes the rate of taxation for any year at a mill rate, the resolution shall also include a statement expressing the rate of taxation in dollars and cents on each one hundred dollars ($100) of assessed valuation of taxable property.

§ 3209. Tax Duplicates.—The board of supervisors shall require a duplicate to be made designating the amount of township tax levied against each taxpayer of the township, and also duplicates for all other taxes levied and assessed under this act, and deliver the duplicate within thirty days after the adoption of the budget or within thirty days after receipt of the assessment roll from the county, whichever is later, to the township tax collector.

§ 3210. Additions and Revisions to Duplicates.—(a) When there is any construction of a building or buildings not otherwise exempt as a dwelling after the first day of January of any year and the building is not included in the tax duplicate of the township, the authority responsible for assessments in the township shall upon the request of the board of supervisors inspect and reassess, subject to the right of appeal and adjustment by the State law under which assessments are made, all taxable property in the township to which major improvements have been made after the first day of January of any year and to give notice of the reassessments within ten days to the authority responsible for assessments, the township and the property owner. The property shall be added to the duplicate and is taxable for township purposes at the reassessed valuation for that proportionate part of the fiscal year of the township remaining after the property was improved. Any improvement made during the month shall be computed as having been made on the first day of the month. A certified copy of the additions or revisions to the duplicate shall be furnished by the board of supervisors to the township tax collector, together with its warrant for collection of the taxes, and within ten days the township tax collector shall notify the owner of the property of the taxes due in the township.

(b) When an assessment is made for a portion of a year, the assessment shall be added to the duplicate of the following or succeeding year unless the value of the improvements has already been included in that duplicate.

ARTICLE XXXIII
COLLECTION OF ASSESSMENTS

53 P.S. § 68301–68303

§ 3301. Assessments Collected by Tax Collector.—(a) When any assessment for street lights, fire hydrant service, police protection or other service is implemented by the board of supervisors and charged to the tax collector for collection, assessments for the service shall be filed with the township tax collector. The tax collector shall give thirty days' notice that the assessments are due and payable. The notice shall state the due date to each party assessed and be served by mailing notice to the owner of the property. The tax collector is entitled to the same commission for the collection of these assessments as for the collection of the general township tax. If any assessment remains unpaid ninety days after the due date, it shall be turned over to the township solicitor for collection by means of an action in assumpsit for recovery or a municipal lien filed against the property of the delinquent owner for the amount of the unpaid assessment, plus interest established by the board of supervisors from the date the assessment was due. If an owner has two or more lots against which there is an assessment for the same year, the lots shall be embraced in one claim. Assessments, when collected, shall be paid over to the township treasurer, who shall deposit and keep them in a separate account, to be paid out only for expenses incurred in providing the service. Each special assessment account shall be audited by the board of auditors of the township.

(b) When any assessment for refuse collection in special districts or other service is charged against the owners, occupants or tenants of property within the township, the collection of which is charged to the tax collector, the assessments for the service shall be filed with the tax collector. The tax collector shall give thirty days' notice that the assessments are due and payable. The notice shall state the due date to each party assessed and be served by mailing to the owner, occupant or tenant of the property. The tax collector is entitled to the same commission for the collection of these assessments as for the collection of the general township tax. If any assessment remains unpaid ninety days after the due date, it shall be turned over to the township solicitor for collection by action in assumpsit for the amount of the unpaid assessment, plus interest established by the board of supervisors from the date the assessment was due and all costs incurred in the collection of the assessment. Assessments, when collected, shall be paid over to the township treasurer, who shall deposit and keep them in a separate account, to be paid out only for expenses incurred in providing the service. Each special assessment account shall be audited by the board of auditors of the township.

§ 3302. Assessments Collected by Township Treasurer.—(a) When any assessment for construction, maintenance and repair of street, sewer, water, sidewalks, curbs or other service is implemented by the board of supervisors, the collection of which is not charged to the tax collector, the assessments for the service shall be filed with the township treasurer. The township treasurer shall give thirty days' notice that the assessments are due and payable. The notice shall state the due date to each party assessed and shall be served by mailing it to the owner of the property. If any assessment remains unpaid ninety days after the due date, it shall be turned over to the township solicitor for collection by means of an action in assumpsit for recovery or a municipal lien filed against the property of the delinquent owner for the amount of the unpaid assessment, plus interest established by the board of supervisors from the date the assessment was due. If an owner has two or more lots against which there is an assessment for the same year, the lots shall be embraced in one claim. Upon receipt of payment of assessments, the township treasurer shall deposit the assessments in a separate account, to be paid out only for expenses incurred in providing the service. Each special assessment account shall be audited by the board of auditors of the township.

(b) When any assessment for refuse collection or other service is charged against the owners, occupants or tenants of property within the township, the collection of which is not charged to the tax collector, the assessments shall be filed with the township treasurer. The township treasurer shall give thirty days' notice that the assessments are due and payable. The notice shall state the due date to each party assessed and be served by mailing it to the owner, occupant or tenant of the property. If any assessment remains unpaid ninety days after the due date, it shall be turned over to the township solicitor for collection by action in assumpsit for the amount of the unpaid assessment, plus interest established by the board of supervisors from the date the assessment was due and all costs incurred in the collection of the assessment. Upon receipt of the assessments, the township treasurer shall deposit and keep them in a separate account, to be paid out only for expenses incurred in providing the service. Each special assessment account shall be audited by the board of auditors of the township.

§ 3303. Installment Payments.—(a) When any township authorizes the construction or acquisition of any sanitary sewer or system of sanitary sewers, or the improvement of any street or portion thereof, or the installation of curbing or sidewalks, or a water supply or water systems, and all or part of the cost is assessed against the properties benefited, improved or accommodated by the sewer or system of sewers, or curbing or sidewalks, or water supply, or abutting upon the street or portion thereof, the board of supervisors may authorize the payment of the assessment in equal annual or more frequent installments. The ordinance shall specify the length of time over which the installments may be extended and whether payments are to be made by annual or more frequent installments. Installments shall bear interest at a rate not to exceed six percent or a higher amount equal to the amount of interest on the indebtedness, if any, commencing at the time established by ordinance. If bonds have been issued and sold to provide for the payment of any street improvement, the assessments shall not be payable beyond the term for which the bonds are issued, and the expenses for the improvements and interest thereon to the first day when interest is payable on the bonds shall be taken as the cost of the improvement to be assessed on the property benefited.

(b) Claims to secure the assessments shall be entered in the prothonotary's office of the county at the same time and in the same form and shall be collected in the same manner as municipal claims are filed and collected.

(c) Assessments are payable to the township treasurer in quarterly, semiannual or annual installments, with interest from the date from which interest is computed on the amount of the assessments.

(d) If there is a default in the payment of any installment and interest for a period of sixty days after it becomes due, the entire assessment and accrued interest shall become due, and the township solicitor shall proceed to collect the assessment under the general laws relating to the collection of municipal claims.

(e) Any owner of property against whom any assessment is made may pay the assessment in full, at any time, with interest and costs thereon to the due date of the next installment, and that payment shall discharge the lien.

ARTICLE XXXIV

EMINENT DOMAIN; ASSESSMENT OF DAMAGES AND BENEFITS

53 P.S. § 68401–68407

§ 3401. Scope of Article.—When the right of eminent domain or the ascertainment and assessment of damages and benefits in viewer proceedings is exercised by a township, the proceeding shall be as set forth in this article. In addition to any of the provisions of this act, all eminent domain proceedings shall conform to the act of June 22, 1964 (Sp.Sess., P.L. 84, No. 6), known as the "Eminent Domain Code."

§ 3402. Restrictions as to Certain Property.—(a) In addition to the restrictions made by other provisions of this act in particular cases, no township shall, except as provided in subsection (b), exercise the right of eminent domain against land now occupied by any building which was used during the Colonial or Revolutionary period as a place of Assembly by the Council of the Colony of Pennsylvania, the Supreme Executive Council of the Commonwealth of Pennsylvania or the Congress of the United States; or against the land occupied by any fort, redoubt or blockhouse erected during the Colonial or Revolutionary period or any building used as headquarters by the Commander-in-Chief of the Continental Army; or against the site of any building, fort, redoubt, blockhouse or headquarters, which are preserved for their historic associations and not for private profit. The Colonial and Revolutionary period is taken as ended on September 3, 1783.

(b) The restriction on eminent domain provided in subsection (a) shall not apply:

(1) if a township in a county of the second class A obtains a statement from the Pennsylvania Historical and Museum Commission or the historical society of the county where the land is situate certifying that the building or other structure, the existence of which would otherwise restrict the township from exercising the right of eminent domain, is not being maintained in a manner appropriate to an historical structure; and

(2) if the purpose of the acquisition of the land and structures by a township in a county of the second class A is to ensure the preservation and maintenance of the historical site and structure sought to be protected by subsection (a).

§ 3403. Value of Land or Property Not to be Assessed as Benefits.—In the appropriation of land or property for public use, other than for roads, it is not lawful to assess any portion of the damage done to or value of the land or property so appropriated against the other property adjoining or in the vicinity of the land or property so appropriated.

§ 3404. Title Acquired.—When land or property is taken under eminent domain proceedings, other than for road purposes, or is acquired by gift, purchase or otherwise, the title obtained by the township is in fee simple. In particular instances, a different title may by agreement be acquired.

§ 3405. Assessment of Damages and Benefits.—The damages may be paid in whole or in part by the township or may be assessed in whole or in part upon the property benefited. In the latter case, the viewers, having first determined the damages apart from the benefits, shall assess the total cost of the improvement, or so much thereof as may be just and reasonable, upon the properties peculiarly benefited, including in the assessment all parties for which damages have been allowed, and shall report the findings to the court. The total assessment for benefits shall not exceed the total damages awarded or agreed upon.

§ 3406. Assessment Awards.—In proceedings to assess damages and benefits, if the land or property is both benefited and damaged by the improvements, the excess of damages over benefits or the excess of benefits over damages, or nothing if the benefits and damages are equal, shall be awarded to or assessed against the owner of land or property affected thereby.

§ 3407. Assessments to Bear Interest.—All assessments for benefits and costs shall bear interest at six percent annually from the expiration of thirty days after they have been finally ascertained and shall be payable to the township treasurer.

ARTICLE XXXV

VIOLATION OF ACT GENERALLY

53 P.S. § 68501

§ 3501. Violation of Act Generally; Penalty.—Any township supervisor, elected or appointed township official or employe, roadmaster or contractor or any other person, including any corporation officer or employe, who violates any of the provisions of this act, other than those for which specific penalties are provided, or who fails to carry out the provisions of this act commits a summary offense. All fines collected for violation of this act shall be paid to the township treasurer and credited to the general township fund.

ARTICLE XXXVI
ACTIONS BY TOWNSHIPS

53 P.S. § 68601

§ 3601. Recovery of Municipal Claims.—(a) In addition to the remedies under law for the filing of liens for the collection of municipal claims, a township may proceed for the recovery and collection of any municipal claim by action of assumpsit against the person who was the owner of the property when the improvement was completed, even if there was a failure on the part of the township or its agents to enter the municipal claim as a lien against the property assessed for the improvement, and for the recovery of which the action of assumpsit was brought.

(b) Any action in assumpsit shall be commenced within three years after the completion of the improvement from which the claim arises.

ARTICLE XXXVII
REPEALS

53 P.S. § 68701

§ 3701. Repeals.—(a) Nothing contained in this act revives any act, or part of any act, repealed by the act reenacted, amended or revised by this act.

(b) The following additional acts or parts of acts are hereby repealed as respectively indicated:

Act of May 1, 1913 (P.L. 155, No. 104), entitled "An act regulating the letting of certain contracts for the erection, construction, and alteration of public buildings," insofar as it relates to townships of the second class.

Act of May 10, 1923 (P.L. 198, No. 144), entitled "An act authorizing courts of quarter sessions to commit the care of certain burial grounds to the councils of boroughs, township commissioners and township supervisors of townships; and requiring boroughs and townships to pay the expenses in connection therewith," insofar as it relates to townships of the second class.

Act of June 22, 1931 (P.L. 844, No. 274), entitled, as amended, "An act authorizing the Commonwealth of Pennsylvania, or any department or division thereof, and counties, cities, boroughs, incorporated towns, townships, school districts, vocational school districts, and institution districts to make contracts of life, health, hospitalization, medical services, and accident policies for the benefit of employes thereof, and contracts for pensions for such employes; and providing for the payment of the cost thereof," insofar as it relates to townships of the second class.

Act of May 1, 1935 (P.L. 124, No. 47), entitled "An act authorizing the insurance of deposits of funds, of this Commonwealth and of the political subdivisions thereof, with the Federal Deposit Insurance Corporation or other similar agency; and prohibiting requiring further security for amounts so insured," insofar as it relates to townships of the second class.

Act of July 18, 1935 (P.L. 1173, No. 382), entitled "An act to prohibit discrimination on account of race, creed or color in employment under contracts for public buildings or public works," insofar as it relates to townships of the second class.

Act of March 16, 1937 (P.L. 98, No. 26), entitled "An act authorizing political subdivisions to stipulate in specifications, upon which contracts for the construction, alteration or repairs of any public work or improvement are entered into, the minimum wages to be paid to laborers and mechanics, and providing for the stipulation of penalties in such contracts where such minimum wage stipulations are violated, and for the recovery of such penalties, and their return in certain cases," insofar as it relates to townships of the second class.

(c) All other acts and parts of acts inconsistent with this act are repealed.

(d) This act does not repeal or modify any of the provisions of 66 Pa.C.S. (relating to public utilities); nor any local or special law; nor any law relating to the Board of Commissioners of Navigation for the River Delaware and its navigable tributaries; nor the provisions of any law the enforcement of which is vested in the Department of Health or the Department of Environmental Resources; nor does this act repeal or modify any of the provisions of any statute amendatory of law in force at the time of the passage of this act or otherwise enacted at the session of the General Assembly of 1995, whether the acts were adopted before the passage of this act or after the passage of this act; nor does this act repeal any act, or part thereof, in force at the time of the passage of this act which is amended by any statute enacted at the session of the General Assembly of 1995.

CHAPTER 36

THE BOROUGH CODE

8 Pa.C.S.A. §§ 101–3501

PART I
BOROUGHS

Chapter 1
Preliminary Provisions

---

§ 101. Short title of part.

This part shall be known and may be cited as the Borough Code.

§ 101.1. Definitions.

The following words and phrases when used in this part shall have the meanings given to them in this section unless the context clearly indicates otherwise:

"Abutting property" or **"abutting real estate."** In reference to any street, the term shall mean any property physically adjoining the street, regardless of what the reversion rights in the street may be and regardless of where the lot lines may be in relation to the street.

"Council." A borough council.

"Highway." A State highway of this Commonwealth.

"Latest official census." The later of any of the following:

(1) The most recent Federal decennial census.

(2) A census conducted later in time than the census under paragraph (1) by the United States Census Bureau.

"Municipal corporation." A city, borough, incorporated town, township of the first or second class or any home rule municipality other than a county.

"Municipality." A municipal corporation or a county.

"Pennsylvania Construction Code." The act of November 10, 1999 (P.L.491, No.45), known as the Pennsylvania Construction Code Act.

"Pennsylvania Municipalities Planning Code." The act of July 31, 1968 (P.L.805, No.247), known as the Pennsylvania Municipalities Planning Code.

"Street." Any street, road, lane, court, cul-de-sac, alley, public way and public square.

§ 102. Excluded provisions.

This part shall not include any provisions and shall not be construed to repeal any acts relating to:

(1) The assessment and valuation of property and persons for the purpose of taxation and the collection of taxes, except as provided in this part.

(2) The collection of municipal claims by liens.

(3) The method of incurring or increasing indebtedness.

(4) Conduct of elections.

(5) Public schools.

(6) The powers and duties of borough and ward constables.

(7) Magisterial district judges.

(8) The giving of municipal consent to public utilities.

(9) State highways.

(10) Validations of elections, bonds, ordinances and acts of corporate officers.

(11) 18 Pa.C.S. (relating to crimes and offenses).

(12) 75 Pa.C.S. (relating to vehicles).

§ 103. Construction of part.

(a) Continuation.—The following shall apply:

(1) The provisions of this part that are the same as those of laws existing on January 1, 1966, are intended as a continuation of laws existing on January 1, 1966, and not as new enactments.

(2) The repeal by this part of any act or part of an act shall not revive any act or part repealed or superseded nor affect the corporate existence of any incorporated borough.

(3) The provisions of this part shall not affect any of the following:

(i) Any act done, liability incurred or right accrued or vested.

(ii) Any suit or prosecution pending or to be instituted to enforce any right or penalty or punish any offense under the authority of the repealed laws.

(4) All ordinances, resolutions, regulations and rules made under any act repealed under this part shall continue with the same force and effect as if the act had not been repealed to the extent that the ordinances, resolutions, regulations and rules could have been made under this part.

(5) Any individual holding office under any act repealed by this part shall continue to hold office until the expiration of the term, subject to the conditions attached to the office prior to January 1, 1966.

(b) Powers and duties.—Borough council shall have the corporate powers and duties and borough officials shall have the powers and duties under this part and as provided in other laws to the extent that the powers and duties are not repealed under this part.

§ 104. Constitutional construction.

The provisions of this part are severable. If any provision of this part or its application to any person or circumstance is held invalid, the invalidity shall not affect other provisions or applications of this part which can be given effect without the invalid provision or application.

§ 105. Construction of references.

If reference is made in this part to any act, the reference shall apply to and include any codification in which the provisions of the act referred to are substantially reenacted.

§ 106. Application.

(a) General.—This part shall apply to all boroughs.

(b) Prior acts.—This part shall not annul or repeal any local or special act or part of a local or special act in force on January 1, 1966.

(c) Local law.—The following shall apply:

(1) The provisions of this part similar to the provisions of the former act of May 14, 1915 (P.L.312, No.192), entitled "An act providing a system of government for boroughs, and revising, amending, and consolidating the law relating to boroughs," shall apply to boroughs incorporated under local laws in the same manner as similar provisions of the former act of May 4, 1927 (P.L.519, No.336), entitled "An act concerning boroughs, and revising, amending and consolidating the law relating to boroughs," were extended to boroughs acting under local laws.

Table of Contents | Part I Ch. 1–3 Ethics, Records, Open Meetings | Part II Ch. 4–10 Taxation | Part III Ch. 11–18 Torts, Contracts & Civil Rules | Part IV Ch. 19–24 Zoning & Planning | Part V Ch. 25–30 Construction and Emergency Codes | Part VI Ch. 31–39 Municipal Codes | Index

(2) If a provision of this part conflicts with a special or local law applicable to a borough that has not been surrendered, the provisions shall be construed so that effect may be given to both. If the conflict between the provisions is irreconcilable, the provision in the local or special law shall prevail.

§ 107. Acceptance.

(a) **Petition.**—The following shall apply:

(1) A borough incorporated or acting under any local or special act may surrender the provisions of its special and local acts in their entirety or as they are inconsistent with this part and be governed by this part by presenting a petition to the court of common pleas of the county setting forth the desire of the borough to accept the provisions of this part.

(2) The petition under paragraph (1) shall indicate whether it is the desire of the borough to surrender all of its special and local acts or to retain its special and local acts that are not inconsistent with this part.

(3) If the petition indicates a desire to retain local or special acts, it shall indicate the local or special acts to be retained. The petition shall be made by the council or by at least 10% of the registered electors of the borough as of the date the petition is filed.

(b) **Hearing.**—The following shall apply:

(1) Upon the presentation of a petition under subsection (a), the court shall set and provide notice of a hearing date. An inhabitant of the borough may remonstrate against the granting of the petition at the hearing.

(2) If the court grants the petition, the decree of the court shall be recorded in the office for the recording of deeds, and the borough shall be subject to this part and any local or special acts retained as set forth in the petition. On and after the date of the decree, any local or special act applicable to the borough shall no longer apply to the borough if it is inconsistent with this part or has been surrendered.

(c) **Force and effect.**—If a borough accepts this part under this section, all of the following shall continue with the same force and effect as if no acceptance had been made:

(1) Liabilities incurred.

(2) Rights accrued or vested.

(3) Obligations issued or contracted.

(4) Suits and prosecutions pending or to be instituted to enforce any right or penalty accrued or to punish any offense committed prior to the acceptance.

(5) Ordinances.

§ 107.1. Acceptance by incorporated towns.

(a) **Partial acceptance.**—The following shall apply:

(1) An incorporated town incorporated or acting under a local or special act may, by ordinance, elect to be governed by the provisions of this part and shall surrender any provisions of its special and local acts that are inconsistent with this part adopted by the incorporated town.

(2) An ordinance under paragraph (1) shall indicate the provisions of this part to be adopted and, if applicable, the provisions of the incorporated town's special and local acts to be surrendered.

(3) On and after the effective date of the ordinance and until the ordinance may be repealed or amended, the provisions of this part indicated in the ordinance shall be the law applicable to the incorporated town, and the provisions of any local or special acts, to the extent surrendered as indicated in the ordinance, shall not apply to the incorporated town.

(b) Full acceptance.—An incorporated town incorporated or acting under any local or special act may elect to accept this part in its entirety and surrender all local and special acts by petition as set forth in section 107 (relating to acceptance). If an incorporated town accepts this part in its entirety and surrenders all local and special acts, the incorporated town shall become a borough, and the decree of the court permitting the acceptance shall indicate the name of the new borough.

(c) Force and effect.—The following shall apply:

(1) If an incorporated town accepts this part under this section, all of the following shall continue with the same force and effect as if no acceptance had been made:

(i) Liabilities incurred.

(ii) Rights accrued or vested.

(iii) Obligations issued or contracted.

(iv) Suits and prosecutions pending or to be instituted to enforce any right or penalty accrued or punish any offense committed prior to acceptance.

(v) Ordinances.

(2) An incorporated town shall not have the power to alter or amend any provision of this part that has been adopted in accordance with this section or section 107.

§ 108. (Reserved).

§ 109. Publication of notices.

(a) Newspaper of general circulation.—If in this part notice is required to be given in one newspaper of general circulation, the notice shall be published in one of the following:

(1) A newspaper of general circulation as defined in 45 Pa.C.S. § 101 (relating to definitions) which is published and circulated in each borough affected.

(2) A newspaper of general circulation, circulated in each borough affected, which has a bona fide paid circulation equal to or greater than any newspaper published in each borough affected by the notice.

(b) Legal newspaper.—Unless dispensed with by special order of court, the notice required to be published in a newspaper of general circulation shall also be published in the legal newspaper for the county of the borough affected, if the notice refers to any of the following:

(1) Any proceeding in any court.

(2) The holding of elections for the increase of indebtedness or the sale of bonds.

§ 110. Terms of existing officers.

This part shall not be construed as affecting or terminating the term of any officer of a borough holding office on January 1, 1966.

CHAPTER 2
CREATION AND ALTERATION

Subchapter

SUBCHAPTER A
INCORPORATION

Sec.

§ 200. Definitions.

The following words and phrases when used in this subchapter shall have the meanings given to them in this section unless the context clearly indicates otherwise:

"Committee." A borough advisory committee.

"Freeholder." A person enjoying a continuous right of ownership and possession of real property for an indeterminate period by fee simple or life estate.

"Township." A township of the first or second class or any home rule township.

§ 201. Contiguous areas.

A court of common pleas may incorporate as a borough any contiguous area from one or more townships within the court's jurisdiction having a population of at least 500 residents. After having been incorporated as a borough, the area shall be a body corporate and politic and shall have the name decreed by the court.

§ 202. Applications.

(a) Petition.—The following shall apply:

(1) The application for incorporation shall be by a petition signed by a majority of the freeholders residing within the limits of the proposed borough and by the freeholders of a majority of the territory within the limits of the proposed borough, if all parts of the proposed borough are in the same township.

(2) If portions of the proposed borough are in different townships, the petition shall be signed by a majority of the freeholders residing in each of the separate portions and by the freeholders of a majority of the territory in each of the separate portions. The following shall apply:

(i) The signatures must be secured within three months immediately preceding the presentation of the signatures to the court.

(ii) The petition shall be subscribed by and sworn to by at least one of the signers.

(iii) The number of signers required to sign the petition shall be ascertained as of the date the petition was presented to court.

(b) (Reserved).

(c) (Reserved).

(d) (Reserved).

(e) **Filing and notice.**—Upon presentation to the court, a petition shall be filed with the clerk of court, and notice of the petition shall be published under section 109 (relating to publication of notices) once a week for four consecutive weeks immediately following the filing of the petition, during which time exceptions may be filed to the petition by any person interested. The notice shall state when and where the petition was filed and the time during which exceptions may be filed to the petition.

(f) **Contents of petition.**—The petition under subsection (e) shall indicate the name of the proposed borough with a particular description of the boundaries of the borough and be accompanied with a plot of the proposed borough. The following shall apply:

(1) If the boundaries of the proposed borough are not the same as an existing township the description shall contain the courses and distances of the boundaries.

(2) If the boundaries of the proposed borough are the same as an existing township, the description:

(i) may contain the courses and distances of the boundaries; and

(ii) shall refer to the name and location of the existing township.

§ 202.1. Borough advisory committee.

(a) **Establishment.**—The court shall establish a borough advisory committee when a petition is received by the court for the creation of a borough. The following shall apply to committee members:

(1) Members shall be appointed by and shall serve at the pleasure of the court.

(2) The committee shall consist of the following:

(i) Two residents of the proposed borough.

(ii) Two residents from each of the existing townships recommended by the respective governing body of the township who are not residing within the proposed borough.

(iii) One resident of the county not residing in any area under subparagraphs (i) and (ii) who shall serve as the chair of the committee.

(3) Members shall serve without salary. The court may entitle each member to reimbursement for the member's actual and necessary expenses incurred in the performance of the member's official duties.

(4) Members may consult with the director of the county planning commission who may advise the committee.

(b) **Duties.**—The committee shall, within 60 days of its creation, advise the court in relation to the establishment of the proposed borough. The committee shall render expert advice and findings of fact relating to the desirability of an incorporation, including advice as to:

(1) The proposed borough's ability to obtain or provide adequate and reasonable community support services such as police protection, fire protection and other appropriate community facility services.

Table of Contents
Part I Ch. 1–3 Ethics, Records, Open Meetings
Part II Ch. 4–10 Taxation
Part III Ch. 11–18 Torts, Contracts & Civil Rules
Part IV Ch. 19–24 Zoning & Planning
Part V Ch. 25–30 Construction and Emergency Codes
Part VI Ch. 31–39 Municipal Codes
Index

(2) Whether the proposed borough constitutes a harmonious whole with common interests and needs that can best be served by a borough government. In examining this factor, the committee shall consider whether the proposed borough represents a distinct community with features different from those of the existing township.

(3) The existing and potential commercial, residential and industrial development of the proposed borough.

(4) Whether the proposed borough would provide for land use regulations to meet the legitimate needs for all categories of residents or whether the plan is exclusionary or would result in economic segregation.

(5) The financial or tax effect on the proposed borough and existing township.

§ 202.2. Advisability of incorporation, certification of question for referendum and decree.

(a) Process.—After receiving the findings-of-fact and the advice of the committee, the court shall conduct a hearing. If, after the hearing, the court deems further investigation necessary to determine the advisability of incorporation, it may issue an order to obtain the additional information. When the court has obtained all reasonably necessary information and has determined that the conditions required under this section have been met, the court shall determine the desirability of the proposed incorporation based upon the following:

(1) The evidence submitted at the hearing and by the committee.

(2) Any additional information obtained after the hearing.

(3) Any other applicable factors the court deems relevant.

(b) Determination.—If the court determines that the desirability of the proposed incorporation is not supported by a preponderance of the evidence, the court shall enter a final decree denying the request of the petitioners and no other proceedings may be held. If the court determines that the desirability of the proposed incorporation is supported by a preponderance of the evidence, the court shall certify the question of the proposed incorporation to the board of election of the county for a referendum vote of the residents of the proposed borough. Upon receipt of the certified election results, the court shall enter a final decree granting or denying the request of the petitioners.

(c) Expenses.—The petition and the final decree granting or denying the petition shall be recorded in the recorder of deeds office of the county at the expense of the petitioners. The petitioners shall pay all other expenses and costs in connection with the proceedings.

§ 203. (Reserved).

§ 204. (Reserved).

§ 205. Borough government and requisites of charter.

(a) Time.—When the petition and the final decree granting the petition have been recorded, the area shall become an incorporated borough and shall be entitled to the rights, privileges and immunities conferred under this part, except as provided under section 211 (relating to temporary preservation, organization and election of officers).

(b) Charter.—The final decree of the court granting the petition shall constitute the charter of the borough. All charters granted under this part shall include:

(1) The corporate name of the borough.

(2) The boundaries of the borough.

§ 206. Farmlands.

If, in any petition for the incorporation of a borough, the boundaries fixed by the petitioners embrace lands exclusively used for the purposes of farming, the court may, if it deems the land does not properly belong to the proposed borough and at the request of any party aggrieved, change the boundaries to exclude the land used for farming.

§ 207. Corporate name.

The corporate name of a borough incorporated under this part shall be "The Borough of ."

§ 208. (Reserved).

§ 209. (Reserved).

§ 210. Certificates.

(a) **Decree.**—When a borough is created, the clerk of courts in each county affected shall, within 30 days of the creation, certify to the Department of State, the Department of Transportation, the Department of Community and Economic Development and the county planning commission a copy of the decree of court incorporating the borough. The clerk may impose a fee of $3.50 as part of the costs of the proceeding for the services under this subsection.

(b) **Penalty.**—Any clerk of the court who fails, neglects or refuses to furnish the certifications as provided under this part commits a summary offense and shall pay a fine of not more than $50.

§ 211. Temporary preservation, organization and election of officers.

(a) **Government.**—The following shall apply:

(1) A newly incorporated area under section 201 (relating to contiguous areas) shall continue to be governed as before the incorporation until the first Monday of January following the municipal election after the issuance of the final decree establishing the new borough.

(2) After a newly incorporated area is no longer governed as before the incorporation under paragraph (1), the officers of the borough who are elected, under section 805 (relating to election after creation), at the municipal or special election shall begin their terms of office, and the borough government shall be considered to be duly organized under this part.

(b) **Election.**—Borough officers shall be elected at:

(1) the next municipal election occurring at least 90 days following the issuance of the decree establishing the borough; or

(2) at the request of the petitioners, a special election called by the court of common pleas.

(c) **Special election.**—If a special election is held under subsection (b)(2), the court shall do all of the following:

(1) Fix the time, place and manner of holding the special election.

(2) Designate an individual to give notice of the special election and the manner of the special election.

(3) Appoint from among the electors of the newly established borough a judge and inspectors to hold the election.

(d) **Terms.**—The following shall apply:

(1) Municipal officers elected at a special election held under subsection (c) shall serve until the first Monday in January following the next succeeding municipal election.

(2) The successors of municipal officers under paragraph (1) shall be elected as provided under section 805 and shall take office upon completion of municipal officer's service under paragraph (1).

§ 212. Boundaries.

The boundaries of the borough shall, as soon as practicable after its incorporation, be appropriately marked. Prior to marking the boundaries, notice shall be provided, as directed by the court, to the governing bodies of adjoining municipal corporations.

§ 213. Adjustment of indebtedness.

(a) Property.—The following shall apply:

(1) After the election of a council under section 211 (relating to temporary preservation, organization and election of officers) when a borough is newly incorporated, the council and the governing body of the township from which the borough was created shall make an equitable adjustment and apportionment of all the public real and personal property owned by the township at the time of the incorporation of the borough.

(2) Except as provided under paragraph (3), the property under paragraph (1) shall include funds and indebtedness.

(3) If adjusting property and indebtedness under paragraph (1), streets, sewers and utilities may not be considered except to the extent that current and unpaid indebtedness was incurred for the construction and improvement of the property.

(b) Proportion.—In making the adjustment and apportionment under subsection (a), the following shall apply:

(1) The borough shall be entitled to a division of the property and indebtedness in the same proportion that the assessed valuation of the taxable real estate included within the territorial limits of the newly incorporated borough bears to the assessed valuation of the taxable real estate in the entire township immediately prior to the incorporation of the borough. The township shall be entitled to the remainder of the property and indebtedness.

(2) If indebtedness was incurred by the township for an improvement located wholly within the territorial limits of the newly incorporated borough, the indebtedness shall be assumed by the borough.

(3) If only part of the improvement is located within the newly incorporated borough, the part of the indebtedness representing the part of the improvement located within the borough shall be assumed by the borough, and the adjustment and apportionment of any remaining debt shall be retained by the township.

(c) Form.—The adjustment and apportionment made under this section must meet all of the following:

(1) Be in writing and duly executed and acknowledged by the secretary or clerk of the township and the secretary of the borough.

(2) Be filed in the office of the clerk of the court of common pleas of the county.

(3) Be filed as a copy with the Department of Community and Economic Development.

§ 214. Judicial adjustment.

(a) Petition.—If the governing bodies of the township and the borough cannot make an amicable adjustment and apportionment of the property and indebtedness within six months after the government of the newly incorporated borough is established, the supervisors or commissioners of the township or the council of the borough may present a petition to the court of common pleas requesting a judicial adjustment.

(b) Appointment.—After receiving a petition under subsection (a), the court shall appoint three disinterested commissioners who meet all of the following requirements:

(1) Are residents and taxpayers of the county.

(2) Are not residents of or own real estate in the township or borough.

(c) Report.—The individuals appointed under subsection (b) shall hold a hearing and make a report to the court containing an adjustment and apportionment of all the property and the indebtedness between the township and the borough. Notice shall be made to the township and borough as provided by the court. The report shall state the amount due and payable from the borough or the township to the other entity and the amount of indebtedness that shall be assumed by the borough or the township.

§ 215. Judicial adjustment award proceedings.

(a) Notice.—The commissioners shall give the township and the borough at least five days' notice of the filing of the report under section 214(c) (relating to judicial adjustment).

(b) Exceptions.—Unless exceptions are filed to the report within 30 days after the date of the filing, the report shall be confirmed by the court.

(c) Effect.—The following shall apply:

(1) Any sum awarded by the report to the township or borough shall be a legal and valid claim in its favor against the borough or township charged with the sum.

(2) Any real or personal property given to the township or borough shall become its respective property.

(3) Any claim or indebtedness charged against the borough or township may be collected from the borough or the township.

§ 216. Exceptions.

If exceptions are filed to the report under section 214(c) (relating to judicial adjustment), the court shall dispose of the exceptions and shall enter its decree confirming or modifying the award.

§ 217. Compensation, expenses and costs.

The commissioners under section 214(b) (relating to judicial adjustment) shall receive compensation and expenses for their services as provided by the court. The costs of the proceedings, including the compensation and expenses of the commissioners, shall be apportioned by the court between the borough and township.

§ 218. Territory located in multiple counties.

If territory included within the limits of a newly incorporated borough is located in at least two counties, the court of common pleas of the county where the larger part of the territory of the borough is located shall have exclusive jurisdiction over the proceedings to adjust and apportion the indebtedness between the borough and township.

§ 219. Bond issues and taxation.

In any proceeding to adjust and apportion indebtedness, the township or the borough shall have power to issue and deliver to the borough or township interest-bearing bonds in liquidation of the indebtedness ascertained, to be its proportionate share payable, if the bonds are acceptable to the borough or township or townships entitled to receive the bonds. The court may make necessary orders for the collection and payment by the township or townships or borough of the amount needed to pay its share of any indebtedness apportioned to it by special taxes to be collected in one year, or by annual installments.

SUBCHAPTER B
CONSOLIDATION
(Reserved)

SUBCHAPTER C
CREATION FROM CITIES OF THE THIRD CLASS

§ 231. Procedure.

(a) Petition.—The court of common pleas shall, upon petition of at least 10% of the registered electors of any city of the third class, order an election to be held at the next general, municipal or primary election occurring at least 90 days after the presentation of the petition.

(b) Vote.—The electors shall, at the election under subsection (a), vote for or against the change of the charter of the city to a borough charter and the adoption of the borough form of government.

(c) Contents.—A petition under subsection (a) shall indicate all of the following:

(1) The inhabitants of the city desire to do all of the following:

(i) Change the charter of the city to a borough charter.

(ii) Be governed by the laws of the Commonwealth relating to boroughs.

(2) The city has had a city form of government for a period of at least five years.

(3) The name of the proposed borough.

(d) Required electors.—The number of registered electors required to sign the petition shall be determined as of the date the petition is filed.

§ 232. Filing, notice and return.

(a) Filing.—Upon presentation of a petition under section 231 (relating to procedure), the court shall determine whether the petition meets the requirements under section 231. If the requirements are met, the court shall:

(1) Enter an appropriate order requiring an election.

(2) Direct that the petition shall be filed with the clerk of the court and that a copy of the petition and order of court shall be filed with the county board of elections.

(b) Notice.—Notice of the time and purpose of the election under subsection (a) shall be given in at least one newspaper of general circulation of the proper county once a week for four consecutive weeks. The publication of the notice shall be made on behalf of the petitioners and shall be in the form approved by the court.

(c) **Return.**—The following shall apply:

(1) The county board of elections shall frame the proper question to be submitted to the electors at the election ordered by the court.

(2) The county board of elections shall make a return of the vote cast on the question submitted to the clerk of the court of common pleas. The return shall be filed with the petition.

(3) If a majority of those voting on the question submitted were in favor of the change of the city charter to a borough charter, the court shall order that the record of the proceedings be recorded in the office for the recording of deeds of the county, and the record shall constitute the charter of the borough under the name provided in the petition. The recorder of deeds in each county affected shall certify to the Department of State, the Department of Transportation, the Department of Community and Economic Development and the county planning commission a copy of the record constituting the charter of the borough.

(4) If a majority of those voting on the question submitted were against the change of the city charter to a borough charter, the same question may not be submitted for a period of five years following the election.

§ 233. Borough government.

(a) **City.**—When the record of the proceedings under section 232 (relating to filing, notice and return) is recorded, the city form of government shall continue in operation until the first Monday of January after the first municipal election, occurring at least 90 days after the recording of the record.

(b) **Borough.**—After the city form of government is no longer in operation under subsection (a), the borough government shall be organized by the officers elected at the municipal election in accordance with section 805 (relating to election after creation).

§ 234. Effect.

(a) **Property.**—When the borough government is formed, the property and assets of the city shall become the property of the borough, and the change of government shall not do any of the following:

(1) Affect any of the following:

(i) Liabilities incurred.

(ii) Rights accrued or vested.

(iii) Obligations issued or contracted.

(iv) Suits or prosecutions pending or instituted to enforce any right or penalty accrued.

(2) Punish any offense committed prior to the formation.

(b) **Ordinances.**—Ordinances of the former city shall continue in force in the new borough until altered or repealed.

(c) **Wards and districts.**—Wards and election districts of the city shall become the wards and election districts of the borough until altered or changed. In the election of members of council from the several wards, two members of council shall be elected from each ward, unless changed as provided by law.

(d) Office.—All constables and election officers in office in the city at the time the borough government is organized shall remain in office until the expiration of their respective terms of office.

§ 235. Costs and expenses.

(a) Petitioners.—Except as provided under subsection (b), the costs and expenses of proceedings to change the charter of a city to a borough, including all costs of advertising, shall be paid by the petitioners.

(b) Exception.—If the vote of electors to change the charter of a city to a borough is in favor of the change, the cost and expenses under subsection (a) shall be paid by the city.

SUBCHAPTER D
CONSOLIDATION OR MERGER AND CHANGE OF CORPORATE NAME

---

§ 241. Consolidation or merger.

A borough may be merged or consolidated into a new or existing municipal corporation in accordance with 53 Pa.C.S. Ch. 7 Subch. C (relating to consolidation and merger).

§ 242. Change of corporate name.

(a) General rule.—The following shall apply:

(1) If the corporate name of a borough differs from the name of the borough in general usage or from the post office designation due to minor discrepancies in spelling, capitalization or the manner of compounding the elements of the name, the court of common pleas, upon petition, may change the name of the borough to conform to the name in general usage or to the post office designation.

(2) The petition under paragraph (1) may be presented by any of the following:

(i) Council, pursuant to a resolution.

(ii) At least 5% of the registered electors of the borough.

(b) Petition.—The following shall apply:

(1) Upon the presentation of a petition under subsection (a), the court shall set and provide notice of a hearing date. An inhabitant of the borough may remonstrate against the granting of the petition at the hearing.

(2) If the court grants the petition, the decree of the court shall be recorded, and the corporate name of the borough shall be as provided in the petition from the date of recording.

(c) Dissemination of decree.—The recorder of deeds in each county affected shall certify to the Department of State, the Department of Transportation, the Department of Community and Economic Development and the county planning commission a copy of the decree changing the corporate name of the borough.

(d) Force and effect.—A change of corporate name shall not affect any of the following:

(1) Liabilities incurred.

(2) Rights accrued or vested.

(3) Obligations issued or contracted.

(4) Any suits or prosecutions pending or instituted to enforce any right or penalty accrued or to punish any offense committed prior to the change.

CHAPTER 3
ANNULMENT OF CHARTERS AND CHANGE OF CORPORATE NAMES
(Reserved)

CHAPTER 4
CHANGE OF LIMITS
(Reserved)

CHAPTER 5
BOUNDARIES [REPEALED]

§ 501. Repealed by 2022, July 7, P.L. 455, NO. 41—§ 4(2)(VIII), Effective in 60 Days [Sept. 6, 2022]

§ 502. Repealed by 2022, July 7, P.L. 455, NO. 41—§ 4(2)(VIII), Effective in 60 Days [Sept. 6, 2022]

§ 503. Repealed by 2022, July 7, P.L. 455, NO. 41—§ 4(2)(VIII), Effective in 60 Days [Sept. 6, 2022]

§ 504. Repealed by 2022, July 7, P.L. 455, NO. 41—§ 4(2)(VIII), Effective in 60 Days [Sept. 6, 2022]

§ 505. Repealed by 2022, July 7, P.L. 455, NO. 41—§ 4(2)(VIII), Effective in 60 Days [Sept. 6, 2022]

§ 506. Repealed by 2022, July 7, P.L. 455, NO. 41—§ 4(2)(VIII), Effective in 60 Days [Sept. 6, 2022]

CHAPTER 6
WARDS

---

§ 601. Creation and alteration.

(a) Council.—In addition to reapportionment initiated in accordance with 53 Pa.C.S. Pt. II Ch. 9 (relating to municipal reapportionment) and section 11 of Article IX of the Constitution of Pennsylvania, a council may, by ordinance, do any of the following:

(1) Divide boroughs into wards.

(2) Erect new wards out of two or more adjoining wards or parts of wards.

(3) Consolidate two or more wards into one ward.

(4) Divide any ward already erected into two or more wards.

(5) Alter the lines of two or more adjoining wards or cause the lines or boundaries of wards to be ascertained or established.

(6) Abolish all wards.

(b) Restrictions.—The following shall apply:

(1) No borough may be divided or redivided into more than 13 wards.

(2) The following shall apply:

(i) No ward may be created containing less than 300 registered electors.

(ii) Any ward which contains less than 350 registered electors after December 31, 1965, may be abolished, and the territory of the ward shall be distributed among the remaining wards as determined by council.

(iii) All wards in existence prior to January 1, 1966, shall remain as established, until altered or divided as provided under this chapter.

(c) Members of council.—If a ward is abolished under this section and the number of wards in a borough is reduced to less than five, a member of council in an abolished ward shall continue in office for his elected term and shall become a member of council at large from the borough.

(d) Composition.—All wards in the borough shall be numbered and composed of compact and contiguous territory as nearly equal in population as practicable as officially and finally reported in the latest official census.

§ 602. Petition of electors.

(a) Council.—At least 5% of registered electors of the borough or, for a proposal affecting only a portion of the borough, at least 5% of the registered electors of the ward which would be affected by the proposal may petition council to initiate proceedings under section 601 (relating to creation and alteration) and may present to council a plot showing the boundaries of the proposed wards of the borough. Council shall, by motion approved by a majority of council and within 90 days of presentment of the petition, determine whether to initiate proceedings under section 601.

(b) Court of common pleas.—If council has not approved a motion within 90 days after the presentment of a petition under subsection (a), ten registered electors may petition the court of common pleas and contest the existing apportionment as violating section 601(b) or (d). The proceedings before the court shall be conducted in accordance with 53 Pa.C.S. §§ 906 (relating to contest of reapportionment by governing body) and 907 (relating to costs and expenses of contest).

§ 603. Notice of ordinance.

(a) Requirement.—Notice of an ordinance enacted in accordance with section 601 (relating to creation and alteration) shall be given by publication once in a newspaper of general circulation.

(b) County board of elections.—A copy of the ordinance, along with a plot showing the boundaries of the wards established, shall be forwarded to the county board of elections.

§ 604. (Reserved).

§ 605. (Reserved).

§ 606. Terms of officers.

(a) Appointment.—Except as provided under subsection (b), if council divides a borough into wards, it shall request the court of common pleas to appoint for each ward a judge and two inspectors of election to hold elections until the officers of the ward may be elected.

(b) Expiration.—Except as provided under subsection (a), officers in office at the time any changes are made under this chapter shall remain in office until the expiration of the terms for which they have been elected. If a vacancy occurs, the vacancy shall be filled by the council, until the first Monday of January next succeeding the election at which the officers are to be elected, as provided under Chapter 8 (relating to elections of officers).

§ 606.1. Construction of chapter.

Nothing under this chapter shall be construed as affecting any of the following:

(1) The powers and duties of the court of common pleas or the county board of elections.

(2) Restrictions on alteration of election districts as provided under Article V of the act of June 3, 1937 (P.L.1333, No.320), known as the Pennsylvania Election Code.

§ 607. (Reserved).

CHAPTER 7
ASSOCIATIONS AND ORGANIZATIONS

Sec.

§ 701. State Association of Boroughs.

(a) Organization.—The boroughs of the Commonwealth may organize a State Association of Boroughs for the purpose of advancing the interests of the boroughs. A borough may join the State Association of Boroughs by motion of council and payment of the annual dues. Each borough, after becoming a member, shall pay reasonable dues as determined by the State Association of Boroughs.

(b) Revenue.—Revenue received by the State Association of Boroughs shall be used to pay for services, publications and other expenses authorized or ratified by the State Association of Boroughs, or incurred on behalf of the State Association of Boroughs by its officers and committees.

§ 701.1. Authorization and expenses.

(a) Delegates.—Council may, by motion, designate one or more delegates from the elected or appointed officers of the borough to attend the annual meeting of the State Association of Boroughs, which shall be held in this Commonwealth in accordance with the procedure adopted by the State Association of Boroughs.

(b) Nondelegates.—Council may, by motion, designate one or more elected or appointed officers or employees of the borough to attend the annual meeting of the State Association of Boroughs as nondelegates or to attend a conference, educational training or committee meeting of the State Association of Boroughs.

(c) Expenses.—The following shall apply:

(1) In addition to any compensation allowed under section 701.2 (relating to compensation), council may, for each delegate, elected or appointed officer or employee under subsection (a) or (b), pay the following expenses upon receipt of an itemized account of expenses:

(i) The registration fee.

(ii) Mileage for use of a personal vehicle or reimbursement of actual transportation expenses going to and returning from the annual meeting, conference, educational training or committee meeting of the State Association of Boroughs.

(iii) Any actual expenses that the council may have agreed to pay.

(2) Notwithstanding this subsection, at least one member of council shall be allowed the following expenses:

(i) The registration fee.

(ii) Lodging, meals, mileage for use of a personal vehicle or reimbursement of actual transportation expenses going to and returning from the meeting.

(iii) Any actual expenses that the council may have agreed to pay.

§ 701.2. Compensation.

(a) Employees.—Council may authorize borough employees, including the mayor and members of council if they are employees of the borough, to be compensated at their regular employee rates during their attendance at the annual meeting or a conference, educational training or committee meeting of the State Association of Boroughs.

(b) Nonemployees.—Council may authorize the mayor and any council member who is not employed by the borough to receive total or partial reimbursement for lost wages or salary, including those from self-employment, while attending the annual meeting or a conference, educational training or committee meeting of the State Association of Boroughs if sufficient documentation is presented to council to justify the reimbursement.

(c) Amount.—The maximum time for which a borough employee or mayor or council member not employed by the borough shall be reimbursed for lost wages or salary while attending the annual meeting or a conference, educational training or committee meeting of the State Association of Boroughs shall be not more than four days, including time spent traveling to and from the event.

(d) Executive members.—The council may authorize a mayor or any council member employed by the borough to be compensated at the mayor's or council member's regular employee rate and a mayor or council member who is not employed by the borough to receive total or partial reimbursement for lost wages or salary, including those from self-employment, if the mayor or council member attends a meeting for which the mayor or council member is an officer, a member of the board of directors, a member of the executive committee, a member of a standing committee or a trustee of the State Association of Boroughs, subject to the following which shall include time spent traveling to and from the event:

(1) The compensation of a mayor or council member for attending a meeting of a standing committee of the State Association of Boroughs shall be limited to two days per year of regular employee rate compensation or lost wages or salary.

(2) The compensation of a mayor or council member for attending a meeting for which the mayor or council member is a trustee for the State Association of Boroughs shall be limited to four days per year of regular employee rate compensation or lost wages or salary.

(3) The compensation of a mayor or council member for attending a meeting for which the mayor or council member is an officer, member of the board of directors or a member of the executive committee of the State Association of Boroughs shall be limited to 15 days per year of regular employee rate compensation or lost wages or salary.

(4) A mayor or council member identified under paragraph (1), (2) or (3) may not be compensated by the borough under this subsection if the mayor or council member receives compensation from the State Association of Boroughs or a board or committee of the State Association of Boroughs for attending the meeting.

§ 702. County and regional associations of boroughs.

(a) Organization.—The boroughs of any county or of two or more adjoining or nearby counties may organize a county or regional association of boroughs, composed of elected and appointed borough officers in the county, organized for the purpose of furthering the interests of the boroughs in the county or regional association of boroughs and their inhabitants.

(b) Appropriation.—A borough may annually appropriate no more than $100 for the support of the county or regional association of boroughs.

(c) Expenses.—The following shall apply:

(1) The borough may pay the following expenses of each delegate for attendance at a meeting of the county or regional association of which the borough is a member:

(i) The registration fee.

(ii) Mileage for use of a personal vehicle or reimbursement of actual transportation expense going to and returning from the meeting.

(iii) Any actual expenses that the council may have agreed to pay.

(2) Every delegate attending the meeting shall submit to the council an itemized account of expenses incurred.

(d) Compensation.—The council may authorize borough employees to be compensated at their regular employee rate during their attendance at a meeting of the county or regional association. The council solely may authorize the mayor

Table of Contents
Part I Ch. 1–3 Ethics, Records, Open Meetings
Part II Ch. 4–10 Taxation
Part III Ch. 11–18 Torts, Contracts & Civil Rules
Part IV Ch. 19–24 Zoning & Planning
Part V Ch. 25–30 Construction and Emergency Codes
Part VI Ch. 31–39 Municipal Codes
Index

and any council member who is not employed by the borough to receive total or partial reimbursement for lost wages or salary while attending the meeting if sufficient documentation is presented to the council to justify the reimbursement.

(e) Other members.—A county or regional association of boroughs may admit representatives of political subdivisions other than boroughs within the county as members. Members admitted under this subsection shall may not participate in any matter of concern solely to boroughs.

§ 703. Other associations and organizations.

(a) Authorization.—A borough, by motion of council, may do any of the following:

(1) Join associations and organizations other than associations and organizations referred to under this chapter concerned with municipal or governmental affairs.

(2) Pay dues to and appropriate funds for the support of and participation in associations and organizations under paragraph (1).

(3) Send delegates to meetings or conferences of associations and organizations under paragraph (1).

(a.1) Compensation and expenses.—The following shall apply:

(1) In addition to any compensation allowed by law for a delegate, the borough may pay the following expenses for each delegate under subsection (a)(3):

(i) The registration fee.

(ii) Mileage for use of a personal vehicle or reimbursement of actual transportation expense going to and returning from the meeting or conference.

(iii) Any expenses that the council may have agreed to pay.

(2) Every delegate under subsection (a)(3) shall submit to the council an itemized account of expenses incurred.

(3) The council may authorize borough employees to be compensated at their regular employee rate during their attendance at an annual meeting or conference of an association or organization under paragraph (1). The time spent in attending the meeting or conference may not be more than four days, including the time traveling to and from the meeting or conference.

(b) Professional and educational meetings.—A borough may, by motion of council, do any of the following:

(1) Authorize any of its officers and employees to attend any of the following:

(i) Meetings of professional organizations and associations.

(ii) Educational training sessions for individuals holding the same or similar office or employment.

(2) Pay all or a portion of the necessary expenses incident to an individual's attendance at meetings or sessions under paragraph (1).

(c) Itemized account.—Every individual attending a conference, meeting or educational training session under this section shall submit to the council an itemized account of the individual's expenses, including traveling expenses or mileage, that council may have agreed to pay.

§ 704. Associations and organizations for mayors.

(a) Authorization.—A mayor may join any mayors' association in Pennsylvania. Council shall pay reasonable dues not to exceed $100 if requested by the mayor. The mayor may attend the annual meeting of the mayors' association,

Chap. 39 Res. During Mil. Service
Chap. 38 Intergov. Coop.
Chap. 37 3rd Class City Code
Chap. 36 Bor. Code
Chap. 35 2nd Class Twp. Code
Chap. 34 1st Class Twp. Code
Chap. 33 Home Rule Chart. Opt. Plans Law
Chap. 32 Water Serv. Act
Chap. 31 Munic. Auth. Act

which shall be held in this Commonwealth in accordance with the procedure adopted by the mayors' association.

(b) Expenses.—A mayor shall, if requested, receive the following expenses for attending the annual meeting under subsection (a):

(1) The registration fee.

(2) Lodging, meals and mileage for use of a personal vehicle or reimbursement of actual transportation expenses going to and returning from the meeting.

(3) Any actual expenses that the council may have agreed to pay.

(c) Itemized account.—Every mayor attending the annual meeting under subsection (a) shall submit to the council an itemized account of expenses incurred at the annual meeting of the mayors' association. The time spent in attending the annual meeting may not be more than four days, including time traveling to and from the meeting.

§ 705. National or State lodge of police officers.

(a) Authorization.—A council may grant a borough employee who is a duly elected representative of a State lodge of police officers or a local lodge which is a part of any national or State lodge of police officers a leave of absence with pay to attend an annual national or State convention or conference of the lodge, for a period not to exceed four days, including necessary time for travel to and from the convention or conference.

(b) Certification.—An employee receiving time off with pay under subsection (a) shall, upon return, submit to the employee's immediate superior a certificate testifying to the employee's attendance at the convention or conference, signed by at least two responsible officers of the convention or conference.

(c) Limitation.—No more than two elected representatives who are employees of the same borough may attend a convention or conference on behalf of a lodge under this section.

CHAPTER 8
ELECTIONS OF OFFICERS

Subchapter

Table of Contents
Part I Ch. 1–3 Ethics, Records, Open Meetings
Part II Ch. 4–10 Taxation
Part III Ch. 11–18 Torts, Contracts & Civil Rules
Part IV Ch. 19–24 Zoning & Planning
Part V Ch. 25–30 Construction and Emergency Codes
Part VI Ch. 31–39 Municipal Codes
Index

SUBCHAPTER A
GENERAL PROVISIONS

§ 801. Eligibility.

(a) Residency.—The following shall apply:

(1) Only registered electors of the borough shall be eligible to elective borough offices.

(2) Except as provided under subsection (c) and 53 Pa.C.S. § 1142 (relating to residency during military service), before being sworn into office, each elected borough officer shall present a signed affidavit to the borough secretary that states that the officer resides in the borough, or within the ward in the case of a ward office, from which elected and has resided in the borough continuously for at least one year immediately prior to the officer's election.

(b) Incompatible offices.—A school director or a trustee of a charter school may not be elected to an elective borough office. No individual may hold more than one elective borough office at the same time.

(c) Exception.—A borough with a population of less than 150 may permit residents that have not resided in the borough continuously for at least one year immediately before the election to be eligible to hold office.

§ 802. Time and place.

Elections for borough officers shall be at the time and place designated by law for the holding of municipal elections.

§ 803. Certificates.

Certificates of election of all borough officers shall be filed with the borough secretary and preserved among the records of the borough for a period of six years.

§ 804. Term and bonds.

(a) Terms.—The following shall apply:

(1) Except as provided under paragraph (2), an individual elected to a borough office shall serve for the term for which the individual was elected.

(2) If a vacancy in office occurs, it shall be filled in the manner provided under this part.

(b) Bonds.—The following shall apply:

(1) Except as provided under paragraph (2), if an elected official of a borough is required to give a bond for the faithful performance of the elected official's duties, the borough may pay the premium for the bond.

(2) A borough shall pay a proportionate share of the cost of a tax collector's bond within the same ratio as the amount of borough taxes bears to the total amount of all taxes indicated by the tax duplicate to be collected by the tax collector during the year preceding the date the premium is due.

§ 805. Election after creation.

(a) **Officers.**—The officers of a borough provided for under section 806 (relating to officers elected) shall be elected at the appropriate municipal election and take office on the first Monday of January succeeding the election if any of the following occur:

(1) A borough is incorporated under Subchapter A of Chapter 2 (relating to incorporation).

(2) At least two boroughs are consolidated under 53 Pa.C.S. Ch. 7 Subch. C (relating to consolidation and merger).

(3) A borough is created from a city of the third class under Subchapter C of Chapter 2 (relating to creation from cities of the third class).

(b) **Terms.**—The following shall apply:

(1) Except as provided under paragraph (2) and at the election under subsection (a), if a borough is not divided into wards, the following members shall be elected to coincide with the number of members of council elected in boroughs existing on January 1, 1966, under section 811 (relating to election):

(i) Three or four members of council shall be elected for terms of two years each.

(ii) Three or four members of council shall be elected for terms of four years each.

(2) One member of council shall be elected from each ward for a term of two years and one member of council shall be elected from each ward for a term of four years in any of the following:

(i) A consolidation of two or more boroughs into one borough.

(ii) The creation of a borough from a city of the third class.

(iii) If two members of council are to be elected from each ward.

(3) In any borough under subsection (a), three auditors shall be elected as follows:

(i) One for a term of two years.

(ii) One for a term of four years.

(iii) One for a term of six years.

(4) Any officers of a borough not listed under this section shall be elected for terms of two or four years to coincide with the terms of officers elected under this part in the existing boroughs.

§ 806. Officers elected.

(a) **Officers.**—The electors of the borough may elect:

(1) A mayor, who shall be elected at municipal elections every four years.

(2) A tax collector, who shall be elected at municipal elections every four years and must be a properly qualified individual. A magisterial district judge may not hold the office of tax collector and the office of magisterial district judge at the same time.

(3) Unless the borough provides for one appointed auditor under section 1005(7) (relating to powers of council), three auditors or one controller. The following shall apply:

(i) In boroughs providing for three elected auditors, one auditor shall be elected at each municipal election for a term of six years.

(ii) In boroughs providing for one elected controller, the controller shall:

(A) be elected at the municipal election;

Chap. 39 Res. During Mil. Service
Chap. 38 Intergov. Coop.
Chap. 37 3rd Class City Code
Chap. 36 Bor. Code
Chap. 35 2nd Class Twp. Code
Chap. 34 1st Class Twp. Code
Chap. 33 Home Rule Chart. Opt. Plans Law
Chap. 32 Water Serv. Act
Chap. 31 Munic. Auth. Act

(B) be a competent accountant and a registered elector of the borough for at least four years prior to the individual's election; and

(C) serve for a term of four years.

(4) Except as provided in section 818 (relating to change in number of members of council), in boroughs not divided into wards, seven members of council.

(5) As follows:

(i) Except as provided under subparagraph (ii), in boroughs divided into wards, at least one and not more than two members of council in each ward.

(ii) In boroughs in which prior to January 1, 1966, three members of council were elected in each ward, three members of council in each ward unless the number is reduced as provided under this part. Members of council shall:

(A) be residents of the ward from which they are elected; and

(B) be chosen by the electors of the ward.

(b) Terms.—The term of an elected officer under this section shall begin the first Monday of January succeeding the individual's election.

SUBCHAPTER B
MEMBERS OF COUNCIL

Sec.

---

§ 811. Election.

Biennially, at the municipal election, a sufficient number of members of council shall be elected to fill the places of members whose terms shall, under this part, expire on the first Monday of January following the election. Members elected under this section shall serve for a term of four years from the first Monday of January succeeding the municipal election.

§ 812. Election of members of council.

(a) General rule.—If council, by ordinance, divides any borough into wards, erects new wards out of two or more wards or parts of wards or divides a ward already erected into two or more wards, the ordinance shall provide for the election of an equal number of members of council, in each of the wards, in a manner as not to interfere with the terms of those previously elected.

(b) Election of members.—The following shall apply:

(1) If a borough is first divided into wards, the ordinance providing for the division shall fix the number of members of council in each ward at not more than two. If the entire number of council is to be composed of an even number, one-half of the entire number must be elected at each municipal election. If the entire number of council is to be an odd number, the ordinance shall establish two classes and provide that one-half of the entire number of members of coun-

cil, less one, shall, as soon as possible, take their office in a year divisible by four, and the remaining number of members of council shall take their office in an even-numbered year not divisible by four.

(2) The apportionment under paragraph (1) shall be equal or as nearly equal as possible representation by wards in each class. Biennially, at each municipal election, a sufficient number of members of council shall be elected, for the term of four years from the first Monday of January succeeding the election, to fill the places of those whose terms shall expire on the first Monday of January following the election.

§ 813. Fixing number of members of council.

If, upon the division of a borough into wards or the creation of a new ward, the number of members of council cannot be equally divided among the wards of the borough, it shall be lawful for council to increase the number of council members to and not exceeding a number that will enable equal apportionment of the members among the several wards of the borough. If a borough is first divided into wards, the number of members of council provided for a ward may not exceed two.

§ 814. Increase in number of ward council members.

Council may, upon petition of at least 5% of the registered electors of the borough, increase the number of members of council to any number not exceeding two for each ward. The sufficiency of the number of signers to the petition shall be ascertained as of the date when the petition is presented to council.

§ 815. Decrease of number of ward council members.

(a) General rule.—If, in any borough divided into wards, the council consists of more than seven members, at least 5% of the registered electors of the borough shall have the power to petition council for a decrease in the number of members of council from each ward, except that the council may not consist of less than seven members. The purpose of the decrease may be to achieve any of the following results:

(1) A council which is less unwieldy in size.

(2) A council which is comparable in size to those in boroughs not divided into wards.

(3) A council consisting of an odd number of members instead of an even number.

(4) A reduction in borough expenditures.

(5) The expedition of the conduct of council meetings.

(b) Petitions.—A petition under subsection (a) shall clearly state whether the petitioners request that the number of members of the council to be elected in each ward shall be reduced from two to one, or from three to two or one, and the reasons why the reduction in number is desired. The petition may state whether it is necessary to add a council member or members to be elected at large in order to achieve or maintain a council consisting of at least seven members or to achieve or maintain a council consisting of an odd number of members. The sufficiency of the number of signers to the petition shall be ascertained as of the date the petition is presented to council.

(c) Notice.—The council shall give notice of the filing of the petition by advertisement in the legal newspaper of the county, if one is published in the county, and in one newspaper of general circulation, and a day and time for a public meeting. After the public meeting council may, by ordinance, decrease the number of council members elected from each ward from two to one, or from three to two or one, and may also provide for the election at large of a member or members of council.

(d) Terms.—Council shall, if necessary, establish a schedule for the subsequent at-large election of council members. The schedule may provide that the initial term of one or more of the council members subsequently elected at large shall be reduced to accommodate a schedule of staggered at-large elections to eventually ensure that, as nearly as possible, one-half of the members of council elected at large will be elected at each municipal election. The following shall apply:

(1) At each municipal election in the borough, if there are two members from each ward, the electors of each ward shall elect one council member to hold office for a term of four years from the first Monday of January succeeding the election.

(2) At each municipal election in the borough, if there is one member from each ward, the electors from each of the odd-numbered wards shall, at the first municipal election, elect one council member for a term of four years, and the electors from each of the even-numbered wards shall elect one council member for a term of two years. At each succeeding municipal election, the electors of the even-numbered wards or odd-numbered wards shall each elect one council member for a term of four years to take the place of those whose terms are about to expire. The council members shall take office on the first Monday of January following their election.

(e) Reduction.—In a borough where, under this section, the number of council members shall be reduced, the council members then in office shall remain in office until the end of their respective terms.

§ 816. Election of members of council where wards abolished.

(a) Abolishing.—If council, by ordinance, abolishes all wards in a borough, the ordinance shall provide for the election of seven members of council at large for the borough in a manner as not to interfere with the terms of those ward members of council previously elected. If there were previously:

(1) Seven members of council, the ordinance shall provide that, at the first municipal election, the electors shall elect three or four members of council, as the case may be, the number to be elected shall be that which, when added to the number of members of council already in office whose terms are not about to expire, shall bring the membership of the council to seven. The newly elected members of council shall serve for terms of four years from the first Monday of January following the first municipal election, except that, in any case where the election of four members of council shall be required to bring the membership of council to its full complement of seven and only three members of council are elected at the municipal election in the other boroughs of the Commonwealth not divided into wards, three members of council shall be elected for four-year terms and one for a two-year term. At every succeeding municipal election, the electors shall elect three or four members of council, as the case may be, each to serve for a term of four years from the first Monday of January following the municipal election.

(2) Eight or more members of council, the ordinance shall provide that, at the first municipal election, the electors shall elect a sufficient number of members of council that, when added to the number of members of council already in office whose terms are not about to expire, will bring the membership of the council to seven. The following shall apply:

(i) The newly elected members of council shall serve for terms of four years from the first Monday of January following the first municipal election. At the second municipal election after the effective date of the ordinance, the electors shall elect a sufficient number of members of council, that, when added to the number of members of council elected at the previous municipal election, shall bring the membership of council to its full complement of seven. Some of the members of council elected at the second municipal election shall serve for a four-year term following the first Monday of January following the municipal election and the remainder shall serve for a two-year term, in an amount to bring the number to be elected in the borough in succeeding municipal elections into conformity with the number elected in the other boroughs of the Commonwealth not divided into wards.

(ii) In the third and all subsequent municipal elections following the effective date of the ordinance, the electors shall elect three or four members of council, as the case may be, each to serve for a term of four years from the first Monday of January following the municipal election.

(iii) In any borough in which, under the ward system of electing members of council, there shall be seven or more members of council whose terms shall not expire on the first Monday of January following the first municipal election after the effective date of the ordinance, no members of council shall be elected at the first municipal election, and the members of council remaining in office shall constitute the council until the first Monday of January following the second municipal election following the effective date of the ordinance.

(iv) At the second municipal election, seven members of council shall be elected in the borough, some to serve for a four-year term of office from the first Monday of January following the second municipal election and the remainder to serve for a two-year term, in an amount to bring the number of members of council to be elected in the borough in succeeding elections into conformity with the number elected in other boroughs of the Commonwealth not divided into wards.

(v) At the third and all subsequent municipal elections following the effective date of the ordinance, the electors shall elect three or four members of council, as the case may be, each to serve for a term of four years from the first Monday of January following the subsequent municipal election.

(3) Six or fewer members of council, the ordinance shall provide that, at the first municipal election, the electors shall elect a sufficient number of members of council that, when added to the number of members of council already in office whose terms are not about to expire, shall bring the membership of council to its full complement of seven. Of the newly elected members of council, either three or four, as necessary to bring the number of members of council to be elected in the borough in succeeding municipal elections into conformity with the number elected in other boroughs of the Commonwealth not divided into wards, shall be elected for four-year terms of office, beginning the first Monday of January following the first municipal election, and the balance shall be elected for two-year terms. At the second municipal election following the effective date of the ordinance and at all subsequent municipal elections, the electors shall elect three or four members of council, as the case may be, to serve for a term of four years from the first Monday of January following the subsequent municipal election.

(b) Vacancies.—At any time following the effective date of the ordinance, when a vacancy may occur in the office of a member of council originally elected or appointed from a particular ward, the individual appointed to fill the vacancy shall not be required to be a resident of the area formerly comprising the ward but shall be otherwise qualified for office as provided in section 801 (relating to eligibility).

§ 817. Vacancies created after a primary election.

If a vacancy is created in the office of a member of council by any ordinance or decree of court as provided in this subchapter after a primary election, it may be filled by nomination made by the committee as is authorized by the rules of the party to make nominations in the event of vacancies on the party ticket.

§ 818. Change in number of members of council.

(a) Petition by electors.—The court of common pleas shall, upon petition of at least 5% of the registered electors of any borough not divided into wards, certify the question of a proposal to reduce the total number of members of council for the borough to five or three or increase the total number of members of council for the borough to five or seven, as specified by the petition, to the board of election of the county for a referendum vote of the residents at the next general election held not sooner than the thirteenth Tuesday after the date of the petition. The sufficiency of the number of signers to the petition shall be ascertained as of the date when the petition is presented to court. Upon receipt of the certified election results, the court shall enter a final decree granting or denying the request of the petitioners. A petition under this section may not be considered more than once in five years.

(b) Deleted by 2020, June 5, P.L. 211, No. 28, § 2, effective in 60 days [Aug. 4, 2020].

(c) Number to be elected by decree.—In its decree under subsection (a), the court shall establish a schedule for the subsequent election of council members at the next two municipal elections. The members of council then in office shall remain in office until the end of their respective terms. Thereafter, the schedule may provide that the initial term of one or more of the council members subsequently elected be reduced to accommodate a schedule of staggered at-large elections to eventually ensure that, as nearly as possible, one-half of the members of council elected will be elected at each municipal election. At all following municipal elections, the proper number of members of council shall be elected to correspond to the number of members of council whose terms are to expire the first Monday of the following January.

(d) (Reserved).

(e) Terms.—In any borough in which, under this section, the number of members of council shall be reduced or increased, the members of council then in office shall remain in office until the end of their respective terms.

SUBCHAPTER C
MAYOR
(Reserved)

SUBCHAPTER D
AUDITORS
(Reserved)

SUBCHAPTER E
CONTROLLER
(Reserved)

SUBCHAPTER F
ASSESSORS
(Reserved)

SUBCHAPTER G
TAX COLLECTOR
(Reserved)

CHAPTER 9

VACANCIES IN OFFICE

---

§ 901. Filling vacancies in elective borough offices.

(a) Vacancies.—If any vacancy occurs in the office of the mayor, member of council, auditor, controller or tax collector, by death, resignation under subsection (a.1) or termination of residency from the borough, or from a ward in the case of a ward office, or by failure to take the required oath, to give bond as provided by law or ordinance or to provide the affidavit required under section 801 (relating to eligibility), or in any other manner whatsoever, the council shall fill the vacancy within 30 days by appointing, by resolution, a registered elector of the borough, or of the ward in case of a ward office, to hold the office, if the term continues that long, until the first Monday in January after the first municipal election occurring more than 60 days after the vacancy occurs, at which election an eligible individual shall be elected to the office for the remainder of the term. Except as provided in section 801(c), no individual shall be appointed to fill a vacancy in an elected borough or ward office unless the individual has resided within the borough, or within the ward in the case of a ward office, continuously for at least one year immediately prior to the individual's appointment.

(a.1) Vacancy by resignation.—

(1) A vacancy shall not be created by a resignation until the date that the resignation is accepted by a majority vote of a quorum of council at a public meeting or the effective date of the tendered resignation, whichever is later. A council must accept a resignation no later than 45 days after it has been tendered in writing to council, unless it is withdrawn in writing prior to acceptance.

(2) A resignation which is not accepted as provided under paragraph (1) shall be deemed accepted after 45 days.

(b) Bond.—The individual appointed shall give bond if required by law or ordinance. If the individual elected to the office fails to give any bond required, to provide the affidavit required under section 801 or to take the required oath, the council, before making the appointment, shall declare the office vacant.

(c) Unfilled vacancies.—If the council of any borough refuses, fails, neglects or is unable, for any reason whatsoever, to fill any vacancy within 30 days after the vacancy happens, as provided in this section, the vacancy shall be filled within 15 additional days by the vacancy board. The vacancy board shall consist of the council, exclusive of the mayor, and one registered elector of the borough who shall be appointed by the council at the council's first meeting each calendar year or as soon as practical and who shall act as chair of the vacancy board. The vacancy board shall appoint a registered elector of the borough, or ward in the case of a ward office, to hold the office, if the term continues that long, until the first Monday in January after the first municipal election occurring more than 60 days after the vacancy occurs, at which election an eligible individual shall be elected to the office for the remainder of the term.

Table of Contents | Part I Ch. 1–3 Ethics, Records, Open Meetings | Part II Ch. 4–10 Taxation | Part III Ch. 11–18 Torts, Contracts & Civil Rules | Part IV Ch. 19–24 Zoning & Planning | Part V Ch. 25–30 Construction and Emergency Codes | Part VI Ch. 31–39 Municipal Codes | Index

(d) Board petition.—If the vacancy is not filled by the vacancy board within 15 days, the chair shall, or in the case of a vacancy in the chair, the remaining members of the vacancy board shall petition the court of common pleas to fill the vacancy by the appointment of a registered elector of the borough, or ward in the case of a ward, to hold the office, if the term continues that long, until the first Monday in January after the first municipal election occurring more than 60 days after the vacancy occurs, at which election an eligible individual shall be elected to the office for the remainder of the term.

(e) Elector petition.—If vacancies exist in more than a majority of the offices of council, the court of common pleas shall fill the vacancies upon presentation of petition signed by not less than 15 registered electors of the borough.

§ 902. Collection of taxes where vacancy in office of tax collector not filled.

If a vacancy in the office of tax collector exists and no registered elector of the borough has, within 30 days, received the appointment to fill the vacancy, the county commissioners, the council and the board of school directors of the school district shall collect the tax for the county, the borough and the school district, respectively, through their respective treasurers, or for school districts, at the option of the district, through their secretaries, and for boroughs, at the option of the council, through their secretaries or borough managers. Nothing in this section shall prohibit a borough from providing for agreements or the joint collection of taxes in accordance with sections 4.2 and 4.4 of the act of May 25, 1945 (P.L.1050, No.394), known as the Local Tax Collection Law.

§ 903. Right of council to declare seat of member vacant for failure to qualify.

If an individual, elected or appointed as a member of council and notified of election or appointment refuses or neglects to qualify as a member of council within ten days following the beginning of the individual's term of office, unless prevented by sickness or necessary absence from the borough, the council, acting without the individual, may declare the individual's office as member of council vacant and may fill the vacancy as provided in section 901 (relating to filling vacancies in elective borough offices). For these actions, a majority of the remaining members of the council shall constitute a quorum.

§ 904. (Reserved).

§ 904.1. Removal of elected official and appointee.

(a) Rule.—A borough officer who is elected or appointed to fill a vacancy in elective office may be removed from office as follows:

(1) By impeachment.

(2) By the Governor for reasonable cause after notice and full hearing on the advice of two-thirds of the Senate.

(3) On conviction of misbehavior in office or of an infamous crime.

(b) Title.—The title to office of a borough officer under subsection (a) may be tried by quo warranto.

§ 905. Temporary auditor.

If for any reason two or three vacancies exist in the office of borough auditors, the council may temporarily appoint and reasonably compensate a qualified individual, who need not be an elector of the borough, who shall have all the powers and duties of the two or three auditors whose offices are vacated.

CHAPTER 10

POWERS AND DUTIES OF ELECTED OFFICIALS

SUBCHAPTER A

COUNCIL

---

§ 1001. Organization of council, quorum, participation by telecommunication device, voting, compensation and eligibility.

(a) Organization.—The council shall organize on the first Monday of January of each even-numbered year by electing one member as president and one member as vice-president, who shall hold the offices at the pleasure of the council. If the first Monday is a legal holiday, the meeting and organization shall take place the following day. Any action taken by any council at any time between 12:01 a.m. on January 1 of an even-numbered year and the organization of council in that year shall be subject to reconsideration by the new council at any time within ten days after organization. The council may, at the organizational meeting, appoint other officers as may be provided for by law or ordinance, or as may be deemed necessary for the conduct of affairs of the borough, and may transact any other business as may come before the meeting. The president, and during the president's absence or incapacity, the vice-president, shall preside over the meetings of council and perform other duties as are prescribed by this part or by ordinance.

(b) Quorum.—A majority of the membership of council then in office shall constitute a quorum. Except as provided in subsection (c), only council members physically present at a meeting place within the borough shall be counted in establishing a quorum.

(c) Telecommunication.—Council may provide for the participation of council members in council meetings by means of telecommunication devices, such as telephones or computer terminals, which permit, at a minimum, audio communication between locations, if the following apply:

(1) A majority of the membership of council then in office is physically present at the advertised meeting place within the borough and a quorum is established at the convening or reconvening of the meeting. If, after the convening or reconvening of a meeting, a member has been disqualified from voting as a matter of law, but is still physically present, council members participating by telecommunication device in accordance with this section shall be counted to maintain a quorum.

(2) The telecommunication device used permits the member or members of council not physically present at the meeting to:

(i) speak to and hear the comments and votes, if any, of the members of council who are physically present, as well as other members of council who may not be physically present and are also using a telecommunication device to participate in the meeting; and

(ii) speak to and hear the comments of the public who are physically present at the meeting.

(3) The telecommunication device used permits the members of council and the members of the public who are physically present at the meeting to speak to and hear the comments and the vote, if any, of the member or members of council who are not physically present at the meeting.

(4) Physical absence of a council member. Council may only authorize participation by telecommunication device for one or more of the following reasons:

(i) illness or disability of the member of council;

(ii) care for the ill or newborn in the member's immediate family;

(iii) emergency; and

(iv) family or business travel.

(5) Nothing in this subsection shall be construed to limit the protections and prohibitions contained in any law or regulation relating to the rights of the disabled.

(d) Voting.—A member of the council shall not be disqualified from voting on any issue before the council solely because the member has previously expressed an opinion on the issue in either an official or unofficial capacity.

(e) Compensation.—Members of council may receive compensation to be fixed by ordinance as follows:

(1) In boroughs with a population of less than 5,000, a maximum of $3,145 per year.

(2) In boroughs with a population of 5,000 or more but less than 10,000, a maximum of $4,190 per year.

(3) In boroughs with a population of 10,000 or more but less than 15,000, a maximum of $5,450 per year.

(4) In boroughs with a population of 15,000 or more but less than 25,000, a maximum of $6,915 per year.

(5) In boroughs with a population of 25,000 or more but less than 35,000, a maximum of $7,335 per year.

(6) In boroughs with a population of 35,000 or more, a maximum of $8,385 per year.

The salaries shall be payable monthly or quarterly for the duties imposed by this part. Benefits provided to members of council under section 1202(26) (relating to specific powers) shall not be considered pay, salary or compensation, but payment for all or a part of the premiums or charges for the benefits shall be in accordance with section 1202(26). Any change in salary, compensation or emoluments of the elected office shall become effective at the beginning of the next term of the member of council.

(e.1) Alternative compensation.—Notwithstanding subsection (e), the council may provide that members of the council shall receive compensation on a per-meeting basis based on attendance of members of council. Total annual compensation may not exceed the amounts specified in subsection (e). Compensation shall only be payable for duly advertised public meetings in which a member of council participated, except compensation is not payable if a member of council is absent from a meeting and the absence is not excused. Excused absence from a meeting shall be determined by council and shall include, but not be limited to, an emergency or illness of the member of council or the member's immediate family, as well as family or business travel. Council may require documentation to support an excused absence.

(f) Eligibility for compensation.—The population shall be determined by the latest available official census figures, except that a borough shall not be required to reduce the salary of a mayor or member of council as a result of a decrease in population. In no case shall the compensation for any member of council exceed that of the mayor in any given borough, but, if the mayor's compensation exceeds that authorized by this section for members of council, the president of council may receive compensation not to exceed that of the office of mayor.

§ 1002. Oath of members of council.

Before entering upon the duties of their offices, the members of council shall take and subscribe an oath or affirmation of office under 53 Pa.C.S. § 1141 (relating to form of oaths of office). The oath or affirmation may be taken before any judge or magisterial district judge of the county, a notary public or the mayor of the borough when the individual has qualified, and the oath or affirmation shall be filed with the borough secretary and preserved among the records of the borough for a period of six years.

§ 1003. When the mayor may preside over council and vote, attendance of mayor at council meetings and breaking tie votes.

(a) Presiding over meetings.—The mayor shall preside over the organization of the council until it is organized as provided in section 1001 (relating to organization of council, quorum, participation by telecommunication device, voting, compensation and eligibility), and shall be deemed a member of council at the organizational meeting if the mayor's membership becomes necessary to constitute a quorum.

(b) Voting at meetings.—The mayor shall not vote at the meeting unless the mayor's vote shall, for any reason, be required to effect the organization of council or to elect any officer who is required to be or may be elected at the organizational meeting. If the mayor is absent from the organizational meeting, one of the members of council physically present at the meeting and chosen by the members eligible to vote at the meeting shall preside.

(c) Attendance.—The mayor may attend any or all regular and special meetings of council and take part in the discussions of the council on matters pertaining to borough affairs, subject to any restrictions applicable to members of council contained in the rules of order or bylaws of the council.

(d) Tie votes.—

(1) If, by reason of a tie or split vote, the council shall be unable to:

(i) enact or pass any ordinance, resolution or motion;

Chap. 39 Res. During Mil. Service
Chap. 38 Intergov. Coop.
Chap. 37 3rd Class City Code
Chap. 36 Bor. Code
Chap. 35 2nd Class Twp. Code
Chap. 34 1st Class Twp. Code
Chap. 33 Home Rule Chart. Opt. Plans Law
Chap. 32 Water Serv. Act
Chap. 31 Munic. Auth. Act

(ii) declare any vacancy pursuant to section 903 (relating to right of council to declare seat of member vacant for failure to qualify);

(iii) fill any other vacancy in its membership or in any other borough office.

(iv) take any action on any matter lawfully brought before it;

the mayor, if in attendance at the meeting, may, at the mayor's option, cast the deciding vote or shall direct that the matter be tabled until a special meeting of council.

(2) The special meeting of council shall be held within not less than five days or more than ten days at which time the matter shall be reconsidered by council.

(3) If a tie or split vote still exists, it shall be the duty of the mayor at that time to cast the deciding vote.

(4) If a tie or split vote occurs at any meeting when the mayor is not in attendance, the matter shall be tabled to a special meeting to be held within not less than five days or more than ten days as set by the president of council, and the mayor shall be given at least five days' notice of the meeting, at which meeting it shall be the duty of the mayor to cast the tie-breaking vote.

§ 1004. Failure of council to organize.

If the council of any borough fails to organize within ten days from the time prescribed in this chapter, the court of common pleas, upon the petition of at least ten registered electors of the borough verified by the affidavit of one of the petitioners, shall issue a rule upon the delinquent members of council to show cause why their seats should not be declared vacant. The rule shall be returnable not less than five days from the time of its issue, and, after hearing, the court may declare the seats of the members of council responsible for the failure to organize vacant and shall appoint others in their place, who shall hold office for the respective unexpired terms.

§ 1005. Powers of council.

The council shall have power:

(1) To, by motion, ordinance or resolution, create the offices of and appoint, a treasurer, a secretary, a solicitor, an engineer, a street commissioner and other officers as it deems necessary. The treasurer and the secretary shall not be members of council. A bank or bank and trust company may be appointed as treasurer. All officers and employees appointed by the council, with the exception of those who under this part or any other act are under civil service or have a definite term of office, shall serve for an indefinite term at the pleasure of the council.

(2) To mitigate or remit fines and forfeitures in reasonable cases.

(3) By resolution, to make temporary loans on the credit of the borough in anticipation of taxes to be collected and issue certificates of indebtedness. The loans shall be repaid from the first money available from taxes in anticipation of which the loans were made.

(4) With respect to depositories and securities, to:

(i) Appoint and revoke the appointment of one or more depositories for borough funds and to fix and approve security to be furnished by the depository. The security may be bonds with corporate or individual securities to be approved by council, or collateral security consisting of obligations of the United States or the Commonwealth or any political subdivision, deposited with the borough or with any bank or trust company within this Commonwealth and of a market value of 120% of the amount of the deposit to be secured. Any deposit of collateral shall be under proper agreement and be accompanied by proper assignment or power of attorney for the transfer of the collateral. The borough treasurer shall deposit all borough funds in a depository designated under this subparagraph. If borough funds are deposited under this subparagraph, the borough treasurer shall be released and discharged from further liability on account of the deposit.

(ii) Subparagraph (i) shall not be construed to require a depository to furnish bond or collateral security to cover the amount of any deposit to the extent that the deposit is insured with the Federal Deposit Insurance Corporation.

(5) To secure indemnity bonds or policies of insurance as it may deem necessary to protect the borough from loss by reason of fire, flood, windstorm, burglary, larceny, negligence or dishonesty or insolvency of a depository, or otherwise, and to pay for the protection the usual or customary costs.

(6) With respect to investments, to:

(i) make investment of borough sinking funds as authorized by 53 Pa.C.S. Pt. VII Subpt. B (relating to indebtedness and borrowing);

(ii) make investment of money in the general fund and in special funds of the borough other than the sinking funds as authorized by Chapter 13 (relating to taxation and finance); and

(iii) liquidate any investment, in whole or in part, by disposing of securities or withdrawing funds on deposit. Any action taken to make or to liquidate any investment shall be made by the officers designated by action of the council.

(7) To provide, by ordinance passed by a two-thirds vote of the entire number of members of council elected, for the appointment of an independent auditor who shall be a certified public accountant registered in this Commonwealth, a firm of certified public accountants registered in this Commonwealth or a competent public accountant or a competent firm of public accountants.

(i) When an ordinance has been adopted, an independent auditor shall be appointed annually, by resolution before the close of the fiscal year, to make an independent examination of the accounting records of the borough for the fiscal year, and the independent auditor shall also perform the other duties and exercise the powers as conferred upon the independent auditor under Subchapter C (relating to auditors).

(ii) When an independent auditor is appointed as provided in this paragraph, the office of elected borough auditor or controller is abolished, but the borough auditors or controller then in office shall continue to hold their office during the term for which elected, and the borough auditors or controller shall not audit, settle or adjust the accounts audited by the independent auditor, but shall perform the other duties of their office.

(iii) If any borough has provided by ordinance for the audit of its accounts by an appointed auditor, the borough shall have the right at any time to repeal the ordinance, and the office of appointed auditor shall be abolished as of the date set in the ordinance. The borough shall have the further right at the next municipal election following the repeal of the ordinance to elect three auditors, one for a term of two years, one for a term of four years and one for a term of six years, from the first Monday of January following the election, which auditors shall succeed the appointed auditor and shall have and possess all the powers and perform all the duties provided in this part for elected auditors. If, at any time after the effective date of any ordinance abolishing the office of appointed auditor, there shall be a vacancy in the office of elected auditor, council shall fill the vacancies in the manner prescribed in section 901 (relating to filling vacancies in elective borough offices).

Table of Contents
Part I Ch. 1–3 Ethics, Records, Open Meetings
Part II Ch. 4–10 Taxation
Part III Ch. 11–18 Torts, Contracts & Civil Rules
Part IV Ch. 19–24 Zoning & Planning
Part V Ch. 25–30 Construction and Emergency Codes
Part VI Ch. 31–39 Municipal Codes
Index

(8) To make, authorize and ratify expenditures for lawful purposes from funds available or from funds borrowed within legal limits.

(9) To pay authorized expenses incurred by elected and appointed borough officers in connection with their duties or other borough business.

§ 1006. Duties of council.

It shall be the duty of the council:

(1) To organize, under section 1001 (relating to organization of council, quorum, participation by telecommunication device, voting, compensation and eligibility), in even-numbered years.

(2) To meet at a stated time at least once a month. Council may adjourn to a stated time for general business or for special businesses. If no quorum is present at a regular, special or reconvened meeting, a majority of those who do meet may agree upon another date for like business in a manner consistent with 65 Pa.C.S. Ch. 7 (relating to open meetings). Special meetings may be called by the president of council or upon written request of at least one-third of the members of council. Members shall have at least 24 hours' notice of the special meetings. The notice shall state whether it is for general or special purposes, and, if it is for special purposes, the notice shall contain a general statement of the nature of the business to be transacted. Presence at a meeting constitutes waiver of notice. Council may adopt rules relating to the calling and holding of special meetings, which rules shall supersede the provisions of this section, provided that the rules comply with the provisions of 65 Pa.C.S. Ch. 7.

(3) To make and preserve records of its proceedings.

(4) To enact, revise, repeal and amend ordinances and resolutions under Chapter 33 (relating to ordinances), and bylaws, rules and regulations, not inconsistent with the laws of this Commonwealth, as it deems beneficial to the borough and to provide for the enforcement of the same. Unless otherwise provided, all powers shall be exercised by vote of the majority of council eligible to vote at a meeting. Routine, ministerial or administrative purchases and powers may be made and exercised by officers or committees if authority for the action was previously given or if the action is subsequently ratified by council. If any action by the council results in a specific written contract or agreement, the contract or agreement shall be signed by the president of the council.

(5) To cause notices to be served, as required by law or ordinance, in a manner council may by motion or other action decide.

(6) To fix the compensation of all of the borough officers, appointees and employees.

(7) To fix the amount of security to be given by the treasurer, and of other officers, appointees and employees as it may designate.

§ 1007. (Reserved).

§ 1008. (Reserved).

§ 1009. Typewritten, printed, photocopied, microfilmed and electronically or digitally stored records valid and recording or transcribing records.

(a) Validity.—All borough records required to be recorded or transcribed shall be deemed valid if typewritten, printed, photocopied, microfilmed or electronically or digitally stored or retained by any other process that accurately reproduces the original and forms a durable medium for recording, storing and reproducing in accordance with the act of May 9, 1949 (P.L.908, No.250), entitled "An act relating to public records of political subdivisions other than cities and counties of the first class; authorizing the recording and copying of documents, plats, papers and instruments of writing by digital, photostatic, photographic, microfilm or other process, and the admissibility and enlargements in evidence; providing for the storage of duplicates and sale of microfilm and digital copies of official records and for the destruction of other records deemed valueless; and providing for the services of the Pennsylvania Historical and Museum Commission to political subdivisions."

(b) Requirements.—If recording or transcribing in a specified book of record is required, including minutes of the proceedings of the council, the records shall be recorded or transcribed as follows:

(1) in a mechanical post binder book capable of being permanently sealed with consecutively numbered pages with a security code printed on it and a permanent locking device with the borough seal being impressed upon each page; or

(2) in a bound book with pages being consecutively numbered by transcribing directly upon the pages of the book of record or by permanently attaching the records or copies to the book of record with the borough seal being impressed upon each page to which the record is attached, with each impression covering both a portion of the attached record and a portion of the page of the book of record to which the record is attached.

(c) Previously recorded documents.—All records previously recorded or transcribed in any manner authorized by this part at the time the records were recorded or transcribed are validated.

§ 1010. (Reserved).

§ 1011. (Reserved).

§ 1012. (Reserved).

§ 1013. (Reserved).

§ 1014. Hearings before council; witnesses.

Councils may compel the attendance of witnesses and the production of books, papers or other evidence at any meeting of the council or any committee of the council and for that purpose may issue subpoenas, signed by the president of council or the chair of the committee, which shall be served in any part of this Commonwealth. If a witness refuses to testify to any fact within the witness's knowledge or to produce any books or papers in the witness's possession or control required to be used as evidence in any case, the borough solicitor shall report the facts relating to the refusal to the court of common pleas. If the court determines the evidence required of the witness to be legal and competent, it shall order the witness to testify or produce the evidence required.

§ 1015. Witness fees and mileage.

No individual residing outside the borough and subpoenaed under section 1014 (relating to hearings before council, witnesses) shall be required to respond to the subpoena until mileage to and from the borough at the rate established by the council under the act of July 20, 1979 (P.L.156, No.51), referred to as the Uniform Mileage Fee Law, and witness fees as required by law relating to witnesses have been paid.

§ 1016. Examination of witnesses; penalty.

An individual called as a witness, as provided in this chapter, may be examined under oath, administered by the president of council or chair of the committee and, for the giving of false testimony, shall be liable for prosecution under applicable laws for perjury.

SUBCHAPTER B
MAYOR
(Reserved)

SUBCHAPTER C
AUDITORS

Sec.

---

§ 1041. Auditors to meet yearly and audit accounts.

(a) **First meeting.**—The auditors of the borough shall meet on the first Tuesday of January of each year and shall organize by the election of a chair and a secretary. If the first Tuesday is a legal holiday, the meeting and organization shall take place the following day. Two auditors shall constitute a quorum.

(b) **Audits.**—The auditors:

(1) Shall audit, adjust and settle the accounts of the tax collectors, the magisterial district judge and all officers of the borough.

(2) May audit, adjust and settle the accounts of any person, corporation, association, organization, committee or commission receiving or expending borough funds.

(3) Audit and report to the council, upon the accounts of every officer of the borough, upon the death, resignation, removal or expiration of the term of the officer.

Unless otherwise agreed to by the auditors and the person being audited, the audit shall be conducted at the place the records of the person are normally kept.

(b.1) **Cancellation.**—All orders, vouchers and certificates of indebtedness which have been paid shall, on their presentation to the auditors, be canceled by writing or stamping the word "audited" on the face of the documents.

(c) (Reserved).

(d) (Reserved).

(e) (Reserved).

(f) (Reserved).

(g) (Reserved).

§ 1042. (Reserved).

§ 1043. (Reserved).

§ 1044. (Reserved).

§ 1045. (Reserved).

§ 1046. (Reserved).

§ 1047. (Reserved).

§ 1048. (Reserved).

§ 1049. (Reserved).

§ 1050. (Reserved).

§ 1051. (Reserved).

§ 1052. (Reserved).

§ 1053. Compensation of auditors.

(a) General compensation.—Subject to the limitations set forth in subsection (b), each auditor shall receive $10 per hour for each hour or portion of an hour necessarily employed in the discharge of the auditor's duties, to be paid by the borough.

(b) Limits.—No auditor in a borough having a population of 10,000 or less shall be entitled to receive more than $1,000 for completing the annual audit, settlement and adjustment. No auditor in a borough having a population in excess of 10,000 shall be entitled to receive more than $2,000 for completing the annual audit, settlement and adjustment.

(c) Reimbursements.—Each auditor shall be reimbursed for travel costs incurred in the performance of the auditing duties at the rate established by the council under the act of July 20, 1979 (P.L.156, No.51), referred to as the Uniform Mileage Fee Law, and for other actual expenses, including postage, notary fees or publication costs, necessarily incurred during the audit.

§ 1054. (Reserved).

§ 1055. Subpoenas, oath and perjury.

(a) Subpoenas.—A majority of the auditors of any borough shall have the power to issue subpoenas to obtain the attendance of the persons whose accounts they are required to adjust, their executors and administrators, and of any persons whom it may be necessary to examine as witnesses and to compel their attendance, and may also compel the production of all documents, including books, vouchers and papers relative to borough accounts. If any person refuses or neglects to appear, to produce documents or to testify, the auditors shall petition the court of common pleas of the county to issue a subpoena to the person and to require the person to produce documents or to appear and to testify before the court. The court shall issue the subpoena if it deems the documents or testimony relevant to the issue.

(b) Oaths.—The auditors of any borough shall have power to administer oaths and affirmations to all persons brought or appearing before them, whether accountants, witnesses or otherwise. Persons guilty of swearing or affirming falsely on the examination commits perjury.

§ 1056. (Reserved).

§ 1057. (Reserved).

Chap. 39 Res. During Mil. Service
Chap. 38 Intergov. Coop.
Chap. 37 3rd Class City Code
Chap. 36 Bor. Code
Chap. 35 2nd Class Twp. Code
Chap. 34 1st Class Twp. Code
Chap. 33 Home Rule Chart. Opt. Plans Law
Chap. 32 Water Serv. Act
Chap. 31 Munic. Auth. Act

§ 1058. Pay of witnesses.

Witnesses, other than officers of the borough, appearing before the auditors and individuals or officers serving subpoenas shall be paid, out of the borough treasury upon authorization signed by a majority of the auditors and orders drawn on the borough treasury, the same fees as are payable for rendering similar services in civil proceedings before a magisterial district judge. The amount paid shall be made a part of the charge against any officer who shall be charged by the auditors with any balance, if the costs have been incurred in establishing the balance. The costs collected from any officer shall be repaid into the borough treasury.

§ 1059. Auditors to settle accounts where witnesses do not appear.

If any person in possession of documents relative to public accounts before auditors refuses to produce the same or if any officer whose accounts are to be settled and adjusted by the auditors refuses to appear or submit to examination as directed by this subchapter, the auditors or a majority of them may proceed, by the examination of witnesses and other evidence, to ascertain and settle, as near as may be, the amount of public money received by the officer and its application to public purposes or otherwise.

§ 1059.1. Completion, filing and publication of auditor's report and financial statement.

(a) Reports.—The auditors shall complete the annual audit, adjustment and settlement as soon as possible after the end of the fiscal year. The auditors shall, within ten days after completing the annual audit, publish once, in at least one newspaper of general circulation, concise financial information prepared or approved by the auditors and consistent with the audited financial statements for total assets, total liabilities and total net position at the end of the fiscal year and total revenue, total expenses and changes in total net position for that fiscal year and a reference to a place within the borough where copies of the financial statements and accompanying audit report may be examined. If the full financial statements and accompanying audit report are not published, copies shall be supplied to the publishing newspaper when the request for publication is submitted.

(b) Details.—The auditors shall prepare a report which shall contain an audit of the accounts of the last fiscal year and shall also show a complete statement of the financial condition of the borough, giving in detail all of the following:

(1) The actual indebtedness.

(2) The amount of funded debt.

(3) The amount of floating debt.

(4) The valuation of taxable property in the borough.

(5) The assets of the borough with their character and value.

(6) The date of maturity of the respective forms of funded debt of the borough.

(b.1) Filing of report and penalties.—The report shall be prepared no later than 90 days after the close of the fiscal year. It shall be the duty of the secretary of the auditors to file a copy of the report with the secretary of the borough, with the clerk of the court of common pleas of the county or the prothonotary under local rules of court, with the Department of Transportation and with the Department of Community and Economic Development no later than 90 days after the close of the fiscal year. Any secretary of the auditors refusing or willfully neglecting to file the report commits a summary offense. If the failure to file the report within the period specified is due to the failure of any or all of the auditors to prepare the statement upon which the report is to be based, the auditor commits a summary offense.

(c) Service of report.—The secretary of the auditors shall serve, by registered or certified mail, notice to every elected or appointed official against whom a balance or shortage appears in the report required under subsection (b). The notice shall be served prior to the filing of the report and shall indicate the amount of the balance or shortage and a brief description of how the balance or shortage was derived. The notice shall indicate that the balance or shortage is deemed a surcharge under section 1059.3 (relating to surcharge by auditors) and shall apprise the officer served of the right to appeal under section 1059.4 (relating to appeals from audit). Service of notice is complete when the notice is properly addressed, postage prepaid and mailed. Failure to receive the notice required by this subsection shall not constitute grounds for relief from any judgment entered under this chapter.

(d) Presentation.—The annual auditors report and the annual financial statement shall be presented on a uniform form prepared by a committee as provided in Chapter 13 (relating to taxation and finance).

§ 1059.2. Attorney to auditors.

The borough auditors may employ an attorney if deemed advisable by a majority of the auditors. The auditors, with the agreement of council, shall determine the compensation to be paid to the attorney. If the auditors and council cannot agree on the compensation, upon petition of the auditors, the court of common pleas shall establish the compensation for the attorney employed by the auditors. The compensation for the attorney shall be paid out of the borough general fund.

§ 1059.3. Surcharge by auditors.

(a) Surcharges.—

(1) The amount of any balance or shortage or of any expenditure of a kind or made in a manner prohibited or not authorized by statute which causes a financial loss to the borough shall be a surcharge against any officer against whom the balance or shortage shall appear, or who by vote, act or neglect has permitted or approved the expenditure.

(2) The following shall apply:

(i) No elected or appointed official of a borough may be surcharged for any act, error or omission in excess of the actual financial loss sustained by the borough.

(ii) A surcharge shall take into consideration as its basis the results of the act, error or omission and the results had the procedure been strictly in accordance with law.

(iii) Subparagraph (i) shall not apply to cases involving fraud or collusion on the part of officers nor to any penalty enuring to the benefit of or payable to the Commonwealth. Notwithstanding this section, the procedures in the act of May 25, 1945 (P.L.1050, No.394), known as the Local Tax Collection Law, shall apply to balances and shortages in the tax accounts of the tax collector.

(iv) No elected or appointed official of a borough may be surcharged if the official acted in good faith reliance on a written, nonconfidential opinion of the solicitor of the borough or on an opinion of the borough solicitor publicly stated at an open meeting of the borough and recorded in the official minutes of the meeting. This subparagraph shall not apply if a solicitor's opinion has been rendered under duress or if the parties seeking and rendering the solicitor's opinion have colluded to purposefully commit a violation of law. As used in this subparagraph, the term "solicitor" shall include a special counsel appointed by the borough for a specific matter.

(b) Illegal acts.—In any matter involving a financial transaction, any official knowingly and willfully acting contrary to law commits a misdemeanor and, upon conviction, may be sentenced to pay a fine not exceeding $100.

§ 1059.4. Appeals from audit.

It shall be lawful for the borough, or any taxpayer of the borough on its behalf, or any person whose account is settled or audited, to appeal from the settlement or audit, as shown in the auditors report, to the court of common pleas of the county no later than 40 days from the date of the filing of the auditor's report with the clerk of common pleas.

§ 1059.5. Taxpayers appealing to enter bond.

No appeal by a taxpayer or officer may be allowed unless, within the time of taking the appeal, the appellant secures a bond in the sum of $1,000 with sufficient surety to prosecute the appeal and to pay all costs of appeal, in case, if the appellant is a taxpayer, the appellant fails to obtain a final decision more favorable to the borough than that awarded by the auditors or, in case, if the appellant is an accounting officer, the appellant fails to obtain a final decision more favorable to the officer than that awarded by the auditors. Unless the bond is filed as provided in this section, the court of common pleas, upon application, shall set aside the appeal.

§ 1059.6. Procedure on appeals.

(a) Evidence and burden.—In any proceeding upon an appeal from a report of the auditors, the accounts of the office or officers or the person, corporation, association, organization, committee or commission in question may be investigated de novo, and the burden shall be upon each officer, person, corporation, association, organization, committee or commission whose accounts are involved in the appeal of establishing the person's right to credits claimed by the person, but the opposing party in the appeal may use any facts, figures or findings of the report of the auditors as prima facie evidence against any officer or other entity.

(b) Multiple appeals.—If more than one appeal from a report of the auditors has been taken, the court shall, on its own motion or upon motion of any interested party, direct the several appeals to be disposed of in a single proceeding.

§ 1059.7. Findings of fact and law, judgment and appeals.

After the hearing, the court shall file its findings of fact and law and enter judgment accordingly, and the judgment so entered may be enforced by the prevailing party by any appropriate proceeding. Appeals from the court's ruling may be taken in accordance with law.

§ 1059.8. Attorney fees.

(a) Fees awarded.—Upon final determination of an appeal taken under section 1059.4 (relating to appeals from audit) from any report, audit or settlement of the account of any borough officer, attorney fees shall be awarded as follows:

(1) If, in the opinion of the court the final determination is more favorable to the borough officer involved than that awarded by the auditors, the borough shall pay reasonable attorney fees or, under paragraph (3), a portion of reasonable attorney fees incurred by the officer in connection with the surcharge proceeding.

(2) If, in the opinion of the court, the final determination is more favorable to the borough than that awarded by the auditors in the case of an appeal taken by the borough or a taxpayer, the borough officer who is the subject of the surcharge proceeding shall pay reasonable attorney fees or, under paragraph (3), a portion of reasonable attorney fees incurred by the borough, elector or taxpayer in connection with the surcharge proceeding.

(3) If, in the opinion of the court, the final determination is in part more favorable to the borough and in part more favorable to the borough officer involved in the surcharge proceeding than that awarded by the auditors, the court may order:

(i) the borough to pay a portion of reasonable attorney fees incurred by the officer in connection with the surcharge proceeding; or

(ii) the borough officer who is the subject of the surcharge proceeding to pay a portion of reasonable attorney fees incurred by the borough or taxpayer in connection with the surcharge proceeding.

(b) Other accounts.—The attorney fees in case of appeals involving accounts other than those of borough officers shall be allocated in the court's discretion.

§ 1059.9. Balances due to be entered as judgments.

A balance in a report of the auditors against an officer of the borough shall constitute a surcharge against the officer as fully as if expressly stated in the report to be a surcharge. The amount of a balance and of any express surcharge shall, if no appeal is taken or after an appeal has been finally determined in favor of the borough, be entered by the prothonotary as a judgment against the officer. The clerk of the court of common pleas shall certify the amount of every balance or surcharge contained in a report from which no appeal has been taken within the time provided under this chapter to the court of common pleas for entry by the prothonotary as a judgment. Any taxpayer of the borough may enforce the collection of the balance or surcharge for the benefit of the borough, by action or execution, upon filing in the court of common pleas a bond, in the sum of $1,000 with one or more sureties, conditioned to indemnify the borough from all costs of the proceedings undertaken by the taxpayer, subject to all rights of appeal from the report of auditors granted by this part. If a person has been or shall be surcharged for an illegal purchase and no fraud or collusion is shown and the surcharge is paid to the borough, the article purchased shall become the property of the person surcharged.

§ 1059.10. Penalty for failure to comply with law.

(a) Neglect.—An auditor neglecting or refusing to comply with this chapter commits a summary offense.

(b) Financial interest.—An auditor who is financially interested, directly or indirectly, in a borough transaction commits a summary offense.

§ 1059.11. General powers and duties of independent auditor.

(a) Powers and duties.—If an independent auditor is appointed under section 1005(7) (relating to powers of council), the independent auditor shall have the same powers and duties and be subject to the same penalties as the auditors under this chapter. The independent auditor shall annually examine, audit and settle all accounts in which the borough is concerned. The audit shall consist of an examination in accordance with generally accepted auditing standards and shall include tests of the accounting records and other auditing procedures as the independent auditor considers necessary in the circumstances. The independent auditor shall make and publish the annual financial report in the same form and manner and at the same time as required in this part of the auditors of the borough.

(b) Reporting.—The independent auditor shall audit the accounting records of the borough for the fiscal year and shall prepare a report on the examination which shall be subject to appeal in the same manner as reports of the auditors under this chapter. The report shall set forth:

(1) The scope of the examination.

(2) The independent auditor's opinion of the fairness of the presentation of the financial statement of the borough, which shall show a complete statement of the financial condition of the borough, giving in detail the actual indebtedness, the amount of funded debt, the amount of floating debt, the valuation of the taxable property in the borough, the assets of the borough with their character and value and the date of the maturity of the respective forms of funded debt of the borough.

(3) The amount of any balance or shortage or any expenditure of any kind or made in a manner prohibited or not authorized by a statute which came

to the independent auditor's attention during the course of the examination and which, in the independent auditor's opinion, causes a financial loss to the borough as provided in section 1059.3 (relating to surcharge by auditors) shall be a surcharge against an officer against whom the balance or shortage shall appear, subject to appeal, entry as judgment, certification and enforcement as provided in this chapter.

(c) **Hiring attorney.**—The independent auditor may employ an attorney subject to the provisions of section 1059.8 (relating to attorney fees), except that the employment shall be with the consent of council.

(d) **Other applicable laws.**—Sections 1055 (relating to subpoenas, oath, perjury), 1058 (relating to pay of witnesses) and 1059 (relating to auditors to settle accounts where witnesses do not appear) shall apply to proceedings initiated by independent auditors.

(e) **Compensation.**—The compensation of the independent auditor shall be determined by council and paid by borough funds.

SUBCHAPTER D
CONTROLLER

Sec.

§ 1061. Oath and bond of controller.

The borough controller shall, before entering upon the duties of office, take the required oath or affirmation of office under 53 Pa.C.S. § 1141 (relating to form of oaths of office). The controller shall give bond to the borough with a surety company to be approved by the council, in a sum as council may direct by ordinance, conditioned for the faithful discharge of the controller's duties. The amount of the bond shall be sufficient to adequately protect the borough from any illegal or unfaithful action by the controller. The cost of the bond shall be paid by the borough.

§ 1062. Salary of controller.

The council shall fix the annual salary of the controller. Any change in salary, compensation or emoluments of the elected office shall become effective at the beginning of the next term of the controller.

§ 1063. General powers and duties of controller.

(a) **General duties and powers.**—The borough controller shall manage the fiscal affairs of the borough. The controller shall examine, audit and settle all accounts in which the borough is concerned either as debtor or creditor if provision for the settlement is made by law. If no provision or an insufficient provision has been made, the controller shall examine the accounts and report to the council the relevant facts and opinion on the accounts.

(b) Accounts.—In the examination, audit and settlement of accounts, the controller shall have all of the powers and perform all of the duties vested in and imposed on the auditors by this part. A person guilty of swearing or affirming falsely before the controller commits perjury. The controller shall make and file an annual report of the audit and make and publish the annual financial report in the same form and manner and at the same time as required in this part of the auditors of the borough.

(c) Scope.—The controller shall:

(1) have supervision and control of the accounts of all departments, bureaus and officers of the borough authorized to collect, receive or disburse the public money or who are charged with the management or custody of the accounts;

(2) audit their respective accounts and may at any time require from any of them a statement in writing of any money or property of the borough in their possession or under their control, showing the amount of cash on hand and the amount deposited in banks and banking institutions together with the names of the institutions;

(3) have power to examine every account of a borough officer in any bank or banking institution to verify the accuracy of the statement of the borough, department, bureau or officer, and it shall be the duty of every department, bureau or officer, and of every bank and banking institution, its officers and agents, to furnish full information to the controller in relation to the account. No banker or banking institution, its officers or agents shall be subject to prosecution under other laws of this Commonwealth for disclosing information with respect to an account;

(4) immediately upon the discovery of any default, irregularity or delinquency, report the discovery to the council; and

(5) audit and report upon the accounts of an officer upon the death, resignation, removal or expiration of the term of the officer.

§ 1064. (Reserved).

§ 1065. Countersigned warrants.

The controller shall countersign all warrants upon the borough treasurer, with the form of the warrant to be prescribed by council, except that no warrant shall be countersigned unless there is money in the treasury to pay the warrant. If a warrant on the treasurer shall be presented to the controller to be countersigned, the person presenting the warrant shall, if the controller requires, produce evidence that:

(1) The amount expressed in the warrant is due to the person in whose favor it is drawn.

(2) The supplies or service for payment of which the warrant is drawn have been furnished or performed according to law and the terms of the contract.

§ 1066. Prevention of appropriation overdrafts.

The controller shall not permit any appropriation made by the council to be overdrawn. If an appropriation is exhausted, the object of which is not complete, the controller shall immediately report the fact to the council and accompany the report with a statement of the money which have been drawn on the appropriation and the particular purpose for which they are drawn.

§ 1067. Amount of contracts to be charged against appropriations.

(a) General rule.—A contract involving appropriation of money shall designate the item of appropriation on which it is founded, and the estimated amount of the expenditure which shall be charged against the item, and certified by the borough controller on the contract, before it shall take effect as a contract. Payment required by the contract shall be made from the fund appropriated.

Chap. 39 Res. During Mil. Service
Chap. 38 Intergov. Coop.
Chap. 37 3rd Class City Code
Chap. 36 Bor. Code
Chap. 35 2nd Class Twp. Code
Chap. 34 1st Class Twp. Code
Chap. 33 Home Rule Chart. Opt. Plans Law
Chap. 32 Water Serv. Act
Chap. 31 Munic. Auth. Act

(b) Liability for excess.—If the controller certifies a contract in excess of the appropriation made, the borough shall not be liable for the excess, but the controller and the controller's sureties shall be liable for the same, which may be recovered in an action at law by the aggrieved contracting party.

(c) Certification by controller.—The controller shall certify contracts for the payment of which sufficient appropriations have been made.

§ 1068. Controller's recommendations on borough finances.

The borough controller shall, as often as the controller may deem expedient or the council shall direct, suggest plans to the council for the management and improvement of the borough finances.

§ 1069. Books to be kept by controller.

The borough controller shall keep a regular set of books which shall be opened and keep as many accounts, under appropriate titles, as may be necessary to show separately and distinctly all the estates and property, real and personal, vested in the borough, all trusts in the care of the borough, all debts due and owing the borough, all receipts and expenditures of the various departments of the borough government and all appropriations made by council and the sums under the same, respectively.

§ 1070. Appeals from controller's report.

Appeals may be taken from the settlement and audit of the controller, as shown in the controller's report to the court of common pleas of the county, by the same persons in the same manner within the same time subject to the same conditions and procedure and with like effect in every respect as provided in this part in the cases of appeals from the settlement and audit of the auditors as shown in their report.

§ 1071. Acceptance by ordinance.

(a) General rule.—This subchapter shall not become operative or effective in any borough not having a controller until the borough shall, by ordinance, accept this chapter. If a borough accepts this subchapter, the court of common pleas, upon petition of council, shall appoint a controller to hold office until the first Monday of January following the next municipal election at which a controller shall be elected under this part.

(b) Continuation of borough auditors.—In all boroughs accepting this subchapter, the borough auditors then in office or the appointed auditor serving as borough auditor shall continue to hold their offices until the first day of January following the election of a borough controller after which date the office of borough auditor shall be abolished.

(c) Discontinuation.—A borough may discontinue the office of controller and either reestablish the office of elected auditors or the position of appointed auditor by repealing the ordinance under which the office of controller was created. The controller in office at the time of the repeal shall continue in office until the end of the controller's term.

SUBCHAPTER E
(Reserved)

SUBCHAPTER F
TAX COLLECTOR

---

§ 1086. Powers and duties of tax collector.

(a) General rule.—Except as otherwise provided in subsection (b), the tax collector shall be the collector of all State, county, borough, school, institution district and other taxes levied within the borough by the authorities empowered to levy taxes.

(b) Exception.—

(1) No tax collector may collect any tax levied and imposed under the act of December 31, 1965 (P.L.1257, No.511), known as The Local Tax Enabling Act, unless the ordinance imposing the tax provides that the tax collector shall be the collector of the tax.

(2) No ordinance, however, may authorize the collection of income taxes in a manner other than that provided in Chapter 5 of The Local Tax Enabling Act.

(c) Other laws.—The tax collector shall, in addition to the powers, authority, duties and responsibilities provided for by this part, have all the powers, perform all the duties and be subject to all the obligations and responsibilities for the collection of taxes as are now vested in, conferred upon or imposed upon tax collectors by law.

CHAPTER 10A
MAYOR

---

§ 10A01. Eligibility of mayor.

No mayor may hold any other borough office or appointment during the term for which the mayor is elected, except as is permitted under section 1104 (relating to appointments and incompatible offices). The mayor shall be eligible to succeed himself. The mayor shall not be a member of council, nor shall the mayor preside over or vote at any meeting of council, except as provided in section 1003 (relating to when the mayor may preside over council and vote, attendance of mayor at council meetings and breaking tie votes).

§ 10A02. Incompatible offices.

No member of Congress or any person holding any office or appointment of profit or trust under the Federal Government or any person holding the office of magisterial district judge may at the same time be capable of holding the office of mayor.

Table of Contents
Part I Ch. 1–3 Ethics, Records, Open Meetings
Part II Ch. 4–10 Taxation
Part III Ch. 11–18 Torts, Contracts & Civil Rules
Part IV Ch. 19–24 Zoning & Planning
Part V Ch. 25–30 Construction and Emergency Codes
Part VI Ch. 31–39 Municipal Codes
Index

§ 10A03. Oath of mayor.

The mayor, before exercising the duties of office, shall take and subscribe an oath or affirmation of office under 53 Pa.C.S. § 1141 (relating to form of oaths of office). The oath or affirmation may be taken before a judge or magisterial district judge of the county or a notary public and shall be filed with the borough secretary and be preserved among the records of the borough for a period of six years.

§ 10A04. Salary of mayor.

(a) General rule.—The salary of the mayor shall be established by ordinance and shall not exceed the following:

(1) In a borough with a population of less than 5,000, a maximum of $4,190 per year.

(2) In a borough with a population of 5,000 or more but less than 10,000, a maximum of $8,385 per year.

(3) In a borough with a population of 10,000 or more but less than 15,000, a maximum of $12,575 per year.

(4) In a borough with a population in excess of 15,000, a maximum of $840 per year per 1,000 residents or fraction of 1,000, the population to be determined by the latest official census figures.

(a.1) Treatment of benefits.—Benefits provided to the mayor under section 1202(26) (relating to specific powers) shall not be considered pay, salary or compensation, but payment for all or a part of the premiums or charges for the benefits shall be in accordance with section 1202(26).

(b) Change in salary.—A change in salary, compensation or emoluments of the elected office shall become effective at the beginning of the next term of the mayor.

§ 10A05. Salaried mayor not to receive certain fees.

(a) General rule.—Except as provided in subsection (b), any salary paid under an ordinance shall be in lieu of all costs and fees allowed by a mayor. Costs and fees shall be collected by the mayor and deposited into the borough treasury.

(b) Marriage ceremony fees.—

(1) Nothing in this part shall be construed to prevent a mayor from receiving a monetary fee for the performance of a marriage ceremony in this Commonwealth, if the fee does not exceed $150 for each ceremony performed.

(2) Prior to performing these ceremonies, the mayor shall notify council in writing of the mayor's intention to perform marriage ceremonies.

(3) The notification to council shall remain in effect for the term of the mayor or until the notification is rescinded by the mayor.

(4) The mayor shall maintain accurate accounts of the fees received relating to the performance of marriage ceremonies and provide council each quarter with a report of money received for that period. The quarterly report shall include the amount of money received and the names of persons from whom money was received, along with the date and the location of the performed ceremony, and the quarterly report shall be considered a public record.

(5) The receipt of a fee under this subsection shall not be considered a violation of 65 Pa.C.S. Ch. 11 (relating to ethics standards and financial disclosure) and shall not be considered compensation under this part.

§ 10A06. General powers of mayor.

(a) Oaths and affirmations.—The mayor may administer oaths and affirmations in matters pertaining to borough affairs.

(b) Emergencies.—

(1) In addition to the power granted to mayors by 35 Pa.C.S. Pt. V (relating to emergency management services) and in order to enable the mayor to

effectually preserve the public peace within the borough, the mayor shall have the power to prevent and suppress mobs, riots and unlawful and tumultuous assemblies.

(2) In the event that a state of emergency exists, a mayor shall have the authority to request aid and assistance from law enforcement officers and agencies from a neighboring municipality.

(3) In response to a request of a mayor made in accordance with this subsection, a municipal police officer shall, within the borough from which the request was made, have the power and authority to enforce the laws of this Commonwealth or otherwise perform the functions of that office as if enforcing those laws or performing those functions within the territorial limits of the officer's primary jurisdiction, subject to the limitations and conditions set forth in 42 Pa.C.S. § 8953(b), (c), (d) and (e) (relating to Statewide municipal police jurisdiction).

(4) If the mayor considers that a state of emergency exists, the mayor may issue a proclamation, which shall be in writing and posted in one or more conspicuous places and the contents of which shall be made available to all news media, declaring a state of emergency for a period not to exceed seven days unless sooner rescinded, modified or ratified or extended by resolution of council.

(5) The mayor may prohibit in the proclamation for all or part of the borough:

(i) Any person being on the public streets or in the public parks or at any other public place during the hours declared by the mayor to be a period of curfew.

(ii) The entry or departure of persons into or from any restricted area.

(iii) The sale, purchase or dispensing of any commodities or goods as designated by the mayor.

(iv) The transportation, possession or use of gasoline, kerosene or other combustible, flammable or explosive liquids or materials except in connection with the normal operation of motor vehicles, normal home use or legitimate commercial use.

(v) Any other activities as the mayor reasonably believes should be prohibited to help preserve life, health, property or the public peace.

(6) The proclamation shall describe the specific restricted area with particularity and shall specify the hours when restrictions are to be in effect.

(7) A person violating the proclamation of emergency commits a summary offense and shall, upon conviction, be sentenced to pay a fine not to exceed $300 and costs or to a term of imprisonment not to exceed 30 days.

§ 10A07. Duties of mayor.

The mayor shall have the following duties:

(1) To preserve order in the borough, to enforce the ordinances and regulations, to remove nuisances, to exact a faithful performance of the duties of the officers appointed and to perform any other duties as shall be vested in the mayor's office by law or ordinance.

(2) Except as provided in section 1006(4) (relating to duties of council), to sign papers, contracts, obligations and documents as may be required by law.

(3) To collect any costs and fees received and to pay the money into the treasury, except as provided in section 10A05(b) (relating to salaried mayor not to receive certain fees), to report to the council from time to time on the state of the borough and to make recommendations to the council on matters of borough concern. The borough shall furnish the mayor with the necessary dockets, books, forms and files as are necessary for the conduct of the mayor's

Chap. 39 Res. During Mil. Service
Chap. 38 Intergov. Coop.
Chap. 37 3rd Class City Code
Chap. 36 Bor. Code
Chap. 35 2nd Class Twp. Code
Chap. 34 1st Class Twp. Code
Chap. 33 Home Rule Chart. Opt. Plans Law
Chap. 32 Water Serv. Act
Chap. 31 Munic. Auth. Act

office and which shall be and remain the property of the borough and be surrendered to the mayor's successor in office.

§ 10A08. President or vice president of council to act as mayor.

(a) General rule.—If the mayor is absent or incapacitated or there is a vacancy in the office, the duties of the office shall be discharged by the president of council or, in the absence or incapacity of the president of council or if there is a vacancy in the office, by the vice president of council.

(b) Salary.—While discharging the duties of mayor, the president or vice president of council shall be entitled to the same salary as the mayor would receive and, during the time the salary is paid to the president or vice president of council as acting mayor, the mayor shall not be paid compensation.

(c) Veto and voting power.—The president or vice president of council while acting as mayor shall have power to veto a proposed ordinance or the annual tax resolution under section 1302(a) (relating to tax levy) or to break a tie but shall not have power to vote as a member of council.

CHAPTER 11

POWERS, DUTIES AND RIGHTS OF APPOINTED OFFICERS AND EMPLOYEES

Subchapter

SUBCHAPTER A

GENERAL PROVISIONS

Sec.

---

§ 1101. Compensation, hours and days of work and outside employment.

Appointed officers and employees of the borough shall receive compensation for their services as the council shall prescribe. Council may also establish the hours and days of work and may restrict the outside employment of borough employees or any class or category of employment.

§ 1102. Accounts.

All officers and employees appointed by a council shall, if directed, render their accounts to the council for settlement.

§ 1103. Bonds.

If an appointed officer or employee of a borough is required by law or action of council to give bond for the faithful performance of the officer's or employee's duties, the borough may pay the premium on the bond. All bonds required to be given by borough officials or employees shall be with a surety company authorized by law to act as surety. The borough shall pay a proportionate share of the cost of the bond of an appointed tax collector in the same ratio as provided in section 804 (relating to term and bonds) for elected tax collectors.

§ 1104. Appointments and incompatible offices.

(a) General rule.—Unless there is incompatibility in fact, an elective or appointive officer of the borough shall be eligible to serve on any board, commission, bureau or other agency created by or for the borough or any borough office created or authorized by statute and may accept appointments under the statute.

(b) Prohibition.—

(1) Except as set forth in paragraph (2), no elected borough official of a borough with a population of 3,000 or more may serve as an employee of that borough.

(2) Paragraph (1) shall not apply to a borough official serving as an employee of that borough prior to the certification of the 2010 official census or a subsequent latest official census which indicates an increase in the population of that borough to 3,000 or more.

(c) Multiple offices.—If there is no incompatibility in fact and subject to subsection (a) as to compensation, appointees of council may hold two or more appointive borough offices, but no mayor or member of council may serve as borough manager, secretary or treasurer.

(d) Magisterial district judges.—No person holding the office of magisterial district judge may at the same time hold any elected or appointed borough office.

(e) Secretary and treasurer.—The offices of secretary and treasurer may be held by the same person if authorized by ordinance.

(f) Police officers and firefighters.—

(1) No police officer or firefighter may hold an elective office of the borough that employs the police officer or firefighter.

(2) No police officer or firefighter who is employed by a regional department, council of government or other cooperative venture may hold an elective office of any municipality that participates in the regional department, council of government or other cooperative venture.

(3) No police officer or firefighter may hold an elective office of the borough in which the police officer or firefighter resides if the department employing the police officer or firefighter is providing police or fire protection service to that borough by contract.

(g) Majority vote required.—All appointments to be made by the council shall be made by a majority of the members of council unless a different vote is required by statute.

(h) Construction.—Nothing contained in this section shall be construed to affect the eligibility of a borough official to hold any other public office or receive compensation.

Chap. 39 Res. During Mil. Service
Chap. 38 Intergov. Coop.
Chap. 37 3rd Class City Code
Chap. 36 Bor. Code
Chap. 35 2nd Class Twp. Code
Chap. 34 1st Class Twp. Code
Chap. 33 Home Rule Chart. Opt. Plans Law
Chap. 32 Water Serv. Act
Chap. 31 Munic. Auth. Act

§ 1105. Compensation of certain employees.

(a) **General rule.**—A borough may provide, by ordinance, to appointees and employees of not less than ten years of satisfactory service and who are not less than 60 years of age upon termination of active employment with the borough, a proportion of the compensation last paid to them but not in excess of 50% of the compensation, including benefits received under the Social Security Act (49 Stat. 620, 42 U.S.C. § 301 et seq.), if any, as fixed in the ordinance or amendment of the ordinance.

(b) **Postretirement compensation.**—Any arrangement to provide postretirement compensation to retired appointees and employees under this section shall be a pension plan within the meaning of that term under the act of December 18, 1984 (P.L.1005, No.205), known as the Municipal Pension Plan Funding Standard and Recovery Act, and the borough establishing such plan shall provide funding of the pension plan in an amount sufficient to meet the minimum obligation of the municipality with respect to the pension plan under that act.

(c) **Funding.**—The expenditures authorized in this section shall be paid out of the general tax levy for the current expenditures of the year and not by any special tax.

(d) **Construction.**—Nothing in this section shall be construed to preclude an appointee or employee of the borough from joining in any pension system or municipal retirement system that the borough may adopt.

§ 1105.1. Retirement benefits of employees transferred to authorities.

(a) **Required membership.**—The following employees of municipal authorities shall be members of the borough retirement system upon a written election as provided in this section:

(1) An employee of a wastewater authority created by a borough and one or more townships under 53 Pa.C.S. Ch. 56 (relating to municipal authorities) that commenced operations after December 1, 2001, who satisfies the requirements of subsection (b), has past service credits under the borough retirement plan and has filed a written election to be a member of the borough retirement system with council and the wastewater authority prior to September 14, 2005.

(2) An employee of a municipal authority created by a borough under 53 Pa.C.S. Ch. 56 that commenced operations after October 4, 2010, who satisfies the requirements of subsection (b), has past service credits under the borough retirement plan and files a written election with the council and the authority to be a member of the borough retirement system within one year of July 16, 2012.

(b) **Eligibility criteria.**—

(1) In order to qualify for the option under subsection (a), the employee must satisfy both of the following requirements:

(i) Immediately prior to the date of transfer of employment to the authority, be an employee of the borough that, either alone or together with one or more municipalities, established the authority.

(ii) Be an active member of the borough's retirement system on the date that the employee's employment was transferred to the authority.

(2) For an employee who files an election under subsection (a), the affected authority shall:

(i) Deduct from the employee's salary an amount equal to the employee contribution that would have been deducted had the employee continued to be a borough employee and shall pay the deducted amount to the borough's retirement fund.

(ii) Pay to the borough's retirement fund an employer contribution equal to the employer normal cost plus anticipated administrative expenses and amortization payments less general municipal pension system State aid expressed as a percentage of the system's total payroll as calculated by the borough under the act of December 18, 1984 (P.L.1005, No.205), known as the Municipal Pension Plan Funding Standard and Recovery Act, and applied to the payroll of the employee.

(c) **State aid calculation.**—All employees who elect to be members of the borough retirement system under this section shall be treated as borough employees in determining the borough's annual allocation of general municipal pension system State aid under section 402(e) of the Municipal Pension Plan Funding Standard and Recovery Act, and the annual allocation of general municipal pension system State aid under section 402(e) of the Municipal Pension Plan Funding Standard and Recovery Act shall be payable to the borough.

SUBCHAPTER B
TREASURER

§ 1106. Bond and duties.

(a) **General rule.**—The borough treasurer shall, before entering upon the duties of office, give bond in an amount determined by council, conditioned for the faithful performance of the treasurer's duties.

(b) **Specific duties.**—The treasurer shall:

(1) Receive all money due the borough and deposit the money promptly in a designated depository in the name of the borough.

(2) Keep distinct and accurate accounts of all sums received from taxes and other sources, which accounts shall be open to the inspection of council and any citizen of this Commonwealth.

(3)(i) Pay out all money only on direction by the council, upon an order signed by the president of council and the borough secretary and also by the borough controller, if any. The order shall not be executed unless there is money in the treasury available.

(ii) Nothing in this part shall be construed to preclude the use of electronic signatures and transactions to the extent authorized by the act of December 16, 1999 (P.L.971, No.69), known as the Electronic Transactions Act, or any other law.

(4) Annually submit the accounts to the elected auditors, independent auditor or controller for settlement.

(5) Preserve the account books, papers, documents and other records of the office and turn them over to the successor in office.

(c) **Payment of all other money.**—All money received by any officer or other person for the use of the borough shall be paid to the borough treasurer.

§ 1107. Assistant treasurer.

A council may, by resolution, appoint an assistant treasurer who may not be a member of the council. Council may appoint the assistant treasurer as the assistant secretary if the assistant treasurer is not a member of council. The assistant treasurer shall assist the treasurer in the performance of the treasurer's duties

Chap. 39 Res. During Mil. Service
Chap. 38 Intergov. Coop.
Chap. 37 3rd Class City Code
Chap. 36 Bor. Code
Chap. 35 2nd Class Twp. Code
Chap. 34 1st Class Twp. Code
Chap. 33 Home Rule Chart. Opt. Plans Law
Chap. 32 Water Serv. Act
Chap. 31 Munic. Auth. Act

and, in case of absence or disability of the treasurer, shall perform the duties and may exercise the powers of the treasurer.

SUBCHAPTER C
SECRETARY

---

§ 1111. Duties.

(a) **Attendance at meetings and maintenance of minutes.**—The secretary shall attend all meetings of the council and shall maintain full minutes of its proceedings.

(b) **Other duties.**—The secretary shall:

(1) Record or transcribe the bylaws, rules, regulations, resolutions and ordinances of the borough in accordance with section 1009 (relating to typewritten, printed, photocopied, microfilmed and electronically or digitally stored records valid and recording or transcribing records).

(2) Preserve the records and documents of the borough, have custody of the corporate seal and deliver to the secretary's successor the seal and all books, papers and other records and things belonging to the borough.

(3) Certify copies of any book, paper, record, bylaw, rule, regulation, resolution, ordinance or proceeding of the borough under the seal of the borough. The copies, if certified, shall be admissible in evidence in any court of this Commonwealth.

(4) Attest the execution of all instruments, record all ordinances and attest the same by the secretary's signature and file of record proof of service of all notices required by law. The secretary's certificate shall be good evidence of notice.

(5) Inform council and the public as required by 65 Pa.C.S. Ch. 7 (relating to open meetings) of all borough meetings, including special meetings of council.

(c) **Necessary documents.**—The borough shall furnish the secretary with the necessary dockets, books, forms and files as are necessary for the conduct of the office, which documents shall be and remain the property of the borough.

§ 1112. Assistant secretary.

A council may, by resolution, appoint an assistant secretary. The assistant secretary shall assist the secretary in the performance of the secretary's duties and, in case of absence or disability of the secretary, perform the duties and may exercise the powers of the secretary. The assistant secretary may be appointed from the membership of the council but shall not be any other officer of the council. Council may appoint the assistant secretary as the assistant treasurer if the assistant secretary is not a member of council.

§ 1113. Records open to inspection.

The fiscal records and documents and the minute book and other records and documents of every borough shall be open in accordance with the act of February 14, 2008 (P.L.6, No.3), known as the Right-to-Know Law.

SUBCHAPTER D
SOLICITOR

---

§ 1116. Solicitor to have control of legal matters.

The legal matters of the borough shall be under the control of the borough solicitor. No department or officer of the borough, except as otherwise provided by law, shall employ an additional counsel without the assent or ratification of the council. The borough solicitor must be licensed to practice law in this Commonwealth and may be one person or a law firm, partnership, association or professional corporation. The borough solicitor serves at the pleasure of council. In the absence of the solicitor, the law firm of which the solicitor is a member or associate may perform any of the duties or functions of the solicitor.

§ 1117. Duties of solicitor and outside counsel.

(a) **General rule.**—The borough solicitor shall:

(1) Prepare or approve, if directed or requested to do so by council or the mayor, any bonds, obligations, contracts, leases, conveyances, ordinances and assurances to which the borough or any department of the borough may be a party.

(2) Commence and prosecute all actions brought by the borough for or on account of any of the estates, rights, trusts, privileges, claims or demands of the borough, as well as defend the borough or any borough officer against all actions or suits brought against the borough or borough officer in which any of the estates, rights, privileges, trusts, ordinances or accounts of the borough may be brought in question before any court in this Commonwealth.

(3) Furnish the council or committees of the council, the mayor or the head of a department, upon request, with an opinion in writing upon any question of law which may be submitted by any of them in their official capacities.

(4) Perform every other professional act incident to the office which the borough solicitor may be authorized or required to do by the council or the mayor.

(b) **Outside counsel.**—In the case of a legal dispute between the mayor and council or in any other case in which representation of the mayor and council by the borough solicitor would create a conflict of interest for the borough solicitor, the mayor may employ outside counsel at borough expense, not to exceed $4,000 in any 12-month period, to perform necessary legal services.

§ 1118. Assistant solicitor.

A council may, by resolution, appoint an assistant solicitor to assist the solicitor in the performance of the solicitor's duties and, in the absence or disability of the solicitor, to perform the duties and exercise the powers of the solicitor.

SUBCHAPTER E
POLICE

§ 1121. Council's powers concerning police.

(a) Establishment of police department.—Council may, by ordinance, establish a police department. If council establishes a police department, the following shall apply:

(1) Council may appoint police officers, subject to Subchapter J (relating to civil service for police and fire apparatus operators).

(2) Council may remove, suspend or reduce in rank any police officer:

(i) in accordance with the act of June 15, 1951 (P.L.586, No.144), entitled "An act regulating the suspension, removal, furloughing and reinstatement of police officers in boroughs and townships of the first class having police forces of less than three members, and in townships of the second class"; or

(ii) subject to Subchapter J.

(3) Council shall designate the ranks in the police department and the duties of each rank and may designate one of the police officers as chief of police.

(4) Council may assign any member of the police department to attend training classes offered by the Federal or State Government and may pay the police officer's expenses while attending the school.

(5) Council shall determine the total weekly hours of employment that shall apply to the police officers.

(b) Powers of borough police officers.—A borough police officer shall have those powers and abilities as are granted to police officers under the laws of this Commonwealth, the rules of the Supreme Court or the ordinances of the borough for which a fine or penalty is imposed unless otherwise excepted in this part.

(c) Ratification.—In any case in which a borough has previously appointed police officers or established a police department by action of council but not under an ordinance regularly enacted, the action shall be deemed to have been a valid exercise of the legislative power of the borough, and all police officers appointed shall occupy the same status and shall have the same rights and privileges as in the case of police officers appointed under authority of an ordinance.

(d) Political participation.—No police officer may participate in any political or election campaign while on duty or in uniform or while using borough property otherwise than to exercise the officer's right of suffrage.

§ 1122. Police serving under cooperative agreement or contract.

(a) General rule.—If a borough enters into a cooperative agreement or contract with any municipal corporation, regional police force or other governmental entity created by two or more municipal corporations under 53 Pa.C.S. Ch. 23 Subch. A (relating to intergovernmental cooperation) for the furnishing or receiving of police protection as authorized by section 1202(24) (relating to specific powers), the police force of the municipal corporation, regional police force or other governmental entity furnishing the police protection shall be appointed and accepted as the police force of the borough receiving the police service by resolution of the council.

(b) Employment status.—Police officers of the police force of a municipal corporation, regional police force or other government entity so appointed shall, insofar as civil service and pensions are concerned, be deemed to be appointees and employees only of the municipal corporation, regional police force or other government entity furnishing their service and making the original appointment.

§ 1123. Police badge.

Borough police officers shall wear a shield or badge with the word "Police" when on duty.

§ 1123.1. Mayor's powers concerning police.

(a) General rule.—The mayor shall have full charge and control of the chief of police and the police force.

(b) Direction.—The mayor shall direct the time during which, the place where and the manner in which the chief of police and the police force perform the duties of their rank.

(c) Delegation of duties.—The mayor may delegate to the chief of police or other officer supervision over and instruction to subordinate officers in the manner of performing their duties.

(d) Appointment of special police.—The mayor may appoint special police during an emergency in which the safety and welfare of the borough and the public is endangered.

(e) Auxiliary police.—The mayor may activate auxiliary police in accordance with general law and, notwithstanding any other provision of law, may activate auxiliary police for purposes of crowd and traffic control for limited periods during events if, in the mayor's discretion, public safety is promoted by the activation of the auxiliary police.

§ 1124. Suspension by mayor.

(a) General rule.—In addition to the powers of council to suspend police officers, the mayor may, for cause and without pay, suspend any police officers until the succeeding regular meeting of the council at which time or later the council may, subject to Subchapter J (relating to civil service for police and fire apparatus operators), if they are in effect at the time, suspend, discharge, reduce in rank or reinstate with pay the police officers.

(b) Reinstatement.—

(1) A police officer suspended by the mayor may not be reinstated by council at a date earlier than ten working days from the date fixed by the mayor for the suspension to commence.

(2) In any case in which the council has reinstated a police officer after having been suspended by the mayor, the mayor shall not suspend the police officer for reasons:

(i) arising from the same act for which the first suspension was made; or

(ii) that the council, in reinstating the police officer, determined not to be grounds for suspension.

§ 1125. Compensation.

Borough police and special police appointed by the mayor shall receive compensation as fixed by the council.

§ 1126. (Reserved).

§ 1127. School crossing guards.

(a) Appointment.—

(1) Upon request by the board of school directors of the school district in which a borough is wholly or partially located, the council may appoint school crossing guards who shall have the duty of controlling and directing traffic and pedestrians at or near schools and who shall be in suitable and distinctive uniform.

(2) While on duty, school crossing guards shall be under and subject to the direction of the mayor, shall serve at the pleasure of the council, except as noted in subsection (b), shall not be subject to Subchapter J (relating to civil service for police and fire apparatus operators) and shall not be entitled to participate in any borough pension plan or plans.

(3)(i) The compensation of the school crossing guards, if any, shall be fixed by the council and shall be jointly paid by the council and the board of school directors, in a ratio to be determined by the council and board of school directors.

(ii) If the council and board of school directors are unable to determine the ratio of compensation of the school crossing guards to be paid by the council and the board, each shall pay one-half of the compensation of the crossing guards.

(4) Notwithstanding any other provision of law, auxiliary police officers, appointed as prescribed by general law, may be designated to serve as crossing guards.

(b) Ordinance.—

(1) The council may enact an ordinance allowing a board of school directors to assume hiring and oversight of school crossing guards. Before the council may enact the ordinance, the board of directors of the school district must adopt a resolution requesting the authority to assume the hiring and oversight of school crossing guards.

(2) The ordinance enacted by the council shall outline how the police department will provide any necessary training and assistance of the school crossing guards while on duty.

(3) School crossing guards shall be authorized in the management of traffic and pedestrians in and around areas identified by the police department and the school district superintendent or the superintendent's designees.

(4) School crossing guards shall not:

(i) Be subject to the civil service provisions of this part.

(ii) Be considered part of the bargaining unit of the school district.

(iii) Be considered:

(A) An employee as defined under section 1101-A of the act of March 10, 1949 (P.L.30, No.14), known as the Public School Code of 1949.

(B) A school employee as defined under 24 Pa.C.S. § 8102 (relating to definitions).

(C) An employee under any plan.

(5) After the ordinance is enacted by the council, the school district shall assume the cost of compensation, including fixing compensation, if any, of the school crossing guards.

(6) Notwithstanding any other provision of law, auxiliary police officers, appointed as prescribed by general law, may be hired by the school district to serve as school crossing guards.

(7) The board of school directors shall notify the council of the individuals hired to serve as school crossing guards and request the necessary training or assistance be provided as outlined by the ordinance.

SUBCHAPTER F
POLICE PENSION FUND IN BOROUGHS HAVING POLICE FORCE OF LESS THAN THREE MEMBERS

§ 1131. Police pension fund.

(a) Authorization to establish.—If a police force of less than three full-time members is being maintained, the borough may, unless there is a private organization or association constituting and managing an existing pension fund for the members of the police force in the borough, by ordinance, establish a police pension fund into which each member of the police force shall pay an equal and proportionate monthly charge to be withheld from the pay of the member.

(b) Investment and insurance instruments as alternative.—In lieu of establishing a pension fund in accordance with subsection (a), the borough may, by ordinance, provide investment or insurance instruments for the purpose of the payment of pensions or annuities to the members of the police force who receive honorable discharge by reason of age or disability and to the families of police officers injured or killed in service.

(c) Administration.—

(1) All pension funds or investment or insurance instruments established under this section shall be under the direction of the council, or a committee as it may designate, and shall be applied under regulations as the council may, by ordinance, prescribe for the benefit of the members of the police force who receive honorable discharge by reason of age or disability and the families of police officers injured or killed in service.

(2) Council shall appoint by resolution a chief administrative officer who shall have the primary responsibility for the execution of the administrative affairs of the pension plan, subject to the direction of council.

(3) Any allowances made to individuals who retire by reason of disability or age shall be in conformity with a uniform scale.

(d) Eligibility.—The ordinance establishing the police pension fund shall prescribe a minimum period of total service, a minimum age or both after which members of the force may be eligible for retirement from active duty.

(e) Obligation of payments.—Payments made on account of police pensions shall not be a charge on any fund in the treasury of the borough or under its control except the police pension fund.

(f) Funding.—A borough establishing a police pension fund by ordinance under this section shall provide from any available borough revenue source funding of the police pension fund in an amount sufficient to meet the minimum obligation of the borough with respect to the police pension fund under the act of December 18, 1984 (P.L.1005, No.205), known as the Municipal Pension Plan Funding Standard and Recovery Act.

(g) Management.—

(1) A borough may take, by gift, grant, devise or bequest, any money or property, real, personal or mixed, in trust for the benefit of the police pension fund.

(2) The care, management, investment and disposal of the trust funds or property shall be vested in the officers as the borough shall direct by ordinance and shall be governed by the officers, subject to any directions not inconsistent with the ordinance as the donors of the funds and property may prescribe.

(h) Right to equal and proportionate share.—No person participating in the police pension fund and becoming entitled to receive a benefit from the fund may be deprived of the person's right to an equal and proportionate share of the fund upon the basis upon which the person first became entitled to the benefit.

(i) Applicable law.—The act of May 29, 1956 (1955 P.L.1804, No.600), referred to as the Municipal Police Pension Law, or the act of February 1, 1974 (P.L.34, No.15), known as the Pennsylvania Municipal Retirement Law, shall govern any borough police pension fund not established under the provisions of this section.

§ 1132. Private police pension funds and optional transfers.

(a) General rule.—If there is a private organization or association constituting and managing an existing pension fund for the members of the police force in any borough, the borough shall establish a police pension for the purpose of paying pensions to the members of its police force if the membership of the organization or association by a two-thirds vote elects to transfer its funds with all its assets and liabilities into a borough pension fund as required to be established by this part.

(b) Assumption of liability.—The transfer in subsection (a) may be made by the transfer of securities. After the transfer, the borough police pension fund shall assume the liability of continuing the payment of pensions to members of the police force retired prior to the transfer, in accordance with the laws and regulations under which the members were retired.

SUBCHAPTER G

MANAGER

Sec.

§ 1141. Borough manager created by ordinance and election.

(a) General rule.—The council of a borough may, at its discretion at any time, create by ordinance the office of borough manager and may, in like manner, abolish the office. While the office exists, the council shall, from time to time, and if there is a vacancy, elect, by a vote of a majority of all the members, one individual, partnership, limited partnership, association or professional corporation as the borough manager.

(b) Subject to agreement.—The borough manager shall serve at the pleasure of council, subject to contractual rights that may arise under an employment agreement or professional services agreement that may be entered in accordance with section 1142 (relating to powers and duties).

§ 1142. Powers and duties.

(a) General rule.—The powers and duties of the borough manager shall be regulated by ordinance.

(b) Employment or professional services agreement.—

(1) Council may enter into an employment or professional services agreement with the borough manager that specifies the terms and conditions of employment.

(2) The employment or professional services agreement may remain in effect for a specified period terminating no later than two years after the effective date of the agreement or the date of the organizational meeting of council following the next municipal election, whichever occurs first.

(3) An employment or professional services agreement entered into under this section may specify conditions under which a borough manager who is an individual will be entitled to severance compensation or, in the case of a partnership, a limited partnership, an association or a professional corporation, payments for the termination of appointment. In no event may the employment or professional services agreement guarantee retention or employment through the term of the agreement or confer upon the borough manager any legal remedy based on specific performance.

(4) An employment or professional services agreement with a borough manager executed on or after a municipal election but before the first meeting in January the year after the municipal election shall be void.

(5) The council may delegate to the borough manager, by ordinance and subject to recall, any of the nonlegislative and nonjudicial powers and duties of the council, the planning commission and the shade tree commission. With approval of council, the mayor may delegate to the borough manager any of the mayor's nonlegislative and nonjudicial powers and duties.

(c) **Status as public official.**—The borough manager, if an individual, and, for a partnership, limited partnership, association or professional corporation appointed as the borough manager, each officer and employee directly providing services as required or authorized by the agreement shall be considered a public official for purposes of the provisions of 65 Pa.C.S. § 1103 (relating to restricted activities).

§ 1143. Other offices not incompatible.

(a) **General rule.**—The offices of borough manager, street commissioner, secretary, treasurer and chief of police shall not be incompatible, and any two or more or all of the offices may be held by one person. Neither the mayor nor any member of the council shall be eligible to hold the office of borough manager.

(b) **Applicability.**—In the case of a partnership, limited partnership, association or professional corporation appointed as the borough manager, the restriction under subsection (a) shall apply to each officer and employee who directly provides services as required or authorized by the agreement.

SUBCHAPTER H

PLANNING COMMISSION

(Reserved)

SUBCHAPTER I

MINE AND QUARRY INSPECTION AND SURFACE SUPPORT

(Reserved)

SUBCHAPTER J
CIVIL SERVICE FOR POLICE AND FIRE APPARATUS OPERATORS

---

§ 1170. Definitions.

The following words and phrases when used in in this subchapter shall have the meanings given to them in this section unless the context clearly indicates otherwise:

"Fire apparatus operator." A person who operates fire apparatus and devotes his normal working hours to operating any piece of fire apparatus or other services connected with fire protection work and who is paid a stated salary or compensation for the work by the borough.

"Police force." A police force organized and operating as prescribed by law, the members of which devote their normal working hours to police duty or duty in connection with the bureau, agencies and services connected with police protection work and who are paid a stated salary or compensation for the work by the borough. As used in this subchapter, the term shall not include any of the following:

(1) Special police appointed by the mayor to act in emergencies.

(2) A person appointed solely for parking meter enforcement duties.

(3) Special school police.

(4) Extra police serving from time to time or on an hourly or daily basis.

(5) An auxiliary policeman appointed under the act of January 14, 1952 (1951 P.L.2016, No.561), entitled "An act providing for supplementing the police forces of cities, boroughs, towns and townships, for the appointment, powers and control of auxiliary police therein, and for the transfer during

disasters and emergencies of such auxiliary police, members of the regular police forces, and police equipment thereof."

§ 1171. Appointments of police and fire apparatus operators.

(a) Nonapplicability of subchapter.—This subchapter shall not apply to:

(1) a borough that has a police force of less than three members;

(2) a borough that has a police force of three or more members if those members in excess of two are appointed on a temporary basis through a federally funded program;

(3) a volunteer fire department or company that employs its own operators; or

(4) a borough that has less than three salaried fire apparatus operators.

(b) Compensation.—This subchapter is subject to the power of council to determine compensation.

(c) Appointments and promotions.—An appointment to and promotion in the police force or as fire apparatus operator paid directly by a borough and in the borough shall be made only according to qualifications and fitness, to be ascertained by examinations which shall be competitive as provided in this part.

(d) Suspension, removal and reduction in rank.—No person shall be suspended, removed or reduced in rank as a paid employee in any police force or as a paid fire apparatus operator of a borough, except in accordance with this subchapter.

(e) Retirement.—Nothing in this subchapter shall apply to retirement, nor shall anything in this subchapter be construed to prevent a borough from adopting a compulsory retirement age for its employees or for any class of employees and from retiring all employees automatically when they reach that age.

§ 1172. Civil service commission.

(a) Establishment.—A civil service commission is established in each borough where a police force or paid fire apparatus operators are maintained.

(b) Membership and terms.—The commission shall consist of three commissioners who shall be qualified electors of the borough and appointed by the council initially to serve for the terms of two, four and six years. As terms expire, the commissioners shall be appointed for terms of six years.

(c) Vacancies.—A vacancy occurring in the commission for any reason shall be filled by the council for the unexpired term within the period of 30 days after the vacancy occurs.

(d) Alternate members.—

(1) Council may appoint no more than three qualified electors of the borough to serve as alternate members of the commission. The term of office of the alternate members shall be six years.

(2) If seated under section 1174 (relating to organization of commission), an alternate shall be entitled to participate in all proceedings and discussions of the commission to the same and full extent as provided by law for commission members, including specifically the right to cast a vote as a voting member during the proceedings, and shall have all the powers and duties specified in this part and as otherwise provided by law.

(3) An alternate member may not hold another office in the borough.

(4) An alternate may participate in any proceeding or discussion of the commission but may not vote as a member of the commission unless designated as a voting alternate member under section 1174.

(e) Oath or affirmation of office.—Each member of the commission, before entering upon the discharge of the duties of office, shall take an oath or affirmation of office under 53 Pa.C.S. § 1141 (relating to form of oaths of office).

(f) **Compensation prohibited.**—The civil service commissioners shall receive no compensation.

§ 1173. Offices incompatible with civil service commissioner.

No commissioner shall at the same time hold an elective or appointed office under the Federal Government, this Commonwealth or any political subdivision of the Commonwealth, except that one member of the commission may be a member of the council and one may be a member of the teaching profession.

§ 1174. Organization of commission.

(a) **General rule.**—The commission first appointed shall organize within ten days of its appointment and shall elect one of its members as the chair and one as the secretary. Thereafter, the commission shall meet and organize within 30 days of the first Monday of each even-numbered year. Each commissioner shall be notified in writing of each and every meeting.

(b) **Quorum.**—Three members of the commission shall constitute a quorum. If, by reason of absence or disqualification of a member a quorum is not reached, the chair shall designate as many alternate members of the commission to sit on the commission as may be needed to provide a quorum.

(c) **Alternate members.**—

(1) An alternate member of the commission shall continue to serve on the commission in all proceedings involving the matter or case for which the alternate was initially designated until the commission has made a final determination of the matter or case.

(2) Designation of an alternate member under this section shall be made on a case-by-case basis in rotation according to declining seniority among the alternates.

(d) **Validity of commission action.**—No action of the commission may be valid unless it shall have the concurrence of at least two members.

§ 1175. Clerks, supplies and solicitor.

The borough shall:

(1) Furnish to the commission, on its requisition, clerical assistance that may be necessary for the work of the commission.

(2) Provide a suitable and convenient room for the use of the commission. The commission shall order from the borough the necessary stationery, postage, printing and supplies.

(3) Provide the services of a solicitor for the commission to be appointed by the commission and paid by the borough. The borough may place a reasonable limit on the amount allowed each year for the services of the commission solicitor.

(4) Through its elected and appointed officials, aid the commission in all proper ways in carrying out the provisions of this subchapter relating to civil service.

§ 1176. Rules and regulations.

(a) **General rule.**—The commission may prescribe, amend and enforce rules and regulations for carrying into effect this subchapter and shall be governed by the rules and regulations. Before the effective date of the rules and regulations or amendments to them, they shall be first approved by council. If the rules and regulations or amendments have been approved, they shall not be annulled, amended or added to without the approval of council.

(b) **Public distribution and inspection.**—All rules and regulations and modifications shall be made available by the borough for public distribution or inspection.

Chap. 39 Res. During Mil. Service
Chap. 38 Intergov. Coop.
Chap. 37 3rd Class City Code
Chap. 36 Bor. Code
Chap. 35 2nd Class Twp. Code
Chap. 34 1st Class Twp. Code
Chap. 33 Home Rule Chart. Opt. Plans Law
Chap. 32 Water Serv. Act
Chap. 31 Munic. Auth. Act

§ 1177. Minutes and records.

The commission shall maintain minutes of its proceedings and records of examinations and other official actions. All recommendations of applicants for appointment received by the commission shall be kept and preserved for a period of five years, and all records and all written causes of removal filed with the commission, except as otherwise provided in section 1191 (relating to hearings on dismissals and reductions), shall be open to public inspection and subject to reasonable regulation.

§ 1178. Investigations.

The commission may conduct investigations concerning all matters touching the administration and enforcement of this subchapter and rules and regulations adopted under this subchapter. The chair of the commission may administer oaths and affirmations in connection with the investigations.

§ 1179. Subpoenas.

(a) General rule.—The commission may issue subpoenas over the signature of the chair to require the attendance of witnesses and the production of records and papers pertaining to any investigation or inquiry. The fees of witnesses for attendance and travel shall be the same as for witnesses appearing in the courts and shall be paid from appropriations for the incidental expenses of the commission.

(b) Persons required to attend.—All officers in public service and employees shall attend and testify if required to do so by the commission.

(c) Penalty for violation.—If any person refuses or neglects to obey a subpoena issued by the commission, the person shall, upon conviction, be sentenced to pay a fine not to exceed $100 and, in default of the payment of the fine and costs, shall be imprisoned for a term not to exceed 30 days.

(d) Petition to court.—If a person refuses or neglects to obey a subpoena issued by the commission, the commission may apply by petition to the court of common pleas of the county for its subpoena requiring the attendance of the person before the commission or the court to testify and to produce any records and papers necessary and, if the person defaults, the person shall be held in contempt of court.

§ 1180. Annual report.

The commission shall make an annual report to the council containing a brief summary of its work during the year which shall be available for public inspection.

§ 1181. General provisions relating to examinations.

(a) Rules and regulations.—

(1) The commission shall make rules and regulations, to be approved as provided in section 1176 (relating to rules and regulations), providing for the examination of applicants for positions in the police force and as paid fire apparatus operators and for promotions, which rules and regulations shall prescribe the minimum qualifications of all applicants to be examined and the passing grades.

(2) All examinations for positions or promotions shall be practical in character and shall relate to matters and include inquiries as will fairly test the merit and fitness of the persons examined to discharge the duties of the employment sought by them.

(3) All examinations shall be open to all applicants who have the minimum qualifications required by the rules and regulations.

(4) Each applicant for an original position shall:

(i) Be subject to the regulations adopted by the commission.

(ii) Either before or after the written examination, submit to a physical fitness or agility examination that is job related and consistent with business necessity.

(iii) If made a conditional offer of employment, be given a physical and psychological medical examination as provided in section 1189 (relating to physical and psychological medical examination).

(iv) Be subject to a background investigation. Background investigations may be restricted to those candidates on an eligibility list or those to be certified to council for appointment in accordance with section 1184 (relating to eligibility list and manner of filling appointments).

(a.1) Promotions.—

(1) An applicant for promotion shall be subject to the regulations adopted by the commission and to examination and selection in accordance with section 1188 (relating to promotions).

(2) A physical fitness or agility examination that is job related and consistent with business necessity and physical and psychological medical examinations may, but need not, be required for a promotion.

(b) Public notice.—Public notice of the time and place of every examination, together with the information as to the kind of position to be filled, shall be given by publication once in a newspaper of general circulation, at least two weeks prior to each examination, and a copy of the notice shall be prominently posted in the office of the commission or other public place.

(c) Posting of eligibility list.—The commission shall post in its office the eligibility list containing the names and grades of those who have passed the examination.

§ 1182. Application for examination.

A person who desires to apply for examination must file with the commission a formal application in which the applicant shall provide, under oath or affirmation, the following information:

(1) Full name and residence or post office address.

(2) Citizenship and place and date of birth.

(3) Condition of health and physical capacity for public service.

(4) Business or employment and the applicant's residence for the past five years.

(5) Other information as may be required by the commission's rules and regulations, showing the applicant's qualifications for the position for which the applicant is being examined.

§ 1183. Rejection of applicant and hearing.

(a) General rule.—The commission may refuse to examine or, if examined, may refuse to certify after examination as eligible any applicant who:

(1) is found to lack any of the minimum qualifications for examination prescribed in the rules and regulations adopted for the position or employment for which the applicant has applied;

(2) is physically unfit for the performance of the duties of the position to which the applicant seeks employment;

(3) is illegally using a controlled substance, as defined in section 102 of the Controlled Substances Act (Public Law 91-513, 21 U.S.C. § 802);

(4) has been guilty of any crime involving moral turpitude or of infamous or notoriously disgraceful conduct;

(5) has been dismissed from public service for delinquency or misconduct of office; or

Chap. 39 Res. During Mil. Service
Chap. 38 Intergov. Coop.
Chap. 37 3rd Class City Code
Chap. 36 Bor. Code
Chap. 35 2nd Class Twp. Code
Chap. 34 1st Class Twp. Code
Chap. 33 Home Rule Chart. Opt. Plans Law
Chap. 32 Water Serv. Act
Chap. 31 Munic. Auth. Act

(6) is affiliated with any group whose policies or activities are subversive to the form of government enumerated in the Constitutions and laws of the United States and this Commonwealth.

(b) Hearing requirements.—

(1) If an applicant is aggrieved by the refusal of the commission to certify the applicant as eligible after examination or a person is aggrieved by refusal of the commission to examine the person, the commission shall, at the request of the applicant or person aggrieved, within ten days, appoint a time and place for a public hearing.

(2) At the hearing, the applicant or person aggrieved may appear with or without counsel, and the commission shall take testimony and review its refusal to provide examination or certification.

(3) The deliberations of the commission, including interim rulings on evidentiary or procedural issues, may be held in the nature of a closed executive session.

(4) The commission's disposition of the matter shall constitute official action which shall occur at a public meeting held under 65 Pa.C.S. Ch. 7 (relating to open meetings).

(5) The decision of the commission shall be final.

§ 1184. Eligibility list and manner of filling appointments.

(a) Ranking of candidates.—

(1) At the completion of the testing process, including a physical agility or other examination, with the exception of a background investigation to be conducted after the establishment of an eligibility list and physical and psychological medical examination under section 1189 (relating to physical and psychological medical examination), the commission shall rank the candidates who have satisfied the minimum requirements for appointment on an eligibility list.

(2) The eligibility list shall contain the names of individuals eligible for appointment listed from highest to lowest based on their scores on the examinations administered by the commission and any points for which an applicant was entitled by virtue of 51 Pa.C.S. Ch. 71 (relating to veterans' preference).

(3) The eligibility list will be valid for one year from the date the commission formally adopts the eligibility list.

(4) Prior to expiration of the one-year period, the commission may extend the validity of the eligibility list for up to an additional 12 months by a majority vote of the commission at a duly authorized commission meeting.

(5) In the absence of a lawful extension by the commission under paragraph (4), the list shall expire.

(b) Procedure for filling positions.—Except as provided in subsection (c), every original position or employment in the police force or as paid fire apparatus operators, except that of chief of police or chief of the fire department, or equivalent, shall be filled only in the following manner:

(1) The council shall notify the commission of any vacancy which is to be filled and shall request the certification of an eligibility list.

(2) The commission shall certify for each existing vacancy from the eligibility list the names of the three persons or a lesser number, if three are not available, who have received the highest average.

(3) The council shall make a conditional appointment from the three names certified, based solely on the merits and fitness of the candidates, unless council makes objections to the commission regarding one or more of the certified persons for any of the reasons stated in section 1183 (relating to rejection of applicant and hearing).

Chap. 39 Res. During Mil. Service
Chap. 38 Intergov. Coop.
Chap. 37 3rd Class City Code
Chap. 36 Bor. Code
Chap. 35 2nd Class Twp. Code
Chap. 34 1st Class Twp. Code
Chap. 33 Home Rule Chart. Opt. Plans Law
Chap. 32 Water Serv. Act
Chap. 31 Munic. Auth. Act

(4) If the objections are sustained by the commission as provided in section 1183 or the conditional appointee is determined to be unqualified in accordance with the procedures specified in section 1189, the commission shall strike the name of the person from the eligibility list and certify the next highest name for each name stricken from the eligibility list.

(5) As each subsequent vacancy occurs in the same or another position, the same procedure shall be followed.

(c) Vacancies in existing positions.—

(1) Any vacancy in an existing position in the police force or as a paid fire apparatus operator which occurs as a result of retirement, resignation, disability or death may be filled by council by the reappointment or reinstatement of a former employee of the police force or fire department who had previously complied with this section.

(2) No examination, other than a physical examination as directed by the civil service commission, shall be required in any case of reappointment or reinstatement.

(d) Vacancies in certain offices.—

(1) In the case of a vacancy in the office of chief of police or chief of the fire department, or equivalent official, the council may nominate a person to the commission.

(2) The commission shall subject the nominated person to a noncompetitive examination and, if the person is certified by the commission as qualified, the person may then be appointed to the position and shall be subject to this subchapter.

§ 1185. Age and residency of applicants.

No person shall be eligible to apply for examination unless the person is at least 18 years of age at the date of application. An applicant need not be a resident of the borough. The council of the borough may authorize the commission, by rule or regulation, to require police officers and paid fire apparatus operators to become residents of the borough after appointment to the positions.

§ 1186. Probationary period.

(a) General rule.—An original appointment to a position in the police force or as a paid fire apparatus operator shall be for a probationary period of not less than six months and not more than one year, but during the probationary period an appointee may be dismissed only for a cause specified in section 1183 (relating to rejection of applicant and hearing) or because of incapacity for duty due to the use of alcohol or drugs.

(b) Notice denying permanent appointment.—

(1) If, at the close of a probationary period, the conduct or fitness of the probationer has not been satisfactory to the council, the probationer shall be notified in writing that the probationer will not receive a permanent appointment and the appointment shall cease.

(2) If the probationer is not notified or dismissed in accordance with this section, the probationer's retention shall be equivalent to a permanent appointment.

(c) Finality of decision.—The decision of a borough to suspend or discharge a probationer shall be final and shall not be subject to the hearing provisions of section 1191 (relating to hearings on dismissals and reductions).

§ 1187. Provisional appointments.

(a) General rule.—If there are urgent reasons for the filling of a vacancy in a position in the police force and there are no names on the eligibility list for the appointment, the council may nominate a person to the commission for noncompetitive examination, and, if the nominee shall be certified by the commission as qualified after noncompetitive examination, the nominee may be appointed provisionally to fill the vacancy.

(b) Competitive examination required.—

(1) Within three weeks of the provisional appointment, the commission shall hold a competitive examination and certify an eligibility list. A regular appointment shall then be made from the name or names submitted by the commission.

(2) Nothing in this section shall be construed to prevent the appointment, without examination, of persons temporarily as police officers in cases of riot or other emergencies or as fire apparatus operators in emergency cases.

§ 1188. Promotions.

(a) General rule.—A promotion shall be based on merit to be ascertained by an examination to be prescribed by the commission. All questions relative to a promotion shall be practical in character and fairly test the merit and fitness of persons seeking promotion.

(b) Notification of vacancy.—Council shall notify the commission of a vacancy in the police force or as a paid fire apparatus operator in the borough which is to be filled by promotion and shall request the certification of an eligibility list.

(c) Certification required.—

(1) The commission shall certify for each vacancy the names of three persons on the eligibility list who have received the highest average in the last preceding promotional examination held within a period of two years preceding the date of the request for the eligibility list.

(2) If three names are not available, the commission shall certify the names remaining on the eligibility list.

(3) The council shall make an appointment from the names certified, based solely on the merits and fitness of the candidate, unless council makes objections to the commission regarding one or more of the persons so certified for any reason provided under section 1183 (relating to rejection of applicant and hearing).

(d) Increase in salary as promotion.—The council may determine in each instance whether an increase in salary constitutes a promotion.

§ 1189. Physical and psychological medical examination.

(a) Conditional offer of employment.—

(1) An applicant selected from the eligibility list shall receive a conditional offer of employment. The offer of employment shall be conditioned upon the conditional appointee undergoing a physical and psychological medical examination and a determination that the conditional appointee is capable of performing all the essential functions of the position.

(2) Physical medical examinations shall be conducted under the direction of a physician or other qualified medical professional.

(3) Psychological medical examinations shall be conducted under the direction of a psychiatrist or psychologist.

(b) Opinion to be rendered.—The physician, other qualified medical professional, psychiatrist or psychologist must be appointed by council and shall render an opinion as to whether the conditional appointee has a physical or mental condition which calls into question the person's ability to perform all of the essential functions of the position for which the person was conditionally appointed.

(c) Interactive discussion with conditional appointee.—If the opinion rendered by the physician, other qualified medical professional, psychiatrist or psychologist calls into question the conditional appointee's ability to perform all essential functions of a position, the person designated by council shall meet with the conditional appointee for the purpose of having one or more interactive discussions on whether the conditional appointee can, with or without reasonable accommodation, perform all the essential functions of the position.

(d) Written notice after interactive discussion.—If, at the conclusion of the interactive discussion conducted under subsection (c), council determines that the conditional appointee is not qualified, council shall give written notice to the conditional appointee and the commission.

(e) Construction.—Nothing in this part shall be construed to authorize physical or psychological medical examinations prior to conditional appointment.

(f) Definitions.—The following words and phrases used in this section shall have the meanings given to them in this subsection unless the context clearly indicates otherwise:

"Medical examination." An examination, procedure, inquiry or test designed to obtain information about medical history or a physical or mental condition which might disqualify an applicant for a position if it would prevent the applicant from performing, with or without a reasonable accommodation, all of the essential functions of the position.

"Physician." The term shall have the meaning given to it under 1 Pa.C.S. § 1991 (relating to definitions).

"Qualified medical professional." An individual, in collaboration with or under the supervision or direction of a physician, as may be required by law, who is licensed:

(1) as a physician assistant under the act of December 20, 1985 (P.L.457, No.112), known as the Medical Practice Act of 1985, or the act of October 5, 1978 (P.L.1109, No.261), known as the Osteopathic Medical Practice Act; or

(2) as a certified registered nurse practitioner under the act of May 22, 1951 (P.L.317, No.69), known as The Professional Nursing Law.

§ 1190. Removals.

(a) General rule.—No person employed in any police or fire force of any borough may be suspended without pay, removed or reduced in rank except for the following reasons:

(1) Physical or mental disability affecting the person's ability to continue in service, in which cases the person shall receive an honorable discharge from service.

(2) Neglect or violation of any official duty.

(3) Violation of any law if the violation constitutes a misdemeanor or felony.

(4) Inefficiency, neglect, intemperance, immorality, disobedience of orders or conduct unbecoming of an officer.

(5) Intoxication while on duty.

(6) Engaging or participating in the conduct of a political or election campaign while on duty or in uniform or while using borough property otherwise than to exercise the person's own right of suffrage.

(7) Engaging or participating in the conduct of a political or election campaign for an incompatible office as provided in section 1104(f) (relating to appointments and incompatible offices).

(b) Restriction.—A person employed by a police or fire force shall not be removed for religious, racial or political reasons.

(c) Statement of charges.—A written statement of charges made against a person shall be furnished to the person within five days after the statement of charges is filed. The person shall have ten days from the date of receiving the notice to submit a written request for a hearing to the civil service commission under section 1191 (relating to hearings on dismissals and reductions).

(d) Furlough.—If, for reasons of economy or other reasons, it shall be deemed necessary by any borough to reduce the number of paid employees of the police or fire force, the borough shall furlough the person, including a probationer, last appointed to the respective force. The removal shall be accomplished by furloughing in numerical order commencing with the person last appointed until the reduction shall have been accomplished. In the event the police force or fire force shall again be increased, the employees furloughed shall be reinstated in the order of their seniority in the service. This subsection as to reductions in force is not applicable to a chief of police.

§ 1191. Hearings on dismissals and reductions.

(a) Time of answer and hearing.—A person suspended, removed or reduced in rank may make written answers to any charges filed against the person not later than the day scheduled for the hearing. The commission shall grant the person a hearing that shall be held within a period of ten days from the filing of written charges, unless continued by the commission for cause at the request of the council or the accused. The failure of the commission to hold a hearing within ten days from the filing of the written charges shall not result in the dismissal of the charges filed.

(b) Conduct of hearing.—At any hearing, the person against whom the charges are made may be present in person and by counsel. The council may suspend the person, without pay, pending the determination of the charges against the person, but, in the event the commission fails to uphold the charges, the person sought to be suspended, removed or reduced in rank shall be reinstated with full pay for the period during which the person was suspended, removed or reduced in rank, and no charges shall be officially recorded against the person's record. A stenographic record of all testimony taken at the hearings shall be filed with and preserved by the commission, which record shall be sealed and not be available for public inspection in the event the charges are dismissed.

(c) Appeal.—All parties shall have an immediate right of appeal to the court of common pleas of the county, and the case shall there be determined as the court deems proper. No order of suspension made by the commission may be for a longer period than one year. The appeal shall be taken within 30 days from the date of entry by the commission of its final order and shall be by petition. Upon the appeal being taken and docketed, the court of common pleas shall schedule a day for a hearing and shall proceed to hear the appeal on the original record and additional proof or testimony as the parties concerned may desire to offer in evidence. The decision of the court affirming or revising the decision of the commission shall be final, and the employee shall be suspended, discharged, reduced in rank or reinstated in accordance with the order of court.

(d) Proceedings.—The council and the person sought to be suspended, removed or reduced in rank shall at all times have the right to employ counsel before the commission and upon appeal to the court of common pleas. Unless the council or the person sought to be suspended, removed or reduced in rank requests that the proceedings before the commission be open to the public, the proceedings before the commission under this section shall be held in the nature of a closed executive session that shall not be open to the public. The request shall be presented to the commission before the civil service hearing commences. The deliberations of the commission, including interim rulings on evidentiary or procedural issues, may be held in private and shall not be subject to a request for being open to the public, the council or the person sought to be suspended, removed or reduced in rank. The commission's disposition of the disciplinary action shall constitute official action which shall occur at a public meeting held pursuant to 65 Pa.C.S. Ch. 7 (relating to open meetings).

§ 1192. Employees exempted.

All appointments in the police or fire forces of boroughs, including the chief of police or equivalent official, prior to the creation of a commission, shall continue to hold their positions and shall not be required to take any examination under the provisions of this subchapter, except that which may be required for promotion. This section shall not be construed to apply to persons employed temporarily in emergency cases.

§ 1193. Discrimination on account of political or religious affiliations.

(a) **Information.**—No question in any form of application for examination or in any examination shall be so framed as to elicit information concerning the political or religious opinions or affiliations of any applicant nor shall inquiry be made concerning the opinions or affiliations, and all disclosures of opinions or affiliations shall be ignored.

(b) **Prohibition.**—No discrimination shall be exercised, threatened or promised by any person against or in favor of any applicant or employee because of political or religious opinions or affiliations or race, and no offer or promise or reward, favor or benefit, directly or indirectly, shall be made to or received by any person for any act done or duty omitted or to be done under this subchapter.

§ 1194. Penalty.

A member of council who, by vote, appoints any person to the police force or as a fire apparatus operator contrary to the provisions of this subchapter, or a member of council or member of the commission who willfully refuses to comply with or conform to the provisions of this subchapter, commits a misdemeanor and, upon conviction, shall be sentenced to pay a fine not exceeding $100 or to imprisonment not exceeding 90 days, or both.

SUBCHAPTER K
INDEPENDENT AUDITOR
(Reserved)

CHAPTER 12
CORPORATE POWERS

Sec.

§ 1201. General powers.

A borough may:

(1) Have succession perpetually by its corporate name.

(2) Sue and be sued and complain and defend in the courts of this Commonwealth.

(3) Make and use a common seal and alter the same at its discretion.

(4) Purchase, exchange, acquire by gift or otherwise, hold, lease, let and convey, by sale or lease, real and personal property deemed to be in the best interest of the borough, subject to the restrictions, limitations or exceptions as set forth in this chapter.

§ 1201.1. Real property.

(a) **Sale.**—No real estate owned by the borough may be sold except upon approval of council by resolution. Additionally, no real estate owned by the borough may be sold for a consideration in excess of $6,000, except to the highest bidder after due notice by advertisement for bids or advertisement of a public auction.

(a.1) **Advertisement.**—The advertisement shall be published once in one newspaper of general circulation not less than ten days prior to the date scheduled for the opening of bids or public auction. The date for opening bids or public auction shall be announced in the advertisement.

(a.2) **Award of contracts.**—The award of contracts shall be made only by public announcement at a regular or special meeting of council or at the public auction. All bids shall be accepted on the condition that payment of the purchase price in full shall be made within 60 days of the acceptance of bids. If no compliant bids are received after advertisement, the applicable procedures in the act of October 27, 1979 (P.L.241, No.78), entitled, "An act authorizing political subdivisions, municipality authorities and transportation authorities to enter into contracts for the purchase of goods and the sale of real and personal property where no bids are received," shall be followed.

(b) **Rejection of bids.**—The council shall have the authority to reject all bids if the bids are deemed to be less than the fair market value of the real property. In the case of a public auction, the council may establish a minimum bid based on the fair market value of the real property.

(c) **Exception.**—Real estate owned by a borough may be sold at a consideration of $6,000 or less without advertisement or competitive bidding only after council estimates the value of the property upon receipt of an appraisal by a qualified real estate appraiser. Prior to selling real estate valued at $6,000 or less without advertisement or competitive bidding, council shall make a public announcement of the council's intention to sell the real estate at a regular or special meeting of council at least 30 days prior to the sale.

(d) **Exchange of real property.**—

(1) Notwithstanding this section, council shall have the authority to exchange real property for real property of equal or greater value without complying with this section, if the property being acquired by the borough is to be used for municipal purposes. Municipal purposes as used in this subsection include a subsequent sale or lease of the property to any of the entities listed in section 1201.3 (relating to exceptions).

(2) Any conveyance of real property acquired in an exchange to an entity listed in section 1201.3 may contain a clause under which the lands and buildings will revert to the borough if they are no longer being used for the purposes of the entity.

(3) If council chooses to exercise its power of real property exchange under this section, it shall be by resolution adopted by council. Notice of the resolution, including a description of the properties to be exchanged, shall be published once in one newspaper of general circulation not more than 60 days nor fewer than seven days prior to adoption.

(4) Participation in a real property exchange shall not prohibit the application of the requirements of the act of October 4, 1978 (P.L.851, No.166), known as the Flood Plain Management Act.

§ 1201.2. Personal property.

(a) **Sale.**—Except as provided in subsection (b), no borough personal property may be disposed of, by sale or otherwise, except upon approval of council by resolution. In cases when council approves a sale of the property, council shall estimate the fair market value of the entire lot to be disposed of. If council estimates the fair market value to be $2,000 or more, the entire lot shall be advertised for sale once in at least one newspaper of general circulation not less than ten days prior to the date scheduled for the opening of bids or public auction. The date of opening of bids or public auction shall be announced in the advertisement, and sale of the property advertised shall be made to the best responsible bidder.

(a.1) Electronic auction sale.—A public auction of personal property may be conducted by means of an online or electronic auction sale. During an electronic auction sale, bids shall be accepted electronically at the time and in the manner designated in the advertisement. During the electronic auction, each bidder shall have the capability to view the bidder's bid rank or the high bid price. Bidders may increase their bid prices during the electronic auction. The record of the electronic auction shall be accessible for public inspection. The purchase price shall be paid by the highest bidder immediately or at a reasonable time after the conclusion of the electronic auction as determined by council. In the event that shipping costs are incurred, they shall be paid by the highest bidder. A borough that has complied with the advertising requirements of this section may provide additional public notice of the sale by bids or public auction in any manner deemed appropriate by council. The advertisement for electronic auction sales authorized in this paragraph shall include the Internet address or means of accessing the electronic auction and the date, time and duration of the electronic auction.

(a.2) Rejection of bids.—Council may reject any bids received if the bids are believed to be less than the fair market value of the property. If no bids are received after advertisement, the applicable procedures in the act of October 27, 1979 (P.L.241, No.78), entitled, "An act authorizing political subdivisions, municipality authorities and transportation authorities to enter into contracts for the purchase of goods and the sale of real and personal property where no bids are received," shall be followed.

(b) Exception for small value sales.—Council shall, by resolution, adopt a procedure for the sale of surplus personal property, either individual items or lots of items, of an estimated fair market value of less than $2,000. The approval of council shall not be required for any individual sale that shall be made in conformity to the procedure.

(c) Exchange of personal property.—This section shall not be mandatory when borough personal property is to be traded in or exchanged for new or used personal property being acquired by the borough, except that the trade or exchange shall be by resolution.

§ 1201.3. Exceptions.

(a) Sale of property.—Nothing under this chapter requiring advertising for bids or sale at public auction and sale to the highest bidder shall apply if borough real or personal property is to be sold to any of the following:

(1) A county, city, borough, town, township, institution district, school district, volunteer fire company, volunteer ambulance service or volunteer rescue squad located within the borough.

(2) A council of government, consortium, cooperative or other similar entity created pursuant to 53 Pa.C.S. Ch. 23 Subch. A (relating to intergovernmental cooperation).

(3) An authority as defined in 53 Pa.C.S. § 5602 (relating to definitions).

(4) A nonprofit corporation engaged in community development or reuse only upon entering into a written agreement with the nonprofit corporation that requires the property to be used for industrial, commercial or affordable housing purposes. This exemption shall not apply to property on which existing governmental functions are conducted. This exemption shall also not apply

to property owned and operated by the borough or subcontracted or operated on behalf of the borough in order to conduct existing government functions.

(5) A person for the person's exclusive use in an industrial development program.

(6) A nonprofit corporation organized as a public library for its exclusive use as a library.

(7) A nonprofit medical service corporation as authorized under section 1202(50) (relating to specific powers).

(8) A nonprofit housing corporation as authorized by section 1202(51).

(9) The Federal Government or the Commonwealth.

(10) A nonprofit museum or historical society for its exclusive use as a nonprofit museum or historical society.

(b) Sales to certain nonprofit corporations.—When real property is to be sold to a nonprofit corporation organized as a public library for its exclusive use as a library or to a nonprofit medical service corporation or to a nonprofit housing corporation, council may elect to accept nominal consideration for the sale as it shall deem appropriate.

(c) Reversion.—Real property sold under this section to a volunteer fire company, volunteer ambulance service or volunteer rescue squad, nonprofit medical service corporation or nonprofit housing corporation shall be subject to the condition that when the property is not used for the purposes of the company, service, squad or corporation the property shall revert to the borough.

§ 1202. Specific powers.

The powers of the borough shall be vested in the council. In the exercise of any specific powers involving the enactment of an ordinance or the making of any regulation, restriction or prohibition, the borough may provide for enforcement and penalties for violations. The specific powers of the borough shall include the following:

(1) To prescribe reasonable fees for the services of the borough's officers and to enforce the payment of the fees. This paragraph shall not be applicable to the services rendered by borough police officers in responding to motor vehicle accidents pursuant to 53 Pa.C.S. § 1392 (relating to prohibition of fees for police services).

(2) In the operation of its utilities, parking meters, parking lots, recreational facilities and other facilities and services, to make and regulate charges for them for general borough purposes.

(3) To impose fines and penalties, incurring partial or total forfeiture, or to remit the same.

(4) To prohibit and remove any nuisance or dangerous structure on public or private grounds, including, but not limited to, accumulations of garbage and rubbish, the storage of abandoned or junked automobiles and obstructions or nuisances in the streets of the borough. The borough may require the removal of any nuisance or dangerous structure by the owner or occupier of the grounds or remove the nuisance or dangerous structure itself and collect the cost of removal, together with a penalty of 10% of the cost, in the manner provided by law for the collection of municipal claims, or by action of assumpsit, or the borough may seek relief by bill in equity.

(5) To make regulations as may be necessary for the health, safety, morals, general welfare and cleanliness and beauty, convenience, comfort and safety of the borough.

(6) To make regulations respecting vaults, cesspools and drains.

Table of Contents
Part I Ch. 1–3 Ethics, Records, Open Meetings
Part II Ch. 4–10 Taxation
Part III Ch. 11–18 Torts, Contracts & Civil Rules
Part IV Ch. 19–24 Zoning & Planning
Part V Ch. 25–30 Construction and Emergency Codes
Part VI Ch. 31–39 Municipal Codes
Index

(7) To make regulations relative to the accumulation of manure, compost and the like to the extent authorized by 3 Pa.C.S. Ch. 5 (relating to nutrient management and odor management).

(8) (Reserved).

(9) To the extent not otherwise prohibited by the act of December 7, 1982 (P.L.784, No.225), known as the Dog Law, to destroy dogs found at large contrary to laws of this Commonwealth, to prohibit or regulate, by ordinance, the running at large of dogs, cats or other pets and, in the enforcement of the regulations, to direct the seizure, detention or killing of dogs, cats or other pets, prescribing reasonable charges for their seizure and detention and to provide for their sale for the benefit of the borough in default of the redemption of the pet by its owners.

(10) To enact ordinances prohibiting or regulating the keeping or running at large of livestock and fowls and any other animals not covered in paragraph (9) and authorizing their seizure, detention or, in the case of unowned pigeons, humane destruction. The borough may prescribe reasonable charges for the seizure and detention of the animals and provide for their sale for the benefit of the borough in default of the redemption of the animals by their owners. Ordinances enacted under this paragraph shall not unreasonably interfere with any agricultural operation to the extent prohibited by applicable State law.

(11) To regulate the emission of smoke from chimneys, smokestacks and other sources to the extent the regulation is not otherwise prohibited by applicable Federal or State law. This paragraph shall not apply to locomotive smokestacks.

(12) To regulate the streets, sewers, public squares, common grounds, sidewalks, curbs, gutters, culverts and drains, and the heights, grades, widths, slopes and their construction, and to prohibit the erection or construction of any building or other obstruction to the convenient use of the same.

(13) To prohibit or regulate the riding, driving, parking or other passage of any animal or vehicle over, along and across sidewalks. As used in this paragraph, the term "vehicle" shall include any device in, upon or by which any person or property may be transported. The term shall not include a self-propelled wheelchair or an electrical mobility device operated by and designed for the exclusive use of a person with a mobility-related disability.

(14) To adopt ordinances defining disorderly conduct or disturbing the peace within the limits of the borough and to provide for the imposition of penalties for the conduct in amounts, without limitation except as provided under this part, as council shall establish, and notwithstanding any laws of this Commonwealth upon disorderly conduct or disturbing the peace and the penalties.

(15) To adopt and enforce a construction code, a property maintenance code and a fire prevention code and exercise any additional reserved powers pursuant to Chapter 32A (relating to uniform construction code, property maintenance code and reserved powers).

(16) To prohibit and regulate the smoking or carrying of lighted cigarettes, cigars, pipes or matches and the use of matches or fire-producing devices. An ordinance enacted or regulation or resolution adopted under this paragraph shall not regulate smoking in a manner that conflicts with the act of June 13, 2008 (P.L.182, No.27), known as the Clean Indoor Air Act.

(17) To provide for fireworks and inflammable articles as follows:

(i) To regulate and prohibit, by ordinance, the manufacture of fireworks or inflammable or dangerous articles.

(ii) To grant permits for supervised public displays of fireworks and adopt rules and regulations governing the displays.

(iii) To adopt, by ordinance, rules and regulations not inconsistent with State regulations relating to the storage of inflammable articles.

(iv) To impose, by ordinance, other safeguards concerning inflammable articles as may be necessary.

(18) To require and regulate the numbering of buildings and lots.

(19) To make regulations respecting partition fences and the foundations and party walls of buildings.

(20) To provide for the prohibition, licensing and regulation of business as follows:

(i) In addition to licensing in accordance with Chapter 29 (relating to licenses and license fees), to prohibit, license and regulate by ordinance the following:

(A) The carrying on of any manufacture, art, trade or business which may be noxious or offensive and prejudicial to the public health or safety of the inhabitants.

(B) The establishment and maintenance of junk yards, salvage yards and other places used and maintained for the collection, storage and disposal of used or second-hand goods and materials.

(C) With respect to marketplaces:

(I) regulate markets whether for individual use or for resale;

(II) purchase and own ground;

(III) erect, establish and maintain marketplaces for which purposes parts of a street or sidewalk may be temporarily used;

(IV) contract with a person or association of persons, companies or corporations for the erection, maintenance and regulation of marketplaces, on terms and conditions, and in a manner, as the council may prescribe;

(V) provide and enforce suitable regulations respecting marketplaces;

(VI) provide for the payment of the cost or expense of marketplaces, either in whole or in part, out of the funds of the borough; and

(VII) levy and collect a suitable license fee from every person who may be authorized by council to occupy any portion of marketplaces or any portion of the streets or sidewalks for temporary market purposes.

(ii) Notwithstanding subparagraph (i), boroughs may prohibit, license and regulate businesses unless prohibited by law.

(iii) To issue licenses under the act of July 31, 1963 (P.L.410, No.217), entitled "An act regulating and licensing all sales at retail when such sales are advertised as 'Closing Out Sale,' 'Fire, Smoke or Water Damage Sale,' or 'Defunct Business Sale,' with exceptions; requiring filing of inventory and bond; and providing for appeals and penalties."

(21) To plan for and regulate the development of the borough by:

(i) establishing and maintaining uniform building lines upon any or all borough streets under applicable law; and

(ii) utilizing powers delegated by the Pennsylvania Municipalities Planning Code and other applicable laws by adopting zoning, subdivision and land use and development regulations.

(22)(i) To provide for the creation of capital reserve fund for anticipated capital expenditures as follows:

(A) Create and maintain a separate capital reserve fund for anticipated legal capital expenditures. The money in the fund shall be used, from time to time, for the construction, purchase, replacement of or expansion of municipal buildings, equipment, machinery, motor vehicles or other capital assets of the borough and for no other purpose.

(B) Appropriate money from the general borough funds to be paid into the capital reserve fund or place in the fund any money received from the sale, lease or other disposition of any borough property or from any other source, unless received or acquired for a particular purpose. The fund shall be controlled, invested, reinvested and administered and the money expended for any of the purposes for which the fund is created in a manner as may be determined by council. The money in the fund, when invested, shall be invested in securities designated by 53 Pa.C.S. Pt. VII Subpt. B (relating to indebtedness and borrowing) as legal investments for sinking funds of municipalities.

(ii) This paragraph shall not be construed to limit the powers of the borough to the use of money in the capital reserve fund in making lawful capital expenditures.

(23) To create and maintain a separate operating reserve fund from which appropriations may be made to meet emergencies involving the health, safety and welfare of the residents of the borough, to counterbalance potential budget deficits resulting from shortfalls in anticipated revenues or program receipts from whatever source, to counterbalance potential budget deficits resulting from increases in anticipated costs for goods or services or to provide anticipated operating expenditures related either to the planned growth of existing projects or programs or to the establishment of new projects or programs if, for a project or program appropriations, have been made and allocated to a separate restricted account established within the operating reserve fund. Council may annually make appropriations from the general fund to the operating reserve fund, but no appropriation may be made to the operating reserve fund if the effect of the appropriation would cause the fund to exceed 25% of the estimated revenues of the borough's general fund in the current fiscal year. The operating reserve fund shall be invested, reinvested and administered in a manner consistent with the provisions of section 1316 (relating to investment of funds).

(24) To enter into agreements with other political subdivisions, in accordance with existing laws, in making joint purchases of materials, supplies or equipment and in performing governmental powers, duties and functions and in carrying into effect provisions of 53 Pa.C.S. Ch. 23 Subch. A (relating to intergovernmental cooperation), and agreements with the proper authorities of municipal corporations, regional police or fire forces or other public safety or governmental entities created by two or more municipal corporations under 53 Pa.C.S. Ch. 23 Subch. A (relating to intergovernmental cooperation), either for mutual aid or assistance in police and fire protection or any other public safety services, or for the furnishing to or receiving from the municipal corporations or governmental entities police and fire protection or any other public safety services, and to make appropriations for public safety services. In connection with agreements for police or fire protection or any other public safety services, it shall not be necessary to advertise for bids or receive bonds as required for contracts under existing law. When an agreement has been entered into, the police, firefighters, fire police or any other public safety services of the employing municipal corporation or governmental entity shall have the powers and authority conferred by law on police, firefighters, fire police or any other public safety services in the territory of the municipal corporation which has contracted to secure the service.

(25) To make contracts of insurance, with any mutual or other fire insurance company, association or exchange, duly authorized by law to transact insurance business in this Commonwealth, on any building or property owned or leased by the borough.

(26) To provide for other insurance as follows:

(i) To appropriate an amount as may be necessary to secure insurance or compensation in accordance with Article VI of the act of June 2, 1915 (P.L.736, No.338), known as the Workers' Compensation Act, for:

(A) volunteer firefighters of companies duly recognized by the borough, by motion or resolution, killed or injured while going to, returning from or attending fires or while performing their duties as special fire police; and

(B) other borough employees as "employe" is defined in section 601 of the Workers' Compensation Act.

(ii) To make contracts of insurance with any insurance company, association or exchange authorized to transact business in this Commonwealth insuring borough employees or any class or classes of employees, or mayor and council or their dependents, under a policy or policies of insurance covering life, health, hospitalization, medical and surgical service or accident insurance.

(iii) To contract with an insurance company, granting annuities or pensions, for the pensioning of borough employees or any class or classes of employees, and to agree to pay part or all of the premiums or charges for carrying the contracts and to appropriate money from the borough treasury for those purposes.

(iv) To make contracts with any insurance company, association or exchange authorized to transact business in this Commonwealth to insure any public liability of the borough and to appropriate money from the borough treasury for that purpose.

(v) Nothing in this paragraph shall affect any contract, right or coverage of insurance vested or existing on July 16, 2012. Contract, as used in this paragraph, includes an annuity contract if the option to renew continues to provide the same rights to the annuitant that existed on July 16, 2012.

(27) To contract with a company owning, leasing or operating a light rail or similar transportation system, whether surface, elevated or underground, within the limits of the borough, for the acquisition, leasing or regulation of the franchises, properties, powers, duties and liabilities of the company for the purpose of providing public transportation. A contract may provide that the companies may make payments to the borough in lieu of the performance of certain duties or may include a provision that municipal consent shall not be granted to any other company for the same services covered by the contract. A contract may also provide, subject to any required approval by the Pennsylvania Public Utility Commission and consistent with the jurisdictional limits established under 49 U.S.C. (relating to transportation), for the laying, installation or removal of tracks or lines, to prevent the laying or installation of otherwise authorized tracks or lines or to change the route of any tracks or lines for the consideration and upon conditions as may be agreed upon. Council may acquire, maintain and operate any existing inclined plane passenger transportation facilities and may acquire or may establish vehicular feeder lines for those facilities.

(28) To do any of the following:

(i) Acquire land or buildings by purchase, gift, exchange or eminent domain.

(ii) Erect a building or lease land or buildings, within the borough limits, for community purposes or for public facilities such as comfort and waiting stations and drinking fountains.

(iii) Erect watering troughs.

(iv) Maintain the public facilities.

(v) Provide for the payment of the cost and maintenance of the items under this paragraph from the funds of the borough.

(29) To provide a lockup for the temporary detention of persons.

(30) To display the flag of the United States or of the Commonwealth, the official POW/MIA flag or the flag of any county, city, borough or other municipality in this Commonwealth on the public buildings or grounds and in public places of the borough.

(31) To provide for parking as follows:

(i) to acquire by lease, purchase or eminent domain any land that the council may deem necessary or desirable for the purpose of establishing and maintaining parking lots;

(ii) to regulate the use of parking lots;

(iii) to regulate parking and provide parking accommodations to promote the convenience and protection of the public; and

(iv) to establish or designate, at the discretion of the council, areas exclusively reserved for parking by handicapped individuals and to post signs regulating the areas.

The right to regulate the use of the lots shall include the right to impose fines and fees for violation of any law or ordinance regulating parking. Regulation of parking lots shall be consistent with 75 Pa.C.S. (relating to vehicles) and the act of October 27, 1955 (P.L.744, No.222), known as the Pennsylvania Human Relations Act.

(32) To acquire by purchase or by gift and to repair, supervise, operate and maintain ancient landmarks and other property of historical or antiquarian interest and to make appropriations to nonprofit associations or corporations organized for the purpose of acquiring and maintaining historical properties. The appropriations shall only be used by the association or corporation for the acquisition, restoration and maintenance of the historical properties.

(33) To provide against all hazards of war, terrorism and other disasters and their consequences, and for those purposes to have the power of eminent domain, to cooperate with any other unit and agency of government, Federal, State or local in every lawful way for purposes of defense against the hazards of war and terrorism and to further provide against the hazards of manmade or natural disasters in conjunction with the powers applicable to boroughs in 35 Pa.C.S. Pt. V (relating to emergency management services).

(34)(i) To purchase vehicles and other equipment necessary for the towing of motor vehicles, tractors, trailers, recreational trailers and other vehicles from highways, roads, streets and public property of the borough.

(ii) To impose fees for towing if the towing equipment is used for the lawful removal of motor vehicles, tractors, trailers, recreational trailers and other vehicles from highways, roads, streets and public property of the borough.

(iii) To authorize or contract with commercial towers that agree to tow vehicles for a negotiated price as the official towers for the borough for the lawful removal of motor vehicles, tractors, trailers, recreational trailers and other vehicles from highways, roads, streets and public property of the borough in accordance with Federal and State law.

(iv) To impose fees in the same manner as authorized when the towing is performed with borough vehicles and equipment.

A commercial tower that agrees not to charge in excess of the negotiated price and is otherwise lawfully authorized to tow vehicles in accordance with Federal and State law shall be put on an official rotation list for the borough if council provides for a list. This paragraph shall apply only when the borough is requesting a vehicle to be towed. In all other cases, the owner or operator of a vehicle shall be permitted to select and pay for the tower.

(35) To purchase or contribute to the purchase of fire engines and fire apparatus, boats, rescue and lifesaving equipment and supplies for the use of the borough for fire, rescue and lifesaving services, including community ambulance service, and to appropriate money for fire companies and rescue units located within the borough, including for the construction, repair and maintenance of buildings for fire companies and rescue units, and to acquire land for those purposes. Appropriations may include funds to establish, equip, maintain and operate lawfully organized or incorporated fire training schools within the county or regional firefighters' associations or an entity created pursuant to 53 Pa.C.S. Ch. 23 Subch. A for the purpose of giving instruction and practical training in the prevention, control and fighting of fire and related fire department emergencies to the members of fire departments and volunteer fire companies in any municipal corporation within this Commonwealth. Annual appropriations may also be made to an ambulance service, or council may enter into contracts for use in providing community ambulance service.

(36) To appropriate money for the expense of municipal music.

(37) To accept, purchase and plant or contribute to the purchasing and planting of shade trees along the streets and sidewalks of the borough and to have the care, custody and control of shade trees pursuant to Chapter 27 (relating to recreation places, shade trees and forests).

(38) To appropriate money for the support of any incorporated hospital that is engaged in charitable work and extends treatment and medical attention to residents of the borough, but no appropriation shall exceed in any year the cost of free service extended to residents of the borough that is in excess of any amount paid by the Commonwealth towards free service.

(39) To appropriate money toward the maintenance and support of any medical center or hospital building and further appropriate from the funds toward the purchase and erection of medical or hospital facilities. When the total cost of the purchase or erection exceeds $100,000, it will necessitate approval by the appropriate health planning agency.

(40) To appropriate money annually for the expense of community nurse services to any nonprofit associations or corporations that provide community nursing services for the elderly and other needy persons, the control of communicable disease, the immunization of children, the operation of child health centers (Well-Baby Clinics), instructive visits to parents of new babies, beginning in the prenatal period, and family health guidance, including nutrition, detection and correction of defects all of which relate to the responsibilities of local boards of health.

(41) To appropriate in any year out of the general funds of the borough for the observance of holidays or centennials or other anniversaries or for borough celebrations or other civic projects or programs.

(42) To appropriate from borough funds money for the handling, storage and distribution of surplus foods obtained through either a Federal, State or local agency. All appropriations of money made by any borough for the handling, storage and distribution of surplus foods obtained through either a Federal, State or local agency are validated.

(43) To make appropriations to an industrial development agency.

(44) To appropriate money annually to any tourist promotion agency, as defined in the act of July 4, 2008 (P.L.621, No.50), known as the Tourism Promotion Act, to assist the agencies in carrying out tourist promotional activities.

Table of Contents
Part I Ch. 1–3 Ethics, Records, Open Meetings
Part II Ch. 4–10 Taxation
Part III Ch. 11–18 Torts, Contracts & Civil Rules
Part IV Ch. 19–24 Zoning & Planning
Part V Ch. 25–30 Construction and Emergency Codes
Part VI Ch. 31–39 Municipal Codes
Index

Chap. 39 Res. During Mil. Service
Chap. 38 Intergov. Coop.
Chap. 37 3rd Class City Code
Chap. 36 Bor. Code
Chap. 35 2nd Class Twp. Code
Chap. 34 1st Class Twp. Code
Chap. 33 Home Rule Chart. Opt. Plans Law
Chap. 32 Water Serv. Act
Chap. 31 Munic. Auth. Act

(45) To appropriate money to assist any municipality or municipal airport authority to acquire, establish, operate and maintain any and all air navigation facilities lying either within or without the limits of the borough.

(46) To issue nondebt revenue bonds pursuant to provisions of 53 Pa.C.S. Pt. VII Subpt. B to provide sufficient money for and toward the acquisition, construction, reconstruction, extension or improvement of municipal facilities, including water systems or facilities, sewers, sewer systems and sewage disposal systems or facilities, systems for the treatment or disposal of garbage and refuse, gas plants, gas distribution systems or other FOR ITS OWN MUNICIPAL PURPOSES, MUNICIPAL GAS DISTRIBUTION SYSTEMS OR MUNICIPAL gas works, electric light or power plants or power distribution systems, aeronautical facilities, including, but not limited to, airports, terminals and hangars and park and recreational facilities and parking lots and facilities to be secured solely by the pledge of the whole or part of the rent, toll or charge for the use or services of the facilities. Included in the cost of the issue may be any costs and expenses incident to construction and financing the facilities and selling and distributing the bonds.

(47) To offer rewards for the arrest and conviction of persons guilty of capital or other crimes within the borough.

(48) To appropriate funds for urban common carrier mass transportation purposes from current revenues and to make annual contributions to county departments of transportation or to urban common carrier mass transportation authorities to assist the departments or the authorities to meet costs of operation, maintenance, capital improvements and debt service and to enter into long-term agreements providing for the payment of the contributions.

(49) To undertake community development programs, including, but not limited to, urban renewal, public housing, model cities programs and neighborhood development projects.

(50) To sell to a nonprofit medical service corporation borough-owned:

(i) real property for its exclusive use as a site for a medical service facility; and

(ii) personal property for use at the medical service facility.

(51) To sell to a nonprofit housing corporation borough-owned:

(i) real property for its exclusive use for housing for the elderly; and

(ii) personal property for its use at the nonprofit housing corporation.

(52) To make grants annually to nonprofit art corporations for the conduct of their artistic and cultural activities. For the purposes of this paragraph, the term "nonprofit art corporation" shall mean a local arts council, commission or coordinating agency or any other nonprofit corporation engaged in the production or display of works of art, including the visual, written or performing arts. Artistic and cultural activities include the display or production of theater, music, dance, painting, architecture, sculpture, arts and crafts, photography, film, graphic arts and design and creative writing.

(53) To appropriate annually an amount toward a neighborhood crime watch program. Notwithstanding any other provision of law, no borough or official of a borough may become subject to contractual, tort or other liability as a result of having made an appropriation under this paragraph.

(54) To appropriate funds for programs that benefit senior citizens or make grants to civic organizations that represent senior citizens, provide services to senior citizens or of which its members are senior citizens.

(55) To appropriate money to nonprofit watershed associations for watersheds serving the borough. Appropriations may not be used to undertake

litigation against any municipality or to seek redress against any individual landowner.

(56) To ensure that fire and emergency medical services are provided within the borough by the means and to the extent determined by the borough, including the appropriate financial and administrative assistance for these services. The borough shall consult with fire and emergency medical services providers to discuss the emergency services needs of the borough. The borough shall require any emergency services organization receiving borough funds to provide to the borough an annual itemized listing of all expenditures of these funds before the borough may consider budgeting additional funding to the organization.

(57) To appropriate money to the conservation district, as defined in the act of May 15, 1945 (P.L.547, No.217), known as the Conservation District Law, in which the borough is located.

(58) To require the owner, operator or superintendent of every mine, colliery or quarry located wholly or partially within the limits of the borough to furnish to the borough maps, plans and drawings of workings, excavations and surface support as the council may require. In the case of coal mines and collieries, the map or plan shall exhibit the workings or excavations in every seam of coal on a separate sheet and the tunnels and passages connecting with the workings or excavations. It shall show in degrees the general inclination of the strata, with any material deflection in the strata in the workings or excavations, and shall also show the tidal elevations of the bottom of every shaft, slope, tunnel and gangway and of any other point in the mine or on the surface where the elevation shall be deemed necessary by the borough. The map or plan shall show the number of the last survey on the gangways or the most advanced workings. Every owner, operator or superintendent of a mine, colliery or quarry shall update, at least once every three months, the pertinent maps, plans and drawings to reflect any extensions made in any mine, colliery or quarry during the three preceding months, except those made within 30 days immediately preceding the time of placing the extensions upon the map or drawing. A borough engineer, assistant or other person authorized by council may enter and survey any mine, colliery or quarry within the limits of the borough, at all reasonable times, but not so as to impede or obstruct the workings of the mine, colliery or quarry. The owner, operator or superintendent of the mine, colliery or quarry shall furnish the means necessary for the entry, survey and exit.

(59) To petition the court of common pleas for the appointment of viewers to assess the total cost of an improvement as set forth in Chapter 21A (relating to assessments and charges for public improvements). The viewers shall assess the total cost of the improvement, or so much of the cost as may be just and reasonable, upon the lands or properties peculiarly benefited.

(60) To authorize any borough to:

(i) purchase, own, use, operate and control any

(60) To authorize:

(i) Any borough to purchase, own, use, operate and control any natural gas well or wells for the purpose of supplying natural gas for its own municipal purposes; and

(ii) purchase, own, use, operate and control natural gas works. A borough owning or operating a municipal gas distribution system on the effective date of this section to purchase, own, use, operate and control municipal gas distribution systems.

(61) To establish, by ordinance, and maintain a real estate registry for the purpose of procuring accurate information in reference to the ownership of real estate in the borough in a manner not inconsistent with the act of October 9, 2008

Chap. 39 Res. During Mil. Service
Chap. 38 Intergov. Coop.
Chap. 37 3rd Class City Code
Chap. 36 Bor. Code
Chap. 35 2nd Class Twp. Code
Chap. 34 1st Class Twp. Code
Chap. 33 Home Rule Chart. Opt. Plans Law
Chap. 32 Water Serv. Act
Chap. 31 Munic. Auth. Act

(P.L.1400, No.110), known as the Uniform Municipal Deed Registration Act. Council shall designate a person to have charge of the registry who shall cause to be made and carefully preserve all necessary books, maps and plans as may show the location and ownership of every lot, piece of real estate and subdivision of real estate. For purposes of establishing or maintaining the registry, the person in charge of the registry shall have access to public records without charge. Information contained within a real estate registry shall not affect the validity of any municipal claim or tax claim of the borough. Nothing in this paragraph shall prohibit a borough from requiring owners to provide information relevant to the enforcement of any borough ordinance in accordance with law.

(62) To manufacture, purchase or otherwise supply electricity pursuant to Chapter 24A (relating to manufacture and supply of electricity).

(63) To provide the following:

(i) telecommunications services to the extent that provision of services is not inconsistent with 66 Pa.C.S. Ch. 30 (relating to alternative form of regulation of telecommunications services); and

(ii) cable television services in a manner consistent with Federal law.

(64) To acquire, by purchase or condemnation, or to construct underground conduits within which electrical, communication and other types of wires shall be placed and, by ordinance and subject to approval by the Pennsylvania Public Utility Commission, to regulate the manner and terms and conditions of the use of any underground conduits. Council may define reasonable districts of the borough within which underground conduits shall be used for the placement of wires without the approval of the Pennsylvania Public Utility Commission. The powers reserved by this paragraph shall not be bartered away or surrendered by the borough.

(65) In addition to the remedies provided by law for the filing of liens for the collection of municipal claims, including, but not limited to, water rates, sewer rates and the removal of nuisances, to proceed for the recovery and collection of claims by action of assumpsit against the person or persons who were the owner or owners of the property at the time of the completion of the improvement or at the time the water or sewer rates or the cost of the removal of nuisances first became payable, notwithstanding the fact that there was a failure on the part of the borough or its agents to enter the municipal claim as a lien against the property assessed for the improvement, or for the furnishing of water or sewer services and for the removal of nuisances and for the recovery of which the action of assumpsit was brought. The action in assumpsit shall be commenced either within six years after the completion of the improvement from which the claim arises or within six years after the water or sewer rates or the cost of abating a nuisance first became payable.

§ 1203. Reserved powers.

The council may make and adopt all ordinances, bylaws, rules and regulations not inconsistent with or restrained by the Constitution of Pennsylvania and laws of this Commonwealth as may be expedient or necessary for the proper management, care and control of the borough and its finances and the maintenance of peace, good government, safety and welfare of the borough and its trade, commerce and manufactures.

CHAPTER 13

TAXATION AND FINANCE

---

§ 1301. Fiscal year.

The fiscal year of every borough shall coincide with the calendar year, beginning January 1 and ending December 31.

§ 1302. Tax levy.

(a) **Authority.**—The council of the borough shall have power, by resolution for taxes levied at the same rate as or a rate lower than the previous fiscal year, and by ordinance if the tax rate increases from the previous fiscal year, to levy and collect annually a tax not exceeding 30 mills for general borough purposes, unless the council by majority action, upon due cause shown by resolution, petitions the court of common pleas, in which case the court may order a rate of not more than five mills additional to be levied and in addition any of the following taxes:

(1) An annual tax sufficient to pay interest and principal on any indebtedness incurred pursuant to 53 Pa.C.S. Pt. VII Subpt. B (relating to indebtedness and borrowing) or any prior or subsequent act governing the incurrence of indebtedness of the borough.

(2) To provide for pensions, retirement or the purchase of annuity contracts for borough employees, not exceeding one-half mill.

(3) To defray the cost and expenses of caring for shade trees as provided in section 2720.1 (relating to maintenance by borough and tax levy) and the expense of publishing the notice referred to in section 2720.1, not exceeding one-tenth mill.

(4) For lighting and illuminating the streets, highways and other public places, not exceeding eight mills.

(5) For gas, water and electric, not exceeding eight mills, additional millage permitted only following a favorable referendum on the matter held in accordance with the election laws of this Commonwealth.

Table of Contents
Part I Ch. 1–3 Ethics, Records, Open Meetings
Part II Ch. 4–10 Taxation
Part III Ch. 11–18 Torts, Contracts & Civil Rules
Part IV Ch. 19–24 Zoning & Planning
Part V Ch. 25–30 Construction and Emergency Codes
Part VI Ch. 31–39 Municipal Codes
Index

(6) For the purchase of fire engines, fire apparatus and fire hose for the use of the borough or for assisting any fire company in the borough in the purchase, renewal or repair of any of its fire engines, fire apparatus or fire hose, for the purposes of making appropriations to fire companies both within and without the borough and of contracting with adjacent municipalities or volunteer fire companies in adjacent municipalities for fire protection, for the training of fire personnel and payments to fire training schools and centers or for the purchase of land upon which to erect a firehouse, or for the erection and maintenance of a firehouse or fire training school and center, not exceeding three mills. The following shall apply:

(i) The borough may appropriate up to one-half, but not to exceed one mill, of the revenue generated from a tax under this paragraph for the purpose of paying salaries, benefits or other compensation of fire suppression employees of the borough or a fire company serving the borough. For any calendar year, the council may waive the appropriation limitation under this subparagraph by resolution.

(ii) If an annual tax for the purposes specified in this paragraph is proposed to be set at a level higher than three mills, the question shall be submitted to the voters of the borough, and the county board of elections shall frame the question in accordance with the election laws of this Commonwealth for submission to the voters of the borough.

(7) For building a firehouse, fire training school and center, lockup or municipal building, not exceeding two mills, additional millage permitted only following a favorable referendum on the matter held in accordance with the election laws of this Commonwealth.

(8) To establish and maintain a local library or to maintain or aid in the maintenance of a local library established by deed, gift or testamentary provision, for the use of the residents of the borough, in accordance with 24 Pa.C.S. Ch. 93 (relating to public library code).

(9) (i) For the purpose of supporting ambulance, rescue and other emergency services serving the borough, not to exceed one-half mill, except as provided in subsection (e).

(ii) The borough may appropriate up to one-half of the revenue generated from a tax under subparagraph (i) for the purpose of paying salaries, benefits or other compensation of employees of the ambulance, rescue or other emergency service. For any calendar year, the council may waive the appropriation limitation under this subparagraph by resolution.

(10) An annual tax sufficient for the purpose of maintaining and operating recreation places or for paying the borough's share of a joint action with one or more political subdivisions, in accordance with section 2701 (relating to general powers).

(b) Amount.—The taxes shall be levied on the dollar on the valuation assessed for county purposes, as now is or may be provided by law. All real property, offices, professions and persons made taxable by the laws of this Commonwealth for county rates and levies may, in the discretion of council, be taxed after the same manner for those purposes. An action on the part of the borough authorities fixing the tax rate for any year at a mill rate shall include a statement expressing the rate of taxation in dollars and cents on each $100 of assessed valuation of taxable property.

(c) Use of taxes for general purposes.—Nothing contained in this section may prevent the application of money received from taxes levied for general purposes to the purposes of paying interest and sinking fund charges on indebtedness.

(d) Proceeds.—The proceeds of all taxes for which additional millage is authorized under this section shall be kept in a separate fund and used only for the purposes provided under this section. The additional taxes authorized by referendum shall continue to be levied annually for the period provided under this section in the question submitted in the referendum and, if any taxes for which the question voted upon shall not have stated the duration of the tax, until the tax shall be abolished by vote of the electors in a subsequent referendum.

(e) Tax for ambulance and rescue squads.—The tax for supporting ambulance and rescue squads serving the borough shall not exceed the rate specified in subsection (a)(9) except when the question is submitted to the voters of the borough in the form of a referendum which will appear on the ballot in accordance with the election laws of the Commonwealth, in which case the rate shall not exceed two mills. The county board of elections shall frame the question to be submitted to the voters of the borough in accordance with the election laws of this Commonwealth.

§ 1302.1. Different and separate tax levies.

(a) General rule.—A borough may in any year levy separate and different rates of taxation for municipal purposes on all real estate classified as nonfarmland, exclusive of the buildings on the real estate, and on all real estate classified as either buildings on land or farmland. When real estate tax rates are so levied:

(1) The rates shall be determined by the requirements of the borough budget.

(2) A higher rate may be levied on real estate classified as nonfarmland than on real estate classified as either buildings on land or farmland if the respective rates on nonfarmland and on buildings or farmland are so fixed as not to constitute a greater levy in the aggregate than the levy to result from the maximum rate allowed by law on all real estate.

(3) The rates shall be uniform as to all real estate within the classification.

(b) Nonseverability.—Notwithstanding section 104 (relating to constitutional construction), the provisions of this section are nonseverable. If any provision of this section or its application to any person or circumstance is held invalid, the remaining provisions or applications of this section are void.

(c) Definitions.—As used in this section, the following words and phrases shall have the meanings given to them in this subsection:

"Farmland." Any tract of land that is actively devoted to agricultural use, including, but not limited to, the commercial production of crops, livestock and livestock products as defined in section 3 of the act of June 30, 1981 (P.L.128, No.43), known as the Agricultural Area Security Law.

"Nonfarmland." Any tract of land that is not farmland.

§ 1303. Special levy to pay debts.

In addition to the levies provided for in section 1302.1 (relating to different and separate tax levies) if the council refuses or neglects to levy a sufficient tax to pay the debts due by the borough, a court may, after ascertaining the amount of the indebtedness of the borough, direct a writ of mandamus to the proper officers of the borough to collect by special taxation an amount sufficient to pay the indebtedness in one or more annual installments, as determined reasonable by the court.

§ 1304. Special road fund tax.

(a) Authority.—Any borough shall be empowered, within its general power to levy taxes, to collect annually a tax upon all real property taxable for borough purposes, not to exceed five mills on the dollar in any one year, for the purpose of creating and maintaining a special fund to be used by its borough in making permanent street improvements and to pay contract prices for paving and other permanent street improvements, prior to the collection of the cost and expense

Chap. 39 Res. During Mil. Service
Chap. 38 Intergov. Coop.
Chap. 37 3rd Class City Code
Chap. 36 Bor. Code
Chap. 35 2nd Class Twp. Code
Chap. 34 1st Class Twp. Code
Chap. 33 Home Rule Chart. Opt. Plans Law
Chap. 32 Water Serv. Act
Chap. 31 Munic. Auth. Act

from the property owners adjoining or abutting the property by the borough under existing laws.

(b) Application.—If the cost and expense or any part of the cost and expense of the construction of any permanent street improvement, which has been made under existing laws and which has been aided in its construction from the special fund provided for under this section, has been assessed and collected from the owners of the real property adjoining or abutting upon the improvement, it shall be applied to the credit of the special fund, to the extent of the withdrawal from the special fund for that purpose.

§ 1305. Date tax duplicate to issue.

Council shall, within 30 days after adoption of the budget or within 30 days after receipt of the assessment roll from the county, whichever is later, issue their duplicate of taxes assessed to the collector of taxes of the borough.

§ 1306. Additions and revisions to duplicates.

(a) Inspection and reassessment.—If in any borough there is any construction of a building or buildings not otherwise exempt as a dwelling after the council has prepared a duplicate of the assessment of borough taxes and the building is not included in the tax duplicate of the borough, the county assessment office shall, upon the request of the council, direct the assessor in the county assessment office to inspect and reassess, subject to the right of appeal and adjustment provided by statute, all taxable property in the borough to which major improvements have been made after the original duplicates were prepared and to give notice of the reassessments within ten days to the authority responsible for assessments, the borough and the property owner. The real property shall then be added to the duplicate and shall be taxable for borough purposes at the reassessed valuation for that proportionate part of the fiscal year of the borough remaining after the real property was improved. Any improvement made during the month shall be computed as having been made on the first of the month.

(b) Copy of additions or revisions.—A certified copy of the additions or revisions to the duplicate shall be furnished by the council to the borough tax collector, together with their warrant for collection of the taxes, and, within ten days, the borough tax collector shall notify the owner of the real property of the taxes due to the borough.

§ 1307. Preparation of budget.

Prior to the adoption of the budget, a proposed budget or annual estimate of revenues and expenditures for the ensuing year shall be prepared in a manner designated by the council. The proposed budget shall be kept on file with the borough secretary and be made available for public inspection by the borough secretary for a period of ten days.

§ 1308. Notice of proposed budget and penalty.

(a) Notice.—Notice that the proposed budget is available for inspection shall be published by the borough secretary in a newspaper of general circulation, except in boroughs in which the estimated budget receipts are less than $50,000 in 2012, where, in lieu of the newspaper publications, notice may be conspicuously posted during the ten-day period in a place readily viewable by the public at the office of the borough secretary and with further notice as shall be prescribed by council.

(b) Failure.—Any borough secretary who fails or refuses to give the notice that the proposed budget is available for inspection, as required, shall, upon conviction in a summary proceeding, be sentenced to pay a fine not exceeding $100 and costs of prosecution.

§ 1309. Revision and completion of budget.

After the expiration of the ten days, council shall make the revision in the budget as deemed advisable. The budget must be as comprehensive and exact as the information available will permit. In addition to expenditures proposed for the current fiscal year, council may include as proposed expenditures a sum sufficient to pay any existing indebtedness and to pay the ordinary operating expenses for the subsequent year until the taxes of the subsequent year are received and may also include a sum to provide in whole or in part for any deferred maintenance, depreciation and replacements. Within the tax levy and debt limitations, council may also include, in whole or in part, expenditures for capital investments and purchases. Expenditures of a legislative character must be made, authorized or ratified by ordinance. Other expenditures allowed by law may be made or ratified by motion in council. The expenditures, whether by ordinance or motion, must then be considered as appropriations affecting the budget. A balance of revenues over expenditures may be expended in a subsequent year for a lawful purpose.

§ 1310. Adoption of budget.

Upon completion of the budget containing the estimated receipts and expenditures, the council shall adopt the budget by motion of the council, which may not be later than December 31.

§ 1310.1. Tax ordinance or resolution.

After council has adopted the budget, it is the duty of the council to adopt a resolution levying the taxes referred to in this part for the fiscal year for taxes levied at the same rate as or a rate lower than the previous fiscal year, and to enact an ordinance if the tax rate increases from the previous fiscal year, subject to approval of the mayor or enactment over the mayor's veto under the procedure established in section 3301.3(c) (relating to enactment, approval and veto).

§ 1311. Amending budget and notice.

During the month of January next following a municipal election, the council of a borough may amend the budget and the levy and tax rate to conform with its amended budget. A period of ten days' public inspection at the office of the borough secretary of the proposed amended budget, after notice by the borough secretary to that effect is published once in a newspaper of general circulation, must intervene between the proposed amended budget and its adoption. An amended budget must be adopted by council on or before the 15th day of February.

§ 1312. Modification of budget and supplemental appropriations and transfers.

The council in its reasonable discretion may, in any year, by motion, modify the budget after its final adoption. New appropriations, supplementary appropriations and transfers from one appropriation to another may be made during the fiscal year, either before or after the expenditure is authorized or ratified after the expenditure is made, if it is within the current year's revenues, or the money is promptly made available through borrowing as allowed by law.

§ 1313. Payment from borough funds.

The payments made by the council from the borough funds must be made by proper borough orders, drawn upon the treasurer. No borough order may be authorized by council or signed by the president or secretary of a council unless there are sufficient funds in the treasury of the borough to pay the order, and no orders may be made payable at any time in the future or draw interest. A separate borough order must be drawn for each account or payment.

§ 1313.1. Creation of special funds and investments.

Council may set aside in a separate fund any money received out of or from the sale, lease or other disposition of any borough property or received from any source unless the money was received or acquired for a particular purpose. The fund must be controlled, invested and administered, and the income arising from the fund expended, in the manner as may be determined by action of the council under the ordinance creating the fund. The ordinance may provide that only the

Table of Contents
Part I Ch. 1–3 Ethics, Records, Open Meetings
Part II Ch. 4–10 Taxation
Part III Ch. 11–18 Torts, Contracts & Civil Rules
Part IV Ch. 19–24 Zoning & Planning
Part V Ch. 25–30 Construction and Emergency Codes
Part VI Ch. 31–39 Municipal Codes
Index

income from the fund may be used or expended, and that neither principal nor any part of the principal may be used or expended unless upon authorization of a majority vote of the qualified electors of the borough. The ordinances previously enacted by a borough creating and establishing a separate fund as authorized by this section must be deemed and taken as valid and effectual for all purposes if the other requirements of law concerning the enactment of the separate fund have been complied with.

§ 1314. Uniform financial report and forms.

(a) Preparation of uniform forms.—The uniform forms for the annual financial statement required to be made by the auditors or the controller must be prepared by a committee consisting of four representatives from the Pennsylvania State Association of Boroughs, the Secretary of Community and Economic Development, or the secretary's designee, and any additional members appointed under statute.

(b) Appointment of representatives.—The representatives of boroughs must be appointed by the president of the Pennsylvania State Association of Boroughs. The representatives shall be chosen from among the finance officers or other officers of the borough who have knowledge of the borough's fiscal procedures. As far as possible, they must be chosen to represent boroughs in the various population groups. The president of the organization shall supply to the Department of Community and Economic Development the names and addresses of the representatives immediately upon their appointment.

(c) Compensation of representatives.—The representatives shall serve without compensation but shall be reimbursed by the Commonwealth for the necessary expenses incurred in attending meetings of the committee.

(d) Meetings.—The committee shall meet from time to time as conditions may warrant at the call of the Secretary of Community and Economic Development, or the secretary's designee, who shall serve as chair of the committee.

(e) Duty of secretary and cooperation.—It shall be the duty of the Secretary of Community and Economic Development, or the secretary's designee, to ensure that the forms required by this chapter are prepared in cooperation with the committee. In the event that the committee should for any reason fail to furnish the cooperation, the Secretary of Community and Economic Development, or the secretary's designee, shall prepare the forms. After their preparation, the secretary shall issue the forms and distribute them annually, as needed to the proper officers of each borough.

§ 1315. Capital improvements to certain public service facilities.

(a) Authority.—For the purpose of financing the cost and expense or its share of the cost and expense of capital improvements, including the purchase and installation of machinery and equipment, by altering, improving or enlarging any of the following, a borough owning the plant or facility may issue nondebt revenue bonds as provided in section 1202(46) (relating to specific powers):

(1) its sewer, sewer system or sewage treatment works, either singly or jointly, with other municipalities;

(2) its water works, either singly or jointly, with other municipalities;

(3) its electric power plant or power distribution system; or

(4) its gas plant, gas distribution system or other for its own municipal purposes, municipal gas distribution system or municipal gas works.

(b) Rates.—A borough issuing nondebt revenue bonds under the authority of this section shall adjust and, when necessary, increase the rates of rentals or charges pledged as security for the bonds in order to provide sufficient revenue. The revenue must be set aside as reserve funds to cover depreciation of the properties involved and for future improvements to the plant or facility involved as well as for the payment of the interest on the bonds and the principal at the time of maturity.

§ 1316. Investment of funds.

(a) Duty of council.—Council shall invest borough funds consistent with sound business practice.

(b) Investment program.—Council shall provide for an investment program subject to restrictions contained in this part and in another applicable statute and any rules and regulations adopted by council.

(c) Authorized types of investments.—Authorized types of investments for borough funds are:

(1) United States Treasury bills.

(2) Short-term obligations of the United States Government or its agencies or instrumentalities.

(3) Deposits in savings accounts or time deposits, other than certificates of deposit, or share accounts of institutions insured by the Federal Deposit Insurance Corporation or the National Credit Union Share Insurance Fund to the extent that the accounts are so insured, and, for the amounts above the insured maximum, if approved collateral as provided by law shall be pledged by the depository.

(4) Obligations of:

(i) the United States or its agencies or instrumentalities backed by the full faith and credit of the United States;

(ii) the Commonwealth or its agencies or instrumentalities backed by the full faith and credit of the Commonwealth; or

(iii) a political subdivision of the Commonwealth or its agencies or instrumentalities backed by the full faith and credit of the political subdivision.

(5) Shares of an investment company registered under the Investment Company Act of 1940 (54 Stat. 789, 15 U.S.C. § 80a-1 et seq.), whose shares are registered under the Securities Act of 1933 (48 Stat. 74, 15 U.S.C. § 77a et seq.), if the only investments of the company are in the authorized investments for borough funds listed in paragraphs (1) through (4).

(6) Certificates of deposit purchased from institutions insured by the Federal Deposit Insurance Corporation or the National Credit Union Share Insurance Fund to the extent that the accounts are so insured. For amounts above the insured maximum, the certificates of deposit must be collateralized by a pledge or assignment of assets of the institution, and the collateral may include loans, including interest in pools of loans, secured by first mortgage liens on real property. Certificates of deposit purchased from commercial banks must be limited to an amount equal to 20% of a bank's total capital and surplus. Certificates of deposit purchased from savings and loan associations or savings banks must be limited to an amount equal to 20% of an institution's assets minus liabilities.

(7) An investment authorized by 20 Pa.C.S. Ch. 73 (relating to municipalities investments) must be an authorized investment for a pension or retirement fund.

(8) Bonds of a municipal authority or parking authority created solely by the borough for the purpose of either investment or possible retirement of the bonds and acquisition of authority projects at an earlier date than originally contemplated, using for the purpose either surplus funds of the borough or money appropriated in the annual budget for the purpose.

Table of Contents
Part I Ch. 1–3 Ethics, Records, Open Meetings
Part II Ch. 4–10 Taxation
Part III Ch. 11–18 Torts, Contracts & Civil Rules
Part IV Ch. 19–24 Zoning & Planning
Part V Ch. 25–30 Construction and Emergency Codes
Part VI Ch. 31–39 Municipal Codes
Index

(9) An investment authorized by the act of July 25, 1973 (P.L.217, No.53), entitled "An act authorizing cities of the first class and second class to invest all funds received and deposited with the city treasurer in certain commercial paper under certain terms and conditions; and providing for investment of public corporation or municipal authority funds."

(d) In making investments of borough funds, council has authority to:

(1) Permit assets pledged as collateral under subsection (c)(3), to be pooled in accordance with the act of August 6, 1971 (P.L.281, No.72), entitled "An act standardizing the procedures for pledges of assets to secure deposits of public funds with banking institutions pursuant to other laws; establishing a standard rule for the types, amounts and valuations of assets eligible to be used as collateral for deposits of public funds; permitting assets to be pledged against deposits on a pooled basis; and authorizing the appointment of custodians to act as pledgees of assets."

(2) Combine money from more than one fund under borough control for the purchase of a single investment, if each of the funds combined for the purpose shall be accounted for separately in all respects and the earnings from the investment are separately and individually computed and recorded and credited to the accounts from which the investment was purchased.

(3) Join with one or more other political subdivisions and municipal authorities in accordance with 53 Pa.C.S. Ch. 23 Subch. A (relating to intergovernmental cooperation) in the purchase of a single investment, provided the requirements of paragraph (2) are adhered to regarding separate accounting of individual funds and separate computation, recording and crediting of the earnings from the funds.

§ 1317. (Reserved).

CHAPTER 14
CONTRACTS

Sec.

---

§ 1401. Power to make contracts.

(a) Authority of borough.—Each borough may make contracts for lawful purposes and for the purposes of carrying into execution this part and laws of this Commonwealth.

(b) Contracts and purchases.—Except as otherwise specifically provided in this title, all contracts and purchases must be made with and from the lowest qualified and responsible bidder. In awarding contracts and making purchases, council has the right to take into consideration such factors as the availability, cost and quality of service and may establish prequalification standards for contracts and purchases. A prequalification standard must be reasonably designed to assist council in determining the ability of a bidder to successfully complete a contract or purchase.

(c) Electronic submission of bids.—A borough may permit the electronic submission of bids and may receive bids electronically for competitively bid purchases and contracts pursuant to 62 Pa.C.S. Ch. 46 (relating to electronic bidding by local government units).

§ 1402. Regulation of contracts.

(a) Requirements.—All contracts or purchases in excess of the base amount of $18,500, subject to adjustment under subsection (a.2), except those mentioned in this section and except as provided by the act of October 27, 1979 (P.L.241, No.78), entitled, as amended, "An act authorizing political subdivisions, municipality authorities and transportation authorities to enter into contracts for the purchase of goods and the sale of real and personal property where no bids are received," shall not be made except with and from the lowest qualified and responsible bidder after due notice in one newspaper of general circulation, at least two times at intervals of not less than three days where daily newspapers of general circulation are available for publication and, in case of weekly newspapers, notice once a week for two successive weeks. The first advertisement shall be published not more than 45 days and the second advertisement not less than ten days prior to the date fixed for the opening of bids. Advertisements for contracts or purchases must also be posted in a conspicuous place within the borough. Advertisements for contracts and purchases must contain the date, time and location for opening of bids and must state the amount of the performance bond determined under subsection (c). The amount of the contract must in all cases, whether of straight sale price, conditional sale, lease, lease purchase or otherwise, be the entire amount which the borough pays to the successful bidder or the bidder's assigns in order to obtain the services or property, or both, and may not be construed to mean only the amount that is paid to acquire title or to receive another particular benefit of the whole bargain.

(a.1) Price quotations.—Written or telephonic price quotations from at least three qualified and responsible contractors must be requested for contracts in excess of the base amount of $10,000, subject to adjustment under subsection (a.2), and less than the amount requiring advertisement and competitive bidding, or, in lieu of price quotations, a memorandum must be kept on file showing that fewer than three qualified contractors exist in the market area within which it is practicable to obtain quotations. A written record of telephonic price quotations must be made and must contain at least the date of the quotation, the name of the contractor and the contractor's representative, the construction, reconstruction, repair, maintenance or work that was the subject of the quotation and the price. Written price quotations, written records of telephonic price quotations and memoranda must be retained for a period of three years. Written price quotations as used throughout this section include electronic mail.

(a.2) Adjustments to base amounts.—Adjustments to the base amounts specified under subsections (a) and (a.1) must be made as follows:

(1) The Department of Labor and Industry shall determine the percentage change in the Consumer Price Index for All Urban Consumers: All Items (CPI-U) for the United States City Average as published by the United States Department of Labor, Bureau of Labor Statistics, for the 12-month period ending September 30, 2012, and for each successive 12-month period.

(2) If the department determines that there is no positive percentage change, then no adjustment to the base amounts may occur for the relevant time period provided for in this subsection.

Table of Contents
Part I Ch. 1–3 Ethics, Records, Open Meetings
Part II Ch. 4–10 Taxation
Part III Ch. 11–18 Torts, Contracts & Civil Rules
Part IV Ch. 19–24 Zoning & Planning
Part V Ch. 25–30 Construction and Emergency Codes
Part VI Ch. 31–39 Municipal Codes
Index

(3)(i) If the department determines that there is a positive percentage change in the first year that the determination is made under paragraph (1), the positive percentage change must be multiplied by each base amount, and the products must be added to the base amounts, respectively, and the sums must be preliminary adjusted amounts.

(ii) The preliminary adjusted amounts must be rounded to the nearest $100 to determine the final adjusted base amounts for purposes of subsections (a) and (a.1).

(4) In each successive year in which there is a positive percentage change in the CPI-U for the United States City Average, the positive percentage change must be multiplied by the most recent preliminary adjusted amounts, and the products must be added to the preliminary adjusted amount of the prior year to calculate the preliminary adjusted amounts for the current year. The sums must be rounded to the nearest $100 to determine the new final adjusted base amounts for purposes of subsections (a) and (a.1).

(5) The determinations and adjustments required under this subsection must be made in the period between October 1 and November 15 of each year.

(6) The final adjusted base amounts and new final adjusted base amounts obtained under paragraphs (3) and (4) become effective January 1 for the calendar year following the year in which the determination required under paragraph (1) is made.

(7) The department shall publish notice in the Pennsylvania Bulletin prior to January 1 of each calendar year of the annual percentage change determined under paragraph (1) and the unadjusted or final adjusted base amounts determined under paragraphs (3) and (4) at which competitive bidding is required under subsection (a) and written or telephonic price quotations are required under subsection (a.1), respectively, for the calendar year beginning January 1 after publication of the notice. The notice must include a written and illustrative explanation of the calculations performed by the department in establishing the unadjusted or final adjusted base amounts under this subsection for the ensuing calendar year.

(8) The annual increase in the preliminary adjusted base amounts obtained under paragraphs (3) and (4) may not exceed 3%.

(b) Awarding contracts and authority of council.—

(1) The award of contracts must be made by public announcement at the meeting at which bids are received, or at a subsequent meeting, the time and place of which shall be publicly announced when bids are received. If for any reason one or both of the meetings are not held, the same business may be transacted at a subsequent meeting if at least five days' notice shall be published in the newspaper of general circulation. At council's request, the bids advertised for must be accompanied by cash, money order, a certified or cashier's good faith check or other irrevocable letter of credit drawn upon a bank authorized to do business in this Commonwealth or by a bond with corporate surety in the amount as council determines, and, when requested, no bid may be considered unless so accompanied.

(2) Notwithstanding paragraph (1), council may direct that a committee of council, a member of council or a member of the borough staff receive, open and review bids during normal business hours and forward the information to council for subsequent award at a public meeting. Bidders must be notified and other interested parties, upon request, must be notified of the date, time and location of the opening of bids and may be present when the bids are opened.

(c) Security.—The successful bidder when advertising is required may, at the discretion of council, be required to furnish a bond or irrevocable letter of credit

Chap. 39 Res. During Mil. Service
Chap. 38 Intergov. Coop.
Chap. 37 3rd Class City Code
Chap. 36 Bor. Code
Chap. 35 2nd Class Twp. Code
Chap. 34 1st Class Twp. Code
Chap. 33 Home Rule Chart. Opt. Plans Law
Chap. 32 Water Serv. Act
Chap. 31 Munic. Auth. Act

or other security with suitable reasonable requirements guaranteeing the work to be done with sufficient surety in an amount as determined by council that must be not less than 10% nor more than 100% of the amount of the liability under the contract within 20 days after the contract has been awarded, unless council shall prescribe a shorter period of not less than ten days, and, upon failure to furnish the security within the time, the previous award is void. Deliveries, accomplishment and guarantees may be required in all cases of expenditures.

(d) **Contracts or purchases.**—The contracts or purchases made by council, which shall not require advertising, bidding or price quotations as provided in this part, are as follows:

(1) Those for routine maintenance, repairs or replacements for water, electricity or public works of the borough, if they do not constitute new additions, extensions or enlargements of existing facilities and equipment, but security may be required by council, as in other cases of work done.

(1.1) Those for emergency maintenance, repairs or replacements for water, electricity or public works of the borough, if they do not constitute new additions, extensions or enlargements of existing facilities and equipment, but security may be required by council, as in other cases of work done. The actual emergency and the nature of the procurement shall be stated in a resolution by council and adopted at the next public meeting.

(1.2) Those for the mitigation of a real or potential emergency involving a clear and present danger to the health, safety and welfare of the residents of the borough. For those contracts or purchases made in cases of emergencies, the actual emergency and the nature of the procurement shall be stated in a resolution by council and adopted at the next public meeting.

(2) Those made for improvements, repairs and maintenance of any kind, made or provided by a borough, through its own employees, if the materials used for street improvement, maintenance or construction in excess of the amount specified or adjusted under subsection (a.1) are subject to the relevant price quotation or advertising requirements contained in this section.

(3) Those under which particular types, models or pieces of new equipment, articles, apparatus, appliances, computer software, vehicles or parts of vehicles are desired by council, which are patented and manufactured or copyrighted products.

(3.1) Those for used personal property, such as equipment, articles, apparatus, appliances, vehicles or parts of vehicles being purchased from a public utility, municipal corporation, county, school district, municipal authority, council of government, volunteer fire company, volunteer ambulance service, volunteer rescue squad or Federal or State Government.

(4)(i) Those involving a policy of insurance or a surety company bond.

(ii) Those made for utility service for borough purposes, including, but not limited to, those made for natural gas or telecommunications services and electricity.

(iii) Deleted by amendment.

(iv) Those made with another political subdivision, or a county, or council of government, consortium, cooperative or other similar entity created under 53 Pa.C.S. Ch. 23 Subch. A (relating to intergovernmental cooperation) or the Commonwealth, the Federal Government, an agency of the Commonwealth or the Federal Government, or a municipal authority, including the sale, lease or loan of any supplies or materials by the Commonwealth or the Federal Government or their agencies. The price may not be in excess of that fixed by the Commonwealth, the Federal Government or their agencies.

(5) Those involving personal or professional services.

(6) Those made relating to the purchase of electricity and associated energy and related services by a borough owning or operating electric generation or distribution facilities with any of the following:

(i) A political subdivision.

(ii) Another state.

(iii) The Commonwealth or a Commonwealth agency.

(iv) The Federal Government.

(v) A private corporation.

(vi) An electric cooperative corporation under 15 Pa.C.S. Ch. 73 (relating to electric cooperative corporations).

(vii) A nonprofit membership corporation. As used in this subparagraph, the term "nonprofit membership corporation" means an entity, the membership of which:

(A) consists solely of Commonwealth boroughs, such as a consortium, buying group or municipal power agency under section 24A04 (relating to municipal power agencies); or

(B) consists of Commonwealth boroughs and political subdivisions of another state.

(viii) An electric cooperative of another state.

Nothing in this paragraph prohibits council from engaging in advertising, bidding or price quotations if the council determines that the advertising, bidding or price quotations are in the public interest.

(7) Those made for materials and supplies or equipment rental under emergency conditions under 35 Pa.C.S. Pt. V (relating to emergency management services).

(e) Council shall award contracts subject to the requirements of and may exercise any powers granted by the following acts to the extent applicable:

(1) The act of August 15, 1961 (P.L.987, No.442), known as the Pennsylvania Prevailing Wage Act.

(2) The act of December 20, 1967 (P.L.869, No.385), known as the Public Works Contractors' Bond Law of 1967.

(3) The act of January 17, 1968 (P.L.11, No.5), known as The Minimum Wage Act of 1968.

(4) The act of January 23, 1974 (P.L.9, No.4), referred to as the Public Contract Bid Withdrawal Law.

(5) The act of March 3, 1978 (P.L.6, No.3), known as the Steel Products Procurement Act.

(6) The act of February 17, 1994 (P.L.73, No.7), known as the Contractor and Subcontractor Payment Act.

(7) 62 Pa.C.S. Pt. II (relating to general procurement provisions).

(f) Prohibition.—No person, consultant, firm or corporation contracting with the borough for purposes of rendering personal or professional services to the borough may share with a borough officer or employee, and no borough officer or employee may accept, a portion of the compensation or fees paid by the borough for the contracted services provided to the borough except under the following terms or conditions:

(1) Full disclosure of the relevant information regarding the sharing of the compensation or fees must be made to the council of the borough.

(2) The council of the borough must approve the sharing of a fee or compensation for personal or professional services prior to the performance of the services.

(3) No fee or compensation for personal or professional services may be shared except for work actually performed.

(4) No shared fee or compensation for personal or professional services may be paid at a rate in excess of that commensurate for similar personal or professional services.

§ 1403. Evasion of advertising requirements.

(a) Prohibition.—

(1) No member of council may evade section 1402 (relating to regulation of contracts) as to advertising for bids by purchasing or contracting for services and personal properties piecemeal for the purpose of obtaining prices under the amount specified or adjusted under section 1402(a) upon transactions, which transactions should, in the exercise of reasonable discretion and prudence, be conducted as one transaction amounting to more than the amount specified or adjusted under section 1402(a).

(2) This subsection is intended to make unlawful the evading of advertising requirements by making a series of purchases or contracts, each for less than the advertising requirement price, or by making several simultaneous purchases or contracts, each below the price, when, in either case, the transactions involved should have been made as one transaction for one price.

(3) Any members of council who vote in violation of this subsection and know that the transaction upon which they vote is or should be a part of a larger transaction and is being divided in order to evade the requirements as to advertising for bids shall be jointly and severally subject to surcharge for 10% of the full amount of the contract or purchase.

(4) If it appears that a member of council may have voted in violation of this section, but the purchase or contract on which the member of council voted was not approved by council, this section shall not apply.

(b) Penalty.—Any council member who votes to unlawfully evade the provisions of section 1402 and knows that the transaction upon which the member voted is or should be a part of a larger transaction and is being divided in order to evade the requirements as to advertising for bids commits a misdemeanor of the third degree for each contract entered into as a direct result of that vote. The penalty under this subsection shall be in addition to a surcharge that may be assessed under subsection (a).

§ 1404. Personal interest in contracts or purchases.

Elected and appointed borough officials and borough employees are restricted from an interest in borough contracts and purchases to the extent provided in 65 Pa.C.S. Ch. 11 (relating to ethics standards and financial disclosure).

§ 1404.1. Purchase contracts for petroleum products and fire company, etc., participation.

The council of each borough shall have power to permit, subject to terms and conditions as it may and, as specifically provided, shall, prescribe, a paid or volunteer fire company, paid or volunteer rescue company and paid or volunteer ambulance company in the borough to participate in purchase contracts for petroleum products entered into by the borough. A company desiring to participate in purchase contracts shall file with the borough secretary a request to authorize it to participate in contracts for the purchase of petroleum products of the borough and agreeing that it will be bound by the terms and conditions as the borough may and, as specifically provided, shall, prescribe and that it will be responsible for payment directly to the vendor under each purchase contract. Among the terms and conditions, the borough shall prescribe that the prices must be F.O.B. destination.

Table of Contents
Part I Ch. 1–3 Ethics, Records, Open Meetings
Part II Ch. 4–10 Taxation
Part III Ch. 11–18 Torts, Contracts & Civil Rules
Part IV Ch. 19–24 Zoning & Planning
Part V Ch. 25–30 Construction and Emergency Codes
Part VI Ch. 31–39 Municipal Codes
Index

§ 1405. Separate bids for plumbing, heating, ventilating and electrical work.

If, in the preparation for the erection, construction and alteration of a public building, the entire cost of the work exceeds the amount specified or adjusted under section 1402(a) (relating to regulation of contracts), the architect, engineer or other person preparing the specifications may, if requested by the council, prepare separate specifications for the plumbing, heating, ventilating and electrical work. The person authorized to enter into contracts for the erection, construction or alteration of the public buildings may, if the separate specifications have been proposed, receive separate bids upon each of the branches of work and shall award the contract to the lowest responsible bidder for each of the branches.

§ 1406. Bonds for the protection of labor and materials.

Before a contract exceeding $10,000 is awarded to a prime contractor or construction manager for the construction, erection, installation, completion, alteration, repair of or addition to a public work or improvement of any kind, the contractor shall furnish to the borough a payment bond for the protection of claimants supplying labor or materials to the prime contractor to whom the contract is awarded, at 100% of the contract amount, conditioned for the prompt payment of the materials furnished or labor supplied or performed in the prosecution of the contract under the act of December 20, 1967 (P.L.869, No.385), known as the Public Works Contractors' Bond Law of 1967. The bond requirement is in addition to any other bond requirement required by law to be given in connection with the contract.

§ 1407. (Reserved).

§ 1408. (Reserved).

§ 1409. (Reserved).

§ 1410. Acceptance by contractor of Workers' Compensation Act.

(a) Contract provision.—A contract executed by a borough or an officer of a borough, which involves the construction or doing of work involving the employment of labor, must contain a provision that the contractor shall accept, insofar as the work covered by the contract is concerned, the provisions of the act of June 2, 1915 (P.L.736, No.338), known as the Workers' Compensation Act, and the supplements and amendments to the Workers' Compensation Act, and that the contractor will insure his liability under the act and will file with the borough with which the contract is made a certificate of insurance providing evidence of the coverage or file with the borough with which the contract is made a certificate of exemption from insurance from the Bureau of Workers' Compensation of the Department of Labor and Industry. The certificate of exemption from insurance may be issued on the basis of either individual self-insurance or group self-insurance. Additionally, a contractor shall file with the borough with which the contract is made any applications to be excepted by the provisions of the Workers' Compensation Act in respect to certain employees on religious grounds if the applications have been accepted by the Department of Labor and Industry.

(b) Violation.—A contract executed in violation of subsection (a) is null and void.

§ 1411. (Reserved).

CHAPTER 15
EMINENT DOMAIN, ASSESSMENT OF DAMAGES AND DAMAGES FOR INJURY TO PROPERTY

SUBCHAPTER A
GENERAL PROVISIONS RELATING TO EMINENT DOMAIN

§ 1501. Exercise of eminent domain.

A borough may enter upon, appropriate, injure or destroy private lands, property or material, or lands previously granted or dedicated to public use that are no longer used for the purpose for which the lands were granted, according to the proceedings set forth in 26 Pa.C.S. (relating to eminent domain), for any of the following purposes:

(1) The laying out, opening, widening, extending, vacating, grading or changing the grades or lines of streets.

(2) The construction of bridges and the piers and abutments for bridges.

(3) The construction of slopes, embankments and sewers.

(4) The erection and extension of water systems, wharves and docks, public buildings, public auditoriums, memorials, monuments, public works, filtration plants, sewerage systems, sewage treatment works, refuse disposal or incineration plants, sanitary landfills, gas plants, electric plants and libraries.

(5) The establishing of parks, playgrounds and recreation places, the changing of watercourses.

(6) For all other purposes authorized by this part.

§ 1502. Restrictions as to certain property.

(a) Historically significant property.—In addition to a restriction made by another provision of this part in a particular case, no borough may exercise the right of eminent domain against:

(1) land now occupied by a building that was used during the Colonial or Revolutionary period as a place of assembly by the Council of the Colony of Pennsylvania, the Supreme Executive Council of the Commonwealth of Pennsylvania or the Congress of the United States;

(2) the land occupied by a fort, redoubt or blockhouse erected during the Colonial or Revolutionary period or a building used as headquarters by the Commander-in-Chief of the Continental Army; or

(3) the site of a building, fort, redoubt, blockhouse, or headquarters that is preserved for its historic associations and not for private profit.

(a.1) Colonial or Revolutionary period.—For the purposes of subsection (a), the Colonial and Revolutionary period terminates on September 3, 1783.

(b) Prohibition.—No land or property used for a cemetery, burying ground or place of public worship may be taken or appropriated by virtue of a power contained in this chapter.

§ 1502.1. Declaration of intention.

A borough shall declare its intention to acquire, enter upon, take, use and appropriate any private property or land for any of the purposes authorized by this chapter through a duly enacted ordinance.

§ 1503. Application of 26 Pa.C.S.

Eminent domain proceedings must conform to the provisions of 26 Pa.C.S. (relating to eminent domain), including, but not limited to, payment of damages and costs.

SUBCHAPTER B
PROCEDURE FOR ASSESSMENT OF BENEFITS BY VIEWERS
(Reserved)

SUBCHAPTER C
DAMAGES FOR INJURY TO PROPERTY

Sec.
1561. Right to damages given in certain cases.
1562. (Reserved).
1563. (Reserved).
1564. (Reserved).
1565. (Reserved).

---

§ 1561. Right to damages given in certain cases.

The right to damages against a borough is given to an owner or tenant of land, property or material, abutting on, or through which pass, streets, injured by the vacating of the streets, or the vacation of bridges and piers, abutments and approaches.

§ 1562. (Reserved).

§ 1563. (Reserved).

§ 1564. (Reserved).

§ 1565. (Reserved).

CHAPTER 16
LAND SUBDIVISION
(RESERVED)

CHAPTER 17
STREETS

Subchapter

SUBCHAPTER A
GENERAL PROVISIONS

Sec.

---

§ 1701. Definitions.

The following words and phrases when used in this chapter shall have the meanings given to them in this section unless the context clearly indicates otherwise:

"Improving a street." The term includes work upon a street or portion thereof done or proposed to be done in order to open the street, if the street has not previously been opened or, if previously opened, to make the street more usable or more suitable for use by the traveling public or safer for the use. The term includes, but is not limited to, grading, paving, curbing and macadamizing.

"Laying out." The term includes the plotting of:

(1) An unopened street or portion of the street on a borough plan or official map adopted in accordance with the Pennsylvania Municipalities Planning Code on a subdivision or land development plan or by the enactment of an ordinance adopted in accordance with this chapter.

(2) An unopened street in a case where any of the lines of the street are proposed to be revised or in a case where the street was never previously laid out although the street may have been opened and used.

"Opened streets." The term includes the streets within the borough used as public passageways.

"Opening a street." The term includes the construction and grading of a street or portion thereof and the act of physically taking possession of an area or laid-out street for the purpose of making the same usable to the traveling public.

"Person." The term includes a natural person, association, firm, corporation or political subdivision.

"Personal notice." The term includes notice upon the owner of a premises either by personal service upon the owner or by certified mail to the owner at the owner's last known address. Where service has not been successfully made by either of the two methods first mentioned, it may be made by leaving the notice at or upon the premises.

"Portion." The term includes a portion either of the width or length of a street. Opening a portion of a street may mean extending or widening a street and vacating a portion of a street may mean closing or narrowing a street.

"Street." The term includes a street, road, lane, court, cul-de-sac, alley, public way and public square, either for or intended for public use, and includes the cartway, sidewalk, gutter and the right-of-way area, whether or not the street or a part of the street is owned in fee by others than the borough. Streets are of two classes, opened and unopened.

"Unopened streets." The term includes the streets within the borough neither used as a public passageway, nor accepted or maintained, but plotted in one of the following:

(1) a borough plan or official map adopted in accordance with the Pennsylvania Municipalities Planning Code;

(2) an ordinance laying out the street in accordance with this chapter;

(3) a subdivision or land development plan; or

(4) an individual deed.

§ 1702. (Reserved).

§ 1703. (Reserved).

§ 1704. Streets connecting with street of other municipality.

No action may be taken under this chapter that would result in the change of location or grade or the vacation of a street or portion thereof that connects with a street of another municipality, without approval of the court of common pleas of the county in which the municipality is located, unless the municipality first files with the borough secretary its approval of the proposed action.

§ 1705. Entry on land to maintain marks and monuments.

The council, its agents and employees, may enter upon any land or property and maintain marks and monuments, so far as the council may deem necessary, in carrying out its powers and duties under this chapter.

§ 1706. Exclusive nature of provisions.

No street may be dedicated, accepted, acquired, laid out, opened or vacated by a borough except under this chapter.

§ 1707. Failure of council to hold hearing.

If, after the filing of a petition under this chapter, council fails to hold a required hearing, an aggrieved party may file a mandamus action in the court of common pleas requesting that a hearing be held.

§ 1708. Street lighting, ornamental lighting and traffic control signals and devices.

Council may provide street lights and ornamental lighting and make regulations for the protection of lighting. Council may assess the costs for the erection of lighting in accordance with Chapter 21A (relating to assessments and charges for public improvements). Council may provide for the erection, maintenance and operation of traffic control signals and devices in accordance with 75 Pa.C.S. (relating to vehicles).

SUBCHAPTER B

PLAN OF STREETS

§ 1711. (Reserved).

§ 1712. Borough street plan.

(a) Adoption of plan.—A borough that has not maintained an accurate plan of borough streets adopted in accordance with this part prior to July 16, 2012, may only adopt a plan of streets under the Pennsylvania Municipalities Planning Code, governing the adoption of an official map.

(b) Amendments to plan.—If a borough maintains a plan of streets adopted prior to July 16, 2012, or maintains an official map containing opened and unopened streets, a street laid out in accordance with this part by ordinance or by final approval of a subdivision or land development plan must be deemed an amendment to the plan. Notwithstanding any other provision of law, a deemed amendment as provided in this section and a subsequent placement of the street on a plan may not be subject to public notice or public hearing, if the street has been laid out in accordance with the requirements of this chapter.

(c) Prohibition.—The maintenance of a plan of streets or official map shall not be required in order for a borough to lay out streets in accordance with section 1721.2(b) (relating to laying out streets and procedure) or lay out and open a street in accordance with section 1724 (relating to effect of laying out street).

SUBCHAPTER C
LAYING OUT STREETS

§ 1721. (Reserved).

§ 1721.1. Power to lay out, open, etc.

(a) Authority of borough.—In accordance with the provisions of this chapter, boroughs may, with or without petition of abutting property owners, lay out, open, widen, straighten, alter, extend and improve, and may establish or reestablish the grades of, and keep in order and repair and in safe passable condition, a street or portion of a street within the borough limits or may vacate the street or portion of a street if deemed expedient for the public good and provide for the costs of alteration.

(b) Laying out or opening streets.—Boroughs may lay out or open:

(1) a street or portion of a street as it appears upon a borough plan or an official map adopted in accordance with the Pennsylvania Municipalities Planning Code or is described in an ordinance adopted in accordance with this chapter;

(2) a street or portion of a street that the borough determines to acquire by eminent domain;

(3) a street to which the public has acquired rights by constant use over a period exceeding 21 years; or

(4) a street or portion of a street, laid out or constructed by a person that the borough sees fit to open or accept as provided in this chapter.

§ 1721.2. Laying out streets and procedure.

(a) Streets deemed to be laid out.—A street identified in a plan of streets, an official map adopted in accordance with the Pennsylvania Municipalities Planning Code or a recorded subdivision or land development plan is deemed to be laid out for purposes of this part.

(b) Future street opening.—A borough has the authority, by ordinance, to lay out an area for future opening as a public street. The proposed ordinance laying out the street must be advertised in a newspaper of general circulation once a week for two successive weeks. On or before the publication of the first advertisement, personal notice must be provided to the owners of a property abutting the proposed street or through which the proposed street is to be laid out, and, if the proposed street will lead into an adjacent municipality, a copy of the proposed ordinance must be sent to the adjacent municipality. The proposed ordinance must have appended to the ordinance or referenced a map sufficient to apprise the public of the proposed location, profile and dimensions of the street and must list the names of the owners of a property through which the proposed street has been laid out.

(c) Hearing, notice and enactment.—Within ten days after the second publication of the notice required under subsection (b), an interested party may petition council for a hearing, which council shall hold within 60 days after the date of the petition. Council shall give at least 15 days' notice of the hearing in a newspaper of general circulation and by personal notice to persons entitled to the notice under subsection (b). Council may enact the ordinance no later than 30 days following the date of the hearing or, where no timely petition has been filed, within 30 days of the second publication of the notice required by subsection (b). The enactment of the ordinance constitutes public notice of the borough's intent to recognize the street within the system of borough streets and the borough's rights in the street. Within 30 days of the enactment of the ordinance, a party aggrieved by council's action may appeal to the court of common pleas.

(d) Filing of ordinance.—If, at the time of the enactment of an ordinance in accordance with subsection (c), the lines of the laid out street include property not subject to use as a public passageway, the ordinance must be filed with the recorder of deeds of the county where the borough is located. The recorder of deeds shall index the ordinance by name of borough, name of the property owner and, if applicable, parcel number of the property through which the proposed street is laid out.

(e) Landowners.—If a street has been laid out by ordinance as provided in this section, the owner or subsequent owner has no right to damages for buildings or improvements placed on streets after the date of enactment, and the buildings or improvements must be removed at the expense of the landowner after the opening of the street in accordance with this part.

(f) Laying out without opening.—The laying out of a street, without opening the street, creates no right to public use of the street and does not constitute the taking or acceptance of a property or obligate the borough to improve or maintain the street or the property on which the street has been laid out.

(g) Previously laid out streets.—Nothing in this section may affect the validity or legal effect of a street laid out in accordance with law prior to July 16, 2012.

§ 1722. (Reserved).

§ 1723. (Reserved).

§ 1724. Effect of laying out street.

(a) Street unopened after ten years.—At any time after a street or portion of the street has remained laid out but not opened for a period of ten years or longer, an owner of 50% of the front feet of the land over which the street or portion of the street was laid out may petition the council to cancel the laying out of the street. Following at least 15 days' notice in a newspaper of general circulation and at least 15 days' personal notice to the owners of the real estate abutting upon the land over which the street or portion of the street was laid out, council shall hold a public hearing on the matter. Council may, on motion, deny the petition or, by ordinance, grant the petition and cancel the laying out of the street. A person aggrieved by the decision of the council, either granting or denying the petition, may appeal it. The ordinance providing for the cancellation of the laying out of a street must be filed with the recorder of deeds in accordance with section 1721.2(d) (relating to laying out streets and procedure).

(b) Street unopened after 21 years.—If a street has been laid out and has not been opened to or used by the public for a period of 21 years, the street may not thereafter be opened without the consent of at least 51% percent of the number of owners of the abutting real estate and without the consent of the owners of at least 51% of the property abutting the street, based on a front foot basis.

SUBCHAPTER D
OPENING, ACCEPTANCE AND VACATION OF STREETS

Sec.

---

§ 1731. Authority to open and vacate streets and procedure.

(a) Authority of council authority.—By ordinance, council has the authority to:

(1) Open a street or portion of a street previously laid out or simultaneously to lay out and open a street or portion thereof. A street or portion of a street so opened is a public street of the borough.

(2) Vacate or close a street or portion of a street previously opened or laid out provided that no street or portion of a street providing the sole means of access to a tract of land is vacated without the consent of those to whom access would be denied. Vacation of a street terminates the public right in or to the street but does not affect a private right acquired by an owner of abutting property.

(b) Notice.—The proposed ordinance opening or vacating a street or portion of a street must be advertised in a newspaper of general circulation once a week for two successive weeks. On or before the publication of the first advertisement, personal notice must be provided to the owners of a property abutting the street proposed to be opened or vacated. The proposed ordinance must have appended to it or reference a map or survey sufficient to apprise the public of the proposed location, profile and dimensions of the street and must list the names of the owners of a property abutting the street.

(c) Hearing.—Within ten days after the second publication of the notice required under subsection (b), an interested party may petition council for a hearing, which council shall hold within 60 days after the date of the petition. Council shall give at least 15 days' notice of the hearing in a newspaper of general circulation and by personal notice to persons entitled to notice under subsection (b). Council may enact the ordinance no later than 30 days following the date of the hearing or, where no timely petition has been filed, within 30 days of the second publication of the notice required under subsection (b). Within 30 days of the enactment of the ordinance, any party aggrieved by council's action may appeal to the court of common pleas.

§ 1732. Petition for opening or vacating street and action thereon.

(a) Petitioning council.—Any person or persons constituting a majority in number and interest of the owner of the real estate abutting upon an area not opened as a street or abutting upon an existing street or portion of a street may petition the council to:

(1) Open or lay out and open the area as a street or portion of a street.

(2) Vacate a street or portion of a street.

(b) Hearing and decision.—Council shall hold a hearing after receiving a petition filed with council in accordance with subsection (a), following at least 15 days' personal notice to the owners of abutting real estate not joining in the petition and following at least 15 days' notice thereof in a newspaper of general circulation. Following the hearing, council shall either by motion deny the petition or by ordinance open, lay out and open or vacate the street or portion of the street. The provisions of section 1731 (relating to authority to open and vacate streets and procedure) applicable to ordinances enacted by authority of that section apply to ordinances enacted by authority of this section.

(c) Release.—A petition for the vacation of a street or portion of a street may release the borough from the damages sustained as a result of the vacation if the petition is signed by the owners of the property abutting upon the street or portion of the street. Where the release has been included in the petition, no proceedings for award of damages may be had, and no damages as a result of the vacation may, under any conditions, be awarded to an abutting property owner.

§ 1733. Action for damages and benefits and award.

(a) Authority of borough.—Upon the effective date of an ordinance enacted to open a street or portion of a street by authority of section 1731 (relating to authority to open and vacate streets and procedure) or 1732 (relating to petition for opening or vacating street and action thereon), the borough has authority to enter upon and take possession of the street or portion of the street opened by the ordinance, if no structures are upon the street. If a structure has been located upon the street or portion of the street so opened, prior to the laying out of the street or prior to the simultaneous laying out and opening of the street, the street may not be opened until the owner of the structure has been given 60 days' personal notice to vacate the structure. Council may not be required to file any bond or security for the exercise of the right granted by this section.

(b) Limitation.—The parties whose ground is taken in the opening of a street or portion of the street have three years from and after the effective date of the ordinance opening the street or portion of the street in which to bring an action for damages resulting from the opening of the street or portion of the street. In case of the assessment of damages for the opening of a street or portion of the street, the award of damages, if any, includes:

(1) the damages resulting from the grade at which the street or portion of the street is to be opened; and

(2) the plan attached to the report of the viewers awarding the damages must include a profile plan showing the existing grade as well as the grade to which the street or portion of the street is to be opened.

Costs and expenses that cannot be assessed upon property benefited must be paid by the borough.

(c) No agreement on damages.—If the parties cannot agree upon damages sustained by reason of the opening or vacation of any street or portion of a street, the damages shall be assessed by a jury of view under the law governing eminent domain.

§ 1734. Acceptance and dedication of streets.

(a) Accept an opened street.—A borough may, by ordinance, accept an opened street not previously dedicated to or laid out by the borough by following the procedure set forth in section 1731 (relating to authority to open and vacate streets and procedure) or 1732 (relating to petition for opening or vacating street and action thereon), and the effect of the acceptance shall be the same as of opening the street. No street may be accepted unless the street connects with at least one other previously opened street or State highway.

(b) Prohibition.—No borough may acquire a right in or responsibility for a street privately constructed until dedication of the street has been presented to and accepted by the borough and until the dedication has been recorded in the county office for the recording of deeds.

§ 1735. Streets not to be constructed, dedicated or opened to travel without the approval of council.

(a) Requirements.—No person may construct, dedicate or open to travel a street or a drainage facility in connection with the street for public use or travel or for the common use of occupants of buildings abutting thereon in a borough without first submitting suitable plans to the council and obtaining its approval. The plans must:

(1) be prepared in accordance with rules and regulations as may be prescribed by the council; and

(2) show the profiles of the street, the course, structure and capacity of a drainage facility, and the method of drainage of the adjacent or contiguous territory, and any other or further details that may be required under the rules or regulations adopted by the council.

(b) Pennsylvania Municipalities Planning Code.—The Pennsylvania Municipalities Planning Code shall apply to the construction, security requirements and dedication of streets and connected drainage facilities if the streets proposed to be constructed are part of a plan required by an ordinance adopted under the Pennsylvania Municipalities Planning Code.

(c) Authority and duties of council.—

(1) Before acting upon plans not subject to review under subsection (b), council may, at its discretion, arrange for a public hearing after giving the notice as it may deem desirable in each case. Council may alter the plans and specify changes or modifications of any kind and may make its approval of the plans subject to alterations, changes or modifications. Plans, when so approved, must be:

(i) signed on behalf of the borough by the officer as the council may designate; and

(ii) must be filed where the plans are available for public inspection among the records of the borough at reasonable times.

(2) No approval of plans by council may obligate or require the borough to construct, reconstruct, maintain, repair or grade a street or drainage facilities associated therewith.

(d) No plan approved.—If the council refuses to approve any plans submitted to it, a person aggrieved by the action of council may, within 30 days after the action, appeal from the action by petition to the court of common pleas of the county, and the court shall hear the matter de novo. After hearing, the court may enter a decree affirming, reversing or modifying the action of the council as may appear just. The court shall designate the manner in which notice of the hearing of an appeal shall be given to all parties interested. The decision of the court shall be final. A plan approved by the action of council or by the court on appeal must be recorded by the person applying for approval in the office of the recorder of deeds in the county.

(e) **Restriction.**—If a street or a drainage facility in connection with the street is opened, constructed or dedicated for public use or travel, except in strict accordance with a plan approved by the council or the court on appeal as provided in this chapter, neither the council nor any other public authority may place, construct or operate a sewer, drain, water pipe or other facility or do any work in or upon the street. Neither council nor any other public authority has a responsibility with respect to the street or drainage facility, notwithstanding the use of the street or drainage facility by the public. Nothing in this chapter prevents the laying of a trunk sewer, drain or water or gas main, if required by engineering necessity for the accommodation of other territory.

(f) **Failure to comply with chapter.**—A person who constructs, opens or dedicates a street or drainage facility in connection with a street, for public use or travel in a borough, without having first complied with this chapter is guilty of a misdemeanor of the third degree and is subject to a suit for the costs and damages incurred by the borough or property owners in the course of correcting the substantive violations of State law or borough ordinance resulting from or arising out of the unlawfully constructed street or facility. Nothing under this section may be construed to apply to the Department of Transportation.

§ 1736. (Reserved).

§ 1737. (Reserved).

SUBCHAPTER E
VACATING STREETS
(Reserved)

SUBCHAPTER F
STRAIGHTENING AND RELOCATING STREETS

Sec.

§ 1751. Authority to straighten and relocate streets and procedure.

Council may, by ordinance, provide for straightening or relocating any street previously opened which involves the opening of a portion of the straightened or relocated street over land not previously a portion of the street or the vacation of a portion of the previously opened street no longer to be used for street purposes. The straightening or relocation shall be considered as an opening or vacation and shall be effected in the same manner and by the same procedure as provided in section 1731 (relating to authority to open and vacate streets and procedure) but may be considered as a single proceeding to be effected by enactment of a single ordinance.

SUBCHAPTER G
IMPROVEMENT OF BOROUGH STREETS

§ 1761. Proceedings with or without petition.

Boroughs may improve streets, parts of streets or a particular width or additional widths of streets, with or without the assistance or contribution of the Federal Government, the Commonwealth, the county or a corporation occupying the thoroughfare, and may assess and collect the whole cost of improvement, the whole cost not aided or contributed or any part of the cost from the owners of real estate abutting on the improvement in accordance with Chapter 21A (relating to assessments and charges for public improvements).

§ 1762. (Reserved).

§ 1763. (Reserved).

SUBCHAPTER H
IMPROVEMENT OF STREETS OUTSIDE OR PARTLY OUTSIDE BOROUGH LIMITS

§ 1771. Improvement of streets outside or partly outside borough limits.

(a) General rule.—

(1) Any borough may enter into a written agreement with an adjoining municipality for improving streets, including streets that are boundaries between the borough and the municipality and may provide in the contract for the division of the damages, costs and expenses of the improvement.

(2) The borough may assess its share of the costs against the owner of property abutting upon the borough's side of the improvement in the manner provided in Chapter 21A (relating to assessments and charges for public improvements) or may agree to pay any part of the costs, damages and expenses of the improvements out of the general funds.

(3) The portion of the damages, costs and expenses agreed to be paid by the borough shall be ascertained as provided in the law governing eminent domain.

(b) Street dividing borough and township.—

(1) If the center line of any street constitutes the dividing line between a borough and a township located in the same county, any agreement to improve

Table of Contents
Part I Ch. 1–3 Ethics, Records, Open Meetings
Part II Ch. 4–10 Taxation
Part III Ch. 11–18 Torts, Contracts & Civil Rules
Part IV Ch. 19–24 Zoning & Planning
Part V Ch. 25–30 Construction and Emergency Codes
Part VI Ch. 31–39 Municipal Codes
Index

and maintain the street shall be made with the governing bodies of the township and, if necessary, the county.

(2) The improvement shall be constructed and subsequent repairs shall be made under the supervision of the borough and in compliance with plans to be agreed upon, in writing, by the parties.

(3) One-half of the cost of the repairs shall be borne by the borough. The borough may assess its share of costs against the owners of real property abutting on the borough's side of the improvement in the manner provided in Chapter 21A.

(c) Street dividing borough and any other municipality.—

(1) If any street, more than one-half the width or the entire width of which is within the limits of any borough, divides the borough from any other municipality, the street may be improved by the borough.

(2) The property abutting on the side of the street which is located outside the limits of the borough making the improvements may, for a depth of 150 feet, plus one-half the width of the street, from its center line, be assessed for any and all municipal improvements to or on the street in accordance with Chapter 21A.

(d) Street outside limits of borough.—A borough may appropriate and expend money for the improvement of a street, not to exceed one mile in length, outside the limits of the borough for the purpose of connecting improved streets in the borough with State highways, interstate highways and county roads.

§ 1772. (Reserved).

§ 1773. (Reserved).

§ 1774. (Reserved).

§ 1775. (Reserved).

SUBCHAPTER I
ACQUISITION OR USE OF ABUTTING LANDS

§ 1781. (Reserved).

§ 1782. Acquisition of property for unobstructed view.

(a) General rule.—Any borough may, singly or jointly with another municipality, acquire, by purchase or by the right of eminent domain, a free and unobstructed view down and across lands located at or near the intersection of any two streets or highways or a street or highway and a railroad or railway or at a curve in any street or highway as may be necessary to accomplish the following:

(1) Assure a free and unobstructed view in all directions at the crossings.

(2) Prevent the use of the lands for any purpose or in any manner which may interfere with or obstruct the view of persons traveling upon the street or highway.

(b) Obstructions to be abated or removed.—After condemnation, the borough may abate or remove or cause to be abated or removed any obstruction to the view over and across the lands except poles used in furnishing service to the public.

(c) Condemnation proceedings.—The proceedings for the condemnation of the view over and across lands and for the assessment of damages for property taken, injured or destroyed, or the portion thereof agreed to be paid by the borough if the taking is jointly with another municipality, shall be taken in the manner provided in the law governing eminent domain.

(d) Use of lands.—Upon the purchase or condemnation of a view, the owner of the lands may make every use of the lands as will not interfere with a free and unobstructed view at the dangerous crossing or curve.

CHAPTER 18
SIDEWALKS

Sec.

---

§ 1800. Definitions.

The following words and phrases when used in this chapter shall have the meanings given to them in this section unless the context clearly indicates otherwise:

"Sidewalk." The portion of a street located outside the cartway and may include paved footway, unpaved grasslot, curb and gutter.

§ 1801. Power to lay out, establish and compel construction of sidewalks.

(a) General rule.—

(1) Any borough may, by ordinance, lay out and establish sidewalks, curbs, gutters and surface water drains along any street and, with the consent of the Secretary of Transportation, along any State highway.

(2) The borough may also require owners of property abutting on any street or State highway to grade, construct, drain, pave and repave the sidewalk, curb or gutter and keep them in repair and in safe and usable condition along the property at the grades and under the regulations and specifications as council may prescribe.

(b)(Reserved).

§ 1802. Sidewalks on land abutting State highways and along roads outside borough.

Any borough may, by ordinance, lay out sidewalks, gutters, and surface water drains upon land abutting the sides of State highways and upon land abutting the sides of public roads, where the roads are outside the borough limits, but the land upon which the sidewalks, gutters and surface water drains are to be laid out is within the borough limits.

Table of Contents
Part I Ch. 1–3 Ethics, Records, Open Meetings
Part II Ch. 4–10 Taxation
Part III Ch. 11–18 Torts, Contracts & Civil Rules
Part IV Ch. 19–24 Zoning & Planning
Part V Ch. 25–30 Construction and Emergency Codes
Part VI Ch. 31–39 Municipal Codes
Index

§ 1803. Establishment of grades.

Any borough may establish a grade or grades for sidewalks, which may be separate and apart from the grade or grades established for the cartway or roadway.

§ 1804. Boroughs may pay all or part of cost of grading and curbing.

The borough may pay all or any part of the cost and expenses of grading and curbing any sidewalk.

§ 1805. Borough may do work and collect cost.

(a) General rule.—Upon the failure of any property owner to comply with any of the requirements in sections 1801 (relating to power to lay out, establish and compel the construction of sidewalks), 1802 (relating to sidewalks on land abutting State highways and along roads outside borough), 1803 (relating to establishment of grades) and 1804 (relating to boroughs may pay all or part of cost of grading and curbing), the borough may, after notice, cause the grading, paving, repairing, curbing and guttering to be done at the cost of the owner. The borough may collect the cost of the work and an additional 10% of the cost, together with all charges and expenses, from the owner and may file a municipal claim for the amounts or collect the amounts by action in assumpsit.

(b) Notices.—

(1) All notices shall be served upon the owner of the premises to which the notice refers, if the owner is a resident of the borough. If the owner is not a resident, then the notice may be served upon the agent or tenant of the owner or upon the occupant of the premises. If the owner has no agent or tenant or there is no occupier of the premises, then service shall be by notice posted upon the premises.

(2) The notice required by this section shall specify a period of time of not less than 30 days for the owner to complete the specified work. If the work has not been completed after the specified time has elapsed, the owner shall be deemed to have failed to comply.

§ 1806. Emergency repairs to sidewalks.

(a) General rule.—

(1) In addition to the remedies now vested in boroughs to make repairs to sidewalks, any borough shall have power to make emergency repairs to any sidewalks within the borough if an inspection of the sidewalk discloses that, and a certificate made by the officer or head of the department or committee lawfully having charge of sidewalk repairs specifies that, a dangerous condition exists that can be repaired by an expenditure of not more than $1,000.

(2) Before repairs are made, a notice to make the repairs within 48 hours shall be served upon the owner of the property. If the owner cannot be served within the county, notice may be served upon the agent of the owner or the party in possession or, if there is no agent or party in possession, the notice may be served by posting the same upon the premises.

(b) Cost.—

(1) Upon the completion of the work, the cost shall be a charge against the owner of the property and shall be a lien, until paid, upon the abutting property if a claim is filed. The charge may also be collected by action of assumpsit.

(2) This section is intended to provide an additional remedy for boroughs in connection with emergency repairs, where the actual cost of doing the work does not exceed $1,000. The certificate of the officer or head of the department or committee in charge of repairs to sidewalks shall be conclusive evidence of the existence of the emergency justifying the repair under the terms of this section.

CHAPTER 19
BRIDGES, VIADUCTS AND UNDERGROUND PASSAGEWAYS

---

§ 1901. Construction or acquisition and maintenance of bridges and viaducts.

(a) Authority.—Any borough may locate and build, or acquire by purchase, condemnation or otherwise, any bridge or viaduct and the piers, approaches and abutments for the bridge or viaduct, to be used and thereafter improved and maintained as a street, over any river, creek, stream, railroad or public or private property or over and across a combination of any of them, whether the bridge or viaduct shall be wholly or partly within the borough limits.

(b) Proceedings.—The proceedings for laying out and opening a bridge or viaduct shall be the same as provided by this part for the laying out and opening of streets, and the bridge or viaduct or portion of the bridge or viaduct may thereafter be vacated under the same procedure as provided in this part for the relocation or vacation of streets or portions of streets.

§ 1902. Right to appropriate property and assessment of damages.

In any case where the borough does not agree with the owner or owners for damages done or likely to be done by the erection of a bridge or viaduct, the borough may take and appropriate the land and property necessary to erect the bridge or viaduct. The damages caused by the taking and appropriation shall be assessed according to 26 Pa.C.S. (relating to eminent domain).

§ 1903. Boundary bridges.

If a bridge or viaduct crosses the boundary line of a borough and another municipality, the borough may enter into an intergovernmental cooperation agreement in accordance with 53 Pa.C.S. Ch. 23 Subch. A (relating to intergovernmental cooperation) with the municipality in the construction and maintenance of the bridge and shall apportion the costs according to the intergovernmental agreement.

§ 1904. Contracts with railroads, other companies and counties.

(a) General rule.—

(1) The borough may enter into a contract with the county commissioners, railroads, street railways and other companies or interested parties for the building and maintenance of bridges or viaducts and for the payment of any damages caused by the location or erection thereof.

(2) The contracts may stipulate that the county, borough, railroad company, street railway or other company or interested party shall pay a certain part of the contract price of the work, including damages, or may stipulate that each shall construct a certain portion of the work and may provide otherwise for the payment of damages.

(b) Payment.—

(1) When any railroad company, street railway or other company or interested party agrees to pay a certain portion of the cost of the work, it shall pay the portion into the borough treasury. The borough treasurer shall pay the amount over to the contractor, as may be provided in the contract. The amount to be paid by the county shall be paid directly to the contractor.

(2) The agreement may provide for the maintenance of the bridges and viaducts after their erection. Nothing under this section shall authorize any borough to contract with a county for the maintenance of any bridge or viaduct which does not cross a place over which the county is authorized to build bridges. The bridge or viaduct shall be maintained as a borough structure, and the borough may contract with any party interested, except the county, for the maintenance of the bridge or viaduct.

(3) Nothing in this section shall affect the powers or duties of the Pennsylvania Public Utility Commission to the extent otherwise provided by law.

§ 1905. Overhead and underground passageways.

If the comfort and safety of the residents of a borough and an adjoining municipality are enhanced by any overhead or underground passageway connecting with adjoining streets in either the borough or the municipality and extending to any plant or place of business where residents of the borough are employed, the borough may, jointly with each adjoining municipality, construct and maintain any passageway or may join with other interests in the construction and maintenance of the passageway.

CHAPTER 20
SANITARY SEWERS

SUBCHAPTER A
LAYING OUT, CONSTRUCTION AND OPERATION OF SANITARY SEWERS AND CONSTRUCTION OF SEWAGE TREATMENT WORKS

§ 2000. Definitions.

The following words and phrases when used in this chapter shall have the meanings given to them in this section unless the context clearly indicates otherwise:

"Combined sewer." A sewer used for the receiving and collecting of sewage and liquid waste from the inside of buildings and structures, storm water, roof or surface drainage, sump pump discharge and draining from foundation drains.

"Sanitary sewer" or "sanitary sewer system." A sewer or sewers used for receiving and collecting sewage matter and liquid waste from the inside of buildings and structures. Storm water shall not be permitted to enter into a sanitary sewer. A sanitary sewer or sanitary sewer system does not include a combined sewer.

"Sewer system." Either a sanitary sewer or a combined sewer and includes pump stations and force mains.

§ 2001. Power to lay out and construct.

(a) General rule.—

(1) Upon enactment of an ordinance, boroughs may lay out and construct sanitary sewers and branches of sanitary sewers in streets and on public or private property and may construct sewage treatment works on land owned or acquired for those purposes. Boroughs may pay the costs and expenses of sanitary sewer systems and treatment works out of borough funds or may assess the costs and expenses pursuant to Chapter 21A (relating to assessments and charges for public improvements).

(2) Boroughs may determine the location and the manner in which sanitary sewer systems shall be constructed. Sanitary sewers laid and constructed in streets may be located in the center of the street or in the right-of-way or the curb lines of the street and may be for the service and use of properties on both sides of the street or on only one side of the street in which they are laid, as directed by the council. Boroughs shall have the authority to lay out and construct sanitary sewers in any street, any portion of which is within the limits of the borough and which forms a portion of the boundary dividing the borough from any other municipal corporation within the same county, in the same manner and to the same extent as if the whole of the street was within the limits of the borough.

(3) If any borough is maintaining and operating a sanitary sewer system and sewage treatment works, it shall be lawful for the borough to supply sewerage service to municipalities, persons and corporations outside the limits of the borough and to enter into contracts for service at rates not less than those required to be paid by persons and corporations within the limits of the borough. This privilege shall not conflict with the rights of any sewer company or the rights of any other borough.

(b) Consent.—

(1) If required by other law, a borough shall obtain the consent and permit of the Department of Environmental Protection or other Federal, State or county entity, including the Pennsylvania Turnpike Commission, for the laying out and construction of a sanitary sewer and treatment works.

(2) Where construction beyond the limits of the borough is entirely within the limits of a State or county highway or the turnpike, a sanitary sewer may be constructed in or under the State or county highway or turnpike if written notice is given to the Department of Transportation, county commissioners or Pennsylvania Turnpike Commission, respectively, and consent is obtained before construction is commenced. Permission shall not be unreasonably withheld.

(c) **Regulations.**—Council may, by ordinance, make regulations respecting the use and maintenance of the sanitary sewer system and treatment works. Violations of the ordinance may be enforced by penalties. The regulations may do all of the following:

(1) Specify materials and substances which may or may not enter the public sewer or sewer system.

(2) Require that certain types or classes of waste be subjected to treatment or to grinding or other reduction in size before entering into the sewer.

(3) Restrict the quantity of waste material that may enter a sanitary sewer from any premises within any time interval.

(4) Require that property owners provide means other than the public sanitary sewers for disposal of storm, surface and roof water originating or accumulating upon their property.

§ 2002. Assessments.

Assessments, whether based according to benefits conferred or by the front foot basis, and assessment awards, if any, shall be calculated pursuant to Chapter 21A (relating to assessments and charges for public improvements).

§ 2003. (Reserved).

§ 2004. (Reserved).

§ 2005. (Reserved).

§ 2006. (Reserved).

§ 2007. (Reserved).

§ 2008. (Reserved).

§ 2009. Extensions beyond borough limits and eminent domain.

The borough may extend the necessary sewer mains, pipes and outlets beyond the limits of the borough to a point where the sewage is to be disposed or collected and received. The borough shall have power to enter upon and condemn land for the construction of all sewer mains, outlets and treatment works as may be necessary for the disposal or the collection of the sewage, if the extension is in conformity with 26 Pa.C.S. § 206 (relating to extraterritorial takings) and any other applicable requirement of 26 Pa.C.S. (relating to eminent domain).

§ 2010. Notice of certain ordinances.

No ordinance for any construction of sewers or treatment works beyond the limits of the borough shall be enacted until notice of the ordinance has been given in all of the following manners:

(1) By publication of the proposed ordinance, once a week for four weeks in one newspaper of general circulation.

(2) By serving copies of the proposed ordinance at least ten days before the enactment of the ordinance upon all land owners through whose land the sewer is to pass or on whose lands any treatment works are to be located.

§ 2011. (Reserved).

§ 2012. Unlawful to build within right-of-way of sanitary sewers.

It shall be unlawful for any person to erect any building or make any improvement within the right-of-way of any sanitary sewer after due notice of the laying out of the sanitary sewer, and, if any erection or improvement shall be made, no allowance shall be had for the building or improvement in the assessment of damages.

§ 2013. Opening sanitary sewers.

(a) General rule.—A proceeding to open a sanitary sewer shall be void if a borough:

(1) lays out any sanitary sewer over or under private property which is located in whole or in part within the limits of the borough; and

(2) does not proceed to open the sanitary sewer and to assess the damage arising therefrom within two years from the enactment of the ordinance.

(b) Exception.—If a borough has laid out a sanitary sewer without the enactment of an ordinance prior to July 16, 2012, and has not opened the sanitary sewer, the proceedings shall not be deemed to be void. The borough shall have two years from July 16, 2012, to open the sanitary sewer or the whole proceeding shall be void.

SUBCHAPTER B
JOINT SANITARY SEWERS

---

§ 2021. Joint sanitary sewer systems.

(a) General rule.—Pursuant to 53 Pa.C.S. Ch. 23 Subch. A (relating to intergovernmental cooperation), boroughs may contract with other municipal corporations providing for the joint construction or maintenance of sanitary sewer systems and for the joint construction onto existing sanitary sewer systems. The agreement shall provide for the apportionment of costs among the municipal corporations. The council may assess the borough's respective portion of the costs, as may be legally assessable, upon property benefited by the facilities pursuant to Chapter 21A (relating to assessments and charges for public improvements). Any portion of the cost not assessed or assessable shall be paid by the respective municipal corporations under the agreement.

(b) Composition of joint sanitary sewer board.—

(1) The municipal corporations joining or contemplating joining in any improvement, in order to facilitate the building of the sanitary sewer system and in securing preliminary surveys and estimates, may, by ordinance, provide for the appointment of a joint sanitary sewer board composed of one representative from each of the municipal corporations joining. The board shall act as the advisory and administrative agency in the construction of the improvement and its subsequent operation and maintenance.

(2) Members of the joint sanitary sewer board shall serve for terms of six years each from the dates of their respective appointments and until their successors are appointed. The joint sanitary sewer board shall organize by the election of a chair, secretary and treasurer. The secretary and treasurer may be the same person.

(3) The municipal corporations may in the ordinances creating the joint sanitary sewer board authorize the board to appoint an engineer, a solicitor and other assistants as are deemed necessary and agree to the share of the compensation of those persons each municipal corporation is to pay.

(4) The members of the joint sanitary sewer board shall receive compensation for attending board meetings as established in the budget that is prepared by the joint sanitary sewer board and submitted to and adopted by the municipal corporations. The members shall be entitled to actual expenses to be paid by the respective municipal corporations the members represent.

(c) Powers of the joint sanitary sewer board.—

(1) The joint sanitary sewer board may adopt rules and regulations consistent with the requirements of this part to govern its proceedings and shall prepare and suggest any practical measures and plans by which the joint improvement may be carried to successful completion and plan the future development of the system, so as to conform to a general plan.

(2) The joint sanitary sewer board may prepare a joint agreement or agreements for submission to and adoption by the municipal corporations defining the advisory and administrative powers of the joint sanitary sewer board and setting forth the following:

(i) Consents of the municipal corporations to the proposed improvement.

(ii) The manner in which preliminary and final plans, specifications and estimates for the proposed improvement shall be prepared and adopted.

(iii) How proposals for bids shall be advertised and contracts awarded.

(iv) The manner in which the costs of the improvement and other incidental and preliminary expenses in connection with the improvement and the future cost of operation and maintenance shall be equitably shared, apportioned and paid.

(v) All other matters, including the preparation and submission of annual and other budgets, as may be deemed necessary or required by law to complete the proposed improvement and to assure future maintenance and operation thereof.

(3) The joint sanitary sewer board may not make any improvement or spend any public money which has not first been authorized by all of the municipal corporations proceeding with the improvement.

(d) Eminent domain.—

(1) When it is necessary to acquire, appropriate, injure or destroy private property to build a joint sanitary sewer system or improvement and the property cannot be acquired by purchase or gift, the right of eminent domain shall vest in the municipal corporation where the property is located.

(2) When it is necessary to acquire, injure or destroy property in any territory not within the limits of any of the municipal corporations joining in the improvement, the right of eminent domain shall be vested in the municipal corporation adjacent to the territory where the property is located subject to 26 Pa.C.S. § 206 (relating to extraterritorial takings).

(3) Damages for any property taken, injured or destroyed shall be assessed under laws relating to the municipal corporation exercising the right of eminent domain and shall be paid by the municipal corporations joining in the same proportion as other costs of the improvements.

(e) Indebtedness.—Each of the boroughs joining in the improvement shall have power to incur or increase its indebtedness, not exceeding the constitutional limits, for the purpose of paying its share or portion of the cost of the improvement in the manner now provided by law for the incurring of indebtedness.

§ 2022. (Reserved).

§ 2023. Connections with sanitary sewers of adjacent municipalities.

A borough may connect with an existing sanitary sewer, owned by an adjacent municipality, for sewerage purposes in the manner prescribed in sections 2024 (relating to applications to court), 2025 (relating to appointment of viewers) and 2026 (relating to report of viewers and appeals to court).

§ 2024. Applications to court.

If a borough desires to connect with the existing sanitary sewer of an adjacent municipality and no agreement, either upon the basis of a rental payment for the use of an existing sanitary sewer or a division of the cost of the construction or maintenance of the sanitary sewer, has been reached between the borough and the adjacent municipality, an application shall be made by council to the court of common pleas of the county where the proposed connection is to be located, setting forth that fact.

§ 2025. Appointment of viewers.

If the court determines that the connection can be made without impairing the usefulness of the existing sanitary sewer, it shall appoint three viewers who shall:

(1) View the premises and investigate the facts of the case.

(2) Assess the proportionate part of the expense of building the original sanitary sewer upon the borough.

(3) Fix the proportion of the expense for repairs which each municipality shall thereafter bear.

(4) Determine all other questions liable to arise in connection with the sanitary sewer.

§ 2026. Report of viewers and appeals to court.

The viewers shall report to the court the result of their investigation. The report shall be confirmed within 30 days unless exceptions are filed. After confirmation of the report or the disposal of any exceptions, any party interested may appeal from the decision of the court of common pleas.

SUBCHAPTER C
POWER TO SUPPLY SEWERAGE SERVICE OUTSIDE BOROUGH LIMITS
(Reserved)

SUBCHAPTER D
ACQUISITION OF COMMUNITY COLLECTION OR DISPOSAL SYSTEMS

§ 2040. Definitions.

The following words and phrases when used in this subchapter shall have the meanings given to them in this section unless the context clearly indicates otherwise:

"Community sewage collection or disposal system." All or part of a device or devices installed on any privately or publicly owned parcel of land intended to treat or dispose of the sewage or equivalent volume of domestic sewage from two or more residences, buildings or occupied parcels of land, or any system of piping used in collection and conveyance of sewage on private or public property.

§ 2041. (Reserved).

§ 2041.1. Power to acquire community sewage collection or disposal systems.

(a) General rule.—A borough may, by ordinance, acquire ownership of a community sewage collection or disposal system by purchase or by the exercise of eminent domain pursuant to 26 Pa.C.S. (relating to eminent domain) or by gift from the owner or owners.

(b) Assessment of costs and expenses.—In eminent domain proceedings, the viewers shall assess the costs and expenses of the community sewage collection or disposal system acquired by the borough upon the property or properties benefited according to benefits. Any deficiency that is not assessed upon the benefited property or properties shall be paid by the borough.

§ 2042. (Reserved).

§ 2043. Community sewage collection or disposal systems.

(a) General rule.—After a community sewage collection or disposal system has been acquired under this subchapter by the borough, the council shall have the power to enlarge the system if it deems it advisable. The cost and expenses of the enlargement may be distributed or assessed in the same manner as if the enlargement was a regular sewer constructed by the borough under other provisions of this part.

(b) Acquisition and ownership.—If a community sewage collection or disposal system is established or constructed within a borough by a private owner or owners and the council is thereafter empowered by ordinance to acquire the ownership of the sewage disposal system, or when the system has been enlarged by the borough, the acquisition and ownership shall be subject to the following provisions:

(1) An agreement shall be considered a valid agreement by the owners of the sewage collection or disposal system and shall be a transfer of ownership to the borough when any of the following enter into an agreement with the borough for the acquisition of the system by the borough:

(i) The person or persons having established or constructed a community sewage collection or disposal system.

(ii) More than one-half of the number of owners of properties which are connected with, have a right to use and are using a community collection or disposal system.

(2) The borough shall operate and maintain any sewage collection or disposal system acquired and any enlargement or addition thereto for the use of the following:

(i) Persons having acquired from the borough or from the former owner or owners the right to use the system.

(ii) Other owners of property accessible to the system up to the capacity of the sewage collection or disposal system.

(3) All persons whose property connects with the sewage collection or disposal system acquired or constructed by the borough shall pay to the borough treasurer a monthly, quarterly, semiannual or annual charge prescribed by a resolution of the council. The amount of the charges shall not be in excess of the estimated amount necessary to maintain and operate the system and to establish a reserve fund sufficient for its future replacement.

(4) All sewer rentals or charges imposed by the council against properties connected with a community sewage collection or disposal system under this section shall constitute liens against the properties and may be collected in the same manner as other sewer charges.

(5) All money received from the sewer charges shall be deposited as a special reserve fund and shall be used only for the payment of the cost of operating and maintaining the sewage collection or disposal system and the replacement of the collection or disposal system, if necessary and economically desirable. If, at any time after the acquisition or enlargement of the community sewage system, a regular sewer system is made available by the borough for connection with the properties using the community sewage collection or disposal system, the owners of the properties shall be subject to the other provisions of this part relating to sewers, and all money at that time in the reserve fund which was received from charges for the use of that particular sewage collection or disposal system and which is over and above the amount expended for the operation and maintenance of that particular sewage collection or disposal system shall be used towards the payment of any sewer assessments charged against the properties under other sections of this part.

(c) **Construction.**—Nothing in this section may be construed to supersede the requirements of the act of January 24, 1966 (1965 P.L.1535, No.537), known as the Pennsylvania Sewage Facilities Act.

SUBCHAPTER E

CONNECTION AND USE OF SANITARY SEWERS

---

§ 2051. Ordinances to require sanitary sewer connections.

A borough may, by ordinance, require any owner of property benefited, improved or accommodated by a sanitary sewer to make connections with the sanitary sewer, in the manner as the borough may order, for the purpose of discharge of drainage or waste matter as the borough may specify. All connections required shall be uniform. The owner shall be given at least 45 days' notice of any ordinance requiring a sanitary sewer connection. Upon failure of the owner to make the connection, the borough may make the connection and collect the cost from the owner by a municipal claim or by an action of assumpsit. The borough may by penalties enforce any ordinance it enacts with reference to any sanitary sewer connections.

§ 2052. (Reserved).

§ 2053. Tapping fees.

The following shall apply to tapping fees:

(1) Any borough may, by ordinance, provide for charging a tapping fee if the owner of any property connects the property with a sanitary sewer system constructed or acquired by the borough if the tapping fee is calculated in accordance with 53 Pa.C.S. § 5607 (relating to purposes and powers). The tapping fee shall be in addition to any charges assessed and collected against the property in the construction or acquisition of the sanitary sewer by the borough.

(2) If a sanitary sewer system or any part or extension of a sanitary sewer system owned by a borough has been constructed by the borough at the expense of a private person or corporation or has been constructed by a private person or corporation under the supervision of the borough at the expense of the private person or corporation, the borough shall have the right to charge a tapping fee calculated in accordance with 53 Pa.C.S. § 5607 and refund the tapping fee or any part of the fee to the person or corporation who has paid for the construction of the sanitary sewer system or any part or extension of the sanitary sewer system in accordance with 53 Pa.C.S. § 5607. The total of the refunds shall never exceed the cost of the system or any part or extension of the system to the person or corporation paying for the construction of the system or any part or extension of the system.

(3) Where the property connected or to be connected with the sanitary sewer system of the borough is not equipped with a water meter, the borough may install a meter at its own cost and expense. If the property is supplied with water from the facilities of a public water supply agency, the borough shall not install a meter without the consent and approval of the public water supply agency.

§ 2054. (Reserved).

SUBCHAPTER F

MONTHLY, QUARTERLY OR ANNUAL RENTALS

Sec.

---

§ 2061. Ordinance for monthly, quarterly or annual rental.

If a borough constructs any sanitary sewer, sewer system or sewage treatment works or acquires, wholly or partially, the same at public expense, as authorized in this chapter, the council may provide, by ordinance, for the collection of a monthly, quarterly or annual rental or charge or a fixed sum for the use of the sanitary sewer, sewer system or sewage treatment works from the owner of property served by it.

§ 2062. Rental amount.

(a) **Included amounts.**—The monthly, quarterly or annual rental may include:

(1) The amount expended monthly, quarterly or annually by the borough in maintenance, repair, alteration, inspection, depreciation or other expense of the sanitary sewer, sewer system or sewage treatment works.

(2) Interest on money expended or borrowed by the borough in the construction of the sanitary sewer, sewer system or sewage treatment works or in the acquisition, enlargement or extension of the sanitary sewer or sewer system.

(3) An amount sufficient for the amortization of debt incurred by the borough for the purpose of construction of a sanitary sewer, sewer system or sewage treatment works or for the purpose of acquisition, enlargement or extension of a sanitary sewer or sewer system.

(b) Apportionment.—The monthly, quarterly or annual amount or fixed sum shall be apportioned equitably among the properties served by the sanitary sewers, sewer system or sewage treatment works.

§ 2063. Collection of rental.

(a) General rule.—The monthly, quarterly or annual rental or charge or the fixed sum shall be authorized and collected as provided by general ordinances and, if levied and charged, shall be a lien on the properties charged from the date set forth in the ordinance. If the rental, charge or fixed sum is not paid after 30 days' notice, it may be collected by an action of assumpsit in the name of the borough against the owner of the property charged or by a lien filed in the nature of a municipal lien.

(b) Collection.—The council shall execute a warrant or warrants, authorizing the collection of the monthly, quarterly or annual sewer rentals or charges, or the fixed sum, to the officer employed by council to collect the same. The officer shall have the authority now vested by law for the collection of borough taxes.

§ 2064. (Reserved).

SUBCHAPTER G
SEWERS ON BOUNDARY STREETS
(Reserved)

CHAPTER 21
COLLECTION BY INSTALLMENT OF STREET AND SEWER ASSESSMENTS
(Reserved)

CHAPTER 21A
ASSESSMENTS AND CHARGES FOR PUBLIC IMPROVEMENTS

Sec.

---

§ 21A00. Definitions.

The following words and phrases when used in this chapter shall have the meanings given to them in this section unless the context clearly indicates otherwise:

"Personal notice." The term shall mean and include notice upon the owner of a property either by personal service upon the owner or by certified mail to the owner at the owner's last known address or where service, after a reasonable attempt, shall not have been successfully made by either of these two methods, then by leaving notice at or upon the property.

§ 21A01. Authority to assess.

(a) General rule.—Council shall have the power to pay the cost, in whole or in part, of any and all public improvements of all natures and descriptions, including, but not limited to, the grading, building, paving, regrading, rebuilding and repaving of streets as defined in section 1701 (relating to definitions), the creation, extension, renovation or enlargement of water mains and sewage collection, transmission, treatment and disposal systems and the creation, extension and renovation of storm, surface and subsurface drainage systems, the construction, reconstruction and repair of wharves and docks, the installation of ornamental street lighting or the planting, removal, maintenance and protection of shade trees by any of the following methods:

(1) from general borough funds;

(2) from special borough funds created for that purpose; or

(3) by assessment of costs against the benefited properties either on the front foot or benefit conferred method of assessment.

Except as provided in subsection (c), the costs and expenses of sanitary sewers may be assessed against properties benefited, accommodated or improved regardless of the property line location and regardless of whether any portion of a property benefited, accommodated or physically improved abuts upon the sanitary sewer.

(b) Payment of indebtedness.—

(1) If a borough that incurs authorized indebtedness under 53 Pa.C.S. Pt. VII Subpt. B (relating to indebtedness and borrowing) for the purposes of funding the cost and expense of making public improvements for which assessments can be made in accordance with this chapter, payments made on the assessment must be applied to pay the debt service for the indebtedness incurred for funding the cost and expense of making the public improvement.

(2) Notwithstanding section 21A07 (relating to payment of assessments in installments), when bonds are issued in a manner provided by law and an assessment is to be paid in installments, the assessment shall be payable in equal installments during the term for which the bond is issued, and the cost of the improvement plus interest beginning the first day when interest is payable on the bond shall be the cost of the improvement to be assessed on a property.

(c) Property outside borough.—Property benefited, improved or accommodated which is located outside the limits of the borough that constructed a sanitary sewer may, if located no more than 150 feet from the sewer main, be assessed for the cost of the sewer in the same manner as the property would be assessed under the laws of this Commonwealth if it were entirely located within the limits of the borough, if the property is given permission to use the sanitary sewer and is not, at the time the sanitary sewer is constructed, provided with sanitary sewer facilities.

(d) Water mains.—Boroughs shall have power to assess the whole cost or any part of the cost of construction of new water mains built in connection with the establishment or extension of a municipally owned water supply system, even if the mains are located outside the limits of the borough, and that serve abutting properties, against the properties abutting the boundary line. The borough may provide that the assessment be rebated to the owner of the assessed property out of rates charged for water consumed in serving the assessed property. The borough may also issue a negotiable credit memorandum in the amount of the assessment which may be used for the payment of any water service to the extent of the assessment.

§ 21A02. Notice of assessments.

The borough secretary shall cause 30 days' personal notice of the assessment to be served upon each property owner assessed. If a certificate is required to be filed with council relating to the public improvement as otherwise provided in this part, then a copy of the certificate shall accompany the notice.

§ 21A03. Assessment based on front foot basis.

(a) General rule.—If council elects to collect the cost, including any administrative fees, of any improvement on the front foot basis, the cost to be collected shall be divided by the total number of linear feet of street frontage of each property benefited, and there shall be assessed against each property that portion of the cost which is determined by multiplying the dividend of the prior calculation by the number of linear feet for street frontage of that property.

(b) Certificate of assessment.—Council shall issue a certificate of assessment when assessing on the front foot basis duly certified under the seal of the borough and attested by the president of council and secretary. The certificate of assessment shall be prima facie evidence in any suit for recovery of the same of the correctness and validity of the assessment.

(c) Adjustments in assessments.—Notwithstanding subsection (a), council may make equitable adjustments for corner lots, lots of irregular shape or, where special conditions exist, where an assessment for full frontage would be unjust.

§ 21A04. Assessment of benefits conferred.

(a) General rule.—In lieu of the front foot basis, council may elect to have the benefits of public improvements assessed, in whole or in part, upon property benefited, improved or accommodated by assessing an equal assessment on the properties benefited, improved or accommodated in proportion to the total cost of construction of the improvement. The amount of the charge on each property shall be determined by council.

(b) Certificate.—Council shall issue a certificate of assessment when assessing benefits upon property benefited, improved or accommodated, duly certified under the seal of the borough and attested by the president of council and secretary. The certificate of assessment shall be prima facie evidence in any suit for recovery of the same of the correctness and validity of the assessment.

§ 21A05. Assessment awards.

In proceedings to assess benefits, if the land or property is both benefited and damaged by the public improvements, the excess of damages over benefits, the excess of benefits over damages or nothing in case the benefits and damages are equal shall be awarded to or assessed against the owner of land and property affected. Damages shall be calculated pursuant to 26 Pa.C.S. (relating to eminent domain).

§ 21A06. Petition for viewers.

(a) Petition.—Taxpayers of the borough whose property is being assessed for benefits for a public improvement may present a petition to the court of common pleas stating that the assessment insufficiently represents the benefits accruing to abutting, benefited or accommodated properties. The petition may include a request for the appointment of viewers to assess benefits if at least 50% of the taxpayers whose parcels are abutting, benefited or accommodated by the public improvement in question join the petition or if taxpayers whose property valuation as assessed for taxable purposes within the borough amounts to at least 50% of the total property valuation of the properties being assessed for the public improvement join the petition. The petition must be presented within three months of the enactment of the ordinance levying the assessment.

Table of Contents
Part I Ch. 1–3 Ethics, Records, Open Meetings
Part II Ch. 4–10 Taxation
Part III Ch. 11–18 Torts, Contracts & Civil Rules
Part IV Ch. 19–24 Zoning & Planning
Part V Ch. 25–30 Construction and Emergency Codes
Part VI Ch. 31–39 Municipal Codes
Index

(b) Viewers.—The court shall appoint three disinterested viewers, none of whom shall be a resident of that portion of the borough that is benefited or accommodated by the public improvement in question, and the viewers shall proceed under this part and 26 Pa.C.S. (relating to eminent domain) for the assessment of damages and benefits by viewers. Upon the filing of the petition by taxpayers for the appointment of viewers, any assessment made by the council and any proceedings shall be stayed pending the disposition of the petition by the court.

§ 21A07. Payment of assessments in installments.

(a) Installments.—If an ordinance is passed providing for a public improvement, the expense of which is to be defrayed by an assessment against properties benefited by the improvement, either by the front foot or benefit conferred method, the ordinance shall specify the length of time over which the installments may be extended and whether payments are to be made by equal annual or more frequent installments. If the provisions of section 21A01(b)(2) (relating to authority to assess) and this subsection conflict, the provisions of section 21A01(b)(2) shall prevail to the extent of the conflict.

(b) Commencement of payments and rate of interest.—The ordinance shall set a time when the installment payments shall commence and shall set forth the rate of interest for the installments which shall not be more than 6% per year.

(c) Installment agreement.—The borough shall enter into a written installment agreement with each property owner, subject to the requirements of the ordinance pertaining to the agreements and this chapter.

(d) Unpaid installments.—If an installment remains unpaid for 60 days after it has become due and payable, the entire unpaid assessment, plus unpaid accrued interest and any costs, shall be due and payable, and the borough solicitor shall proceed to collect it by filing a lien in the same manner as municipal claims are filed or by action in assumpsit.

(e) Prepayment.—A property owner upon whom an assessment has been made may pay all or as many of the installments before they are due, with interest and costs to the due date of the next installment.

§ 21A08. Collection of assessments.

(a) Collection methods.—If an assessment remains unpaid at the expiration of the 30-day personal notice and an installment agreement has not been entered into pursuant to section 21A06 (relating to petition for viewers), the borough solicitor shall collect the unpaid assessment, with interest from the time of completion of the improvement or from the time of filing a certificate of assessment with council, plus costs, by filing a lien to be collected in the same manner as municipal claims or by action in assumpsit. When a property owner has two or more lots against which there is an assessment for the same improvement, all of the lots may be embraced in one claim.

(b) Payment location.—Assessments, whether paid one time or by installments, shall be payable at the office of the borough treasurer or any other place as the applicable ordinance shall provide.

CHAPTER 22
STORM SEWERS AND WATERCOURSES

Sec.

---

§ 2201. Authority of boroughs.

(a) General rule.—Any borough may, by ordinance, after obtaining any required permit from the Department of Environmental Protection or other Federal or State entity do the following:

(1) Widen and deepen any watercourse running through or within the borough and erect dykes, retaining walls and embankments along the watercourse as may be necessary to prevent the water from overflowing the banks.

(2) Confine and pave any watercourse or portion thereof, other than a navigable stream.

(3) Engage in channel improvement through the construction and maintenance of storm sewers and the accumulation and discharge of water into storm sewers.

(4) Vacate or alter the course or channel of any watercourse, other than a navigable stream.

(5) Acquire, operate and maintain areas for the infiltration, detention or retention of storm water and for other methods of storm water management authorized by the Department of Environmental Protection.

(b) Authorization and consent.—For any purpose set forth in subsection (a), a borough may enter upon and condemn property and materials as may be necessary. No borough may confine and pave, vacate or alter any watercourse used by any municipality, municipal authority or water company as a source of supply unless the municipality, municipal authority or water company shall first consent to the confining and paving, vacation or alteration.

§ 2202. Right of entry upon lands.

A borough may enter upon any land lying near a watercourse and secure the material as may be necessary for the purpose of making and repairing the embankments along the watercourse when the material cannot be obtained by contract at a reasonable price. The borough shall cause no unnecessary damage to the owners of the land, shall repair any fences, structures or damage to the land that is caused by the borough and shall compensate the owner, either by agreement or in accordance with 26 Pa.C.S. (relating to eminent domain), for any materials obtained under this section.

§ 2203. Manner of financing work.

A borough may pay for the costs and expenses of any work authorized under section 2201 (relating to authority of boroughs) wholly or in part from money of the borough available for the purpose. To the extent that a borough does not receive assistance from the Federal, State or county government for the costs and expenses of the work, the borough may assess the benefited properties located within the drainage area of the watercourse in accordance with Chapter 21A (relating to assessments and charges for public improvements).

§ 2204. Proceedings to assess damages.

Any person aggrieved by any ordinance enacted or action taken pursuant to sections 2201 (relating to authority of boroughs), 2202 (relating to right of entry upon lands) and 2203 (relating to manner of financing work) may file a complaint with the court of common pleas to fix and determine the damages for property taken, injured or destroyed under 26 Pa.C.S. (relating to eminent domain).

§ 2205. Unlawful to build within right-of-way of storm sewers.

It shall be unlawful for a person to erect a building or make an improvement within the right-of-way of a storm sewer laid out after due notice of the laying out of the storm sewer. If the erection or improvement is made, no allowance shall be made in the assessment of damages.

§ 2206. Power to acquire storm sewer systems.

(a) **General rule.**—A borough may, by ordinance, acquire ownership of storm sewers, culverts and the necessary inlets and appliances for surface, under surface and storm sewer drainage by purchase, by the exercise of eminent domain pursuant to 26 Pa.C.S. (relating to eminent domain) or by gift from the owner or owners.

(b) **Eminent domain.**—In eminent domain proceedings, the viewers shall assess the costs and expenses of the storm sewer, culverts, inlets and appliances acquired by the borough upon the property or properties benefited according to benefits. Any deficiency that is not assessed upon the benefited property or properties shall be paid by the borough.

CHAPTER 23
UNDERGROUND CONDUITS
(Reserved)

CHAPTER 24
WATER SYSTEM

Subchapter

SUBCHAPTER A
GENERAL POWERS TO SUPPLY WATER

Sec.

---

§ 2401. Power to supply water and make regulations.

(a) Supply of water.—Boroughs may supply water for the use of the public within the borough by constructing or purchasing and operating a water system, by entering into contract with persons or corporations authorized to supply water within the limits of the borough or partly by constructing or purchasing and operating a water system and partly by entering into a contract.

(b) Regulations.—Council may make regulations for the protection of water pipes, reservoirs and other apparatus used in the supplying or storing of water, for the prevention of the waste of water supplied and for the drilling of water wells within the borough.

(c) Rates.—Council shall fix the rates to be charged for the water furnished to individuals, partnerships, associations or corporations and shall provide for the collection of water rents from users of water supplied by the borough. The borough's provision of water to users outside the borough limits as to character of service, extensions and rates shall be subject to any applicable approval, regulation or control imposed by 66 Pa.C.S. Pt. I (relating to Public Utility Code).

§ 2402. Contracts not to abridge powers.

A borough's power to construct and operate a water system as provided in section 2401 (relating to power to supply water and make regulations) shall not be abridged by the borough entering into a contract with a person or corporation for the supply of water, but the power shall remain in force as though the contract had not been made.

§ 2403. Issue of bonds where water system acquired.

Where the price and terms are agreed upon, a borough may become the owner of and operate any water system owned and operated by a corporation furnishing water within the acquiring borough and in nearby municipal corporations. The borough may pay for the water system from the revenues derived from general obligation bonds or utility bonds issued in the manner provided by 53 Pa.C.S. Pt. VII Subpt. B (relating to indebtedness and borrowing).

§ 2404. Refunding bonds.

(a) General rule.—If a borough acquires a water system subject to any existing lien or liens and, at the time of acquisition, issues utility bonds secured by the liens on the water system and which impose no municipal liability, then, when the utility bonds mature or at any time prior, the borough may issue and sell utility bonds for the purposes of refunding the outstanding bonds. The refunding bonds shall be issued as utility bonds pursuant to 53 Pa.C.S. Pt. VII Subpt. B (relating to indebtedness and borrowing). The issued bonds shall not be deemed to be the creation of new obligations but shall be deemed a continuation of the bonds existing or created at the time of the original acquisition of the water system.

(b) Time, interest rate and amount.—The bonds shall not be refunded for a longer period than 20 years, and the refunding lien bonds issued shall not bear interest at a rate exceeding 6%. The aggregate amount of the issued refunding lien bonds shall not exceed the amount of the bonds to be refunded. Any money placed in any fund by the borough or by any commission of the water system for the purpose of redeeming or paying the bonds at maturity shall be first applied to the payment of the principal of the bonds to be refunded and the balance of the bonds only shall be refunded by the issue of new bonds.

§ 2405. (Reserved).

§ 2406. Contracts to supply water for municipal purposes.

Boroughs may receive bids from water companies and municipal authorities authorized to do business within the borough and from other municipalities operating a water system for the supply of water for fire protection and for other municipal purposes. The borough may contract for the supply of water with the water company.

Table of Contents | Part I Ch. 1–3 Ethics, Records, Open Meetings | Part II Ch. 4–10 Taxation | Part III Ch. 11–18 Torts, Contracts & Civil Rules | Part IV Ch. 19–24 Zoning & Planning | Part V Ch. 25–30 Construction and Emergency Codes | Part VI Ch. 31–39 Municipal Codes | Index

§ 2407. Power to supply water beyond limits of borough.

If a borough maintains a water system, it shall be lawful for the borough to supply water to persons and corporations outside the limits of the borough, but the supply of water shall be subject to any applicable approval or regulation imposed by 66 Pa.C.S. Pt. I (relating to Public Utility Code). The privilege shall not conflict with the corporate rights of any water company or the rights of any other municipality or municipal authority.

§ 2408. Assessment for water mains.

Boroughs shall have power to assess the whole cost or any part of the cost of construction of new water mains built in connection with the establishment or extension of a municipally owned water supply system in accordance with Chapter 21A (relating to assessments and charges for public improvements), notwithstanding if the mains are located within or without the limits of the borough.

§ 2409. Sale of water system.

(a) **General rule.**—By ordinance, a borough may sell all or part of its water system to a purchaser at an agreed upon price, and, thereafter, for all purposes that price shall be deemed to be the purchaser's original cost less accrued depreciation of the plant at the date of purchase. No ordinance shall take effect until the expiration of ten days following its enactment and if, within that ten-day period, a protest signed by at least 10% of the registered electors of the borough is filed with the council, the sale shall be stayed pending a referendum on the ordinance.

(b) **Protest.**—The following shall apply to a protest:

(1) The borough secretary, within five days following the filing of the protest, shall certify to the county board of elections a copy of the ordinance and the fact of the protest, together with the number of signers of the protest, and the county board of elections shall direct a referendum to be held on the matter at a special election to be held at the time of the next general or municipal or primary election occurring not less than 60 days from the date of the certification by the borough secretary.

(2) The referendum shall be conducted by the county board of elections in the manner provided by the act of June 3, 1937 (P.L.1333, No.320), known as the Pennsylvania Election Code, for the holding of special elections. The ballot used when voting upon the question shall contain a question stating the nature and purpose of the ordinance and provide that a "yes" vote shall be to sustain the ordinance and a "no" vote shall be to reject it.

(3) If more electors vote to sustain the ordinance than to reject it, the ordinance shall take effect immediately. If more electors shall vote to reject the ordinance than to sustain it, the ordinance shall be null and void and shall not take effect.

SUBCHAPTER A.1
ACQUISITION BY EMINENT DOMAIN

Sec.

---

§ 2411. Appropriation of lands and waters.

A borough desiring to build a water system or to improve its water supply may appropriate springs, streams, rivers or creeks and lands, easements and rights-of-way, within or without its limits. If the appropriation is outside its limits, the appropriation shall be in compliance with 26 Pa.C.S. § 206 (relating to extraterritorial takings). For the purpose of conducting water obtained outside its limits, a borough may lay pipes under and over any lands, rivers, streams, bridges, highways and under railroads. No water appropriated under this section shall be used in a manner as to deprive the owner of the water of the free use and enjoyment of the water for domestic or farm purposes. The exercise of the powers in this section shall be subject to any required approvals or permits from the Department of Environmental Protection or other Federal or State entity.

§ 2412. Agreements as to damages.

Prior to any appropriation under section 2411 (relating to appropriation of lands and waters), the borough shall attempt to agree with the owner as to the damage done or likely to be done. If the parties cannot agree, the borough shall proceed pursuant to 26 Pa.C.S. (relating to eminent domain).

§ 2413. (Reserved).

SUBCHAPTER A.2
ACQUISITION BY PURCHASE AFTER APPRAISEMENT

§ 2421. Petition to court.

If a borough desires to own and operate a water system owned by any person, firm or corporation, the borough may present its petition to the court of common pleas of the county where the water system is located, setting forth that:

(1) The borough desires to own the water system.

(2) It will be necessary to issue bonds.

(3) A value should be placed upon the water system, including all property, real and personal, used in connection with the water system.

§ 2422. Appointment of appraisers.

(a) Valuation.—The court of common pleas shall appoint three civil engineers as appraisers to value and appraise:

(1) The water system.

(2) The property used in connection with the water system.

(3) The contracts or agreements with municipalities.

(b) Report.—The civil engineers shall file their report in the court within three months after their appointment unless the time is extended by the court.

§ 2423. Powers of appraisers.

The appraisers shall have the following powers:

(1) To access the books and records of the person, firm or corporation owning the water system to inform themselves as to the income and value of the water system.

(2) To administer oaths and to take the testimony of witnesses.

(b) **Report.**—The report of the appraisers shall be final unless the report is appealed.

§ 2424. Appeal from appraisement.

(a) **Filing of petition.**—Within ten days after notice of the filing of any report in the court of common pleas, either party may appeal from the appraisement by filing a petition for a hearing before the court alleging an undervaluation or overvaluation of the property.

(b) **Hearing.**—The court shall fix a time when the appeal may be heard, giving at least ten days' notice to the parties, and, upon hearing, the court of common pleas shall have power to affirm or modify the report as the court deems just and proper.

§ 2425. Authority to purchase and consent to sell.

(a) **Authority to purchase.**—After the value is finally determined, the borough is authorized to buy the water system at the valuation fixed.

(b) **Consent to sell.**—The person, firm or corporation owning the water system shall, within ten days after notice, file in the court of common pleas its consent to sell and convey its water system and property to the borough at the valuation fixed. In default of the filing of the consent, the person, firm, or corporation shall cease to have any exclusive privilege of supplying the borough or the citizens of the borough with water, and the borough may install the water system as may be necessary for the accommodation of the public.

§ 2426. Bond issue and limitations.

(a) **Bond issue.**—For the purpose of purchasing a water system, the borough may issue utility bonds in the manner provided by 53 Pa.C.S. Pt. VII Subpt. B (relating to indebtedness and borrowing).

(b) **Limitations.**—The bonds shall not exceed in amount the value fixed by the appraisers or the court of common pleas. The proceeds of the sale of the bonds shall be used exclusively for the purpose of paying for the property acquired.

§ 2427. (Reserved).

SUBCHAPTER A.3

POWER TO LEASE WATER SYSTEM

Sec.

---

§ 2431. Lease of water system.

The council of a borough may enter into a contract with any individual, partnership, association or corporation for the leasing of a water system of the individual, partnership, association or corporation.

§ 2432. Term of lease and rental.

The lease term may be for a term of years and at a rental price as shall be agreed upon by the borough and the individual, copartnership, association or corporation.

§ 2433. Operation of property.

A borough shall have the same powers in operating a leased water system as it would have in operating a purchased or condemned water system.

§ 2434. (Reserved).

SUBCHAPTER A.4
JOINT WATER SYSTEM

---

§ 2436. Joint acquisition and construction.

A borough may join with one or more municipal corporations in the construction or acquisition and maintenance of a water system.

§ 2437. Permits.

The construction of a water system shall be commenced only after plans for the water system have been filed with the Department of Environmental Protection and, if required by law, other Federal or State entities and permits issued in accordance with law.

§ 2438. Joint commission.

(a) General rule.—The municipal corporations joining in the construction or acquisition and maintenance of a water system may, by ordinance, provide for the appointment of a joint commission of a water system in order to facilitate the construction, operation and maintenance of the water system and to secure preliminary surveys and estimates.

(b) Function.—The joint commission shall act generally as the advisory and administrative agency in the construction of the improvement and its subsequent operation and maintenance.

(c) Composition.—The joint commission shall be composed of one representative from each of the joining municipal corporations.

(d) Term of members.—The members of the joint commission shall serve for terms of six years each from the dates of their respective appointments and until their successors are appointed.

(e) Officers.—The joint commission shall organize by the election of a chair, secretary and treasurer. The secretary and treasurer may be the same person.

(f) Ordinance provisions.—The municipal corporations may, in the ordinances creating the joint commission, authorize it to appoint an engineer, a solicitor and other assistants as are deemed necessary and agree to share the compensation for attending its meetings as shall be fixed in the budget prepared by the commission and submitted to and adopted by the joining municipal corporations.

(g) Compensation limitation and expenses.—The budget item providing for the compensation to the members for attending meetings shall not exceed $500 per year, but members shall be entitled to actual expenses to be paid by the respective municipal corporations that the members represent. The fee for each attendance at meetings shall be stipulated, and no member shall be paid a fee for any meeting the member does not attend.

SUBCHAPTER A.5
CONDEMNATION OF LANDS FOR ROAD PURPOSES AND TO PREVENT CONTAMINATION

---

§ 2441. Acquisition of land.

(a) Acquisition for construction of roads.—If a borough finds it necessary, when storing water for supply to the public, to occupy and overflow portions of any public road with water or if any public road leads into or crosses over any reservoir used for the storage of water, the borough shall, at its own expense, reconstruct or build a road in a favorable location, which shall be in the same or better condition as the original road. A borough is authorized to condemn land for these purposes if an agreement as to price cannot be reached with the landowner.

(b) Land outside borough limits.—A condemnation of land outside the borough limits shall be in conformity with 26 Pa.C.S. § 206 (relating to extraterritorial takings).

(c) Acquisition to prevent contamination.—A borough may acquire, by purchase or condemnation, land along and contiguous to streams of water or reservoirs from which water is taken for public use if necessary to preserve the water from contamination.

§ 2442. Filing maps and plans.

If a change is made under section 2441(a) (relating to acquisition of land), the borough shall file in the court of common pleas a map or plan showing the change of road, and, if the road is outside the limits of the borough, it shall furnish to the governing body of the municipal corporation a copy of the map.

§ 2443. (Reserved).

§ 2444. (Reserved).

SUBCHAPTER A.6
COMMISSION OF WATER SYSTEM

---

§ 2451. Commission.

(a) Establishment.—If a borough owns and maintains a water system, there may be established in the borough, by ordinance, a commission of the water system, which shall have the power of a nonprofit corporation, to be composed of either three or five citizens of the borough appointed by the council who shall be known as commissioners of the water system.

(b) Abolishment.—At any time after three years from the first appointment of the commissioners of the water system, the borough may abolish the commission by repealing the ordinance establishing the commission, which shall terminate the terms of the commissioners then in office.

§ 2452. Terms of commissioners and compensation.

(a) General rule.—If a borough establishes a commission of the water system, it shall be the duty of the council to appoint the commissioners of the water system.

(b) Commissions with three commissioners.—If there are three commissioners, one shall be appointed to serve for one year, one for two years and one for three years. Annually thereafter, the council shall appoint one commissioner of the water system to serve a term of three years.

(c) Commissions with five commissioners.—If there are five commissioners, one shall be appointed to serve for one year, one for two years, one for three years, one for four years and one for five years. Annually thereafter, the council shall appoint one commissioner of the water system to serve a term of five years.

(d) Vacancy.—In case of a vacancy, the council shall fill the vacancy for the unexpired term.

(e) Salary and expenses.—The commissioners of the water system may receive a salary for their services and shall be reimbursed by the borough for all expenses necessarily incurred in the performance of their duties.

(f) Salary limitations.—The salary of the commissioners shall not exceed the following:

(1) In service areas with fewer than 5,000 metered accounts, a maximum of $1,875 per year or $156.25 per month.

(2) In service areas with 5,000 but fewer than 10,000 metered accounts, a maximum of $2,500 per year or $208.33 per month.

(3) In service areas with 10,000 but fewer than 15,000 metered accounts, a maximum of $3,250 per year or $270.83 per month.

(4) In service areas with 15,000 but fewer than 25,000 metered accounts, a maximum of $4,125 per year or $343.75 per month.

(5) In service areas with 25,000 but fewer than 35,000 metered accounts, a maximum of $4,375 per year or $364.58 per month.

(6) In service areas with 35,000 or more metered accounts, a maximum of $5,000 per year or $416.67 per month.

§ 2453. Organization of commissioners.

The commissioners of the water system shall meet within ten days after their first appointment and annually thereafter and organize by electing a president and secretary.

§ 2454. Powers of commission.

After organization, the commissioners shall take charge and control of the water system of the borough. The commission shall have the following powers:

(1) To appoint all necessary officers and agents and take from the officers and agents security for the faithful performance of their duties as the commission deems proper.

(2) To fix the salaries and wages of the officers and agents.

(3) To provide for the repair, extension, improvement and maintenance of the water system and the construction of a new water system.

(4) To collect water rents.

(5) To make and establish the rates and conditions upon which water will be furnished to applicants, subject to any applicable approval, regulation or control imposed by 66 Pa.C.S. Pt. I (relating to Public Utility Code).

(6) To make bylaws and regulations for the economic and efficient management of the water system, which shall not be inconsistent with any of the laws of this Commonwealth or the rules and regulations of the Department of Environmental Protection. No bylaws or regulations shall become effective until they have been approved by the council and enacted as ordinances of the borough.

§ 2455. Issue of bonds.

The borough may, upon the request of the commissioners of the water system, issue general obligation or nondebt revenue bonds for the extension of the water system or the erection of a new water system. The bonds shall be designated "water system bonds" and shall be issued and sold in the manner provided by 53 Pa.C.S. Pt. VII Subpt. B (relating to indebtedness and borrowing).

§ 2456. Preparation of plans and specifications and contracts.

(a) Preparation of plans and specifications.—The commissioners shall prepare plans and specifications of all work to be performed and materials necessary for the repair, maintenance and extension of the water system or the construction of a new water system.

(b) Contracts.—The commissioners shall, after plans and specifications for the extension or the construction of a water system have been submitted to and approved by the Department of Environmental Protection and a permit has been granted as may be required by law:

(1) Invite proposals for the performing of the work and the furnishing of materials.

(2) Advertise for bids as required by law.

(3) Let contracts to the lowest qualified and responsible bidder.

(4) Take adequate security for the performance of the contracts and for the payment of all labor and materials.

§ 2457. Reports by commission.

The commissioners shall make a monthly report to the council of the receipts and disbursements during the preceding month and annually make a detailed report of the condition of the water system. Both the monthly and annual reports shall be deemed to be public records.

§ 2458. Care of funds.

(a) Collectors.—Collectors shall be appointed by the commissioners, in accordance with section 2454 (relating to powers of commission), who shall collect all money for water rents.

(b) Deposits.—The money collected shall be deposited weekly with the borough treasurer who shall return a receipt to the commissioners.

(c) Use.—All money collected shall be kept in a separate fund and shall be used for the purpose of repairing, maintaining and extending the water system and the construction of a new water system. All money remaining after the expenditures shall be used solely for the payment of any indebtedness on the water system and any indebtedness incurred by the borough for constructing, maintaining, improving, enlarging or extending the water system.

(d) Withdrawals.—No money shall be drawn from the fund except upon order countersigned by the president and secretary of the commission.

SUBCHAPTER A.7
WATER CONNECTIONS

---

§ 2461. Ordinance.

(a) General rule.—Council may, by ordinance, require any owner of property to connect with and use a water system of the borough or municipal authority or a joint water board in either of the following cases:

(1) Except as provided in subsection (b), if the property owner's principal building is located within 150 feet of a water system or any part or extension of the system.

(2) If the property owner's principal building has no supply of water which is safe for human consumption.

(b) Exception.—A property owner who after July 16, 2012, is subject to mandatory connection under subsection (a)(1) shall not be required to connect to the water system in accordance with subsection (a) if all of the following conditions exist:

(1) The water system or part or extension of the system that is within 150 feet of the principal building was in existence on July 16, 2012.

(2) The principal building has its own supply of water which is safe for human consumption.

(3) Prior to July 16, 2012, the property owner was not required to connect to the existing system.

(c) Backflow prevention.—A borough may require any owner of property to install and maintain a backflow prevention device based on the degree of potential hazard of the connected property in accordance with the Pennsylvania Construction Code and regulations promulgated under that act.

(d) Penalties.—A borough may assess penalties for the violation of ordinances pertaining to water connections or backflow prevention devices.

§ 2462. Notice and failure to make required connection.

An owner shall be given at least 45 days' notice of any ordinance requiring a water connection, and, upon failure of the owner to make the required connection, the borough may make the connection and collect the cost from the owner by a municipal claim or in an action of assumpsit. All connections required shall be uniform.

§ 2463. Water main tapping fees.

(a) General rule.—A borough may, by ordinance, provide for charging a tapping fee calculated in accordance with 53 Pa.C.S. § 5607 (relating to purposes and powers) if the owner of any property connects the property with a water main constructed or acquired by the borough. The tapping fee shall be in addition to any charges assessed and collected against the property in the construction or acquisition of the water main by the borough.

Table of Contents
Part I Ch. 1–3 Ethics, Records, Open Meetings
Part II Ch. 4–10 Taxation
Part III Ch. 11–18 Torts, Contracts & Civil Rules
Part IV Ch. 19–24 Zoning & Planning
Part V Ch. 25–30 Construction and Emergency Codes
Part VI Ch. 31–39 Municipal Codes
Index

Chap. 39 Res. During Mil. Service
Chap. 38 Intergov. Coop.
Chap. 37 3rd Class City Code
Chap. 36 Bor. Code
Chap. 35 2nd Class Twp. Code
Chap. 34 1st Class Twp. Code
Chap. 33 Home Rule Chart. Opt. Plans Law
Chap. 32 Water Serv. Act
Chap. 31 Munic. Auth. Act

(b) Refund.—If a water main or part or extension owned by a borough has been constructed by the borough at the expense of a private person or corporation or has been constructed by a private person or corporation under the supervision of the borough at the expense of the private person or corporation, the borough shall have the right to charge a tapping fee calculated in accordance with 53 Pa.C.S. § 5607 and refund the tapping fee or any part of the tapping fee to the person or corporation who has paid for the construction of the water main or any part or extension. The total of the refunds shall never exceed the cost of the system or any part or extension to the person or corporation paying for the construction.

SUBCHAPTER B
(Reserved)

SUBCHAPTER C
(Reserved)

SUBCHAPTER D
(Reserved)

CHAPTER 24A
MANUFACTURE AND SUPPLY OF ELECTRICITY

Sec.

---

§ 24A01. Definitions.

The following words and phrases when used in this chapter shall have the meanings given to them in this section unless the context clearly indicates otherwise:

"Municipal power agency." A separate body politic and corporate under the laws of this Commonwealth created by agreement between or among two or more boroughs pursuant to section 24A04 (relating to municipal power agencies).

"Project." Electric plants, hydroelectric plant works, system, facilities or real or personal property, together with their parts and appurtenances, used or useful in connection with the generation, production, transmission, purchase, sale, exchange or interchange of electric power or energy, or any interest therein or right to capacity thereof.

"Revenue bond." An instrument imposing an obligation for the repayment of money borrowed, payable as to both principal and interest exclusively from the income and revenues derived from an interest in an electric plant or project.

§ 24A02. General powers.

(a) Electric plants and projects.—A borough may, either singly or jointly, manufacture or purchase electricity for the use of its inhabitants, own, construct, acquire by lease, purchase or otherwise gain an interest in, operate and manage or cause to be operated and managed an electric plant or project located within or without this Commonwealth. In the exercise of these powers, a borough may join with any other borough, political subdivision, agency or instrumentality of the Federal Government, State government, political subdivision of another state, private corporation empowered to supply electricity, electric cooperative corporation formed under 15 Pa.C.S. Ch. 73 Subchs. A (relating to preliminary provisions) and B (relating to powers, duties and safeguards) or previously formed under the former act of June 21, 1937 (P.L.1969, No.389), known as the Electric Cooperative Corporation Act, or an electric cooperative corporation in another state.

(b) Contracts for supplying electricity.—A borough owning or operating an electric plant may make contracts for supplying electricity for commercial purposes outside the limits of the borough, if the borough has received the consent of the other municipal governing body and, if applicable, subject to 66 Pa.C.S. Pt. I (relating to Public Utility Code).

(c) Additional sources.—A borough may conduct studies as necessary to determine the feasibility and cost of any additional sources and supplies of electric power and energy and may cooperate with private power companies, other boroughs, electric cooperative corporations and other public or private electric power entities, within or without this Commonwealth, in the development of electric power and energy.

(d) Consent of borough to supply electricity.—No person, partnership or corporation may introduce electric current for light, heat or power purposes, without the consent of the council, into the limits of any borough that is furnishing electric current to its inhabitants. This subsection shall not apply to any person, partnership or corporation manufacturing electricity exclusively for its own use.

(e) Corporate rights.—Nothing in this chapter may conflict with the corporate rights of a corporation empowered to supply electricity in the territory adjacent to the borough or with the rights of any other municipality.

(f) Restrictions.—A borough shall not become a stockholder in, obtain or appropriate money for or loan its credit to a corporation, association, institution or individual or otherwise act contrary to the provisions of section 9 of Article IX of the Constitution of Pennsylvania.

(g) General powers.—A borough, through its governing body, shall have the power to do and accomplish all actions reasonably necessary and incident to the administration, operation and management of a plant or project.

§ 24A03. Specific powers.

(a) Specific powers enumerated.—In addition to exercising its general powers under section 24A02 (relating to general powers), a borough, through its governing body, shall have the following powers:

(1) To contract for the purchase, sale, exchange, interchange, wheeling, pooling or transmission of electric power and energy or for the right to the capacity of electric power, inside and outside of this Commonwealth, to and from any public or private power entities, private power companies, other boroughs and electric cooperative corporations. The sale of electric power to a borough for resale inside the limits of the borough and the sale of electric power by a borough inside the limits of the borough shall be exempt from the tax imposed under section 1101 of the act of March 4, 1971 (P.L.6, No.2), known as the Tax Reform Code of 1971.[1]

(2) To regulate the use of and the charge for electricity furnished by the borough for use throughout the borough. A borough may fix, establish, maintain and collect or authorize by contract or otherwise the establishment, levying and collection of the rates, fees, rental or other charges, including connection charges, for the services afforded by or in connection with any properties which the borough constructs, erects, owns, acquires, operates or manages and for the sale or transmission of electric energy and power as it deems necessary, proper, desirable and reasonable.

1. Act 28 of 2020 amended subsec. (a)(1). Section 3(1) of Act 28 provided that the amendment of subsec. (a)(1) shall apply to gross receipts received after December 31, 2016. Section 3(2) of Act 28 provided that the amendment of subsec. (a)(1) shall apply to sales to or by a municipal power agency or any borough owned or operated utility established on or before the effective date of section 3.

Table of Contents
Part I Ch. 1–3 Ethics, Records, Open Meetings
Part II Ch. 4–10 Taxation
Part III Ch. 11–18 Torts, Contracts & Civil Rules
Part IV Ch. 19–24 Zoning & Planning
Part V Ch. 25–30 Construction and Emergency Codes
Part VI Ch. 31–39 Municipal Codes
Index

(3) To procure insurance against any losses in connection with its property, operations or assets in the amounts and from the insurers as the governing body or bodies deem desirable.

(4) To contract for and to accept any gifts, grants or loans of funds, property or financial or other aid in any form, from the United States or any agency or instrumentality of the United States, or from any other source.

(5) To lease, or otherwise grant the use of, and to make charges for the use of any property or facility owned or controlled by the borough.

(6) To procure from the United States or any agency or instrumentality of the United States, or from any state or agency or instrumentality of a state, any consents, authorizations or approvals which may be requisite to enable ownership, operation, construction or repair.

(7) To borrow money and from time to time to issue revenue bonds and to enter into agreements with the purchasers of the revenue bonds. A borough that incurs debt for the construction or purchase of an electric plant, or land on which to construct an electric plant, or gains an interest in an electric plant or project under section 24A02 shall incur the debt in accordance with and to the extent permitted by 53 Pa.C.S. Pt. VII Subpt. B (relating to indebtedness and borrowing). Interest and principal paid on revenue bonds issued by a borough under this chapter shall be exempt from all State taxes of any kind or nature.

(8) To mortgage a property acquired or owned under section 24A02 to secure the payment of its revenue bonds or other obligations issued to finance the acquisition, ownership or repair.

(9) To sell, by ordinance, all or part of its electric works to a purchaser for the sale price agreed upon by the parties. After the sale, the price shall be deemed to be the purchaser's original cost less accrued depreciation of the plant at the date of purchase.

(10) To purchase the electric works of any person, partnership or electric company organized under the laws of this Commonwealth that is furnishing electricity to the borough or the public within the borough. The borough and the person, partnership or a majority in value of the stockholders of a corporation may agree upon the purchase price, except that, upon failure of the parties to agree on the price, the borough may proceed according to 26 Pa.C.S. (relating to eminent domain).

(b) Eminent domain.—In the erection and extension of an electric plant or project under this chapter and for all other purposes authorized by this part, a borough may enter upon, appropriate, injure or destroy private lands, property or material according to the proceedings set forth in 26 Pa.C.S. A borough shall not have the power of condemnation with regard to any property of a private or public retail electric supplier which geographically lies beyond the boundaries of the corporate limits of the borough.

§ 24A04. Municipal power agencies.

(a) General rule.—Two or more boroughs may form a municipal power agency by the execution of an agency agreement authorized by an ordinance of the governing bodies of each borough. The agency agreement shall state:

(1) The name of the agency, which shall include the words "municipal power agency."

(2) The names of the boroughs which have approved the agency agreement and are initial members of the municipal power agency.

(3) That the municipal power agency is created pursuant to the authority granted by this part.

Chap. 39 Res. During Mil. Service
Chap. 38 Intergov. Coop.
Chap. 37 3rd Class City Code
Chap. 36 Bor. Code
Chap. 35 2nd Class Twp. Code
Chap. 34 1st Class Twp. Code
Chap. 33 Home Rule Chart. Opt. Plans Law
Chap. 32 Water Serv. Act
Chap. 31 Munic. Auth. Act

(4) The names and addresses of the persons initially appointed by the governing bodies to act as representatives to the municipal power agency from the member boroughs.

(5) The limitations, if any, placed on the powers or terms of representatives appointed by the governing bodies of the member boroughs.

(6) The names and addresses of the initial board of directors of the municipal power agency, if known by the time of filing, which shall be constituted by not less than five persons who are representatives of the member boroughs, selected by the vote of a majority of the representatives.

(b) Certificate of incorporation.—The agency agreement under subsection (a) and a certified copy of the ordinance of the governing body of each borough shall be filed for record with the Secretary of the Commonwealth. If the agency agreement meets the requirements of this section, the Secretary of the Commonwealth shall record the agreement and issue and record a certificate of incorporation which shall be conclusive proof of substantial compliance with the requirements of this section. The certificate shall state the name of the municipal power agency and the fact and date of incorporation. Upon the issuance of the certificate of incorporation, the existence of the municipal power agency as a political instrumentality of the Commonwealth shall begin.

(b.1) Open meetings.—Regular and special meetings of the representatives of member boroughs and the board of directors as provided in this section shall be subject to 65 Pa.C.S. Ch. 7 (relating to open meetings).

(c) Bylaws.—The bylaws of the municipal power agency and any amendments shall be proposed by the board of directors and shall be adopted by a majority vote of the representatives of the member boroughs unless the agency agreement requires a greater vote at a meeting held after notice. Subject to the provisions of the agency agreement, the requirements of this part and the laws of this Commonwealth, the bylaws shall state:

(1) The qualifications of member boroughs and limitations, if any, upon their number.

(2) Conditions of membership, if any.

(3) The manner and time of calling regular meetings of representatives of member boroughs.

(4) The manner and conditions of termination of membership.

(5) Other provisions for regulating the affairs of the municipal power agency as the representatives of the member boroughs shall determine to be necessary.

(d) Registered office.—Every municipal power agency shall maintain an office in this Commonwealth to be known as its registered office. When a municipal power agency desires to change the location of its registered office, it shall file with the Secretary of the Commonwealth a certificate of change of location of registered office, stating the new location by address, including street and number, if any, and the effective date of change. When the certificate of change of location has been duly filed, the board of directors may make the change without any further action.

(e) Directors.—The following apply:

(1) Each of the directors shall hold office for the term for which the director has been selected and until a successor has been selected and has qualified. Directors shall discharge their duties in good faith and with that diligence and care which an ordinary prudent person in a like position would exercise under similar circumstances.

(2) The agency agreement or the bylaws may prescribe the number, term of office, powers, authority and duties of directors, the time and place of their

meetings and other regulations concerning directors in a manner consistent with law.

(3) Except where the agency agreement or bylaws prescribe otherwise, the term of office of a director shall be for one year.

(4) Except where the agency agreement or bylaws prescribe otherwise, a meeting of the board of directors may be held at any place within this Commonwealth designated by the board, after notice, and an act of the majority of the directors present at a meeting at which a quorum is present is the act of the board.

(5) Except where the agency agreement or bylaws prescribe otherwise, any vacancy occurring on the board shall be filled by a person nominated by the remaining members of the board and elected by a majority of representatives of the member boroughs.

(f) Officers.—Except where the agency agreement or bylaws prescribe otherwise, the board of directors shall appoint a president from its membership and a secretary, treasurer and any other officers or agents deemed necessary who may, but need not be, borough representatives or directors. An officer may be removed with or without cause by the board of directors. Officers of the municipal power agency shall have the authority and duties in the management of the business of the municipal power agency that the agency agreement or bylaws prescribe or, in the absence of the prescription, as the board of directors determines.

(g) Representatives of member boroughs.—The following apply:

(1) Except as otherwise provided in the agency agreement or the bylaws, the duly authorized representatives of each member borough shall act as and vote on behalf of that borough.

(2) Except where the agency agreement or bylaws provide otherwise, representatives of the member boroughs shall hold at least one meeting each year for the election of directors and for the transaction of any other business.

(3) Except where the agency agreement or bylaws prescribe otherwise, special meetings of the representatives may be called for any purpose upon written request to the president or secretary to call the meeting. The officer shall give notice of the meeting to be held between ten and 60 days after receipt of the request.

(4) Unless the agency agreement or bylaws provide for a different percentage, a quorum for a meeting of the representatives of the member boroughs is a majority of the total members, and a quorum for meetings of the board of directors is a majority of the membership of the board.

(h) Amendment of agency agreement.—The agency agreement may be amended as proposed at any meeting of the representatives of the members for which notice stating the purpose shall be given to each representative and, unless the agency agreement or bylaws require otherwise, shall become effective when ratified by ordinances of a majority of the governing bodies of the member boroughs. Each amendment and the ordinances approving it shall be filed for record with the Secretary of the Commonwealth.

(i) Appropriations.—Each member borough shall have full power and authority, within budgetary limits applicable to it, to appropriate money for the payment of expenses of the formation of the municipal power agency and of its representative in exercising its functions as a member of the agency.

(j) General powers.—A municipal power agency may own, construct, acquire by lease, purchase or otherwise gain an interest by itself or as co-owner or tenant in common and operate and manage or cause to be operated and managed an electric plant or project located within or without this Commonwealth jointly with any political subdivision, subdivision of the Federal Government, State government, political subdivision of another state, private corporation empowered to supply electricity, electric cooperative corporation formed under the former act of June 21, 1937 (P.L.1969, No.389), known as the Electric Cooperative Corporation Act, or electric cooperative corporation in another state.

(k) Specific powers.—All powers of a municipal power agency shall be exercised by its board of directors, unless otherwise provided by the agency agreement or bylaws. A municipal power agency shall have the power to do and accomplish all actions reasonably necessary and incident to the ownership, construction, acquisition, administration, operation and management of an electric plant or project. Among the specific powers of a municipal power agency shall be the following:

(1) To sue and be sued.

(2) To enter into contracts.

(3) To cooperate with private power companies, boroughs, electric cooperative corporations and other public or private electric power entities inside and outside of this Commonwealth in the development of electric power and energy.

(4) To make the studies as may be necessary to determine the feasibility and cost of any additional sources and supplies of electric power and energy.

(5) To contract for the purchase, sale, exchange, interchange, wheeling, pooling or transmission of electric power and energy or for the right to the capacity thereof, inside and outside of this Commonwealth, to and from any public or private power entities, private power companies, other boroughs and electric cooperative corporations.

(6) To procure insurance against any losses in connection with its property, operations or assets in amounts and from insurers as the board of directors deems desirable.

(7) To contract for and to accept any gifts, grants or loans of funds, property or financial or other aid in any form from the United States or any agency or instrumentality of the United States or from any other source.

(8) To acquire, hold, use, operate and dispose of personal property.

(9) To acquire, hold, use and dispose of its income, revenues, funds and money.

(10) To acquire, own, use, lease, operate and dispose of real property and interests in real property and to make improvements to the real property.

(11) To grant the use, by lease or otherwise, and to make charges for the use of any property or facility owned or controlled by it.

(12) To procure from the United States or any agency or instrumentality of the United States, or from any state or agency or instrumentality of a state, any consents, authorizations or approvals which may be requisite to enable ownership, operation, construction or repair.

(13) To borrow money and from time to time to issue revenue bonds and to enter into agreements with the purchasers of the revenue bonds.

(14) To invest funds not required for immediate use, including, but not limited to, proceeds from the sale of revenue bonds. The power of a municipal power agency to invest shall be the same as that of a borough, as exercised by the council pursuant to sections 1005(6) (relating to powers of council) and 1316 (relating to investment of funds).

(15) To mortgage any property acquired or owned to secure the payment of its revenue bonds or other obligations issued to finance the acquisition, ownership or repair.

(l) Eminent domain.—

(1) Except as provided under paragraph (2), in the erection and extension of an electric plant or project and for all other purposes authorized by this part, a municipal power agency may enter upon, appropriate, injure or destroy private lands, property or material according to the proceedings set forth in 26 Pa.C.S. (relating to eminent domain).

(2) A municipal power agency shall not have the power of condemnation with regard to any property of a private or public retail electric supplier which geographically lies beyond the boundaries of the corporate limits of its member boroughs.

(m) Revenue bonds.—A municipal power agency which gains an interest in an electric plant or project may pay all or part of the cost from the revenues derived from the sale of revenue bonds issued in the manner provided by 53 Pa.C.S. Pt. VII Subpt. B (relating to indebtedness and borrowing).

(n) Bylaws.—A municipal power agency may make and enforce bylaws or rules which it deems necessary or desirable. A municipal power agency may establish, fix, levy and collect or may authorize, by contract, franchise, lease or otherwise, the establishment, levying and collection of rents, rates and other charges for the services afforded by the municipal power agency, including connection for the services afforded by the municipal power agency, including connection charges or by or in connection with any project or properties which it may construct, erect, acquire, own, operate or control, or with respect to which it may have any interest or any right to capacity thereof, and for the sale of electric energy or of generation or transmission capacity or services as it may deem necessary, proper, desirable and reasonable. Rents, rates and other charges shall be at least sufficient to meet expenses thereof, including reasonable reserves, interest and principal payments.

(o) State tax exemptions.—Interest and principal paid on revenue bonds issued by a municipal power agency shall be exempt from all State taxes of whatsoever kind or nature.

§ 24A05. Additional contracting authority.

(a) Additional contracting authority.—In addition to the authority provided under section 24A02 (relating to general powers), a borough that, on October 27, 2010, owned or operated electric generation or distribution facilities and a borough that is a member of a nonprofit membership corporation may contract with the nonprofit membership corporation for the following:

(1) The development of electric power and associated energy, including the conduct of investigations or studies necessary to determine the feasibility and cost of additional sources and supplies of electric power and associated energy.

(2) The purchase, sale, exchange, interchange, wheeling, pooling or transmission of electric power and associated energy or the right to the capacity from sources and projects in this Commonwealth or another state for a period not to exceed 50 years.

(b) Contract requirements.—A contract under subsection (a)(2) shall include the purpose of the contract, the duration of the contract and available procedures to terminate the contract subsequent to the repayment of all indebtedness secured under the contract.

(c) Minimum quantity of electric power and energy.—If a borough is a member of a nonprofit membership corporation, a contract under subsection (a)(2) may, if specifically set forth in the contract, obligate the borough to:

(1) Take and pay for a minimum quantity of electric power and associated energy if the power and energy are available for delivery.

(2) In connection with a project owned by the nonprofit membership corporation or in which the nonprofit membership corporation obtains an undivided

ownership interest, take or pay for a minimum amount of electric power and energy.

(3) Pay for electric power and energy only if utilized by the borough.

(d) Applicability of minimum requirements.—

(1) The authority under subsection (c)(1) shall apply whether or not the borough accepts delivery of the power and energy.

(2) The authority under subsection (c)(2) shall apply notwithstanding the suspension, interruption, interference or reduction or curtailment of the output of the project or the electric power and energy contracted for and whether or not:

(i) the electric power and energy is available for delivery to the borough; or

(ii) the borough accepts delivery of the electric power and energy.

(e) Take-or-pay or take-and-pay arrangements.—No borough may be obligated under a take-or-pay or take-and-pay arrangement entered into with a nonprofit membership corporation in which the borough maintains membership unless that obligation is expressly authorized by an act of the council.

(f) Restrictions.—A nonprofit membership corporation shall not:

(1) Condition membership in the nonprofit membership corporation on the inclusion of any take-or-pay or take-and-pay obligations in a contract under subsection (a)(2).

(2) Except as set forth in subsection (g), require take-or-pay or take-and-pay obligations in a contract with a borough unless the contract meets the criteria of subsection (c)(1) or (2).

(g) Future contracts.—A borough that is a member of a nonprofit membership corporation may enter into future power supply contracts, contract renewals or contract extensions with the nonprofit membership corporation under subsection (c)(3):

(1) with no take-or-pay or take-and-pay obligations as permitted by subsection (c)(1) and (2); and

(2) without prejudice or discrimination as compared to any other borough which chooses to enter into contracts permitted by subsection (c)(1) and (2) with the nonprofit membership corporation.

(h) Future power supply contract terms.—In order to carry out subsection (g), a nonprofit membership corporation which provides or offers electric power and associated energy to a member borough in this Commonwealth under subsection (a)(2) shall offer, to all of its member boroughs in this Commonwealth, future power supply contract terms, contract renewals or contract extensions under subsection (c)(3) on a comparable and nondiscriminatory basis and with similar terms and conditions to future power supply contract terms, contract renewals or contract extensions that would be appropriate under subsection (c)(3) which the nonprofit membership corporation contemporaneously offers to its members in other states.

(i) Payments.—All obligations under a contract under subsection (a)(2) shall be paid from revenues derived from the operation of the borough's electric system, and payments shall be an operating expense of the borough's electric system.

(j) Obligations of other entities.—If explicitly set forth in a contract under subsection (a)(2), a borough may agree to assume, prorate or otherwise become liable for the obligations of another borough of this Commonwealth or of a political subdivision of another state that is a member of the nonprofit membership corporation if the borough or other political subdivision defaults in the payment of its obligations for the purchase of the electric power and associated energy. The contract may include provisions to permit a borough to succeed to the rights and interests of the defaulting borough or political subdivision to purchase electric power and associated energy. A borough's liability for the obligations of a defaulting borough of this Commonwealth or a political subdivision of another state shall not exceed 25% of a borough's initial nominal entitlement to electric power and associated energy under the contract.

(k) Pledge of borough property prohibited.—None of the obligations under the contract may constitute a legal or equitable pledge, charge, lien or encumbrance on any property of the borough or on any of its income, receipts or revenues, except revenues of its electric system. The full faith and credit and the taxing power of the borough shall not be pledged for the payment of an obligation under the contract.

(l) Construction.—This section is intended to add to the powers and rights of a borough, and nothing in this section may be construed to limit either the general or specific powers or rights of a borough set forth in this title.

(m) Definition.—As used in this section, the term "nonprofit membership corporation" means an entity the membership of which:

(1) consists solely of Pennsylvania boroughs, such as a consortium, buying group or municipal power agency under section 24A04 (relating to municipal power agencies); or

(2) consists of Pennsylvania boroughs and political subdivisions of another state or states.

CHAPTER 25

(Reserved)

CHAPTER 25A

AIRPORTS

---

§ 25A01. Authority to secure lands for airports.

A borough is authorized and empowered to acquire by lease, purchase or condemnation any land lying either within or without the limits of the borough which, in the judgment of the council, may be necessary and desirable for the purpose of establishing and maintaining municipal airport facilities. The proceedings for the condemnation of land under the provisions of this chapter and for the assessment of damages for property taken, injured or destroyed shall be conducted in the manner provided by 26 Pa.C.S. (relating to eminent domain). The title acquired by the borough exercising the power of condemnation shall be a title in fee simple.

§ 25A02. Authority to establish and lease airports.

A borough acquiring land under the provisions of this chapter is authorized and empowered to establish, equip, condition, operate and maintain the land as a municipal airport and may lease the land, or any part, to any individual or corporation desiring to use the same for aviation purposes. A borough may enter into a contract, in the form of a lease, providing for the use of the land, or any part, by the Federal Government for its use of the land for aviation purposes upon nominal rental or without consideration.

Chap. 39 Res. During Mil. Service
Chap. 38 Intergov. Coop.
Chap. 37 3rd Class City Code
Chap. 36 Bor. Code
Chap. 35 2nd Class Twp. Code
Chap. 34 1st Class Twp. Code
Chap. 33 Home Rule Chart. Opt. Plans Law
Chap. 32 Water Serv. Act
Chap. 31 Munic. Auth. Act

§ 25A03. Joint airports.

In accordance with the powers in this chapter, a borough may, jointly with another municipality, acquire land for aviation purposes and may jointly operate and maintain the airport on the terms and conditions as agreed upon by the governing bodies of the borough and other municipality.

CHAPTER 25B
SOLID WASTE COLLECTION AND DISPOSITION

---

§ 25B01. Definitions.

The following words and phrases when used in this chapter shall have the meanings given to them in this section unless the context clearly indicates otherwise:

"Municipal authority." A body politic and corporate created under 53 Pa.C.S. Ch. 56 (relating to municipal authorities).

"Municipal waste." As defined in section 103 of the act of July 28, 1988 (P.L.556, No.101), known as the Municipal Waste Planning, Recycling and Waste Reduction Act.

§ 25B02. Accumulation of municipal waste.

Council, in the manner authorized by the act of July 7, 1980 (P.L.380, No.97), known as the Solid Waste Management Act, and the act of July 28, 1988 (P.L.556, No.101), known as the Municipal Waste Planning, Recycling and Waste Reduction Act, may prohibit accumulations of municipal waste upon public and private property, including the imposition and collection of reasonable fees and charges for the collection, removal and disposal of municipal waste.

§ 25B03. Collection and removal.

(a) General rule.—Council may collect and remove, by contract or otherwise, municipal waste and recyclables and prescribe penalties for the enforcement of the collection and removal.

(b) Contract length.—A contract with refuse haulers may be made for an initial period not to exceed five years with optional renewal periods of up to five years.

(c) Limitation.—The limitation under subsection (b) does not apply to a contract with a political subdivision or municipal authority.

§ 25B04. Disposal.

(a) General rule.—Council may dispose of, by contract or otherwise, municipal waste.

(b) Contract length.—A contract with the owner of a private facility for the disposal or incineration of municipal waste may be made for a period not to exceed 20 years.

Table of Contents
Part I Ch. 1–3 Ethics, Records, Open Meetings
Part II Ch. 4–10 Taxation
Part III Ch. 11–18 Torts, Contracts & Civil Rules
Part IV Ch. 19–24 Zoning & Planning
Part V Ch. 25–30 Construction and Emergency Codes
Part VI Ch. 31–39 Municipal Codes
Index

(c) **Exemption.**—The limitation under subsection (b) shall not apply to a contract with a political subdivision or municipal authority.

§ 25B05. Acquisition of real property and facilities.

The following shall apply:

(1) Council may acquire real property and erect, maintain, improve, operate and lease, either as lessor or lessee, facilities for incineration, landfill or other methods of disposal, either inside or outside the limits of the borough, including equipment, either separately or jointly, with a political subdivision or municipal authority in order to provide for the collection, removal, disposal and destruction of municipal waste, for the collection and storage of recyclable materials or for the composting of leaf and yard waste.

(2) Council may provide for the payment of the cost, either in whole or part, out of the funds of the borough.

(3) Council may acquire land for landfill purposes, either amicably or by exercising the power of eminent domain, and may maintain lands and places for the dumping of municipal waste.

(4) If council acquires land outside the limits of the borough by exercising the power of eminent domain, the taking shall be subject to the limitations in 26 Pa.C.S. § 206 (relating to extraterritorial takings).

§ 25B06. Rates and charges.

(a) **Council authorization.**—Council may establish, alter, charge and collect rates and other charges for the:

(1) collection, removal and disposal of municipal waste and recyclable materials;

(2) cost of including the payment of any indebtedness incurred for the construction, purchase, improvement, repair, maintenance and operation of any facilities for collection, removal and disposal; and

(3) amount due under a contract with a political subdivision or municipal authority furnishing the services or facilities.

(b) **Method of collection.**—The rates and other charges shall be collected under the act of May 16, 1923 (P.L.207, No.153), referred to as the Municipal Claim and Tax Lien Law, by a civil action or any other collection method authorized by law.

§ 25B07. Appropriations.

Council may make appropriations to a political subdivision or municipal authority for the construction, purchase, improvement, repair, maintenance and operation of a facility for the collection, removal, disposal or marketing of municipal waste, recyclable materials or composted leaf and yard waste.

§ 25B08. Exclusion from other laws.

A borough may not be subject to requirements otherwise imposed by law for the sale of personal property owned by the borough when selling recyclable materials or materials separated, collected, recovered or created by recycling, as provided in the act of April 9, 1992 (P.L.70, No.21), entitled "An act excluding the sale of recyclable material from political subdivision personal property sale restrictions relating to advertising and bidding."

CHAPTER 26
WHARVES AND DOCKS

---

§ 2601. Powers.

(a) Construction and repair.—Boroughs shall have the power to construct and repair wharves and docks and may acquire, by purchase or condemnation, real estate along navigable waters and within the borough limits as needed for the construction. Prior to any condemnation, a borough shall enact an ordinance authorizing the same.

(b) Additional powers.—Boroughs have the following additional powers:

(1) To regulate, fix and enforce the collection of the rate of wharfage for all public wharves and docks within its limits.

(2) To regulate the anchoring of vessels, boats or rafts within the borough limits.

(3) To regulate the depositing of freight on the public wharves.

§ 2602. (Reserved).

§ 2603. Proceedings.

The proceedings before the viewers for the assessment of damages for property taken, injured or destroyed under this chapter and the proceedings on their report shall be as provided in 26 Pa.C.S. (relating to eminent domain). The costs of all proceedings, including the compensation of the viewers, shall be paid by the borough.

§ 2604. Assessment of damages.

(a) General rule.—The damages for the taking or injury of any property for use as a wharf, pier or bulkhead shall include full compensation for the value of the property taken or injured.

(b) Partial taking.—If the property taken or injured shall constitute a part of a plant used as an entirety, the damage to the owner or tenant shall be assessed by taking the difference in market value of the plant as a whole, including buildings and all equipment installed and used in the plant, before and after taking or injury, and notwithstanding that part of the plant may be separated by a street or highway.

§ 2605. Leases.

Any borough may lease any wharf or part and collect rent by distress or otherwise. No one term of a lease shall be for a period longer than three years.

§ 2606. Market houses, terminal sheds, tracks and facilities.

(a) Market houses and terminal sheds.—Boroughs may erect and maintain market houses and terminal sheds on wharves for the receipt and distribution of freight and express.

(b) Tracks and facilities.—Boroughs may construct railroad and street railway tracks or other facilities on wharves to provide for the convenient hauling

Table of Contents
Part I Ch. 1–3 Ethics, Records, Open Meetings
Part II Ch. 4–10 Taxation
Part III Ch. 11–18 Torts, Contracts & Civil Rules
Part IV Ch. 19–24 Zoning & Planning
Part V Ch. 25–30 Construction and Emergency Codes
Part VI Ch. 31–39 Municipal Codes
Index

of freight or express matter and may collect rents, tolls or charges for the use of market houses, terminal sheds, tracks and facilities. No permit other than a license revocable at will shall be granted, and no exclusive permit for the use of the facilities shall be granted.

§ 2607. Public use preserved.

No structure erected and no right granted under the powers conferred under this chapter shall interfere with the public use of wharves for waterborne commerce.

§ 2608. Saving clause.

Nothing contained in this chapter shall be construed as conferring upon boroughs any power conferred by existing law on the Navigation Commission for the Delaware River and its Navigable Tributaries or to permit boroughs to do any act or to enact any ordinance inconsistent with the laws, rules and regulations relating to the commission.

CHAPTER 27

RECREATION PLACES, SHADE TREES AND FORESTS

Subchapter

SUBCHAPTER A

PARKS AND PLAYGROUNDS

Sec.

§ 2700. Definitions.

The following words and phrases when used in this chapter shall have the meanings given to them in this section unless the context clearly indicates otherwise:

"Recreation places." Public parks, parkways and playgrounds, playfields, swimming pools, public baths, bathing places, indoor recreation centers and gymnasiums.

§ 2701. General powers.

(a) General rule.—A borough may provide, improve, maintain and regulate recreation places within the borough limits or in any adjacent municipal corporation if the other municipal corporation shall, by ordinance, signify its consent to the provision, improvement, maintenance or regulation.

(b) Acquisition.—A borough may enter upon, appropriate and acquire by gift, devise, purchase, lease or otherwise private property or may designate and set apart any lands or buildings owned by the borough and not dedicated or devoted to other public uses for the purpose of making, enlarging and maintaining recreation places.

(c) Joint action.—A borough may join with one or more political subdivisions to acquire, create, equip, improve, regulate, maintain and operate any recreation place in accordance with 53 Pa.C.S. Ch. 23 Subch. A (relating to intergovernmental cooperation).

(d) Limitation.—No borough, acting individually or jointly, may acquire private property within the limits of another municipal corporation for the purposes designated in this section without the consent of the governing body of the municipal corporation in which the property is located in accordance with 26 Pa.C.S. (relating to eminent domain).

(e) Expenses.—All expenses incurred in the maintenance, improvement, acquisition or operation of recreation places, as provided in this section, shall be payable from the treasury of the borough or the borough and other political subdivisions as may be provided for by agreement of the governing bodies. The council may annually appropriate, and cause to be raised by taxation as provided under section 1302(a)(10) (relating to tax levy), an amount necessary for the purpose of maintaining and operating recreation places or for paying its share of the amount.

§ 2702. Power to acquire.

A borough may enter upon, appropriate and acquire by gift, devise, purchase, lease or otherwise private property within the limits of the borough or in any adjacent township. A borough may designate and set apart any lands or buildings owned by the borough and not dedicated or devoted to other public uses.

(b) Joint acquisition.—Two or more boroughs may jointly appropriate and acquire by gift, devise, purchase, lease or otherwise private property within the limits of any township adjacent to any of the boroughs for the purpose of making, enlarging and maintaining recreation places. All the costs and expenses relative to the property acquired by two or more boroughs jointly shall be paid by the respective boroughs in the proportions as may be agreed upon by the respective councils.

(c) Private property of other borough or city.—Any borough may likewise acquire private property within the limits of another borough or city for the purposes designated in this section if the other borough or city shall, by ordinance, signify its consent to the acquisition.

§ 2703. Appropriation of private property.

The appropriation of private property for the purpose of making, enlarging and maintaining recreation places is declared to be the taking of private property for public use, and, for all damage suffered by the owners of any property taken in that manner, the funds of the borough raised by taxation shall be pledged as security. The proceedings for the taking of private property and the assessment of damages for private property taken, injured or destroyed under this chapter shall be as provided in 26 Pa.C.S. (relating to eminent domain).

§ 2704. (Reserved).

§ 2705. (Reserved).

§ 2706. (Reserved).

§ 2707. (Reserved).

Table of Contents
Part I Ch. 1–3 Ethics, Records, Open Meetings
Part II Ch. 4–10 Taxation
Part III Ch. 11–18 Torts, Contracts & Civil Rules
Part IV Ch. 19–24 Zoning & Planning
Part V Ch. 25–30 Construction and Emergency Codes
Part VI Ch. 31–39 Municipal Codes
Index

§ 2708. Recreation board or other authority.

(a) Recreation board or other authority.—The authority to supervise and maintain recreation places may be vested in any existing body or board, including the council, or in a recreation board, as the council shall determine. The council of the borough may equip, operate and maintain the recreation places, as authorized by this chapter, and may, for the purpose of carrying out the provisions of this chapter, employ any officers or employees as it may deem proper.

(b) (Reserved).

(c) Joint recreation board.—Any borough may join or create, with one or more municipalities, a joint recreation board in accordance with 53 Pa.C.S. Ch. 23 Subch. A (relating to intergovernmental cooperation). The composition of the board and its powers and duties shall be as provided by agreement of the governing bodies of the municipalities.

§ 2709. Establishment of recreation board.

(a) Establishment.—If the council determines that the power to equip, operate and maintain recreation places shall be exercised by a recreation board, the council may, by ordinance, establish in the borough a recreation board which shall possess those powers and duties as may be delegated to it by ordinance.

(b) Composition.—The board shall consist of a minimum of five and a maximum of nine persons. Two of the members may be members or appointees of the school board of the school district in which the borough is located. If the board consists of seven members, three of the members may be members or appointees of the school board. The borough members of the board shall be appointed by the council and shall serve terms not longer than five years. The terms of the members shall be staggered in a manner that at least one member's term expires annually.

(c) Compensation.—Members of the board shall serve without pay.

(d) Vacancies.—Vacancies in the board, occurring otherwise than by expiration of term, shall be filled for the unexpired term in the same manner as original appointments.

§ 2710. Organization of board and employees.

The members of a recreation board established under this chapter shall elect their own chair and secretary and select all other necessary officers to serve for a period of one year. The recreation board may, with the approval of council, establish employment positions and hire employees to fill the approved positions. The board shall have power to adopt rules and regulations for the conduct of all business within its jurisdiction.

§ 2711. (Reserved).

§ 2712. (Reserved).

§ 2713. Lease for school athletics.

(a) Lease.—A borough maintaining a recreation place may lease a recreation place, or a portion of a recreation place, suitable for athletic sports and athletic games to any school board or school athletic association organized by a school board and organized for the purpose of conducting amateur athletic sports and games among pupils of the public school.

(b) Admission charge.—The borough maintaining a recreation place may permit a school board or school athletic association to charge admission to sports and games and to deny persons refusing to pay admission access to the grounds where sports or games are being conducted, if sports and games are not conducted for individual profit.

SUBCHAPTER B
SHADE TREES

---

§ 2720. Care, custody and control.

(a) Council authority.—Council shall have exclusive care, custody and control of shade trees in the borough. Council may:

(1) Plant, transplant, remove, maintain and protect shade trees on the streets and highways in the borough.

(2) Employ and pay persons and make and enforce regulations as may be necessary for the care and protection of the shade trees of the borough.

(b) Planting, transplanting or removal.—Council may, by ordinance, and with or without the petition of a majority of the property owners, upon any public street in the borough, plant, transplant or remove shade trees. Council may, with or without petition, require the planting and replanting of suitable shade trees along and upon the sides of the streets, upon alignment and at points as may be designated by ordinance, by the owners of property abutting the street at the points designated.

(c) Limitation.—Nothing in this part may authorize council to plant or replant, or require the planting or replanting of, trees at any point which may interfere with the necessary or reasonable use of any street or abutting property or the business conducted on the property.

(d) Assessment of costs.—On failure of any owner, after reasonable notice, to comply with the terms of an ordinance requiring the planting or replanting of shade trees, the borough may cause the trees to be planted or replanted and assess the cost against the owner in accordance with section 2720.2 (relating to payment by owners and assessments).

(e) Diseased plants, shrubs and trees.—Council may, upon notice as may be provided by ordinance, require owners of property to cut and remove plants, shrubs and trees afflicted with any disease that threatens to injure or destroy plants, shrubs and shade trees in the borough under regulations prescribed by ordinance. Upon failure of any owner to comply with the notice, the borough may cause the work to be done by the borough and assess the cost against the owner in accordance with section 2720.2.

§ 2720.1. Maintenance by borough and tax levy.

(a) Cost and expenses.—The cost and expenses of caring for shade trees after having been planted or transplanted and the expense of publishing any notice required by this subchapter shall be paid by the borough.

(b) Tax levy or appropriation.—Council may levy a general tax, not to exceed the sum of one-tenth of one mill on the dollar on the assessed valuation of the property in the borough taxable for county purposes, for the purpose of defraying the cost and expenses of caring for the shade trees and the expense of publishing notices, or it may provide for the expense of the caring for trees already planted and of publishing the notice by appropriations.

§ 2720.2. Payment by owners and assessments.

(a) Payment by owners.—The cost of planting, transplanting or removing any shade trees or the necessary and suitable guards, curbing or grading for their protection and of the replacing of pavement or sidewalk necessarily disturbed in the execution of the work shall be paid by the owners of the real estate abutting the location of the work.

(b) Assessment and collection.—In the event that the borough undertakes the work described in this section, costs shall be certified, assessed against the abutting owners and collected in accordance with Chapter 21A (relating to assessments and charges for public improvements).

§ 2720.3. Notice of work.

If council proposes to plant, transplant or remove shade trees on any street, notice of the time and place of the meeting at which the work is to be considered shall be given in one newspaper of general circulation once a week for two weeks immediately preceding the time of the meeting. The notice shall specify in detail the streets or portions upon which trees are proposed to be planted, transplanted or removed. In the event that a shade tree commission is to undertake the work, the commission shall provide the notice.

§ 2720.4. Penalties.

(a) Penalties for violation.—To the extent provided by ordinance, council may assess penalties for the violation of regulations relating to shade trees or delegate the power to assess penalties to a shade tree commission. Any penalty assessed shall be a lien upon the real estate of the offender and may be collected as municipal claims are collected.

(b) Separate fund.—All penalties or assessments imposed under this subchapter shall be paid to the borough treasurer, to be kept in a separate fund and utilized only for the purposes authorized by this subchapter.

§ 2721. Shade tree commission.

(a) Establishment.—Council by ordinance may establish a shade tree commission and delegate to the shade tree commission the exclusive care, custody and control of shade trees and authorization to plant, transplant, remove, maintain and protect shade trees on the streets and highways in the borough.

(b) Commission authority.—The shade tree commission may make and enforce regulations for the care and protection of shade trees. No regulation may be in force until it has been approved by the council and enacted as an ordinance.

(c) Park commission.—If in any borough there exists a commission for the care of public parks, the council may, by ordinance, confer on the park commission all the powers and all the duties prescribed by this chapter for a shade tree commission.

§ 2722. Composition of commission.

(a) General.—Except as provided in subsection (b), a shade tree commission shall be composed of three residents of the borough who shall be appointed by the council and shall serve without compensation.

(b) Council option.—The council, by ordinance, may provide that a shade tree commission be composed of five members who shall be residents of the borough, shall be appointed by the council and shall serve without compensation.

(c) Three-member commission.—If a shade tree commission of three members is established by any borough, the council shall appoint one member for a term of three years, one for a term of four years and one for a term of five years. On the expiration of the term of any commissioner, a successor shall be appointed by the council to serve for a term of five years.

(d) Five-member commission.—If a shade tree commission of five members is established by any borough, the council shall appoint members to staggered terms so that one term expires every year. On the expiration of the term of any commissioner, a successor shall be appointed by the council to serve for a term of five years.

(e) Vacancies.—Vacancies in the office of commissioner shall be filled by the council for the unexpired term.

§ 2723. (Reserved).

§ 2724. (Reserved).

§ 2724.1. Duties of commission.

(a) Annual report.—A shade tree commission shall annually report in full to the council its transactions and expenses for the last fiscal year of the borough.

(b) Notice.—If a shade tree commission proposes to plant, transplant or remove shade trees on any street, notice of the time and place of the meeting at which the work is to be considered shall be given by the shade tree commission in accordance with section 2720.3 (relating to notice of work).

(c) Certification of amounts required.—The shade tree commission shall each year certify to council an amount needed for the care of shade trees and for the publication of notices required by this subchapter. The shade tree commission shall use funds appropriated or raised by taxation in accordance with section 2720.1 (relating to maintenance by borough and tax levy) for any purpose authorized by council.

(d) Certification of assessments.—The shade tree commission shall ascertain and certify to council and the borough treasurer the amount of any assessment imposed in accordance with this subchapter for the planting, transplanting or removal of plants, shrubs and trees.

§ 2725. (Reserved).

§ 2726. (Reserved).

§ 2727. (Reserved).

§ 2728. (Reserved).

§ 2729. (Reserved).

§ 2730. (Reserved).

SUBCHAPTER C
FORESTS

§ 2751. Acquisition of land for forest purposes.

A borough may acquire by purchase, gift or lease tracts of land covered with forest or tree growth or suitable for the growth of trees and administer the tracts in accordance with the practices and principles of scientific forestry, for the benefit of the borough. The tracts may be of any size suitable for the purpose and may be located within or without the borough limits.

§ 2752. (Reserved).

§ 2753. Ordinance of acquisition.

If the council deems it expedient to acquire land for the purposes of a municipal forest, it shall enact an ordinance setting forth the facts and conditions relating to the proposed action.

§ 2754. Appropriations.

Money necessary for the purchase of the tracts shall be appropriated in the same manner as appropriations for borough purposes. Money may be provided from the current revenue or by the proceeds of a sale of general obligation bonds in accordance with existing law.

§ 2755. Regulations.

Upon the acquisition of a municipal forest or land suitable for a municipal forest, the council may promulgate regulations for the government and proper administration of the same as necessary to produce continuing borough revenue by the sale of forest products.

§ 2756. Appropriations and revenue.

Money necessary for the administration, maintenance, protection and development of forests shall be appropriated and applied as is now done for borough purposes. The revenue and return on the revenue arising from the forests shall be paid into the borough treasury to be used for general borough purposes.

§ 2757. Use of forests.

A municipal forest may be used by the public as general outing or recreation grounds subject to the regulations under section 2755 (relating to regulations).

§ 2758. Ordinance of sale.

(a) Requirement.—If the council deems it expedient to sell or lease a municipal forest, a part of a municipal forest or a product from a municipal forest, it shall enact an ordinance setting forth the facts and conditions relating to the proposed action.

(b) Conditions.—In order to enact an ordinance under this section, there must be compliance with the advertising and bidding requirements of section 1201.1 (relating to real estate).

§ 2759. Pruning and thinning.

(a) Authority.—To comply with the practices and principles of scientific forestry, the council has the following powers:

(1) To pass a resolution to prune or thin out a municipal forest or portion of a municipal forest.

(2) To sell the products of the pruning or thinning out.

(b) Personnel.—To carry out subsection (a), the borough may use its own personnel or contract with skilled personnel.

(c) Bidding and advertising.—The bidding and advertising requirements of this part do not apply to any of the following:

(1) Sales under subsection (a)(2).

(2) Contracts under subsection (b).

CHAPTER 28

CEMETERIES

Sec.

---

§ 2800. Appropriations for burial ground maintenance.

A borough may appropriate annually, out of the general funds of the borough, a sum for the care, upkeep, maintenance and beautifying of:

(1) cemeteries and burial grounds lying wholly or partly within the boundary limits of the borough or in the territory immediately adjacent to the borough; and

(2) private roads in or leading to property under paragraph (1).

§ 2800.1. Burial of deceased persons.

A borough may prohibit the burial or interment of deceased persons anywhere within borough limits.

§ 2801. Management by cemetery commission.

If the title and management of a cemetery is vested in a borough, the council may, by ordinance, vest the care, management and operation of the cemetery in a cemetery commission of three citizens to be appointed by the council. The ordinance shall provide for the terms of the cemetery commissioners.

§ 2802. Transfer from borough to company.

(a) Authority.—Upon petition of at least 10% of living cemetery lot owners, the council may transfer the cemetery and its management to an incorporated cemetery company.

(b) Procedure.—Upon presentation of a petition under subsection (a), the council may enact an ordinance declaring that, upon the acceptance of the ordinance by the incorporated cemetery company and filed with the borough secretary, the title and control of the cemetery shall vest in the incorporated cemetery company.

(c) Recording.—A copy of the ordinance and the acceptance by the incorporated cemetery company, certified by the borough secretary, shall be recorded in the office of the recorder of deeds of the county.

§ 2803. (Reserved).

§ 2804. (Reserved).

§ 2805. Transfer from company to borough.

(a) Judicial action.—

(1) Upon the petition of an incorporated cemetery company and the owners of a majority of the taxable real estate in the borough, the court of common pleas may authorize the transfer of a cemetery to the borough where the cemetery is located or is adjacent to the borough.

(2) A copy of the court order under paragraph (1) shall be filed with the recorder of deeds.

(b) Cost.—The transfer shall be made without cost to the borough.

(c) Effect.—Upon transfer, the following apply:

(1) The borough shall exercise the powers and privileges of the incorporated company.

(2) The borough may do all of the following:

(i) Purchase up to 30 acres of land within or adjacent to the borough limits for the extension of the cemetery;

(ii) Pay for the purchase under subparagraph (i) by:

(A) sale of lots or otherwise; or

(B) any means other than taxation.

(iii) Lay out lots purchased and alter the original plot of the cemetery.

(iv) Dispose of the grounds in the same manner as the incorporated company could have done.

(d) Deeds.—

(1) A deed for a lot, made by the borough, shall have the same validity as the deed of the incorporated cemetery company.

(2) The borough may make a deed to a person that, prior to transfer under this section:

(i) purchased a lot; but

(ii) did not receive a deed.

§ 2805.1. Neglected or abandoned cemeteries.

(a) Maintenance.—The council may, upon compliance with subsection (b), direct the removal of weeds, refuse and debris from an abandoned or neglected cemetery.

(b) Notice.—

(1) To exercise the power under subsection (a), the council must give notice to the owner directing the removal of weeds, refuse and debris from the cemetery within 30 days of service under paragraph (2).

(2) Notice must be effected by any of the following means:

(i) Personal service on the owner.

(ii) Certified mail, addressee only, return receipt requested, to the owner at the owner's last known address.

(iii) After reasonable attempts to give notice under subparagraph (i) or (ii) have failed, posting notice at or upon the property.

(c) Action.—

(1) If the removal is not completed within 30 days after the notice is effected under subsection (b)(2), the council shall provide for the removal to be done by employees of the borough or by a contractor at the expense of the borough.

(2) The costs of removal under paragraph (1) shall be assessed against the owner of the cemetery and collected under Chapter 21A (relating to assessments and charges for public improvements).

§ 2806. (Reserved).

§ 2807. (Reserved).

§ 2808. Removing bodies to alter plots.

In altering the plot of a cemetery, bodies may be removed and reinterred in a suitable place but without cost to surviving relatives.

§ 2809. Removal of bodies to other cemeteries.

(a) Authority.—

(1) This subsection applies to a privately owned cemetery, a borough-owned cemetery or a cemetery affiliated with a religious society or church or any other organization, when the cemetery:

(i) has ceased to be used for interments;

(ii) has become so neglected as to become a public nuisance;

(iii) hinders the improvement and progressive interests of the borough; or

(iv) is desired by the borough as a site for any public purpose.

(2) The court of common pleas may, upon compliance with subsection (b), direct the removal of the remains of the dead from a cemetery.

(b) Procedure.—

(1) A petition under this section must be made to the court by any of the following:

(i) The manager of the cemetery in charge of a religious society or church or an other organization. The following are required to utilize this subparagraph:

(A) Public notice of a meeting of the entity on the petition must be given two weeks before the meeting.

(B) At the meeting, a majority of the members of the entity must approve the petition.

(C) The petition must set forth that the cemetery has ceased to be used for interments.

(ii) If the cemetery is not under the charge of anyone, 50 residents of the borough. A petition under this subparagraph must set forth that the improvements and progressive interests of the borough are hampered and the welfare of the borough is injured by the presence of the cemetery.

(iii) The council. A petition under this subparagraph must set forth that:

(A) the cemetery has become so neglected as to become a public nuisance;

(B) the improvements and progressive interests of the borough are hampered and the welfare of the borough is injured by the presence of the cemetery; or

(C) the land is desired for a public purpose.

(2) Notice must be given by advertisement in a newspaper of general circulation once a week for three successive weeks.

(c) Private action.—A relative of the deceased individual subject to removal or another interested party of the dead may, prior to action under subsection (d), remove the remains at private expense.

(d) Public action.—

(1) The removal shall be made by:

(i) the manager of the cemetery;

(ii) the borough if the cemetery is:

(A) not in charge of a manager; or

(B) owned by the borough.

(2) The removal shall be made at the expense of the removing party in a careful manner.

(3) The removal shall be made:

(i) except as set forth in subparagraph (ii), to a cemetery selected by the person that makes the removal; or

(ii) upon request of a relative of the deceased individual subject to removal or another interested party, to a designated cemetery in the vicinity.

(4) Each body removed shall be placed in a separate casket and grave, and the marker over the remains of the body shall be placed as near as possible in the same relative position as before removal.

(e) Effect.—After the removal of all dead bodies from a cemetery, the land shall cease to be a cemetery or burial ground and may be acquired by the borough as other real estate is acquired for borough purposes.

§ 2810. (Reserved).

§ 2811. (Reserved).

§ 2812. (Reserved).

§ 2813. (Reserved).

§ 2814. (Reserved).

§ 2815. (Reserved).

§ 2816. Purchase of plots for burial of deceased service members.

(a) Authority.—A borough may purchase plots of ground in a cemetery or burial ground within its limits for the interment of deceased members of the armed forces who:

(1) die within the borough or have a legal residence within the borough at the time of death; and

(2) are entitled to be buried by the county under the provisions of existing law.

(b) Cost.—Plots purchased under this section shall be paid for out of the borough treasury.

CHAPTER 29
LICENSES AND LICENSE FEES

§ 2901. Licensing transient retail business.

(a) Authority.—A borough may, by ordinance, regulate and license transient merchants engaged in any transient retail business within the borough.

(b) Licensure.—The following shall apply:

(1) An ordinance under this section may prohibit the transient retail business without a license and provide for enforcement by penalties or other appropriate means.

(2) Except as set forth in paragraph (3), an ordinance under this section may set a license fee which bears a reasonable relationship to the cost of administering the ordinance and regulating and inspecting the transient retail business.

(3) Paragraph (2) does not apply as follows:

(i) Except as set forth in paragraph (ii), the ordinance may not impose a license fee on the following transient merchants:

(A) A farmer selling the farmer's own produce.

(B) A person selling personal property if the proceeds of the sale are to be applied to a charitable or philanthropic purpose.

(C) A manufacturer or producer in the sale of any of the following:

(I) Bread. This subclause includes a bakery product.

(II) Meat. This subclause includes a meat product.

(III) Milk. This subclause includes a milk product. This subclause does not include ice cream or another frozen dessert.

(ii) The exception under this paragraph does not apply to a transient merchant that is also selling other personal property not excepted under subparagraph (i).

(c) Registration.—An ordinance under this section may require that a transient merchant exempt under subsection (b)(2) register with the borough and otherwise be subject to all other provisions of the ordinance.

(d) Definition.—As used in this section, the term "transient merchant" means a person engaged in transient retail business for the sale of personal property, whether the business is conducted from a fixed location within the borough or by an individual engaged in peddling, soliciting or the taking of orders from house to house.

§ 2902. Licensure saved.

(a) Commonwealth.—Nothing contained in this chapter shall be construed to relieve a person from a statutorily imposed:

(1) licensure requirement;

(2) license tax; or

(3) license fee.

(b) Boroughs.—A Commonwealth license tax or fee shall not preempt the registration, licensing or regulatory powers of a borough in accordance with this chapter unless the preemption is expressly authorized.

§ 2903. Licensing parking lots and parking garages operated for profit.

(a) Authority.—

(1) A borough may, by ordinance, regulate the business of operating parking lots or parking garages for profit within the borough and may require the lots or garages to reserve areas exclusively for parking by handicapped individuals. Under the ordinance:

(i) License or permit fees may be charged and collected from the operators of the parking lots or parking garages.

(ii) Security is subject to the following:

(A) Except as set forth in clause (B), the borough shall require from each operator of a parking lot or parking garage a bond to be approved by the council for the protection of the public from loss of or damage to vehicles parked, stored or placed under the jurisdiction of a parking lot or parking garage operator.

(B) Clause (A) shall not apply to parking lots or parking garages operated by a municipal authority or a parking authority.

(2) An ordinance under paragraph (1) must be consistent with 75 Pa.C.S. (relating to vehicles).

(b) Individuals with disabilities.—Nothing in this section may be construed to limit statutory and regulatory protections and prohibitions contained relating to the rights of disabled individuals.

§ 2904. Persons taking orders by samples.

(a) Prohibition.—A borough may not impose, levy or collect a license fee or mercantile tax upon a person that takes, by sample, from a dealer or merchant an order for merchandise on behalf of an individual or company that pays a license fee or mercantile tax at the individual's or company's chief place of business.

(b) Limitation.—Nothing in this section shall authorize a person to sell by retail to a person other than a dealer or merchant without payment of a license or permit fee.

§ 2905. Equality of residents and nonresidents.

A borough may not enact an ordinance imposing a license fee upon a manufacturer, including an agent and employee, that is a resident of this Commonwealth and solicits orders for or sells personal property manufactured in this Commonwealth if the borough could not legally impose the same license fee upon a manufacturer, including an agent and employee, that is a nonresident of this Commonwealth and solicits orders for or sells personal property manufactured outside this Commonwealth.

§ 2906. Insurance business.

A borough may not impose a license fee upon an insurance company, including an agent, or an insurance broker authorized to transact business under the act of May 17, 1921 (P.L.682, No.284), known as The Insurance Company Law of 1921.

CHAPTER 29A
VETERANS' AFFAIRS

SUBCHAPTER A
PENNSYLVANIA NATIONAL GUARD

§ 29A01. Eminent domain for National Guard purposes.

(a) Authority.—Except as set forth in subsection (b), the council may take, by right of eminent domain, for the purpose of appropriating to the borough for the use of the Pennsylvania National Guard, public lands, easements and property as may be in its possession or control and used or held by the borough for any other purpose.

(b) Exception.—Eminent domain may not be exercised as to a street or wharf.

§ 29A02. Land for armory purposes.

(a) Authority.—Except as set forth in subsection (b), the council may acquire, by purchase or by gift or by the right of eminent domain, land for the use of the Pennsylvania National Guard, to be conveyed to the Commonwealth in order to assist the State Armory Board in the erection of armories.

(b) Exception.—The power under subsection (a) may not be exercised to take any of the following:

(1) Church property.

(2) A graveyard or cemetery.

(3) A dwelling house or the curtilage of property:

(i) designated in paragraph (1) or (2); and

(ii) in the actual occupancy of the owner.

§ 29A03. Appropriation to assist in erection of armories.

The council has the following powers:

(1) To appropriate money or convey land, either independently or in conjunction with another municipality, to:

(i) assist the State Armory Board in the erection of armories for the use of the Pennsylvania National Guard; and

(ii) furnish water, sewer service, light or fuel free of cost to the Commonwealth for use in any armory of the Pennsylvania National Guard.

(2) To do all things necessary to accomplish the purpose of this section.

§ 29A04. Support of Pennsylvania National Guard units.

(a) Appropriation.—The council may appropriate annually a sum to be used and expended exclusively for the support and maintenance, discipline and training of a unit of the Pennsylvania National Guard.

Table of Contents
Part I Ch. 1–3 Ethics, Records, Open Meetings
Part II Ch. 4–10 Taxation
Part III Ch. 11–18 Torts, Contracts & Civil Rules
Part IV Ch. 19–24 Zoning & Planning
Part V Ch. 25–30 Construction and Emergency Codes
Part VI Ch. 31–39 Municipal Codes
Index

(b) Payment.—

(1) The money appropriated shall be paid by warrant drawn to the order of the commanding officer of the unit upon certification to the borough, by the Adjutant General, that the unit has satisfactorily passed the annual inspection provided by law.

(2) The commanding officer shall account, by proper vouchers to the borough each year, for the expenditure of the money appropriated. No appropriation shall be made for any subsequent year until the expenditure of the previous year is accounted for. The accounts of the expenditures shall be subject to the inspection of the Department of Military and Veterans Affairs and shall be audited by the Auditor General in accordance with law.

SUBCHAPTER B
SUPPORT OF VETERANS' ORGANIZATIONS

§ 29A11. Appropriations to organizations and American Gold Star Mothers, Inc.

(a) Appropriation.—

(1) The council may appropriate annually money to aid in defraying the expenses of Memorial Day, Veterans' Day or a similar day provided for by Federal or State law.

(2) The appropriation shall be divided in amounts as council deems proper to:

(i) an organization composed of veterans of a war in which the United States was engaged; and

(ii) American Gold Star Mothers, Inc.

(3) The money shall be appropriated to defray actual expenses only.

(b) Payment.—Before payment is made, the organization receiving the appropriation must submit verified accounts of its expenditures.

§ 29A12. Payment of rent for meetings.

The council may appropriate annually a sum to an incorporated organization of American veterans of a war in which the United States was engaged, to be used in the payment of the rent for a facility in which the organization has its regular meetings.

§ 29A13. Rooms for veterans' organizations and children.

The council may furnish without charge to an organization composed of American veterans of a war in which the United States was engaged and children of the veterans a room in a public building of the borough.

§ 29A14. Care and erection of memorials.

(a) Authority.—The council may control and maintain a soldier's memorial which is:

(1) situated in the borough;

(2) not controlled and maintained by an individual or entity; and

(3) not placed by the Federal Government, the Commonwealth, the county or another state.

(b) Funding.—The council may receive and expend any money to be used for the maintenance of the memorials.

(c) Contributions.—The council may contribute to the erection and maintenance of a memorial in honor of those who served in a war in which the United States was engaged.

CHAPTER 30

REAL ESTATE REGISTRY

(Reserved)

CHAPTER 31

HEALTH AND SANITATION

Sec.

---

§ 3100. Definitions.

The following words and phrases when used in this chapter shall have the meanings given to them in this section unless the context clearly indicates otherwise:

"Board." A board of health established under section 3101(a) (relating to administration).

"Board secretary." The secretary of a board.

"Department." The Department of Health of the Commonwealth.

"Health officer." An individual appointed under section 3101(a) (relating to administration) or 3103(b)(1)(iii) (relating to oaths, officers and security).

"Professional health care provider." An individual who is licensed, certified or registered to practice or operate in the health care field under the laws of this Commonwealth. The term includes:

(1) A physician.

(2) A dentist.

(3) A podiatrist.

(4) A chiropractor.

Table of Contents
Part I Ch. 1–3 Ethics, Records, Open Meetings
Part II Ch. 4–10 Taxation
Part III Ch. 11–18 Torts, Contracts & Civil Rules
Part IV Ch. 19–24 Zoning & Planning
Part V Ch. 25–30 Construction and Emergency Codes
Part VI Ch. 31–39 Municipal Codes
Index

(5) An optometrist.

(6) A psychologist.

(7) A pharmacist.

(8) A registered or practical nurse.

(9) A physical therapist.

(10) A physician's assistant.

(11) A paramedic.

(12) An administrator of any hospital, nursing or convalescent home or other health care facility.

(13) A veterinarian.

§ 3101. Administration.

(a) Establishment.—The council may, by ordinance, appoint a board of health or a health officer to administer and enforce the health ordinances and related ordinances of the borough. A health officer must have experience or training in public health work and must, within six months of taking the oath of office, be certified for the office of health officer by the department.

(b) Expenses.—Expenses incurred by the board or a health officer shall be paid by the borough.

(c) Dissolution.—A borough may, by ordinance, dissolve a board and decide to become subject to the jurisdiction of a county department of health or joint county department of health under the act of August 24, 1951 (P.L.1304, No.315), known as the Local Health Administration Law.

§ 3102. Board.

(a) Membership.—

(1) A board appointed by a council shall be composed of three or five members, subject to the following:

(i) Except as set forth in subparagraph (ii), at least one member must be a professional health care provider with not less than two years' experience in the practice of the member's respective profession.

(ii) If subparagraph (i) cannot be met, at least one member must have had experience in or be knowledgeable of public health issues.

(b) Terms.—

(1) Initial terms shall be staggered as follows:

(i) For a three-member board:

(A) one member shall serve a term of one year;

(B) one member shall serve a term of two years; and

(C) one member shall serve a term of three years.

(ii) For a five-member board:

(A) one member shall serve a term of one year;

(B) one member shall serve a term of two years;

(C) one member shall serve a term of three years;

(D) one member shall serve a term of four years; and

(E) one member shall serve a term of five years.

(2) Subsequent terms shall be staggered as follows:

(i) For a three-member board, a subsequent term shall be three years.

(ii) For a five-member board, a subsequent term shall be five years.

(c) Compensation.—

(1) Except as set forth in paragraph (2), the members of the board shall serve without compensation.

(2) Paragraph (1) shall not apply to a member of the board who is elected board secretary under section 3103(b)(2) (relating to oaths, officers and security).

§ 3103. Oaths, officers and security.

(a) Oath of office.—A member of the board must take the oath prescribed for borough members of council.

(b) Officers.—

(1) The board shall annually organize by electing:

(i) a president from among the members of the board;

(ii) a board secretary who may or may not be a member of the board; and

(iii) a health officer.

(2) The board secretary and the health officer shall receive salaries fixed by the board and ratified by the council.

(3) The board secretary and health officer shall serve until a successor is elected and qualified.

(c) Security.—The council may require the board secretary and health officer to furnish a bond to the borough in a prescribed amount for the faithful discharge of their duties.

§ 3104. Duties of board secretary.

The board secretary has the following duties:

(1) To maintain, under 53 Pa.C.S. Ch. 13 Subch. F (relating to records), the minutes of the proceedings of the board and keep accurate accounts of the expenditures of the board.

(2) To draw requisitions for the payment of money on account of the board from appropriations made by the council to the board and present the requisitions to the president of the board for the president's approval.

(3) To render statements of the expenditures to the board at each stated meeting or as frequently as the board requires.

(4) To prepare, under the direction of the board, the annual report to the council and the estimate of appropriation needed for the ensuing year.

(5) To report to the department at statutory or regulatory intervals the cases of communicable disease reported to the board on the form provided by the department and make an annual report to the department.

(6) To perform other duties required by the board.

§ 3105. Powers and duties of health officer.

(a) Powers.—A health officer may issue a citation for violation of a health ordinance or related law.

(b) Duties.—A health officer has the following duties:

(1) Administer and enforce the health ordinances of the borough and related law.

(2) Perform the duties as are vested in local health officers by Statute or regulation.

(3) Make sanitary inspections.

(4) Execute the orders of the board.

(5) To attend all regular and special meetings of the board of health.

Table of Contents
Part I Ch. 1–3 Ethics, Records, Open Meetings
Part II Ch. 4–10 Taxation
Part III Ch. 11–18 Torts, Contracts & Civil Rules
Part IV Ch. 19–24 Zoning & Planning
Part V Ch. 25–30 Construction and Emergency Codes
Part VI Ch. 31–39 Municipal Codes
Index

Chap. 39 Res. During Mil. Service
Chap. 38 Intergov. Coop.
Chap. 37 3rd Class City Code
Chap. 36 Bor. Code
Chap. 35 2nd Class Twp. Code
Chap. 34 1st Class Twp. Code
Chap. 33 Home Rule Chart. Opt. Plans Law
Chap. 32 Water Serv. Act
Chap. 31 Munic. Auth. Act

§ 3106. Powers and duties of board.

(a) Powers.—A board has the following powers to:

(1) Recommend to the council rules and regulations necessary for the preservation of the public health and for carrying into effect the functions of the board.

(2) Appoint a health officer. A health officer must have experience or training in public health work and must, within six months of taking the oath of office, be certified for the office of health officer by the department.

(3) Abate and remove nuisances the board deems detrimental to the public health.

(4) Mark infected premises.

(b) Duties.—A board has the duty to enforce all of the following related to promotion of public health and prevention of the introduction and spread of infectious or contagious disease:

(1) A statute.

(2) A regulation of the department.

(3) An ordinance of the borough.

§ 3107. Entry upon premises.

(a) Authority.—

(1) This subsection applies to all of the following:

(i) A member of a board.

(ii) A health officer.

(iii) An employee of a board or a health officer.

(iv) An agent of a board or health officer.

(2) An individual subject to paragraph (1) may, upon order of the board:

(i) enter premises in the borough where an infectious or contagious disease or a nuisance detrimental to the public health is suspected; and

(ii) examine and abate the disease or nuisance.

(b) Warrant.—If entry under subsection (a)(2)(i) is prevented, the board of health or health officer may obtain an administrative search warrant from a magisterial district judge with jurisdiction over the premises upon a showing of any of the following:

(1) Reasonable standards and an administrative plan for conducting inspections.

(2) The condition of the premises or general area and the passage of time since the last inspection.

(3) Probable cause of a violation of a law specified in section 3106(b) (relating to powers and duties of board).

§ 3108. Abatement of nuisances.

(a) Initial order.—If the board finds a condition or premises to be a nuisance to the health of the people of the borough, it shall issue a written order of abatement directed to the owner or agent of the owner of the premises. The order shall:

(1) state that the conditions specified in the premises constitute the nuisance; and

(2) order an abatement of the nuisance within a specified reasonable time.

(b) Subsequent order.—

(1) Upon noncompliance of the order under subsection (a), the board shall issue a written order to the health officer directing removal or abatement of the nuisance.

(2) An order under paragraph (1) shall be executed by the health officer or an agent of the health officer.

(3) The expense of execution under paragraph (2) shall be recoverable as a municipal claim from the owner of the premises, with a 10% penalty.

(c) Legal action.—In lieu of or in addition to the procedure under subsections (a) and (b), council may seek relief from a nuisance or threatened nuisance by an action at law or in equity. Council may seek guidance of the board or the health officer in determining the nature of the relief requested.

§ 3109. Expenditures.

(a) Estimate.—The board or the health officer shall submit to council, before commencement of the borough's fiscal year, an estimate of the probable expenditures of the board or the health officer during the ensuing fiscal year.

(b) Appropriation.—Council shall make appropriations based on the estimate as deemed necessary.

(c) Report.—The board or the health officer shall, each January, submit a report to council on:

(1) the appropriation and the expenditures for the preceding fiscal year; and

(2) information on subjects relative to the sanitary conditions or requirements of the borough.

§ 3110. Cooperation.

A borough may cooperate in the administration and enforcement of health laws with:

(1) the department;

(2) a county in which the borough is located; and

(3) a municipal corporation.

§ 3111. Department.

(a) No limitation.—Nothing in this part may be construed to limit the powers and duties of the department, including the powers and duties under Article XXI of the act of April 9, 1929 (P.L.177, No.175), known as The Administrative Code of 1929.

(b) Expenses.—

(1) Expenses of the department for which the borough is liable shall be paid by the borough where the expenses have been incurred.

(2) If expenses under paragraph (1) are unpaid for a period of more than three months after a statement of the expense has been rendered to the borough and demand for payment is made, the Secretary of Health shall, with the approval of the Governor, institute an action against the borough for the collection of the expense. The reasonableness of the expenditures made by the secretary shall be submitted to the jury for its determination.

(3) Upon payment, the department shall return the money to the State Treasurer, who shall credit the amount to the appropriation made to the department.

§ 3112. (Reserved).

§ 3113. (Reserved).

§ 3114. (Reserved).

CHAPTER 32
ZONING
(Reserved)

CHAPTER 32A

UNIFORM CONSTRUCTION CODE, PROPERTY MAINTENANCE CODE AND RESERVED POWERS

Sec.

§ 32A01. Primacy of Uniform Construction Code.

(a) General rule.—The following shall apply to the construction, alteration, repair and occupancy of all buildings and structures within a borough:

(1) The Pennsylvania Construction Code.

(2) The Uniform Construction Code adopted under section 301 of the Pennsylvania Construction Code.

(b) Primacy.—This section and any ordinance, rule or regulation adopted under this section shall not supersede or abrogate the Pennsylvania Construction Code or the Uniform Construction Code and shall be construed and read in pari materia with the Pennsylvania Construction Code and the Uniform Construction Code.

§ 32A02. Changes in Uniform Construction Code.

A borough may propose and enact an ordinance to equal or exceed the minimum requirements of the Uniform Construction Code in accordance with section 503 of the Pennsylvania Construction Code. Any ordinance exceeding the provisions of the Uniform Construction Code shall be required to meet the standards under section 503(j)(2) of the Pennsylvania Construction Code.

§ 32A03. Public nuisance.

(a) Abatement.—Except as provided under subsection (b), any building, housing or property or a part of any building, housing or property erected, altered, extended, reconstructed, removed or maintained, contrary to the provisions of an ordinance passed for the purposes specified under this chapter, may be declared, by a court of law, a public nuisance and may be abatable.

(b) Exception.—A violation of the Uniform Construction Code or any ordinance that equals or exceeds the Uniform Construction Code shall be subject to the Pennsylvania Construction Code and the regulations adopted under the Pennsylvania Construction Code Act relating to enforcement for noncompliance.

§ 32A04. Property maintenance code.

(a) Enactment.—Notwithstanding the primacy of the Uniform Construction Code, a borough may enact one of the following:

(1) A property maintenance ordinance and may incorporate a standard or nationally recognized property maintenance code, or any variations or changes or parts of the code, published and printed in book form, without incorporating the text of the code in the ordinance.

(2) A standard or nationally recognized property maintenance code or any variations or changes or parts as its property maintenance ordinance.

(a.1) Notice.—The following shall apply:

(1) An ordinance or any variations or changes or parts under subsection (a) shall not be required to be advertised after passage. Notice of the consideration of an ordinance or any variations or changes or parts under subsection (a) shall be published in a manner that will give adequate notice of its contents and a reference to the place within the borough where copies of the proposed property maintenance code may be examined or obtained.

(2) The notice required under paragraph (1) shall be published once in one newspaper of general circulation at least one week and not more than three weeks prior to the presentation of the proposed property maintenance code to council.

(a.2) Inspection.—At least three copies of the ordinance adopted by council:

(1) shall be made available:

(i) for public inspection and use during business hours; or

(ii) to any interested party who pays the cost of copying; or

(2) may be furnished or lent without charge.

(a.3) A property maintenance code adopted by reference shall:

(1) not be required to be recorded in or attached to an ordinance book; and

(2) be deemed to have been legally recorded if the ordinance by which the code was adopted by reference has been recorded with an accompanying notation stating where the full text of the code has been filed.

(a.4) Fines and penalties.—An ordinance under this section may provide for reasonable property fines and penalties for violations of the ordinance.

(a.5) Procedure.—The procedure under this section relating to the adoption of an ordinance under this section may be used in amending, supplementing or repealing any of the provisions of the ordinance.

(b) Property maintenance inspectors.—Council may appoint property maintenance inspectors who may enter, subject to constitutional standards in a similar manner as provided under section 3107 (relating to entry upon premises), and inspect any premises at reasonable hours and in a reasonable manner for the administration and enforcement of the borough's property maintenance code or ordinance under subsection (a). Any fees payable to property maintenance inspectors under the ordinance shall be paid by the property maintenance inspectors as soon as possible to the borough treasurer for the use of the borough.

(c) Legal actions.—In addition to the penalties provided by a property maintenance ordinance, a borough may institute appropriate actions or proceedings at law or in equity to prevent or restrain property maintenance violations.

(d) Construction.—The powers of a borough under this section shall be in addition to the powers provided under the following:

(1) The act of November 26, 2008 (P.L.1672, No.135), known as the Abandoned and Blighted Property Conservatorship Act.

(2) 53 Pa.C.S. Ch. 61 (relating to neighborhood blight reclamation and revitalization).

(3) 68 Pa.C.S. Ch. 21 (relating to land banks).

§ 32A05. Reserved powers.

(a) Power.—If, as a result of legislative action or final order of court which is not subject to appellate review, the Uniform Construction Code or any replacement code is no longer applicable in boroughs, a borough may:

(1) Enact and enforce ordinances to govern and regulate the following in relation to a building and housing, parts of a building and housing or a facility and service in or about a building or housing:

(i) Construction, reconstruction, alteration, extension, repair and conversion.

(ii) Maintenance.

(iii) Occupation.

(iv) Sanitation.

(v) Ventilation, heating, egress, lighting, electrical wiring, water supply, toilet facilities, drainage, plumbing, fire prevention and fireproofing, including limitations under which only buildings of noncombustible material and fireproofed roofs are used in construction.

(vi) Erection or substantial reconstruction.

(vii) Use and inspection.

(viii) Sanitation and inspection of land attached to a building or housing.

(2) Require that the approval of plans and specifications are secured before construction, reconstruction, alteration, extension, repair or conversion of a building is started.

(3) Appoint and determine the compensation of the following:

(i) Building inspectors.

(ii) Housing inspectors.

(iii) Property maintenance inspectors.

(iv) Fire prevention inspectors.

(v) Electrical inspectors.

(vi) Plumbing inspectors.

(4) In addition to penalties provided by an ordinance, institute actions to do any of the following:

(i) Prevent or restrain the unlawful construction, reconstruction, alteration, extension, repair, conversion, maintenance, use or occupation of property located within the borough.

(ii) Restrain, correct or abate a violation.

(iii) Prevent the use or occupancy of a building, housing or structure.

(b) **Codes.**—The following shall apply:

(1) A code under subsection (a)(1) may be combined or separately enacted or combined with a property maintenance code.

(2) A borough may adopt, amend or incorporate by reference any standard or nationally recognized code or any variations or changes or parts of the code as its ordinance as provided under section 32A04 (relating to property maintenance code).

(3) An ordinance under subsection (a)(1) may provide for reasonable fines and penalties for violations of the ordinance in compliance with Chapter 33 (relating to ordinances).

(c) **Inspectors.**—An inspector under subsection (a)(3) may enter, subject to constitutional standards in a similar manner as provided under section 3107 (relating to entry upon premises), and inspect a premises at reasonable hours and in a reasonable manner for the administration and enforcement of the borough's adopted codes or ordinances incorporating standard or nationally recognized codes. Any fees payable to inspectors under the ordinances shall be paid by the inspectors as soon as possible to the borough treasurer for the use of the borough.

CHAPTER 33
ORDINANCES

SUBCHAPTER A
GENERAL PROVISIONS

---

§ 3301.1. Ordinances and resolutions.

(a) General rule.—Council shall enact ordinances in accordance with this part and the laws of this Commonwealth in which the powers of the borough shall be exercised as deemed beneficial to the borough and to provide for the enforcement of the powers of the borough. Council may amend, repeal or revise existing ordinances by the enactment of subsequent ordinances.

(b) Legislative acts.—Every legislative act of council must be by ordinance. Legislative acts shall include, but not be limited to:

(1) Tax ordinances.

(2) Deleted by 2024, March 28, P.L. 2, No. 2, § 4, effective in 60 days [May 28, 2024].

(3) Capital expenditures not payable out of current funds

(4) Legislation doing any of the following:

(i) Exercising the police power of the borough.

(ii) Regulating land use, development and subdivision.

(iii) Imposing building, plumbing, electrical, property maintenance, housing and similar standards.

(iv) Regulating the conduct of a person or entity within the borough and imposing penalties for violation of the regulated conduct.

(5) Imposing assessments on benefited property for public improvements in accordance with Chapter 21A (relating to assessments and charges for public improvements).

(c) Resolutions.—Council shall adopt resolutions in accordance with this part and the laws of this Commonwealth. Resolutions may be adopted for any purpose, including, but not limited to, the following:

Table of Contents
Part I Ch. 1–3 Ethics, Records, Open Meetings
Part II Ch. 4–10 Taxation
Part III Ch. 11–18 Torts, Contracts & Civil Rules
Part IV Ch. 19–24 Zoning & Planning
Part V Ch. 25–30 Construction and Emergency Codes
Part VI Ch. 31–39 Municipal Codes
Index

(1) Ceremonial or congratulatory expressions of the good will of the council.

(2) Statements of public policy of the council.

(3) Approval of formal agreements of the borough, except for agreements arising under an established purchasing system of the borough.

(4) Approval, if required, of administrative rules, regulations and bylaws arising under State statutes or borough ordinances.

(5) The filling of borough-appointed positions and of vacancies of elected officials, except as otherwise provided.

(6) Annual tax millage rate in accordance with section 1302(a) (relating to tax levy).

(d) Real and personal property.—Council's approval of the acquisition, disposition and leasing of real or personal property shall be by adoption of a resolution in a manner consistent with this part.

§ 3301.2. Publication.

(a) Requirements.—Except as provided under this part or other law, council shall publish every proposed ordinance once in one newspaper of general circulation no less than seven days and no more than 60 days prior to the day when council shall vote on the proposed ordinance. Publication of any proposed ordinance shall include all of the following:

(1) The full text or the title of the ordinance and a brief summary prepared by the borough solicitor setting forth all the provisions in reasonable detail.

(2) A reference to the borough office or other place where borough records are kept where copies of the proposed ordinance may be examined.

(b) Summary.—If the full text is not included in the publication of the proposed ordinance, the following shall apply:

(1) The newspaper in which the proposed ordinance is published shall, upon request, be furnished a copy of the full text.

(2) The following shall apply:

(i) In addition to copies of the full text of the proposed ordinance retained where borough records are kept in accordance with subsection (a), an attested copy of the full text shall be filed in the county law library or other county office designated by the county commissioners.

(ii) The county commissioners may impose a fee not greater than the actual costs of storing the proposed ordinance.

(iii) Filing with the county may be completed by the submission of an electronic copy of the ordinance through a method available, in the sole discretion of the county, to permit receipt by the office storing municipal ordinances.

(iv) Upon request by the borough, the county shall notify the borough of the method by which electronic copies may be submitted.

(v) The county may store the ordinance electronically, if the public is able to access the electronically stored borough ordinances during regular business hours at the office or at a remote location.

(vi) The borough shall retain a printed copy of the email and ordinance as transmitted.

(3) The date of the filing with the county under paragraph (2) shall not affect the effective date of the ordinance and shall not be deemed a defect in the process of the enactment of the ordinance.

(c) Notice of amendments.—If substantial amendments are made in the proposed ordinance, before voting upon enactment, council shall, within ten days, readvertise in one newspaper of general circulation a brief summary setting forth all the provisions in reasonable detail together with a summary of the amendments. A copy of the full text of the amended proposed ordinance shall be retained where borough records are kept.

§ 3301.3. Enactment, approval and veto.

(a) Approval by mayor.—

(1) Every ordinance enacted by council shall be presented to the mayor for the mayor's approval. Presentation to the mayor shall be deemed to mean delivery to the mayor by hand delivery or certified mail, addressee only, to the mayor at the mayor's last known address. Delivery shall be deemed complete upon depositing in the mail, postage or charges prepaid, as evidenced by a certificate of mailing.

(2) The following shall apply:

(i) If the mayor approves the ordinance, the mayor shall sign it.

(ii) If the mayor does not approve the ordinance, the mayor shall return it with objections, which shall be entered upon the minutes, to the council at its next scheduled meeting occurring at least ten days after the meeting at which the ordinance was enacted by council.

(iii) Council shall reconsider the ordinance either at the meeting at which the vetoed ordinance was returned or not later than ten days after the meeting at any other scheduled meeting. If, after reconsideration, a majority of all elected council members plus one votes to override the mayor's veto, the ordinance shall have full force and effect as if it had received the approval of the mayor. The vote shall be determined by yeas and nays and the names and votes of the members shall be entered upon the minutes.

(iv) A scheduled meeting, as used in this section, may be either a regular, special or reconvened meeting.

(3) If an ordinance is not returned by the mayor at council's next scheduled meeting occurring at least ten days after its presentation to the mayor, the ordinance shall have full force and effect as if it had been approved by the mayor.

(b) Effective date.—The effective date of an enacted ordinance, except as provided in the ordinance, shall be one of the following:

(1) The date when the mayor approves the ordinance.

(2) The date of enactment by the council over the veto of the mayor.

(3) For an ordinance not returned by the mayor at the next scheduled meeting of council occurring at least ten days after the meeting at which the ordinance was enacted by the council, the date of the succeeding scheduled meeting of council.

(c) Tax ordinance or resolution.—The following shall apply:

(1) If council presents the mayor with the annual tax ordinance or resolution under section 1310.1 (relating to tax ordinance or resolution), the mayor shall, within ten days of receiving the tax ordinance or resolution, approve or return the tax ordinance or resolution to the borough secretary with a statement setting forth the mayor's objections.

(2) Council shall reconsider the tax ordinance or resolution at any scheduled meeting held not later than ten days after the mayor has returned the tax ordinance or resolution to the secretary with the mayor's objections. The mayor's objections shall be entered upon the minutes of the meeting.

(3) A veto of the tax ordinance or resolution of the borough may be overridden by a vote of a majority of all elected council members plus one. If the veto is overridden, the ordinance or resolution shall have full force and effect as if it had received the approval of the mayor.

(4) If the mayor neither approves the tax ordinance or resolution nor returns it with objections, the date of enactment of the tax ordinance or resolution shall be the date of the adoption of the tax ordinance or resolution by council.

Chap. 39 Res. During Mil. Service
Chap. 38 Intergov. Coop.
Chap. 37 3rd Class City Code
Chap. 36 Bor. Code
Chap. 35 2nd Class Twp. Code
Chap. 34 1st Class Twp. Code
Chap. 33 Home Rule Chart. Opt. Plans Law
Chap. 32 Water Serv. Act
Chap. 31 Munic. Auth. Act

§ 3301.4. Recording, advertising and proof.

(a) **Recording.**—All borough ordinances shall, within 30 days after approval by the mayor, the council's override of the mayor's veto or council's next scheduled meeting after its presentation to the mayor, be recorded by the borough secretary in an ordinance book. All borough resolutions pertaining to tax levies shall, within 30 days after approval by the mayor, the council's override of the mayor's veto or the council's next scheduled meeting after its presentation to the mayor, be recorded by the borough secretary in an ordinance book. The ordinance book shall be open to the inspection of citizens during normal business hours.

(b) **Proof.**—All ordinances may be proved by the certificate of the borough secretary under the corporate seal. If an ordinance is printed or published in book or pamphlet form by the authority of the borough, the ordinance shall be accepted as evidence without further proof. The entry of the borough ordinance or the entry of a borough resolution pertaining to a tax levy in the ordinance book shall be sufficient without the signature of the president of council, mayor or member of council.

(c) **Prior ordinances.**—The text of a borough ordinance or a portion of an ordinance which was attached to the ordinance book before January 1, 1966, shall be considered in force as if the ordinances or portions of ordinances had been recorded in the ordinance book if all other requirements of this part applicable to the enactment, approval, advertising and recording of the ordinances or portions of ordinances were complied with within the time limits prescribed under this part.

§ 3301.5. Codification of ordinances.

(a) **Consolidation, codification and revision.**—The borough council, under section 3301.1(a) (relating to ordinances and resolutions), may:

(1) enact a consolidation, codification or revision of borough ordinances or recorded resolutions as a single ordinance of the borough; and

(2) enact a complete group ordinance, repealing or amending existing ordinances as necessary.

(b) **Enactment.**—For a consolidation, codification or revision under subsection (a), the following apply:

(1) The ordinance must be introduced in the council at least 30 days before its final enactment.

(2) At least 15 days before final enactment, notice of the introduction of the ordinance must be given by advertisement in a newspaper of general circulation. For enactment under subsection (a)(2), the notice must list, in lieu of a table of contents, the titles of each of the ordinances in the complete group.

(c) **Subsequent notice.**—When any consolidation, codification or revision under subsection (a) has been enacted as an ordinance, it shall not be necessary to advertise the entire text, but it shall be sufficient to publish a notice referring to notice under subsection (b)(2) and stating final enactment.

§ 3301.6. Appeals from ordinances.

Complaint as to the legality of any ordinance or resolution must be made to the court of common pleas. In cases of ordinances laying out streets over private lands, the court shall have jurisdiction to review the propriety as well as the legality of the ordinance.

§ 3301.7. Replacement of ordinance books.

(a) **Ordinance.**—

(1) If an ordinance book is unserviceable, the council may provide by ordinance for the secretary of the borough to establish a replacement ordinance book recording all ordinances affected by the replacement.

(2) The following apply to an ordinance under this subsection:

(i) The ordinance must be recorded in the ordinance book immediately following the recorded ordinances affected by the replacement.

(ii) The ordinance must direct the secretary, upon completion of the recording, to publish once, in one newspaper of general circulation, a notice:

(A) identifying the ordinances contained in the unserviceable ordinance book; and

(B) stating that the old books and records of borough ordinances and the replacement ordinance book are open to public inspection for the purpose of verification and correction for a period of 30 days from the date of the notice.

(b) Secretary.—

(1) The secretary, in recording the ordinances, must make complete copies of the ordinances, including the date of enactment and approval and the names of the officers who signed them.

(2) After notice and corrections under subsection (a)(2)(ii), the secretary must certify each ordinance as a correct copy of the original.

(c) Effect.—Upon compliance with subsection (b), the recorded replacement ordinance shall replace the original ordinance as the ordinances of the borough for the period covered by the new ordinance book.

§ 3302. (Reserved).

§ 3303. (Reserved).

§ 3304. (Reserved).

§ 3305. (Reserved).

§ 3306. (Reserved).

§ 3307. (Reserved).

§ 3308. (Reserved).

§ 3309. (Reserved).

SUBCHAPTER B
ENFORCEMENT

Sec.

---

§ 3321. Fines and penalties.

(a) Prescription.—

(1) A borough ordinance shall prescribe fines and penalties for violation.

(2) A civil penalty may not exceed $600 per violation.

(3) The council may prescribe a criminal fine not to exceed $1,000 per violation and may prescribe imprisonment to the extent allowed by law for the punishment of a summary offense.

(4) An ordinance under this subsection may provide that a separate violation under paragraph (2) or (3) shall arise for:

(i) each day of violation; and

(ii) each applicable section of the ordinance.

(5) An ordinance may provide for assessment of court costs and reasonable attorney fees incurred by the borough in the enforcement proceedings.

(6) The council may delegate the initial determination of ordinance violation and the service of notice of violation to a qualified officer or agent.

(b) Enforcement at law.—Unless otherwise provided by statute, a borough ordinance shall set forth the method of its enforcement in accordance with the following:

(1) Except as provided in paragraph (2), if the penalty is not paid, the borough shall initiate a civil action for collection in accordance with the Pennsylvania Rules of Civil Procedure. A borough shall be exempt from the payment of costs in an action under this paragraph.

(2) For an ordinance regulating building, housing, property maintenance, health, fire, public safety, parking, solicitation, curfew, water or air or noise pollution, enforcement shall be by a criminal action in the same manner provided for the enforcement of summary offenses under the Pennsylvania Rules of Criminal Procedure. The municipal solicitor may assume charge of the prosecution without the consent of the district attorney as required under Pa.R.Crim.P. No. 454 (relating to trial in summary cases). Violations of the property maintenance code or ordinance may also be enforced under section 32A04(c) (relating to property maintenance code).

(3) Except for an ordinance subject to paragraph (2), an ordinance enacted prior to July 16, 2012, shall be deemed automatically amended so that it shall be enforced under paragraph (1).

(4) If a civil claim under this subsection, exclusive of interest, costs or fees, exceeds the monetary jurisdiction of a magisterial district judge under 42 Pa.C.S. § 1515(a) (relating to jurisdiction and venue), the borough may:

(i) bring the action in a court of common pleas; or

(ii) make a waiver under 42 Pa.C.S. § 1515(a)(3).

(c) Enforcement in equity.—In addition to or in lieu of enforcement under subsection (b), a borough may enforce an ordinance in equity in a court of common pleas of the county where the borough is situate.

(d) Payment.—Money collected under subsection (b) shall be paid to the borough treasurer.

§ 3322. Commitment pending trial.

An individual arrested for the violation of a borough ordinance may, pending trial, be committed to:

(1) the borough correctional facility; or

(2) if there is no suitable borough correctional facility, to a county correctional facility.

§ 3323. Commitment after trial.

A defendant sentenced to imprisonment for a violation of a borough ordinance may be committed to:

(1) the borough correctional facility for up to ten days; or

(2) a county correctional facility for up to 30 days.

§ 3324. Payment of costs by borough.

If a prisoner is committed to a county correctional facility under section 3322(2) (relating to commitment pending trial) or 3323(2) (relating to commitment after trial), the expenses of maintaining the prisoner during confinement shall be paid by the borough, and the county shall not be liable for the maintenance.

CHAPTER 34
ACTIONS BY AND AGAINST BOROUGHS
(Reserved)

CHAPTER 35
ACTS OF ASSEMBLY REPEALED AND SAVING CLAUSE

§ 3501. Repeals.

(a) (Reserved).

(b) Inconsistent repeal.—All acts or parts of acts inconsistent with this part are repealed. This part shall furnish a complete and exclusive system for the government and regulation of boroughs, except as enumerated under section 102 (relating to excluded provisions).

(c) Law not repealed.—Nothing under this part shall be construed to repeal any of the following:

(1) A local or special law.

(2) A law relating to the Navigation Commission for the Delaware River and its navigable tributaries.

(3) A law, the enforcement of which is vested in the Department of Health.

(3.1) A law, the enforcement of which is vested in the Department of Environmental Protection.

(4) A law, the enforcement of which is vested in the Department of Conservation and Natural Resources.

(5) The act of December 31, 1965 (P.L.1257, No.511), known as The Local Tax Enabling Act.

(6) The act of February 14, 2008 (P.L.6, No.3), known as the Right-to-Know Law.

(7) 45 Pa.C.S. (relating to legal notices).

(8) 65 Pa.C.S. (relating to public officers).

(9) 66 Pa.C.S. Pt. I (relating to Public Utility Code).

(d) Revival.—Nothing under this part shall be construed to revive any act or part of a repealed act.

ADDITIONAL PROVISIONS OF ACT 37 OF 2014 pertaining to the reenacted Borough Code:

Section 2. Section 7132(b) of Title 44 is amended to read:

§ 7132. Police officers.

* * *

(b) Exception.—Unless prevented from doing so by the operation of 8 Pa.C.S. Ch. 11 Subch. J (relating to civil service for police and fire apparatus operators), borough policemen who reside in the borough may hold and exercise the office of constable in the borough, or in any ward thereof, and receive all costs, fees and emoluments pertaining to such office.

Table of Contents
Part I Ch. 1–3 Ethics, Records, Open Meetings
Part II Ch. 4–10 Taxation
Part III Ch. 11–18 Torts, Contracts & Civil Rules
Part IV Ch. 19–24 Zoning & Planning
Part V Ch. 25–30 Construction and Emergency Codes
Part VI Ch. 31–39 Municipal Codes
Index

Section 3. Repeals are as follows:

(1) The General Assembly declares that the repeal under paragraph (2) is necessary to effectuate the addition of 8 Pa.C.S. Pt. I.

(2) The act of February 1, 1966 (1965 P.L.1656, No.581), known as The Borough Code, is repealed.

Section 4. The addition of 8 Pa.C.S. Pt. I is a continuation of the act of February 1, 1966 (1965 P.L.1656, No.581), known as The Borough Code. The following apply:

(1) Except as otherwise provided in 8 Pa.C.S. Pt. I, all activities initiated under The Borough Code shall continue and remain in full force and effect and may be completed under 8 Pa.C.S. Pt. I. Orders, regulations, rules and decisions which were made under The Borough Code and which are in effect on the effective date of section 3(2) of this act shall remain in full force and effect until revoked, vacated or modified under 8 Pa.C.S. Pt. I. Contracts, obligations and collective bargaining agreements entered into under The Borough Code are not affected nor impaired by the repeal of The Borough Code.

(2) Except as set forth in paragraph (3), any difference in language between 8 Pa.C.S. Pt. I and The Borough Code is intended only to conform to the style of the Pennsylvania Consolidated Statutes and is not intended to change or affect the legislative intent, judicial construction or administration and implementation of The Borough Code.

(3) Paragraph (2) does not apply to the addition of the following provisions of 8 Pa.C.S.:

(i) The definition of "freeholders" in section 200.

(ii) Section 202(a)(3).

(iii) Section 210(a).

(iv) Section 801.

(v) Section 901(a.1).

(vi) Section 902.

(vii) Section 904.1.

(viii) Section 1104(a) and (f)(3).

(ix) Section 1121(a)(5).

(x) SECTION 1202(20), (23), (35), (46) and (60).

(xi) Section 1302(a)(10).

(xii) section SECTION 1315(a)(4).

(xiii) Section 21A06.

(xiv) Section 2456(b)(3).

(xv) Section 2701(e).

(xvi) Section 2708(b).

(xvii) Section 3301.1(b)(5).

(xviii) Section 3301.2(a)(2), (b)(2) and (c).

Section 5. The addition of 8 Pa.C.S. §§ 801(b) and 1104(f)(3) shall apply to officials elected or appointed to fill a vacancy in an elected office after the effective date of this section.

Section 6. This act shall take effect in 60 days. [Enacted April 18, 2014]

CHAPTER 37-A

THE THIRD CLASS CITY CODE

11 Pa.C.S. §§ 101–14702

Chapter

CHAPTER 101
PRELIMINARY PROVISIONS

Sec.

Table of Contents
Part I Ch. 1–3 Ethics, Records, Open Meetings
Part II Ch. 4–10 Taxation
Part III Ch. 11–18 Torts, Contracts & Civil Rules
Part IV Ch. 19–24 Zoning & Planning
Part V Ch. 25–30 Construction and Emergency Codes
Part VI Ch. 31–39 Municipal Codes
Index

---

§ 10101. Short title of part.

This part shall be known and may be cited as the Third Class City Code.

§ 10102. Definitions.

The following words and phrases when used in this part shall have the meanings given to them in this section unless the context clearly indicates otherwise:

"Bill." A proposed ordinance introduced in council.

"City." A city of the third class.

"Council." A council of a city.

"Highway." A State highway of the Commonwealth.

"Home Rule Charter and Optional Plans Law." The provisions of 53 Pa.C.S. Pt. III Subpt. E (relating to home rule and optional plan government) and, where applicable, the former act of April 13, 1972 (P.L.184, No.62), known as the Home Rule Charter and Optional Plans Law.

"Municipal authority" or **"municipality authority."** A body politic and corporate created under any of the following:

(1) 53 Pa.C.S. Ch. 56 (relating to municipal authorities).

(2) The former act of May 2, 1945 (P.L.382, No.164), known as the Municipality Authorities Act of 1945.

(3) The former act of June 28, 1935 (P.L.463, No.191), known as the Municipality Authorities Act of one thousand nine hundred and thirty-five.

"Municipal Claim and Tax Lien Law." The act of May 16, 1923 (P.L.207, No.153), referred to as the Municipal Claim and Tax Lien Law.

"Municipal corporation." A city, borough, incorporated town or township.

"Municipalities Planning Code." The act of July 31, 1968 (P.L.805, No.247), known as the Pennsylvania Municipalities Planning Code.

"Municipality." A county, city, borough, incorporated town or township.

"Newspaper of general circulation." As defined in 45 Pa.C.S. § 101 (relating to definitions).

"Pennsylvania Construction Code Act." The act of November 10, 1999 (P.L.491, No.45), known as the Pennsylvania Construction Code Act.

"Pennsylvania Election Code." The act of June 3, 1937 (P.L.1333, No.320), known as the Pennsylvania Election Code.

"Street." Any of the following:

(1) A street, avenue, boulevard, parkway, road, lane, court, alley or public square within a city.

(2) A highway within a city to the extent that the city is legally responsible for it, pursuant to agreement or by other means.

§ 10103. Excluded provisions.

This part shall not be construed to repeal an act relating to:

Chap. 39 Res. During Mil. Service
Chap. 38 Intergov. Coop.
Chap. 37 3rd Class City Code
Chap. 36 Bor. Code
Chap. 35 2nd Class Twp. Code
Chap. 34 1st Class Twp. Code
Chap. 33 Home Rule Chart. Opt. Plans Law
Chap. 32 Water Serv. Act
Chap. 31 Munic. Auth. Act

(1) The collection of municipal and tax claims by lien.

(2) The method of incurring and increasing city indebtedness.

(3) The conduct of an election.

(4) A public school, except for the collection of a school tax by the city treasurer.

(5) (Reserved).

(6) A constable.

(7) The provision of municipal consent to a public utility.

(8) A weight and measure.

(9) A validation of an election, bond, ordinance and act of a corporate officer.

(10) A joint city and county building.

(11) A library.

(12) A highway.

(13) A joint or several authority or duty which applies to a city and to other classes of political subdivisions by virtue of general acts of Assembly.

§ 10104. Construction of part.

(a) Existing law.—

(1) The provisions of this part that are the same as the provisions of existing laws are intended as a continuation of the existing laws and not as new enactments.

(2) The repeal under this part of a statutory provision shall not revive a repealed or superseded statutory provision or affect the corporate existence of an incorporated city.

(3) The provisions of this part shall not affect any of the following:

(i) An act that was taken, a liability that was incurred or a right that accrued or vested.

(ii) A suit or prosecution that is pending or to be instituted to enforce a right or penalty or punish an offense under the authority of the repealed law.

(4) Each ordinance, resolution, regulation and rule made under a statute repealed under this part shall continue with the same force and effect as if the statute had not been repealed.

(5) An individual holding an office or position under or by virtue of a statute repealed under this part shall continue to hold the office or position until the expiration of the term of office, subject to the conditions and tenure attached to the office or position prior to July 1, 1931.

(b) Powers.—A city shall possess, and council and other city officials may execute, the corporate powers and duties as provided in this part and in other laws to the extent that the powers and duties are not repealed by this part.

§ 10105. Constitutional construction.

The provisions of this part are severable. If any provision of this part or its application to any person or circumstance is held invalid, the invalidity shall not affect other provisions or applications of this part which can be given effect without the invalid provision or application.

§ 10106. (Reserved).

§ 10107. Applicability and ability.

(a) Applicability.—This part shall apply to:

(1) All cities which have been incorporated under or which have accepted the provisions of the act of May 23, 1874 (P.L.230, No.152), entitled "An act

dividing cities of this State into three classes; regulating the passage of ordinances; providing for contracts for supplies and work for said cities; authorizing the increase of indebtedness, and the creation of a sinking fund to redeem the same; defining and punishing certain offenses in all of said cities; and providing for the incorporation and government of the cities of the third class."

(2) All cities which have been incorporated under the provisions of the former act of May 23, 1889 (P.L.277, No.247), entitled "An act providing for the incorporation and government of cities of the third class."

(3) All cities which have been incorporated under the provisions of the former act of June 27, 1913 (P.L.568, No.367), entitled "An act providing for the incorporation, regulation, and government of cities of the third class; regulating nomination and election of municipal officers therein; and repealing, consolidating, and extending existing laws in relation thereto."

(4) All cities formed by the consolidation of boroughs having voted separately to become cities in accordance with the provisions of the former act of May 24, 1917 (P.L.262, No.143), entitled "An act to enable two or more boroughs that are contiguous or in close proximity to be united and to become one city, wherever each of said boroughs shall have heretofore voted or shall hereafter vote to become a city of the third class, under laws now enacted or which may hereafter be enacted; and wherever each of said boroughs has duly received or shall hereafter duly receive letters patent constituting it a city of the third class, but where sufficient time shall not have elapsed after the granting of such letters patent for the holding of a municipal election; providing for the consequences of such consolidation, the government of such consolidated city, the payment of the indebtedness of each of the united territories and the enforcement of debts and claims due to and from each, and fixing the jurisdiction over the said consolidated city in the courts of the county in which the majority of its inhabitants shall reside."

(5) All cities incorporated under the provisions of the former act of June 23, 1931 (P.L.932, No.317), known as The Third Class City Code.

(6) All cities incorporated under the provisions of this part.

(b) Ability.—This part shall not be construed as a limitation on the ability of a city to do any of the following:

(1) To continue operating under the form of government previously selected and exercising powers previously acquired by the city in accordance with the act of July 15, 1957 (P.L.901, No.399), known as the Optional Third Class City Charter Law.

(2) To adopt or continue utilizing a form of government and to acquire or continue exercising powers pursuant to an optional plan or a home rule charter which has been or may be adopted in accordance with the Home Rule Charter and Optional Plans Law.

§ 10108. (Reserved).

§ 10109. Publication of notices.

(a) General newspaper.—

(1) If advertisement, notice or publication is required to be published in a newspaper under this part, the publication must be made one time, unless the provision requiring publication specifies other times, in at least one newspaper of general circulation published in the city. If a newspaper of general circulation published in the city does not exist, publication must be made in a newspaper of general circulation in the city.

(2) If notice is required to be published in more than one newspaper, it must be published in at least one newspaper of general circulation published in the city. If a newspaper of general circulation published in the city does not exist, publication must be made in a newspaper of general circulation in the city.

(b) Legal newspaper.—

(1) Except as provided under paragraph (2) and in addition to the requirements of subsection (a), if a notice relates to a proceeding or matter in a court, the holding of an election for the increase of indebtedness or the issue and sale of bonds to be financed by taxation, the notice must be published in the legal newspaper designated by the rules of court of the proper county for the publication of legal notices and advertisements, unless publication is not required by special order of court.

(2) An ordinance, auditor's statement, summary of an auditor's statement, advertisement inviting a proposal for public contract and for bid for material and supplies or a list of delinquent taxpayers shall be published only in newspapers of general circulation.

CHAPTER 102
PROCEDURES FOR INCORPORATION

---

§ 10200. Definitions.

The following words and phrases when used in this chapter shall have the meanings given to them in this section unless the context clearly indicates otherwise:

"Incorporation resolution." A resolution to submit at a general or municipal election a referendum question to the registered voters of a municipal corporation.

"Municipal corporation." A borough, a township of the first class, a township of the second class or an incorporated town.

"Referendum question." The question of whether a municipal corporation shall become incorporated as a city of the third class to be known as the "City of ...."

§ 10201. Creation of cities.

A city shall be chartered as follows:

(1) A single municipal corporation having a population of at least 10,000 according to the last preceding United States census may be incorporated as a city in accordance with this chapter if a majority of the registered voters in the municipal corporation cast an affirmative vote in favor of the referendum question.

(2) Two or more contiguous municipal corporations having a combined population of at least 10,000 according to the last preceding United States census may, under 53 Pa.C.S. Ch. 7 Subch. C (relating to consolidation and merger), incorporate as a city and determine whether the newly incorporated

city shall be governed by this part and other general laws applicable to and governing cities.

§ 10203.1. Incorporating resolution.

(a) Governing body.—The governing body of a municipal corporation may adopt an incorporation resolution.

(b) Petition.—If at least 200 registered voters of a municipal corporation petition the governing body of the municipal corporation for the adoption of an incorporation resolution, the governing body shall adopt the incorporation resolution.

§ 10204. Resolution certification and form.

The governing body of a municipal corporation that adopts an incorporation resolution shall certify the incorporation resolution to the county board of elections of each proper county. The county board of elections shall, at the general or municipal election in the manner required by the Pennsylvania Election Code, submit a referendum question to the registered voters of the municipal corporation that has certified an incorporation resolution.

§ 10204.1. Notice of election.

Notice of the election at which registered voters of a municipal corporation will be voting on a referendum question shall be given by the secretary or other person designated by the municipal corporation. The notice required under this section shall be published once a week for four successive weeks in a newspaper of general circulation in the municipal corporation in which the referendum question will be submitted to the registered voters.

§ 10205. Returns of election.

In each county in which a referendum question is submitted to the registered voters of a municipal corporation, the county board of elections shall return the vote cast on the referendum question to the following:

(1) The clerk of the court for the county.

(2) The governing body of the municipal corporation in which registered voters voted on a referendum question.

(3) If a majority of the votes cast by the registered voters of the municipal corporation are in favor of incorporating as a city, the Secretary of the Commonwealth and the Department of Community and Economic Development.

§ 10206. Vote against incorporating as city.

If the returns of an election under section 10204.1 (relating to notice of election) show that a majority of registered voters in a municipal corporation voted "no" on the referendum question, further proceedings may not occur and another election on the referendum question may not be held in the municipal corporation until the third ensuing general or municipal election.

§ 10207. Letters patent and boundaries.

If the returns of an election under section 10204.1 (relating to notice of election) show that a majority of registered voters in a municipal corporation voted "yes" on the referendum question, within 60 days after the election the governing body of the municipal corporation shall furnish to the Secretary of the Commonwealth the necessary information with respect to the boundaries of the new city and the Governor shall issue letters patent, under the Great Seal of the Commonwealth, reciting the facts, defining the boundaries of the city and constituting the city as a body corporate and politic by the name of the City of........................

§ 10208. Property of entities vested in city.

The property and estates of the municipal corporations which have become a city in accordance with this chapter are severally and respectively vested in the corporation or body politic of the city for the use and benefit of the citizens of the city.

§ 10209. Temporary preservation and city organization.

(a) Existing government.—The government of the municipal corporation shall continue in full force and operation until the first Monday of January next succeeding the municipal election under section 10702 (relating to first elections in newly created cities). On the first Monday of January next succeeding the municipal election under section 10702, the officers of the city chosen at the municipal election shall begin their terms of service and the city government shall be organized under this part.

(b) Service.—If, in the organization of the city government of a newly incorporated city, an individual is appointed by council to an office which, under this part, has a definite term and a definite time for the election of an individual to the office, the individual appointed shall serve only for the time intervening between the individual's appointment and the day set under this part for the regular election or appointment of the officer for a full term.

§ 10210. Existing liabilities, debts and claims.

If a municipal corporation is incorporated as a city in accordance with this part, the following shall apply:

(1) Each suit, prosecution, debt and claim shall be transferred to the newly incorporated city.

(2) Each pending suit involving the municipal corporation shall be under the management and control of the newly incorporated city which shall be substituted as a party in the suit.

(3) Each valid claim and demand existing against the municipal corporation shall be enforceable against the city.

(4) Each bond and floating indebtedness and the interest on a bond and floating indebtedness existing at the time a municipal corporation became incorporated as a city in accordance with this part must be paid by the newly incorporated city in a manner that taxes are uniform throughout the territorial limits of the whole city.

CHAPTER 103
CHANGE OF CORPORATE TITLE

---

§ 10301. Resolution and petition.

Council may initiate proceedings to change the corporate title of a city by doing all of the following:

(1) Adopting a resolution proposing to make the change in the corporate title of a city.

(2) Presenting to the court of common pleas of the county in which the city is located a petition, along with a certified copy of the resolution, requesting the change in the corporate title of the city.

§ 10302. Hearing and decree.

(a) Date and publication.—Upon presentation to the court of the petition and resolution under section 10301 (relating to resolution and petition), the court shall set a day for a hearing on the question of the change in the corporate title of the city and shall direct that notice of the hearing be published once a week for three weeks in a newspaper of general circulation.

(b) Testimony.—A court shall permit a resident of the city to give testimony at the hearing in support of or in opposition to the change of the corporate title of the city.

(c) Order.—A court shall order a change of the corporate title of the city in accordance with the petition and resolution of council or dismiss the petition.

§ 10303. Recording decree.

A change in the corporate title of a city that is ordered in accordance with section 10302(c) (relating to hearing and decree) may not take effect until a certified copy of the decree of court is filed in the office of the Secretary of the Commonwealth and is recorded in the office of the recorder of deeds of the county in which the city is located.

§ 10304. Existing rights and liabilities.

A change in the corporate title of a city shall not affect any of the following:

(1) A liability incurred.

(2) A right accrued or vested.

(3) An obligation issued or contracted.

(4) A suit or prosecution pending or instituted to enforce a right or penalty accrued or to punish an offense committed prior to the change.

CHAPTER 104
CREATION AND DIVISION OF WARDS

Sec.

---

§ 10401. General power of council.

(a) Power.—In addition to reapportionment of wards under 53 Pa.C.S. Ch. 9 (relating to municipal reapportionment) and section 11 of Article IX of the Constitution of Pennsylvania, a council may, with or without a petition as provided under section 10401.1 (relating to petition of registered voters) and subject to approval by the registered voters as provided under section 10407 (relating to voting procedures), create a new ward, divide a ward or detach part of a ward and attach it to another ward, in accordance with this chapter.

(b) Registered voter requirement.—A new ward must contain at least 300 registered voters according to the last general or municipal election.

(c) Size.—Each ward in a city shall be numbered and composed of compact and contiguous territory as nearly equal in population as practicable and as officially and finally reported in the most recent Federal decennial or special census.

§ 10401.1. Petition of registered voters.

(a) Initiation of proceedings.—Registered voters may petition council to initiate proceedings under section 10401 (relating to general power of council) to create new wards, divide a ward or wards or detach part of a ward and attach it to another ward as follows:

(1) One hundred registered voters may petition council to create or divide a ward if:

(i) In the case of a petition proposing to create a ward, the petitioners reside in the portion of the city which the petition proposes to create as a ward.

(ii) In the case of a petition proposing to divide a ward, the petitioners reside in the ward which the petition proposes to divide.

(2) Twenty-five registered voters may petition to detach part of one ward and attach the detached part to another ward if the petitioners reside in the part of the ward that is proposed to be detached.

(b) Council.—Council shall determine, by motion approved by a majority of council and within 90 days of presentment of the petition, whether to initiate proceedings under section 10401. If the motion is in favor of initiating proceedings, council shall appoint a commission in accordance with section 10403 (relating to appointment of commission).

(c) Court of common pleas.—If council has not approved a motion within 90 days after the presentment of a petition under subsection (a), 10 registered voters may petition the court of common pleas and contest the existing apportionment as violating section 10401. The proceedings before the court shall be conducted in accordance with 53 Pa.C.S. §§ 906 (relating to contest of reapportionment by governing body) and 907 (relating to costs and expenses of contest).

§ 10402. (Reserved).

§ 10403. Appointment of commission.

(a) Report and recommendation.—If council initiates proceedings under section 10401 (relating to general power of council), council shall appoint as commissioners five impartial registered voters who are residents of the city to make a report and recommendation concerning the necessity, desirability and feasibility of proposed wards.

(b) Residency.—Except as provided under subsection (c), a commissioner under subsection (a) may not be a resident of a ward which will be affected by the petition.

(c) Exception.—If a city has less than four wards, a commissioner appointed under subsection (a) must be selected from the city at large and may be a resident of a ward which will be affected by the petition.

§ 10403.1. Expenses of commissioners.

Council must make an appropriation for reasonable expenses incurred by commissioners for service under this chapter. Each commissioner shall submit for approval an itemized account of the commissioner's expenses to the city controller.

§ 10403.2. Report.

(a) Contents.—

(1) The commissioners appointed by council under section 10403(a) (relating to appointment of commission) shall examine the premises and prepare a report which shall include a draft of each ward affected by the proposed creation, division or detachment showing the following:

(i) The division or change or the lines of each ward as affected by the separation and attachment.

(ii) The population contained within each affected ward using figures officially and finally reported in the most recent Federal decennial or special census.

(2) The report under paragraph (1) shall be submitted to council and shall include a recommendation reflecting the decision of a majority of the commissioners concerning the proposed creation, division or detachment of a ward.

(b) **Territory.**—Consistent with the standards applied in municipal reapportionment under 53 Pa.C.S. § 903(b) (relating to reapportionment by governing body), a report under subsection (a) may not recommend the creation, division or detachment of a ward unless the result of implementing the report and recommendation would be that each ward in the city is composed of compact and contiguous territory as nearly equal in population as practicable as officially and finally reported in the most recent Federal decennial or special census.

(c) **Submittal.**—Upon receipt of a report under subsection (a), council shall, by motion, determine whether to submit the question of the proposed creation, division or detachment of a ward as provided in the report to the registered voters of the city in accordance with section 10404 (relating to election).

§ 10404. Election.

(a) **Certification.**—If, based upon the report under section 10403.2 (relating to report), council decides to proceed, council shall certify to the county board of elections the question of the creation, division or detachment of the ward to be submitted to the registered voters of each ward which are the subject of the report at the general or municipal election occurring not less than 90 days after the report was approved by council.

(b) **Ballot.**—The county board of elections shall place the question of approving the creation, division or detachment of a ward on the ballot in each ward or parts of a ward that will be affected by the question at the appropriate election in the manner provided under the Pennsylvania Election Code.

§ 10405. Notice of election and review of report.

(a) **Publication.**—A city must publish a notice of election in a newspaper of general circulation at least 15 days prior to the date that the question of approving the creation, division or detachment of a ward is to be presented at the specified general or municipal election.

(b) **Contents.**—An election notice under subsection (a) must contain a statement of the issue to be submitted to the registered voters at the election, including each ward or parts of a ward to be affected and the date on which the election is to be held. The notice shall reference the report and specify that it is available for review and copying as a public record under the act of February 14, 2008 (P.L.6, No.3), known as the Right-to-Know Law.

§ 10406. Election laws.

Each matter relating to the election at which the question of approving the creation, division or detachment of a ward or is to be presented to the voters shall be governed by the Pennsylvania Election Code.

§ 10407. Voting procedures.

(a) **Publication.**—The county board of elections must tabulate and publish the results of the referendum in a newspaper of general circulation within 30 days of the election. A certified copy of the results shall be placed on record with the minutes of council.

(b) **Positive vote.**—If a majority voted in favor of creating or dividing a ward or the detachment of a part of a ward to be attached to another ward, council shall proceed to create or divide a ward or detach a part of a ward to be attached to another ward in accordance with the report and shall number the new wards if necessary.

(c) Negative vote.—If a majority voted against creating or dividing a ward or the detachment of a part of a ward to be attached to another ward, further action may not be taken and a new petition on the same question may not be resubmitted until two years from the date of the election.

§ 10408. Change of ward lines by council.

If council determines during proceedings for the division or creation of a ward that any of the boundaries or divisions are uncertain, council must determine the relocation of the line to conform as nearly as possible to the previously determined boundary lines so that each ward in the city is composed of compact and contiguous territory as nearly equal in population as practicable as officially and finally reported in the most recent Federal decennial or special census.

§ 10409. Pennsylvania Election Code.

Nothing under this chapter shall be construed as affecting the powers and duties of the court of common pleas or the county board of elections and restrictions on alteration of election districts as provided under Article V of the Pennsylvania Election Code.

CHAPTER 106

CITY BOUNDARIES [REPEALED]

§ 10601. Repealed by 2022, July 7, P.L. 455, NO. 41—§ 4(2)(IX), Effective in 60 Days [Sept. 6, 2022]

§ 10602. Repealed by 2022, July 7, P.L. 455, NO. 41—§ 4(2)(IX), Effective in 60 Days [Sept. 6, 2022]

§ 10603. Repealed by 2022, July 7, P.L. 455, NO. 41—§ 4(2)(IX), Effective in 60 Days [Sept. 6, 2022]

§ 10604. Repealed by 2022, July 7, P.L. 455, NO. 41—§ 4(2)(IX), Effective in 60 Days [Sept. 6, 2022]

§ 10605. Repealed by 2022, July 7, P.L. 455, NO. 41—§ 4(2)(IX), Effective in 60 Days [Sept. 6, 2022]

§ 10606. Repealed by 2022, July 7, P.L. 455, NO. 41—§ 4(2)(IX), Effective in 60 Days [Sept. 6, 2022]

CHAPTER 107

ELECTED OFFICERS AND ELECTIONS

Sec.

§ 10701. Elected officers, term, reelection and vacancy.

(a) Elected officer and term.—

(1) Except as provided under subsection (c), the elected officers of a city shall be a mayor, four council members, a controller and a treasurer.

(2) Except as provided under section 10702 (relating to first elections in newly created cities) with respect to the first election of members of council, each elected officer shall serve for a term of four years from the first Monday of January next succeeding the officer's election.

(3) An officer shall be eligible for reelection.

(b) Disqualification.—A individual elected to a city office who fails to qualify in accordance with sections 10904 (relating to offices to be held until qualification of successors) and 10905 (relating to oath of office, violation of oath and penalty) and, as applicable, section 11101 (relating to executive departments), 11201 (relating to qualifications), 11401 (relating to qualifications) or 11701 (relating to qualifications, bond and compensation) shall be ineligible to qualify. A vacancy shall exist in the office and a individual shall be appointed to fill the vacancy in the manner provided under this part.

(c) Addition of council members.—Two additional council members may be elected to form a seven-member council comprised of six council members and the mayor, as follows:

(1) After petition of at least 5% of the registered voters of the city or pursuant to a resolution of council, and approval by a majority of voters at the next municipal or general election, two additional council members shall be elected.

(2) The referendum petition or resolution of council certified by the city clerk must be filed with the county board of elections not later than the thirteenth Tuesday before the next municipal or general election. The county board of elections must place the question before the electors as provided under the Pennsylvania Election Code. The form of the question shall be as follows:

Should two additional council members be elected to serve in this city, so that council shall be comprised of six council members and the mayor?

Yes No

(3) The county board of elections must tabulate and publish in a newspaper of general circulation the results of the referendum within 30 days of the election.

(4) The question of additional council members may not be voted on more than once in a three-year period.

(5) The terms of a council member elected under this subsection shall be as follows:

(i) At the first municipal election following approval at a general election of the question providing for the election of two additional council members, one of the additional council members shall be elected for a term of four years and one for a term of two years. Each council member shall serve from the first Monday of January after the election.

(ii) At the first general election following approval at a municipal election of the question providing for the election of two additional council members, one of the additional council members shall be elected for a term of three years and one for a term of one year. Each council member shall serve from the first Monday of January after the election.

(iii) After the term listed under subparagraph (i) or (ii), each additional council member shall be elected for a term of four years beginning service from the first Monday of January after the election.

(6) In a city divided into wards, each council member elected under paragraph (5) shall represent the city at large. No earlier than four years after the election adding two additional council members, the city may change the representation of either or both of the two additional seats from at large to

ward representation in accordance with Chapter 104 (relating to creation and division of wards) or any other law.

(d) Reduction of council members.—A city that has opted for a seven-member council may reestablish a five-member council comprised of four council members and the mayor, as follows:

(1) In a city in which the electorate has opted for a seven-member council, comprised of six council members and the mayor, the city must return to a five-member council, including the mayor, upon petition of at least 5% of the registered voters of the city or pursuant to a resolution of council and after approval by a majority of electors voting at the next municipal or general election. The referendum petition or resolution must be filed with the county board of elections not later than the thirteenth Tuesday before the next municipal or general election. The county board of elections shall place the question before the electors as provided under the Pennsylvania Election Code. The form of the question shall be as follows:

Should this city return to a five-member council, comprised of four council members and the mayor?

Yes No

(2) The county board of elections shall tabulate and publish in a newspaper of general circulation the results of the referendum within 30 days of the election. The question of reducing the seven-member council may not be voted on more than once in a five-year period.

(3) The following shall apply:

(i) At the first municipal election following approval of the question providing for the return to a five-member council, comprised of four council members and the mayor, four council members shall be elected to serve from the first Monday of January after the election.

(ii) The terms of the six council members serving on the seven-member council shall cease on the first Monday of January after the election under subparagraph (i).

(iii) The four candidates receiving the highest number of votes for the office of council member shall be elected.

(iv) The two candidates receiving the first and second highest number of votes shall serve for a term of four years.

(v) The two candidates receiving the third and fourth highest number of votes shall serve for a term of two years.

(vi) After the terms listed under subparagraphs (iv) and (v), a council member shall serve a term provided under subsection (a).

§ 10702. First elections in newly created cities.

(a) Election.—At the first municipal election occurring at least 90 days after the date of the letters patent issued by the Governor incorporating the city, the registered voters of the city shall elect city officials as provided under section 10701(a)(1) (relating to elected officers, term, reelection and vacancy).

(b) Highest votes.—The two candidates for council receiving the highest number of votes at the election shall serve for a term of four years from the first Monday of January next succeeding the candidate's election.

(c) Next highest votes.—The two candidates for council receiving the next highest number of votes shall serve for a term of two years from the first Monday of January next succeeding the election.

Table of Contents
Part I Ch. 1–3 Ethics, Records, Open Meetings
Part II Ch. 4–10 Taxation
Part III Ch. 11–18 Torts, Contracts & Civil Rules
Part IV Ch. 19–24 Zoning & Planning
Part V Ch. 25–30 Construction and Emergency Codes
Part VI Ch. 31–39 Municipal Codes
Index

§ 10703. Nominations and elections.

Each matter relating to a nomination of a candidate and election of a city officer shall be governed by the Pennsylvania Election Code.

§ 10704. Certificates of election.

After the election of city officers under this chapter, the county board of elections must issue and the officer-elect must procure a certificate of election. The officer-elect must present the certificate of election to council on the date and time provided under law for council's organization. The certificate must be filed with the city archives and the certificate's presentation must be noted in the minutes.

CHAPTER 108

VACANCIES IN OFFICE

---

§ 10801. Council and office of mayor.

(a) Appointment.—Within 30 days of a vacancy in the office of mayor or other member of council or if an elected mayor or council member has failed to qualify under section 10701 (relating to elected officers, term, reelection and vacancy) prior to taking office, council must, by a majority of council's remaining members, appoint a qualified individual to fill the vacant office.

(b) President judge.—If a council does not fill a vacancy within 30 days under subsection (a) or if a vacancy exists in the offices of at least a majority of the members of council, including the position of mayor, the president judge of the court of common pleas having jurisdiction within the city, must fill each vacancy upon either the petition of at least 10 qualified electors of the city or the petition of a majority of the remaining members of council.

(c) Term.—A individual appointed under subsection (a) or (b) shall serve for the lesser of the following terms:

(1) The remainder of the unexpired term of the office to which the individual is appointed.

(2) Until the first Monday of January after the next municipal election occurring at least 30 days after the vacancy occurred.

(d) Unexpired term.—If necessary to fill the unexpired term of the individual originally elected to an office that has become vacant, an individual shall be elected at the municipal election referred to under subsection (c)(2) to serve from the first Monday of January after the election for the remainder of the unexpired term.

§ 10802. Controller and treasurer.

(a) Appointment.—Within 30 days after a vacancy occurs in the office of city controller or in the office of city treasurer or if an elected city controller or city treasurer has failed to qualify under section 10701 (relating to elected officers, term, reelection and vacancy) prior to taking office, council must appoint a qualified individual to fill the vacant office.

(b) President judge.—If a council does not fill a vacancy within 30 days under subsection (a), the president judge of the court of common pleas having jurisdiction within the city must fill the vacancy upon the petition of at least 10 registered voters of the city.

(c) **Term.**—An individual appointed under subsection (a) or (b) shall serve for the lesser of the following terms:

(1) For the remainder of the unexpired term of the controller or treasurer whose office has become vacant.

(2) Until the first Monday of January after the next municipal election occurring at least 200 days after the vacancy occurs.

(d) **Unexpired term.**—If necessary to fill the unexpired term of the controller or treasurer whose office has become vacant, an individual shall be elected at the municipal election referred to under subsection (c)(2) to serve from the first Monday of January after the election for the remainder of the unexpired term.

(e) **Bond.**—If an individual is elected or appointed to fill an office for which a bond is required and if within 14 days of the date the individual is scheduled to take the oath of office at the organizational meeting of council the individual fails to post a bond, the office shall be deemed to be vacant and the resulting vacancy shall be filled as provided under this chapter.

CHAPTER 109

CITY OFFICERS AND EMPLOYEES

---

§ 10901. Appointment, removal and prohibition.

(a) **Powers and duties.**—Council:

(1) May appoint and dismiss any city officer and employee, except for an elected officer.

(2) Shall provide for the removal of an officer of the city whose office is established by ordinance, except as provided under this chapter.

(b) **Elective city office.**—The following shall apply to an individual holding an elective city office:

(1) The individual must be removed from office in accordance with the Constitution of Pennsylvania as follows:

(i) by impeachment;

(ii) by the Governor for reasonable cause after due notice and full hearing on the advice of two-thirds of the Senate; or

(iii) upon conviction of misbehavior in office or of any infamous crime.

(2) This chapter and other provisions of law requiring a forfeiture of office upon the conviction of a crime shall apply only if the court determines that the conviction is for misbehavior in office or for an infamous crime.

(3) Nothing under this section shall prevent title to an elected city office from being tried by proceedings of quo warranto as provided under law.

(c) Appointed office or position.—The following shall apply to an individual who is appointed to a city office or position, except for elective offices:

(1) The individual may be removed by the appointing power, except as limited under law or the Constitution of Pennsylvania.

(2) The individual must be removed on conviction of misbehavior in office or of an infamous crime.

(d) Prohibition.—Except as otherwise provided under law, an individual may not concurrently hold elective city office and be an employee of the same city.

§ 10902. Number, duties and compensation.

(a) Prescription.—Except as otherwise provided under this chapter, council may prescribe, by ordinance, the number, duties and compensation of the officers and employees of the city.

(b) Limitations.—The following shall apply to compensation paid to an officer or employee of the city:

(1) A payment may not be authorized from the city treasury to an officer or employee of the city unless that officer or employee has been elected or appointed in accordance with law.

(2) Unless previously authorized under law, an ordinance may not give extra compensation to an officer or employee of the city.

(c) Offense.—An officer drawing or countersigning a document authorizing payment or passing or paying a voucher contrary to this section commits a misdemeanor and shall, upon conviction, be:

(1) subject to forfeiting office in accordance with section 10901(b)(2) (relating to appointment, removal and prohibition); and

(2) sentenced to pay a fine of not more than $5,000 or to imprisonment for not more than one year, or both.

§ 10903. Salary, compensation and emoluments of officers.

(a) Prohibition.—A city may not increase or diminish the salary, compensation or emoluments of an elected officer after the officer's election. A change in salary, compensation or emoluments of an elected office shall take effect at the beginning of the next term of the member of council or other elected official.

(b) Retirement benefits.—Nothing under subsection (a) shall be construed to limit retirement benefits applicable to each employee and officer.

§ 10904. Offices to be held until qualification of successors.

(a) Successor.—An officer of a city, who has been elected or appointed and has qualified under this chapter, shall hold office until the officer's successor meets all of the following:

(1) Is elected or appointed and takes the oath of office.

(2) Provides the necessary bond.

(3) Takes other necessary actions required by law to qualify to assume office.

(b) Failure to appear.—If an elected official fails to appear at the organizational meeting of council to demonstrate the official's qualifications for office and to take the oath of office either:

(1) the official must fully qualify for office and take the oath of office within 14 days of the date of the organizational meeting of council; or

(2) the office of that elected official shall be deemed to be vacant and the vacancy shall be filled in the manner provided by this chapter.

(c) Multiple terms expiring.—Members whose terms have expired and who are to be replaced shall draw lots to determine which of the members shall continue to serve on council until the member's successor duly qualifies or takes the oath of office when all of the following apply:

(1) The terms of office of more than one council at-large member expire.

(2) More than one seated council member is to be replaced as the result of an election.

(3) Only one of the newly elected council members fails to qualify to assume office.

(d) Continuing to hold office.—An individual continuing to hold office under this section after the first Monday of January, which would have marked the end of the individual's term, may not participate in:

(1) The deliberations concerning the individual's successor.

(2) A vote appointing the individual's successor.

§ 10905. Oath of office, violation of oath and penalty.

(a) Oath required.—Each officer of the city, whether elected or appointed, shall, before entering upon the officer's respective duties, take and subscribe an oath or affirmation of office pursuant to 53 Pa.C.S. § 1141 (relating to form of oaths of office).

(b) Oath as qualification.—An individual who refuses to take the oath shall be deemed not to have met the qualifications to hold office.

(c) Violation.—An individual who violates the individual's oath:

(1) commits a misdemeanor; and

(2) upon conviction shall be:

(i) sentenced to pay a fine of not more than $1,000 or to imprisonment for not more than one year, or both; and

(ii) subject to forfeiting office in accordance with section 10901 (relating to appointment, removal and prohibition).

§ 10906. Bond to be given by officers and agents.

(a) Bond.—In addition to the requirements for bonding that may be imposed by this chapter or any other law, council may require from each elected or appointed officer and agent of the city a lawful bond with corporate surety for the faithful performance of his or her duties.

(b) Requirement.—An officer or agent required by law or ordinance to give bond may not be sworn into office or enter upon the duties of office until the bond has been approved by the proper authority.

§ 10907. Surety bonds, insurance and premiums.

(a) Bonds.—Unless otherwise provided by this chapter or any other provision of law, the following shall apply when an elected or appointed officer or employee of a city is required to give a bond:

(1) The bond shall be for the faithful performance of the duties of the elected or appointed officer or employee.

(2) The bond shall be endorsed by a surety or other company that is:

(i) Authorized by law to act as a surety.

(ii) Qualified to do business in this Commonwealth.

(3) The bond of an elected or appointed officer or employee shall be with a corporate surety and not with an individual or personal surety.

(4) The city shall pay the premium on the bond, unless either:

(i) all or a portion of the premium on the bond is to be paid by the Commonwealth or political subdivisions other than the city; or

(ii) provisions are otherwise made in law for payment of the premium on the bond, in which case the city shall pay the unpaid portion of the premium.

(5) The bond shall be approved by the city solicitor.

(6) In addition to any other conditions required by law, the bond shall be in the sum and with conditions as council may direct.

(b) Exception.—Except as may be otherwise provided in section 11402 (relating to bond, insurance and salary), when an elected or appointed officer or employee of a city is required to give a bond for the faithful performance of the officer's or employee's duties, in lieu of the bond council may:

(1) Purchase one or more blanket bonds for elected or appointed officers or employees.

(2) Purchase insurance provided that the insurance covers the same events of loss and insures the city against the same misconduct as the bond required under this chapter.

(c) Insurance.—In addition to a bond required by this chapter or insurance in lieu of the bond, council may require insurance in accordance with the following:

(1) A city officer or employee who as part of their official duties handle money or have money in their possession may be required to be covered by adequate insurance which provides the types of protection against loss as may be designated by council.

(2) Council may require the insurance to include protection against loss through robbery, burglary or larceny.

(3) The cost of the insurance shall be paid by the city and the amount of the insurance shall be fixed by council.

§ 10908. Officers not to become surety on bonds given to city and penalty.

(a) Surety.—A city officer or member of council may not become the surety on a bond or obligation given to the city by an agent or contractor for the faithful performance of a trust, agency or contract.

(b) Penalty.—An individual violating a provision of this section commits a misdemeanor and shall, upon conviction, be:

(1) Subject to forfeiting office in accordance with section 10901 (relating to appointment, removal and prohibition).

(2) Sentenced to pay a fine of not more than $100.

§ 10909. Money and accounts to be delivered by officer to successor.

(a) Delivered.—All money, accounts, property, documents or effects belonging to the city in the possession of an officer of the city shall be either:

(1) returned to the city upon the officer's termination of office; or

(2) delivered to the officer's qualified successor.

(b) Violation.—An individual violating the provisions of this section shall be subject to prosecution in accordance with the applicable provisions of 18 Pa.C.S. (relating to crimes and offenses).

(c) Limitation.—Nothing set forth in this section may limit any other remedies at law or in equity available to the city.

§ 10916. Pennsylvania municipal league and other municipal affairs organizations.

(a) Unification.—A city may:

(1) unite with:

(i) one or more city;

(ii) cities of two or more classes; and

(iii) one or more municipality;

(2) form and organize a league of cities and municipalities; and

(3) hold annual conventions for the study and consideration of municipal affairs of concern that pertain to the cities and municipalities comprising the league.

(b) Delegates.—A city that is a member of the league may do the following:

(1) Send delegates to the league.

(2) Pay the necessary expenses, including:

(i) Incidental expenses to attend the annual convention.

(ii) Dues to the league.

(iii) Appropriate money to join and participate in any of the various business and training programs of the league designed to address municipal needs in a cost-efficient manner.

(3) Provide a fund for the necessary costs and expenses of the league and league conventions.

(c) Accounting.—Each delegate shall submit to the city controller for approval an itemized account of the delegate's expenses to be paid under the authority of this section.

(d) Appropriation.—Council is authorized to appropriate money for support of and participation in other organizations at the national and State level concerned with municipal affairs.

§ 10917. Powers of subpoena and compelling testimony.

(a) Applicability.—This section shall apply to any of the following which are specifically empowered to conduct hearings and investigations:

(1) an officer or official of the city; or

(2) a city agency created or authorized to be created by this part.

(b) Issuance.—For the purposes of a hearing or investigation, the officer, official or city agency under subsection (a) shall have the authority to issue subpoenas for the following:

(1) attendance and giving of testimony by witnesses as are subject to the subpoenas of the courts of record of this Commonwealth; and

(2) as duces tecum as to the witnesses.

(c) Format.—In the case of a city agency, the subpoenas shall be issued in the name of the city and of the agency upon the signature of the presiding officer of the city and the official seal, if any, of the agency.

(d) Service.—Subpoenas shall be served by an individual 18 years of age or older as directed by the city or city agency, in accordance with the Rules of Civil Procedure, and return of service shall be filed in accordance with law and applicable rules of court.

(e) Enforcement.—Subpoenas issued by an officer or official of the city or a city agency shall be enforced in the same manner, and violations of a subpoena shall be subject to the same penalties, as provided by general law for subpoenas of the courts of common pleas of the Commonwealth.

§ 10918. Consolidation or integration of fire and police personnel prohibited.

A city may not consolidate, integrate or reorganize the paid members of the fire force and the paid members of the police force into one bureau or organization.

CHAPTER 110
COUNCIL

Subchapter

SUBCHAPTER A
GENERAL PROVISIONS

Sec.

---

§ 11001. Qualifications of council members.

(a) Requirements.—A council member shall:

(1) Be at least 18 years of age.

(2) Be elected by the electors at large, subject to the creation of wards pursuant to Chapter 104 (relating to creation and division of wards).

(b) Residency.—

(1) A council member shall reside in the city from which elected and shall have resided in the city continuously for at least one year before their election.

(2) Prior to being sworn into office and as a condition to qualifying for office, each elected council member shall present a signed affidavit to the city clerk that either:

(i) states the individual resides in the city and has resided in the city continuously for at least one year preceding the individual's election; or

(ii) in the case of election to a ward office, states the individual resides in the ward from which elected and has resided in the ward continuously for at least one year preceding the individual's election.

(c) Incompatible offices.—The following individuals may not serve as a council member while continuing to hold the incompatible office or employment, except as provided in this chapter:

(1) An officer of the United States or of the Commonwealth, except notaries public or officers of the militia.

(2) A county officer.

(3) An officer of a school district located in the city.

(4) An officer or employee of the city or of a department of the city.

§ 11002. Vesting of legislative power.

The legislative power of every city shall be vested in a council composed of the mayor and council members.

§ 11003. Organization of council.

(a) Organization.—On the first Monday of the January following the regular municipal election, the members of council shall assemble at the usual place of meeting for the purpose of organizing.

(b) Holiday.—If the first Monday is a legal holiday, the meeting shall be held the first day following.

(c) Mayor.—The mayor shall:

(1) Be the president of council.

(2) Be a member of council.

(3) Have the same rights and duties, including introducing bills and making motions, as pertain to other council members.

(d) Vice president.—Unless otherwise provided by ordinance in accordance with section 11101 (relating to executive departments), the vice president of council shall either be:

(1) the member of council designated as the director of the department of accounts and finance; or

(2) the member of council appointed by council as its vice president, if the member of council is not the director of the department of accounts and finance.

§ 11004. Oath of council members, quorum and rules.

(a) Oath.—The members of council shall take the oath of office provided for in section 10905 (relating to oath of office, violation of oath and penalty).

(b) Quorum.—

(1) A majority of the number of members of council shall constitute a quorum.

(2) A smaller number may compel the attendance of absent members, under penalties to be prescribed by ordinance.

(3) Only members physically present at a meeting place within the city shall be counted in establishing a quorum.

(c) Rules.—In accordance with law, council may determine and adopt rules for procedure and conduct of business.

§ 11005. Meetings of council, notice and participation by telecommunication device.

(a) Meetings.—

(1) Council shall hold stated meetings at least once each month, and at other times as may be fixed by ordinance, and continue them so long as the transaction of the public business demands.

(2) Special meetings must be held in accordance with the following:

(i) The mayor, as president of council, may call special meetings of council.

(ii) A special meeting of council shall be called by the mayor upon the request of:

(A) Two council members in the case of a five-member council; or

(B) three council members in the case of a seven-member council.

(iii) In addition to any notice required by 65 Pa.C.S. Ch. 7 (relating to open meetings), 24-hour notice of a special meeting shall be given to each member.

Table of Contents
Part I Ch. 1–3 Ethics, Records, Open Meetings
Part II Ch. 4–10 Taxation
Part III Ch. 11–18 Torts, Contracts & Civil Rules
Part IV Ch. 19–24 Zoning & Planning
Part V Ch. 25–30 Construction and Emergency Codes
Part VI Ch. 31–39 Municipal Codes
Index

(iv) A special meeting can be a special purpose meeting or a general purpose meeting, as advertised.

(v) Notice of a special meeting shall state the nature of the business to be conducted at the meeting.

(b) **Telecommunication.**—Council may provide for the participation of council members in meetings of council by means of telecommunication devices, including telephones or computer terminals which permit audio communication, between locations if:

(1) A quorum under section 11004 (relating to oath of council members, quorum and rules) is established at the convening or reconvening of the meeting. If after the convening or reconvening of the meeting a member has been disqualified from voting as a matter of law but is still physically present, council members participating by telecommunication device in accordance with this section shall be counted to maintain a quorum.

(2) The telecommunication device used permits the member or members of council not physically present at the meeting to:

(i) speak to and hear the comments and votes, if any, of the members of council who are physically present as well as other members of council who may not be physically present and who are also using a telecommunication device to participate in the meeting; and

(ii) speak to and hear the comments of the public who are physically present at the meeting.

(3) The telecommunication device used permits members of council and the members of the public who are physically present at the meeting to speak to and hear the comments and votes, if any, of the member or members of council who are not physically present at the meeting.

(4) Council may only authorize participation by telecommunication device for any of the following reasons for physical absence:

(i) Illness or disability of the member of council.

(ii) Care for the ill or newborn in the member's immediate family.

(iii) Emergency.

(iv) Family or business travel.

(5) Nothing in this subsection may be construed to limit the protection and prohibition contained in any law or regulation relating to the rights of the disabled.

(c) **Public access.**—All meetings of council, whether regular or special, shall be open to the public.

(d) **Previous councils.**—Council shall be a continuous body and it shall be lawful for a council to complete unfinished business or legislation begun by the preceding council.

§ 11015. Attendance of witnesses and production of books before council or committee of council.

(a) **Subpoenas.**—Council may compel the attendance of witnesses and the production of books, papers and other evidence at a meeting of the body or a committee of council. A subpoena signed by the mayor or the chairperson of the committee may be issued in a pending case of inquiry or investigation. The subpoena may be served and executed in this Commonwealth.

(b) **Oaths.**—A member of council and the city clerk shall have power to administer oaths to the witnesses.

(c) **Refusal.**—

(1) If a witness refuses to testify as to a fact within the witness' knowledge, or to produce a book or paper within the witness' possession or under the witness' control required to be used as evidence in the case, the city clerk shall report the facts relating to the refusal to the court of common pleas. The court:

(i) May hear new evidence which may be offered on behalf of or against the witness.

(ii) Shall hear all questions arising from the refusal and new evidence not included in the clerk's report.

(2) If the court determines that the testimony or evidence required by the witness is legal, properly competent and ought to be given or produced by the witness, the court shall order the witness to testify or produce books or papers, or both, as the case may be.

(3) If the witness refuses to testify or to produce the books or papers, the court shall have power to hold the witness for contempt.

(d) Penalties and reimbursement.—An individual called as a witness and examined under oath shall be liable to indictment, conviction and punishment for perjury as if the witness had been called and examined before a committee of the General Assembly or in a judicial proceeding before a court of record, in accordance with existing laws. An individual outside of the city subpoenaed under this section, shall be entitled to:

(1) Be reimbursed for mileage to and from the city at the maximum mileage rate periodically established by the United States Internal Revenue Service.

(2) A per diem allowance as established by council for the individual's time in the city.

§ 11016. Salaries.

(a) Salary.—Except as provided in subsection (b), a council member shall receive an annual salary for the member's service during the member's term. The salary shall be fixed by ordinance and payable in regular installments. Council may, by an ordinance fixing the salaries, provide for the assessment and retention from the salaries of reasonable fines for absence from regular or special meetings of council or committees of council.

(b) Compensation.—As an alternative to the annual salary method in subsection (a), council may provide that a member of council will receive compensation, based on attendance, on a per-meeting basis. The compensation shall only be payable for duly advertised public meetings in which a council member participated. If council has provided that members of council will receive compensation on a per-meeting basis, council may provide for the forfeiture of up to 1/12th of the annual compensation of a council member or impose another appropriate penalty for each unexcused absence from a regularly scheduled meeting.

(c) Range.—The salary paid to a council member shall be in accordance with the following:

(1) Until changed by ordinance, for the term of council members in newly created cities, each council member may receive a salary as follows:

(i) Not more than $1,875 per year in cities having a population of less than 5,000.

(ii) Not more than $2,500 per year in cities having a population of 5,000 or more but less than 10,000.

(iii) Not more than $3,250 per year in cities having a population of 10,000 or more but less than 15,000.

(iv) Not more than $4,125 per year in cities having a population of 15,000 or more but less than 25,000.

(v) Not more than $4,375 per year in cities having a population of 25,000 or more but less than 35,000.

(vi) Not more than $5,000 per year in cities having a population of 35,000 or more.

(2) The compensation to be received by council members and elected officials in cities other than newly created cities shall be fixed by ordinance of council finally enacted at least two days prior to the last day fixed by law for candidates to withdraw their names from nominating petitions.

§ 11016.1. Appointment of city clerk.

(a) Appointment.—Council shall appoint a city clerk, whose compensation shall be fixed by ordinance, who meets all the following criteria:

(1) Is an at-will employee.

(2) Has no property interest in the city clerk's position.

(b) Powers and duties.—Council may, by ordinance or resolution, prescribe duties of the city clerk in addition to those established by law. The city clerk shall have the power of a notary public to administer oaths in any matter pertaining to the business of the city or in a legal proceeding in which the city is interested.

(c) Custody.—The records of council shall be in the actual or constructive custody of the city clerk and shall be subject to inspection and copying in accordance with the act of February 14, 2008 (P.L.6, No.3), known as the Right-to-Know Law.

SUBCHAPTER A.1
ORDINANCES

Sec.

---

§ 11018.1. Ordinances and resolutions.

(a) Ordinances.—With regard to ordinances, the following shall apply:

(1) Council shall enact ordinances as may be necessary to carry out the requirements of this part and impose fines and penalties for the violation of the ordinances, recoverable in the manner provided in this part and subject to limitations as to the amount of the fines and penalties.

(2) Every legislative act of council shall be by ordinance and the legislative acts shall include:

(i) Certain tax ordinances.

(ii) General appropriation ordinances.

(iii) All ordinances that:

(A) Exercise the police power of the city.

(B) Regulate land use, development and subdivision.

(C) Impose building, plumbing, electrical, property maintenance, housing and similar standards.

(D) Otherwise regulate the conduct of persons within the city.

(iv) Imposition of penalties for the violation of ordinances.

(3) A proposed ordinance may be introduced by a council member and council may require that the introduction of a proposed ordinance by a council member be by motion.

(b) **Resolutions.**—With regard to resolutions, the following shall apply:

(1) Council shall adopt resolutions in accordance with the provisions of this part.

(2) The purposes for which resolutions may be adopted shall include, but not be limited to, the following:

(i) Ceremonial or congratulatory expressions of the goodwill of council.

(ii) Statements of public policy of council.

(iii) Approval of formal agreements of the city, except when an agreement arises under a previously approved purchasing system of the city.

(iv) Approval of the acquisition, disposition and leasing of real property.

(v) Approval of administrative rules and regulations arising under State statutes or city ordinances.

(vi) Annual tax millage rate in accordance with section 12531 (relating to tax levies).

(3) When eminent domain proceedings are instituted by resolution, notice of the resolution, including a description of the subject properties, must be published once in a newspaper of general circulation not more than 60 days nor fewer than seven days prior to adoption.

§ 11018.2. Voting, no veto and vote necessary to enact ordinances or adopt resolutions.

(a) **Voting generally.**—Members of council present or participating via a telecommunication device shall vote on each question before council, except:

(1) As may be required by the provisions of a public official ethics law which may be applicable to members of council.

(2) As may be excused by a simple majority vote of the members of council present at a council meeting, for cause, which shall be entered in the journal, as may be deemed appropriate.

(b) **Veto.**—The mayor shall have no right of veto.

(c) **Majority vote.**—Except as otherwise provided in this part, an ordinance may not be enacted and a resolution may not be adopted by council without an affirmative vote of a majority of the number of the members of council.

§ 11018.3. Journal of proceedings, recording and withholding of vote.

(a) **Journal.**—Council shall keep a journal of the proceedings. The journal shall be in the possession of the city clerk and shall, at all times, be open to public inspection.

(b) **Recording.**—For every vote, the yeas and nays shall be called and recorded by the city clerk. An ordinance shall and a resolution may be reduced to writing before the vote is taken on the ordinance or resolution. A resolution pertaining to tax levies shall be reduced to writing before the vote is taken.

(c) **Withholding.**—A member of council shall not withhold the member's vote on a question before council, unless permitted to do so in accordance with section 11018.2(a) (relating to voting, no veto and vote necessary to enact ordinances or adopt resolutions).

§ 11018.4. Signing and attesting ordinances.

A legislative act of council shall be by ordinance. An ordinance enacted by council shall be signed by the mayor and attested by the city clerk.

§ 11018.5. Proposed ordinances and titles.

(a) **Format.**—A proposed ordinance shall be presented to council in written form as a bill and shall be numbered sequentially for the calendar year.

(b) **Single subject.**—An ordinance, except for a general appropriation ordinance, may not be enacted containing more than one subject, which shall be reasonably identified in the title.

(c) **Original purpose.**—An ordinance may not be altered or amended upon enactment by council as to change the original purpose.

(d) **Title.**—The title of an ordinance shall not be considered in the construction or interpretation of the ordinance by a court of competent jurisdiction.

§ 11018.6. Reading of proposed ordinances and final enactment.

(a) **Reading.**—The title of every proposed ordinance shall be read at least twice, once when introduced and again before final enactment by council. Amendments or other changes to the proposed ordinance shall be read in their entirety.

(b) **Public availability.**—A complete copy of every ordinance introduced shall be available for public inspection at the city clerk's office during regular office hours.

(c) **Time frame.**—An ordinance may not be finally enacted by council the same day it was introduced. At least three days shall intervene between the ordinance's introduction and final enactment by council.

(d) **Numbering.**—Upon enactment, ordinances shall be numbered sequentially.

§ 11018.7. Payments not authorized by law.

An ordinance may not be enacted and a resolution may not be adopted providing for the payment of money by the city without previous authority of law. An officer executing a document authorizing payment, making a payment or passing a voucher for a payment not authorized by law commits a misdemeanor. The officer shall, upon conviction, be sentenced to pay a fine of not more than $5,000 and to imprisonment for not more than one year.

§ 11018.8. Time of taking effect of ordinances.

Unless otherwise provided by law, an ordinance, except those pertaining to the subjects set forth in section 11050(b) (relating to time ordinances go into effect), shall take effect after:

(1) The tenth day after enactment.

(2) Being signed by the mayor.

(3) Being attested by the city clerk.

§ 11018.9. Publication of proposed ordinances.

(a) **Publication required.**—A proposed ordinance, except as otherwise provided in this chapter, shall be published in a newspaper of general circulation not more than 60 days nor fewer than seven days prior to enactment.

(b) **Contents.**—

(1) Except as otherwise provided by law, the publication of a proposed ordinance shall include either:

(i) the full text; or

(ii) the title and a summary of the ordinance setting forth the provisions in reasonable detail and a reference to a place within the city where copies of the proposed ordinance may be examined.

(2) If the full text is not published, the newspaper in which the proposed ordinance is published shall be furnished a copy of the ordinance, upon request.

(c) Readvertisement.—In the event substantial amendments are made in the proposed ordinance, before voting upon enactment council shall, within 10 days, readvertise in one newspaper of general circulation a brief summary setting forth all provisions and amendments in reasonable detail.

§ 11018.10. Filing of proposed ordinances.

(a) Place of filing.—If the full text is not published, an attested copy of the proposed ordinance shall be filed when the summary of the ordinance is published in the county law library or other county office designated by the county commissioners. The county commissioners may impose a fee no greater than necessary to cover the actual costs of storing the proposed ordinances. Filing with the county may be completed by the submission of an electronic copy of the ordinance through a method available, in the sole discretion of the county, to permit receipt by the office storing municipal ordinances. Upon request by the city, the county shall notify the city of the method by which electronic copies may be submitted. The county may store the ordinance electronically, provided that the public is able to access the electronically stored city ordinances during regular business hours at the office or at a remote location. The city shall retain a printed copy of the e-mail and ordinance as transmitted.

(b) Date of filing.—The date of filing the proposed ordinance with the county shall not affect the effective date of the ordinance or the validity of the process of enactment of the ordinance.

§ 11018.11. Records of ordinances maintained by city clerk.

(a) Records.—Within Within one month after enactment, each ordinance shall be certified and recorded by the city clerk in a book provided by the city which shall, at all times, be open to the inspection of the public. Within one month after adoption, each resolution pertaining to a tax levy shall be certified and recorded by the city clerk in a book provided by the city which shall, at all times, be open to the inspection of the public. A standard or nationally recognized code or a portion of the standard or nationally recognized code enacted by reference need not be recorded in or attached to the ordinance book but shall be deemed to have been legally recorded if the ordinance by which the code was enacted by reference is recorded, with an accompanying notation stating where the full text of the code is filed. A failure to record within the time provided shall not be deemed a defect in the process of the enactment or adoption of the ordinance or of the resolution that pertains to a tax levy.

(b) Compilation or codification.—At the close of each year, with the advice and assistance of the city solicitor, the city clerk shall bind, compile or codify all the ordinances or recorded resolutions of the city, or true copies of the ordinances or recorded resolutions, which remain in force and effect.

(c) Indexing.—The city clerk shall also properly index the record books, compilation or codification of ordinances or resolutions.

(d) Retention.—The retention of ordinances and recorded resolutions shall be in accordance with 53 Pa.C.S. Ch. 13 Subch. F (relating to records).

(e) Attachment.—A city ordinance or portion of a city ordinance which prior to June 6, 1963, is attached to the city ordinance book shall be considered in force as if the ordinance or portions of the ordinance were recorded directly upon the pages of the ordinance book.

§ 11018.12. Proof and evidence.

(a) Proof.—An ordinance, resolution, motion or other proceeding of council may be proved by the certificate of the city clerk under the corporate seal.

(b) Evidence.—When an ordinance, resolution, motion or proceeding of council is printed or published in book or pamphlet form by authority of the city, it shall be read and received as evidence in all courts and elsewhere without further proof.

§ 11018.13. Standard or nationally recognized codes.

(a) Authority to enact.—In the same manner as other ordinances, and except as otherwise provided in this chapter or the Pennsylvania Construction Code Act, council may enact, by reference to a standard or nationally recognized code, all or a portion of the standard or nationally recognized code as an ordinance of the city. Three copies of the proposed standard or nationally recognized code, portion of the code or amendment to the code shall be filed in the office of the city clerk at least 10 days before council considers the proposed ordinance. Upon enactment, a copy shall be kept with the ordinance book and available for public use, inspection and examination.

(b) Time frame.—

(1) Except as otherwise provided by the Pennsylvania Construction Code Act and regulations adopted pursuant to the act, an ordinance adopting, by reference, a standard or nationally recognized code shall be enacted within 60 days after introduction and shall encompass subsequent changes in the code unless otherwise specified in the ordinance.

(2) An ordinance which incorporates standard or nationally recognized code amendments by reference shall become effective after the same procedure and in the same manner as is specified in this section for original adoption of the code.

(c) Technical regulations or code.—An ordinance that incorporates, by reference, standard technical regulations or code shall be subject to the provisions of the Pennsylvania Construction Code Act, if applicable.

§ 11018.14. Maps, plans or drawings.

(a) Adoption.—Except as otherwise provided under the Municipalities Planning Code, if maps, plans or drawings are to be adopted as part of an ordinance, council, instead of publishing the maps, plans or drawings as part of the ordinance may make reference in publishing the ordinance or a summary of the ordinance, the location where the maps, plans or drawings are on file and may be examined.

(b) Amending.—Once enacted as part of an ordinance, a map, plan or drawing shall be amended by ordinance.

§ 11018.15. Codification of ordinances.

(a) Preparation authorized.—Council may prepare a consolidation or codification of the general body of city ordinances or the ordinances on a particular subject. Council may adopt the consolidation or codification as an ordinance of the city in the same manner prescribed for the adoption of an ordinance, except as follows:

(1) A consolidation or codification to be enacted as a single ordinance shall be introduced in council at least 30 days before its final enactment. At least 15 days before final enactment, notice of introduction of the consolidation or codification specifying the general nature and content shall be given, by advertisement, in a newspaper of general circulation.

(2) The required advertised notice of the proposed adoption of the consolidation or codification shall include:

(i) A listing of the table of contents.

(ii) A place within the city where a copy of the proposed consolidation or codification may be examined.

(b) Additional procedure.—The procedure for the consolidation or codification of city ordinances as a single ordinance may also be followed in enacting a complete group or body of ordinances repealing or amending existing ordinances as may be necessary in the course of preparing a consolidation or codification of the city ordinances. The advertisement giving notice of the proposed adoption shall list, in lieu of a table of contents, only the titles of each of the ordinances in the complete group or body of ordinances.

(c) Adoption by reference.—The consolidation or codification may contain provisions which will operate to adopt, by reference, a building, fire prevention or other standard or model code or zoning ordinance and zoning map in accordance with section 11018.13 (relating to standard or nationally recognized codes) and, if applicable, section 11018.14 (relating to maps, plans or drawings).

§ 11018.16. Enforcement of ordinances, recovery and payment of fines and penalties.

(a) Enforcement.—An action, prosecution, complaint or proceeding for the violation of an ordinance of the city and for the fine, penalty and forfeiture imposed shall be instituted in the corporate name of the city and be conducted in the manner prescribed by law.

(b) Proceedings.—Unless otherwise provided by law, a proceeding for the violation of the ordinances of the city shall be conducted as a summary conviction proceeding, or a proceeding for the recovery of penalties, before a magisterial district judge with the same right of appeal from a final judgment entered.

§ 11018.17. Penalty.

A person who violates an ordinance enacted under the authority of this chapter for which no penalty is specified commits a summary offense and upon conviction shall be sentenced to pay a fine of not more than $1,000 or to imprisonment for not more than 90 days, or both.

SUBCHAPTER B
INITIATING ORDINANCES BY ELECTORS

Sec.

---

§ 11030. Initiation of proposed ordinances by petition and exceptions.

(a) Submission.—Except as provided in subsection (b), a proposed ordinance may be submitted to council by a petition signed by the electors of a city in accordance with this subchapter.

(b) Exclusions.—The following proposed ordinances may not be submitted by petition to council in accordance with this subchapter:

Table of Contents
Part I Ch. 1–3 Ethics, Records, Open Meetings
Part II Ch. 4–10 Taxation
Part III Ch. 11–18 Torts, Contracts & Civil Rules
Part IV Ch. 19–24 Zoning & Planning
Part V Ch. 25–30 Construction and Emergency Codes
Part VI Ch. 31–39 Municipal Codes
Index

Chap. 39 Res. During Mil. Service
Chap. 38 Intergov. Coop.
Chap. 37 3rd Class City Code
Chap. 36 Bor. Code
Chap. 35 2nd Class Twp. Code
Chap. 34 1st Class Twp. Code
Chap. 33 Home Rule Chart. Opt. Plans Law
Chap. 32 Water Serv. Act
Chap. 31 Munic. Auth. Act

(1) Proposed ordinances dealing with the subjects set forth in section 11050(b) (relating to time ordinances go into effect).

(2) Proposed ordinances to repeal, amend or modify an ordinance which took effect after having been subject to the provisions of the referendum for reconsideration of the ordinance.

§ 11031. Petition and notice.

If the city clerk receives a written request for the preparation of a petition for the submission of a proposed ordinance to council by at least 100 qualified electors of the city and the request is accompanied by a copy of the proposed ordinance, within 10 days of receipt the city clerk shall do each of the following:

(1) Prepare the requested petition.

(2) Publish notice at least once in a newspaper of general circulation that provides at least the following information:

(i) The date on which the request for the petition was received and that the petition will be ready for signing at the expiration of 10 days from that date.

(ii) The purpose for which the petition is made.

(iii) The place at which and the dates and times during which the petition may be signed, with 15 business days being allowed for signatures.

§ 11032. Signing and oath.

(a) Petition.—A petition for the submission of a proposed ordinance shall be signed in the city clerk's office. The petition shall be retained in the city clerk's office at all times for a period of 15 days. Each signer shall:

(1) Add to the signer's signature the signer's address.

(2) Make oath before the city clerk that the signer is a qualified elector of the city and resides at the address given.

(b) Hours.—The city clerk shall keep the city clerk's office open, at a minimum, from 9 a.m. through 7 p.m. Monday through Friday, except holidays, for the purpose of permitting electors to sign the petition. The city clerk shall not permit an individual to sign the petition after 7 p.m. on the last day for signing the petition.

§ 11033. Number of signatures, examination and certificate by city clerk.

(a) Signatures.—Within 10 days after the period of time for signing the petition has elapsed, the city clerk shall:

(1) Examine the petition.

(2) Ascertain whether or not the petition is signed by electors of the city, equal in number to at least 20% of the entire votes cast by registered electors for all candidates for mayor at the last preceding municipal election at which a mayor was elected.

(b) Employees.—If necessary, council may allow the city clerk additional help for the purpose of complying with this section.

(c) Results.—The city clerk shall attach to the petition the clerk's certificate showing the result of the examination.

(d) Failure.—If less than the required 20% under subsection (a)(2) is certified, the petition shall fail and shall be filed in the office of the city clerk.

§ 11034. Submission to council.

If the petition is certified to contain signatures as required in section 11033(a)(2) (relating to number of signatures, examination and certificate by city clerk), the city clerk shall submit the petition to council without delay.

§ 11035. Actions by council and notices.

If the petition accompanying the proposed ordinance is signed by electors of the city as required in section 11033(a)(2) (relating to number of signatures, examination and certificate by city clerk), council shall do one of the following:

(1) Enact the proposed ordinance without alteration within 20 days, except as otherwise provided in this chapter, after attachment of the city clerk's certificate to the accompanying petition.

(2) Call for a referendum to be held at the time of the next general, municipal or primary election occurring at least 90 days thereafter, at which election the proposed ordinance must be submitted, without alteration, to the electors of the city for a vote, after attachment of the city clerk's certificate to the accompanying petition. Notice of the election and the text of the question to be submitted to the electors shall be published in the same manner as publication is required in section 1201 of the Pennsylvania Election Code.

§ 11036. Form of ballot on submission to vote.

The question to be submitted to the electors on the proposed ordinance shall be framed to state the nature of the proposed ordinance, followed by the words "yes" and "no". The question shall be placed on the ballot which shall be counted, returned and computed in accordance with section 11062 (relating to computing and filing returns) and the election laws of the Commonwealth.

§ 11037. Effect of majority vote.

If the majority of the qualified electors voting on the proposed ordinance vote in favor of the ordinance, the ordinance shall become a valid and binding ordinance of the city.

§ 11038. No repeal within two years.

An ordinance proposed by petition, whether enacted by council or adopted by a vote of the electors, shall not be repealed or amended within two years of the effective date except by a vote of the electors.

§ 11039. Number of proposed ordinances to be submitted and elections limited.

Any number of proposed ordinances may be voted upon at the same election, in accordance with the provisions of this subchapter. Proposed ordinances on the same subject matter shall not be submitted by petition more frequently than once every three years.

§ 11040. Submission for repeal by council.

Council may submit a proposition for the repeal or amendment of an ordinance to be voted upon at a succeeding municipal, general or primary election occurring at least 90 days after council's submission of the proposition. Should the submitted proposition receive a majority of the votes cast on the proposition at the election, the ordinance shall be repealed or amended accordingly.

§ 11041. Publication of proposed ordinance, repeal or amendment.

Whenever a proposed ordinance is to be submitted to the electors of the city at an election or an ordinance is submitted by council for repeal or amendment, notice of the election and text of the question to be submitted to the electors shall be published in the same manner as publication is required in section 1201 of the Pennsylvania Election Code.

SUBCHAPTER C

RECONSIDERING ORDINANCES BY ELECTORS

§ 11050. Time ordinances go into effect.

(a) **Timing.**—Except as provided in subsection (b), an ordinance enacted by council may not go into effect before 10 days from the time of the ordinance's final enactment by council.

(b) **Immediate enactment.**—The following may be made effective upon final enactment:

(1) An ordinance:

(i) Expressly required to be enacted by the general laws of the Commonwealth.

(ii) Expressly required to be enacted by the provisions of any act of the General Assembly.

(iii) That contains provisions and matters which are subject to the approval of an officer or tribunal of the Commonwealth.

(2) An ordinance or resolution where permitted providing for any of the following:

(i) Tax levies or fees.

(ii) Annual and other appropriations.

(iii) The exercise of the right of eminent domain.

(3) An ordinance providing for any of the following:

(i) The preservation of the public peace, health, morals and safety.

(ii) The exercise of the police powers of the city government.

(iii) The prevention and abatement of nuisances.

(4) An ordinance providing for an election to increase indebtedness and any other ordinance which by law must be submitted to an election before it shall take effect.

(5) An ordinance providing for the opening, paving, grading or other improvement of streets or highways if the improvement is petitioned for by a majority, in number or interest, of the abutting property owners.

(6) An ordinance providing for either:

(i) the construction of sewers; or

(ii) streets, highways and sidewalks to be kept in:

(A) Good order and repair.

(B) In a safe and passable condition.

§ 11051. Petition and reconsideration of ordinance.

With the exception of an ordinance dealing with the subjects set forth in section 11050(b) (relating to time ordinances go into effect), an ordinance shall be suspended from going into operation and shall be reconsidered by council if all of the following occur:

(1) A petition is presented to council:

(i) within 10 days after the ordinance's final enactment;

(ii) in accordance with this subchapter; and

(iii) which protests against enactment of the ordinance.

(2) The petition must be signed by electors as required in section 11033(a)(2) (relating to number of signatures, examination and certificate by city clerk).

§ 11052. Preparation of petition by city clerk and notice.

(a) Petition.—A petition under section 11051 (relating to petition and reconsideration of ordinance) shall be prepared by the city clerk immediately upon receipt by the clerk of the written request of 100 qualified electors of the city asking that the petition be prepared. Upon preparation of the petition, the clerk shall give notice by publication in a newspaper of general circulation:

(1) That the petition is ready for signing.

(2) The purpose of the petition.

(3) The place and time when the petition may be signed.

(b) Signing.—The signing shall be done only in the city clerk's office where the petition shall be retained during the period of 10 days after the enactment of the ordinance.

§ 11053. Additional petitions.

(a) Petitions.—In order to facilitate the signing of the petition, the city clerk shall make at least two additional similar petitions for signing by the qualified electors. Signing an additional similar petition shall have the same force and effect as signing the original petition. The city clerk is authorized to employ at least two individuals to take charge of the additional petitions.

(b) Employees.—The city clerk and employees hired under this section are empowered to administer the oath required to be taken by the electors. This section also shall apply to petitions initiating ordinances under Subchapter B (relating to initiating ordinances by electors).

§ 11054. Signatures, oath and time of signing.

(a) Signers.—Each signer of a petition under section 11051 (relating to petition and reconsideration of ordinance) shall also do all the following:

(1) Include the signer's address.

(2) Make an oath before the city clerk or other person authorized under section 11053 (relating to additional petitions) that the signer:

(i) Is a qualified elector of the city.

(ii) Resides at the address given.

(b) Office hours.—The city clerk shall keep the city clerk's office open, at a minimum, from 9 a.m. through 7 p.m. Monday through Friday, except holidays, for the purpose of receiving signatures to the petitions. The city clerk shall not permit an individual to sign a petition after 7 p.m. of the tenth day following the enactment of the ordinance on which the referendum vote is requested.

§ 11055. Presentation of petition to council.

At the expiration of 10 days, the petition shall be filed with council and presented by the city clerk at council's next meeting.

§ 11056. Ascertainment of number of signers and report.

After presentation of the petition to council, the city clerk shall ascertain whether or not the referendum petition is signed by a number of registered electors equal to 20% of all the votes cast for all candidates for mayor at the last preceding municipal election at which a mayor was elected. Council may allow the clerk additional help for that purpose. After the clerk has made the examination, the clerk shall report the result to council.

§ 11059. Effect of petition and submission to electors.

(a) Petition lacking signatures.—If it appears that the petition under this subchapter has not been signed by the required number of electors, no action shall be taken. The ordinance shall be taken to be in full force from the time or times it would have gone into effect had there been no petition against the ordinance.

(b) Reconsideration.—Council must reconsider an ordinance if the petition is signed by a number of electors equal to 20% of all the votes cast for mayor. If the ordinance is not entirely repealed by council on reconsideration, council must call a referendum to be held at the time of the next general, municipal or primary election occurring at least 60 days after the reconsideration.

(c) Submission.—At the election, the ordinance shall be submitted without alteration in accordance with the Pennsylvania Election Code.

§ 11060. Certification to county board of elections, ballots or ballot labels and expense of elections.

(a) Certification.—The city clerk, after consultation with the city solicitor, shall certify to the county board of elections a copy of the ordinance and the proceedings of council directing the referendum vote. The county board of elections shall cause the question to be printed for use in the election districts of the city.

(b) Preparation.—The preparation of ballots or ballot labels for and the holding of a referendum shall be conducted in the manner as provided in the Pennsylvania Election Code.

(c) Number.—Any number of ordinances may be referred and voted on at the same election.

§ 11061. Form of ballot or ballot label.

The ballot used when voting on the ordinance shall contain a question stating the nature of the referred ordinance followed by the words "yes" and "no" and shall be conducted in the manner as provided in the Pennsylvania Election Code.

§ 11062. Computing and filing returns.

(a) Computing.—An officer holding an election shall keep a tally sheet and make a return of votes on the referendum question in the same manner as a tally sheet is kept and a return is made in an election of officers and the submission of other questions as provided by the Pennsylvania Election Code.

(b) Filing.—A return shall be filed with the county board of elections which shall compute the return and certify the results to council. The return and certification of a referendum question shall be conducted in the manner as provided in the Pennsylvania Election Code.

§ 11063. Effect of the vote.

If a majority of the electors vote in favor of the ordinance, the ordinance shall take effect when the results of the election are certified by council. If a majority of the electors vote against the ordinance, the ordinance shall be nullified.

§ 11064. Publication of ordinance before election.

Before any referendum is held on any ordinance in accordance with this subchapter, the city shall provide notice of the ordinance by publishing a copy of the ordinance in a newspaper of general circulation. Publication in accordance with this section shall be in addition to the publication requirements of the Pennsylvania Election Code.

CHAPTER 111
EXECUTIVE DEPARTMENT

§ 11101. Executive departments.

The city may enact an ordinance establishing departments to implement administrative functions of the city. If the city fails to adopt an ordinance, powers and duties of the city shall be allocated and assigned among the following:

(1) The department of public affairs.

(2) The department of accounts and finance.

(3) The department of public safety.

(4) The department of streets and public improvements.

(5) The department of parks and public property.

§ 11102. Determination of powers and duties of departments.

Council may, by ordinance, do all of the following:

(1) Determine the powers and duties to be performed by each department.

(2) Prescribe the powers and duties of officers and employees.

(3) Assign particular officers and employees, including directors of departments, to one or more of the departments.

(4) Require an officer or employee to perform duties in two or more departments.

(5) Adopt rules and regulations as deemed necessary for the efficient and economical conduct of the business of the city.

§ 11103. Designation of department directors.

(a) Duties of mayor.—

(1) If a department of public affairs is established by ordinance, the mayor shall be director of the department of public affairs.

(2) Regardless of whether or not a department of public affairs is established by ordinance, the mayor shall supervise city police.

(b) Designations.—

Table of Contents
Part I Ch. 1–3 Ethics, Records, Open Meetings
Part II Ch. 4–10 Taxation
Part III Ch. 11–18 Torts, Contracts & Civil Rules
Part IV Ch. 19–24 Zoning & Planning
Part V Ch. 25–30 Construction and Emergency Codes
Part VI Ch. 31–39 Municipal Codes
Index

(1) Council shall, at its organization meeting, designate, by resolution, a council member to be a director of any of the following, if established by ordinance:

(i) The department of accounts and finance.

(ii) The department of public safety.

(iii) The department of streets and public improvements.

(iv) The department of parks and public property.

(2) A designation under paragraph (1) may be changed at council's discretion.

§ 11104. Department directors responsible for city property and supplies and reports.

A department director shall be responsible for the property and supplies of the city within the director's department. The department director shall prepare and maintain a perpetual inventory of the property and supplies for which the department director is responsible and, from time to time during the fiscal year, file the inventory with the city clerk or other official designated by council. The city clerk or other designated official with whom the inventory is filed shall, upon request, transmit a copy of the inventory to the chief fiscal officer and council.

§ 11105. Quarterly reports from department directors.

(a) Report.—At the close of each quarter of the fiscal year, a department director shall prepare and submit to the director of the department of accounts and finance, if a department of accounts and finance is established by ordinance, or to the business administrator or other official designated by council, a comprehensive and detailed report of all expenditures and operations of the director's department during the quarter.

(b) Review.—Not later than the date of the second meeting of council, the director of the department of accounts and finance, if the department of accounts and finance is established by ordinance, or the business administrator or other official designated by council, shall:

(1) review and consolidate the quarterly reports submitted under subsection (a); and

(2) prepare and submit to council a consolidated report on the expenditures and operations of the city government, including recommendations.

CHAPTER 112
MAYOR

Sec.

§ 11201. Qualifications.

The qualifications for office of mayor shall be as follows:

(1) An individual must be at least 18 years of age.

(2) An individual must be elected at large by the qualified electors of the city.

(3) An individual must be a resident of the city where the individual was elected for not less than one year before the date of the individual's election.

(4) Before being sworn into the office of mayor, an individual elected to mayor must present a signed affidavit to the city clerk certifying that the individual is in accordance with the requirement under paragraph (3).

(5) An individual elected to the office of mayor must reside in the city for the duration of the individual's term of service.

§ 11202. Inauguration.

The mayor shall be the chief executive of the city. The mayor shall be inaugurated and take the oath of office in accordance with sections 10904 (relating to offices to be held until qualification of successors) and 10905 (relating to oath of office, violation of oath and penalty) on the first Monday of January after the regular municipal election. If the first Monday is a legal holiday, the mayor shall be inaugurated and take the oath the first day after that day or as soon after that day as possible.

§ 11203. Execution of laws, powers of sheriff conferred and emergency powers.

(a) Execution.—The mayor shall execute and enforce the ordinances of the city and all general laws applicable to the ordinances.

(b) Report.—The mayor shall submit an annual report to council and the public that includes recommendations on ways to improve efficiency of the city government based on the prior fiscal year and any other recommendations the mayor deems to be in the public interest.

(c) Police powers.—In order to enable the mayor to effectively preserve the public peace within the city, all the powers conferred by the law upon sheriffs to prevent and suppress mobs, riots and unlawful and tumultuous assemblies shall be conferred upon the mayor.

(d) Emergency proclamations issuance.—If the mayor determines that a state of emergency exists, the mayor may issue a proclamation in writing declaring a state of emergency. The mayor shall provide notice of the contents of the proclamation to council and to the news media within the city.

(e) Emergency proclamations contents.—Upon the issuance of a proclamation declaring a state of emergency under subsection (d), the following shall apply:

(1) The state of emergency shall not exceed five days, unless extended by council.

(2) In the case of a declaration of a state of emergency by the mayor for a citywide or site-specific emergency, a city department may temporarily implement the department's emergency assignments without complying with procedures required by law pertaining to the incurring of obligations and the employment of temporary workers.

(3) The proclamation may prohibit, for all or any part of the city where there is a clear and present danger to life or property through civil disorder:

(i) an individual from being on public streets, in public parks or at any other public place during the hours declared by the mayor to be a period of curfew;

(ii) the assembling or gathering of a group of individuals, in numbers to be designated by the mayor, upon public streets, parks or other public places;

(iii) the entry or departure of an individual into or from any restricted area;

(iv) the sale, purchase or dispensing of any commodities or goods designated by the mayor;

(v) the transportation, possession or use of gasoline, kerosene or other combustible, flammable or explosive liquids or materials, except in connection with the normal operation of motor vehicles, normal home use or legitimate commercial use; and

(vi) any other activities as the mayor reasonably believes would cause a clear and present danger to the preservation of life, health, property or the public peace.

(f) Time and location.—A proclamation declaring a state of emergency shall describe any restricted area with particularity and specify the hours when the restrictions are to be in effect.

(g) Penalties.—An individual who violates a proclamation declaring a state of emergency commits a summary offense and shall, upon conviction, be sentenced as provided by law.

§ 11204. Official seal of mayor.

Council shall provide an official seal for the mayor in a form, as reasonably requested by the mayor, which shall not be changed during the mayor's term of office.

§ 11205. Supervision of conduct of city officers.

(a) Supervision.—The mayor shall supervise the conduct of all city officers, examine the grounds of all reasonable complaints against them and cause all of their violations or neglect of duty to be promptly punished or reported for correction as council may direct.

(b) Implementation.—In order to implement the provisions of subsection (a), the mayor may issue subpoenas and compulsory processes, under the mayor's official seal, for the attendance of individuals and the production of documentation. A subpoena shall be enforced in the manner as provided for council under section 11015 (relating to attendance of witnesses and production of books before council or committee of council).

§ 11206. City government reports.

The mayor may request a report from a city official or department director containing information pertaining to administrative functions under the control and management of the city official or department director. The mayor may submit a report pertaining to all matters of city government to council as the mayor deems necessary.

§ 11207. Acknowledgments and oaths.

The mayor may take acknowledgments of any instruments in writing pertaining to the business of the city, solemnize marriages and administer oaths and affirmations as to city business and shall attest all the mayor's acts with the mayor's official seal.

§ 11208. Salary.

(a) Payment.—

(1) The mayor shall receive for the mayor's services during the term of service an annual salary to be fixed by ordinance, payable in equal installments as council shall provide.

(2) Council shall, by ordinance, fix the amount of salary to be paid to the mayor for the mayor's services and may provide for the assessment and retention from the salary of reasonable fines for absence from regular or special meetings of council or committees of council.

(3) The amount of the mayor's salary shall be at least $2,500 annually.

(b) Amounts.—Until changed by ordinance, the salary of mayors in newly created cities shall be as follows:

Chap. 39 Res. During Mil. Service
Chap. 38 Intergov. Coop.
Chap. 37 3rd Class City Code
Chap. 36 Bor. Code
Chap. 35 2nd Class Twp. Code
Chap. 34 1st Class Twp. Code
Chap. 33 Home Rule Chart. Opt. Plans Law
Chap. 32 Water Serv. Act
Chap. 31 Munic. Auth. Act

(1) In cities with a population of less than 5,000, a maximum of $2,500 per year.

(2) In cities with a population of 5,000 or more but less than 10,000, a maximum of $5,000 per year.

(3) In cities with a population of 10,000 or more but less than 15,000, a maximum of $7,500 year.

(4) In cities with a population of more than 15,000, a maximum of $500 per every thousand residents per year as determined by the most recent census data provided by the United States Census Bureau.

(c) Administration.—

(1) The salary to be received by a mayor in a city other than a newly created city shall be fixed by ordinance of council enacted not less than two days before the last day fixed by law for candidates to withdraw their names from nominating petitions.

(2) The compensation to be received by the mayor shall not be increased or diminished after the mayor's election unless the increase or decrease was included in an ordinance enacted not less than two days before the last day fixed by law for candidates to withdraw their names from nominating petitions.

(d) Marriage ceremonies.—

(1) Subject to paragraph (2) and notwithstanding any other provisions of law, a mayor may receive a honorarium, fee or reimbursement of expenses related to the performance of a marriage ceremony in this Commonwealth if the mayor first notifies council in writing of the mayor's intention to perform a marriage ceremony. Notice under this paragraph shall remain in effect for the term of the mayor or until the notification is rescinded by the mayor.

(2) The honorarium, fee or reimbursement under paragraph (1) shall not exceed $150 for each ceremony performed. The mayor shall keep accurate accounts of the fees received relating to the performance of marriage ceremonies and submit a quarterly report of money received for that period to council. The quarterly report shall include the amount of money received, the names of individuals from whom money was received and the date and location of the performed ceremony. The quarterly report shall be a public record in accordance with the act of February 14, 2008 (P.L.6, No.3), known as the Right-to-Know Law.

(3) The receipt of a honorarium, fee or reimbursement under this subsection shall not be a violation of 65 Pa.C.S. Ch. 11 (relating to ethics standards and financial disclosure) and shall not be part of a salary received in accordance with this section.

§ 11209. Powers and duties of acting mayor.

(a) Absence or inability to act.—During the absence of the mayor or the inability of the mayor to act, the vice president of council shall be the acting mayor who shall exercise all the rights and powers of the mayor.

(b) Death, resignation or otherwise.—In the event of a vacancy in the office of the mayor by reason of death, resignation or otherwise, the vice president of council shall be the acting mayor. The vice president of council shall receive the salary of mayor as specified under section 11208 (relating to salary), but may not receive a salary as a council member until the successor of the mayor is duly appointed and qualified in accordance with section 10901 (relating to appointment, removal and prohibition).

(c) Acting mayor designation.—During the absence or inability of the vice president of council to act as mayor, council shall designate another one of its members to act as mayor.

CHAPTER 112A

CITY ADMINISTRATOR

---

§ 112A00. Definitions.

The following words and phrases when used in this chapter shall have the meanings given to them in this section unless the context clearly indicates otherwise:

"City administrator." The term includes a city administrator or a city manager.

"Office of city administrator." The term includes an office of a city administrator or an office of a city manager.

§ 112A01. Office of city administrator.

(a) **Establishment.**—Council may enact an ordinance by a majority vote of all the members of council establishing the office of city administrator.

(b) **Abolishment.**—Council may enact an ordinance by a majority vote of all the members of council abolishing the office of city administrator.

§ 112A02. Appointment of city administrator.

(a) **Appointment.**—In a city that has established an office of city administrator, council shall appoint an individual, partnership, limited partnership, an association or professional corporation to be city administrator. The appointment of a city administrator shall be by a majority vote of all the members of council.

(b) **Selection.**—Council shall select a city administrator on the basis of executive and administrative qualifications, education and experience and may give special consideration to applicants with training and experience in municipal government operation. The city administrator shall serve at the pleasure of council, subject to contractual rights that may arise under an employment or professional services agreement that may be entered in accordance with section 112A03 (relating to employment or professional services agreement).

§ 112A03. Employment or professional services agreement.

(a) **Agreement.**—Council may enter into an employment or professional services agreement with the city administrator. The agreement may set forth the terms and conditions of employment. The agreement shall remain in effect for a specified period terminating not later than two years after the effective date of the agreement or the date of the organizational meeting of council after the next municipal election, whichever is earlier.

(b) **Conditions.**—

(1) An agreement under subsection (a) may specify conditions under which a city administrator may be entitled to severance compensation if the city administrator is an individual or payments for the termination of appointment if the city administrator is a partnership, limited partnership, an association or professional corporation.

(2) An agreement under subsection (a) may not guarantee retention or employment through the term of the agreement or confer upon the city administrator any legal remedy based on specific performance.

(3) An agreement under subsection (a), executed on or after a municipal election but before the first meeting in January the year after the municipal election, shall be void.

(c) Status as public official.—The city administrator, if an individual, and, for a partnership, limited partnership, an association or professional corporation appointed as the city administrator, each officer and employee directly providing services as required or authorized by the agreement shall be considered a public official for purposes of the provisions of 65 Pa.C.S. § 1103 (relating to restricted activities).

§ 112A04. Residency and elective city office.

(a) Residence of city administrator who is an individual.—At the time an individual is appointed to fill the office of city administrator, the appointee does not have to be a resident of the city. After appointment, a city administrator who is an individual may reside outside the city only with the approval of council.

(b) Incompatibility.—The city administrator may not hold any elective city office. In the case of a partnership, limited partnership, an association or professional corporation appointed as city administrator, the restriction under this subsection shall apply to all officers and employees who directly provide services as required or authorized by the agreement.

§ 112A05. Powers and duties.

(a) Powers and duties generally.—Council may, by ordinance, vest in the city administrator powers and duties relating to the general management of city business and to the enforcement of city ordinances and regulations. Nothing in this section shall be construed to diminish the powers granted to other city officers by law.

(b) Specific powers.—The powers and duties conferred upon a city administrator by council may include the following:

(1) Appointment as chief administrative officer of the city, responsible to council for the proper and efficient administration of the affairs of the city.

(2) Directing and supervising the administration of all departments and functions of the city, except as otherwise provided by law.

(3) Except as otherwise provided by this chapter, appointing city employees on the basis of merit system principles and suspending, removing or otherwise disciplining employees, in accordance with the following:

(i) The city administrator may make recommendations to council concerning appointments or removals at the department-head level.

(ii) Before taking any action with regard to appointments or removals at the department-head level, the city administrator shall confer with council.

(iii) Council shall confirm appointments or removals at the department-head level.

(4) If the city administrator is an individual, designating a qualified administrative officer of the city to perform the city administrator's duties during the city administrator's temporary absence or disability. In the event the city administrator fails or is unable to make the designation or if the city administrator's absence or disability continues more than 30 days, council may, by resolution, appoint an officer of the city to perform the duties of the city

administrator during the city administrator's absence or disability until the city administrator is able to return to work.

(5) Negotiating contracts for the city, subject to the approval of council, making recommendations concerning the nature and location of municipal improvements and executing municipal improvements as determined by council.

(6) Ensuring that all terms and conditions imposed in favor of the city or its residents in any law, franchise or contract are faithfully kept and performed, and upon knowledge of any violation, informing council.

(7) Attending all meetings of council and participating in discussions with council. Nothing in this paragraph shall be construed to permit the city administrator to vote with council.

(8) Recommending the adoption of measures to council as the city administrator may deem necessary or expedient, keeping council advised of the financial condition of the city and making reports to council as requested by council.

(9) Investigating, at any time, the affairs of any officer or department of the city that is under the city administrator's jurisdiction.

(10) Preparing and submitting the annual city budget for review and approval by council. The recommended budget and an enabling ordinance shall be submitted to council for its review not later than the last stated meeting in November of each year. The city administrator may include an explanatory comment or statement of the recommended budget. The recommended budget shall be in a form as required by law for city budgets and shall contain information explaining the various items of expenditure and revenue as may be required by council.

(11) Performing other duties as may be designated by council by ordinance.

CHAPTER 114
CITY TREASURER

Sec.

---

§ 11401. Qualifications.

The qualifications for the office of city treasurer shall be as follows:

(1) An individual must be an accountant.

(2) An individual must be at least 21 years of age.

(3) An individual must be a resident of the city for at least one year before the individual's election.

(4) Before being sworn into office, an elected city treasurer must present a signed affidavit to the city clerk certifying that the individual is in accordance with the requirements under paragraph (3).

(5) An elected city treasurer must reside in the city throughout the city treasurer's term of office.

(6) An individual must be a qualified tax collector or, in the case of an individual appointed to fill a vacancy in the office of treasurer, become a qualified tax collector, in accordance with the act of May 25, 1945 (P.L.1050, No.394), known as the Local Tax Collection Law.

§ 11402. Bond, insurance and salary.

(a) Conditioning.—The city treasurer shall provide lawful fidelity bond, covering the full term of office, for the faithful performance of official duties, including duties as tax collector of city, county, institution district and school taxes. In addition to being subject to other conditions as council may direct, the bond of the city treasurer shall be conditioned upon the following:

(1) The accounting for and paying over of all money received as city treasurer.

(2) The accounting for and paying over of all money received, including taxes, penalties and interest, as tax collector of city, county, institution district and school taxes.

(3) The safekeeping and paying over of all public money entrusted to the city treasurer's care.

(b) Required bonds.—

(1) Except as provided for in paragraph (2), council may require the following bonds from the city treasurer:

(i) A bond for the faithful performance by the city treasurer of official duties other than those of tax collector.

(ii) A bond covering the duties of the city treasurer as collector of city, county, institution district and school taxes.

(2) In lieu of the bond required for the faithful performance by the city treasurer of official duties other than those of tax collector under paragraph (1)(i), council may purchase insurance that covers the same events of loss and insures the city against the same misconduct as the bond under paragraph (1)(i) in compliance with this chapter.

(c) Liability discharged.—The city treasurer and the city treasurer's surety shall be discharged from further liability on any bond as tax collector if:

(1) the tax items contained in the duplicates delivered to the city treasurer under section 11402.2 (relating to delivery of duplicates of taxes) have been:

(i) collected and paid over;

(ii) assigned to third-party assignees;

(iii) certified to council for entry as liens in the office of the prothonotary or as claims in the tax claim bureau; or

(iv) returned to the county treasurer or city treasurer for sale; or

(2) in the case of taxes not levied upon real estate, a record of the taxes which remain uncollected have been filed with the tax authority.

(d) Insurance protection.—Council may require the city treasurer to be covered by insurance protection in accordance with section 10907(c) (relating to surety bonds, insurance and premiums).

(e) Bond insurance petition.—

(1) The taxing district may petition the court of common pleas having jurisdiction in the city to have the city treasurer furnish an additional bond and insurance. Upon petition, the city treasurer shall furnish an additional bond and insurance as the court may prescribe. The premium on the bond and

Table of Contents
Part I Ch. 1–3 Ethics, Records, Open Meetings
Part II Ch. 4–10 Taxation
Part III Ch. 11–18 Torts, Contracts & Civil Rules
Part IV Ch. 19–24 Zoning & Planning
Part V Ch. 25–30 Construction and Emergency Codes
Part VI Ch. 31–39 Municipal Codes
Index

insurance shall be shared on a pro rata basis by the taxing districts interested, according to each taxing district's respective tax interests under the act of May 25, 1945 (P.L.1050, No.394), known as the Local Tax Collection Law.

(2) The city treasurer shall not be required to provide bond and insurance in an amount in excess of the taxes to be collected by the treasurer. The bond and insurance provided by the city treasurer shall be for the use of the city and the taxing districts involved.

(f) Salary.—The city treasurer shall receive a fixed annual salary as provided by ordinance. The salary as a tax collector for the city, county, institution district and school district shall be as provided under the Local Tax Collection Law.

§ 11402.1. City treasurer to be tax collector.

Except as otherwise provided by the act of December 31, 1965 (P.L.1257, No.511), known as The Local Tax Enabling Act, the city treasurer, by virtue of the city treasurer's office, shall be the collector of the city, county, school and institution district taxes assessed or levied in the city by the proper authorities in the city. As tax collector, the city treasurer shall maintain and keep an office which may be the same as that of the city treasurer for the purpose of receiving taxes during regular business hours.

§ 11402.2. Delivery of duplicates of taxes.

(a) Duplicate delivery.—

(1) Not later than 30 days after the adoption of the budget or not later than 30 days after receipt of the assessment roll from the county, whichever is later, council and county and county institution district authorities shall compile and deliver the duplicates of taxes assessed to the city treasurer to be collected.

(2) The proper school authorities shall compile and deliver the school duplicates of taxes in the city at the time and in the manner as provided by law.

(b) Inspection.—All duplicates of taxes provided to or received by the city treasurer shall be open to proper inspection by the public and auditing and examining officers of the city, county or school district and shall be delivered by the city treasurer at the expiration of the city treasurer's term to the city treasurer's successor.

§ 11402.3. Tax liens and liability for false returns.

(a) Tax liens.—Upon the settlement of the duplicates of city, county, institution district and school taxes which by law are made a lien on real estate, the city treasurer as tax collector shall make out schedules of the city, county, school or institution district taxes uncollected upon the duplicates, including a brief description of the properties against which the taxes are assessed for the purpose of entering a lien or selling the properties.

(b) Failure to collect.—The failure of the city treasurer to collect the taxes from personal property shall not impair the lien of the taxes or affect any sale made for the collection of the taxes.

(c) False returns.—If the city treasurer makes a willfully false return, the city treasurer shall be liable to any individual injured by the false return.

§ 11403. Receipt and payment of money.

(a) Payments.—The city treasurer shall receive all money payable to the city from the sources as council may assign. Upon request, the city treasurer shall issue a receipt to an individual making the payment. The city treasurer shall pay all documents authorizing payment duly countersigned.

(b) Duplicates.—All receipts for money received on behalf of the city by the city treasurer shall be numbered serially and made in duplicate. Not later than the next succeeding business day, the city treasurer shall transmit the duplicates to the city controller.

§ 11404. Method of keeping accounts.

The accounts of the city treasurer shall clearly exhibit all the items of receipts and expenditures of the city, the sources from which the money are received and the objects for which the expenditures are disbursed. The city treasurer shall keep separate and distinct accounts of the receipts and expenditures of the city, including the sinking fund, each department providing a utility service and each special fund.

§ 11405. Restrictions on money paid out.

Money may not be paid out of the city treasury unless the money has been previously approved, duly authorized and appropriated by council for its intended purposes as explicitly mentioned in the document authorizing payment.

§ 11406. Depositories of city funds.

(a) Depositories.—The city treasurer shall keep public funds in banks or financial depositories as directed by council and under the restrictions and safeguards as provided by council. The city treasurer shall verify the city treasurer's accounts as requested by council.

(b) Liability prohibited.—The city treasurer, acting in accordance with law, shall not be liable for the loss of city funds caused by the insolvency or negligence of any city depositories.

§ 11407. Delivery of city property.

The city treasurer shall, upon leaving office, deliver to the city or to the city treasurer's duly qualified successor all money, accounts, property or effects in the city treasurer's possession belonging to the city.

§ 11408. Appointment of deputy city treasurer and employees.

(a) Appointments.—The city treasurer may appoint the following:

(1) A deputy city treasurer who, in the case of the sickness, absence or inability of the city treasurer to act, shall have the same powers and shall perform the same duties as are imposed by law upon the city treasurer. The appointment under this paragraph shall be in compliance with the requirements of the act of May 25, 1945 (P.L.1050, No.394), known as the Local Tax Collection Law.

(2) Employees of the city treasurer's office. The number and compensation of the assistants shall be fixed by council and the assistants shall be employees of the city.

(b) Insurance.—Individuals appointed under subsection (a) shall be covered by bond, blanket bond or insurance in accordance with section 10907 (relating to surety bonds, insurance and premiums).

CHAPTER 115
CITY ENGINEER

§ 11501. Appointment of city engineer.

Council shall provide for the manner of appointment and compensation of the city engineer. The city engineer shall be a registered professional engineer in this Commonwealth and shall serve at the pleasure of council. Nothing in this section shall be construed to prohibit council from designating an engineering firm of registered professional engineers from performing the duties and functions of the city engineer.

§ 11502. Control of engineering matters.

The city engineer shall have the supervision, direction and control of the engineering matters of the city. Unless authorized by council, a department of the city may not employ or retain any additional engineers.

§ 11503. Duties.

As authorized by council, engineering work undertaken by the city shall be performed or supervised by the city engineer or by another registered professional engineer employed by the city for a particular purpose. The duties of the city engineer may include all of the following:

(1) Preparing plans, specifications and estimates and undertaking other engineering work relating to constructing, reconstructing, maintaining and repairing streets, pavements, sewers, bridges, culverts and other municipal improvements.

(2) Making reports, giving estimates, supplying information and responding to questions concerning city engineering work to city officials and employees. Council may regulate the manner, number and method of making questions under this paragraph.

(3) Conducting, supervising or directing surveys relating to city property and improvements authorized by law or as directed by council.

(4) Preparing a topographical survey of the city or a general plan of city streets, marking the lines of streets, including streets already opened and streets intended to be opened for public use, as council may deem necessary.

(5) Surveying, making a draft or plan of and laying out new or proposed streets, as council may deem necessary.

(6) Reporting a grade for any proposed or new streets, as council may deem necessary.

(7) Making reports, as deemed expedient by the city engineer or as council shall direct, of the surveys and plans of city streets in convenient locations without awaiting the completion of the entire survey.

(8) Keeping and maintaining books and records and providing for certified copies of books and records, as provided by council or required by law.

§ 11504. Certifying commencement and completion of municipal improvements.

(a) Certification.—Within a reasonable time after the completion of any municipal improvement, the cost and expense of which, in whole or in part, is to be paid by the abutting property owner, the city engineer or employees designated by the city engineer shall:

(1) certify the day or time of the completion of work;

(2) file the certification under paragraph (1) with the city clerk, who shall maintain a centralized book or listing of certifications; and

(3) provide notice of the filing to the city solicitor.

(b) Evidence of completion.—Information filed with the city clerk under subsection (a)(2) shall be conclusive evidence of the day or time when the improvement commenced and was completed.

(c) **Definition.**—As used in this section, the term "the day or time of the completion of the work" means the time of the completion of the whole contract for the improvement.

§ 11505. Entering upon property for surveys.

For the purposes of carrying out authorized surveys, laying out streets or other engineering work of the city, the city engineer or other persons engaged in city engineering work may enter upon any property occupied by any person within the city.

CHAPTER 116
CITY SOLICITOR

Sec.

---

§ 11601. Appointment of city solicitor.

Council shall provide, by ordinance, for the manner of appointment and compensation of the city solicitor, which may be a law firm.

§ 11602. Direction of legal matters.

The city solicitor shall have the direction and control of the legal matters of the city. Unless authorized by council, a department of the city may not employ or retain any additional counsel in any matter or cause.

§ 11603. Duties.

The city solicitor shall have the following duties:

(1) Overseeing, as directed by resolution or ordinance, the preparation of all bonds, obligations, contracts, leases, conveyances and assurances to which the city or a municipal department is a party.

(2) Overseeing litigation by or against the city or a municipal officer, in the municipal officer's official capacity, including:

(i) filing of a municipal claim or lien; and

(ii) administrative practice.

(3) Performing any action incident to the office which the city solicitor may be lawfully authorized and required to do by the mayor or by any ordinance or resolution of council.

(4) Performing duties as council directs.

§ 11604. Written opinions to be furnished.

(a) **Opinions.**—Subject to regulation by council in accordance with subsection (b), the city solicitor shall submit a written opinion on questions of law submitted by any of the following:

(1) Council.

(2) The mayor.

Table of Contents
Part I Ch. 1–3 Ethics, Records, Open Meetings
Part II Ch. 4–10 Taxation
Part III Ch. 11–18 Torts, Contracts & Civil Rules
Part IV Ch. 19–24 Zoning & Planning
Part V Ch. 25–30 Construction and Emergency Codes
Part VI Ch. 31–39 Municipal Codes
Index

(3) Any other elected city official.

(4) Any appointed city official designated by council as authorized to request a written legal opinion.

(b) Regulation.—Council may provide for the regulation of the manner in which questions are presented to the city solicitor by any elected or appointed city official and may limit the questions submitted in the manner as council may direct.

§ 11607. Satisfaction of liens due city.

Upon the payment of any lien or other debt of record due to the city to a city employee, city official or any other person authorized to receive the payment, the person who received the payment shall, as soon as practicable, notify the city solicitor. The city solicitor or the solicitor's designee, as soon as practicable, shall cause the satisfaction to be entered upon the proper record of the lien or debt of record.

§ 11609. Assistant solicitor.

Council may appoint one or more assistant city solicitors to assist the city solicitor in the performance of all duties and shall provide for the compensation of assistant solicitors by resolution.

§ 11610. Special counsel.

Council may retain special counsel for particular proceedings or matters of the city and shall provide for the compensation of special counsel by resolution.

CHAPTER 117
CITY CONTROLLER AND INDEPENDENT AUDITOR

Subchapter

SUBCHAPTER A
CITY CONTROLLER

Sec.

§ 11701. Qualifications, bond and compensation.

(a) Qualifications.—The qualifications for the position of city controller shall be as follows:

(1) The individual must be an accountant.

(2) The individual must be at least 21 years of age.

(3) The individual must be a resident of the city for at least one year before the individual's election to the position of city controller.

(4) Before being sworn into office, the elected city controller must present a signed affidavit to the city clerk certifying that the individual is in accordance with the requirement under paragraph (3).

(5) An elected city controller must reside in the city throughout the individual's term of office.

(b) Bond.—The city controller shall provide a bond in accordance with section 10907 (relating to surety bonds, insurance and premiums) for the faithful performance of official duties as the city controller. The bond shall cover the full term of office and shall be conditioned upon the following:

(1) The accounting for and paying over of all money received as city controller.

(2) The safekeeping and payment over of all public money entrusted to the city controller's care.

(c) Salary.—The city controller shall receive a fixed annual salary set by ordinance in an amount not less than the compensation paid to members of council.

§ 11704. Powers and duties of city controller.

(a) Payment authorization.—The city controller shall countersign all documents authorizing the payment of money from the city treasury, if satisfied of the legality of the payment.

(b) Oaths or affirmations.—The city controller may administer oaths or affirmations in relation to any matter pertaining to the authentication of any account, claim or demand of or against the city. The city controller may not receive any fee for administering oaths or affirmations under this subsection.

(c) Account examination.—The city controller may examine the following accounts:

(1) The accounts in which the city is concerned, either as a debtor or creditor.

(2) The accounts of all city bureaus, officers and departments which collect, receive and disburse public money or are charged with management, control or custody of public money.

(3) The accounts of a city officer upon the death, resignation, removal or expiration of the term of the officer.

(4) The accounts of any library to which the city makes appropriations, any institution owned by the city and any Pennsylvania National Guard units to which the city makes an appropriation.

(d) Subpoenas.—In the same manner in which subpoenas may be issued and enforced in accordance with section 10917 (relating to powers of subpoena and compelling testimony), the city controller may issue subpoenas to obtain the attendance of officers whose accounts the city controller is authorized to examine and any other individuals whom it may be necessary to examine as witnesses.

(e) Statements.—The city controller may present council with annual or periodic statements concerning the results of the city controller's examination of accounts, which shall be public records in accordance with the act of February 14, 2008 (P.L.6, No.3), known as the Right-to-Know Law.

§ 11704.1. Deputy controller and employees.

The city controller may appoint a deputy controller and may select individuals to serve as assistants and employees in the city controller's office. The number of assistants and employees permitted, if any, shall be fixed by council. Assistants and employees in the city controller's office shall, in all other respects, be considered employees of the city. The deputy controller, assistants and employees appointed under this section shall be bonded and their compensation shall be fixed by council.

§ 11704.2. Temporary deputy controller.

In case of the sickness, absence or inability of a city controller to perform the city controller's duties, if no deputy controller has been appointed by the city

Chap. 39 Res. During Mil. Service
Chap. 38 Intergov. Coop.
Chap. 37 3rd Class City Code
Chap. 36 Bor. Code
Chap. 35 2nd Class Twp. Code
Chap. 34 1st Class Twp. Code
Chap. 33 Home Rule Chart. Opt. Plans Law
Chap. 32 Water Serv. Act
Chap. 31 Munic. Auth. Act

controller, council may appoint a temporary deputy controller to serve during the sickness, absence or inability of the city controller or until the city controller shall appoint a deputy controller. A deputy controller shall be bonded and receive the compensation fixed by council.

§ 11704.3. Continuation of office.

The appointment of an independent auditor in accordance with Subchapter B (relating to independent auditor) shall not abolish the office of city controller. The elected controller shall continue to exercise the powers retained for the controller in this subchapter.

SUBCHAPTER B
INDEPENDENT AUDITOR

Sec.

§ 11704.11. Appointment of independent auditor.

Council shall provide, by resolution, for the appointment of an independent auditor. The independent auditor may be a certified public accountant or a firm of certified public accountants.

§ 11704.12. Powers and duties of independent auditor.

(a) Annual audit.—The independent auditor shall conduct an annual audit of all accounts of city officers, departments and offices which collect, receive and disburse public money or are authorized with the management, control or custody of public money on which the independent auditor is required to report under this subchapter. The annual audit, as directed by council, shall also include any accounts subject to examination by the city controller under Subchapter A (relating to city controller).

(b) Subpoenas.—The independent auditor may issue subpoenas to obtain the attendance of officers whose accounts the independent auditor is authorized to examine and any other individuals whom it may be necessary to examine as witnesses.

§ 11705. Annual report to council and appeals.

(a) Audit report.—

(1) At council's first meeting in March of each year, the independent auditor shall submit a report to council that includes the audits made of the accounts of the officers authorized with the custody, control or disbursement of public money. The report shall provide the balance of each officer's accounts.

(2) Within 90 days of the end of each fiscal year, the independent auditor shall file a copy of the annual report under paragraph (1) with the clerk of court or the prothonotary, as provided by local rule of court.

(b) Financial condition report.—The independent auditor shall submit an annual report to council summarizing the fiscal condition of the affairs of the city. Council may require advisory interim reports from the independent auditor.

(b.1) Right-to-know.—Reports prepared under this section shall be public in accordance with the act of February 14, 2008 (P.L.6, No.3), known as the Right-to-Know Law.

(c) Appeals.—Not later than 45 days after the annual report to council has been filed, the city, a taxpayer of the city on the city's behalf or any officer whose account is settled or audited may file an appeal from the settlement or audit to the court of common pleas of the county in which the city is located. If the appellant is a taxpayer of the city or an officer, the taxpayer of the city or the officer shall file a bond, with one or more sufficient sureties, conditioned to pay reasonable attorney fees and court costs if the appellant fails in the appeal.

CHAPTER 118
ACCOUNTS AND FINANCES

§ 11801. Fiscal year.

The fiscal year of each city shall begin on January 1 and end on December 31.

§ 11802. Powers and duties of chief fiscal officer.

(a) Appointment.—Council shall appoint a chief fiscal officer. In filling the position of chief fiscal officer, council may appoint the director of the department of accounts and finance or the city administrator if one is an individual appointed under Chapter 111 (relating to the executive department) or 112A (relating to city administrator).

(b) Bond.—The chief fiscal officer shall furnish a bond in accordance with section 10907 (relating to surety bonds, insurance and premiums).

(c) Powers.—

(1) The chief fiscal officer may administer oaths and affirmations pertaining to the authentication of an account with the city or a claim by or demand against the city.

(2) The chief fiscal officer may not receive any additional compensation for the administration or oath and affirmations under paragraph (1).

§ 11803. Deputy chief fiscal officer.

(a) Appointment.—Council may authorize the chief fiscal officer to appoint, subject to the approval of council, a deputy chief fiscal officer whose compensation shall be fixed by council.

(b) Bond.—The deputy chief fiscal officer shall furnish a bond in accordance with section 10907 (relating to surety bonds, insurance and premiums).

(c) Powers.—

(1) The deputy chief fiscal officer may administer oaths and affirmations pertaining to the authentication of an account with the city or a claim by or demand against the city.

(2) The deputy chief fiscal officer may not receive any additional compensation for the administration or oath and affirmations under paragraph (1).

(d) Temporary deputy chief fiscal officer.—If no deputy chief fiscal officer has been appointed, council may appoint a temporary deputy chief fiscal officer to serve during the chief fiscal officer's illness, absence or inability to serve. The temporary deputy chief fiscal officer may be required to furnish a bond as required by council.

§ 11804. Regulations concerning appropriation.

(a) Debt.—Debt may not be incurred by any department of the city except in accordance with law.

(b) Appropriations.—Money may not be paid out of the city treasury except by an appropriation made in accordance with law and a document authorizing payment drawn by the proper officer.

(c) Expenditures.—The city may not hire employees, purchase materials, execute contracts or issue orders for the payment of any money if it would result in the total expenditure of money for a specific purpose to exceed the amount appropriated for that purpose.

(d) Expense reports.—If an appropriation is entirely expended and the object of the appropriation is not completed, not later than the next regularly scheduled council meeting, the chief fiscal officer shall report the fact to council and accompany the report with a statement of the money which have been drawn on the appropriation and the particular purpose for which the money were drawn.

(e) Supplemental appropriations.—Council may, by ordinance, make supplemental appropriations for any lawful purpose from any money in the city treasury or estimated to be deposited in the city treasury within the fiscal year and not appropriated for any other purpose, including the proceeds of any borrowing authorized by law.

(f) Transfers.—

(1) Council may authorize the transfer of any unexpended balance of an appropriation item.

(2) Before authorizing a transfer under paragraph (1), council shall seek comments from any director of a department negatively affected by the proposed transfer.

(g) Methods of transfers.—Council shall determine the manner and method of all intradepartmental and interdepartmental financial transfers.

§ 11804.1. Investment of city money.

(a) General rule.—Council shall have power to provide the following:

(1) The investment of city sinking funds as authorized by 53 Pa.C.S. Pt. VII Subpt. B (relating to indebtedness and borrowing).

(2) The investment of money in the general fund and in special funds of the city, other than the sinking funds as authorized by this chapter.

(3) The liquidation of any investment, in whole or in part, by disposing of securities or withdrawing money on deposit. Any action taken to make or to liquidate any investment shall be made by the officers designated by action of council.

(b) **Investment.**—Council shall invest city money consistent with sound business practices.

(c) **Restrictions.**—Council shall provide for an investment program subject to restrictions contained in this chapter and in any other applicable statute and any rules and regulations adopted by council.

(d) **Authorized investments.**—Authorized types of investments of city money shall be any of the following:

(1) United States Treasury bills.

(2) Short-term obligations of the United States Government or its agencies or instrumentalities.

(3) Deposits in savings accounts, time deposits, other than certificates of deposit, or share accounts of institutions insured by the Federal Deposit Insurance Corporation or the National Credit Union Share Insurance Fund to the extent that the accounts are so insured and, for any amounts above the insured maximum, provided that approved collateral as prescribed by law shall be pledged by the depository.

(4) Obligations of:

(i) The United States Government or any of its agencies or instrumentalities backed by the full faith and credit of the United States.

(ii) The Commonwealth or any of its agencies or instrumentalities backed by the full faith and credit of the Commonwealth.

(iii) Any political subdivision of the Commonwealth or any of its agencies or instrumentalities backed by the full faith and credit of the political subdivision.

(5) Shares of an investment company registered under the Investment Company Act of 1940 (54 Stat. 789, 15 U.S.C. § 80a-1 et seq.), whose shares are registered under the Securities Act of 1933 (48 Stat. 74, 15 U.S.C. § 77a et seq.), provided that the only investments of the company are in the authorized investments of city money under paragraphs (1), (2), (3) and (4).

(6) Certificates of deposit purchased from institutions insured by the Federal Deposit Insurance Corporation or the National Credit Union Share Insurance Fund to the extent that the accounts are so insured. However, for any amounts above the insured maximum, the certificates of deposit shall be collateralized by a pledge or assignment of assets of the institution and the collateral may include loans, including interest in pools of loans, secured by first mortgage liens on real property. Certificates of deposit purchased from commercial banks shall be limited to an amount equal to 20% of a bank's total capital and surplus. Certificates of deposit purchased from savings and loan associations or savings banks shall be limited to an amount equal to 20% of an institution's assets minus liabilities.

(7) For any pension or retirement fund, any investment authorized by 20 Pa.C.S. Ch. 73 (relating to municipalities investments).

(8) Repurchase agreements which are fully collateralized by obligations of the United States Government or its agencies or instrumentalities, which are free from other liens and backed by the full faith and credit of the United States or are rated in the highest category by a nationally recognized statistical rating organization.

(9) Deposits in investment pools established by the State Treasurer or established by local governments pursuant to 53 Pa.C.S. Ch. 23 Subch. A (relating to intergovernmental cooperation) and related statutes, provided that the investment pools are rated in the highest category by a nationally recognized statistical rating organization.

(e) **Authority.**—In making investments of city money, council shall have authority to do any of the following:

(1) Permit assets pledged as collateral under subsection (d)(3) to be pooled in accordance with the act of August 6, 1971 (P.L.281, No.72), entitled "An act standardizing the procedures for pledges of assets to secure deposits of public funds with banking institutions pursuant to other laws; establishing a standard rule for the types, amounts and valuations of assets eligible to be used as collateral for deposits of public funds; permitting assets to be pledged against deposits on a pooled basis; and authorizing the appointment of custodians to act as pledgees of assets."

(2) Combine money from more than one fund under city control for the purchase of a single investment, provided that each of the funds shall be accounted for separately in all respects and that the earnings from the investment are separately and individually computed and recorded and credited to the accounts from which the investment was purchased.

(3) Join with one or more other political subdivisions and municipal authorities in accordance with 53 Pa.C.S. Ch. 23, Subch. A, in the purchase of a single investment, provided that the requirements of paragraph (2) are adhered to.

§ 11805. Countersigning documents, money available and evidence required.

(a) **General rule.**—The chief fiscal officer shall countersign all documents, in the form approved by council, authorizing payment from the city treasury.

(b) **Prohibition.**—In countersigning documents authorizing payment from the city treasury, the chief fiscal officer shall not permit any appropriation made by council to be overdrawn and shall not countersign unless there is money in the treasury to pay the appropriation.

(c) **Evidence.**—Except in the case of documents authorizing payment to volunteer fire companies, whenever a document authorizing payment from the city treasury is presented to the chief fiscal officer to be countersigned, the person presenting the document shall be required to produce evidence of each of the following:

(1) That the amount expressed in the document is due to the person in whose favor it is drawn.

(2) That the supplies, services or other consideration for payment have been furnished, performed or given according to law and the terms of the contract, if any, were satisfied.

§ 11806. Record of assets, property, trusts, debts due, receipts and expenditures.

The chief fiscal officer or other official or employee of the city designated by council shall have charge and keep a record of accounts, under appropriate titles, to show separately and distinctly the following:

(1) All of the assets and property vested in the city.

(2) All trusts in care of the city.

(3) Debts owed by the city.

(4) All of the receipts and expenditures of the various departments.

§ 11807. Supervision of accounts of departments.

The chief fiscal officer shall have the supervision and control of the accounts of all of the departments and may require at any time a statement in writing of all money or property of the city under any department's control.

§ 11808. Suggestions for improvement of city finances.

The chief fiscal officer may, and when council directs shall, suggest plans to council for the management and improvement of the city finances.

§ 11809. Annual budget, presentation to council, notice, revision and adoption.

(a) Introduction.—Each year at the last stated meeting in November, the chief fiscal officer shall, on behalf of council, present to council for introduction a proposed budget ordinance. The proposed budget ordinance shall show the estimated receipts, expenditures and liabilities for the ensuing year, with the balance of unexpended appropriations and all other information of value as a basis for fixing the levy and tax rate for the next fiscal year. Council shall, upon introducing the proposed budget ordinance, fix a date for adoption, which shall be not later than December 31 of that year.

(b) Estimate.—The departments of the city government shall, before the proposed budget ordinance is introduced as provided under subsection (a), furnish to council an estimate of the probable receipts and expenditures and an estimate of the amount required by each of the departments for public service during the ensuing fiscal year as a basis for making the annual appropriations.

(c) Inspection.—

(1) When the proposed budget ordinance is submitted to council and has been introduced, the city clerk shall immediately make the proposed budget ordinance available for public inspection at the city clerk's office and shall publish a notice to that effect once in a newspaper of general circulation in accordance with the provisions of section 10109 (relating to publication of notices).

(2) The notice shall state the date fixed by council for enactment of the proposed budget ordinance and notice shall be published at least 20 days prior to the time fixed by council for enactment of the proposed budget ordinance. The proposed budget ordinance shall be available for public inspection at the city clerk's office for at least 10 days after the newspaper notice is published.

(d) Enactment.—Council shall, after making the changes and modifications as appear proper, enact the budget and any appropriation measures required to put it into effect upon the date fixed for enactment. The budget shall reflect as nearly as possible the estimated revenues and expenditures of the city for the year for which the budget is prepared. Should it appear upon any revision of the budget that the estimated expenditures in the enacted budget would be increased more than 10% in the aggregate or more than 25% in any individual item over the proposed budget, the budget shall not be enacted with any of the increases unless the budget is made available for public inspection for a period of at least 10 days after notice to that effect is published as provided under subsection (c).

§ 11810. Amending budget and notice.

(a) General rule.—During the month of January following the expiration of a past fiscal year, in furthering its fiduciary responsibility, council may amend the budget and the levy and tax rate to conform to its amended budget ordinance. A period of 10 days' public inspection at the city clerk's office of the proposed amended budget ordinance, after notice by the city clerk to that effect is published in a newspaper of general circulation as provided in section 10109 (relating to publication of notices), shall intervene between council's introduction of the proposed amended budget ordinance and its enactment. Any amended budget ordinance must be enacted by council on or before February 15.

(b) Prohibition.—After introduction, no proposed amended budget ordinance shall be revised upward in excess of 10% in the aggregate or as to an individual item in excess of 25% of the amount of the individual item in the proposed amended budget ordinance.

§ 11811. Appropriations, tax rate and limitations.

(a) General rule.—When all estimates for the receipts, liabilities and expenditures for the ensuing year are made, council shall proceed to make the annual

appropriations and shall fix the tax rate at the figure that will, in combination with all other estimated receipts of the city, fully meet and cover the aggregate amount of the estimates of liabilities and expenditures for the ensuing year.

(b) Exceptions.—

(1) No appropriation shall be made for any purpose until the following are provided for:

(i) Interest accruing on the funded debt of the city and the principal of that part of the debt as may be coming due in that fiscal year.

(ii) The salaries of officers.

(iii) The ordinary and necessary expenses of the city.

(2) No appropriation shall be made for any purpose in excess of the estimated receipts and revenues for the fiscal year for which the appropriations are made.

§ 11811.2. Borrowing in anticipation of current revenue.

In accordance with 53 Pa.C.S. Pt. VII Subpt. B (relating to indebtedness and borrowing), cities may:

(1) borrow money in anticipation of current revenues to an amount of not more than the anticipated current revenues, which shall be pledged for the payment of the loan or loans; and

(2) issue notes or other forms of obligation in evidence of the debt.

§ 11812. Annual reports, publication, filing report with Department of Community and Economic Development and penalty.

(a) Annual report.—The chief fiscal officer shall make a report, verified by oath or affirmation to council at a stated meeting in April in each year, of the public accounts of the city and of the trusts in its care for the preceding fiscal year, exhibiting all of the expenditures of the accounts, respectively, and the sources from which the revenue and funds are derived and in what measures the revenue and funds have been disbursed. Each account shall be accompanied by a statement detailing all of the following:

(1) The appropriations made by council.

(2) The amount drawn and encumbered on each appropriation.

(3) The unencumbered balance outstanding to the debit or credit of the appropriation at the close of the fiscal year.

(b) Publication.—

(1) The report shall be accompanied by a concise financial statement setting forth all of the following:

(i) The balance in the treasury at the beginning of the fiscal year.

(ii) All revenues received during the fiscal year, by major classifications.

(iii) All expenditures made during the fiscal year, by major functions.

(iv) The current resources and liabilities of the city at the end of the fiscal year.

(v) The gross liability and the net debt of the city.

(vi) The amount of the assessed valuation of the taxable property in the city.

(vii) The assets of the city.

(viii) The character and value of the assets.

(ix) The date of the last maturity of the respective forms of funded debt.

(x) The assets in each sinking fund.

(2) The concise financial information approved by the independent auditor and consistent with the audited financial statements for total assets, total liabilities and total net position at the end of the fiscal year and total revenue, total expenses and changes in total net position for that fiscal year and a reference to a place within the city where copies of the financial statements and accompanying auditor's report may be examined shall be published in a newspaper of general circulation as required by section 10109 (relating to publication of notices) at least 10 days prior to the April meeting scheduled pursuant to subsection (a). If the full financial statements and accompanying auditor's report are not published, copies shall be supplied to the publishing newspaper when the request for publication is submitted.

(3) Before the report or statement is made or the concise financial information is published, it shall be approved by the independent auditor, who may approve it, subject to exceptions. Council may cause the statement to be printed in pamphlet form in addition to the publications made.

(c) **Filing.**—The chief fiscal officer shall annually report the financial condition of the city to the Department of Community and Economic Development within 90 days after the close of the fiscal year. The report shall be signed and duly verified by the oath of the chief fiscal officer and approved by the independent auditor, as provided above. Any chief fiscal officer appointed by the city refusing or willfully neglecting to file the report shall, upon conviction in a summary proceeding brought by the Department of Community and Economic Development, be sentenced to pay a fine of $5 for each day delayed beyond 90 days and costs. All fines recovered shall be for use by the Commonwealth.

(d) **Form.**—The report to the Department of Community and Economic Development shall be presented in a form as provided for in section 11813 (relating to committee to prepare uniform forms).

§ 11813. Committee to prepare uniform forms.

(a) **General rule.**—The uniform financial report forms under this chapter shall be prepared by a committee consisting of four representatives of the Pennsylvania Municipal League and the Secretary of Community and Economic Development, or the secretary's agent or designee who shall be an individual trained in the field of municipal finance.

(b) **Appointment.**—The representatives shall be appointed by the president of the Pennsylvania Municipal League within 60 days of notification by the Secretary of Community and Economic Development or the secretary's agent or designee that the committee will convene. The representatives shall be chosen from among chief fiscal officers of cities or other officers of cities who have knowledge of fiscal procedures and shall be chosen to represent cities in the various population groups. The president of the Pennsylvania Municipal League and other designated participants shall supply to the Secretary of Community and Economic Development the names and addresses of the representatives immediately upon their appointment.

(c) **Compensation and meetings.**—The representatives shall serve without compensation, but they shall be reimbursed by the Commonwealth for all necessary expenses incurred in attending meetings of the committee. The committee shall meet at the call of the Secretary of Community and Economic Development, or the secretary's agent or designee, who shall serve as chairperson of the committee.

(d) **Duty of secretary.**—It shall be the duty of the Secretary of Community and Economic Development, or the secretary's agent or designee, to ensure the forms required by this chapter are prepared in cooperation with the committee. In the event that the committee should for any reason fail to furnish the cooperation, the Secretary of Community and Economic Development, or the secretary's agent or designee, shall complete the preparation of the forms. After their preparation, the Secretary of Community and Economic Development, or the secretary's agent or designee, shall issue the forms and distribute them annually, as needed, to the designated officers of each city.

(e) Change or alteration.—No change or alteration in the forms prescribed shall be made by the Secretary of Community and Economic Development or the secretary's agent or designee, except by a majority approval of the committee, unless upon reasonable notice two or more representatives of the committee fail to attend the committee meetings. In voting upon any change or alteration, each representative and the chairperson of the committee shall have one vote.

§ 11814. Annual reports to council on insurance and bonds.

The chief fiscal officer shall prepare or cause to be prepared and submit to council, as council shall direct, a complete and itemized report of all policies of insurance contracted by the city for the information and consideration of council. The chief fiscal officer shall prepare a report, as council shall direct, of all bonds given for the protection of the city in whole or in part.

CHAPTER 119

CONTRACTS

Sec.

---

§ 11901. Power to make and regulate contracts.

(a) General rule.—Each city may execute contracts for the purpose of carrying out the provisions of this part and the laws of the Commonwealth. In addition to and consistent with the requirements of this chapter, council shall, by ordinance, provide for and regulate the procedures for the award of all contracts, including the purchase of supplies and materials.

(b) Real and personal property.—Contracts for the sale of real and personal property shall conform to the provisions of section 12402.1 (relating to city property and affairs).

Table of Contents
Part I Ch. 1–3 Ethics, Records, Open Meetings
Part II Ch. 4–10 Taxation
Part III Ch. 11–18 Torts, Contracts & Civil Rules
Part IV Ch. 19–24 Zoning & Planning
Part V Ch. 25–30 Construction and Emergency Codes
Part VI Ch. 31–39 Municipal Codes
Index

§ 11901.1. Contracts or purchases in excess of base amount of $18,500.

(a) General rule.—Except as provided in section 11901.4(b) (relating to contracts or purchases not requiring advertising or bidding), all contracts or purchases in excess of the base amount of $18,500, subject to adjustment under section 11903.1 (relating to adjustments to base amount based on Consumer Price Index for All Urban Consumers), shall be subject to advertising and competitive bidding as provided in this chapter.

(b) Contract.—All services and personal properties required by any city municipal department, where the amount exceeds the base amount of $18,500, subject to adjustment under section 11903.1, shall be furnished and performed under written contract. The contract shall be awarded and given to the lowest responsible bidder after advertising two times, each publication on a different day, in not more than two newspapers of general circulation, in accordance with the provisions of section 10109 (relating to publication of notices). The bids shall not be opened until at least 10 days have elapsed after the first advertisement is published. A copy of the advertisement for contracts or purchases shall be posted in the city office designated by council.

§ 11901.2. Contracts or purchases not in excess of base amount of $18,500.

With regard to all contracts or purchases not in excess of the base amount of $18,500, subject to adjustment under section 11903.1 (relating to adjustments to base amount based on Consumer Price Index for All Urban Consumers), the following shall apply:

(1) The purchases or contracts shall be evidenced by note or memorandum in writing, signed by the officer or employee making the purchase or contract.

(2) Council, or the officer designated by council, shall approve all purchases or contracts, except council need not approve those purchases or contracts within the category of small or routine purchases or incidental expenses, as defined by ordinance.

§ 11901.3. Determining amount of contract.

The amount of the contract shall be the entire amount which the city pays to the successful bidder or the successful bidder's assigns in order to obtain the services or property, or both, and shall not be construed to mean only the amount which is paid to acquire title or to receive any other particular benefit or benefits of the whole bargain.

§ 11901.4. Contracts or purchases not requiring advertising or bidding.

(a) Not in excess of base amount.—City contracts or purchases, if not in excess of the base amount of $18,500, subject to adjustment under section 11903.1 (relating to adjustments to base amount based on Consumer Price Index for All Urban Consumers), shall not require advertising or bidding.

(b) In excess of base amount.—The following city contracts or purchases involving an expenditure over the base amount of $18,500, subject to adjustment under section 11903.1, do not require advertising or bidding:

(1) Contracts for maintenance, repairs or replacements for water, electric light or other public works of the city, provided they do not constitute new additions, extensions or enlargements of existing facilities and equipment. Security may be required by council as in other cases of work done.

(2) Contracts for improvements, repairs and maintenance of any kind made or provided by any city through its own employees, except that this exception shall not apply to construction materials used in a street improvement.

(3) Contracts for new equipment, articles, apparatus, appliances or vehicles which are patented or copyrighted products.

Chap. 39 Res. During Mil. Service
Chap. 38 Intergov. Coop.
Chap. 37 3rd Class City Code
Chap. 36 Bor. Code
Chap. 35 2nd Class Twp. Code
Chap. 34 1st Class Twp. Code
Chap. 33 Home Rule Chart. Opt. Plans Law
Chap. 32 Water Serv. Act
Chap. 31 Munic. Auth. Act

(4) Contracts involving any policies of insurance or surety company bonds.

(5) Contracts for public utility service and electricity, natural gas or telecommunication services, provided that, in the case of utilities not under tariff with the Pennsylvania Public Utility Commission, contracts made without advertising and bidding shall be made only after receiving written or telephonic price quotations from at least three qualified and responsible providers. In lieu of price quotations, a memorandum shall be kept on file showing that fewer than three qualified providers exist in the market area within which it is practicable to obtain quotations. A written record of telephonic price quotations shall be made and shall contain at least the date of the quotation, the name of the provider and the provider's representative, the type of service that was the subject of the quotation and the price. Written price quotations, written records of telephonic price quotations and memoranda shall be retained for a period of three years.

(6) Contracts entered into with the Federal Government, the Commonwealth, another political subdivision or a county, any agency of the Federal Government or the Commonwealth, any municipal authority, including the sale, leasing or loan of any supplies or materials by the Federal Government or the Commonwealth, or their agencies, but the price shall not be in excess of that fixed by the Federal Government, the Commonwealth or their agencies.

(7) Contracts involving personal or professional services.

(8) Contracts executed during a state of emergency declared by the mayor in accordance with section 11203 (relating to execution of laws, powers of sheriff conferred and emergency powers) or those made during a disaster emergency declared by the Governor or during a local emergency in accordance with 35 Pa.C.S. Pt. V (relating to emergency management services).

(9) Those for used personal property, such as equipment, articles, apparatus, appliances, vehicles or parts of vehicles being purchased from a volunteer fire company, volunteer ambulance service or volunteer rescue squad.

§ 11901.5. Receipt, opening, award or rejection of bids.

(a) Advertisement.—If advertisement and bidding are required, the advertisement shall specify the time and place bids will be received and the time and place for the opening of bids.

(b) Bids.—Bids received pursuant to advertisement shall be opened publicly by council or its designated agent. The amount of each bid and any other relevant information as may be specified by council, together with the name of each bidder, shall be disclosed and recorded and the record shall be open to public inspection.

(c) Award or rejection.—At a public meeting of council, not more than 60 days after the receipt of bids, council shall either award the contract or reject all bids.

§ 11901.6. Bid, performance and payment security.

(a) Bid security.—The following shall apply to bid security:

(1) Council may require that bids received pursuant to advertisement be accompanied by bid security, in a reasonable amount, which shall be in the form of a certified or bank check or a bond provided by a surety company authorized to do business in this Commonwealth or another form of security as specified in the advertisement for bids.

(2) In the event the successful bidder shall, upon award of the contract, fail to comply with the requirements of subsection (b) as to performance security, the bid security shall be forfeited to the city as liquidated damages.

(b) Performance security.—The following shall apply to performance security:

(1) In the case of a contract that had been subject to advertising and bidding, the successful bidder shall be required to furnish performance security in the form of a bond or irrevocable letter of credit in an amount equal to 100% of the contract price with suitable reasonable requirements guaranteeing the performance of the contract. Performance security shall be provided within 20 days after the contract has been awarded, unless council prescribes a shorter period of not less than 10 days. Failure to furnish the security within the required time period shall void the award.

(2) The provisions of this subsection requiring successful bidders to furnish performance security shall not be mandatory as to contracts for the purchase of motor vehicles or other pieces of equipment but only as to those contracts which involve furnishing of labor and materials. Council may, in all cases of contracts or purchases, require security for performance, delivery or other terms.

(c) **Payment security.**—The following shall apply to payment security:

(1) In conformity with the act of December 20, 1967 (P.L.869, No.385), known as the Public Works Contractors' Bond Law of 1967, it shall be the duty of every city to require any individual, partnership, association or corporation entering into a contract with the city for the construction, erection, installation, completion, alteration, repair of or addition to any public work or improvement of any kind, where the amount of the contract is in excess of $10,000, before commencing work under the contract, to provide payment security in a form acceptable to and approved by the city, which may include, but need not be limited to, any of the following equal to 100% of the contract amount:

(i) A bond.

(ii) Federal or Commonwealth-chartered lending institution irrevocable letters of credit.

(iii) Restrictive or escrow accounts in the lending institutions under subparagraph (ii).

(2) The payment security shall be solely for the protection of claimants supplying labor or materials to the prime contractor to whom the contract was awarded, or to any of the prime contractor's subcontractors, in the execution of the work provided for in the contract. The payment security shall be conditioned for the prompt payment of all material furnished or labor supplied or performed in the execution of the work under the contract.

§ 11901.7. Compliance with other laws.

Every contract subject to this chapter shall comply, as applicable, with the provisions of the act of August 15, 1961 (P.L.987, No.442), known as the Pennsylvania Prevailing Wage Act, the act of December 20, 1967 (P.L.869, No.385), known as the Public Works Contractors' Bond Law of 1967, the act of January 23, 1974 (P.L.9, No.4), referred to as the Public Contract Bid Withdrawal Law, the act of March 3, 1978 (P.L.6, No.3), known as the Steel Products Procurement Act, the act of February 17, 1994 (P.L.73, No.7), known as the Contractor and Subcontractor Payment Act, and 62 Pa.C.S. Chs. 37 Subch. B (relating to motor vehicles), 39 (relating to contracts for public works) and 45 (relating to antibid-rigging).

§ 11901.8. Prohibitions.

No individual, consultant, firm or corporation contracting with a city for purposes of rendering personal or professional services to the city shall share with any city officer or employee, and no city officer or employee shall accept, any portion of the compensation or fees paid by the city for the contracted services provided to the city.

§ 11901.9. Lowest responsible bidder.

For purposes of this chapter, the lowest responsible bidder need not be the bidder submitting the lowest dollar amount bid. The city may also consider the quality of goods or services supplied, ease of repair, compatibility with other city equipment or services, responsiveness, past performance of the bidder and any other reasonable factors specified in the advertisement for bids.

§ 11902. Evasion of advertising requirements.

The following shall apply:

(1) No elected or appointed official or officials of any city shall evade the provisions of this chapter requiring advertising for bids by purchasing or contracting for services and personal properties piecemeal for the purpose of obtaining prices under the base amount of $18,500, subject to adjustment under section 11903.1 (relating to adjustments to base amount based on Consumer Price Index for All Urban Consumers), upon transactions which should, in the exercise of reasonable discretion and prudence, be conducted as one transaction amounting to more than the base amount of $18,500, subject to adjustment under section 11903.1.

(2) Paragraph (1) is intended to make unlawful the practice of evading advertising requirements by making a series of purchases or contracts, each for less than the advertising requirement price, or by making several simultaneous purchases or contracts, each below the price, when, in either case, the transactions involved should have been made as one transaction for one price.

(3) Any elected or appointed official who acts in violation of paragraph (1), knowing that the transaction upon which the elected or appointed official acts is or ought to be a part of a larger transaction and that it is being divided in order to evade the requirements as to advertising for bids, shall be jointly and severally subject to surcharge for 10% of the full amount of the contract or purchase. Wherever it shall appear that an elected or appointed official may have acted in violation of this section but the purchase or contract on which the elected or appointed official acted was not executed, this section shall be inapplicable.

§ 11903.1. Adjustments to base amount based on Consumer Price Index for All Urban Consumers.

Adjustments to the base amounts specified under sections 11901.1 (relating to contracts or purchases in excess of base amount of $18,500), 11902 (relating to evasion of advertising requirements) and 11909 (relating to separate bids for plumbing, heating, ventilating and electrical work, elevators and escalators) shall be made as follows:

(1) The Department of Labor and Industry shall determine the percentage change in the Consumer Price Index for All Urban Consumers: All Items (CPI-U) for the United States City Average as published by the United States Department of Labor, Bureau of Labor Statistics, for the 12-month period ending September 30.

(2) If the Department of Labor and Industry determines that there is no positive percentage change, no adjustment to the base amounts shall occur for the relevant time period provided for in this section.

(3)(i) If the Department of Labor and Industry determines that there is a positive percentage change in the first year that the determination is made under paragraph (1), the positive percentage change shall be multiplied by each base amount, the products shall be added to the base amounts, respectively, and the sums shall be preliminary adjusted amounts.

(ii) The preliminary adjusted amounts shall be rounded to the nearest $100 to determine the final adjusted base amounts for purposes of sections 11901.1 and 11902.

(4) In each successive year in which there is a positive percentage change in the CPI-U for the United States City Average, the positive percentage change shall be multiplied by the most recent preliminary adjusted amounts and the products shall be added to the preliminary adjusted amount of the prior year to calculate the preliminary adjusted amounts for the current year. The sums shall be rounded to the nearest $100 to determine the new final adjusted base amounts for purposes of sections 11901.1 and 11902.

(5) The determinations and adjustments required under this section shall be made annually after October 1 and before November 15.

(6) The final adjusted base amounts and new final adjusted base amounts obtained under paragraphs (3) and (4) shall become effective January 1 for the calendar year following the year in which the determination required under paragraph (1) is made.

(7) The Department of Labor and Industry shall publish notice in the Pennsylvania Bulletin prior to January 1 of each calendar year of the annual percentage change determined under paragraph (1) and the unadjusted or final adjusted base amounts determined under paragraphs (3) and (4) at which competitive bidding is required under section 11901.1 and advertising is required under section 11902 or separate bids are required under section 11909 for the calendar year beginning the first day of January after publication of the notice. The notice shall include a written and illustrative explanation of the calculations performed by the Department of Labor and Industry in establishing the unadjusted or final adjusted base amounts under this section for the ensuing calendar year.

(8) The annual increase in the preliminary adjusted base amounts obtained under paragraphs (3) and (4) shall not exceed 3%.

§ 11906. Designation of appropriations, certification in excess of appropriation and contracts for governmental services for more than one year.

With regard to any contract, council may direct the city administrator, chief fiscal officer or other designated official or employee to furnish information concerning the availability of appropriated money to satisfy required payments under the contract. Nothing in this section shall prevent the making of contracts for governmental services for a period exceeding one year, but any contract shall be executed only for the amounts agreed to be paid for the services to be rendered in succeeding fiscal years.

§ 11908.1. Purchase contracts for petroleum products, fire company and participation.

Council of each city shall have power to permit, subject to any terms and conditions as the city may impose, any fire company, rescue company and ambulance company in the city to participate in purchase contracts for petroleum products entered into by the city. Fire company, rescue company and ambulance company participation in purchase contracts for petroleum products shall be subject to the condition that all prices shall be F.O.B. If permitted by council, a fire company, rescue company or ambulance company may participate in designated petroleum product contracts entered into by the city, subject to the fire company, rescue company or ambulance company:

(1) Having filed with the city clerk a request that it be authorized to participate in contracts for the purchase of petroleum products of the city.

(2) Having agreed that it will be bound by any terms and conditions imposed by the city.

Table of Contents
Part I Ch. 1–3 Ethics, Records, Open Meetings
Part II Ch. 4–10 Taxation
Part III Ch. 11–18 Torts, Contracts & Civil Rules
Part IV Ch. 19–24 Zoning & Planning
Part V Ch. 25–30 Construction and Emergency Codes
Part VI Ch. 31–39 Municipal Codes
Index

(3) Having agreed that it will be responsible for payment directly to the vendor under each purchase contract.

§ 11909. Separate bids for plumbing, heating, ventilating and electrical work, elevators and escalators.

The following shall apply:

(1) In the preparation of specifications for the erection, construction and alteration of any public building, when the entire cost of the work shall exceed the base amount of $18,500, subject to adjustment under section 11903.1 (relating to adjustments to base amount based on Consumer Price Index for All Urban Consumers), the architect, engineer or other person preparing the specifications shall prepare only the following separate specifications:

(i) Plumbing.

(ii) Heating.

(iii) Ventilating.

(iv) Electrical work.

(v) Elevators and escalators.

(vi) One complete set of specifications for all the other work to be done in the erection, construction and alteration.

(2) The project manager, construction manager or other person authorized by council to enter into contracts for the erection, construction or alteration of the public buildings shall receive separate bids upon each of the branches of work and council or the appropriate city officer shall award the contract to the lowest responsible bidder for each of the branches, including the balance of the work, in addition to the plumbing, heating, ventilating and electrical work and elevators and escalators. Where it is desired to install an air conditioning unit, the heating and ventilating may be regarded as one branch of work having only one set of specifications, and bids may be received and a contract awarded on that set as provided under this chapter.

§ 11910. Acceptance by contractor of Workers' Compensation Act.

(a) General rule.—All contracts executed by any city which involve the construction or performance of any work involving the employment of labor shall contain a provision that the contractor shall accept and file with the city, proof of compliance with or exemption from the act of June 2, 1915 (P.L.736, No.338), known as the Workers' Compensation Act, insofar as the work covered by the contract is concerned.

(b) Certificate of exemption.—A certificate of exemption from issuance may be issued on the basis of either individual self-insurance or group self-insurance.

(c) Exception.—A contractor shall file with the city any proof that the Department of Labor and Industry, with respect to certain employees, has accepted the application to be excepted from the provisions of the Workers' Compensation Act on religious grounds.

(d) Violation.—Any contract executed in violation of this section is void.

§ 11911. Contracts for improvements and assignment of assessments.

Where the whole or any part of the cost of an improvement is to be paid by assessments upon the property abutting or benefited, the city may enter into an agreement with the contractor, pursuant to which the contractor shall take an assignment of the assessments in payment of the amount due under the terms of the contract and the city shall not be otherwise liable under the contract.

§ 11912. Architects and engineers in employ of city, prohibitions from bidding on public works and penalty.

(a) Bidding.—It shall be unlawful for any architect or engineer in the employ of any city to bid on any public work of the city.

(b) Award.—It shall be unlawful for the officers of any city, charged with the duty of letting any public work, to award a contract to any architect or engineer in the employ of the city.

(c) Violation.—Any person violating these provisions commits a misdemeanor and shall, upon conviction, be subject to forfeiting office, in accordance with section 10901 (relating to appointment, removal and prohibition), and sentenced to pay a fine of not more than $500, or to imprisonment for not less than six months, or both. Any contract made in violation of the provisions of this section shall be null and void.

(d) Construction.—The provisions of this section shall be in addition to any prohibition in 65 Pa.C.S. Ch. 11 (relating to ethics standards and financial disclosure).

§ 11916. Contracts with passenger or transportation companies.

Except as may be prohibited by 66 Pa.C.S. Pt. I (relating to public utility code) or Federal or other State regulation of transportation or commerce, a city may, as it deems necessary for the public benefit and convenience, contract with a person owning a public transportation service, railroad company, street railway, motor power company or passenger or transportation company.

CHAPTER 120

POLICE FORCE

---

§ 12001. Appointment, number, rank, compensation and qualifications of police officers.

(a) General rule.—Council shall fix, by ordinance, the number, grades and compensation of the members of the city police force, who shall, except as provided in section 12002 (relating to designation of chief), be appointed in accordance with the civil service provisions of this chapter.

(b) Demotion.—No member of the city police force having been promoted in conformity with the civil service provisions of this chapter shall be demoted in rank or discharged from the police force except upon proper cause shown as set forth under the civil service provisions of this chapter and section 12002.

(c) Prohibition.—No police officer, after the police officer's appointment and qualification, shall hold at the same time the office of constable.

Table of Contents
Part I Ch. 1–3 Ethics, Records, Open Meetings
Part II Ch. 4–10 Taxation
Part III Ch. 11–18 Torts, Contracts & Civil Rules
Part IV Ch. 19–24 Zoning & Planning
Part V Ch. 25–30 Construction and Emergency Codes
Part VI Ch. 31–39 Municipal Codes
Index

(d) Rules and regulations.—Council shall promulgate rules and regulations for the organization and governing of the police force.

§ 12002. Designation of chief.

The chief of police shall be designated by the mayor from within the ranks and may be demoted without cause in the same manner, but not to any rank lower than the rank which was held at the time of designation as chief of police. In the event that no qualified officer from within the ranks has applied for the designation, the chief of police shall be designated by the mayor from outside the ranks. The officers, other than the chief of police, shall be designated in accordance with Chapter 144 (relating to civil service).

§ 12003. Extra police officers and compensation.

The mayor may appoint extra police officers, whenever it is necessary in the judgment of the mayor for the public safety or to preserve order, to serve for a period designated by council, not to exceed 30 days and whose compensation shall be fixed by council.

§ 12005. Powers of police officers to arrest.

Police officers shall be ex-officio constables of the city, and shall enforce the laws of the Commonwealth or otherwise perform the functions of their office in accordance with 42 Pa.C.S. §§ 8952 (relating to primary municipal police jurisdiction) and 8953 (relating to Statewide municipal police jurisdiction) and upon property owned or controlled by the city or by a municipal authority created by the city. A police officer may, without warrant and upon view, arrest and commit for hearing any and all individuals:

(1) Guilty of:

(i) breach of the peace;

(ii) vagrancy;

(iii) riotous or disorderly conduct; or

(iv) drunkenness.

(2) Engaged in the commission of any unlawful act tending to imperil the personal security or endanger the property of the citizens.

(3) Violating any of the ordinances of the city for the violation of which a fine or penalty is imposed.

§ 12006. Service of process, fees and payment into treasury.

Police officers shall have authority to serve and to execute criminal process or processes issued for the violation of city ordinances and shall charge the same fees and costs as pertain by law to the constables of the city for similar services, but the fees and costs shall be paid into the city treasury monthly.

§ 12007. Supervision by mayor.

The chief of police shall obey the orders of the mayor and make report to the mayor, which shall be presented monthly by the mayor to council.

§ 12008. Extra compensation prohibited, exception and penalty.

No police officer shall ask, demand or receive any compensation or reward for the police officer's services other than compensation provided by ordinance, except rewards offered for the arrest of persons accused of crimes committed outside of the city in which the police officer is employed. A police officer violating any of the provisions of this section commits a misdemeanor of the third degree and shall, upon conviction, be sentenced to pay a fine or imprisonment, or both, to be followed by dismissal from office.

§ 12009. Compensation or insurance for volunteer police officer.

Each city may make necessary appropriations to provide compensation or insurance for volunteer police officers injured or killed while engaged in the performance of duties as may be assigned to them in the city.

§ 12010. School crossing guards.

(a) Request.—Upon request of the board of school directors of the school district in which a city is located, council may appoint school crossing guards who shall control and direct traffic at or near schools. They shall serve at the pleasure of council, except as provided for in subsection (b). The compensation of the school crossing guards, if any, shall be fixed by council and shall be jointly paid by council and the board of school directors, in a ratio to be determined by council and the board of school directors. If council and the board of school directors are unable to determine the ratio of compensation of the school crossing guards to be paid by council and the board, each shall pay one-half of the compensation of the school crossing guards.

(b) Ordinance.—

(1) Council may enact an ordinance allowing a board of school directors to assume the hiring and oversight of the school crossing guards. Before council may enact the ordinance, the board of directors of the school district shall adopt a resolution requesting the authority to assume the hiring and oversight of the school crossing guards. The ordinance enacted by council shall outline how the city police department will provide any necessary training and assistance to the school crossing guards while on duty.

(2) School crossing guards shall not fall under the bargaining unit of the school district or be classified as an employee or under any benefits as provided under the act of March 10, 1949 (P.L.30, No.14), known as the Public School Code of 1949. For the purposes of this paragraph, the term employee shall have the same meaning given to the term "employe" under section 1101-A of the Public School Code of 1949.

(3) After the ordinance is enacted by council, the school district shall assume the cost of compensation, including fixing the compensation, if any, of the school crossing guards. The board of school directors shall notify council, the mayor and the police chief or commissioner of those hired to serve as school crossing guards and request the necessary training or assistance be provided as outlined by the ordinance.

(c) Duties.—Whether council appoints school crossing guards upon the request of the board of school directors or whether council enacts an ordinance allowing a board of school directors to assume the hiring and oversight of the school crossing guards, the following shall apply to school crossing guards:

(1) Their duties and authority shall be restricted to the management of traffic and pedestrians in and around areas identified by the city police force and the school district superintendent or a designee.

(2) They shall be in suitable and distinctive uniforms while performing their duties as school crossing guards.

(3) They shall not be subject to the civil service provisions of this chapter.

(4) They shall not be entitled to participate in any city or school district pension or benefit plan or plans.

(5) Auxiliary police officers lawfully appointed may be designated by council or hired by the school district, as applicable, to serve as school crossing guards.

CHAPTER 121

FIRE BUREAU

Sec.

---

§ 12101. Organization of fire bureau, maintenance and apparatus.

With regard to a city fire bureau, council shall have the authority to:

(1) establish and organize a fire bureau by ordinance;

(2) make appropriations for the maintenance of the fire bureau;

(3) promulgate regulations for the governing of the officers and companies belonging to the fire bureau; and

(4) purchase equipment and apparatus for the extinguishment, prevention and investigation of fires and for the public safety.

§ 12101.1. Appointment and demotion of fire chief.

The mayor, by and with approval and consent of council, shall appoint the fire chief who may be demoted without cause but not to any rank lower than the rank which the fire chief held within the fire bureau at the time of designation as fire chief. In the event that no qualified employee of the fire bureau has applied for the appointment, the fire chief shall be appointed by the mayor, by and with approval and consent of council, from outside the ranks.

§ 12102. Paid fire bureau, election of officers and companies.

When a paid fire bureau is organized by any city, council, except as provided by section 12101.1 (relating to appointment and demotion of fire chief), may provide for the election or appointment of the officers and companies belonging to the fire bureau by ordinance in accordance with civil service provisions, where applicable. The minimum annual starting salary or compensation to be paid to officers and firefighters by any city shall be established by council.

§ 12103. Platoon system and hours of service.

(a) **General rule.**—The director of the department having charge of the fire bureau in a city may divide the officers and members of companies of the uniformed fire force in the employ of the city, and any other firefighters and drivers regularly employed and paid by the city, except the chief engineer and assistant chiefs, and those employed subject to call, into shifts, bodies or platoons to perform service during the hours as the director shall fix. In cases of riot, serious conflagration, times of war, public celebrations or other emergency, the fire chief or officer in charge at any fire shall have the power to assign all the members of the fire force to continuous duty or to continue any member of the fire force on duty, if necessary.

(b) **Schedule after May 19, 2014.**—Except as provided in subsection (c), no schedule shall require a member of any shift, body or platoon to perform continu-

Chap. 39 Res. During Mil. Service
Chap. 38 Intergov. Coop.
Chap. 37 3rd Class City Code
Chap. 36 Bor. Code
Chap. 35 2nd Class Twp. Code
Chap. 34 1st Class Twp. Code
Chap. 33 Home Rule Chart. Opt. Plans Law
Chap. 32 Water Serv. Act
Chap. 31 Munic. Auth. Act

ous service for a consecutive period of 24 hours, except in cases of emergency or as otherwise agreed to through collective bargaining or an award pursuant to the act of June 24, 1968 (P.L.237, No.111), referred to as the Policemen and Firemen Collective Bargaining Act. The provisions of this subsection shall not be deemed to alter or affect any schedules in existence prior to May 19, 2014.

(c) Schedule before May 19, 2014.—In a city where the work schedule in existence prior to May 19, 2014, required a work shift of less than 24 hours, no schedule shall require a member of any shift, body or platoon to perform continuous service for a consecutive period of 24 hours, except in cases of emergency or as otherwise voluntarily agreed through collective bargaining. Once so modified, no further work schedule may contain provisions reinstituting a restriction on duty of less than 24 hours of continuous service.

§ 12104. Fire marshal.

(a) General rule.—A city may, by ordinance, provide for the creation of the office of fire marshal who shall be appointed by the mayor, by and with the approval and consent of council, biennially.

(b) Powers.—

(1) The fire marshal and any authorized assistant shall inspect all construction or buildings within the city or upon property owned or controlled by the city or a municipal authority of the city within this Commonwealth and shall enforce all laws of the Commonwealth and ordinances of the city relating to the construction or buildings, for the prevention, containment or investigation of fire and fire hazards, both as to the construction or buildings and as to their contents or occupancies.

(2) The fire marshal or the fire marshal's assistants shall report to the director of public safety or to council or other designated official, as council shall by ordinance provide, any faulty or dangerous construction or building or like condition in any building that may constitute a fire hazard or any proposed use or occupation of any construction, building or premises which would create or increase a hazard of fire.

(3) The fire marshal shall investigate and keep a permanent record of the cause, origin and circumstances of every fire and the damage resulting from the fire occurring within the fire marshal's jurisdiction immediately after the occurrence of the fire.

(4) The records of the fire marshal shall be open to public inspection, except as exempted in accordance with the act of February 14, 2008 (P.L.6, No.3), known as the Right-to-Know Law. The fire marshal shall submit to council an annual report consolidating the information contained in the records as directed by council.

(5) If a fire is deemed suspicious, the fire marshal shall have the authority to investigate the fire.

§ 12105. Obstructing fire marshal.

(a) General rule.—It shall be unlawful for any person to obstruct or prevent or attempt to obstruct or prevent the fire marshal in the discharge of the fire marshal's duties.

(b) Penalties.—Council may, by ordinance, establish the types or grades of the criminal conduct and may establish fines or imprisonment, or both, for the violations. No fine may exceed $1,000 for any single violation and no imprisonment shall exceed 90 days.

§ 12106. Investigation of cause of fire and power of mayor.

The mayor of any city may issue a subpoena in the name of the Commonwealth to an individual requiring the attendance of the individual before the mayor or the fire marshal at the time and place as may be named in the subpoena, then and there to testify, under oath or affirmation, which the fire marshal in the absence of the mayor is empowered to administer, as to:

(1) the origin of any fire occurring within the bounds of the city; and

(2) any facts or circumstances that may be deemed important to secure the detection and conviction of any party guilty of the offense of arson or attempted arson.

§ 12107. Fire chief ex-officio fire marshal.

The fire chief of a city shall be ex-officio fire marshal if the office is not separately filled pursuant to ordinance in the city and, in that case, all the powers and duties given to or imposed upon the fire marshal under this chapter shall be enjoyed and exercised by the fire chief.

§ 12108. Compensation insurance for injured volunteer firefighters or special fire police.

A city may make appropriations to secure insurance or compensation for volunteer firefighters killed or injured while engaged in the performance of their duties or as special fire police.

§ 12109. Salary of nonunion city fire officers.

A fire chief or head of a fire department of a city who has been removed from bargaining units under the act of June 24, 1968 (P.L.237, No.111), referred to as the Policemen and Firemen Collective Bargaining Act, by rulings of the Pennsylvania Labor Relations Board shall receive not less than the same dollar increase, including fringe benefits but excluding overtime and holiday pay, as received by the highest-ranking fire officer participating in the bargaining unit.

CHAPTER 122
SURVEYS AND SURFACE SUPPORT IN COAL MINING AREAS

---

§ 12203. Survey of mines.

(a) General rule.—For the purpose of conducting a survey as may be required by council, the city engineer or other registered professional engineer employed by the city may:

(1) enter and survey a mine or colliery within the limits of the city, in whole or in part, at all reasonable times, either by day or night, without impeding or obstructing the workings of the mine or colliery; and

(2) take with them other persons necessary for the purpose of making a survey.

(b) Duty to provide entry, survey and exit.—The owner, operator or superintendent of the mine or colliery shall furnish the means necessary for the entry, survey and exit.

§ 12204. Operators to furnish maps and contents.

The owner, operator or superintendent of a coal mine or colliery within the limits of the city, in whole or in part, shall, at the request of council, make or cause to be made and furnished to the city engineer an accurate map or plan of the workings or excavations of each coal mine or colliery within the limits of the city.

§ 12205. Extensions to be placed on maps.

(a) Duty to update.—Not less than once every three months, a map that has been provided to a city, at the request of council, pursuant to section 12204 (relating to operators to furnish maps and contents) shall be updated at the direction of the mine owner, operator or superintendent.

(b) Contents.—The updated map shall show all the extensions made in any mine within the limits of the city, in whole or in part, and not already so placed upon the map, except those made within 30 days immediately preceding the time of placing the extensions upon the map.

§ 12206. Certain surface supports not to be removed.

It shall be unlawful for an individual, partnership, association or corporation to dig, mine, remove or carry away the coal, rock, earth or other minerals or materials forming the natural support of the surface beneath the streets and places of a city to an extent and in a manner as to remove the necessary support of the surface, without having first placed or constructed an artificial permanent support sufficient to uphold and preserve the stability of the surfaces of the streets and places.

§ 12207. Penalty for surface support violations.

An individual, corporation or association violating the provisions of this chapter concerning surface support of streets and places within the city commits a misdemeanor and shall, upon conviction, be sentenced to pay a fine not to exceed $1,000 or imprisonment for a period not to exceed 90 days, or both. Each day in which the violation continues shall constitute an additional and separate offense.

§ 12209. Enactment of ordinances.

Council may enact ordinances necessary for the enforcement of the provisions of this chapter and provide penalties for the violation.

CHAPTER 123
PUBLIC HEALTH

Subchapter

SUBCHAPTER A
BOARD OF HEALTH

Sec.

§ 12300. Definitions.

The following words and phrases when used in this chapter shall have the meanings given to them in this section unless the context clearly indicates otherwise:

"Public nuisance" or "nuisance." A nuisance detrimental to the public health, unless a different meaning is specified.

§ 12301. Board of health.

A city shall have a board of health. Council may, by ordinance, create a board of health or council shall be the board of health. If council is the board of health, members of council shall receive no additional compensation for serving on the board.

§ 12302. Members of appointed boards of health.

(a) **General rule.**—Council shall appoint five members to a board of health created by ordinance. Appointed members shall serve without compensation. Except in the case of an appointed member who is a licensed or certified health care professional with a principal office in the city, members of the appointed board of health must be residents of the city.

(b) **Qualifications.**—

(1) Two members of the board must be licensed or certified health care professionals, unless council cannot identify two professionals who are willing to serve, in which case, one member must be a licensed or certified health care professional.

(2) If no licensed or certified health care professional can be identified to serve on the board, council may appoint an individual who has experience or is knowledgeable of public health issues.

(c) **Licensure and certification required.**—Health care professionals pursuant to this section must be licensed or certified by:

(1) the State Board of Medicine;

(2) the State Board of Examiners of Nursing Home Administrators;

(3) the State Board of Podiatry;

(4) the State Board of Veterinary Medicine;

(5) the State Board of Occupational Therapy Education and Licensure;

(6) the State Board of Osteopathic Medicine;

(7) the State Board of Pharmacy;

(8) the State Board of Physical Therapy;

(9) the State Board of Nursing;

(10) the State Board of Social Workers, Marriage and Family Therapists and Professional Counselors;

(11) the State Board of Chiropractic;

(12) the State Board of Dentistry;

(13) the State Board of Optometry;

(14) the State Board of Psychology; or

(15) the State Board of Examiners in Speech-Language and Audiology.

(d) Terms.—After the creation of the board, for initial membership, council shall, by ordinance, designate one appointee for a term of one year, one for a term of two years, one for a term of three years, one for a term of four years and one for a term of five years. For subsequent membership, one member of the board shall be appointed annually to serve for a term of five years from the first Monday of January succeeding the member's appointment.

(e) Removal.—Council may remove appointed members of the board for official misconduct or neglect of duty.

(f) Vacancies.—A vacancy on an appointed board shall be filled by council. Council shall appoint a qualified individual to membership on the board for the unexpired term of the individual whose membership had been vacated.

§ 12303. Oath of office.

(a) General rule.—Each member of the board of health shall take the oath of office prescribed in section 10905 (relating to oath of office, violation of oath and penalty).

(b) Organization.—The board of health shall organize annually on the first Monday of January and shall elect a president annually from among its members.

(c) Appointment of secretary.—Council shall appoint a secretary of the board of health who is not a member of the board of health. The secretary shall receive a salary as approved by council.

§ 12304. Duties of secretary.

The secretary of the board shall:

(1) Keep the minutes of the proceedings of the board and accurate accounts of the expenditures of the board.

(2) Draw all requisitions for the payment of money on account of the board of health from appropriations made by council to the board and shall present the requisitions to the president of the board for the president's approval.

(3) Render statements of the expenditures to the board at each stated meeting or as frequently as the board may require.

(4) Prepare, under the direction of the board, the annual report to council, together with the estimate of appropriations needed for the ensuing year.

(5) Make reports to the Department of Health as required by law, rule or regulation of the department.

(6) Make other reports and perform other duties as required by law or by the board of health.

§ 12305. Health officer.

(a) Selection and oath.—

(1) Council shall, by ordinance, determine the manner and method of selection of a health officer who shall be an individual with experience or training in public health work and who shall be or shall become certified for the office of health officer by the State Department of Health within six months of taking the oath of office.

(2) The health officer shall take the oath required of members of the board.

(3) The health officer shall be the agent of the board of health, but shall not serve as a member of the board of health.

(b) Qualifications.—

(1) Council may appoint, as the principal health officer of the city, the manager or chief administrator employed and compensated by a nonprofit corporation which may be appointed as a board of health in accordance with Subchapter C (relating to corporations acting as boards of health).

(2) The manager or chief administrator, to be eligible for appointment, must be a reputable physician with at least five years' experience in the practice of the physician's profession or in public health work.

(3) The principal health officer, appointed pursuant to this subsection, shall have all the powers, authority and duties prescribed by law upon principal health officers.

§ 12306. Duties of health officer.

(a) **General rule.**—The health officer shall:

(1) Attend all regular and special meetings of the board of health.

(2) Be available for the prompt performance of the health officer's official duties.

(3) Quarantine places of communicable diseases in accordance with law and with the rules and regulations of the Department of Health or of the city board of health.

(4) Execute all laws, rules and regulations for the disinfection of quarantined places.

(5) Serve written notice on teachers and persons in charge of public, parochial, Sunday and other schools requiring the exclusion of children from school who are suffering from or who reside with individuals who are suffering from communicable diseases.

(6) Make sanitary inspections subject to constitutional standards in a similar manner as provided in section 12308 (relating to powers of board of health).

(7) Execute the orders of the board of health and all other laws, rules, regulations and orders pertaining to the health officer's office.

(b) **Issuance of citations.**—The health officer shall, to the extent the health officer's duties allow, have the power to issue citations for the violation of applicable laws or ordinances.

§ 12307. Duties of board of health.

(a) **General rule.**—The board of health shall prevent or diminish the introduction or further spread of infectious or contagious diseases and otherwise to protect and increase the public health by:

(1) regulating access to places of infection or contagion;

(2) isolating carriers of infection or contagion or individuals who have been exposed to any infectious or contagious disease;

(3) abating or removing all nuisances which the board deems prejudicial to the public health; and

(4) enforcing vaccination laws.

(5) promulgating regulations, as it deems proper, for the preservation or improvement of public health, consistent with this chapter and the laws of the Commonwealth.

(b) **Enforcement.**—In carrying out its duties under this chapter, the board of health shall, if authorized, enforce the laws of the Commonwealth that are relevant to and relate to its duties.

(c) **Transmittal of information.**—The board of health shall transmit to the Department of Health all of its reports and publications and other information regarding public health in the city as may be requested or required by the department.

§ 12308. Powers of board of health.

The board of health shall:

(1) If authorized by council, employ agents and employees at rates of compensation approved by council.

(2) Enter upon any premises within the city, as a body or by committee or by its agents or employees, which are suspected of infectious or contagious disease or of any other nuisance prejudicial to the public health or which pose danger, for the purpose of examining the premises or of preventing, confining or abating public nuisances. The following apply:

(i) In the event that entry upon any premises is refused by an owner, an agent of an owner or tenant, the board of health shall obtain an administrative search warrant from a magisterial district judge within the judicial district where the premises to be inspected is located.

(ii) It shall be sufficient to support the issuance of a warrant for the board of health to provide to the magisterial district judge evidence of any of the following:

(A) Reasonable standards and an administrative plan for conducting inspections.

(B) The condition of the premises or general area and the passage of time since the last inspection.

(C) Facts, supported by an oath or affirmation, alleging that probable cause exists that a law, regulation or ordinance subject to enforcement by the board of health has been violated.

(3) Conduct investigations and hold public hearings in the performance of its duties and powers. In a hearing under this paragraph, the president and secretary of the board may administer oaths and affirmations, but shall receive no fee for administration, and the board of health may require the attendance of witnesses and their books and papers in accordance with section 10917 (relating to powers of subpoena and compelling testimony).

(4) Publish and enforce its rules and regulations as approved by council.

(5) If approved by council, provide for or cooperate in providing for general and gratuitous vaccination, disinfection and other public health control programs and make medical relief available to benefit public health.

(6) Provide, in accordance with Subchapter B (relating to public nuisances detrimental to public health), for the prevention, abatement and removal of conditions found to be detrimental to public health as public nuisances or to declare and certify to council that the premises or places harboring the detrimental condition are public, not private, nuisances.

§ 12309. Effect of rules and regulations.

Rules and regulations adopted by the board of health shall be presented to council for its approval subject to the following:

(1) Council may approve, by ordinance, the rules and regulations submitted by the board of health.

(2) Upon approval by council, the rules and regulations of the board of health shall have the force and effect of ordinances of the city.

(3) The ordinance approving the rules and regulations may incorporate them by reference.

(4) Council shall provide a place for the public to view the rules and regulations.

(5) The ordinance approving the rules and regulations shall prescribe the penalties, fines or imprisonment for violations.

Table of Contents
Part I Ch. 1–3 Ethics, Records, Open Meetings
Part II Ch. 4–10 Taxation
Part III Ch. 11–18 Torts, Contracts & Civil Rules
Part IV Ch. 19–24 Zoning & Planning
Part V Ch. 25–30 Construction and Emergency Codes
Part VI Ch. 31–39 Municipal Codes
Index

§ 12310. Fees and penalties.

All fees and penalties collected or received by the board of health or a board officer acting in an official capacity shall be paid to the city treasurer for use by the city.

§ 12311. Proceedings of board of health to be public.

The proceedings of the board of health shall be public and its journal of proceedings shall be open to public inspection.

SUBCHAPTER B

PUBLIC NUISANCES DETRIMENTAL TO PUBLIC HEALTH

Sec.

§ 12320. Determination of public nuisances.

(a) General rule.—A condition or usage in a city, whether public or private, determined by the board of health to be detrimental to the public health shall constitute a public nuisance.

(b) Powers.—The powers of investigation and entering upon premises vested in the board of health and its agents and employees pursuant to its orders shall be available for the determination of public nuisances.

§ 12321. Abatement of public nuisances by designated department.

(a) Duty to report.—If, in accordance with this subchapter, the board of health determines that a public nuisance exists, it shall report its determination, along with any request for summary abatement, to the department designated by council in section 127A02 (relating to report and investigation of public nuisance).

(b) Procedure.—The report to the designated department that the board of health has determined that a public nuisance exists shall be deemed a determination by the designated department that a public nuisance exists as required by section 127A02(d)(1). Notwithstanding any other provision of Chapter 127A (relating to nuisance abatement), the department designated to abate public nuisances shall proceed as follows:

(1) Summary abatement, if requested by the board of health, shall be pursued if the criteria set forth in section 127A02(d)(2) exists.

(2) If summary abatement is not pursued, proceed with abatement with prior notice in accordance with Chapter 127A.

SUBCHAPTER C

CORPORATIONS ACTING AS BOARDS OF HEALTH

Sec.

---

§ 12330. Board of directors of corporation to be appointed members of board of health.

(a) General rule.—Council may, by ordinance, appoint the members of a board of directors of a nonprofit corporation as the board of health for the city for a term of five years, provided that the nonprofit corporation:

(1) Has as its principal purpose to substantially preserve and promote the public health of the city and to control and eliminate disease.

(2) Has sufficient means to render valuable assistance to the city's public health affairs, in the opinion of council and the Department of Health.

(3) Is properly organized and managed.

(4) Has not fewer than five and not more than nine members on the board of directors.

(5) Has at least two reputable physicians on the board, each of whom has not less than five years' experience in the practice of the physician's profession.

(b) Vacancies.—When the office of any member of the board of directors is terminated, pursuant to the nonprofit corporation's charter or bylaws, the office of the member of the board of health shall also terminate with the resulting vacancy to be filled under subsection (c).

(c) Additional members to board of health.—

(1) If the number of the board of directors of the nonprofit corporation increases, subject to the limitation of a maximum of nine members, council may appoint any individual added to the corporation's board of directors as an additional member of the board of health for a term equal to the unexpired term of the other members.

(2) An additional appointment under this subsection shall be subject to any subsequent termination resulting from a limitation in the corporation's charter and bylaws.

§ 12332. Power of board.

The board of health under this subchapter shall have all the power and authority and perform the duties prescribed by law upon boards of health of cities.

§ 12333. Health officer.

Pursuant to section 12305(b) (relating to health officer), council may appoint the manager or chief administrator of a nonprofit corporation as the principal health officer of the city.

§ 12334. Secretary.

The secretary of the board of directors of the nonprofit corporation under this subchapter may serve as secretary of the board of health.

§ 12335. Filling of vacancies.

(a) General rule.—Council may appoint successors for vacancies on the board of health that occur:

(1) As five-year terms of board members expire. The successors shall serve for five-year terms.

(2) For any other reason, but a successor appointment shall be for the unexpired portion of the five-year term.

Table of Contents
Part I Ch. 1–3 Ethics, Records, Open Meetings
Part II Ch. 4–10 Taxation
Part III Ch. 11–18 Torts, Contracts & Civil Rules
Part IV Ch. 19–24 Zoning & Planning
Part V Ch. 25–30 Construction and Emergency Codes
Part VI Ch. 31–39 Municipal Codes
Index

(b) **Selection.**—Successors, whether appointed for a five-year term or the unexpired portion of a five-year term, shall be selected from the members of the nonprofit corporation's board of directors.

§ 12337. No compensation for members.

The members of the board of health under this subchapter shall serve without compensation from the city.

§ 12338. Applicability of Subchapter.

This subchapter shall be effective only under the circumstances set forth in section 12330 (relating to board of directors of corporation to be appointed members of board of health).

SUBCHAPTER D

PENALTY

Sec.

---

§ 12340. Penalty.

Any person who:

(1) violates any provision of this chapter or any order or regulation of the board of health made under the authority of this chapter;

(2) violates any law, regulation or ordinance referred to or authorized by this chapter;

(3) obstructs or interferes with any person in the execution of any order or regulation of the board; or

(4) willfully and illegally refuses to obey any order or regulation of the board;

commits a summary offense punishable in accordance with sections 11018.16 (relating to enforcement of ordinances, recovery and payment of fines and penalties) and 11018.17 (relating to penalty).

CHAPTER 124

CORPORATE POWERS

Sec.

Chap. 39 Res. During Mil. Service
Chap. 38 Intergov. Coop.
Chap. 37 3rd Class City Code
Chap. 36 Bor. Code
Chap. 35 2nd Class Twp. Code
Chap. 34 1st Class Twp. Code
Chap. 33 Home Rule Chart. Opt. Plans Law
Chap. 32 Water Serv. Act
Chap. 31 Munic. Auth. Act

---

§ 12402. Powers of cities.

(a) General rule.—A city is declared to be a body corporate and politic, shall have perpetual succession and may:

(1) Sue and be sued.

(2) Have and use a corporate seal and alter the seal. The seal shall have upon it the word "Pennsylvania," the name of the city and the year of its original incorporation.

(3) Display the flag of the United States, the Commonwealth or of any county, city, borough or other municipality in this Commonwealth on the public buildings of the city.

(4) Appropriate money and accept gifts or grants of money, other property or services from public or private sources for the exercise of powers expressed or implied in this chapter or any other applicable law.

(b) Exercise of powers.—The powers granted in this chapter shall be exercised in the manner provided in this chapter.

§ 12402.1. City property and affairs.

(a) General rule.—In exercising its discretion to make decisions that further the public interest under terms it deems most beneficial to the city, council may, subject to any restrictions, limitations or exceptions stated in this chapter:

Table of Contents
Part I Ch. 1–3 Ethics, Records, Open Meetings
Part II Ch. 4–10 Taxation
Part III Ch. 11–18 Torts, Contracts & Civil Rules
Part IV Ch. 19–24 Zoning & Planning
Part V Ch. 25–30 Construction and Emergency Codes
Part VI Ch. 31–39 Municipal Codes
Index

(1) Purchase, hold, use and manage real and personal property.

(2) Exchange personal property.

(3) Lease, sell and convey real and personal property owned by the city.

(4) Make contracts and do all other acts respecting city property and affairs as council may deem conducive to the public interest and necessary to the exercise of the city's corporate and administrative powers.

(b) Sales of real estate.—

(1) No real estate owned by the city may be sold except upon approval of council by resolution, and no real estate owned by the city may be sold for a consideration in excess of $6,000, except to the highest bidder after due notice by advertisement for bids or advertisement of a public auction in one newspaper of general circulation in the city.

(2) The advertisement shall be published once not less than 10 days prior to the date fixed for the opening of bids or public auction and the date for opening bids or public auction shall be announced in the advertisement.

(3) The award of contracts shall be made only by public announcement at a regular or special meeting of council or at the public auction.

(4) All bids shall be accepted on the condition that payment of the purchase price in full shall be made within 60 days of the acceptance of bids.

(5) Council may reject all bids which it deems to be less than the fair market value of the real property.

(6) In the case of a public auction, council may establish a minimum bid based on the fair market value of the real property.

(7) If no compliant bids are received after advertisement, the applicable procedures in the act of October 27, 1979 (P.L.241, No.78), entitled "An act authorizing political subdivisions, municipality authorities and transportation authorities to enter into contracts for the purchase of goods and the sale of real and personal property where no bids are received," shall be followed.

(8) Real estate owned by a city may be sold at a consideration of $6,000 or less without advertisement or competitive bidding only after council estimates the value of the real estate upon receipt of an appraisal by a qualified real estate appraiser. Prior to selling real estate valued at $6,000 or less without advertisement or competitive bidding, council shall make a public announcement of the council's intention to sell the real estate at a regular or special meeting of council at least 30 days prior to the sale.

(9)(i) This section shall not apply if council exercises its authority to exchange real property of the city for real property of equal or greater value, provided that the property being acquired by the city is to be used for municipal purposes.

(ii) If council chooses to exercise its power of real property exchange pursuant to this section, it shall be by resolution adopted by council.

(iii) Notice of the resolution, including a description of the properties to be exchanged, shall be published once in one newspaper of general circulation not more than 60 days nor fewer than seven days prior to adoption.

(c) Sale of personal property.—

(1) No personal property of the city shall be disposed of, by sale or otherwise, except upon approval of council by resolution.

(2) Council shall estimate the sale value of the entire lot to be disposed of.

(3) If council estimates the sale value to be less than $2,000, council may sell the property, in whole or in part, for the best price or prices obtainable.

(4) If council estimates the sale value to be $2,000 or more, the entire lot shall be advertised for sale in at least one newspaper of general circulation in accordance with the provisions of section 10109 (relating to publication of

notices) and sale of the property advertised shall be made to the best responsible bidder.

(5) The bids shall not be opened until at least 10 days after the newspaper advertisement is published.

(6) The provisions of this subsection shall not be mandatory where personal property of the city is to be traded in or exchanged for other personal property.

(7) Council may sell any personal property of the city at auction pursuant to subsection (d), but shall observe the same notice requirements as contained in this subsection.

(d) Online or electronic auction of personal property.—In regards to the sale of personal property of the city, an auction may be conducted by means of an online or electronic auction sale subject to the following:

(1) Bids shall be accepted electronically at the time and in the manner designated in the advertisement pursuant to the notice requirements in subsection (c).

(2) Each bidder shall have the capability to view the bidder's bid rank or the high bid price.

(3) Bidders may increase their bid prices during the electronic auction.

(4) The record of the electronic auction shall be available for public inspection.

(5) The purchase price shall be paid by the high bidder immediately or at a reasonable time after the conclusion of the electronic auction, as determined by council.

(6) In the event that shipping costs are incurred, they shall be paid by the high bidder.

(7) A city that has complied with the advertising requirements of subsection (c) may provide additional public notice of the sale by bid or auction in any manner deemed appropriate by council.

(8) The newspaper advertisement for electronic auction sales authorized in this section shall include the Internet address or means of accessing the electronic auction and the date, time and duration of the electronic auction.

(e) Nonapplicability.—Any requirement for advertising for bids and sale to the highest bidder imposed by this part or by a city pursuant to this section shall not apply where real or personal property of the city is sold to the following, provided that when any real property is no longer used for the purpose of the conveyance, the real property shall revert to the city:

(1) The Federal Government, the Commonwealth, a municipality, home rule municipality, institution district or school district.

(2) A volunteer fire company, volunteer ambulance service or volunteer rescue squad located within the city or providing emergency services in the city.

(3) A municipal authority, a housing authority created pursuant to the act of May 28, 1937 (P.L.955, No.265), known as the Housing Authorities Law, an urban redevelopment authority created pursuant to the act of May 24, 1945 (P.L.991, No.385), known as the Urban Redevelopment Law, a parking authority created under 53 Pa.C.S. Ch. 55 (relating to parking authorities) or under the former act of June 5, 1947 (P.L.458, No.208), known as the Parking Authority Law, or a port authority created pursuant to the act of December 6, 1972 (P.L.1392, No.298), known as the Third Class City Port Authority Act.

(4) A nonprofit corporation engaged in community industrial development.

(5) A nonprofit corporation organized as a public library.

(6) A nonprofit medical service corporation.

(7) A nonprofit housing corporation.

(8) A nonprofit museum or historical organization.

(f) Nominal consideration acceptable.—When real or personal property is sold pursuant to subsection (e)(5), (6) or (7), the city may accept nominal consideration as it shall deem appropriate.

§ 12403. Payment of debts and expenses.

Council may provide for the payment of the debts and expenses of the city and appropriate money for the payment.

§ 12404. Creation of reserve funds.

(a) Capital reserve fund.—

(1) Council may create and maintain a separate capital reserve fund for any anticipated capital expenses, which shall be designated for a specific purpose or purposes when created. The money in the fund shall be used for no other purpose unless council declares that conditions in the city make other expenses more urgent than those for which the fund was created.

(2) Council may appropriate money from the general city fund to be paid into the capital reserve fund or place in the fund any money received from the sale, lease or other disposition of any property of the city or from any other source.

(b) Operating reserve fund.—With regard to an operating reserve fund, the following shall apply:

(1) Council shall have the power to create and maintain a separate operating reserve fund in order to:

(i) minimize future revenue shortfalls and deficits;

(ii) provide greater continuity and predictability in the funding of vital government services;

(iii) minimize the need to increase taxes to balance the budget in times of fiscal distress; and

(iv) provide the capacity to undertake long-range financial planning and to develop fiscal resources to meet long-term needs.

(2) Council may annually make appropriations from the general city fund to the operating reserve fund, but no appropriation shall be made to the operating reserve fund if the effect of the appropriation would cause the fund to exceed 25% of the estimated revenues of the city's general fund in the current fiscal year.

(3) Council may, at any time by resolution, make appropriations from the operating reserve fund for the following purposes only:

(i) to address emergencies involving the health, safety or welfare of the residents of the city;

(ii) to counterbalance potential budget deficits resulting from shortfalls in anticipated revenues or program receipts from any source;

(iii) to counterbalance potential budget deficits resulting from increases in anticipated costs for goods or services; or

(iv) to provide for anticipated operating expenditures related either to the planned growth of existing projects or programs or to the establishment of new projects or programs if, for each project or program, appropriations have been made and allocated to a separate restricted account established within the operating reserve fund.

(c) Investment and administration.—The operating reserve fund shall be invested, reinvested and administered in a manner consistent with the provisions of this part relating to the investment of city funds generally.

§ 12405. Hiring of employees and salaries.

Council may provide for and regulate the manner of hiring and discharging employees and the fixing of their salaries or compensation, consistent with applicable Federal and State law.

§ 12406. Creation of necessary offices or boards.

In addition to the city departments established in accordance with Chapter 111 (relating to the executive department), council may create any city office, public board, bureau or commission, which it may deem necessary for the good of government and interests of the city, and, with regard to an office or membership on a board, bureau or commission, unless otherwise provided by this part, council may make appointments and regulate and prescribe the terms, duties and compensation.

§ 12407. Lockups.

(a) **General rule.**—Council may provide for lockup facilities as deemed necessary for the detention and confinement of individuals.

(b) **Restriction.**—No city shall erect or construct a city jail or lockup or use any existing building or lockup for the first time that will be or is located within 500 feet of a public school building.

§ 12408. Market places.

Council may:

(1) Purchase, lease and own ground for market places.

(2) Erect, maintain and establish market places.

(3) Provide for and enforce suitable general market regulations.

(4) Contract with any person for the erection and regulation of market places on terms and conditions and in the manner as council may prescribe.

(5) Levy and collect a license fee from every person who may be authorized by council to occupy any portion of the streets, sidewalks or city property for temporary market purposes.

§ 12409. Accumulation of ashes, garbage, solid waste and refuse materials.

(a) **General rule.**—Council in the manner authorized by the act of July 7, 1980 (P.L.380, No.97), known as the Solid Waste Management Act, and the act of July 28, 1988 (P.L.556, No.101), known as the Municipal Waste Planning, Recycling and Waste Reduction Act, may prohibit accumulations of ashes, garbage, solid waste and other refuse materials upon private property, including the imposition and collection of reasonable fees and charges for the collection, removal and disposal.

(b) **Collection and removal.**—

(1) Council may collect and remove, by contract or otherwise, ashes, garbage, solid waste and other refuse materials and recyclables and prescribe penalties for the enforcement.

(2) A contract with refuse haulers may be made for an initial period not to exceed five years with optional renewal periods of up to five years.

(3) The limitation in paragraph (2) does not apply to a contract with a county or municipal corporation.

(c) **Disposal.**—

(1) Council may dispose of, by contract or otherwise, ashes, garbage, solid waste or other refuse materials.

(2) A contract with the owner of a private facility for the disposal or incineration of ashes, garbage, solid waste or other refuse materials may be made for a period not to exceed 20 years.

(3) The limitation in paragraph (2) does not apply to a contract with a county or municipal corporation.

(d) Acquisition of real property and facilities.—

(1) Council may acquire any real property and erect, maintain, improve, operate and lease, either as lessor or lessee, facilities for incineration, landfill or other methods of disposal, either inside or outside the limits of the city, including equipment, either separately or jointly, with a county or municipal corporation in order to provide for the collection, removal, disposal and destruction of ashes, garbage, solid waste or other refuse materials, for the collection and storage of recyclable materials or for the composting of leaf and yard waste.

(2) Council may provide for the payment of the cost out of the funds of the city.

(3) Council may acquire land for landfill purposes, either amicably or by exercising the power of eminent domain, and may maintain lands and places for the dumping of ashes, garbage, solid waste or other refuse materials.

(4) If council acquires land outside the limits of the city by exercising the power of eminent domain, the taking shall be subject to the limitations in 26 Pa.C.S. § 206 (relating to extraterritorial takings).

(e) Rates and charges.—

(1) Council may establish, alter, charge and collect rates and other charges for:

(i) the collection, removal and disposal of ashes, garbage, solid waste, other refuse materials and recyclable materials; and

(ii) the cost of including the payment of any indebtedness incurred for the construction, purchase, improvement, repair, maintenance and operation of any facilities for collection, removal and disposal; and

(iii) the amount due under a contract with a county or municipal corporation furnishing the services or facilities.

(2) The rates and other charges shall be collected pursuant to the Municipal Claim and Tax Lien Law or by a civil action.

(f) Appropriations.—Council may make appropriations to a county or municipal corporation for the construction, purchase, improvement, repair, maintenance and operation of a facility for the collection, removal, disposal or marketing of ashes, garbage, solid waste, other refuse materials, recyclable materials or composted leaf and yard waste.

(g) Exclusion from other laws.—A city shall not be subject to requirements otherwise imposed by law for the sale of personal property owned by the city when selling recyclable materials or materials separated, collected, recovered or created by recycling, as provided in the act of April 9, 1992 (P.L.70, No.21), entitled "An act excluding the sale of recyclable material from political subdivision personal property sale restrictions relating to advertising and bidding."

§ 12410. Regulation of pets and feral animals.

Council may, by ordinance, prohibit and regulate the running at large of dogs, cats, other pets and feral animals.

§ 12411. Inspection and regulation of fireplaces and chimneys and smoke regulations.

In conformity with Federal and State laws and regulations, council may regulate and inspect fireplaces, chimneys and other sources of smoke and fly-ash to control the production and emission of unnecessary smoke and fly-ash.

§ 12412. Fireworks and inflammable articles.

In conformity with Federal and State laws and regulations, council may:

(1) Regulate and prohibit the manufacture of fireworks or inflammable or dangerous articles.

(2) Grant permits for supervised public displays of fireworks and adopt rules and regulations governing the displays.

(3) Adopt rules and regulations not inconsistent with State regulations relating to the storage of inflammable articles.

(4) Impose other safeguards concerning inflammable articles as may be necessary.

§ 12413. Regulation of division fences, party walls and foundations.

(a) Authority.—

(1) Subject to the provisions of and regulations adopted pursuant to the Pennsylvania Construction Code Act and other applicable law, council may provide regulations for party walls and division fences, the foundations of buildings and entering upon the land or lands, lot or lots, of any person within the city at all reasonable hours by its duly appointed city engineer or building inspectors in order to enforce the regulations and set out foundations.

(2) Council may prescribe reasonable fees for the service of city officers in the inspection and regulation of party walls, division fences and foundations and may enforce the payment of the fees.

(3) Council may provide fines or penalties for violations of an ordinance enacted pursuant to this section.

(b) Specifications.—

(1) In setting out foundations and regulating party walls as to breadth and thickness, the city shall require the foundations to be laid equally upon the lands of the persons between whom the party wall is to be made.

(2) The cost of the foundation and party wall shall be divided proportionately among the property owners sharing the wall. The property owners shall either share the expense when the foundation is laid and the party wall is erected or when the subsequent building is erected if all buildings are not erected at the same time.

§ 12414. Nuisances.

Council may prohibit and abate public nuisances in accordance with Subchapter B of Chapter 123 (relating to public nuisances detrimental to public health).

§ 12415. Regulation of encroachments.

In compliance with applicable State laws and city ordinances, council may provide for the regulation of all encroachments in, under or upon sidewalks or other portions of streets in the city.

§ 12416. Shade trees.

(a) Power to regulate.—

(1) Council may, by ordinance, regulate the manner and method, if any, for the planting, trimming, removing, maintaining and protection of shade trees in, on and along or extending over the public streets, sidewalks and rights-of-way of the city and provide for penalties for violations.

(2) The cost of the activities under paragraph (1) may, at council's discretion, be assessed against the owners of the properties abutting the street, sidewalk or right-of-way upon which any tree is located pursuant to Chapter 145A (relating to assessments for public improvements), except that the cost and expense of caring for trees after they have been planted shall be paid by the city.

Chap. 39 Res. During Mil. Service
Chap. 38 Intergov. Coop.
Chap. 37 3rd Class City Code
Chap. 36 Bor. Code
Chap. 35 2nd Class Twp. Code
Chap. 34 1st Class Twp. Code
Chap. 33 Home Rule Chart. Opt. Plans Law
Chap. 32 Water Serv. Act
Chap. 31 Munic. Auth. Act

(b) Shade tree commission.—

(1) Council may, by ordinance, provide for the creation of a shade tree commission, its composition, powers and duties and delegate council's authority for regulating shade trees to the commission.

(2) In lieu of an ordinance under paragraph (1), council may delegate its regulatory powers for shade trees to an existing department.

(3) If a shade tree commission is established, its meeting shall be subject to the provisions of 65 Pa.C.S. Ch. 7 (relating to open meetings).

§ 12417. Numbering of buildings.

Council may require and regulate the numbering of buildings and lots.

§ 12418. Transportation stands.

Council may establish stands for taxis, buses, automobiles and other vehicles for hire and enforce the observance and use of the stands.

§ 12419. Police force.

(a) General rule.—Council may establish and maintain a police force and define the duties of the force in accordance with Chapter 120 (relating to police force).

(b) Method of providing police services.—Subject to the requirements of 53 Pa.C.S. Ch. 23 Subch. A (relating to intergovernmental cooperation), council may provide for police services as follows:

(1) by municipal police officers under a contract;

(2) through the purchase of the police services; or

(3) by joining or developing a consolidated regional police service.

§ 12420. Police regulations.

Council may establish and enforce suitable police regulations for the protection of individuals and property.

§ 12421. Rewards.

Council may offer rewards for the arrest and conviction of individuals guilty of capital or other crimes within the city.

§ 12422. Prevent riots.

Council may prevent and restrain riots, noises, disturbances or disorderly assemblies in any street, house or place in the city.

§ 12423. Regulate discharge of guns and deadly weapons.

To the extent permitted by Federal and other State law, council may regulate, prohibit and prevent the discharge of guns and prevent the carrying of concealed deadly weapons.

§ 12424. Racing and dangerous practices.

With regard to streets and public places in the city, council may regulate or prohibit racing or fast driving of vehicles and all games, practices or amusements likely to result in danger or damage to any individual or property.

§ 12425. Bathing, recreational swimming establishments and boat houses and bath houses.

To the extent permitted by the act of June 23, 1931 (P.L.899, No.299), known as the Public Bathing Law, council may regulate the time and place of bathing in rivers and other public water in and adjoining the city and may construct, maintain and manage municipal boat houses, bath houses and recreational swimming establishments.

§ 12426. Musical entertainment.

Council may appropriate money to defray the expenses of musical entertainment held under the auspices of the city and for the purpose of having music in any public park or place.

§ 12427. Aid to historical societies.

Council may make annual appropriations for the support and maintenance of the principal historical society located in the city, which shall be incorporated under the laws of the Commonwealth, and shall maintain permanent quarters for the society and keep them open to the public.

§ 12428. Establishment of institutions to collect educational collections.

(a) General rule.—Council may establish institutions authorized to collect and hold certain scientific, educational and economic collections, the object of each being the instruction of the public concerning commerce, manufacturing, mining and agriculture.

(b) Powers.—The institutions may purchase or accept, by gift, any real estate, money or personal property necessary for use and promotion. The institutions may use, convey or transfer the property as if they were bodies corporate and shall be governed by boards of trustees, nominated, appointed and confirmed in the manner council may determine.

§ 12429. Ambulances and rescue and lifesaving services.

Council may:

(1) Acquire, operate and maintain motor vehicles for the purposes of transporting sick and injured individuals to and from hospitals.

(2) Appropriate money toward ambulances and rescue and lifesaving services.

(3) Make contracts relating to rescue and lifesaving services.

§ 12430. Insurance.

(a) Contracts authorized.—Council, in its discretion or as required by law or a collective bargaining agreement, may make contracts of insurance and contracts for annuities or pensions, including the following:

(1) Contracts of insurance with any mutual or other fire insurance company, association or exchange, duly authorized by law to transact insurance business in this Commonwealth, on any building or property owned by the city and contracts to insure against burglary or theft of city property, fire, other disaster and public liability.

(2) Contracts of insurance with any insurance company, nonprofit hospitalization corporation or nonprofit medical service corporation authorized to transact insurance business within this Commonwealth, insuring elected or appointed officers, officials and employees of the city, or their dependents, under a policy or policies of group insurance covering life, health, hospitalization, medical service or accident insurance.

(3) Contracts to purchase annuities or pensions for elected or appointed officers, officials and employees.

(b) Payment of premium and charges.—In the case of a contract for the benefit of elected or appointed officers, officials and employees of the city, or their dependents, the city may, as determined by council or as required by law or a collective bargaining agreement, pay part or all of the premiums or charges for the contract.

§ 12431. Parking lots.

Council may acquire, by lease, purchase or condemnation proceedings, land that in its judgment may be necessary and desirable for the purpose of establishing and maintaining lots for the sole purpose of parking motor vehicles. Council may regulate the use of the land, including the posting of signs, and may establish or designate areas exclusively reserved for parking by individuals with disabilities. Regulation of parking lots shall be consistent with 75 Pa.C.S. (relating to vehicles) and the act of October 27, 1955 (P.L.744, No.222), known as the Pennsylvania Human Relations Act.

§ 12432. Disorderly conduct.

Council may, by ordinance, prohibit disorderly conduct within the limits of the city and provide for the imposition of penalties in accordance with this part. If an ordinance is enacted, it shall define disorderly conduct in a manner substantially similar to the provisions of 18 Pa.C.S. § 5503 (relating to disorderly conduct).

§ 12433. Official expenses on city business.

Council may make appropriations for the reasonable expenses of city officials incurred in the conduct of city business.

§ 12434. Municipal authorities and cooperation with other political subdivisions.

(a) Municipal authorities.—Council may, by ordinance, individually or in cooperation with other municipalities or school districts, form municipal authorities as authorized under 53 Pa.C.S. Ch. 56 (relating to municipal authorities).

(b) Cooperative agreements.—Council may make cooperative agreements with regard to the performance of a city's powers, duties and functions in accordance with the provisions of 53 Pa.C.S. Ch. 23 Subch. A (relating to intergovernmental cooperation).

§ 12435. Local self-government.

Council shall have the power to enact, make, adopt, modify, repeal and enforce, in accordance with this part, ordinances, resolutions, rules and regulations not inconsistent with or restrained by the Constitution of Pennsylvania and laws of the Commonwealth that are either of the following:

(1) Expedient or necessary for the proper management, care and control of the city and its finances and the maintenance of the peace, good government, safety and welfare of the city and its trade, commerce and manufactures.

(2) Necessary to the exercise of the powers and authority of local self-government in municipal affairs.

§ 12436. Historical property.

Council may acquire, by purchase or gift, repair, supervise, operate and maintain landmarks and other historical properties that are either eligible for listing or listed in the National Register of Historic Places or certified by the Pennsylvania Historical and Museum Commission as having historical significance.

§ 12437. Appropriations for handling, storage and distribution of surplus foods.

(a) Appropriations.—Council may appropriate from city funds money for the handling, storage and distribution of surplus foods obtained through a Federal, State or local agency.

(b) Validity of previous appropriations.—All appropriations of money previously made by council for the handling, storage and distribution of surplus foods obtained, through a Federal, State or local agency, are validated.

§ 12438. Junk dealers and junk yards.

Council may regulate and license junk dealers and the establishment and maintenance of junk yards and scrap yards, including automobile junk or grave yards.

§ 12439. Appropriations for industrial development.

Council may make appropriations to an industrial development organization as defined in section 2301 of the act of June 29, 1996 (P.L.434, No.67), known as the Job Enhancement Act, when the city is located within the area for which the industrial development organization has been authorized to make application to and receive grants from the Department of Community and Economic Development for the purposes specified in Chapter 23 of the Job Enhancement Act.

§ 12440. Nondebt revenue bonds.

Consistent with and without limitation of any power conferred or duty imposed by 53 Pa.C.S. Pt. VII Subpt. B (relating to indebtedness and borrowing), council may issue nondebt revenue bonds pursuant to the provisions of 53 Pa.C.S. Pt. VII Subpt. B.

§ 12441. Appropriations for urban common carrier mass transportation.

Council may make appropriations for urban common carrier mass transportation from current revenues and make annual contributions to county departments of transportation or to urban common carrier mass transportation authorities to assist the departments or the authorities to meet costs of operation, maintenance, capital improvements and debt service and to enter into long-term agreements providing for the payment of the contributions.

§ 12442. Appropriation for nonprofit art corporation.

(a) Appropriation.—Council may appropriate money annually, of not more than an amount equal to one mill of the real estate tax, to any nonprofit art corporation for the conduct of its artistic and cultural activities.

(b) Definitions.—As used in this section, the following words and phrases shall have the meanings given to them in this subsection:

"Artistic and cultural activities." Shall include the display or production of theater, music, dance, painting, architecture, sculpture, arts and crafts, photography, film, graphic arts and design and creative writing.

"Nonprofit art corporation." A local arts council, commission or coordinating agency or any other nonprofit corporation engaged in the production or display of works of art, including the visual, written or performing arts.

§ 12443. Ratification and validation of real estate sales.

(a) Ratification and validation.—A deed conveying title to real estate or interests in real estate from a city to any other party is valid and conveys the property and interests described in the deed in accordance with the terms of the deed if:

(1) the deed is executed and delivered pursuant to an ordinance or resolution of council; and

(2) the deed is not contested by an action filed in the court of common pleas of the county in which the city is located within six years of the date the deed is recorded.

(b) Incontestability.—A deed shall not, after the time period specified in subsection (a), be subject to attack in any court, agency or proceeding.

§ 12444. Validation and maintenance of certain records.

(a) Validation of records.—Except as otherwise provided by law, city records that are required to be recorded or copied shall be deemed valid if recorded or transcribed by any digital, photostatic, photographic, microphotographic, microfilm, microcard, miniature photographic, optical, electronic or other process

Chap. 39 Res. During Mil. Service
Chap. 38 Intergov. Coop.
Chap. 37 3rd Class City Code
Chap. 36 Bor. Code
Chap. 35 2nd Class Twp. Code
Chap. 34 1st Class Twp. Code
Chap. 33 Home Rule Chart. Opt. Plans Law
Chap. 32 Water Serv. Act
Chap. 31 Munic. Auth. Act

that accurately reproduces the original and forms a durable medium for recording, storing and reproducing the original in accordance with standards, policies and procedures for the creation, maintenance, transmission or reproduction of images of records approved by the county or local government records committees, as applicable, and as otherwise provided by law. Where recording in a specific book is required, except for minutes or the proceedings of council, the records may be recorded, transcribed or otherwise assembled in an appropriate book, disk or other medium approved by resolution of council, and all records recorded and assembled in any manner are validated.

(b) Maintenance of records.—A city shall not be required to retain original or paper copies of documents after the documents are archived by any of the methods provided for in subsection (a) or as otherwise provided by law.

§ 12445. Rights within streets and rights-of-way.

(a) Rights within streets.—Council may consent to a person using city streets and other properties, whether the use is within, on or over the streets or public property in question, for transportation purposes or for the purpose of installing and maintaining pipes, wires, fibers, cables or any other utility or service medium. Council may define a reasonable district within which all electric or telephone wires, cables or any other utility or service medium are to be placed underground.

(b) Compliance with other law.—The power granted to a city in subsection (a) shall be exercised in compliance with Federal and State law and shall be subject to the power of the Pennsylvania Public Utility Commission under 66 Pa.C.S. Pt. I (relating to public utility code) to regulate the business, facilities and service of public utilities, including determining the location and installation of utility facilities.

(c) Rights-of-way.—A city shall pay just compensation to any property owner whose land has been acquired by the city for use as a right-of-way for purposes of this section. Just compensation shall be determined pursuant to 26 Pa.C.S. (relating to eminent domain).

§ 12446. Emergency services.

(a) Provision of emergency services.—A city shall be responsible for ensuring that fire and emergency medical services are provided within the city by the means and to the extent determined by the city, including the appropriate financial and administrative assistance for these services.

(b) Consultation with providers.—The city shall consult with fire and emergency medical services providers to discuss the emergency service needs of the city.

(c) Expenditure report.—The city shall require any emergency services providers receiving city money to provide an annual itemized listing of all expenditures of city money before the city may consider budgeting additional funding to the provider.

§ 12447. Charitable purposes.

(a) Creation of city bureau or agency.—Council may, by ordinance, create a city bureau or agency to receive, in trust, all property bestowed upon the bureau or agency for charitable purposes. Council may control the property for the purposes of the trust.

(b) Appropriations.—Council may make appropriations to the agency or bureau for charitable purposes, except as limited by the Constitution of Pennsylvania and laws of the Commonwealth.

(c) Definition.—As used in this section, the term "charitable purposes" shall mean the relief of poverty, the advancement of education, the promotion of

health, governmental or municipal purposes and other purposes which benefit the community.

§ 12448. Observances, celebrations and recognition.

(a) **Appropriation.**—Council may appropriate funds for any of the following:

(1) The observance of a holiday, centennial or other anniversary, for a city celebration or for a civic project or program.

(2) Flowers, a plaque or other token of tangible personal property other than cash, gift certificates or equivalent items, in an amount not to exceed $100, recognizing the service or passing of a city official, employee or volunteer.

(b) **Value.**—The value of tangible personal property received by a public official, employee or volunteer as provided under subsection (a)(2) shall be considered of de minimis economic impact, as defined in 65 Pa.C.S. § 1102 (relating to definitions), and shall not be subject to reporting under 65 Pa.C.S. § 1105 (relating to statement of financial interests).

CHAPTER 125

TAXATION

Subchapter

SUBCHAPTER A

ASSESSMENTS OF PROPERTY FOR TAXATION

Sec.

---

§ 12522. Assessment powers.

(a) **Power to appoint assessors.**—With regard to the valuing and assessing of property for taxation within a city, the following shall apply:

(1) If, on May 19, 2014, a city is utilizing the county assessment office for the valuation and assessment of property, the city shall continue to utilize the county assessment office for this purpose.

(2) If paragraph (1) does not apply, council may appoint and employ persons to value and assess property for taxation within a city, following the procedures and methodologies set forth in the assessment law applicable in the county in which the city is located, provided that the act of April 16, 1992 (P.L.155, No.28), known as the Assessors Certification Act, shall apply to persons hired pursuant to this paragraph.

(3) If paragraph (2) applies, a city may subsequently elect to utilize the county assessment office to value and assess property.

(4) The following shall apply with respect to the established predetermined ratio:

(i) A city, conducting its own assessments as authorized by paragraph (2), or utilizing the county assessment office pursuant to paragraph (1) or (3), may, by ordinance, adopt an established predetermined ratio different from that used by the county. The city shall apply the ratio selected to the actual valuation supplied by the county to determine assessed value for tax purposes. The established predetermined ratio selected by the city may not exceed 100% of actual value.

(ii) As used in this paragraph, the term "established predetermined ratio" shall mean the ratio of assessed value to market value established by council and uniformly applied in determining assessed value in any year.

(5) A city that is utilizing the county assessment office in accordance with paragraph (1) or that elects to utilize the county assessment office in accordance with paragraph (3) may not appoint and employ persons to value and assess property in accordance with paragraph (2).

(b) City-appointed assessors.—In any case in which a city appoints persons to value and assess property, the following shall apply:

(1) If the property being assessed is not wholly within the city limits, it shall be assessed in the same manner and within the same jurisdiction as if the property were being assessed for county purposes.

(2) If a city has established a registry of real estate for purposes of assessment, a city may obtain, from the official in charge of the registry, available information as to the registered owners of real estate, under rules and regulations as may be established by ordinance. It shall be a sufficient description of any real estate in any assessment books or duplicates to designate the real estate by the city lot number, other number or designation, as is used on the registry.

(3) For purposes of assessment appeals, council shall constitute the board of revision of taxes and appeals and the city clerk shall serve as clerk of the board.

(4) Except as authorized in this section, the city shall not exercise powers contrary to or in limitation or expansion of powers granted by statutes that provide the substantive rules governing the making of assessments and valuations of property that are applicable to the assessment of property for taxation purposes under the county assessment law applicable in the county in which the city is located.

(5) A city conducting its own assessments pursuant to subsection (a)(2) shall establish and follow procedures that are consistent with similar procedures provided in the assessment law or laws applicable in the county in which the city is located, including providing notice of an opportunity to appeal assessments, for taking appeals to and from the board of revision of taxes and appeals and for the conduct of proceedings before the board.

(c) Temporary tax exemption for residential construction.—A temporary tax exemption for residential construction shall be subject to the following:

(1) New single and multiple dwellings constructed for residential purposes and improvements to existing unoccupied dwellings or improvements to existing structures for purposes of conversion to dwellings shall not be valued or assessed for purposes of real property taxes until:

(i) occupied;

(ii) conveyed to a bona fide purchaser; or

(iii) one year from the first day of the month in which falls the 60th day after the building permit was issued or, if no building permit or other notification of improvement was required, then from the date construction commenced.

(2) The assessment of any multiple dwelling because of occupancy shall be upon the proportion which the value of the occupied portion bears to the value of the entire multiple dwelling.

(3) As used in this subsection, the term "dwelling" means a building or portion of a building intended for permanent use as a home or residence.

Table of Contents
Part I Ch. 1–3 Ethics, Records, Open Meetings
Part II Ch. 4–10 Taxation
Part III Ch. 11–18 Torts, Contracts & Civil Rules
Part IV Ch. 19–24 Zoning & Planning
Part V Ch. 25–30 Construction and Emergency Codes
Part VI Ch. 31–39 Municipal Codes
Index

SUBCHAPTER B

LEVY AND COLLECTION

---

§ 12531. Tax levies.

(a) Property tax.—Council may, by resolution for taxes levied at the same rate as or a rate lower than the previous fiscal year, and by ordinance if the tax rate increases from the previous fiscal year, levy and, in accordance with this part, provide for the collection of taxes on all property within the city that is made taxable for city purposes and subject to valuation and assessment by the county assessment office or the city, as provided in Subchapter A (relating to assessments of property for taxation), as follows:

(1) A tax for general revenue purposes of not more than 30 mills.

(2) An annual tax sufficient to pay interest and principal on any indebtedness incurred pursuant to 53 Pa.C.S. Pt. VII Subpt. B (relating to indebtedness and borrowing) or any prior or subsequent act governing the incurrence of indebtedness of the city.

(3) An annual tax, not to exceed five mills, to light the highways, roads and other public places in the city.

(4) An annual tax for the purpose of maintaining and operating recreation places and programs.

(5) An annual tax, not to exceed the sum of one-tenth of one mill, for the purpose of defraying the cost and expense of caring for shade trees and the administrative expenses connected with the care, or council may provide for the expenses by appropriation from the city general fund.

(b) Residence tax.—Council may, by ordinance, levy and, in accordance with this part, provide for the collection of a residence tax for general revenue purposes, of not more than $5 annually, on all inhabitants who are 18 years of age or older.

(c) Property tax rules.—With regard to the taxes authorized in subsection (a), the following shall apply:

(1) Special purpose levies authorized in this section shall not be included in calculating the 30-mill limit imposed by subsection (a).

(2) Any ordinance or resolution fixing the rate of taxation for any year at a millage rate shall also include a statement expressing the rate of taxation in dollars and cents on each $100 of assessed valuation of taxable property.

(3) Council may, by resolution for taxes levied at the same rate as or a rate lower than the previous fiscal year, and by ordinance if the tax rate increases from the previous fiscal year, in any year levy separate and different rates of taxation for city purposes on all real estate classified as land, exclusive of the buildings on the real estate, and on all real estate classified as buildings on land. When real estate tax rates are so levied:

(i) The rates shall be determined by the requirements of the city budget as approved by council.

(ii) The respective rates levied on land and buildings do not have to be equal but must be fixed so as not to constitute a greater levy in the aggregate than a rate of 30 mills on both land and buildings.

(iii) The rates shall be uniform as to all real estate within the classification.

(4) Where council, by a majority action upon due cause shown, petitions the court of common pleas for the right to levy additional millage for general revenue purposes, the court, after public notice as it may direct and after hearing, may order a greater rate than 30 mills but not more than five additional mills to be levied.

(5)(i) Notwithstanding council's power to authorize the transfer of an unexpended balance of an appropriation item pursuant to section 11804 (relating to regulations concerning appropriation), when money are collected for any special purpose, a city treasurer or council member may not apply the money for any purpose other than that for which it was collected.

(ii) Any city treasurer or council member who violates subparagraph (i) commits a misdemeanor of the third degree and, in addition to the fine or penalty that may be imposed upon conviction, shall be required to pay restitution in the amount of money improperly spent.

§ 12531.1. Exemptions from taxation.

Council may, by ordinance or resolution, exempt any individual whose total income from all sources is less than $12,000 per annum from any per capita or residence tax levied under this chapter. This exemption shall not apply to real property taxes.

§ 12531.2. Certification of schedule.

For the purpose of delinquent tax collection and the filing of liens on property upon which the taxes, assessed and levied, have not been paid and have become delinquent, the city treasurer shall certify schedules of unpaid taxes. The certification shall be made to the person designated by each taxing district for which the city treasurer collects taxes.

SUBCHAPTER C
SALES OF REAL ESTATE FOR DELINQUENT TAXES

Sec.

---

§ 12542.1. Public sale of property to satisfy tax claims.

(a) Public sale.—Property upon which city real estate taxes have not been paid and have become delinquent may become subject to public sale in accordance with one of the following:

(1) The act of July 7, 1947 (P.L.1368, No.542), known as the Real Estate Tax Sale Law.

(2) The Municipal Claim and Tax Lien Law.

(b) Other remedies.—The remedies authorized in this section shall be in addition to other remedies provided for the collection of delinquent city taxes, including an action in assumpsit.

(c) Date of delinquency.—Unless otherwise provided for under the statutes listed under subsection (a), taxes shall become delinquent 30 days after the final deadline for payment of the taxes for the current tax year.

§ 12543. Certification of schedules to city treasurer.

At the request of the city treasurer, any person acting on behalf of the city who possesses a schedule of unpaid city taxes shall certify the schedule to the city treasurer along with the description of property against which the unpaid taxes were assessed.

§ 12546. Record of sales, purchase and resale.

(a) Record of sales.—The city treasurer shall keep in the treasurer's office, or in another place as council may direct, a record of all the sales made pursuant to section 12542.1 (relating to public sale of property to satisfy tax claims).

(b) Purchase of property at tax sale.—Notwithstanding any other provision of law, the city shall have the right to bid on and purchase properties sold pursuant to section 12542.1.

(c) Resale of property.—Properties purchased by the city under subsection (b) may be sold in accordance with section 12402.1(b) (relating to city property and affairs).

§ 12552.1. Conduct of tax sales.

The procedures and requirements relating to the sale of property for delinquent taxes, including the advertisement for and the time and conduct of the sale, the payment of the purchase price, the distribution of proceeds, making the return and confirmation of sale and the delivery of deed, shall be governed by the act of July 7, 1947 (P.L.1368, No.542), known as the Real Estate Tax Sale Law, or the Municipal Claim and Tax Lien Law as utilized by the city in accordance with section 12542.1 (relating to public sale of property to satisfy tax claims) and by any applicable rules of court governing procedures for tax sales.

CHAPTER 126

LICENSES AND LICENSE FEES

---

§ 12601. Licensing and regulatory powers.

In addition to all other powers granted by this part and other laws, a city shall have the specific licensing and regulatory authority provided by this chapter.

§ 12601.1. Registration of businesses or occupations.

(a) Registration.—Council may, by ordinance, designate the types or kinds of businesses or occupations located or carried out within the city that are subject to annual registration with the city.

(b) Annual fee.—Unless otherwise provided in this chapter, an ordinance requiring registration in accordance with this section may provide for an annual fee on businesses and occupations in an amount reasonably related to the administration of the registration program, not to exceed $100.

§ 12602. Regulation of motor vehicles.

(a) General rule.—Subject to subsection (b), a city may regulate transportation by motor vehicle.

(b) Exception.—A city shall have no authority to and shall not regulate transportation by motor vehicle in a manner that is preempted by or is inconsistent with applicable Federal and State laws and regulations, policies or orders of Federal and State regulatory agencies.

(c) Definitions.—The following words and phrases when used in this section shall have the meanings given to them in this subsection unless the context clearly indicates otherwise:

"Regulate." Licensing and making regulations for transportation by motor vehicle, including the designation of streets for transportation by motor vehicle.

"Transportation by motor vehicle." The transportation for pay of passengers and property, within the limits of the city or from points in the city to points beyond the limits of the city, by a motor vehicle that is not operated on tracks.

§ 12603. Licensing of plumbers.

Council may, as provided by ordinance or the laws of the Commonwealth, license and provide for the collection of a license fee from all persons certified as being qualified to engage in the business of plumbing or house drainage.

§ 12604. Power to regulate and license transient merchants.

(a) General rule.—With regard to transient merchants, a city shall have power, by ordinance, to regulate and license the transient merchant, including requiring that a license be procured prior to commencement of transient merchant activity.

(b) Penalty.—An ordinance adopted pursuant to subsection (a) may impose a penalty of not more than $500 for a violation of its provisions and may provide for other means of enforcement.

(c) License fee.—The fee for a transient merchant license shall not exceed $250 for each month during which any sale or solicitation is continued.

(d) Definition.—As used in this section, the term "transient merchant" shall:

(1) include all of the following:

(i) Transient wholesale and transient retail businesses for the sale of goods, wares or merchandise within the city.

(ii) Transient charitable solicitors for the solicitation of charitable contributions within the city.

(2) not include any of the following:

(i) Farmers selling their own produce.

(ii) Persons selling donated goods, wares and merchandise if the proceeds of the sale are to be applied to any charitable or philanthropic purpose.

(iii) A person selling bakery products, meat and meat products or milk and milk products, if that person is the manufacturer or producer of the products sold.

§ 12605. Regulation of special events.

(a) Special events.—In addition to other licensing and regulatory powers authorized by this chapter, council shall have the authority, by ordinance, to require a permit for and to reasonably regulate the conduct of a special event, which may include, but are not limited to, the following:

(1) Music festivals.

(2) Concerts.

(3) Dances.

(4) Circuses.

(5) Carnivals.

(6) Arts and craft shows.

(7) Parades.

(8) Public assemblies.

(9) Demonstrations.

(10) Performances.

(11) Exhibitions.

(12) Community events.

(13) Block parties.

(b) Purpose of regulation.—Regulation of a special event pursuant to this section shall be for the purpose of protecting and preserving city and public property or for the purpose of promoting or protecting public health, safety or welfare.

(c) Permit requirement.—Pursuant to this section, a city may reasonably regulate and require a permit for any of the following:

(1) A special event that will result in the obstruction of a city street or sidewalk or that would compromise the ability of the city to respond to a public safety emergency.

(2) A special event on any property wholly or partially owned or maintained by the city.

(3) A special event on private property, if, in connection with the event, the city will be providing city services, including those relating to public safety, fire and sanitary facilities, beyond what is routinely provided by the city.

§ 12650. Regulation of parking lot and parking garage operators.

(a) General rule.—For the purpose of protecting the public, a city may enact suitable ordinances regulating the business of operating for-profit parking lots and for-profit parking garages within the city. Ordinances shall be consistent with 75 Pa.C.S. (relating to vehicles). A city may require for-profit parking lots and for-profit parking garages to reserve areas exclusively for parking by handicapped individuals. Nothing in this section shall be construed to limit the protections and prohibitions contained in section 202 of the Americans with Disabilities Act of 1990 (Public Law 101-336, 104 Stat. 327), the act of October 27, 1955 (P.L.744, No.222), known as the Pennsylvania Human Relations Act, and Federal and State rules and regulations implementing those acts. License and permit requirements may be imposed on for-profit parking lots and for-profit parking garages and license or permit fees may be charged and collected from the operators of the parking lots and parking garages.

(b) Liability insurance.—A city adopting a regulatory plan applicable to for-profit parking lots and for-profit parking garages shall have the authority to require that each operator maintain insurance from an insurer legally authorized to conduct business in this Commonwealth in amounts not less than that which are prescribed by council for the protection of the public from loss of or damage to the vehicles parked, stored or placed under the jurisdiction of the operator and against liability arising out of the ownership or use of the parking lot or parking garage.

§ 12651. Farmers.

A city may not levy or collect a license fee from a farmer upon sales of the farmer's own produce in or about the streets of the city. This section shall not restrict a city's power to regulate the conduct of a farmer's business.

Table of Contents
Part I Ch. 1–3 Ethics, Records, Open Meetings
Part II Ch. 4–10 Taxation
Part III Ch. 11–18 Torts, Contracts & Civil Rules
Part IV Ch. 19–24 Zoning & Planning
Part V Ch. 25–30 Construction and Emergency Codes
Part VI Ch. 31–39 Municipal Codes
Index

§ 12652. Insurance business.

A city may not levy or collect a license fee upon an insurance company or its agents or an insurance broker authorized to transact business under the laws of the Commonwealth.

§ 12653. Persons taking orders by samples.

A city may not levy or collect a license fee or mercantile tax upon a person taking orders for merchandise by sample from a dealer or merchant for persons who pay a license or mercantile tax at their primary places of business. Nothing in this section shall authorize a person to sell by retail to persons other than dealers or merchants without payment of a license or permit fee.

§ 12654. Commonwealth licenses.

This chapter shall not be construed to relieve a person from the duty of taking out a license or from the payment of any license tax or fee imposed or authorized by any other statute, nor shall any Commonwealth license tax or fee preempt the registration, licensure or regulatory powers of a city in accordance with this chapter, unless the preemption is expressly authorized.

CHAPTER 127
REAL ESTATE REGISTRY

Sec.

§ 12704. Real estate registry.

(a) Registration requirement.—For the purpose of procuring accurate information on the ownership of all real estate, council may provide, by ordinance, for a real estate registry in accordance with the act of October 9, 2008 (P.L.1400, No.110), known as the Uniform Municipal Deed Registration Act. If required by the ordinance, every owner, subsequent purchaser, devisee or person acquiring title by partition, or otherwise, to real estate in the city shall furnish, at the designated city office, descriptions of their respective properties upon blanks to be furnished by the city and, at the same time, present their conveyance to be stamped by the designated city official or employee, without charge, as evidence of its registration. A person who fails to register real estate as required by this chapter shall be liable for a penalty established by ordinance, with costs of suit, in the name and for the use of the city, as penalties for the violation of city ordinances are recoverable.

(b) Registry.—A registry established in accordance with this section shall be in the form provided by council and may include books, maps and plans. The registry shall show the location and dimensions of each property in the city, as well as the street number of and the name of the owner of the properties, and shall allow for the inclusion of the names of future owners and dates of future transfer of title.

(c) Access to records by city officials.—A city official or employee charged with acquiring information necessary to establish and maintain the registry shall have free access, without charge, to any of the public records where the information may be obtained. The official or employee may also search in any other place for documentary or other evidence of title not reported to the city official or employee pursuant to this section if it is necessary for the completion of the registry.

(d) Preservation of registry.—The registry shall be preserved in the manner council shall designate in accordance with 53 Pa.C.S. Ch. 13 Subch. F (relating to records).

(e) Certified copies of registry.—The city official or employee charged with the duty of maintaining the registry shall provide certified copies of any entries to the registry and the copies shall be received in evidence in the same manner as the original registry would be admissible. Certified copies also shall be furnished to any person for a reasonable fee.

(f) Properties sold at judicial sales.—The sheriff of the county in which the city is situated shall present for registry the deeds of all properties within the city limits sold by the sheriff at judicial sales, whether by execution, in partition or otherwise.

(g) Use of registry as source of owners' names.—A city's registry may be used as the lawful and proper source of property owners' or reputed owners' names for all lawful purposes, including the filing of municipal claims.

(h) Municipal and tax claims.—Nothing in this section shall invalidate any municipal or tax claim by reason of the fact that the claim is not assessed or levied against the registered owner.

CHAPTER 127A
NUISANCE ABATEMENT

Sec.

§ 127A01. Definitions.

The following words and phrases when used in this chapter shall have the meanings given to them in this section unless the context clearly indicates otherwise:

"Abatement." The removal, stoppage or destruction by any reasonable means of the cause or constitution of a public nuisance.

"Department." The department designated by council to determine the existence of and to abate a public nuisance in accordance with this chapter.

"Owner." With regard to the property on which the alleged public nuisance exists, the owner of record, based upon the city's real estate registry if the city maintains a registry, or, if the city does not maintain a real estate registry on the tax assessment records of the city, or of the county in which the city is located. The term may include any person in whom is vested all or any part of the legal or equitable title to the property or who has charge, care or control of the property as agent, executor, administrator, assignee, receiver, trustee, guardian, lessee or mortgagee in possession.

"Property." Personal property or real property and any improvements to real property.

"Public nuisance."

(1) Conduct or property, or the condition or use of property, defined or declared to be a public nuisance under any provision of this part or other law.

(2) Conduct or property, or the condition or use of property, if the department determines that it endangers the health or safety of, or causes hurt, harm, inconvenience, discomfort, damage or injury to, a person or property in the city, by reason of the conduct or property, or the condition or use of the property, being any of the following:

(i) A menace, threat or hazard to the general health and safety of the community.

(ii) A fire hazard.

(iii) A building or structure that is unsafe for occupancy or use.

(iv) Property that is so inadequately or insufficiently maintained that it diminishes or depreciates the enjoyment and use of other property in its immediate vicinity to the extent that it is harmful to the community in which the property is situated.

(3) Unauthorized accumulations of garbage and rubbish and the unauthorized storage of abandoned or junked automobiles or other vehicles on private or public property, and the carrying on of any offensive manufacture or business.

"Summary abatement." Abatement of a public nuisance by the city without prior notice to the owner of the property in accordance with this chapter.

§ 127A02. Report and investigation of public nuisance.

(a) Designation of department.—Council shall designate the department to which reports of the existence of a possible public nuisance shall be made.

(b) Criteria for investigating reports.—The department shall establish criteria for investigating reports to determine the existence of a public nuisance. The reports may be submitted by a member of the public, city employee or elected or appointed city official or result from inspections made by the department.

(c) Notification.—If the department, either as a result of a report or an investigation, reasonably believes the reported property involves a building that appears to be structurally unsafe, the department shall notify the city's building inspector or other appropriate official who shall cause the property to be inspected, subject to constitutional standards in a similar manner as provided in section 12308 (relating to powers of board of health) and submit a written report to the department.

(d) Determination.—Upon completing its investigation and receiving any written reports required under subsection (c), the department shall determine all of the following:

(1) If a public nuisance exists.

(2) If the public nuisance is of such a severe and substantial nature that it presents a clear, immediate and substantial danger to public health or safety or to the health or safety of any occupant of a property on which a public nuisance exists or of any property in the vicinity of the public nuisance that it is sufficient to justify extraordinary and immediate action without prior notice to the owner of the property to avoid personal injury, death or substantial loss of property.

(e) Retention of records.—Following an investigation, the department shall retain a copy of its findings, including any reports and any photographs of the property or condition investigated, pursuant to 53 Pa.C.S. Ch. 13 Subch. F (relating to records).

§ 127A03. Summary abatement.

(a) General rule.—A city shall have the power to utilize summary abatement in accordance with this section.

(b) Conditions.—In the case of a reported public nuisance, the department shall have authority to utilize summary abatement if all of the following occur:

(1) The department determines the existence of the criteria in section 127A02(d) (relating to report and investigation of public nuisance).

(2) The mayor or the mayor's designee provides express authorization to utilize summary abatement.

(c) Notice not required.—If summary abatement is implemented pursuant to subsection (b), the department shall have the authority to enter upon the property for the purpose of abatement without prior notice to the owner of the property or to the holders of liens on the property.

(d) Procedure.—The following shall apply:

(1) Within 10 days following a summary abatement, the department shall post on the property upon which the abatement has occurred a notice describing the action taken to abate the nuisance.

(2) Within 20 days following a summary abatement, the department shall determine the identity of the owner of the property by reference to the city's real estate registry if the city maintains a registry, or, in the absence of a registry, by reference to county assessment records, and the identity of the holders of all liens upon the property which are properly indexed among the records of the county and provide to the owner and to all lienholders written notice, by first class mail or hand delivery, of the action taken to abate the nuisance.

(3) Within 30 days following a summary abatement, the department shall file with the city treasurer or other financial officer of the city designated by council a statement of costs of the abatement, which shall include the administrative fee and civil penalty provided by this chapter. After filing with the city treasurer, notice of the statement of costs shall be provided to the owner and lienholders in accordance with section 127A04(b) (relating to prior notice of abatement).

§ 127A04. Prior notice of abatement.

(a) Abatement authority.—The department shall have the authority to abate a public nuisance with prior notice as provided by this section if, after inspecting the property or condition reported to be a public nuisance, subject to constitutional standards in a similar manner as provided in section 12308 (relating to powers of board of health), the department determines, as provided for in section 127A02(d)(1) (relating to report and investigation of public nuisance), that the public nuisance exists.

(b) Method of notice.—

(1) If the department proceeds with abatement pursuant to this section, it shall identify the owner of the property by reference to the city's real estate registry if the city maintains a registry, or, in the absence of a registry, by reference to county assessment records, and shall immediately serve a written notice on the owner by any of the following methods:

(i) Personal service.

(ii) Leaving a copy of the notice at the place of residence or business of the owner or the address of the owner shown in the city's real estate registry or in the records in the office of the recorder of deeds.

Table of Contents | Part I Ch. 1–3 Ethics, Records, Open Meetings | Part II Ch. 4–10 Taxation | Part III Ch. 11–18 Torts, Contracts & Civil Rules | Part IV Ch. 19–24 Zoning & Planning | Part V Ch. 25–30 Construction and Emergency Codes | Part VI Ch. 31–39 Municipal Codes | Index

(iii) Mailing a copy by United States certified mail, return receipt requested, to the owner at the owner's current address shown in the city's real estate registry or in the records in the office of the recorder of deeds.

(2) If service of the written notice is unable to be perfected by any of the methods under paragraph (1), the department shall publish a copy of the notice in a newspaper of general circulation once a week for two consecutive weeks and shall provide a copy of the notice to the individual in possession of the property on which the department has determined that the public nuisance exists, or, if there is no individual in possession of the property, the department shall post a copy of the notice at the structure, location or premises.

(3) The department shall determine from the records in the offices of the recorder of deeds the identities of all lienholders of the property and serve a written notice on all lienholders by United States certified mail, return receipt requested.

(c) Contents of notice.—The notice to the owner and lienholders shall state clearly and concisely the findings and determination of the department with respect to the existence of a public nuisance. The notice shall further state that the public nuisance shall be abated by the city at the expense of the owner unless it is otherwise abated within 30 days of the notice or within any extension of that period granted by the department.

(d) Liability.—A person who is the owner of the premises, location or structure at the time a notice to abate a public nuisance is issued and served upon the person shall be responsible for complying with the notice and shall be liable for any costs incurred by the city in connection with the notice, notwithstanding if the person conveyed the person's interest in the property to another after the notice was issued and served.

(e) Defense.—It shall not be a defense to the determination that a public nuisance exists that the property is boarded up or otherwise enclosed.

§ 127A05. Abatement by owner.

(a) Duty of owner.—Within 30 days after written notice has been provided pursuant to section 127A04(b)(1) or (2) (relating to prior notice of abatement), the owner shall remove and abate the nuisance.

(b) Extension.—The department, upon written application by the owner within the 30-day period referred to in subsection (a), may grant additional time for the owner to effect the abatement of the public nuisance, if the extension is limited to a specific time period.

§ 127A06. Appeal after notice and hearing.

(a) Hearing.—A city shall, by ordinance, provide a procedure by which an owner of the property who has been served with a notice pursuant to section 127A04(b)(1) or (2) (relating to prior notice of abatement) may request and have a timely hearing on the question of whether a public nuisance, in fact, exists.

(b) Appeal board.—Council, or a committee of three council members appointed by council, shall constitute the public nuisance appeals board which, if an appeal is taken, shall conduct the hearing on the question of whether a public nuisance, in fact, exists. The appeals board may uphold, amend or modify the determination of the department or extend the time for compliance with the department's order if the extension is limited to a specific time period.

(c) Time limitations.—An appeal under this section shall suspend the period of time within which the nuisance is to be abated until a decision is rendered by the appeals board.

§ 127A07. Abatement by city after notice and statement of costs.

(a) Abatement by city after notice.—If a public nuisance has not been abated at the expiration of 30 days after notice has been provided or within additional time as the department or appeals board may grant, taking into consideration the provisions of section 127A06(c) (relating to appeal after notice and hearing), the department shall have the authority to enter upon the property for the purpose of abatement.

(b) Statement of costs.—Upon abatement in accordance with this section, the department shall file with the city treasurer or other financial officer of the city designated by council a statement of costs of the abatement, which shall include the administrative fee and civil penalty provided by this chapter.

§ 127A08. Assistance in abatement.

In abating a public nuisance, the department may call upon any of the city departments or divisions for assistance, as shall be deemed necessary, or may abate the public nuisance by private contract.

§ 127A09. Salvage of material.

If deemed practicable by the department, the department may salvage and sell at private or public sale any material derived from an abatement of a public nuisance. Pursuant to ordinance, all of the following shall apply to the proceeds obtained from the sale of any material salvaged as a result of an abatement:

(1) The proceeds shall be deposited as directed by ordinance.

(2) The proceeds may be applied against the amount of the costs, fees and penalties relating to the abatement.

(3) If the amount of the proceeds exceeds the amount of the costs, fees and penalties, any excess shall be paid to the owner.

§ 127A10. Notice of assessment and appeal of charges.

(a) Notice of assessment.—Upon receipt of the statement of costs from the department, either for a summary abatement pursuant to section 127A03 (relating to summary abatement) or for an abatement with notice pursuant to section 127A04 (relating to prior notice of abatement), the city treasurer or other financial officer of the city designated by council shall, in accordance with section 127A04(b), give notice of the amount set forth in the statement of costs to the owner and lienholders of the property upon which the public nuisance has been abated. The notice shall state that the city proposes to assess against the property the amount set forth in the notice and that objections to the proposed assessment must be made in writing and received by the designated officer within 20 days from the date of mailing the notice.

(b) Lien.—Upon the expiration of the 20-day period, if no written objections have been received by the officer, the total amount of costs, fees and penalties specified in the statement of costs may be entered as a lien against the property on which the nuisance was abated and shall be collected in the manner provided for the collection of municipal claims and liens, subject to rights of appeal provided in this section.

(c) Administrative review.—If objections of the owner or a lienholder are received by the designated officer prior to the expiration of the 20-day period, the officer shall refer the matter to the department for administrative review.

(d) Procedure.—The city shall, by ordinance, provide a procedure by which the department shall make a determination regarding any timely filed objection and by which an appeal of the department's determination may be made to the appeals board referred to in section 127A06(b) (relating to appeal after notice and hearing).

(e) **Final administrative decision.**—The determination of the appeals board shall be a final administrative decision within the city.

(f) **Reduction or cancellation of assessment.**—The department, in administrative review, or the appeals board, on appeal, may reduce or cancel a proposed assessment if it is determined that any of the following did not conform to the provisions of this chapter:

(1) The notice to remove the nuisance.

(2) The work performed in abating the nuisance.

(3) The computation of charges.

(g) **Elimination of civil penalty.**—The department, in administrative review, or the appeals board, on appeal, may reduce a proposed assessment by eliminating the civil penalty portion of the statement of costs if any of the following apply:

(1) The current owner did not own the property at the time the notice required in section 127A04 (relating to prior notice of abatement) was posted.

(2) The owner did not receive the notice to remove the public nuisance, did not have knowledge of the public nuisance and could not, with the exercise of reasonable diligence, have had knowledge of the public nuisance.

§ 127A11. Personal liability of owner.

Notwithstanding the right of the city to utilize in rem proceedings to pursue collection of the costs, fees and penalties in the statement of costs as a municipal claim, the person who is the owner of the property at the time of a summary abatement at which the notice required is given, or, in the case of an abatement pursuant to section 127A04 (relating to prior notice of abatement), the person who was the owner of the property at the time notice of the existence of the public nuisance was given, shall be personally liable for the amount of the assessment, including all interest, other charges and, except as provided in section 127A10(g) (relating to notice of assessment and appeal of charges), civil penalties.

§ 127A12. Administrative fee and civil penalties.

Whenever a public nuisance is abated by the city, the statement of the costs of the public nuisance shall include the city's actual cost of abatement, plus an administrative fee, not to exceed 10%, and a civil penalty. For the first abatement of a public nuisance upon any owner's property within the city in any two-year period, the civil penalty shall be $250. For second and subsequent abatements upon any properties of any owner within the city during any two-year period, the civil penalty shall be $500. The increased civil penalty shall be imposed and collected regardless of whether the second and subsequent public nuisances upon property or properties of an owner involve the same property or the public nuisances are of the same or different character.

CHAPTER 128
EMINENT DOMAIN

Sec.

§ 12801. Exercise of eminent domain.

(a) General rule.—In addition to all other purposes for which a city may exercise the power of eminent domain as authorized by this part or by other laws of the Commonwealth and subject to the duty to provide just compensation, a city may acquire property by eminent domain, including entering upon, appropriating, taking, using and occupying private lands and property for any of the following public purposes:

(1) The laying out, opening, widening, extending, vacating, grading or changing the grades or lines of streets.

(2) The construction of bridges and the piers, abutments and approaches for bridges.

(3) The construction of slopes, embankments and storm water sewers, including storm water drains.

(4) The erection and extension of waterworks, wharves and docks, public buildings, public works, filtration plants, sewage systems, sewage treatment works, waste disposal plants, including disposal of garbage, ashes and other refuse materials and transfer facilities, gas plants, electric power and light plants, fire houses, hospitals, public auditoriums, memorial buildings, public transportation facilities, comfort stations, homeless shelters, waiting stations, communications facilities, drinking fountains, libraries and other public buildings and public works.

(5) The establishing of recreation places.

(6) The changing of watercourses.

(7) The acquisition of lands, easements and property for use of the Pennsylvania National Guard in accordance with sections 144A13 (relating to eminent domain for National Guard purposes) and 144A14 (relating to land for armory purposes).

(b) Eminent domain proceedings.—Eminent domain proceedings shall be subject to and conform with the provisions of 26 Pa.C.S. (relating to eminent domain).

§ 12802. Restrictions as to certain property.

(a) General rule.—In addition to the restrictions made by other provisions of this part in particular cases or by any other provision of law, no city shall exercise the right of eminent domain against:

(1) Land now occupied by any building which was used during the Colonial or Revolutionary period as a place of assembly by the Council of the Colony of Pennsylvania, the Supreme Executive Council of the Commonwealth of Pennsylvania or the Congress of the United States.

(2) Land occupied by any fort, redoubt or blockhouse erected during the Colonial or Revolutionary period or any building used as headquarters by the Commander-in-Chief of the Continental Army.

(3) The site of any building, fort, redoubt, blockhouse or headquarters, which are preserved for their historic associations and not for private profit.

(b) Colonial and Revolutionary period.—The Colonial and Revolutionary period shall be deemed to have ended on September 3, 1783.

§ 12803. Title acquired.

Except as otherwise provided by law, if land or other real or personal property is acquired by a city in eminent domain proceedings or is acquired by gift, purchase or otherwise, the title obtained by the city shall be in fee simple absolute or like absolute ownership unless the parties agree otherwise in writing and the agreement expressly appears in a recorded deed affecting any real property acquired by the city or in the notice of condemnation.

§ 12824. Assessment awards.

In proceedings to assess damages and benefits, one of the following shall be awarded to or assessed against the owner of land and affected property:

(1) The excess of damages over benefits.

(2) The excess of benefits over damages.

(3) Nothing, if the benefits and damages are equal.

CHAPTER 129

STREETS

---

§ 12901. Map of streets.

(a) General rule.—Council may authorize and approve a comprehensive map of city streets, which may be part of an official map adopted in accordance with the Municipalities Planning Code.

(b) Amendment to comprehensive map.—If council adopts a comprehensive map of city streets, any street subsequently laid out in accordance with this chapter shall be deemed an amendment to the comprehensive map.

§ 12902. Laying out streets.

(a) General rule.—A city may lay out streets by any of the following means:

(1) Identifying the street on a comprehensive map of city streets.

(2) Identifying the street in an amendment to the comprehensive map.

(3) Identifying the street in a recorded subdivision or land development plan.

(4) An ordinance laying out any area for future opening as a public street.

(b) Filing of ordinance.—If, at the time of the enactment of an ordinance in accordance with subsection (a)(4), the lines of the laid-out street include property not subject to use as a public passageway, the ordinance shall be filed with the recorder of deeds of the county where the city is located.

(c) Indexing of ordinances.—The recorder of deeds shall index the ordinance by the name of the city, the name of the property owner and, if applicable, the parcel number of the property through which the proposed street is laid out.

§ 12903. Effect of laying out street.

With regard to land not previously used by the city as a passageway for public travel, the laying out and locating of a street in accordance with this chapter shall not in and of itself do any of the following:

(1) Authorize the entry upon or the appropriation of any property.

(2) Constitute the opening of any street or the taking or acceptance of any land.

(3) Obligate the city to improve or maintain the street or land.

§ 12904. Improvements within laid-out streets.

(a) General rule.—No permit shall be issued for any building within the lines of any street laid out pursuant to this chapter.

(b) Damages.—No person shall recover damages for the taking for public use of any building or improvements constructed within the lines of any street after the street has been included in the general plan or official map, and any building or improvement shall be removed at the expense of the owner.

§ 12915. Power to open and alter streets.

(a) General rule.—With regard to any street or any part of a street within city limits, a city may, with or without any petition of property owners, do any of the following:

(1) Open, widen, straighten, alter, extend and improve.

(2) Establish or reestablish the grades.

(3) Keep in order and repair and in safe passable condition.

(4) Vacate and discontinue when deemed expedient for the public good.

(5) With the approval of the Department of Transportation, vacate highways laid out by the Commonwealth within the city limits which have remained unopened for 30 years.

(b) Payment.—A city may pay for any of the actions authorized in subsection (a), either in whole or in part, from the general revenues of the city.

§ 12916. Ordinances when no petition is presented.

(a) General rule.—An ordinance shall be enacted for the opening, widening, straightening, extending or vacating of any street without petition of property owners by the affirmative vote of a majority of the whole number of members of council, plus one.

(b) Enactment of ordinance.—The following shall apply prior to the enactment of an ordinance pursuant to subsection (a):

(1) The expiration of 28 days from the date of its introduction.

(2) Prior to the end of the 28-day period in paragraph (1), copies of the ordinance shall be published in a newspaper of general circulation in the city once a week for three consecutive weeks immediately following the introduction of the ordinance.

Table of Contents
Part I Ch. 1–3 Ethics, Records, Open Meetings
Part II Ch. 4–10 Taxation
Part III Ch. 11–18 Torts, Contracts & Civil Rules
Part IV Ch. 19–24 Zoning & Planning
Part V Ch. 25–30 Construction and Emergency Codes
Part VI Ch. 31–39 Municipal Codes
Index

(3) In case no newspaper is published in the city, then in the same manner in one newspaper published in the county as required by section 10109 (relating to publication of notices).

§ 12917. Erection of improvements restricted.

(a) **General rule.**—Any ordinance widening or straightening any street shall fix the new line or lines.

(b) **Conformation to new lines.**—The ordinance may require that no owner or builder shall erect any new building or rebuild or alter the front of any building already erected without making it conform to the new lines.

(c) **Right of action.**—A land owner's right of action shall accrue only when the city actually enters on and occupies the land within the lines or the building is located or relocated to conform to the lines.

§ 12918. Petition for opening.

(a) **Presentment to council.**—A petition may be presented to council for the opening, widening, straightening, altering, extending, vacating, establishing or reestablishing of the grade of any street.

(b) **Majority of property owners required.**—A petition made pursuant to this section shall be:

(1) Signed by a majority, in number and interest, of the owners of property abutting on the line of the proposed improvement or vacation as fixed at the time of presentation of the petition.

(2) Verified by affidavit of one or more of the petitioners.

(c) **Majority in interest.**—The majority in interest of owners of undivided interests in any piece of property shall be deemed as one person for the purposes of the petition.

§ 12919. Notice of petition.

(a) **General rule.**—After a petition has been presented in accordance with section 12918 (relating to petition for opening) and council has determined the adequacy of the petition, but before final enactment of any ordinance enacted pursuant to the petition, notice shall be published in a newspaper of general circulation once a week for three consecutive weeks as required by section 10109 (relating to publication of notices), and handbills shall be posted in conspicuous places along the line of the proposed improvement.

(b) **Requirements.**—The notice and handbills shall state that:

(1) The petition for the improvement was signed by a majority, in interest and number, of the owners of property abutting the line of the proposed improvement.

(2) Any person interested may provide comments at a public hearing to be held at a date, time and place as stated in the published notice and handbills.

(c) **Notice of determination to proceed.**—If, after a hearing, council determines to proceed with the consideration of an ordinance pursuant to the petition, it shall publish notice of the ordinance and incorporate reference to any maps or drawing, in accordance with Subchapter A.1 of Chapter 110 (relating to ordinances).

§ 12922. Assessment of damages and benefits.

If necessary, in any proceedings to exercise one of the powers given in section 12915 (relating to power to open and alter streets), viewers shall be appointed, damages awarded and benefits assessed as provided in 26 Pa.C.S. (relating to eminent domain) or as provided in this chapter for the assessment of benefits.

§ 12930. Power to grade, pave and macadamize.

(a) General rule.—A city may grade, pave, macadamize or otherwise improve any street and the sidewalks of the street when included as a part of the improvement, have them set with curbs and provide for drainage.

(b) Improvement.—A city may provide for the following improvements of any street, in length, in the space between the curb, gutter or cartway and the property line:

(1) An original work or improvement.

(2) A change, repair, renewal or alteration in the street or curb.

(3) Parking spaces.

(4) Shade trees.

(5) Changing, altering, renewing, replanting, pruning or otherwise making improvements in an item listed under paragraph (1), (2), (3) or (4).

§ 12931. Payment of cost of improvement.

(a) General rule.—The costs and expenses of the improvements done under section 12930 (relating to power to grade, pave and macadamize) shall be paid, in whole or in part, by the city or by the owners of real estate bounding and abutting the improvement.

(b) Assessment.—Cost and expense upon the abutting real estate shall be assessed in accordance with Chapter 145A (relating to assessments for public improvements).

§ 12938. Preparation of streets for paving or repairing.

(a) General rule.—Council may provide, by ordinance, for the laying, renewing and repairing of all gas, water, steam or other pipes or conduits in any street before the paving, repaving or repairing of the street and for making the necessary connections with the pipes.

(b) Sewer improvement.—Council may provide for the necessary connections and branches leading into main or lateral sewers.

(c) Private utility companies.—With regard to connections requiring extensions from sewers or from gas, water, steam or other pipes or conduits, council may not require private utility companies to make extensions beyond the inner line of the curbstone of the street unless it determines that it is necessary to do so as a sanitary measure.

(d) Recoupment of cost.—If, after notice to all persons and owners affected of the necessity for the laying, renewing and repairing of gas, water, steam or other pipes or conduits in a street and the necessity of making necessary connections prior to the proposed paving, repaving or repairing of the street, there is a failure to comply, council may perform work and may collect the cost of paving, repaving or repairing of the pipes or conduits, with interest, from the persons and owners affected.

(e) Liens.—The cost of the sewer connections shall be a first lien against the land for whose benefit the connections are made. A separate lien may be filed for the cost, or the sewer connection cost may be included in any lien filed for the cost of the street improvement, and the lien and the proceedings on the lien shall be as in the case of other municipal liens.

§ 12939. Highways in cities.

(a) Power over highways.—Powers, rights and duties given to a city over its streets shall extend to highways to the extent that the city is legally responsible for them, pursuant to agreement or otherwise.

(b) Damages.—A city shall not be responsible for damages to property owners abutting a highway under subsection (a) for acts of the Commonwealth unless the

Chap. 39 Res. During Mil. Service
Chap. 38 Intergov. Coop.
Chap. 37 3rd Class City Code
Chap. 36 Bor. Code
Chap. 35 2nd Class Twp. Code
Chap. 34 1st Class Twp. Code
Chap. 33 Home Rule Chart. Opt. Plans Law
Chap. 32 Water Serv. Act
Chap. 31 Munic. Auth. Act

city shall assume them, under this chapter or the act of June 1, 1945 (P.L.1242, No.428), known as the State Highway Law.

§ 12950. Grade crossing.

(a) Railroad crossings.—A city constructing a street across a railroad shall construct the street above or below the grade of the railroad, unless permitted by the Pennsylvania Public Utility Commission to construct the street at grade.

(b) New construction.—Any new construction of a street crossing a railroad or any vacation of any street crossing a railroad shall be constructed or vacated only in a manner consistent with the rules and regulations and under the jurisdiction of the Pennsylvania Public Utility Commission.

(c) Compensation to owners.—The compensation for damages to the owners of adjacent property taken, injured or destroyed by the construction of a street crossing a railroad or any vacation of any street crossing a railroad shall be ascertained, fixed and paid according to 66 Pa.C.S. Pt. I (relating to public utility code).

§ 12955. Acquisition of unobstructed views.

Any city may acquire, by purchase or by the right of eminent domain, a free and unobstructed view down and across lands located at or near intersections or curves of streets, railroads or railways to assure a free and unobstructed view in all directions at the intersections or curves and to prevent the use of the lands over and across which the view was acquired for any purpose or in any manner which may interfere with or obstruct the vision of any person traveling upon any street within the city.

§ 12960. Use of abutting lands for embankments, slopes, fills and culverts.

(a) General rule.—In the grading of any street, a city may use so much of the lots and lands abutting on the street for the construction of embankments, slopes, fills and culverts, as may be necessary for the completion of the improvement.

(b) Compensation.—Compensation for damages, costs and expenses resulting from the use of lots and lands abutting on the street for the construction of embankments, slopes, fills and culverts shall be made in the same manner as compensation for using and occupying private lands for the grading of streets under section 12801 (relating to exercise of eminent domain).

§ 12970. Appropriation for connections with highways.

A city may, singly or jointly with other political subdivisions, appropriate money for the improvement of streets or roads beyond the limits of a city for the purpose of connecting improved streets in a city with a highway.

§ 12975. Street closings and detours.

(a) General rule.—The following shall apply to the closing of a street to vehicular traffic:

(1) No street shall be closed to vehicular traffic, except upon order of the department of streets and public improvements or other department of the city having jurisdiction over public streets, or, in cases of emergency, when immediate action is necessary to protect public safety, by order of the mayor, the police or the fire marshal.

(2) A street may not remain closed for a longer period than is necessary for the purpose for which the order to close was issued.

(3) Except in cases of emergency, when immediate action is necessary to protect public safety, no street shall be closed to vehicular traffic when the street has been designated as a detour by the Department of Transportation, unless the Secretary of Transportation has provided written consent or council has, by resolution duly recorded on its minutes, declared the closing necessary for the safety of the public.

(4) When any street which forms a part or section of a State highway or has been designated as a detour by the Department of Transportation is closed to vehicular traffic, the city shall at once notify the Department of Transportation of the creation of a detour under this section. The Department of Transportation shall be notified immediately after the detour is removed.

(5) When any street is to be closed, it shall be the duty of the official or department that authorized the closing to designate a detour.

(6) While the detour is in use, legible signs shall be erected and maintained at reasonable intervals, indicating the proper direction and the detour shall be maintained in safe and passable condition.

(7) When the street that had been closed is opened for traffic, all detour signs shall be removed.

(b) Agreements with owners of private land.—A city may enter into an agreement with the owners of private lands covering the acquisition of right-of-way privileges for a detour over private property for the period when a street shall be closed to traffic. If the parties cannot reach an agreement, the city may proceed with the construction of the detour, with the owner of the property taken for the detour entitled to seek damages, if any, in the same manner as damages are now ascertained for the opening of streets in the city.

(c) Payment.—In the exercise of the rights conferred by this section relating to detours, council is empowered to pay for the necessary maintenance, subsequent repair and land rental out of money available for the construction and maintenance of city streets.

(d) Penalty.—Any individual who willfully removes, defaces, destroys or disregards any barricade, light, danger sign, detour sign, signal or warning of any other type legally erected or placed or who drives on, over or across any street which has been closed by proper authority commits a summary offense punishable upon conviction in accordance with section 11018.16 (relating to enforcement of ordinances, recovery and payment of fines and penalties).

(e) Fine for multiple offenses.—In addition to subsection (d), a person shall pay a fine of not less than $500 or more than the maximum fine authorized in section 11018.17 (relating to penalty) for the second or any subsequent offense.

(f) Costs of prosecution.—An individual punished under subsection (d) or (e) shall pay the costs of prosecution together with the value of the property so removed, defaced or destroyed.

(g) Exception.—An individual who has no outlet due to the closing of a street may drive on, over or across the street, subject to reasonable conditions as may be prescribed by the city without being subject to the penalties imposed by this section.

(h) Collection of fines.—All fines collected under the provisions of this section shall be paid over to the city treasurer.

(i) Civil damages.—In addition to the penalties provided in subsections (d) and (e), the city, its agents or contractors may, in an action at law, recover damages from any person who damages a street when it is closed to vehicular traffic.

§ 12985. Maintenance of streets forming boundaries.

(a) General rule.—A street on the boundary line between a city and another municipal corporation shall be maintained jointly by the city and the other municipal corporation.

(b) Maintenance agreement.—The officers of the city and the municipal corporation maintaining a street under subsection (a) shall enter into an agreement

Table of Contents
Part I Ch. 1–3 Ethics, Records, Open Meetings
Part II Ch. 4–10 Taxation
Part III Ch. 11–18 Torts, Contracts & Civil Rules
Part IV Ch. 19–24 Zoning & Planning
Part V Ch. 25–30 Construction and Emergency Codes
Part VI Ch. 31–39 Municipal Codes
Index

providing for the division of the cost of maintenance between the city and other municipal corporation.

(c) Refusal to participate.—If a municipal corporation shall fail or refuse to enter into a contract under this section, the city or any taxpayer of the noncontracting municipal corporation may petition the court of common pleas of the county, setting forth the facts.

(d) Court decision.—The court, after hearing of which notice shall be given to all parties interested as the court may direct, shall make an order directing the manner of the maintenance and the division of the cost of maintenance between the city and the other municipal corporation.

§ 12986. Streets, the center line of which is the boundary between city and another municipal corporation.

(a) General rule.—A city may enter into a contract with a municipal corporation to provide for the grading, curbing, draining, paving and macadamizing of any street that constitutes the dividing line between the city and the municipal corporation.

(b) Supervision.—The alterations and improvements shall be made under the supervision of the city or municipal corporation, or by contract let by the city or the municipal corporation, as may be provided for in the contract between the city and the municipal corporation.

§ 12988. Streets more than half of whose width is within city.

(a) Authority to improve entire street.—Whenever any street, more than one-half the width of which is within the limits of the city, shall divide the city from any other municipal corporation, the street may be improved by the city in the same manner as if the street were entirely located within the limits of the city.

(b) Assessment.—The property, within or outside the city, that abuts the street and benefits from the improvements may, for a depth of 150 feet plus one-half the width of the street measured from its center line, be assessed for any and all municipal improvements to or on the street in the same manner as the property would be assessed under the provisions of this chapter if it were entirely located within the limits of the city.

§ 12989. Assessment for improvements on property outside limits where street entirely within city.

Whenever any street, entirely within the limits of any city, shall divide the city from any other municipal corporation, the property on the side of the street, within or outside the city, that abuts the street and benefits from the improvement may, for a depth of 150 feet from its center line, be assessed for any and all municipal improvements to or on the streets on which the property abuts, in the same manner as the property would be assessed under the provisions of this part if it were entirely located within the limits of the city.

CHAPTER 130
SIDEWALKS

Sec.

§ 13001. Power to lay out and grade sidewalks and compel construction of sidewalks.

(a) General rule.—Any city may lay out, ordain and establish sidewalks, curbs, gutters and drains along any street, and may, with or without petition, require owners of property abutting any street to construct, pave, curb, repave and recurb the sidewalks and keep the sidewalks in good repair along their property at grades and under regulations and specifications as council may provide.

(b) State highways.—A city shall obtain written consent from the Department of Transportation if the highway is a State highway.

§ 13002. Construction by cities upon failure of owner and collection of cost.

(a) General rule.—Upon failure of any owner of property abutting any street to construct, pave, curb, repave, recurb or maintain any sidewalk, in accordance with the notice required in subsection (f), the city, itself or by contract, may complete the construction, paving, curbing, repaving, recurbing or maintenance.

(b) Recoupment of costs.—A city may collect the following from an owner who has failed to complete the construction, paving, curbing, repaving, recurbing or maintenance of the sidewalk pursuant to notice to do so:

(1) Costs incurred by the city pursuant to subsection (a).

(2) A penalty of 10% of the costs.

(3) All charges and expenses.

(c) Liens upon the property.—The costs, penalties, charges and expenses provided for in subsection (b) shall be a lien upon the property for which the notice to construct, pave, curb, repave, recurb or maintain the sidewalk was given.

(d) Duration of the lien.—The lien shall exist from the time of the completion of the work, which shall be certified in accordance with section 11504 (relating to certifying commencement and completion of municipal improvements).

(e) Filing of the lien.—The lien may be filed and proceeded in as provided by law in the case of municipal liens or may be collected from the owner by action in assumpsit. Alternatively, the cost may be borne by the city, in whole or in part, and, if in part, the rest to be collected as provided by this section.

(f) Service of notice.—Notice of the lien shall be served upon one of the following:

(1) The owner of property to construct, pave, curb, repave, recurb or maintain a sidewalk, if that can be done within the county.

(2) If service cannot be made under paragraph (1), then notice may be served upon the owner's agent or the party in possession.

(3) If service cannot be made under paragraph (1) or (2), notice may be served by posting conspicuously upon the premises.

(g) Failure to comply.—Council may, by ordinance, provide that an owner shall be deemed to have failed to comply if the work is not completed within a specified period, which may be more but shall not be less than 45 days after the service or posting.

§ 13002.1. Ordinances.

All reconstruction, repaving and recurbing of sidewalks may be included in the ordinance providing for the original construction, paving and curbing of sidewalks without the necessity for adopting a new ordinance.

§ 13003. Emergency repairs.

(a) General rule.—Any city may make emergency repairs to sidewalks, within its corporate limits, if an officer or designated individual representing the department in charge of repairs to sidewalks upon inspection determines that a substantial and immediate danger exists to public health, safety and welfare.

(b) Written report.—The officer or individual shall prepare a written report of those conditions which shall be conclusive evidence of the existence of the emergency justifying the repair.

(c) Additional remedy for city.—This section is intended to provide an additional remedy for cities in connection with emergency repairs of sidewalks.

(d) Notice.—The following shall apply:

(1) A copy of the written report shall be served upon the abutting property owner, along with a notice to make emergency repairs to the sidewalk within 48 hours of service of the notice and report.

(2) The notice and copy of the report shall be served as provided in this chapter for constructing and maintaining sidewalks and curbs.

(3) The report shall expressly state that emergency repairs are required.

(4) If the owner fails to make the emergency repairs within the prescribed time, the city may make the emergency repairs to the sidewalk.

(e) Costs.—Upon the completion of any emergency repairs, the cost of the repairs shall be a charge against the owner of the abutting property and shall be a lien, until paid, upon the abutting property, provided a claim is filed for the lien in accordance with the law providing for the filing and collection of municipal claims.

(f) Action in assumpsit.—The amount of the claim against the owner of the abutting property may also be collected from the owner by an action in assumpsit.

CHAPTER 131

BRIDGES

Sec.

§ 13101. Construction and maintenance of bridges.

(a) General rule.—Cities may locate, build and maintain bridges, wholly or partially within the city limits, along with the piers, abutments and approaches appurtenant to the bridges, to be used as public streets.

(b) Definition.—As used in this chapter, the term "bridge" shall mean a structure built to span and provide passage over a valley, road, railroad track, private property, river, creek, stream or any other body of water or physical obstacle and shall include viaducts constructed from a series of spans or arches.

§ 13102. Ordinance for location of bridges.

(a) General rule.—Cities may enact ordinances fixing the location and providing for the laying out and opening of the routes or locations for bridges, which shall be public streets.

(b) Procedure.—The procedure for the laying out and opening of the routes or locations of bridges shall be the same as is provided by this chapter for the laying out and opening of streets.

§ 13103. Right to appropriate property.

(a) Failure to agree on damages.—A city that has not agreed with an owner regarding damages done, or likely to be done, by the erection of the bridge may take and appropriate the lands and property necessary to erect the bridge.

(b) Assessment of damages.—The measure of damages for the taking and appropriation shall be assessed in the same manner and with like proceedings as provided for property taken, injured or destroyed under 26 Pa.C.S. (relating to eminent domain).

§ 13110. Agreement for joint construction and maintenance.

(a) General rule.—The city may enter into an agreement with any political subdivision, public agency, public utility or any other person interested and by law authorized to enter into an agreement, or with any or all of them, for the laying out, construction, improvement and maintenance of any bridge and for the payment of any damages caused by the action.

(b) Requirements of agreement.—An agreement authorized under subsection (a) shall provide for the following:

(1) Respective duties, obligations and responsibilities of the parties to the agreement, including construction and maintenance of the bridge.

(2) Payments relating to and damages caused by the construction and maintenance.

(c) Contract.—After an agreement authorized under subsection (a) has been entered into, the city and the other parties to the agreement shall have the authority to do the following:

(1) Prepare plans or specifications of the entire work.

(2) Advertise for bids in the manner required by law.

(3) Award the contract to the lowest responsible bidder.

(d) Liability.—The city shall be liable to the contractor for only the part of the contract price as it has agreed to pay by the agreement under subsection (a) but it shall, in addition, be liable to the contractor for any money actually paid into the city treasury by the other parties pursuant to the terms of the agreement.

§ 13114. Recording of contract.

Any of the contracts provided for under this chapter may be recorded in the office of the recorder of deeds in the proper county. The record shall be notice to all persons who might be affected by the contract.

§ 13115. Power to construct boundary bridges.

Whenever a creek, over which a bridge may be necessary, shall be on the division line of a city and another municipality, the city may enter into an intergovernmental agreement pursuant to 53 Pa.C.S. Ch. 23 Subch. A (relating to intergovernmental cooperation) with the municipality for the construction and maintenance of a bridge and for apportionment of the costs.

§ 13135. Acquisition of existing bridges.

(a) **General rule.**—A city may purchase, condemn, maintain and use any public toll bridge crossing any river or stream within the limits of the municipality, together with the approaches and appurtenances to the toll bridge.

(b) **Cost.**—A city may enter into contracts with the county commissioners or the legislative body in a county that has adopted a home rule charter of the proper county for the county to pay a portion of the cost of purchase, condemnation and maintenance.

CHAPTER 132

SANITARY SEWERS

§ 13201. Construction of sanitary sewers, cost and eminent domain.

(a) **General rule.**—A city shall have the power to construct and reconstruct, or cause to be constructed or reconstructed, in its streets and over and across public and private lands or property, sanitary sewers of all kinds, main or local, with extensions and with lateral and branch sewers, including house connections to the curb.

(b) **Cost.**—The cost and expense of construction and reconstruction in accordance with subsection (a) may be paid out of the general revenues or special money raised for that purpose, or assessed, in whole or in part, upon property benefited, improved or accommodated, as provided for in Chapter 145A (relating to assessments for public improvements).

(c) **Eminent domain.**—The city shall have the right of eminent domain to effectuate the purposes of this section. The damages for property taken, injured or destroyed shall be ascertained and paid as provided in 26 Pa.C.S. (relating to eminent domain).

§ 13201.1. Required connection and fees.

(a) **General rule.**—In addition to paying for the cost and expense of construction or reconstruction in accordance with section 13201(b) (relating to construction of sanitary sewers, cost and eminent domain), a city may, by ordinance, require connection to a sanitary sewer system provided by the city or a municipal authority serving the city.

(b) **Cost.**—As a condition of connection to a city-owned sewer collection, treatment or disposal facility, a city may impose and charge the following to property owners who desire to or are required to connect to the sanitary sewer system:

(1) A connection fee.

(2) A customer facilities fee.

(3) A tapping fee.

(4) Similar fees, as enumerated and defined by 53 Pa.C.S. § 5607(d)(24) (relating to purposes and powers).

§ 13206. Construction of sanitary sewage treatment works.

(a) General rule.—A city may construct, or cause to be constructed, sanitary sewage treatment works, which may be part of the same improvement and under the same contract as sanitary sewers.

(b) Location of construction.—Sewage treatment works may be erected within or outside the limits of the city.

(c) Eminent domain.—The city shall have authority to acquire, by eminent domain or otherwise, property within or, subject to the limitations in 26 Pa.C.S. § 206 (relating to extraterritorial takings), outside the limits of the city deemed necessary for the treatment works and the sewers leading to the treatment works.

§ 13213.1. Rental fees or charges.

(a) General rule.—All persons whose property is connected to a sanitary sewer system shall pay a monthly, quarterly, semiannual or annual charge to the city, in addition to the cost of making the connection. The charges shall be imposed by the city in accordance with procedures approved by council. Until paid, a charge shall constitute a lien against the property connected to the sanitary sewer system and the amount of the charge may be recovered by due process of law through an action in assumpsit in the name of the city against the owner of the property charged or by a lien filed in the nature of a municipal lien.

(b) Calculation of fees.—All water utilities supplying water to users within the boundaries of any city shall, at the request of council, furnish to the city, at reasonable times agreed to by the city and water utilities, a list of all water meter readings and flat-rate water bills and the basis for each flat-rate water charge so that the data may be used in calculating sewer rental fees. The city may reimburse utilities for clerical and other expenses incurred in the preparation of the lists.

(c) Limitation of section.—Nothing in this section shall be construed to repeal or modify any of the provisions of 66 Pa.C.S. (relating to public utilities).

(d) Fund.—Subject to subsection (e), all sanitary sewer rentals received shall be deposited in a special fund to be used only for the payment of the cost of administration, construction, reconstruction, repair, operation and maintenance of the sanitary sewer system.

(e) Transfer of funds.—Notwithstanding the provisions of the act of July 18, 1935 (P.L.1286, No.402), entitled "An act empowering counties, cities, boroughs, incorporated towns, and townships to charge and collect from owners of and water users in property served thereby, annual rentals, rates or charges for the use of certain sewers, sewerage systems and sewage treatment works, including charges for operation, inspection, maintenance, repair, depreciation, and the amortization of indebtedness and interest thereon; empowering counties, cities, boroughs, incorporated towns and townships to contract with authorities organized by cities of the second class, by cities of the second class A, by counties or by cities of the third class for sewer, sewerage and sewage treatment services; to grant, convey, lease, transfer, encumber, mortgage and pledge to such authorities, their sewers, sewerage systems and sewage treatment works; to assign and pledge to such authorities rentals, rates and charges charged and collected by them for the use thereof, and to assign to such authorities their power to charge and collect the same; and validating all the contracts, grants, conveyances, leases, transfers, assignments, encumbrances, mortgages and pledges heretofore made," or any other law, council may transfer part of the sanitary sewer rentals in the special fund to the city general fund to meet immediate general financial obligations or to ensure adequate cash flow for city operations, provided that money transferred from the special fund to the city general fund shall be repaid to the special fund prior to the end of the fiscal year or at a date as council may determine.

(f) Notification of service.—If a city has agreed to provide sanitary sewer service to a residential dwelling unit in which the owner does not reside, the city shall notify the owner and the tenant within 30 days after the tenant's bill for that service first becomes overdue. The notification shall be provided by first class mail to the address of the owner provided to the city by the owner and to the billing address of the tenant, respectively.

(g) Construction.—Nothing in this subsection shall be construed to relieve the owner of liability for the service unless the city fails to provide the notice under this section.

§ 13222.1. Acquisition of existing sanitary sewer systems.

(a) General rule.—A city may, by ordinance, acquire all or part of an existing sanitary sewer system or community subsurface sanitary sewage collection and treatment system.

(b) Means of acquisition.—A city may acquire a sewer system under subsection (a) by any of the following means:

(1) By purchase, when the city and the owner can agree on a price of not more than the actual value of the sanitary sewer system or part of the system to be transferred.

(2) By deed of dedication to the city by the owner of the sanitary sewer system or part of the system.

(3) If the facilities are within the city, by the exercise of eminent domain.

(c) Distribution of assessment costs.—If any sanitary sewer system or community subsurface sanitary disposal collection and treatment system is acquired by purchase or eminent domain under this section, the cost of acquisition may be distributed or assessed under this part when a sanitary sewer system is constructed by the city.

(d) Acquired systems.—A city has the same rights, powers and duties with respect to acquired sanitary sewer systems as the city would have with respect to sanitary sewer systems constructed by the city.

§ 13230. Sewers outside cartway and curb lines.

(a) General rule.—Cities may require and permit sanitary sewers and sewer pipes to be laid and constructed outside the cartway and the curb lines of the cartway in any street or highway.

(b) Use.—The sanitary sewers shall be for the service and use of the property on the side of the street or highway in which they are laid.

(c) Recoupment of costs.—The costs and expenses of any sanitary sewer laid and constructed in accordance with subsection (a) may be assessed against the property benefited, improved and accommodated by the sanitary sewer.

§ 13240. Building joint sewers.

(a) General rule.—Cities may, jointly with other municipalities or municipal authorities, do the following:

(1) Build and construct sanitary sewers, including trunk-line sewers or drains and sewage treatment works.

(2) Connect into the system existing sanitary sewers.

(3) Assess respective portions of the cost of an action under this subsection, or so much of the cost as may be legally assessable, upon the property benefited,

improved and accommodated by the improvement pursuant to Chapter 145A (relating to assessments for public improvements).

(b) Costs.—Any portion of the cost of an improvement not assessed or not assessable shall be paid as agreed upon by the respective cities and other municipalities or municipal authorities.

(c) Joint sewer board.—The cities and other municipalities or municipal authorities joining or contemplating joining in an improvement under subsection (a) in order to facilitate the securing of preliminary surveys and estimates and the building of the improvement may, by ordinance or resolution, provide for the appointment of a joint sewer board composed of one representative from each of the cities and other municipalities or municipal authorities joining, which shall act generally as the advisory and administrative agency in securing surveys and estimates, the construction of the improvement and its subsequent operation and maintenance.

(d) Length of service on board.—Members of the board shall serve for a term of six years from the date of appointment and continue to serve until successors are appointed.

(e) Membership.—The joint sewer board shall organize by the election of a chair, vice chair, secretary and treasurer.

(f) Agreement of parties.—Cities and other municipalities or municipal authorities may, in the ordinances and resolutions creating the joint sewer board, authorize the board to:

(1) Appoint an engineer, a solicitor and other assistants as are deemed necessary.

(2) Enter into an agreement with respect to the share of compensation of an appointee under paragraph (1) the city, municipality or municipal authority is responsible for.

(g) Compensation for board members.—The members of the joint sewer board shall receive compensation for attending meetings of the board, as shall be fixed in the budget prepared by the board for submission to and adoption by the cities and other municipalities or municipal authorities as provided in subsection (h).

(h) Budget.—The budget item providing for the compensation to members for attending meetings shall not exceed a total of $250 per year and the following shall apply:

(1) No member shall be paid unless the member attends a meeting of the board.

(2) The fee for each attendance shall be stipulated.

(3) Members shall be entitled to actual expenses to be paid by the respective cities and other municipalities or municipal authorities which the members represent.

(i) Power of board.—The joint sewer board shall have the power to adopt rules and regulations to govern its proceedings and shall prepare and suggest any practical measures and plans by means of which the joint improvement may be carried to successful completion, and the future development of the system, so as to conform to a general plan, is assured and safeguarded.

(j) Submission of joint assessment.—

(1) The joint sewer board shall have power to prepare a joint agreement or agreements for submission to and adoption by cities and other municipalities or municipal authorities which shall set forth:

Chap. 39 Res. During Mil. Service
Chap. 38 Intergov. Coop.
Chap. 37 3rd Class City Code
Chap. 36 Bor. Code
Chap. 35 2nd Class Twp. Code
Chap. 34 1st Class Twp. Code
Chap. 33 Home Rule Chart. Opt. Plans Law
Chap. 32 Water Serv. Act
Chap. 31 Munic. Auth. Act

(i) The advisory and administrative powers of the board.

(ii) The consent of each city and other municipality or municipal authority to the proposed improvement.

(iii) The manner in which preliminary and final plans, specifications and estimates for the proposed improvement shall be prepared and adopted.

(iv) How proposals for bids shall be advertised and contracts let.

(v) The manner in which the costs of the improvement and other incidental and preliminary expenses in connection with the improvement, and the future cost of operation and maintenance, shall be equitably shared, apportioned and paid.

(vi) Other matters including the preparation and submission of annual and other budgets as may be deemed necessary or required by law to carry the proposed improvement to completion and to assure future maintenance and operation of the improvement.

(2) Nothing contained in this subsection shall authorize the board to make any improvement or expend any public money which has not first been authorized by all of the cities and other municipalities or municipal authorities proceeding with the improvement.

(k) Eminent domain.—

(1) If it is necessary to acquire, appropriate, injure or destroy private property of any kind to build any joint sewer improvement and the private property cannot be acquired by purchase or gift, the right of eminent domain shall vest in the city or other municipalities or municipal authorities where the property is located.

(2) If it is necessary to acquire, injure or destroy property of any kind in any territory not within the limits of any of the cities and other municipalities or municipal authorities joining in the improvement, subject to the limitations in 26 Pa.C.S. § 206 (relating to extraterritorial takings), the right of eminent domain shall be vested in any city and other municipalities or municipal authorities joining in the sewer improvement.

(l) Damages.—Damages for any property taken, injured or destroyed shall be assessed as provided by the general laws relating to the cities and other municipalities or municipal authorities exercising the right of eminent domain and, pursuant to the procedures of 26 Pa.C.S. (relating to eminent domain) if applicable, shall be paid by cities and other municipalities or municipal authorities joining in the same proportion as other costs of the improvement.

(m) Indebtedness.—Each of the cities joining in an improvement authorized by this section shall have power to incur or increase its indebtedness in accordance with 53 Pa.C.S. Pt. VII Subpt. B (relating to indebtedness and borrowing), for the purpose of paying its share or portion of the costs of the improvement.

§ 13241. Approval of Department of Environmental Protection.

No sewer or plant shall be constructed until plans and specifications have been submitted to the Department of Environmental Protection and approved in accordance with provisions of applicable law.

§ 13245.1. Connection to existing municipal sanitary sewer.

(a) General rule.—A city may, by agreement, connect with an existing sanitary sewer owned by any municipal corporation or municipal authority for either sanitary sewage collection or treatment purposes.

(b) Petition court of common pleas.—When a city desires to connect with the existing sewer of any municipal corporation or municipal authority and no agreement has been reached between the city and the municipal corporation or municipal authority, council shall present a petition to the court of common pleas setting forth those facts. The court shall fix a date for a hearing and notify all interested parties of the date.

(c) Appointment of viewers.—If, after the hearing the court determines that the connection can be made without impairing the usefulness of the existing sanitary sewer system, the court shall appoint three viewers to:

(1) View the premises.

(2) Investigate the facts of the case.

(3) Assess the necessary costs and expenses of making the connection.

(4) Assess the proportionate part of the expense of building the original sanitary sewer system upon the city.

(d) Determination of the court.—The court shall determine the proportion of the expense for repairs that each city, municipal corporation and municipal authority bears and shall determine all other questions liable to arise in connection with the repairs.

(e) Report.—The viewers shall submit a report to the court with the result of their investigation, which shall be confirmed within 30 days, unless exceptions to the report are filed.

(f) Appeal.—After confirmation of the report or the disposal of any exceptions, any party interested may appeal the decision of the court of common pleas.

§ 13250. Sewers extended outside of city.

(a) General rule.—A city with a sanitary sewer system may extend the system and construct sewers beyond the city's boundaries into adjoining municipalities in the county where the city is located and furnish sewer facilities to, and permit the tapping and the connection with the sewer facilities by, any person and municipality in the county where the city is located in accordance with law and the rules and regulations of the Pennsylvania Public Utility Commission.

(b) Limitation.—This section does not authorize a city to extend a sewerage system or construct sewers in territory outside the boundaries of the cities in which sewerage facilities are furnished by a private company or by a municipality authority.

CHAPTER 134

WATERCOURSES, FLOOD PROTECTION PROJECTS AND STORM WATER SYSTEMS

Sec.

---

§ 13401. Establishing and changing watercourses, flood protection projects and storm water systems.

(a) General rule.—Subject to obtaining, if required, the authorization of the Federal Government and the Department of Environmental Protection, a city may, by ordinance, do any of the following:

(1) Realign, change or vacate the channels, beds and mouths of watercourses through lands, marshes or waters in or adjacent to the city, subject to the limitations in the act of August 7, 1936 (1st Sp.Sess., P.L.106, No.46),

referred to as the Flood Control Law, the act of June 22, 1937 (P.L.1987, No.394), known as The Clean Streams Law, the act of November 26, 1978 (P.L.1375, No.325), known as the Dam Safety and Encroachments Act, and 26 Pa.C.S. § 206 (relating to extraterritorial takings).

(2) Confine, pave or completely enclose watercourses within the city.

(3) Prevent and remove obstructions and encroachments from watercourses and the banks of streams that threaten or injure the city or property in the city at the expense of those that caused the obstruction or encroachment through proceedings at law or equity.

(4) Construct and maintain dams in a watercourse flowing through the city, or partly within and partly outside its corporate limits, for the purpose of improving the public health, safety and welfare in the city.

(5) Plan and provide for projects, infrastructure and improvements as a means of managing and controlling storm water, which may include, but need not be limited to, the transport, storage and infiltration of storm water and other innovative techniques identified in the county-prepared watershed plans pursuant to the act of October 4, 1978 (P.L.864, No.167), known as the Storm Water Management Act.

(6) Plan and provide for projects, infrastructure and improvements as a means of providing flood protection pursuant to the Flood Control Law.

(b) Condemnation and taking of property.—A city may, for the purpose of this section, purchase, acquire, enter upon, take, use and appropriate private property and materials as necessary. Condemnation proceedings shall be pursuant to the procedures in 26 Pa.C.S. (relating to eminent domain) and any takings of property outside the limits of the city shall be subject to the limitations in 26 Pa.C.S. § 206.

§ 13407. Assessment of benefits and liens.

(a) General rule.—With regard to improvements made pursuant to section 13401(a) (relating to establishing and changing watercourses, flood protection projects and storm water systems), a city may, if feasible, assess the benefits upon property benefited by the improvements pursuant to Chapter 145A (relating to assessments for public improvements).

(b) Lien.—The assessments of benefits shall become liens upon the property assessed.

(c) Collection of claim.—Claims for the benefits may be collected in the same manner as municipal claims are collected or they may be collected by action of assumpsit, however, the lien of the judgment is limited to the property assessed.

§ 13408. Waters excepted.

Nothing contained in this chapter shall apply to any watercourse used by any municipality or water company as a source of supply, unless the municipality or water company shall consent to the vacation or alteration.

CHAPTER 135

UTILITY SERVICE

Sec.

§ 13501.1. Right to furnish water, lighting, electric, gas or other similar utility service.

(a) Authority of city.—A city may supply water, lighting, electric, gas or other similar utility service for public and private uses within the city. For these purposes, a city may install, maintain and operate the necessary facilities and acquire property and make improvements as needed. In carrying out the authority granted by this section, a city may exercise the powers granted to it under this chapter or another law deemed necessary to carry out the purposes of this section, including the power to acquire, by eminent domain or otherwise, and the power to temporarily use or lease property.

(b) Rates and charges.—A city supplying water, lighting, electric, gas or other similar utility service may fix the rates and charges applicable to the service in accordance with section 13587 (relating to fixing rates).

(c) Incurring debt.—For the purposes of this section, a city may incur debt in accordance with 53 Pa.C.S. Pt. VII Subpt. B (relating to indebtedness and borrowing).

§ 13540.1. Power to furnish utilities to consumers outside city.

A city that provides utility service in accordance with section 13501.1 (relating to right to furnish water, lighting, electric, gas or other similar utility service) may provide utility service in a surrounding municipality that is not provided with utility service by another municipality, local or regional public authority or private company, subject to and in accordance with applicable law and the rules and regulations of the Pennsylvania Public Utility Commission with regard to the character of service, extensions and rates.

§ 13585. Payment of cost of extensions.

When an extension of pipes, wires or conduits is made to permit a city to supply water, light, electric, gas or other similar utility service to a portion of the city not previously supplied with the service, an assessment of the cost of the service may be made in accordance with Chapter 145A (relating to assessments for public improvements).

§ 13587. Fixing rates.

Council shall fix, or may delegate to a city department the power to fix, with the approval of council, rates for the use of water, light, electric, gas or other similar utility service, and, in the case of consumers outside the city, the fixing of rates shall be subject to and in accordance with applicable law and the rules and regulations of the Pennsylvania Public Utility Commission.

§ 13588. Collection of utility charges.

(a) Authority for ordinance.—Council shall provide, by ordinance, for the collection of charges for the use of water, light, electric, gas or other similar utility service that may accrue to the city, fixing the time when the charges are payable and the penalties for nonpayment. The charges shall be assessed to the respective owners of the real estate on which the utility service is used. If the charges are not paid in accordance with the provisions of the ordinance, a claim for the amount due may be filed as a lien and collected in accordance with the Municipal Claim and Tax Lien Law.

(b) Owner liability.—

(1) If a city that has agreed to provide water service through a separate meter and separate service line to a residential dwelling unit in which the owner does not reside, the owner shall be liable to pay the tenant's bill for service rendered to the tenant by the city only if the city notifies the owner and the tenant within 30 days after the bill first becomes overdue. Notification must be provided by first class mail to the address of the owner provided to the city by the owner and to the billing address of the tenant, respectively.

(2) This subsection may not be construed to require a city to terminate service to a tenant. An owner shall not be liable for any service which the city provides to the tenant 90 or more days after the tenant's bill first becomes overdue unless the city has been prevented by court order from terminating service to that tenant.

§ 13590. Disposition of revenues.

The revenues derived from the city's furnishing of water, light, electric, gas or other similar utility service shall be applied as follows:

(1) to the purposes of the respective departments under the direction of which the utility service is provided;

(2) for the reduction of debt related to the provision of the service provided under paragraph (1); and

(3) to another city department that provides labor or materials for the maintenance and repair of property or facilities relating to the city's provision of a utility service.

CHAPTER 136
PUBLIC BUILDINGS AND WORKS

§ 13601. Public buildings generally.

(a) **Authority of city.**—With regard to a public building, a city may, by ordinance, do any of the following:

(1) erect, purchase, establish or maintain the public buildings; or

(2) purchase, take, use, occupy or acquire, by any lawful means, including eminent domain, private land, buildings and property in order to erect, establish or maintain a public building.

(b) **Included structures.**—For purposes of this chapter, a public building includes not only a building or structure that council deems necessary for the use of the city, but also another building and structure to be used for a public purpose, including a public auditorium, public library, public memorial building and monument.

§ 13603. Payment of erection and maintenance costs.

A city may:

(1) Appropriate money and incur debt in accordance with 53 Pa.C.S. Pt. VII Subpt. B (relating to indebtedness and borrowing) for the purchase or acquisition of private land, buildings and property through eminent domain in order to erect or establish a public building.

(2) Appropriate money for the operation and maintenance of a public building.

§ 13605. Donation of land by city for library purposes and contributions toward maintenance.

In addition to the power to make an appropriation, donation or gift for a library purpose in accordance with 24 Pa.C.S. Ch. 93 (relating to public library code), a city may acquire and donate land for library purposes to a local library as defined in 24 Pa.C.S. § 9302 (relating to definitions).

§ 13606. Rental of public auditorium and disposition of proceeds.

In the case of a public auditorium, a city may, by order of council, charge a rental fee for the use of the public auditorium. The money derived from the rental of the public auditorium shall be paid into the city general fund.

§ 13607. Long-term improvement lease.

(a) Authority of city.—A city may lease city real estate on a long-term improvement lease, at a nominal rental fee or otherwise, to a nonprofit corporation for the purpose of providing an auditorium for a dramatic, musical, artistic, literary, scientific or patriotic society or event or for another purpose as may be approved by council.

(b) Term.—A long-term improvement lease:

(1) May not be for a term of more than 99 years.

(2) May provide for a right of renewal for a like term.

(3) Shall contain provisions for the improvement of the real estate by the lessee by the erection of a suitable building of dignified and appropriate architecture. The absolute ownership of the building shall revert to the city, free of claim or charge, at the end of the term of the lease or a renewal of the lease.

(c) Use of building.—A building erected under a long-term improvement lease may be used for a public purpose, including as an auditorium for a dramatic, musical, artistic, literary or scientific event and for the accommodation of a patriotic society or group or other accommodation and feature, as may be approved by the city.

(d) Title and local taxation.—The title to property subject to a long-term improvement lease shall remain with the city. For purposes of local taxation, the property subject to a long-term improvement lease and the leasehold estate created by the lease shall be deemed to be devoted to a public purpose and public use.

(e) Lessee.—The lessee under a long-term improvement lease shall be exclusively liable for the maintenance and upkeep of the demised premises and shall be solely responsible for the maintenance and operation of the demised premises.

(f) Lessor.—A long-term improvement lease may provide that the lessor is entitled to receive a sum equal to the net income of the demised premises after reasonable reserves and proper amortization charges.

CHAPTER 137

PARKS, PLAYGROUNDS AND RECREATION CENTERS

Sec.

Chap. 39 Res. During Mil. Service
Chap. 38 Intergov. Coop.
Chap. 37 3rd Class City Code
Chap. 36 Bor. Code
Chap. 35 2nd Class Twp. Code
Chap. 34 1st Class Twp. Code
Chap. 33 Home Rule Chart. Opt. Plans Law
Chap. 32 Water Serv. Act
Chap. 31 Munic. Auth. Act

§ 13703. Acquisition of lands and buildings.

By purchase, gift or right of eminent domain, a city may enter upon, take, use and acquire land, property or a building for the purpose of making, extending, enlarging and maintaining a recreation place. The recreation place shall consist of a public park, parkway, playground, field, gymnasium, public bath, swimming pool or indoor recreation center. A city may:

(1) Levy and collect a special tax as may be necessary to pay for the recreation place.

(2) Make appropriations for the improvement, maintenance, care, regulation and governing of the recreation place.

(3) Designate and set apart for use, for a purpose specified in this section, land and a building owned by the city and not dedicated or devoted to other public use.

(4) Lease land and a building in the city for temporary use for a purpose specified under this section. Land, property and a building outside the limits of the city may be purchased or acquired for the recreation place with the consent of the governing body of the municipal corporation in which the land, property or building is situated.

§ 13703.1. Powers of council and delegation.

(a) **Council.**—Council may equip, operate, supervise and maintain a recreation place and employ a recreation director or other officer or employee deemed necessary in order to carry out the provisions of this chapter.

(b) **Supervision and maintenance.**—When more than one-half the full cost of the supervision and maintenance of the recreation place, including the compensation of an officer or employee hired to carry out the provisions of this chapter, are borne by the city, council may fix the compensation of the officer or employee.

(c) **Delegation.**—Council may delegate all or part of its power under subsection (a) to an existing body or board or to a recreation board, as council shall determine.

§ 13705. Creation and composition of recreation board.

(a) **Establishment.**—Council may establish in the city a recreation board.

(b) **Power and responsibilities.**—The recreation board shall possess the powers and responsibilities delegated to it by council in accordance with section 13703.1(c) (relating to powers of council and delegation).

(c) **Composition.**—When established, the recreation board shall consist of five or seven individuals.

(d) **Appointment and terms.**—The members of the recreation board shall be appointed by the mayor, with the approval of council, and shall serve for terms no longer than five years. The terms of the members shall be staggered in a manner that at least one expires annually.

(e) **Compensation.**—The members of the recreation board shall serve without pay.

(f) **Vacancy.**—A vacancy in the board, other than by expiration of term, shall be for the unexpired term and shall be filled in the same manner as the original appointment.

§ 13706. Organization of board.

The members of a recreation board established under this chapter shall elect a chair and secretary and select the other necessary officers to serve for a period of one year. The board may adopt rules and regulations for the conduct of all business within its jurisdiction. A meeting of the board shall be subject to the provisions of 65 Pa.C.S. Ch. 7 (relating to open meetings).

§ 13707. Joint ownership and maintenance.

A city may acquire, jointly with one or more other municipalities, property for and operate and maintain a recreation place. A city may join with a school district and appropriate money for equipping, operating and maintaining a recreation place.

§ 13708. Borrowing.

Council may borrow money and incur debt in accordance with 53 Pa.C.S. Pt. VII Subpt. B (relating to indebtedness and borrowing) for the purpose of acquiring land, a building and equipment for a recreation place.

§ 13709. Maintenance and tax levy.

An expense incurred in the maintenance and operation of a recreation place established under this chapter, including the operation of a recreation program in the recreation place, may be paid from the city treasury. Council may annually appropriate, and cause to be raised by taxation in accordance with section 12531(a)(4) (relating to tax levies), a tax for this purpose. The funds may be appropriated for the purposes of this section to an existing body or board or to a recreation board.

§ 13709.1. City trust.

(a) Authority of city and council.—The following shall apply:

(1) A city may receive in trust the estate, money, assets and real and personal property that has been or will be bestowed upon the city by donation, gift, legacy, endowment, bequest, devise, conveyance or other means for:

(i) the purpose of establishing or maintaining a public park; or

(ii) another public purpose for the use and benefit of the residents of the city.

(2) For the purposes of the trust, council may control the estate, money, assets and real and personal property received under this subsection.

(3) The authority provided under this subsection shall be in addition to the other powers conferred by law.

(b) Transfer of control.—The following shall apply:

(1) Control of a city trust shall be transferred to council if the trust has been or is created as a result of a property or estate having been conveyed, bequeathed or devised or otherwise given or donated to a city in trust for:

(i) the purpose of establishing or maintaining a public park; or

(ii) another public purpose for the use and benefit of the residents of the city.

(2) Upon petition of council, the court of common pleas in the county where a city is located may transfer control of the trust to council if necessary to carry out the intention of this section.

(c) Delegation.—Council may delegate the supervision and operation of recreation places subject to the trust to a recreation board in accordance with section 13703.1 (relating to powers of council and delegation).

(d) Power of the court.—This section shall not limit a power of the court to terminate or reform a trust under existing law.

§ 13718. Park rangers.

(a) Authority of council.—Under the provisions of this chapter, council may provide, by ordinance, for the selection and employment of the number of individuals deemed necessary to act as park rangers, fix compensation and duties and provide for uniforms.

(b) Authority of park ranger.—To the extent authorized by 53 Pa.C.S. Ch. 21 Subch. D (relating to municipal police education and training), an individual appointed as a park ranger under an ordinance passed under the provisions of subsection (a) shall have, in a park and playground and other public place in the city and beyond the limits of the city when the city has acquired land, property and a building for a park and playground or another public purpose, the same power in preserving the peace, maintaining order and making arrests as a police officer has in the city.

(c) Supervision, control and direction.—A park ranger shall be under the supervision, control and direction of the director of the department of parks and public property or, if none exists, another department as council directs.

(d) Definition.—For purposes of the act of June 28, 1935 (P.L.477, No.193), referred to as the Enforcement Officer Disability Benefits Law (Heart and Lung Act), the term "park ranger," as used in this section, shall mean a park guard.

CHAPTER 141A
UNIFORM CONSTRUCTION CODE, PROPERTY MAINTENANCE CODE AND RESERVED POWERS

Sec.

---

§ 141A01. Primacy of certain codes.

(a) Applicability.—The Pennsylvania Construction Code Act and the Uniform Construction Code adopted under section 301 of the Pennsylvania Construction Code Act shall apply to the construction, alteration, repair and occupancy of the buildings and structures within a city.

(b) Construction.—This chapter and an ordinance, rule or regulation adopted under this chapter shall not supersede or abrogate the Pennsylvania Construction Code Act or the Uniform Construction Code and shall be construed and read in pari materia with them.

§ 141A02. Changes in Uniform Construction Code.

A city may propose and enact an ordinance to equal or exceed the minimum requirements of the Uniform Construction Code in accordance with and subject to the requirements of section 503 of the Pennsylvania Construction Code Act. An ordinance exceeding the provisions of the Uniform Construction Code must meet the standards provided in section 503(j)(2) of the Pennsylvania Construction Code Act.

§ 141A03. Public nuisance.

A building, housing or property erected, altered, extended, reconstructed, removed or maintained contrary to a provision of an ordinance enacted for a purpose specified in this chapter may be reported in accordance with Chapter 127A (relating to nuisance abatement) to the department designated to determine whether a public nuisance exists. If a public nuisance is determined to exist, the public nuisance may be abated in accordance with that chapter, provided that a violation of the Uniform Construction Code or an ordinance that equals or exceeds the Uniform Construction Code is subject to:

(1) The provisions of the Pennsylvania Construction Code Act.

(2) The regulations adopted under that act by the Department of Labor and Industry relating to enforcement for noncompliance.

§ 141A04. Property maintenance code.

(a) Enactment.—Notwithstanding the primacy of the Uniform Construction Code, a city may enact a property maintenance ordinance, including a standard or nationally recognized property maintenance code or a change or variation. In accordance with section 11018.13 (relating to standard or nationally recognized codes), the ordinance may, by reference, incorporate a standard or nationally recognized property maintenance code or a variation or change, published and printed in book form, without setting forth the text of the code in the ordinance.

(b) Public availability.—The full text of the property maintenance code need not be published, but, in accordance with section 11018.9 (relating to publication of proposed ordinances), it shall be sufficient to publish a summary setting forth the provisions of the ordinance in reasonable detail and a reference to a place within the city where copies of the proposed ordinance may be examined. Not fewer than three copies of the proposed property maintenance code shall be made available to public inspection and use during business hours. Copies shall also be made available to an interested party in accordance with the act of February 14, 2008 (P.L.6, No.3), known as the Right-to-Know Law, or may be furnished or loaned without charge.

(c) Violations.—A property maintenance code ordinance may provide for fines and penalties of not more than $1,000 or imprisonment for not more than 90 days, or both, for violations. The procedure set forth under this chapter relating to the enactment of the ordinance may be utilized in amending, supplementing or repealing any of the provisions of the ordinance.

(d) Inspectors.—Council may appoint property maintenance inspectors who may, subject to constitutional standards in a similar manner as provided in section 12308 (relating to powers of board of health), enter upon and inspect the premises at reasonable hours for the administration and enforcement of the city's property maintenance code or ordinance incorporating a standard or nationally recognized property maintenance code. A fee payable to a property maintenance inspector under the ordinance must be paid by the property maintenance inspector to the city treasurer for the use of the city as promptly as possible.

(e) Additional remedies.—In addition to the penalties provided by the property maintenance ordinance, the city may institute an appropriate action or proceeding at law or in equity to prevent or restrain a property maintenance violation.

(f) Relation to other acts.—The powers of a city as provided in this section shall be in addition to, but not limited to, the powers provided in:

(1) The act of November 26, 2008 (P.L.1672, No.135), known as the Abandoned and Blighted Property Conservatorship Act.

(2) 53 Pa.C.S. Ch. 61 (relating to neighborhood blight reclamation and revitalization).

(3) 68 Pa.C.S. Ch. 21 (relating to land banks).

§ 141A05. Reserved powers.

If, as a result of legislative action or final order of court for which the time for appeal has expired and no appeal has been taken or from which there is no pending appeal, the Uniform Construction Code or a replacement code is no longer applicable in a city, a city may:

(1) Enact and enforce an ordinance to govern and regulate:

(i) construction;

(ii) reconstruction;

(iii) alteration;

(iv) extension;

(v) repair;

(vi) conversion;

(vii) maintenance;

(viii) occupation;

(ix) sanitation;

(x) ventilation;

(xi) heating;

(xii) egress;

(xiii) lighting;

(xiv) electric wiring;

(xv) water supply;

(xvi) toilet facilities;

(xvii) drainage;

(xviii) plumbing;

(xix) fire prevention;

(xx) fireproofing, including prescribing limitations under which only buildings of noncombustible material and fireproofed roofs are used in construction, erection or substantial reconstruction;

(xxi) use and inspection of all buildings and housing or parts of buildings and housing, and the roofs, walls and foundations of the buildings and housing and all facilities and services in or about the buildings or housing constructed, erected, altered, designed or used, in whole or in part, for any use or occupancy; and

(xxii) the sanitation and inspection of land appurtenant to the buildings and housing.

(1.1) Combine or separately enact or combine the ordinances under paragraph (1) with the property maintenance code.

(2) Require that, before any work of construction, reconstruction, alteration, extension, repair or conversion of a building begins, approval of the plans and specifications is secured.

(3) Incorporate a standard or nationally recognized code or a variation or change, published and printed in book form, without incorporating the text of the code as provided in Subchapter A.1 of Chapter 110 (relating to ordinances). The ordinance may provide for fines and penalties of not more than $1,000 or imprisonment for not more than 90 days, or both, for violations. The procedure set forth under this chapter relating to the enactment of the ordinance may be utilized in amending, supplementing or repealing a provision of an ordinance that incorporates all or a part of a standard or nationally recognized code or a variation or change.

(4) Appoint a building inspector, housing inspector, property maintenance inspector, fire prevention inspector, electrical inspector and plumbing inspector and fix inspectors' compensation. Subject to constitutional standards in a similar manner as provided in section 12308 (relating to powers of board of health), the inspector may enter upon and inspect a premises at reasonable

hours for the administration and enforcement of the city's enacted codes or ordinances incorporating standard or nationally recognized codes. A fee payable to an inspector under the ordinance shall be paid by the inspector to the city treasurer for the use of the city as promptly as possible.

(5) In addition to the penalties provided by an ordinance, institute an appropriate action or proceeding at law or in equity to prevent or restrain the unlawful construction, reconstruction, alteration, extension, repair, conversion, maintenance or use or occupation of property located within the city, to restrain, correct or abate the violation and to prevent the use or occupancy of the building, housing or structure.

CHAPTER 142
AERONAUTICS

Sec.

---

§ 14201. Power to acquire land for aeronautical purposes and maintenance of municipal airports.

A city may establish and maintain a municipal airport and may acquire by lease, purchase or condemnation proceedings, subject to the limitations in 26 Pa.C.S. § 206 (relating to extraterritorial takings), land lying either within or outside the territorial limits of the city and within or outside the territorial limits of the county in which the city is located, that in the judgment of council may be necessary and desirable for the purpose of establishing and maintaining a municipal airport, landing field, aviation easement or intermediate landing field and other air navigation facilities.

§ 14203. Leasing of land acquired for aeronautical purposes.

A city acquiring land for aeronautical purposes may lease the land or part of the land to an individual or corporation desiring to use the same for aeronautical purposes.

§ 14204. Operation of facilities jointly.

A city may operate and maintain a municipal airport, landing field or intermediate landing fields and other air navigation facility jointly in accordance with 53 Pa.C.S. Ch. 23 Subch. A (relating to intergovernmental cooperation).

§ 14205. Appropriation for support of air navigation facilities.

A city that does not own, lease or operate a municipal airport, landing field or intermediate landing field or other air navigation facility may appropriate money for the support and maintenance of any of the facilities, situate either within or outside the boundaries of the city or of the county or counties in which the city is located.

CHAPTER 143
PENSIONS

SUBCHAPTER A
POLICE

---

§ 14300. Definitions.

(a) Chapter.—The following words and phrases when used in this chapter shall have the meanings given to them in this subsection unless the context clearly indicates otherwise:

"Joint coverage member." A city employee who becomes a member of the retirement system subsequent to the last date permitted by the city for statement or preference concerning Social Security coverage, or who, having become a member on or before that date, filed a written statement with a city's retirement board that the member elects Social Security coverage under an agreement with the Secretary of Health and Human Services entered into by the Commonwealth.

"Single coverage member." A city employee who becomes a member of the retirement system on or before the last date permitted by the city for statement of preference concerning Social Security coverage and who either filed a written statement with the retirement board that the member does not elect Social Security coverage under any agreement with the Secretary of Health and Human Services entered into by the Commonwealth or did not file any written statement with the retirement board.

(b) Subchapter.—The following words and phrases when used in this subchapter shall have the meanings given to them in this subsection unless the context clearly indicates otherwise:

"Salary." The fixed amount of compensation paid at regular, periodic intervals by the city to the member and from which pension contributions have been deducted.

§ 14301. Police pension fund.

(a) Establishment.—By ordinance, a city shall establish a police pension fund.

(b) Requirements.—The following shall apply to a police pension fund established under this section:

(1) The fund shall be maintained by an equal and proportionate monthly charge against each member of the police force that may not exceed annually 4% of the pay of the member and an additional amount not to exceed 1% of the pay of the member.

(2) The charges under paragraph (1) shall be paid by the member or the municipal corporation to provide sufficient funds for payments required by section 14303(f) (relating to allowances and service increments).

(3) The payments under paragraph (2) shall be made to a surviving spouse even if the spouse remarries or, if no spouse survives or if the individual survives and subsequently dies, to the children under 18 years of age of:

(i) a member of the police force;

(ii) a member retired on pension; or

(iii) a member who died in service.

(4) The fund shall be under the direction and control of council but may be committed to the custody and management of an officer of the city or to another person, as may be designated by council by ordinance.

(5) Under regulations as council may prescribe by ordinance, the fund shall be applied for the benefit of:

(i) members of the police force that have received honorable discharge from the police force by reason of age or disability;

(ii) surviving spouses even if they remarry; or

(iii) if no spouse survives or if the individual survives and subsequently dies, the child or children under 18 years of age of:

(A) members of the police force; or

(B) members retired on pension.

(6) An allowance made to an individual who retired by reason of a disability or age shall be in conformity with a uniform scale, together with a service increment as provided under this chapter.

(7) Compensation paid to a corporate custodian of the police pension fund shall be paid from the city general fund.

§ 14302. Retirement and final discharge.

(a) Requirements for ordinance.—With regard to continuous service and minimum retirement age requirements, the ordinance establishing the police pension fund shall prescribe as follows:

(1) A minimum period of continuous service of not less than 20 years.

(2) If a minimum retirement age is prescribed, a minimum age of 50 years.

(b) Retired member.—If not unfit by reason of age, disability or otherwise, a retired member shall be subject to service as a police reserve under terms and conditions as may be established by council.

(c) Military service.—With the approval of council, a member of the police pension fund shall be entitled to have full credit for each year or fraction of a year, not to exceed five years, of the service upon the member's payment to:

(1) the police pension fund of an amount equal to that which the member would have paid had the member been a member during the period for which credit is desired; and

Table of Contents
Part I Ch. 1–3 Ethics, Records, Open Meetings
Part II Ch. 4–10 Taxation
Part III Ch. 11–18 Torts, Contracts & Civil Rules
Part IV Ch. 19–24 Zoning & Planning
Part V Ch. 25–30 Construction and Emergency Codes
Part VI Ch. 31–39 Municipal Codes
Index

(2) the fund of an additional amount as the equivalent of the contributions of the city on account of the military service.

To be eligible under this subsection, the member must be a contributor who served in the armed forces of the United States after September 1, 1940, and was not a member of the police pension fund prior to the military service.

§ 14302.1. Limited vested benefit.

(a) Ordinance.—The ordinance establishing a police pension fund may provide for a limited vested benefit if the benefit would conform to section 305 of the act of December 18, 1984 (P.L.1005, No.205), known as the Municipal Pension Plan Funding Standard and Recovery Act.

(b) Requirements.—Under a limited vested benefit, a member of the police pension fund who has not completed the minimum period of continuous service requirement and satisfied an applicable minimum age requirement, but who has completed 12 years of full-time service shall be entitled to vest the member's retirement benefits subject to the following conditions:

(1) The member must file with the management board of the police pension fund a written notice of the member's intention to vest.

(2) The member must include in the notice the date the member intends to terminate the member's service as a full-time police officer.

(3) The termination date shall be at least 30 days later than the date of notice to vest.

(4) The member must be in good standing with the police department on the date of the notice to vest.

(5) The board shall indicate on the notice to vest the rate of the monthly pay of the member as of the date of the notice to vest or the highest average annual salary which the member received during any five years of service preceding that date, whichever is higher.

(c) Notification.—Upon reaching the date that would have been the member's retirement date if the member continued full-time employment with the police department, the member shall notify the board, in writing, that the member desires to collect the member's pension.

(d) Amount of retirement benefits.—The amount of retirement benefits the member is entitled to receive under this section shall be computed as follows:

(1) The initial determination of the member's base retirement benefits shall be computed on the salary indicated on the notice to vest.

(2) The portion of the base retirement benefits due the member shall be determined by applying to the base amount the percentage that the member's years of service rendered bears to the years of service that would have been rendered if the member continued to be employed by the department until the member's minimum retirement date.

§ 14303. Allowance and service increments.

(a) Allowance.—A payment for an allowance shall only be a charge on the police pension fund and may not be a charge on another fund under the control or in the city treasury.

(b) Apportionment of the pension.—The basis of the apportionment of the pension:

(1) shall be determined by the rate of the monthly pay of the member at the date of injury, death, honorable discharge, vesting under section 14302.1 (relating to limited vested benefit) or retirement, or the highest average annual salary that the member received during any five years of service preceding

injury, death, honorable discharge, vesting under section 14302.1 or retirement, whichever is higher.

(2) except as to service increments provided for in subsection (d), may not exceed in a year one-half the annual pay of the member computed at the monthly or average annual rate, whichever is higher.

(c) Limitation.—

(1) The provisions of subsection (b)(2) may not apply to a city operating under:

(i) an optional charter adopted in accordance with the act of July 15, 1957 (P.L.901, No.399), known as the Optional Third Class City Charter Law; or

(ii) a home rule charter adopted in accordance with 53 Pa.C.S. Pt. III Subpt. E (relating to home rule and optional plan government).

(2) This subsection is applicable only to a city that had a pension plan in effect prior to July 1, 1931, that provided pensions in an amount greater than 50% of salary.

(d) Conditions.—In addition to the retirement allowance authorized to be paid from the police pension fund by this chapter and notwithstanding the limitations placed upon the retirement allowances and upon contributions, a contributor who becomes entitled to the retirement allowance shall be entitled to the payment of a service increment in accordance with and subject to the following conditions:

(1) The following shall apply:

(i) Service increment shall be the sum obtained by computing:

(A) the number of whole years after having served the minimum required by this chapter during which a contributor has been employed by the city and paid out of the city treasury, including credit for military service as provided in section 14302 (relating to retirement and final discharge); and

(B) multiplying the number of years computed under clause (A) by an amount equal to 0.025% of the retirement allowance that has become payable to the contributor in accordance with the provisions of this chapter.

(ii) In computing the service increment, employment after the contributor has reached 65 years of age may not be included and a service increment may not be paid in excess of $100 per month.

(2) From and after January 1, 1952, a contributor shall pay into the retirement fund a monthly sum in addition to the contributor's retirement contribution that shall be equal to one-half of 1% of the contributor's salary, provided that:

(i) the payment may not exceed the sum of $1 per month; and

(ii) the service increment contribution may not be paid after a contributor has reached 65 years of age.

(3) An individual who is a contributor on January 1, 1952, and has reached 65 years of age shall have the contributor's service increment computed on the years of employment prior to the date the contributor reached 65 years of age.

(4) A service increment contribution shall be paid at the same time and in the same manner as a retirement contribution. A service increment contribution may be withdrawn in full without interest by an individual who:

(i) left the employment of the city, subject to the same conditions by which a retirement contribution may be withdrawn; or

(ii) retires before becoming entitled to a service increment.

(5) The members of the police force who are now contributors to the retirement fund and the members employed by the city after January 1, 1952, if required to become contributors to the retirement fund, shall be subject to the provisions of this part.

(6) After June 19, 2002, a city may agree to make service increment payments in excess of $100 per month as long as the payments do not exceed $500 per month. In computing the service increments, employment after the contributor has reached 65 years of age may not be included, provided that an agreement to provide an increase in service increment payments shall include a proportionate increase in the amount a contributor shall pay into the retirement fund under paragraph (2), not to exceed $5 per month.

(e) Spouse and children.—The spouse of a member of the police force or a member who retires on pension who dies or, if no spouse survives or if the spouse survives and subsequently dies or remarries, the child or children under 18 years of age of a member of the police force or a member who retires on pension who dies on or after August 1, 1963, shall, during the lifetime of the surviving spouse, even if the surviving spouse remarries, or until reaching 18 years of age in the case of a child or children, be entitled to receive a pension calculated at the rate of 50% of the pension the member was receiving or would have been receiving if the member was retired at the time of the member's death and may receive the pension the member was receiving or would have been receiving had the member been retired at the time of the member's death.

(f) Certain police officers.—A police officer who has less than 10 years of service and who dies or is totally disabled due to injuries or mental incapacities not in the line of duty and is unable to perform the duties of a police officer may be entitled to a pension of 25% of the police officer's annual compensation. For death or injuries received after 10 years of service, the compensation may be 50% of the police officer's annual compensation.

(g) Disability pension.—The disability pension may be payable to the police officer during the police officer's lifetime and, if the police officer dies, the pension payment that the police officer was receiving may be continued to be paid to:

(1) the police officer's spouse if the spouse survives; or

(2) if the spouse subsequently dies or remarries, the child or children under 18 years of age of the police officer.

§ 14303.1. Increase of allowances after retirement.

(a) Increase of allowance.—Upon the recommendation of the persons having custody and management of the police pension fund, a city may, at its discretion, increase the allowance of individuals receiving an allowance from the police pension fund by reason of and after the termination of the services of a member of the fund.

(b) Limitation.—An increase made under this section must be in conformity with a uniform scale that may be based on the cost of living, but the total of the allowance may not exceed one-half of the current salary being paid patrol persons of the highest pay grade.

§ 14303.2. Total disability.

(a) Injury sustained in the line of duty.—Notwithstanding any provision of this chapter, a police officer who becomes totally disabled due to an injury sustained in the line of duty shall be deemed to be fully vested in the police pension fund, regardless of the actual number of years of credited service, and shall be eligible for immediate retirement benefits.

(b) Claim and proof.—The governing body of the city shall decide a claim under this section. Proof of disability shall be by competent medical evidence provided by the claimant. The governing body of the city may, at any time, have the claimant examined by its own physician.

(c) Procedure.—A claim under this section may be initiated as the regulations of council prescribe. Hearings and appeals shall be as provided in 2 Pa.C.S. (relating to administrative law and procedure).

(d) Subrogation.—The police pension fund shall be subrogated to the right of the claimant to the extent of a payment made under the act of June 2, 1915 (P.L.736, No.338), known as the Workers' Compensation Act, or the act of June 28, 1935 (P.L.477, No.193), referred to as the Enforcement Officer Disability Benefits Law (Heart and Lung Act).

(e) Definition.—As used in this section, the term "total disability" means permanent mental or physical impairment that renders the police officer unable to perform the officer's duties.

§ 14304. Inalienable rights in fund.

Whenever an individual becomes entitled to receive an allowance from the police pension fund and has been admitted to participate in the fund, the individual may not be deprived of the individual's right to equal and proportionate participation in the fund on the basis upon which the individual first became entitled to participation.

§ 14305. Payments to police pension fund by city.

Unless otherwise required by the act of December 18, 1984 (P.L.1005, No.205), known as the Municipal Pension Plan Funding Standard and Recovery Act, or another provision of law, this section shall govern the payment to the police pension fund of money raised by a tax levied by the city. The following shall apply:

(1) A city shall pay annually to the police pension fund a sum of money sufficient to meet the requirements of and to maintain the fund. In any year, the sum may not be less than one-half of 1% or more than 3% of the taxes levied by the city, other than a tax levied to pay interest on or extinguish the debt of the city.

(2) Council may exceed the limitation imposed by this section if an additional amount is deemed necessary to provide sufficient funds for payments to surviving spouses of members retired on pension, killed or who die in the service, provided that the city may annually pay into the fund not less than one-half of 1% of the taxes levied by the city, other than a tax levied to pay interest on or extinguish the debt of the city.

§ 14306. Management of police pension fund.

Only a person designated in accordance with section 14301(b)(4) (relating to police pension fund) shall be authorized to make decisions to hold, receive and distribute the money of the police pension fund.

§ 14307. Trust for benefit of police pension fund.

By gift, grant, devise or bequest, a city may take money or real, personal or mixed property in trust for the benefit of the pension fund. The care, management, investment and disposal of the body of the trust shall be vested in the officer or officers of the city for the time the council designates. The care, management and disposal shall be directed by ordinance and the body of the trust shall be governed by the ordinance, subject to the directions that are not inconsistent with the ordinance, as the settlor of the trust may prescribe.

§ 14308. Repayment before retirement.

(a) Refund.—If a contributing member of the police pension fund ceases to be a member of the police force before becoming entitled to a pension, the total amount of the contributions paid into the pension fund by the member shall be refunded to the member in full, without interest.

Table of Contents
Part I Ch. 1–3 Ethics, Records, Open Meetings
Part II Ch. 4–10 Taxation
Part III Ch. 11–18 Torts, Contracts & Civil Rules
Part IV Ch. 19–24 Zoning & Planning
Part V Ch. 25–30 Construction and Emergency Codes
Part VI Ch. 31–39 Municipal Codes
Index

(b) Return of amount contributed.—If the fund has returned to the member the amount contributed and afterward the individual again becomes a member of the police force, the member shall not be entitled to the pension designated until 20 years after the member's reemployment, unless the member returns to the police pension fund the amount withdrawn. If a member returns to the pension fund the amount withdrawn, the period of 20 years shall be computed from the time the member first became a member of the police force, excluding the period of time during which the member was not employed by the police force.

(c) Payment to member's estate.—If a member of the police force dies not in the line of service before the member becomes entitled to a pension and the member is not survived by a spouse or family entitled to payments as provided in this subchapter, the total amount of contributions paid into the pension fund by the member shall be paid over to the member's estate.

§ 14309. (Reserved).

SUBCHAPTER B
FIREFIGHTERS

Sec.

---

§ 14319. Definitions.

The following words and phrases when used in this subchapter shall have the meanings given to them in this section unless the context clearly indicates otherwise:

"Salary." The fixed amount of compensation paid at regular, periodic intervals by the city to the member and from which pension contributions have been deducted.

§ 14320. Firefighters' pension fund, management and annuity contracts.

(a) Duty of city.—Except as provided in this subchapter, a city shall provide an annuity contract or establish, by ordinance, a firefighters' pension fund.

(b) Monthly charge.—The annuity contract or firefighters' pension fund shall be maintained, in part, by an equal and proportionate monthly charge against each member of the fire department. The charge may not exceed annually 4% of the pay of the member and an additional amount not to exceed 1% if deemed necessary by council to provide sufficient funds for payments to surviving spouses of members retired on pension, killed or who die in service.

(c) Existing organization or association.—If there is an existing organization or association for the benefit of fully paid firefighters, constituting and having in charge the distribution of firefighters' pension money, an annuity contract may not be provided and a firefighters' pension fund may not be established under the provisions of this section unless and until the members of the organization or association, by a two-thirds vote, elect to transfer the existing fund into the pension fund required under this section.

(d) Pension fund board.—A firefighters' pension fund established under the provisions of this section shall be under the direction and control of a board of managers that shall consist of the following:

(1) Ex-officio members as follows:

(i) the mayor;

(ii) the director of the department of accounts and finance;

(iii) the director of the department having charge of the fire department or, in a city where the mayor is also the director of the department having charge of the fire department, the director of the department of public safety;

(iv) the city controller; and

(v) the chief of the bureau of fire.

(2) Two members of the fire department to be chosen by the members of the fire department.

(e) Substitution.—If a city does not establish a department whose director is named as an ex-officio member of the board of managers, the director of another department or the officers of the city as may be designated by council shall be substituted on the board of managers.

(f) Terms and vacancy.—Of the first members chosen by the members of the fire department to the board of managers, one shall be chosen for a term of two years and one for a term of four years. Biennially after the initial choices, one fire department member shall be chosen for a term of four years to take the place of the one whose term expires. In case of vacancy among the managers chosen by the fire department, a successor shall be chosen for the unexpired term.

(g) Requirements.—Under regulations prescribed by the board of managers, the firefighters' pension fund shall be applied for the benefit of the members of the fire department who receive honorable discharge from the fire department by reason of service, age or disability, surviving spouses of retired members and the families of members who are killed or who die in the service. A pension to an individual who is retired by reason of disability, service or age must be in conformity with a uniform scale, together with service increments as provided under this subchapter. A benefit from the fund to the family of a member who was killed or who died in service shall take into consideration the member's surviving spouse and the member's minor children under 18 years of age, if any.

§ 14320.1. Limited vested benefit for firefighters.

(a) Ordinance.—The ordinance establishing a firefighters' pension fund may provide for a limited vested benefit if the benefit would conform to section 305 of the act of December 18, 1984 (P.L.1005, No.205), known as the Municipal Pension Plan Funding Standard and Recovery Act.

(b) Conditions.—Under a limited vested benefit, if a member of the firefighters' pension fund has not completed the minimum period of continuous service and the applicable minimum age requirement but has completed 12 years of full-time service and ceased to be employed as a full-time firefighter, the member shall be entitled to vest the member's retirement benefits subject to the following conditions:

(1) The member must file with the management board of the firefighters' pension fund a written notice of the member's intention to vest.

(2) The member must include in the notice the date the member intends to terminate service as a full-time firefighter.

(3) The termination date shall be at least 30 days later than the date of notice to vest.

(4) The member must be in good standing with the fire department on the date of notice to vest.

(5) The board shall indicate on the notice to vest the rate of the monthly pay of the member as of the date of the notice to vest or the highest average annual salary which the member received during any five years of service preceding the date, whichever is higher.

(c) Notification.—Upon reaching the date that would have been the member's retirement date had the member continued full-time employment with the fire department, the member shall notify the board in writing that the member desires to collect the member's pension.

(d) Computation.—The amount of retirement benefits the member is entitled to receive under this section shall be computed as follows:

(1) The initial determination of the member's base retirement benefits shall be computed on the salary indicated on the notice to vest.

(2) The portion of the base retirement benefits due the member shall be determined by applying to the base amount the percentage that the member's years of service rendered bears to the years of service that would have been rendered had the member continued to be employed by the department until the member's minimum retirement date.

§ 14321. Retirement and final discharge.

(a) Ordinance.—With regard to continuous service and minimum age requirements, the ordinance establishing or regulations governing the firefighters' pension fund shall prescribe as follows:

(1) A minimum period of continuous service of not less than 20 years.

(2) If a minimum age is prescribed, a minimum of 50 years of age.

(b) Retired member.—If not unfit by reason of age, disability or otherwise, a retired member shall be subject to service as a firefighter reserve in a case of emergency under terms and conditions as may be established by council.

(c) Military service.—With the approval of council, a member of the firefighters' pension fund shall be entitled to have full credit for each year or fraction of a year, not to exceed five years, of service upon:

(1) the member's payment to the firefighters' pension fund of an amount equal to that which the member would have paid had the member been a member during the period for which the member desires credit; and

(2) the member's payment to the fund of an additional amount as the equivalent of the contributions of the city plus the interest the city would have been required to pay on the contributions on account of the military service. To be eligible under this paragraph, the member must be a contributor who served in the armed forces of the United States after September 1, 1940, and was not a member of the firefighters' pension fund prior to the military service.

(d) Payments to surviving spouse.—Upon the death of a member who retires on pension or is killed in service on or after January 1, 1960, or who dies in the service on or after January 1, 1968, payments as provided under this subchapter shall be made to the member's surviving spouse during the life of the spouse.

§ 14322. Pensions and service increments.

(a) Payments.—The following apply:

(1) Payments of pensions shall only be a charge on the firefighters' pension fund and shall not be a charge on any other fund under the control, or in the treasury, of the city.

(2) The basis of the pension of a member shall be determined by the monthly salary of the member at the date of vesting under section 14320.1 (relating to limited vested benefit for firefighters) or retirement, or the highest average annual salary which the member received during any five years of service preceding retirement, whichever is higher, whether for disability, or by reason of age or service, and except as to service increments provided for in subsection (b), shall be one-half the annual salary of the member at the time of vesting under section 14320.1 or retirement computed at the monthly or average annual rate, whichever is higher.

(3) For payment of pensions to members for permanent injury incurred in service and to families of members killed or who die in service, the amount and commencement of the payment of pensions shall be fixed by regulations of the board of managers. These regulations shall not take into consideration the amount and duration of workers' compensation allowed by law. Payments to surviving spouses of members retired on pension or killed in service on or after January 1, 1960, or who die in service on or after January 1, 1968, shall be the amount payable to the member or which would have been payable had the member been retired at the time of the member's death.

(a.1) Home rule and optional charter plans.—The provisions of subsection (a)(2) shall not apply to a city, whether operating under an optional charter adopted in accordance with the act of July 15, 1957 (P.L.901, No.399), known as the Optional Third Class City Charter Law or under a home rule charter adopted in accordance with 53 Pa.C.S. Pt. III Subpt. E (relating to home rule and optional plan government), which had pension plans in effect prior to June 19, 2002, that provided pensions in an amount greater than 50% of salary.

(b) Service increment.—In addition to the pension which is authorized to be paid from the firefighters' pension fund under this chapter and notwithstanding the limitations placed upon the pensions and upon contributions under this chapter, every contributor entitled to the pension shall also be entitled to the payment of a service increment in accordance with and subject to the conditions imposed under this chapter.

(1) A service increment shall be the sum obtained by computing the number of whole years after having served the minimum required by this chapter during which a contributor has been employed by the city and paid out of the city treasury, including credit for military service as provided in section 14321 (relating to retirement and final discharge), and multiplying the number of years by an amount equal to 0.025% of the retirement allowance which has become payable to the contributor in accordance with the provisions of this chapter. In computing the service increment, no employment after the contributor has reached 65 years of age shall be included and no service increment shall be paid in excess of $100 per month.

(2) After September 18, 1968, each contributor shall pay into the pension fund a monthly sum in addition to the contributor's pension contribution which shall not exceed the sum of $1 per month, provided that the service increment contribution shall not be paid after a contributor has reached 65 years of age.

(3) Any individual who is a member of the department on September 18, 1968, and who has reached 65 years of age shall have the individual's service increment computed on the years of employment prior to the member reaching 65 years of age.

(4) Service increment contributions shall be paid at the same time and in the same manner as pensions and may be withdrawn in full, without interest,

Table of Contents
Part I Ch. 1–3 Ethics, Records, Open Meetings
Part II Ch. 4–10 Taxation
Part III Ch. 11–18 Torts, Contracts & Civil Rules
Part IV Ch. 19–24 Zoning & Planning
Part V Ch. 25–30 Construction and Emergency Codes
Part VI Ch. 31–39 Municipal Codes
Index

by individuals who leave the employment of the city, subject to the same conditions by which retirement contributions may be withdrawn, or by individuals who retire before becoming entitled to any service increment.

(5) All members of the fire department who are now contributors to the pension fund and all those employed by the city after September 18, 1968, if required to become contributors to the pension fund, shall be subject to the provisions of this chapter.

(6) After June 19, 2002, a city may agree to make service increment payments in excess of $100 per month as long as the payments do not exceed $500 per month, and, in computing the service increments, no employment after the contributor has reached 65 years of age shall be included, provided that any agreement to provide an increase in service increment payments shall include a proportionate increase in the amount each contributor shall pay into the retirement fund under paragraph (2), not to exceed $5 per month.

§ 14322.1. Increase of allowances after retirement.

(a) Recommendation.—A city may, at any time, at its discretion and upon the recommendation of the persons having custody and management of the firefighters' pension fund, increase the allowances of individuals receiving allowances of any kind from the fund by reason of and after the termination of the services of any member of the fund.

(b) Uniform scale.—Increases made pursuant to this section shall be in conformity with a uniform scale, which may be based on the cost of living, but the total of the allowances shall not, at any time, exceed one-half of the current salary being paid firefighters of the highest pay grade.

§ 14323. Causes for forfeiture of rights in fund and other employments.

(a) Requirement.—Whenever an individual becomes entitled to receive a pension from the firefighters' pension fund and has been admitted to participate in the pension fund, the individual shall not be deprived of the individual's right to participation in the pension fund on the basis upon which the individual first became entitled to participation, unless otherwise required by the act of July 8, 1978 (P.L.752, No.140), known as the Public Employee Pension Forfeiture Act.

(b) Notice and hearing.—Any termination of a pension shall be only after due notice and hearing as prescribed by regulation of the managers of the fund.

§ 14324. Payments to firefighters' pension fund by city.

Unless otherwise required by the act of December 18, 1984 (P.L.1005, No.205), known as the Municipal Pension Plan Funding Standard and Recovery Act, or by any other provision of law, this section shall govern the payment of money raised by taxes levied by the city to the firefighters' pension fund. The following shall apply:

(1) A city shall pay to the firefighters' pension fund annually a sum of money not less than one-half of 1% nor more than 3% of all taxes levied by the city, other than taxes levied to pay interest on or extinguish the debt of the city.

(2) Council may exceed the limitations imposed by this section if an additional amount is deemed necessary to provide sufficient money for payments to surviving spouses of members retired on pension, killed or who die in service, provided that the city shall annually pay into the fund not less than one-half of 1% of all taxes levied by the city, other than taxes levied to pay interest on or extinguish the debt of the city.

§ 14325. Transfers from other pension funds.

(a) Transfers.—In any city where the members of the fire department are members of a pension fund not established solely for the purpose of pensioning members of the fire department, an amount equal to the money contributed to the other pension fund by members of the fire department who have not retired and a just and equitable proportion of the money contributed by the city to the other pension fund for the future retirement of members of the fire department shall be transferred from the other pension fund into the firefighters' pension fund required under this chapter. The transfers may be made by the transfer of securities. The amounts to be transferred shall be amicably adjusted by the managers of the firefighters' pension fund and the pension board having the charge of the other pension fund. In case of disagreement as to the amount to be transferred, the disagreement shall be resolved by council, whose action on the matter shall be final.

(b) Continuation.—Nothing under this section shall be construed to relieve any existing pension fund of its liability to continue the payment of pensions to retired members of the fire department in accordance with the laws and regulations under which the members were retired.

§ 14326. Trusts for benefit of firefighters' pension fund.

A city may take, by gift, grant, devise or bequest, any money or property, real, personal or mixed, in trust for the benefit of the pension fund. The care, management, investment and disposal of the body of the trust shall be vested in the officer or officers of the city as the city may designate. The care, management and disposal shall be directed by ordinance and the body of the trust shall be governed by the ordinance, subject to directions not inconsistent with the ordinance, as the settlor of the trust may prescribe.

§ 14327. Repayment before retirement.

(a) Refund.—If a contributing member of the firefighters' pension fund ceases to be a member of the fire department before the member becomes entitled to a pension, the total amount of the contributions paid into the pension fund by the member shall be refunded in full without interest.

(b) Withdrawals.—If the fund returns to the member the amount contributed and afterward the individual again becomes a member of the fire department, the member shall not be entitled to the pension designated until 20 years after the member's reemployment, unless the member returns to the pension fund the amount withdrawn, in which event the period of 20 years shall be computed from the time the member first became a member of the fire department, excluding any period of time during which the member was not employed by the fire department.

(c) Death of a member.—In the event of the death of a member of the fire department, the total amount of contributions paid into the pension fund by the member shall be paid over to the member's estate if any of the following apply:

(1) the death did not occur in the line of duty;

(2) the death occurs before the member becomes entitled to a pension; and

(3) the member has no surviving spouse or family entitled to payments as provided in this subchapter.

§ 14328. (Reserved).

SUBCHAPTER C

PENSION FOR EMPLOYEES OTHER THAN POLICE OFFICERS AND CITY-PAID FIREFIGHTERS

Sec.

Table of Contents
Part I Ch. 1–3 Ethics, Records, Open Meetings
Part II Ch. 4–10 Taxation
Part III Ch. 11–18 Torts, Contracts & Civil Rules
Part IV Ch. 19–24 Zoning & Planning
Part V Ch. 25–30 Construction and Emergency Codes
Part VI Ch. 31–39 Municipal Codes
Index

---

§ 14339. Definitions.

The following words and phrases when used in this subchapter shall have the meanings given to them in this section unless the context clearly indicates otherwise:

"Board." A pension board created by a city under section 14341(a) (relating to pension board and duties).

"Employed," "employed by the city" or "in the employment of any city." The terms include:

(1) Each individual in the service of cities creating a pension fund and a pension board in accordance with this subchapter, who are not, on June 28, 1951, otherwise protected by pensions authorized under this chapter.

(2) A volunteer firefighter who becomes a member of the pension fund.

"Employees." The term includes:

(1) Each individual in the service of cities creating a pension fund and a pension board in accordance with this subchapter, who are not, on June 28, 1951, otherwise protected by pensions authorized under this chapter.

(2) A volunteer firefighter who becomes a member of the pension fund.

(3) Officers and officials of the city, whether elected or appointed.

"Fund." A pension fund created by a city under section 14340(a) (relating to pension for employees other than police or city-paid firefighters).

"Volunteer firefighter." A driver of firefighting apparatus or ambulances, regularly employed and paid by a volunteer fire company rendering services recognized and accepted by a city.

§ 14340. Pension for employees other than police or city-paid firefighters.

(a) Nonmembers.—Cities may create a pension fund for employees who are not members of the police force or city-paid fire department and surviving spouses of retired members if council so elects and the families of employees that are injured or killed in service in the manner, under the conditions and subject to the qualifications set forth in this subchapter.

(b) (Reserved).

§ 14341. Pension board and duties.

(a) Members.—Any city which creates a pension fund in accordance with this subchapter shall establish a pension board consisting of the mayor, the city controller, the superintendent of finance, two employees to be chosen by the employees contributing to the pension fund and, if members of council participate in the pension fund and are members of the fund, a member of council chosen by council.

(b) Duties.—It shall be the duty of the board to register all individuals employed by the city, administer the collections and distribution of the pension fund and make reasonable rules as the board may deem necessary.

§ 14342. Retirement age.

In a city which has created a pension fund and board in accordance with this subchapter, an employee 60 years of age or older who has been employed for a period of 20 years or more shall, upon application to the board, be retired from service and shall, subject to qualifications provided in this subchapter during the remainder of the employee's life, receive the pension or compensation fixed by this subchapter.

§ 14343. Retirement allowance, proof of disability and joint and single coverage members defined.

(a) Entitlement.—

(1) During the lifetime of an individual employed by a city creating a fund and board in accordance with this subchapter shall be entitled to receive 50% of the amount which would constitute the highest average annual salary or wages which the individual received during the last or any five years of the individual's employment by the city as a pension annually, which shall be paid in semi-monthly payments.

(2) Should an individual with 20 or more years of service be dismissed, voluntarily retired or be in any manner deprived of the individual's position or employment before attaining 60 years of age and upon continuing a monthly payment to the fund equal to the last amount due and paid monthly while in active service, the individual shall be entitled to the pension, notwithstanding that the individual has not attained 60 years of age at the time of the individual's separation from the service of the city, but the pension shall not commence until the individual has attained 60 years of age.

(3) If any employee becomes totally and permanently disabled after 10 years of service and before attaining 60 years of age, the individual shall be entitled to the pension. Proof of total and permanent disability shall consist of the sworn statement of three practicing physicians, designated by the board, that the employee is in a permanent condition of health which would permanently disable the individual from performing the duties of the individual's position or office.

(b) (Reserved).

(c) Reduction.—If a city has entered into an agreement with the Commonwealth to place certain employees under the Social Security Act (49 Stat. 620, 42 U.S.C. § 301 et seq.), the pension to be paid joint coverage members according to the provisions of this section payable after the age and upon that portion of annual compensation on which Social Security benefits are payable shall be reduced by an amount equal to 40% of the primary insurance amount of Social Security paid or payable to the member. The reduction shall be subject to the following provisions:

(1) Upon attainment of the age at which Social Security benefits are payable by a beneficiary receiving a pension or upon retirement of a contributor after attaining that age, the individual's eligibility to the benefits commonly referred to as the old age insurance benefit and the primary insurance amount of Social Security upon which the reduction in the pension shall be based, shall be computed by the board in the manner specified in the Social Security Act, except that in determining the eligibility and the amount, only wages or compensation for services performed in the employ of the city shall be included.

(2) The reduction shall not apply to a pension for total and permanent disability payable under this section.

(3) Whenever the amount of the reduction from the pension is determined, it shall remain fixed for the duration of the pension, except that any decrease in the primary insurance amount under the Social Security Act shall result in a corresponding decrease in the amount of the reduction from the pension.

(4) The total sum, including Social Security benefits, to be received upon retirement by an employee who is a member of the system at the time of the agreement shall not be less than the allowance that would be paid by the retirement system in the absence of the agreement.

(d) Surviving spouse payments.—If council elects, by ordinance, to make the payments, the surviving spouse of an employee who retired on pension or is killed in service on or after January 1, 1960, shall, during the surviving spouse's lifetime or so long as the surviving spouse does not remarry, be entitled to receive a pension calculated at the rate of 50% of the pension the member was receiving or would have been entitled to receive had the member been retired at the time of the member's death.

§ 14343.1. Retirement allowances, full coverage and payments.

(a) Allowance.—If a city has entered into an agreement with the Commonwealth to place certain employees under the Social Security Act (49 Stat. 620, 42 U.S.C. § 301 et seq.), the board may authorize any joint coverage member of the retirement system to elect, according to the provisions of this section, to receive compensation without the reduction provided for in section 14343 (relating to retirement allowance, proof of disability and joint and single coverage members defined), provided the member shall make a lump-sum payment to the board or installment payments, as may be approved by the board, equal to the difference between the amount of the accumulated fund to the member's credit in the fund as of the last date for which salary or wages was paid and the amount which would have been to the member's credit in the fund if contributions had been made on that portion of the member's salary or wages on which Social Security allowances are payable at the same rate as made on that portion of the member's salary or wages in excess of that on which Social Security allowances are payable, from the time that the salary or wages became subject to Social Security coverage. Election shall be made in writing, in the form prescribed by the board, and shall be accompanied by the lump-sum payment or an agreement as to installment payments.

(b) Election.—The board may authorize a member to make the election under subsection (a) at any time, and, if made prior to retirement, the member shall, in addition to any lump-sum or installment payments required, pay to the board contributions on the member's entire salary or wages received after the election at the rate provided in this subchapter for monthly salary or wages in excess of that on which Social Security allowances are payable.

§ 14343.2. Limited vested benefit.

(a) Ordinance.—In accordance with this subchapter, an ordinance creating a fund may provide for a limited vested benefit if it would conform to section 305 of the act of December 18, 1984 (P.L.1005, No.205), known as the Municipal Pension Plan Funding Standard and Recovery Act.

(a.1) Vesting.—Under a limited vested benefit, if a member of the fund terminates employment before reaching the date which would have been the member's earliest retirement date had the member continued employment by meeting the minimum age and minimum period of continuous service requirements but after having completed 12 years of full-time service, the member shall be entitled to vest the member's retirement benefits subject to the following conditions:

Chap. 39 Res. During Mil. Service
Chap. 38 Intergov. Coop.
Chap. 37 3rd Class City Code
Chap. 36 Bor. Code
Chap. 35 2nd Class Twp. Code
Chap. 34 1st Class Twp. Code
Chap. 33 Home Rule Chart. Opt. Plans Law
Chap. 32 Water Serv. Act
Chap. 31 Munic. Auth. Act

(1) The member must file with the management board of the fund a written notice of the member's intention to vest.

(2) The member must include in the notice the date the member intends to terminate the member's service as an employee.

(3) The termination date shall be at least 30 days later than the date of notice to vest.

(4) The member must be in good standing with the city on the date of notice to vest.

(5) The board shall indicate on the notice to vest the rate of monthly pay of the member as of the date of the notice to vest or the highest average annual salary which the member received during any five years of service preceding the date, whichever is higher.

(b) Collection.—Upon reaching the date which would have been the member's earliest retirement date had the member continued the member's employment with the city, the member shall notify the board, in writing, that the member desires to collect the member's pension. The amount of retirement benefits the member is entitled to receive under this section shall be computed as follows:

(1) The initial determination of the member's base retirement benefits shall be computed on the salary indicated on the notice to vest.

(2) The portion of the base retirement benefits due the member shall be determined by applying to the base amount the percentage that the member's years of service actually rendered bears to the years of service which would have been rendered had the member continued to be employed by the city until the member's earliest retirement date.

§ 14344. Amount of payments into fund and repayment before retirement.

The employees of any city creating a fund and board in accordance with this subchapter shall pay monthly to the board an amount equal to 2% of their monthly salaries or wages, and, if council elects by ordinance to make payments, an additional amount not to exceed 1% if deemed necessary by council to provide sufficient funds for payments to the surviving spouses of members who were retired on pension or killed in service, which shall be applied to the purposes of the fund. Payment of the monthly amount or contribution under this section shall cease and be discontinued at the time the beneficiary receives their pension. If, for any cause, an employee contributing to the fund ceases to be an employee of the city before the employee becomes entitled to a pension, the total amount of the contributions paid into the fund by the employee shall be refunded to the employee in full, without interest. If an employer returns to the employee the amount contributed and reenters the employ of the city, the employee shall not be entitled to the pension designated until 20 years after reemployment, unless the employee shall return to the fund the amount withdrawn, in which event that period of 20 years shall be computed from the time the employee first enters the service of the city. In the event of the death of an employee before the employee becomes entitled to the pension, the total amount of contributions paid into the fund by the employee shall be paid over to the estate of the deceased employee.

§ 14344.1. Determination of liability upon extension of Social Security.

(a) Determination.—If a city has entered into an agreement with the Commonwealth to place its employees under the Social Security Act (49 Stat. 620, 42 U.S.C § 301 et seq.), the board shall appoint an actuary and may fix the employee's compensation. The actuary shall determine the present value of the liability on account of pensions payable under the provisions of section 14343 (relating to retirement allowance, proof of disability and joint and single coverage members defined) to employees who are members of the system on the effective date of the agreement and shall offset the value of any assets in the fund

Table of Contents
Part I Ch. 1–3 Ethics, Records, Open Meetings
Part II Ch. 4–10 Taxation
Part III Ch. 11–18 Torts, Contracts & Civil Rules
Part IV Ch. 19–24 Zoning & Planning
Part V Ch. 25–30 Construction and Emergency Codes
Part VI Ch. 31–39 Municipal Codes
Index

to determine the unfunded liability. The city may make payments toward the unfunded liability until the accumulated reserve equals the present value of the liability. The actuary shall also determine the amount which shall be contributed annually into the fund on account of service of all new and original members subsequent to the effective date of the agreement.

(b) Contribution.—Employees shall pay into the board, monthly, an amount equal to 3.5% of that portion of monthly compensation on which Social Security allowances are payable and 5% of any monthly compensation in excess of that on which Social Security allowances are payable. The remainder of the needed annual contribution for service subsequent to the date of the agreement, as determined by the actuary, shall become the obligation of the city and shall be paid by it to the board by annual appropriations. The provisions of this section shall, in all applicable cases, supersede the provisions relating to contributions in section 14344 (relating to amount of payments into fund and repayment before retirement) and section 14348 (relating to appropriations and contributions to fund).

§ 14345. Payments by laborers optional.

Any individual holding a position in a city as a laborer at a per diem wage shall not be compelled to pay or contribute toward the fund, but shall have the option of so doing and, in that event only, of becoming entitled to the pension provided for under this subchapter.

§ 14346. Heads of departments to certify list of employees.

The head of every department and office employing individuals entitled to receive a pension shall certify to the board all employees so employed and the amount of salary or wages which is paid to employees, together with dismissals, resignations or terminations of service and, from office or department records, furnish other relevant information as the board requires. In the case of a volunteer fire company, "head of department or office" shall mean the president or secretary of the board of trustees of the volunteer fire company.

§ 14347. Receipt, investment and payment of funds.

When deemed advisable, it shall be the duty of the board to receive, retain and invest the funds payable in accordance with the provisions of this subchapter and pay over, by warrant or check, the amount due to employees.

§ 14348. Appropriations and contributions to fund.

Council may annually set aside, apportion and appropriate, out of all taxes and income of the city, to the board a sum sufficient to maintain the pensions or compensations due on account of the city contributions for all employees, except volunteer firefighters. The board of trustees of the volunteer fire company employing and paying members shall annually contribute to the board a sum equal to the same percentage of its participating payroll as the amount contributed by the city for the same year bears to its participating payroll for each volunteer firefighter member becoming a member of the fund.

§ 14349. Application.

(a) Applicability.—The benefits provided for by this subchapter shall apply to all individuals employed in any capacity or holding positions in, or, in the case of a volunteer firefighter, rendering services recognized and accepted by, a city creating a fund and board in accordance with provisions of this subchapter. This subchapter shall not apply to employees of departments, bureaus or offices which are otherwise protected by pensions authorized by this chapter.

(b) Membership.—Any volunteer firefighter may become a member of a fund as of the date of the volunteer firefighter's original employment or of the inception of the fund, whichever is later, upon the volunteer firefighter making back contributions and if the volunteer fire company or its board of trustees employing and paying the volunteer firefighter agrees to contribute and contributes to the fund the required sums.

§ 14350. Computation of time of service.

The time of service of 20 years shall be computed from the time of the first or original employment, which shall consist of service to the city and need not be continuous.

§ 14351. Funds payable to be free of attachment.

The compensation or pension shall not be subject to attachment or execution, shall be payable only to the beneficiary designated and shall not be subject to assignment or transfer.

§ 14352. (Reserved).

§ 14353. Beneficiaries of fund not to be employed by city.

No individual who becomes a beneficiary shall be employed by the the city in any capacity. Subject to the provisions of section 14361 (relating to right to a pension if salary refused), nothing in this section shall be construed to prohibit an individual who becomes a beneficiary from serving in an elective city office.

SUBCHAPTER D
BENEFICIARIES SERVING IN ELECTIVE OFFICE

Sec.

---

§ 14361. Right to a pension if salary refused.

In a city governed by the provisions of this part, the act of July 15, 1957 (P.L.901, No.399), known as the Optional Third Class City Charter Law or 53 Pa.C.S. Pt. III Subpt. E (relating to home rule and optional plan government), a beneficiary serving in an elective city office shall not be prohibited from receiving a pension for any month in which the beneficiary does not accept a salary from serving in the elective office.

CHAPTER 144
CIVIL SERVICE

Sec.

---

§ 14401. Examinations required of all appointees.

No individual may be appointed to any uniformed position in the police or fire departments, excluding chiefs, unless all of the following apply:

(1) The individual passed all examinations as provided for under this chapter.

(2) The individual was appointed in the manner and according to the terms, provisions and conditions of this chapter.

§ 14402. Appointment of civil service board.

Cities shall establish a civil service board that shall provide for and oversee the examination of applicants for appointment and promotion to any position in the police or fire departments. Council shall appoint three city residents to the board who shall serve four-year terms or until their successors are appointed and qualified, except for the initial appointment of board members as provided for in section 14403 (relating to civil service board and quorum). Any individual who is a registered elector of the city may be appointed to the board. No city officer, official or employee shall be eligible for appointment to the civil service board.

§ 14402.1. Existing civil service positions.

All nonuniformed employees in city positions that were subject to civil service regulation immediately prior to May 19, 2014, shall continue to be subject to civil service regulation otherwise provided in this chapter for uniformed employees with regard to the nonuniformed positions.

§ 14403. Civil service board and quorum.

(a) **Terms.**—In a city in which the civil service board is first established, terms of members of the board shall be staggered. Council shall initially appoint to the board one individual to serve for two years, one individual to serve for three years and one individual to serve for four years.

(b) **Vacancies.**—Upon the expiration of the term of any member, a successor shall be appointed by council to serve on the civil service board for a term of four years. If any vacancies occur, they shall be filled by council for the unexpired term. Before entering upon the duties of office, each member shall take and subscribe to the oath of office prescribed by 53 Pa.C.S. § 1141 (relating to form of oaths of office) and file the oath, duly certified by the officer administering it, with the city administrator or, in cities without a city administrator, the city clerk.

(c) **Compensation.**—No salary or other compensation shall be paid to any member of the civil service board.

(d) **Quorum.**—Two members of the civil service board shall constitute a quorum necessary for the transaction of business of the board.

(e) **Organization.**—The civil service board shall organize for the purpose of transacting all business immediately after the first appointments and as new appointments to the board are made. After organizing, the board shall elect one of its members as chairperson and one member as secretary.

§ 14403.1. Alternate board members.

Council may appoint not more than three qualified electors of the city to serve as alternate members of the civil service board. The term of office of the alternate members shall be four years. If, by reason of absence or disqualification of a member, a quorum is not reached, the chairperson shall designate as many alternate members of the board to sit on the board as may be needed to provide a quorum. When seated pursuant to this section, an alternate shall be entitled to participate in all proceedings and discussions of the board to the extent as provided by law for board members, including the right to cast a vote as a voting member during the proceedings and shall have all the powers and duties set forth in this chapter and as otherwise provided by law. Any alternate member of the board shall continue to serve on the board in all proceedings involving the matter or case for which the alternate was initially designated until the board has made a final determination of the matter or case. Designation of an alternate pursuant to this section shall be made on a case-by-case basis in rotation according to declining seniority among all alternates. Alternates shall hold no other office in the city. Any alternate may participate in any proceeding or discussion of the board but shall not be entitled to vote as a member of the board unless designated as a voting alternate member pursuant to this section.

§ 14403.2. Investigations and subpoenas.

(a) Investigations.—The civil service board shall have the power to conduct investigations concerning all matters relating to the administration and enforcement of its rules and regulations. The chairperson shall be authorized to administer oaths and affirmations for witnesses testifying in matters before the board.

(b) Subpoenas.—The civil service board shall have the power to issue subpoenas over the signature of the chairperson or designee and to require the attendance of witnesses and the production of records and papers pertaining to matters before the board, including any background investigation conducted pursuant to any applicable rules and regulations.

§ 14404. Rules, regulations and examinations.

(a) Duties.—The civil service board shall have the power and its duty shall be to prepare and adopt rules and regulations, subject to approval by council, which, in the board's discretion, secure and maintain the best service for the public for the selection, appointment and promotion of individuals who are qualified to perform the work which is the subject of the civil service examination as provided in this chapter and who are to be employed, appointed or promoted by the city. The rules and regulations adopted by the board shall provide for ascertaining and determining, so far as possible, the knowledge, skills, aptitude, mental and physical abilities, experience, education and character of all applicants as these criteria would reasonably apply to the respective positions. The rules and regulations shall also provide for examinations upon any and all subjects deemed proper or necessary by the board for the purpose of determining the qualifications of applicants for the respective positions sought and for which application is made.

(b) Subjects.—The civil service board shall, in accordance with this part, adopt rules and regulations concerning the following matters:

(1) minutes of proceedings;

(2) rules of procedure;

(3) records of examinations;

(4) annual report to council;

(5) notice of rules and regulations and any amendments or repeals to rules and regulations;

(6) application forms;

(7) further provisions concerning the duties of the chairperson and secretary;

(8) appointment of examiners; and

(9) other administrative matters.

§ 14404.1. Physical and psychological medical examinations.

(a) Requirement.—The civil service board may require that an applicant conditionally appointed in accordance with section 14406 (relating to selection of appointee from certified list of applicants) undergo a physical or psychological medical examination as a condition of permanent appointment. Physical medical examinations, if required, shall be under the direction of a physician or other qualified medical professional. Psychological medical examinations, if required, shall be under the direction of a psychiatrist or psychologist.

(b) **Professional opinion.**—A physician, other qualified medical professional, psychiatrist or psychologist shall be appointed by council and shall render an opinion as to whether the conditional appointee has a physical or mental condition which calls into question the individual's ability to perform all the essential functions of the position for which the individual was conditionally appointed.

(c) **Performance.**—If the opinion rendered by the physician, other qualified medical professional, psychiatrist or psychologist calls into question the conditional appointee's ability to perform all essential functions of a position, the director of the department within which the position is to be filled shall meet with the conditional appointee for the purpose of having one or more interactive discussions on whether the conditional appointee can, with or without reasonable accommodation, perform all the essential functions of the position.

(d) **Determination.**—If, at the conclusion of the interactive discussion under subsection (c), the director of the department determines that the conditional appointee is not qualified, the director shall give written notice to the conditional appointee and the civil service board.

(e) **Authorization.**—Nothing in this chapter shall be construed to authorize physical or psychological medical examinations prior to conditional appointment in accordance with section 14406.

(f) **Definitions.**—As used in this section, the following words and phrases shall have the meanings given to them in this subsection unless the context clearly indicates otherwise:

"Medical examination." Any examination, procedure, inquiry or test designed to obtain information about medical history or a physical or mental condition which might disqualify an applicant if it would prevent the applicant from performing, with or without reasonable accommodation, all of the essential functions of the position.

"Qualified medical professional." An individual, in collaboration with or under the supervision or direction of a physician, as may be required by law, who is licensed:

(1) as a physician assistant pursuant to the act of December 20, 1985 (P.L.457, No.112), known as the Medical Practice Act of 1985, or the act of October 5, 1978 (P.L.1109, No.261), known as the Osteopathic Medical Practice Act; or

(2) as a certified registered nurse practitioner pursuant to the act of May 22, 1951 (P.L.317, No.69), known as The Professional Nursing Law.

§ 14405.1. Veterans' preference.

In accordance with 51 Pa.C.S. Ch. 71 (relating to veterans' preference), the following shall apply to the appointment of a uniformed civil service position:

(1) A veteran who meets the qualifications for and conditions of the position under uniform eligibility rules, which include successful passage of an examination, shall receive an additional 10 points on the examination pursuant to 51 Pa.C.S. § 7103(a) (relating to additional points in grading civil service examinations).

(2) If, after the additional 10 points are granted, a veteran is on the list of three eligible applicants, the veteran shall receive a preference in hiring over nonveterans on that list.

(3) The preference provided by this section shall constitute the only preference with regard to a uniformed civil service position to which a veteran is entitled under this chapter.

§ 14406. Selection of appointee from certified list of applicants.

The following shall apply to civil service selection, conditional appointments and appointments and shall be incorporated by reference in the rules and regulations of the civil service board:

(1) The civil service board shall make and keep, in numerical order, a list containing the names of all applicants for civil service positions in the city who pass the required examinations, including any required physical fitness or agility examinations that are job related and consistent with business necessity.

(2) Physical fitness and agility examinations shall be conducted on a pass-fail basis.

(3) Written and oral examinations used to establish an eligibility list shall offer the opportunity to achieve 100 points.

(4) If both written and oral examination methods are used in conjunction with each other, the board, prior to initiating testing, shall establish what constitutes a passing score on each portion of the examination. If only a written examination method is used, the board shall establish the passing score before the examination is conducted.

(5) When more than one individual takes examinations for any position at the same time, the names of all those successfully passing the examination shall be entered on the eligibility list in the order of their respective point totals, the highest coming first.

(6) The board shall furnish to council a certified copy of all lists prepared and kept. Lists are public records and shall be maintained for a period of two years or until a new list is certified to council, whichever occurs first.

(7) Whenever council determines an initial appointment is to be made to a civil service position in the city, the director of the department in which the appointment is to be made shall make written application to the chairperson of the board, who shall certify to council, in writing, the three names on the eligibility list of applicants for the position having the highest number of points, unless there are less than three eligible names on the list, in which event the board shall certify the names. The director of the department in which the appointment is to be made shall nominate to council an individual from the eligibility list submitted to fill the vacancy.

(8) If council approves the nomination, the individual nominated shall be conditionally appointed by council to fill the vacancy and shall be assigned for service in the department, subject to any required physical or psychological medical examinations that may be required by the board as a condition of permanent appointment in accordance with section 14404.1 (relating to physical and psychological medical examinations).

(9) If council does not approve the nomination, or if the appointee is determined by the medical examination process to be unqualified, the director of the department in which the appointment is to be made shall submit another nomination for the position from the remaining names, if any. If the second nomination is not approved by council, or if the appointee is determined by the medical examination process to be unqualified, the director shall submit the third name, if any.

(10) The individual whose nomination by the director is approved by council shall be appointed to fill the civil service position under consideration.

(11) The name of the individual appointed shall be immediately stricken from the certified list of the board, and, except as otherwise provided in this subsection, the names of the nonappointed individuals shall immediately be restored to their proper place on the certified list. Names shall be stricken from the certified list if:

(i) the name of any applicant has been submitted to council and been rejected three times;

(ii) the conditional applicant has not been appointed three times; or

(iii) the conditional applicant has been determined by the medical examination process to be unqualified.

(12) Examinations for promotions for civil service positions in the city shall be made pursuant to section 14406.1 (relating to promotions).

(13) As used in this section, the term "medical examination" shall have the meaning given to it in section 14404.1(f).

§ 14406.1. Promotions.

(a) Certification.—Council shall notify the civil service board of a civil service vacancy in the city which is to be filled by promotion and shall request the certification of an eligibility list as provided in this chapter. For each vacancy, the board shall certify the names of three individuals on the eligibility list who have received the highest average in the last preceding promotional examination held within the period of two years preceding the date of the request for the eligibility list. If three names are not available, the board shall certify the names remaining on the list. Council shall make an appointment from the names certified based solely on the merits and fitness of the candidates unless council makes objections to the board regarding one or more of the individuals on the eligibility list. Council shall have power to determine whether an increase in salary shall constitute a promotion.

(b) Additional powers.—Notwithstanding subsection (a), the mayor or other elected or appointed official of a city that has adopted one of the following shall retain the power to promote a candidate pursuant to that law:

(1) An optional charter pursuant to the act of July 15, 1957 (P.L.901, No.399), known as the Optional Third Class City Charter Law.

(2) An optional plan pursuant to 53 Pa.C.S. Chs. 30 (relating to types of optional plans of government) and 31 (relating to general provisions common to optional plans).

(3) Any other law authorizing or permitting the mayor or other elected or appointed official to promote a candidate.

(c) Exceptions.—The provisions of this section shall not apply to the mayor's designation or appointment of the chief of police pursuant to section 12002 (relating to designation of chief) or the mayor's designation or appointment of a fire chief pursuant to section 12101.1 (relating to appointment and demotion of fire chief).

§ 14407. Tenure and temporary appointments.

(a) Standard.—All appointments made pursuant to the provisions of this chapter shall be for and during good behavior, and no employee hired pursuant to the provisions of this chapter shall be removed or transferred for any political reasons.

(b) Temporary appointments.—In case of riot or emergency, temporary appointments to positions in the civil service may be made without complying with the provisions of this chapter.

§ 14408. Suspension, discharge and discipline, reduction of employees and appeals.

(a) Provisions.—

(1) All employees subject to civil service shall be subject to suspension, discharge and discipline by the director of the department in which the employee works for misconduct or violation of any law of the Commonwealth, ordinance of the city or regulation of the department. If it should become necessary to reduce

the number of employees in the department for economic purposes, the following apply:

(i) Seniority rights shall prevail.

(ii) Any and all removals for cause or causes shall be from the members last appointed.

(iii) The member or members serving the shortest time shall be removed first, however members with longer times of service may be discharged for cause.

(2) Any employee aggrieved by the suspension, discharge or discipline imposed by a department director more serious than a suspension of three days without pay may request a hearing before council or the civil service board, if designated by ordinance. At the hearing, the employee may be represented by counsel.

(a.1) Appeal.—Any civil service employee aggrieved by the decision of council or the civil service board shall have the right to appeal in accordance with 2 Pa.C.S. Ch. 7 Subch. B (relating to judicial review of local agency action). This review shall be exclusive. When no appeal is taken within the time prescribed by law, the decision by council or the civil service board shall become final in accordance with law. The issue before the court shall be whether the action of council or the civil service board shall be affirmed or modified in any respect, whether the charges should be dismissed or whether the suspension or demotion made by the director shall be affirmed or rescinded. If any employee has been suspended and the charges are dismissed or the suspension rescinded on appeal, the employee shall receive full compensation for the entire period of suspension.

(b) Challenge.—In any case in which a police officer or firefighter who is a member of a bargaining unit is subject to suspension, discharge or discipline, the police officer or firefighter shall have the option of challenging the suspension, discharge or discipline imposed by using the procedures provided in subsection (a)(2) or by a proceeding in grievance arbitration. A choice to proceed either by the procedures provided for in subsection (a)(2) or by grievance arbitration shall foreclose the opportunity to proceed in the alternative method.

§ 14409. Secretary and compensation.

The civil service board shall appoint a secretary and prescribe the secretary's duties and shall have the power to change these duties. The secretary shall be subject to removal, at any time, by the board. Council shall establish the compensation to be paid to the secretary and all necessary supplies for the use of the board shall be supplied by the city.

§ 14410. Review of eligibility lists.

The lists of eligible names kept by the civil service board shall be annually examined by the board for the purpose of deleting individuals from the list who are permanently unavailable for or disqualified for the position or positions involved, either by death, permanent removal from the area, written desire to be removed from the list or by other permanent cause in conformity with the board's rules and regulations adopted pursuant to section 14404 (relating to rules, regulations and examinations).

CHAPTER 144A
VETERANS' AFFAIRS

Subchapter

SUBCHAPTER A

SUPPORT OF VETERANS' ORGANIZATIONS

---

§ 144A00. Definitions.

The following words and phrases when used in this subchapter shall have the meanings given to them in this section unless the context clearly indicates otherwise:

"Veterans' organization." An incorporated organization of veterans of the armed forces of the United States or an organization comprising veterans' parents or children.

§ 144A01. Appropriations to veterans' organizations.

(a) **Annual appropriation.**—Council may make annual appropriations to veterans' organizations to aid in defraying the following expenses:

(1) Expenses relating to Memorial Day and Veterans Day.

(2) Other expenses, such as payment of rent of any building or rooms where the organization has its regular meetings.

(b) **Requirements.**—Payments shall be made to defray actual expenses only. Before any payment is made, the veterans' organization receiving the payment shall submit verified accounts of its expenditures.

§ 144A02. Rooms for meetings of veterans.

Council may provide to a veterans' organization, upon application of the organization, a facility in any public building of the city that is sufficient for periodic meetings of the organization.

SUBCHAPTER B

PENNSYLVANIA NATIONAL GUARD

---

§ 144A11. Support of Pennsylvania National Guard units.

(a) **Annual appropriation.**—Council may appropriate annually a sum for the support and maintenance, discipline and training of any troop, company or similar unit of the Pennsylvania National Guard. If the units are organized as a battalion, regiment or similar organization, the total amount due may be paid to the commanding officer of the battalion, regiment or similar organization.

(b) **Condition.**—Any money appropriated shall be paid by warrant drawn to the order of the commanding officer of the company, battalion, regiment or similar organization and conditioned upon certification by the Adjutant General of the Commonwealth to the city that the company has satisfactorily passed the annual inspection provided by law.

Chap. 39 Res. During Mil. Service
Chap. 38 Intergov. Coop.
Chap. 37 3rd Class City Code
Chap. 36 Bor. Code
Chap. 35 2nd Class Twp. Code
Chap. 34 1st Class Twp. Code
Chap. 33 Home Rule Chart. Opt. Plans Law
Chap. 32 Water Serv. Act
Chap. 31 Munic. Auth. Act

(c) Use of funds.—The money appropriated shall be used and expended solely and exclusively for the support, maintenance, discipline and training of the company, battalion, regiment or similar organization.

(d) Accounting required.—The commanding officer shall account, by proper vouchers to the city each year, for the expenditure of the money appropriated. No appropriation shall be made for any subsequent year until the expenditure of the previous year is duly and satisfactorily accounted for. The accounts of the expenditures shall be subject to the inspection of the Department of Military and Veterans Affairs and shall be audited by the independent auditor in the manner provided by this chapter for the audit of accounts of city money.

§ 144A12. Assistance of armories.

(a) Assistance.—Council may appropriate money or convey land, either independently or in conjunction with any other political subdivision, to the Commonwealth for the following purposes:

(1) To assist the State Armory Board in the erection of armories for the use of the Pennsylvania National Guard.

(2) To furnish water, sewer services, light or fuel free of cost to the Commonwealth for use in any armory of the Pennsylvania National Guard.

(b) Council authority.—Council may do all things necessary to accomplish the purpose of this section.

§ 144A13. Eminent domain for National Guard purposes.

Council may take, by right of eminent domain for the purpose of appropriating to itself for the use of the Pennsylvania National Guard, public lands, easements and public property in its possession or control and used or held by it for any other purpose. However, the right of eminent domain shall not be exercised as to any street or wharf.

§ 144A14. Land for armory purposes.

(a) General rule.—Council may acquire, by purchase, gift or the right of eminent domain, any land for the use of the Pennsylvania National Guard and may convey lands so acquired to the Commonwealth in order to assist the State Armory Board in the erection of armories.

(b) Limitations.—The power conferred by this section shall not be exercised to take any church property, graveyard or cemetery.

(c) Lands outside city limits.—Lands within three miles outside the limits of the city may be acquired in accordance with this section for the use of the Pennsylvania National Guard. However, if the land outside the limits of the city is acquired by eminent domain, the taking shall be subject to the limitations in 26 Pa.C.S. § 206 (relating to extraterritorial takings).

SUBCHAPTER C
BURIALS AND MEMORIALS

Sec.

---

§ 144A21. Purchase of burial grounds for deceased servicepersons.

Council may appropriate money for and purchase plots of ground in any cemetery or burial ground within its respective city limits for the interment of deceased servicepersons:

(1) who:

(i) die within the city; or

(ii) die beyond the city limits but have a legal residence within the city at the time of death; and

(2) whose bodies are entitled to be buried by the county under the provisions of existing law.

§ 144A22. Care of memorials.

(a) Council authority.—Council may take charge of, care for, maintain and keep in good order and repair, at the expense of the city, any soldier's monument, gun or carriage or similar memorial, if the memorial:

(1) Is situate in the city.

(2) Is not in the charge or care of any individual, body or organization.

(3) Is not put up or placed by the Federal Government, the Commonwealth or the commissioners of the county or by the direction or authority of any other state.

(b) Donations.—Council may receive money from any individual or organization and may expend the money for the benefit of memorials.

§ 144A23. Memorial trees.

Council may provide for or authorize provision for memorial trees for residents of the city who died while in the military service of the United States or in consequence of that service. Council may make appropriations or accept contributions for this purpose. Trees shall bear some permanent indication of their purpose.

§ 144A24. Penalty for injury to memorial trees.

Any individual who willfully, maliciously or negligently destroys or injures any tree planted pursuant to section 144A23 (relating to memorial trees) commits a misdemeanor of the third degree and shall, upon conviction, be sentenced to pay a fine of not more than $500, or to imprisonment for not more than three months, or both.

CHAPTER 145A

ASSESSMENTS FOR PUBLIC IMPROVEMENTS

Sec.

---

§ 145A00. Definitions.

The following words and phrases when used in this chapter shall have the meanings given to them in this section unless the context clearly indicates otherwise:

"Public improvement." The term includes, but is not limited to, the following:

(1) The building, paving, grading, rebuilding, repaving and regrading of streets, sidewalks, curbs and gutters.

(2) The creation, extension and renovation of water and sewerage collection, transmission, treatment and disposal systems.

(3) The creation, extension and renovation of storm, surface and subsurface drainage systems.

(4) The construction, reconstruction and repair of wharves and docks.

(5) The installation of pipes, wires and conduits relating to city-supplied utility services.

(6) The installation, maintenance or operation of lighting that services the streets and sidewalks within the city.

(7) The planting, maintaining, trimming, transplanting, removal and protection of shade trees.

§ 145A01. Authority to assess.

(a) Authority.—Unless otherwise provided for in this part, a city is authorized to assess all or any portion of the costs of a public improvement, including any related administrative fees, against any properties that are benefited by the public improvement.

(b) Payment of costs.—Unless otherwise provided in this chapter, in addition to the authority to assess the cost of public improvements against properties benefited, a city may pay for the cost of public improvements, in whole or in part, from the city general fund or, if authorized, from a special city fund dedicated to that purpose.

(c) Indebtedness.—If a city incurs indebtedness pursuant to 53 Pa.C.S. Pt. VII Subpt. B (relating to indebtedness and borrowing) for the purposes of funding the cost and expense of making public improvements for which assessments are made in accordance with this chapter, payments made on the assessments must be applied to pay the debt service for the indebtedness incurred for funding the cost and expense of making the public improvements.

§ 145A02. Method of assessment.

(a) Ordinance.—In any case in which council elects to exercise the power to make assessments for a given public improvement as authorized in section 145A01 (relating to authority to assess), council shall, by ordinance and in conformity with this chapter, establish the method and procedure pursuant to which assessments shall be made.

(b) Allocation of costs and expenses.—Council may, by ordinance, make the assessment by any means that results in fairly allocating all or a portion of the costs and expenses of the public improvement among all properties benefited by the improvement in reasonable proportion to the benefits conferred upon each property. The methods that may be used to make assessments in accordance with this subsection may include, but are not limited to:

(1) An equal assessment per front foot, lot, parcel, dwelling unit or square foot.

(2) An assessment made by viewers.

Table of Contents | Part I Ch. 1–3 Ethics, Records, Open Meetings | Part II Ch. 4–10 Taxation | Part III Ch. 11–18 Torts, Contracts & Civil Rules | Part IV Ch. 19–24 Zoning & Planning | Part V Ch. 25–30 Construction and Emergency Codes | Part VI Ch. 31–39 Municipal Codes | Index

(c) **Front foot method.**—If the front foot method is used:

(1) The cost to be collected shall be divided by the total number of linear feet of street frontage of all properties benefited.

(2) The assessment against each property shall be that portion of the cost which is determined by multiplying the dividend under paragraph (1) by the number of linear feet for street frontage of that property.

(3) In the case of corner or irregularly shaped lots or where special conditions exist, council shall have the power and its duty shall be to provide for an equitable adjustment, as necessary, to prevent an unjust or excessive assessment.

(d) **Assessment based on report of viewers.**—In order to pay for all or a portion of the cost or expenses of a public improvement, council may determine to assess properties benefited based upon a report of viewers. Three disinterested persons shall be appointed by council as viewers. A majority of the viewers shall assess the cost against each property benefited in reasonable proportion to the benefits conferred upon each property. The viewers, or a majority of them, shall:

(1) Make a report, in writing, which shall specify the amount assessed upon each property.

(2) Present the report directly to council or file it with the city clerk as council directs.

§ 145A03. Notice of assessment.

(a) **Personal notice.**—After the amounts to be assessed against the properties to be benefited by the public improvement have been calculated pursuant to the method and procedures as prescribed by ordinance, the city shall give personal notice of the assessment to the owner of each property that is being assessed. The notice shall also state that the owner has 30 days from receipt of the notice to appeal the assessment.

(b) **Assessment effective.**—An assessment made pursuant to this chapter shall become effective 30 days after personal notice is given by any of the following means:

(1) Personal service on the owner.

(2) Certified mail, addressee only, return receipt requested, to the owner at the owner's last known address.

(3) Posting notice at or upon the property after reasonable attempts to give personal notice pursuant to paragraphs (1) and (2) have failed.

§ 145A04. Appeals to court.

Within 30 days after receipt of the notice of assessment, an owner of property shall have the right to appeal the assessment to the court of common pleas in the county in which the assessed property is located. On appeal, unless the court finds fraud, mistake or illegality, the court shall be restricted to determining the following questions:

(1) Whether the property assessed received any special benefits from the improvement.

(2) Whether the assessment made exceeds the special benefits received.

§ 145A05. Benefits and damages.

In any proceeding in which damages to property are being sought as a result of a public improvement for which an assessment of benefits has been made, the excess of damages over benefits, or the excess of benefits over damages, or nothing in case the benefits and damages are equal, shall be awarded to or assessed against the owner of land and property affected by the public improvement.

§ 145A06. Return by city of assessments paid on property unlawfully assessed.

The following shall apply with regard to the return of payments made on an unlawful assessment:

(1) If, after a timely appeal, a court makes a final determination that a property was unlawfully assessed or that the amount assessed exceeded, to a substantial amount, the benefits received by the property assessed from the public improvement, a city that received money in payment of the assessment shall repay the money in an amount as ordered by the court.

(2) Within two years of receiving payment of an assessment, the city may repay the money voluntarily if the city determines that the assessment was made erroneously.

(3) Repayments to property owners pursuant to paragraph (1) or (2) shall include interest from the date of payment of the unlawful or erroneous assessment at the rate of interest that is provided for in 53 Pa.C.S. § 8426 (relating to interest on overpayment).

§ 145A07. Payment of assessments in installments.

(a) Authorization.—An ordinance providing for a public improvement, the expense of which is to be defrayed by an assessment against properties benefited by the public improvement, may authorize payment of the assessment in installments. The ordinance shall:

(1) Set a time when the installment payments shall commence.

(2) Specify the length of time over which the installments may be extended. The period during which installments may be paid shall not exceed the lesser of 10 years or the number of years equal to the period of maturity of the bonds issued to fund the public improvement.

(3) Specify whether payments are to be made by equal annual or more frequent installments.

(b) Interest rate.—The ordinance shall set forth the rate of interest for the installments, which shall not be more than 10% per year unless a bond is issued for the improvement, in which case the maximum interest rate on the installment payments shall be in accordance with section 9 of the Municipal Claim and Tax Lien Law.

(c) Written agreement.—The city shall enter into a written installment agreement with each property owner that will pay the assessment in installments, subject to the requirements of the ordinance pertaining to the agreements and this chapter.

(d) Installments not paid.—If any of the installments remain unpaid for 60 days after the installments have become due and payable:

(1) The entire unpaid assessment, plus unpaid accrued interest and any costs, shall be due and payable.

(2) The city may proceed to collect the installments by filing a lien in the same manner as municipal claims are filed under the Municipal Claim and Tax Lien Law or by instituting a civil action.

(e) Advance payments.—Any property owner upon whom an assessment has been made may pay all or as many of the installments before they are due, with interest and costs, on or before the due date of the next installment.

§ 145A08. Collection of assessments.

(a) Authority.—Council shall have the power to authorize the city treasurer or other city official to collect assessments.

(b) Procedure.—The following shall apply to the collection of assessments:

(1) A city may collect an assessment that remains unpaid for 60 days after personal notice was given pursuant to section 145A03 (relating to notice of assessment) unless an installment agreement has been entered into pursuant to section 145A07 (relating to payment of assessments in installments).

(2) An assessment made under this chapter may be collected in the same manner as municipal claims under the Municipal Claim and Tax Lien Law or by instituting a civil action against the owner of the property benefited.

(3) Interest on an unpaid assessment shall begin to accrue from the time of completion of the improvement at a rate of 10% per year unless a bond is issued for the improvement, in which case the maximum interest rate shall be pursuant to section 9 of the Municipal Claim and Tax Lien Law.

(4) If a property owner has two or more lots against which there is an assessment for the same improvement, all of the lots may be embraced in one claim.

(5) Assessments, whether paid one time or by installments, shall be payable at the office of the city treasurer or any other place designated by ordinance.

CHAPTER 146
COLLECTION OF MUNICIPAL CLAIMS AND COMPROMISE OF CLAIMS

Sec.

---

§ 14601. Collection of municipal claims.

(a) Civil action.—In addition to the remedies provided by this part or any other law for the filing of liens for the collection of municipal claims, including water rates, sewer rates and the removal of nuisances, a city may proceed for the recovery and collection of municipal claims by civil action as follows:

(1) The action shall be brought against the person who was the owner of the property at the time:

(i) of the completion of the improvement; or

(ii) the water or sewer rates or the cost of the removal of nuisances first became payable.

(2) A city may bring a civil action, notwithstanding the failure on the part of the city or its agents to enter the municipal claim as a lien against the property assessed for the improvement, for the furnishing of water or sewer services or for the removal of nuisances and for the recovery of which the action was brought.

(b) Limitation period.—The civil action shall be commenced either within six years after the completion of the improvement from which the claim arises or within six years after the water or sewer rates or the cost of abating a nuisance first became payable.

§ 14602. Compromise of municipal claims.

(a) Agreement.—Council may agree with the owner of the real estate to accept a sum less than the whole of the amount of a municipal claim due, in compromise or reduction of the amount of the claim and the interest charges, expenses and fees added to and due on the claim, if:

(1) the city had entered the claim in the office of the prothonotary as a lien against real estate; and

(2) the claim has existed for 10 years or more.

(b) Satisfaction of lien.—Upon receipt of the compromise amount as agreed upon:

(1) The city shall cause the lien to be properly satisfied on the record, which shall be as effective as if the whole amount of the claim, interest, charges, expenses and fees had been paid.

(2) The claim shall no longer be a lien against the real estate or a claim against the owner of the real estate.

(c) Applicability.—The provisions of this section permitting compromise of municipal claims shall not apply to or in any manner affect any claims, the assessments for which:

(1) Are:

(i) the sole basis of improvement bonds issued by any political subdivision; and

(ii) the security for the payment of the bonds.

(2) Have been assigned by any political subdivision to any contractor in payment of the amount due the contractor under terms of the contract for the improvement for which the assessments were levied.

CHAPTER 147

MISCELLANEOUS PROVISIONS

§ 14701. Intent.

It is intended that this part furnish a complete and exclusive system for the government and regulation of cities, except as provided for in section 10103 (relating to excluded provisions).

§ 14702. Construction.

Nothing contained in this part shall be construed to repeal:

(1) The provisions of the act of May 23, 1945 (P.L.903, No.362), entitled "An act authorizing cities of the third class to establish an optional retirement system for officers and employes independently of any pension system or systems existing in such cities."

(2) The act of February 14, 2008 (P.L.6, No.3), known as the Right-to-Know Law.

(3) The provisions of 45 Pa.C.S. (relating to legal notices).

(4) The provisions of 65 Pa.C.S. (relating to public officers).

(5) The provisions of 66 Pa.C.S. Pt. I (relating to Public Utility Code).

(6) The provisions of 74 Pa.C.S. Ch. 59 Subch. B (relating to airport zoning).

(7) Any local or special laws.

(8) Any law relating to the Navigation Commission for the Delaware River and its Navigable Tributaries.

(9) The provisions of any law, the enforcement of which is vested in the Department of Health or the Department of Environmental Protection.

(10) The provisions of any law, the enforcement of which is vested in the Department of Conservation and Natural Resources.

(11) Any laws or parts of laws pertaining to civil defense.

(12) A supplement to any act under this section.

PART VI
MISCELLANEOUS PROVISIONS (RESERVED)

Section 2. Repeals are as follows:

(1) The General Assembly declares that the repeal under paragraph (2) is necessary to effectuate the addition of 11 Pa.C.S. Pt. V.

(2) The act of June 23, 1931 (P.L.932, No.317), known as The Third Class City Code, is repealed.

Section 3. The addition of 11 Pa.C.S. Pt. V is a continuation of the act of June 23, 1931 (P.L.932, No.317), known as The Third Class City Code. The following apply:

(1) Except as otherwise provided in 11 Pa.C.S. Pt. V, all activities initiated under The Third Class City Code shall continue and remain in full force and effect and may be completed under 11 Pa.C.S. Pt. V. Orders, regulations, rules and decisions which were made under The Third Class City Code and which are in effect on the effective date of section 2(2) of this act shall remain in full force and effect until revoked, vacated or modified under 11 Pa.C.S. Pt. V. Contracts, obligations and collective bargaining agreements entered into under The Third Class City Code are not affected nor impaired by the repeal of The Third Class City Code.

(2) Except as set forth in paragraph (3), any difference in language between 11 Pa.C.S. Pt. V and The Third Class City Code is intended only to conform to the style of the Pennsylvania Consolidated Statutes and is not intended to change or affect the legislative intent, judicial construction or administration and implementation of The Third Class City Code.

(3) Paragraph (2) does not apply to the addition of the following provisions:

(i) 11 Pa.C.S. § 11018.11(e).

(ii) 11 Pa.C.S. § 11401(6).

(iii) 11 Pa.C.S. § 11402(b)(2).

(iv) 11 Pa.C.S. § 11813(b).

(v) 11 Pa.C.S. § 12448.

(vi) 11 Pa.C.S. § 14406(11)(ii).

(vii) 11 Pa.C.S. § 144A11(d).

CHAPTER 37-B

OPTIONAL THIRD CLASS CITY CHARTER LAW

53 P.S. §§ 41101–41625

TABLE OF CONTENTS

ARTICLE I.
PRELIMINARY PROVISION

§ 41101. Short title

This act shall be known and may be cited as the "Optional Third Class City Charter Law."

§ 41102. Definitions

The following words and terms as used in this act, unless the context clearly indicates otherwise, shall mean:

"City," a city of the third class.

§ 41103. Partial invalidity

If any clause, sentence, paragraph, section or part of this act shall be adjudged by any court of competent jurisdiction to be invalid, such judgment shall not affect, impair or invalidate the remainder thereof, but shall be confined in its operation to the clause, sentence, paragraph, section or part thereof directly involved in the controversy in which such judgment shall have rendered.

ARTICLE II.
PROCEDURE FOR ADOPTION OF OPTIONAL CHARTER PLANS

A. Charter Commission

§ 41201. Initiation of proceedings; ordinance; petition; question; election

(a) Whenever authorized by ordinance of the council, or upon petition of the registered voters of any city to the county board of elections of the county wherein the city is located, an election shall be held in the city upon the question: "Shall a charter commission of seven members (or any designated number up to and including fifteen) be elected to study the charter and form of government of the city of and to consider a new charter and to make recommendations thereon". The petition calling for such election shall be in the form required by subsection (b) hereof, and shall be signed by at least fifteen per centum of the registered voters of the city.

Within five days after the final enactment of an ordinance authorizing such election, the city clerk shall file a certified copy of the ordinance with the county board of elections, together with a copy of the question to be submitted to the electors. At the next municipal or general election occurring not less than sixty days after the filing of the ordinance or the petition with the county election board, it shall cause the question above stated to be submitted to the electors of the city as other questions are submitted under the provisions of the Pennsylvania Election Code.[1]

(b) A petition under this section shall be filed at least sixty-four days prior to the municipal or general election, and the petition and the proceedings therein shall be in the manner and subject to the provisions of the election laws which relate to the signing, filing and adjudication of nomination petitions in so far as such provisions are applicable, except that no petition shall be signed or circulated prior to thirty days before the last day on which such petition may be filed.

---

1. 25 P.S. § 2601 et seq.

§ 41202. Charter commission; election; candidates; nomination and listing; instructions

A charter commission of seven members or other number designated in the question shall be elected by the qualified voters at the same election the question is submitted to the electors or at the next succeeding primary or municipal election. Candidates for the office of charter commissioner shall be nominated and placed upon the ballot containing the question or if not placed upon such ballot shall be placed upon the ballot at the next succeeding primary or municipal election and the proceedings thereon adjudicated in the manner provided by and subject to the provisions of the Pennsylvania Election Code[2] which relate to the nomination of candidates nominated by nomination papers filed by political bodies for other offices elective by the voters of a city, except that they shall be nominated and listed without any political designation or slogan, and no nomination paper shall be signed or circulated prior to thirty days before the last day on which such papers may be filed. Each voter shall be instructed to vote on the question and, regardless of the manner of his vote on the question, to vote for the designated number of members of a charter commission who shall serve if the question is or has been determined in the affirmative.

§ 41203. Qualification of candidates; nomination papers; acceptance of nomination

(a) Candidates for the charter commission shall be registered voters of the city. They may be nominated by nomination papers signed by a number of qualified electors of the city equal at least to two per centum of the largest entire vote cast for any city officer elected at the last preceding municipal election in the city and filed with the county board of elections not less than forty-four days prior to the date of the election.

(b) Each nominating paper shall set forth the names, places of residence, and post-office addresses of the candidate or candidates thereby nominated, that the nomination is for the office of charter commissioner, and that the signers are legally qualified to vote for such candidate or candidates. Every voter signing a nominating paper shall add to his signature his place of residence, post-office address and street number, if any. No voter shall sign a nomination paper or papers for more than the designated number of candidates.

(c) Each nominating paper shall, before it may be filed with the county board of elections, contain an acceptance of such nomination in writing, signed by the candidate or candidates therein nominated, upon or annexed to such paper, or if the same person or persons be named in more than one paper, upon or annexed to one of such papers. Such acceptance shall certify that the candidate is a registered voter of the city, that the nominee consents to stand as a candidate at the election, and that if elected he agrees to take office and serve.

(d) Each nominating paper shall be verified by an oath or affirmation of one or more of the signers thereof, taken and subscribed before a person qualified under the laws of Pennsylvania to administer an oath, to the effect that the paper was signed by each of the signers thereof in his proper handwriting, that the signers are, to the best knowledge and belief of the affiant, registered voters of the city, and that the nomination paper is prepared and filed in good faith for the sole purpose of endorsing the person or persons named therein for election as stated in the paper.

§ 41204. Returns and canvass of elections; candidates elected; tie vote

The result of the votes cast for and against the question as to the election of a charter commission shall be returned by the election officers, and a canvass of

2. 25 P.S. 2601 et seq.

such election had, as is provided by law in the case of other public questions put to the voters of a single city. The votes cast for members of the charter commission shall be counted, and the result thereof returned by the election officers, and a canvass of such election had, as is provided by law in the case of election of members of city council. The designated number of candidates receiving the greatest number of votes shall be elected and shall constitute the charter commission: Provided, That if a majority of those voting on said question shall vote against the election of a charter commission, none of the candidates shall be elected. If two or more candidates shall be equal and greatest in number of votes, they shall draw lots to determine which one shall be elected.

§ 41205. Organization of commission; chairman; meetings; rules; quorum; majority vote

As soon as possible and in any event no later than fifteen days after its election, the charter commission shall organize and hold its first meeting and elect one of its members as chairman, fix its hours and place of meeting, and adopt such rules for the conduct of its business as it may deem necessary and advisable. A majority of the members of said commission shall constitute a quorum for the transaction of business, but no recommendation of said commission shall have any legal effect unless adopted by a majority of the whole number of the members of the commission.

§ 41206. Vacancies

In case of any vacancy in the charter commission, the remaining members of such commission shall fill it by appointing thereto some other properly qualified elector.

§ 41207. Functions and duties

It shall be the function and duty of the charter commission to study the form of government of the city, to compare it with other available forms under the laws of this State, to determine whether or not in its judgment the government of the city could be strengthened, made more clearly responsive or accountable to the people, or whether its operation could become more economical or efficient under a changed form of government.

§ 41208. Compensation; expenses; appropriation

Members of the charter commission shall serve without compensation, but shall be reimbursed by the city for their necessary expenses incurred in the performance of their duties. Council shall appropriate moneys necessary for such purpose.

Within the limits of such appropriations and privately contributed funds and services as shall be made available to it, the charter commission may appoint one or more consultants and clerical and other assistants to serve at the pleasure of the commission and may fix a reasonable compensation to be paid such consultants and clerical and other assistants.

§ 41209. Hearings; forums; discussion

The charter commission shall hold public hearings, may hold private hearings and sponsor public forums, and generally shall provide for the widest possible public information and discussion respecting the purposes and progress of its work.

§ 41210. Report; plans; publication; copies

The charter commission shall report its findings and recommendations to the citizens of the city within nine calendar months from the date of its election. It shall publish or cause to be published sufficient copies of its final report for public study and information, and shall deliver to the city clerk sufficient copies of the report to supply it to any interested citizen upon request. If the charter commission shall recommend the adoption of any of the optional plans of government as authorized in this act, the report shall contain the complete plan as recommended.

§ 41211. Discharge; amended report

(a) The charter commission shall be discharged upon the filing of its report: Provided, That if the commission's recommendations require further procedure on the part of city council or the people of the city, the commission shall not be discharged until a copy of the report has been certified to the county board of elections. Any time before such procedure has been finally concluded but not later than one year from the date of the publication of its final report, the commission may modify or change any recommendation set forth in said final report by publishing an amended report.

(b) Whenever a charter commission issues an amended report pursuant to subsection (a) above, such amended report shall supersede the final report and such final report shall cease to have any legal effect under this act.

(c) The procedure to be taken under the amended report shall be governed by all provisions of Article II of this act[3] applicable to the final report of a charter commission submitted pursuant to section 210 of this act.[4]

§ 41212. Alternative recommendations

The charter commission may report and recommend:

(1) that a referendum shall be held to submit to the qualified voters of the city the question of adopting one of the optional forms of government authorized by this act to be specified by the commission; or

(2) that the form of government of the city shall remain unchanged; or

(3) such other action as it may deem advisable consistent with its functions as set forth in this article.

§ 41213. Election of mayor; number of councilmen

If the charter commission shall recommend the adoption of any of the optional forms of government set forth in this act, it may also specify that the mayor be elected directly by the voters of the city or chosen by council and that the city council shall consist of seven or nine members instead of five members as provided in said optional forms. If the charter commission shall recommend the adoption of the council-manager form of government, it may specify that the mayor be elected directly by the voters of the city or by council.

§ 41214. Question submitted to voters

The question to be submitted to the voters for the adoption of any of the optional plans of government authorized by this act shall be submitted in the following form or such part thereof as shall be applicable:

---

3. Section 41201 et seq. of this title.

4. Section 41210 of this title.

Chap. 39 Res. During Mil. Service
Chap. 38 Intergov. Coop.
Chap. 37 3rd Class City Code
Chap. 36 Bor. Code
Chap. 35 2nd Class Twp. Code
Chap. 34 1st Class Twp. Code
Chap. 33 Home Rule Chart. Opt. Plans Law
Chap. 32 Water Serv. Act
Chap. 31 Munic. Auth. Act

"Shall ....(insert name of plan)........... of the Optional Third Class City Charter Law providing for ....(insert number).......... councilmen to be elected at large be adopted by the city of ....(insert name of city)..............?"

§ 41215. Commission's report certified to election board; submitting question to voters

If the charter commission shall recommend that the question of adopting one of the optional forms of government authorized by this act shall be submitted to the voters of the city, it shall be the duty of the city clerk, within five days thereafter, to certify a copy of the commission's report to the county election board, which shall cause the question of adoption or rejection to be placed upon the ballot or voting machines at such time as the commission shall in its report specify. The commission may cause the question to be submitted to the people at the next general or municipal election, occurring not less than sixty days following the filing of a copy of the commission's report with the county board of elections, or at a special election occurring not less than sixty days or more than one hundred twenty days after the filing of the report, at such time as the commission's report shall direct. At such election, the question of adopting that form of government recommended by the charter commission shall be submitted to the voters of the city by the county board of elections in the same manner as other questions are submitted to the voters of a city under the provisions of the Pennsylvania Election Code.[5] The charter commission shall frame the question to be placed upon the ballot as herein provided, and if it deems appropriate an interpretative statement to accompany such question.

§ 41216. Pending and subsequent proceedings; notice of petition

(a) No ordinance may be passed and no petition may be filed for the election of a charter commission pursuant to section 201 of this act[6] while proceedings are pending under any other petition or ordinance filed or passed under the authority of section 201, nor within four years after an election shall have been held pursuant to any such ordinance or petition passed or filed under section 201 hereof.

(b) For the purpose of this section, proceedings shall be considered as having started (i) in the case of an ordinance upon the final vote of council in favor of the ordinance, notwithstanding the fact that the ordinance cannot take effect until a certain number of days thereafter; or (ii) in the case of a petition, as soon as it is properly signed by one-third of the number of registered voters required for such petition and written notice thereof filed in the office of the county board of elections and in the office of the city clerk, who shall cause the same to be immediately posted in a conspicuous place in said office, open to public inspection.

§ 41217. Proposed charter; majority vote; manner of taking effect

Whenever the legally qualified voters of any city by a majority of those voting on the question vote in favor of adopting a change in their form of government pursuant to this act, the proposed charter shall take effect according to its terms and the provisions of this act.

§ 41218. Subsequent change in government

The voters of any city which has adopted an optional charter plan of government pursuant to this act may not vote on the question of adopting another form of government until four years after the optional charter plan became effective.

---

5. 25 P.S. § 2601 et seq.

6. Section 41201 of this title.

§ 41219. Complete form of government

For the purposes of this act, each of the optional forms of government provided by this act and each of said optional forms as modified by any available provisions concerning size of council is hereby declared to be a complete and separate form of government provided by the Legislature for submission to the voters of the city.

B. Abandonment of an Optional Plan and Reversion to a Prior Form

§ 41231. Petition; referendum; reversion; subsequent submission

Any city may, subject to the provisions of section 218 of this act,[7] abandon its optional plan and revert to the form of government under which it was governed immediately prior thereto, upon the filing of a petition and referendum, as follows:

(1) Upon petition to the county board of elections of the registered voters of the city, signed by the same number thereof as required in section 201,[8] for an election to submit the question of abandonment and reversion as herein provided, the county board of elections shall provide for submission of the question to the voters of the city at the first general election to be held not less than sixty days after the filing of the petition as provided in the Pennsylvania Election Code.[9]

(2) The form of the question shall be as follows:

Shall the city of ....
(name of city) abandon its present form of government and revert to its prior form of government, known as ....
.... (popular name of plan) as provided by The Third Class City Code?

(3) If a majority of those voting on the question vote in the affirmative, the city shall revert to its prior form of government on the first Monday of January following the next regular municipal election.

If a majority of those voting on the question vote in the negative, the question of abandonment and reversion shall not again be submitted for five years.

(4) The reversion to a prior form of government shall take effect as provided in Article VI, of this act[10] for transition to an optional plan hereunder in so far as applicable.

C. Conduct of Elections

§ 41241. Returns; computation; certificates

All elections provided for in this act shall be conducted by the election officers for such city in accordance with the Pennsylvania Election Code.[11] The election officers shall count the votes cast and make return thereof to the county board of elections. The result of any such election shall be computed by the county board of elections in the same manner as is provided by law for the computation of similar returns. Certificates of the result of any such election shall be filed by the county board of elections with the city council of the city and with the Secretary of the Commonwealth.

7. Section 41218 of this title.
8. Section 41201 of this title.
9. 25 P.S. § 2601 et seq.
10. Section 41601 et seq. of this title.
11. 25 P.S. § 2601 et seq.

§ 41242. Notice; proclamation; posting

At least thirty days' notice of each election herein provided for shall be given by proclamation of the mayor of the city. A copy of such proclamation shall be posted at each polling place of the city on the day of the election, and shall be published in at least two newspapers of general circulation in the city once a week for three consecutive weeks during the period of thirty days prior of the election.

ARTICLE III.
GENERAL POWERS AND LIMITATIONS

A. Powers (Refs & Annos)

§ 41301. Governing law; organic law; existing charters, laws and ordinances

Upon the adoption by the qualified voters of any city of any of the optional plans of government set forth in this act, the city shall thereafter be governed by the plan adopted and by the provisions of this act common to optional plans and by all applicable provisions of general law, subject to the transitional provisions of Article VI of this act,[12] unless and until the city should adopt another form of government as provided by law. The plan adopted and the provisions of this act common to optional plans shall become the organic law of the city at the time fixed by this act. So far as they are consistent with the grant of powers and the limitations, restrictions and regulations hereinafter prescribed, they shall supersede any existing charter, and all acts and parts of acts, local, special or general, affecting the organization, government and powers of such city to the extent that they are inconsistent or in conflict therein. All existing acts or parts of acts and ordinances affecting the organization, government and powers of the city not inconsistent or in conflict with the organic law so adopted shall remain in full force until modified or repealed as provided by law.

§ 41302. New charter; recording; filing

The city clerk of the city shall forthwith cause the new charter as approved by the qualified electors to be recorded in the ordinance book of the city. He shall also file a certified copy thereof in the office of the Secretary of the Commonwealth.

§ 41303. General powers

Each city governed by an optional form of government pursuant to this act shall, subject to the provisions of and limitations prescribed by this act, have full power to:

(1) Organize and regulate its internal affairs, and to establish, alter, and abolish offices, positions and employments and to define the functions, powers and duties thereof and fix their term, tenure and compensation;

(2) Adopt and enforce local ordinances;

(2.1) Impose penalties of fine not exceeding one per month on a property and limited to no more than one thousand dollars ($1,000) for the first two continual and uncorrected violations and not exceeding five thousand dollars ($5,000) for the third and any subsequent continual and uncorrected violation of the same subsection of a building ordinance, housing ordinance, property maintenance ordinance, fire prevention ordinance, electrical ordinance or plumbing ordinance on the same property, unless the violation is found to pose a threat to the public's health, safety or property, then penalties of fine may be provided for as follows:

12. Section 41601 et seq. of this title.

(i) not exceeding one citation per five calendar days for a continual and uncorrected violation of the same subsection of such ordinance on the same property;

(ii) limited to no less than five hundred dollars ($500) and no more than one thousand dollars ($1,000) for the first two continual and uncorrected violations of the same subsection of such ordinance on the same property and no less than one thousand dollars ($1,000) and not exceeding ten thousand dollars ($10,000) for the third and any subsequent continual and uncorrected violation of the same subsection of such ordinance on the same property, or imprisonment for any term not exceeding ninety days, or both;

(2.2) Impose penalties of fine not exceeding one thousand dollars ($1,000) or a term of imprisonment not exceeding ninety days, or both, for violations of any section of any other ordinance;

(2.3) Construct, acquire, operate or maintain any and all public improvements, projects or enterprises for any public purpose, subject to referendum requirements otherwise imposed by law, and to exercise all powers of local government in such manner as its governing body may determine;

(3) Sue and be sued, to have a corporate seal, to contract and be contracted with, to buy, sell, lease, hold and dispose of real and personal property, to appropriate and expend moneys, and to adopt, amend and repeal such ordinances and resolutions as may be required for the good government thereof;

(4) Exercise powers of condemnation, borrowing and taxation in the manner provided by general law applicable to cities of the third class.

§ 41304. Interpretation of powers; liberal construction

The general grant of municipal power contained in this article is intended to confer the greatest power of local self-government consistent with the Constitution of this State. Any specific enumeration of municipal powers contained in this act or in any other law shall not be construed in any way to limit the general description of power contained in this article, and any such specifically enumerated municipal powers shall be construed as in addition and supplementary to the powers conferred in general terms by this article. All grants of municipal power to cities governed by an optional plan under this act, whether in the form of specific enumeration or general terms, shall be liberally construed in favor of the city.

B. Limitations

§ 41305. Pension or retirement rights; terms of office; extraterritorial powers; proprietary or private business; powers granted by legislature

The charter of any city adopted in accordance with this act shall not give any power or authority to diminish any rights or privileges of any present city employe in his pension or retirement system. Terms of office of a mayor, treasurer, controller or members of council elected to or holding office prior to adoption of a charter shall not be terminated prior to the time for which elected. No city shall exercise any powers or authority beyond the city limits except such as are conferred by an act of the General Assembly, and no city shall engage in any proprietary or private business except as authorized by the General Assembly. Notwithstanding the grant of powers contained in this act, no city shall exercise powers contrary to or in limitation or enlargement of powers granted to the city by acts of the General Assembly which are:

(1) Applicable to a class or classes of cities on the following subjects:

(i) Providing for the filing and collection of municipal and tax claims or liens and for the sale of real or personal property in satisfaction thereof:

Table of Contents | Part I Ch. 1–3 Ethics, Records, Open Meetings | Part II Ch. 4–10 Taxation | Part III Ch. 11–18 Torts, Contracts & Civil Rules | Part IV Ch. 19–24 Zoning & Planning | Part V Ch. 25–30 Construction and Emergency Codes | Part VI Ch. 31–39 Municipal Codes | Index

Chap. 39 Res. During Mil. Service
Chap. 38 Intergov. Coop.
Chap. 37 3rd Class City Code
Chap. 36 Bor. Code
Chap. 35 2nd Class Twp. Code
Chap. 34 1st Class Twp. Code
Chap. 33 Home Rule Chart. Opt. Plans Law
Chap. 32 Water Serv. Act
Chap. 31 Munic. Auth. Act

(ii) Providing for the exercise of the power of eminent domain and the procedure for the condemnation of property for public purposes.

(iii) Providing for the assessment of damages and benefits for property taken, injured or destroyed.

(iv) Providing methods for the incurring or increasing of indebtedness.

(v) Providing for the annexation or exclusion or detachment of territory.

(vi) Regulating public schools.

(vii) Providing for the personal registration of electors.

(viii) Limiting rates and fixing subjects of taxation.

(ix) Providing for the assessment of real or personal property and persons for taxation purposes, except that any city adopting one of the optional charter plans provided under this act which has not elected to become subject to the provisions of the act of May 21, 1943 (P.L. 571), known as "The Fourth to Eighth Class County Assessment Law,"[13] may, by ordinance, provide for the hearing of appeals from assessments made by the city assessor and the revision thereof by an administrative agency rather than by council: Provided, That in so doing such city shall adhere to the requirements of general law regarding notice to taxables and the right of a person to appeal.

(x) Relating to civil service.

(xi) Relating to public health.

(2) Applicable in every part of the Commonwealth.

(3) Applicable to all the cities of the Commonwealth.

§ 41401. Name; cities governed

The form of government provided in this article shall be known as the "mayor-council plan A" and shall, together with Articles III.[14] and VI.,[15] govern any city, the voters of which have adopted it pursuant to this act.

§ 41402. Governing personnel

Each city hereunder shall be governed by an elected council, an elected mayor, an elected treasurer and an elected controller and by such other officers and employes as may be duly appointed pursuant to this article, general law or ordinance.

B. Elected Officials (Refs & Annos)

§ 41403. Mayor; treasurer; controller; election; term

The mayor, the treasurer and the controller shall be elected by the voters of the city at a regular municipal election, and shall serve for a term of four years beginning on the first Monday of January next following his election.

§ 41404. Councilmen; number; election; term

The council shall consist of five members, unless pursuant to the authority granted under section 213 of this act,[16] the city shall be governed by a council of seven or nine members. Members of the council shall be elected at large by the voters of the city at a regular municipal election and shall serve for a term of four years, except as hereinafter provided for those first elected beginning on the first Monday of January next following their election.

13. 71 P.S. § 5453.101 et seq.

14. Section 41301 et seq. of this title.

15. Section 41601 et seq. of this title.

16. 53 P.S. § 41213.

§ 41405. First council; election; term

At the first municipal election following the adoption by a city of this plan, councilmen shall be elected and shall serve for the terms as provided in section 622 of this act.[17]

§ 41406. Vacancies

(a) If a vacancy exists in the city council, the city council shall, by a majority of its remaining members, fill such vacancy, within thirty days thereafter, by electing a qualified person to serve until that first Monday of January when his successor who shall have been elected by the qualified electors at the next municipal election, occurring at least thirty days after such vacancy exists, is duly sworn into office for the remainder of the term of the person originally elected to said office.

In case vacancies should exist whereby the offices of a majority or more members of the city council become vacant, the remaining members shall fill such vacancies, one at a time, giving each new appointee such reasonable notice of his appointment as will enable him to meet and act with the then qualified member or members of the city council in making further appointments until a bare majority of members of city council have been qualified, whereupon the said members shall fill the remaining vacancies at a meeting attended by the said majority members of city council, such appointees to receive a majority of the votes of the members present at any such meeting. The person or persons selected to fill such vacancy or vacancies shall hold their offices as herein provided.

If, by reason of a tie vote, or otherwise, such vacancy shall not have been filled by the remaining members of city council within the time as limited herein, the court of common pleas, upon the petition of ten or more qualified electors, shall fill such vacancy by the appointment of a qualified person, for the portion of the unexpired term as above provided.

If, at any time, vacancies should occur or exist in the membership of all members of city council, the court of common pleas shall appoint a city council, of persons properly qualified, who shall serve as herein provided.

(b) If a vacancy occurs in the office of mayor, city treasurer or city controller, the city council shall fill such vacancy, within thirty days thereafter, by choosing a mayor, a city treasurer or a city controller, as the case may be, to serve until his successor is elected by the qualified electors at the next municipal election, occurring at least two hundred days after such vacancy occurs, and is duly sworn into office. The person so elected shall serve from the first Monday of January next succeeding his election for the remainder of the term of the person originally elected to such office.

If, by reason of a tie vote or otherwise, a vacancy in the office of mayor, treasurer or controller shall not have been filled by council within the time as limited herein, the court of common pleas, upon petition of ten or more qualified electors, shall fill such vacancy by the appointment of a qualified person for the portion of the unexpired term as herein provided.

C. Council

§ 41407. Legislative power

The legislative power of the city shall be exercised by the city council, except as may be otherwise provided by general law.

§ 41408. Organization; president; presiding officer

On the first Monday of January following the regular municipal election, the members of council shall assemble at the usual place of meeting and organize and

17. 53 P.S. § 41622.

Table of Contents
Part I Ch. 1–3 Ethics, Records, Open Meetings
Part II Ch. 4–10 Taxation
Part III Ch. 11–18 Torts, Contracts & Civil Rules
Part IV Ch. 19–24 Zoning & Planning
Part V Ch. 25–30 Construction and Emergency Codes
Part VI Ch. 31–39 Municipal Codes
Index

elect a president of the council from among its members, who shall preside at its meetings and perform such other duties as council may prescribe. If the first Monday is a legal holiday, the meeting shall be held on the first day following. In the absence of the president, the council shall elect a temporary presiding officer.

§ 41409. Officers' statements of duties; investigations

The council, in addition to such other powers and duties as may be conferred upon it by this charter or otherwise by general law, may require any city officer, in its discretion, to prepare and submit sworn statements regarding his official duties in the performance thereof, and may otherwise investigate the conduct of any department office or agency of the city government.

§ 41410. City clerk; solicitor; planning board; zoning board of adjustment; personnel board; advisory bodies

(a) The council shall appoint a city clerk, who shall serve as clerk of the council, its minutes and records of its proceedings, maintain and compile its ordinances and resolutions as this act requires, and perform such functions as may be required by law. The city clerk shall, prior to his appointment, have been qualified by training or experience to perform the duties of the office.

(b) The council may provide for the manner of appointment of a city solicitor, any planning board, zoning board of adjustment or personnel board in the city, and may create commissions and other bodies with advisory powers.

D. Mayor and Administration

§ 41411. Executive power

The executive power of the city shall be exercised by the mayor.

§ 41412. Enforcement and supervisory powers; reports; recommendations

The mayor shall enforce the charter and ordinances of the city and all general laws applicable thereto. He shall, annually, report to the council and the public on the work of the previous year and on the condition and requirements of the city government and shall, from time to time, make such recommendations for action by the council as he may deem in the public interest. He shall supervise all of the departments of the city government, and shall require each department to make an annual and such other reports of its work as he may deem desirable.

§ 41413. Ordinances; council meetings; vote; bonds; notes; contracts; written obligations

(a) Ordinances adopted by the council shall be submitted to the mayor and he shall, within ten days after receiving any ordinance, either approve the ordinance by affixing his signature thereto, or return it to the council by delivering it to the city clerk together with a statement setting forth his objections thereto or to any item or part thereof. No ordinance or any item or part thereof shall take effect without the mayor's approval, unless the mayor fails to return an ordinance to the council within ten days after it has been presented to him, or unless council upon reconsideration thereof, on or after the third day following its return by the mayor, shall by a vote of two-thirds of the members resolve to override the mayor's veto.

(b) The mayor may attend meetings of council and may take part in discussions of council but shall have no vote except in the case of a tie on the question of filling a vacancy in the council, in which case he may cast the deciding vote.

(c) All bonds, notes, contracts and written obligations of the city shall be executed on its behalf by the mayor and the controller.

(d) The mayor, or a person designated under section 414[18] to act as mayor, may require that bids be accompanied by a good faith tender of either cash, a certified check, a cashier's check, a corporate surety bond or other irrevocable letter of credit in a reasonable amount. The advertisement soliciting bids shall set forth the requirement, when applicable, and the amount to be tendered. If a bidder is selected but is unable to perform, the city may retain the amount tendered with the bid as damages.

§ 41414. Acting mayor

The mayor shall designate any department head, or the city clerk, to act as mayor whenever the mayor shall be prevented, by absence from the city, disability or other cause, from attending to the duties of his office. During such time the person so designated by the mayor shall possess all the rights, powers, and duties of mayor. Whenever the mayor shall have been unable to attend to the duties of his office for a period of sixty consecutive days for any of the above stated reasons, a member of council shall be appointed by the council as acting mayor, who shall succeed to all the rights, powers and duties of the mayor or the then acting mayor.

§ 41415. City treasurer; departments; department heads; subordinate officers and employees

(a) The city treasurer shall perform such functions and duties and have such powers relating to the collection, receiving, safe keeping and payment over of public moneys including city, county, institution district and school district taxes as provided by general law and shall have such other functions, powers and duties as may be assigned to him by council.

(b) The city may have a department of administration and shall have such other departments, not exceeding a total of nine, as council may establish by ordinance. All of the administrative functions, powers and duties of the city, other than those vested in the office of the city clerk, city treasurer and city controller, shall be allocated and assigned among and within such departments.

(c) Each department shall be headed by a director who shall be appointed by the mayor with the advice and consent of the council. Each department head shall serve during the term of office of the mayor appointing him, and until the appointment and qualification of his successor. No member of city council shall head a department.

(d) The mayor may, in his discretion, remove any department head after notice and an opportunity to be heard. Prior to removing a department head, the mayor shall first file written notice of his intention with the council, and such removal shall become effective on the twentieth day after the filing of such notice.

(e) Subject to the provisions of Article XLIV. of the act of June 23, 1931 (P.L. 932), known as the "Third Class City Code"[19] and the provisions of the act of May 31, 1933 (P.L. 1108), entitled "An act providing for the appointment, promotion, reduction, removal and reinstatement of paid officers, firemen and employes of fire departments and of fire alarm operators and fire box inspectors in the bureaus of electricity in cities of the second and third class; defining the powers and duties of civil service commissions for such purposes; and fixing penalties",[20] department heads shall appoint subordinate officers and employes within their respective departments and may, with approval of the mayor, remove such officers and employes.

18. 53 P.S. § 41414.

19. 53 P.S. §§ 39401 to 39410.

20. 53 P.S. §§ 39861 to 39877.

§ 41416. Business administrator; qualifications; residence; powers and duties; budget; purchasing system

Where a department of administration is established, it shall be headed by a director who shall be known and designated as business administrator. He shall be chosen solely on the basis of his executive and administrative qualifications with special reference to his actual experience in, or his knowledge of, accepted practice in respect to the duties of his office as hereinafter set forth. At the time of his appointment, he need not be a resident of the city or State, but during his tenure of office he may reside outside the city only with the approval of council. He shall have, exercise and discharge the functions, powers and duties of the department. The department, under the direction and supervision of the mayor, shall:

(1) Assist in the preparation of the budget;

(2) Administer a centralized purchasing system; and

(3) Perform such other duties as council may prescribe.

E. Budget and Control

§ 41417. Preparation; requests for appropriations; hearings

The city budget shall be prepared by the mayor with the assistance of the business administrator or other officer designated by the mayor. Except for the budget for the first budget year after adoption of the Mayor-Council Plan A, the mayor shall, not later than the month of November, require all department heads to submit requests for appropriations for the ensuing budget year, and to appear before the mayor or the business administrator or other officer at public hearings, which shall be held during that month, on the various requests. In preparation of the budget for the first budget year after adoption of the Mayor-Council Plan A, such requests shall be made and such hearings shall be held in February of the first budget year.

§ 41418. Recommended budget; explanations; form; analysis; reductions; increases; adoption date

Except as hereafter provided for submission of the first recommended budget after adoption of the Mayor-Council Plan A, at the last stated meeting in November, the mayor shall submit to council his recommended budget in the form of an ordinance, together with such explanatory comment or statement as he may deem desirable. After adoption of the Mayor-Council Plan A, the first recommended budget together with the explanatory comment or statement, shall be submitted by the mayor in the form of an ordinance to council not later than the first day of March and shall be adopted by council not later than the first meeting in March of the first budget year, or, if the mayor elects to do so, he may recommend the amendment and adoption of the annual budget and the levy of a tax rate under sections 1809, 1810 and 1811 of the act of June 23, 1931 (P.L. 932), known as "The Third Class City Code", reenacted and amended June 28, 1951 (P.L. 662).[21] The budget shall be in such form as is required the council for city budgets, and shall in addition have appended thereto a detailed analysis of the various items of expenditure and revenue. Council may reduce any item or items in the mayor's budget by a vote of a majority of the council, but an increase in any item or items therein shall become effective only upon an affirmative vote of two-thirds of the members of council.

Council shall, upon passing the proposed budget ordinance on first reading, fix a date for adoption thereof, which shall except as otherwise provided be not later than the 31st day of December immediately following.

21. 53 P.S. §§ 36809 to 36811.

§ 41419. Work program; quarterly allotments; unit costs

The council shall, where practicable, provide for the maintenance of a system of work programs and quarterly allotments, for operation of the budget. It shall be the duty of the officer or department administering any such program to develop and report appropriate unit costs of budgeted expenditures.

§ 41420. Control function; encumbrance system; requisitions; preaudits; individual warrants

The council shall provide by ordinance for the exercise of a control function, in the management of the finances of the city, by the city controller. The control function shall include provision for an encumbrance system of budget operation, for expenditures only upon written requisition, for the pre-audit by the city controller of all claims and demands against the city prior to payment, and for the control of all payments out of any public funds by individual warrants for each payment to the official having custody thereof.

§ 41421. Audits; public accountants

The council may provide for annual post audits of all accounts by an outside certified public accountant to be appointed by council.

ARTICLE V. COUNCIL-MANAGER PLAN

A. Form of Government; Election of Councilmen and Controller

§ 41501. Name; cities governed

The form of government provided in this article shall be known as the "council-manager plan" and shall, together with Articles III.[22] and VI.,[23] govern any city, the voters of which have adopted this plan pursuant to this act.

§ 41502. Governing personnel

Each city under this article shall be governed by a mayor chosen as provided in sections 213 and 507,[24] an elected council, an elected controller, an appointed city manager, an elected treasurer and by such other officers and employes as may be duly appointed pursuant to this article, general law or ordinance.

§ 41503. Controller; treasurer; election; term

The controller and the treasurer shall be elected by the voters of the city at a regular municipal election, and shall serve for a term of four years beginning the first Monday of January next following his election.

§ 41504. Councilmen; number; election; term

The city council shall consist of five members unless, pursuant to the authority granted under section 213 of this act,[25] the city shall be governed by a council of seven or nine members. Members of the city council shall be elected, at large, by the voters of the city at a regular municipal election, and shall serve for a term of four years, except as hereinafter provided for those first elected, beginning on the first Monday of January next following their election.

22. 53 P.S. § 41301 et seq.

23. 53 P.S. § 41601 et seq.

24. 53 P.S. §§ 41213, 41507.

25. 53 P.S. § 41213.

§ 41505. First council; election; term

At the first municipal election following the adoption by a city of this charter plan, councilmen shall be elected and shall serve for the terms as provided in section 622 of this act.[26]

§ 41506. Vacancies

(a) If a vacancy exists in the city council, council shall, by a majority of its remaining members, fill such vacancy within thirty days thereafter by electing a qualified person to serve until that first Monday of January, when his successor who shall have been elected by the qualified electors at the next municipal election occurring at least thirty days after such vacancy exists, is duly sworn into office for the remainder of the term of the person originally elected to said office.

In case vacancies should exist whereby the offices of a majority or more of the members of the city council become vacant, the remaining members shall fill such vacancies, one at a time, giving each new appointee such reasonable notice of his appointment as will enable him to meet and act with the then qualified member or members of the city council in making further appointments until a bare majority of members of city council have been qualified, whereupon said members shall fill the remaining vacancies at a meeting attended by the said members, such appointees to receive a majority of the votes of the members present at such meeting. The person or persons selected to fill such vacancy or vacancies shall hold their offices as herein provided.

If, by reason of a tie vote or otherwise, such vacancy shall not have been filled by the remaining members of city council within the time as limited herein, the court of common pleas, upon the petition of ten or more qualified electors, shall fill such vacancy by the appointment of a qualified person for the portion of the unexpired term as above provided.

If, at any time, vacancies should occur or exist in the membership of all members of city council, the court of common pleas shall appoint a city council of persons properly qualified, who shall serve as herein provided.

(b) If a vacancy occurs in the office of city controller or city treasurer, the city council shall fill such vacancy, within thirty days thereafter, by choosing a city controller or city treasurer to serve until his successor is elected by the qualified electors at the next municipal election, occurring at least two hundred days after such vacancy occurs, and is duly sworn into office. The person so elected shall serve from the first Monday of January next succeeding his election for the remainder of the term of the person originally elected to such office.

If, by reason of a tie vote or otherwise, such vacancy shall not have been filled by council within the time as limited herein, the court of common pleas, upon petition of ten or more qualified electors, shall fill such vacancy by the appointment of a qualified person for the portion of the unexpired term as herein provided.

B. Council

§ 41507. Organization; election of mayor

(a) On the first Monday of January following the regular municipal election, the members of the city council shall assemble at the usual place of meeting and organize and choose one of their number as mayor unless otherwise provided. The mayor shall be chosen by ballot by majority within five ballots to be taken within[27] two days of said organization meeting, to elect a mayor, then the member who in the election for members of to elect a mayor, then the member who in the election

26. 53 P.S. § 41622.

27. "with" in original.

for members of the city council received the greatest number of votes shall be the mayor. Should such person decline to accept the office, then the person receiving the next highest vote shall be the mayor, and so on, until the office is filled.

(b) On the recommendation of the charter commission as provided in section 213,[28] the mayor shall be elected directly by the voters of the city at the regular municipal election, in lieu of being chosen as provided in subsection (a) of this section 507.

(c) In cities wherein the mayor is chosen by council, on petition of thirty per centum of the number of residents of the city who voted at the last preceding general election, there shall be placed on the ballot at the next succeeding primary, municipal or general election a question on choosing of the mayor by council or election directly by the voters of the city. Should a majority of those voting on the question be in favor of electing the mayor directly by the voters of the city, the office of mayor shall be filled by the election of a mayor at the next municipal election.

§ 41508. Mayor's powers and duties; bonds; notes; contracts; written obligations

The mayor shall preside at all meetings of the city council and shall have a voice and vote in its proceedings. All bonds, notes, contracts and written obligations of the city shall be executed on its behalf by the mayor and controller or, in the event of the mayor's inability to act, by the controller and such councilman as the city council shall designate to act as mayor during his absence or disability. The powers and duties of the mayor shall be only such as are expressly conferred upon him by this article.

§ 41509. General powers and policy

All powers of the city and the determination of all matters of policy shall be vested in the city council, except as otherwise provided by this act or by general law.

§ 41510. Appointed personnel; advisory bodies

The city council shall appoint a city manager and a city clerk. The office of city manager and city clerk may be held by the same person. The council may provide for the manner of appointment of a city solicitor, any planning board, zoning board of adjustment or personnel board in the city, and may create commissions and other bodies with advisory powers.

§ 41511. Executive and administrative departments, boards and offices; deputy manager

The city council shall continue or create, and determine and define, the powers and duties of such executive and administrative departments, boards and offices, in addition to those provided for herein, as it may deem necessary for the proper and efficient conduct of the affairs of the city, including the office of deputy manager. Any department, board or office so continued or created may, at any time, be abolished by the city council. No member of city council shall head an administrative department.

§ 41512. Council to act as a body; individual influence or interference; dealing through manager; investigating committees or commissions; misdemeanor; forfeiture of office

It is the intention of this article that the city council shall act in all matters as a body, and it is contrary to the spirit of this article for any of its members to seek individually to influence the official acts of the city manager, or any other officer, or for the council or any of its members to direct or request the appoint-

28. 53 P.S. § 41213.

ment of any person to, or his removal from, office or to interfere in any way with the performance by such officers of their duties. The council and its members shall deal with the administrative service solely through the manager and shall not give orders to any subordinates of the manager, either publicly or privately. Nothing herein contained shall prevent the city council from appointing committees or commissions of its own members or of citizens to conduct investigations into the conduct of any officer or department, or any matter relating to the welfare of the city, and delegating to such committees or commissions such powers of inquiry as the city council may deem necessary. Any councilman violating any of the provisions of this section is guilty of misdemeanor in office, and upon conviction thereof in a court of competent jurisdiction, shall be disqualified and forfeit his office as councilman.

C. City Manager

§ 41513. Qualifications; residence; office-holder

The city manager shall be chosen by the council solely on the basis of his executive and administrative qualifications with special reference to his actual experience in, or his knowledge of, accepted practice in respect to the duties of his office as hereinafter set forth. At the time of his appointment, he need not be a resident of the city or State, but during his tenure of office he may reside outside the city only with the approval of council. The city manager shall not hold any elective city office.

§ 41514. Term; removal; hearing; suspension; salary

The city manager shall hold office for an indefinite term, and may be removed by a majority vote of the council. At least thirty days before such removal shall become effective, the council shall, by a majority vote of its members, adopt a preliminary resolution stating the reasons for his removal. The manager may reply in writing and may request a public hearing, which shall be held not earlier than twenty days nor later than thirty days after the filing of such request. After such public hearing, if one be requested, and after full consideration, the council by majority vote of its members may adopt a final resolution of removal. By the preliminary resolution, the council may suspend the manager from duty, but shall, in any case, cause to be paid him forthwith any unpaid balance of his salary and his salary for the next three calendar months following adoption of the preliminary resolution.

§ 41515. Absence or disability

The manager may designate a qualified administrative officer of the city to perform his duties during his temporary absence or disability. In the event of his failure to make such designation, or if the absence or disability continues more than thirty days, the council may, by resolution, appoint an officer of the city to perform the duties of the manager during such absence or disability until he shall return or his disability shall cease.

§ 41516. Powers and duties; reports; recommendations; investigations; responsibility to council

(a) The city manager shall:

(1) Be the chief executive and administrative official of the city;

(2) Execute all laws and ordinances of the city;

(3) Appoint and have power to remove a deputy manager, if one be authorized by the council, all department heads and all other officers, subordinates, and assistants for whose selection or removal no other method is provided in this article, except that he may authorize the head of a department to appoint and remove subordinates in such department, supervise and control his appoin-

tees, and report all appointments or removals at the next meeting thereafter of the city council;

(4) Negotiate contracts for the city, subject to the approval of the city council, make recommendations concerning the nature and location of municipal improvements, and execute municipal improvements as determined by the city council;

(5) See that all terms and conditions imposed in favor of the city or its inhabitants in any statute, public utility franchise or other contract are faithfully kept and performed, and upon knowledge of any violation, call the same to the attention of the city council;

(6) Attend all meetings of the city council with the right to take part in the discussions, but without the right to vote;

(7) Recommend to the city council for adoption such measures as he may deem necessary or expedient, keep the council advised of the financial condition of the city, make reports to the council as requested by it, and at least once a year make an annual report of his work for the benefit of the council and the public;

(8) Investigate at any time the affairs of any officer or department of the city which is under his jurisdiction;

(9) Perform such other duties as may be required of the city manager by ordinance or resolution of the city council;

(10) The city manager shall be responsible to the council for carrying out all policies established by it and for the proper administration of all affairs of the city within the jurisdiction of the council.

(b) The city manager may require that bids be accompanied by a good faith tender of either cash, a certified check, a cashier's check, a corporate surety bond or other irrevocable letter of credit in a reasonable amount. The advertisement soliciting bids shall set forth the requirement, when applicable, and the amount to be tendered. If a bidder is selected but is unable to perform, the city may retain the amount tendered with the bid as damages.

§ 41517. Budget; requests for appropriations

The city budget shall be prepared by the city manager. Not later than the month of November of each year, the city manager shall require all department heads to submit requests for appropriations for the ensuing budget year.

§ 41518. Recommended budget; explanations; form; analysis; hearings; adoption date; work programs; quarterly allotments; unit costs

At the last stated meeting in November, the city manager shall submit to council his recommended budget in the form of an ordinance, together with such explanatory comment or statement as he may deem desirable. The budget shall be in such form as is required by law for city budgets, and shall in addition have appended thereto detailed analysis of the various items of expenditure and revenue. Public hearings shall be held on the recommended budget before action thereon is taken by council. Council[29] shall upon passing the proposed budget ordinance on first reading fix a date for adoption thereof which shall be not later than the 31st day of December immediately following.

The council shall, where practicable, provide by ordinance for the operation of a system of work programs and quarterly allotments for operation of the budget and for development and reporting of appropriate unit costs of budgeted expenditures.

29. "Council" omitted in original.

§ 41519. Control function; encumbrance system; requisitions; preaudit; individual warrants

The council shall provide by ordinance for the exercise of a control function, in the management of the finances of the city, by the city controller. The control function shall include provision for an encumbrance system of budget operation, for expenditures only upon written requisition, for the pre-audit by the city controller of all claims and demands against the city prior to payment, for the control of all payments out of any public funds by individual warrants for each payment to the official having custody thereof.

§ 41520. Audits; public accountants

The council shall provide for annual post audits of all accounts by an outside certified public accountant to be appointed by council.

§ 41521. Power of mayor or other executive head

Any provision of general law now or hereafter enacted conferring the appointing power or other power upon the mayor or other executive head of the city shall be construed as meaning the city manager in a city governed under this article, and the appointments or the power exercised by the city manager in accordance with such provision shall be classified and given the same force and effect as if executed by the official named therein.

D. City Treasurer

§ 41522. Powers; duties; functions

The city treasurer shall have all the powers, duties and functions relating to the collection, receiving, safekeeping, accounting for, and payment over of public moneys including county, city, institution district and school district taxes, as provided by general law, and shall perform such other functions and duties as may be required of him by the city council.

ARTICLE VI. GENERAL PROVISIONS COMMON TO OPTIONAL PLANS

A. Officers and Employes

§ 41601. Interest in contracts with city or public utilities

No officer or employe elected or appointed in any city shall be interested, directly or indirectly, in any contract or job for work or materials or the profits thereof, to be furnished or performed for the city, and no such officer or employe shall be interested, directly or indirectly, in any contract or job for work or materials or the profits thereof, to be furnished or performed for any person operating any interurban railway, street railway, bus line, gas works, waterworks, electric light or power plant, heating plant, telegraph line, telephone exchange, or other public utility within the territorial limits of such city.

§ 41602. Frank; free passes, tickets or service; favors

No officer or employe shall accept or receive, directly or indirectly, from any person operating within the territorial limits of a city any interurban railway, bus line, street railway, gas works, waterworks, electric light or power plant, heating plant, telegraph line, telephone exchange or other business using or operating under a public franchise, any frank, free pass, free ticket or free service, or accept or receive, directly or indirectly, from any person, any other service upon terms more favorable than is granted to the public generally, except that such prohibition of free transportation shall not apply to policemen or firemen in uniform. Nor shall any free service to the city officials heretofore provided by any franchise or ordinance be affected by this section.

§ 41603. Gifts or promises for political support

No candidate for office, appointment or employment and no officer, appointee or employe in any city shall, directly or indirectly, give or promise any person any office, position, employment, benefit or anything of value for the purpose of influencing or obtaining the political support, aid or vote of any person, under the penalty of being disqualified to hold the office or employment to which he may be or may have been elected or appointed.

§ 41604. Ineligibility; forfeiture of office; misdemeanor in office

Any person convicted of a crime or offense involving moral turpitude shall be ineligible to assume any city office, position or employment in a city governed pursuant to this act, and upon conviction thereof, while in office, shall forfeit his office. Any person who shall violate any of the provisions of sections 601, 602 or[30] 603 of this act[31] shall be guilty of a misdemeanor in office, and upon conviction thereof in a court of competent jurisdiction, shall forfeit his office.

§ 41605. Refusal to appear; defense of self incrimination; waiving immunity from prosecution

If any person hereafter elected or appointed to any office or position in a city governed under this act shall, after lawful notice or process, wilfully refuse or fail to appear before any court, any legislative committee, or the Governor, or having appeared shall refuse to testify or to answer any question regarding the property, government or affairs of the city, or regarding his nomination, election, appointment or official conduct on the ground that his answer would tend to incriminate him, or shall refuse to waive immunity from prosecution[32] on account of any such matter in relation to which he may be asked to testify, may be removed from office by the council of the city in its discretion. Any person removed from office pursuant to this section shall not thereafter be eligible for election or appointment to any office or employment in such city.

B. Legislation by Council

§ 41606. Meetings; special meetings; journal; record

The council shall, by ordinance or resolution, designate the time of holding regular meetings which shall be at least monthly. The mayor or the president of council, as the case may be, may and, upon written request of a majority of the members of the council, shall call a special meeting of the council. In the call, he shall designate the purpose of the special meeting and no other business shall be considered. All meetings of the council shall be open to the public. The city clerk shall keep a journal of its proceedings and record the minutes of every meeting.

§ 41607. Rules of procedure; quorum; majority vote; procedure on ordinance or resolution; signing minutes; officials compensation

(a) Council shall determine its own rules of procedure, not inconsistent with ordinance or statute. A majority of the whole number of members of the council shall constitute a quorum, but no ordinance shall be adopted by the council without the affirmative vote of a majority of all the members of the council.

(b) Each ordinance or resolution shall be introduced in written or typewritten form, and shall be read and considered as provided by general law. The vote upon every motion, resolution or ordinance shall be taken by roll call and the yeas and nays shall be entered on the minutes. The minutes of each meeting shall be signed by the officer presiding at such meeting and by the city clerk.

30. "or" omitted in original.

31. 53 P.S. §§ 41601 to 41603.

32. "prosceution" in original.

(c) The compensation of the controller, treasurer and department heads shall be fixed by the council.

The compensation of the mayor and councilmen elected to their offices in the year prior to the transition year to the mayor council plan A pursuant to this act shall be as follows:

1970 Population	Mayor	Councilmen	President of Council
Cities under 25,000	$ 8,000	$1,800	$2,100
Cities from 25,000 to 49,999	$13,500	$2,200	$2,500
Cities from 50,000 to 74,999	$15,000	$2,500	$2,800
Cities of 75,000 to 124,999	$18,000	$2,800	$3,000
Cities of 125,000 and over	$20,000	$3,100	$3,300

The compensation of the mayor and councilmen elected to their offices in the year prior to the transition year to the council-manager plan pursuant to this act shall be as follows:

1970 Population	Mayor	Councilmen
Cities under 25,000	$1,800	$1,200
Cities under 25,000 to 49,999	$2,100	$1,500
Cities from 50,000 to 74,999	$2,400	$1,800
Cities of 75,000 and over	$3,000	$2,400

The compensation of the mayor, councilmen, controller and treasurer elected to their offices subsequent to the transition year to the mayor-council plan A or to the council-manager plan pursuant to this act shall be fixed by ordinance of council finally passed or adopted at least two days prior to the last day fixed by law for candidates to withdraw their names from nominating petitions previous to the day of the municipal election. After such compensation is once fixed by ordinance only an increase or decrease thereof need be fixed by such ordinance.

§ 41608. Ordinances; adoption; publication; incorporation by reference; effective date

(a) Except as may otherwise be provided in this act all ordinances shall be adopted and published in the manner required by general law: Provided, however, That any ordinance may incorporate by reference any standard technical regulations or code, official or unofficial, which need not be so published whenever ten copies of said regulations or code have been placed on file in the office of the city clerk and in the office of the body or department charged with the enforcement of said ordinance for the examination of the public so long as said ordinance is in effect.

(b) No ordinance other than the local budget ordinance shall take effect less than twenty days after its final passage by council and approval by the mayor where such approval is required, unless the council shall adopt a resolution declaring an emergency and at least two-thirds of all the members of the council vote in favor of such resolution.

Chap. 39 Res. During Mil. Service
Chap. 38 Intergov. Coop.
Chap. 37 3rd Class City Code
Chap. 36 Bor. Code
Chap. 35 2nd Class Twp. Code
Chap. 34 1st Class Twp. Code
Chap. 33 Home Rule Chart. Opt. Plans Law
Chap. 32 Water Serv. Act
Chap. 31 Munic. Auth. Act

§ 41609. Ordinances and resolutions; record; binding; codification; indexes

The city clerk shall record all ordinances and resolutions adopted by council and at the close of each year, with the advice and assistance of the city attorney, shall bind, compile or codify all the ordinances and resolutions, or true copies thereof, of the city which then remain in force and effect. He shall also properly index the record books, compilation or codification of ordinances and resolutions.

§ 41610. Regulations; filing; publication

No rule or regulation made by any department, officer, agency or authority of the city, except such as relates to the organization or internal management of the city government or a part thereof, shall take effect until it is filed either with the city clerk or in such other manner as may be provided by ordinance. The council shall provide for the prompt publication of such rules and regulations.

C. Transition to Optional Charter Plan

§ 41620. Effective date of adopted plan; discontinuance date

(a) Whenever the electors of a city adopt any of the optional charter plans provided by this act at any election for that purpose, such city shall be governed under the provisions of such charter plan and this act from the first Monday in January following the next succeeding municipal election.

(b) Whenever the electors of a city vote to discontinue such optional plan at any election for that purpose, the city shall cease to be governed by the provisions of such charter plan and this act on the first Monday of January following the next succeeding municipal election.

§ 41621. Hold-over officials; term and compensation; new treasurer and controller

(a) The mayor, the members of council, the treasurer and the controller in office at the time of the adoption of any charter plan provided by this act shall continue in office until the expiration of their terms and shall receive the compensation provided by law at that time. Any such officer may, by writing filed with the city treasurer, direct that any portion of his compensation be returned to the city treasury.

(b) If an elected city treasurer or city controller is in office at the time of the adoption of an optional charter plan under the provisions of this act, a treasurer or controller, as the case may be, shall not be elected to take office until after the resignation, death, removal or expiration of the term of said treasurer or controller.

§ 41622. First council; terms; vacancies; new mayor

(a) At the municipal election next succeeding the adoption of one of the optional charter plans provided for in this act, the number of councilmen prescribed by the terms of the charter less the number of councilmen then in office whose terms do not expire on the first Monday of January next following, shall be elected. For the purpose of this section, an existing mayor shall be considered as a member of council, and after the new charter plan goes into effect, his duties shall be only those of a member of council as prescribed by the new charter plan and a new mayor shall be elected at this election or appointed as provided by the plan adopted.

(b) At such election, if two, three or four councilmen are elected, they shall each serve for terms of four years. If five are elected, the four candidates receiving the highest number of votes shall serve for terms of four years, and the candidate receiving the next highest number of votes shall serve for a term of two years. If six or seven are elected, the five candidates receiving the highest number of votes shall serve for terms of four years, and the one or two candidates, as the case may be, receiving the next highest number of votes shall serve for a

Table of Contents | Part I Ch. 1–3 Ethics, Records, Open Meetings | Part II Ch. 4–10 Taxation | Part III Ch. 11–18 Torts, Contracts & Civil Rules | Part IV Ch. 19–24 Zoning & Planning | Part V Ch. 25–30 Construction and Emergency Codes | Part VI Ch. 31–39 Municipal Codes | Index

term of two years. Thereafter, all councilmen shall be elected for terms of four years.

(c) If any vacancies in council occurring by reason of resignation, death or removal shall exist ninety days or more before such election, they shall be filled for the remainder of the term of the person originally elected to that office.

§ 41623. Existing ordinances and resolutions

Upon the effective date of an optional charter adopted pursuant to this act, all ordinances and resolutions of the city to the extent that they are not inconsistent with the provisions of this act shall remain in full force and effect until modified or repealed as provided by law.

§ 41624. Existing offices; organization and administration resolutions

(a) On the effective date of an optional plan adopted pursuant to this act, all appointive offices then existing in such city shall be abolished and the terms of all appointed officers shall immediately cease and determine: Provided, That nothing in this section shall be construed to abolish the office or terminate the terms of office of any alderman or constable or of any official or employe now protected[33] by any tenure of office or civil service law, or of any policeman or fireman, whether or not protected by a tenure of office law.

(b) Provision for officers and for the organization and administration of the city government under the optional plan may be made by resolution pending the adoption of ordinances, but any such resolution shall expire not later than sixty days after the effective date of the optional plan.

§ 41625. Pending actions and proceedings

All actions and proceedings of a legislative, executive or judicial character, which are pending upon the effective date of an optional plan adopted pursuant to this act, may continue and the appropriate officer or employe under such optional plan shall be substituted for the officer or employe theretofore exercising or discharging the function, power or duty involved in such action or proceeding.

33. "protested" in original.

CHAPTER 38
INTERGOVERNMENTAL COOPERATION

53 Pa.C.S. §§ 2301-2317

Title 53
Chapter 23. General Provisions
Subchapter A. Intergovernmental Cooperation

Sec.

Cross References. Subchapter A is referred to in sections 305, 5611, 6103, 8002 of this title; sections 1122, 1201.3, 1202, 1316, 1402, 1903, 2021, 2701, 2708 of Title 8 (Boroughs and Incorporated Towns); sections 11804.1, 12419, 12434, 13115, 14204 of Title 11 (Cities); sections 8501, 8955 of Title 42 (Judiciary and Judicial Procedure); section 2107 of Title 68 (Real and Personal Property).

§ 2301. Scope of subchapter.

This subchapter applies to all local governments.

§ 2302. Definitions.

The following words and phrases when used in this subchapter shall have the meanings given to them in this section unless the context clearly indicates otherwise:

"Local government." A county, city of the second class, second class A and third class, borough, incorporated town, township, school district or any other similar general purpose unit of government created by the General Assembly after July 12, 1972.

§ 2303. Intergovernmental cooperation authorized.

(a) General rule.—Two or more local governments in this Commonwealth may jointly cooperate, or any local government may jointly cooperate with any similar entities located in any other state, in the exercise or in the performance of their respective governmental functions, powers or responsibilities.

Table of Contents
Part I Ch. 1–3 Ethics, Records, Open Meetings
Part II Ch. 4–10 Taxation
Part III Ch. 11–18 Torts, Contracts & Civil Rules
Part IV Ch. 19–24 Zoning & Planning
Part V Ch. 25–30 Construction and Emergency Codes
Part VI Ch. 31–39 Municipal Codes
Index

(b) Joint agreements.—For the purpose of carrying the provisions of this subchapter into effect, the local governments or other entities so cooperating shall enter into any joint agreements as may be deemed appropriate for those purposes.

§ 2304. Intergovernmental cooperation.

A municipality by act of its governing body may, or upon being required by initiative and referendum in the area affected shall, cooperate or agree in the exercise of any function, power or responsibility with or delegate or transfer any function, power or responsibility to one or more other local governments, the Federal Government or any other state or its government.

§ 2305. Adoption of ordinance or resolution.

(a) Ordinance or resolution.—A local government may enter into intergovernmental cooperation with or delegate any functions, powers or responsibilities to another governmental unit, local government or authority as defined in section 5602 (relating to definitions) upon the passage of an ordinance or resolution by its governing body. If mandated by initiative and referendum in the area affected, the local government shall adopt such an ordinance or resolution.

(b) Compliance by authorities.—An authority as defined in section 5602 may not share or be delegated any function, power or responsibility through an agreement under this subchapter unless the function, power or responsibility is authorized by both the law under which the authority was created and the powers or purposes of the authority contained within its articles of incorporation.

(c) Council of governing bodies.—An intergovernmental agreement creating a council or consortium of governing bodies or similar entity separate from the organizing governing bodies may not be entered into unless by ordinance. A municipality may join an existing intergovernmental cooperation agreement of other municipalities whereby such an entity was created by resolution or by ordinance.

§ 2306. Initiative and referendum.

(a) Initiative.—An initiative under this subchapter shall be commenced by filing with the appropriate election officials at least 90 days prior to the next primary or general election a petition containing a proposal for referendum signed by electors comprising 5% of the number of electors voting for the office of Governor in the last gubernatorial election in each local government or area affected. The applicable election officials shall place the proposal on the ballot in a manner fairly representing the content of the petition for decision by referendum at the election. Initiative on a similar question shall not be submitted more often than once in five years.

(b) Referendum.—The question shall be placed on the ballot as a referendum and shall become effective by a majority vote of the electors voting thereon.

§ 2307. Content of ordinance or resolution.

The ordinance or resolution adopted by the governing body of a local government entering into intergovernmental cooperation or delegating or transferring any functions, powers or responsibilities to another local government, an authority as defined in section 5602 (relating to definitions) or to a council of governments, consortium or any other similar entity shall specify:

(1) The conditions of agreement in the case of cooperation with or delegation to other local governments, the Commonwealth, other states or the Federal Government.

(2) The duration of the term of the agreement.

(3) The purpose and objectives of the agreement, including the powers and scope of authority delegated in the agreement.

(4) The manner and extent of financing the agreement.

(5) The organizational structure necessary to implement the agreement.

(6) The manner in which real or personal property shall be acquired, managed, licensed or disposed of.

(7) That the entity created under this section shall be empowered to enter into contracts for policies of group insurance and employee benefits, including Social Security, for its employees.

§ 2308. Bids for certain joint purchases.

(a) **Notice.**—All joint purchases involving an expenditure of more than a base amount of $18,500, subject to adjustment under subsection (b), shall be made by contract, in writing, only after notice for bids once a week for two weeks in at least one and not more than two newspapers of general circulation in the joining local governments. All contracts shall be let to the lowest responsible bidder. Every contract for the construction, reconstruction, alteration, repair, improvement or maintenance of public works shall comply with the provisions of the act of March 3, 1978 (P.L.6, No.3), known as the Steel Products Procurement Act.

(b) **Adjustments.**—Adjustments to the base amounts specified under subsection (a) shall be made as follows:

(1) The Department of Labor and Industry shall determine the percentage change in the Consumer Price Index for All Urban Consumers: All Items (CPI-U) for the United States City Average as published by the United States Department of Labor, Bureau of Labor Statistics, for the 12-month period ending September 30, 2012, and for each successive 12-month period thereafter.

(2) If the department determines that there is no positive percentage change, then no adjustment to the base amounts shall occur for the relevant time period provided for in this subsection.

(3)(i) If the department determines that there is a positive percentage change in the first year that the determination is made under paragraph (1), the positive percentage change shall be multiplied by each base amount, and the products shall be added to the base amounts, respectively, and the sums shall be preliminary adjusted amounts.

(ii) The preliminary adjusted amounts shall be rounded to the nearest $100 to determine the final adjusted base amounts for purposes of subsection (a).

(4) In each successive year in which there is a positive percentage change in the CPI-U for the United States City Average, the positive percentage change shall be multiplied by the most recent preliminary adjusted amounts, and the products shall be added to the preliminary adjusted amount of the prior year to calculate the preliminary adjusted amounts for the current year. The sums thereof shall be rounded to the nearest $100 to determine the new final adjusted base amounts for purposes of subsection (a).

(5) The determinations and adjustments required under this subsection shall be made in the period between October 1 and November 15 of the year following the effective date of this subsection and annually between October 1 and November 15 of each year thereafter.

(6) The final adjusted base amounts and new final adjusted base amounts obtained under paragraphs (3) and (4) shall become effective January 1 for the calendar year following the year in which the determination required under paragraph (1) is made.

(7) The department shall publish notice in the Pennsylvania Bulletin prior to January 1 of each calendar year of the annual percentage change determined under paragraph (1) and the unadjusted or final adjusted base amounts deter-

Chap. 39 Res. During Mil. Service
Chap. 38 Intergov. Coop.
Chap. 37 3rd Class City Code
Chap. 36 Bor. Code
Chap. 35 2nd Class Twp. Code
Chap. 34 1st Class Twp. Code
Chap. 33 Home Rule Chart. Opt. Plans Law
Chap. 32 Water Serv. Act
Chap. 31 Munic. Auth. Act

mined under paragraphs (3) and (4) at which competitive bidding is required under subsection (a) for the calendar year beginning the first day of January after publication of the notice. The notice shall include a written and illustrative explanation of the calculations performed by the department in establishing the unadjusted or final adjusted base amounts under this subsection for the ensuing calendar year.

(8) The annual increase in the preliminary adjusted base amounts obtained under paragraphs (3) and (4) shall not exceed 3%.

§ 2309. Direct purchases.

In addition to joint purchases authorized by section 2308 (relating to bids for certain joint purchases), local governments may make direct purchases from vendors or suppliers of goods, materials or equipment without compliance with existing and otherwise applicable statutory requirements governing competitive bidding and execution of contracts as follows:

(1) Any county may by appropriate resolution, and subject to such reasonable regulations as it may prescribe, permit any local government within the county to participate in or purchase off contracts for goods, materials or equipment entered into by the county.

(2) Any local government desiring to participate in purchase contracts shall file with the county purchasing agency and with the county solicitor a certified copy of an ordinance or resolution of its governing body requesting that it be authorized to participate in purchase contracts of the county and agreeing that it will be bound by the terms and conditions as the county prescribes and that it will be responsible for payment directly to the vendor under each purchase contract.

(3) The county may permit participation by local governments only where the solicitation for bids and specifications for the county contracts, and the contracts themselves, expressly provide for and inform prospective and successful bidders that the contract to be let is intended to be subject to this subchapter and to regulations adopted by the county.

(4) Among the terms and conditions as the county may specify, it shall prescribe that all prices shall be F.O.B. destination.

§ 2310. Joint purchases with private educational establishments.

Any local government may, by ordinance or resolution, authorize joint purchases of materials, supplies and equipment with any private school, parochial school, private college or university or nonprofit human services agency within the local government. The ordinance or resolution shall require that the school, college or agency shall be bound by the terms and conditions of purchasing agreements which the local government prescribes and that the school, college or agency shall be responsible for payment directly to the vendor under each purchase contract. Schools, colleges and agencies shall be exempt from any existing statutory requirements governing competitive bidding and execution of contracts with respect to purchases under this section.

§ 2311. Written or telephonic price quotations required.

(a) Amount.—Written or telephonic price quotations from at least three qualified and responsible contractors shall be requested for all contracts in excess of the base amount of $10,000, subject to adjustment under subsection (b), but are less than the amount requiring advertisement and competitive bidding, or, in lieu of price quotations, a memorandum shall be kept on file showing that fewer than three qualified contractors exist in the market area within which it is practicable to obtain quotations. A written record of telephonic price quotations shall be made and shall contain at least the date of the quotation, the name of the contractor and the contractor's representative, the construction, reconstruction, repair, maintenance or work which was the subject of the quotation and the price, written price quotations, written records of telephonic price quotations, and memoranda shall be retained for a period of three years.

(b) **Adjustments.**—Adjustments to the base amounts specified under subsection (a) shall be made as follows:

(1) The Department of Labor and Industry shall determine the percentage change in the Consumer Price Index for All Urban Consumers: All Items (CPI-U) for the United States City Average as published by the United States Department of Labor, Bureau of Labor Statistics, for the 12-month period ending September 30, 2012, and for each successive 12-month period thereafter.

(2) If the department determines that there is no positive percentage change, then no adjustment to the base amounts shall occur for the relevant time period provided for in this subsection.

(3)(i) If the department determines that there is a positive percentage change in the first year that the determination is made under paragraph (1), the positive percentage change shall be multiplied by each base amount, and the products shall be added to the base amounts, respectively, and the sums shall be preliminary adjusted amounts.

(ii) The preliminary adjusted amounts shall be rounded to the nearest $100 to determine the final adjusted base amounts for purposes of subsection (a).

(4) In each successive year in which there is a positive percentage change in the CPI-U for the United States City Average, the positive percentage change shall be multiplied by the most recent preliminary adjusted amounts, and the products shall be added to the preliminary adjusted amount of the prior year to calculate the preliminary adjusted amounts for the current year. The sums thereof shall be rounded to the nearest $100 to determine the new final adjusted base amounts for purposes of subsection (a).

(5) The determinations and adjustments required under this subsection shall be made in the period between October 1 and November 15 of the year following the effective date of this subsection and annually between October 1 and November 15 of each year thereafter.

(6) The final adjusted base amounts and new final adjusted base amounts obtained under paragraphs (3) and (4) shall become effective January 1 for the calendar year following the year in which the determination required under paragraph (1) is made.

(7) The department shall publish notice in the Pennsylvania Bulletin prior to January 1 of each calendar year of the annual percentage change determined under paragraph (1) and the unadjusted or final adjusted base amounts determined under paragraphs (3) and (4) at which written or telephonic price quotations are required under subsection (a), for the calendar year beginning the first day of January after publication of the notice. The notice shall include a written and illustrative explanation of the calculations performed by the department in establishing the unadjusted or final adjusted base amounts under this subsection for the ensuing calendar year.

(8) The annual increase in the preliminary adjusted base amounts obtained under paragraphs (3) and (4) shall not exceed 3%.

§ 2312. Division of transactions provided.

No local government shall evade the provisions of section 2308 (relating to bids for certain joint purchases) as to advertising for bids or purchasing materials or contracting for services piecemeal for the purpose of obtaining prices under a base amount of $18,500, subject to adjustment under section 2308(b), upon transactions which should in the exercise of reasonable discretion and prudence be conducted as one transaction amounting to more than a base amount of $18,500, subject to adjustment under section 2308(b). This provision is intended to make unlawful the practice of evading advertising requirements by making a series of purchases or contracts each for less than the advertising requirement price or by making several simultaneous purchases or contracts each below such price when in either case the transaction involved should have been made as one transaction for one price.

§ 2313. Penalty.

Any member of a governing body of a local government who votes to unlawfully evade the provisions of section 2308 (relating to bids for certain joint purchases) and who knows that the transaction upon which he so votes is or ought to be a part of a larger transaction and that it is being divided in order to evade the requirements as to advertising for bids commits a misdemeanor of the third degree for each contract entered into as a direct result of that vote.

§ 2314. Required review of specified agreements.

(a) General rule.—An agreement between a local government and the Federal Government, the Commonwealth, any other state or government of another state under the provisions of this subchapter shall, prior to and as a condition precedent to enactment of an ordinance or resolution, be submitted to the Local Government Commission for review and recommendation. An agreement exclusively between a local government and an authority as defined in section 5602 (relating to definitions) shall not be subject to the requirements under this section.

(b) Commission review.—

(1) The commission shall, within 90 days of receipt of the agreement, provide to the local government or other party submitting the agreement an advisory written response of its review of, and any recommended changes to, the agreement with regard to form and compatibility with the laws of this Commonwealth.

(2) If an agreement has been submitted to the commission for review as required by this subsection, the failure of the commission to provide an advisory written response within 90 days of receipt of the agreement shall not bar or impede the effectiveness or implementation of the agreement.

(c) Exceptions.—This section shall not apply to the following contracts, agreements or transactions:

(1) Contracts or agreements between a local government and the Commonwealth that are of a routine nature or are performed on a periodic basis, such as those for public improvements or maintenance.

(2) State grants and loans that are administered by the Commonwealth pursuant to statute or regulation.

(3) Contracts or agreements for cooperative purchasing.

(4) Contracts, agreements or memoranda of understanding between the Commonwealth and a local government that are expressly authorized by statute or regulation and by which the Commonwealth delegates all or a portion of its enforcement duties or responsibilities to a local government.

(5) Contracts or agreements between the Commonwealth and a local government that are expressly authorized by statute or regulation and through which the local government provides a service on behalf of the Commonwealth.

(6) Contracts or agreements relating to the purchase, right to capacity, sale, exchange, interchange, wheeling, pooling, transmission or development of electric power and associated energy and related services.

§ 2315. Effect of joint cooperation agreements.

Any joint cooperation agreement shall be deemed in force as to any local government when the agreement has been adopted by ordinance or resolution by all cooperating local governments. After adoption by all cooperating local governments, the agreement shall be binding upon the local government, and its covenants may be enforced by appropriate remedy by any one or more of the local governments against any other local government which is a party to the agreement.

§ 2316. Recognition by Commonwealth departments and agencies.

All Commonwealth departments and agencies in the performance of their administrative duties shall deem a council of governments, consortiums or other similar entities established by two or more municipalities under this subchapter as a legal entity.

§ 2317. Agreements for fire protection services in cities of the second class.

(a) Absorption of certain firefighters.—Notwithstanding the provisions of the act of May 23, 1907 (P.L.206, No.167), entitled "An act to regulate and improve the civil service of the cities of the second class in the Commonwealth of Pennsylvania; making violations of its provisions to be misdemeanors, and providing penalties for violations thereof," and the act of June 27, 1939 (P.L.1207, No.405), entitled, as amended, "An act regulating the appointment, promotion, suspension, reduction, removal, and reinstatement of employes (except chiefs and chief clerks) in bureaus of fire and fire alarm operators and fire box inspectors in bureaus of electricity, in cities of the second class; defining the powers and duties of Civil Service Commissions for such purpose in said cities; and repealing inconsistent legislation," in the case of an original appointment of a full-time firefighter in a borough with a population between 18,000 and 19,500 according to the 2000 census that is located in a county of the second class and is contiguous with a city of the second class, when the full-time firefighter is absorbed by appointment into the classified service in the bureau of fire of a city of a second class under an intergovernmental cooperation agreement for fire protective services, the full-time firefighter shall be:

(1) Subject only to a physical examination of the scope given for promotion.

(2) Subject to a probationary period of six months.

(3) Appointed from outside a certified eligibility list.

(4) Exempted from an eligibility examination.

(5) Exempted from a residency requirement at the time of original appointment. The firefighter shall be required, however, to become a bona fide resident of the city of the second class on or before the first anniversary of the original appointment.

(b) Eligible lists and appointments.—Under this section only, the civil service commission of the city of the second class shall not be required to generate eligible lists or indicate appointment thereon, and no individual who is on an existing eligibility list for original appointment into the classified service of the bureau of fire of a city of a second class shall have a right to be appointed until the eligible full-time firefighters of the borough are appointed under the intergovernmental cooperation agreement.

CHAPTER 39

RESIDENCY DURING MILITARY SERVICE

53 Pa.C.S. § 1142

---

§ 1142. Residency during military service.

(a) General rule.—A person's active military duty shall not disqualify the person from fulfilling a residency requirement imposed by a municipal code or charter as a qualification of elected office or to fill a vacancy of elected office.

(b) Deemed residency.—For purposes of subsection (a), a person who is a resident of a municipality for at least one year immediately prior to the person's absence due to active military duty shall be deemed to be an ongoing resident of the municipality unless and until the person demonstrates an intent to establish a new domicile outside of the municipality.

(c) Definition.—As used in this section, the term "active military duty" shall include active service in any of the armed forces of the United States, including a National Guard or reserve component.

INDEX

Table of Contents
Part I Ch. 1–3 Ethics, Records, Open Meetings
Part II Ch. 4–10 Taxation
Part III Ch. 11–18 Torts, Contracts & Civil Rules
Part IV Ch. 19–24 Zoning & Planning
Part V Ch. 25–30 Construction and Emergency Codes
Part VI Ch. 31–39 Municipal Codes
Index

Table of Contents
Part I Ch. 1–3 Ethics, Records, Open Meetings
Part II Ch. 4–10 Taxation
Part III Ch. 11–18 Torts, Contracts & Civil Rules
Part IV Ch. 19–24 Zoning & Planning
Part V Ch. 25–30 Construction and Emergency Codes
Part VI Ch. 31–39 Municipal Codes
Index

Table of Contents
Part I Ch. 1–3 Ethics, Records, Open Meetings
Part II Ch. 4–10 Taxation
Part III Ch. 11–18 Torts, Contracts & Civil Rules
Part IV Ch. 19–24 Zoning & Planning
Part V Ch. 25–30 Construction and Emergency Codes
Part VI Ch. 31–39 Municipal Codes
Index

Table of Contents
Part I Ch. 1–3 Ethics, Records, Open Meetings
Part II Ch. 4–10 Taxation
Part III Ch. 11–18 Torts, Contracts & Civil Rules
Part IV Ch. 19–24 Zoning & Planning
Part V Ch. 25–30 Construction and Emergency Codes
Part VI Ch. 31–39 Municipal Codes
Index

INDEX

NEIGHBORHOOD BLIGHT RECLAMATION AND REVITALIZATION ACT

OPEN RECORDS LAW

Table of Contents
Part I Ch. 1–3 Ethics, Records, Open Meetings
Part II Ch. 4–10 Taxation
Part III Ch. 11–18 Torts, Contracts & Civil Rules
Part IV Ch. 19–24 Zoning & Planning
Part V Ch. 25–30 Construction and Emergency Codes
Part VI Ch. 31–39 Municipal Codes
Index

Table of Contents
Part I Ch. 1–3 Ethics, Records, Open Meetings
Part II Ch. 4–10 Taxation
Part III Ch. 11–18 Torts, Contracts & Civil Rules
Part IV Ch. 19–24 Zoning & Planning
Part V Ch. 25–30 Construction and Emergency Codes
Part VI Ch. 31–39 Municipal Codes
Index

INDEX

INDEX

Table of Contents
Part I Ch. 1–3 Ethics, Records, Open Meetings
Part II Ch. 4–10 Taxation
Part III Ch. 11–18 Torts, Contracts & Civil Rules
Part IV Ch. 19–24 Zoning & Planning
Part V Ch. 25–30 Construction and Emergency Codes
Part VI Ch. 31–39 Municipal Codes
Index

Table of Contents
Part I Ch. 1–3 Ethics, Records, Open Meetings
Part II Ch. 4–10 Taxation
Part III Ch. 11–18 Torts, Contracts & Civil Rules
Part IV Ch. 19–24 Zoning & Planning
Part V Ch. 25–30 Construction and Emergency Codes
Part VI Ch. 31–39 Municipal Codes
Index

Table of Contents
Part I Ch. 1–3 Ethics, Records, Open Meetings
Part II Ch. 4–10 Taxation
Part III Ch. 11–18 Torts, Contracts & Civil Rules
Part IV Ch. 19–24 Zoning & Planning
Part V Ch. 25–30 Construction and Emergency Codes
Part VI Ch. 31–39 Municipal Codes
Index

INDEX

SMALL WIRELESS FACILITIES DEPLOYMENT ACT

SOCIAL SECURITY NUMBER PRIVACY ACT

SUNSHINE ACT

INDEX